1994
CATHOLIC ALMANAC

Felician A. Foy, O.F.M.
EDITOR

Rose M. Avato
ASSOCIATE EDITOR

Our Sunday Visitor Publishing Division
Our Sunday Visitor, Inc.
HUNTINGTON • INDIANA

D0232827

ACKNOWLEDGMENTS: Catholic News Service, for coverage of news and documentary texts; *The Documents of Vatican II*, ed. W. M. Abbott (Herder and Herder, America Press: New York 1966), for quotations of Council documents; *Annuario Pontificio* (1993); *Statistical Yearbook of the Church* (1991); *L'Osservatore Romano* (English editions); *The Official Catholic Directory* — Excerpts of statistical data (and other noted material) reprinted with permission of *The Official Catholic Directory*,™ © 1993 by Reed Reference Publishing, a division of Reed Publishing (USA) Inc. Trademark used under license from Reed Publishing (Nederland) B.V.; *The Papal Encyclicals*, 5 vols., ed. C. Carlen (Pierian Press, Ann Arbor, Mich.); Newsletter of the U.S. Bishops' Committee on the Liturgy; The United States Catholic Mission Assoc. (3029 Fourth St. N.E., Washington, D.C. 20017), for U.S. overseas-mission compilations and statistics; Catholic Press Directory (1993); Canadian Conference of Catholic Bishops, for latest available Canadian Catholic statistics; Rev. Thomas J. Reese, S.J., for names of dioceses for which U.S. bishops were ordained; other sources as credited in particular entries.

1994 Catholic Almanac

Copyright © Our Sunday Visitor Publishing Division, Our Sunday Visitor, Inc., 1993
Published annually by Our Sunday Visitor Publishing Division, Our Sunday Visitor, Inc., 200 Noll Plaza, Huntington, IN 46750
Address editorial queries to The Catholic Almanac, P.O. Box 3765, Wallington, NJ 07057; all other queries to the Publisher.
ISBN 0-87973-271-7 (Kivar edition)
ISBN 0-87973-272-5 (cloth edition)
Library of Congress Catalog Card No. 73-641001
International Standard Serial Number (ISSN) 0069-1208

TABLE OF CONTENTS

INDEX

Carolines and Marshalls, 431, 532
Carpatho-Russians (Ruthenians), 268, 270
Carpino, Francesco, Card., 155, 167, 168
Carroll, Charles, 395
Carroll, Eamon, O. Carm., Rev., 260
Carroll, John, Bp., 395, 473
Carroll, Mark K., Bp., 473
Carroll Center for the Blind, 562
Carter, Alexander, Bp., 384
Carter, Gerald Emmett, Card., 155, 167, 168
Carthusians, Order of, 494
Casaroli, Agostino, Card., 155, 167, 168
Casey, Luis Morgan, Bp., 448
Casey, Robert P., Gov., 64, 81
Casimir, St., 250
Casimir, Sisters of St., 504
Casoria, Giuseppe, Card., 155, 167, 168
Cassian, St., 250
Cassidy, Edward I., Card., 91, 106, 155, 167, 168
Cassock, 215
Castel Gandolfo, 175
Castillo, John de, St., 389
Castillo Lara, Rosalio Jose, Card., 155, 167, 168
Catacombs, 300
Catala, Magin, 389
Catechesis, 300
Catechetics (Bishops' Synod), 145
Catechism, 300
Catechism of the Catholic Church, 39-41, 68, 88
   Commission, 152
Catechists, World Statistics, 367
Catechumen, 300
   See also Baptism
Catechumenate (RCIA), 224
Catechumens, Mass, 213
Catechumens, Oil of, 319
Catharism, **see** Manichaeism
Cathedra, 300
   See also Ex Cathedra
Cathedral, 436
Cathedrals, Canada (Jurisdictions, Hierarchy), 375-80
Cathedrals, U.S., 436-38
Cathedraticum, 300
Catherine Laboure, St., 250-51
   Miraculous Medal, 265
Catherine of Bologna, St., 251
Catherine of Siena, St., 198
Catholic, 300
   Action, **see** Lay Apostolate
   Actors' Guild of America, 595
   Aid Association, 574
   Alumni Clubs International, 574
   Answers, 574
   Associations, 573-81
   Awards, 544, 569, 596-99
   Baptisms, **see** Baptisms
   Belief, **see** Doctrine, Catholic
   Biblical Assn. of America, 574
   Book Publishers Association, 574
   Central Union, 571
   Charities, USA, 64, 69, 545
   Chronology in U.S., 398-411
   Church Extension Society, 527
   Colleges, U.S., 533-38
   Commission on Intellectual and Cultural Affairs, 574
   Committee of Appalachia, 574
   Communications Campaign, 105
   Communications Foundation, 596
   Conferences, State, 444
   Conferences, U.S., 441-44
   Daughters of the Americas, 574
   Dictionary, **see** Glossary
   Doctrine, **see** Doctrine, Catholic
   Eastern Churches, 266-73
   Education, **see** Education, Catholic
   Forester Youth Program, 572
   Golden Age, 574
   Guardian Society, 574
   Health Association, 545
   Hierarchy, **see** Hierarchy

Catholic
   History in the U.S., 395-411
   Home Bureau, 575
   Home Study Service, 575
   Hospitals, **see** Hospitals, Catholic
   Interracial Council of New York, 575
   Knights of America, 575
   Knights of Ohio, 575
   Kolping Society, 575
   League, 575
   League for Religious and Civil Rights, 108, 575
   Library Association, 575
   Major Markets, 97
   Medical Mission Board, 571
   Men, National Council of, 578
   Missions, 524-27
   Movement for Intellectual and Cultural Affairs, 571
   Near East Welfare Association, 575
   Negro-American Mission Board, 527
   Network of Volunteer Service, 572
   News Agencies, 594
   News Service, 594
   Order of Foresters, 575
   Organizations (U.S.), 573-81
   Organizations, International, 371-73
   Pamphlet Society, 575
   Peace Fellowship, 575
   Periodicals, Foreign, 593-94
   Periodicals, U.S., 582-93
   Population, **see** Statistics, Catholic
   Press, **see** Press, Catholic
   Press Association, 93, 569, 575
   Radio Programs, U.S., 595
   Relief Services, 82, 100, 102, 523
   Schools, **see** Schools, Catholic
   Social Doctrine, 201-09
   Social Service Facilities, World, 367
   Social Services, U.S., 545-62
   Societies in U.S., 573-81
   Statistics, **see** Statistics, Catholic
   Supreme Court Justices, 412
   Telecommunications Network of America, 97, 596
   Television Network, 596
   Television Programs, 595, 596
   Theatre, U.S., 595
   Theological Society of America, 575
   Union of Texas, 575
   Universities, Pontifical, 540-41
   Universities, U.S., 533-38
   University of America, 534, 541, 599
   Views Broadcast, 595
   Volunteers in Florida, 571
   War Veterans, 575
   Women, National Council of, 579
   Worker Movement, 575
   Workman, 575
   Youth Organization (CYO), 572
   Youth Organizations, 572-73
      See also Church, Catholic
Catholic-Jewish Relations, 290-93
   Commission (Vatican), 152, 291
Catholic Lutheran Relations, 66
   Scandinavia, 106
Catholic-Muslim Relations, 293-94
   Vatican Commission, 152
Catholic-Orthodox Relations, 63, 64, 67, 75, 85, 95, 276
   Balamand Document, 95, 276
   Declarations of Popes, Other Prelates, 285, 286
   Developments, 276
   Dialogue, 64, 67, 276
   Dialogues, U.S., 285, 287
   International Theological Commission, 286
      See also Orthodox Churches, Eastern
Catholics
   in Presidents' Cabinets, U.S., 411-12
   in Supreme Court, U.S., 412
   in Statuary Hall, 412
   in U.S. Congress, 72-3
Catholics against Capital Punishment, 575

Catholics United for Spiritual Action, 575
Catholics United for the Faith, 575
Causality, **see** Existence of God
Causes of Saints, Congregation, 147
Cavazos, Lauro (Catholics in Presidents' Cabinets), 412
Cayenne, **see** French Guiana
Cayman Islands, 336
Cazabon, Gilles, Bp., 384
CBS Program, Objections, 80
Cé, Marco, Card., 155, 167, 168
Cecilia, St., 251
CELAM (Latin American Bishops' Conference), 49-50, 50-1, 371
   General Assembly (1992), Papal Address, 49-50
   Message to Peoples of Region, 50-1
Celebret, 300
Celebrezze, Anthony (Catholics in Presidents' Cabinets), 412
Celibacy, 57, 300-01
   John Paul II on, 67
Cenacle, 301
Cenacle, Congregation of Our Lady of Retreat in the, 504
Cenobitic Life (318), 113
Censer, 301
Censorship of Books, 301
Censures, 301
Centenary (Fifth) of Evangelization of America, **see** Quincentenary
Center for Applied Research in the Apostolate, (CARA), 72, 85, 571
   Seminary Statistics, 85
Center of Concern, 572
Centesimus Annus, Encyclical Letter of John Paul II, 202-09
Central African Republic, 336, 368
Central America
   American Missionary Bishops, 427
   Cardinals, 168
   Episcopal Conferences, 371
      See also El Salvador; Guatemala; Nicaragua
Central Association of the Miraculous Medal, 575
Central Statistics Office, 151, 177
Ceremonies, Master of, 301
Cerularius, Michael (1043-1059), 116
Ceuta, 337
Ceylon, **see** Sri Lanka
Chabanel, Noel, St., 389
Chad, 337, 368
Chair of Peter (Feast), 246
Chalcedon, Council of (451), 114, 123
Chaldean Rite, 268-69
   in U.S., 271
Chalice, 216
"The Challenge of Peace: God's Promise and Our Response" (U.S. Bishops' Pastoral), 209
Chamber, Apostolic, 150
Chamberlain, 301
Chancellor, 301
Chancery, 301
Chancery Offices, U.S., 439-41
Chant, Gregorian, 211
Chapel, 302
Chaplain, 302
Chaplains, National Association of Catholic, 545
Chaplains Aid Association, 575
Chaplet, 302
Chapter, 302
Chaput, Charles J., O.F.M. Cap., Bp., 448
Charbonneau, Paul E., Bp., 384
Charismatic Renewal, Catholic, 302
Charisms, 302
Charities, Catholic, National Conference, **see** Charities USA, Catholic
Charities, Office of Papal, 151
Charities, Pontifical Council, Cor Unum, 71, 150
Charities USA, Catholic, 72, 73, 545
Charity, 302
   Heroic Act, 311

Ethelbert, St., 252
Ethics, 307
  Situational, 327-28
Ethiopia, 342, 368
Ethiopian Orthodox Patriarch-Papal
  Meeting, 276
Ethiopian Rite Catholics, 267
Etsou-Nzabi-Bamungwabi, Frédéric,
  Card., 157, 167, 168
Ethnic Conflicts, see
  Bosnia-Herzegovina, Croatia,
  Yugoslavia
Euangelion (Gospel), 192
Eucharist (Holy), 223, 225-27
  Administration to Non-Catholics, 227
  and Evangelization, 59
  Central Place of, 124
  Devotion Outside of Mass, 226
  Exposition, 222, 309
  Fast, 309
  John Paul II on, 88
  Ministers, Special, 220
  Reservation of, see Tabernacle
  Sacrifice, see Mass
  See also Communion, Holy;
    Transubstantiation
Eucharist, Religious of, 507
Eucharistic Congresses, 308
  45th International, 58-9
Eucharistic Franciscan Missionary
  Sisters, 508
Eucharistic Liturgy, 213-14
Eucharistic Prayers (Mass), 214, 218
Eucharistic Sharing (Intercommunion),
  226-27, 314
Eudes, John, St., 254
Eudists (Congregation of Jesus and
  Mary), 495
Eugenics, 308
Euphrasia Pelletier, St., 252
Europe, 71, 93-4
  Bishops' Conference, 87, 371
  Cardinals, 168
  Catholic Statistics, 367
  Eastern Rite Jurisdictions, 269
  Missionary Bishops (U.S.), 427
Eusebius of Vercelli, St., 252
Euthanasia, 308
  Assisted Suicide, 61-2
  England, 101
  Michigan Catholic Conference
    Statement, 61-2
  Netherlands, 80
Eutychianism (451), 114
Evangelical Counsels, 304
Evangelicalism, 281
Evangelion, 272
Evangelists, 193, 195-97
Evangelization, 308
Evangelization (John Paul II), 35
Evangelization of the Americas, Fifth
  Centenary, 46-9
Evangelization ot Peoples, Congregation
  of, 148
Everson v. Board of Education (Bus
  Transportation), 413
Evolution, 308
Ex Cathedra, 182
  See also Infallibility
Exaltation (Triumph) of the Holy Cross,
  249
Examen, Particular (Examination of
  Conscience), 304
Exarch, 144
Exceptional Children, see Handicapped,
  Facilities for
Excommunication, 308
Exegesis, 194
Existentialism, 308-09
Exner, Adam, O.M.I., Abp., 384-85
Exodus, 188
Exorcism, 309
Exorcist, 229
Exposition of the Blessed Sacrament,
  222, 309
  for Extended Periods of Time, 222
Extension Society, 527

External Forum, 310
Extreme Unction, see Anointing of the
  Sick
Ezekiel, 191
Ezra, 189

F

Fabian, St., 252
Fabric of St. Peter, 151
Faculties, 309
  of Ecclesiastical Studies, 541-42
Fagan, Harry A., 600
Faith, 309
  Congregation for Doctrine of, 147
  Congregation for Propagation
    (Evangelization of Peoples), 148
  Mysteries, 318
  Privilege of (Petrine Privilege), 234
  Promoter of, 323
  Rule of, 309
  See also Creed; Doctrine
  Society for Propagation of, 580
Faith and Order Conference, 103, 106,
  331
Faithful, Communion of, 303
Faithful, Mass of, 213
Faithful, Prayer of the, 213
Falcao, Jose Freire, Card., 157, 168
Falconio, Diomede, O.F.M. (U.S.
  Cardinals), 169, 475
Falkland Islands, 342
False Decretals (847-852), 115
Family, 74, 99
  Council for, 150
Family, Holy (Feast), 247
FamilyFest Conference, 95
Family Movement, Christian, 571
Family Rosary, Inc., 576
Family Rosary Center, Africa, 82
Family Theater, 595
Famine, International Conference,
  74
Fan Xueyan, Peter Joseph, Bp., 102
Farley, James A. (Catholics in
  Presidents' Cabinets), 412
Farley, John (U.S. Cardinals), 168, 475
Farmer, Ferdinand, 390
Faroe Islands, 342
Fasani, Francis, St., 252
Fast, Eucharistic, 309
Fast Days, 238
Father, 309
Father Flanagan's Boys Town, 556
Father Justin Rosary Hour, 595
Father McKenna Award, 598
Fathers, Church, 197
Fathers of Mercy, 498
Fatima, 264
Favalora, John C., Bp., 39, 451
Fear, 309
Feast Days, 238, 246-49
Feast of Weeks, 290
Feasts, Movable, 238, 239
Febres Cordero, Miguel, St., 255
Febronianism (1764), 119
Fecteau, Clement, Bp., 385
Federal, Joseph L., Bp., 451
Federal Aid to Education, 528
  See also Church-State Decisions
Federation of Diocesan Liturgical
  Commissions, 576
Felhauer, David E., Bp., 451¡
Felici, Angelo, Card., 157, 167, 168
Felician Sisters (Sisters of St. Felix),
  508
Felicity, St. (Perpetua and Felicity, Sts.),
  256
Fellowship of Catholic Scholars, 576,
  598
  Cardinal Wright Award, 598
Feminism, Extreme, 99
Ferdinand III, St., 252
Fernandez, Joseph A., 81
Fernando Po, see Equatorial Guinea
Ferrario, Joseph A., Bp., 100, 451
Festival of Lights (Hanukkah), 290
Fetus, Tissue Transplant Network, 84,

Fiacre (Fiachra), St., 252
Fidei Despositum (Catechism of the
  Catholic Church), 39-40
Fidelis of Sigmaringen, St., 252
Fidelitas Medal, 598
Fides (Mission News Service), 594
Fifth Centenary of Evangelization of
  Americas, 46-9
Fiji, 342
Filevich, Basil (Wasyl), Bp., 385
Filippini, Religious Teachers, 508
Films, Catholic, see Television
Finger Towel, 216
Finland, 342
Finlay, James C., S.J., Rev., 600
Fiorenza, Joseph A., Bp., 451
First Amendment (Wall of Separation),
  416
  See also Church-State Decisions
First Catholic Slovak Ladies
  Association, 576
First Catholic Slovak Union (Jednota),
  576
First Friday, 309
First Saturday, 309
Fisher, Carl, S.S.J., Bp. (Death), 600
Fisher, John, St., 254
Fisherman's Ring, 309
Fitzmyer, Joseph A., S.J., 80
Fitzpatrick, John J., Bp., 451
Fitzsimons, George K., Bp., 451
FitzSimons, Thomas, 395
Flag, Papal, 176
Flaget, Benedict, 390
Flanagan, Bernard J., Bp., 451
Flavin, Glennon P., Bp., 451
Fliss, Raphael M., Bp., 451
Flood Relief, 101
Florence, Council (1431-45), 118, 123
Flores, Patrick, Abp., 451
Florida, 393, 400, 428, 432, 434, 438,
  444, 529, 538, 546-47, 556, 558, 564
  Shrine to Mary, Queen of Universe,
    105, 427
  Hurricane Andrew, 108
Floyd, John B. (Catholics in Presidents'
  Cabinets), 411
Flynn, Harry J., Bp., 451
Flynn, Raymond, 100, 108, 178
Focolare Movement, 95, 372, 522
Foi et Lumiere, 372
Foley, David E., Bp., 451-52
Foley, John Patrick, Abp., 150, 452
  See also Social Communications
    Council
Foreign Mission Society of America,
  Catholic (Maryknoll), 498
Foreign Missions, U.S. Personnel, 524-26
  American Bishops, 427
Foreign Missions, St. Joseph's Society
  for (Mill Hill Missionaries), 498
Forester Youth Program, 572
Foresters, Catholic Order of, 575
Forgiveness of Sin, 309
  See also Confession; Penance
Formosa, see Taiwan
Forst, Marion F., Bp., 452
Fortier, Jean-Marie, Abp., 385
Fortitude, 309
Fortune Telling, 309
Forty Hours Devotion, 309-10
Forum, 310
Foster, Vincent W., Jr., 600
Fougere, Joseph Vernon, Bp., 385
Foundations and Donors Interested in
  Catholic Activities, 576
Four Books of Sentences (1160), 117
Fox, Matthew, Rev., 42-3, 83
France, 342-43, 368
  Anti-Immigrant Attitudes, 98
  Religious Sanctions (1901), 121
  Revolution (1789), 120
Frances of Rome, St., 252
Frances Xavier Cabrini, St., 85, 252
Francis, Joseph A., S.V.D., Bp., 452
Francis, St., Assisi, 252
  See also Crib; Portiuncula

Ryan, Daniel L., Bp., 465
Ryan, James C., O.F.M., Bp., 465
Ryan, Joseph T., Abp., 465
Ryan, Sylvester D., Bp., 465

S

Sabatini, Lawrence, C.S., Bp., 387
Sabattani, Aurelio, Card., 164, 167, 168
Sabbah, Michel, Patriarch, 74, 89-90,
    106, 178
Sabbath, 324
Sabbath (Jewish), 290
Sabellianism (c. 260), 113
Sacrament, Blessed, see Blessed
    Sacrament
Sacrament, Sisters of Most Holy, 518
Sacramental Forum, see Forum
Sacramentals, 210
Sacramentary, 219, 324
Sacramentine Nuns, 518
Sacraments, 223-33
    Congregation, 147
    Eastern Churches, 266
    Grace, 311
    Liturgical Developments, 220
Sacraments and Polish National
    Catholics, 289
Sacrarium, 324
Sacred Heart (June 10, 1994), 242, 249
    Enthronement, 324
    Promises, 324-25
Sacred Heart, Brothers of, 499
Sacred Heart, Missionaries of, 499
Sacred Heart Catholic Univ. (Italy), 540
Sacred Heart Fathers and Brothers,
    499-500
Sacred Heart League, 580
Sacred Heart, Sisters (list), 518
Sacred Heart of Mary, Religious, 518
Sacred Heart Program, 595
Sacred Hearts of Jesus and Mary, Congr.
    of, 500
Sacred Scripture, see Bible
Sacrifice of Mass, see Mass
Sacrilege, 325
Sacristy, 325
Sacrosanctum Concilium, 123
    See also Liturgy Constitution
Sacrum Diaconatus Ordinem, see
    Deacon, Permanent
Sadducees, 325
Sahagun, Bernardino de, 391
Saint
    Anne de Beaupre, Shrine, 388
    Ann's Church, Vatican City, 176
    Ansgar's Scandinavian Catholic
        League, 580
    Anthony's Guild, 562, 580
    Christopher and Nevis, 358
    Elizabeth Ann Seton Medal, 599
    Francis de Sales Award, 599
    Genesius Award, 598
    Gregory Foundation for Latin Liturgy,
        580
    Helena, 358
    Joan's International Alliance, 373
    Joseph's Oratory Shrine, 388
    Joseph's University of Beirut, 540
    Jude League, 580
    Lucia, 358
    Margaret of Scotland Guild, 580
    Martin de Porres Guild, 580
    Patrick's College, Maynooth (Ireland),
        540
    Patrick's Day, 81
    Paul's University, Ottawa, 540
    Pierre and Miquelon, 358
    Thomas of Villanueva Univ. (Cuba),
        540
    Vincent and Grenadines (West Indies),
        358
    Vincent de Paul Medal, 599
    Vincent de Paul Society, 545
Saint-Antoine, Jude, Bp., 387
Saint-Gelais, Raymond, Bp., 387
Saints, 325
    Biographical Sketches, 249-57

Saints
    Canonization, 299-300
    Canonized since Leo XIII, 140-42
    Commemorations in Calendar, 237-38,
        240-45
    Communion of, 303
    Congregation for Causes of, 147
    Cult, 325
    Emblems, 259-60
    Patrons, 257-59
    Veneration, 325
    See also Proper Names of Individual
        Saints
Salamanca, University of (Spain), 540
Salatka, Charles, Abp., 465
Saldarini, Giovanni, Card., 164, 167, 168
Sales, Eugenio de Araujo, Card., 164,
    167, 168
Salesian Cooperators, 573
Salesian Sisters (Daughters of Mary
    Help of Christians), 514
Salesians of St. John Bosco, 500
Salesianum, Pontifical University, 542
Salinas de Gortari, Carlos, Pres.
    (Mexico), see Mexico, Papal Visit
Saltarelli, Michael A., Bp., 465
Salvation, 325
Salvation History, 325
Salvation outside the Church, 325
Salvatorian Fathers, Basilian, 493
Salvatorians, 500
Samoa, American, 358, 431, 532
Samoa, Western, 359
Samra, Nicholas J., Bp., 465
Samuel, 189
San Marino, 359
Sanchez, Jose T., Card., 164, 167, 168
Sanchez, Robert, Abp., 88, 465
    Resignation, 88
Sanctifying Grace, 311
    See also Sacraments
Sanctuary, 217
Sanctuary Lamp, 217
San Pedro, Enrique, S.J., Bp., 465
Sanschagrin, Albert, O.M.I., Bp., 387
Santo Tomas University (Philippines),
    540
Santeria Rituals, 97
Santos, Alexandre Maria dos, O.F.M.,
    Card., 164, 167, 168
Sao Paulo University (Brazil), 540
Sao Tome and Principe, 358, 368
Sarajevo, see Bosnia
Satan (Devil), 306
Satanism, 325
Satowaki, Joseph Asajiro, Card., 164,
    167, 168
Saudi Arabia, 359
Saul (Historical Books of the Bible), 189
Savior, see Jesus
Savior, Company of the, 518
Scalabrinians (Missionaries of St.
    Charles), 498
Scalia, Antonin (Catholic Justice,
    Supreme Court), 412
Scandal, 325
Scandinavia, Catholic-Lutheran
    Relations, 106
Scandinavia, Episcopal Conference, 370
Scanlan, John J., Bp., 465
Scapular, 325
    Medal, 326
    Promise, 326
Scarpone Caporale, Gerald, O.F.M., Bp.,
    465
Schad, James L., Bp., 465
Schaluck, Hermann, O.F.M., Rev., 90
Scheiber, Richard P., 600
Scherer, Alfred Vicente, Card., 165, 167,
    168
Scheut Fathers, see Immaculate Heart
    Missioners
Schism, Schismatic, 326
Schism, Western, 129
Schladweiler, Alphonse, Bp., 465
Schlaefer Berg, Salvator, O.F.M. Cap.,
    Bp., 465

Schlarman, Stanley G., Bp., 465
Schlotterback, Edward, O.S.F.S., Bp.,
    465
Schmidt, Firmin M., O.F.M. Cap., Bp.,
    465
Schmitt, Bernard W., Bp., 465
Schmitt, Mark, Bp., 465-66
Schmitz Simon, Paul, O.F.M. Cap., Bp.,
    466
Schoenherr, Walter J., Bp., 466
Schoenstatt Sisters of Mary, 522
Scholastica, St., 256
Scholasticism, 326
Schools, Catholic (U.S.), 528-39
    Aid, 528
    Blue Ribbon, 101
    Colleges and Universities, 533-38
    for Handicapped, 555-60
    Legal Status, 528
    NCEA, 528
    Remedial Education (Aguilar v.
        Felton), 415
    Shared Time, 528
    Statistics, 529-32
    See also Religious Education;
        Seminaries
Schools, Public, see Public Schools
Schuck, James A., O.F.M., Bp., 600
Schulte, Francis B., Abp., 466
Schuster, Eldon, Bp., 466
Schwery, Henri, Card., 165, 167,
    168
Schweitz, Roger L., O.M.I., Bp., 466
Science and Religion, 88
Sciences, Pontifical Academy, 543-44
Scotland, 358-59, 370
Scribes, 326
Scripture, see Bible
Scruple, 326
Sea, Apostleship of, 571
Seal of Confession, 326
Seasons, Church, 237
Sebastian, St., 256
Sebastian Aparicio, Bl., 389
Second Vatican Council, see Council,
    Second Vatican
Secretariat of State, Vatican, 146-47
Sects, Guatemala, 78
Secular (Diocesan) Clergy, 303
    Statistics (World), 367
    See also Individual Countries
Secular Institutes, 520-22
    Congregation (Institutes of
        Consecrated Life and Societies of
        Apostolic Life), 148
    World Conference, 521
Secular (Third) Orders, 523
Secularism, 326
Sede Vacante, see Interregnum
See, 326
Seelos, Francis X., 391
Seghers, Charles J., 391
Sellinger, Joseph A., S.J., 600
Seminarians
    Countries of the World, 332-66
    United States, 76, 85, 436
    World (Summary), 367
Seminaries, U.S., 538-39
Seminaries and Institutes of Study,
    Congregation, 148
Seminary, 326
Semi-Pelagianism (431, 529), 114
Senegal, 359, 370
Senses of the Bible (Interpretation),
    194-95
Sensi, Giuseppe Maria, Card., 165, 167,
    168
Separated and Divorced Catholics,
    Pastoral Ministry, 235-36
Separation, Marriage, 234
Septuagint Bible, 187
Seraphim (Angels), 296-97
Serbs, see Bosnia-Herzegovina, Croatia,
    Yugoslavia
Serbs (Byzantine Rite), 268
Sermon on the Mount, 326
Serra, Junipero, Bl., 391

VERITATIS SPLENDOR: ENCYCLICAL ON MORAL THEOLOGY

Veritatis Splendor ("The Splendor of Truth") is the title of Pope John Paul's 10th encyclical letter, the first of its kind ever issued on the foundations of moral theology.

The letter is focused on Scripture — the commandments and discipleship of Christ — as the central framework for understanding Christian morality. It is a repudiation of moral theories that would relativize truth or universal norms and/or would absolutize freedom.

The letter, published Oct. 5, 1993, is addressed to bishops as the Church's chief teachers and guardians of doctrine.

In introductory comments, the Pope said he wrote the encyclical because today "certain fundamental truths of Catholic doctrine . . . risk being distorted or denied" by flawed moral theories. "It is no longer a matter of limited and occasional dissent, but of an overall and systematic calling into question of traditional moral doctrine on the basis of certain anthropological and ethical presuppositions. . . . The enduring absoluteness of any moral value" is called into question, and "man is no longer convinced that only in the truth can he find salvation."

Among moral theories repudiated by the Pope are any which would allow exceptions to the "negative precepts" of natural law and the commandments, such as prohibitions against murder, stealing and adultery. "The negative commandments oblige always and under all circumstances. . . . Jesus himself affirms that these prohibitions allow no exceptions," he wrote. He reaffirmed church teaching that certain acts are "intrinsically evil" and therefore always wrong.

90TH YEAR OF THE ALMANAC

The 1994 edition of the *Catholic Almanac*, published by Our Sunday Visitor, Inc., marks the 90th anniversary of its printing history. It is the 87th edition; no volumes were published in 1930, 1934 and 1935.

The *Catholic Almanac* originated remotely from *St. Antony's Almanac*, a 64-page annual with calendar, feature and devotional contents, published by the Franciscans of Holy Name Province from 1904 to 1929. *The Franciscan Almanac* was the title of the completely revised work published in 1931 by *The Franciscan Magazine*. A volume of 320 pages, it represented a radical change from previous edi-

tions and inaugurated content development that has continued to the present time.

The current 600-page edition is a one-of-a-kind factual handbook of basic and contemporary information on an encyclopedic range of subjects pertaining to the Catholic Church and its activity in the world.

St. Anthony's Guild published the book from 1936 to 71. Editions from 1940 to 1968 were issued under the title *The National Catholic Almanac;* the present title was adopted in 1969. Editions from 1959 to 1971 were produced jointly by St. Anthony's Guild and Doubleday & Co., Inc.

POPE JOHN PAUL IN JAMAICA, MEXICO AND DENVER

Pope John Paul, on the 60th foreign trip of his pontificate Aug. 9 to 15, 1993, visited Jamaica, Mexico and Denver, Colorado — where he encountered several hundreds of thousands of young people for the celebration of World Youth Day '93.

ITINERARY

In Jamaica

Aug. 9: Arrival at Norman Manley International Airport, Kingston; visit to house for the poor run by Mother Teresa's Missionaries of Charity; meetings with government officials.

Aug. 10: In Kingston, prayer service with priests, deacons, seminarians, men and women religious at the Cathedral of the Most Holy Trinity; meeting with lay people at St. George College; ecumenical Liturgy of the Word at Holy Cross Church; celebration of Mass at National Stadium.

In Mexico

Aug. 11: Departure from Kingston, arrival at Merida airport. At Izamal, meeting with representatives of indigenous communities at the Sanctuary of Our Lady of Izamal. In Merida, meeting with President Carlos Salinas de Gortari; celebration of Mass.

In Mexico, Denver

Aug. 12: Departure from Merida, arrival in Denver. Meeting with President Clinton at Regis University; welcome by 90,000 youths in Mile High Stadium.

From the time of his arrival, Pope John Paul's agenda was closely related to the program of the Youth Day celebration.

Young people had their own round of activities ranging from quiet time alone and group time for prayer, reception of the sacraments of penance and the Eucharist, catechetical discussions, making friends, enjoying music and other youthful diversions. Two exceptional events were their observance of Friday as a day of sacrifice, resulting in contributions to a Uganda hospital treating children with AIDS, and participation by many in a 15-mile pilgrimage-hike to the site of the all-night vigil of Aug. 14.

In Denver

Aug. 13: Celebration of Mass with U.S. bishops at the Denver cathedral; time for privacy and rest at Camp St. Malo, an archdiocesan retreat 70 miles north of Denver; his taped message was broadcast to 70,000 youths making the Way of the Cross at Mile High Stadium.

Aug. 14: Celebration of Mass for delegates to the International Youth Forum and representatives of U.S. dioceses; Liturgy of the Word for 18,000 people of the Archdiocese of Denver; participation in all-night vigil of 250,000 youths at Cherry Creek State Park.

Aug. 15: Celebration of Mass for youths attended by 400,000 people at Cherry Creek State Park; meeting with 10,000 Vietnamese Catholics; visit with children at Mt. St. Vincent Home; meeting with Vice President Al Gore before evening departure from Stapleton International Airport for Rome.

REPORT BY THE POPE

The following report on the trip to Jamaica, Mexico and Denver was made by the Pope during a general audience Aug. 18, 1993.

These excerpts are from the text published in the Aug. 25 English edition of "L'Osservatore Romano." Subheads have been added.

"I have come that they may have life, and have it abundantly" (Jn. 10:10).

This was the main theme of the world youth meeting that took place several days ago in Denver, Colorado, in the center of the United States of America.

On 12 October last year, America initiated the celebrations commemorating the fifth centenary of the evangelization that had begun precisely on 12 October 1492 in Santo Domingo. The youth meeting in Denver took place toward the end of the jubilee year commemorating this important event. Therefore, it is an integral part of the celebrations for that fifth centenary, taking its point of departure precisely from that very theme: Evangelization, Life in Christ, the Fullness of Life.

The first stop on the apostolic journey was Kingston, the capital of Jamaica. The visit to the home of the poor run by Mother Teresa of Calcutta's sisters was particularly moving; and there were warm meetings with priests and religious in Holy Trinity Cathedral, with the laity in the auditorium of St. George's College, and with representatives of the Anglican and Protestant denominations and of the Jewish community in the parish church of Holy Cross.

My stay in Jamaica concluded with a solemn Eucharistic celebration in the National Stadium. In recalling the great evils caused by the slave trade, which trampled on the dignity of the human person, the image of God, I emphasized in the homily the basic values of marriage and the Christian family, values proclaimed by the Gospel and constantly reiterated by the Church's magisterium.

Church Worked To Support the Indigenous

I then went to the Mexican Peninsula of Yucatan, specifically, to Izamal and Merida, where, in the context of the fifth centenary of the evangelization of the New World, I wanted to pay due homage to the descendants of those living on the American continent at the time when the cross of Christ was erected there, 12 October 1492. A "pilgrim" for the third time in Mexico, I wanted to reconfirm my solidarity and that of the whole Church with the joys and sufferings of the great, noble Mexican people.

At the shrine of Our Lady of Izamal, dedicated to the Immaculate Conception, "Queen and Patroness of Yucatan," and built on the foundations of a

Mayan pyramid, a significant meeting took place with the indigenous people. I extended my greeting to the peoples and ethnic groups of America, from North to South, from Alaska to Tierra del Fuego, naming each of them. In mentioning the Mayan culture, as well as the Aztec and Incan, I intended to underscore how the ancestral values and sacred vision of life were open to the Gospel message and, at the same time, to recall the Church's work in defending the Indios and in supporting the local people when they were threatened with mistreatment and abuse.

The solemn Eucharistic celebration in Merida on the esplanade of Xoclan-Mulsay concluded my stay in Mexico.

World Youth Days

The stop in Denver was important, for it allowed me to meet thousands and thousands of young people, who were more numerous than expected. I prayed and reflected with them on the theme of the life flowing from Christ. With them I was able to look hopefully at the present and, particularly, to the future, despite the difficulties humanity is experiencing in this unique period of its history.

In fact the World Youth Days arose from the desire to offer young people significant "rest stops" on their continuing pilgrimage of faith, which is also nourished by meeting contemporaries from other countries and comparing respective experiences.

The annual celebrations of this "Day" mark, as it were, pauses for reflection and examination on this journey of faith and evangelization, times for common prayer and meditation on themes studied in advance within youth associations, movements and groups at the parish and diocesan levels.

Thus, young people feel they are on a continual pilgrimage on the highways of the world. In them, the Church sees herself and her mission in the midst of mankind; with them, she welcomes the great challenges of the future, aware that all humanity needs a renewed youthfulness of spirit.

How could we not thank God for the fruits of the genuine renewal produced by these World Youth Days? From the first meeting, held at St. Peter's Square on Palm Sunday of 1986, a tradition began that has seen world and diocesan meetings in alternating years, as if to emphasize the indispensable vigor of young peoples' apostolic commitment at both the local and universal level. Since that time there has been a meeting every two years: in Buenos Aires, Argentina; Santiago de Compostela, Spain; and Czestochowa, Poland.

Appropriate Meeting Place

It was fitting for us to meet this year in America at the end of the fifth centenary of the evangelization of that continent, in order to give witness to the urgent need to break down the "walls" of poverty and injustice, of indifference and selfishness, so that an open and welcoming world can be built, one based on Christ, who came to earth so that mankind "may have life and have it abundantly."

The most interesting aspect of the Denver gathering was certainly the response of the young people, who came from all the dioceses of the United States and from every continent to show their openness to the life that is Christ. They came to pray. At the various meetings they showed a deep awareness of God's presence in their lives. Significant moments were the Way of the Cross, the Mass for the delegates to the International Youth Forum and, especially, the vigil and the solemn Mass on the feast of the Assumption.

This great pilgrimage of young people did not have a shrine for its destination, but a modern city. In the heart of this "metropolis," the world's young people proclaimed their identity as Catholics and their desire to build human relationships based on the truth and values of the Gospel. They gathered in Denver to say "yes" to life and to peace, against the threats of death that jeopardize the culture of life. The true center of the Eighth World Youth Day was the young people themselves.

I entrust the expectations and spiritual fruits of World Youth Day to the intercession of Mary assumed into heaven. May she lead and encourage young people to continue their pilgrimage of faith and prepare them for the next World Youth Day, which will take place in Manila at the beginning of 1995.

EXCERPTS FROM ADDRESSES IN JAMAICA AND MEXICO

These two excerpts—from addresses delivered by the Pope on his arrival Aug. 9 at Kingston and at the Marian shrine at Izamal Aug. 11 — are from texts published Aug. 18 and 25, respectively, in English editions of "L'Osservatore Romano."

Christian Witness and Fault

The first evangelization of the Americas was the beginning of the Church's presence in this part of the world, a presence made up of holiness of life and the witness of Christian charity on the part of many, but also of the faults and sins of others. In fact, last year divine Providence also enabled me to visit Goree in Senegal where there is a striking monument to the tragic enslavement of millions of African men, women and children, uprooted from their homes and separated from their loved ones to be sold as merchandise. The immensity of their suffering corresponds to the enormity of the crime committed against them: the denial of their human dignity. Goree was the appropriate place to implore heaven's forgiveness in the name of humanity, and to pray that human beings will learn to look at one another and respect one another as God's image, in order to love one another as sons and daughters of their common Father in heaven.

Now, here in Jamaica, I wish to remember the original Arawak people and your ancestors who were brought here from Africa. Let us pray that the wounds of past experiences will at last be healed and that everyone will work, with full respect for each person's dignity, for a future in which justice, peace and solidarity will leave no room for hatred or discrimination.

Ethnic Fellowship without Frontiers

Today's message is addressed not only to those present, but goes far beyond the borders of the Yucatan to embrace all the communities, ethnic groups and indigenous peoples of America: from the Peninsula of Alaska to Tierra del Fuego.

With the eyes of faith I see in you the generations of men and women who have preceded you throughout history, and I want to express once again all the love the Church has for you. You are the heirs of the peoples — the Tupi-Guarani, Aymara, Maya, Quechua, Chibcha, Nahualt, Mixtec, Araucan, Yanomami, Guajiro, Inuit, Apache and so many others — who were the creators of glorious cultures such as the Aztec, Mayan, and Incan. Your ancestral values and your vision of life, which recognizes the sacredness of the human being and the world, led you, through the Gospel, to open your hearts to Jesus, who is "the Way, the Truth and the Life" (Jn. 14:6).

I feel it is my duty to call for solidarity, for fellowship without frontiers. The knowledge that we are all children of the same God, redeemed by the blood of Jesus Christ, must move you, under the impulse of faith, to foster in solidarity the necessary conditions which can make the societies in which you live a place that is more just and fraternal for all. This solidarity, to which I invite you as Pastor of the universal Church, has its roots not in doubtful or passing ideologies, but in the lasting truth of the Good News which Jesus brings us.

YOUTH DAY CELEBRATIONS: EVENTS AND ADDRESSES

The following excerpts are from texts circulated by the CNS Documentary Service, Origins, Aug. 26, 1993 (Vol. 23, No. 11).

The President and the Pope

Pope John Paul was greeted by President Clinton on his arrival Aug. 12 at Denver's Stapleton International Airport. The President said:

"America is a better, stronger, more just nation because of the influence that you have had on our world in recent years and because of the influence that American Catholics have had on our nation from the very beginning."

"We know that you were the force to light the spark of freedom over communism in your native Poland and throughout Eastern Europe — that you have been an advocate for peace and justice among nations and peoples."

After their meeting, Clinton welcomed "the Vatican's commitment to human rights, including religious freedom for all." He also alluded to some of the international topics they talked about.

Pope John Paul responded:

"I greatly appreciate your generous words of welcome. The World Youth Day being celebrated this year in Denver gives me the opportunity to meet you, and through you to express once again to the American people my sentiments of deep esteem and friendship."

"The well-being of the world's children and young people must be of immense concern to all who have public responsibilities. In my pastoral visits to the Church in every part of the world, I have been deeply moved by the almost universal conditions of difficulty in which young people grow up and live. Too many sufferings are visited upon them . . ."

"But how do we help them? Only by instilling a high moral vision can a society ensure that its young people are given the possibility to mature as free and intelligent human beings, endowed with a robust sense of responsibility to the common good, capable of working with others to create a community and a nation with a strong moral fiber."

After their private meeting at Regis University, the Pope said he was pleased at the opportunity to speak with the President, and added:

"The inalienable dignity of every human being and the rights which flow from that dignity — in the first place, the right to life and the defense of life — as well as the well-being and full human development of individuals and peoples, are at the heart of the themes on which the Church seeks a sincere and constructive dialogue with the leaders of the world's nations and representatives of the international community. I look forward to further contacts in the future, in the same spirit of mutual understanding and esteem which has always characterized relations between the United States and the Holy See."

Pilgrimage to Metropolis

At Mile High Stadium before an enthusiastic, cheering throng of 90,000 young people, the Pope said:

"Pilgrims set out for a destination. In our case, it is not so much a place or a shrine that we seek to honor. Ours is a pilgrimage to a modern city, a symbolic destination. The 'metropolis' is the place which determines the life-style and the history of a large part of the human family at the end of the 20th century. This modern city of Denver is set in the beautiful natural surroundings of the Rocky Mountains, as if to put the work of human hands in relationship with the work of the Creator. We are therefore searching for the reflection of God not only in the beauty of nature but also in humanity's achievements and in each individual person. On this pilgrimage our steps are guided by the words of Jesus Christ: 'I came that they may have life, and have it abundantly (Jn. 10:10).'"

"The World Youth Day challenges you to be fully conscious of who you are as God's dearly beloved sons and daughters."

"Each one must have the courage to go and spread the Good News among the people of the last part of the 20th century, in particular among young people of your own age, who will take the Church and society into the next century."

Readiness To Help

At Mass with cardinals and bishops from various countries, the Pope asked:

"Are we always ready to help the young people discover the transcendent elements of the Christian life? From our words and actions do they conclude that the Church is indeed a mystery of communion with the blessed Trinity, and not just a human institution with temporal aims? Through our ministry, the young people present here need to be able to discover, above all, that they are temples of God and that the Spirit of God dwells in them (cf. 1 Cor. 3:16)."

Courage Needed

In a taped message broadcast to 70,000 youths taking part in the Way of the Cross in Mile High Stadium, the Pope urged them to "take courage in the face of life's difficulties and injustices," and commit themselves "to the struggle for justice, solidarity and peace in the world." He exhorted them to be "witnesses of God's love for the innocent and the weak, for the poor and the oppressed."

Youth Apostolate in the Church

In an address to about 300 International Youth Forum delegates and a greater number of diocesan representatives, the Pope observed:

"Young people need to be able to see the practical relevance of their efforts to meet the real needs of people, especially the poor and neglected. They should be able to see that their apostolate belongs fully to the Church's mission in the world."

"As leaders in the field of the youth apostolate, (forum personnel) will have to find ways of involving young people in projects and activities of formation, spirituality and service, giving them responsibility for themselves and their work, and taking care to avoid isolating them and their apostolate from the rest of the ecclesial community."

In making a commitment to the new evangelization, "it is not enough to offer a 'merely human wisdom, a pseudoscience of well-being.' We must be convinced that we have 'a pearl of great price,'a great treasure.'"

Moral Questions

Sexual abuse of children by clergy and moral questions were among the themes of a talk by the Holy Father to a congregation of people from Colorado.

The Church in the United States is vital and dynamic, rich in "faith and love and holiness" (1 Tm. 2:15), the Pope said. " By far the vast majority of her bishops, priests, religious and laity are dedicated followers of Christ and generous servants of the Gospel message of love. Nevertheless, at a time when all institutions are suspect, the Church herself has not escaped reproach. I have already written to the bishops of the United States about the pain of the suffering and scandal caused by the sins of some ministers of the altar. Sad situations such as these invite us anew to look at the mystery of the Church with the eyes of faith. While every human means for responding to this evil must be implemented, we cannot forget that the first and most important means is prayer: ardent, humble, confident prayer. America needs much prayer — lest it lose its soul."

On many questions, especially with regard to moral questions, "the teaching of the Church in our day is placed in a social and cultural context which renders it more difficult to understand and yet more urgent and irreplaceable for promoting the true good of men and women (*Familiaris Consortio*, 30). Nowhere is this more evident than in questions relating to the transmission of human life and to the inalienable right to life of the unborn."

"When the question is asked, What is to be done (about contemporary moral and social problems)? everybody must be committed to fostering a profound sense of the value of life and the dignity of the human person. The whole of society must work to change the structural conditions which lead people, especially the young, to the lack of vision, the loss of esteem for themselves and for others which leads to violence. But, since the root of violence is in the human heart, society will be condemned to go on causing it, feeding it and even, to an extent, glorifying it, unless it reaffirms the moral and religious truths which alone are an effective barrier to lawlessness and violence, because these truths alone are capable of enlightening and strengthening conscience. Ultimately, it is the victory of grace over sin that leads to fraternal harmony and reconciliation."

Responsibility for the World

During the prayer vigil in Cherry Creek State Park, the Pope said:

"The special place of human beings in all that God made lies in their being given a share in God's own concern and providence for the whole of creation. The Creator has entrusted the world to us as a gift and as a responsibility. He who is eternal Providence, the one who guides the entire universe toward its final destiny, made us in his image and likeness so that we too should become 'providence' — a wise and intelligent providence, guiding human development and the development of the world along the path of harmony with the Creator's will, for the well-being of the human family and the fulfillment of each individual's transcendent calling."

"False models of progress have led to endangering the earth's proper ecological balance. Man — made in the image and likeness of the Creator — was meant to be the good shepherd of the environment in which he exists and lives. . . . In recent times man himself has become the destroyer of his own natural environment. In some places this has already happened or is happening."

Anti-Life Mentality

"But not only that. There is spreading, too, an anti-life mentality — an attitude of hostility to life in the womb and life in its last stages. Precisely when science and medicine are achieving a greater capacity to safeguard health and life, the threats against life are becoming more insidious. Abortion and euthanasia — the actual killing of another human being — are hailed as 'rights' and solutions to 'problems' — an individual's problem, or society's. The slaughter of the innocents is no less sinful and devastating simply because it is done in a legal and scientific way. In the modern metropolis, life — God's first gift, and the fundamental right of every individual, on which all other rights are based — is often treated as just one more commodity to be organized, commercialized and manipulated according to convenience."

"Christ the Good Shepherd ... sees so many young people throwing away their lives in a flight into irresponsibility and falsehood. Drug and alcohol abuse, pornography and sexual disorder, violence: these are grave social problems which call for a serious response from the whole of society, within each country and on the international level. But they are also personal tragedies, and they need to be met with concrete interpersonal acts of love and solidarity in a great rebirth of the sense of personal answerability before God, before others and before our own conscience. We are our brothers' keepers! (cf. Gn. 4:9)."

Manipulation of Conscience

"In a technological culture in which people are used to dominating matter, discovering its laws and mechanisms in order to transform it according to their wishes, the danger arises of also wanting to manipulate conscience and its demands. In a culture which holds that no universally valid truths are possible, nothing is absolute. Therefore, in the end — they say — objective goodness and evil no longer really matter. Good comes to mean what is pleasing or useful at a particular moment. Evil means what contradicts our subjective wishes. Each person can build a private system of values."

"Young people, do not give in to this widespread false morality. Do not stifle your conscience."

"A rebirth of conscience must come from two sources: first, the effort to know objective truth with certainty, including the truth about God; and second, the light of faith in Jesus Christ, who alone has the words of life."

"In order to have life and have it abundantly, in order to restore the original harmony of creation, we must respect that divine image in all of creation and, in a special way, in human life itself."

Youth Day a Celebration of Life

At Cherry Creek State Park Aug. 15, the Holy Father celebrated Mass before one of the largest-ever assemblies of young people in the United States. He called the Youth Day event a celebration of life.

"The Eighth World Youth Day is a celebration of life. This gathering has been the occasion for a serious reflection on the words of Jesus Christ: 'I came that they may have life, and have it abundantly' (Jn. 10:10). Young people from every corner of the world, in ardent prayer you have opened your hearts to the truth of Christ's promise of new life. Through the sacraments, especially penance and the Eucharist, and by means of the unity and friendship created among so many, you have had a real and transforming experience of the new life which only Christ can give. You, young pilgrims, have also shown that you understand that Christ's gift of life is not for you alone. You have become more conscious of your vocation and mission in the Church and in the world."

A Culture of Death

"A 'culture of death' seeks to impose itself on our desire to live and live to the full. There are those who reject the light of life, preferring 'the fruitless works of darkness' (Eph. 5:11). Their harvest is injustice, discrimination, exploitation, deceit, violence. In every age, a measure of their apparent success is the death of innocents. In our own century, as at no other time in history, the 'culture of death' has assumed a social and institutional form of legality to justify the most horrible crimes against humanity: genocide, 'final solutions,' 'ethnic cleansings,' and the massive 'taking of lives of human beings even before they are born or before they reach the natural point of death.'"

"In much of contemporary thinking, any reference to a 'law' guaranteed by the Creator is absent. There remains only each individual's choice of this or that objective as convenient or useful in a given set of circumstances. No longer is anything considered intrinsically 'good' and 'universally binding.' Rights are affirmed but, because they are without any reference to an objective truth, they are deprived of any solid basis. ... Vast sectors of society are confused about what is right and what is wrong, and are at the mercy of those with the power to 'create' opinion and impose it on others."

Mission To Evangelize

"At this stage of history, the liberating message of the Gospel of life has been put into your hands. And the mission of proclaiming it to the ends of the earth is now passing to your generation. Like the great Apostle Paul, you too must feel the full urgency of the task. 'Woe to me if I do not evangelize' (1 Cor. 9:16). Woe to you if you do not succeed in defending life. The Church needs your energies, your enthusiasm, your youthful ideals, in order to make the Gospel of life penetrate the fabric of society, transforming peoples' hearts and the structures of society in order to create a civilization of true justice and love. Now more than ever, in a world that is often without light and without the courage of noble ideals, people need the fresh, vital spirituality of the Gospel."

"Do not be afraid to go out on the streets and into public places like the first Apostles, who preached Christ and the Good News of salvation in the squares of cities, towns and villages. This is no time to be ashamed of the Gospel (cf. Rom. 1:16). It is the time to preach it from the rooftops (cf. Mt 10:27). Do not be afraid to break out of comfortable and routine modes of living in order to take up the challenge of making Christ known in the modern 'metropolis.' It is you who 'must go out into the byroads' (Mt. 22:9) and invite everyone you meet to the banquet which God has prepared for his people. The Gospel must not be kept hidden because of fear or indifference. It was never meant to be hidden away in private. It has to be put on a stand so that people may see its light and give praise to our heavenly Father (cf. Mt. 5:15-16)."

The Challenge of Healing

In an address to 10,000 Vietnamese, the Pope said: "Perhaps the greatest challenge of the present is to heal any ill feeling or divisions which have grown up between citizens of the same country. Too much suffering has left profound wounds."

He urged Vietnamese-American Catholics,

thought to number about 150,000 in the US, to "help restore and rebuild churches, seminaries, convents, schools, hospitals and other institutions which have no other aim but to serve the needs of the Vietnamese people" in Vietnam. Reconstruction would be possible only "with the cooperation of everyone, and this in turn calls for mutual respect, forgiveness and unity of purpose."

Concern for Children

The Pope's last visit of the trip was to St. Vincent's Home, run by Sisters of Charity of Leavenworth, for children aged 5 to 14 with emotional and behavioral problems. He said:

"Concern for the child even before birth, from the first moment of conception and then throughout the years of infancy and youth, is the primary and fundamental test of the relationship of one human being to another."

He appealed to national and international leaders to protect the rights of children: "There exists the Convention on the Rights of the Child, adopted at the United Nations in 1989 and already signed by many states, including the Holy See. I hope that more and more states will ensure the juridical force and practical application of the convention, so that no child on earth will be left without the legal guarantee of his or her fundamental rights."

Farewell

Vice President Al Gore bade farewell to the Pope Aug. 15, saying that Americans shared his concern about human needs that have not been met throughout the world. He said: "We do not only want change. What good is change if it is devoid of vision? Rather, we want to be guided by tradition and the timeless values like those contained within the teachings of the church."

Gore, a leading environmentalist, called the Pope "a powerful and penetrating ally for those who make ecological awareness our cause."

A Culture of Life

"For believers," said the Holy Father, "commitment to the spiritual and moral renewal which society needs is a gift of the Spirit of the Lord, who fills the whole earth, for it is the Spirit who offers man the light and the strength to measure up to his supreme destiny. This has been particularly evident in the prayer-filled attitude of the young people gathered here. As a result, they go away more committed to the victory of the culture of life over the culture of death."

"The culture of life means respect for nature and protection of God's work of creation. In a special way it means respect for human life from the first moment of conception until its natural end. A genuine culture of life is all the more essential when — as I have written in the social encyclical *Centesimus Annus* — 'human ingenuity seems to be directed more toward limiting, suppressing or destroying the sources of life — including recourse to abortion, which unfortunately is so widespread in the world — than toward defending and opening up the possibilities of life (No.39).' "

"A culture of life means service to the underprivileged, the poor and the oppressed, because justice and freedom are inseparable and exist only if they exist for everyone. The culture of life means thanking God every day for his gift of life, for our worth and dignity as human beings, and for the friendship and fellowship he offers us as we make our pilgrim way toward our eternal destiny."

Gratitude

"I leave the United States with gratitude to God in my heart. ... I pray that America will continue to believe in its own noble ideals, and I express the hope that the United States will be a wise and helpful partner in the multilateral efforts being made to resolve some of the more difficult questions facing the international community."

"My gratitude becomes an ardent prayer for the people of this great country, for the fulfillment of Americas's destiny as one nation, under God, with liberty and justice for all."

"America, defend life so that you may live in peace and harmony."

INTERNATIONAL YOUTH FORUM

About 300 delegates to the International Youth Forum met Aug. 8 to 11, 1993, in advance of and in conjunction with the World Youth Day celebration in Denver. The young adults from some 70 countries focused attention on a variety of subjects, including social issues, challenges to youths in the practice and application of their Catholic faith, and ways to evangelize young people. It was the fourth meeting of the forum, under the sponsorship of the Pontifical Council for the Laity.

Members of the forum composed a message addressed to their contemporaries. It said in part:

Message to Youth

"We recognize that in the Church we are born in faith and continue to be revived. We ask the pastors to continue to help us discover our vocation, our direction in society and in the Church, by giving us the formation we need as young Christians."

"We recognize that, united with our brothers and sisters, we are the Church of today and the Church of tomorrow. We share with believers and nonbelievers alike a thirst for truth, a hunger for solidarity and a desire for self-giving. As youth, we tend to be demanding, critical and inquisitive. We do not ask the young people to abandon their uncertainties, questions or criticisms. Rather, we ask all those who call themselves Christians to allow themselves to be guided by grace to encounter Christ in the Church, through the sacraments, prayer and reception of the word. With the help of these means we strive to live mercy and solidarity and thus always be open to our neighbors. We are confident that the first place where this spirit can be lived, experienced and felt is through the family."

"From our Christian experience, we want to share with all the world's youth our desire to build a new society, a society of love. We strive to develop our personal gifts to the best of our ability so as to better serve society. We strive to serve, in particular, the weakest, the poorest and the most vulnerable among us. To make this a reality, we need to walk together, hand in hand, with all the youth and all people of the world who love life."

"We thank Pope John Paul II, Peter's successor, for his encouragement, and we pledge to him to be the new evangelizers and the living stones of the Church. We are convinced of one thing: In Christ we can change the world. But, before we can change the world, each one us has to change his heart through humility."

U.S. BISHOPS AT VATICAN: PAPAL TALKS

Bishops of dioceses are required to visit the Vatican every five years. During the year of their visit, they are required to report to the Pope on the state of the Church in their dioceses, to appear before the Pope and to venerate the tombs of the Apostles Sts. Peter and Paul. Groups of bishops from dioceses of the United States made *ad limina* visits ("to the threshold" of the tombs of the Apostles) in 1993.

This article was written by John Thavis, CNS Rome correspondent. Subheads have been added.

Variety of Subjects

During the first half of the 1993 *ad limina* visits, Pope John Paul II's talks to U.S. bishops focused largely on the need for clear and firm presentation of church teaching.

At the same time, the meetings prompted an important papal reflection on the problem of sex abuse by clergy — a chief concern of U.S. prelates as they came into the consultative sessions.

The bishops described the visits as fruitful and encouraging. They said they were impressed with the Pope's willingness to give up hours of his time in one-on-one encounters, informal group lunches, concelebrated Masses and speeches.

"The most important thing about these visits is deepening our connection with the Holy Father. We feel that keenly here — a real sense of solidarity," said Bishop David B. Thompson, of Charleston, S.C.

Clear Teaching

In his talk to the first group of prelates in March, the Pope quickly went to his dominant theme, saying the greatest contribution bishops can make to the Church today is to teach the faith unambiguously. In this way, they can help end the "disharmony and confusion" produced by dissenting views, he said.

The Pope said he recognized that most American Catholics give the "assent of faith" to church truths, but some "assume the right to decide themselves . . . which teachings to accept." This kind of selectivity is unacceptable, he added.

The Pope's message was not peculiar to the United States; he had made the same points in foreign trips or to various groups at the Vatican. A papal encyclical due out in the fall was expected to focus on the worldwide implications of selective adherence to moral teachings.

In his remarks to U.S bishops, the Pope repeatedly emphasized the importance of the new *Catechism of the Catholic Church* as a tool of teaching that could help launch a "national re-catechizing endeavor" in the United States.

But the bishops faced an awkward practical problem: the English translation of the catechism had been held up at the Vatican for months. The bishops told the Pope and other Vatican officials they were eagerly awaiting final approval; but, as of midsummer, they still had no clear idea of when it would be out.

Catholic Education

Speaking in April, the Pope stressed that the U.S. Catholic educational system must be strengthened and preserved. Again, he balanced praise for the "excellent" services offered by church-run schools with apprehension about the institutions' financial future and Catholic identity.

The Church's vitality depends on its ability to defend and spread authentic doctrine, he said. When an educational system defines itself as Catholic, he said, it must respect church teaching in every aspect of its activity — from scholarship and research to the behavior of the faculty.

In May, the Pope explored another aspect of the theme when he said that only a complete presentation of church teaching can curb the influence of sects and New Age ideas. These ideas, based on borrowings from Eastern spirituality and psychology, reject the concept of sin and the need for redemption, yet are finding their way into preaching, catechesis and workshops, he warned.

The answer is for Catholic teaching and preaching to emphasize the basics of the faith: supernatural life, the reality of sin and the Church's "unfailing hope in her Lord," he said.

Birth Control

In June, the Pope turned to what he acknowledged was one of the most difficult teachings to follow: the teaching against artificial birth control. One reason Catholics have problems with the birth control issue is "inadequate and insufficient explanation" by church authorities, he said.

The Pope called on bishops to promote this teaching in programs before and after marriage, and to defend the "sacred reality" of the family against such threats as "domestic partnership" laws, which recognize homosexual unions.

For the bishops, the *ad limina* visits offered an opportunity to discuss a wide range of pastoral problems, in particular the recent cases of sexual abuse by clergy. In their meetings with the Pope and Vatican officials, many pointed out that church law often makes defrocking known sex offenders a long and difficult process.

Sexual Abuse by Clergy

The Pope responded in June with a letter expressing concern for the problem and support for the bishops, and announcing a joint U.S.-Vatican commission to consider more efficient ways to deal with offenders. The bishops were pleased that direct access to the Pope achieved results on a difficult issue.

The selecting, training and ministry of the priest were topics in several papal speeches and in private discussions between bishops and the Pope.

In June, the Pope said one response to cases of sexual misconduct by clergy must be close screening of seminarians. He praised the U.S. bishops' revised program for priestly formation, and urged bishops to be demanding in the selection of priestly candidates.

Several bishops found the Pope inquiring about vocations programs in their dioceses and about ministry in priestless parishes. While praising the strong lay participation in administrative and liturgical life of parishes, the Pope insisted that the priest's ministerial powers must be recognized as distinct.

He said local church communities should view priestless Sunday services as a temporary solution and not as the norm. No truly living church community can resign itself to being without a priest, he said.

Feminism

In a July talk, the Pope focused on the role of women in the Church. His message was twofold:

While the Church must defend women's legitimate rights in society and the Church, there should be no compromise with an "extreme" feminism that divides people along "bitter, ideological lines."

He said this type of feminism had ushered in forms of "nature worship" and other pagan practices that take the place of Christian worship. He said he was particularly concerned that some U.S. nuns were encouraging this kind of feminism, and he asked the bishops to call them to "honest and sincere dialogue."

Ad Limina Process

The papal speeches were only part of the *ad limina* process, which includes extensive meetings with a number of Vatican officials and the more informal encounters with the Pope. But Vatican officials have said the Pope's talks, taken as a whole, will provide a good overall view of pastoral concerns in the United States — seen from a Vatican perspective.

Beginning in September and continuing through December, five more groups of bishops were scheduled to visit the Vatican. The visits would give them a chance to explain their ministry face-to-face with the Pope, and give the Pontiff a chance to suggest solutions and provide encouragement.

SEXUAL ABUSE BY CLERGY

In a newspaper column published during Holy Week 1993, Archbishop Rembert G. Weakland of Milwaukee called the barrage of news about sexual misconduct by priests the contemporary "Good Friday" of the Catholic Church. He especially focused on the issue of sexual abuse of children by priests, and said: "We have a problem in our Church today with pedophilia and we must face it. It is not enough to say that we have less pedophilia than other groups in society. What we have is real, and it impedes our ministry as a Church."

At the same time, in the Apr. 8 edition of the *Catholic Herald*, Archbishop Weakland asked people to recognize and support "the multitude of good and faithful priests" who are not involved in sexual misconduct.

Estimate of Number of Cases

The number of priests involved nationwide in the sexual abuse of minors has been variously estimated: 2,500 abusers of 100,000 in the previous 25 years, according to sociologist Father Andrew M. Greeley; 1,060 abusers of about 15,000 victims between 1951 and 1991, according to Father Philip J. Murnion, director of the National Pastoral Life Center in New York. Everyone agrees that even one case of clerical abuse of one child is one too many.

A leading priest-psychiatrist, Jesuit Father James J. Gill, cited the case of Father Gilbert Gauthe as "a wake-up call" that alerted the nation's church and mental health officials to the nature and extent of child molestation by priests. Father Gauthe, a priest of the Diocese of Lafayette, La., was sentenced in 1985 to 20 years at hard labor for sexually abusing small boys. In retrospect, said Father Gill, the case marked the start of far-reaching reforms in the way the Church in the U.S. deals with this issue.

Before that, bishops "did not ignore it" when a priest was accused of sexual activity with a minor, but they approached it primarily as a moral issue of temptation and sin, not as a psychological or psychiatric problem. "Bishops thought they were doing the best they could by moving the priest to a new situation," away from the child to whom he had been attracted.

But, as the Gauthe case unfolded, Father Gill said "a lot of us became aware (that) not only does this happen but, when it happens, the implications are monumental — not just financially, but in how many people are involved (as victims), the harm to them and to their families."

Steps Being Taken

Because of the awareness provoked by the Gauthe case and other incidents uncovered at that time, "church officials began to realize that the old way (giving a priest a few sessions with a counselor and then moving him) was inadequate," Father Gill said.

Since that time, Catholic News Service reported that bishops and superiors of religious orders have taken major steps to:

• investigate immediately and thoroughly any allegation of child molestation by a priest;

• remove the priest from his post immediately if an allegation appears substantial, and place him under professional evaluation and treatment;

• recognize the serious impact abuse can have on victims and offer immediate pastoral care and other appropriate assistance to them and their families;

• deal with the likelihood of other victims, taking account of research that shows most offenders have had multiple victims before discovery;

• assure that a priest diagnosed as a pedophile will either be barred from ministry or placed in a limited ministry with supervision and restrictions designed to prevent any risk to children;

• establish and publicize clear, strict guidelines for reporting suspected cases of child sex abuse and responding to such reports;

• improve screening and supervision of candidates for the priesthood in order to weed out those with serious psychosexual disorders and improve the formation of others.

• cooperate with law enforcement authorities.

Efforts by bishops to deal with clerical sexual abuse of children in their own dioceses gained momentum from sometime in the 1980s and became the subject of discussions at the national level by the National Conference of Catholic Bishops, particularly in 1992 and 1993.

Papal Concern

Pope John Paul, in a June 11, 1993, letter to U.S. bishops said in part: "During these last months I have become aware of how much you, the pastors of the Church in the United States, together with all the faithful, are suffering because of certain cases of scandal given by members of the clergy. During the *ad lamina* visits (by the bishops to the Holy See in 1993), many times the conversation has turned to this problem of how the sins of clerics have shocked the moral sensibilities of many and become an occasion of sin for others. The Gospel word, 'woe,' has a special meaning, especially when Christ applies it to cases of scandal, and first of all to the scandal 'of the little ones' (cf. Mt. 18:6). How severe are Christ's words when he speaks of such scandal."

"The vast majority of bishops and priests are devoted followers of Christ, ardent workers in his vineyard and men who are deeply sensitive to the needs of their brothers and sisters. That is why I am deeply pained, like you, when it seems that the words of Christ can be applied to some ministers of the altar. . . . I fully share your sorrow and your concern, especially your concern for the victims so seriously hurt by these misdeeds."

The Pope also said in his letter that "a joint committee of experts from the Holy See and the bishops' conference has just been established to study how the universal canonical reforms can best be applied to the particular situation of the United States."

The joint committee, at a meeting in the spring, produced a document addressing several areas of church law with a bearing on ways and means of disciplining sex offenders among the clergy.

Committee Agenda

The establishment of an eight-member U.S. bishops' Ad Hoc Committee on Sexual Abuse was announced during the meeting of the National Conference of Catholic Bishops June 17 to 18, 1993, in New Orleans. Bishop John Kinney of Bismarck, N.D., chairman, said the committee would investigate: what the conference can do "to stand beside

the victims and their families"; how to "aid bishops in working with priests who have been abusers"; means of strengthening the screening of candidates for the priesthood and other ministries; ways of assessing the risks or possibilities of "any future assignments for priest-perpetrators"; sexual misconduct of other church employees or volunteers; what the Church can share from its experience with the rest of society.

Bishop Kinney also said he wanted "to make sure that all of us bishops understand the depth and the seriousness, the pain and the agony of this problem, and why it strikes at the very heart of the Church's trust level and credibility level."

During an organizational meeting early in August, the bishops' ad hoc committee outlined four areas on which it intended to focus its concern: (1) appropriate response to guilty or accused priests, victims or potential victims and their families; (2) prevention of future abuse through screening of seminary candidates; (3) reassignment of priests who have been involved in sexual abuse; (4) education of clergy and the public about sexual abuse.

Public Perception Not Accurate

Bishop Favalora of St. Petersburg, a committee member, said the group hoped its work would benefit the general public as well as the Church. One particular concern was the public perception that the Church had done little to address problems of sexual abuse. Actually, he said, the subject had been the focus of attention within the Church since the early 1980s. "There is probably no single institution or agency in the country that has gathered more information on this subject. We're probably the only major group discussing this topic," he said.

Archbishop John Quinn of San Francisco referred to this matter Apr. 10, 1993, according to an article, "Sins of a Father," in the June 19 edition of *America*. He said: "Outrage and bitter recriminations are being visited upon bishops for inept handling of these problems (of sexual abuse of minors). Yet until the middle 1980s, hardly 10 years ago, the subject of child abuse was not part of the required training of mental health professionals, and in the national qualifying examinations not one question dealt with this topic. The mental health field until recently knew little about this problem, yet bishops are somehow expected to have known what the professionals did not."

Late in the spring of 1993 Cardinal John J. O'-Connor addressed the more than 2,000 priests in the Archdiocese of New York on the topic of sexual abuse of children, underscoring its scandalous effect on the Church and detailing the manner in which the archdiocese — like other U.S. dioceses — planned to deal with the matter. Later, in a homily at Mass June 20, he said: "The Church is going through a period of trial by fire; and, when fire doesn't destroy, it purifies."

CATECHISM OF THE CATHOLIC CHURCH

Following are excerpts from the apostolic constitution *Fidei Depositum* ("Deposit of Faith") with which Pope John Paul formally presented the new

Catechism of the Catholic Church to the world Dec. 7, 1992. The Catechism was approved June 25 and the constitution was dated Oct. 11, 1992.

These excerpts are from the text circulated in the Nov. 25, 1992, English edition of "L'Osservatore Romano."

1. Introduction

On 25 January 1985 I convoked an Extraordinary Assembly of the Synod of Bishops for the 25th anniversary of the close of the (Second Vatican) Council. The purpose of this assembly was to celebrate the graces and spiritual fruits of Vatican II, to study its teaching in greater depth in order the better to adhere to it and to promote knowledge and application of it.

On that occasion the Synod Fathers stated: "Very many have expressed the desire that a catechism or compendium of all Catholic doctrine regarding both faith and morals be composed, that it might be, as it were, a point of reference for the catechisms or compendiums that are prepared in various regions. The presentation of doctrine must be biblical and liturgical. It must be sound doctrine suited to the present life of Christians." After the Synod ended, I made this desire my own, considering it as fully responding to a real need both of the universal Church and of the particular churches.

For this reason we thank the Lord wholeheartedly on this day when we can offer the entire Church this "reference text" entitled the *Catechism of the Catholic Church,* for a catechesis renewed at the living source of the faith.

Following the renewal of the liturgy and the new codification of the canon law of the Latin Church and that of the Oriental Catholic Churches, this catechism will make a very important contribution to that work of renewing the whole life of the Church, as desired and begun by the Second Vatican Council.

2. The Process and Spirit of Drafting the Text

The *Catechism of the Catholic Church* is the result of very extensive collaboration: it was prepared over six years of intense work done in a spirit of complete openness and fervent zeal.

In 1986 I entrusted a commission of 12 cardinals and bishops, chaired by Cardinal Joseph Ratzinger, with the task of preparing a draft of the catechism requested by the Synod Fathers. An editorial committee of seven diocesan bishops, experts in theology and catechesis, assisted the commission in its work.

The commission, charged with giving directives and with overseeing the course of the work, attentively followed all the stages in editing the nine subsequent drafts. The editorial committee, for its part, assumed responsibility for writing the text, making the emendations requested by the commission and examining the observations of numerous theologians, exegetes and catechists, and, above all, of the bishops of the whole world, in order to improve the text. The committee was a place of fruitful and enriching exchanges of opinion to ensure the unity and homogeneity of the text.

The project was the object of extensive consultation among all Catholic bishops, their episcopal conferences or synods, and of theological and catechetical institutes. As a whole, it received a broadly favorable acceptance on the part of the episcopate. It can be said that this catechism is the result of the collaboration of the whole episcopate of the Catholic Church.

3. Arrangement of the Material

The *Catechism of the Catholic Church* on the one hand repeats the "old" traditional order already followed by the Catechism of St. Pius V, arranging the material in four parts: the Creed; the Sacred Liturgy, with pride of place being given to the sacraments; the Christian Way of Life, explained beginning with the Ten Commandments; and, finally, Christian Prayer. At the same time, however, the contents are often expressed in a "new" way in order to respond to the questions of our age.

The four parts are related one to the other: the Christian mystery is the object of faith (first part); it is celebrated and communicated in liturgical actions (second part); it is present to enlighten and sustain the children of God in their actions (third part); it is the basis for our prayer, the privileged expression of which is the Our Father, and it represents the object of our supplication, our praise and our intercession (fourth part).

4. The Doctrinal Value of the Text

The *Catechism of the Catholic Church* ... is a statement of the Church's faith and of Catholic doctrine, attested to or illumined by Sacred Scripture, apostolic tradition and the Church's magisterium. I declare it to be a valid and legitimate instrument for ecclesial communion and a sure norm for teaching the faith. May it serve the renewal to which the Holy Spirit ceaselessly calls the Church of God, the Body of Christ, on her pilgrimage to the undiminished light of the kingdom!

I ask the Church's pastors and the Christian faithful to receive this catechism in a spirit of communion and to use it assiduously in fulfilling their mission of proclaiming the faith and calling people to the Gospel life. This catechism is given to them that it might be a sure and authentic reference text for teaching Catholic doctrine, and particularly for preparing local catechisms. It is also offered to all the faithful who wish to deepen their knowledge of the unfathomable riches of salvation. It is meant to support ecumenical efforts that are moved by the holy desire for the unity of all Christians, showing carefully the content and wondrous harmony of the Catholic faith. The *Catechism of the Catholic Church,* lastly, is offered to every individual who asks us to give an account of the hope that is in us and who wants to know what the Catholic Church believes.

This catechism is not intended to replace the local catechisms duly approved by the ecclesiastical authorities, the diocesan bishops and the episcopal conferences, especially if they have been approved by the Apostolic See. It is meant to encourage and assist in the writing of new local catechisms, which must take into account various situations and cultures, while carefully preserving the unity of faith and fidelity to Catholic doctrine.

Additional Notes

The new *Catechism of the Catholic Church* is the first of its kind since 1566, the year of publication of the *Roman Catechism* by Pope Pius V in the wake of the Council of Trent.

Requests of the catechetical commission for suggestions and critical comments regarding subject matter and related details elicited 24,000 recommendations from various sources.

The French edition of the catechism was the first published, Nov. 11, 1992. Spanish, Italian and German editions were published by June 18, 1993. Work was still progressing on the English edition late in the summer of 1993, due apparently to concern about the fidelity of translation and problems related to the use of inclusive language. Work was also continuing toward completion and approval of the master Latin text.

It was reported that 13 U.S. publishers would issue editions of the catechism. Overall coordination of publication would be handled by the Office of Publication and Promotion Services, U.S. Catholic Conference.

NEW AGE MOVEMENT

The following excerpts are from an article by Archbishop J. Francis Stafford of Denver, published in the Jan. 27, 1993, English edition of "L'-Osservatore Romano."

A Perversion of Christian Faith

"The New Age (movement or philosophy) . . . is presented . . . as a salvific wisdom. It approximates to the gnostic enthusiasms which have troubled the Church from her inception, and which in fact ground all heresy. Gnosticism consists, in all its varied presentations, in a reversion to paganism under pseudo-Christian auspices. This camouflaging of an absolute and comprehensive antagonism to Christianity has characterized Gnosticism from its origins, as it did in the flower children of the Age of Aquarius, and as it does in the New Age disciples today. The New Age movement is only the current Western version of this perennial perversion of the Christian faith."

"The Protestant church historian, Sydney Ahlstrohm, has pointed to the emergence of the Beatles in the fall of 1962 as the beginning of the Age of Aquarius, the proximate predecessor of the New Age. The Aquarians, following the Beatles' prophetic lines, were anti-Christians, fascinated with Hindu and Buddhist mysticism, with astrology, and with counter-cultural insurrection generally. Their political sympathies were of the far left; their theological expression was the radical 'Death of God' theology of the late 1960s, whose ground is . . . a condemnation of 'religion' and a consequent exaltation of secularity as the valid contemporary expression of a mature Christianity."

Remote Origins

"More remote predecessors of the Aquarian Age may be found in the Rosicrucians, in the occultism of Madame Blavatsky and Mrs. Annie Besant, in Christian Science, . . . in Renaissance humanism, . . . in medieval gnostic sects such as Catharism and Cabalism, in the aberrant Joachimite spirituality, . . . and ultimately in the mix of Middle Platonism, hermeticism and pagan mystery religion which constituted the Gnosticism of the first Christian centuries. The recent contribution of Hindu and Buddhist speculation cannot be ignored "along with their nihilistic and pessimistic currents of thought."

Believing in Anything

"The New Age movement appears to have its specific historical inception, or perhaps its catalyst, in the theosophist and occultist speculations of Alice Anne Bailey (1880-1949), whose copious and repetitive publications have been in print over the past 70 years in numerous editions, most of them recent. The contemporary rediscovery of and fascination with her New Age doctrine owes a great deal to the deracination of those millions of unchurched people in the Western world who, once anchored in certitudes of the Christian faith, have lost that spiritual security under the pervasive and corrosive influence of a counter-Catholic symbolism of modernity, and now, seeking another spiritual haven, find themselves in the position described by G. K. Chesterton, of the apostate from Christianity who, instead of now believing nothing, believes anything."

"The range of the 'anything'that is the subject of the credo of this (New Age) cult is currently illustrated by the works of its better known contemporary adepts, e.g., Shirley MacLaine (*Out on a Limb*) and Father Matthew Fox (*Creation Spirituality*), both representatives of that vice of pseudo-Christian 'enthusiasm' which Ronald Knox excoriated more than 40 years ago. But it is not at all accidental that Catholic circles should find to their taste such 'theology' as Father Fox represents: his doctrine is that of the bulk of the feminist theologians now writing, and of that Catholic Neo-Modernist 'dissent' whose focus is on the rejection of sacramental realism. Once that refusal of Catholic historical optimism is in place, all that remains is the negotiation of terms of surrender to a *Zeitgeist* now well on the way to becoming the *Weltgeist*."

Impersonal Cosmic Responsibility

"Gnostic enthusiasms, however popularized, have always displayed a generous flexibility: they are capable of indefinitely numerous expressions, and are open to a variety of applications: utopian, ecological, liberationist, therapeutic, feminist, romantic, deconstructionist. The characteristic feature of the various expressions of the New Age movement is their common reversion to the ancient pagan morality of responsibility to the cosmos, with its correlative refusal of any personal historical responsibility for the here and now. It is this entirely faceless and impersonal cosmological responsibility for the safeguarding of the universe — rather than the notion of personal responsibility traditional in the Western world, viz., for the salvation of mankind in the Kingdom of God — that is criteriological for virtue in the New Age."

"The explicitly anti-Christian and anti-Catholic thrust of the New Age movement is indispensable to it; over against the gnostic denial of the significance of history stands the Christ and his worshiping Church. ... An eager willingness to reinterpret the historical Jesus in the service of their version of a pagan mysticism marks alike the works of Mrs. Bailey and those of such devotees of her New Age as Ms. MacLaine, Father Fox and the doctrinaire promoters of feminine liberation."

Devaluation of Catholicism

"The movement is today the more dangerous in that a great deal of academic theology, as well as the postulatory atheism still infecting much of modern science, lends support not so much to the imaginative transports of Mrs. Bailey's theosophy as to the general devaluation of historical Catholicism, which now as always is seen to present the single effective opposition to Gnosticism. Whether as doctrine, as moral practice or as public institution, Catholicism is seen to stand athwart the program alike of academic and of New Age freedom."

"As always, a major target ... is the Church's sacramental worship, in and by which the freedom which is sustained by the nuptial and historical order of the New Covenant is made effective in the public life of the world. The destructive rationalism of the New Age, and of the new academy, offers an alternative ... counter-historical symbolism (at variance with Catholic doctrine and practice regarding the nature of human beings, the Trinity, the sacraments, moral responsibility, etc.)."

"In the end, the New Age is no more than one more pagan soteriology. It looks to the extinction of the good creation that is in Christ, the Image of God, in order that one may image nothing."

ANOTHER VIEW

The Tablet, the British international Catholic weekly, reported May 8, 1993, that a study group set up by the Church of Scotland's Board of Social Responsibility had issued a warning against the dangers of the New Age movement. The article said in part as follows.

"The report pointed out that the term New Age was used to shelter a vast range of therapies, ideologies, cultural trends and beliefs drawn from many world religions and cults. But there would appear to be three central beliefs running through all New Age thinking: the idea that all is one ('reality consists of one basic substance and there is no difference between a rock, a person or a carrot'); that all is God ('God is an impersonal energy or force and thus permeates everything'); and that humanity needs a change in consciousness (which is what all the techniques and therapies are designed to achieve). In addition, another major unifying factor was belief in reincarnation."

CREATION SPIRITUALITY

One expression of the New Age movement is Creation Spirituality as formulated and popularized by Dominican Father Matthew Fox, founder and director of the Institute of Culture and Creative Spirituality.

Father Fox, born in 1940, ordained to the priesthood in the Dominican Order in 1967 and the recipient of a doctorate in theology from the *Institut Catolique de Paris,* founded his institute in 1977 and affiliated it with Mundelein College in Chicago. Six years later he moved it to the College of the Holy Names in Oakland, California.

Father Fox is the author of more than 10 books, editor-in-chief of the bimonthly *Creation Spirituality* and lecturer on the national and international circuit. Three of his books are *The Magical, Mystical Bear; Whee, We, Wee All the Way Home;* and *Original Blessing: A Primer in Creation Spirituality.*

Findings of Three Theologians

These three books and the program of Father Fox's institute drew the attention of Cardinal Joseph Ratzinger, prefect of the Congregation for the Doctrine of the Faith. He requested in July, 1984, that an examination be made of these works by Dominican theologians of the St. Albert the Great Province. On completion of their examination of the books and unspecified activities of Father Fox in May, 1985, three theologians said they had found nothing "to warrant condemnation," but "agreed that certain spiritual traditions of the Catholic Church and certain traditional doctrines ('Fall-Redemption theology' and its perspectives on sin, the cross, ascetical discipline, for example) could be better integrated with his own perspectives and insights concerning the goodness of the original creation."

It became apparent, according to a statement released by the central U.S. province of the Dominican Order Oct. 19, 1988, "that one activity of Fox and the Institute of Culture and Creative Spirituality which was causing a vehement reaction was the presence on his part-time staff of Starhawk, a well-known social activist, feminist and practitioner of wicca (witchcraft)."

Cardinal Ratzinger Not Convinced

Cardinal Ratzinger, in a Dec. 9, 1985, letter to Father Damian Byrne, master general of the Dominicans, said he had reservations about the conclusions reached by the theologians and raised a question about permitting Father Fox to publish and to continue his institute-related work. He suggested that measures might be undertaken "which will not only preclude future difficulties but will publicly redress the present scandal of Father Fox's seeming espousal of witchcraft and the harm which his published books and teaching activities have already brought to the faithful."

In another letter, dated Sept. 17, 1987, Cardinal Ratzinger instructed Father Byrne "to use your good offices to assure that Father Fox's present assignment as director of the Institute for Creation Spirituality ... be terminated and that he be instructed to cease from further dissemination of the central thesis of his book, *Original Blessing,* either in writing or in the form of speeches or workshops, etc. It appears also necessary that he dissociate himself from 'wicca,' the ideology of 'Starhawk,' a self-styled witch."

In view of the congregation's concern, Father Byrne required that Father Fox take a sabbatical year and refrain from teaching and lecturing during that time. The sabbatical was to begin Dec. 15, 1988. Father Fox, on receiving the order, acceded to its requirement but indicated that the sabbatical might be of less than a year's duration.

Statements by Father Fox

At a press conference Oct. 20, 1988, Father Fox called creation spirituality "the oldest spiritual tradition in the Bible." It offers a way of "reclaiming the Western mystical tradition. It furnishes common ground on which many persons and movements can gather. Among these are those working for justice toward native peoples, gender justice, justice to lesbian and gay people, and the liberation of the so-called Third World and First World peoples."

He said he does not deny the doctrine of original sin but decries what he claims is "the exaggerated importance given that doctrine in the Western Church." This opinion, along with other elements in his writing and teaching, could be considered open to an interpretation not in agreement with doctrine concerning the need and role of grace for salvation.

Creation-centered spirituality, according to Father Fox, "re-grounds us in our own Western mystical roots. It liberates us from sexism and dualism between body and spirit. It liberates us from boring worship because it re-sets worship in a cosmological context."

This form of spirituality combines a variety of elements drawn from Catholic mysticism, liberation theologies, Eastern and Native American religions, environmentalism, feminism, modern science and other sources.

The Congregation for the Doctrine of the Faith expressed particular concern regarding Father Fox's treatment of the doctrine of original sin. Objections were also raised about his references to God as "Mother" and his commitment to "fervent" feminism.

Dismissal from Dominican Order

In August, 1992, Father Fox refused to comply with orders that he leave his institute-related work and return to community life with his province in Chicago. He said his conscience dictated that he remain in California and continue his work, which "must go on no matter what the opposition." His dismissal by the master general of the Dominican Order in June, 1992, was confirmed Feb. 22, 1993, by the Congregation for Institutes of Consecrated Life and Societies of Apostolic Life. The reason was his "illegitimate absence from his religious community."

Dominican spokesman Father Malachy O'Dwyer said the decision to dismiss Father Fox from the Order had "absolutely nothing to do with his work" but with his refusal to return to community life. Father Fox claimed the dismissal process was "an effort to silence my work and stigmatize it." He called the dismissal an "act of institutional violence" against him.

The dismissal did not affect Father Fox's standing as a priest but did involve his need of authorization by a bishop for pastoral ministry.

HEALTH CARE REFORM

The bishops of the United States adopted June 18, 1993, a resolution on health care reform entitled,"A Framework for Comprehensive Health Care Reform: Protecting Human Life, Promoting Human Dignity, Pursuing the Common Good."

The text of the resolution was circulated by the CNS Documentary Service, Origins, July 1, 1993 (Vol.23, No. 7).

I. INTRODUCTION

Our nation's health care system serves too few and costs too much. A major national debate on how to assure access for all, restrain costs and increase quality is moving to the center of American public life. This resolution is addressed to the Catholic community and the leaders of our nation. We seek to outline the values, criteria and priorities which are guiding our conference's participation in this vital dialogue. We hope to offer a constructive and distinctive contribution reflecting the Catholic community's strong convictions and broad experience in health care.

The debate and decisions will not be easy. They will touch every family and business, every community and parish. Health care reform represents an effort to redirect a seventh of our national economy and to reshape our society's response to a basic

human need. It is not only an economic challenge, it is a moral imperative.

The Catholic community has much at stake and much to contribute to this vital national dialogue. For decades, we have advocated sweeping reform. In communities across our land we serve the sick and pick up the pieces of a failing system. We are pastors, teachers and leaders of a community deeply committed to comprehensive health reform. Our urgency for reform reflects both on our traditional principles and everyday experience.

A. A Tradition of Teaching

Our approach to health care is shaped by a simple but fundamental principle: "Every person has a right to adequate health care. This right flows from the sanctity of human life and the dignity that belongs to all human persons, who are made in the image of God." Health care is more than a commodity; it is a basic human right, an essential safeguard of human life and dignity. We believe our people's health care should not depend on where they work, how much their parents earn or where they live. Our constant teaching that each human life must be protected and human dignity promoted leads us to insist that all people have a right to health care. This right is explicitly affirmed in (the papal encyclical letter)

Pacem in Terris and is the foundation of our advocacy for health care reform. When millions of Americans are without health coverage, when rising costs threaten the coverage of millions more, when infant mortality remains shockingly high, the right to health care is seriously undermined and our health care system is in need of fundamental reform.

Our call for health care reform is rooted in the biblical call to heal the sick and to serve "the least of these," the priorities of social justice and the principle of the common good. The existing patterns of health care in the United States do not meet the minimal standard of social justice and the common good. The substantial inequity of our health care system can no longer be ignored or explained away. The principal defect is that more than 35 million persons do not have guaranteed access to basic health care. Others have some access, but their coverage is too limited or too costly to offer health security for their families. High health care costs contribute to a declining standard of living for many American families. The current health care system is so inequitable, and the disparities between rich and poor and those with access and those without are so great that it is clearly unjust.

The burdens of this system are not shared equally. One out of three Hispanics and one of five African-Americans are uninsured. The health care in our inner cities and some rural communities leads to Third World rates of infant mortality. The virtue of solidarity and our teaching on the option for the poor and vulnerable require us to measure our health system in terms of how it affects the weak and disadvantaged. In seeking the fundamental changes which are necessary, we focus especially on the impact of national health policies on the poor and the vulnerable.

The traditional value of stewardship also contributes to our call for reform. It is predicted that health care costs will more than double between 1980 and 2000. Our nation pays far more for health care than other industrialized countries and that strains the private economy and leaves too few resources for housing, education and other economic and social needs. Stewardship demands that we address the duplication, waste and other factors that make our system so expensive.

For three-quarters of a century, the Catholic bishops of the United States have called for national action to assure decent health care for all Americans. We seek to bring a moral perspective in an intensely political debate; we offer an ethical framework in an arena dominated by powerful economic interests.

B. A Community of Caring

The Catholic community in states, cities and towns all across the country, brings not only strong convictions, but also broad experience as providers and purchasers of health care. The Church has been involved in the delivery of health services since the early days of this nation. Catholic health care facilities are now the largest network of nonprofit hospitals and nursing homes in the United States, serving more than 20 million people in a single year. As pastors, we see the strains and stresses related to inadequate health care, the human consequences

of a failing system. In approximately 600 Catholic hospitals and 1,500 long-term and specialized care settings, in our parishes and schools, Catholic Charities shelters and services, Campaign for Human Development-funded groups, we see the consequences of failed and confused policy: families without insurance, sick without options, children without care, the plight of real people behind the statistics. We seek to offer a human perspective in an often overly technical discussion

C. Our Experience as Employers

Catholic dioceses, parishes, schools, agencies and hospitals are major purchasers of insurance and health care. The rapidly escalating costs of coverage are impacting almost every diocese, agency, parish and school. The increasing resources we spend on health care are dollars that don't fund much needed ministry, services and personnel. We know well the fiscal consequences of the rising health costs which are hurting our economy and diverting precious resources.

D. A Capacity for Advocacy

Our community also brings to this debate expertise and credibility rooted in our experience and values, a history and record of active support for health care reform which goes back decades, active ministry in inner city, suburban and rural communities, an institutional presence in every state and congressional district. We are a very diverse community of believers and citizens who could make a big difference in the health care debate.

The Catholic Health Association, which serves Catholic-sponsored health care facilities, has developed a comprehensive framework for a reformed health care system. This plan reflects the experience and expertise of Catholic leaders who are deeply involved in meeting the health care needs of the nation. We welcome CHA's impressive initiative in developing this plan which includes important values and policy directions to help guide the debate and decisions in the months ahead.

Health care reform is an issue that unites the Catholic community. We need to continue to work together to help make the case for comprehensive reform, share our values and experience, and urge our representatives to adopt health care reform which will protect the life and dignity of all. We offer a potential constituency of conscience in the midst of a debate too often dominated by special interests and partisan needs. The debate over national health care reform will test both our Church and our country.

II. CRITERIA FOR REFORM

Applying our experience and principles to the choices before the nation, our bishops conference strongly supports comprehensive reform that will ensure a decent level of health care for all without regard to their ability to pay. This will require concerted action by federal and other levels of government and by the diverse providers and consumers of health care. We believe government, an instrument of our common purpose called to pursue the common good, has an essential role to play in assuring that the rights of all people to adequate health care are respected.

We believe reform of the health care system which is truly fundamental and enduring must be rooted in values which reflect the essential dignity of each person, ensure that basic human rights are protected, and recognize the unique needs and claims of the poor. We commend to the leaders of our nation the following criteria for reform.

● Respect for Life. Whether it preserves and enhances the sanctity and dignity of human life from conception to natural death.

● Priority Concern for the Poor. Whether it gives special priority to meeting the most pressing health care needs of the poor and underserved, ensuring that they receive quality health services.

● Universal Access. Whether it provides ready universal access to comprehensive health care for every person living in the United States.

● Comprehensive Benefits. Whether it provides comprehensive benefits sufficient to maintain and promote good health, to provide preventive care, to treat disease, injury and disability appropriately, and to care for persons who are chronically ill or dying.

● Pluralism. Whether it allows and encourages the involvement of the public and private sectors, including the voluntary, religious and nonprofit sectors, in the delivery of care and services; and whether it ensures respect for religious and ethical values in the delivery of health care for consumers and for individual and institutional providers.

● Quality. Whether it promotes the development of processes and standards that will help to achieve quality and equity in health services, in the training of providers and in the informed participation of consumers in decision making on health care.

● Cost Containment and Controls. Whether it creates effective cost containment measures that reduce waste, inefficiency and unnecessary care; measures that control rising costs of competition, commercialism and administration; and measures that provide incentives to individuals and providers for effective and economical use of limited resources.

● Equitable Financing. Whether it assures society's obligation to finance universal access to comprehensive health care in an equitable fashion, based on ability to pay; and whether proposed cost-sharing arrangements are designed to avoid creating barriers to effective care for the poor and vulnerable.

III. KEY POLICY PRIORITIES

We hope Catholics and others will use these criteria to assess proposals for reform. In applying these criteria, we have chosen to focus our advocacy on several essential priorities.

Priority Concern for the Poor/Universal Access: We look at health care reform from the bottom up, how it touches the unserved and underserved. Genuine health care reform must especially focus on the basic health needs of the poor (i.e., those who are unable through private resources, employer support or public aid to provide payment for health care services, or those unable to gain access to health care because of limited resources, inadequate education or discrimination).

When there is a question of allocating scarce resources, the vulnerable and the poor have a compelling claim to first consideration. Special attention must be given to ensuring that those who have suffered from inaccessible and inadequate health care (e.g., in central cities, isolated rural areas and migrant camps) are first brought back into an effective system of quality care. Therefore, we will strongly support measures to ensure true universal access and rapid steps to improve the health care of the poor and unserved. Universal access must not be significantly postponed, since coverage delayed may well be coverage denied. We do not support a two-tiered health system since separate health care coverage for the poor usually results in poor health care. Linking the health care of poor and working-class families to the health care of those with greater resources is probably the best assurance of comprehensive benefits and quality care.

Respect for Human Life and Human Dignity: Real health care reform must protect and enhance human life and human dignity. Every member of the human family has the right to life and to the means which are suitable for the full development of life. This is why we insist that every human being has the right to quality health services, regardless of age, income, illness or condition of life. Government statistics on infant mortality are evidence that lack of access and inadequate care are literally matters of life and death. The needs of the frail elderly, the unborn child, the person living with AIDS and the undocumented immigrant must be addressed by health care reform.

Neither the violence of abortion and euthanasia nor the growing advocacy for assisted suicide is consistent with respect for human life. When destructive practices such as abortion or euthanasia seek acceptance as aspects of "health care" alongside genuine elements of the healing art, the very meaning of health care is distorted and threatened. A consistent concern for human dignity is strongly demonstrated by providing access to quality care from the prenatal period throughout infancy and childhood, into adult life and at the end of life when care is possible even if cure is not. Therefore, we are convinced it would be a moral tragedy, a serious policy misjudgment and a major political mistake to burden health care reform with abortion coverage that most Americans oppose and the federal government has not funded for the last 17 years. Consequently, we continue to oppose unequivocally the inclusion of abortion as a health care benefit, as do three out of four Americans (April 6, 1993, *New York Times* poll).

As longtime advocates of health care reform, we appeal to the leaders of the nation to avoid a divisive and polarizing dispute which could jeopardize passage of national health care reform. We strongly believe it would be morally wrong and counterproductive to compel individuals, institutions or states to pay for or participate in procedures that fundamentally violate basic moral principles and the consciences of millions of Americans. The common good is not advanced when advocates of so-called "choice" compel taxpayers to fund what we and many others are convinced is the destruction of human life.

Pursuing the Common Good and Preserving Pluralism: We fear the cause of real reform can be undermined by special interest conflict and the resistance of powerful forces who have a major stake in maintaining the status quo. It also can be thwarted by unnecessary partisan political combat. We believe the debate can be advanced by a continuing focus on the common good and a healthy respect for genuine pluralism. A reformed system must encourage the creative and renewed involvement of both the public and private sectors, including voluntary, religious and nonprofit providers of care. It must also respect the religious and ethical values of both individuals and institutions involved in the health care system. We are deeply concerned that Catholic and other institutions with strong moral foundations may face increasing economic and regulatory pressures to compromise their moral principles and to participate in practices inconsistent with their commitment to human life. The Catholic community is strongly committed to continuing to meet the health needs of the nation in a framework of genuine reform, which respects the essential role and values of religiously affiliated providers of health care.

Restraining Costs: We have the best health care technology in the world, but tens of millions have little or no access to it and the costs of the system are straining our nation, our economy, our families and our Church to the breaking point. We insist that any acceptable plan must include effective mechanisms to restrain rising health care costs. By bringing health care cost inflation down, we could cut the federal deficit, improve economic competitiveness, and help stem the decline in living standards for many working families. Without cost containment, we cannot hope to make health care affordable and direct scarce national resources to other pressing problems which, in turn, worsen health problems (e.g., inadequate housing, poverty, joblessness and poor education).

IV. CONCLUSION

The Catholic bishops' conference will continue to work with our people and others for reform of the U.S. health care system, especially on these key priorities. In our view, the best measure of any proposed health care initiative is the extent to which it combines universal access to comprehensive quality health care with cost control, while ensuring quality care for the poor and preserving human life and dignity.

We welcome the signs that our nation and our leaders are beginning to face up to the challenge of reform. We will assess the Clinton administration's plan and the alternatives to it on the basis of our criteria and experience. We will be active and involved participants in this vital national debate.

New public policy is essential to address the health care crisis, but it is not sufficient. Each of us must examine how we contribute to this crisis — how our own attitudes and behavior demonstrate a lack of respect for our own health and the dignity of all. Are we prepared to make the changes, address the neglect, accept the sacrifices and practice the discipline that can lead to better health care for all Americans? In our own lives and in this vital health care debate, we are all called to protect human life, promote human dignity and pursue the common good. In particular, we call on Catholics involved in the health care system to play leadership roles in shaping health care reform which respects human life and enhances human dignity.

Now is the time for real health care reform. It is a matter of fundamental justice. For so many, it is literally a matter of life and death, of lives cut short and dignity denied. We urge our national leaders to look beyond special interest claims and partisan differences to unite our nation in a new commitment to meeting the health care needs of our people, especially the poor and vulnerable. This is a major political task, a significant policy challenge, and a moral imperative.

FIFTH CENTENARY OF EVANGELIZATION OF AMERICAS

Pope John Paul, on his 56th foreign pastoral trip, visited the Dominican Republic for the third time Oct. 9 to 14, 1992, for the celebration of the 500th anniversary of evangelization in the Americas.

ITINERARY

October 9: Flight from Rome and arrival at Las Americas Airport, Santo Domingo.

October 10: In Santo Domingo, visit to the president of the Dominican Republic; Mass with clergy and religious at the Cathedral of Our Lady of the Incarnation, the first cathedral in the Americas.

October 11: In Santo Domingo, Mass near the new Columbus monument; canonization of Blessed Ezequiel Moreno y Diaz; recitation of the Angelus; meeting with the diplomatic corps.

October 12: In Higuey, Mass at the Marian shrine of Altagracia; Act of Entrustment to Mary. In Santo Domingo, opening of the Fourth General Assembly of the Latin American Bishops' Conference (CELAM). **October 13:** In Santo Domingo, Mass; meetings with Amerindians, African Americans and Haitians; attendance at sessions of the CELAM assembly.

October 14: Return to Rome.

EXCERPTS FROM ADDRESSES

The following excerpts are from texts in the English editions of "L'Osservatore Romano" for Oct. 14 and 21, 1992.

On Arrival

"I have come to celebrate, first and foremost, Jesus Christ, the first and greatest Evangelist, who entrusted his Church with the task of proclaiming his message of salvation throughout the world. I come as a herald of Christ, fulfilling the mission entrusted to the Apostle Peter and his successors to confirm the brethren in the faith. I also come to share your faith, your desires, joys and suffering."

"Moved by pastoral concern for the whole Church and in intimate communion with my brother bishops of the continent, I wanted to convoke the Fourth

General Conference of the Latin American episcopate (and to inaugurate) on the 12th of this month (the celebration) marking the 500th anniversary of the date on which Christ's cross was implanted in the New World."

"During this half millennium the Church has accompanied the Latin American peoples on their journey, sharing their joys and desires. Today they are at a crossroads of history and pause to look at urgent, difficult problems. The Church feels challenged by the dramatic condition of so many of her sons and daughters who are looking for a word of encouragement and hope from her. Therefore, together with the pastors of the Church gathered together in this assembly in Santo Domingo, I want to reaffirm once again our essential vocation of service to the Latin American people and proclaim each individual's inalienable dignity as a child of God, redeemed by Jesus Christ."

Christ Must Be Your Passion
This was the theme the Pope's address to priests, deacons and religious, Oct. 10.

"To everyone here and to all those in the various fields of pastoral and apostolic work in Latin America who work closely with the bishops in the immense task of the new evangelization, I urge you to be the light and salt that enlightens and seasons everything around you with Christian virtues. Your life of witness as priests and consecrated persons must always be evangelizing in nature, so that those who need the light of faith may accept the word of salvation joyfully; so that the poor and most neglected may feel the closeness of fraternal solidarity; so that the marginalized and abandoned may experience the love of Christ; so that those without a voice may be heard; so that those treated unjustly may be defended and helped."

"Jesus Christ and the Church must be your life's passion. You cannot love and serve Christ if you do not love and serve the Church, her pastors and her faithful. Be the 'living stones' of the Church in Latin America."

Challenge to All
The Pope commemorated five centuries of evangelization, challenged all sectors of Latin American society to work together for the solution of their problems, and canonized Ezequiel Moreno y Diaz during Mass Oct. 11 near the Columbus lighthouse-monument.

"Gathered around the altar in Santo Domingo to give thanks to God, we are celebrating the arrival of the light which shed life and hope on the journey of those peoples who, 500 years ago, were born to the Christian faith. By the power of the Holy Spirit, Christ's redemptive work was made present through that multitude of missionaries who ... crossed the ocean to proclaim the message of salvation to their brothers and sisters."

"Today, in union with the whole Church, let us offer thanks for the five centuries of evangelization."

At the same time, he appealed: "America, open your doors to Christ! Let the seed planted five centuries ago make all areas of your life fruitful: in-

dividuals and families, culture and work, economics and politics, the present and future."

Eradication of Poverty
At a meeting with the diplomatic corps Oct. 11, the Pope addressed "those who have responsibility for the government of Latin America," asking that they "give a determined thrust to the process of Latin American integration which will allow their peoples to take their rightful place on the global scene." He appealed for the peaceful solution of controversies, respect for human rights and moves toward the disposition of problems connected with external debt and spending for arms. On the subject of poverty, he said:

"On a continent where the process of impoverishment cannot be contained, where the levels of unemployment and underemployment are so high and which, in contrast, has great potential and abundant resources, we cannot put off an adequate investment of capital, making it available to create new jobs and increase production. Poverty is inhuman and unjust; it must be eradicated. Therefore, we must make full use of human resources; this is the key factor in a people's progress. Indeed, investing in the education of children and young people means assuring a better future for all."

Roles in New Evangelization
The Pope entrusted the peoples of the Americas to Mary at the shrine of Altagracia in Higuey Oct. 12 during a Mass commemorating the 500th anniversary of the arrival of the Gospel in the Americas. He also spoke about the roles of all Christians in the new evangelization.

"As believers, the Dominican laity are called on to make the Gospel values present in the various sectors of the life and culture of their people. It is precisely their Christian vocation that makes them live in the midst of temporal realities as builders of peace and harmony, always cooperating in the common good of the nation. Everyone must promote justice and solidarity in the fields of their concrete social responsibilities: in the economic sector, in trade unions and political activity, in the area of culture, in the media and in charitable and educational work. All are called to cooperate in the great task of the new evangelization."

Special Messages
Indigenous Peoples: The Pope told descendants of the original inhabitants that the values of their ancestors were "seeds of the word" which "were purified, deepened and completed by the Christian message, which proclaims universal brotherhood and defends justice." He recognized abuses committed against them by "individuals who did not see their indigenous brothers and sisters as children of God, their Father." He urged them to maintain and promote their culture with legitimate pride.

Amerindians: The Pope said he hoped the quincentenary events would "confirm them in the Christian faith and sustain their legitimate aspirations for achieving their rightful place in society and the Church."

African-Americans: "Everyone is aware of the

serious injustice committed against those black peoples of the African continent who were violently torn from their land, their culture and their traditions, and who were shipped to America as slaves. . . . These men and women were the victims of a disgraceful trade in which people who were baptized, but who did not live their faith, took part. How can we forget the enormous suffering inflicted, the violation of the most basic human rights, on those people deported from the African continent? How can we forget the human lives destroyed by slavery?" The Holy Father urged African-Americans "to defend your identity, to be conscious of your values and to make them bear fruit."

Haitians: The Pope expressed his sympathy and concern for "the sufferings of you all. I pray for those who have been forced to flee to other lands, for those who feel persecuted, for those who are disoriented, without work or security, and for all those whose rights have been ignored."

He also said: "It is my hope that Haiti, following the lead of other Latin American countries, will develop a great apostolic thrust and an enormous catechetical activity so that the baptized may attain a better knowledge of the Christian faith and may yield genuine fruits of holiness. I would also hope to see the development of a profound concern for humanity, an effort to incarnate the Gospel in the culture of the people, and I would like people to help one another to establish and maintain truly human relationships."

PAPAL REFLECTIONS ON HIS VISIT TO SANTO DOMINGO

Following are excerpts from the address delivered by Pope John Paul at a general audience Oct. 21 and published in the Oct. 28, 1992, English edition of "L'Osservatore Romano."

"Jesus Christ is the same yesterday, today and forever!" (Heb. 13:8).

"These words have a special meaning in connection with the date of 12 October 1492. Christopher Columbus, who left Spain heading West to search for a new route to the Indies (thus, toward Asia), discovered a new continent on that date. The discovery of America began with the islands of the Antilles, in particular, that which was then named Hispaniola. Precisely on that island the cross, symbol of redemption, was erected for the first time — and from there evangelization began."

"On 12 October 1992, the Bishop, of Rome, together with the whole Church and especially with the American Episcopate, went on pilgrimage to that cross from where — 500 years ago — the evangelization of this new land began, first toward the South and then toward the North. This was primarily a pilgrimage of thanksgiving. The itinerary included Santo Domingo and the shrine of Our Lady of Altagracia."

Missionaries of Love and Humility

"After 500 years, words of thanksgiving must be offered with the Mother of God for the 'great things' which the Father, the Son and the Holy Spirit have done for the people of the American continent through the ministry of so many messengers and stewards of the mysteries of God. Evangelization is a work of the love of Christ, who acts through human beings. America was evangelized by missionaries full of love, whose humility, courage, dedication and holiness, and even the very sacrifice of their lives, gave witness to him who is the Way the Truth and the Life."

"Through my pilgrimage to the place where evangelization began, a pilgrimage characterized by thanksgiving, we wanted at the same time to make an act of atonement before the infinite holiness of God for everything which during that advance toward the American continent was marred by sin, injustice and violence. Some of the missionaries have left us an impressive witness. One need only recall the names of Montesinos, las Casas, Cordoba, Fray Juan del Valle and many others."

Plea for Forgiveness

"After 500 years, we stand before Christ, who is the Lord of all history, to address those words to the Father that Christ himself taught us: 'Forgive us our trespasses, as we forgive . . .'" (cf. Mt. 6:12).

"The Redeemer's prayer is addressed to the Father and at the same time to all who suffered various injustices. We do not cease asking these people for 'forgiveness.' This request for pardon is primarily addressed to the first inhabitants of the new land, to the Indios — and then to those who were brought from Africa as slaves to do heavy labor."

" 'Forgive us our trespasses . . .' — this prayer is also part of evangelization. It should also be mentioned that the injustices perpetrated were the occasion for the first draft of a code of human rights — a task in which the University of Salamanca distinguished itself. This work gradually bore fruit. In our time, these rights are commonly recognized as principles of universal morality."

" 'Forgive us our trespasses . . .' Teach us to conquer evil with good" (cf. Rom. 12:21).

Not a New Gospel

" 'Jesus Christ is the same yesterday, today and forever!' (Heb. 13:8). The fifth centenary of evangelization — as a celebration of thanksgiving and atonement — at the same time represents a new beginning. In close connection with the date of 12 October 1992, the bishops of all Latin America opened a conference devoted to the new evangelization. The Santo Domingo conference is a continuation of the ones held in Rio de Janeiro, Medellin and Puebla.

"The new evangelization does not mean a 'new Gospel' because 'Christ is the same yesterday, today and forever.' A new evangelization means an appropriate response to the 'signs of the times,' to the needs of individuals and peoples at the close of the Second Christian Millenium. It also means promoting a new dimension of justice and peace, as well as a culture profoundly rooted in the Gospel — a new man in Jesus Christ."

"May Santo Domingo be a new Upper Room

where the successors of the Apostles, gathered in prayer with the Mother of Christ, prepare the way for the new evangelization of all America. On the threshold of the Third Christian Millenium, may the pastors know how to offer the world 'Christ, who is the same yesterday, today and forever.' "

CELAM GENERAL ASSEMBLY: PAPAL ADDRESS

The following excerpts are from the address delivered by Pope John Paul at the opening of the Fourth General Conference of the Latin American Bishops Oct. 12, 1993, in Santo Domingo.
These excerpts are from the text circulated by the CNS Documentary Service, Origins, Oct. 22, 1992 (Vol. 22, No. 19).

Purpose

"This conference is meeting to celebrate Jesus Christ, to thank God for his presence in these lands of the Americas where the message of salvation began to spread 500 years ago. It is meeting to celebrate the planting of the Church, which has furnished the New World with such abundant fruits of holiness and love during these five centuries."

"This general conference is meeting to trace guidelines for an evangelizing activity that will place Christ in the heart and on the lips of all Latin Americans. This is our task: to make the truth about Christ and the truth about the human being penetrate ever more deeply into all strata of society and to transform it."

"This conference must know how to combine the three doctrinal and pastoral elements that constitute the three axes of the new evangelization: Christology, ecclesiology and anthropology. The challenges to the Church's evangelizing activity in the Americas today must be met through a deep and solid Christology, and on the basis of a sound anthropology and a clear and correct ecclesiological vision."

New Evangelization

"The new evangelization is the central idea within the whole set of issues to be addressed in this conference."

"The new evangelization does not consist in a 'new Gospel,' which would always arise from ourselves, our culture, our analysis of human need. Hence, it would not be the 'Gospel' but mere human invention, and there would be no salvation in it. Nor does it consist of trimming away from the Gospel everything that seems difficult for the contemporary mind-set to accept. Culture is not the measure of the Gospel; rather, Jesus Christ is the measure of all culture and all human endeavor. No, the new evangelization does not arise from the desire 'to curry favor with human beings' or to 'please people' (Gal. 1:10), but from responsibility for the gift that God has made to us in Christ, in which we accede to the truth about God and about the human being, and to the possibility of true life."

"The starting point for the new evangelization is the certainty that in Christ are 'inscrutable riches' (Eph. 3:8) that are not exhausted by any culture or any age and that we human beings can always approach in order to be enriched. ... That wealth is first and foremost Christ himself, his person, for he himself is our salvation."

"Newness does not touch the content of the Gospel message, which is unchangeable, for Christ is 'the same, yesterday, today and forever.' Hence, the Gospel is to be preached with complete faithfulness and purity as it has been guarded and transmitted by the tradition of the Church. ... Reductive Christologies ... cannot be accepted as instruments for the new evangelization."

New Attitude toward Evangelization

"The newness of the evangelizing activity that we have called for is a matter of attitude, style, effort and planning. ... An evangelization new in its ardor means a solid faith, an intense pastoral charity and a steadfast fidelity that, under the action of the Spirit, generate a spirituality, an irrepressible enthusiasm for the task of announcing the Gospel."

"The new times demand that the Christian message reach people today through new methods of apostolate and that it be expressed in language and forms that are accessible to Latin Americans."

Human Development

"Stimulating human development must be the logical outcome of evangelization, which tends toward the comprehensive liberation of the person."

"Concern for the social dimension is 'part of the Church's evangelizing mission' and is also 'an essential part of the Christian message, since this doctrine points out the direct consequences of that message in the life of society and situates daily work and struggles for justice in the context of bearing witness to Christ the Savior.' "

"The problem of human development cannot be considered apart from human relationship with God. ... Genuine efforts at human betterment must always respect the truth about God and the truth about the human being, and respect both God's rights and the rights of the human being."

Like Medellin and Puebla

"In continuity with the Medellin and Puebla conferences, the Church reaffirms the preferential option on behalf of the poor. That option is not exclusive or excluding, since the message of salvation is intended for all. It is 'an option, moreover, that is based essentially on God's word, and not on criteria provided by human sciences or opposed ideologies, which often reduce the poor to abstract sociopolitical and economic categories. But it is a firm and irrevocable option.' "

"The genuine praxis of liberation must always be inspired by the doctrine of the Church as set forth in the two instructions by the Congregation for the Doctrine of the Faith (*Libertatis Nuntius*, 1984; *Libertatis Conscientia*, 1986). ... The Church can in no way allow any ideology or political current to snatch away the banner of justice, for it is one of the primary demands of the Gospel and at the same time a fruit of the coming of God's kingdom."

"This general conference might consider the desirability of celebrating in the near future a meeting of representatives of the episcopacies of the Americas — which might even have a synodal character — in order to increase cooperation among the various local churches in different fields of pastoral activity. In the framework of the new evangelization and as an expression of episcopal communion, such a meeting could also deal with issues of justice and solidarity among all the nations of the Americas."

Dignity of the Person

"There is no genuine human development, true liberation or preferential option for the poor unless it is based on the very foundations of the dignity of the person and of the surroundings in which the person must develop, according to the Creator's design. Hence, among the topics and options that require the entire attention of the Church, I cannot fail to recall those of the family and of life: two things that are closely interrelated, since the family is 'the sanctuary of life.'"

The Pope cited a number of problems related to the family, including common-law arrangements, divorce, the plight of street children and the culture of death "manifested in abortion, euthanasia, war, guerrilla warfare, kidnapping, terrorism and other forms of violence or exploitation."

"We cannot forget that comprehensive human advancement is critically important for the development of the peoples of Latin America. For 'a people's development does not derive primarily from money, material assistance or technological means, but from the formation of consciences and the gradual maturing of ways of thinking and patterns of behavior. The human being is the principal agent of development, not money or technology.' Latin America's greatest wealth is its peoples. By 'awakening their consciences through the Gospel,' the Church contributes to the awakening of dormant energies that can be put to work in building a new civilization."

Christian Culture

"Although the Gospel is not identified with any particular culture, it certainly should provide cultures with inspiration to transform themselves from within by enriching them with the Christian values that derive from faith. Indeed, the evangelization of cultures represents the deepest and most comprehensive way to evangelize a society, since the message of Christ thereby permeates people's awareness and is projected into the ethos of a people, its essential attitudes, its institutions and all its structures."

"To proclaim Jesus Christ in all cultures is the Church's central concern and the object of its mission."

"The absence of fundamental Christian values in the culture of modernity has not only obscured the transcendent dimension and inclined many people — even in Latin America — toward religious indifference, but it is also the key reason for the social disillusionment that has given rise to the crisis of that culture. As a result of the autonomy introduced by rationalism, today values tend to be based primarily on a subjective social consensus that often leads to positions contrary even to natural ethics. Consider the drama of abortion, abuses in genetic engineering and attacks on life and on the dignity of the person."

"The plurality of options available today demands that there be a deep pastoral renewal through the Gospel discernment of the prevailing values, attitudes and collective behavior patterns which often are a decisive factor in choosing either good or evil."

Evangelization of Culture

" 'The evangelization of culture is an effort to understand the mind-sets and attitudes of the contemporary world and to shine the light of the Gospel on them. It is the intention to reach all levels of human life in order to make it more worthy.' However, this effort at understanding and shedding light must always be accompanied by the proclamation of the Good News. Thus, the Gospel's penetration of cultures will not be a mere external adaptation but 'a profound and all-embracing one, which involves Christian message and also the Church's reflection and practice,' and will always respect the characteristics and integrity of the faith."

"The moment has come to commit all of the Church's energies to the new evangelization and the mission ad gentes (among those who have not yet received the Gospel). No believer in Christ, no institution of the Church, can avoid this supreme duty: to proclaim Christ to all peoples."

"The greatest sign of gratitude for receiving Christ 500 years ago and the greatest sign of its Christian vitality is to become committed to mission."

"We must not forget that the primary form of evangelization is witness, that is, proclaiming the message of salvation through one's works and the consistency of one's life, thus making it incarnate in the everyday history of human beings."

CELAM MESSAGE TO PEOPLES OF LATIN AMERICA AND CARIBBEAN

The bishops of Latin America issued a message to the people of the region at the conclusion of their Fourth General Assembly, Oct. 12 to 28, 1992, in Santo Domingo.

The following excerpts are from the text circulated by the CNS Documentary Service, Origins, Jan. 14, 1993 (Vol. 22, No. 31).

Purpose

"The Fourth General Conference of the Latin American Episcopate has sought to provide a basic outline for a new impetus to evangelization that will put Christ into the hearts, on the lips and in the activities and lives of all Latin Americans. Our task is to ensure that the truth about Christ, the Church and humanity penetrate the strata of society ever more deeply, seeking its gradual transformation. Our work has mainly focused on the new evangelization."

"Our meeting is closely related to and in continuity with those of the same kind that preceded it: the first was held in Rio de Janeiro, Brazil, in 1955, the second in Medellin, Colombia, in 1968, and the third in Puebla, Mexico, in 1979. We fully confirm the same choices that marked those meetings and embody their more substantive conclusions."

"We wish to convert our desire to evangelize into concrete action that makes it possible for people to overcome their problems and recover from their pain . . . and to have primary responsibility for their own lives through their saving encounter with the Lord."

Pastoral Priorities

The bishops proposed a set of guidelines for pastoral activity in connection with the new evangelization. They included the following.

"So that Christ may be the center of our people's life, we call all the faithful to a new evangelization and appeal especially to the laity, and particularly the young people among them."

• "A renewed catechesis and a living liturgy in a Church constantly concerned with mission will increasingly attract and sanctify all Christians, particularly those who are distant and indifferent to the Church."

• "The new evangelization will intensify the missionary apostolate in all our churches and will make us feel responsible for going beyond our frontiers to bring to other peoples the faith that reached us 500 years ago."

"As an expression of the new evangelization, we also commit ourselves to working for the integral development of the Latin American and Caribbean peoples, with the poor as our main concern."

• "In this human development, the family, where life originates, will occupy a privileged and fundamental place. Today it is urgently necessary to promote and protect life from the many attacks upon it from various sectors of modern society."

• "We should promote an evangelization that penetrates to the deepest roots of our peoples' common culture, paying special attention to the growing urban culture."

• "We have devoted particular attention to an authentic incarnation of the Gospel in the indigenous and African-American cultures of our continent."

• "For this inculturation of the Gospel, effective educational programs and the use of the modern means of communication are most important."

Necessary Elements

"Besides its primarily religious objective, the new evangelization launched by the Fourth General Conference offers the necessary elements for the birth of the Great Homeland."

Reconciliation: "The indispensable reconciliation whereby, in the logic of the Our Father, past and present divisions will be healed, former and recent injustices will be mutually forgiven, and peace will be restored."

Solidarity: "People helping others to bear their burden and sharing with them their own aspirations. 'The new ideal of solidarity must prevail over the old desire to control.'"

Integration: "To achieve the integration of our countries, the barriers of isolation, discrimination and mutual indifference must be overcome. 'Latin American integration is a factor which can significantly help in overcoming the pressing problems which affect the continent today.'"

Communion: "Deep communion in the Church concerning the political will for progress and well-being."

"The social and spiritual heritage contained in these four words — reconciliation, solidarity, integration and communion —could be transformed into Latin America's greatest resource. These are the wishes and prayers of the bishops of the Fourth General Conference of the Latin American Episcopate."

"We entrust our work to Our Lady of Guadalupe, Star of the New Evangelization."

PAPAL VISIT TO BENIN, UGANDA, SUDAN

Pope John Paul, on his 10th apostolic trip to Africa, visited Benin, Uganda and Sudan Feb. 3 to 10, 1993. It was the 57th foreign trip of his pontificate.

Excerpts from papal addresses are from texts published in the Feb. 10 and 17, 1993, English editions of "L'Osservatore Romano."

ITINERARY

In Benin

February 3: At Cotonou, celebration of Mass and ordination of priests, meeting with members of the bishops' conference.

• *New Evangelization:* This, together with the nature of their ministry, was the principal theme of the Pope's homily during the Mass at which he ordained 12 deacons to the priesthood.

He elaborated on the subject in a written message presented to members' of the nation's episcopal conference.

"Today more than ever the world needs the proclamation of the Good News. The Church wants

to bring the Gospel not only to the geographic areas where it has not yet reached, but also, and especially, to the milieus of the human family, which it should endow with life from within. The goal of evangelization is, through the acceptance of the faith, interior change, the conversion of the personal and collective conscience of mankind."

• *Inculturation:* "Evangelization ... comes through inculturation of the faith."

"The Gospel message plays a prophetic and critical role. It is meant to give new life, to sift what is ambiguous or tarnished in ancestral customs as well as in practices recently imported from foreign lands. Everything that is good, noble and true can be accepted, so that the Christian mystery may be expressed according to the African genius."

"The Second Vatican Council gave three criteria for discernment in accepting the cultural values of peoples, namely: their ability to contribute to the glory of God the Creator; their ability to show forth the grace of the Savior; and, finally, their ability to be ordered to Christian life."

February 4: At Parakou, meeting with Muslims,

celebration of Mass. At Cotonou, meetings with the president, voodoo practitioners, priests, men and women religious, seminarians, lay persons and members of other Christian communities.

● *Christian-Muslim Cooperation:* At a meeting with Muslim leaders, the Pope said: "Many points common to Muslims and Christians are related to religious piety, such as the importance given to prayer, a regard for morality and a sense of the dignity of the human person open to the transcendent."

"All Beninese, without distinction of tribe or religion are called to join efforts for its reconstruction. The development of Benin, in which Muslims, Christians and members of the traditional religion must participate, should benefit all segments of the population, avoiding all forms of moral, physical or psychological violence."

The Holy Father emphasized the importance of efforts to foster family values, the education of the young, the quest for peace, and ways and means of eliminating poverty.

● *Christian Unity:* "The first step toward unity is welcoming the message of Christ with the necessary conversion of heart that this involves," the Pope said during Mass at Parakou.

"Christians must enter with everyone into the dialogue of salvation which God offers the world through the ages, and which the Church pursues, faithful to the divine initiative."

"The dialogue which you must seek is that of daily life, where each tries to cultivate a spirit of good neighborliness, sharing joys and pains, common problems and concerns. This attitude is fundamental: it requires a balanced attitude, deep religious conviction and openness to truth."

The Pope cited the Eucharist as the sacrament and sign of unity.

● *Seeds of the Word in Voodoo:* In addressing adherents of Voodooism, the Pope said: "The Catholic Church looks favorably upon dialogue. ... She wants to establish positive and constructive relationships with individuals and with the human groups of various faiths in view of a mutual enrichment."

"The Second Vatican Council ... recognized that in the diverse religious traditions there is something true and good, the seeds of the word."

"These are the foundations for a fruitful dialogue."

"You have a strong attachment to the traditions handed on by your ancestors. It is legitimate to be grateful to your forefathers who passed on this sense of the sacred, belief in a single God who is good, a sense of celebration, esteem for the moral life and for harmony in society."

"The ancestors of (the) missionaries who came from Europe had themselves received the Gospel when they already had another religion and a worship. In receiving the message of God, they did not lose anything. On the contrary, they gained by knowing Jesus Christ and, by baptism, through him they became sons and daughters of the God of love and mercy."

In Uganda

February 5: Afternoon arrival at Entebbe, after flight from Cotonou. At Kampala, visit to the president.

February 6: At Gulu, celebration of Mass. At Kampala, meeting with youths.

● *Youths:* The Pope challenged young people to prepare for their future responsibilities in society by seeking the truth in education, by preparing for marriage and family life in honest and chaste relationships, and by forging a "chain of solidarity" extending to every level of social life.

February 7: At Namugongo, ecumenical meeting at the Anglican shrine of the Ugandan martyrs, veneration of the relics of St. Charles Lwanga at the national Catholic shrine of the martyrs, celebration of Mass. At Nsambya, meetings with the sick at St. Francis Hospital and with the bishops' conference.

● *Ugandan Martyrs:* At their shrine, the Pope called the Uganda martyrs the "truest of Africans." (They were several Anglicans and 22 Catholics put to death between 1885 and 1887 for their refusal to participate in the corrupt life-style of King Mwanga.) While paying tribute to them, the Holy Father spoke also about the Christian heritage of the country and praised the many lay men and women striving for holiness; he made special mention of women, Christian families, and various associations and movements of lay persons.

● *AIDS:* With the sick at St. Francis Hospital, the Pope spoke about the redemptive value of suffering. Addressing the subject of AIDS, he said: "The church, together with all men and women of good will, is deeply distressed at the great number of individuals in Uganda, particularly children and young people, who are suffering from AIDS, and at the untold hardship which this disease has brought to families, communities and the nation itself. Today I wish to make my own the words of your bishops, who wrote: 'The situation which is affecting everybody in the country needs to be confronted with solidarity, with much love and care for the victims, with much generosity to the orphans and with much commitment to a renewed way of Christian moral living.' The sick too have a special role to play in meeting the challenge of AIDS: You can offer your suffering for the spread of Christ's truth and love throughout this beloved nation."

● *Church as Reconciling Community:* This was a major theme of the Pope's address to members of the nation's episcopal conference. "At this moment in Uganda's history (with spiritual goods and the 'culture of peace' remaining under attack) it falls to the Church to answer with greater fidelity God's injunction to be a reconciling community. ... Awareness (of this responsibility) should bear fruit in a readiness on the part of all the faithful of Uganda to put aside hatred and thus testify to the truth that the spirit of mercy is stronger than the spirit of revenge. In this regard we cannot fail to mention the specific role of Catholic lay leaders. To them are entrusted the affairs of the temporal order: politics, economics, the direction of society. In these fields they 'are called upon to engage directly in dialogue or to work for dialogue aimed at reconciliation.'"

"No one, of course, should imagine that, by inviting the Catholic citizens of Uganda to work for community renewal, you are implying that this duty is theirs alone. No, the cooperation of Christians of all churches and ecclesial communities with one another, as with followers of other religions, is not only welcome but indispensable."

February 8: At Kasese, celebration of Mass. At Kampala, meeting with the diplomatic corps.

• *Called To Be One:* At Mass, the Pope reminded his hearers that the unity of civil society in Uganda needed to be built up and that the renewal of family life — which requires pastoral care and support from the Christian community — contributes to strengthening unity.

• *Africa Needs the Help of Other Nations:* The Pope told diplomats that, although Africa is beset by conflicts of various kinds, famine and the mass dislocations of people, there are signs of a growth in democratic government and of a recovery of supportive values. He said Africans are responsible for developing their own future, but they need help from the international community.

February 9: At Soroti, celebration of Mass. At Kampala, Vespers celebration for opening of the third meeting in Africa of the permanent council for preparation of the forthcoming Synod of Bishops for Africa.

• *Evangelization Priorities:* During Mass, the Pope told priests, men and women religious, and lay persons: "The present generation of Ugandan Catholics must not let the light which the martyrs caused to shine upon this land be dimmed." In first place among their priorities is the "fundamental task of evangelization."

"The mission to evangelize implies that Ugandan Christians must listen to the cries of all those in this country and throughout Africa pleading to be freed from so many forms of slavery: from ignorance, and from the oppression that weighs so heavily on the poor, the elderly and lonely, the sick, refugees, the defenseless young, and, in particular, the orphans of war and the orphans left by the AIDS epidemic. They all need your preferential and practical love. Whatever you do for them, you do to Christ himself."

"Your bishops have also urged the Church in Uganda to defend courageously human life and human dignity. Christians must make a clear and active option for justice. ... Only by overcoming rivalry and hatred, only by putting aside the desire for revenge, only by forgiving and being reconciled, will the Christians of Uganda bear witness to the Light. Improving ecumenical relations, praying for Christian unity, fostering greater understanding and cooperation with the followers of Islam in human development and in building a new Uganda founded on justice and respect for human rights: all this is part of the task that lies before the Catholic community at the approach of a new Christian millennium. ... Your bishops have indicated the way forward. May the whole Catholic community respond, like a lamp on a lampstand where it gives light to all in the household."

• *African Synod:* "The immediate future of the Church's life on this continent will be profoundly influenced by the Special Assembly for Africa of the Synod of Bishops. This important event (to begin Apr. 10, 1994) is meant to help the particular churches in Africa to pass on the light of the Gospel in all its fullness to the men and women of the next generation."

In Sudan

Feb. 10: At Khartoum, meeting with priests, men and women religious, seminarians, novices and catechists; visit to the president; meeting with Christian and other religious leaders, celebration of Mass, departure and flight to Rome.

• *Protection of Minorities:* At a meeting with President Omar Hassan Ahmed al Bashir, the Pope said he had come to Sudan "to offer the message of reconciliation and hope which is at the heart of Catholicism and which I bring to all the Sudanese people, irrespective of differences of religion or ethnic origin."

The Pope recalled an address to diplomats Jan. 16, 1993, in which he "felt the need to make specific reference to the war which continues to set the peoples of the North and South of Sudan against each other. I expressed the sincere hope 'that the Sudanese, with freedom to choose, will succeed in finding a constitutional formula which will make it possible to overcome contradictions and struggles, with proper respect paid to the specific characteristics of each community.'"

"Only a legally guaranteed respect for human rights in a system of equal justice for all can create the right conditions for peaceful coexistence and cooperation in serving the common good."

• *Fundamental Principles:* "Two fundamental principles underlie the universal obligation to understand and respect the variety and richness of other peoples, societies, cultures and religions. First, the inalienable dignity of every human person, irrespective of racial, ethnic, cultural or national origin or religious belief, means that, when people coalesce in groups, they have a right to enjoy a collective identity. Thus, minorities within a country have the right to exist, with their own language, culture and traditions, and the state is morally obliged to leave room for their identity and self-expression. Secondly, the fundamental unity of the human race, which takes its origin from God the Creator of all, requires that no group should consider itself superior to another. It likewise requires that integration should be built on effective solidarity and freedom from discrimination. Consequently, the state has a duty to respect and defend the differences existing among its citizens, and to permit their diversity to serve the common good. Experience shows that peace and internal security can only be guaranteed through respect for the rights of all those for whom the state has responsibility."

• *Religious Freedom:* "In such a perspective, the freedom of individuals and communities to profess and practice their religion is an essential element for peaceful human coexistence. Freedom of conscience and freedom to seek the truth and to act according to one's personal religious beliefs are so fundamentally human that any effort to restrict them almost inevitably leads to bitter conflict."

"Where relations between groups within a nation have broken down, dialogue and negotiation are the obligatory paths to peace. Reconciliation, in accordance with justice and respect for the legitimate aspirations of all sectors of the national community must be the rule."

"My good wishes for the Sudan become an earnest

prayer that God's gift of peace will become a reality in your midst, that harmony and cooperation between North and South, between Christians and Muslims, will take the place of conflict, that obstacles to religious freedom will soon be a thing of the past."

POPE JOHN PAUL IN ALBANIA

Pope John Paul, on the 58th foreign trip of his pontificate, visited Albania Apr. 25. The key event of the visit was the ordination of four bishops and the reestablishment of the hierarchy in the country which in 1967 officially declared itself atheistic. The two cities on the papal itinerary were Shkoder and Tirana.

The following excerpts are from texts published in the Apr. 28 and May 5, 1993, English editions of "L'Osservatore Romano."

ADDRESSES

Desire to Contribute

On arrival at Tirana, the Pope said: "Just as she shared in the recent trials (of nearly 50 years of rigid communist control), so now the Church wishes to share in the joy and responsibility of the new season of freedom that has just begun. It is her great desire to make a significant contribution to the achievement of Albania's integral progress and its active insertion into the European context, toward which its ancient historical roots naturally lead it."

Ordination of Bishops

During the Mass in Shkoder at which he ordained four bishops, the Holy Father declared: "Behold, the Eucharist is returning to your land. The Church is returning, coming out of the catacombs as in the time of the Roman Empire; and, full of joy for the freedom she has regained, she proclaims: 'The Lord is risen. . . . The Lord is truly risen.'"

Addressing the priests about to be ordained bishops, the Pope said: "It is therefore a very moving time, which also stirs the depths of our heart because, with your episcopal ordination, the Albanian Church begins anew to live in fullness; to express the life that is hers, in which every aspect of the apostolic inheritance is manifest."

Bishops' Backgrounds

"I greet you, Archbishop Frano Illia of Shkodre, on the very day on which, 25 years ago, you were condemned to death, a sentence which was later commuted to hard labor, which you served for 20 years."

"I greet your Auxiliary, Bishop Zef Simoni, also condemned a year before you, on 25 April, 1967, to 15 years' imprisonment. Providence also chose 15 April as the date of your episcopal ordination."

"I greet you, Archbishop Rrok K. Mirdita of Durres-Tirane, who have so generously agreed to face the challenges and hardships of a demanding, tiring pastoral service."

"Last of all, I greet you, Bishop Robert Ashta of Pult, to whom the people of this land are also grateful for the suffering you have borne in the difficult past."

Hierarchy Reestablished

"With your ordination, dear brothers, the Catholic community regains stability and security in its hierarchical structure and, through your support and your enlightened pastoral care, it can look to the future with greater serenity and confidence. Thus, it will be ready generously to offer its own contribution, as it never failed to do in the past, to the spiritual, cultural and social development of the Albanian nation."

"You, the new pastors of this flock of Christ, are entrusted today with the ministry of keeping it in fidelity, of administering it in the truth, of leading it to holiness and to full communion in the sanctifying Spirit, so that it may express the wealth of its charisms and bear the plentiful fruit of solidarity and peace."

Address to the Nation

The Pope addressed all Albanians during formal farewell ceremonies in Tirana in the square dedicated to the honor of their national hero, George Castriota Skanderbeg, who led a strong defense against Turkish invaders in the 15th century.

Of religious freedom, the Pope said: "You have regained your freedom virtually without bloodshed. You have almost miraculously risen from an abyss of tyranny and death."

"The religious freedom which you finally enjoy today, however, is not only a precious gift of the Lord for those who have the grace of faith. It is a gift for all, because it is the basic guarantee of every other expression of freedom. It intimately touches the individual in that inviolable sanctuary of the conscience, where the human being encounters the Creator and is fully aware of his own dignity. Correctly used, there is no social disorder to be feared from such freedom. In fact, sincere faith does not divide people but rather unites them despite their differences. There is nothing like faith to remind us that, if we have one Creator, we are all brothers and sisters. Thus, religious freedom is a shield against totalitarianism and a decisive contribution to human brotherhood. True religious freedom rejects any temptation to intolerance and sectarianism, and fosters attitudes of respectful and constructive dialogue."

Patriotism and Harmony

The Holy Father warned against misguided patriotism. "May the strong patriotic feelings which you are experiencing at this time never degenerate into that intolerant and aggressive nationalism which still claims victims today and is provoking ferocious animosity in many parts of the world, in fact, not very far from here" (for example, in Bosnia-Herzegovina).

"Instead, may your harmony in coexistence continue to grow. It is necessary to learn the art of dialogue and listening, even when it requires an effort. It is the price of freedom, the secret of genuine moral and civil progress."

The Pope also asked "the international community to turn its full attention to the needs of integral (Albanian) development. Only in this way will it be possible to build peace in this Balkan region, stained with the blood of ignoble and senseless fratricidal conflicts."

PAPAL COMMENT

The resurrection of the Church in Albania was the theme of the Pope's address at the general audience of Apr. 28. He said, in part as follows.

Albania Was Like a Tomb

" 'Who will roll back the stone for us from the entrance to the tomb?' " (Mk. 16:3).

"These words of the women who had rushed to Christ's tomb on the day after the Sabbath come to mind when one considers the recent history of the country I was able to visit last Sunday. For years Albania had become synonymous with the particular oppression established by a totalitarian, atheistic system in which the rejection of God was pushed to its furthest limits. There the right to freedom of conscience and religion had been trampled upon most brutally; those who simply administered baptism, or engaged in any religious practices were threatened with the death penalty. The persecution raged against Christians and Muslims alike."

"The country thus became like the tomb in which the Jews buried Christ, putting a stone against its entrance."

"But behold, the women who came to the tomb 'found the stone rolled away' (Lk. 24:2). For Albania, too, as a result of the events beginning in 1989, the tombstone was rolled away and a period of changes began. Human rights, including that of freedom of conscience and religion, have now become the basis of social life. In these circumstances it became possible — and in a certain sense even necessary, especially with respect to the Catholic community — for the Pope to visit. This took place on 25 April last."

"The Church in Albania is now living a new spring."

"My visit last Sunday was meant to hallow this event by consecrating new bishops."

Hope and Encouragement

"My departure discourse, addressed to the whole nation, was meant to be a message of hope and encouragement. I invited them not to forget easily the sufferings endured by Albanians in the decades past."

"I indicated to the people of Albania their future challenges. Their regained religious freedom will certainly by the leaven of a democratic society if the value and primary importance of the human person are recognized, and if all social, political and economic relations are marked by authentic solidarity."

"In addition, I expressed the wish that Albania, with the assistance of the international community, may overcome the serious crisis of the present moment. It will be helped by its sense of family and acceptance, and especially by its faith. It will receive great support from a continually renewed understanding between Catholics, the Orthodox and Muslims. Albania has reopened its doors to God, and God does not abandon those who trust in him."

PAPAL VISIT TO SPAIN

Pope John Paul, on the 59th foreign trip of his pontificate, visited Spain for the fourth time June 12 to 17, 1993.

Excerpts from the Pope's addresses are from the texts published in June 23 and 30, 1993, English editions of "L'Osservatore Romano."

ITINERARY AND ADDRESSES

June 12: Late morning arrival at the Seville airport; visit to the cathedral, the fourth largest church in the world; celebration of Mass and the ordination of 38 deacons to the priesthood.

Total Mystery of the Eucharist

In an address to bishops, priests and religious at the cathedral in Seville, the Pope said: "It is important for us to live and teach others how to live the total mystery of the Eucharist: the sacrament of sacrifice, of the Banquet and of the abiding Presence of Jesus Christ the Savior. You know well that the various forms of Eucharistic devotion are both an extension of the sacrifice and of Communion, and a preparation for them. Is it necessary to stress once again the deep theological and spiritual motivations which underlie devotion to the Blessed Sacrament outside the celebration of Mass? It is true that the reservation of the Sacrament was begun in order to take Communion to the sick and those absent from the celebration. However, as the *Catechism of the Catholic Church* says, 'to deepen faith in the real presence of Christ in the Eucharist, the Church is aware of the meaning of silent adoration of the Lord present under the Eucharistic species' (No. 1379)."

Ministry of Priests

This was the theme of the Pope's homily as he ordained 38 deacons to the priesthood. He said: "I want to exhort you in the ministry that you are beginning today, not to neglect the sacrament of reconciliation, in which all Christians receive forgiveness of their sins. Conduct a pastoral activity that will lead the faithful to personal conversion, for which you must devote to the ministry of forgiveness all the time necessary, with the generosity and patience of true 'fishers of men.'"

He also said: "See to it that your preaching is always inspired by the word of God, transmitted by tradition and authoritatively proposed by the teaching authority of the Church. Speak out valiantly, preach with deep faith, inspiring hope always, as witnesses of the risen Lord."

"Your witness as priests should always be evangelizing, in order that those who are deprived of the light of the faith may welcome with joy the word of salvation; so that the poor and the most neglected may feel the closeness of brotherly solidarity; so that the alienated and desolate may experience Christ's love; so that the voiceless may feel they are heard; so that those who have been unjustly treated may find protection and help."

June 13: In Seville, celebration of the *Statio Orbis* Mass concluding the 45th International Eucharistic Congress, concelebrated by 200 cardinals, archbishops and bishops along with 1,200 priests, and attended by 300,000 or more people from many countries; meeting with the international group of 150 delegates involved in preparations and related arrangements for the congress. At Dos Hermanas, official opening of the San Rafael Residence for the Elderly, a social works project of the congress. (See separate entry on the congress.)

June 14: In Huelva, celebration of Mass; visits to churches in Moguer and Palos de la Frontera; coronation of Our Lady of the Miracles at the monastery in La Rabida. In El Rocio, visit to the Marian shrine and meeting with the faithful; return to Seville. Events of the day were related to places and circumstances connected with the voyages of Columbus and the departure of the first missionaries to the New World.

Society and Evangelization

At Mass in Huelva, the Pope spoke about the state of contemporary society and called for "a renewed creative effort" of evangelization.

The Pope prefaced his remarks about contemporary society by saying: "With grateful and joyful remembrance we have celebrated the fifth centenary of that great epic of the Spanish missionaries, to whom by my presence in Huelva, the cradle of discovery, I want to render homage in the name of the whole Church. However, the Church cannot limit herself to recalling her glorious past. For her, the commemoration of what took place 500 years ago is 'a call to a new creative force in her evangelization.' The remembrance of the past should serve as a stimulus and an incentive for the task of facing the challenges of the present with apostolic determination and courage."

Secularization

Our society, "despite its deep Christian roots, has seen the spread within its ranks of the phenomena of secularization and of de-Christianization — a society which 'continually calls for a re-evangelization,' without delay. The Church ... cannot close in on herself. She must listen to and make her own the prayer of Mary, who continues to intercede as a mother on behalf of human beings who, even though unaware of it, thirst for the 'new and improved' wine of the Gospel. The signs of de-Christianization which we observe cannot become a pretext for a conformist resignation or a paralyzing discouragement; indeed, the Church sees in these signs the voice of God who is calling us to enlighten consciences with the light of the Gospel."

"The neglect of God, the absence of moral values of which he alone can be the foundation, are at the root of the economic systems which forget the dignity of the person and the moral law, and which consider gain as the primary goal and the only motivation of one's own life project. This basic reality is not unrelated to the painful socio-economic phenomena which have repercussions on so many families, such as the drama of unemployment, as many of you know from painful personal experience, and by which many men and women, deprived of the means of personal fulfillment through honest employment, are led to desperation or added to the list of those marginalized from society."

Harm to Family and Society

"Alienation from God, the eclipse of moral values, has also caused the deterioration of family life, which is today profoundly afflicted by the growing trend of separation and divorce, by the systematic decline in the birth-rate — even through the abominable crime of abortion — by the growing tendency to abandon the elderly who are often deprived of the warmth of a family environment and of the necessary interchange between generations. This whole phenomenon of the obscuring of Christian moral values has most devastating repercussions on the youth, the object of subtle manipulation today, many of whom are victims of drugs and alcohol, or pornography or other forms of degrading consumerism, which futilely claim to fill the void of spiritual values with a style of life directed toward having rather than being, and which wants to have more, not in order to be more but in order to spend life in enjoyment as an end in itself. The idolatry of profit and the unbridled consumerism of having and enjoying are also at the root of the irresponsible destruction of the environment, inasmuch as they drive man to make arbitrary use of the earth, subjecting it without restraint to his will, as though it did not have its own requisites and a prior God-given purpose, which man can indeed develop but must not betray."

"It is the call of this society which desperately needs the light and the truth of the Gospel. ... A new creative effort of evangelization of our world is necessary and urgent. The challenge is decisive and does allow for delay or waiting."

Popular Expressions of Religion

At the shrine of Our Lady of El Rocio the Holy Father spoke about popular expressions of piety and their relation to authentic faith. The shrine, visited by an average of 10,000 pilgrims every Sunday, is the center of devotion in Andalusia and the locale of 87 devotional confraternities.

"Your devotion to the Blessed Virgin represents a key experience in popular piety and, at the same time, constitutes a complex socio-cultural and religious phenomenon. ... In the deep roots of this religious and cultural phenomenon we can see the authentic spiritual values of faith in God and the acknowledgment of Christ as the Son of God and the Savior of mankind, of love and of devotion to the Blessed Virgin, and of Christian fellowship, which is born of the knowledge that we are children of the same heavenly Father."

"Your devotion to the Blessed Virgin, as shown in ... your pilgrimages to the shrine and in your activities in the confraternities, has much that is positive and encouraging, but it has also gathered, as you say, 'the dust of the road,' of which it must be cleansed. It is necessary, therefore, that, by drawing from the roots of this devotion, you give these sources of faith their evangelical fullness; that is, that you discover the profound reasons for the presence of Mary in your lives as the model in your pilgrimage of faith, and that the true reasons for devotion, which have their basis in the Gospel's teaching, may be evident on a personal and community level."

"In fact, separating the expression of popular piety from the Gospel roots of the faith, thus reducing it to a mere expression of folklore or of custom, would mean betraying its true essence. It is the Christian faith, devotion to Mary, the desire to imitate her, that bestows authenticity on the religious and Marian expressions of our people. But this Marian devotion ... needs to be continually enlightened and nourished through listening to and meditating on the word of God, making it the inspirational model of our conduct in all the areas of our daily existence."

June 15: In Madrid, visit to King Juan Carlos and his family; meeting with members of the Spanish bishops' conference; celebration of Mass and consecration of the Cathedral of La Almudena.

Life Enlightened by the Gospel

This was the theme of the Holy Father's address to the 78 members of the Spanish bishops' conference.

"I am very happy to learn that the joint work of the conference and the pastoral plans of your dioceses are focusing on the proposal to give a determined impulse to a vigorous evangelization apostolate. ... The time has come to develop the Church's pastoral activity in all its fullness with internal unity, spiritual firmness and apostolic boldness. The new evangelization needs new witnesses, persons who have experienced the real transformation of their lives by contact with Jesus Christ and who are capable of transmitting that experience to others. This is God's hour, a time for the hope that does not disappoint. This is the time to renew the interior life of your ecclesial communities and to undertake a courageous pastoral and evangelizing activity in Spanish society as a whole."

"Together with faith in God the Creator, modern man needs to know and accept the divine grace offered in Jesus Christ to free us from sin and from the power of death. The best contribution which the Church can make to the solution of the problems which afflict your society —such as the economic crisis, the unemployment which plagues so many families and so many young people, violence, terrorism and drug addiction — is to help all to discover the presence and the grace of God in us, to be renewed in the depths of their heart, putting on the new man who is Christ."

"The new evangelization to which I invite you requires a singular effort of purification and of holiness. For this reason, by reviving the best traditions of the many bishop-evangelizers and saints whom

your Church has given in the past, you should be tireless heralds of the Gospel, preaching the truth of Christ . . ., convinced that in this way you will offer the best possible service to the Church and to the whole society. The proclamation of the word should be sustained by a holy life, held together by prayer and lived day by day in charity, that is, in the humble service of love and of mercy toward all those in need."

Crisis of Moral Values

"I am aware of the grave crisis of moral values present in an alarming manner in various sectors of individual and social life, which strikes in a particular way the family and youth, and which has repercussions known to all in the management of public affairs. The existence of a growing process of secularization cannot be denied, a process which finds immediate echo in certain means of social communication, favoring in this way the spread of a religious indifferentism which becomes embedded in the personal and collective conscience, so that for many people God is no longer the origin and goal, the meaning and ultimate explanation of life."

"The Church is called to enlighten every sector of human and social living through the Gospel. And she must do this on the basis of a purpose which is her own, which 'is a religious one.' ... The Church, through her vocation of service to man in all of his dimensions, makes an effort to contribute to the pursuit of those objectives which promote the common good of society, above all in order to be 'at once the sign and the safeguard of the transcendental dimension of the human person.' Therefore, (as the Second Vatican Council) points out, 'the Church, by reason of her role and competence, is not identified with any political community, nor bound by ties to any political system.' However, this does not mean that she has nothing to say to the political community by way of enlightening it on the basis of the values and criteria of the Gospel."

The Pope called on the bishops to revitalize "the Christian roots of the old Continent," to stand by their "preferential concern for youth ministry" and to "listen carefully" to their priests.

He urged them not to "be afraid of the powers of this world" and said: "The Church's true progress requires as something essential the preservation of the whole of her tradition, defended by the living teaching authority of the pope and the bishops in communion with him."

June 16: In Madrid, prayer service with priests and seminarians; meeting with Prime Minister Felipe Gonzalez and Jose Maria Aznar, leader of the conservative Popular Party; meeting with the diplomatic corps; celebration of Mass and canonization of St. Enrique de Osso, founder of the Society of St. Teresa.

Formation of Men for the Priesthood

This was the central subject of the Popes address to students for the priesthood.

"The secret of your whole formation — human, spiritual, intellectual and pastoral — is to be found in your configuration to Christ. In fact, the priest is an *alter Christus*. It is only by identifying with him that you will find your own identity, your own joy and your own apostolic effectiveness. Therefore, the formation you receive in the seminary must be aimed at preparing you 'to enter into communion with the charity of Christ, the Good Shepherd.' The covenant of Christ, his total gift — even giving his life — expresses the charity of the Good Shepherd who gives his life in abundance for his sheep. The same charity must shape, therefore, the life of the pastors of the Church."

"The focal point of the spiritual life of the candidate for the priesthood must be the daily Eucharist. ... By the redeeming mystery of Christ, renewed in the Eucharist, the sense of mission, the ardent love for mankind, is nourished. From the Eucharist one also understands that all participation in the priesthood of Christ has a universal dimension. It is necessary to educate the heart in this perspective, so that we experience the drama of those peoples and multitudes who still do not know Christ, and so that we may always be ready to go to any part of the world to proclaim him to 'all nations.' This readiness ... is especially necessary today, before the vast horizons which are open to the mission of the Church and before the challenges of the new evangelization."

"The priest, who is called to make Christ's redemption present through the sacraments, must always live with the same concern as the Lord: the salvation of man. The priestly ministry would be empty of content if, in pastoral contact with people, its Christian soteriological dimension were forgotten. This happens, unfortunately, in the reductive forms of exercise of ministry, as if it were a function of mere human, social or psychological support. The priest, like Jesus, is sent to mankind to help people discover their vocation as children of God, to awaken in them — as Jesus did in the Samaritan woman — a yearning for the supernatural life. The priest is sent to move hearts to conversion, educating the moral conscience and reconciling people with God through the sacrament of penance."

New Saint

At Mass in Madrid the Pope canonized Father Enrique de Osso and Cervello and addressed a message of hope and encouragement to families.

Enrique de Osso, born Oct. 16, 1840, near Tarragona, was ordained to the priesthood in 1873. Deeply involved and very active in catechetical work, he organized two apostolic groups before founding in 1876 the Society of St. Teresa of Jesus, dedicated to Christian education. He died Jan. 27, 1896, at a Franciscan friary in Gilet, near Valencia.

The Family

The Pope prefaced his remarks about the family with the general comment: "Today more than ever people feel the need for God. The more the outlook on life is secularized, the more society is dehumanized because it loses the proper perspective on relationships between people; and, when the sense of the transcendent is weakened, the very vision of life and history is diminished, and there is a threat to the dignity and freedom of the human person, who has his origin and goal in God, his Creator."

Of the family, the Pope said: "I want to address a special message of encouragement and hope to Spanish families. I urge them, the sanctuaries of love and life, to be true 'domestic churches,' places of encounter with God, centers for the spread of the faith, schools of Christian living. ... We are all aware of the problems threatening marriage and the family institution in our day; therefore, it is necessary to present authentically the ideal of the Christian family, based on unity and fidelity in marriage, open to children, guided by love. And how could we fail to express great support for the repeated statements of the Spanish episcopate on behalf of life and on the illicitness of abortion. I urge everyone not to desist in the defense of the dignity of every human life, of the indissolubility of marriage, the fidelity of conjugal love, the education of children and young people according to Christian principles, in the face of blind ideologies which deny the transcendent and which recent history has exposed, by showing their true face."

June 17: Late morning departure for Rome.

45TH INTERNATIONAL EUCHARISTIC CONGRESS

The 45th International Eucharistic Congress, held June 7 to 13, 1993, in Seville focused attention on the overall theme of Eucharist and Evangelization in a varied program of special Masses, 24-hour exposition of the Blessed Sacrament in churches, processions in the Spanish tradition, formal addresses, discussions and workshops on such topics as theology, religious education, liturgy, pastoral endeavors and social action.

The climax of the proceedings was the concluding Mass celebrated on the solemnity of Corpus Christi by Pope John Paul with 200 cardinals, archbishops and bishops, and 1,200 priests before a throng of hundreds of thousands of worshipers.

Action Sacrament

The Pope called attention to the fact that the Eucharist is an "action" sacrament that orients Catholics toward love and leads to a recognition that modern society must respond in a better way to the needy. He said that social projects connected with the congress — including a drug rehabilitation program, education projects, centers for the sick, the formally opened San Rafael Residence for the elderly at Dos Hermanas — were not merely symbolic add-ons. "These works of charity are not something superfluous and incidental; they represent the very demand of the sacrament."

A final message issued by the congress emphasized the obligation of the First World nations to use their wealth to overcome problems in developing countries. "The unbridled race for well-being that causes people of the North to possess a second home should transform itself into a just concern for providing a home to all those lacking one in the Southern Hemisphere," the message said.

"The Eucharistic table implies solidarity and participation with the poor, along with the announcement of a more just and more fraternal world," said Bishop Miguel Oliver Roman, secretary general of the congress.

Cardinal Joachim Meissner of Cologne, one of several keynote speakers, stated succinctly: "Christians cannot be terminal consumers of the Eucharist," but must "participate in the life-style of Christ."

The congress was held under the auspices of the Pontifical Commission for International Eucharistic Congresses, headed by Cardinal Edouard Gagnon. Key assistants in the work of preparation and conduct of the congress were 6,200 or more official delegates appointed by episcopal conferences in about 70 countries.

The commission announced that the 46th congress would be held in 1997 in Wroclaw, Poland.

Papal Homily

The Holy Father began his homily with one of the traditional Divine Praises, "Blessed Be the Most Holy Sacrament of the Altar," thus emphasizing the focus of the congress. He said: "I join in spirit with all of you, beloved brothers and sisters, gathered around this altar which today is like the heart of the whole Church: *Statio orbis*, the station of the whole world, the meeting place of the Christian assembly, which today makes Seville the privileged center of adoration and worship in this holy Mass closing the 45th International Eucharistic Congress."

"This celebration invites us .. to pause and reflect how Christ, who was crucified for our sins on the altar of the cross and rose for our redemption, has conquered death and 'lives forever' (cf. Rv. 1:18).

"This is the great truth which inspires all who believe in Christ. In this solemn celebration ... I remember in a special way the many brothers and sisters of other Christian churches who want to receive the sacred Eucharist. The Church recognizes all that unites us with these beloved brothers and

sisters in baptism, but she also knows that the Eucharistic communion is the sign of the Church's full unity in the faith. She prays intently to the Lord that the long-awaited day will arrive on which, united in the faith, we can all participate together in the Eucharistic Banquet."

Eucharist and Evangelization

"The theme of the Eucharistic Congress ... places before our eyes the intimate relationship between the Eucharist and evangelization, and proclaims the missionary yearning which the Holy Spirit has aroused in the Church of our time. The relationship between Eucharist and evangelization also becomes a memorial for us, a memorial of an historical event of special significance and consequence for the Catholic Church: the fifth centenary of the evangelization of America, the commemoration of which has once more emphasized the crucial role played by Spanish missionaries in implanting the Gospel in the New World."

"Our world, although it has an undeniable desire for unity and cries out more than ever the need for justice, is marked by so much injustice, is broken by differences. This situation is contrary to the ideal of 'koinonia' or communion of life and love, of faith and of resources, of Eucharistic bread and natural bread, about which the New Testament speaks to us precisely in relation to the Eucharist. As St. Paul exhorted the faithful of Corinth, it is an unacceptable contradiction to eat the Body of Christ unworthily in division and discrimination (1 Cor. 11:18-21). The sacrament of the Eucharist cannot be separated from the commandment of love. One cannot receive the Body of Christ and feel remote from those who are hungry or thirsty, who are exploited or strangers, who are imprisoned or suffering from infirmity (cf. Mt. 25:41-44). As the *Catechism of the Catholic Church* states: 'The Eucharist involves a commitment on behalf of the poor. In order truly to receive the Body and Blood of Christ given up for us, we must recognize Christ in the poor, his brothers and sisters" (n. 1397).

"Eucharistic communion must create within us such a strength of faith and love that we live open to others, with hearts filled with mercy for all their needs."

RESPONSE TO ORDINATION DECISION BY THE CHURCH OF ENGLAND

The General Synod of the Church of England decided by majority vote Nov. 11, 1992, to approve the ordination of women to the priesthood. A significant number of church members were and remain opposed to the decision, and some have indicated desire and intention to be received into full communion with the Catholic Church. Against this background, the Catholic bishops of England and Wales issued a pastoral message which was read in parish churches May 1, 1993. The major part of the message is given below.

This lengthy excerpt of the bishops' message is from the text circulated by the CNS Documentary Service, Origins, May 6, 1993 (Vol. 22, No. 47).

Reaction to the Decision

Last November, the General Synod of the Church of England passed a resolution authorizing the ordination of women to the priesthood. Although this measure was agreed by a two-thirds

majority, it left a number of Anglican clergy and lay people not only opposed to the decision itself but also deeply troubled in conscience. As has been well publicized, some have turned toward the Catholic Church and begun to consider whether they might seek full communion with our Church. The extent of reaction has taken many by surprise. The uncertainty about the numbers involved has helped to fuel rumor and misunderstanding.

Many different hopes and anxieties have been expressed in the nation at large as well as within the Church of England and within our own Catholic community. As your bishops, we have listened to these and have reflected together on the sensitive pastoral and ecumenical issues which are involved. . . We have been able to agree on certain principles which must guide our response, and we have begun to set out some practical ways forward. More detailed reports will be available through the media, but we also wish to send this pastoral message to all our priests and people. Our purpose is to explain these principles and invite you to share with us the process of prayer and reflection which is needed at this time.

Basic Question: Authority

It is important, first of all, to understand that for many of those Anglicans now looking toward the Catholic Church the synod vote last November brought to a head some long-felt difficulties. These people, by no means all clergy, are concerned particularly about authority. They do not believe that the General Synod has the authority to admit women to the priesthood.They believe that decisions about a matter of such doctrinal importance should not be taken by the Church of England alone. Even though much discussion has focused on attitudes to women and ordination, it is the issue of the teaching authority claimed by the Church of England which is at the heart of present anxieties. It is to this that we, as Catholics, must respond.

We believe that, while the gift of the Holy Spirit is given to all Christians by virtue of their baptism, it is the bishops of the Catholic Church, together with the pope, who have the task of teaching with authority those things which Christ has revealed to us as saving truth. It is this understanding of authority, as the sure way to truth, which in recent years led us to explain that the Anglican vote to ordain women would in fact change our relationship with the Church of England, adding a real obstacle to our hopes for unity. It is this same teaching authority, expressed especially in the ministry of the pope, which some Anglicans now wish to recognize and adhere to.

Our response must reflect our deep pastoral concern. As a Catholic community, one of our first responsibilities is to welcome those who seek with a sincere heart to belong to our Church. Each person's journey into the Catholic Church is unique, but in the present circumstances we shall wish to acknowledge the value of the ministry and life of faith which those who now seek to join us have already experienced.

Total Integration Sought

In the light of some fears which have been expressed, let it be clearly understood that this does not mean bargaining with truth nor a wholesale abandonment of the disciplines of our Church. Nor is compromise sought in what is expected of those seeking full communion with the Catholic Church. We gladly welcome their rich devotion and personal holiness, but we look toward their eventual total integration into the life and mission of the Catholic Church. This remains true whether they approach us as individuals or in groups. Our response will be generous and understanding. It will be guided by the same principles, even if in the difficult period of transition these may be expressed in different practical forms suited to various situations in our different dioceses.

We repeat: We shall look forward toward eventual total integration into the Catholic Church. But this is a new situation, and we must feel our way forward sensitively, courageously, with understanding and faith. Of course it will also, in general terms, be after due consultation with the Holy See. It is communion with the one universal Catholic Church which those troubled at this time are seeking, not some negotiated change of membership at the local level.

We hope that those who join us as a result of these events will come to live happily a truly Catholic way of life in accordance with the teachings of the Second Vatican Council. But we cannot expect that the issues and concerns of the present time can be resolved quickly, not least because of the uncertainty created by the parliamentary legislation now needed by the Church of England to implement the decision of last November's synod. For our part, we must proceed patiently and with prayer.

Whatever the outcome of this process, our ecumenical relationships continue because they are central to our response to the Lord's will for the Church. The real bond of baptism still unites us, and we must make every effort to build upon that bond, not only with our Anglican brothers and sisters but also with other Christian communities. Together we are called to serve God's kingdom in our world. Together we have a mission to proclaim the Gospel in the circumstances of our own society in this country, as well as in the wider world. Our ecumenical commitment must always keep in mind this larger purpose.

BONDS OF PEACE

The bishops of the Church of England announced in June, 1993, that there would be no discrimination against priests who oppose the ordination of women to the priesthood. The announcement came in the form of a document entitled "Bonds of Peace." Its purpose is to protect the rights of, and provide pastoral support for, clergy whose views on women's ordination are different from those of their bishop.

ABORTION DEVELOPMENTS

Pro-Abortion Executive Orders

Abortion developments in 1993 included President Clinton's executive orders of Jan. 22 which reversed:

● regulations prohibiting abortion counseling in federally funded family planning clinics;

● a ban on fetal tissue research;

● restrictions on access to abortion in U.S. military hospitals overseas;

● the "Mexico City Policy" which denied U.S. foreign aid to programs overseas that promoted abortion.

The President also ordered a study of the French abortion pill RU-486, but did not immediately lift the ban on its importation for personal use.

As he signed the orders, the President said: "We must free science and medicine from the grasp of politics. Our vision should be of an America where abortion is safe and legal, but rare.'"

How abortion would be rendered "rare" was open to serious question, according to various commentators.

Additional Developments

Among additional developments were:

● modification of the Hyde Amendment, in force

since 1977, to permit federal funding of abortion not only in cases of danger of maternal death but also in cases of incest and rape;

• abortion coverage in insurance plans of federal employees.

Inchoate attempts were made to move forward a Freedom of Choice Act which would supersede and prohibit any kind of national or state regulation with respect to the practice of abortion.

None of these or other developments brought about any essential change in the constitutional status of the right to or practice of abortion.

Four Major Decisions

Planned Parenthood v. Casey: The most important recent U.S. Supreme Court decision on abortion was handed down June 29, 1992, in the case of Planned Parenthood v. Casey. The court declared constitutional provisions of a 1989 Pennsylvania law regulating the practice of abortion.

In a fragmented decision with five separate opinions, the court upheld these provisions of Pennsylvania's Abortion Control Law:

• Women seeking abortion must receive information about risks, fetal development and alternatives to abortion, and must wait at least 24 hours after receiving such information before having an abortion.

• Medical offices must file detailed, confidential reports about each abortion performed.

• Minors must get permission from one parent or a judge before having an abortion.

The court struck down a requirement that married women notify their husbands before having an abortion.

The court did not revisit or overturn the radical pro-abortion Roe v. Wade decision of 1973.

Three of the most important Supreme Court decisions on abortion prior to Planned Parenthood v. Casey were Roe v. Wade, Webster v. Reproductive Health Services and Rust v. Sullivan.

Roe v. Wade: The key abortion-related decision was handed down by the Supreme Court in the case of Roe v. Wade. The court ruled 7-to-2 Jan. 22, 1973:

(1) During the first three months of pregnancy, a woman's right to privacy is paramount; accordingly, she has an unrestricted right to abortion with the consent and cooperation of a physician.

(2) In the second trimester, the principle controlling legislation is the health or welfare of the mother.

(3) In the third trimester, the "state subsequent to viability," the controlling principles of legislation are the State's "interest in the potentiality of human life" and "the preservation of the life or health of the mother."

The decision legalized abortion nationwide; practically, on demand.

In the 20 years subsequent to the Roe v. Wade decision, an estimated 32 to 35 million legal abortions have been performed in the United States.

Webster v. Reproductive Health Services: The court upheld, July 3, 1989, 5-to-4, provisions of the Missouri law:

(1) forbidding public employees to perform or assist in abortions;

(2) barring the use of public facilities for abortion;

(3) requiring physicians to take steps to determine fetal viability when a woman 20 or more weeks pregnant seeks an abortion.

At issue was an appeal of a lower court ruling in Webster v. Reproductive Health Services, Inc., with respect to the statute, Missouri Senate Committee Substitute for House Bill No. 1596, which was signed into law in June, 1986.

The court did not overturn Roe v. Wade because the case afforded no occasion to revisit the 1973 decision. Neither did the court rule on the preamble of the Missouri law, which states that human life begins at conception.

Rust v. Sullivan: The U.S. Supreme Court ruled 5-to-4 May 23, 1991 that provisions of Title X (the National Family Planning Program) of the 1970 Public Health Service Act were in accord with the U.S. Constitution. Pertinent regulations forbade family planning clinics from counseling or advising abortion if they received federal funds disbursed under Title X.

The Court observed:

(1) Abortion cannot be equated with family planning. The family planning legislation of 1970 distinguished between abortion and family planning, and intended to restrict federal funding to planning human life, not destroying it.

(2) The admission of a legal right (in this case, abortion) does not necessarily imply a government duty to promote the right.

(3) The fact that abortion is a legal right does not mean the government and those who do not subscribe to this right have to pay for it.

The Court ruled that the government has the right to establish rules for funding only family planning programs which do not "encourage, promote or advocate abortion."

BIRTHRIGHT

Birthright is an interdenominational guidance and referral service organization offering pregnant women alternatives to abortion, in line with the motto, "It is the right of every pregnant woman to give birth and the right of every child to be born." Started in 1968, it has chapters in Canada, the United States, the United Kingdom, Ireland, New Zealand, Australia, Hong Kong and South Africa. The executive director of Birthright, U.S.A., is Mrs. D. Cocciolone, 686 N. Broad St., Woodbury, N.J. 08096. Birthright has a national 800 number.

PHYSICIAN-ASSISTED SUICIDE AND EUTHANASIA

The following statement, issued Apr. 19, 1993, by the Board of Directors of the Michigan Catholic Conference, was circulated by the CNS Documentary Service, Origins, June 10, 1993 (Vol. 23, No. 4).

Realistic View

Death, quite understandably, is a frightening prospect, although differently for different people. This is not necessarily a sign of weakness or wavering faith; actually it is realistic to face something so monumental and mysterious as death with a certain amount of wonderment and awe.

Now, in addition to the natural ambivalence to death, we have come to fear dying, for dying is often accompanied by suffering and we have been conditioned to avoid suffering at all costs. There are some sufferings, however, which cannot be avoided. Growing up is one, dying is another.

We believe that dying is a human act. We can and should try to minimize the suffering, but we cannot take away the risk and the letting-go that is involved. Experience tells us that there is something beneficial about this precious stage of human existence. For the dying and those who are committed to them, the end of life can be a time of intimacy, healing, soul-searching, wonder and awe. From a merely sociological and psychological point of view, dying is not something to be avoided at all costs.

It is appropriate and desireable to take every reasonable human means possible to alleviate or eliminate pain and suffering for the chronically ill or the dying. We believe that "everything that blossoms dies," and that we are not required to take extreme measures to squeeze every second of earthly life from our earthly sojourn.

Death with Dignity

In other words, we believe that people should be allowed to die, and to die with dignity. We believe that it is not necessary to take unreasonable means to prolong human life. It might be noted that "unreasonable means" can include family members or friends who tell a dying person to "keep fighting" or try to create a false hope of recovery instead of handing on the truth.

For millennia, people have looked to their faith to find the answers to the "profound mysteries of the human condition." With hope in the risen Christ, many of us have found peace and understanding of life, death and eternal life. On the other hand, there are many today who argue for the right to exercise what they perceive as the "ultimate freedom of choice": suicide. A few, for a great variety of reasons, seek solutions to the existential conditions of pain, suffering and loss in self-imposed or assisted death.

There are those in our society today who believe that euthanasia (literally, "good death") protects those who wish to die with dignity. They are wrong. Euthanasia and suicide are an outgrowth of what our Holy Father, Pope John Paul II, has called "a false love." In 1979, prior to his election to the papacy, Cardinal Karol Wojtyla wrote in Love and Responsibility: "True love perfects and develops personal existence. . . ."

This "false love" causes those who lose hope to become victims of a culture which tolerates mercy killing and physician-assisted suicide.

Serious Considerations

Society must be very careful when it puts its hand on the switch of human life. Euthanasia would add an entirely different category of permissible killing, and it raises very serious problems that have not been carefully considered.

• What sort of fear will this cause in persons who are chronically ill, aged or disabled?

• What sort of subtle pressure will this create among those who feel (or are) unwanted?

• Would it not mean that individuals would be handing over control of their lives and destinies without any possibility of calling it back?

• Who determines and how do we determine when unavoidable pain and suffering are too much? All of us can think of times in our lives when we thought our burden too heavy to bear another step.

We shape our society, and our society shapes us. If we sanction euthanasia or physician-assisted suicide, we can be absolutely sure it will have consequences far beyond the individual case we may have in mind. Physician-assisted suicide and euthanasia are more than one-on-one killing. It is societal killing and will affect how we think about ourselves and others, about life and death, far beyond this issue.

Life with Dignity and Faith

We believe that a just society promotes and enhances the dignity of all human life for the common good.

• We invite the Catholic community to prayerful reflection and thoughtful action on this subject.

• We urge the medical and legal professions to study the issue with discipline, integrity and compassion. The medical community particularly, trained to heal, must conform to the strictest canons of healing as an art and as a science. The desire to control pain has always been valid, but not the desire to push control so far as to directly cause death.

• We challenge the media not to capitalize on people's confusion, ambivalence and even fear about the use of modern life-prolonging technologies, but to provide thorough research to clarify and enlighten.

We have thus far spoken on a human plane, and we believe that our reasons at that level are compelling. But we cannot speak about life and death without including our faith. We believe in God.

We believe that our following of Jesus is most of all to die as he died — freely, with trust in God's plan and God's timetable, not ours!

What we really believe in is life, not death. We arrive at life by dying, which means letting go of all that we hold dear. For Christians, dying is not an ultimate evil to be avoided at all costs; it is a step toward the fullness of life. It is just a piece of the journey, and not the entire journey.

Dying is part of our ultimate power to say how we will respond to the mystery of who we are and who God is. It is at the core of our freedom. True freedom does not claim the power to die as we choose — which is what euthanasia attempts to do. We claim only the freedom to choose how we will accept death as it is presented to each of us. Our logo is the cross, for Jesus freely responded to a death he did not choose and made it the path to life.

Therefore, we call upon all people of good will to reflect on the value of life and its ultimate meaning. Let us follow the exhortation the dying Moses spoke to the Jewish people: "I set before you life and death. . . . Choose life!

OCTOBER 1992

VATICAN

Praise for Courageous Fidelity in Sudan — Pope John Paul praised Catholics for their "courageous fidelity" in the face of anti-Christian policies and practices of the Muslim government. Addressing visiting Sudanese bishops Oct. 2, he said the application of Islamic law to non-Muslims had "set the stage for the loss of many civil liberties," resulting in "discrimination in education, the harassment of priests, religious and catechists, and the expulsion of missionaries." He also said "the baptized are characterized as 'foreigners' in their own homeland." Islamic law, in force since 1984, was a central factor in the years-long civil war between the Muslim North and largely Christian and traditionally African South. The Pope spoke a month after bishops from Sudan and six other East African countries appealed to the United Nations and the Organization of African Unity to help stop "callous and cynical oppression of Christian citizens and religious leaders in Sudan." They said, however, that direct appeals to Sudanese officials "only seem to increase the indignities on non-Muslims."

Synod of Diocese of Rome — At the opening of a synod for the Diocese of Rome, the Pope said Oct. 3 that the church there should have great concern for people "who have the greatest need." He convoked the synod so the local church could "renew and purify itself in order better to reflect the light of Christ.

Trip to Dominican Republic — Pope John Paul, visiting the Dominican Republic Oct. 10 to 13, took part in ceremonies marking the 500th anniversary of the introduction of Christianity in the Americas and attended the opening of the fourth general assembly of the Latin American Bishops' Conference. (See separate entries.)

Missionary Involvement — The Pope called for greater participation by lay persons in the missionary activity of the Church. "Every baptized person is called to effectively participate in mission activity through the precious offering of prayers and suffering, and with material aid," he said in a Mission Day statement Oct. 18.

Respect for Persons — The fundamentally ethical character of business decisions, social policies and models of development makes it imperative that leaders in these areas be guided by more than purely economic considerations." So stated the Pope Oct. 19 at a meeting with the World Business Council. "Today more than ever there is an urgent need for generous cooperation between all forces in society in promoting the common good in a way that respects the dignity of individuals and social groups while fostering an effective solidarity which transcends mere self-interest. . . . Great efforts are needed to rethink material development in terms of service to the integral well-being of people."

Catholic-Orthodox Relations in Romania — Dialogue and a common commitment to efforts for the solution of social and economic problems should mark relations between the churches, said the Pope Oct. 24. "I hope that a peaceful and fruitful dialogue will develop between the Orthodox Church and the Catholic Church in Romania to solve the questions that have arisen and still exist after a half century of tragic persecution against Christians." The new situation in the country "calls for a rigorous reflection on the commitment of Christians in society. If it is done together, this reflection will help all Christians to see their specific tasks more clearly; it could lay the foundations of an active cooperation and a common witness of faith and life."

Aid for Bosnians — War victims in Bosnia-Herzegovina, "exposed to unheard-of violence that menaces the very existence of individuals and entire populations," were in dire need of aid "so they can survive," declared Pope John Paul during a general audience Oct. 21. Unrestricted violence was frustrating efforts to provide the needed aid.

Christian Environmental Obligation — Recognizing God as the source of all life and the understanding of humanity's place in the order of creation inspire the Christian obligation to protect the environment. So stated the Pope Oct. 22 at a meeting with members of the organizing committee of the international St. Francis Prize for the Environment.

Beatifications — The Holy Father beatified 122 male religious (71 Hospitallers of St. John of God and 51 Claretians) who were murdered in 1936 during the early months of the Spanish Civil War. He said they symbolized all persons killed for preserving their faith in 20th century prisons and concentration camps. Also beatified was Narcisa de Jesus Martilo Moran of Ecuador, a lay woman of Ecuador.

Anti-Semitism Condemned — Anti-Semitism and every other form of racism are sins and must be condemned, the Pope said Oct. 28 as he marked the 27th anniversary of the promulgation of the Second Vatican Council's document dealing with Catholic-Jewish relations. "I point out this anniversary deeply saddened by news of attacks and profanations which for some time have been insulting the memory of the victims of the Shoah (Holocaust) in those very places which witnessed the suffering of millions of innocent people," he said.

Galileo Case — Pope John Paul formally acknowledged that church judges erred when they condemned 17th-century astronomer Galilei Galileo for maintaining that the earth revolves around the sun. "This sad misunderstanding now belongs to the past," he told members of the Pontifical Academy of Sciences Oct. 31.

General Audience Topics:

● Together with the Pope, and never apart from him, the College of Bishops reflects both the universality and unity of the people of God (Oct. 7).

● Reflections on his Oct. 9 to 14 visit to the Dominican Republic (Oct. 21).

● In carrying out their apostolic mission, bishops must bear witness to Christ before the people of their dioceses and those outside the Church (Oct. 28).

Briefs:

● Christians must be patient and tireless in their efforts to heal centuries-long interreligious divisions, said Cardinal Edward I. Cassidy, president of the Pontifical Council for Promoting Christian Unity, Oct. 7 in Vadstena, Sweden.

• A new pension plan for Vatican employees, along with a permanent pension fund, was unveiled Oct. 6. It was estimated that retiring mid-level employees would receive from $18,000 to $23,000 annually under the plan. The Vatican had 3,365 active employees and 1,259 retirees.

Invitation to Visit Jerusalem

Israeli Foreign Minister Shimon Peres, at a 45-minute private meeting Oct. 23, invited Pope John Paul to visit Jerusalem. A Vatican statement issued after the meeting said the Pope reiterated his wish to make a pilgrimage to "the Holy Land and to Jerusalem, Holy City for all Jewish, Christian and Muslim believers," but did not indicate either time or manner of such a visit.

NATIONAL

Red Mass — President George Bush, members of the Supreme Court and other government officials were among the 1,300 persons who attended a Red Mass Oct. 4 at St. Matthew's Cathedral in Washington. Cardinal Roger M. Mahony of Los Angeles urged them and others in public life to work for reconciliation and the healing of divisions in the country. "We servants of both God and our country are doubly bound to this duty . . . to promote justice and equality," he said in a homily. The 40th annual Red Mass, so called because of the red vestments worn by the celebrants, was celebrated the day before the opening of the fall term of the U.S. Supreme Court. The celebration of such a Mass, for the blessing and guidance of those who administer justice, dates back to the Middle Ages in Europe.

Catholic-Orthodox Dialogue — Members of the Joint Committee of Orthodox and Roman Catholic Bishops, in a joint communique released Oct. 6, "reaffirmed their commitment to (their) annual dialogues and their conviction that, through dialogue, mutual understanding, good will and trust, they are following the teachings of the Lord." They reaffirmed their commitment despite the so-called "severe strain" in relations "because of recent events in Eastern Europe." The events in question included the "manipulation of religion" for the purpose of rekindling ethnic hatred in the civil war of Serbians, Croatians and others in the Balkans, and the "deepest reservations" of the Orthodox concerning a Vatican letter on the theme of the Church as communion.

Cause for Cardinal Cooke — Cardinal John J. O'Connor announced Oct. 6 that the Vatican had approved opening of the cause for the canonization of Cardinal Terence J. Cooke, his predecessor as archbishop of New York. The announcement was made on the ninth anniversary of Cardinal Cooke's death.

Change Public Opinion — The Church's primary task regarding abortion is to change public opinion, not to gain passage of a law prohibiting abortion, said Jesuit Father Avery Dulles Oct. 6 in an address at Fordham University. Anti-abortion law would be fruitless without the backing of public opinion. On the subject of "Religion and the Transformation of Politics," Father Dulles also observed:

• U.S. bishops had gone too far in placing their religious authority behind specific positions in the political sphere. It would be better for them to stick to general principles of Catholic teaching, as distinguished from prudential judgments on various subjects.

• "The Church can make its best contribution to the political order by being itself, by being the community of faith and worship that it was from its earliest days."

• "The Church, even without directly intervening in the political process, can make a major contribution to the political order by shaping the ideas and habits of the persons who constitute the society, making them morally and spiritually capable of responsible self-government."

• The "major crisis of our day" is the conflict between a culture contending for "a transcendent, God-given order of justice and morality," and a "progessivist" culture that rejects the idea of permanent truths and moral principles.

Catholic Charities USA — One thousand delegates attending the national convention of Catholic Charities USA Oct. 9 to 13 in Philadelphia heard the keynote speaker say it was wrong for governments to expect churches to take on the responsibility of clearing up the chaos caused by the default of social policy and the withdrawal of federal resources. Robert Kuttner, economist and journalist, said churches, and Catholic Charities in particular, were being asked "to carry a much heavier load. . . . If you, look at who is doing real hands-on work in needy communities — who's there for the long haul, and not because it's fashionable but because it's rooted in a deeper spiritual commitment — a lot of what you find is rooted in Catholic social teaching." Outgoing president Father Thomas J. Harvey reported that Catholic Charities agencies nationwide helped 12.3 million people in the previous year, as compared with 3.4 million 10 years earlier. His successor, Jesuit Father Fred Kammer, noted that 68 percent of social services provided by member agencies were for basic food and shelter, as compared with 23 percent a decade earlier. He said social services would continue to be a growth industry unless political decisions made at national, state and local levels change.

Liberal Intolerance — Pennsylvania Governor Robert P. Casey, addressing the Al Smith dinner in New York Oct. 15, warned against a "new liberal intolerance" that denies a hearing to views such as his pro-life position. Disturbing signs indicated that such intolerance had extended to religious belief and had reached the stage of anti-Catholicism, he said. Backgrounding his remarks were the refusal of Democratic Party officials to let him address their national convention in July, and the heckling that shouted him down during a forum Oct. 2 at the Cooper Union for the Advancement of Science and Art.

Josephites' 100th Anniversary — Priests and brothers of the Society of St. Joseph of the Sacred Heart began a year-long centennial celebration Oct. 17 with a Mass in Baltimore. The community, whose sole apostolate was and remains evangelization of African-Americans, had a 100-year record of ministry in 174 parishes in 37 U.S. dioceses.

Violence against Women — "Violence in any form — physical, sexual, psychological or verbal — is sinful; many times it is a crime as well." So declared a statement issued during the month by two committees of the U.S. bishops, on Women in Society and in the Church, and on Marriage and Family Life. The bishops said they hoped their statement, entitled "When I Call for Help: A Pastoral Response to Domestic Violence against Women," would be an initial step in a continuing effort by the Church to combat domestic violence.

Education for Chastity — It is an essential component of sex education because chastity "is a virtue that develops a person's authentic maturity," said Bishop Thomas V. Daily of Brooklyn at a press conference introducing new diocesan "Sexuality Education Guidelines." The 66-page booklet said "the Church must become more actively involved" in education on sexuality, in part because the "efforts of the public schools to undertake this responsibility are proving to be disastrous." Backgrounding this view was opposition to the morally objectionable "rainbow" curriculum on sex education for New York City public schools, which had the effect of ratifying homosexual and lesbian life-styles.

Intellectual Commitment of Nuns — This was a subject of discussion at an Oct. 15-to-17 conference of nuns in Washington. "The educational levels of women religious are exceedingly high when compared with the total population," reported Franciscan Sister Katarina Schuth on the findings of a survey of 1,000 nuns, of whom 93 percent held bachelor's degrees and 80 percent had master's or higher degrees. The principal question raised during the conference was how future intellectual life in religious orders of women would be influenced by such factors as:

• a major shift in emphasis from educational apostolates to other ministries, especially service to the poor;

• shifts in understanding the place of order-sponsored or order-staffed institutions;

• declines in the number of members and increases in the average age of nuns;

• financial constraints accompanying the foregoing demographic factors;

• the influence of feminism in and outside the Church.

Briefs:

• Maritime ministers attended the 19th World Congress of the Apostleship of the Sea early in the month in Houston, with concern for total pastoral service to seafarers and dock workers.

• In the second month of enforcement in Mississippi of the first state law requiring a 24-hour wait before an abortion, the weekly average of 220 abortions was cut in half. The number of abortion-seekers who went elsewhere was not known.

• Three bishops on the U.S.-Mexican border urged "every person of conscience" to join in efforts for justice for migrant farm workers. In a joint statement Oct. 16, they called it a "moral imperative" to change farm workers' "unacceptable" living and working conditions.

• The Wisconsin Catholic Conference issued a set of guidelines Oct. 27 advising church institutions on ways and means of implementing the new Americans with Disabilities Act.

• Honored: Mother Teresa of Calcutta, with the University of Notre Dame Award for Humanitarian Service; Carl Anderson, dean of the John Paul II Institute for Studies on Marriage and Family, with the 1992 Thomas Linacre Award of the National Federation of Catholic Physicians' Guilds; Lakota Indian Harry Blue Thunder, with the Lumen Christi Award of the Catholic Church Extension Society, for 60 years of service as a catechist.

Life Chains against Abortion

An estimated 950,000 people nationwide linked arms to form life chains against abortion and other threats to life on Respect Life Sunday, Oct. 4. The comprehensive theme of the day was struck by Bishop John C. Reiss of Trenton who wrote in a pastoral letter: "Insist that your legislators respond to a vision of human existence which does not discount whole groups of human beings, such as the unborn, the handicapped, the elderly, the poor, the mentally and physically disabled." Life chains were formed in many cities, including Atlanta, Arlington (Va.), Boston, Chicago, Cleveland, Dallas, Mobile, San Francisco, St. Petersburg, Trenton and Tulsa.

INTERNATIONAL

Mozambique Accord — Government and guerrilla leaders signed a peace accord Oct. 4 calling for an end to 16 years of civil war and opening the way for massive foreign assistance to one of Africa's poorest countries. The treaty, mediated by Catholic officials, was praised by Pope John Paul as a positive step toward stable peace throughout southern Africa. The agreement called for a cease-fire and implementation by the parliament of agreed-upon measures leading to multiparty elections within one year, and also provided for a restructuring of the military and national security forces to keep them from being tools of the government.

Sex Tours to Thailand — Sex tours by foreigners were not only immoral but were also contributing to enslavement of the poor, according to Cardinal Michael Michai Kitbunchu of Bangkok. Speaking early in the month in Milan, he said travel agencies organizing "red-light" trips catered mostly to Germans, Japanese, people from Taiwan and Muslim countries, as well as some from Italy. He said there were more than 500,000 prostitutes in Thailand.

No Sacraments for Mafiosi — A southern Italian archbishop instructed priests to refuse sacraments to known Mafia members in an effort to break the "code of silence" protecting organized crime. Archbishop Giuseppe Agostino of Crotone-Santa Severina issued the order in a pastoral letter Oct. 9. Convicted or "notorious" Mafiosi were to be denied Communion or marriage in the Church, and were declared ineligible to be godparents or leaders of parish activities. Those wishing to return to the sacraments would be required to make a sincere request to do so and take part in a program of spiritual rehabilitation.

CELAM Assembly — The fourth General Assembly of the Latin American Bishops' Conference was held Oct. 12 to 28 in Santo Domingo. (See separate entry.)

Religious Affiliation on I.D. Cards — The Pakistani government drew intense minority-community criticism for its Oct. 13 decision to require notice of religious affiliation on national identity cards. "Now the truth has dawned on us — we are aliens in our own country," Martin Aslam, coordinator of the Ecumenical Institute for Justice and Peace in Karachi, said at a press conference after the announcement by the Religious Affairs Ministry. Bishop John Joseph of Faisalabad, chairman of the commission, said Oct. 17: "When Pakistan came into being (in 1971), the maulanas (Muslim religious leaders) opposed the creation of Pakistan, and it was the Christians who voted with the liberal Muslims for the creation of Pakistan. . . . But today, without even taking one minority member into confidence, a committee of maulanas has decided to change the national identity card into a religious card." Including a religion column on the national identity card "is the worst form of apartheid in the name of religion," said the bishops' conference in a letter to the prime minister the previous April.

Media Blasted — The bishops of Poland charged the secular print and electronic media with attacks on religious education and insults to Pope John Paul. "Every bid to criticize Christian values is greeted with an exaggerated clamor by the media," they said in a message read in churches Oct. 18. "Much talk shows a disgraceful attitude toward Christ, toward prayer, and to the fundamental moral principles accepted by the great majority of our society."

Skeletons in El Salvador — Forensic experts unearthed 22 skeletons of children and babies in the remote hamlet of El Mozote, uncovering evidence in support of claims that soldiers had killed civilians in the largest massacre in the nation's civil war. The skeletons were exhumed Oct. 19 from the ruins of a church building where the U.S.-trained Atlacatl Battalion allegedly began a three-day slaughter of more than 800 people in December, 1981. Maria Julia Hernandez of Tutela Legal, the human rights office of the San Salvador archdiocese, claimed there was a governmental cover-up of information about those who ordered and participated in the massacre.

Nobel Prizewinner — Rigoberta Menchu of Guatemala, social activist and former head of the National Coordinating Commission for the United Peasants Committee, was notified Oct. 16 that she had been named the winner of the 1992 Nobel Peace Prize. She said she planned to use the $1.2 million prize money to establish a fund in memory of her father, Vicente Menchu, who was killed in 1980 while taking part in a demonstration for human rights in Guatemala City.

American Nuns Slain — Five American nuns were killed by rebels Oct. 20 near Monrovia, Liberia. Members of the Adorers of the Blood of Christ, based in Ruma, Ill., they were Sisters: Shirley Kolmer, 61, Kathleen McGuire, 54, Agnes Mueller, 62, Mary Joel Kolmer, 58, and Barbara Muttra, 69. (See November entry.)

Opposition to Neo-Nazis — The Justice and Peace Commission of the Archdiocese of Sao Paulo, Brazil, said it was prepared to enlist in the campaign of the Democratic Movement against Nazism and All Forms of Discrimination, formed in the wake of several attacks by white-power skinhead groups. In a letter to Rabbi Henry Sobel, a founder of the movement, the commission said it was "profoundly indignant about the recent violations of human rights in Sao Paulo and expresses its solidarity with all of the victims — Jews, blacks, Northeasterners, poor and unemployed."

Nuclear Deterrence Outmoded — The Vatican nuncio to the United Nations declared Oct. 28 that "the dangerous strategy of nuclear deterrence is outmoded." Archbishop Renato R. Martino told the General Assembly committee dealing with disarmament and international security: "It is no longer enough merely to reduce nuclear stocks. . . . The world must move to the abolition of nuclear weapons through a universal, non-discriminatory ban with intensive inspection by a universal authority. . . . Nuclear weapons are unneeded. War itself has no place in a world in which common security has become the dominant characteristic." Archbishop Martino called on the international community to develop "a comprehensive approach to world peace, social justice, economic development and environmental protection."

Briefs:

● Lebanese Bishop Bechara Rai of Jubayl said Oct. 5 that, despite a 1989 agreement that ended 15 years of civil war, the continued presence of foreign forces in the country had made genuine political reform impossible.

● Archbishop Marcel Gervais of Ottawa, head of the Canadian Bishops' Conference, protested the harassment and attempted detention of Haitian Bishop Willy Romelus of Jeremie by members of the nation's armed forces. Bishop Romelus was a critic of the regime in power since the expulsion of democratically elected Father Jean-Bertrand Aristide in September, 1991.

● The Council of the Lutheran World Federation, of 114 churches and 70 million believers, praised the accomplishments of 25 years of Catholic-Lutheran relations and committed itself "to continue with the Roman Catholic Church on the path to visible unity."

Wiped Out

Organized Catholic life in Banja Luka, about 150 miles northwest of Sarajevo, Bosnia-Herzegovina, was wiped out by Serbian occupation forces, according to a local priest recently allowed to visit Croatia. He confirmed that 40 percent of Catholic churches in and around Banja Luka had been totally destroyed while all the rest, including St. Bonaventure Cathedral, had suffered heavy damage. Catholics faced constant harassment and intimidation, most parishes were without priests, and lay persons were usually barred from attending church. The priest said: "Most are afraid to speak out publicly and are forced to identify with Serbian policy. Prominent Serbs who tried to stand against it have since disappeared. Meanwhile, most ordinary Serbs are living much better than their Croatian or Muslim neighbors, who have been thrown out of their jobs and can now obtain hardly anything."

NOVEMBER 1992

VATICAN

Ordination of Women in Church of England — "This decision by the Anglican Communion constitutes a new and grave obstacle to the entire process of reconciliation with the Catholic Church," Vatican spokesman Joaquin Navarro-Valls said in a statement issued shortly after the Nov. 11 decision by the General Synod of the Church of England. Cardinal George Basil Hume of Westminster said, however, that the Catholic-Anglican dialogue would continue on the basis of "a real but partial communion in virtue of our baptism, of much that we believe in common (and) of our allegiance to Jesus Christ as true God and true Man." (See separate entry.)

Availability of Mass — The Pope said Nov. 11 that making regular Mass available to as many of his people as possible is a top priority for every bishop. "It is well known that there are difficulties in satisfying this need in many areas . . . because of the lack of priests and for other reasons." But that should make bishops "even more attentive to the problem of vocations and the wise distribution of available clergy. . . . It is necessary to make sure that the greatest number of faithful may partake in the body and blood of Christ in the Eucharistic Celebration, which culminates in Communion."

Challenge To Fill the Void — Filling the ideological void left by communism is one of the "new challenges" facing promoters of Catholic social teaching. East Europeans must not replace communism with unbridled freedom and the "cult of individual economic success." So stated the Pope Nov. 12 at a meeting with members of the Pontifical Council for Justice and Peace. He asked: "Doesn't this risk replacing one servitude with another?"

Racism and Nationalism in Germany — The Pope, warning about "racism and nationalist tendencies" in Germany, told bishops they should take the lead in protecting Jews from extremists. "You should work hard so that everything possible is done to prevent racist and nationalist tendencies from spreading, especially among the young. . . . In no case should Christians give in to indifference and apathy. That would be no less dangerous than violence itself. . . . I encourage you to work in a particular way to protect your Jewish brethren. One can never tolerate the desecration of synagogues and attacks on commemorative (cemetery) monuments which, because of their painful history, are of great importance to the Jews."

Celibacy Defended — Celibacy signifies the "unconditional acceptance" of priestly ministry, a fact which contemporary society — "no longer marked by Christian values " — does not understand. So stated the Holy Father as he declared Nov. 14 that the Church cannot adjust its rules to match the "different set of values" in vogue in today's society.

Respect for and Acceptance of the Disabled — International health and medical experts told participants in a Vatican conference that people with disabilities deserve respect and full acceptance in society. The Nov. 19-to-21 conference, sponsored by the Pontifical Council for Pastoral Assistance to Health Care Workers and attended by about 7,000 persons, examined the needs and special gifts of the disabled and said greater attention should be paid to both. Msgr. Thomas Cribbin, recently retired board chairman of the National Catholic Office for Persons with Disabilities, said the disabled were seeking "respect and acceptance," above all. "They want to get away from this concept of sympathy. They want equality, for the doors to open wide — whether it's the doors of a church, a religion, a world of work or recreation."

Pope John Paul said in an address that many disabled persons "feel ignored in their difficulties and are in fact pushed to lead a marginalized life." While legislation increasingly promotes social integration of the disabled, "much still remains to be done so that the cultural, social and architectural barriers keeping the disabled from satisfying their legitimate aspirations will be definitively overcome. They must attain full integration into the life of the family of believers."

The majority of the estimated 500 million disabled persons in the world were among the poorest and weakest inhabitants. Eighty-five percent of them were in the Third World, according to Cardinal Fiorenzo Angelini, president of the Pontifical Council for Pastoral Assistance to Health Care Workers.

Armenian Synod — Pope John Paul, at the start of the Armenian Catholic Bishops' Synod Nov. 19, prayed for the day when Armenian Catholic and Orthodox bishops might deliberate together. "For now," he said, "we offer to God our suffering for that which still divides us, in the certainty that he who creates every unity will one day make our desire a reality." He told the bishops to remain faithful to the heritage they share with their Orthodox counterparts and to preserve the unique elements of their rite while responding to the contemporary needs of their people. He encouraged the prelates to undertake a serious study of their liturgy, and said "it would be significant if such a process could take place in communion" with the bishops of the much larger Armenian Orthodox Church. The Pope also praised Armenian Catholics for their fidelity to the faith during 70 years under communist rule in the former Soviet Union.

Mexican Beatifications — The Pope beatified 26 Mexicans Nov. 22 — 22 priests and three laymen, martyrs, and Sister Maria Natividad Venegas, who founded the Daughters of the Sacred Heart of Jesus.

"Unbridled Butchery" — Democracies must respect life and end the "unbridled butchery of innocents" caused by abortion, declared the Pope Nov. 27 at a meeting with visiting bishops from Portugal. States must legally recognize human rights, "the first of which is the right to life. . . . Democracy demands respect for these rights, which at the same time form the limitations on democracy."

Dialogue with Orthodox — The Pope said the troubled dialogue between Catholics and Orthodox needed to be re-stimulated and pursued with "prudence and courage," in a traditional message to Ecumenical Orthodox Patriarch Bartholomeos I Nov. 30, the feast of St. Andrew, whom the Orthodox regard as the founder of their church.

General Audience Topics:

• When bishops in union with the Pope universally and definitively teach Catholic doctrine, their teaching enjoys infallible authority (Nov. 4).

• The sacramental ministry of bishops, which is centered on the Eucharist, involves responsibility for the promotion of vocations to the priesthood and the wise distribution of clergy (Nov. 11).

• As vicars and legates of Christ, bishops govern their churches not only by counsel and persuasion but also by authority and sacred power (Nov. 18).

• The papal ministry is based on the mandate which Simon Peter received from Jesus himself after Peter made his divinely inspired profession of faith (Nov. 25).

Briefs:

• Pope John Paul called on Croatia's bishops Nov. 9 to be "apostles of peace and renewal" in the midst of ethnic war, and appealed Nov. 29 for an end to two years of tribal warfare in Rwanda.

• At least 192 missionaries were killed between 1980 and 1992, reported Cardinal Jozef Tomko, head of the Congregation for the Evangelization of Peoples, during a memorial service Nov. 21.

Catechism of the Catholic Church

The new *Catechism of the Catholic Church* was released in its French edition Nov. 16 along with an accompanying apostolic constitution entitled *Fidei Depositum* ("Deposit of Faith"). It is the first universal collection of Catholic doctrine issued since 1566. (See separate entry.)

NATIONAL

Catholic-Jewish Ignorance — Christian and Jewish leaders meeting Nov. 2 and 3 at Sacred Heart University in Fairfield, Conn., called for efforts to banish the ignorance of Christians and Jews about each other's faith. "We have enormous ignorance of each other's religions. We should study each other's faith, our aims and patterns of life in a whole human context," said Schubert Ogden, a theology professor at Southern Methodist University. "Jews should learn about the role that Jesus plays in the life of Christians, and a Christian must come to understand the role that Torah plays in the life of a Jew." Dominican Father Joseph A. Di Nola, another theologian, said in a statement: "Our lack of knowledge about each other is enormous, despite the fact that we live side by side as neighbors and business associates." Rabbi Jack Bemporad, head of the Sacred Heart Center for Christian-Jewish Understanding, said that progress in relations had been "accomplished through intensive work, consultations and dialogues, but was done on the highest level with only limited filtering down to grass-roots clergy and laity. This is the task we now face."

Election Results — The nation's economic situation was apparently the dominant factor for voters who elected a Democrat to the presidency Nov. 3 for the first time in 12 years. Catholics voted for Bill Clinton in larger numbers than they did for President Bush or Ross Perot, according to Election Day exit polling conducted at 300 voting places nationwide. On state ballot measures, voters upheld a Maryland law prohibiting restrictions on abortion and rejected an Arizona initiative that would have outlawed most abortions. In California, they rejected Proposition 161 which would have legalized physician-assisted suicide. Opponents of abortion called Clinton's election a purely economic decision by voters. They voiced fears that, as a campaign strategy, Clinton "committed himself to an abortion policy far more extreme than that favored by the majority of Americans," said Wanda Franz, president of the National Right to Life Committee.

More Forceful Pro-Life Movement — "We call upon President-elect Clinton and Vice President-elect Gore to exercise the same compassion toward the unborn that they pleaded for during the campaign on behalf of the unemployed and other disenfranchised," said Cardinal John J. O'Connor in a statement issued Nov. 4. "The pro-life movement must demand of all elected officials and those who will campaign for office in the future that they recognize the grave moral obligation to do everything within their power to stop the slaughter of the innocents and to stop mouthing platitudes asserting that anyone can morally exercise the 'choice' to kill an unborn baby."

Assisted Suicide — An official of the bishops' Secretariat for Pro-Life Activities criticized two articles in *The New England Journal of Medicine* for proposing criteria under which physician-assisted suicide should be permitted. The articles were published Nov. 5, two days after a proposal to legalize such action was defeated in California by a 54-to-46 percent margin. "Naive is the kindest word I have" for the articles, said Richard M. Doerflinger. "They ignore fundamental facts about human nature and our own embattled health care system." The criteria in question were similar to the guidelines used in The Netherlands for physician-assisted suicide.

Abortion: Most Lethal Epidemic — Cancer and AIDS are "terrifying words" that bring to mind diseases that kill people, but abortion is an even "more frightful word for death," said Archbishop Edward A. McCarthy in an early November letter to all parishes in the Archdiocese of Miami. He called abortion "more lethal than the greatest of epidemics" and an opening of the way to "euthanasia and other attacks on the sacredness of life that can be devastating to our civilized society." Abortion is accompanied by "a degeneration of conscience," particularly among those who employ such euphemisms as "freedom of choice" and "respect for the rights of women." He called the "lucrative abortion industry an abomination."

Sisters' Ministries — A recently published national study of more than 72,000 women religious indicated that they were moving more and more to serving people with the greatest needs, such as the poor, elderly, terminally ill, homeless, and minorities of all kinds. There were still more nuns in elementary and secondary education than in any other field, but parish ministries were reported to be their second-largest and fastest-growing field of work. Peacemaking, work for justice, insertion among the poor, empowering others, developing lay leadership and working for systemic change ranked high in the nuns' priorities, according to findings of the study, conducted in 1991 under the auspices of the Leadership Conference of Women Religious. Sisters were turning away from:

• serving schoolchildren, toward serving adults;

• working in institutions they own or sponsor, toward a greater diversity of ministries;

• service in affluent or middle-class communities, toward service with the poor.

NCCB-USCC Meeting — About 250 bishops attended the annual meeting of the National Conference of Catholic Bishops and the U.S. Catholic Conference Nov. 16 to 19 in Washington. Actions included the following:

• defeat of a controversial pastoral letter on the concerns of women in Church and society;

• passage of a resolution on sex abuse by clergy;

• approval of a pastoral letter on stewardship and of a national plan for evangelization;

• election of new officers, headed by Archbishop William H. Keeler of Baltimore.

(See separate entry.)

Missal Changes: Too Much — Some of the proposed changes in a revised English translation of the Roman Missal (Sacramentary) were exaggerated beyond measure in an effort to eliminate sexist language. So stated Cardinal Roger M. Mahony in an interview published in *The Tidings*, newspaper of the Archdiocese of Los Angeles. His criticism came after release of the "Third Progress Report on the Revision of the Roman Missal" by the International Commission on English in the Liturgy. While praising various aspects of the revision, he said in a related letter to Archbishop Daniel E. Pilarczyk that many of the changes were "far beyond what most bishops of the episcopal conferences understand as 'translation.'" He called for wider participation by bishops in coming up "with what we feel is a translation that maintains the integrity of the Latin version's theology and ecclesiology while giving it to us in inspiring English."

Critique of Condom Distribution — The bishops of New York, in a pastoral statement critical of condom distribution, called on parents to counsel their children not to turn the "life-giving, wondrous act" of sex into an act of death and destruction. The statement, entitled "On Condom Distribution in Public Schools," urged parents, educators, policymakers and others to convey to adolescents the message that "human sexuality is beautiful, powerful, sacred and good, ... and must be used responsibly" in marriage. The bishops also cited the estimated 17 percent failure rate of condoms.

Court Actions:

• The Supreme Court heard arguments Nov. 4 in a case testing the constitutionality of ritual animal sacrifice that had the potential of setting new guidelines regarding religious freedom.

The case involved the right of the Santeria Church of Lukumi Babalu Aye to practice animal sacrifice and the right of the Miami suburb of Hialeah to outlaw animal sacrifice for reasons of public health.

• The U.S. Supreme Court decided 6 to 3 Nov. 30 not to review lower court rulings which overturned the Guam law which prohibited almost all abortions.

Briefs:

• Jesuit Father Arthur F. Shea, 86, active since 1940 as a missionary in the Philippines, was honored Nov. 6 at the 50th annual Jesuit Mission Dinner in New York.

• Three bishops were among 1,500 signers of an advertisement decrying a Vatican memorandum on gay rights legislation: Bishop Walter F. Sullivan of Richmond, Auxiliary Bishop Thomas J. Gumbleton of Detroit and retired Bishop Charles A. Buswell of Pueblo, Colo. They called the memorandum discriminatory.

• Catholic Charities USA made the first of several grants to hurricane-damaged areas in the dioceses of Miami ($430,000), Lafayette, La. ($80,000), Houma-Thibodaux ($10,000) and Honolulu ($10,000). Additional grants were under consideration.

Tributes to Murdered Nuns

Memorial services were held in various places during the month for five nuns who were slain in October by rebels in Liberia. The nuns — members of the community of Adorers of the Blood of Christ, based in Ruma, Ill. — were Sisters Shirley Kolmer, 61, Kathleen McGuire, 54, Agnes Mueller, 62, Mary Joel Kolmer, 58, and Barbara Muttra, 69. (Burial of the five in Ruma was completed Jan. 17, 1993.)

• Pope John Paul prayed Nov. 1 that the murders of the five American nuns, reported the previous day, might be a catalyst for peace in that nation. He said they were "brutally murdered outside Monrovia where they (had) dedicated their lives to announcing the Gospel and serving their brothers and sisters."

• Cardinal Jozef Tomko, prefect of the Congregation for the Evangelization of Peoples, presided at a Mass for the sisters Nov. 21 in Rome. He said in a homily: "These five American sisters go to join the numerous other missionaries killed in different parts of the world. The history of the Church is accompanied by an unbroken chain of martyrs and our century, which seemed to be an 'enlightened' one, has added no small contribution. ... Few people realize just how many modern martyrs have given their lives for Christ in the past few years in the missions. Since 1992 up to today, 192 missionaries, men and women, have been killed, and it is feared that the actual number could be higher."

• William Twaddell, U.S. ambassador to Liberia, said in a cable message to the nuns' motherhouse that the sisters had been "acting in the most noble tradition of their order and their faith. The safety and welfare of the wounded and the defenseless motivated them and were their only concerns in the midst of war."

INTERNATIONAL

Religion Is Essential to Society — Although religion is always personal, it is never private, and it has social implications that are often overlooked, declared Cardinal George Basil Hume of Westminster Nov. 4 in a lecture at Surrey University, Oxford. "Religion is an essential constituent of a society's identity and is its very soul." Recent years witnessed a decline in the public role and influence of institutional religion, he remarked, noting that many people no longer believed in objective norms of morality. "Morality has become, in our individualistic age, a matter of opinion. It is essential for the future of our society to escape from moral subjectivism."

Compassion for Victims of AIDS — Officials of Catholic medical and charitable agencies called for compassion for Asian victims of AIDS during the 10th Congress of the Asian Federation of Catholic Medical Associations, held early in the month in Bangkok. "HIV is not a selective virus; it does not bypass Christians and Catholics," said Father Robert Vitillo of Caritas Internationalis, the Church's development and emergency aid agency.

Anti-Semitism Condemned — Cardinal Camillo Ruini of Rome and Bishop Karl Lehmann of the German Bishops' Conference condemned recent acts of anti-Semitism in their respective countries. Bishop Lehmann called on "all Catholic Christians to reject actions of intolerance. . . . Anti-Semitism is a sin against God and humanity. It can have no place among Christians and their communities." Cardinal Ruini said Nov. 7 that the Church "firmly condemns the repeated episodes of intolerance and violence that have occurred recently" against Jews in Rome. Thousands of people marched in Rome and Germany to protest what was perceived to be a general increase in anti-Semitism.

Ordination of Women — The General Synod of the Church of England voted Nov. 11 to ordain women to the priesthood, an action requiring ratification by Parliament and the Queen of England. Dr. George Carey, archbishop of Canterbury and spiritual head of the Church of England supported the legislation. It was called a serious obstacle in the way of Anglican-Catholic unity by Cardinal Edward I. Cassidy, president of the Pontifical Council for Promoting Christian Unity. (See separate entry.)

Hindu Attack — The bishops of India protested the beatings of a priest and five nuns by five attackers identified as Hindu militants in the Diocese of Ujjain. The attack was the latest attempt by Hindu fundamentalists to "scare away" missionaries, according to Father Jose Kondoor, chancellor of the diocese. He also said the Church in Madhya Pradesh had been having troubles caused by Hindus since their party came to power in May, 1990.

Poor and Refugees — "Listen to the cry of the poor" and respond with "generous solidarity" were the themes of a statement presented Nov. 13 by Vatican representative Archbishop Renato R. Martino to the U.N. General Assembly committee dealing with economic questions. "The fact that in today's world, with all its scientific resources and progress, so many people live in poverty, is a grave affront to human dignity" and "a real challenge to the conscience of humanity." He called for reforms to ensure long-range development of nations as well as "immediate intervention for those whose suffering is acute."

Archbishop Martino also urged changes in international law to provide refugee status to some people who leave their countries for economic reasons "that threaten their lives and physical safety." He said: "Those who flee economic conditions that threaten their lives and physical safety must be treated differently than those who emigrate simply to improve their financial or social position." He noted that current practice under the Geneva Convention designated as refugees those fleeing persecution for race, religion or membership in social or political groups. The international community, he said, should now add "the victims of armed conflicts, erroneous economic policies and natural disasters." He added: Refugees are not merely "mouths to be fed," but persons who come "with hands that can produce and minds that can create. . . . Emphasis on their dignity and rights not only gives a humane dimension to the initiatives taken on their behalf, but also prevents anyone from using or exploiting their tragedy for political or extraneous purposes."

Birth Control Development Programs — Economic development programs that include pressure to control birth rates violate the religious identity of Latin America and the human dignity of its people, the region's bishops said in a letter to the United Nations. "We know that a demographic problem exists in some of our countries, but it is not licit to confront the problem in ways at odds with ethics. . . . It is necessary to strengthen the culture of life against the culture of death, which claims so many victims among our peoples." All too often economic development and progress are sought as ends in themselves without regard for the dignity of the people and the sacredness of individual human lives. "Systematic campaigns against birth organized by international institutions and governments," which use pressure and go "against the culture and religious identity of our nations," cannot be accepted. The bishops' letter was released Nov. 19 at the Vatican.

Briefs:

• Catholics in Hong Kong reported that many asylum-seekers from Vietnam were being forced unfairly into return trips home because of flaws in procedures for determining their refugees status.

• Jesuits in El Salvador said they wanted conditional reprieves (from jail but not from charges) for jailed military officers convicted in the murders of six Jesuit priests in 1989. It was thought the real authors of the crimes were still free.

Wipe-out Urged

Chinese officials and members of the Communist Party were urged to take measures to wipe out underground religious movements in the country, reported Asian UCA News. According to documents obtained by the agency, the principal target of the campaign was the underground church of Catholics loyal to the Holy See. "Completely Destroying the Organizations and Systems of the Underground Religious Force" was the title of the one of the documents. It listed a number of actions to curb the influence of the underground church, including:

• Clerics and core members of the underground church should be harassed by persistent arrests to keep them in suspense.

• Underground priests should be re-educated while being restrained from unauthorized preaching.

• Services at unauthorized locations should be banned.

• Followers of underground priests should be re-educated and made members of the government-sanctioned church as soon as possible.

DECEMBER 1992

VATICAN

Concern for Europe — Concern about the role of the Church in Europe was the motive for Pope John Paul's call for a prayer-for-peace meeting at Assisi in January. At a meeting with presidents of European bishops' conferences Dec. 1, he spelled out some of his worries, including ethnic unrest erupting into warfare, a persistent "counter-evangelization" trend in European society, and new tensions in interfaith relations. Such developments required the Church to "renew itself and strengthen its capacity to give clear witness in favor of Christ."

Sterilization a Grave Offense — Sterilization for the purpose of avoiding child-bearing is a "grave offense" against human dignity, the Pope told members of the Italian Society of Gynecology and Obstetrics Dec. 5. The practice violates God's plan for sexual intercourse to be a means of uniting spouses and possibly creating new life. "By asserting the dignity of life, of every unborn life, the Church is obeying the supreme command of God."

Humanitarian Aid — As U.S. troops launched a relief-protection operation in Somalia, Pope John Paul said the international community should make sure that humanitarian aid reaches suffering populations. "War between nations or internal conflicts must not condemn defenseless citizens to death by hunger," he said Dec. 5. While not specifically endorsing military operations, the Pope said relief must get through, even if it means intervention in the internal affairs of a country. The Pope made his appeal in Rome at the opening of the International Conference on Nutrition, sponsored by the U.N. Food and Agriculture Organization.

Natural Family Planning — The Church and governments should increase their efforts to promote natural methods of family planning because they are morally acceptable, safe and reliable ways to achieve or avoid pregnancy, said participants in a Vatican meeting. "We recommend that natural methods should be available to all couples everywhere," declared 45 educators, physicians, scientists and theologians who participated in the Dec. 9-to-11 meeting sponsored by the Pontifical Council for the Family. They also said: "We express our gratitude to the Catholic Church, which has strongly encouraged responsible parenthood through the use of natural methods of regulating fertility."

Church Teaching vs. Capitalist Excess — In an address to members of an Italian Catholic labor organization, the Pope said Dec. 12 that, after the collapse of Marxism, the social teaching of the Church was needed more than ever to help stem excesses of the free market system. The Church must constantly try to place the economy at the service of the human being. "This message has become even more urgent now that the collapse of Marxism has left an open field to the free trade ideology, which tends to undervalue the ethical demands to which even the market economy must submit in order to serve the human being. . . . Christians, faced with the threat of a corrosive dissolving of fundamental values, are called upon to commit themselves personally and as a community to announce the Gospel and make real-life applications of the social doctrine of the Church." This forms the nucleus of what the Church is calling the "new evangelization" of the late 20th century.

Free Gift — Christmas marks God's gift of himself to humanity, but the gift is not forced on anyone. "It can be said that the coming of God (as man) stops at the threshold of human will," the Pope said Dec. 15 during an annual pre-Christmas Mass for university students, professors and administrators. The time of Advent "is given to us so that we might become more and more aware of the presence of him who is always coming, who stands at the door and knocks." Those who believe in God and accept the salvation his Son brings are called to do God's work in the world, which is "the evangelical vineyard" of God.

Accept Refugees — The Pope urged Germany to continue accepting refugees in spite of anti-foreigner violence in the country. At the same time, he said Dec. 19, the Church must be aware that there are limits on the amount of hospitality a single nation can offer. His remarks echoed the position of the German bishops, who had condemned attacks on foreigners while proposing more realistic controls on some forms of immigration. He noted that Germany had welcomed far more refugees than any other European nation.

Poor Interpretation — Media descriptions of the Second Vatican Council as a power struggle between conservatives and progressives in the Church were partial and "very unjust" interpretations, said the Pope Dec. 22 at a meeting with members of the Roman Curia. During the council, he observed, the Church extracted "some old and new things" from "the great treasury confided to it by God" in order to put new life in humanity's divine relationship. "Any attempts to reduce the reality of the Church to dimensions which are solely sociological become inadequate." Vatican II generated "great interest in the mass media," but the media "frequently indulged in a rather partial interpretation of the activities, presenting the council as a place of conflict between conservative and progressive tendencies." It is wrong "to reduce that historic event to such an opposition and struggle among rival groups."

$1.2 Million Given Away — With funds donated for use at his discretion, the Pope gave more than $1.2 million to victims of disasters in 1992, reported the Pontifical Council Cor Unum, which coordinates Catholic relief work throughout the world.

General Audience Topics:

● Peter, after repenting of his human weakness in denying Christ, was strengthened by grace and enabled to confirm the other Apostles (Dec. 2).

● The Lord entrusted Peter with the mandate to feed his sheep and made him the universal shepherd of his flock, the Church Dec. 9).

● Peter exercised a particular authority which was recognized in the early Church (Dec. 16).

● Devotion to Mary honors Christ (Dec. 30).

Briefs:

● The Vatican announced Dec. 2 that a symbolic contribution of $20,000 would be made to the 1993 budget of the U.N. Relief and Works Agency for Palestinian Refugees.

• The Pope met with: Episcopal Bishop Frank T. Griswold of Chicago, co-chairman of the U.S. Anglican-Roman Catholic Consultation, Dec 4; the Rev. Kathleen Richardson, president of the Methodist Conference of Great Britain, Dec. 17.

• The Holy Father expressed his sadness and concern at the plight of victims of disasters in Bolivia (avalanche, Dec. 9), Indonesia (earthquake, Dec. 12) and Portugal (plane crash, Dec. 21).

Christmas Themes

Prayers for global peace and respect for human life were principal themes of Pope John Paul's celebration of the birth of Jesus.

"Come, we beg you, that your love, the gift of peace, may triumph," he prayed in his blessing to the City of Rome and the World on Christmas Day. He said nothing could prevent the Prince of Peace from coming into the world, "even in the martyred parts of the world where killing is still going on and evil seems to reign unchallenged." He called on the leaders of nations to practice solidarity as the highway to justice and peace. He asked people to "listen to the voice of love, both sweet and powerful, especially you who brandish violent and murderous arms." His thoughts were of those living in fear, sadness and pain.

At midnight Mass, the Pope said the light of Christ's birth could not and cannot be dimmed by "the shadows of poverty or the gloom of neglect and humiliation." In view of the birth of Jesus, "could there be a more convincing proof of the fact that God loves mankind?" Christmas reveals to people of good will God's plan for peace in the world. "But," the Holy Father asked, "can peace truly prevail on earth when there is no good will, when people do not care that God loves them?"

Millions of people in more than 50 countries were able to watch the televised midnight Mass celebrated by the Pope. His traditional Christmas Day message and greeting (in 54 languages) were broadcast in about 65 countries.

NATIONAL

AIDS Crisis — People in communities confronted with the AIDS crisis should come together to pray for better understanding of the disease and of one another, said Auxiliary Bishop Joseph M. Sullivan of Brooklyn in observance of World AIDS Day Dec. 1 in New York. While noting that communities are torn apart not only by the "ravaging disease" but also by the "alienation" that accompanies it, he appealed for perseverance in efforts to gain further insight into the AIDS crisis and to confront it "as people who will not give up on each other." Members of the community should "call upon God to heal us all" of blindness to one another. "Let us pray that God will not abandon us, and that we will not abandon one another." With another message, Bishop Thomas V. Daily of Brooklyn said the Church "must always reflect Christ's compassion, understanding and healing. ... It is the person that we, as church, pledge to nourish and support, as best we can, with Christian love, action and prayer."

AIDS-related services were a priority of Caritas Internationalis, reported Father Robert J. Vitillo, director and executive with special responsibility for such activity. Speaking in New York, he said about 125 projects were in operation in Africa, Asia, Latin America and Eastern Europe. He called attention to the fact that the response of the Church to the AIDS pandemic was extensive, even though many people were unaware of it. He observed that some people think the Church writes off people with AIDS as under punishment from God. The untold story, he said, is that the Church has been providing AIDS victims with a global ministry of education, social service and spiritual support.

End U.S.-Vatican Relations — The leader of a Southern Baptist organization urged President-elect Bill Clinton to "redress a wrong" done by President Ronald Reagan and stop the practice of appointing a U.S. ambassador to the Vatican. Richard D. Land, executive director of the Christian Life Commission of the Southern Baptist Convention, asked Clinton in a letter Dec. 2 to revoke the diplomatic status of the U.S. representative to the Vatican. Barry Lynn, executive director of Americans United for Separation of Church and State, also called for an end to the diplomatic exchange. A 1984 lawsuit for that purpose was dismissed by the 3rd U.S. Circuit Court of Appeals.

Fewer Women Entering Religious Life — Fewer U.S. women than men were entering religious life each year, according to findings of a study conducted by the Center for Applied Research in the Apostolate. The "CARA Formation Directory for Men and Women Religious 1993," released Dec. 2, reported: "On the average, the number of men in initial formation per community in 1989 was 8.9; in spring, 1992, the average number of men in formation was 9.8. ... In contrast, in 1992 women's congregations had an average of 4.0 women in initial formation, down from 5.6 in 1989." Data for the 1993 directory came from responses to an April, 1992, questionnaire by 786 of the 984 congregations, provinces and monasteries of U.S. men and women religious, or 78 percent of the religious institutes in the country. The combined membership of the responding institutes for the 1993 directory was 107,526, or 87 percent of the 123,929 men and women religious in the country.

Covenant House Vigils — The Covenant House ministry to homeless youths held simultaneous candlelight vigils in nine cities Dec. 3 to call attention to the plight of the young people it shelters. The vigils were held in New York, Los Angeles, Houston, New Orleans, Toronto, Anchorage, Fort Lauderdale, Newark and Atlantic City. Covenant House President Sister Mary Rose McGeady told vigil participants that the lives of many youths could not brighten without help. "It is our hope that, as we hold our candles high, the light will serve as a beacon to our country to focus its attention on our homeless kids, kids who without help may very well not survive. ... We must all work toward the day when even one homeless kid is a statistic that is unacceptable to us as a nation."

Catholics in Congress — One hundred and 41 Catholics were to be members of the 103rd U.S. Congress, due to go into session in January: 23 Senators (16 Democrats and seven Republicans) and

118 Representatives (77 Democrats and 41 Republicans).

Abortion Regulations — The U.S. Supreme Court left intact Dec. 7 a ruling upholding Mississippi's law requiring women to wait 24 hours before having an abortion. The court also let stand the state's informed consent requirement, under which physicians must tell women about the risks of and alternatives to abortion. The earlier ruling was made by the 5th U.S. Circuit Court of Appeals.

Respect for Abortion Opponents — More than 60 organizations and individuals asked President-elect Clinton not to "disenfranchise" the millions of Americans who oppose abortion. In advertisements published Dec. 8 in *The New York Times* and *Boston Herald*, they specifically asked Clinton not to resume a federal subsidy of abortion. "It would indeed create a moral crisis if citizens, against deeply held moral and religious beliefs, were forced to subsidize with federal tax dollars the wanton destruction of defenseless unborn human beings."

Hispanic Pastoral Plan — The Spanish Apostolate of the Diocese of Rockville Center inaugurated a new pastoral plan emphasizing implementation at parish levels. The plan, *Un Pueblo en Cristo* ("A People United in Christ"), was approved by Auxiliary Bishop John C. Dunne at a special liturgy Dec. 13. He said it represented "clear evidence that the Hispanic community of the diocese has found its true identity and cultural value, and is now being recognized officially as such," said Father Pablo M. Rodriguez, vicar for Hispanics. The plan, developed through meetings with 30 Hispanic faith communities since June, 1990, pinpointed five priorities: evangelization, formation, family ministry, youth ministry and social/pastoral ministry. It was estimated that more than 180,000 Hispanics lived in the Long Island diocese.

Norplant Plan Opposed — Archbishop William H. Keeler of Baltimore criticized a proposal by city officials to promote the use of Norplant, a long-term contraceptive implant, among the city's teen-age school girls. "I say we should give moral education a chance. . . . I'm concerned because it seems that the people formulating these policies have given up on teaching young people basic moral values, including respect for self and respect for others. . . . I am unaware of serious efforts here to teach young people in the schools, girls and boys alike, positively about abstinence from sexual relations. Such programs have been introduced in other parts of the country, including inner-city settings, with measurable and positive results. . . . Moral values would give moral foundation and provide a new cultural setting in the school, along with the example of many dedicated teachers and the support of parents."

Bosnian Rapes Denounced — The heads of three U.S. bishops' committees denounced the systematic rape and murder of Bosnian women by Serbs. In a joint statement Dec. 21 they called the organized, systematic rapes part of the Serbian "ethnic cleansing" campaign, which they described as a "hideous new contribution to the roster of crimes against humanity." Such attacks not only degrade the victims and subject them to life-long torment, but are an apparently intentional effort to destroy "the very structure of family and community life" among the Muslim and Croat populace in the region. The bishops

called for trial of the perpetrators, urged international efforts to aid the violated women and their babies, and asked people to pray for the victims and their families. The statement was issued by Cardinal Joseph L. Bernardin, chairman of the Committee on Marriage and the Family; Archbishop John R. Roach, chairman of the Committee on International Policy; and Bishop John J. Snyder, chairman of the Committee on Women in Society and in the Church.

Briefs:

● The Sisters of the Holy Family, founded by Henriette Delille and two companions, celebrated the completion of 150 years of service to black people and others in need.

● About 800 participants in a meeting of the National Federation of Catholic Youth Ministry focused attention Dec. 2 to 5 on work with families, schools and the media to improve their service to young people.

● The Tekakwitha Conference announced the launching of a new outreach program for Native American Catholics living in urban areas.

Leading News Stories of 1992

The following were among leading news stories of the year.

● Observance of the 500th anniversary of the introduction of Christianity in the Americas, coupled with the fourth general assembly of the Latin American Bishops' Conference.

● Publication of the *Catechism of the Catholic Church,* the first of its kind in more than 400 years.

● Failure of the U.S. bishops to develop an acceptable pastoral letter on the concerns of women in society and in the Church.

● Mass famine in Somalia and the beginning of U.N. efforts to safeguard relief operations.

● The murder of five American nuns in Liberia.

● The decision by the General Synod of the Church of England to authorize the ordination of women to the priesthood.

● Reports of sexual abuse of minors by priests.

● The genocidal war and "ethnic cleansing" in former Yugoslavia.

● Surgery on Pope John Paul for the removal of a benign tumor.

INTERNATIONAL

Widespread Religious Intolerance — The Vatican nuncio to the United Nations said in a Dec. 1 statement to a General Assembly committee that religious intolerance remained a widespread problem despite improved conditions in Central and Eastern Europe. Archbishop Renato R. Martino said political changes had reduced "the number of countries holding official ideologically-inspired policies of religious persecution or repression." However, "all too often, even to this day, the banner of religion has been waved to mask and to fan enmities rooted in interests or vindications that have little or nothing to do with religion itself, such as economic disparities, social tensions and racial intolerance."

Marginal Citizens — Christians risked becoming marginal citizens if religious affiliation ceased being a determining factor of political power in Lebanon, said Maronite Patriarch Nasrallah P. Sfeir. Ending the system under which power is divided among religious groups would threaten the prospects for harmony among Muslims and Christians. "It will open the way for the more numerous community to dominate the minority, causing its marginalization." The Patriarch, whose address was reported by Vatican Radio, spoke at the opening of a general assembly of Lebanon's patriarchs and bishops.

Families Need Pastoral Help — Bishop-heads of European national family life commissions said that urgent pastoral responses were needed to meet contemporary challenges to Christian family life. The challenges included a rising divorce rate, remarriage while a spouse is still alive, a diminishing birth rate and pressures in favor of abortion. They were called examples of "the seriousness and size of the challenges launched at the indissolubility of marriage and of the attempts against life." At the same time, the bishops said in a statement made public Dec. 3, the challenges pointed to "the urgency of a deeper and more systematic evangelization before and after marriage."

To Prevent Famine — With world attention focused on emergency relief for Somalia's starving multitudes, government officials and nutrition experts in Rome were discussing ways and means of warding off similar disasters in the future. At a Dec. 5-to-11 International Conference on Nutrition, sponsored by the U.N. Food and Agriculture Organization and the World Health Organization, a final declaration pledged a new global effort to end famine and all forms of malnutrition. The declaration said: "Hunger and malnutrition are unacceptable in a world that has both the knowledge and the resources to end this human catastrophe. ... We recognize that globally there is enough food for all; inequitable access is the main problem." The statement echoed many of the concerns listed by Pope John Paul in his opening address to the conference, which was attended by representatives from scores of governments and international organizations.

Praise for Somalia Operation — A Vatican official praised the U.S.-led operation in Somalia, saying that armed protection of relief programs was a necessary first step in restoring justice to the country. "I personally think this (operation) is protecting and feeding people — the poor, the hungry and the truly suffering. This is a real social and charitable work that the Americans are doing." Archbishop Alois Wagner, the Vatican representative to the U.N. Food and Agriculture Organization, said Dec. 10 that bringing food to the starving would in turn help in bringing about justice and "a real social understanding" in the country.

Senseless Violence in South Africa — Recent deaths and injuries in a restaurant bombing and a hand grenade attack at a golf club party brought "to the fore the senseless violence that continues to ravage" the country, said the Southern African Bishops' Conference Dec. 8. "It is a sad reflection on our society that it takes a massacre or a new form of violence to jolt us out of our apparent complacency with the killings that occur all too regularly." One person was killed and 18 were injured in the bombing of a Queenstown restaurant Dec. 3. Four people were killed and 17 injured in the Nov. 28 attack at the King William's Town Golf Club.

Fear of Hindu Zealots — The demolition of an historic mosque by Hindu zealots in Ayodyah, northern India, caused religious minorities in general to fear for their safety. By Dec. 10, more than 600 people had been killed in the country by rioting and police actions intended to control the chaos. Catholic and Protestant leaders issued a statement in which they demanded safeguarding of minority rights and protection for all places of worship.

Rosary Crusade — Cardinal Roger M. Mahony, at a Mass attended by more than a million people in Manila, stressed the role of prayer in helping to unite families and overcome spiritual and physical hardships. The Mass marked the 50th anniversary of the Family Rosary Crusade.

Rights of Asylum — Caritas Europe condemned a European Community proposal on migration as an attack on the human rights of asylum seekers. The principal objection was to a section of a draft plan that would urge citizens of countries with poor records on rights to stay in their homelands and try to improve conditions there. The suggestion, said the group, "ignores the fact that, in most countries where human rights abuses are prevalent, legislation is weak and security forces are known to have very little regard for civilized standards."

Guatemalan Church-State Relations — Relations deteriorated throughout 1992 in confrontations over human rights. A special target of government hostility was the archdiocesan Human Rights Office, which registered 470 rights violations, including 190 state-linked murders, in the first half of the year.

Briefs:

● Maltese Dominican Father Mark F. Montebello was silenced by his order after expressing deviant opinions on radio favoring homosexual marriage and questioning Christ's reasons for remaining single.

● Jerusalem Patriarch Michel Sabbah's Christmas message included a special greeting to 417 Palestinians stranded on the Lebanese border after being deported from Israel Dec. 17.

● Polish sources reported the 1992 theft of church goods valued at an estimated $3.6 million.

Church Needs in Former U.S.S.R.

The needs of churches in the former Soviet Union were discussed and assessed at a meeting of representatives of 32 Catholic aid agencies and churches in the republics of the Commonwealth of Independent States. The meeting was held at the Vatican under the auspices of Cor Unum. According to a delayed report of the Nov. 27 and 28 assembly, participants concluded:

● All church aid should be sent to individual republics, not to the Commonwealth.

● Emphasis should be on strengthening fledgling church programs and structures rather than short-term relief.

● There was an acute need for spiritual formation, with due regard for interfaith sensitivity.

● Churches needed to take charge of their own programs.

● Local churches could not attempt to substitute for the state in dealing with serious social and economic problems.

JANUARY 1993

VATICAN

Peace Day Message — Pope John Paul began 1993 with a plea for peace in the world's trouble spots, from the Balkans to the Middle East. At a Mass marking World Peace Day Jan. 1, he said the persistence of conflicts across the globe illustrated a great challenge facing the Church: to "eradicate hatred — the first enemy of peace — from the depth of the human being." Citing the theme — "If you want peace, reach out to the poor" — he said poverty represented a "constant threat to peace" in many places. "We must become aware that in many parts of the world there is still violence and injustice, to which we cannot remain indifferent and passive." He called attention to the fact that the plight of the poor, who suffer most from hatred and warfare, made clear one of the best reasons for peace: that war does not serve the common good.

Moral Dimension of Therapy — Psychiatric therapy must help patients develop morally as well as psychologically, the Pope said Jan. 4 in an address to members of the World Psychiatric Association, the American Psychiatric Association and the American Psychoanalytic Association. "No adequate assessment of the nature of the human person or the requirements for human fulfillment and psycho-social well-being can be made without respect for man's spiritual dimension." Psychiatric practice "involves a sensitivity to the often-tangled working of the human mind and heart, and an openness to the ultimate concerns which give meaning to peoples' lives." This creates the "urgent need for a constructive dialogue" between religion and psychiatry. The Pope added that psychiatry also has social ramifications because of "a relationship between the appearance and aggravation of certain illnesses and mental disturbances and the crisis of values" in society.

Ordination of Bishops — Bishops are called to unite their people in faith, said the Pope Jan. 6 at the ordination of 11 bishops — three from Italy, two from Poland, and one each from Ghana, Hungary, Peru, Slovenia, Sri Lanka and the United States. He asked the bishops to "bring the offering of the Christian people to the feet of the divine Savior, that is, the gifts of your churches together with your pastoral efforts. In this way the most holy gift which God has bestowed on the world in Jesus Christ will increasingly reveal itself, and humanity will come to know how much God has loved it, not hesitating to give his only begotten Son for it."

Prayer for Peace at Assisi — Pope John Paul was joined by more than 120 Christian, Muslim and Jewish representatives for two days of prayer for peace Jan. 9 and 10. The Holy Father, speaking at a prayer vigil, said in part: "The first aim of this vigil is that all men and women in Europe who are open to religious values might feel the wounds of war as if they were inflicted on their own flesh — anguish, loneliness, powerlessness, grief, pain and death. Perhaps even despair. . . . In the face of such a tragedy we cannot remain indifferent; we cannot sleep. We must, in fact, watch and pray, like the Lord Jesus in the Garden of Olives when he took upon himself our sins. . . . Peace on earth is our task, a task for men and women 'of good will.' In particular, it is a task for Christians. It is our responsibility before the world and in the world, which remains without true peace unless Jesus Christ bestows it through his 'instruments of peace,' through 'peacemakers.'" Quoting Pope Paul VI, he added: "'Our mission is to teach men to love one another, to be reconciled, to train themselves for peace.'"

Speakers during the observance included: Muslim leader Jacub Selimoski, Archbishop Vinko Puljic of Sarajevo, and Rabbi David Rosen, director of interfaith relations for the Anti-Defamation League of B'nai B'rith in Jerusalem. Cardinal Anthony J. Bevilacqua took part in the prayer meeting.

When Talks Fail — In a major address to diplomats Jan. 16, the Pope said that, when negotiations for peace have failed and whole populations are threatened, the international community has a duty to step in and "disarm the aggressor." Outside nations do not have the "right to indifference" when they see unjust attacks continuing, he told more than 100 diplomats accredited to the Vatican. He coupled his assessment of trouble spots with an impassioned plea for the people of Bosnia-Herzegovina, urging the international community to refuse to accept territorial conquest by force and the campaign for "ethnic cleansing" being waged by Serbian Orthodox forces against Muslims and mostly Catholic Croatians.

In the same address the Pope asked the world not to forget the suffering people of Iraq, as U.S. warplanes led reprisal raids against installations in the country in mid-month. It must be remembered, he said against the apparent background of the 1991 Persian Gulf War, that "war has long-term consequences" and "forces civilian populations to endure heavy sufferings."

Catholic-Orthodox Relations — At the conclusion Jan. 25 of the Week of Prayer for Christian Unity, Pope John Paul pledged increased cooperation with Orthodox Christians, especially in Eastern Europe. He said: "It is the firm intention of the Catholic Church to make every possible effort so that, with the barriers of misunderstanding knocked down and the stumbling blocks present on the way of dialogue overcome, the whole body of Christ before long can breathe with 'the two lungs' of the church communities of East and West totally reconciled."

Efforts against Misuse of Religion — The Pope, in a meeting with officials of the World Islamic League, said Christians and Muslims should join in efforts against the "misuse of religion" to fuel animosity and strife. Muslim representatives, in turn, asked for the Pope's help in prodding peace moves in the Middle East and in Bosnia-Herzegovina. One Muslim leader said he agreed that religion was often a pretext for political conflict. The exchange came Jan. 28 during a visit to the Vatican by Islamic League Secretary-General Abdullah Omar Nasseef and several other league officials.

General Audience Topics:

● St. Peter's decision to baptize Cornelius was a critical step in the Church's realization that the Gentiles were called to share in God's saving plan (Jan. 13).

• The fruit of the Holy Spirit is seen in the variety of gifts, virtues and charisms which he bestows in order to promote the unity of Christians (Jan. 20).

• It was the will of Christ that there should be successors of Peter to continue his mission as the visible principle of the Church's unity in faith (Jan. 27).

Briefs:

• The Vatican announced Jan. 4 the establishment of diplomatic relations with two countries, the Czech Republic and Slovakia, formed in the breakup of Czechoslovakia.

• The Vatican joined 125 nations Jan. 14 in signing a treaty banning chemical weapons.

• Tests conducted Jan. 18 showed that "the Pope's health is excellent," reported Vatican spokesman Joaquin Navarro-Valls Jan. 25, six months after the Pontiff underwent surgery for the removal of a tumor in the colon.

• The Pope accepted the resignation of controversial Dutch Bishop Johannes M. Gijsen of Roermond.

Clinton's Pro-Abortion Moves

The Vatican newspaper sharply criticized President Clinton for revoking pro-life policies and said his administration had started down "the pathway of death and violence." The strongly worded commentary came less than 24 hours after Clinton cancelled several restrictions on the practice of abortion. The action was a "big disappointment" to those who had hoped that his policy decisions would be based on defense of human rights, said *L'Osservatore Romano* Jan. 23. "With these steps, the announced 'renewal' is starting out on the pathway of death and violence against innocent human beings. . . . This is not progress, neither for the United States nor for humanity, which once again must suffer a humiliating defeat." The new President's executive orders (see item in National section below) reversed policies of Presidents Reagan and Bush.

NATIONAL

Vatican-U.S. Relations — The U.S. ambassador to the Vatican said Jan. 7 that he would not comment on recent calls by some U.S. church organizations for President-elect Clinton to abolish diplomatic relations with the Vatican, but he added that such opposition was not new. Thomas Melady, U.S. ambassador since 1989, said the decision rested solely with the new President. "It would be inappropriate for me to comment on what he'll do," said Melady. Evangelical, Southern Baptist and Protestant organizations were in support of a campaign to persuade Clinton to break the diplomatic ties, which were established formally by President Reagan in 1984.

Unfair INS Policy — In arguments before the U.S. Supreme Court Jan. 11, a disputed U.S. Immigration and Naturalization Service policy was likened to hanging signs saying, "No Irish need apply" or "No blacks wanted." The comparison was related to an INS appeal of a lower court ruling providing for extension of the period for applying for amnesty under the 1986 Immigration Reform and Control Act. In a suit filed by Catholic Social Services on behalf of clients, a U.S. District Court in California ruled that the INS wrongly informed people that they were ineligible to apply for amnesty because they had left the United States for brief periods of time after arriving here. The 9th U.S. Circuit Court of Appeals upheld the lower court ruling and ordered the extension.

Operation Rescue and KKK Law — The U.S. Supreme Court ruled 6-to-3 Jan. 13 that abortion clinic blockades do not violate a 122-year-old civil rights law and therefore are not subject to federal intervention to stop them. Justice Antonin Scalia, writing for the majority, said "opposition to abortion cannot possibly be considered . . . opposition to women. Whatever one thinks of abortion, it cannot be denied that there are common and respectable reasons for opposing it, other than hatred of or condescension toward" women. The Alexandria Women's Health Clinic in Virginia claimed that blockades by abortion protesters, including Jane Bray and members of Operation Rescue, violated the 1871 Civil Rights Act, also known as the Ku Klux Klan Act because it was used to safeguard the rights of blacks targeted by the Klan.

Today's Seminarians Are Different — New theology students are more diverse than they were in the past, according to 169 U.S. Catholic faculty members, from 39 theological seminaries, surveyed in a study entitled "Readiness for Theological Studies: A Study of Faculty Perceptions on the Readiness of Seminarians." Faculty members viewed new theology students as:

• more diverse than in the past in age and background, with respect to race, ethnicity, culture, education, and spiritual, religious and family experience;

• generally strong in the spirit of service, sensitivity to others, spirituality and pastoral concern, but weak academically.

• more frequently from dysfunctional family backgrounds, lacking in a shared "Catholic culture" and more conservative.

Surrogate Life-Death Decisions — The bishops of New York said the state should include strict safeguards to protect terminally ill, incapacitated patients if it decides to adopt a new law giving designated surrogates authority to make decisions for them. Bishop Howard J. Hubbard of Albany testified on behalf of the bishops before the New York State Assembly's Health Committee Jan. 13. He said the bishops agreed in principle with the idea of surrogate decision-making for incapacitated patients, but they had a number of concerns about the bill under consideration. Among the concerns was an apparently growing acceptance in society of the idea "that a person should have absolute autonomy in making decisions regarding health care treatments without consideration for objective moral principles and values." Against the notion of absolute autonomy, he argued that "no one — no patient, no health care agent and no surrogate — has the right to make or request" euthanasia, an act or omission directly causing or intended to cause a person's death in order to end suffering.

Religion in the U.S. — "Religion itself is a vital part of life in the United States," Cardinal James A. Hickey of Washington said three days before the inauguration Jan. 20 of President Bill Clinton. Speaking at Mass in St. Matthew's Cathedral, the Cardinal said believers "can and must contribute to the national dialogue; first by pointing to the need for a public morality and second by a spirit of willing service. . . . As men and women of faith, we are obligated to speak clearly of those moral principles and values which are so necessary for the common good of our society. . . . We imperil our ability to live and work together when we conclude that morality is a private concern unrelated to the well-being of our society."

Toward Fuller Communion in Christ — This was the theme of the Week of Prayer for Christian Unity Jan. 18 to 25. In one of several statements issued during the week, Archbishop Rembert G. Weakland of Milwaukee and Episcopal Bishop Theodore Eastman of Baltimore said the quest for unity requires patience, commitment and a willingness to listen and pray. "The quest is central to the identity of all of us who confess Jesus Christ," said Christian Brother Jeffrey Gros, associate director of the Committee for Ecumenical and Interreligious Affairs, National Conference of Catholic Bishops.

March for Life — Seventy-five thousand or more people from all across the country converged on Washington for the annual March for Life Jan. 22, the 20th anniversary of the abortion-on-demand decision of the U.S. Supreme Court in Roe v. Wade and Doe v. Bolton. They were seriously affronted by President Clinton who on the same day not only refused to address them but also issued executive orders ending a number of restrictions on the practice of abortion. (See item below.) His actions were called a "slap in the face" and an "insult" to people demonstrating in defense of the life of the unborn.

Briefs:

• Eternal Word Television Network reported that its new station was broadcasting 24 hours a day in about 20 languages.

• The Collection for the Church in Latin America allocated more than $4 million in 1992 to Catholic projects in the region.

• One hundred and fifty years after its inception, the international Apostleship of Prayer reported continuing growth.

Pro-Abortion Executive Orders

On the 20th anniversary of the pro-abortion decision of the U.S. Supreme Court in Roe v. Wade, President Clinton issued orders reversing:

• regulations prohibiting abortion counseling in federally funded family planning clinics;

• a ban on fetal tissue research;

• restrictions on access to abortion in U.S. military hospitals overseas;

• the "Mexico City Policy," which denied U.S. foreign aid to programs overseas that promoted abortion.

The President also ordered a study of the French abortion pill RU-486, but did not immediately lift the ban on its importation for personal use.

As he signed the orders, the President said: "We must free science and medicine from the grasp of politics. Our vision should be of an America where abortion is safe and legal, but rare." How abortion would be rendered "rare" was open to serious question, according to various commentators.

Republican Representative Chris Smith of New Jersey, co-chairman of the Congressional Pro-Life Caucus, said in an address in the House Jan 25: "Mr. Clinton, a captive of the abortion industry, says he wants abortions to be 'rare,' and then turns around and aggressively promotes new anti-baby policies that will lead to more abortions." In a message to the President, Smith said: "Executive orders promoting abortion for teen-agers and using baby brains and body parts for transplantation undermine the carefully orchestrated illusion of Mr. Clinton and Mr. Gore as child advocates. You don't protect children by killing some of them, Mr. President."

Cardinal Anthony J. Bevilacqua said he was "gravely disappointed" at Clinton's actions, especially that the new President chose the day of the annual March for Life "to antagonize and divide our nation, rather than to seek reconciliation and support for human life. . . . I call on all people who know the natural value of all human life to promote even more vigorously the numerous alternatives to abortion and let their elected officials know of their opposition to all pro-abortion legislation."

INTERNATIONAL

Beatings in Haiti — Mass-goers were clubbed with sticks and rifle butts, and a Haitian priest was threatened by soldiers and an armed mob as he celebrated Mass early in January at the Church of the Nativity in L'Acul du Nord. The Haitian Platform for Human Rights reported that the attack was one of the latest in a campaign aimed at priests who were critical of the government. According to a source who did not want to be identified for fear of reprisals, during the Mass Father Francois Renaud had accused the regime, headed by de facto Prime Minister Marc Bazin, of constitutional violations and of fomenting institutionalized violence that was terrorizing the country.

In another development, a delegation of the World Council of Churches confirmed reports of widespread violations of human rights in Haiti. Since the coup of Sept. 30, 1991, it was estimated that 3,000 people had been killed, 4,500 had been detained illegally and perhaps 400,000 had left the capital, according to the Jan. 9 edition of *The Tablet*, the British weekly.

Pastors without Borders — Church leaders meeting in Africa proposed the creation of a mobile force of "Pastors without Borders" to respond to the suffering of the continent's six million refugees and 16 million internally displaced persons. The recommendation came in a document issued at the conclusion of a Jan. 6-to-9 consultation in Lusaka, Zambia, under the sponsorship of the Pontifical Council for Migrants and Travelers. Participants said the suffering of refugees and displaced persons represented "perhaps the greatest of the tragedies of our time." They recommended:

• better pastoral preparation for resettlement and repatriation;

• special training programs for lay leaders and catechists from refugee communities;

• emphasis on small Christian communities within the refugee population;

• pastoral assistance in the language of the refugees;

• special church-sponsored programs for women, children, the elderly and disabled, who represented the majority of refugees.

Real Need of Sudanese — Providing food aid to southern Sudanese without pressuring their government to respect human rights was like fattening cattle for the slaughter, according to a Sudanese bishop at the Lusaka meeting Jan. 6 to 9. "I ask for our people something greater than money and food. I ask for assistance to help us gain our human rights and dignity, and our human identity," said Bishop Parides Taban of Torit.

Sects in Guatemala — Archbishop Prospero Penados de Barrio of Guatemala City said in a message that one resolution for the new year should concern ways and means of stopping the spread of evangelical sects in the country. "Proselytizing of the sects suffocates the Christian faith," and their message "dilutes the coherence and the unity of God's word," he said. More than 30 percent of the Guatemalan population was Protestant.

Negative Attitudes in Russia — The head of Russia's newly inaugurated Jesuit region said that Catholics faced a rough road in many of the former Soviet republics. Father Stanislaw Opiela said popular attitudes toward Catholics were "generally negative" and warned that some Orthodox Church leaders wanted Orthodoxy declared the official state religion. There were numbers of Catholic baptisms, but serious interest in the faith was limited. "Besides lacking any confessional expression, religious feelings usually have no clear ethical consequences for everyday behavior. Most ordinary Russians would say they believe in God, when what they really believe in is some entity connected with their extrasensory interests."

Desecrations in Pakistan — Bishop John Joseph of Faisalabad accused the government of allowing Christian churches and Hindu temples to be ransacked in violence sweeping the country since the previous month. About 40 people died in rioting in December; at least 80 temples and five churches were ransacked. The bishop said: "The police were silent spectators to the desecrations. . . . The prime minister should have directed punitive measures against the police and the civil government over their culpable negligence. Cases should have also been registered against the demonstrators."

Sectarian Violence in India — Police were not doing enough to stop outbreaks of violence between Hindus and Muslims, according to Father Myron Pereira of Bombay, who was interviewed Jan. 13 on Vatican Radio. He reported that the predominantly Hindu and "highly politicized" police force was doing very little to curb interreligious fighting which had left hundreds dead since December. He said there was a prevailing attitude of vendetta against Muslims; their businesses and properties were being burned and individuals were being targeted and killed. A

bridge-building effort between all religious communities in the country was sorely needed.

Assisted Suicide — The president of the Canadian bishops' conference warned that assisted suicide and euthanasia are wrong and that it is wrong for anyone to participate in them. Archbishop Marcel Gervais of Ottawa said Jan. 13: "It is a cruel irony that 'death with dignity,' a pro-life phrase, has been taken over to justify killing. . . . Individual situations are tragic and very compelling, but they cannot justify disregard of basic values that are critical to the maintenance of a just and humane society. . . . The killing of another person, even with that person's consent, is a very public matter. To accept killing as a private matter of individual choice is to diminish respect for human life, dull our consciences and dehumanize society."

Support for Churches in Former USSR — The bishops of Poland called for practical support for Catholic communities in the former Soviet Union, to ensure their "spiritual development and improved material conditions." In a mid-month appeal, the bishops' Office for Helping Catholics in the East said current priorities included the rebuilding of Catholic churches in the European part of Russia and the development of parish activities in Siberia and Kazakhstan. The bishops said: "Although for protocol reasons our aid is officially earmarked for Catholics, in practice Christians of all denominations obtain equal benefits from it." Thirty-three priests were working in European Russia's 36 registered parishes; 19 of the priests were from Poland.

Briefs:

• More than 110,000 pilgrims, mostly older teenagers and young adults, took part in the 15th annual interfaith Taize meeting in Vienna.

• Since Jews and Christians are brothers and sisters in faith, so-called Christian anti-Semitism is a contradiction in terms, said Cardinal Johannes Willebrands Jan. 13 at a meeting in Rome.

• Maryknoll Fathers and Brothers announced Jan. 15 the official establishment of a formal mission program in Vietnam.

• Eastern Europe's first church-approved Catholic daily newspaper began publishing Jan. 22 in Warsaw with an initial run of 210,000 copies.

Conditions in The Netherlands

Against the background of years-long controversy and avant-garde difficulties in The Netherlands, Pope John Paul told bishops of that country Jan. 11: "Signs of hope for the future are not lacking. Many Catholics are still faithful and they sincerely live their faith in God and they are involved, in their parishes and in the diocesan structure too, in initiatives which reflect Christ's love for mankind. Furthermore, the aggressiveness of the critical fringes is weakening, and encouraging signs of coming together in communion around the bishop are evident. The publication of the new *Catechism of the Catholic Church* will not fail to reassure and strengthen the faithful who have become disoriented in the theological ferment of recent years, bringing back to the true sources of the faith those who went astray following false prophets."

FEBRUARY 1993

VATICAN

10th Trip to Africa — Pope John Paul visited Benin, Uganda and Sudan on an eight-day trip, Feb. 3 to 10. (See separate entry.)

World Day of the Sick — Pope John Paul observed the first annual World Day of the Sick Feb. 11, in connection with the commemoration of Our Lady of Lourdes.

African Synod Agenda — This was the subject of a 119-page working paper released by the Vatican Feb. 10. The overall theme of the synod, scheduled to be held in April 1994, was to be evangelization, with five sub-themes: proclaiming the Gospel, inculturation, dialogue with Islam and traditional religions, justice and peace, and social communication. The document described Africa as a continent rich in human resources but devastated by economic disaster in many countries. It said the Church must help mend the social fabric if it is to be credible to modern Africans.

Three-Month Jubilee — The Pope declared a three-month jubilee observance for Spain and Latin America to mark the 500th anniversary of the first missionaries' arrival in the New World. He decreed the grant of a plenary indulgence to persons participating in special liturgical ceremonies organized by local churches during the period of Feb. 28, the first Sunday of Lent, to May 30, the solemnity of Pentecost.

Annulment Protest — With a diplomatic note presented to the Italian government Feb. 17, the Vatican protested an Italian appellate court decision allowing state courts to annul the civil bonds of a Catholic marriage. Archbishop Zenon Grocholewski, secretary of the Apostolic Signatura, the Church's supreme court, said: "The Church can never accept the authority of the state to declare canonical marriages null." This is true "even in cases where the declaration of nullity was motivated by the same cause foreseen in canon law, such as impotency" or the inability of parties to understand the seriousness of the obligations of Catholic marriage.

Development for Human Needs, Religious Bias — Development programs should improve opportunities for education, health and nutrition services as well as a country's productivity, a Vatican official told participants in an international meeting of human rights experts. "One must insist on a concept of development that goes beyond a mere increase in per capita productivity. It should have as its primary reference the human being in all his or her dimensions." So stated Archbishop Paul F. Tabet, head of a Vatican delegation at the 49th session of the U.N. Commission for Human Rights in Geneva. His remarks were released Feb. 20. The archbishop said economic development should be understood as implementation of a broad spectrum of rights: to adequate housing, improved education, better levels of health care and nutrition, a healthier environment and fair distribution systems. Economic progress should also lead to increased opportunity for groups and individuals to take part in the social, economic and cultural life of their country; in effect, to put into practice an effective democracy.

Reason instead of Rockets — "Silence the weapons and let the use of reason prevail" for settling conflicts in Angola and Rwanda, said the Pope Feb. 21. With memories of his trip to three African countries still fresh, he said he wanted to share his "growing concern . . . over the grave events afflicting other dear countries of that continent. . . . Recent serious internal rivalries have led to thousands of deaths in Angola," where the peace process broke down when rebels of the National Union for Total Independence of Angola rejected the results of multiparty elections the previous September. The Pope said: "I turn once again to those who have at heart concern for the authentic development of nations, so that they work for peace in Angola. . . . Nowhere in the world have violence and war brought solutions to the problems of individual and collective life."

Commission for Eastern Europe — The Pope created a new commission to help the Church throughout Eastern Europe rebuild itself and its relationship with neighboring Orthodox Churches. The Permanent Interdicasterial Commission for the Church in Eastern Europe, replacing the Pontifical Commission for Russia, was formally established Jan. 15; the decree of establishment was released Feb. 23. The main tasks of the commission are:

- to help local Catholic communities "consolidate their recomposition after decades of persecution";
- to oversee the relations of Catholic communities with other churches in the region;
- to promote and coordinate the activities of various institutions which had been helping Catholic communities in Eastern Europe for a long time.

Precious Time of Lent — The Holy Father called Lent a precious time of prayer and penance meant to lead Christians to a deeper love for God and neighbor. On Ash Wednesday, Feb. 24, he asked Catholics to join him in "opening ourselves to beginning this journey of spiritual renewal, welcoming the invitation of the Church to turn inward and seek a deeper contact with the Lord through regularly listening to his word, a more intense commitment to prayer and penance, and greater attention to the poor and suffering. . . . We cannot let this time of special graces pass in vain."

Priest Exchange — Where priests are in short supply, churches in other parts of the world must help fill the gap through exchange programs, said the Pope Feb. 26 during the first plenary session of the Permanent Commission for the Equal Distribution of Priests in the World. Noting that the Vatican continually received requests from dioceses where priests were scarce, he said: "It is indispensable that church communities with the most clergy be open to some form of exchange in order to guarantee priests for the neediest churches. . . . Those who can give cannot remain indifferent. The future of the Church depends on this generosity."

Care for Rape Victims, Babies — The Pope called for compassion for rape victims in war-ravaged Bosnia-Herzegovina and said that babies born of assaulted women also deserved respect and love. In a letter published in the Feb. 26 edition of *L'Osservatore Romano*, he asked pastors to give urgent aid to "the mothers, wives and young girls who, through a venting of racial hatred or brutal lust, have suffered violence." He also said: "The whole community must draw close to these women who have been so painfully offended and to their families, to help them transform an act of violence into an act of love and welcome." Reports from Bosnia said that thousands of women, particularly Muslims, had been raped by Serbian soldiers.

General Audience Topics:

There were no general audiences on Feb. 3 and 10, while the Pope was traveling in Africa.

● Recollections of his trip to Benin, Uganda and Sudan (Feb. 17).

● The successor of Peter enjoys full and supreme power of jurisdiction in faith and morals, and in all that concerns the Church's governance (Feb. 24).

Briefs:

● The Pope offered prayers and condolences to victims and survivors of the Feb. 17 Haitian ferry disaster in which hundreds of persons lost their lives.

● "Christians cannot remain impassive when so many of their brothers and sisters are struggling in a situation of misery or when their rights as persons and members of society are not respected," the Pope told visiting bishops from Equatorial Guinea Feb. 18.

● The Pope told the president of Slovenia Feb. 19 that national autonomy is a good thing, but new nations must be sure their citizens' patriotism does not "degenerate into closed and aggressive nationalism."

● Twice during the month Vatican diplomats at major international meetings called for the world community to hold people responsible for "crimes against humanity" in the republics of former Yugoslavia. War does not excuse either crimes or personal responsibility or blind obedience in carrying out orders to commit crimes.

Euthanasia in The Netherlands

The Dutch Parliament approved legislation Feb. 9 authorizing assisted suicide by doctors under the following conditions:

● The patient must be terminally ill and suffering unbearable pain.

● The patient must request death.

● Another doctor should be consulted prior to the assisted suicide.

● All cases must be reported to the coroner with a detailed account of circumstances.

A front-page editorial in the Feb. 21 edition of *L'-Osservatore Romano* said that through such legislation on euthanasia "legal principles and universal ethics are overturned by aberrant applications." The legislation was called the result of a "neo-capitalistic culture, which values the quality of life on the basis of efficiency. . . . Euthanasia and abortion, whether voluntary or imposed, are the barbaric, but horrendously logical, effects of that premise." The editorial reported remarks of Bishop Elio Sgreccia, vice president of the Pontifical Council for the Family, who compared the legislation to the extermination policies of Adolf Hitler. His criticism elicited a diplomatic protest from the Dutch government.

NATIONAL

Parish Closing Upheld — The Vatican turned down an appeal from a group of Catholics seeking to reverse the decision of Bishop Timothy J. Harrington of Worcester to close St. Joseph's Church in the see city and to merge it with a neighboring parish. Cardinal Jose T. Sanchez, prefect of the Congregation for the Clergy, wrote that the bishop followed proper procedure in merging the parishes, and that those who opposed the decision "conducted themselves badly, seizing the properties of the church and holding in custody even the Blessed Sacrament. . . . Even the civil courts of that district of the United States have ruled in favor of the bishop's right to end the unlawful occupation and detention of church properties."

CBS Programs Pulled — Two CBS-affiliated television stations owned by the Mormon Church pulled the drama, "Picket Fences," from their prime-time schedule because of the content of some episodes. Incidents that stations KIRO of Seattle and KSL of Salt Lake City found objectionable included a man dancing with his wife's corpse, a woman experiencing orgasm through some kind of psychic phenomenon, and a suspected incestuous relationship which turned out to be polygamous among people calling themselves Mormons. KSL president Bruce Reese said the Mormon episode "grossly misrepresented" the Mormon stand on polygamy and that CBS declined to try and get rid of "misrepresentation and enforcement of old stereotypes." A spokesman for KIRO said the station would review "Picket Fences" in advance and make decisions about the shows on a case-by-case basis.

A November episode of the series was criticized by Richard Doerflinger, associate director of the U.S. Bishops' Secretariat for Pro-Life Activities. He complained that the program in question portrayed a nun performing a mercy killing while singing "Killing Me Softly." He said the euthanasia episode, scheduled for broadcast during the month, "takes the case of (assisted- suicide practitioner) Jack Kevorkian, and transforms him into a black Catholic woman — a nun, no less — and makes her into a hero by giving (someone) a lethal injection." He called the series "bizarre" and said it featured themes that offend almost everyone.

Indian Religious Rites Bill — Sixteen religious organizations asked Congress to amend the 1978 Indian Religious Freedom Act.

The bill in question would:

● require that tribes be advised and consulted when federal agencies plan to change the uses of land considered sacred;

● protect the use of peyote in worship;

● give Native Americans in prison the same access to religious services as that provided prisoners of other faiths;

● reduce the red tape involved in obtaining permission for the use of eagle feathers and other parts of federally protected animals for religious purposes.

Hispanic Evangelization — Evangelization efforts among Hispanics should target professionals as well as the poor and needy, directors of Hispanic ministry were told at a national conference in Houston Feb. 8 to 11. Sister Lourdes Toro, associate director of the Hispanic Apostolate of the Archdiocese of Newark, said it was the responsibility of church workers to "ensure that the Good

News is reaching and including the most needy and alienated of our Church. But, on the other hand, have we not failed by not taking care of the professional class? The Gospel is for everyone." If Hispanic professionals "have strong Gospel values, they can influence and transform from within." Sister Lourdes made the comments in a speech given at the first National Convocation of Diocesan Directors of Hispanic Ministry.

Vote against Fernandez — Cardinal John J. O'-Connor praised Feb. 14 members of the New York City Board of Education who voted not to renew the contract of the controversial chancellor of the city's public school system. Joseph A. Fernandez had come under attack from many Catholics and others, especially for promoting condom distribution in schools and introducing a "Children of the Rainbow" curriculum teaching acceptance and validation of homosexual behavior.

St. Patrick's Day Parade Decision — Federal Judge Kevin Thomas ruled Feb. 26 that the Ancient Order of Hibernians had the right to its traditional parade in New York City and to exclude homosexuals marching under their identifying banners. The ruling overturned an Oct. 27, 1992, decision by the New York City Human Rights Commission that said the parade fell under the category of public accommodations, like a hotel or restaurant, and that parade discrimination violated the city's Human Rights Law. The Thomas decision ended months of controversy provoked and prolonged by Mayor David N. Dinkins. The public accommodations argument was regarded as specious by the court, the Hibernians, the local chapter of the American Civil Liberties Union and others.

Clinton Policies Criticized — Archbishop Joseph T. Dimino, head of the Archdiocese for the Military Services U.S.A., said in a letter addressed to President Bill Clinton: "As the Archbishop responsible for the religious welfare of all Catholic men, women and children associated with the armed forces, and as a former military chaplain familiar with the realities of military life, I urge you to heed the advice of the Joint Chiefs of Staff to maintain the traditional Defense Department policy concerning homosexuality. ... The acceptance of homosexuality as an appropriate alternate life-style for the military will in my judgment have disastrous consequences for all concerned." Two days after the archbishop's letter, Clinton announced that an executive order to lift the 50-year ban on homosexuals in the military would be drafted by July 15.

With reference to an executive order signed by the President Jan. 22, allowing women to pay for their own abortions in military hospitals, the archbishop said in another letter: It "poses a grave matter of conscience" for Catholic members of the armed forces whose religious beliefs forbid participation in abortions. Because of the dictates of conscience, they shall be forced to refuse participation."

Briefs:

● Bishop James W. Malone of Youngstown was named chairman of the board of directors of the Catholic Telecommunications Network of America.

● George Noonan, director of the Center for Pastoral Life and Ministry of the Diocese of Kansas City-St. Joseph, was honored with Yale University's Distinction in Lay Ministry in the Church Award Feb. 10.

● Participants in a national symposium at Boys Town agreed that effective ministry with youths from different cultures was rooted in understanding of the cultural issues affecting them.

● "Howard's End" and "Lorenzo's Oil" were among movies honored with Christopher Awards Feb. 25.

Divisive Freedom of Choice Act

Passage of the Freedom of Choice Act would "only fan the flames of controversy and further divide our nation," Pennsylvania Governor Robert P. Casey told the House Judiciary Subcommittee on Civil and Constitutional Rights Feb. 23. "You cannot stifle this debate (about the unrestricted practice of abortion) with a piece of paper." He said the federal bill would make abortion the least-regulated industry in the country and would "mandate an abortion-on-demand regime for the entire country in a way which goes against the expressed will of the overwhelming majority of the American people. It would repeal reasonable limitations on the practice of abortion enacted by the people in the states and prohibit them from enacting any similar limitations in the future. It would bind the people in a legal straightjacket that would only provoke more confrontation and controversy."

INTERNATIONAL

Refugees' Plight — Vatican officials and other experts meeting Feb.1 to 4 in Budapest focused attention on the plight of an increasing number of refugees, especially with respect to East Europeans seeking safe haven or employment elsewhere on the Continent. Conferees said Europe's economic refugees should be given individual consideration and should not be subject to categorical expulsion. They expressed special concern over deportations of Gypsies, who had no home territory. While noting that some limits on immigration were inevitable, they said the criteria used to establish the "level of supportability" must take into account the human needs of new arrivals. Refugees should not be denied admission simply to protect local prosperity. The meeting was sponsored by the Pontifical Council for Migrants and Travelers.

Religious Sites Attacked in Poland — Attacks and thefts at Polish religious sites were reported to be increasing, as police in Warsaw launched a major hunt for the perpetrators of the worst vandalism suffered by a cemetery in the city's memory. More than 500 graves were destroyed or damaged at the Wawrzyszew Catholic cemetery in what police said was the work of at least a dozen vandals. A police inspector, Jozef Kazubek, confirmed that a "big hunt" was under way to apprehend those responsible for the outrage. "This is the first time in Poland that the devastation of graves has occurred on such a scale, and it can only have been the work of pathologically sick people," he said. Other incidents of vandalism included the profanation of a statue of the Virgin Mary and the theft of 18 historic icons.

Environmental Concern — This was the subject under discussion during a six-day colloquium held in Tagaytay, The Philippines, under the sponsorship of the Office of Education and Student Chaplaincy of the Federation of Asian Bishops' Conferences. Church representatives and scientists called for ways of adding a faith dimension to scientific efforts to safeguard and improve the environment. They said the root causes of environmental crisis were "abject poverty, consumerism brought about by human greed and people's ignorance about ecological issues."

Haitian Solution from Within — Bishop Guire Poulard of Jacmel believed Haiti's 16-month-long crisis could not be solved by an internationally-brokered agreement. "The only solution to the present situation has to be a Haitian one," he said. This would involve finding a consensus among all parties, including the army and the legislative, judicial and executive branches of government. Backgrounding his remarks was the crisis situation triggered by the military coup which ousted democratically elected President Jean-Bertrand Aristide in September, 1991.

Child Labor — Instead of halting child labor in South Africa, new government rules appeared likely to result in more exploitation, said a network of children's rights groups. Government-led discussions of children at work were said to be leaning toward "legislating what we are trying to work against," said Sister Shellagh Mary Waspe, who represented the Johannesburg diocesan justice and peace commission on the Network against Child Labor. Loopholes in the new guidelines would "allow employers to continue exploiting children," said Jackie Loffell of the Johannesburg Child Welfare Society. She cited one rule that would allow children to be employed for "pocket money."

Dissident Anglicans — Cardinal George Basil Hume of Westminster reminded Anglicans considering leaving the Church of England over the issue of women's ordination to the priesthood that any decision about union with Catholics would be made by the Holy See. He issued a brief statement following press reports that Anglican dissidents were close to agreement on setting up a national network of former Anglican parishes in communion with Rome. Catholic sources said that such a move would be premature; also, that an acceptable model for such groups had not yet been developed.

Famine and Refugees — Sudan was in a "continuing cycle of spiraling famine," reported Catholic Relief Services' senior director for Africa Feb.23. "Sudan is being described as Africa's 'silent crisis' because so much attention recently has been focused on Somalia," said Peter Shiras at a round table discussion called by the U.S. House Select Committee on Hunger. The country was in the midst of a 10-year civil war pitting the mostly Arab-Muslim North against black Christians and animists in the South. It was estimated that four million Sudanese had been displaced because of the war, and that several hundred thousand might face starvation in coming months, according to the U.S. Office of Foreign Disaster Assistance. Catholic Relief Services was the only American relief agency working in the Eastern Equatorial region of southern Sudan, where most of the fighting was taking place. CRS was providing food for more than 120,000 people in the region.

Haitian Bishop Beaten — U.N. observers and diplomats rescued Bishop Willy Romelus of Jeremie Feb. 25 from being beaten by a mob of 40 attackers as he left a Mass for several hundred victims of a ferry boat disaster. "Had we not been there, Bishop Romelus might have been killed," said Michael Moller, the Danish coordinator of a joint United Nations-Organization of American States team monitoring human rights in Haiti. Bishop Romelus was shaken and bruised but not seriously hurt.

Briefs:

● The establishment of the first African center of the Family Rosary in Nairobi, Kenya, was reported early in the month.

● Muslim gunmen freed two kidnapped Spanish nuns Feb. 5 after 20 days in captivity in the southern Philippines.

● The human rights office of the Archdiocese of Guatemala was the recipient of the National French Commission's Human Rights Award for its work with refugees and on behalf of persons deprived of rights.

● "Muslims, Orthodox and Catholics live in harmony, consult with one another regularly and exchange visits on the occasion of religious feasts or when a new church or mosque is opened," said Aleko Dhima, secretary general of the Albanian Orthodox Church.

Who Ordered Jesuit Murders in El Salvador?

The Lawyers' Committee for Human Rights called on the Clinton administration to help uncover the masterminds behind the 1989 murders of six Jesuit priests, their cook and her daughter in San Salvador. "Though a trial took place, the Salvadoran government has never seriously investigated the key questions of who gave the ultimate orders to kill the Jesuits and who orchestrated the coverup," wrote Michael H. Posner, director of the New York-based organization. "We believe that these issues now deserve renewed attention by the Clinton administration." "A Chronicle of Death Foretold: The Jesuit Murders in El Salvador," charged that the Bush administration withheld information that could have led to the prosecution of those who planned the murders.

In another development, Auxiliary Bishop Gregorio Rosa Chavez of San Salvador said that "selective violence" was endemic in the country despite the end of 12 years of brutal civil war. "There are enough unexplained cases, and they point to something we could call selective violence," he said. The killings "make one think of a premeditated plan to impose again the law of the jungle. . . . But, for the moment, I would not dare to point out in what direction we think investigations should go." Bishop Rosa faulted the government of President Alfredo Cristiani for failing to carry out a proper investigation of the killings.

MARCH 1993

VATICAN

Healing Action — Pope John Paul appointed two auxiliary bishops for the Swiss Diocese of Chur in an effort to heal divisions associated with the controversial ministry of Bishop Wolfgang Haas. The Pope took the action after "long reflection and prayer," and with an appeal to the bishops of the country to welcome the new prelates and help them, along with Bishop Haas, to "win the hearts of the people." In a letter made public Mar. 4, he said he wanted the entire church in Switzerland to "help reestablish full communion" in a diocese torn by pastoral discord. The new auxiliaries were Father Peter Henrici, S.J., 64, dean of the theological faculty of the Gregorian University in Rome; and Father Paul Vollmar, 58, provincial of the Marianist Fathers.

Fox Dismissal Confirmed — Father Matthew Fox received notice Mar. 3 that the Vatican had confirmed the decision of his Dominican superiors to dismiss him from the order because of his refusal to return to community life in Chicago. Father Malachy O'Dwyer, liaison for Vatican-Dominican relations, said the decision had "absolutely nothing to do with his work" as the founder of the Institute of Culture and Creative Spirituality at Holy Names College in Oakland, Calif.

Maximum Effort To End Conflict in Bosnia — The Pope urged the United Nations to use its "right of intervention" to save populations from further fighting in Bosnia-Herzegovina. In a Mar. 11 letter to Secretary-General Boutros Boutros-Ghali, he said the U.N. was the most appropriate forum for action when members of the international community were "incapable of coping with their differences." Citing the human suffering in Bosnia, the Pope called urgent attention to the fact that there was a legal and moral basis for "the right of intervention in order to protect populations taken hostage by the insanity of warmakers. . . . As Pastor of the Catholic Church, I implore the people of good will who work at the U.N. headquarters to do all that is in their power to stop this conflict."

Encouragement of the Media — The Catholic Church must encourage morally right and informative works by the media as well as protest what is morally objectionable, said the Pope Mar. 12 at a meeting with members and consultors of the Pontifical Council for Social Communications. He said the media have an endless potential to inform, to create and to communicate art and culture, to refresh the human spirit and to spread and strengthen God's kingdom. But the Church is also "painfully aware of the damage which can be inflicted on individuals and society by the misuse of these instruments. . . . In concrete situations, it is the duty of the Church, her pastors and members, to acknowledge and encourage programs and publications which promote unity, peace, virtue and true brotherly love." It is also the duty of members of the Church "to protest against programs and publications which are morally objectionable and which threaten to violate personal and public integrity and the sanctity of family life."

Lebanon Synod, Working Paper — "Christ Is Our Hope: Renewed by His Spirit, We Witness to His Love," was the title and stated theme of the working paper for the future Lebanese Synod of Bishops. The 99-page document, released Mar. 13, dealt with pastoral aspects and problems related to the political, economic and social conditions of the battered country. It noted that national unity was the primary objective of the church and of the majority of Lebanese. The date and place of the synod had not been set at the time of writing.

Special Training for Latin America — Pope John Paul told bishops of the region that the Church in their countries needed special training programs for ministers and lay persons in order to enable them to resist threats to women, the family and innocent life. There was need to place the family and human life at the center of the "new evangelization" of the continent, he said Mar. 18. "This choice must be the subject of a serious and systematic reflection in seminaries, in formation houses and in institutes." Preparation of ministers of all kinds should deepen knowledge of the "theology of the family" as well as familiarity with issues of family rights, bioethics, marriage preparation, sex education and demographic questions.

Saints and Blesseds — The Pope beatified Canadian Sister Dina Belanger (1897-1929) and publicly confirmed the cult of Blessed John Duns Scotus (1266-1308) Mar. 20. He canonized Saints Claudine Thevenet (Sister Marie of St. Ignatius, 1774-1839) and Juana Fernandez (Sister Teresa of Los Andes, the first Chilean saint, 1900-1920) Mar. 21.

Respect for the Name of God — Taking the name of God in vain is not only a sin but also a violation of the respect which must be due to those who believe in God, the Pope said Mar. 21. God's name is holy and must be treated with reverence and love. "Unfortunately, one frequently notices an attitude of thoughtlessness, sometimes crossing the line into open contempt" of God's name in swearing, sacrilegious usage and mockery.

General Audience Topics:

• The Successor of Peter imparts authoritative teaching on faith and morals to the whole Church (Mar. 10).

• The Pope's extraordinary magisterium (teaching authority) is exercised when he passes solemn judgment on points of doctrine belonging to the deposit of faith (Mar. 17).

• In exercising his magisterium, the Holy Father receives the assistance of the Holy Spirit promised him in the person of Blessed Peter himself (Mar.24).

• In the sacrament of holy orders, priests receive a share in the pastoral authority by which Christ builds up, sanctifies and rules his Church (Mar. 31).

Briefs:

• The Pope thanked Knights of Columbus Mar. 20 for their efforts to promote high standards in family and public life.

• Serious potential difficulties in marriages between Catholics and Muslims were cited by Vatican official Father Thomas Michel and Auxiliary Bishop Clemente Riva of Rome.

• The Pope told 8,000 youthful members of the Neocatechumenal Way Mar. 28 that the vocations of Christian marriage, priesthood and religious life flow from the grace received at baptism.

Address to U.S. Bishops

The greatest service the bishops can give the Church right now is to teach the faith unambiguously and thus end "disharmony and confusion" produced by dissenting views. So stated the Pope Mar. 20 in an address to the first group of U.S. bishops making their required *ad limina* visits in 1993. He was particularly concerned about Catholics who go their own way on matters of doctrine. While recognizing that a majority of U.S. Catholics understand that an "assent of faith" is needed, he said the cultural climate in the United States is often suspicious or hostile to religious truths. "In a climate of individualism, some assume the right to decide for themselves, even in important matters of faith, which teachings to accept, while ignoring those they find unacceptable. . . . Selectivity in adhering to authoritative church teaching . . . is incompatible with being a good Catholic." The bishop's task is to insist on full acceptance of church teaching, clearly and unambiguously, so that it will "rise above the clash of conflicting notions with the forcefulness and power of the truth." The Holy Father hoped the new "Catechism of the Catholic Church" would help launch a "national re-catechizing endeavor" in the United States.

NATIONAL

Assisted Suicide — An official of the U.S. bishops' Pro-Life Secretariat told elderly and seriously ill persons that legal efforts to assure their "right" to assisted suicide would "not advance their freedom but would cheapen their lives." So commented Richard Doerflinger with reference to a lawsuit filed Mar. 1 by the American Civil Liberties Union against Michigan's new ban on assisted suicide. The suit charged that the law violated the privacy and due process clauses of the state and federal constitutions. Doerflinger said the ACLU arguments promoted "the euthanasia agenda in its most extreme form. . . . By invoking a 'right to privacy' like the one used 20 years ago to legalize abortion, the ACLU also invites analogies to a policy of unlimited abortion that has claimed 29 million unborn lives."

Fetal Tissue Transplant Network — A research team proposed that U.S. Catholic health care facilities form a national network for transplantation of fetal tissue obtained by means other than induced abortions. The network "would collect, process, store and distribute fetal tissue for transplantation," said Peter J. Cataldo, director of research at the Pope John XXIII Medical-Moral Research and Education Center. The key ethical provision behind the proposal was that "fetal tissues from induced abortions are not to be used." Only tissues from ectopic pregnancies or miscarriages would be used, in contrast to the practice of using tissue from induced abortions.

Meeting with President Clinton — Three bishops and an official of the bishops' conferences met with President Bill Clinton Mar. 5 "as pastors, not political leaders," to open channels of communication with the administration on major public issues. Attending the meeting were Archbishops William Keeler of Baltimore and Theodore E. McCarrick of Newark, Bishop Anthony M. Pilla of Cleveland, and Msgr. Robert N. Lynch, general secretary of the conferences. In a statement issued shortly after the hour-long meeting at the White House, Archbishop Keeler said the Church wants "to work with the administration in a constructive way. We offer cooperation and common ground wherever possible, and civil and respectful disagreement when it may be necessary." He acknowledged that on abortion "there are significant differences" dividing the Church and the President. He hoped, however, that dialogue on the issue might continue. He added that the Church's "advocacy efforts are focused on protecting the weak and the vulnerable — the unborn child, poor families and children, the victims of injustice and violence here and abroad."

No Pro-Life Connection — Pro-life officials condemned the killing of Doctor David Gunn at an abortion clinic in Pensacola, Fla. Michael F. Griffin surrendered to police immediately after shooting the abortionist and was ordered held without bond on murder charges Mar. 11. "It makes a mockery of the pro-life ethic and the pro-life cause to say that killing can ever be right in its name," said Helen Alvare,, director of planning and information of the bishops' Secretariat for Pro-Life Activities. She said Griffin had no known ties to any organized pro-life group and that the man had shown by his actions that he was "not just out of line but completely in opposition" to the pro-life movement.

Templeton Prize — Chuck Colson, founder and director of Prison Fellowship, was the winner of the 1993 Templeton Prize for Progress in Religion. His seven-month jail term for involvement in Watergate prompted him to form the 17-year-old prison outreach ministry to help convicted criminals change their lives by evangelism and practical assistance.

Judeo-Christian Institute — Priests and rabbis commemorated the 40th anniversary of Seton Hall University's Institute of Judeo-Christian Studies Mar. 21. Rabbi John Lewis Eron, of Temple B'nai Abraham in Livingston, N.J., congratulated the institute for "providing an intellectual foundation for honest dialogue" which brings Jews and Christians together with the goal of "appreciating each other's faith" and knowing "each other as real people with strong religious feelings." Msgr. John M. Oesterreicher, founder of the institute, recalled its "birth pangs" and criticisms directed at it during the early days. "All attacks on it," he said, "whether born of ignorance or malice, have been offset by words and deeds of leading bishops who put the seal of approval on the theological vision that guided the institute."

Women Religious and Synod '94 — The National Board of the Leadership Conference of Women Religious, in a statement released Mar. 26, asked that women religious "be included as full participants in the deliberations" of the 1994 Synod of Bishops. "If the work of the synod (regarding religious life) is to be credible to women religious of the Church, who are the largest number of those committed to religious life, the uniqueness of women's reality must be brought to bear upon the deliberations," said the board. Under synod rules, only selected bishops and a few priests who head religious orders are eligible to be voting delegates. Women have attended synods as papally appointed observers or theological experts, but never as voting members.

Seminary Statistics — The Center for Applied Research in the Apostolate reported Mar. 26 fall enrollment statistics for the 1992-93 school year:

• The total number of seminarians rose from 6,677 in 1991 to 6,698.

• The number of high school seminarians dropped from 1,217 to 1,150.

• The number of college seminarians declined from 1,757 to 1,582.

• Seminarians in post-college programs increased from 3,467 to 3,651.

• The number of novices in religious orders preparing for the priesthood increased from 236 to 315.

Force in the Balkans — The Administrative Board of the U.S. Catholic Conference, decrying "the litany of horrors" in the Balkan war, said in a statement Mar. 29 it was "time for religious believers and the international community to act with new resolve" in the conflict. The statement approved "strictly limited" use of force, a political solution to the war, the creation of a war-crimes tribunal, and help for refugees and nations accepting them. "The world cannot stand aside as innocent people are destroyed, as aggression shapes a new world, as the hopes of freedom turn into the violence of war," the board said.

Briefs:

• Dorothy Day, founder of the Catholic Worker Movement, and St. Frances Xavier Cabrini were among the leading choices in a survey of the most influential women of the 20th century. The survey was conducted by a research branch of Siena College.

• The lack of a religious or spiritual foundation was regarded as the greatest threat to family life, according to a survey of 2,126 adult Kentuckians conducted by Peggy Meszaros, dean of the University of Kentucky's College of Human and Environmental Sciences.

• "Environment: A Southern Baptist and Roman Catholic Perspective," was the title of a joint study brochure issued after the most recent round of U.S. Southern Baptist-Roman Catholic conversations.

RCIA Participants

Tens of thousands of Americans across the country were in the final phase of initiation in the Catholic Church. They were catechumens preparing for baptism who had participated in the Rite of Election and (already baptized) candidates who had responded to the Call to Continuing Conversion on the first Sunday of Lent. All were participants in programs and ceremonies related to the Rite of Christian Initiation of Adults. The total number of those involved was not known, but 47 dioceses reported a total of more than 23,400 catechumens and candidates.

The RCIA, developed along with other liturgical reforms following the Second Vatican Council, is a revival and adaptation of the catechumenate in the early Church; it integrates the instructional and spiritual formation of catechumens with the liturgy. The formation program has been adapted for use with baptized non-Catholics wanting to join the Church and with already baptized Catholics who have not received the other sacraments of initiation, i.e., first Communion and confirmation.

INTERNATIONAL

Contempt toward Christianity — Maryknoll missionaries released a statement Mar. 5 which said the bishops of Tanzania had protested "open and deliberate contempts, slanders and blasphemies against Christianity." The bishops, deciding that it was the "right time" to speak, said the government had been "keeping quiet," thereby condoning blasphemies made against Christianity in "public speeches, cassette tapes and some newspapers that are constantly carrying derogatory and insulting contents." Such actions had brought about a "new situation" after 30 years of peace and mutual understanding in the country despite religious and other differences. The bishops called for the "government to safeguard the right of independence and respect for religious worship of all Tanzanians without any discrimination."

Assisted Suicide — Canadian pro-life leaders hailed the decision of the British Columbia Court of Appeals against physician-assisted suicide in the case of terminally ill Sue Rodriguez, who was suffering from Lou Gehrig's disease. "We are relieved that the decision has come down against physician-assisted suicide and that society is going to protect the vulnerable," said Dr. Robert Pancratz, vice president of the Compassionate Healthcare Network of Canada. Network president Cheryl Eckstein said: "We hope that Sue Rodriguez will understand that, while we lament that she has a serious disease, we must continue to resist any decision that would drastically affect society as a whole."

Catholic-Orthodox Relations — While relations remained strained on upper levels over charges of proselytism by Catholics and Catholic efforts to reclaim property, members of both churches on local levels were reported to be cooperating in ventures of mutual concern. Catholics and Orthodox agreed, for example, that disputes had not prevented their communicants from working together to rebuild Russia's long-suppressed Christian culture and spiritual life. Paulist Father Ronald G. Roberson, a former staff member of the Pontifical Council for Promoting Christian Unity, spoke Mar. 18 about the need for mutual trust and reconciliation among Catholics and Orthodox.

Priests Released in China — It was unofficially reported that Chinese authorities had released from prison between 15 and 20 priests in recent months. Also reported unofficially was the continuing detention of nearly 4,000 political prisoners.

IRA Bombings Condemned — Two cardinals issued their first-ever joint statement Mar. 26 to express outrage at the Irish Republican Army bombing that killed two children and injured more than 50 people at a Warrington, England, shopping center Mar. 20. "The outrage was so appalling in its indifference to the lives of men, women and children that we issue this joint statement to express the sense of horror we both feel," said Cardinal Cahal Daly of Armagh and Cardinal George Basil Hume of Westminster. "Such actions by the IRA are utterly inhuman and barbaric. They are totally incompatible with the teaching of the Catholic Church and are to be unreservedly condemned. . . . We know our feeling of revulsion is shared by the overwhelming majority of people in Ireland, as well as in Britain, who bear no responsibility for such outrageous acts perpetrated by a very small faction."

Abortion, Birth Control In Latin America — Latin American bishops meeting on family issues at the Vatican denounced abortion, birth control and other threats to human life. In a set of recommendations made public Mar. 22, they said the Church needed to improve its education of church personnel and clearly affirm church teaching in order to counteract anti-family trends on the continent. Their statement said the Church must denounce the moral impoverishment that results in countries that accept the "anti-birth" arguments of organizations like the International Planned Parenthood Federation. The statement called attention to the fact that important economic and political interests are involved in the worldwide marketing of contraceptives and abortion-causing agents.

More Dialogue Needed in Poland — "Generally speaking, the Church is not open enough" and is in need of "new thinking and an openness to dialogue." So stated Auxiliary Bishop Tadeusz Pieronek of Sosnowiec in an interview published in the Warsaw daily newspaper, Wycie Warszawy. "Accepting criticism is always hard, especially for someone at the top," he said. But, "even in the worst critic, we should always look for a seed of truth, since the most malicious critic always touches what is weakest and most painful. . . . The Church in Poland . . . must look for new ways."

Refusal To Step Down — Father Eugenio Pizarro declared that he would defy his archbishop and provisions of canon law in refusing to withdraw from political activity and his campaign for the presidency of Chile. "My candidacy is not negotiable," he told Catholic News Service in Santiago. He had asked for a year's leave of absence to campaign, but instead was suspended from pastoral ministry in February, said Archbishop Carlos Oviedo Cavada of Santiago.

Chilean Saint — Approximately 25,000 people gathered at the sanctuary of Auco, north of Santiago, to celebrate the canonization Mar. 21 of Chile's first saint, Sister Teresa de los Andes.

Radio Pulpit — A cardinal from the Philippines and a nun from Ghana said radio is the Church's most effective and far-reaching pulpit in Asia and Africa. God's word is "transmitted through the air waves to the remotest areas where even the absence of electricity cannot stop what can be heard from a transistor radio," said Cardinal Jaime L. Sin of Manila. Sister Pierre-Elise Gafah of Accra said: "Radio forms part and parcel of our people's lives." For "a people endowed with the art of oratory, the radio, so to speak, is very much at home in Africa. Through the radio we have been able to move from one oral stage to another without having been able or without having known how to focus on the written aspect."

Church Symbolic in Mideast? — Because of continuing Christian emigration from the Middle East, the Church's presence there may become only symbolic within two decades, said participants in a meeting sponsored by the Middle East and North African region of Caritas. "If things continue in this direction, it is clear that within 15 to 20 years the Christian presence in this area of the world will be nothing but symbolic," said Father Silvano Tomasi, secretary of the Pontifical Council for Pastoral Care of Migrants and Itinerant Peoples. "The churches, monuments, historical documents and literature will remain, but the vitality of the Church as a faith community will vanish."

Briefs:
• The Polish Parliament narrowly rejected a proposal by ex-communist and opposition legislators that would have scrapped the tax exemption on charitable donations to church groups.
• The Vietnamese edition of the Roman Missal turned out to be a best seller (6,000 copies) once the government relaxed its censorship rules and permitted publication of the book.
• Members of Caritas Macao who visited eastern China to monitor joint flood relief projects undertaken with Chinese authorities reported a marked improvement in relations with Chinese officials.

Truth Commission Report on El Salvador

A U.N. Truth Commission report released Mar. 15 named high-ranking Salvadoran military officers it said ordered the killings of six Jesuit priests, their housekeeper and her daughter in 1989, and the assassination of Archbishop Oscar A. Romero of San Salvador in 1980. The report — entitled "From Madness to Hope: The 12-Year War in El Salvador" — called for the immediate dismissal of 40 military officers linked to atrocities and for banning three prominent rebel leaders from holding public office for 10 years. The Truth Commission report also concluded that the U.S.-trained Atlacatl army unit was responsible for the El Mozote massacre of 1,000 men, women and children in December, 1981.

Defense Minister Gen. Rene Emilio Ponce, accused in the report of having ordered the Jesuit murders, called the commission "unfair and prejudiced." The U.S. Jesuit Conference said in a statement that President Alfredo Cristiani should accept Ponce's resignation, offered Mar. 12, and should also remove from office the other officers named in the Truth Commission report. The statement said: "It is true that General Ponce . . . was the one who gave the direct order to Colonel (Guillermo Alfredo) Benavides on the night of Nov. 15-16, 1989, to 'kill Father Ellacuria and leave no witnesses.' (Father Ellacuria was rector of the University of Central America at the time of his assassination.) As long as they remain in office Ponce and his co-conspirators are living symbols of a Salvadoran military which cannot be held accountable for even the most heinous human rights violations."

APRIL 1993

VATICAN

Concern for Anglicans — The Vatican is committed to the search for unity with the Anglican Communion and also to the pastoral care of Anglicans who may want to join the Catholic Church, said Vatican spokesman Joaquin Navarro-Valls Apr. 6. Respecting the freedom of conscience of those Anglicans who do not believe their church has the authority to validly ordain women to the priesthood "is not an obstacle to the ecumenical journey," he stated. Discussion of the matter would be handled by the Bishops' Conference of England and Wales. "At this point the Holy See is not involved in any negotiations in relation to this matter. . . . The National Council for Promoting Christian Unity has emphasized that the fervent desire of the Catholic Church remains the re-establishment of full communion with the whole Anglican Communion and that, consequently, the search for this full and visible union will continue." Navarro-Valls acknowledged that "the ordination of women constitutes a serious obstacle to this search."

Holy Thursday Message to Priests — The gift of the new *Catechism of the Catholic Church*, the nature of priestly ministry centered on the Eucharist, and their state of celibacy were principal themes of the Pope's annual message to priests for Holy Thursday, celebrated this year Apr. 8.

Nuns Should Move — In a letter dated Apr. 9, the Pope told Carmelite nuns living in a convent just outside the Nazi death camp at Auschwitz that they should move to another location. He said: "You should move to another place . . . It remains a matter for the free will of each of you whether you wish to continue living the Carmelite life within the existing community (relocated at a nearby new interfaith cultural center) or whether you wish to return to the mother convent. For each of you, this is also a moment of trial. May it please the crucified and resurrected Christ to enable you to recognize his will and the particular calling to the Carmelite path of life." The several-years presence of the nuns at the Auschwitz convent was a bone of contention in Catholic-Jewish relations. Jewish opinion worldwide objected to the location of the convent, contending that it detracted from the significance of the Holocaust.

Reorganized European Council — The reorganized Council of European Bishops' Conferences should provide a united voice for Christian values on the Continent, Pope John Paul said Apr. 16 at a meeting with former and new members of the body. The council must bring the Gospel message to Europe, "especially in the face of not always hidden attempts to marginalize faith and salvific truth from every manifestation of public life." The reorganization involved a change in council membership, of presidents of national conferences instead of elected delegates. The Pope said the council must help the Church fulfill its "commitment to a renewed evangelization and to an effective contribution to the new Europe, open to universal solidarity." While the council must respect the rights and responsibilities of national episcopal conferences, it can play the necessary role of being "a witness and spokesman" for the Church on the Continent. "In this way the community of believers will have a way to make its voice heard even in civil spheres, the voice of a community in agreement and striving to announce the good news of hope and charity." Archbishop Miloslav Vlk of Prague, head of the Czech conference, was elected president of the council.

Warsaw Ghetto Uprising — Pope John Paul, in a message marking the 50th anniversary of the Warsaw Ghetto Uprising, called Apr. 16 on Christians and Jews to unite against all forms of prejudice and anti-Semitism. He called the 1943 uprising, in which some 25,000 Jews were killed by occupying Nazi forces, a time of horrible suffering that must not be forgotten. "Together with the whole Church, I wish to remember those terrible days of the Second World War, days of contempt for the human person, manifested in the horror of the sufferings endured at that time by so many of our Jewish brothers and sisters. It is with profound grief that we call to mind what happened then, and indeed all that happened in the long black night of the *Shoah*. We remember, and we need to remember, but we need to remember with renewed trust in God and in his healing blessing."

Canon Law in Crisis — Ten years after promulgation of the new Code of Canon Law, a Vatican official said it was in crisis because people did not feel bound to observe it in practice. To improve the situation, it is incumbent on pastors to recognize that its observance is an essential factor in their ministry. So stated Bishop Julian Herranz, secretary of the Pontifical Council for the Interpretation of Legislative Texts, Apr. 19 at the opening of an International Symposium on Canon Law. He described the updated code as "pastoral," but said it faced opposition from those who regard church law as an obstacle to the spontaneity of the faithful and the working of the Holy Spirit. Some view canon law as violating the principle of democracy, forgetting that the authority of church law does not rest on "popular sovereignty." Others are affected by the prevailing trend toward moral relativism in society. All of which has fueled a "crisis of obedience to canonical norms," making it difficult for church law to guide personal conduct and relations among members of the Church. A critical factor is the weakening of the sense of the obligatory character of canon law.

Biblical Studies — Pope John Paul, marking the anniversaries of two encyclical letters on biblical interpretation, said the Church must encourage a continuing study of sacred Scripture. "Biblical thought must be constantly translated into contemporary language so that it can be expressed in a way suited to its listeners," he said Apr. 23. "However, this translation should be faithful to the original and cannot force the texts in order to make them fit an interpretation or an approach in fashion at a given moment." Members of the Pontifical Biblical Commission, cardinals and diplomats accredited to the Vatican attended the ceremony marking the 100th and 50th anniversaries, respectively, of *Providentissimus Deus* by Leo XIII and *Divino Afflante Spiritu* by Pius XII. The Pope said both documents, while responding to concerns of their times, have a permanent validity for the ongoing study and translation of the Scriptures. Taken together, they provide balanced guidelines for reading the Scriptures in the light of faith and with the use of historical, linguistic and other disciplines.

Gypsy Killings Commemorated — In a letter released Apr. 24, the Pope recalled the mass killings of Gypsies at the Nazi death camp of Auschwitz and said the Gypsy population still suffered from intolerance and discrimination. The tragic lesson of Auschwitz must not be forgotten, especially in view of the explosion of new ethnic hatred in Europe, he said. The letter marked the 50th anniversary of the arrival of the first trainload of Gypsies at the concentration camp in southern Poland where thousands of Gypsies were put to death in gas chambers. The Pope said their extermination was carried out "in the name of an insane ideology of hatred and contempt for the human being." Unfortunately, he added, Gypsies remained subject to prejudice, acts of intolerance and even outright discrimination" despite their undeniable right to a place in society and to their own cultural identity.

Trip to Albania — On a one-day visit to Albania Apr. 25, the Pope re-established the hierarchy with the ordination of four bishops for the formerly self-proclaimed atheistic country. (See separate entry.)

General Audience Topics:

• Invitation to the faithful to enter into the spirit of Holy Week (Apr. 7).

• The proclamation of Christ's death and resurrection is the beginning of all authentic discipleship and the source of the Church's mission (Apr. 14).

• Priests must not preach their own word but the word of God that has been entrusted to the Church for proclamation in its integrity (Apr. 21).

• The Pope's impressions of his Apr. 25 visit to Albania (Apr. 28).

Briefs:

• According to a new pay scale announced by the Vatican Central Labor Office Apr. 2, salaries for the Vatican's 3,400 lay employees ranged from $960 to $1,500 a month, plus seniority payments.

• Pope John Paul established a commission to review questions about the *Catechism of the Catholic Church* and to promote its use.

• Italian nuclear physicist Nicola Cabibbo was named president of the Pontifical Academy of Sciences.

• Participants in a Vatican-sponsored conference termed abortion a "grave crime" and called for political commitment to make it illegal, Apr. 23.

• Veteran diplomat Archbishop Gabriel Montalvo was named president of the Pontifical Ecclesiastical Academy, the Vatican's diplomatic training school.

Easter Message

Pope John Paul climaxed the full round of Holy Week ceremonies with Mass and a special message on Easter Sunday. He commemorated Christ's suffering, death and resurrection with calls for peace in the world. He said, in part:

"May the paschal announcement loudly resound, especially wherever violence, anguish and despair still oppress individuals and families, peoples and nations. I am thinking especially of those countries of Africa which feel frustrated in their aspirations to peace, such as Angola, Rwanda and Somalia, or which are moving amid a thousand difficulties toward the goals of democracy and harmony, such as Togo and Zaire. And how can we keep silent today — the day of peace — before the fratricidal struggles causing bloodshed in the region of the Caucasus, before the atrocious drama being relentlessly played out in Bosnia-Herzegovina? ... No one can consider that this tragic situation is not their affair, a situation which humiliates Europe and seriously compromises the future of peace. Leaders of nations, men and women of good will, with my heart overflowing with sorrow, I appeal once more to each of you: Stop this war! Put an end, I beg you, to the unspeakable cruelties whereby human dignity is being violated and God, our just and merciful Father, is being offended!"

NATIONAL

Resignation Accepted — Pope John Paul accepted the resignation of Archbishop Robert F. Sanchez of Santa Fe Apr. 6. The resignation had been tendered Mar. 19 amid allegations that the archbishop had intimate relations with several young women in the 1970s and 1980s. The Pope appealed for compassion and prayer in dealing with the "painful" scandal.

Waco Tragedy Inevitable — The end result of the standoff at the Branch Davidian compound in Waco, Texas, was inevitable because of the group leader's apocalyptic vision, according to Father Paul E. Desmaris, head of the Occult Awareness Ministry of the Providence diocese. He said he was dismayed but not shocked by reports of the deaths of more than 80 sect members Apr. 19. "It was just a matter of time" before the situation came to a head, he said. "The compound had all the elements present for mass suicide, ... a charismatic leader (David Koresh) and followers who had sold body, mind and soul into a dream."

Science and Religion — Bishops have a mandate to reach out to the scientific community for the purpose of promoting understanding of the relationship of science to the spiritual dimension of human nature and to the moral/ethical dimensions of scientific theories and discoveries. So stated Bishop William B. Friend of Shreveport, La., Apr. 14 at the opening of a Notre Dame symposium on "Knowing God, Christ and Nature in the Post-Positivistic Era." The three-day meeting was attended by about 250 theologians, philosophers, scientists, church leaders and university students.

Pro-Abortion Agenda — An announcement by the head of the Food and Drug Administration of a step toward U.S. marketing of the French abortion pill, RU-486, signalled the Clinton administration's "real agenda" on abortion, according to a spokeswoman for the U.S. bishops. "Once again, the administration that pledged to make abortion rare has demonstrated its real agenda — to make abortion more plentiful," said Helen Alvare, director of planning and information for the bishops' Secretariat for Pro-Life Activities. She made the comment after

FDA Commissioner David A. Kessler announced Apr. 20 that Roussel-Uclaf, the French manufacturer of RU-486, had given the New York-based Population Council license to produce the drug in the U.S. She said Kessler's actions constituted "unprecedented pressure" by the Clinton administration on Roussel-Uclaf, which had previously indicated it was not interested in making RU-486 in the United States. Importation of the drug for personal use had been outlawed since June, 1989, but importation for research purposes was allowed.

Circulation Down — Catholic periodicals in the United States and Canada had a total 1992 circulation of 27,493,219; the number was nearly a million short of that reported for 1991. Among figures reported in the 1993 *Catholic Press Directory* were the following: newspapers, 5,956,318; magazines, 16,941,170; newsletters, 3,806,602; other-language publications, 789,129; total number of publications, 679. The most notable circulation losses recorded by individual publications were those of three general-interest national newspapers: *Catholic Twin Circle*, from 47,000 to 22,500; *National Catholic Register*, from 47,223 to 26,000; *Our Sunday Visitor*, from 160,000 to 125,000.

Holocaust Museum — The U.S. Holocaust Museum in Washington not only recounts the deaths of millions of victims of World War II but also presents a lesson for all people, according to Catholic and Jewish commentators. "It tells a crucial story, summing up the underside of the 20th century," said Eugene J. Fisher, associate director of the Secretariat for Ecumenical and Interreligious Affairs, National Conference of Catholic Bishops. He called the new museum's role "extremely important" in "helping all Christians remember what can happen if we're not extremely vigilant." Rabbi A. James Rudin, interreligious affairs director of the American Jewish Committee, said the museum "makes permanent a piece of history that can't be forgotten." The museum was dedicated Apr. 22.

Briefs:

● Father George Hogan was named official circus chaplain by the Migration and Refugee Services, U.S. Catholic Conference.

● More than 13,000 educators attended sessions of the 90th annual convention of the National Catholic Educational Association Apr. 12 to 15 in New Orleans. "Catholic Educators: Telling the Good News Story," was the theme of the convention.

● The fifth annual Day of Prayer for the Faith of Our Children, Apr. 25, was sponsored by the Catholic Church Extension Society.

Population Statistics

The U.S. Catholic population grew by nearly a million in 1992 but other key statistics were in decline, according to the 1993 edition of *The Official Catholic Directory*. The new figures, compared with those of the previous year, indicated:

● The total number of Catholics increased by more than 950,000, from 58,267,424 to 59,220,723.

● There were nearly 1,400 fewer priests, down from 52,277 to 50,907.

● The number of women religious dropped more than 5,300, from 99,337 to 94,022.

● The number of ordinations to the priesthood dropped from 864 to 605 and the number of students reported in diocesan and religious seminaries combined dropped from 6,454 to 5,891.

● The total number of Catholic educational institutions dropped, but the number of students increased slightly

● Catholic college enrollment increased by 1,632, to 660,787.

● There were about 636,000 students in Catholic high schools, a slight decrease.

● For the fourth straight year Catholic elementary school enrollment gained slightly, going above two million.

INTERNATIONAL

Ghetto Uprising Remembrance — The Polish archbishop responsible for relations with Jews called on the nation's Catholics to mark the 50th anniversary of the 1943 Warsaw Ghetto Uprising with prayers for murdered Jews and Poles who "shared their wartime fate." In a message to parishes, Archbishop Henryk Muszynski of Gniezo, said Poles should reflect on "the greatness of the sacrifice made by victims of a generation which should not have been lost." Commemoration of the uprising "should not be limited only to recollecting the time of captivity and humiliation. Remembrance of the sacrifice of these people should generate within us a will to struggle with all forms of injustice, hurtfulness, xenophobia, mutual stereotypes and lack of sympathy, which finds expression both in anti-Semitism and in anti-Polonism."

Refugees Not Welcome — Western Europe appeared to be slamming the door on refugees fleeing from civil wars in more than 30 countries, according to church and government experts on migration issues. As an example, they cited tight restrictions on the more than three million people who had abandoned their homes because of fighting in the former republic of Yugoslavia. Most of them were forced to live in poverty and precarious conditions in breakaway republics. Experts feared that the situation mirrored a growing tendency to keep out foreigners in a post-Cold War era marked by an increase of ethnic, racial and national antagonisms. They also said a declining economy and rising unemployment were igniting fears of foreigners as unwelcome competitors for diminishing numbers of jobs. "Europe is not an area of welcome for refugees," said Franco Foschi, president of the Association for the Study of World Refugee Problems. There were more than 18 million refugees and another 24 million displaced persons in the world, according to U.N. statistics. Less than five percent of the refugees had been absorbed by Western Europe, said Archbishop Giovanni Cheli, president of the Pontifical Council for Migrants and Travelers.

Appeal for End to Violence — Latin-rite Patriarch Michel Sabbah, marking a tense Easter weekend, appealed for an end to violence in the Holy Land. He said that, in the face of stalled Arab-Israeli negotiations, both sides needed to make a serious commitment to dialogue and to reject violence as counterproductive. "It is time to become convinced that, despite all the prejudices fed by a century of conflict, the other (party) was not created in God's image to be the enemy but to be a friend and brother."

In a related development, Archbishop John R. Roach of St. Paul and Minneapolis said in a letter to Patriarch Michel Sabbah: "It grieves us that, due to the closing of the West Bank and Gaza (by Israel), a considerable portion of the community of faith is prevented from celebrating with you this week at the holy sites."

Franciscans Not To Bear Arms — Father Hermann Schaluck, minister general of the Order of Friars Minor, said in a statement Apr. 20 that members of the order in the former Yugoslavian republics may not carry weapons. Christ and St. Francis of Assisi, he said, "would not support friars being part of a military campaign. . . . I do not mean that we should be or can be indifferent," but "we must construct peace without arms. It is a slow process of conversion. This war will be leaving deep emotional and spiritual wounds that will need great care and healing. I hope that the friars can be prepared to assist the people on their long journey of healing and reconciliation." Twenty friars were reported in service as military chaplains in Croatia and Herzegovina.

Education Rules in Poland — The nation's Constitutional Tribunal ruled Apr. 20 that three provisions of law governing religious education in public schools were illegal. The court ordered an end to requirements that:

• parents and pupils not wishing to participate in religion classes must sign a declaration to that effect;

• pupils not attending religion classes must enroll in ethics courses;

• religion teachers must have certification by a bishop.

More Freedom Wanted — The bishops of Vietnam were asking the government for greater freedom in the education of priests, seminarians and teachers, according to a Vatican Radio report Apr. 21. Specifically, the bishops wanted:

• permission for each diocese to send priests abroad for study;

• higher limits on the number of seminarians for larger dioceses;

• approval for a new seminary and two formation centers;

• opportunity to organize summer refresher courses for seminary professors, with the assistance of foreign experts.

Defend Cultural Identity — Four bishops from Mexico's rural and largely indigenous South issued a call for the Church to defend the cultural identity of indigenous peoples and incorporate them more and more in the life of the Church. Basing their declarations on the conclusions reached at the October, 1992, general assembly of the Latin American Bishops' Conference, they said the Church should turn its preferential option for the poor into a concerted effort to understand and support indigenous peoples "so that they can become the builders of their own future." In their pastoral letter, they criticized those who romanticize indigenous culture from a folkloric perspective. On the contrary, they said such culture should be taken seriously and considered "the most solid foundation of the multicultural and multiethnic identity of the (Latin American) continent."

No Special Rite — The bishops of Great Britain, in a statement released Apr. 23, ruled out a special rite for members of the Church of England wanting to become Roman Catholics, rejected conversions based solely on opposition to the church's approval for the ordination of women to the priesthood, and stated there was no consideration of a "personal prelature" for Anglicans-become-Catholics. (See separate entry.)

Liberia's Forgotten War — Calling the civil conflict in Liberia a "forgotten war," Vatican envoy Cardinal Roger Etchegaray appealed to the international community to demonstrate concern for the nation. "Liberia risks sinking into the resigned indifference of the world community," said the cardinal in a statement issued in the Apr. 29 edition of *L'Osservatore Romano*. He said the three-year-old war had been all but forgotten as international attention turned toward "other conflicts considered more serious or more threatening to international peace."

Briefs:

• Chinese Bishop Stephen Liu Difen of Anguo, 80, was the third bishop who died in government custody in three years. News of his death Nov. 14, 1992, was reported this month.

• Col. Guillermo Benavides and Lt. Yusshy Mendoza, jailed for the 1989 murder of six Jesuits, their cook and her daughter, were set free early in the month under a controversial amnesty for El Salvadoran war criminals.

• Evangelizing Europe involves fusing the peoples' desire for freedom and democracy with Gospel values, said Archbishop Miloslav Vlk of Prague Apr. 18. He was the first East European president of the Council of European Bishops' Conferences.

UNICEF, Church, Family Planning

In a statement delivered to the executive board of UNICEF Apr. 27, the Vatican warned that a UNICEF document on family planning contained wording at odds with the moral teaching of the Church. The statement noted that previous UNICEF publications said the agency does not favor any particular method of spacing births. But, "as some of the wording of the family document would (now) suggest otherwise, our delegation places particular importance on ensuring that Catholics not find themselves excluded from participation in or support of UNICEF." The statement was read by New York businessman John Klink, a volunteer assistant to the Vatican's mission to the United Nations. He said "the Holy See notes with satisfaction" statements in the family planning document that UNICEF does not support abortion as a method of family planning and that in practice it "does not provide contraceptive supplies from its resources." The objectionable wording in question concerned possible cooperation of UNICEF with other agencies whose family planning programs are not in accord with the teaching of the Church.

MAY 1993

VATICAN

Departments Merged — Pope John Paul merged two Vatican agencies dealing with cultures and non-believers, and said the new agency would try to heal the "fracture" between contemporary society and the Gospel. Under the reorganization, the Pontifical Council for Dialogue with Non-Believers ended its activity as a separate curial agency and became part of the Pontifical Council for Culture. The council, as announced May 4, was charged with promoting "the encounter between the saving message of the Gospel and the cultures of our time, which are often marked by non-belief and religious indifference."

150th Anniversary — The Holy Childhood Association, established in 1843 and subsequently made a Vatican organization, celebrated its 150th anniversary early in the month. With funds raised by young people throughout the world, it reported the annual distribution of about $15 million annually toward schools, children's homes and other projects in 152 countries. Association officials reported the following at a press conference:

• Over the previous decade, 1.5 million children had been disabled by bombings, mines, firearms and torture.

• Approximately 12 million children had been forced out of their homes by war; five million were growing up in refugee camps.

• The scandal of sexual exploitation of children through prostitution and pornography has become a worldwide phenomenon, often promoted by "sex tours" offered by Western agencies.

• In 50 developing countries, the percentage of children enrolled in primary schools was decreasing at an alarming rate.

Ecumenism a Priority — Calling ecumenism a priority of the Church and not just an area of specialization for interested individuals, Cardinal Edward I. Cassidy said that conversion and education are needed within the Church for all of its members to recognize the importance of Christian unity and efforts to achieve it. The president of the Pontifical Council for Promoting Christian Unity spoke May 10 at the opening of a six-day interfaith meeting attended by representatives of eight Anglican, Orthodox and Protestant churches.

Christian Brothers' Witness — "Your apostolate in the Church makes you primary witnesses of hope in the face of the uncertainties, doubts or problems which give youths anxiety today," said the Pope May 14 at a meeting with Brothers of the Christian Schools and their co-workers. "Your mission is important and difficult. You must accomplish it in an age of considerable changes in society."

Appeal to Women Religious — The Pope asked women religious May 14 to bring their love and dedication to bear on all situations where life is threatened or derided. "Your particular vocation . . . must express itself on the front lines of defending human life throughout its earthly existence, from conception to its natural end," he told 800 women religious attending an assembly of the International Union of Superiors General. An authentic defense of human life requires a proclamation of the Gospel message and includes "the promotion of human rights, the defense of the woman and her dignity, a culture of peace and communion between peoples, and respect for creation, the gift of God which must stimulate blessing and praise of the Creator."

Space for the Handicapped — "The quality of a society and of a civilization is measured by the respect which it shows toward the weakest of its members," said the Pope May 14 at a meeting with 150 persons associated with the International Research Center for the Self-Sufficiency of the Handicapped. Communities must help people with handicapping conditions "integrate themselves fully in civil society and in its economic processes," and must "make real space for their potential," which is often hidden but which must be discovered, encouraged and cultivated.

Beatifications — The Holy Father beatified four persons May 16: Father Maurice Tournay, who was killed by Buddhist monks in 1949; Sister Marie-Louise Trichet, foundress of the Daughters of Wisdom in the early 1700s; Benedictine Sister Colomba Joanna Gabriel, who opened houses in Rome for poor and hungry people in the early 1900s; and Sister Florida Cevoli, known for reforms she initiated in an order of Franciscan nuns in the 18th century.

Priesthood Conference — Gregorian University and the Congregation for the Clergy were sponsors of a May 26-to-28 conference which featured discussions on the biblical roots of priesthood, priesthood and celibacy in the early Church, the difference between ordained priesthood and the priesthood of all the faithful, and various aspects of training of candidates for the priesthood.

General Audience Topics:

• Acting in the name of Christ, priests administer the sacraments which, by the power of the Holy Spirit, bestow the life of grace (May 5).

• Priests carry out their sacred ministry, above all, in the Eucharist when, in the person of Christ, they re-present his eternal sacrifice (May 12).

• In carrying out his pastoral ministry, the priest must strive to promote the spiritual and ecclesial maturity of the community entrusted to him (May 19).

• The Second Vatican Council clearly recognized the importance of priestly holiness for renewing the Church and spreading the Gospel (May 26).

Briefs:

• The Pope ordained 29 priests for the Diocese of Rome May 2, the World Day of Prayer for Vocations.

• The Rome diocesan phase of the canonization cause of Pope Paul VI was initiated May 11.

• Pope John Paul expressed his "strongest condemnation" of bombings in Rome, May 14, and Florence, May 27.

Third Visit to Sicily

Pope John Paul, on his 109th pastoral visit to Italian locales outside of Rome, visited six cities in Sicily May 8 to 10. He celebrated Mass daily before large gatherings of people and in more than 15 homilies and speeches addressed issues of serious concern, including: living the Gospel, prevalent corruption in politics and social life, the need for a "culture of initiative" in business to create jobs and combat poverty, a challenge to youths to renew society with the power of the Gospel. He reserved his strongest comments for an attack on the Mafia. In Agricento on May 9, he said in part:

"The true force capable of overcoming destructive trends (in Sicilian life) comes from the faith which, however, requires not only an interior personal assent, but also a courageous exterior witness which is expressed in condemning evil with conviction. Here, in your land, it demands a clear denunciation of the culture of the Mafia, which is a culture of death, a profoundly inhuman, anti-Gospel foe of human dignity and civil harmony."

"As in the past the people of Sicily have been able to withstand long, painful trials, so too today they have the necessary resources, together with the solid support of the Italian nation, to heal the present wounds, many of which are the result of enduring social conditions. Today as yesterday, the Sicilian Church is called to share the commitment, effort and risks of those who are struggling, even to their personal disadvantage, to lay the foundations of a future of progress, justice and peace for the whole island."

NATIONAL

Challenges to Peace — Cardinal Joseph L. Bernardin of Chicago warned against "the immorality of isolationism" in a speech marking the 10th anniversary of the U.S. bishops' pastoral letter on peace. "After the Cold War, there is an understandable but dangerous temptation to turn inward. . . But this is not an option for believers in the universal Church nor for citizens in the world's last superpower," he said at a symposium May 1 in Uncasville, Conn. "In a world where 40,000 children die every day from hunger and its consequences, in a world with ethnic cleansing and systematic rape in Bosnia, in a world where people are still denied life, dignity and fundamental rights because of their race, ethnicity, religion or economic status — we cannot turn away. . . . There is need for new thinking about the status of peace, the nature of war and effective responses to conflict." The bishops' letter bore the title, "The Challenge of Peace: God's Promise and Our Response."

Third World Debt — "The poor of the Third World are getting poorer, despite the rhetoric about development. . . . It's killing the people and it's killing the earth." So stated Columban Missionary Father Sean McDonagh, a 20-year veteran of missionary work in the Philippines and author of *To Care for the Earth* and *The Greening of the Earth*. Speaking in Chicago May 6, he cited a UNICEF report that attributed 500,000 deaths of children to Third World debt.

Health Care Reform — This was the principal topic under discussion at a closed meeting of U.S. archbishops May 11 in Chicago. A press release described the session as "an informational one, to outline medical-moral, social justice and other issues involved in the national discussion of health care reform." The Catholic Health Association reported that Catholic hospitals, about 10 percent of the U.S. total, treated approximately 56 million people in 1992.

Domestic Partnership — Cardinal Anthony J. Bevilacqua of Philadelphia, in no uncertain terms, declared his opposition to a proposed city ordinance that would give quasi-marital recognition to domestic relationship of homosexuals. He said May 14: The "proposed legislation extends legal recognition to a sexual relationship which I — and I sincerely believe the majority of citizens in this city — consider to be immoral. This legislation gives to those in a homosexual relationship the same legitimacy accorded to those in a marital relationship. . . . The bill is dangerous because it attempts to create a legitimacy which homosexual cohabitation does not and cannot enjoy." The cardinal also said: "If the members of the City Council do not uphold the truth, that committed marriages and stable marriages lie at the heart of a civilized society and serve as the foundation on which it is built, then the consequence of continued social deterioration in our city is all too predictable." (Mayor Edward G. Rendell, in a letter to the City Council June 1, asked the body to "defer consideration" of Bill 531 and another proposal, Bill 552, that would have extended benefits to all unmarried partners, both homosexual and heterosexual.)

In another development, the Hawaii Supreme Court ruled May 5 that a state ban on homosexual marriages might be unconstitutional. With a 3-to-1 vote, the court ordered a lower court to review a state ban on same-sex marriages. Justice Steven H. Levinson wrote that "marriage is a basic civil right" and that the Hawaiian law "denies same-sex couples the marital status and its concomitant rights and benefits." The ruling prompted commentary May 21 from Patrick Downes, editor of the diocesan newspaper: "To allow a man to 'marry' a man or a woman to 'marry' a woman is to grossly deny the inherent procreative nature of marriage and therefore change its very definition. . . . Take away the assumption of procreation, and all that's left is not a marriage but a dry, empty shell of a civil agreement open to anyone's interpretation and use. If you eliminate procreation from the basic definition of marriage, on what legal basis could you stop three people from getting married, or a mother and a son?"

Apology to Indians — During a visit to an historic Indian mission in DeSmet, Idaho, the superior general of the Jesuits apologized to American Indians for past mistakes made by missionaries of his order. Father Peter-Hans Kolvenbach said he wanted to join other religious leaders who had publicly acknowledged insensitivity toward tribal customs, language and spirituality. "I want to take this moment to add my voice to theirs," he said May 16 at Sacred Heart Mission on the Couer d'Alene Indian Reservation. "The Society of Jesus is sorry for the mistakes it has made in the past."

Assisted Suicide — Dominican Sister Sharon Park, associate director of the Washington State Catholic Conference, and Ken VanDerhoef, president of Human Life of Washington, stated their opposition to a new nonprofit organization dedicated to helping terminally ill persons commit suicide. Barbara Dority, president of Compassion in Dying, said at a press conference May 19 in Seattle that the group would offer every kind of assistance to terminally ill persons wanting to commit suicide, short of directly aiding in the act of suicide. VanDerhoef said: "These people, regardless of what they call themselves, are clearly bent on promoting the death ethic."

During the month, Jack Kevorkian assisted in a suicide for the 16th time since 1990.

Churches' Role in Social Welfare — Local church congregations play a crucial role in the social welfare of the country, according to a study conducted by Independent Sector, a Washington-based organization that promotes community service. Highlights of the study report indicated:

● Individual financial contributions to U.S. religious congregations in 1991 amounted to $39.2 billion.

● Congregations used some $6.6 billion of that amount in direct expenditures for community service: almost $4.7 billion to denominational organizations and charities, $1.3 billion to other charitable organizations in the community, and $654 million in direct assistance to individuals.

● Churchgoers donated about 1.8 billion hours of volunteer service to their congregations and to human services.

● Clergy and other paid employees of congregations devoted nearly 750 million hours to human services.

● The total estimated contributions of religious congregations for community services was $27.7 billion.

CPA Convention — Members of the Catholic Press Association, meeting May 26 to 28 in Cincinnati, ratified a statement entitled "Freedom and Responsibility in the Catholic Press." They also announced awards for excellence in various categories of journalistic endeavor (see separate entry). Father John Catoir, director of The Christophers, was honored with the 1993 St. Francis de Sales Award.

Abortion Law Upheld — The 5th U.S. Circuit Court of Appeals in New Orleans upheld the constitutionality of a Mississippi law requiring women under the age of 18 to obtain parental consent before having an abortion. The 2-to-1 ruling May 27 said the law was a constitutionally permissible way for the state to "express profound respect for the life of the unborn" and gave women under 18 enough alternatives (e.g., court approval in stated circumstances) to two-parent consent.

Briefs:

● About 200 priests, religious and lay persons attended the sixth annual pastoring workshop sponsored by the National Black Catholic Congress May 2 to 6 at Hollywood Beach, Florida.

● *The Clarion Herald* published a special supplement marking the 200th anniversary of the Archdiocese of New Orleans.

● The Marian Library on the campus of the University of Dayton was the beneficiary of a $400,000 bequest and a collection of Marian artifacts, from the estate of Arthur W. Clinton, Jr. He also bequeathed $260,000 to the Mariological Society of America.

U.S. Policy on Bosnia

This was the subject of a letter addressed May 11 to U.S. Secretary of State Warren M. Christopher by Archbishop John R. Roach, chairman of the International Policy Committee, U.S. Catholic Conference. The letter said in part as follows.

"We believe that the United States, with the United Nations and other international bodies, should find effective means of protecting innocent people and bringing about a just and lasting political solution to this dreadful conflict."

"How the United States chooses to intervene in Bosnia raises difficult moral questions. ... The strong presumption against the resort to military force may be overridden only if certain strict criteria are met. There must be a just cause, force must be undertaken by a legitimate authority, the intention must be to restore justice and peace and not to seek vengeance, there must be a reasonable probability of success, the comparative justice of the conflicting parties must be weighed, force must be a last resort, the likely overall harm caused by military force must be proportionate to the good likely to be achieved, and particular uses of force must be discriminate and proportionate."

"There is no real military solution in the former Yugoslavia. But, as the Holy See has said (Jan. 16, 1993), governments and the international community have a right and duty to disarm the aggressor. We are convinced that there is just cause to use force to defend largely helpless people in Bosnia against aggression and barbarism that are destroying the very foundations of society and threaten large numbers of people."

"Specifically, we support:

● "implementation, where feasible, of the U.N. Security Council's decision to establish safe havens in Bosnia, as a temporary measure to save lives and protect against 'ethnic cleansing' until a political solution can be found.

● "more concerted measures to protect civilian populations in besieged cities, to protect fleeing refugees and to ensure the delivery of aid to the needy.

● "continued enforcement of economic sanctions.

● "full implementation and enforcement of a political settlement in Bosnia and the cease-fire in Croatia, a step we recognize would probably require the use of U.S. troops."

INTERNATIONAL

Death of Chinese Bishop — Auxiliary Bishop Paul Liu Shuhe of Yixian, secretary-general of the pro-Vatican underground bishops' conference, died May 2 while in hiding from government authorities. His death was reported by UCA News, an Asian agency based in Thailand. The 74-year-old bishop had spent nearly 26 years in jail, detention or under house arrest because of his faith, ministry and refusal to belong to the government-controlled church.

European Search for Identity — After a half century as an ideological battleground, Europe was searching for its cultural identity and, in the process, trying to define its relationship with Christianity, said speakers during a May 12-to-14 forum in Rome. The forum, sponsored by Rome's Beato Angelico Foundation and attended by religious, academic and political leaders from the Continent, focused attention on the tenuous contemporary relationship between culture and faith. In contrast with the optimistic voices heard when European communism began to crumble in 1989, speakers showed deep concern that, despite some signs of religious awakening, there remained a worrisome gap between contemporary societies and Christian values. Cardinal Agostino Casaroli said there was reason to wonder whether Christian civilization on the Continent might succumb to "the weariness of European Christians. ... There are serious worries created by the vertical fall of Christian values in the area of respect for human rights and populations in Europe, and by the frightening rise of selfishness and animosity between ethnic groups and states."

Threat of New Rules — Archbishop Tadeusz Kondrusiewicz, apostolic administrator of European Russia, voiced "grave concern" over a proposal to increase state control over religion. He said in a newspaper interview that all denominations in Russia were against a proposed law which would empower the legislature to re-establish a church-monitoring Experts Consultative Council and to impose tighter restrictions on the registration of foreign-based communities operating in Russia. "In the circumstances, the new regulations will clearly affect Catholics in Russia," said the archbishop. Despite various obstacles, he said that three churches had been reopened this year and estimated that there were between 250,000 and 300,000 practicing Catholics in European Russia.

More than Demographics — A Vatican official told a United Nations committee preparing for a 1994 conference on population that discussions should go beyond demographics to include the family and other topics related to population. In a May 17 statement, Archbishop Renato R. Martino included "responsible planning of family size and spacing of births" among concerns deserving attention. The Catholic Church "does not propose procreation at any cost," he said, repeating a statement he made at the 1992 Rio conference on the environment. But, he noted, the Church insists that couples respect "the objective moral order" and use "licit methods." The International Conference on Population and Development was scheduled for Sept. 5 to 13, 1994, in Cairo. Archbishop Martino said the title of the conference "marks a significant evolution and reflects the correct view of many countries, especially the developing countries," that major issues should not be separated from "integral development. ... A conference on population and development must, above all, place in evidence that sustainable development is about people, about the hopes, anxieties and aspirations of women and men of today and tomorrow, of the various generations of the one human family."

Ethnic Cleansing in Sudan — Slavery, ethnic cleansing, deportation and forced conscription into the army were ongoing realities in Sudan, according to exiled Bishop Macram Max Gassis of El Obeid.

"In the face of these crimes against humanity, I remain horrified and saddened in seeing Christian nations silent and even hesitant to admit that a true religious and ethnic persecution exists" in the country. The bishop spoke during a visit to several Italian cities during the month.

Election Issues in Spain — Heading the list were abortion, corruption and unemployment. So stated the bishops in a 1,000-word statement about elections scheduled for June 6. They cited:
- "the alarming climate of corruption caused by fraudulent and immoral methods in some public and private economic activities";
- warned about the "growing problem of unemployment";
- said that economic decline was producing "important sectors of poverty and marginalization with worrying manifestations of drug addiction, crime and AIDS";
- "respect for the rights of the unborn" and aid programs for children.

Nuns Moving — Five of the 14 Carmelite nuns who had occupied a controversial convent adjoining the Auschwitz concentration camp were reported moved into a new interfaith center nearby. Controversy over the site of the convent dated from 1985, with frequent objections to its presence and activities voiced by representatives of Jewish organizations.

Life Begins at Conception — So stated the supreme court of Germany May 28 as it declared the nation's abortion reform law unconstitutional. The decision required implementation by legislation. The court ruled that the German constitution's protection for all life included unborn life, and barred health plans from paying for abortions or state hospitals from performing them.

Briefs:
- The bishops of Poland appealed May 1 to society to support the Church's defense of Christian values and to resist "nihilism and moral chaos."
- Ten Albanian Franciscan friars who survived their nation's communist persecution were joined by eight foreign friars in re-establishing the Franciscans' Albanian Province.
- Peruvian Father Gustavo Gutierrez, the "Father of Liberation Theology," was made a Knight of the Legion of Honor by French President Francois Mitterand.
- Eastern- and Latin-rite bishops of Ukraine held their first joint meeting May 18 and 19 for the discussion of ways and means of addressing pastoral and social problems of their people.

Cardinal Murdered

Cardinal Juan Jesus Posadas Ocampo was shot to death May 24 in the parking area of the Guadalajara Airport, Mexico. One report said he was killed accidentally in a crossfire between gunmen of rival drug gangs. Another account, verified by the local coroner, said he was struck with 14 bullets fired from point-bank range, a finding which seemed to indicate intentional assassination rather than accidental death. The cardinal, mourned by many, was known as a vigorous opponent of drug traffic and the use of guns.

JUNE 1993

VATICAN

Media Image Bombardment — Pope John Paul said June 4 that the bombardment of families by media images of sex and violence had caused great damage to society, and that the problem required a strong response by families and advocacy groups to obtain "decisive changes" in media content. While acknowledging that the media can educate and entertain, the Pope decried the spread of "programs and written material in which there is a proliferation of every sort of violence. ... A type of bombardment occurs, with messages that undermine moral principles and destroy the serious atmosphere needed to transmit values worthy of the human being."

New Dean — Cardinal Bernardin Gantin, head of the Congregation for Bishops, was elected Dean of the College of Cardinals early in the month. The Italian newspaper, *Il Messaggero*, said the election of the 71-year-old prelate from Benin was "another sign of the universality of the Church and is a consequence of the internationalization of the Roman Curia. The dean presides over the College of Cardinals as the first among equals, and carries out key functions on the death of a pope and in the election of a successor.

FamilyFest — "The values of giving, communion, generosity, love and the sublime tasks of procreation and education, which are born and grow in the family, are grounds for reflection by everyone concerned about the destiny of the human person and of human existence." So stated the Pope June 7 at a FamilyFest Mass in St. Peter's Square. The conference, sponsored by the New Families branch of the Focolare Movement, attracted some 12,000 Christian, Jewish, Muslim and Buddhist family members to Rome and others to satellite reception sites throughout the world. FamilyFest '93 was billed as a preparatory meeting for the 1994 International Year of the Family, declared by the United Nations.

Ethiopian Patriarch Welcomed — The Pope welcomed Ethiopian Orthodox Patriarch Abuna Paulos to his celebration of the Feast of Corpus Christi as a sign of common faith in the Eucharist. He said June 10 in a homily at the Basilica of St. John Lateran: "His participation shows the common faith of our churches in the Eucharist as the living presence of Jesus among his disciples. ... We fervently beg Jesus Christ, present in the sacrament on the altar, to sustain all — Catholics and Orthodox — in the journey toward full (Christian) unity." The Mass at which the Pope spoke was preceded by an evening procession of the Blessed Sacrament through the streets of Rome.

Trip to Spain — The Holy Father visited several cities of Spain June 12 to 17. The high point of the visit was his celebration of the Mass which concluded the 45th International Eucharistic Congress in Seville. (See separate entry.)

World Conference on Human Rights — The Pope voiced support for the conference held June 14 to 25 in Vienna, at which 2,000 delegates from 163 nations reaffirmed the human rights spelled out in the United Nations Charter. He told diplomats in Madrid June 16: "The common conscience of humanity sees an increasingly clear need for international law, solidly founded on ethical principles, to be able to give real protection to the fundamental rights and freedoms of the human person."

Intervention Guidelines Needed — Recent attacks by U.S. and U.N. forces in Somalia showed a need for the international community to develop precise guidelines for armed humanitarian intervention. "Only a precise ethical and moral frame of reference" can orient peacekeeping operations toward just solutions in line with international law. So stated a front-page editorial in the June 16 edition of *L'Osservatore Romano*. "Operation Hope" was aimed at protecting the distribution of humanitarian aid and pacifying "a nation in the hands of armed factions able to add the unbearable weight of their violence to the terrible devastation which famine and hunger had already brought to the martyred country. But, after seven months of 'Restore Hope,' a very different and opposite reality has been superimposed. The same population which expected peace and food aid now finds itself in the midst of an offensive fielding missiles and every type of bombardment." The concept of "humanitarian intervention" was being buried under innocent bodies in Bosnia as well as in Somalia.

Catholic-Orthodox Document — In an important step forward in Catholic-Orthodox relations, theologians from both churches approved a document intended to defuse pastoral tension over the issue of proselytizing. Specifically, the theologians agreed that it was unacceptable to seek conversions from among each other's faithful. The document was produced during the seventh plenary session of the International Commission for Theological Dialogue, held June 17 to 24 in Balamand, Lebanon. The document, with its statement of principles and guidelines regarding the status and activity of Eastern-rite Catholic churches, was to be submitted to authorities of Catholic and Orthodox churches for approval and application.

Needs of Eastern Churches — The churches of the East need to be enriched with "new perspectives and new methodologies" that reflect the influence of the Second Vatican Council, the Pope said June 24 in an address to members of a charity organization connected with the Congregation for the Oriental Churches. After years of "persecution and troubles," and over and above their need for buildings and material resources, local churches "need help in forming consciences in the faith through catechesis, the liturgy, commitment to charity, and love between Christians and among all people of good will."

Mass with Archbishops — At an annual Mass June 29, the solemnity of Sts. Peter and Paul, the Pope presented the pallium (see separate entry) to 27 archbishops who had been appointed to metropolitan sees during the previous year. The ceremony was attended by an Orthodox delegation sent by Ecumenical Patriarch Bartholomeos I of Constantinople, whom the Holy Father welcomed with feelings of "joy and fraternal charity." Addressing the Patriarch, he said: "With your participation in today's celebration, you give witness to the desire for unity that animates all Christ's faithful. At the end of the second millennium, this unity appears increasingly as a particular demand of the faith."

General Audience Topics:
• Priests must be devoted to prayer because of their relation to Christ and mission (June 2).
• In the Eucharist, priests are united with the Lord, grow in pastoral charity, learn to praise God for his blessings (June 9).
• There was no general audience June 16 while the Pope was in Spain.
• Reflections on his visit to Spain (June 23).
• Devotion to Mary is an important part of a priest's spiritual life (June 30).

Briefs:
• The Pope paid tribute to Pope John XXIII on the 30th anniversary of his death, June 3.
• A year after his pastoral visit to Angola, the Pope pleaded June 6 with political forces there to halt the "absurd" war that was devastating the country.
• At a meeting June 19 with Consolata Missionaries, the Pope said many people do not appreciate the hardships and sacrifices experienced by missionaries.
• With 15 Gypsy survivors of World War II death camps June 27, the Pope said the Nazi effort to destroy their people was a "crime against humanity."

New Ecumenical Directory
A new "Directory for the Application of Principles and Norms on Ecumenism" was released June 8 by the Pontifical Council for Promoting Christian Unity. In five chapters, the 100-page directory updates and refines the contents of similar documents issued in 1967 and 1970. One commentator called it "the most significant document on ecumenism for the Catholic Church this decade."

NATIONAL
Social Deficit — The U.S. Catholic Conference joined the National Council of Churches and the Synagogue Council of America in a June 9 statement on the nation's growing "social deficit." In "A Call to the Common Ground for the Common Good," they cited six areas of concern: priority for the poor, focus on basic human dignity and needs, genuine reform of the welfare system, respect for diversity, new politics of community and a commitment to empowerment.

Retirement Fund for Religious — The fifth annual fund appeal raised $24,609,127 to be given in grants to needy religious communities for their aged and infirm members. The appeal was under the sponsorship of the Tri-Conference Retirement Office, a joint project of the National Conference of Catholic Bishops, the Leadership Conference of Women Religious and the Conference of Major Superiors of Men.

Haitian Refugees Resettled — After a waiting period of nearly two years, 46 HIV-infected Haitian refugees cleared to enter the United States were being resettled by the U.S. bishops' Office of Migration and Refugee Services. The order to release the political refugees from detention at Guantanamo Bay, Cuba, was handed down by U.S. District Court Judge Sterling Johnson, Jr. In his 53-page ruling, Judge Johnson said the Bush and Clinton administrations showed "outrageous, callous and reprehensible" behavior by refusing to provide adequate medical care for refugees living in a shantytown on the naval base. He called the area "nothing more than an HIV prison camp."

Clinic Bill Opposed — A bill intended to protect abortion clinics from blockades would unfairly impose harsh penalties on protesters acting on their conscientious beliefs. Bishop James T. McHugh of Camden told the House Judiciary Committee June 10 that the Freedom of Access to Clinic Entrances was not about maintaining public order or protecting patients or employees of abortion clinics from violence. "This bill is about advancing abortion," he said. "It is an expression and validation of a pro-abortion mentality that increasingly attempts to dignify itself with the protection and support of politicans and laws, so as to expand the incidence of abortion and encourage its use." By addressing itself only to "reproductive health" offices, the bill was "a particular danger to the rights of public assembly and free speech guaranteed under the First Amendment," said the bishop.

Health Care Reform — U.S. bishops, in a statement issued at their meeting June 17 to 19 in New Orleans, said the Catholic community must be a "constituency of conscience" in the national health care reform debate. The document, they said, "restates our long-standing support for national health care reform and shares the principles and priorities that guide our advocacy in this area." The document listed "criteria for reform" that the bishops believed should guide the debate: universal access, priority concern for the poor, respect for life, comprehensive benefits, pluralism, equitable financing, cost containment, controls and quality. The statement reiterated opposition to the inclusion of abortion coverage in a national health care plan. "We appeal to the leaders of the nation to avoid a divisive and polarizing dispute by not insisting that millions of pro-life Americans participate in abortion as a part of national health care reform." (For text, see separate entry.)

Anti-Poverty Awards — The Campaign for Human Development announced June 18 the awarding of $7.4 million in grants to 225 community-based, anti-poverty projects across the country in 1993. Jesuit Father Joseph Hacala, executive director of the campaign, said 80 church-based community organizing projects were receiving grants along with a large number of projects relating to children and families. Another trend seen in the year's grants was concern for job quality and job security for persons with low incomes.

Permanent Deacons — Twenty-five years and several months after Pope Paul VI restored the order of permanent deacon, there were about 10,000 of them and nearly 4,000 candidates for ordination in the United States. National Diaconate Day was observed June 20.

Hyde Amendment — The House of Representatives voted 255 to 178 June 30 to forbid federal funding of abortion except in cases of danger of maternal death, rape or incest. The amendment — to a fiscal 1994 funding bill for the departments of Education, Labor, Health and Human Services — was submitted by Rep.. William H. Natcher, D-Ky., but is popularly referred to as the Hyde Amendment, for Rep. Henry J. Hyde, R-Ill., who first proposed the funding ban in effect since 1977. The rape and incest provisions in the Natcher proposal made it slightly less restrictive than the original Hyde Amendment, which limited federal funding only to cases "where the life of the mother would be endangered if the fetus were carried to term." The National Committee for a Human Life Amendment, a Catholic pro-life group, said that only 89 abortions were funded by Medicaid in fiscal 1991. It was predicted that at least 300,000 abortions would be funded annually at a cost of $75 million if the Clinton budget were accepted.

Nuns Returning to Sudan — Maryknoll headquarters announced that four nuns expelled from Sudan in August, 1992, were returning to work with Sudanese refugees along the border with Uganda. They were Sisters: Ruth Greble of Philadelphia, Mary Ellen Manz of Long Island, Nancy Lyons and Marilyn Norris of California.

Meetings — Meetings during the month included those of:

● The Catholic Charismatic Leaders' Conference, June 4 to 6 in Steubenville, Ohio, attended by about 1,200.

● The National Council for Catholic Evangelization, June 9 to 12, in Tempe, Ariz., attended by Native Americans and others.

● The National Association of Pastoral Musicians, June 16 to 19, in St. Louis, attended by 3,800.

Briefs:

● Ukrainians from the New York area gathered at St. Patrick's Cathedral June 1 in remembrance of the Josef Stalin-made famine in which an estimated six million people died of starvation and famine-related diseases in 1932 and 1933.

● Archbishop William H. Keeler, president of the U.S. Catholic Conference, said in a June 10 letter to Israeli Foreign Minister Shimon Peres that the closure of Jerusalem, imposed Apr. 1, was an "unjustified burden on a large population for the offense of a few." He asked for lifting of the ban on access to Jerusalem by Palestinian residents of the Occupied Territories.

● Faced with debts nearing $270,000 and an unresolved lawsuit, Catholic Major Markets, which distributed national advertising to Catholic newspapers, announced its dissolution June 15.

● Bishops agreed June 17 to a plan to turn their Catholic Telecommunications Network of America into a major educational resource feeding directly to parishes throughout the country.

U.S. Supreme Court Decisions

● In Lamb's Chapel v. Center Moriches Union School District, the court reversed June 7 a ruling by the 3rd U.S. Circuit Court of Appeals, declaring that the school district was wrong in excluding the congregation of Lamb's Chapel from using public school meeting space to show a film series that addressed family problems from a religious perspective. Justice Byron White, writing for the court, said that, considering that the district permitted a wide variety of organizations to use school property after hours, "there would have been no realistic danger that the community would think that the district was endorsing religion or any particular creed, and any benefit to religion or to the church would have been no more than incidental." The ruling was unanimous.

● Also on June 7, the court let stand a ruling by the 5th U.S. Circuit Court of Appeals, permitting students in Texas, Mississippi and Louisiana to include prayers in graduation exercises, so long as they are organized and led by students.

● Municipal laws that effectively prohibit a single church from performing its religious rituals are unconstitutional, declared the court unanimously June 11 in the case of Church of Lukumi Babalu Aye v. City of Hialeah. The ordinances at issue amounted to a "religious gerrymander" that singled out one religion, Santeria. The case arose from the efforts of the Hialeah City Council to restrict the congregation's ritual animal sacrifices. Writing for the court, Justice Anthony Kennedy said the laws were contrary to principles allowing free exercise of religion because they were not neutral or generally applicable.

● In Zobrest v. Catalina Foothills School District, the court ruled 5 to 4 June 18 that a public school district may provide a sign-language interpreter for a deaf student attending a Catholic school without violating constitutional separation of church and state. Chief Justice William Rehnquist, writing for the court, said no government funds ever find their way into the coffers of a sectarian school in such a case. "Handicapped children, not sectarian schools, are the primary beneficiaries of the Disabilities Education Act; to the extent sectarian schools benefit at all from (the act), they are only incidental beneficiaries."

INTERNATIONAL

Mass at Site of Massacre —Archbishop Tadeusz Kondrusiewicz, apostolic administrator of Moscow, celebrated Mass late in May in the Katyn forest where more than 5,000 Polish Army officers were massacred by Soviet paramilitary police in April, 1940. The Mass, according to a delayed report, followed a series of Catholic-Orthodox services in Katyn. The Soviet Union finally admitted responsibility for the wartime killings after previously blaming German invaders.

Not the Time for a Party — Less than a week before national elections, the head of the Spanish Bishops' Conference said it was not the time for Spanish Catholics to unite around a political party. For historical reasons, this would be interpreted as a desire to return to the situation under dictator Francisco Franco, when Catholicism was the state religion. "We would open the door to numerous polemics, which certainly would not favor the mission of the Church in our society," said Archbishop Elias Yanes of Zaragoza in a June 1 newspaper interview.

Pornography — Pornography in the United States has seriously undermined moral values and was becoming a major export to former communist countries, said Dean Kaplan June 2 at a Vatican-sponsored conference. The official of the Religious

Alliance against Pornography said U.S. pornography was "an $8 billion to $10 billion per-year industry reaching virtually every neighborhood and every home through magazines, videos, computers and even the telephone." Speaking at the conference on "The Rights of the Family and the Communications Media," Kaplan expressed "sadness" at the influence of U.S. media on the "degradation of families and children around the world."

New Bishops in Troubled See — It was hoped that the appointment of two new auxiliary bishops would, in the words of the Pope, help to "re-establish full communion" in the strife-torn Diocese of Chur, Switzerland. Bishop Wolfgang Haas was at the center of controversy since the time of his appointment in May, 1990. The new auxiliary bishops were Peter Henrici, dean of the theological faculty of Gregorian University, and Paul Vollmar, provincial of the Swiss Marianist Fathers.

Conditions in Bosnia — After visiting Bosnian Catholics May 28 to 31 in the Serb-controlled Diocese of Banja Luka, Cardinal Roger Etchegaray said he felt "humiliated" at Europe's inability to stop gross violations of ethical principles there. "I came back with a deep admiration for the faithful there, but also with extreme repugnance for the conditions under which they are obliged to live," he said on Vatican Radio June 3. Europeans should feel shame not only at the inability to bring peace but at "our weakness in dealing with the contempt for ethical principles, on which we claim to base our society."

Immigrants Are Scapegoats — Immigrants are becoming scapegoats of the economic problems of France, said Archbishop Jacques Delaporte, president of the bishops' Justice and Peace Commission, in criticism of a government-sponsored bill that would seriously limit immigration. "The Catholic Church wants to show its solidarity with immigrants, who are often the first affected by the current socio-economic difficulties," he said in an interview published in the June 3 edition of *La Croix*. On the same day, the government asked Parliament to approve a bill that would make it more difficult for foreigners to enter France, qualify for residency, marry French citizens, get permission to bring family members to France, and remain in France after illegal entry. The archbishop rejected criticisms that the bishops' position was disguised support for opposition parties, The stand was "not ideologically or politically colored," he said, but was simply in favor "of a part of the population in difficulty." There were about five million foreigners in France; many of them were from Third World countries.

Vocation of the Church in South Africa — This was the subject of remarks by Cardinal Jozef Tomko on his return to Rome from a visit to South Africa in May. "We have here a society with many wounds and much frustration, which will take time to heal. . . . The solution proposed by the Church is that of the Gospel: the reconciliation and pacification of this varied and complex society. The Church must now concentrate on the desire for more profound spirituality expressed by the laity, and she must steep her testimony in the evangelical radicalism of the Gospel counsels and beatitudes. This is her vocation. . . . The Gospel, also as a social program, is South Africa's only salvation."

Don't Market RU-486 in U.S — In a letter dated June 19, members and consultants of the U.S. bishops' Committee for Pro-Life Activities urged the German company that owns the abortion pill not to join an "immoral campaign" seeking to market RU-486 in the United States. The letter said in part: "Introducing such a drug into the unregulated American abortion industry would be the height of irresponsibility, even from the standpoint of women's health alone. . . . We urge you not to proceed with plans to license RU-486 as an abortion drug and to allow its manufacture and distribution in our country." The letter sharply criticized the U.S. Food and Drug Administration for its role in encouraging Roussel-Uclaf (a French subsidiary of Hoechst) to make an agreement with the New York-based Population Council.

Property Proposals — Bishops in the Czech Republic protested new government proposals to limit the restitution of church lands and other property confiscated under communist rule. They said their interest in the return of property was not to enrich the Church but "to make it possible to develop charitable and educational activities and the conservation of monuments."

Briefs:
• Catholics in eastern China's Diocese of Fuzhou celebrated the centenary of the beatification of five Spanish Dominicans martyred in 18th century crackdowns on foreign missionaries.

• Engaging in social action in India was difficult for Catholics because of pressure from Hindu fundamentalists who regarded it as an incentive to conversion, said Archbishop Raul N. Gonsalves of Goa in an interview in Spain.

• Russian scientist Dmitri Kouznetsov, at a related conference in Rome, estimated that the Shroud of Turin might be at least 1,900 years old. He said earlier estimates were wrong because of failure to consider variations found in linen and changes in the cloth after it was exposed to intense heat during a fire in 1532.

• A wave of Muslim fundamentalism in Egypt was making life dangerous for the minority Christian community, said Coptic Patriarch Stephanos II Ghattas of Alexandria in a Spanish newspaper interview June 12.

Bonds of Peace

This is the title of a program devised by bishops of the Church of England to keep within the Anglican Communion clergy opposed to the ordination of women to the priesthood. According to the plan, there would be no discrimination against opponents to the ordination of women, and "flying bishops" would provide pastoral care for them in different dioceses. It was thought in some quarters that the plan was ambiguous in that it would permit the ordination of men to the priesthood who disagreed with the stance of the church in favor of the ordination of women. The plan was on hold pending action by Parliament and the Queen with respect to the church's decision of Nov. 11, 1992, to permit the ordination of women to the priesthood.

JULY 1993

VATICAN

No Sign of Cancer — Test results indicated July 2 that Pope John Paul had no traces of cancer, nearly a year after he underwent surgery for removal of an intestinal tumor. "The results of the examination were absolutely normal. There is no trace of anything that would suggest a malignancy," said Vatican spokesman Joaquin Navarro-Valls.

Rights, Yes; Extreme Feminism, No —The Church must support the rights of women and seriously reflect on their role in the Church, but without compromising with an "extreme" and ideological form of feminism. So stated the Pope July 2 at a meeting with about 30 U.S. bishops making *ad limina* visits. "Respect for women's rights is without doubt an essential step toward a more just and mature society, and the Church cannot fail to make her own this worthy objective." The Pope was concerned, however, that in some circles there was dissatisfaction with the Church's position regarding women —especially among those who failed to distinguish between women's human and civil rights in society and ministries and functions in the Church. This could easily lead to "presenting false demands and raising false hopes. ... What is certain is that the questions cannot be resolved through a compromise with a feminism which polarizes along bitter, ideological lines. ... It is not simply that some people claim a right for women to be admitted to the ordained priesthood. In its extreme form" feminism involves the danger of undermining the Christian faith. The Pope said such types of feminism were sometimes marked by forms of "nature worship" and the celebration of myths and symbols in place of true Christian worship

Children as Missionaries — "Children can become missionaries to their peers and to others. With their simple honesty and their generosity, they can attract their small friends to the faith and create in adults the longing for a faith that is more impassioned and joyous," said the Pope in a message for the celebration of World Mission Day Oct. 17, 1993. He encouraged parents and others to emphasize the "missionary formation of children" as a pastoral goal in families, schools and parishes.

Pleas for Peace — The Pope issued another plea for peace in Somalia, July 2; urged a peaceful resolution of a secessionist dispute in Papua New Guinea, July 6; and delivered another impassioned appeal for an end to war in Bosnia-Herzegovina, July 21.

Family, Peace Day Theme — Pope John Paul, concerned at threats to family values throughout the world, chose the family as the theme of his message for the Jan. 1, 1994, observance of World Peace Day. It was reported that the message, entitled "The Family Creates the Peace of the Human Family," would explore the positive contributions of the family in transmitting basic values and moral formation to new generations. It would also examine how war and other social ills break down the family and its ability to help build a peaceful society. The Pope was convinced of the existence of an "intimate connection between peace and healthy family life," according to a Vatican statement. It was also noted that the current array of conflicts between nations and ethnic groups "in almost every corner of the world" raised serious questions about the role of the family in the contemporary world. Such conflicts were based on values opposed to the love and human dignity that should be instilled in the family milieu.

Visitor for Lebanese Migrants — The Pope named July 7 an apostolic visitor — Msgr. Joseph Khoury, a Maronite with years of Vatican experience — to help provide pastoral care to Lebanese who had migrated to European countries in recent years. The move reflected papal concern that Lebanese emigrants might be losing their pastoral traditions and ties to their native church community. It was estimated that 50,000 to 70,000 Lebanese had settled in France, with smaller numbers in England, Switzerland, Italy and Germany.

Somalia Raid a Massacre — *L'Osservatore Romano* said the U.S. helicopter gunship raid on leaders of a Somalia faction in Mogadishu was a "massacre" that compromised progress in negotiations toward peace in the embattled country. The July 12 assault on the command center for warlord Gen. Mohammed Farah Aidid killed 54 Somalis; afterwards, four foreign journalists were killed by angry Somalis. The newspaper said: "This latest bloody intervention by the Americans involved in the U.N. operation demonstrates, if it were necessary, that the original objective of the mission (to protect relief operations) has been abandoned or momentarily forgotten. ... The response by the U.S. forces is considered excessive. ... The massacre leaves a terrible mark on Somalia and on (the U.N. operation). The diehard supporters of Aidid and the fanatical crowds that the general has used against U.N. troops cannot be brought to reason by carnage." Vatican spokesman Joaquin Navarro-Valls said July 14 that the situation in Somalia was shifting from "the logic of assistance to the logic of provocation and escalation. And, where the logic of assistance is, no one knows."

Missionary Murdered — Pope John Paul condemned continuing acts of "unjustified violence" in Colombia, with special reference to the murder of Spanish missionary Father Javier Cirujano Arjona who had been kidnapped May 29 and was found dead July 16. He had been involved in efforts over a four-year period to negotiate the demobilization of leftist rebels in the country.

Poverty of Spirit — The faith calls on all Christians to live a "spirit of poverty" and maintain an attitude of detachment from earthly goods, said the Pope July 21. "The spirit of poverty is necessary for everyone, in every time and every place. To fall short of this, would be to betray the Gospel." Being faithful to this spirit, however, does not require "the practice of a radical poverty with the renunciation of all property, or even the abolition of this human right." The Church seeks to bring "moderation" to the understanding and practice of poverty.

Culture of Death — "The future of humanity very much depends on a vast alliance for life, and young people are called to be on the front lines of this demanding battle for civilization, which is also a battle for authentic progress." So stated the Pope July 25 as he also said: Particularly striking is the existing "tolerance for a culture of death, often presented as a civil conquest for new rights" which bring death to the unborn through abortion and to the sick through euthanasia. Against this background in which the meaning and sense of life remain obscured, often not even cases of suicide — many of which involve young adults or even adolescents and children — are news." It makes no sense to protect animal and plant life on the planet without first vigorously defending, "from the very first stages of existence, the human being, placed by God at the head of creation."

General Audience Topics:

● Those to whom the Lord gives the mission of being shepherds through priestly ordination are called to embody the heroic love of Jesus himself (July 7).

● In the life of celibacy the Church sees a sign of the priest's special consecration to Christ as one who has left everything to follow him (July 17).

● Like all followers of Christ, priests must cultivate an interior detachment from earthly goods and a generous openness to the needs of others (July 21).

● Priests do not have a political mission; Christ was not involved in worldly affairs (July 28).

Briefs:

● Frederic Ozanam, a French layman who founded the Society of St. Vincent de Paul in 1833, was declared Venerable by the Pope, who also acknowledged formally July 6 the heroic virtues of Dominican Father Samuel Mazzuchelli, a 19th century missionary to settlers and Native Americans in the Midwest.

● The Pope returned to Rome July 16 after 10 days of vacation in northern Italy.

● Raymond Flynn, the new U.S. ambassador to the Holy See, presented his credentials July 17 to Cardinal Angelo Sodano, secretary of state.

● The Pope visited July 28 two churches damaged by bombs, the Basilica of St. John Lateran and the Church of St. George in Velabro. A Vatican source said: "The Holy See does not consider the bombings to be an act against the Church, but sees them in the framework of the political destabilization under way in Italy."

Lefebvre Followers Adamant

Five years after the late dissident Archbishop Marcel Lefebvre led them into schism, his followers remained adamant in refusing to be reconciled with the Church. Despite an aggressive program of pre-Vatican II liturgical permissions and other overtures, Vatican personnel said that only a handful of priests and few lay persons had returned to the Church, and the movement was continuing to grow.

Archbishop Lefebvre, former head of the Archdiocese of Dakar, Senegal, refused to accept key enactments of the Second Vatican Council, particularly with respect to liturgical reform, religious liberty and ecumenism. He was suspended from the exercise of holy orders in July, 1976, after ordaining 13 priests without authorization. He was excommunicated following the irregular ordination of four bishops in 1988 and remained recalcitrant thereafter to the time of his death, Mar. 25, 1991. He left behind an organization claiming a million members

(500,000 according to Vatican estimates), 250 or more priests and about as many seminarians. In 1993, the movement remained strong in French-, English- and German-speaking countries. Its biggest base was France, where it had about 500 pastoral centers and 20 schools. There were numerous installations in the United States. Lefebvrist priests belong to the Priestly Society of St. Pius X, headed by Father Franz Schmidberger since 1983.

NATIONAL

Excommunication Overturned — Bishop Joseph A. Ferrario of Honolulu announced July 2 that the Congregation for the Doctrine of the Faith had overturned his excommunication of six dissident Catholics who had set up and operated an independent chapel, hosting worship services celebrated by schismatic clergy and publicly rejecting the bishop's authority. "In the judgment of the congregation," said Bishop Ferrario, "it was not sufficiently demonstrated that these individuals were schismatic according to the Church's strict definition of what formally constitutes this offense. At the same time, the congregation has stated that 'those same facts (about the groups' activities) referred to in the decree on the whole do not conform to the liturgical and canonical norms' of the Church. Likewise, the congregation has stated that the behavior of these persons has caused a 'grave nuisance, putting in danger the common good of the local church.'" Members of the group could be held liable to the penalty of interdict, which would bar them from receiving the sacraments even though it would not banish them from the Church as excommunicated persons.

Balkan Efforts Criticized — The senior director of Catholic Relief Services' Eurasian Region criticized the United Nations' peacemaking effort in former Yugoslavia and called for stronger interventionist moves to ensure "a viable Bosnia." David Holdridge said: "The whole tenor of the U.N. operation is no-risk safety. . . . I think it is in our best interests to intervene. Secure Bosnia by any means necessary." He said intervention was necessary "if you don't want a situation where you have two million people being polarized and radicalized, groups growing up in these camps. You've got the P.L.O. all over again."

Operation Rescue Campaign — Operation Rescue abortion protests got a mixed reception from Catholics in cities targeted for the "Cities of Refuge" campaign of July 9 to 18. The cities included Dallas, Philadelphia, Minneapolis and Cleveland. Operation Rescue's national headquarters reported that more than 10,500 people had officially registered to take part in protests, 593 protesters were arrested, and 39 pregnant women decided not to have abortions as a result of the protests.

Informed Consent before Abortion — The Michigan State Senate joined the House July 13 in passing a bill requiring informed consent and a 24-hour waiting period before abortions. Governor John Engler announced he would sign the bill into law. Michigan thus became the sixth state to enact such requirements; the others were Mississippi, Nebraska, North Dakota, Pennsylvania and Utah. The Pennsylvania and Utah laws were under court challenge.

Clinton Administration Out of Order — Bishop James T. McHugh of Camden blasted the Clinton administration for hosting a meeting June 25 at the White House with a coalition of dissident Catholic groups. It is wrong, he said, for government officials to give "even the appearance of taking sides in matters of church policy or doctrine." Writing in mid-July, he said the coalition, Catholic Organizations for Renewal, had among its members "organizations that are diametrically opposed to specific Catholic doctrines or moral teachings, often hostile and openly political in trying to undermine church teachings and policies. The organizations included CORPUS and the Women's Ordination Conference, both of which oppose church laws against married or female priests; Catholics for a Free Choice, which advocates abortion rights; and Catholics Speak Out, formed before the Pope's 1987 visit to the U.S. as a forum for organized opposition to various decisions and policies of the Vatican. The groups involved "seek to destroy the unity of the Church and engage in a misrepresentation of church positions," noted Bishop McHugh.

Flood Relief — Church agencies of all kinds were involved in efforts to forestall flood and to extend emergency relief to thousands of people in stricken areas of Minnesota, Wisconsin, Iowa, Illinois, Missouri and South Dakota. By July 19, six weeks of flooding in the Midwest had caused at least 30 deaths and $10 billion in damage, and had left some 16,000 square miles of farmland under water. The American Red Cross estimated that at least 22,000 homes were damaged or destroyed.

***Humanae Vitae* Conference** — Nearly 1,500 people attended the International *Humanae Vitae* Conference July 25 to 30 in Omaha, held under the sponsorship of the Pope Paul VI Institute for the Study of Human Reproduction. The conference marked the 25th anniversary of the Pope's encyclical letter "Of Human Life." (See separate entry.)

Black Catholics Meet — About 250 African-American Catholics gathered in Louisville July 25 to 31 to celebrate their blackness, Catholicity and contributions to the Church on the 25th anniversary of the founding of two black Catholic organizations. Several bishops and scores of priests, nuns, seminarians, permanent deacons and deacons' wives attended the joint conference of the National Black Catholic Clergy Caucus, the National Black Sisters' Conference and the National Black Catholic Seminarians' Association. As the clergy caucus and the sisters' conference celebrated their 25th anniversaries, a National Association of African-American Catholic Deacons was formed, with Frederick Mason of Chicago as president. Conference delegates represented various church ministries, including education, parish work, youth ministry, and inner-city outreach. Sister Amedee Maxwell, a Louisville native, said it was "a time to share the gifts that we have and also to hear the needs of the people; to make sure we are tuned to the needs of the people in various ministries."

In another event, the Junior Knights and Daughters of Peter Claver held a biennial convention July 8 to 11 in Kansas City, Mo. One attendant, Tenisha Kent, said of the gathering: "We are promoting our faith in God."

Meetings — Groups holding meetings during the month included:

● National Catholic Home Education Convention, July 2 to 3 in Manassas, Va., attended by more than 800 persons.

● North America Conference of Separated and Divorced Catholics, July 8 to 11 in Washington, attended by about 250.

● National Catholic Charismatic Renewal, July 9 to 11 in Seattle, attended by 2,500, and in Albuquerque, July 30 to Aug. 1.

● National Catholic HIV/AIDS Ministry Conference, July 22 to 27, at Loyola University, Chicago.

Briefs:

● Thirty-six Catholic high schools were among Blue Ribbon Schools recognized by the U.S. Department of Education .

● The Archdiocese of Boston donated a shipment of $500,000 worth of medicines and medical supplies to the poor, needy, elderly, children and mentally ill of Cuba.

● Knights of Columbus gave more than 41 million hours of community service and nearly $93 million to church, community and youth programs in 1992.

Military Policy on Homosexuals

President Clinton's policy on homosexuals in the armed forces, announced July 19, is compatible with Catholic teaching, stated Father Eugene T. Gomulka, deputy chaplain of the Marine Corps, July 20. "I'm pleased that the distinction is there between homosexual orientation and homosexual activity," he said. The "don't ask, don't tell, don't pursue" policy prohibits homosexual conduct by military personnel. It eliminates sexual orientation alone as grounds for separation from the military, "unless manifested by homosexual conduct. . . . Applicants will be informed of the conduct that is proscribed for members of the armed forces, including homosexual conduct." The announced policy was scheduled to take effect by presidential directive Oct. 1, 1993. President Clinton had sought a policy that would have validated the homosexual life-style and affirmed its compatibility with the exigencies of military life and discipline.

INTERNATIONAL

Don't Blame Islam — Blaming Islam for recent episodes of terrorism was wrong and risked damaging relations between Christians and Muslims. So stated Jesuit Father Thomas Michel head of the Muslim section of the Pontifical Council for Interreligious Dialogue. He said in an interview July 2 that people should realize that "there is no such thing as 'Islamic terrorism'" any more than acts of violence by Christians can be labeled "Christian terrorism."

British Bishops against Euthanasia —There should be no change in Britain's law against euthanasia, said Anglican and Roman Catholic bishops in a rare joint statement issued early in the month. Re-stating Christian belief that human life is a gift from God to be cherished, they said that patients should not be permitted by law to have doctors bring about their deaths. "Both churches," they said, "are resolutely opposed to the legislation of euthanasia, even though it may be put forward as a means of relieving suffering, shortening the anguish of families or friends, or saving scarce resources."

Bible Published in China — The first 50,000 copies of a Chinese-language Bible, part of a planned run of 200,000, was published by the government-approved Catholic organization. The event, which took place early in June, marked the first time the state-sanctioned church had published the entire Bible in Chinese. So stated Anthony Liu Bainian, a vice chairman of the Chinese Catholic Patriotic Association, according to a July 6 report by UCA News, an Asian news agency based in Thailand. The state-approved organization claimed a membership of 3.5 million.

New Auschwitz Happening — As the last Carmelite nuns vacated the convent outside the Auschwitz death camp, the superior stirred up another controversy by renting the building to a Polish nationalist group. Father Marek Glownia, who protested the nun's action, said: "On the one side, the so-called 'convent conflict' (with Jews over the location of the convent) is over. But the head sister has done something which, in my opinion, she had no right to do. I don't know what she was motivated by when she rented the building to the association. But the decision is particularly regrettable, given that this is a small political organization composed mostly of elderly people with an extreme nationalist character."

Concern about NAFTA — Mexican bishops continued to express concern that the North American Free Trade Agreement would ignore the poor as Mexico, Canada and the United States worked toward final agreement on the accord. NAFTA, among other things, would: eliminate tariffs on agricultural products and 10,000 different manufactured goods; phase out tariffs on North American-built automobiles; end limits on bank ownership among nationals of the three countries by the year 2000; allow Canadian and U.S. firms access to the Mexican energy production market; and ease immigration regulations on business executives and professionals.

Racist Attacks in Italy — Bishops of the Naples area criticized what they called race-motivated attacks on African immigrants, many of them seasonal farmworkers. "Racist posters and meetings, malicious burnings of non-European immigrant housing" and the burning of a trailer camp church officials wanted to turn into a residence for immigrants were the latest "tragic evidence" of prejudice, they said, in a July 15 statement. The statement was signed by Cardinal Michele Giordano of Naples and four other bishops. They said immigrants should not be made scapegoats for Italy's economic problems, which included a shortage of government funds for housing and public services. "The consequences of these crises cannot be dumped solely on the immigrants of color who, forced to live on the lower rungs of the social and housing ladder, have provided for years a decisive contribution to the development of agricultural activities."

Abortion Information Ban Upheld — Ireland's Supreme Court upheld July 20 a ruling preventing a clinic from giving women information on where to go to get abortions abroad. The court ruled 4 to 1 to keep the ban despite a 1992 referendum in which most people voted for making abortion information available in the Irish Republic and allowing women to travel abroad to terminate pregnancies.

Homosexuality — The Church's traditional rejection of homosexual acts but not of homosexual persons was reaffirmed by Cardinal George Basil Hume of Westminster in a statement published July 21. "The particular inclination of the homosexual person is not a sin. ... Being a homosexual person ... is neither morally good nor morally bad. It is homosexual acts that are morally wrong." The cardinal said that church teaching is based on two fundamental principles. (1) The sexual expression of love was intended by God to find its place exclusively within marriage between a man and a woman, and (2) this sexual expression of love must always be open to the possible transmission of new life. As a result, the Church cannot equate homosexual partnership with heterosexual marriage, nor condone homosexual acts.

Attack on Anglican Church — The Southern African Catholic Bishops' Conference expressed horror at an attack July 25 on an Anglican church in Cape Town in which at least 11 people were killed and 50 injured. "At a time when South Africa is moving, however painfully, toward a peaceful political settlement, there are those who appear hellbent on sowing division and devastation," the bishops said. "Even a house of worship is no longer a place of safety" in a country struggling toward democracy and the end of apartheid.

Briefs:

● Despite official restrictions, 7,000 Catholics from across China prayed at the grave of Bishop Peter Joseph Fan Xueyan of Baoding who died in police custody Apr. 13, 1992. The commemoration took place June 17, according to a delayed report from the newspaper of the Archdiocese of Taipei, Taiwan.

● The resignation of 75-year-old Bishop Pavo Zanic of Mostar and Duvo was accepted by Pope John Paul. The bishop had been critical and skeptical about the alleged apparitions at Medjugorje.

● Caritas and Catholic Relief Services are running 10-truck convoys of food and other supplies to beleaguered Banja Luka, Bosnia-Herzegovina.

● The Security Council recommended the admission of Andorra to the United Nations as the body's 184th member. The small state in the East Pyrenees between France and Spain was nominally headed by a Catholic bishop and the French president.

Disobey the Government

In a direct challenge to President Fidel Ramos, Cardinal Jaime Sin of Manila urged health workers to disobey government orders and not promote contraception. "We must obey God rather than men!" said the cardinal in the latest of a series of attacks on the government's population control program. The bishops' conference, in a statement released July 13, called the government policy "anti-life" and offensive to Catholic principles and ethics.

AUGUST 1993

VATICAN

More Appeals for Peace — As a cease-fire between Israelis and Arabs in southern Lebanon went into effect, the Pope appealed Aug. 1 to leaders on both sides to renounce violence and commit themselves to negotiations for peace. "Avoid provocation and reactions which, with their terrible logic of violence, could raise new and immense obstacles to the already very troubled peace process, the only real hope for the entire region."

On Aug. 22 the Holy Father called on warring factions in Angola to respect the peace agreement they had signed and stop the killing. "News from Angola, where violent battles continue, move me to unite myself with the recent message of the country's bishops who have denounced the tragic consequences of an absurd and inhumane war," he said Aug. 22. "With them, I turn to all the interested parties so that the population may finally live in peace and freedom." He appealed to all Angolans to "silence the weapons and meet together to seek paths to reconciliation. Open yourselves to talk with one another. Give one another a hand. Be children of the same people." The peace accord mentioned by the Pope was signed in 1991.

Commitment to Ecumenism — The Church's commitment to the quest for Christian unity was reaffirmed by Pope John Paul in a message addressed to the fifth World Conference on Faith and Order, sponsored by the Commission on Faith and Order of the World Council of Churches. Twenty-six Catholics were among the 120 persons attending the 10-day conference which began Aug. 3 in Santiago de Compostela, Spain. The central theme of the meeting was "Toward Communion in Faith, Life and Witness."

Youth Day Celebration — Pope John Paul visited Jamaica, Mexico and Denver on the 60th foreign trip of his pontificate Aug. 9 to 16. The climax of the trip was his celebration of World Youth Day with nearly 400,000 young people from 70 nations. (See separate entry.)

Foundation Grants — The Populorum Progressio Foundation, established by Pope John Paul in April, 1992, announced the allocation of $569,564 to 68 self-help projects designed by indigenous communities in 10 Latin American nations. The foundation was named after the title of Pope Paul VI's encyclical letter of 1967.

Protection of the Environment — The Pope asked scientists to spearhead a movement among their peers throughout the world to educate people about the need to protect the environment and to develop ways and means of safeguarding it. In a message to 60 scientists attending an Aug. 19-to-24 meeting in Erice, Italy, he said: "The enemy which threatens life and the progress of people today is called egoism, lack of love for one's neighbor, and a desire for power in every sector: economic, political and industrial." He called for "a profound change . . . in which the values of science, held in common with and not opposed to those of faith, become the supporting axis of civil, moral and material development, not just for some people but for all men and

women of the earth who, as brothers and sisters, must confront and resolve the problems of planetary emergencies."

Contacts with China — Spokesman Joaquin Navarro-Valls said Aug. 20 that the Vatican and China had an increasing number of unspecified "indirect contacts" aimed at improving relations.

Israeli-PLO Plan — Observers welcomed an Israeli-Palestine Liberation Organization plan for Palestinian self-rule in the occupied Gaza Strip and Jericho as a first step toward lasting peace in the Middle East. "The Holy See looks with satisfaction upon this concrete progress in the peace process, hoping that the whole process will advance on all fronts," said Joaquin Navarro-Valls Aug. 31. (See separate article.)

General Audience Topics:

● The priest's self-denial finds expression in what he does to preserve the communion existing between himself, the bishop and his fellow priests (Aug. 4).

● There was no general audience Aug. 11, with the Pope en route to Jamaica, Mexico and Denver. (See separate entry.)

● The Holy Father reflected on his just completed trip. (See above.)

Briefs:

● The Pope celebrated a Mass Aug. 6 marking the 15th anniversary of the death of Paul VI.

● The Vatican announced Aug. 11 the appointment of Bishop Nicolas Huynh Van Nghi of Phan Thiet as apostolic administrator for the pastoral care of nearly 500,000 Catholics in the Archdiocese of Ho Chi Minh City, Vietnam

● The Pope asked King Albert II, Belgium's new constitutional monarch, to continue his predecessor's policy of fostering unity among the nation's ethnic groups.

1991 Statistics

The *Statistical Yearbook of the Church: 1991* reported a worldwide total of 944 million Catholics, an increase of 16 million over the previous year's total. Catholics, members of the largest single religious body in the world, comprised 18 percent of the world population of almost 5.4 billion. Authors of the yearbook said the Catholic population probably included another five million persons living in China and other unreported areas. The yearbook reported:

● The five countries with the largest Catholic populations were: Brazil (135.2 million), Mexico (83.2 million), Italy (55.7 million), United States (almost 55 million) and The Philippines (52.3 million).

● Diocesan and religious-order priests numbered 404,031, an increase of 858 for the year.

● The numbers of women religious (875,332) and men religious (62,184) were less than those reported for the previous year.

● The number of permanent deacons increased to 18,408; more than half were in North America.

● 608 diocesan priests left the active ministry.

● The number of deacons ordained to the diocesan

priesthood was 6,482, an increase of 544 over the previous year

• Men enrolled in philosophy and theology courses in preparation for the priesthood numbered 99,668.

NATIONAL

Attacks Condemned — The chairman of the bishops' International Policy Committee condemned both Israeli attacks on civilians in southern Lebanon and guerrilla attacks on Israeli settlements. In an Aug. 3 letter Archbishop John R. Roach also called for a more active U.S. role in reviving Mideast peace talks and in rebuilding Lebanon. He noted that "scores of civilians were killed or wounded in the cross-border bombardments" and many villages were severely damaged in Israeli retaliation for attacks by guerrillas based in the region. As a result, Lebanon was "seriously impaired in its efforts to rebuild its society and regain its full integrity. . . . Random attacks by guerrilla groups like Hezbollah on Israeli settlements are terrorism and direct attacks by the Israeli Defense Force on 70 or more Lebanese villages are no less illegitimate. Both are to be condemned."

Respect Life Program — The program for Respect Life Sunday, Oct. 3, 1993, was reported to have a new look while retaining the same "countercultural" theme since it was launched in 1972. "Nowhere is our message more countercultural at this time in history than our belief in and commitment to safeguarding the value and dignity of every single human being — including those human beings waiting to be born that God has already called into existence." So stated Cardinal Roger M. Mahony, chairman of the bishops' Committee for Pro-Life Activities. The committee said in a statement: "Our goal, this year as ever, is to . . . support diocesan and parish leaders as they cooperate with the bishops in teaching the Church's beautiful message of respect for life."

World Youth Day — Hundreds of thousands of young people from 70 nations celebrated World Youth Day with Pope John Paul in Denver in the middle of the month. (See separate entry.)

No ABA Poll on Abortion — The American Bar Association defeated Aug. 10 a resolution that would have forced it to question all 370,000 members about whether they backed the organization's support of abortion rights. The House of Delegates, the ABA's policy-making body, rejected the resolution to hold such a referendum by a vote of 313 to 128. The ABA had flipped-flopped over the controversial issue, with the loss of some members. In February, 1990, the House of Delegates voted to oppose legislation that would regulate or restrict the practice of abortion. However, in August of that year the same body rescinded that vote and adopted a position of neutrality. Then, during the annual ABA meeting in August, 1992, the policy-making body reversed its stand on neutrality and returned to its original stance with passage of a resolution stating that the association opposed any restrictions of abortion rights. *The ABA Journal* reported that the association lost about 1.4 percent of its membership between its 1992 and 1993 billing years because of the economy and policy positions, including the 1992 vote in support of abortion rights.

Shooting Condemned — The shooting and wounding Aug. 19 of Dr. George Tiller outside his abortion clinic in Wichita, Kan., was sharply condemned by Helen M. Alvare, the planning and information director of the bishops' pro-life activities. She said: "There is no room for violence in the pro-life movement. We condemn the shooting of Dr. George Tiller (by Rachelle Shannon) in no uncertain terms. . . . We call on all who oppose abortion to act consistently with our beliefs about the respect owed to every human life."

Priest Suspended — Archbishop Oscar A. Lipscomb of Mobile suspended the priestly faculties of an archdiocesan priest who refused to stop calling the murder of abortionists justifiable homicide. He said in a statement Aug. 23 that he was removing Father David C. Trosch as administrator of St. John's Parish in Magnolia Springs, Ala., because of the priest's "continued public support of an erroneous teaching that the killing of abortionists is morally acceptable."

Post-Abortion Trauma — At least five million women in the United States had suffered severe post-abortion trauma, according to an article in *The Post-Abortion Review,* published by the Springfield (Ill.)-based Elliot Institute for Social Sciences Research. "Pro-choice groups continue to hide the fact that at least 20 percent of women suffer post-abortion psychological problems by describing this problem as occurring among only a 'minority' of women," said David Reardon, director of the institute. "While 20 percent of women is technically a 'minority,' it is heartless to dismiss the suffering and pain of five million women as insignificant." The institute was founded in 1987 to perform original research and education on the impact of abortion on women, men, siblings and society.

Parliament of the World's Religions — How members of the religions of the world should work together to help solve problems of the planet, was the focus of hundreds of events scheduled during the Parliament of the World's Religions which opened Aug. 28 in Chicago. The meeting of about 7,000 leaders and faithful representing 125 faiths was billed as "the greatest gathering of religious and spiritual leaders in history." A 5,000-word "Declaration of a Global Ethic," authored by Hans Kung, was proclaimed at concluding ceremonies Sept. 5.

Common Purpose Sought — President Clinton asked a group of religious leaders to help create a national sense of common purpose. "That does not mean that we have to minimize our diversity, pretend that we don't have deep convictions or run away from our honest disagreements," he said Aug.30. "It means that we must find a way to talk with respect with one another about those things with which we disagree and to find that emotional as well as the intellectual freedom to work together when we can." Among those attending the interfaith breakfast at the White House were four Catholic bishops, the president of the University of Notre Dame and administrators of half a dozen Catholic organizations. Clinton encouraged his guests to speak out about being motivated by faith. "Sometimes I think the environment in which we operate is entirely too secular," he said. "The fact that we have freedom of religion doesn't mean we need to have to try to have freedom from religion."

Meetings — Meetings during the month included those of:

• The Knights of Peter Claver and Ladies Auxiliary, July 31 to Aug. 5, in New Orleans, attended by 2,500.

• Knights of Columbus, Aug. 3 to 5 in Washington, 111th national convention, attended by 2,000 Knights and their families.

• Conference of Major Superiors of Men Religious, Aug. 4 to 7 in Buffalo; Sulpician Father Gerald L. Brown was installed as the new president.

• Leadership Conference of Women Religious, Aug. 14 to 18 in Dallas, attended by more than 800; Sister of Mercy Doris Gottemoeller was installed as the new president.

Briefs:

• Cardinal James A. Hickey presided at a field Mass attended by nearly 7,000 Catholic Boy Scouts and adult leaders at the worldwide Boy Scout Jamboree Aug 8. at Fort A.P. Hill, Va.

• The Catholic Communications Campaign announced Aug. 13 the awarding of $309,000 in grants to eight projects; the largest grant went to National Public Radio for "Wade in the Water," a series of 26 hour-long programs exploring African-American sacred music traditions.

• Amy and Angela Lakeberg, the Siamese twins separated Aug. 20 at Children's Hospital in Philadelphia, were baptized and confirmed before surgery. Amy died in surgery; Angela survived in critical but stable condition.

• About 3,000 people attended the dedication Aug. 22 of the Shrine of Mary, Queen of the Universe, near the Disney theme parks in Florida.

Media Missed the Point

Much of the national media missed the point of the World Youth Day celebration Aug. 12 to 15, according to a cross-section of editorials in Catholic newspapers. Principal criticism focused on the manner in which the celebration was treated in various quarters primarily as a news peg on which to hang, and headline, stale and well-rehearsed stories about dissension and problems of the Church, rather than the events, the message, the people and the spirit of the multi-faceted "Celebration of Life." *The Michigan Catholic* said in an editorial: "It seems that in their rush to denigrate Catholics, television, newspapers and magazines fell all over each other in running from the real story. For some reason, the media could not believe that a quarter million (actually more) Catholic young people from across the world would gather to publicly proclaim their faith. Through ignorance, laziness or prejudice," the media neglected" both the "world" and "youth" aspects of World Youth Day.

INTERNATIONAL

Vatican-Poland Concordat — A new concordat on church-state relations, signed by both parties July 28, was awaiting ratification by the Polish Parliament. Provisions of the agreement would establish the legal equality of church and civil marriages; guarantee the availability of religious education in state schools; and oblige the state to maintain subsidies for the Catholic University of Lublin and the Papal Theology Academy. Treatment of financial matters, including church taxation and property, remained subject to negotiation.

In another development, the bishops urged Catholics to remain loyal to the Church and to resist the country's continuing post-communist "invasion" by the forces of "moral liberalism." In a pastoral letter read in churches Aug. 8, they said: "Even though we have been liberated from the slavery of official atheism, many of our fellow countrymen are living as if God did not exist. We are being poisoned by camouflaged atheism, secularism and organized materialistic liberalism." They also said the Church was considering the best ways of achieving a "still more dynamic witness to the life of the Gospel," and of being "more present in the life of the nation."

Conditions in Bosnia — According to reports from Bosnia:

• In Sarajevo, 350,000 of the archdiocese's 500,000 Catholics had been forced to leave and 100 of the 144 parishes had been occupied by armed forces or destroyed.

• Catholics and Orthodox remaining in Sarajevo were facing increasing discrimination and loss of rights. The same was true of Catholic Croats living in zones of Bosnia controlled by Muslims.

• Several Catholic churches were being used as mosques in Muslim-controlled areas, while others were being ransacked and desecrated.

• Archbishop Francesco Monterisi, Vatican nuncio, said the Pope would increase his efforts for peace. He added that he himself did not have any "illusions" about the extent of church influence for peace.

False Charge — A Sri Lanka bishop rebutted allegations by a prominent Buddhist lay leader that the Church had a secret plot to convert the nation's Buddhists to Catholicism by the year 2000. Auxiliary Bishop Albert Patabendige said the "plot" dealt with deepening the spiritual commitment of priests, not the conversion of Buddhists.

U.S. Troops in El Salvador — Archbishop Arturo Rivera Damas said Aug. 15 that the presence of U.S. troops to participate in joint exercises was a violation of the nation's constitution. Some leading Salvadoran lawyers agreed with him, and some called presence of the troops an affront to national independence. The archbishop said legislators "overstretched the letter and spirit" of the Constitution, which allowed the Assembly to permit foreign soldiers in the country only "in transit."

Filipino Bishops Refuse Dialogue — The nation's bishops refused to participate in a dialogue on the government's population control program, which Cardinal Jaime Sin had already branded as the result of U.S. "demographic imperialism." The bishops "decided to postpone the dialogue to some future date when the time is opportune and the climate favorable," said Bishop Nestor Carino, secretary general of the episcopal conference. Auxiliary Bishop Teodoro Bacani of Manila said Aug.12 that the "government's pushing for artificial birth control is a manifestation of imperialism."

Ukrainian Wounds Are Healing — The Ukrainian Catholic Church's wounds suffered during five decades of illegal existence under communist rule were gradually healing, said Cardinal Myroslav Lubachivsky during a visit to Rome during the month. High-level, informal contacts had begun with the Russian Orthodox to ease tensions, and the more than four million former underground Catholics were becoming integrated into normal church structures, he said. Church-state relations were generally good, although there were still some problems with ex-communist government officials.

Massacre Condemned — The massacre of between 40 and 73 Yanomami Indians in remote Brazil was strongly condemned by the nation's bishops. Archbishop Luciano Mendes de Almeida, president of the episcopal conference, said in a newspaper interview: "The Yanomami people have been subjected to constant attacks by woodcutters and prospectors, and they are unable to stand up to the invasion (of their supposedly protected land), which is driven by profit and contravenes the Constitution." Cardinal Paulo Evaristo Arns of Sao Paulo said: "I regret such a horrifying and inhuman incident where armed people have destroyed the lives of innocent people. I hope justice is applied most vigorously in the case."

Recent violence in Brazil also exacted a toll of death for 21 slum dwellers and an increasing number of street children.

Catholic-Lutheran Relations — Catholic-Lutheran dialogue in Scandinavia was ready to tackle two of the most difficult theological questions related to Christian unity: ministry and the meaning of church. So stated Cardinal Edward I. Cassidy, president of the Pontifical Council for Promoting Christian Unity, during celebrations of the 400th anniversary of the Lutheran Church of Sweden. "Today we can say that, during the last 25 years of dialogue, Lutherans and Catholics have come so close together that we are able to declare the final goal of our ecumenical endeavor as being nothing less than full visible unity," he said in an Aug. 21 presentation in Uppsala. "I am well aware, of course, that this goal is not just around the corner," he added.

Hope in Middle East — Christians and Muslims in the Holy Land shared the same sufferings, but they had renewed hope that negotiations under way would bring about a just peace, said Latin-rite Patriarch Michel Sabbah Aug. 26. Everyone involved in the peace talks seemed to be committed to finding solutions to the issues dividing Arabs and Israelis, he said. "There is great hope. It is the first time that one can perceive such a seriousness of intentions and, I believe, concrete results will be seen soon." He noted that one of the stickiest problems would be the future of the city of Jerusalem and its political and religious identity. The patriarch's views were reported in the Italian newspaper *Avvenire.*

Canadian Bishops — Canadian bishops celebrated the 50th anniversary of their conference during their plenary assembly Aug. 26 to 31 in Ottawa. The bishops discussed pastoral implications of the new *Catechism of the Catholic Church,* along with pastoral priorities in response to the nation's native peoples, health care, agriculture, and preparations for the 1994 assembly of the Synod of Bishops on consecrated life. They elected Bishop Jean-Guy Hamelin of Rouyn-Noranda, Quebec, to succeed Archbishop Marcel Gervais of Ottawa as president of the Canadian Conference of Catholic Bishops.

Mother Teresa Better — Mother Teresa of Calcutta was released from a New Delhi hospital Aug. 27 after suffering from malaria complicated by a heart condition.

Russian Restrictions Eased — After a veto by Russian President Boris Yeltsin and criticisms from world religious leaders, Russian lawmakers toned down restrictions on foreign missionaries and foreign-based religious organizations. A new bill approved by the legislature Aug. 27 removed controversial provisions that would have required foreign-based churches to become affiliated with a Russian church or seek state accreditation. Among critics of the previous bill was Archbishop Tadeusz Kondrusiewicz, apostolic administrator for Catholics in European Russia. The U.S. Catholic Conference had also objected to the former bill.

Muslims Buying Land — A Lebanese bishop warned that his country was being "Islamicized" through land purchases by powerful Muslim groups and the exclusion of Christians from positions in government. "This phenomenon represents a threat to Lebanon, where there has always been coexistence between religious communities," Bishop Bechara Rai of Jbeil said on Vatican Radio Aug. 30.

Briefs:

● The growth of non-Catholic churches, especially evangelical and Pentecostal congregations, among Indians in southeastern Mexico was of special concern to the Church.

● A survey conducted at the Albanian University of Tirana and Shkoder found that about 70 percent of the students said they believed in God. It was said to be a significant finding in the former officially declared atheistic nation.

● Despite isolated attacks, the religious freedom of the Christian minority in Egypt was protected, said Coptic Patriarch Stephanos II Ghattas of Alexandria on Vatican Radio Aug. 28.

Faith and Order Conference

The most diverse and comprehensive gathering in the history of the Faith and Order movement ended Aug. 14 with a renewed commitment to moving toward Christian unity at all levels. "We say to the churches: There is no turning back," said the concluding message of the Fifth World Conference of Faith and Order. The churches cannot turn back, it added, "either from the goal of visible unity or from the single ecumenical movement that unites concern for the unity of the church and concern for engagement in the struggles of the world." The conference was the first of its kind in 30 years and the first ever to include an official Roman Catholic delegation. It was held Aug. 3 to 14 at the ancient Catholic pilgrimage site of Santiago de Compostela, where St. James the Apostle is believed buried. The theme of the meeting, sponsored by the World Council of Churches, was "Toward *Koinonia* (Communion) in Faith, Life and Witness."

SEPTEMBER 1993

PAPAL VISIT TO LITHUANIA, LATVIA AND ESTONIA

(Based on articles by Agostino Bono, CNS Correspondent.)

During his first trip to countries that had been member republics of the Union of Soviet Socialist Republics until they declared independence in the 1990-91 period, Pope John Paul offered advice to the winners and losers of the Cold War.

Winners must be forgiving and losers ready to accept social realities, he said.

The Pope expressed joy at being able to make the Sept. 4-to-10 visit to Lithuania, Latvia and Estonia at "an epoch-making turning point" as the Baltic republics were undergoing transition to democracy.

In Lithuania

He quickly established the themes in his first stop in Lithuania, the only republic of the former Soviet Union where Catholicism was the historically dominant religion.

Repeatedly, the Pope warned that the switch to democracy is not easy and needs Christian moral principles and social values to smooth the way.

Decades of atheistic education would make the Church's role difficult. People might have lost their esteem for religion.

With the defeat of communism, "there must be neither winners nor losers, but rather men and women who need to be helped to leave error behind," he told Lithuanian priests and religious Sept. 4.

"After every significant social upheaval, man bears scars both in patterns of behavior and in his soul," the Pope added.

At a Mass at Vingis Park in Vilnius, Sept. 5, the Pope appealed for peace between Lithuania and Russia, the largest and most dominant republic to emerge from the splintering of the Soviet Union.

Speaking in Russian after Mass, the Pope sent "special greetings to neighboring Russia" and offered prayers to "help Russia find peace both inside and outside her borders."

The same day, the Pope dealt with the thorny issue of the sizeable ethnic Russian population still living in the Baltic countries. Controversy was heavy as to whether they should be granted citizenship, especially the civilians who came as support personnel for the Soviet military and who now wished to stay.

The Pope noted the problem and the bad feelings tied to the Baltics' view of Soviet troops as occupation forces.

The Vatican "recognizes the aspirations of citizens of Russian origin who ask to be able to enjoy their human rights in their country of residence," the Pope told diplomats.

He asked for a "friendly understanding" among all parties and a rejection of the "spirit of revenge" and the "temptation to obtain by force that which can only be established in a lasting manner through good sense and negotiations."

In his talk to the diplomats, the Pope also encouraged democratic nations to provide economic and political aid to the Baltics to ease their transition from communist domination to democracy. Updating the clergy and the formation of lay persons, in line with enactments of the Second Vatican Council, are priorities if the Church is to help physically rebuild society and spiritually revive souls, he said.

At a youth rally Sept. 6 in Kaunas, the Pope urged young people to join lay movements as a way to curb the spread of sects. With the end of religious restrictions,, sects and new religious movements were growing throughout the Baltics, causing worry for the bishops.

On Sept. 7 the Pope celebrated Mass alongside the Hill of Crosses, a centuries-old pilgrimage site where Catholics for years engaged in a see-saw battle of symbols with communist authorities — putting up crosses during the night to replace the ones torn down by communists during the day.

In Latvia

Christians in Latvia must take advantage of an "ecumenical springtime" and base their efforts toward unity on their joint sufferings under communism, the Pope said on his first day in Latvia.

After sharing "the experience of the catacombs, you now want to continue to pray together," he said at an ecumenical meeting Sept. 8.

"The shared experience of the cross has contributed decisively to reinforcing the shared pursuit of values," including the "lofty value of Christian unity," he said.

St. Meinrad, the 12th-century bishop responsible for the region's early Christian evangelization, was a common thread in the Pope's ecumenical activities.

First, he visited St. James Catholic Cathedral to re-establish the public cult to St. Meinrad. Then he went a few blocks away to visit the saint's tomb at the Lutheran church which was the site of an ecumenical meeting.

Interfaith Relations

At the meeting, the Pope praised the different Christian churches "who live together in peace" in Latvia.

But elsewhere, he added, "century after century, groups of Christians refused to extend their hands in brotherhood to other groups of Christians."

What is needed is an "ecumenical spirit which rises above ancient divisions, often originating in a religiosity concerned more with temporal matters than with religious ones," he said.

"The more the permanent elements of faith are affirmed over accidental historical elements, the more the faith will become bright and attractive also for young people today," he said.

At the Catholic cathedral, the Pope prayed that St. Meinrad would "guide and sustain even today the ecumenical path of Latvian Christians.

In Riga Sept. 9, the Pope said that Catholic social doctrine should fill the void left by Marxism in the former Soviet Union. Now that intellectual freedom has been restored, scholars should study Catholic social thought as the paving stone of the future, he said at the University of Latvia.

The fall of Soviet communism "had something of the miraculous, in which it is not difficult to see the hand of God" who is "engaged in a constant and mysterious dialogue with human freedom," he said.

The Pope said that people must use their new freedom during this "sensitive period" to build societies which avoid the defects of Marxism and capitalism.

He praised the university's decision to open a Catholic theology department and said that Catholic social thought should stimulate "scholarly curiosity."

Social Teaching

Pope John Paul gave the first lesson in the social teaching of the Church.

Despite the Church's opposition to communism, "Catholic social doctrine is not a surrogate for capitalism," he said.

"The Church's social teaching is not a third way between capitalism and communism," he added. Nor is it a political or economic doctrine.

Its aim is to cast light on the "inevitable moral implications" of economics and politics, the Pope said.

"Its task is not to draw up a system but to indicate the impassable limits," he added.

"The Church's social teaching does not concern concrete organizational expressions of society but the inspirational principles which must give it direction," he said.

The Pope expressed hope that the University of Latvia might "become a crucible of cultural ecumenism to promote dialogue among believers and their encounter with people of good will."

All must seize the moment to ensure a better tomorrow. "None of us can foresee the future. But we do know that the world will be what we want it to be," he said.

In Estonia

In Tallin, Estonia, on the last day of the trip, the Pope visited two churches, took part in an ecumenical prayer service, met the president of the nation and played the role of host at a dinner for priests and sisters of the diocese.

He celebrated Mass before departing on the four-hour flight back to Rome.

NEWS BRIEFS

U.S. Leadership — U.S. leadership in addressing global problems must be based on moral values, including respect for life, said the Pope Sept. 2 as he received the credentials of Raymond Flynn, new U.S. ambassador to the Vatican.

Meeting with Japanese Emperor — Pope John Paul and Emperor Akihito, meeting Sept. 3, shared their hopes for world peace. The substance of the meeting was symbolized by the gift the 59-year-old Emperor presented to the Pope, a bronze sculpture of a dove with an inscription reading "Peace." At the end of the meeting the Pope said, "We must work together for friendship and peace among peoples." The Emperor answered, "It is absolutely necessary." Vatican spokesman Joaquin Navarro-Valls said of the meeting: "The Emperor paid homage to the Holy Father and to his high moral authority in the world, and expressed his thanks for the notable cultural, social and humanitarian contributions the Catholic Church makes in Japan and in other countries where it is present."

Seminary Visitations — The Congregation for Catholic Education announced Sept. 9 a series of visitations of seminaries in Canada, Britain and Ireland. The primary purpose of the visits was to be evaluation of their programs of study, spiritual formation and other factors involved in the training of candidates for the priesthood. Such evaluations had already been made of seminaries in the United States.

$7.3 Million in Hurricane Relief — Catholic organizations, individuals and religious communities donated more than $7.3 million to help the victims of 1992 Hurricane Andrew, according to Archbishop Edward A. McCarthy of Miami. U.S. dioceses gave the Miami Archdiocese close to $3.7 million, including $440,607 sent directly to Catholic Community Services, the Miami office charged with carrying out relief efforts.

Labor Day Message — Bishop John H. Ricard urged U.S. Catholics observing Labor Day to take up the challenge to recommit themselves "to the Catholic tradition of defending the dignity and rights of workers." He cited "labor priest" Msgr. George G. Higgins as "a symbol of what is best in our social justice tradition." Among quotations from the writings of Msgr. Higgins, the bishop pointed to those related to: his call to the labor movement to focus efforts on organizing low-paid female and immigrant workers; his critique of the "many upwardly mobile Catholics" who had abandoned the worker solidarity ideals of their parents; and his blunt criticism of Catholic institutions that obstructed organizing by their own workers.

Pro-Abortion Surgeon General — The U.S. Senate confirmed Dr. Jocelyn Elders as surgeon general by a 65-to-34 vote Sept. 7 despite efforts by several Catholic and Protestant groups to derail her nomination. At a Sept. 2 news conference called by the Catholic League for Religious and Civil Rights, the religious organizations said Dr. Elders' public remarks belittling the Catholic Church and Christians who oppose abortion should disqualify her from holding public office. Cardinal Anthony J. Bevilacqua called her comments about the Church "clearly insulting, intolerant and inflammatory." Her apology in a letter to Archbishop William H. Keeler, president of the bishops' conference, was called inadequate and "half-hearted." The archbishop had written to President Clinton in July objecting to Ms. Elders' "contemptuous" depiction of Catholic opposition to abortion as coming from "a celibate and male-dominated Church." He also protested her assertions that abortion opponents are unconcerned about life outside the womb — a blatant disregard of the Church's record of social service. Ms. Elders' pro-abortion stance was well known.

POPE JOHN PAUL II

(See many related entries under John Paul II in the Index.)

Cardinal Archbishop Karol Wojtyla of Krakow was elected Bishop of Rome Oct. 16, 1978, on the seventh or eighth ballot cast on the second day of voting at a conclave of 111 cardinals. He chose the name John Paul II and was invested with the pallium, the symbol of his papal office, Oct. 22 in ceremonies attended by more than 250,000 persons in St. Peter's Square.

The 263rd successor of St. Peter as Bishop of Rome and Supreme Pastor of the Universal Church, he is the first non-Italian Pope since Adrian VI (1522-23), the first Polish Pope in the history of the Church, and the youngest at the time of his election since Pius IX (1846-78).

Early Career

Karol Wojtyla was born May 18, 1920, in Wadowice, Poland.

He began higher studies at the age of 18, with major interests in poetry and theater arts. Forced to suspend university courses because of the outbreak of World War II, he went to work in a stone quarry and a chemical plant, thereby earning the later designation of himself as the "Worker Cardinal."

He started studies for the priesthood in 1942 in the underground seminary of Krakow, whose operations had been banned after the Nazi invasion of Poland.

Ordained to the priesthood Nov. 1, 1946, he was immediately sent to Rome for studies at the Angelicum University, where he earned a doctorate in ethics.

Back home in Poland, he worked as an assistant pastor in a village parish and as a chaplain to university students while continuing studies at the Catholic University of Lublin. He was awarded another doctorate there, in moral theology.

He began writing about this time, and eventually produced more than 100 articles and several books on ethical and other themes. Phenomenology was one of his fields of expertise.

University teaching came next, in 1953, with appointment in 1954 to the position of lecturer and later to the chair of ethics at the Catholic University of Lublin, the most prestigious institute of higher learning in Poland.

Bishop and Cardinal

He was ordained Auxiliary Bishop of Krakow Sept. 28, 1958, became Vicar Capitular in 1962 after the death of Apostolic Administrator Eugeniusz Baziak, and was appointed Archbishop Jan. 13, 1964. He was the first residential head of the see since the death of Cardinal Adam Sapieha in 1951. Between then and 1964 the archdiocese was run by administrators because the communist government refused to permit the appointment and ministry of a residential bishop.

Archbishop Wojtyla attended all sessions of the Second Vatican Council from 1962 to 1965, and was one of the writers of the *Pastoral Constitution on the Church in the Modern World.* He also contributed input to the *Declaration on Religious*

Freedom and the *Decree on the Instruments of Social Communication.*

His efforts to put into effect the directives of the council induced him to write a book, *Foundations of Renewal,* in 1972 and to start that same year an archdiocesan synod he saw concluded as Pope during his visit to Poland in 1979.

He was inducted into the College of Cardinals June 26, 1967, as one of the younger members, and subsequently served actively in the Congregation for the Sacraments and Divine Worship, the Congregation for the Clergy, and the Congregation for Catholic Education.

He served as a theological consultant to Pope Paul VI, attended assemblies of the Synod of Bishops as a representative of the Polish Bishops' Conference, and was a member of the Synod's permanent council.

From the beginning of his priestly career, and especially during his episcopate, the Cardinal was vigorous in the defense of human and religious rights, the rights of workers, and rights to religious education.

Close to Cardinal Wyszynski and in company with his fellow bishops, he negotiated the tightrope of Catholic survival in a country under communist control. With them, and as their spokesman at times, he was stalwart in resisting efforts of the regime to impose atheism, materialism and secularism on the people and culture of Poland.

Active Pope

Since the beginning of his pontificate, John Paul has been active as Bishop of Rome, with frequent visits to parishes and institutions of the diocese for the celebration of Mass and participation in other events. During these visits, as well as others to places of pilgrimage and historic significance in Italy, he has had perhaps more personal contact with the faithful than any other pope. The number of attendants at weekly general audiences at the Vatican and Castel Gandolfo has been unprecedented.

Extensive Travels

At the time of writing (Sept. 15, 1993) the Pope had made 61 pastoral trips to more than 100 foreign countries since the start of his pontificate.

● 1979, four trips: Dominican Republic and Mexico, Jan 5 to Feb. 1; Poland, June 2 to 10; Ireland and the United States, Sept. 29 to Oct. 7; Turkey, Nov. 28 to 30.

● 1980, four trips: Africa (Zaire, Congo Republic, Kenya, Ghana, Upper Volta, Ivory Coast), May 2 to 12; France, May 30 to June 2; Brazil (13 cities), June 30 to July 12; West Germany, Nov. 15 to 19.

● 1981, one trip: Philippines, Guam and Japan, with stopovers in Pakistan and Alaska, Feb. 16 to 27.

● 1982, seven trips: Africa (Nigeria, Benin, Gabon, Equatorial Guinea), Feb. 12 to 19; Portugal, May 12 to 15; Great Britain, May 28 to June 2; Argentina, June 11 and 12; Switzerland, June 15; San Marino, Aug. 29; Spain, Oct. 31 to Nov. 9.

● 1983, four trips: Central America (Costa Rica, Nicaragua, Panama, El Salvador, Guatemala, Belize, Honduras) and Haiti, Mar. 2 to 10; Poland, June 16 to 23; Lourdes, France, Aug. 14 and 15; Austria, Sept. 10 to 13.

• 1984, four trips: South Korea, Papua New Guinea, Solomon Islands, Thailand, May 2 to 12; Switzerland, June 12 to 17; Canada, Sept. 9 to 20; Spain, Dominican Republic and Puerto Rico, Oct. 10 to 12.

• 1985, four trips: Venezuela, Ecuador, Peru, Trinidad and Tobago, Jan. 26 to Feb. 6; Belgium, The Netherlands and Luxembourg, May 11 to 21; Africa (Togo, Ivory Coast, Cameroon, Central African Republic, Zaire, Kenya and Morocco), Aug. 8 to 19; Liechtenstein, Sept. 8.

• 1986, four trips: India, Feb. 1 to 10; Colombia and Saint Lucia, July 1 to 7; France, Oct. 4 to 7; Oceania (Australia, New Zealand, Bangladesh, Fiji, Singapore and Seychelles), Nov. 18 to Dec. 1.

• 1987, four trips: Uruguay, Chile and Argentina, Mar. 31 to Apr. 12; West Germany, Apr. 30 to May 4; Poland, June 8 to 14; the United States and Canada, Sept. 10 to 19.

• 1988, four trips: Uruguay, Bolivia, Peru and Paraguay, May 7 to 18; Austria, June 23 to 27; Africa (Zimbabwe, Botswana, Lesotho, Swaziland and Mozambique), Sept. 10 to 19; France, Oct. 8 to 11.

• 1989, four trips: Madagascar, Reunion, Zambia and Malawi, Apr. 28 to May 6; Norway, Ireland, Finland, Denmark and Sweden, June 1 to 10; Spain, Aug. 19 to 21; South Korea, Indonesia, East Timor and Mauritius, Oct. 6 to 16.

• 1990, five trips: Africa (Cape Verde, Guinea Bissau, Mali and Burkina Faso), Jan. 25 to Feb. 1; Czechoslovakia, Apr. 21 and 22; Mexico and Curacao, May 6 to 13; Malta, May 25 to 27; Africa (Tanzania, Burundi, Rwanda and Ivory Coast), Sept. 1 to 10.

• 1991, four trips: Portugal, May 10 to 13; Poland, June 1 to 9; Poland and Hungary, Aug. 13 to 20; Brazil, Oct. 12 to 21.

• 1992, three trips: Africa (Senegal, The Gambia, Guinea), Feb. 10 to 26; Africa (Angola, Sao Tome and Principe), June 4 to 10; Dominican Replublic, Oct. 10 to 14.

• 1993, five trips: Africa (Benin, Uganda, Sudan), Feb. 2 to 10; Albania, April 25; Spain, June 12 to 17; Jamaica, Mexico, Denver (U.S.), Aug. 9 to 15; Lithuania, Latvia, Estonia, Sept. 4 to 10.

Key Writings

Encyclicals: The homilies and addresses delivered by the Pope on these trips covered a wide variety of doctrinal, pastoral and social subjects, all related to the key document of the first year of his pontificate. That was the encyclical letter, *Redemptor Hominis* ("Redeemer of Man"), a treatise on Christian anthropology dealing with the divine and human aspects of redemption and the mission of the Church to carry on a dialogue of salvation with all peoples.

Two other encyclicals published within less than a year of each other were *Dives in Misericordia* ("On the Mercy of God") in 1980 and *Laborem Exercens* ("On Human Work") in 1981. *Slavorum Apostoli* in 1985 honored Sts. Cyril and Methodius, apostles of the Slavic peoples. *Dominum et Vivificantem* ("Lord and Giver of Life") was published in 1986. *Redemptoris Mater* ("Mother of the Redeemer") was published in 1987. The Pope's seventh encyclical, *Sollicitudo Rei Socialis* ("On Social Concerns")

was issued in 1988. Two encyclicals were issued in 1991, *Redemptoris Missio* ("Mission of the Redeemer") and *Centesimus Annus* ("The Hundredth Year").

Other Writings: The Pope published a lengthy exhortation on the family, *Familiaris Consortio* in December, 1981. Writings published in 1984 included two apostolic letters — on suffering, *Salvifici Doloris,* and on Jerusalem; an apostolic exhortation, *Redemptionis Donum,* addressed to and about Religious; a "Charter on the Rights of the Family," and an apostolic exhortation, "Reconciliation and Penance in the Ministry of the Church." In 1986, he issued an apostolic letter on the 1600th anniversary of the conversion of St. Augustine.

Two apostolic letters were published in 1988, on the millennium of Christianity in the Ukraine and the present territory of the Soviet Union.

Writings issued in 1989 included *Christifideles Laici,* an apostolic exhortation on the theme of the 1987 assembly of the Synod of Bishops, and an apostolic letter commemorating the 25th anniversary of Second Vatican Council's *Constitution on the Liturgy.*

In 1990, the Pope issued the first-ever papal statement exclusively on ecology, entitled "Peace with God and All of Creation."

Pastores Dabo Vobis ("I Will Give You Pastors") is the title of an apostolic exhortation issued in 1992; its subject is the formation of priests.

Various Items

Doctrinal Concern: In December, 1980, the Pope directly confronted the controversial writings of Father Hans Kung by giving his approval to a declaration by the Congregation for the Doctrine of the Faith that he could not be regarded as a Catholic theologian.

On Aug. 6, 1983, he authorized release by the Doctrinal Congregation of a letter to bishops throughout the world in refutation of unorthodox views — especially those of Father Edward Schillebeeckx, O.P., — concerning the minister of the Eucharist.

The Holy Father regarded as extremely important a series of talks begun at general audiences in the summer of 1984 on marriage and sexual morality, explaining and firmly supporting traditional doctrine, with emphasis on teaching contained in the encyclical letter, *Humanae Vitae,* by Pope Paul VI.

He approved instructions on liberation theology issued by the Congregation for the Doctrine of the Faith in 1984 and 1986.

He approved the 1986 declaration of the Congregation for the Doctrine of the Faith that U.S. theologian Father Charles E. Curran was not eligible to function as a Catholic theologian.

In 1988, the Pope decreed the excommunication of dissident Archbishop Marcel Lefebvre, the prime mover in the first schism from the Church in nearly 100 years.

He announced approval in May, 1992, of a catechism for the entire Church.

Canon Law: The Pope was deeply involved in the work of completing the revision of the Code of Canon Law, which he ordered into effect as of Nov. 27, 1983. He called it, in effect, the final act of the Second Vatican Council. He emphasized its innovative force in an address Jan. 26, 1984, to personnel of the Roman Rota.

He promulgated the Code of Canon Law for the Eastern Churches Apr. 18, 1990.

Causes of Saints: Pope John Paul has canonized well over 250 saints. (See Canonizations.)

Synods: The Holy Father convoked three of them in 1980.

With the Dutch bishops at the Vatican for a particular synod in January, he called for measures to cope with differences among the prelates and polarization among the people, along with action to remedy doctrinal and disciplinary irregularities. Later reports indicated that results of the synod were less than satisfactory.

Meeting with Ukrainian bishops in March, he named a successor to Cardinal Josyf Slipyi as the ranking bishop and turned down demands of some Ukrainians for a patriarchate.

With more than 200 delegates from episcopal conferences around the world, he held the fifth ordinary assembly of the Synod of Bishops.

He convoked another ordinary assembly of the Synod in 1983 and an extraordinary one that was held Nov. 25 to Dec. 8, 1985. The purpose of the 1985 assembly was to evaluate the effects and implementation of the enactments of the Second Vatican Council, on the occasion of the 20th anniversary of its conclusion. The theme of the 1987 assembly was the role and ministry of lay persons.

The Pope convoked the eighth ordinary assembly of the Synod Sept. 30, 1990, to deal with matters related to priestly formation, before and after ordination. (See Synod of Bishops.)

Since 1989, moves have been initiated for the convocation of particular synodal assemblies for Africa, Europe and Lebanon.

Holy Year: The Holy Father proclaimed a Jubilee celebration of the 1950th anniversary of the Redemption from the Solemnity of the Annunciation of the Lord, Mar. 25, 1983, to Easter Sunday, Apr. 22, 1984, and a Marian Year from Pentecost, 1987, to the Solemnity of the Ascension, 1988.

Cardinals: In June, 1979, the Pope inducted 14 new cardinals into the Sacred College, raising its membership to 135. A second group was inducted Feb. 3, 1983, at which time the total membership was 138. Twenty-eight new cardinals inducted May 25, 1985, brought membership to 152. Twenty-four were inducted in 1988. By late September, 1990, the total was 144. Twenty-two new cardinals were inducted in 1991, along with a cardinal whose name had been held in secret since 1979. There were 148 cardinals as of Sept. 15, 1993. (See College of Cardinals, Biographies of Cardinals.)

Meetings with Bishops: In relations with the hierarchy since becoming Pope, John Paul has met with groups of bishops making required, five-year *ad limina* visits to the Vatican, for first-hand reports and counseling regarding conditions in dioceses all over the world. He has also met with assemblies of bishops in countries he has visited. In 1989, there was a significant meeting of 35 U.S. archbishops with the Pope and 25 Curia officials for the discussion of major topics of pastoral concern.

Ecumenism: He met with Anglican Archbishop Robert Runcie at the Canterbury Cathedral during his visit to Great Britain in May, 1982. The prelates prayed together, renewed their baptismal promises, and issued a joint statement in which they announced the formation of a new joint Catholic-Anglican theological commission for a second round of interfaith dialogue. The Pope has also met with Anglican Archbishop George Carey.

Ever since the beginning of his pontificate, the Pope has maintained contact with Orthodox leaders and officials of other churches and religious bodies, and has encouraged interfaith relations at all levels.

While visiting the headquarters of the World Council of Churches in Geneva June 12, 1984, the Pope said the Church's engagement in the quest for religious unity is irreversible. At the same time, he mentioned two points of extreme significance in Catholic doctrine and practice.

The Church, he said, "entered on the hard ecumenical task, bringing with it a conviction" about the role of the bishop of Rome. "It is convinced that in the ministry of the bishop of Rome it has preserved the visible pole and guarantee of unity in full fidelity to the apostolic tradition and to the faith of the Fathers."

He also reiterated doctrinal opposition to sharing the Eucharist until full unity is achieved. "It is not yet possible for us to celebrate the Eucharist together and communicate at the same table," he said.

Nevertheless, he placed emphasis on things Christians have in common; among them, baptism, reverence for Scripture, prayer, a re-discovery of the "whole role of the Holy Spirit," and cooperation in work for social justice and human rights.

A significant interfaith event of 1986 was the papal visit to the Synagogue of Rome. It was one of a number of events indicative of the Pope's concern for sound relations with Jews.

Audiences and Addresses: The Pope has delivered hundreds of addresses at general and private audiences and on special occasions. All of them have characteristically been grounded in doctrinal essentials coupled with relevance to the people being addressed or the events being commemorated.

World Affairs: In 1984, the Pope agreed to a new concordat with Italy, regulating church-state relations. He agreed also to the establishment of diplomatic relations with the United States. In July, 1989, following years of negotiations, diplomatic relations were re-established with Poland. Relations have also been established with Eastern European countries and Mexico.

In 1991 the Pope repeatedly called for peace in the Middle East, Yugoslavia and other countries, and stressed the need for re-evangelization worldwide, but especially in Europe.

On his travels as well as at the Vatican the Pope has been an outstanding advocate for human rights and dignity, respect for life, peace, nuclear and conventional disarmament, reconciliation among nations, aid and relief for distressed peoples and nations; of people first and things second in all areas of life.

Near Tragedy: The Pope narrowly escaped death May 13, 1981, when he was fired upon at close range by Mehmet Ali Agca, as he entered St. Peter's Square to address a general audience.

DATES AND EVENTS IN CHURCH HISTORY

FIRST CENTURY

c. 33: First Christian Pentecost; descent of the Holy Spirit upon the disciples; preaching of St. Peter in Jerusalem; conversion, baptism and aggregation of some 3,000 persons to the first Christian community.

St. Stephen, deacon, was stoned to death at Jerusalem; he is venerated as the first Christian martyr.

c. 34: St. Paul, formerly Saul the persecutor of Christians, was converted and baptized. After three years of solitude in the desert, he joined the college of the apostles; he made three major missionary journeys and became known as the Apostle to the Gentiles; he was imprisoned twice in Rome and was beheaded there between 64 and 67.

39: Cornelius (the Gentile) and his family were baptized by St. Peter; a significant event signalling the mission of the Church to all peoples.

42: Persecution of Christians in Palestine broke out during the rule of Herod Agrippa; St. James the Greater, the first apostle to die, was beheaded in 44; St. Peter was imprisoned for a short time; many Christians fled to Antioch, marking the beginning of the dispersion of Christians beyond the confines of Palestine. At Antioch, the followers of Christ were called Christians for the first time.

49: Christians at Rome, considered members of a Jewish sect, were adversely affected by a decree of Claudius which forbade Jewish worship there.

51: The Council of Jerusalem, in which all the apostles participated under the presidency of St. Peter, decreed that circumcision, dietary regulations, and various other prescriptions of Mosaic Law were not obligatory for Gentile converts to the Christian community. The crucial decree was issued in opposition to Judaizers who contended that observance of the Mosaic Law in its entirety was necessary for salvation.

64: Persecution broke out at Rome under Nero, the emperor said to have accused Christians of starting the fire which destroyed half of Rome.

64 or 67: Martyrdom of St. Peter at Rome during the Neronian persecution. He established his see and spent his last years there after preaching in and around Jerusalem, establishing a see at Antioch, and presiding at the Council of Jerusalem.

70: Destruction of Jerusalem by Titus.

88-97: Pontificate of St. Clement I, third successor of St. Peter as bishop of Rome, one of the Apostolic Fathers. The *First Epistle of Clement to the Corinthians*, with which he has been identified, was addressed by the Church of Rome to the Church at Corinth, the scene of irregularities and divisions in the Christian community.

95: Domitian persecuted Christians, principally at Rome.

c. 100: Death of St. John, apostle and evangelist, marking the end of the Age of the Apostles and the first generation of the Church.

By the end of the century, Antioch, Alexandria and Ephesus in the East and Rome in the West were established centers of Christian population and influence.

SECOND CENTURY

c. 107: St. Ignatius of Antioch was martyred at Rome. He was the first writer to use the expression, "the Catholic Church."

112: Emperor Trajan, in a rescript to Pliny the Younger, governor of Bithynia, instructed him not to search out Christians but to punish them if they were publicly denounced and refused to do homage to the Roman gods. This rescript set a pattern for Roman magistrates in dealing with Christians.

117-38: Persecution under Hadrian. Many *Acts of Martyrs* date from this period.

c. 125: Spread of Gnosticism, a combination of elements of Platonic philosophy and Eastern mystery religions. Its adherents claimed that its secret-knowledge principle provided a deeper insight into Christian doctrine than divine revelation and faith. One gnostic thesis denied the divinity of Christ; others denied the reality of his humanity, calling it mere appearance (Docetism, Phantasiasm).

c. 144: Excommunication of Marcion, bishop and heretic, who claimed that there was total opposition and no connection at all between the Old Testament and the New Testament, between the God of the Jews and the God of the Christians; and that the Canon (list of inspired writings) of the Bible consisted only of parts of St. Luke's Gospel and 10 letters of St. Paul. Marcionism was checked at Rome by 200 and was condemned by a council held there about 260, but the heresy persisted for several centuries in the East and had some adherents as late as the Middle Ages.

c. 155: St. Polycarp, bishop of Smyrna and disciple of St. John the Evangelist, was martyred.

c. 156: Beginning of Montanism, a form of religious extremism. Its principal tenets were the imminent second coming of Christ, denial of the divine nature of the Church and its power to forgive sin, and excessively rigorous morality. The heresy, preached by Montanus of Phrygia and others, was condemned by Pope St. Zephyrinus (199-217).

161-80: Reign of Marcus Aurelius. His persecution, launched in the wake of natural disasters, was more violent than those of his predecessors.

165: St. Justin, an important early Christian writer, was martyred at Rome.

c. 180: St. Irenaeus, bishop of Lyons and one of the great early theologians, wrote *Adversus Haereses*. He stated that the teaching and tradition of the Roman See was the standard for belief.

196: Easter Controversy, concerning the day of celebration — a Sunday, according to practice in the West, or the 14th of the month of Nisan (in the Hebrew calendar), no matter what day of the week, according to practice in the East. The controversy was not resolved at this time.

The *Didache*, whose extant form dates from the second century, is an important record of Christian belief, practice and governance in the first century.

Latin was introduced as a liturgical language in the West. Other liturgical languages were Aramaic and Greek.

The Catechetical School of Alexandria, founded about the middle of the century, gained increasing influence on doctrinal study and instruction, and interpretation of the Bible.

THIRD CENTURY

202: Persecution under Septimius Severus, who wanted to establish a simple common religion in the Empire.

206: Tertullian, a convert since 197 and the first great ecclesiastical writer in Latin, joined the heretical Montanists; he died in 230.

215: Death of Clement of Alexandria, teacher of Origen and a founding father of the School of Alexandria.

217-35: St. Hippolytus, the first antipope; he was reconciled to the Church while in prison during persecution in 235.

232-54: Origen established the School of Caesarea after being deposed in 231 as head of the School of Alexandria; he died in 254. A scholar and voluminous writer, he was one of the founders of systematic theology and exerted wide influence for many years.

c. 242: Manichaeism originated in Persia: a combination of errors based on the assumption that two supreme principles (good and evil) are operative in creation and life, and that the supreme objective of human endeavor is liberation from evil (matter). The heresy denied the humanity of Christ, the sacramental system, the authority of the Church (and state), and endorsed a moral code which threatened the fabric of society. In the 12th and 13th centuries, it took on the features of Albigensianism and Catharism.

249-51: Persecution under Decius. Many of those who denied the faith *(lapsi)* sought readmission to the Church at the end of the persecution in 251. Pope St. Cornelius agreed with St. Cyprian that *lapsi* were to be readmitted to the Church after satisfying the requirements of appropriate penance. Antipope Novatian, on the other hand, contended that persons who fell away from the Church under persecution and/or those guilty of serious sin after baptism could not be absolved and readmitted to communion with the Church. The heresy was condemned by a Roman synod in 251.

250-300: Neo-Platonism of Plotinus and Porphyry gained followers.

251: Novatian, an antipope, was condemned at Rome.

256: Pope St. Stephen I upheld the validity of baptism properly administered by heretics, in the Rebaptism Controversy.

257: Persecution under Valerian, who attempted to destroy the Church as a social structure.

258: St. Cyprian, bishop of Carthage, was martyred.

c. 260: St. Lucian founded the School of Antioch, a center of influence on biblical studies.

Pope St. Dionysius condemned Sabellianism, a form of modalism (like Monarchianism and Patripassianism). The heresy contended that the Father, Son and Holy Spirit are not distinct divine persons but are only three different modes of being and self-manifestations of the one God.

St. Paul of Thebes became a hermit.

261: Gallienus issued an edict of toleration which ended general persecution for nearly 40 years.

c. 292: Diocletian divided the Roman Empire into East and West. The division emphasized political, cultural and other differences between the two parts of the Empire and influenced different developments in the Church in the East and West. The prestige of Rome began to decline.

FOURTH CENTURY

303: Persecution broke out under Diocletian; it was particularly violent in 304.

305: St. Anthony of Heracles established a foundation for hermits near the Red Sea in Egypt.

c. 306: The first local legislation on clerical celibacy was enacted by a council held at Elvira, Spain; bishops, priests, deacons and other ministers were forbidden to have wives.

311: An edict of toleration issued by Galerius at the urging of Constantine and Licinius officially ended persecution in the West; some persecution continued in the East.

313: The *Edict of Milan* issued by Constantine and Licinius recognized Christianity as a lawful religion in the Roman Empire.

314: A council of Arles condemned Donatism, declaring that baptism properly administered by heretics is valid, in view of the principle that sacraments have their efficacy from Christ, not from the spiritual condition of their human ministers. The heresy was condemned again by a council of Carthage in 411.

318: St. Pachomius established the first foundation of the cenobitic (common) life, as compared with the solitary life of hermits in Upper Egypt.

325: Ecumenical Council of Nicaea (I). Its principal action was the condemnation of Arianism, the most devastating of the early heresies, which denied the divinity of Christ. The heresy was authored by Arius of Alexandria, a priest. Arians and several kinds of Semi-Arians propagandized their tenets widely, established their own hierarchies and churches, and raised havoc in the Church for several centuries. The council contributed to formulation of the Nicene Creed (Creed of Nicaea-Constantinople); fixed the date for the observance of Easter; passed regulations concerning clerical discipline; adopted the civil divisions of the Empire as the model for the jurisdictional organization of the Church.

326: Discovery of the True Cross on which Christ was crucified.

337: Baptism and death of Constantine.

c. 342: Beginning of a 40-year persecution in Persia.

343-44: A council of Sardica reaffirmed doctrine formulated by Nicaea I and declared also that bishops had the right of appeal to the pope as the highest authority in the Church.

361-63: Emperor Julian the Apostate waged an unsuccessful campaign against the Church in an attempt to restore paganism as the religion of the Empire.

c. 365: Persecution under Valens in the East.

c. 376: Beginning of the barbarian invasion in the West.

379: Death of St. Basil, the Father of Monasticism in the East. His writings contributed greatly to the development of rules for the life of Religious.

381: Ecumenical Council of Constantinople (I). It condemned various brands of Arianism as well as Macedonianism, which denied the divinity of the Holy Spirit; contributed to formulation of the Nicene Creed; approved a canon acknowledging Constantinople as the second see after Rome in honor and dignity.

382: The Canon of Sacred Scripture, the official list of the inspired books of the Bible, was contained in the *Decree of Pope St. Damasus* and published by a regional council of Carthage in 397; the Canon was formally defined by the Council of Trent in the 16th century.

382-c. 406: St. Jerome translated the Old and New Testaments into Latin; his work is called the Vulgate version of the Bible.

396: St. Augustine became bishop of Hippo in North Africa.

FIFTH CENTURY

410: Visigoths sacked Rome.

430: St. Augustine, bishop of Hippo for 35 years, died. He was a strong defender of orthodox doctrine against Manichaeism, Donatism and Pelagianism. The depth and range of his writings made him a dominant influence in Christian thought for centuries.

431: Ecumenical Council of Ephesus. It condemned Nestorianism, which denied the unity of the divine and human natures in the Person of Christ; defined *Theotokos* (Bearer of God) as the title of Mary, Mother of the Son of God made Man; condemned Pelagianism. The heresy of Pelagianism, proceeding from the assumption that Adam had a natural right to supernatural life, held that man could attain salvation through the efforts of his natural powers and free will; it involved errors concerning the nature of original sin, the meaning of grace and other matters. Related Semi-Pelagianism was condemned by a council of Orange in 529.

432: St. Patrick arrived in Ireland. By the time of his death in 461 most of the country had been converted, monasteries founded and the hierarchy established.

438: The *Theodosian Code,* a compilation of decrees for the Empire, was issued by Theodosius II; it had great influence on subsequent civil and ecclesiastical law.

449: The Robber Council of Ephesus, which did not have ecclesiastical sanction, declared itself in favor of the opinions of Eutyches who contended that Christ had only one, the divine, nature (Monophysitism).

451: Ecumenical Council of Chalcedon. Its principal action was the condemnation of Monophysitism (also called Eutychianism), which denied the humanity of Christ by holding that he had only one, the divine, nature.

452: Pope St. Leo the Great persuaded Attila the Hun to spare Rome.

455: Vandals sacked Rome. The decline of imperial Rome dates approximately from this time.

484: Patriarch Acacius of Constantinople was excommunicated for signing the *Henoticon*, a document which capitulated to the Monophysite heresy. The excommunication triggered a schism which lasted for 35 years.

494: Pope St. Gelasius I declared in a letter to Emperor Anastasius that the pope had power and authority over the emperor in spiritual matters.

496: Clovis, King of the Franks, was converted and became the defender of Christianity in the West. The Franks became a Catholic people.

SIXTH CENTURY

520 on: Irish monasteries flourished as centers for spiritual life, missionary training and scholarly activity.

529: The Second Council of Orange condemned Semi-Pelagianism.

c. 529: St. Benedict founded the Monte Cassino Abbey. Some years before his death in 543 he wrote a monastic rule which exercised tremendous influence on the form and style of religious life. He is called the Father of Monasticism in the West.

533: John II became the first pope to change his name. The practice did not become general until the time of Sergius IV (1009).

533-34: Emperor Justinian promulgated the *Corpus Juris Civilis* for the Roman world; like the *Theodosian Code,* it influenced subsequent civil and ecclesiastical law.

c. 545: Death of Dionysius Exiguus who was the first to date history from the birth of Christ, a practice which resulted in use of the B.C. and A.D. abbreviations. His calculations were at least four years late.

553: Ecumenical Council of Constantinople (II). It condemned the *Three Chapters,* Nestorian-tainted writings of Theodore of Mopsuestia, Theodoret of Cyrus and Ibas of Edessa.

585: St. Columban founded an influential monastic school at Luxeuil.

589: The most important of several councils of Toledo was held. The Visigoths renounced Arianism, and St. Leander began the organization of the Church in Spain.

590-604: Pontificate of Pope St. Gregory I the Great. He set the form and style of the papacy which prevailed throughout the Middle Ages; exerted great influence on doctrine and liturgy; was strong in support of monastic discipline and clerical celibacy; authored writings on many subjects. Gregorian Chant is named in his honor.

596: Pope St. Gregory I sent St. Augustine of Canterbury and 40 monks to do missionary work in England.

597: St. Columba died. He founded an important monastery at Iona, established schools and did notable missionary work in Scotland. By the end of the century, monasteries of nuns were common; Western monasticism was flourishing; monasticism in the East, under the influence of Monophysitism and other factors, was losing its vigor.

SEVENTH CENTURY

613: St. Columban established the influential monastery of Bobbio in northern Italy; he died there in 615.

622: The Hegira (flight) of Mohammed from Mecca to Medina signalled the beginning of Islam which, by the end of the century, claimed almost all of the southern Mediterranean area.

628: Heraclius, Eastern Emperor, recovered the True Cross from the Persians.

649: A Lateran council condemned two erroneous formulas (*Ecthesis* and *Type*) issued by emperors Heraclius and Constans II as means of reconciling Monophysites with the Church.

664: Actions of the Synod of Whitby advanced the adoption of Roman usages in England, especially regarding the date for the observance of Easter. (See Easter Controversy.)

680-81: Ecumenical Council of Constantinople (III). It condemned Monothelitism, which held that Christ had only one will, the divine; censured Pope Honorius I for a letter to Sergius, bishop of Constantinople, in which he made an ambiguous but not infallible statement about the unity of will and/or operation in Christ.

692: Trullan Synod. Eastern-Church discipline on clerical celibacy was settled, permitting marriage before ordination to the diaconate and continuation in marriage afterwards, but prohibiting marriage following the death of the wife thereafter. Anti-Roman canons contributed to East-West alienation.

During the century, the monastic influence of Ireland and England increased in Western Europe; schools and learning declined; regulations regarding clerical celibacy became more strict in the East.

EIGHTH CENTURY

711: Moslems began the conquest of Spain.

726: Emperor Leo III, the Isaurian, launched a campaign against the veneration of sacred images and relics; called Iconoclasm (image-breaking), it caused turmoil in the East until about 843.

731: Pope Gregory III and a synod at Rome condemned Iconoclasm, with a declaration that the veneration of sacred images was in accord with Catholic tradition.

Venerable Bede issued his *Ecclesiastical History of the English People.*

732: Charles Martel defeated the Moslems at Poitiers, halting their advance in the West.

744: The Monastery of Fulda was established by St. Sturmi, a disciple of St. Boniface; it was influential in the evangelization of Germany.

754: A council of more than 300 Byzantine bishops endorsed Iconoclast errors. This council and its actions were condemned by the Lateran synod of 769.

Stephen II (III) crowned Pepin ruler of the Franks. Pepin twice invaded Italy, in 754 and 756, to defend the pope against the Lombards. His land grants to the papacy, called the Donation of Pepin, were later extended by Charlemagne (773) and formed part of the States of the Church.

c. 755: St. Boniface (Winfrid) was martyred. He was called the Apostle of Germany for his missionary work and organization of the hierarchy there.

781: Alcuin was chosen by Charlemagne to organize a palace school, which became a center of intellectual leadership.

787: Ecumenical Council of Nicaea (II). It condemned Iconoclasm, which held that the use of images was idolatry, and Adoptionism, which claimed that Christ was not the Son of God by nature but only by adoption. This was the last council regarded as ecumenical by Orthodox Churches.

792: A council at Ratisbon condemned Adoptionism.

The famous *Book of Kells* ("The Great Gospel of Columcille") dates from the early eighth or late seventh century.

NINTH CENTURY

800: Charlemagne was crowned Emperor by Pope Leo III on Christmas Day.

Egbert became king of West Saxons; he unified England and strengthened the See of Canterbury.

813: Emperor Leo V, the Armenian, revived Iconoclasm, which persisted until about 843.

814: Charlemagne died.

843: The Treaty of Verdun split the Frankish kingdom among Charlemagne's three grandsons.

844: A Eucharistic controversy involving the writings of St. Paschasius Radbertus, Ratramnus and Rabanus Maurus occasioned the development of terminology regarding the doctrine of the Real Presence.

846: Moslems invaded Italy and attacked Rome.

847-52: Period of composition of the *False Decretals,* a collection of forged documents attributed to popes from St. Clement (88-97) to Gregory II (714-731). The *Decretals,* which strongly supported the autonomy and rights of bishops, were suspect for a long time before being repudiated entirely about 1628.

848: The Council of Mainz condemned Gottschalk for heretical teaching regarding predestination. He was also condemned by the Council of Quierzy in 853.

857: Photius displaced Ignatius as patriarch of Constantinople. This marked the beginning of the Photian Schism, a confused state of East-West relations which has not yet been cleared up by historical research. Photius, a man of exceptional ability, died in 891.

865: St. Ansgar, apostle of Scandinavia, died.

869: St. Cyril died and his brother, St. Methodius (d. 885), was ordained a bishop. The Apostles of the Slavs devised an alphabet and translated the Gospels and liturgy into the Slavonic language.

869-70: Ecumenical Council of Constantinople (IV). It issued a second condemnation of Iconoclasm, condemned and deposed Photius as patriarch of Constantinople and restored Ignatius to the patriarchate. This was the last ecumenical council held in the East. It was first called ecumenical by canonists toward the end of the 11th century.

871-c. 900: Reign of Alfred the Great, the only English king ever anointed by a pope at Rome.

TENTH CENTURY

910: William, duke of Aquitaine, founded the Benedictine Abbey of Cluny, which became a center of monastic and ecclesiastical reform, especially in France.

915: Pope John X played a leading role in the expulsion of Saracens from central and southern Italy.

955: St. Olga, of the Russian royal family, was baptized.

962: Otto I, the Great, crowned by Pope John XII, revived Charlemagne's kingdom, which became the Holy Roman Empire.

966: Mieszko, first of a royal line in Poland, was baptized; he brought Latin Christianity to Poland.

988: Conversion and baptism of St. Vladimir and the people of Kiev which subsequently became part of Russia.

993: John XV was the first pope to decree the official canonization of a saint — Bishop Ulrich (Uldaric) of Augsburg — for the universal Church.

997: St. Stephen became ruler of Hungary. He assisted in organizing the hierarchy and establishing Latin Christianity in that country.

999-1003: Pontificate of Sylvester II (Gerbert of Aquitaine), a Benedictine monk and the first French pope.

ELEVENTH CENTURY

1009: Beginning of lasting East-West Schism in the Church, marked by dropping of the name of Pope Sergius IV from the Byzantine diptychs (the listing of persons prayed for during the liturgy). The deletion was made by Patriarch Sergius II of Constantinople.

1012: St. Romuald founded the Camaldolese Hermits.

1025: The Council of Arras, and other councils later, condemned the Cathari (Neo-Manichaeans, Albigenses).

1027: The Council of Elne proclaimed the Truce of God as a means of stemming violence; it involved armistice periods of varying length, which were later extended.

1038: St. John Gualbert founded the Vallombrosians.

1043-59: Constantinople patriarchate of Michael Cerularius, the key figure in a controversy concerning the primacy of the papacy. His and the Byzantine synod's refusal to acknowledge this primacy in 1054 widened and hardened the East-West Schism in the Church.

1047: Pope Clement II died; he was the only pope ever buried in Germany.

1049-54: Pontificate of St. Leo IX, who inaugurated a movement of papal, diocesan, monastic and clerical reform.

1054: Great East-West Schism, separation of Orthodox Churches from unity with the pope.

1055: Condemnation of the Eucharistic doctrine of Berengarius.

1059: A Lateran council issued new legislation regarding papal elections; voting power was entrusted to the Roman cardinals.

1066: Death of St. Edward the Confessor, king of England from 1042 and restorer of Westminster Abbey.

Defeat, at Hastings, of Harold by William I, who subsequently exerted strong influence on the lifestyle of the Church in England.

1073-85: Pontificate of St. Gregory VII (Hildebrand). A strong pope, he carried forward programs of clerical and general ecclesiastical reform and struggled against Henry IV and other rulers to end the evils of lay investiture. He introduced the Latin liturgy in Spain and set definite dates for the observance of ember days.

1077: Henry IV, excommunicated and suspended from the exercise of imperial powers by Gregory VII, sought absolution from the pope at Canossa. Henry later repudiated this action and in 1084 forced Gregory to leave Rome.

1079: The Council of Rome condemned Eucharistic errors (denial of the Real Presence of Christ under the appearances of bread and wine) of Berengarius, who retracted.

1084: St. Bruno founded the Carthusians.

1097-99: The first of several Crusades undertaken between this time and 1265. Recovery of the Holy Places and gaining free access to them for Christians were the original purposes, but these were diverted to less worthy objectives in various ways. Results included: a Latin Kingdom of Jerusalem, 1099-1187; a military and political misadventure in the form of a Latin Empire of Constantinople, 1204-1261; acquisition, by treaties, of visiting rights for Christians in the Holy Land. East-West economic and cultural relationships increased during the period. In the religious sphere, actions of the Crusaders had the effect of increasing the alienation of the East from the West.

1098: St. Robert founded the Cistercians.

TWELFTH CENTURY

1108: Beginnings of the influential Abbey and School of St. Victor in France.

1115: St. Bernard established the Abbey of Clairvaux and inaugurated the Cistercian Reform.

1118: Christian forces captured Saragossa, Spain; the beginning of the Moslem decline in that country.

1121: St. Norbert established the original monastery of the Praemonstratensians near Laon, France.

1122: The Concordat of Worms *(Pactum Callixtinum)* was formulated and approved by Pope Callistus II and Emperor Henry V to settle controversy concerning the investiture of prelates. The concordat provided that the emperor could invest prelates with symbols of temporal authority but had no right to invest them with spiritual authority, which came from the Church alone, and that the emperor was not to interfere in papal elections. This was the first concordat in history.

1123: Ecumenical Council of the Lateran (I), the first of its kind in the West. It endorsed provisions of the Concordat of Worms concerning the investiture of prelates and approved reform measures in 25 canons.

1139: Ecumenical Council of the Lateran (II). It adopted measures against a schism organized by antipope Anacletus and approved 30 canons related to discipline and other matters; one of the canons stated that holy orders is an invalidating impediment to marriage.

1140: St. Bernard met Abelard in debate at the Council of Sens. Abelard, whose rationalism in theology was condemned for the first time in 1121, died in 1142 at Cluny.

1148: The Synod of Rheims enacted strict disciplinary decrees for communities of women Religious.

1152: The Synod of Kells reorganized the Church in Ireland.

1160: Gratian, whose *Decretum* became a basic text of canon law, died.

Peter Lombard, compiler of the *Four Books of Sentences,* a standard theology text for nearly 200 years, died.

1170: St. Thomas Becket, archbishop of Canterbury, who clashed with Henry II over church-state relations, was murdered in his cathedral.

1171: Pope Alexander III reserved the process of canonization of saints to the Holy See.

1179: Ecumenical Council of the Lateran (III). It enacted measures against Waldensianism and Albigensianism (see year 242 regarding Manichaeism), approved reform decrees in 27 canons, provided that popes be elected by a two-thirds vote of the cardinals.

1184: Waldenses and other heretics were excommunicated by Pope Lucius III.

THIRTEENTH CENTURY

1198-1216: Pontificate of Innocent III, during which the papacy reached its medieval peak of authority, influence and prestige in the Church and in relations with civil rulers.

1208: Innocent III called for a crusade, the first in Christendom itself, against the Albigensians; their beliefs and practices threatened the fabric of society in southern France and northern Italy.

1209: Verbal approval was given by Innocent III to a rule of life for the Order of Friars Minor, started by St. Francis of Assisi.

1212: The Second Order of Franciscans, the Poor Clares, was founded.

1215: Ecumenical Council of the Lateran (IV). It ordered annual reception of the sacraments of penance and the Eucharist; defined and made the first official use of the term transubstantiation to explain the change of bread and wine into the body and blood of Christ; adopted additional measures to counteract teachings and practices of the Albigensians and Cathari; approved 70 canons.

1216: Formal papal approval was given to a rule of life for the Order of Preachers, started by St. Dominic.

The Portiuncula Indulgence was granted by the Holy See at the request of St. Francis of Assisi.

1221: Rule of the Third Order Secular of St. Francis (Secular Franciscan Order) approved verbally by Honorius III.

1226: Death of St. Francis of Assisi.

1231: Pope Gregory IX authorized establishment of the Papal Inquisition for dealing with heretics. It was a creature of its time, when crimes against faith and heretical doctrines of extremists like the Cathari and Albigenses threatened the good of the Christian community, the welfare of the state and the very fabric of society. The institution, which was responsible for excesses in punishment, was most active in the second half of the century in southern France, Italy and Germany.

1245: Ecumenical Council of Lyons (I). It confirmed the deposition of Emperor Frederick II and approved 22 canons.

1247: Preliminary approval was given by the Holy See to a Carmelite rule of life.

1270: St. Louis IX, king of France, died.
Beginning of papal decline.

1274: Ecumenical Council of Lyons (II). It accomplished a temporary reunion of separated Eastern Churches with the Roman Church; issued regulations concerning conclaves for papal elections; approved 31 canons.

Death of St. Thomas Aquinas, Doctor of the Church, of lasting influence.

1280: Pope Nicholas III, who made the *Breviary* the official prayer book for clergy of the Roman Church, died.

1281: The excommunication of Michael Palaeologus by Pope Martin IV ruptured the union effected with the Eastern Church in 1274.

FOURTEENTH CENTURY

1302: Pope Boniface VIII issued the bull *Unam Sanctam,* concerning the unity of the Church and the temporal power of princes, against the background of a struggle with Philip IV of France; it was the most famous medieval document on the subject.

1309-77: For a period of approximately 70 years, seven popes resided at Avignon because of unsettled conditions in Rome and other reasons; see separate entry.

1311-12: Ecumenical Council of Vienne. It suppressed the Knights Templar and enacted a number of reform decrees.

1321: Dante Alighieri died a year after completing the *Divine Comedy.*

1324: Marsilius of Padua completed *Defensor Pacis,* a work condemned by Pope John XXII as heretical because of its denial of papal primacy and the hierarchical structure of the Church, and for other reasons. It was a charter for conciliarism (an ecumenical council is superior to the pope in authority).

1337-1453: Period of the Hundred Years' War, a dynastic struggle between France and England.

1338: Four years after the death of Pope John XXII, who had opposed Louis IV of Bavaria in a years-long controversy, electoral princes declared at the Diet of Rhense that the emperor did not need papal confirmation of his title and right to rule. Charles IV later (1356) said the same thing in a *Golden Bull,* eliminating papal rights in the election of emperors.

1347-50: The Black Death swept across Europe, killing perhaps one-fourth to one-third of the total population; an estimated 40 per cent of the clergy succumbed.

1374: Petrarch, poet and humanist, died.

1377: Return of the papacy from Avignon to Rome.

Beginning of the Western Schism; see separate entry.

FIFTEENTH CENTURY

1409: The Council of Pisa, without canonical authority, tried to end the Western Schism but succeeded only in complicating it by electing a third claimant to the papacy; see Western Schism.

1414-18: Ecumenical Council of Constance. It took successful action to end the Western Schism involving rival claimants to the papacy; rejected the teachings of Wycliff; condemned Hus as a heretic. One decree — passed in the earlier stages of the council but later rejected — asserted the superiority of an ecumenical council over the pope (conciliarism).

1431: St. Joan of Arc was burned at the stake.

1431-45: Ecumenical Council of Florence (also called Basel-Ferrara-Florence). It affirmed the primacy of the pope against the claims of conciliarists that an ecumenical council is superior to the pope. It also formulated and approved decrees of union with several separated Eastern Churches — Greek, Armenian, Jacobite — which failed to gain general or lasting acceptance.

1438: The Pragmatic Sanction of Bourges was enacted by Charles VIII and the French Parliament to curtail papal authority over the Church in France, in the spirit of conciliarism. It found expression in Gallicanism and had effects lasting at least until the French Revolution.

1453: The fall of Constantinople to the Turks.

c. 1456: Gutenberg issued the first edition of the Bible printed from movable type, at Mainz, Germany.

1476: Pope Sixtus IV approved observance of the feast of the Immaculate Conception on Dec. 8 throughout the Church.

1478: Pope Sixtus IV, at the urging of King Ferdinand of Spain, approved establishment of the Spanish Inquisition for dealing with Jewish and Moorish converts accused of heresy. The institution, which was peculiar to Spain and its colonies in America, acquired jurisdiction over other cases as well and fell into disrepute because of its procedures, cruelty and the manner in which it served the Spanish crown, rather than the accused and the good of the Church. Protests by the Holy See failed to curb excesses of the Inquisition, which lingered in Spanish history until early in the 19th century.

1492: Columbus discovered the Americas.

1493: Pope Alexander VI issued a *Bull of Demarcation* which determined spheres of influence for the Spanish and Portuguese in the Americas.

The Renaissance, a humanistic movement which originated in Italy in the 14th century, spread to France, Germany, the Low Countries and England. A transitional period between the medieval world and the modern secular world, it introduced profound changes which affected literature and the other arts, general culture, politics and religion.

SIXTEENTH CENTURY

1512-17: Ecumenical Council of the Lateran (V). It stated the relation and position of the pope with respect to an ecumenical council; acted to counteract the Pragmatic Sanction of Bourges and exaggerated claims of liberty by the Church in France; condemned erroneous teachings concerning the nature of the human soul; stated doctrine concerning indulgences. The council reflected concern for abuses in the Church and the need for reforms but failed to take decisive action in the years immediately preceding the Reformation.

1517: Martin Luther signalled the beginning of the Reformation by posting 95 theses at Wittenberg. Subsequently, he broke completely from doctrinal orthodoxy in discourses and three published works (1519 and 1520); was excommunicated on more than 40 charges of heresy (1521); remained the dominant figure in the Reformation in Germany until his death in 1546.

1519: Zwingli triggered the Reformation in Zurich and became its leading proponent there until his death in combat in 1531.

1524: Luther's encouragement of German princes in putting down the two-year Peasants' Revolt gained political support for his cause.

1528: The Order of Friars Minor Capuchin was approved as an autonomous division of the Franciscan Order; like the Jesuits, the Capuchins became leaders in the Counter-Reformation.

1530: The *Augsburg Confession* of Lutheran faith was issued; it was later supplemented by the *Smalcald Articles,* approved in 1537.

1533: Henry VIII divorced Catherine of Aragon, married Anne Boleyn, was excommunicated. In 1534 he decreed the Act of Supremacy, making the sovereign the head of the Church in England, under which Sts. John Fisher and Thomas More were executed in 1535. Despite his rejection of papal primacy and actions against monastic life in England, he generally maintained doctrinal orthodoxy until his death in 1547.

1536: John Calvin, leader of the Reformation in Switzerland until his death in 1564, issued the first edition of *Institutes of the Christian Religion,* which became the classical text of Reformed (non-Lutheran) theology.

1540: The constitutions of the Society of Jesus (Jesuits), founded by St. Ignatius of Loyola, were approved.

1541: Start of the 11-year career of St. Francis Xavier as a missionary to the East Indies and Japan.

1545-63: Ecumenical Council of Trent. It issued a great number of decrees concerning doctrinal matters opposed by the Reformers, and mobilized the Counter-Reformation. Definitions covered the Canon of the Bible, the rule of faith, the nature of justification, grace, faith, original sin and its effects, the seven sacraments, the sacrificial nature of the Mass, the veneration of saints, use of sacred images, belief in purgatory, the doctrine of indulgences, the jurisdiction of the pope over the whole Church. It initiated many reforms for renewal in the liturgy and general discipline in the Church, the promotion of religious instruction, the education of the clergy through the foundation of seminaries, etc. Trent ranks with Vatican II as the greatest ecumenical council held in the West.

1549: The first Anglican *Book of Common Prayer* was issued by Edward VI. Revised editions were published in 1552, 1559 and 1662 and later.

1553: Start of the five-year reign of Mary Tudor who tried to counteract actions of Henry VIII against the Roman Church.

1555: Enactment of the Peace of Augsburg, an arrangement of religious territorialism rather than toleration, which recognized the existence of Catholicism and Lutheranism in the German Empire and provided that citizens should adopt the religion of their respective rulers.

1558: Beginning of the reign (to 1603) of Queen Elizabeth I of England and Ireland, during which the Church of England took on its definitive form.

1559: Establishment of the hierarchy of the Church of England, with the consecration of Matthew Parker as archbishop of Canterbury.

1563: The first text of the *39 Articles* of the Church of England was issued. Also enacted were a new Act of Supremacy and Oath of Succession to the English throne.

1570: Elizabeth I was excommunicated. Penal measures against Catholics subsequently became more severe.

1571: Defeat of the Turkish armada at Lepanto staved off the invasion of Eastern Europe.

1577: The *Formula of Concord,* the classical statement of Lutheran faith, was issued; it was, generally, a Lutheran counterpart of the canons of the Council of Trent. In 1580, along with other formulas of doctrine, it was included in the *Book of Concord.*

1582: The Gregorian Calendar, named for Pope Gregory XIII, was put into effect and was eventually adopted in most countries: England delayed adoption until 1752.

SEVENTEENTH CENTURY

1605: The Gunpowder Plot, an attempt by Catholic fanatics to blow up James I of England and the houses of Parliament, resulted in an anti-Catholic Oath of Allegiance.

1610: Death of Matteo Ricci, outstanding Jesuit missionary to China, pioneer in cultural relations between China and Europe.

Founding of the first community of Visitation Nuns by Sts. Francis de Sales and Jane de Chantal.

1611: Founding of the Oratorians.

1613: Catholics were banned from Scandinavia.

1625: Founding of the Congregation of the Mission (Vincentians) by St. Vincent de Paul. He founded the Sisters of Charity in 1633.

1642: Death of Galileo, scientist, who was censured by the Congregation of the Holy Office for supporting the Copernican theory of the sun-centered planetary system.

Founding of the Sulpicians by Jacques Olier.

1643: Start of publication of the Bollandist *Acta Sanctorum,* a critical work on lives of the saints.

1648: Provisions in the Peace of Westphalia, ending the Thirty Years' War, extended terms of the Peace of Augsburg (1555) to Calvinists and gave equality to Catholics and Protestants in the 300 states of the Holy Roman Empire.

1649: Oliver Cromwell invaded Ireland and began a severe persecution of the Church there.

1653: Pope Innocent X condemned five propositions of Jansenism, a complex theory which distorted doctrine concerning the relations between divine grace and human freedom. Jansenism was also a rigoristic movement which seriously disturbed the Church in France, the Low Countries and Italy in this and the 18th century.

1673: The Test Act in England barred from public office Catholics who would not deny the doctrine of transubstantiation and receive Communion in the Church of England.

1678: Many English Catholics suffered death as a consequence of the Popish Plot, a false allegation by Titus Oates that Catholics planned to assassinate Charles II, land a French army in the country, burn London, and turn over the government to the Jesuits.

1682: The four Gallican articles, drawn up by Bossuet, asserted political and ecclesiastical immunities of France from papal control. The articles, which rejected the primacy of the pope, were declared null and void by Pope Alexander VIII in 1690.

1689: The Toleration Act granted a measure of freedom of worship to other English dissenters but not to Catholics.

EIGHTEENTH CENTURY

1704: Chinese Rites — involving the Christian adaptation of elements of Confucianism, veneration of ancestors and Chinese terminology in religion — were condemned by Clement XI.

1720: The Passionists were founded by St. Paul of the Cross.

1724: Persecution in China.

1732: The Redemptorists were founded by St. Alphonsus Liguori.

1738: Freemasonry was condemned by Clement XII and Catholics were forbidden to join, under penalty of excommunication; the prohibition was repeated by Benedict XIV in 1751 and by later popes.

1760s: Josephinism, a theory and system of state control of the Church, was initiated in Austria; it remained in force until about 1850.

1764: Febronianism, an unorthodox theory and practice regarding the constitution of the Church and relations between Church and state, was condemned for the first of several times. Proposed by an auxiliary bishop of Trier using the pseudonym Justinus Febronius, it had the effects of minimizing the office of the pope and supporting national churches under state control.

1773: Clement XIV issued a brief of suppression against the Jesuits, following their expulsion from Portugal in 1759, from France in 1764 and from Spain in 1767. Political intrigue and unsubstantiated accusations were principal factors in these developments. The ban, which crippled the society, contained no condemnation of the Jesuit constitutions, particular Jesuits or Jesuit teaching. The society was restored in 1814.

1778: Catholics in England were relieved of some civil disabilities dating back to the time of Henry

VIII, by an act which permitted them to acquire, own and inherit property. Additional liberties were restored by the Roman Catholic Relief Act of 1791 and subsequent enactments of Parliament.

1789: Religious freedom in the United States was guaranteed under the First Amendment to the Constitution.

Beginning of the French Revolution which resulted in: the secularization of church property and the Civil Constitution of the Clergy in 1790; the persecution of priests, religious and lay persons loyal to papal authority; invasion of the Papal States by Napoleon in 1796; renewal of persecution from 1797-1799; attempts to dechristianize France and establish a new religion; the occupation of Rome by French troops and the forced removal of Pius VI to France in 1798.

This century is called the age of Enlightenment or Reason because of the predominating rational and scientific approach of its leading philosophers, scientists and writers with respect to religion, ethics and natural law. This approach downgraded the fact and significance of revealed religion. Also characteristic of the Enlightenment were subjectivism, secularism and optimism regarding human perfectibility.

NINETEENTH CENTURY

1809: Pope Pius VII was made a captive by Napoleon and deported to France where he remained in exile until 1814. During this time he refused to cooperate with Napoleon who sought to bring the Church in France under his own control.

The turbulence in church-state relations in France at the beginning of the century recurred in connection with the Bourbon Restoration, the July Revolution, the second and third Republics, the Second Empire and the Dreyfus case.

1814: The Society of Jesus, suppressed since 1773, was restored.

1817: Reestablishment of the Congregation for the Propagation of the Faith (Propaganda) by Pius VII was an important factor in increasing missionary activity during the century.

1820: Years-long persecution, during which thousands died for the faith, ended in China. Thereafter, communication with the West remained cut off until about 1834. Vigorous missionary work got under way in 1842.

1822: The Pontifical Society for the Propagation of the Faith, inaugurated in France by Pauline Jaricot for the support of missionary activity, was established.

1829: The Catholic Emancipation Act relieved Catholics in England and Ireland of most of the civil disabilities to which they had been subject from the time of Henry VIII.

1832: Gregory XVI, in the encyclical *Mirari vos*, condemned indifferentism, one of the many ideologies at odds with Christian doctrine which were proposed during the century.

1833: Start of the Oxford Movement which affected the Church of England and resulted in some notable conversions, including that of John Henry Newman in 1845, to the Catholic Church.

Frederic Ozanam founded the Society of St. Vincent de Paul in France. The society, whose objective was works of charity, became worldwide.

1848: The *Communist Manifesto,* a revolutionary document symptomatic of socio-economic crisis, was issued.

1850: The hierarchy was reestablished in England and Nicholas Wiseman made the first archbishop of Westminster. He was succeeded in 1865 by Henry Manning, an Oxford convert and proponent of the rights of labor.

1853: The Catholic hierarchy was reestablished in Holland.

1854: Pius IX proclaimed the dogma of the Immaculate Conception in the bull *Ineffabilis Deus.*

1858: The Blessed Virgin Mary appeared to St. Bernadette at Lourdes, France; see separate entry.

1864: Pius IX issued the encyclical *Quanta cura* and the *Syllabus of Errors* in condemnation of some 80 propositions derived from the scientific mentality and rationalism of the century. The subjects in question had deep ramifications in many areas of thought and human endeavor; in religion, they explicitly and/or implicitly rejected divine revelation and the supernatural order.

1867: The first volume of *Das Kapital* was published. Together with the Communist First International, formed in the same year, it had great influence on the subsequent development of communism and socialism.

1869: The Anglican Church was disestablished in Ireland.

1869-70: Ecumenical Council of the Vatican (I). It defined papal primacy and infallibility in a dogmatic constitution on the Church; covered natural religion, revelation, faith, and the relations between faith and reason in a dogmatic constitution on the Catholic faith.

1870-71: Victor Emmanuel II of Sardinia, crowned king of Italy after defeating Austrian and papal forces, marched into Rome in 1870 and expropriated the Papal States after a plebiscite in which Catholics, at the order of Pius IX, did not vote. In 1871, Pius IX refused to accept a Law of Guarantees. Confiscation of church property and hindrance of ecclesiastical administration by the regime followed.

1871: The German Empire, a confederation of 26 states, was formed. Government policy launched a Kulturkampf whose May Laws of 1873 were designed to annul papal jurisdiction in Prussia and other states and to place the Church under imperial control. Resistance to the enactments and the persecution they legalized forced the government to modify its anti-Church policy by 1887.

1878: Beginning of the pontificate of Leo XIII, who was pope until his death in 1903. Leo is best known for the encyclical *Rerum novarum,* which greatly influenced the course of Christian social thought and the labor movement. His other accomplishments included promotion of Scholastic philosophy and the impetus he gave to scriptural studies.

1881: The first International Eucharistic Congress was held in Lille, France.

Alexander II of Russia died. His policies of Russification — as well as those of his two predecessors and a successor during the century — caused great suffering to Catholics, Jews and Protestants in Poland, Lithuania, the Ukraine and Bessarabia.

1882: Charles Darwin died. His theory of evolution by natural selection, one of several scientific highlights of the century, had extensive repercussions in the faith-and-science controversy.

1887: The Catholic University of America was founded in Washington, D.C.

1893: The U.S. apostolic delegation was set up in Washington, D.C.

TWENTIETH CENTURY

1901: Restrictive measures in France forced the Jesuits, Benedictines, Carmelites and other religious orders to leave the country. Subsequently, 14,000 schools were suppressed; religious orders and congregations were expelled; the concordat was renounced in 1905; church property was confiscated in 1906. For some years the Holy See, refusing to comply with government demands for the control of bishops' appointments, left some ecclesiastical offices vacant.

1903-14: Pontificate of St. Pius X. He initiated the codification of canon law, 1904; removed the ban against participation by Catholics in Italian national elections, 1905; issued decrees calling upon the faithful to receive Holy Communion frequently and daily, and stating that children should begin receiving the Eucharist at the age of seven, 1905 and 1910, respectively; ordered the establishment of the Confraternity of Christian Doctrine in all parishes throughout the world, 1905; condemned Modernism in the decree *Lamentabili* and the encyclical *Pascendi*, 1907.

1908: The United States and England, long under the jurisdiction of the Congregation for the Propagation of the Faith as mission territories, were removed from its control and placed under the common law of the Church.

1910: Laws of separation were enacted in Portugal, marking a point of departure in church-state relations.

1911: The Catholic Foreign Mission Society of America — Maryknoll, the first U.S.-founded society of its type — was established.

1914: Start of World War I, which lasted until 1918.

1914-22: Pontificate of Benedict XV. Much of his pontificate was devoted to seeking ways and means of minimizing the material and spiritual havoc of World War I. In 1917 he offered his services as a mediator to the belligerent nations, but his pleas for settlement of the conflict went unheeded.

1917: The Blessed Virgin Mary appeared to three children at Fatima, Portugal; see separate entry.

A new constitution, embodying repressive laws against the Church, was enacted in Mexico. Its implementation resulted in persecution in the 1920s and 1930s.

Bolsheviks seized power in Russia and set up a communist dictatorship. The event marked the rise of communism in Russian and world affairs. One of its immediate, and lasting, results was persecution of the Church, Jews and other segments of the population.

1918: The *Code of Canon Law,* in preparation for more than 10 years, went into effect in the Western Church.

1919: Benedict XV stimulated missionary work through the decree *Maximum Illud*, in which he urged the recruiting and training of native clergy in places where the Church was not firmly established.

1920-22: Ireland was partitioned by two enactments of the British government which (1) made the six counties of Northern Ireland part of the United Kingdom in 1920 and (2) gave dominion status to the Irish Free State in 1922. The Irish Free State became an independent republic in 1949.

1922-39: Pontificate of Pius XI. He subscribed to the Lateran Treaty, 1929, which settled the Roman Question created by the confiscation of the Papal States in 1871; issued the encyclical *Casti connubii,* 1930, an authoritative statement on Christian marriage; resisted the efforts of Benito Mussolini to control Catholic Action and the Church, in the encyclical *Non abbiamo bisogno,* 1931; opposed various fascist policies; issued the encyclicals *Quadragesimo anno,* 1931, developing the social doctrine of Leo XIII's *Rerum novarum,* and *Divini Redemptoris,* 1937, calling for social justice and condemning atheistic communism; condemned anti-Semitism, 1937.

1926: The Catholic Relief Act repealed virtually all legal disabilities of Catholics in England.

1931: Leftists proclaimed Spain a republic and proceeded to disestablish the Church, confiscate church property, deny salaries to the clergy, expel the Jesuits and ban teaching of the Catholic faith. These actions were preludes to the civil war of 1936-1939.

1933: Emergence of Adolf Hitler to power in Germany. By 1935 two of his aims were clear, the elimination of the Jews and control of a single national church. Six million Jews were killed in the Holocaust. The Church was subject to repressive measures, which Pius XI protested futilely in the encyclical *Mit brennender sorge* in 1937.

1936-39: Civil war in Spain between the leftist Loyalist and rightist Franco forces. The Loyalists were defeated and one-man, one-party rule was established. Priests, Religious and lay persons fell victims to Loyalist persecution.

1939-45: World War II.

1939-58: Pontificate of Pius XII. He condemned communism, proclaimed the dogma of the Assumption of Mary in 1950, in various documents and other enactments provided ideological background for many of the accomplishments of the Second Vatican Council. (See Twentieth Century Popes.)

1940: Start of a decade of communist conquest in more than 13 countries, resulting in conditions of persecution for a minimum of 60 million Catholics as well as members of other faiths.

Persecution diminished in Mexico because of non-enforcement of anti-religious laws still on record.

1950: Pius XII proclaimed the dogma of the Assumption of the Blessed Virgin Mary.

1957: The communist regime of China established the Patriotic Association of Chinese Catholics in opposition to the Church in union with the pope.

1958-63: Pontificate of John XXIII. His principal accomplishment was the convocation of the Second Vatican Council, the twenty-first ecumenical council in the history of the Church. (See Twentieth Century Popes.)

1962-65: Ecumenical Council of the Vatican (II). It formulated and promulgated 16 documents — two dogmatic and two pastoral constitutions, nine decrees and three declarations — reflecting pastoral orientation toward renewal and reform in the Church, and making explicit dimensions of doctrine and Christian life requiring emphasis for the full development of the Church and the better accomplishment of its mission in the contemporary world.

1963-78: Pontificate of Paul VI. His main purpose and effort was to give direction and provide guidance for the authentic trends of church renewal set in motion by the Second Vatican Council. (See Twentieth Century Popes.)

1978: The thirty-four-day pontificate of John Paul I. (See Twentieth Century Popes.) Start of the pontificate of John Paul II; see Index.

1983: The revised Code of Canon Law, embodying reforms enacted by the Second Vatican Council, went into effect in the Church of Roman Rite.

1985: Formal ratification of a Vatican-Italy concordat replacing the Lateran Treaty of 1929.

1989-91: Decline and fall of communist influence and control in Middle and Eastern Europe and the Soviet Union.

1991: The Code of Canon Law for Eastern Churches went into effect.

ECUMENICAL COUNCILS

An ecumenical council is an assembly of the college of bishops, with and under the presidency of the pope, which has supreme authority over the Church in matters pertaining to faith, morals, worship and discipline.

The Second Vatican Council stated: "The supreme authority with which this college (of bishops) is empowered over the whole Church is exercised in a solemn way through an ecumenical council. A council is never ecumenical unless it is confirmed or at least accepted as such by the successor of Peter. It is the prerogative of the Roman Pontiff to convoke these councils, to preside over them, and to confirm them" (*Dogmatic Constitution on the Church*, No. 22).

Pope Presides

The pope is the head of an ecumenical council; he presides over it either personally or through legates. Conciliar decrees and other actions have binding force only when confirmed and promulgated by him. If a pope dies during a council, it is suspended until reconvened by another pope. An ecumenical council is not superior to a pope; hence, there is no appeal from a pope to a council.

Collectively, the bishops with the pope represent the whole Church. They do this not as democratic representatives of the faithful in a kind of church parliament, but as the successors of the Apostles with divinely given authority, care and responsibility over the whole Church.

All and only bishops are council participants with deliberative vote. The supreme authority of the Church can invite others and determine the manner of their participation.

Basic legislation concerning ecumenical councils is contained in Canons 337-41 of the Code of Canon Law. Basic doctrinal considerations were stated by the Second Vatican Council in the *Dogmatic Constitution on the Church*.

Background

Ecumenical councils had their prototype in the Council of Jerusalem in 51, at which the Apostles under the leadership of St. Peter decided that converts to the Christian faith were not obliged to observe all the prescriptions of Old Testament law (Acts 15). As early as the second century, bishops got together in regional meetings, synods or councils to take common action for the doctrinal and pastoral good of their communities of faithful. The expansion of such limited assemblies to ecumenical councils was a logical and historical evolution, given the nature and needs of the Church.

Emperors Involved

Emperors were active in summoning or convoking the first eight councils, especially the first five and the eighth. Among reasons for intervention of this kind were the facts that the emperors regarded themselves as guardians of the faith; that the settlement of religious controversies, which had repercussions in political and social turmoil, served the cause of peace in the state; and that the emperors had at their disposal ways and means of facilitating gatherings of bishops. Imperial actions, however, did not account for the formally ecumenical nature of the councils.

Some councils were attended by relatively few bishops, and the ecumenical character of several was open to question for a time. However, confirmation and de facto recognition of their actions by popes and subsequent councils established them as ecumenical.

Role in History

The councils have played a highly significant role in the history of the Church by witnessing to and defining truths of revelation, by shaping forms of worship and discipline, and by promoting measures for the ever-necessary reform and renewal of Catholic life. In general, they have represented attempts of the Church to mobilize itself in times of crisis for self-preservation, self-purification and growth.

The first eight ecumenical councils were held in the East; the other 13, in the West. The majority of separated Eastern Churches — e.g., the Orthodox — recognize the ecumenical character of the first seven councils, which formulated a great deal of basic doctrine. Other separated Eastern Churches acknowledge only the first two or first three ecumenical councils.

The 21 Councils

The 21 ecumenical councils in the history of the Church are listed below, with indication of their names or titles (taken from the names of the places where they were held); the dates; the reigning and/or approving popes; the emperors who were instrumental in convoking the eight councils in the East; the number of bishops who attended, when available; the number of sessions. Significant actions of the first 20 councils are indicated under appropriate dates in Dates and Events in Church History.

1. **Nicaea I,** 325: St. Sylvester I (Emperor Constantine I); attended by approximately 300 bishops; sessions held between May 20 or June 19 to near the end of August.

2. **Constantinople I,** 381: St. Damasus I (Emperor Theodosius I); attended by approximately 150 bishops; sessions held from May to July.

3. **Ephesus,** 431: St. Celestine I (Emperor Theodosius II); attended by 150 to 200 bishops; five sessions held between June 22 and July 17.

4. **Chalcedon,** 451: St. Leo I (Emperor Marcian); attended by approximately 600 bishops; 17 sessions held between Oct. 8 and Nov. 1.

5. **Constantinople II,** 553: Vigilius (Emperor Justinian I); attended by 165 bishops; eight sessions held between May 5 and June 2.

6. **Constantinople III,** 680-681: St. Agatho, St. Leo II (Emperor Constantine IV); attended by approximately 170 bishops; 16 sessions held between Nov. 7, 680, and Sept. 6, 681.

7. **Nicaea II,** 787: Adrian I (Empress Irene); attended by approximately 300 bishops; eight sessions held between Sept. 24 and Oct. 23.

8. **Constantinople IV,** 869-870: Adrian II (Emperor Basil I); attended by 102 bishops; six sessions held between Oct. 5, 869, and Feb. 28, 870.

9. **Lateran I,** 1123: Callistus II; attended by approximately 300 bishops; sessions held between Mar. 8 and Apr. 6.

10. **Lateran II,** 1139: Innocent II; attended by 900 to 1,000 bishops and abbots; three sessions held in April.

11. **Lateran III,** 1179: Alexander III; attended by at least 300 bishops; three sessions held between Mar. 5 and 19.

12. **Lateran IV,** 1215: Innocent III; sessions held between Nov. 11 and 30.

13. **Lyons I,** 1245: Innocent IV; attended by approximately 150 bishops; three sessions held between June 28 and July 17.

14. **Lyons II,** 1274: Gregory X; attended by approximately 500 bishops; six sessions held between May 7 and July 17.

15. **Vienne,** 1311-1312: Clement V; attended by 132 bishops; three sessions held between Oct. 16, 1311, and May 6, 1312.

16. **Constance,** 1414-1418: Gregory XII, Martin V; attended by nearly 200 bishops, plus other prelates and many experts; 45 sessions held between Nov. 5, 1414, and Apr. 22, 1418.

17. **Florence** (also called Basel-Ferrara-Florence), 1431-1445(?): Eugene IV; attended by many Latin-Rite and Eastern-Rite bishops; preliminary sessions were held at Basel and Ferrara before definitive work was accomplished at Florence.

18. **Lateran V,** 1512-1517: Julius II, Leo X; 12 sessions held between May 3, 1512, and Mar. 6, 1517.

19. **Trent,** 1545-1563: Paul III, Julius III, Pius IV; 25 sessions held between Dec. 13, 1545, and Dec. 4, 1563.

20. **Vatican I,** 1869-1870: Pius IX; attended by approximately 800 bishops and other prelates; four public sessions and 89 general meetings held between Dec. 8, 1869, and Sept. 1, 1870.

VATICAN II

The Second Vatican Council, which was forecast by Pope John XXIII Jan. 25, 1959, was held in four sessions in St. Peter's Basilica.

Pope John convoked it and opened the first session, which ran from Oct. 11 to Dec. 8, 1962. Following John's death June 3, 1963, Pope Paul VI reconvened the council for the other three sessions which ran from Sept. 29 to Dec. 4, 1963; Sept. 14 to Nov. 21, 1964; Sept. 14 to Dec. 8, 1965.

A total of 2,860 Fathers participated in council proceedings, and attendance at meetings varied between 2,000 and 2,500. For various reasons, including the denial of exit from Communist-dominated countries, 274 Fathers could not attend.

The council formulated and promulgated 16 documents — two dogmatic and two pastoral constitutions, nine decrees and three declarations — all of which reflect its basic pastoral orientation toward renewal and reform in the Church. Given below are the Latin and English titles of the documents and their dates of promulgation.

- *Lumen Gentium* (Dogmatic Constitution on the Church), Nov. 21, 1964.
- *Dei Verbum* (Dogmatic Constitution on Divine Revelation), Nov. 18, 1965.
- *Sacrosanctum Concilium* (Constitution on the Sacred Liturgy), Dec. 4, 1963.
- *Gaudium et Spes* (Pastoral Constitution on the Church in the Modern World), Dec. 7, 1965.
- *Christus Dominus* (Decree on the Bishops' Pastoral Office in the Church), Oct. 28, 1965.
- *Ad Gentes* (Decree on the Church's Missionary Activity), Dec. 7, 1965.
- *Unitatis Redintegratio* (Decree on Ecumenism), Nov. 21, 1964.
- *Orientalium Ecclesiarum* (Decree on Eastern Catholic Churches), Nov. 21, 1964.
- *Presbyterorum Ordinis* (Decree on the Ministry and Life of Priests), Dec. 7, 1965.
- *Optatam Totius* (Decree on Priestly Formation), Oct. 28, 1965.
- *Perfectae Caritatis* (Decree on the Appropriate Renewal of the Religious Life), Oct. 28, 1965.
- *Apostolicam Actuositatem* (Decree on the Apostolate of the Laity), Nov. 18, 1965.
- *Inter Mirifica* (Decree on the Instruments of Social Communication), Dec. 4, 1963.
- *Dignitatis Humanae* (Declaration on Religious Freedom), Dec. 7, 1965.

- *Nostra Aetate* (Declaration on the Relationship of the Church to Non-Christian Religions), Oct. 28, 1965.
- *Gravissimum Educationis* (Declaration on Christian Education), Oct. 28, 1965.

The key documents were the four constitutions, which set the ideological basis for all the others. To date, the documents with the most visible effects are those on the liturgy, the Church, the Church in the world, ecumenism, the renewal of religious life, the life and ministry of priests, the lay apostolate.

The main business of the council was to explore and make explicit dimensions of doctrine and Christian life requiring emphasis for the full development of the Church and the better accomplishment of its mission in the contemporary world.

THE CHURCH AS COMMUNION

Following are excerpts from a "Letter to the Bishops of the Catholic Church on Some Aspects of the Church Understood as Communion," issued by the Congregation for the Doctrine of the Faith June 15, 1992.

These excerpts are from the Vatican text circulated by the CNS Documentary Service, Origins, June 25, 1992 (Vol. 22, No. 7). Subheads have been added.

Some approaches to ecclesiology suffer from a clearly inadequate awareness of the Church as a mystery of communion, especially insofar as they have not sufficiently integrated the concept of communion with the concepts of the people of God and body of Christ, and have not given due importance to the relationship between the Church as communion and the Church as sacrament.

Invisible and Visible Communion

Ecclesial communion is at the same time both invisible and visible. As an invisible reality, it is the communion of each human being with the Father through Christ in the Holy Spirit, and with the others who are fellow sharers in the divine nature, in the passion of Christ, in the same faith, in the same spirit. In the Church on earth, there is an intimate relationship between this invisible communion and the visible communion in the teaching of the apostles, in the sacraments and in the hierarchical order. ... (The) link between the invisible and the visible elements of ecclesial communion constitutes the Church as the sacrament of salvation.

Ecclesial communion, into which each individual is introduced by faith and by baptism, has its root and center in the holy Eucharist. Indeed, baptism is an incorporation into a body that the risen Lord builds up and keeps alive through the Eucharist, so that this body can truly be called the body of Christ. The Eucharist is the creative force and source of communion among the members of the Church, precisely because it unites each one of them with Christ himself.

Universal and Particular Churches

The Church of Christ, which we profess in the Creed to be one, holy, catholic and apostolic, is the universal Church, that is, the worldwide community of the disciples of the Lord, which is present and active ... (in) those entities which are in themselves churches because, although they are particular (churches), the universal Church becomes present in them with all her essential elements. They are therefore constituted after the model of the universal Church, and each of them is a portion of the people of God entrusted to a bishop to be guided by him with the assistance of his clergy.

The universal Church is therefore the body of the churches. ... Sometimes the idea of a communion of particular churches is presented in such a way as to weaken the concept of the unity of the Church at the visible and institutional level. Thus it is asserted that every particular church is a subject complete in itself, and that the universal Church is the result of a reciprocal recognition on the part of the particular churches. (But) the universal Church cannot be conceived as the sum of the particular churches or as a federation of particular churches.

From the point of view of the Church understood as communion, the universal communion of the faithful and the communion of the churches are not consequences of one another but constitute the same reality from different viewpoints.

Eucharistic and Episcopal Roots

Unity, or communion between the particular churches in the universal Church, is rooted not only in the same faith and in the common baptism, but above all in the Eucharist and in the episcopate. It is rooted in the Eucharist because the Eucharistic Sacrifice, while always offered in a particular community, is never a celebration of that community alone.

Supreme Authority of the Church

For each particular church to be fully church, that is, the particular presence of the universal Church with all its essential elements, and hence constituted after the model of the universal Church, there must be present in it, as a proper element, the supreme authority of the Church: the episcopal college together with their head, the Supreme Pontiff, and never apart from him. The primacy of the bishop of Rome and the episcopal college are proper elements of the universal Church that are not derived from the particularity of the churches, but are nevertheless interior to each particular church. Consequently we must see the ministry of the successor of Peter not only as a global service reaching each particular church from outside, as it were, but as belonging already to the essence of each particular church from within. Indeed, the ministry of the primacy involves, in essence, a truly episcopal power which is not only supreme, full and universal but also immediate, over all, whether pastors or faithful. The ministry of the successor of Peter as something interior to each particular church is a necessary expression of that fundamental mutual interiority between universal Church and particular church.

POPES

Information includes the name of the pope, in many cases his name before becoming pope, his birthplace or country of origin, the date of accession to the papacy, and the date of the end of reign which, in all but a few cases, was the date of death. Double dates indicate date of election and date of solemn beginning of ministry as Pastor of the universal Church.

Source: "Annuario Pontificio."

St. Peter (Simon Bar-Jona): Bethsaida in Galilee; d. c. 64 or 67.

St. Linus: Tuscany; 67-76.

St. Anacletus (Cletus): Rome; 76-88.

St. Clement: Rome; 88-97.

St. Evaristus: Greece; 97-105.

St. Alexander I: Rome; 105-115.

St. Sixtus I: Rome; 115-125.

St. Telesphorus: Greece; 125-136.

St. Hyginus: Greece; 136-140.

St. Pius I: Aquileia; 140-155.

St. Anicetus: Syria; 155-166.

St. Soter: Campania; 166-175.

St. Eleutherius: Nicopolis in Epirus; 175-189.

Up to the time of St. Eleutherius, the years indicated for the beginning and end of pontificates are not absolutely certain. Also, up to the middle of the 11th century, there are some doubts about the exact days and months given in chronological tables.

St. Victor I: Africa; 189-199.

St. Zephyrinus: Rome; 199-217.

St. Callistus I: Rome; 217-222.

St. Urban I: Rome; 222-230.

St. Pontian: Rome; July 21, 230, to Sept. 28, 235.

St. Anterus: Greece; Nov. 21, 235, to Jan. 3, 236.

St. Fabian: Rome; Jan. 10, 236, to Jan. 20, 250.

St. Cornelius: Rome; Mar., 251, to June, 253.

St. Lucius I: Rome; June 25, 253, to Mar. 5, 254.

St. Stephen I: Rome; May 12, 254, to Aug. 2, 257.

St. Sixtus II: Greece; Aug. 30, 257, to Aug. 6, 258.

St. Dionysius: July 22, 259, to Dec. 26, 268.

St. Felix I: Rome; Jan. 5, 269, to Dec. 30, 274.

St. Eutychian: Luni; Jan. 4, 275, to Dec. 7, 283.

St. Caius: Dalmatia; Dec. 17, 283, to Apr. 22, 296.

St. Marcellinus: Rome; June 30, 296, to Oct. 25, 304.

St. Marcellus I: Rome; May 27, 308, or June 26, 308, to Jan. 16, 309.

St. Eusebius: Greece; Apr. 18, 309, to Aug. 17, 309 or 310.

St. Melchiades (Miltiades): Africa; July 2, 311, to Jan. 11, 314.

St. Sylvester I: Rome; Jan. 31, 314, to Dec. 31, 335. (Most of the popes before St. Sylvester I were martyrs.)

St. Marcus: Rome; Jan. 18, 336, to Oct. 7, 336.

St. Julius I: Rome; Feb. 6, 337, to Apr. 12, 352.

Liberius: Rome; May 17, 352, to Sept. 24, 366.

St. Damasus I: Spain; Oct. 1, 366, to Dec. 11, 384.

St. Siricius: Rome; Dec. 15, or 22 or 29, 384, to Nov. 26, 399.

St. Anastasius I: Rome; Nov. 27, 399, to Dec. 19, 401.

St. Innocent I: Albano; Dec. 22, 401, to Mar. 12, 417.

St. Zozimus: Greece; Mar. 18, 417, to Dec. 26, 418.

St. Boniface I: Rome; Dec. 28 or 29, 418, to Sept. 4, 422.

St. Celestine I: Campania; Sept. 10, 422, to July 27, 432.

St. Sixtus III: Rome; July 31, 432, to Aug. 19, 440.

St. Leo I (the Great): Tuscany; Sept. 29, 440, to Nov. 10, 461.

St. Hilary: Sardinia; Nov. 19, 461, to Feb. 29, 468.

St. Simplicius: Tivoli; Mar. 3, 468, to Mar. 10, 483.

St. Felix III (II): Rome; Mar. 13, 483, to Mar. 1, 492.

He should be called Felix II, and his successors of the same name should be numbered accordingly. The discrepancy in the numerical designation of popes named Felix was caused by the erroneous insertion in some lists of the name of St. Felix of Rome, a martyr.

St. Gelasius I: Africa; Mar. 1, 492, to Nov. 21, 496.

Anastasius II: Rome; Nov. 24, 496, to Nov. 19, 498.

St. Symmachus: Sardinia; Nov. 22, 498, to July 19, 514.

St. Hormisdas: Frosinone; July 20, 514, to Aug. 6, 523.

St. John I, Martyr: Tuscany; Aug. 13, 523, to May 18, 526.

St. Felix IV (III): Samnium; July 12, 526, to Sept. 22, 530.

Boniface II: Rome; Sept. 22, 530, to Oct. 17, 532.

John II: Rome; Jan. 2, 533, to May 8, 535.

John II was the first pope to change his name. His given name was Mercury.

St. Agapitus I: Rome; May 13, 535, to Apr. 22, 536.

St. Silverius, Martyr: Campania; June 1 or 8, 536, to Nov. 11, 537 (d. Dec. 2, 537).

St. Silverius was violently deposed in March, 537, and abdicated Nov. 11, 537. His successor, Vigilius, was not recognized as pope by all the Roman clergy until his abdication.

Vigilius: Rome; Mar. 29, 537, to June 7, 555.

Pelagius I: Rome; Apr. 16, 556, to Mar. 4, 561.

John III: Rome; July 17, 561, to July 13, 574.

Benedict I: Rome; June 2, 575, to July 30, 579.

Pelagius II: Rome; Nov. 26, 579, to Feb. 7, 590.

St. Gregory I (the Great): Rome; Sept. 3, 590, to Mar. 12, 604.

Sabinian: Blera in Tuscany; Sept. 13, 604, to Feb. 22, 606.

Boniface III: Rome; Feb. 19, 607, to Nov. 12, 607.

St. Boniface IV: Abruzzi; Aug. 25, 608, to May 8, 615.

St. Deusdedit (Adeodatus I): Rome; Oct. 19, 615, to Nov. 8, 618.

Boniface V: Naples; Dec. 23, 619, to Oct. 25, 625.

Honorius I: Campania; Oct. 27, 625, to Oct. 12, 638.

Severinus: Rome; May 28, 640, to Aug. 2, 640.

John IV: Dalmatia; Dec. 24, 640, to Oct. 12, 642.

Theodore I: Greece; Nov. 24, 642, to May 14, 649.

St. Martin I, Martyr: Todi; July, 649, to Sept. 16, 655 (in exile from June 17, 653).

St. Eugene I: Rome; Aug. 10, 654, to June 2, 657.

St. Eugene I was elected during the exile of St. Martin I, who is believed to have endorsed him as pope.

St. Vitalian: Segni; July 30, 657, to Jan. 27, 672.

Adeodatus II: Rome; Apr. 11, 672, to June 17, 676.

Donus: Rome; Nov. 2, 676, to Apr. 11, 678.

St. Agatho: Sicily; June 27, 678, to Jan. 10, 681.

St. Leo II: Sicily; Aug. 17, 682, to July 3, 683.

St. Benedict II: Rome; June 26, 684, to May 8, 685.

John V: Syria; July 23, 685, to Aug. 2, 686.

Conon: birthplace unknown; Oct. 21, 686, to Sept. 21, 687.

St. Sergius I: Syria; Dec. 15, 687, to Sept. 8, 701.

John VI: Greece; Oct. 30, 701, to Jan. 11, 705.

John VII: Greece; Mar. 1, 705, to Oct. 18, 707.

Sisinnius: Syria; Jan. 15, 708, to Feb. 4, 708.

Constantine: Syria; Mar. 25, 708, to Apr. 9, 715.

St. Gregory II: Rome; May 19, 715, to Feb. 11, 731.

St. Gregory III: Syria; Mar. 18, 731, to Nov., 741.

St. Zachary: Greece; Dec. 10, 741, to Mar. 22, 752.

Stephen II (III): Rome; Mar. 26, 752, to Apr. 26, 757.

After the death of St. Zachary, a Roman priest named Stephen was elected but died (four days later) before his consecration as bishop of Rome, which would have marked the beginning of his pontificate. Another Stephen was elected to succeed Zachary as Stephen II. (The first pope with this name was St. Stephen I, 254-57.) The ordinal III appears in parentheses after the name of Stephen II because the name of the earlier elected but deceased priest was included in some lists. Other Stephens have double numbers.

St. Paul I: Rome; Apr. (May 29), 757, to June 28, 767.

Stephen III (IV): Sicily; Aug. 1 (7), 768, to Jan. 24, 772.

Adrian I: Rome; Feb. 1 (9), 772, to Dec. 25, 795.

St. Leo III: Rome; Dec. 26 (27), 795, to June 12, 816.

Stephen IV (V): Rome; June 22, 816, to Jan. 24, 817.

St. Paschal I: Rome; Jan. 25, 817, to Feb. 11, 824.

Eugene II: Rome; Feb. (May), 824, to Aug., 827.

Valentine: Rome; Aug. 827, to Sept., 827.

Gregory IV: Rome; 827, to Jan., 844.

Sergius II: Rome; Jan., 844 to Jan. 27, 847.

St. Leo IV: Rome; Jan. (Apr. 10), 847, to July 17, 855.

Benedict III: Rome; July (Sept. 29), 855, to Apr. 17, 858.

St. Nicholas I (the Great): Rome; Apr. 24, 858, to Nov. 13, 867.

Adrian II: Rome; Dec. 14, 867, to Dec. 14, 872.

John VIII: Rome; Dec. 14, 872, to Dec. 16, 882.

Marinus I: Gallese; Dec. 16, 882, to May 15, 884.

St. Adrian III: Rome; May 17, 884, to Sept., 885. Cult confirmed June 2, 1891.

Stephen V (VI): Rome; Sept., 885, to Sept. 14, 891.

Formosus: Portus; Oct. 6, 891, to Apr. 4, 896.

Boniface VI: Rome; Apr., 896, to Apr., 896.

Stephen VI (VII): Rome; May, 896, to Aug., 897.

Romanus: Gallese; Aug., 897, to Nov., 897.

Theodore II: Rome; Dec., 897, to Dec., 897.

John IX: Tivoli; Jan., 898, to Jan., 900.

Benedict IV: Rome; Jan. (Feb.), 900, to July, 903.

Leo V: Ardea; July, 903, to Sept., 903.

Sergius III: Rome; Jan. 29, 904, to Apr. 14, 911.

Anastasius III: Rome; Apr., 911, to June, 913.

Landus: Sabina; July, 913, to Feb., 914.

John X: Tossignano (Imola); Mar., 914, to May, 928.

Leo VI: Rome; May, 928, to Dec., 928.

Stephen VII (VIII): Rome; Dec., 928, to Feb., 931.

John XI: Rome; Feb. (Mar.), 931, to Dec., 935.

Leo VII: Rome; Jan. 3, 936, to July 13, 939.

Stephen VIII (IX): Rome; July 14, 939, to Oct., 942.

Marinus II: Rome; Oct. 30, 942, to May, 946.

Agapitus II: Rome; May 10, 946, to Dec., 955.

John XII (Octavius): Tusculum; Dec. 16, 955, to May 14, 964 (date of his death).

Leo VIII: Rome; Dec. 4 (6), 963, to Mar. 1, 965.

Benedict V: Rome; May 22, 964, to July 4, 966.

Confusion exists concerning the legitimacy of claims to the pontificate by Leo VIII and Benedict V. John XII was deposed Dec. 4, 963, by a Roman council. If this deposition was invalid, Leo was an antipope. If the deposition of John was valid, Leo was the legitimate pope and Benedict was an antipope.

John XIII: Rome; Oct. 1, 965, to Sept. 6, 972.

Benedict VI: Rome; Jan. 19, 973, to June, 974.

Benedict VII: Rome; Oct. 974, to July 10, 983.

John XIV (Peter Campenora): Pavia; Dec., 983, to Aug. 20, 984.

John XV: Rome; Aug., 985, to Mar. 996.

Gregory V (Bruno of Carinthia): Saxony; May 3, 996, to Feb. 18, 999.

Sylvester II (Gerbert): Auvergne; Apr. 2, 999, to May 12, 1003.

John XVII (Siccone): Rome; June 1003, to Dec., 1003.

John XVIII (Phasianus): Rome; Jan., 1004, to July, 1009.

Sergius IV (Peter): Rome; July 31, 1009, to May 12, 1012.

The custom of changing one's name on election to the papacy is generally considered to date from the time of Sergius IV. Before his time, several popes had changed their names. After his time, this became a regular practice, with few exceptions; e.g., Adrian VI and Marcellus II.

Benedict VIII (Theophylactus): Tusculum; May 18, 1012, to Apr. 9, 1024.

John XIX (Romanus): Tusculum; Apr. (May), 1024, to 1032.

Benedict IX (Theophylactus): Tusculum; 1032, to 1044.

Sylvester III (John): Rome; Jan. 20, 1045, to Feb. 10, 1045.

Sylvester III was an antipope if the forcible removal of Benedict IX in 1044 was not legitimate.

Benedict IX (second time): Apr. 10, 1045, to May 1, 1045.

Gregory VI (John Gratian): Rome; May 5, 1045, to Dec. 20, 1046.

Clement II (Suitger, Lord of Morsleben and Hornburg): Saxony; Dec. 24 (25), 1046, to Oct. 9, 1047.

If the resignation of Benedict IX in 1045 and his removal at the December, 1046, synod were not legitimate, Gregory VI and Clement II were antipopes.

Benedict IX (third time): Nov. 8, 1047, to July 17, 1048 (d. c. 1055).

Damasus II (Poppo): Bavaria; July 17, 1048, to Aug. 9, 1048.

St. Leo IX (Bruno): Alsace; Feb. 12, 1049, to Apr. 19, 1054.

Victor II (Gebhard): Swabia; Apr. 16, 1055, to July 28, 1057.

Stephen IX (X) (Frederick): Lorraine; Aug. 3, 1057, to Mar. 29, 1058.

Nicholas II (Gerard): Burgundy; Jan. 24, 1059, to July 27, 1061.

Alexander II (Anselmo da Baggio): Milan; Oct. 1, 1061, to Apr. 21, 1073.

St. Gregory VII (Hildebrand): Tuscany; Apr. 22 (June 30), 1073, to May 25, 1085.

Bl. Victor III (Dauferius; Desiderius): Benevento; May 24, 1086, to Sept. 16, 1087. Cult confirmed July 23, 1887.

Bl. Urban II (Otto di Lagery): France; Mar. 12, 1088, to July 29, 1099. Cult confirmed July 14, 1881.

Paschal II (Raniero): Ravenna; Aug. 13 (14), 1099, to Jan. 21, 1118.

Gelasius II (Giovanni Caetani): Gaeta; Jan. 24 (Mar. 10), 1118, to Jan. 28, 1119.

Callistus II (Guido of Burgundy): Burgundy; Feb. 2 (9), 1119, to Dec. 13, 1124.

Honorius II (Lamberto): Fiagnano (Imola); Dec. 15 (21), 1124, to Feb. 13, 1130.

Innocent II (Gregorio Papareschi): Rome; Feb. 14 (23), 1130, to Sept. 24, 1143.

Celestine II (Guido): Citta di Castello; Sept. 26 (Oct. 3), 1143, to Mar. 8, 1144.

Lucius II (Gerardo Caccianemici): Bologna: Mar. 12, 1144, to Feb. 15, 1145.

Bl. Eugene III (Bernardo Paganelli di Montemagno): Pisa; Feb. 15 (18), 1145, to July 8, 1153. Cult confirmed Oct. 3, 1872.

Anastasius IV (Corrado): Rome; July 12, 1153, to Dec, 3, 1154.

Adrian IV (Nicholas Breakspear): England; Dec. 4 (5), 1154, to Sept. 1, 1159.

Alexander III (Rolando Bandinelli): Siena; Sept. 7 (20), 1159, to Aug. 30, 1181.

Lucius III (Ubaldo Allucingoli): Lucca; Sept. 1 (6), 1181, to Sept. 25, 1185.

Urban III (Uberto Crivelli): Milan; Nov. 25 (Dec. 1), 1185, to Oct. 20, 1187.

Gregory VIII (Alberto de Morra): Benevento; Oct. 21 (25), 1187, to Dec. 17, 1187.

Clement III (Paolo Scolari): Rome; Dec. 19 (20), 1187, to Mar., 1191.

Celestine III (Giacinto Bobone): Rome; Mar. 30 (Apr. 14), 1191, to Jan. 8, 1198.

Innocent III (Lotario dei Conti di Segni); Anagni; Jan. 8 (Feb. 22), 1198, to July 16, 1216.

Honorius III (Cencio Savelli): Rome; July 18 (24), 1216, to Mar. 18, 1227.

Gregory IX (Ugolino, Count of Segni): Anagni; Mar. 19 (21), 1227, to Aug. 22, 1241.

Celestine IV (Goffredo Castiglioni): Milan; Oct. 25 (28), 1241, to Nov. 10, 1241.

Innocent IV (Sinibaldo Fieschi): Genoa; June 25 (28), 1243, to Dec. 7, 1254.

Alexander IV (Rinaldo, Count of Segni): Anagni; Dec. 12 (20), 1254, to May 25, 1261.

Urban IV (Jacques Pantaléon): Troyes; Aug. 29 (Sept. 4), 1261, to Oct. 2, 1264.

Clement IV (Guy Foulques or Guido le Gros): France; Feb. 5 (15), 1265, to Nov. 29, 1268.

Bl. Gregory X (Teobaldo Visconti): Piacenza; Sept. 1, 1271 (Mar. 27, 1272), to Jan. 10, 1276. Cult confirmed Sept. 12, 1713.

Bl. Innocent V (Peter of Tarentaise): Savoy; Jan. 21 (Feb. 22), 1276, to June 22, 1276. Cult confirmed Mar. 13, 1898.

Adrian V (Ottobono Fieschi): Genoa: July 11, 1276, to Aug. 18, 1276.

John XXI (Petrus Juliani or Petrus Hispanus): Portugal; Sept. 8 (20), 1276, to May 20, 1277. There is confusion in the numerical designation of popes named John. The error dates back to the time of John XV.

Nicholas III (Giovanni Gaetano Orsini): Rome; Nov. 25 (Dec. 26), 1277, to Aug. 22, 1280.

Martin IV (Simon de Brie): France; Feb. 22 (Mar. 23), 1281, to Mar. 28, 1285. The names of Marinus 1 (882-84) and Marinus II (942-46) were construed as Martin. In view of these two pontificates and the earlier reign of St. Martin I (649-55), this pope was called Martin IV.

Honorius IV (Giacomo Savelli): Rome; Apr. 2 (May 20), 1285, to Apr. 3, 1287.

Nicholas IV (Girolamo Masci): Ascoli; Feb. 22, 1288, to Apr. 4, 1292.

St. Celestine V (Pietro del Murrone): Isernia; July 5 (Aug. 29), 1294, to Dec. 13, 1294; d. 1296. Canonized May 5, 1313.

Boniface VIII (Benedetto Caetani): Anagni; Dec. 24, 1294 (Jan. 23, 1295), to Oct. 11, 1303.

Bl. Benedict XI (Niccolo Boccasini): Treviso; Oct. 22 (27), 1303, to July 7, 1304. Cult confirmed Apr. 24, 1736.

Clement V (Bertrand de Got): France; June 5 (Nov. 14), 1305, to Apr. 20, 1314. (First of Avignon popes.)

John XXII (Jacques d'Euse): Cahors; Aug. 7 (Sept. 5), 1316, to Dec. 4, 1334.

Benedict XII (Jacques Fournier): France; Dec. 20, 1334 (Jan. 8, 1335), to Apr. 25, 1342.

Clement VI (Pierre Roger): France; May 7 (19), 1342, to Dec. 6, 1352.

Innocent VI (Etienne Aubert): France; Dec. 18 (30), 1352, to Sept. 12, 1362.

Bl. Urban V (Guillaume de Grimoard): France; Sept. 28 (Nov. 6), 1362, to Dec. 19, 1370. Cult confirmed Mar. 10, 1870.

Gregory XI (Pierre Roger de Beaufort): France; Dec. 30, 1370 (Jan. 5, 1371), to Mar. 26, 1378. (Last of Avignon popes.)

Urban VI (Bartolomeo Prignano): Naples; Apr. 8 (18), 1378, to Oct. 15, 1389.

Boniface IX (Pietro Tomacelli): Naples; Nov. 2 (9), 1389, to Oct. 1, 1404.

Innocent VII (Cosma Migliorati): Sulmona; Oct. 17 (Nov. 11), 1404, to Nov. 6, 1406.

Gregory XII (Angelo Correr): Venice; Nov. 30 (Dec. 19), 1406, to July 4, 1415, when he voluntarily resigned from the papacy to permit the election of his successor. He died Oct. 18, 1417. (See The Western Schism.)

Martin V (Oddone Colonna): Rome; Nov. 11 (21), 1417, to Feb. 20, 1431.

Eugene IV (Gabriele Condulmer): Venice; Mar. 3 (11), 1431, to Feb. 23, 1447.

Nicholas V (Tommaso Parentucelli): Sarzana; Mar. 6 (19), 1447, to Mar. 24, 1455.

Callistus III (Alfonso Borgia): Jativa (Valencia); Apr. 8 (20), 1455, to Aug. 6, 1458.

Pius II (Enea Silvio Piccolomini): Siena; Aug. 19 (Sept. 3), 1458, to Aug. 14, 1464.

Paul II (Pietro Barbo): Venice; Aug. 30 (Sept. 16), 1464, to July 26, 1471.

Sixtus IV (Francesco della Rovere): Savona; Aug. 9 (25), 1471, to Aug. 12, 1484.

Innocent VIII (Giovanni Battista Cibo): Genoa; Aug. 29 (Sept. 12), 1484, to July 25, 1492.

Alexander VI (Rodrigo Borgia): Jativa (Valencia); Aug. 11 (26), 1492, to Aug. 18, 1503.

Pius III (Francesco Todeschini-Piccolomini): Siena; Sept. 22 (Oct. 1, 8), 1503, to Oct. 18, 1503.

Julius II (Giuliano della Rovere): Savona; Oct. 31 (Nov. 26), 1503, to Feb. 21, 1513.

Leo X (Giovanni de' Medici): Florence; Mar. 9 (19), 1513, to Dec. 1, 1521.

Adrian VI (Adrian Florensz): Utrecht; Jan. 9 (Aug. 31), 1522, to Sept. 14, 1523.

Clement VII (Giulio de' Medici): Florence; Nov. 19 (26), 1523, to Sept. 25, 1534.

Paul III (Alessandro Farnese): Rome; Oct. 13 (Nov. 3), 1534, to Nov. 10, 1549.

Julius III (Giovanni Maria Ciocchi del Monte): Rome; Feb. 7 (22), 1550, to Mar. 23, 1555.

Marcellus II (Marcello Cervini): Montepulciano; Apr. 9 (10), 1555, to May 1, 1555.

Paul IV (Gian Pietro Carafa): Naples; May 23 (26), 1555, to Aug. 18, 1559.

Pius IV (Giovan Angelo de' Medici): Milan; Dec. 25, 1559 (Jan. 6, 1560), to Dec. 9, 1565.

St. Pius V (Antonio-Michele Ghislieri): Bosco (Alexandria); Jan. 7 (17), 1566, to May 1, 1572. Canonized May 22, 1712.

Gregory XIII (Ugo Buoncompagni): Bologna; May 13 (25), 1572, to Apr. 10, 1585.

Sixtus V (Felice Peretti): Grottammare (Ripatransone); Apr. 24 (May 1), 1585, to Aug. 27, 1590.

Urban VII (Giovanni Battista Castagna): Rome; Sept. 15, 1590, to Sept. 27, 1590.

Gregory XIV (Niccolo Sfondrati): Cremona; Dec. 5 (8), 1590, to Oct. 16, 1591.

Innocent IX (Giovanni Antonio Facchinetti): Bologna; Oct. 29 (Nov. 3), 1591, to Dec. 30, 1591.

Clement VIII (Ippolito Aldobrandini): Florence; Jan. 30 (Feb. 9), 1592, to Mar. 3, 1605.

Leo XI (Alessandro de' Medici): Florence; Apr. 1 (10), 1605, to Apr. 27, 1605.

Paul V (Camillo Borghese): Rome; May 16 (29), 1605, to Jan. 28, 1621.

Gregory XV (Alessandro Ludovisi): Bologna; Feb. 9 (14), 1621, to July 8, 1623.

Urban VIII (Maffeo Barberini): Florence; Aug. 6 (Sept. 29), 1623, to July 29, 1644.

Innocent X (Giovanni Battista Pamfili): Rome; Sept. 15 (Oct. 4), 1644, to Jan. 7, 1655.

Alexander VII (Fabio Chigi): Siena; Apr. 7 (18), 1655, to May 22, 1667.

Clement IX (Giulio Rospigliosi): Pistoia; June 20 (26), 1667, to Dec. 9, 1669.

Clement X (Emilio Altieri): Rome; Apr. 29 (May 11), 1670, to July 22, 1676.

Bl. Innocent XI (Benedetto Odescalchi): Como; Sept. 21 (Oct. 4), 1676, to Aug. 12, 1689. Beatified Oct. 7, 1956.

Alexander VIII (Pietro Ottoboni): Venice; Oct. 6 (16), 1689, to Feb. 1, 1691.

Innocent XII (Antonio Pignatelli): Spinazzola; July 12 (15), 1691, to Sept. 27, 1700.

Clement XI (Giovanni Francesco Albani): Nov. 23, 30 (Dec. 8), 1700, to Mar. 19, 1721.

Innocent XIII (Michelangelo dei Conti): Rome; May 8 (18), 1721, to Mar. 7, 1724.

Benedict XIII (Pietro Francesco — Vincenzo Maria — Orsini): Gravina (Bari); May 29 (June 4), 1724, to Feb. 21, 1730.

Clement XII (Lorenzo Corsini): Florence; July 12 (16), 1730, to Feb. 6, 1740.

Benedict XIV (Prospero Lambertini): Bologna; Aug. 17 (22), 1740, to May 3, 1758.

Clement XIII (Carlo Rezzonico): Venice; July 6 (16), 1758, to Feb. 2, 1769.

Clement XIV (Giovanni Vincenzo Antonio — Lorenzo — Ganganelli): Rimini; May 19, 28 (June 4), 1769, to Sept. 22, 1774.

Pius VI (Giovanni Angelo Braschi): Cesena; Feb. 15 (22), 1775, to Aug. 29, 1799.

Pius VII (Barnaba — Gregorio — Chiaramonti): Cesena; Mar. 14 (21), 1800, to Aug. 20, 1823.

Leo XII (Annibale della Genga): Genga (Fabriano); Sept. 28 (Oct. 5), 1823, to Feb. 10, 1829.

Pius VIII (Francesco Saverio Castiglioni): Cingoli; Mar. 31 (Apr. 5), 1829, to Nov. 30, 1830.

Gregory XVI (Bartolomeo Alberto — Mauro — Cappellari): Belluno; Feb. 2 (6), 1831, to June 1, 1846.

Pius IX (Giovanni M. Mastai-Ferretti): Senigallia; June 16 (21), 1846, to Feb. 7, 1878.

Leo XIII (Gioacchino Pecci): Carpineto (Anagni); Feb. 20 (Mar. 3), 1878, to July 20, 1903.

St. Pius X (Giuseppe Sarto): Riese (Treviso); Aug. 4 (9), 1903, to Aug. 20, 1914. Canonized May 29, 1954.

Benedict XV (Giacomo della Chiesa): Genoa; Sept. 3 (6), 1914, to Jan. 22, 1922.

Pius XI (Achille Ratti): Desio (Milan); Feb. 6 (12), 1922, to Feb. 10, 1939.

Pius XII (Eugenio Pacelli): Rome; Mar. 2 (12), 1939, to Oct. 9, 1958.

John XXIII (Angelo Giuseppe Roncalli): Sotto il Monte (Bergamo); Oct. 28 (Nov. 4), 1958, to June 3, 1963.

Paul VI (Giovanni Battista Montini): Concessio (Brescia); June 21 (30), 1963, to Aug. 6, 1978.

John Paul I (Albino Luciani): Forno di Canale (Belluno): Aug. 26 (Sept. 3), 1978, to Sept. 28, 1978.

John Paul II (Karol Wojtyla): Wadowice, Poland; Oct. 16 (22), 1978.

ANTIPOPES

This list of men who claimed or exercised the papal office in an uncanonical manner includes names, birthplaces and dates of alleged reigns.
Source: "Annuario Pontificio."

St. Hippolytus: Rome; 217-235; was reconciled before his death.

Novatian: Rome; 251.

Felix II: Rome; 355 to Nov. 22, 365.

Ursinus: 366-367.

Eulalius: Dec. 27 or 29, 418, to 419.

Lawrence: 498; 501-505.

Dioscorus: Alexandria; Sept. 22, 530, to Oct. 14, 530.

Theodore: ended alleged reign, 687.
Paschal: ended alleged reign, 687.
Constantine: Nepi; June 28 (July 5), 767, to 769.
Philip: July 31, 768; retired to his monastery on the same day.
John: ended alleged reign, Jan., 844.
Anastasius: Aug., 855, to Sept., 855; d. 880.
Christopher: Rome; July or Sept., 903, to Jan., 904.
Boniface VII: Rome; June, 974, to July, 974; Aug., 984, to July, 985.
John XVI: Rossano; Apr., 997, to Feb., 998.
Gregory: ended alleged reign, 1012.
Benedict X: Rome; Apr. 5, 1058, to Jan. 24, 1059.
Honorius II: Verona; Oct. 28, 1061, to 1072.
Clement III: Parma; June 25, 1080 (Mar. 24, 1084), to Sept. 8, 1100.
Theodoric: ended alleged reign, 1100; d. 1102.
Albert: ended alleged reign, 1102.
Sylvester IV: Rome; Nov. 18, 1105, to 1111.
Gregory VIII: France; Mar. 8, 1118, to 1121.
Celestine II: Rome; ended alleged reign, Dec., 1124.
Anacletus II: Rome; Feb. 14 (23), 1130, to Jan. 25, 1138.
Victor IV: Mar., 1138, to May 29, 1138; submitted to Pope Innocent II.
Victor IV: Montecelio; Sept. 7 (Oct. 4), 1159, to Apr. 20, 1164; he did not recognize his predecessor (Victor IV, above).
Paschal III: Apr. 22 (26), 1164, to Sept. 20, 1168.
Callistus III: Arezzo; Sept., 1168, to Aug. 29, 1178; submitted to Pope Alexander III.
Innocent III: Sezze; Sept. 29, 1179, to 1180.
Nicholas V: Corvaro (Rieti); May 12 (22), 1328, to Aug. 25, 1330; d. Oct. 16, 1333.
Four antipopes of the Western Schism:
Clement VII: Sept. 20 (Oct. 31), 1378, to Sept. 16, 1394.
Benedict XIII: Aragon; Sept. 28 (Oct. 11), 1394, to May 23, 1423.
Alexander V: Crete; June 26 (July 7), 1409, to May 3, 1410.
John XXIII: Naples; May 17 (25), 1410, to May 29, 1415. (Date of deposition by Council of Constance which ended the Western Schism; d. Nov. 22, 1419.)
Felix V: Savoy; Nov. 5, 1439 (July 24, 1440), to April 7, 1449; d. 1451.

AVIGNON PAPACY

Avignon was the residence (1309-77) of a series of French popes (Clement V, John XXII, Benedict XII, Clement VI, Innocent VI, Urban V and Gregory XI). Prominent in the period were power struggles over the mixed interests of Church and state with the rulers of France (Philip IV, John II), Bavaria (Lewis IV), England (Edward III); factionalism of French and Italian churchmen; political as well as ecclesiastical turmoil in Italy, a factor of significance in prolonging the stay of popes in Avignon. Despite some positive achievements, the Avignon papacy was a prologue to the Western Schism which began in 1378.

WESTERN SCHISM

The Western Schism was a confused state of affairs which divided Christendom into two and then three papal obediences from 1378 to 1417.

It occurred some 50 years after Marsilius theorized that a general (not ecumenical) council of bishops and other persons was superior to a pope and nearly 30 years before the Council of Florence stated definitively that no kind of council had such authority.

It was a period of disaster preceding the even more disastrous period of the Reformation.

Urban VI, following the return of the papal residence to Rome after approximately 70 years at Avignon, was elected pope Apr. 8, 1378, and reigned until his death in 1389. He was succeeded by Boniface IX (1389-1404), Innocent VII (1404-1406) and Gregory XII (1406-1415). These four are considered the legitimate popes of the period.

Some of the cardinals who chose Urban pope, dissatisfied with his conduct of the office, declared that his election was invalid. They proceeded to elect Clement VII, who claimed the papacy from 1378 to 1394. He was succeeded by Benedict XIII.

Prelates seeking to end the state of divided papal loyalties convoked the Council of Pisa (1409) which, without authority, found Gregory XII and Benedict XIII, in absentia, guilty on 30-odd charges of schism and heresy, deposed them, and elected a third claimant to the papacy, Alexander V (1409-1410). He was succeeded by John XXIII (1410-1415).

The schism was ended by the Council of Constance (1414-1418). This council, although originally called into session in an irregular manner, acquired authority after being convoked by Gregory XII in 1415. In its early irregular phase, it deposed John XXIII whose election to the papacy was uncanonical anyway. After being formally convoked, it accepted the abdication of Gregory in 1415 and dismissed the claims of Benedict XIII two years later, thus clearing the way for the election of Martin V on Nov. 11, 1417. The Council of Constance also rejected the theories of John Wycliff and condemned John Hus as a heretic.

TWENTIETH CENTURY POPES

LEO XIII

Leo XIII (Gioacchino Vincenzo Pecci) was born May 2, 1810, in Carpineto, Italy. Although all but three years of his life and pontificate were of the 19th century, his influence extended well into the 20th century.

He was educated at the Jesuit college in Viterbo, the Roman College, the Academy of Noble Ecclesiastics, and the University of the Sapienza. He was ordained to the priesthood in 1837.

He served as an apostolic delegate to two States of the Church, Benevento from 1838 to 1841 and Perugia in 1841 and 1842. Ordained titular archbishop of Damietta, he was papal nuncio to Belgium from January, 1843, until May, 1846; in the post, he had controversial relations with the government over education issues and acquired his first significant experience of industrialized society.

He was archbishop of Perugia from 1846 to 1878. He became a cardinal in 1853 and chamberlain of the Roman Curia in 1877. He was elected to the papacy Feb. 20, 1878. He died July 20, 1903.

Canonizations: He canonized 18 saints and beatified a group of English martyrs.

Church Administration: He established 300 new dioceses and vicariates; restored the hierarchy in Scotland, set up an English, as contrasted with the Portuguese, hierarchy in India; approved the action of the Congregation for the Propagation of the Faith in reorganizing missions in China.

Encyclicals: He issued 86 encyclicals, on subjects ranging from devotional to social. In the former category were *Annum Sacrum*, on the Sacred Heart, in 1899, and 11 letters on Mary and the Rosary.

Social Questions: Much of Leo's influence stemmed from social doctrine stated in numerous encyclicals, concerning liberalism, liberty, the divine origin of authority; socialism, in *Quod Apostolici Muneris*, 1878; the Christian concept of the family, in *Arcanum*, 1880; socialism and economic liberalism, relations between capital and labor, in *Rerum Novarum*, 1891. Two of his social encyclicals were against the African slave trade.

Interfaith Relations: He was unsuccessful in unity overtures made to Orthodox and Slavic Churches. He declared Anglican orders invalid in the apostolic bull *Apostolicae Curae* Sept. 13, 1896.

International Relations: Leo was frustrated in seeking solutions to the Roman Question arising from the seizure of church lands by the Kingdom of Italy in 1870. He also faced anticlerical situations in Belgium and France and in the Kulturkampf policies of Bismarck in Germany.

Studies: In the encyclical *Aeterni Patris* of Aug. 4, 1879, he ordered a renewal of philosophical and theological studies in seminaries along scholastic, and especially Thomistic, lines, to counteract influential trends of liberalism and Modernism. He issued guidelines for biblical exegesis in *Providentissimus Deus* Nov. 18, 1893, and established the Pontifical Biblical Commission in 1902.

In other actions affecting scholarship and study, he opened the Vatican Archives to scholars in 1883 and established the Vatican Observatory.

United States: He authorized establishment of the apostolic delegation in Washington, D.C., Jan. 24, 1893. He refused to issue a condemnation of the Knights of Labor. With a document entitled *Testem Benevolentiae,* he eased resolution of questions concerning what was called an American heresy in 1899.

ST. PIUS X

St. Pius X (Giuseppe Melchiorre Sarto) was born in 1835 in Riese, Italy. Educated at the college of Castelfranco and the seminary at Padua, he was ordained to the priesthood Sept. 18, 1858. He served as a curate in Trombolo for nine years before beginning an eight-year pastorate at Salzano. He was chancellor of the Treviso diocese from November,

1875, and bishop of Mantua from 1884 until 1893. He was cardinal-patriarch of Venice from that year until his election to the papacy by the conclave held from July 31 to Aug. 4, 1903.

Aims: Pius' principal objectives as pope were "to restore all things in Christ, in order that Christ may be all and in all," and "to teach (and defend) Christian truth and law."

Canonizations, Encyclicals: He canonized four saints and issued 16 encyclicals. One of the encyclicals was issued in commemoration of the 50th anniversary of the proclamation of the dogma of the Immaculate Conception of Mary.

Catechetics: He introduced a whole new era of religious instruction and formation with the encyclical *Acerbo Nimis* of Apr. 15, 1905, in which he called for vigor in establishing and conducting parochial programs of the Confraternity of Christian Doctrine.

Catholic Action: He outlined the role of official Catholic Action in two encyclicals in 1905 and 1906. Favoring organized action by Catholics themselves, he had serious reservations about interconfessional collaboration.

He stoutly maintained claims to papal rights in the anticlerical climate of Italy. He authorized bishops to relax prohibitions against participation by Catholics in some Italian elections.

Church Administration: With the motu proprio *Arduum Sane* of Mar. 19, 1904, he inaugurated the work which resulted in the Code of Canon Law; the code was completed in 1917 and went into effect in the following year. He reorganized and strengthened the Roman Curia with the apostolic constitution *Sapienti Consilio* of June 29, 1908.

While promoting the expansion of missionary work, he removed from the jurisdiction of the Congregation for the Propagation of the Faith the Church in the United States, Canada, Newfoundland, England, Ireland, Holland and Luxembourg.

International Relations: He ended traditional prerogatives of Catholic governments with respect to papal elections, in 1904. He opposed anti-Church and anticlerical actions in several countries: Bolivia in 1905, because of anti-religious legislation; France in 1906, for its 1901 action in annulling its concordat with the Holy See, and for the 1905 Law of Separation by which it decreed separation of Church and state, ordered the confiscation of church property, and blocked religious education and the activities of religious orders; Portugal in 1911, for the separation of Church and state and repressive measures which resulted in persecution later.

In 1912 he called on the bishops of Brazil to work for the improvement of conditions among Indians.

Liturgy: "The Pope of the Eucharist," he strongly recommended the frequent reception of Holy Communion in a decree dated Dec. 20, 1905; in another decree, *Quam Singulari,* of Aug. 8, 1910, he called for the early reception of the sacrament by children. He initiated measures for liturgical reform with new norms for sacred music and the start of work on revision of the *Breviary* for recitation of the Divine Office.

Modernism: Pius was a vigorous opponent of

"the synthesis of all heresies," which threatened the integrity of doctrine through its influence in philosophy, theology and biblical exegesis. In opposition, he condemned 65 of its propositions as erroneous in the decree *Lamentabili* July 3, 1907; issued the encyclical *Pascendi* in the same vein Sept. 8, 1907; backed both of these with censures; and published the Oath against Modernism in September, 1910, to be taken by all the clergy. Ecclesiastical studies suffered to some extent from these actions, necessary as they were at the time.

Pius followed the lead of Leo XIII in promoting the study of scholastic philosophy. He established the Pontifical Biblical Institute May 7, 1909.

His death, Aug. 20, 1914, was hastened by the outbreak of World War I. He was beatified in 1951 and canonized May 29, 1954. His feast is observed Aug. 21.

BENEDICT XV

Benedict XV (Giacomo della Chiesa) was born Nov. 21, 1854, in Pegli, Italy.

He was educated at the Royal University of Genoa and Gregorian University in Rome. He was ordained to the priesthood Dec. 21, 1878.

He served in the papal diplomatic corps from 1882 to 1907; as secretary to the nuncio to Spain from 1882 to 1887, as secretary to the papal secretary of state from 1887, and as undersecretary from 1901.

He was ordained archbishop of Bologna Dec. 22, 1907, and spent four years completing a pastoral visitation there. He was made a cardinal just three months before being elected to the papacy Sept. 3, 1914. He died Jan. 22, 1922. Two key efforts of his pontificate were for peace and the relief of human suffering caused by World War I.

Canonizations: Benedict canonized three saints; one of them was Joan of Arc.

Canon Law: He published the Code of Canon Law, developed by the commission set up by St. Pius X, May 27, 1917; it went into effect the following year.

Curia: He made great changes in the personnel of the Curia. He established the Congregation for the Oriental Churches May 1, 1917, and founded the Pontifical Oriental Institute in Rome later in the year.

Encyclicals: He issued 12 encyclicals. Peace was the theme of three of them. In another, published two years after the cessation of hostilities, he wrote about child victims of the war. He followed the lead of Leo XIII in *Spiritus Paraclitus*, Sept. 15, 1920, on biblical studies.

International Relations: He was largely frustrated on the international level because of the events and attitudes of the war period, but the number of diplomats accredited to the Vatican nearly doubled, from 14 to 26, between the time of his accession to the papacy and his death.

Peace Efforts: Benedict's stance in the war was one of absolute impartiality but not of uninterested neutrality. Because he would not take sides, he was suspected by both sides and the seven-point peace plan he offered to all belligerents Aug. 1, 1917, was turned down. The points of the plan were: recognition of the moral force of right; disarmament; acceptance of arbitration in cases of dispute; guarantee of freedom of the seas; renunciation of war indemnities; evacuation and restoration of occupied territories; examination of territorial claims in dispute.

Relief Efforts: Benedict assumed personal charge of Vatican relief efforts during the war. He set up an international missing persons bureau for contacts between prisoners and their families, but was forced to close it because of the suspicion of warring nations that it was a front for espionage operations. He persuaded the Swiss government to admit into the country military victims of tuberculosis.

Roman Question: Benedict prepared the way for the meetings and negotiations which led to settlement of the question in 1929.

PIUS XI

Pius XI (Ambrogio Damiano Achille Ratti) was born May 31, 1857, in Desio, Italy.

Educated at seminaries in Seviso and Milan, and at the Lombard College, Gregorian University and Academy of St. Thomas in Rome, he was ordained to the priesthood in 1879.

He taught at the major seminary of Milan from 1882 to 1888. Appointed to the staff of the Ambrosian Library in 1888, he remained there until 1911, acquiring a reputation for publishing works on palaeography and serving as director from 1907 to 1911. He then moved to the Vatican Library, of which he was prefect from 1914 to 1918. In 1919, he was named apostolic visitor to Poland in April, nuncio in June, and was made titular archbishop of Lepanto Oct. 28. He was made archbishop of Milan and cardinal June 13, 1921, before being elected to the papacy Feb. 6, 1922. He died Feb. 10, 1939.

Aim: The objective of his pontificate, as stated in the encyclical *Ubi Arcano*, Dec. 23, 1922, was to establish the reign and peace of Christ in society.

Canonizations: He canonized 34 saints, including the Jesuit Martyrs of North America, and conferred the title of Doctor of the Church on Sts. Peter Canisius, John of the Cross, Robert Bellarmine and Albertus Magnus.

Eastern Churches: He called for better understanding of the Eastern Churches in the encyclical *Rerum Orientalium* of Sept. 8, 1928, and developed facilities for the training of Eastern-Rite priests. He inaugurated steps for the codification of Eastern-Church law in 1929. In 1935 he made Syrian Patriarch Tappouni a cardinal.

Encyclicals: His first encyclical, *Ubi Arcano*, in addition to stating the aims of his pontificate, blueprinted Catholic Action and called for its development throughout the Church. In *Quas Primas*, Dec. 11, 1925, he established the feast of Christ the King for universal observance. Subjects of some of his other encyclicals were: Christian education, in *Rappresentanti in Terra*, Dec. 31, 1929; Christian marriage, in *Casti Connubii*, Dec. 31, 1930; social conditions and pressure for social change in line with the teaching in *Rerum Novarum*, in *Quadragesimo Anno*, May 15, 1931; atheistic Communism, in *Divini Redemptoris*, Mar. 19, 1937; the priesthood, in *Ad Catholici Sacerdotii*, Dec. 20, 1935.

Missions: Following the lead of Benedict XV,

Pius called for the training of native clergy in the pattern of their own respective cultures, and promoted missionary developments in various ways. He ordained six native bishops for China in 1926, one for Japan in 1927, and others for regions of Asia, China and India in 1933. He placed the first 40 mission dioceses under native bishops, saw the number of native priests increase from about 2,600 to more than 7,000 and the number of Catholics in missionary areas more than double from nine million.

In the apostolic constitution *Deus Scientiarum Dominus* of May 24, 1931, he ordered the introduction of missiology into theology courses.

Interfaith Relations: Pius was negative to the ecumenical movement among Protestants but approved the Malines Conversations, 1921 to 1926, between Anglicans and Catholics.

International Relations: Relations with the Mussolini government deteriorated from 1931 on, as indicated in the encyclical *Non Abbiamo Bisogno,* when the regime took steps to curb liberties and activities of the Church; they turned critical in 1938 with the emergence of racist policies. Relations deteriorated also in Germany from 1933 on, resulting finally in condemnation of the Nazis in the encyclical *Mit Brennender Sorge,* March, 1937. Pius sparked a revival of the Church in France by encouraging Catholics to work within the democratic framework of the Republic rather than foment trouble over restoration of a monarchy. Pius was powerless to influence developments related to the civil war which erupted in Spain in July, 1936, sporadic persecution and repression by the Calles regime in Mexico, and systematic persecution of the Church in the Soviet Union. Many of the 10 concordats and two agreements reached with European countries after World War I became casualties of World War II.

Roman Question: Pius negotiated for two and one-half years with the Italian government to settle the Roman Question by means of the Lateran Agreement of 1929. The agreement provided independent status for the State of Vatican City; made Catholicism the official religion of Italy, with pastoral and educational freedom and state recognition of Catholic marriages, religious orders and societies; and provided a financial payment to the Vatican for expropriation of the former States of the Church.

PIUS XII

Pius XII (Eugenio Maria Giovanni Pacelli) was born Mar. 2, 1876, in Rome.

Educated at the Gregorian University and the Lateran University, in Rome, he was ordained to the priesthood Apr. 2, 1899.

He entered the Vatican diplomatic service in 1901, worked on the codification of canon law, and was appointed secretary of the Congregation for Ecclesiastical Affairs in 1914. Three years later he was ordained titular archbishop of Sardis and made apostolic nuncio to Bavaria. He was nuncio to Germany from 1920 to 1929, when he was made a cardinal, and took office as papal secretary of state in the following year. His diplomatic negotiations resulted in

concordats between the Vatican and Bavaria (1924), Prussia (1929), Baden (1932), Austria and the German Republic (1933). He took part in negotiations which led to settlement of the Roman Question in 1929.

He was elected to the papacy Mar. 2, 1939. He died Oct. 9, 1958, at Castel Gandolfo after the 12th longest pontificate in history.

Canonizations: He canonized 34 saints, including Mother Frances X. Cabrini, the first U.S. citizen-Saint.

Cardinals: He raised 56 prelates to the rank of cardinal in two consistories held in 1946 and 1953. There were 57 cardinals at the time of his death.

Church Organization and Missions: He increased the number of dioceses from 1,696 to 2,048. He established native hierarchies in China (1946), Burma (1955) and parts of Africa, and extended the native structure of the Church in India. He ordained the first black bishop for Africa.

Communism: In addition to opposing and condemning Communism on numerous occasions, he decreed in 1949 the penalty of excommunication for all Catholics holding formal and willing allegiance to the Communist Party and its policies. During his reign the Church was persecuted in some 15 countries which fell under communist domination.

Doctrine and Liturgy: He proclaimed the dogma of the Assumption of the Blessed Virgin Mary Nov. 1, 1950 (apostolic constitution, *Munificentissimus Deus.*)

In various encyclicals and other enactments, he provided background for the *aggiornamento* introduced by his successor, John XXIII: by his formulations of doctrine and practice regarding the Mystical Body of Christ, the liturgy, sacred music and biblical studies; by the revision of the Rites of Holy Week; by initiation of the work which led to the calendar-missal-breviary reform ordered into effect Jan. 1, 1961; by the first of several modifications of the Eucharistic fast; by extending the time of Mass to the evening. He instituted the feasts of Mary, Queen, and of St. Joseph the Worker, and clarified teaching concerning devotion to the Sacred Heart.

His 41 encyclicals and nearly 1,000 public addresses made Pius one of the greatest teaching popes. His concern in all his communications was to deal with specific points at issue and/or to bring Christian principles to bear on contemporary world problems.

Peace Efforts: Before the start of World War II, he tried unsuccessfully to get the contending nations — Germany and Poland, France and Italy — to settle their differences peaceably. During the war, he offered his services to mediate the widened conflict, spoke out against the horrors of war and the suffering it caused, mobilized relief work for its victims, proposed a five-point program for peace in Christmas messages from 1939 to 1942, and secured a generally open status for the city of Rome. After the war, he endorsed the principles and intent of the United Nations and continued efforts for peace.

United States: Pius appointed more than 200 of the 265 American bishops resident in the U.S. and abroad in 1958, erected 27 dioceses in this country, and raised seven dioceses to archiepiscopal rank.

JOHN XXIII

John XXIII (Angelo Roncalli) was born Nov. 25, 1881, at Sotte il Monte, Italy.

He was educated at the seminary of the Bergamo diocese and the Pontifical Seminary in Rome, where he was ordained to the priesthood Aug. 10, 1904.

He spent the first nine or 10 years of his priesthood as secretary to the bishop of Bergamo and as an instructor in the seminary there. He served as a medic and chaplain in the Italian army during World War I. Afterwards, he resumed duties in his own diocese until he was called to Rome in 1921 for work with the Society for the Propagation of the Faith.

He began diplomatic service in 1925 as titular archbishop of Areopolis and apostolic visitor to Bulgaria. A succession of offices followed: apostolic delegate to Bulgaria (1931-1935); titular archbishop of Mesembria, apostolic delegate to Turkey and Greece, administrator of the Latin vicariate apostolic of Istanbul (1935-1944); apostolic nuncio to France (1944-1953). On these missions, he was engaged in delicate negotiations involving Roman-Rite and Orthodox relations; the needs of people suffering from the consequences of World War II; and unsettling suspicions arising from wartime conditions.

He was made a cardinal Jan. 12, 1953, and three days later was appointed patriarch of Venice, the position he held until his election to the papacy Oct. 28, 1958. He died of stomach cancer June 3, 1963.

John was a strong and vigorous pope whose influence far outmeasured both his age and the shortness of his time in the papacy.

Second Vatican Council: John announced Jan. 25, 1959, his intention of convoking the 21st ecumenical council in history to renew life in the Church, to reform its structures and institutions, and to explore ways and means of promoting unity among Christians. Through the council, which completed its work two and one-half years after his death, he ushered in a new era in the history of the Church.

Canon Law: He established a commission Mar. 28, 1963, for revision of the Code of Canon Law. The revised Code was promulgated in 1983.

Canonizations: He canonized 10 saints and beatified Mother Elizabeth Ann Seton, the first native of the U.S. ever so honored. He named St. Lawrence of Brindisi a Doctor of the Church.

Cardinals: He created 52 cardinals in five consistories, raising membership of the College of Cardinals above the traditional number of 70; at one time in 1962, the membership was 87. He made the college more international in representation than it had ever been, appointing the first cardinals from the Philippines, Japan and Africa. He ordered episcopal ordination for all cardinals. He relieved the suburban bishops of Rome of ordinary jurisdiction over their dioceses so they might devote all their time to business of the Roman Curia.

Eastern Rites: He made all Eastern-Rite patriarchs members of the Congregation for the Oriental Churches.

Ecumenism: He assigned to the Second Vatican Council the task of finding ways and means of promoting unity among Christians. He established

the Vatican Secretariat for Promoting Christian Unity June 5, 1960. He showed his desire for more cordial relations with the Orthodox by sending personal representatives to visit Patriarch Athenagoras I June 27, 1961; approved a mission of five delegates to the General Assembly of the World Council of Churches which met in New Delhi, India, in November, 1961; removed a number of pejorative references to Jews in the Roman-Rite liturgy for Good Friday.

Encyclicals: Of the eight encyclicals he issued, the two outstanding ones were *Mater et Magistra* ("Christianity and Social Progress"), in which he recapitulated, updated and extended the social doctrine stated earlier by Leo XIII and Pius XI; and *Pacem in Terris* ("Peace on Earth"), the first encyclical ever addressed to all men of good will as well as to Catholics, on the natural-law principles of peace.

Liturgy: In forwarding liturgical reforms already begun by Pius XII, he ordered a calendar-missal-breviary reform into effect Jan. 1, 1961. He authorized the use of vernacular languages in the administration of the sacraments and approved giving Holy Communion to the sick in afternoon hours. He selected the liturgy as the first topic of major discussion by the Second Vatican Council.

Missions: He issued an encyclical on the missionary activity of the Church; established native hierarchies in Indonesia, Vietnam and Korea; and called on North American superiors of religious institutes to have one-tenth of their members assigned to work in Latin America by 1971.

Peace: John spoke and used his moral influence for peace in 1961 when tension developed over Berlin, in 1962 during the Algerian revolt from France, and later the same year in the Cuban missile crisis. His efforts were singled out for honor by the Balzan Peace Foundation. In 1963, he was posthumously awarded the U.S. Presidential Medal of Freedom.

PAUL VI

Paul VI (Giovanni Battista Montini) was born Sept. 26, 1897, at Concesio in northern Italy.

Educated at Brescia, he was ordained to the priesthood May 29, 1920. He pursued additional studies at the Pontifical Academy for Noble Ecclesiastics and the Pontifical Gregorian University. In 1924 he began 30 years of service in the Secretariat of State; as undersecretary from 1937 until 1954, he was closely associated with Pius XII and was heavily engaged in organizing informational and relief services during and after World War II.

He was ordained archbishop of Milan Dec. 12, 1954, and was inducted into the College of Cardinals Dec. 15, 1958. He was elected to the papacy June 21, 1963, two days after the conclave began. He died of a heart attack Aug. 6, 1978.

Second Vatican Council: He reconvened the Second Vatican Council after the death of John XXIII, presided over its second, third and fourth sessions, formally promulgated the 16 documents it produced, and devoted the whole of his pontificate to the task of putting them into effect throughout the Church. The main thrust of his pontificate — in a milieu of cultural and other changes in the Church and the world — was toward institutionalization and control of the authentic trends articulated and set in motion by the council.

Canonizations: He canonized 84 saints. They included groups of 22 Ugandan martyrs and 40 martyrs of England and Wales, as well as two Americans — Elizabeth Ann Bayley Seton and John Nepomucene Neumann.

Cardinals: He created 144 cardinals, and gave the Sacred College a more international complexion than it ever had before. He limited participation in papal elections to 120 cardinals under the age of 80.

Collegiality: He established the Synod of Bishops in 1965 and called it into session five times. He stimulated the formation and operation of regional conferences of bishops, and of consultative bodies on other levels.

Creed and Holy Year: On June 30, 1968, he issued a Creed of the People of God in conjunction with the celebration of a Year of Faith. He proclaimed and led the observance of a Holy Year from Christmas Eve of 1974 to Christmas Eve of 1975.

Diplomacy: He met with many world leaders, including Soviet President Nikolai Podgorny in 1967, Marshal Tito of Yugoslavia in 1971 and President Nicolas Ceausescu of Romania in 1973. He worked constantly to reduce tension between the Church and the intransigent regimes of Eastern European countries by means of a detente type of policy called Ostpolitik. He agreed to significant revisions to efforts to revise the concordat with Italy. More then 40 countries established diplomatic relations with the Vatican during his pontificate.

Encyclicals: He issued seven encyclicals, three of which are the best known. In *Populorum Progressio* ("Development of Peoples") he appealed to wealthy countries to take "concrete action" to promote human development and to remedy imbalances between richer and poorer nations; this encyclical, coupled with other documents and related actions, launched the Church into a new depth of involvement as a public advocate for human rights and for humanizing social, political and economic policies. In *Sacerdotalis Caelibatus* ("Priestly Celibacy") he reaffirmed the strict observance of priestly celibacy throughout the Western Church. In *Humanae Vitae* ("Of Human Life") he condemned abortion, sterilization and artificial birth control, in line with traditional teaching and in "defense of life, the gift of God, the glory of the family, the strength of the people."

Interfaith Relations: He initiated formal consultation and informal dialogue on international and national levels between Catholics and non-Catholics — Orthodox, Anglicans, Protestants, Jews, Moslems, Buddhists, Hindus, and unbelievers. He and Greek Orthodox Patriarch Athenagoras I of Constantinople nullified in 1965 the mutual excommunications imposed by their respective churches in 1054.

Liturgy: He carried out the most extensive liturgical reform in history, involving a new Order of the Mass effective in 1969, a revised church calendar in 1970, revisions and translations into vernacular languages of all sacramental rites and other liturgical texts.

Ministries: He authorized the restoration of the permanent diaconate in the Roman Rite and the establishment of new ministries of lay persons.

Peace: In 1968, he instituted the annual observance of a World Day of Peace on New Year's Day as a means of addressing a message of peace to all the world's political leaders and the peoples of all nations. The most dramatic of his many appeals for peace and efforts to ease international tensions was his plea for "No more war!" before the United Nations Oct. 4, 1965.

Pilgrimages: A "Pilgrim Pope," he made pastoral visits to the Holy Land and India in 1964, the United Nations and New York City in 1965, Portugal and Turkey in 1967, Colombia in 1968, Switzerland and Uganda in 1969, and Asia, Pacific islands and Australia in 1970. While in Manila in 1970, he was stabbed by a Bolivian artist who made an attempt on his life.

Roman Curia: He reorganized the central administrative organs of the Church in line with provisions of the apostolic constitution, *Regimini Ecclesiae Universae,* streamlining procedures for more effective service and giving the agencies a more international perspective by drawing officials and consultors from all over the world. He also instituted a number of new commissions and other bodies. Coupled with curial reorganization was a simplification of papal ceremonies.

JOHN PAUL I

John Paul I (Albino Luciani) was born Oct. 17, 1912, in Forno di Canale (now Canale d'Agordo) in northern Italy.

Educated at the minor seminary in Feltre and the major seminary of the Diocese of Belluno, he was ordained to the priesthood July 7, 1935. He pursued further studies at the Pontifical Gregorian University in Rome and was awarded a doctorate in theology. From 1937 to 1947 he was vice rector of the Belluno seminary, where he taught dogmatic and moral theology, canon law and sacred art. He was appointed vicar general of his diocese in 1947 and served as director of catechetics.

Ordained bishop of Vittorio Veneto Dec. 27, 1958, he attended all sessions of the Second Vatican Council, participated in three assemblies of the Synod of Bishops (1971, 1974 and 1977), and was vice president of the Italian Bishops' Conference from 1972 to 1975.

He was appointed archbishop and patriarch of Venice Dec. 15, 1969, and was inducted into the College of Cardinals Mar. 5, 1973.

He was elected to the papacy Aug. 26, 1978, on the fourth ballot cast by the 111 cardinals participating in the largest and one of the shortest conclaves in history. The quickness of his election was matched by the brevity of his pontificate of 33 days, during which he delivered 19 addresses. He died of a heart attack Sept. 28, 1978.

JOHN PAUL II

See separate entry.

PAPAL ENCYCLICALS — BENEDICT XIV (1740) TO JOHN PAUL II

(Source: *The Papal Encyclicals* [5 vols.], Claudia Carlen, I.H.M.; Pieran Press, Ann Arbor, Mich. Used with permission.)

An encyclical letter is a pastoral letter addressed by a pope to the whole Church. In general, it concerns matters of doctrine, morals or discipline. Its formal title consists of the first few words of the official text. A few encyclicals, notably *Pacem in terris* by John XXIII and *Ecclesiam Suam* by Paul VI, have been addressed to "all men of good will" as well as to bishops and the faithful in communion with the Church.

An encyclical epistle, which is like an encyclical letter in many respects, is addressed to part of the Church, that is, to the bishops and faithful of a particular country or area. Its contents may concern other than doctrinal, moral or disciplinary matters of universal significance; for example, the commemoration of historical events, conditions in a certain country.

The authority of encyclicals was stated by Pius XII in the encyclical *Humani generis* Aug. 12, 1950: "Nor must it be thought that what is contained in encyclical letters does not of itself demand assent, on the pretext that the popes do not exercise in them the supreme power of their teaching authority. Rather, such teachings belong to the ordinary magisterium, of which it is true to say: 'He who hears you, hears me' (Lk. 10:16); for the most part, too, what is expounded and inculcated in encyclical letters already appertains to Catholic doctrine for other reasons."

The Second Vatican Council declared: "Religious submission of will and of mind must be shown in a special way to the authentic teaching authority of the Roman Pontiff, even when he is not speaking *ex cathedra*. That is, it must be shown in such a way that his supreme magisterium is acknowledged with reverence, the judgments made by him are sincerely adhered to, according to his manifest mind and will. His mind and will in the matter may be known chiefly either from the character of the documents (one of which could be an encyclical), from his frequent repetition of the same doctrine, or from his manner of speaking" (*Dogmatic Constitution on the Church*, No. 25).

The following list contains the titles and indicates the subject matter of encyclical letters and epistles. The latter are generally distinguishable by the limited scope of their titles or contents.

Benedict XIV
(1740-1758)

1740: *Ubi primum* (On the duties of bishops), Dec. 3.

1741: *Quanta cura* (Forbidding traffic in alms), June 30.

1743: *Nimiam licentiam* (To the bishops of Poland: on validity of marriages), May 18.

1745: *Vix pervenit* (To the bishops of Italy: on usury and other dishonest profit), Nov. 1.

1748: *Magnae Nobis* (To the bishops of Poland: on marriage impediments and dispensations), June 29.

1749: *Peregrinantes* (To all the faithful: proclaiming a Holy Year for 1750), May 5.

Apostolica Constitutio (On preparation for the Holy Year), June 26.

1751: *A quo primum* (To the bishops of Poland: on Jews and Christians living in the same place), June 14.

1754: *Cum Religiosi* (To the bishops of the States of the Church: on catechesis), June 26.

Quod Provinciale (To the bishops of Albania: on Christians using Mohammedan names), Aug. 1.

1755: *Allatae sunt* (To missionaries of the Orient: on the observance of Oriental rites), July 26.

1756: *Ex quo primum* (To bishops of the Greek rite: on the Euchologion), Mar. 1.

Ex omnibus (To the bishops of France: on the apostolic constitution, *Unigenitus), Oct. 16.

Clement XIII
(1758-1769)

1758: *A quo die* (Unity among Christians), Sept. 13.

1759: *Cum primum* (On observing canonical sanctions), Sept. 17.

Appetente Sacro (On the spiritual advantages of fasting), Dec. 20.

1761: *In Dominico agro* (On instruction in the faith), June 14.

1766: *Christianae reipublicae* (On the dangers of anti-Christian writings), Nov. 25.

1768: *Summa quae* (To the bishops of Poland: on the Church in Poland), Jan. 6.

Clement XIV
(1769-1774)

1769: *Decet quam maxime* (To the bishops of Sardinia: on abuses in taxes and benefices), Sept. 21.

Inscrutabili divinae sapientiae (To all Christians: proclaiming a universal jubilee), Dec. 12.

Cum summi (Proclaiming a universal jubilee), Dec. 12.

1774: *Salutis nostrae* (To all Christians: proclaiming a universal jubilee), Apr. 30.

Pius VI
(1775-1799)

1775: *Inscrutabile* (On the problems of the pontificate), Dec. 25.

1791: *Charitas* (To the bishops of France: on the civil oath in France), Apr. 13.

Pius VII
(1800-1823)

1800: *Diu satis* (To the bishops of France: on a return to Gospel principles), May 15.

Leo XII
(1823-1829)

1824: *Ubi primum* (To all bishops: on Leo XII's assuming the pontificate), May 5.

Quod hoc ineunte (Proclaiming a universal jubilee), May 24.

1825: *Charitate Christi* (Extending jubilee to the entire Church), Dec. 25.

Pius VIII
(1829-1830)

1829: *Traditi humilitati* (On Pius VIII's program for the pontificate), May 24.

Gregory XVI
(1831-1846)

1832: *Summo iugiter studio* (To the bishops of Bavaria: on mixed marriages), May 27.

Cum primum (To the bishops of Poland: on civil obedience), June 9.

Mirari vos (On liberalism and religious indifferentism), Aug. 15.

1833: *Quo graviora* (To the bishops of the Rhineland: on the "pragmatic Constitution"), Oct. 4.

1834: *Singulari Nos* (On the errors of Lammenais), June 25.

1835: *Commissum divinitus* (To clergy of Switzerland: on Church and State), May 17.

1840: *Probe nostis* (On the Propagation of the Faith), Sept. 18.

1841: *Quas vestro* (To the bishops of Hungary: on mixed marriages), Apr. 30.

1844: *Inter praecipuas* (On biblical societies), May 8.

Pius IX
(1846-1878)

1846: *Qui pluribus* (On faith and religion), Nov. 9.

1847: *Praedecessores Nostros* (On aid for Ireland), Mar. 25.

Ubi primum (To religious superiors: on discipline for religious), June 17.

1849: *Ubi primum* (On the Immaculate Conception), Feb. 2.

Nostis et Nobiscum (To the bishops of Italy: on the Church in the Pontifical States), Dec. 8.

1851: *Exultavit cor Nostrum* (On the effects of jubilee), Nov. 21.

1852: *Nemo certe ignorat* (To the bishops of Ireland: on the discipline for clergy), Mar. 25.

Probe noscitis Venerabiles (To the bishops of Spain: on the discipline for clergy), May 17.

1853: *Inter multiplices* (To the bishops of France: pleading for unity of spirit), Mar. 21.

1854: *Neminem vestrum* (To clergy and faithful of Constantinople: on the persecution of Armenians), Feb. 2.

Optime noscitis (To the bishops of Ireland: on the proposed Catholic university for Ireland), Mar. 20.

Apostolicae Nostrae caritatis (Urging prayers for peace), Aug. 1.

1855: *Optime noscitis* (To the bishops of Austria: on episcopal meetings), Nov. 5.

1856: *Singulari quidem* (To the bishops of Austria: on the Church in Austria), Mar. 17.

1858: *Cum nuper* (To the bishops of the Kingdom of the Two Sicilies: on care for clerics), Jan. 20.

Amantissimi Redemptoris (On priests and the care of souls), May 3.

1859: *Cum sancta mater Ecclesia* (Pleading for public prayer), Apr. 27.

Qui nuper (On Pontifical States), June 18.

1860: *Nullis certe verbis* (On the need for civil sovereignty), Jan. 19.

1862: *Amantissimus* (To bishops of the Oriental rite: on the care of the churches), Apr. 8.

1863: *Quanto conficiamur moerore* (To the bishops of Italy: on promotion of false doctrines), Aug. 10.

Incredibili (To the bishops of Bogota: on persecution in New Granada), Sept. 17.

1864: *Maximae quidem* (To the bishops of Bavaria: on the Church in Bavaria), Aug. 18.

Quanta cura (Condemning current errors), Dec. 8.

1865: *Meridionali Americae* (To the bishops of South America: on the seminary for native clergy), Sept. 30.

1867: *Levate* (On the afflictions of the Church), Oct. 27.

1870: *Respicientes* (Protesting the taking of the Pontifical States), Nov. 1.

1871: *Ubi Nos* (To all bishops: on Pontifical States), May 15.

Beneficia Dei (On the twenty-fifth anniversary of his pontificate), June 4.

Saepe Venerabiles Fratres (On thanksgiving for twenty-five years of pontificate), Aug. 5.

1872: *Quae in Patriarchatu* (To bishops and people of Chaldea: on the Church in Chaldea), Nov. 16.

1873: *Quartus supra* (To bishops and people of the Armenian rite: on the Church in Armenia), Jan. 6.

Etsi multa (On the Church in Italy, Germany and Switzerland), Nov. 21.

1874: *Vix dum a Nobis* (To the bishops of Austria: on the Church in Austria), Mar. 7.

Omnem sollicitudinem (To the bishops of the Ruthenian rite: on the Greek-Ruthenian rite), May 13.

Gravibus Ecclesiae (To all bishops and faithful: proclaiming a jubilee for 1875), Dec. 24.

1875: *Quod nunquam* (To the bishops of Prussia: on the Church in Prussia), Feb. 5.

Graves ac diuturnae (To the bishops of Switzerland: on the Church in Switzerland), Mar. 23.

Leo XIII
(1878-1903)

1878: *Inscrutabili Dei consilio* (On the evils of society), Apr. 21.

Quod Apostolici muneris (On socialism), Dec. 28.

1879: *Aeterni Patris* (On the restoration of Christian philosophy), Aug. 4.

1880: *Arcanum* (On Christian marriage), Feb. 10.

Grande munus (On Sts. Cyril and Methodius), Sept. 30.

Sancta Dei civitas (On mission societies), Dec. 3.

1881: *Diuturnum* (On the origin of civil power), June 29.

Licet multa (To the bishops of Belgium: on Catholics in Belgium), Aug. 3.

1882: *Etsi Nos* (To the bishops of Italy: on conditions in Italy), Feb. 15.

Auspicato concessum (On St. Francis of Assisi), Sept. 17.

Cum multa (To the bishops of Spain: on conditions in Spain), Dec. 8.

1883: *Supremi Apostolatus officio* (On devotion to the Rosary), Sept. 1.

1884: *Nobilissima Gallorum gens* (To the bishops of France: on the religious question), Feb. 8.

Humanum genus (On Freemasonry), Apr. 20.

Superiore anno (On the recitation of the Rosary), Aug. 30.

1885: *Immortale Dei* (On the Christian constitution of states), Nov. 1.

Spectata fides (To the bishops of England: on Christian education), Nov. 27.

Quod auctoritate (Proclamation of extraordinary Jubilee), Dec. 22.

1886: *Iampridem* (To the bishops of Prussia: on Catholicism in Germany), Jan. 6.

Quod multum (To the bishops of Hungary: on the liberty of the Church), Aug. 22.

Pergrata (To the bishops of Portugal: on the Church in Portugal), Sept. 14.

1887: *Vi e ben noto* (To the bishops of Italy: on the Rosary and public life), Sept. 20.

Officio sanctissimo (To the bishops of Bavaria: on the Church in Bavaria), Dec. 22.

1888: *Quod anniversarius* (On his sacerdotal jubilee), Apr. 1.

In plurimis (To the bishops of Brazil: on the abolition of slavery), May 5.

Libertas (On the nature of human liberty), June 20.

Saepe Nos (To the bishops of Ireland: on boycotting in Ireland), June 24.

Paterna caritas (To the Patriarch of Cilicia and the archbishops and bishops of the Armenian people: on reunion with Rome), July 25.

Quam aerumnosa (To the bishops of America: on Italian immigrants), Dec. 10.

Etsi cunctas (To the bishops of Ireland: on the Church in Ireland), Dec. 21.

Exeunte iam anno (On the right ordering of Christian life), Dec. 25.

1889: *Magni Nobis* (To the bishops of the United States: on the Catholic University of America), Mar. 7.

Quamquam pluries (On devotion to St. Joseph), Aug. 15.

1890: *Sapientiae Christianae* (On Christians as citizens), Jan. 10.

Dall'alto Dell'Apostolico seggio (To the bishops and people of Italy: on Freemasonry in Italy), Oct. 15.

Catholicae Ecclesiae (On slavery in the missions), Nov. 20.

1891: *In ipso* (To the bishops of Austria: on episcopal reunions in Austria), Mar. 3.

Rerum novarum (On capital and labor), May 15.

Pastoralis (To the bishops of Portugal: on religious union), June 25.

Pastoralis officii (To the bishops of Germany and Austria: on the morality of dueling), Sept. 12.

Octobri mense (On the Rosary), Sept. 22.

1892: *Au milieu des sollicitudes* (To the bishops, clergy and faithful of France: on the Church and State in France), Feb. 16.

Quarto abeunte saeculo (To the bishops of Spain, Italy, and the two Americas: on the Columbus quadricentennial), July 16.

Magnae Dei Matris (On the Rosary), Sept. 8.

Inimica vis (To the bishops of Italy: on Freemasonry), Dec. 8.

Custodi di quella fede (To the Italian people: on Freemasonry), Dec. 8.

1893: *Ad extremas* (On seminaries for native clergy), June 24.

Constanti Hungarorum (To the bishops of Hungary: on the Church in Hungary), Sept. 2.

Laetitiae sanctae (Commending devotion to the Rosary), Sept. 8.

Non mediocri (To the bishops of Spain: on the Spanish College in Rome), Oct. 25.

Providentissimus Deus (On the study of Holy Scripture), Nov. 18.

1894: *Caritatis* (To the bishops of Poland: on the Church in Poland), Mar. 19.

Inter graves (To the bishops of Peru: on the Church in Peru), May 1.

Litteras a vobis (To the bishops of Brazil: on the clergy in Brazil), July 2.

Iucunda semper expectatione (On the Rosary), Sept. 8.

Christi nomen (On the propagation of the Faith and Eastern churches), Dec. 24.

1895: *Longinqua* (To the bishops of the United States: on Catholicism in the United States), Jan. 6.

Permoti Nos (To the bishops of Belgium: on social conditions in Belgium), July 10.

Adiutricem (On the Rosary), Sept. 5.

1896: *Insignes* (To the bishops of Hungary: on the Hungarian millennium), May 1.

Satis cognitum (On the unity of the Church), June 29.

Fidentem piumque animum (On the Rosary), Sept. 20.

1897: *Divinum illud munus* (On the Holy Spirit), May 9.

Militantis Ecclesiae (To the bishops of Austria, Germany, and Switzerland: on St. Peter Canisius), Aug. 1.

Augustissimae Virginis Mariae (On the Confraternity of the Holy Rosary), Sept. 12.

Affari vos (To the bishops of Canada: on the Manitoba school question), Dec. 8.

1898: *Caritatis studium* (To the bishops of Scotland: on the Church in Scotland), July 25.

Spesse volte (To the bishops, priests, and people of Italy: on the suppression of Catholic institutions), Aug. 5.

Quam religiosa (To the bishops of Peru: on civil marriage law), Aug. 16.

Diuturni temporis (On the Rosary), Sept. 5.

Quum diuturnum (To the bishops of Latin America: on Latin American bishops' plenary council), Dec. 25.

1899: *Annum Sacrum* (On consecration to the Sacred Heart), May 25.

Depuis le jour (To the archbishops, bishops, and clergy of France: on the education of the clergy), Sept. 8.

Paternae (To the bishops of Brazil: on the education of the clergy), Sept. 18.

1900: *Omnibus compertum* (To the Patriarch and bishops of the Greek-Melkite rite: on unity among the Greek Melkites), July 21.

Tametsi futura prospicientibus (On Jesus Christ the Redeemer), Nov. 1.

1901: *Graves de communi re* (On Christian democracy), Jan. 18.

Gravissimas (To the bishops of Portugal: on religious orders in Portugal), May 16.

Reputantibus (To the bishops of Bohemia and Moravia: on the language question in Bohemia), Aug. 20.

Urbanitatis Veteris (To the bishops of the Latin church in Greece: on the foundation of a seminary in Athens), Nov. 20.

1902: *In amplissimo* (To the bishops of the United States: on the Church in the United States), Apr. 15.

Quod votis (To the bishops of Austria: on the proposed Catholic University), Apr. 30.

Mirae caritatis (On the Holy Eucharist), May 28.

Quae ad Nos (To the bishops of Bohemia and Moravia: on the Church in Bohemia and Moravia), Nov. 22.

Fin dal principio (To the bishops of Italy: on the education of the clergy), Dec. 8.

Dum multa (To the bishops of Ecuador: on marriage legislation), Dec. 24.

Saint Pius X
(1903-1914)

1903: *E supremi* (On the restoration of all things in Christ), Oct. 4.

1904: *Ad diem illum laetissimum* (On the Immaculate Conception), Feb. 2.

Iucunda sane (On Pope Gregory the Great), Mar. 12.

1905: *Acerbo nimis* (On teaching Christian doctrine), Apr. 15.

Il fermo proposito (To the bishops of Italy: on Catholic Action in Italy), June 11.

1906: *Vehementer Nos* (To the bishops, clergy, and people of France: on the French Law of Separation), Feb. 11.

Tribus circiter (On the Mariavites or Mystic Priests of Poland), Apr. 5.

Pieni l'animo (To the bishops of Italy: on the clergy in Italy), July 28.

Gravissimo officio munere (To the bishops of France: on French associations of worship), Aug. 10.

1907: *Une fois encore* (To the bishops, clergy, and people of France: on the separation of Church and State), Jan. 6.

Pascendi dominici gregis (On the doctrines of the Modernists), Sept. 8.

1909: *Communium rerum* (On St. Anselm of Aosta), Apr. 21.

1910: *Editae saepe* (On St. Charles Borromeo), May 26.

1911: *Iamdudum* (On the Law of Separation in Portugal), May 24.

1912: *Lacrimabili statu* (To the bishops of Latin America: on the Indians of South America), June 7.

Singulari quadam (To the bishops of Germany: on labor organizations), Sept. 24.

Benedict XV
(1914-1922)

1914: *Ad beatissimi Apostolorum* (Appeal for peace), Nov. 1.

1917: *Humani generis Redemptionem* (On preaching the Word of God), June 15.

1918: *Quod iam diu* (On the future peace conference), Dec. 1.

1919: *In hac tanta* (To the bishops of Germany: on St. Boniface), May 14.

Paterno iam diu (On children of central Europe), Nov. 24.

1920: *Pacem, Dei munus pulcherrimum* (On peace and Christian reconciliation), May 23.

Spiritus Paraclitus (On St. Jerome), Sept. 15.

Principi Apostolorum Petro (On St. Ephrem the Syrian), Oct. 5.

Annus iam plenus (On children of central Europe), Dec. 1.

1921: *Sacra propediem* (On the Third Order of St. Francis), Jan. 6.

In praeclara summorum (To professors and students of fine arts in Catholic institutions of learning: on Dante), Apr. 30.

Fausto appetente die (On St. Dominic), June 29.

Pius XI
(1922-1939)

1922: *Ubi arcano Dei consilio* (On the peace of Christ in the Kingdom of Christ), Dec. 23.

1923: *Rerum omnium perturbationem* (On St. Francis de Sales), Jan. 26.

Studiorum Ducem (On St. Thomas Aquinas), June 29.

Ecclesiam Dei (On St. Josaphat), Nov. 12.

1924: *Maximam gravissimamque* (To the bishops, clergy, and people of France: on French diocesan associations), Jan. 18.

1925: *Quas primas* (On the feast of Christ the King), Dec. 11.

1926: *Rerum Ecclesiae* (On Catholic missions), Feb. 28.

Rite expiatis (On St. Francis of Assisi), Apr. 30.

Iniquis afflictisque (On the persecution of the Church in Mexico), Nov. 18.

1928: *Mortalium animos* (On religious unity), Jan. 6.

Miserentissimus Redemptor (On reparation to the Sacred Heart), May 8.

Rerum Orientalium (On the promotion of Oriental Studies), Sept. 8.

1929: *Mens Nostra* (On the promotion of Spiritual Exercises), Dec. 20.

Quinquagesimo ante (On his sacerdotal jubilee), Dec. 23.

Rappresentanti in terra (On Christian education), Dec. 31. [Latin text, *Divini illius magistri*, published several months later with minor changes.]

1930: *Ad salutem* (On St. Augustine), Apr. 20.

Casti connubii (On Christian Marriage), Dec. 31.

1931: *Quadragesimo anno* (Commemorating the fortieth anniversary of Leo XIII's *Rerum novarum*: on reconstruction of the soical order), May 15.

Non abbiamo bisogno (On Catholic Action in Italy), June 29.

Nova impendet (On the economic crisis), Oct. 2.

Lux veritatis (On the Council of Ephesus), Dec. 25.

1932: *Caritate Christi compulsi* (On the Sacred Heart), May 3.

Acerba animi (To the bishops of Mexico: on persecution of the Church in Mexico), Sept. 29.

1933: *Dilectissima Nobis* (To the bishops, clergy, and people of Spain: on oppression of the Church in Spain), June 3.

1935: *Ad Catholici sacerdotii* (On the Catholic priesthood), Dec. 20.

1936: *Vigilanti cura* (To the bishops of the United States: on motion pictures), June 29.

1937: *Mit brennender Sorge* (To the bishops of Germany: on the Church and the German Reich), Mar. 14.

Divini Redemptoris (On atheistic communism), Mar. 19.

Nos es muy conocida (To the bishops of Mexico: on the religious situation in Mexico), Mar. 28.

Ingravescentibus malis (On the Rosary) Sept. 29.

Pius XII
(1939-1958)

1939: *Summi Pontificatus* (On the unity of human society), Oct. 20.

Sertum laetitiae (To the bishops of the United States: on the 150th anniversary of the establishment of the hierarchy in the United States), Nov. 1.

1940: *Saeculo exeunte octavo* (To the bishops of Portugal and its colonies: on the eighth centenary of the independence of Portugal), June 13.

1943: *Mystici Corporis Christi* (On the Mystical Body of Christ), June 29.

Divino afflante Spiritu (On promoting biblical studies, commemorating the fiftieth anniversary of *Providentissimus Deus*), Sept. 30.

1944: *Orientalis Ecclesiae* (On St. Cyril, Patriarch of Alexandria), Apr. 9.

1945: *Communium interpretes dolorum* (To the bishops of the world: appealing for prayers for peace during May), Apr. 15.

Orientales omnes Ecclesias (On the 350th anniversary of the reunion of the Ruthenian Church with the Apostolic See), Dec. 23.

1946: *Quemadmodum* (Pleading for the care of the world's destitute children), Jan. 6.

Deiparae Virginis Mariae (To all bishops: on the possibility of defining the Assumption of the Blessed Virgin Mary as a dogma of faith), May 1.

1947: *Fulgens radiatur* (On St. Benedict), Mar. 21.

Mediator Dei (On the sacred liturgy), Nov. 20.

Optatissima pax (Prescribing public prayers for social and world peace), Dec. 18.

1948: *Auspicia quaedam* (On public prayers for world peace and solution of the problem of Palestine), May 1.

In multiplicibus curis (On prayers for peace in Palestine), Oct. 24.

1949: *Redemptoris nostri cruciatus* (On the holy places in Palestine), Apr. 15.

1950: *Anni Sacri* (On the program for combatting atheistic propaganda throughout the world), Mar. 12.

Summi maeroris (On public prayers for peace), July 19.

Humani generis (Concerning some false opinions threatening to undermine the foundations of Catholic doctrine), Aug. 12.

Mirabile illud (On the crusade of prayers for peace), Dec. 6.

1951: *Evangelii praecones* (On the promotion of Catholic missions), June 2.

Sempiternus Rex Christus (On the Council of Chalcedon), Sept. 8.

Ingruentium malorum (On reciting the Rosary), Sept. 15.

1952: *Orientales Ecclesias* (On the persecuted Eastern Church), Dec. 15.

1953: *Doctor Mellifluus* (On St. Bernard of Clairvaux, the last of the fathers), May 24.

Fulgens corona (Proclaiming a Marian Year to commemorate the centenary of the definition of the dogma of the Immaculate Conception), Sept. 8.

1954: *Sacra virginitas* (On consecrated virginity), Mar. 25.

Ecclesiae fastos (To the bishops of Great Britain, Germany, Austria, France, Belgium, and Holland: on St. Boniface), June 5.

Ad Sinarum gentem (To the bishops, clergy, and people of China: on the supranationality of the Church), Oct. 7.

Ad Caeli Reginam (Proclaiming the Queenship of Mary), Oct. 11.

1955: *Musicae sacrae* (On sacred music), Dec. 25.

1956: *Haurietis aquas* (On devotion to the Sacred Heart), May 15.

Luctuosissimi eventus (Urging public prayers for peace and freedom for the people of Hungary), Oct. 28.

Laetamur admodum (Renewing exhortation for prayers for peace for Poland, Hungary, and especially for the Middle East), Nov. 1.

Datis nuperrime (Lamenting the sorrowful events in Hungary and condemning the ruthless use of force), Nov. 5.

1957: *Fidei donum* (On the present condition of the Catholic missions, especially in Africa), Apr. 21.

Invicti athletae (On St. Andrew Bobola), May 16.

Le pelerinage de Lourdes (Warning against materialism on the centenary of the apparitions at Lourdes), July 2.

Miranda prorsus (On the communications field: motion picture, radio, television), Sept. 8.

1958: *Ad Apostolorum Principis* (To the bishops of China; on Communism and the Church in China), June 29.

Meminisse iuvat (On prayers for persecuted Church), July 14.

John XXIII
(1958-1963)

1959: *Ad Petri Cathedram* (On truth, unity, and peace, in a spirit of charity), June 29.

Sacerdotii Nostri primordia (On St. John Vianney), Aug. 1.

Grata recordatio (On the Rosary: prayer for the Church, missions, international and social problems), Sept. 26.

Princeps Pastorum (On the missions, native clergy, lay participation), Nov. 28.

1961: *Mater et Magistra* (On Christianity and social progress), May 15.

Aeterna Dei sapientia (On fifteenth centenary of the death of Pope St. Leo I: the see of Peter as the center of Christian unity), Nov. 11.

1962: *Paenitentiam agere* (On the need for the practice of interior and exterior penance), July 1.

1963: *Pacem in terris* (On establishing universal peace in truth, justice, charity, and liberty), Apr. 11.

Paul VI
(1963-1978)

1964: *Ecclesiam Suam* (On the Church), Aug. 6.

1965: *Mense maio* (On prayers during May for the preservation of peace), Apr. 29.
Mysterium Fidei (On the Holy Eucharist), Sept. 3.
1966: *Christi Matri* (On prayers for peace during October), Sept. 15.
1967: *Populorum progressio* (On the development of peoples), Mar. 26.
Sacerdotalis caelibatus (On the celibacy of the priest), June 24.
1968: *Humanae vitae* (On the regulation of birth), July 25.

John Paul II
(1978-)
1979: *Redemptor hominis* (On redemption and dig nity of the human race), Mar. 4
1980: *Dives in misericordia* (On the mercy of God), Nov. 30.

1981: *Laborem exercens* (On human work), Sept. 14.
1985: *Slavorum Apostoli* (Commemorating Sts. Cyril and Methodius, on the eleventh centenary of the death of St. Methodius), June 2.
1986: *Dominum et Vivificantem* (On the Holy Spirit in the life of the Church and the world), May 18.
1987: *Redemptoris Mater* (On the role of Mary in the mystery of Christ and her active and exemplary presence in the life of the Church), Mar. 25.
Sollicitudo Rei Socialis (On social concerns, on the twentieth anniversary of *Populorum progressio*), Dec. 30.
1991: *Redemptoris missio* (On the permanent validity of the Church's missionary mandate), Jan. 22.
Centesimus annus (Commemorating the centenary of *Rerum novarum* and addressing the social question in a contemporary perspective), May 1.

CANONIZATIONS BY LEO XIII AND HIS SUCCESSORS

Canonization is an infallible declaration by the pope that a person who suffered martyrdom and/or practiced Christian virtue to a heroic degree is in glory with God in heaven and is worthy of public honor by the universal Church and of imitation by the faithful.
(See Canonization entry in Glossary.)

Leo XIII
(1878-1903)
1881: Clare of Montefalco, virgin (d. 1308); John Baptist de Rossi, priest (1698-1764); Lawrence of Brindisi, doctor (d. 1619).
1883: Benedict J. Labre (1748-1783).
1888: Seven Holy Founders of the Servite Order; Peter Claver, priest (1581-1654); John Berchmans (1599-1621); Alphonsus Rodriguez, Jesuit lay brother (1531-1617).
1897: Anthony M. Zaccaria, founder of Barnabites (1502-1539); Peter Fourier, co-founder of Augustinian Canonesses of Our Lady (1565-1640).
1900: John Baptist de La Salle, founder of Christian Brothers (1651-1719); Rita of Cascia (1381-1457).

St. Pius X
(1903-1914)
1904: Alexander Sauli, bishop (1534-1593); Gerard Majella, Redemptorist lay brother (1725-1755).
1909: Joseph Oriol, priest (1650-1702); Clement M. Hofbauer, priest (1751-1820).

Benedict XV
(1914-1922)
1920: Gabriel of the Sorrowful Mother (1838-1862); Margaret Mary Alacoque, virgin (1647-1690); Joan of Arc, virgin (1412-1431).

Pius XI
(1922-1939)
1925: Therese of Lisieux, virgin (1873-1897); Peter Canisius, doctor (1521-1597); Mary Magdalen Postel, foundress of Sisterhood of Christian Schools (1756-1846); Mary Magdalen Sophie Barat, foundress of Society of the Sacred Heart (1779-

1865); John Eudes, founder of Eudist Fathers (1601-1680); John Baptist Vianney (Curé of Ars), priest (1786-1859).
1930: Lucy Filippini, virgin (1672-1732); Catherine Thomas, virgin (1533-1574); Jesuit North American Martyrs (see Index); Robert Bellarmine, bishop-doctor (1542-1621); Theophilus of Corte, priest (1676-1740).
1931: Albert the Great, bishop-doctor (1206-1280) (equivalent canonization).
1933: Andrew Fournet, priest (1752-1834); Bernadette Soubirous, virgin (1844-1879).
1934: Joan Antida Thouret, foundress of Sisters of Charity of St. Joan Antida (1765-1826); Mary Michaeli, foundress of Institute of Handmaids of the Blessed Sacrament (1809-1865); Louise de Marillac, foundress of Sisters of Charity (1591-1660); Joseph Benedict Cottolengo, priest (1786-1842); Pompilius M. Pirotti, priest (1710-1756); Teresa Margaret Redi, virgin (1747-1770); John Bosco, founder of Salesians (1815-1888); Conrad of Parzham, Capuchin lay brother (1818-1894).
1935: John Fisher, bishop-martyr (1469-1535); Thomas More, martyr (1478-1535).
1938: Andrew Bobola, martyr (1592-1657); John Leonardi, founder of Clerics Regular of the Mother of God (c. 1550-1609); Salvatore of Horta, Franciscan lay brother (1520-1567).

Pius XII
(1939-1958)
1940: Gemma Galgani, virgin (1878-1903); Mary Euphrasia Pelletier, foundress of Good Shepherd Sisters (1796-1868).
1943: Margaret of Hungary, virgin (d. 1270) (equivalent canonization).
1946: Frances Xavier Cabrini, foundress of Missionary Sisters of the Sacred Heart (1850-1917).
1947: Nicholas of Flue, hermit (1417-1487); John of Britto, martyr (1647-1693); Bernard Realini, priest (1530-1616); Joseph Cafasso, priest (1811-1860); Michael Garicoits, founder of Auxiliary Priests of the Sacred Heart (1797-1863); Jeanne Elizabeth des Ages, cofoundress of Daughters of the Cross (1773-1838); Louis Marie Grignon de

Montfort, founder of Montfort Fathers (1673-1716); Catherine Laboure, virgin (1806-1876).

1949: Jeanne de Lestonnac, foundress of Religious of Notre Dame of Bordeaux (1556-1640); Maria Josepha Rossello, foundress of Daughters of Our Lady of Pity (1811-1880).

1950: Emily de Rodat, foundress of Congregation of the Holy Family of Villefranche (1787-1852); Anthony Mary Claret, bishop, founder of Claretians (1807-1870); Bartolomea Capitanio (1807-1833) and Vincenza Gerosa (1784-1847), foundresses of Sisters of Charity of Lovere; Jeanne de Valois, foundress of Annonciades of Bourges (1461-1504); Vincenzo M. Strambi, bishop (1745-1824); Maria Goretti, virgin-martyr (1890-1902); Mariana Paredes of Jesus, virgin (1618-1645).

1951: Maria Domenica Mazzarello, co-foundress of Daughters of Our Lady Help of Christians (1837-1881); Emilie de Vialar, foundress of Sisters of St. Joseph "of the Apparition" (1797-1856); Anthony M. Gianelli, bishop (1789-1846); Ignatius of Laconi, Capuchin lay brother (1701-1781); Francis Xavier Bianchi, priest (1743-1815).

1954: Pius X, pope (1835-1914); Dominic Savio (1842-1857); Maria Crocifissa di Rosa, foundress of Handmaids of Charity of Brescia (1813-1855); Peter Chanel, priest-martyr (1803-1841); Gaspar del Bufalo, founder of Missioners of the Most Precious Blood (1786-1837); Joseph M. Pignatelli, priest (1737-1811).

1958: Herman Joseph, O. Praem., priest (1150-1241) (equivalent canonization).

John XXIII
(1958-1963)

1959: Joaquina de Vedruna de Mas, foundress of Carmelite Sisters of Charity (1783-1854); Charles of Sezze, Franciscan lay brother (1613-1670).

1960: Gregory Barbarigo, bishop (1625-1697) (equivalent canonization); John de Ribera, bishop (1532-1611).

1961: Bertilla Boscardin, virgin (1888-1922).

1962: Martin de Porres, lay brother (1579-1639); Peter Julian Eymard, founder of Blessed Sacrament Fathers (1811-1868); Anthony Pucci, priest (1819-1892); Francis Mary of Camporosso, Capuchin lay brother (1804-1866).

1963: Vincent Pallotti, founder of Pallottine Fathers (1795-1850).

Paul VI
(1963-1978)

1964: Charles Lwanga and Twenty-One Companions, Martyrs of Uganda (d. between 1885-1887).

1967: Benilde Romancon, Christian Brother (1805-1862).

1969: Julia Billiart, foundress of Sisters of Notre Dame de Namur (1751-1816).

1970: Maria Della Dolorato Torres Acosta, foundress of Servants Sisters of Mary (1826-1887); Leonard Murialdo, priest, founder of Congregation of St. Joseph (1828-1900); Therese Couderc, foundress of Congregation of Our Lady of the Cenacle (1805-1885); John of Avila, preacher and spiritual director (1499-1569); Nicholas Tavelic, Deodatus of Aquitaine, Peter of Narbonne and

Stephen of Cuneo, martyrs (d. 1391); Forty English and Welsh Martyrs (d. 16th cent.).

1974: Teresa of Jesus Jornet Ibars, foundress of Little Sisters of Abandoned Aged (1843-1897).

1975: Vicenta Maria Lopez y Vicuna, foundress of Institute of Daughters of Mary Immaculate (1847-1890); Elizabeth Bayley Seton, foundress of Sisters of Charity in the U.S. (1774-1821); John Masias, Dominican brother-missionary (1585-1645); Oliver Plunket, archbishop-martyr (1629-1681); Justin de Jacobis, missionary bishop (1800-1860); John Baptist of the Conception, priest, reformer of the Order of the Most Holy Trinity (1561-1613).

1976: Beatrice da Silva, foundress of Congregation of the Immaculate Conception of the BVM (1424 or 1426-1490); John Ogilvie, Scottish Jesuit martyr (1579-1615).

1977: Rafaela Maria Porras y Ayllon, foundress of Handmaids of the Sacred Heart (1850-1925); John Nepomucene Neumann, bishop (1811-1860); Sharbel Makhlouf, Maronite Rite monk (1828-1898).

John Paul II
(1978-)

1982: Crispin of Viterbo, Capuchin brother (1668-1750); Maximilian Kolbe, Conventual Franciscan priest (1894-1941); Marguerite Bourgeoys, foundress of Congregation of Notre Dame (1620-1700); Jeanne Delanoue, foundress of Sisters of St. Anne of Providence of Saumur, France (1666-1736).

1983: Leopold Mandic, Capuchin priest (1866-1942).

1984: Paola Frassinetti, foundress of Sisters of St. Dorothy (1809-1892); 103 Korean Martyrs (d. between 1839-1867); Miguel Febres Cordero, of the Brothers of the Christian Schools (1854-1910).

1986: Francis Anthony Fasani, Conventual Franciscan priest (1681-1742); Giuseppe Maria Tomasi, Theatine, cardinal (1649-1713).

1987: Giuseppe Moscati, layman, physician (d. 1927); Lawrence (Lorenzo) Ruiz and Fifteen Companions (laymen, priests and religious from five countries), Martyrs of Japan (d. 1630s).

1988: Eustochia Calafato, Sicilian Poor Clare (1434-1485); 117 Martyrs of Vietnam (96 Vietnamese, 11 Spanish, 10 French; included 8 bishops, 50 priests, 1 seminarian, 58 lay persons); Roque Gonzalez (1576-1628), Alfonso Rodriguez (1598-1628) and Juan de Castillo (1596-1628), Jesuit martyrs of Paraguay; Rose Philippine Duchesne, French-born foundress of first convent of Society of the Sacred Heart in the U.S. (1796-1852); Simon de Rojas, Trinitarian priest (1552-1624); Magdalen of Canossa, foundress of Canossian Daughters of Charity (1774-1835); Maria Rosa Molas y Vollve, foundress of Sisters of Our Lady of Consolation (d. 1876).

1989: Clelia Barbieri, foundress of Little Sisters of Our Lady of Sorrows (1847-1870); Gaspar Bertoni, priest, founder of Stigmatines (1777-1853); Richard Pampuri, religious (1897-1930); Agnes of Bohemia, virgin (1211-1282); Albert Chmielowski, religious (1845-1916); Mutien-Marie Wiaux, religious (1841-1917).

1990: Marguerite D'Youville, widow, foundress of Grey Nuns; first native Canadian saint (1701-1777).

1991: Raphael (Jozef) Kalinowski, Carmelite priest (1835-1907).

1992: Claude La Colombiere, Jesuit priest (1641-1682); Ezequiel Moreno y Diaz, bishop (1848-1905).

1993 (as of Aug. 25): Marie of St. Ignatius (Claudine Thevenet), foundress (1774-1837); Teresa "de los Andes" (Juana Fernandez Solar), Carmelite, first Chilean saint (1900-20); Enrique de Ossó y Cervelló, priest (1840-96).

BEATIFICATIONS BY POPE JOHN PAUL II, 1979-1993

1979: Francis Coll, O.P., Jacques Laval, S.S.Sp. (Apr. 29); Enrique de Ossó y Cervelló (Oct. 14; canonized June 16, 1993).

1980: Jose de Anchieta, Peter of St. Joseph Betancur, Francois de Montmorency Laval, Kateri Tekakwitha, Marie Guyard of the Incarnation (June 22); Don Luigi Orione, Bartolomea Longo, Maria Anna Sala (Oct. 26).

1981: Sixteen Martyrs of Japan (Lorenzo Ruiz and Companions) (Feb 18; *canonized Oct. 18, 1987*); Maria Repetto, Alan de Solminihac, Richard Pampuri, Claudine Thevenet (canonized 1993), Aloysius (Luigi) Scrosoppi (Oct. 4).

1982: Peter Donders, C.SS.R., Marie Rose Durocher, Andre Bessette, C.S.C., Maria Angela Astorch, Marie Rivier (May 23); Jeanne Jugan, Salvatore Lilli and 7 Armenian Companions (Oct. 3); Sr. Angela of the Cross (Nov. 5).

1983: Maria Gabriella Sagheddu (Jan. 25); Luigi Versiglia, Callisto Caravario (May 15); Ursula Ledochowska (June 20); Raphael (Jozef) Kalinowski (canonized 1991), Bro. Albert (Adam Chmielowski), T.O.R. (June 22); Fra Angelico (equivalent beatification) (July); Giacomo Cusmano, Jeremiah of Valachia, Domingo Iturrate Zubero (Oct. 30); Marie de Jesus Crucified (Marie Baouardy) (Nov. 13).

1984: Fr. William Repin and 98 Companions (Martyrs of Angers during French Revolution), Giovanni Mazzucconi (Feb. 19); Marie Leonie Paradis (Sept. 11); Federico Albert, Clemente Marchisio, Isidore of St. Joseph (Isidore de Loor), Rafaela Ybarra de Villalongo (Sept. 30); Jose Manyanet y Vives, Daniel Brottier, C.S.Sp., Sr. Elizabeth of the Trinity (Elizabeth Catez) (Nov. 25).

1985: Mercedes of Jesus (Feb. 1); Ana de los Angeles Monteagudo (Feb. 2); Pauline von Mallinckrodt, Catherine Troiano (Apr. 14); Benedict Menni, Peter Friedhofen (June 23); Anwarite Nangapeta (Aug. 15); Virginae Centurione Bracelli (Sept. 22); Diego Luis de San Vitores, S.J., Jose M. Rubio y Peralto, S.J., Francisco Garate, S.J. (Oct. 6); Titus Brandsma, O.Carm. (Nov. 3); Pio Campidelli, C.P., Marie Teresa of Jesus Gerhardinger, Rafqa Ar-Rayes (Nov. 17).

1986: Alphonsa Mattathupadathus of the Immaculate Conception, Kuriakose Elias Chavara (Feb. 8); Antoine Chevrier (Oct. 4); Teresa Maria of the Cross Manetti (Oct. 19).

1987: Maria Pilar of St. Francis Borgia, Teresa of the Infant Jesus, Maria Angeles of St. Joseph, Cardinal Marcellis Spinola y Maestre, Emmanuel Domingo y Sol (Mar. 29); Teresa of Jesus "de los Andes" (Apr. 3; canonized Mar. 21, 1993); Edith Stein (Teresa Benedicta of the Cross) (May 1);

Rupert Meyer, S.J. (May 3); Pierre-Francois Jamet, Cardinal Andrea Carlo Ferrari, Benedetta Cambiogio Frasinello, Louis Moreau (May 10); Carolina Kozka, Michal Kozal (June 10); George Matulaitis (Matulewicz) (June 28); Marcel Callo, Pierino Morosoni, Antonia Mesina (Oct. 4); Blandina Marten, Ulricke Nische, Jules Roche (Dro. Arnold) (Nov. 1); 85 Martyrs (d. between 1584-1689) of England, Scotland and Wales (Nov. 22).

1988: John Calabria, Joseph Nascimbeni (Apr. 17); Pietro Bonilli, Kaspar Stanggassinger, Francisco Palau y Quer, Savina Petrilli (Apr. 24), Laura Vicuna (Sept. 3); Joseph Gerard (Sept. 11); Miguel Pro, Giuseppe Benedetto Dusmet, Francisco Faa di Bruno, Junipero Serra, Frederick Janssoone, Josefa Naval Girke (Sept. 25); Bernardo Maria Silvestrelli, Charles Houben, Honoratus Kozminski (Oct. 16); Niels Stensen (Nicolaus Steno) (Oct. 23); Katharine Drexel, 3 Missionary Martyrs of Ethiopia (Liberato Weiss, Samuel Marzorati, Michele Pio Fasoli) (Nov. 20).

1989: Martin of Saint Nicholas, Melchior of St. Augustine, Mary of Jesus of the Good Shepherd, Maria Margaret Caiana, Maria Catherine of St. Augustine (Apr. 23); Victoria Rasoamanarivo (Apr. 30); Bro. Scubilionis (John Bernard Rousseau) (May 2); Elizabeth Renzi, Antonio Lucci (June 17); Niceforo de Jesus y Maria (Vicente Diez Tejerina) and 25 Companions (martyred in Spain), Lorenzo Salvia, Gertrude Caterina Comensoli, Francisca Ana Cirer Carbonell (Oct. 1); 7 Martyrs from Thailand (Philip Sipong, Sr. Agnes Phila, Sr. Lucia Khambang, Agatha Phutta, Cecilia Butsi, Bibiana Khampai, Maria Phon), Timothy Giaccardo, Mother Maria of Jesus Deluil-Martiny (Oct. 22); Giuseppe Baldo (Oct. 31).

1990: 9 Martyrs of Astoria during Spanish Civil War (De la Salle Brothers Cyrill Bertran, Marciano Jose, Julian Alfredo, Victoriano Pio, Benjamin Julian, Augusto Andres, Benito de Jesus, Aniceto Adolfo, and Passionist priest Innocencio Inmaculada), Mercedes Prat, Manuel Barbal Cosan (Brother Jaime), Philip Rinaldi (Apr. 29); Juan Diego (confirmation of Apr. 9 decree), 3 Child Martyrs (Cristobal, Antonio and Juan), Fr. Jose Maria de Yermo y Porres (May 6); Pierre Giorgio Frassati (May 20); Hanibal Maria Di Francia, Joseph Allamano (Oct. 7); Marthe Aimee LeBouteiller, Louise Therese de Montaignac de Chauvance, Maria Schinina, Elisabeth Vendramini (Nov. 4).

1991: Annunciata Cocchetti, Marie Therese Haze, Clara Bosatta (Apr. 21); Jozef Sebastian Pelczar (June 2); Boleslava Lament (June 5); Rafael Chylinski (June 9); Angela Salawa (Aug. 13).

(Continued on page 544.)

HIERARCHY OF THE CATHOLIC CHURCH

ORGANIZATION AND GOVERNMENT

As a structured society, the Catholic Church is organized and governed along lines corresponding mainly to the jurisdictions of the pope and bishops.

The pope is the supreme head of the Church. He has primacy of jurisdiction as well as honor over the entire Church.

Bishops, in union with and in subordination to the pope, are the successors of the Apostles for care of the Church and for the continuation of Christ's mission in the world. They serve the people of their own dioceses, or particular churches, with ordinary authority and jurisdiction. They also share, with the pope and each other, in common concern and effort for the general welfare of the whole Church.

Bishops of exceptional status are patriarchs of Eastern Catholic Churches who, subject only to the pope, are heads of the faithful belonging to their rites throughout the world.

Subject to the Holy Father and directly responsible to him for the exercise of their ministry of service to people in various jurisdictions or divisions of the Church throughout the world are: resident archbishops and metropolitans (heads of archdioceses), diocesan bishops, vicars and prefects apostolic (heads of vicariates apostolic and prefectures apostolic), certain abbots and prelates, apostolic administrators. Each of these, within his respective territory and according to the provisions of canon law, has ordinary jurisdiction over pastors (who are responsible for the administration of parishes), priests, Religious and lay persons.

Also subject to the Holy Father are titular archbishops and bishops, religious orders and congregations of pontifical right, pontifical institutes and faculties, papal nuncios and apostolic delegates.

Assisting the pope and acting in his name in the central government and administration of the Church are cardinals and other officials of the Roman Curia.

THE HIERARCHY

The ministerial hierarchy is the orderly arrangement of the ranks and orders of the clergy to provide for the spiritual care of the faithful, the government of the Church, and the accomplishment of the Church's total mission in the world.

Persons belong to this hierarchy by virtue of ordination and canonical mission.

The term hierarchy is also used to designate an entire body or group of bishops; for example, the hierarchy of the Church, the hierarchy of the United States.

Hierarchy of Order: Consists of the pope, bishops, priests and deacons. Their purpose, for which they are ordained to holy orders, is to carry out the sacramental and pastoral ministry of the Church.

Hierarchy of Jurisdiction: Consists of the pope and bishops by divine institution, and other church officials by ecclesiastical institution and mandate, who have authority to govern and direct the faithful for spiritual ends.

The Pope

His Holiness the Pope is the Bishop of Rome, the Vicar of Jesus Christ, the successor of St. Peter, Prince of the Apostles, the Supreme Pontiff who has the primacy of jurisdiction and not merely of honor over the universal Church, the Patriarch of the West, the Primate of Italy, the Archbishop and Metropolitan of the Roman Province, the Sovereign of the State of Vatican City, Servant of the Servants of God.

Cardinals
(See Index)

Patriarchs

Patriarch, a term which had its origin in the Eastern Church, is the title of a bishop who, second only to the pope, has the highest rank in the hierarchy of jurisdiction. He is the incumbent of one of the sees listed below. Subject only to the pope, a patriarch of the Eastern Church is the head of the faithful belonging to his rite throughout the world. The patriarchal sees are so called because of their special status and dignity in the history of the Church.

The Council of Nicaea (325) recognized three patriarchs — the bishops of Alexandria and Antioch in the East, and of Rome in the West. The First Council of Constantinople (381) added the bishop of Constantinople to the list of patriarchs and gave him rank second only to that of the pope, the bishop of Rome and patriarch of the West; this action was seconded by the Council of Chalcedon (451) and was given full recognition by the Fourth Lateran Council (1215). The Council of Chalcedon also acknowledged patriarchal rights of the bishop of Jerusalem.

Eastern patriarchs are as follows: one of Alexandria, for the Copts; three of Antioch, one each for the Syrians, Maronites and Greek Melkites (the latter also has the personal title of Greek Melkite patriarch of Alexandria and of Jerusalem). The patriarch of Babylonia, for the Chaldeans, and the patriarch of Sis, or Cilicia, for the Armenians, should be called, more properly, *Katholikos* — that is, a prelate delegated for a universality of causes. These patriarchs are elected by bishops of their churches: they receive approval and the pallium, symbolic of their office, from the pope.

Latin Rite patriarchates were established for Antioch, Jerusalem, Alexandria and Constantinople during the Crusades; afterwards, they became patriarchates in name only. Jerusalem, however, was reconstituted as a patriarchate by Pius IX, in virtue of the bull *Nulla Celebrior* of July 23, 1847. In 1964, the Latin titular patriarchates of Constantinople, Alexandria and Antioch, long a bone of contention in relations with Eastern Rites, were abolished.

As of July, 1993, the patriarchs in the Church were:

The Pope, Bishop of Rome, Patriarch of the West; Stephanos II Ghattas, C.M., of Alexandria, for the Copts; Ignace Antoine II Hayek, of Antioch, for the Syrians; Maximos V Hakim, of Antioch, for the Greek Melkites (he also has personal titles of Alexandria and Jerusalem for the Greek Melkites); Nasrallah Pierre Sfeir, of Antioch, for the Maronites; Michel Sabbah, of Jerusalem, for the Latin Rite; Raphael I Bidawid, of Babylon, for the Chaldeans; Jean Pierre XVIII Kasparian, of Cilicia, for the Armenians.

The titular patriarchs (in name only) of the Latin Rite were: Cardinal Antonio Ribeiro, of Lisbon; Cardinal Marco Cé of Venice and Archbishop Raul Nicolau Gonsalves of the East Indies (Archbishop of Goa and Damao, India). The patriarchate of the West Indies has been vacant since 1963.

Archbishops, Metropolitans

Archbishop: A bishop with the title of an archdiocese.

Coadjutor Archbishop: An assistant archbishop with right of succession.

Metropolitan: Archbishop of the principal see, an archdiocese, in an ecclesiastical province consisting of several dioceses. He has the full powers of bishop in his own archdiocese and limited supervisory jurisdiction and influence over the other (suffragan) dioceses in the province. The pallium, conferred by the pope, is the symbol of his status as a metropolitan.

Titular Archbishop: Has the title of an archdiocese which formerly existed in fact but now exists in title only. He does not have ordinary jurisdiction over an archdiocese. Examples are archbishops in the Roman Curia, papal nuncios, apostolic delegates.

Archbishop ad personam: A title of personal honor and distinction granted to some bishops. They do not have ordinary jurisdiction over an archdiocese.

Primate: A title of honor given to the ranking prelate of some countries or regions.

Bishops

Diocesan Bishop: A bishop in charge of a diocese.

Coadjutor Bishop: An assistant (auxiliary) bishop to a diocesan bishop, with right of succession to the see.

Titular Bishops: A bishop with the title of a diocese which formerly existed in fact but now exists in title only; an assistant (auxiliary) bishop to a diocesan bishop.

Episcopal Vicar: An assistant, who may or may not be a bishop, appointed by a residential bishop as his deputy for a certain part of a diocese, a determined type of apostolic work, or the faithful of a certain rite.

Eparch, Exarch: Titles of bishops of Eastern-Rite churches.

Nomination of Bishops: Nominees for episcopal ordination are selected in several ways. Final appointment and/or approval in all cases is subject to decision by the pope.

In the U.S., bishops periodically submit the names of candidates to the archbishop of their province. The names are then considered at a meeting of the bishops of the province, and those receiving a favorable vote are forwarded to the pro-nuncio for transmission to the Holy See. Bishops are free to seek the counsel of priests, religious and lay persons with respect to nominees.

Eastern Catholic churches have their own procedures and synodal regulations for nominating and making final selection of candidates for episcopal ordination. Such selection is subject to approval by the pope.

The Code of Canon Law concedes no rights or privileges to civil authorities with respect to the election, nomination, presentation or designation of candidates for the episcopate.

Ad Limina Visit: Diocesan bishops and apostolic vicars are obliged to make an *ad limina* visit ("to the threshold" of the Apostles) every five years to the tombs of Sts. Peter and Paul, have audience with the Holy Father and consult with appropriate Vatican officials. They are required to send a report on conditions in their jurisdiction to the Congregation for Bishops approximately six — and not less than three — months in advance of the scheduled visit. The most recent regulations concerning the formalities and scheduling of visits by bishops from various countries, generally every five years, were issued by the Congregation for Bishops in a decree dated June 29, 1988.

Others with Ordinary Jurisdiction

Ordinary: One who has the jurisdiction of an office: the pope, diocesan bishops, vicars general, prelates of missionary territories, vicars apostolic prefects apostolic, vicars capitular during the vacancy of a see, superiors general, abbots primate and other major superiors of men Religious.

Some prelates and abbots, with jurisdiction like that of diocesan bishops, are pastors of the people of God in territories (prelatures and abbacies) not under the jurisdiction of diocesan bishops.

Vicar Apostolic: Usually a titular bishop who has ordinary jurisdiction over a mission territory.

Prefect Apostolic: Has ordinary jurisdiction over a mission territory.

Apostolic Administrator: Usually a bishop appointed to administer an ecclesiastical jurisdiction temporarily. Administrators of lesser rank are also appointed for special and more restricted supervisory duties.

Vicar General: A bishop's deputy for the administration of a diocese. Such a vicar does not have to be a bishop.

Honorary Prelates

Honorary prelates belonging to the Pontifical Household are: Apostolic Prothonotaries, Honorary Prelates of His Holiness, and Chaplains of His Holiness. Their title is Reverend Monsignor.

SYNOD OF BISHOPS

The Synod of Bishops was chartered by Pope Paul VI Sept. 15, 1965, in a document he issued on his own initiative under the title, *Apostolica Sollicitudo*. Provisions of this *motu proprio* are contained in Canons 342 to 348 of the Code of Canon Law. According to major provisions of the Synod charter:

• The purposes of the Synod are: "to encourage close union and valued assistance between the Sovereign Pontiff and the bishops of the entire world; to insure that direct and real information is provided on questions and situations touching upon the internal action of the Church and its necessary activity in the world of today; to facilitate agreement on essential points of doctrine and on methods of procedure in the life of the Church."

• The Synod is a central ecclesiastical institution, permanent by nature.

• The Synod is directly and immediately subject to the Pope, who has authority to assign its agenda, to call it into session, and to give its members deliberative as well as advisory authority.

• In addition to a limited number of ex officio members and a few heads of male religious institutes, the majority of the members are elected by and representative of national or regional episcopal conferences. The Pope reserved the right to appoint the general secretary, special secretaries and no more than 15 per cent of the total membership.

The Pope is president of the Synod.

The secretary general is Archbishop Jan Schotte of Belgium.

An advisory council of 15 members (12 elected, three appointed by the pope) provides the secretariat with adequate staff for carrying on liaison with episcopal conferences and for preparing the agenda of synodal assemblies.

Assemblies

1. First Assembly: The first assembly was held from Sept. 29 to Oct. 29, 1967. Its objectives, as stated by Pope Paul VI, were "the preservation and strengthening of the Catholic faith, its integrity, its force, its development, its doctrinal and historical coherence." One result was a recommendation for the establishment of an international commission of theologians to assist the Congregation for the Doctrine of the Faith and to broaden approaches to theological research. Pope Paul set up the commission in 1969.

2. Pope-Bishop Relations: The second assembly held Oct. 11 to 28, 1969, was extraordinary in character. It opened the way toward greater participation by bishops with the pope and each other in the governance of the Church. Proceedings were oriented to three main points: (1) the nature and implications of collegiality; (2) the relationship of bishops and their conferences to the pope; (3) the relationships of bishops and their conferences to each other.

3. Priesthood and Justice: The ministerial priesthood and justice in the world were the principal topics under discussion at the second ordinary assembly, Sept. 30 to Nov. 6, 1971. In one report, the Synod emphasized the primary and permanent dedication of priests in the Church to the ministry of word, sacrament and pastoral service as a full-time vocation. In another report, the assembly stated: "Action on behalf of justice and participation in the transformation of the world fully appear to us as a constitutive dimension of the preaching of the Gospel; or, in other words, of the Church's mission for the redemption of the human race and its liberation from every oppressive situation."

4. Evangelization: The assembly of Sept. 27 to Oct. 26, 1974, produced a general statement on evangelization of the modern world, covering the need for it and its relationship to efforts for total human liberation from personal and social evil. The assembly observed: "The Church does not remain within merely political, social and economic limits (elements which she must certainly take into account) but leads towards freedom under all its forms — liberation from sin, from individual or collective selfishness — and to full communion with God and with men who are like brothers. In this way the Church, in her evangelical way, promotes the true and complete liberation of all men, groups and peoples."

5. Catechetics: The fourth ordinary assembly, Sept. 30 to Oct. 29, 1977, focused attention on catechetics, with special reference to children and young people. The participants issued a "Message to the People of God," the first synodal statement issued since inception of the body, and also presented to Pope Paul VI a set of 34 related propositions and a number of suggestions.

6. Family: "A Message to Christian Families in the Modern World" and a proposal for a "Charter of Family Rights" were produced by the assembly held Sept. 26 to Oct. 25, 1980. The assembly reaffirmed the indissolubility of marriage and the contents of the encyclical letter *Humanae Vitae* (see separate entry), and urged married couples who find it hard to live up to "the difficult but loving demands" of Christ not to be discouraged but to avail themselves of the aid of divine grace. In response to synodal recommendation, Pope John Paul issued a charter of family rights late in 1983.

7. Reconciliation: Penance and reconciliation in the mission of the Church was the theme of the assembly held Sept. 29 to Oct. 29, 1983. Sixty-three propositions related to this theme were formulated on a wide variety of subjects, including: personal sin and so-called systemic or institutional sin; the nature of serious sin; the diminished sense of sin and of the need of redemption, related to decline in the administration and reception of the sacrament of penance; general absolution; individual and social reconciliation; violence and violations of human rights; reconciliation as the basis of peace and justice in society. In a statement issued Oct. 27, the Synod stressed the need of the world to become, increasingly, "a reconciled community of peoples," and said that "the Church, as sacrament of reconciliation to the world, has to be an effective sign of God's mercy."

8. Vatican II Review: The second extraordinary assembly was convened Nov. 24 to Dec. 8, 1985, for the purposes of: (1) recalling the Second Vatican Council; (2) evaluating the implementation of its enactments during the 20 years since its conclusion; (3) seeking ways and means of promoting renewal in the Church in accordance with the spirit and letter of the council. At the conclusion of the assembly the bishops issued two documents. (1) In A Message to the People of God, they noted the need for greater appreciation of the enactments of Vatican II and for greater efforts to put them into effect, so that all members of the Church might discharge their responsibility of proclaiming the good news of salvation. (2) In a Final Report, the first of its kind published by a synodal assembly, the bishops reflected on lights and shadows since Vatican II, stating that negative developments had come from partial and superficial interpretations of conciliar enactments and from incomplete or ineffective implementation thereof. The report also covered a considerable number of subjects discussed during the assembly, ranging from the mystery of the Church to inculturation and the preferential (but not exclusive) option for the poor

9. Vocation and Mission of the Laity in the Church and in the World 20 years after the Second Vatican Council: The seventh ordinary assembly, Oct. 1 to 30, 1987, said in a Message to the People of God: "The majority of the Christian laity live out their vocation as followers and disciples of Christ in all spheres of life which we call 'the world': the family, the field of work, the local community and the like. To permeate this day-to-day living with the spirit of Christ has always been the task of the lay faithful; and it should be with still greater force their challenge today. It is in this way that they sanctify the world and collaborate in the realization of the kingdom of God." The assembly produced a set of 54 propositions which were presented to the Pope for consideration in the preparation of a document of his own on the theme of the assembly. He responded with the apostolic exhortation, *Christifideles Laici*, "The Christian Faithful Laity," released by the Vatican Jan. 30, 1989.

10. Formation of Priests in Circumstances of the Present Day: The eighth general assembly, Sept. 30 to Oct. 28, 1990, dealt principally with the nature and mission of the priesthood; the identity, multi-faceted formation and spirituality of priests; and, in a Message to the People of God, the need on all levels of the Church for the promotion of vocations to the priesthood. Forty-one proposals were presented to the Pope for his consideration in preparing a document of his own on the theme of the assembly. Pope John Paul issued an apostolic exhortation entitled *Pastores Dabo Vobis* ("I Will Give You Shepherds") Apr. 7, 1992, in response to the Synods' recommendations.

The theme of the ninth ordinary assembly, to be held in the fall of 1994, will be "The Consecrated Life and Its Role in the Church and the World."

A special assembly of the Synod for Europe was held Nov. 28 to Dec. 14, 1991. Preparations were under way in 1993 for special assemblies for Lebanon and Africa.

ROMAN CURIA

The Roman Curia is the Church's network of central administrative agencies (called dicasteries) serving the Vatican and the local churches, with authority granted by the Pope.

Background

The Curia evolved gradually from advisory assemblies or synods of the Roman clergy with whose assistance the popes directed church affairs during the first 11 centuries. Its original office was the Apostolic Chancery, established in the fourth century to transmit documents. The antecedents of its permanently functioning agencies and offices were special commissions of cardinals and prelates. Its establishment in a form resembling what it is now dates from the second half of the 16th century.

Pope Paul VI initiated a four-year reorganization study in 1963 which resulted in the constitution *Regimini Ecclesiae Universae*. The document was published Aug. 18, 1967, and went into full effect in March, 1968.

Pope John Paul II, in the apostolic constitution *Pastor Bonus*, published June 28, 1988, and effective Mar. 1, 1989, ordered modifications of the Curia based on the broad outline of Paul VI's reorganization.

Curial Departments

The reorganized Curia (in accordance with Pope John Paul II's reform effective Mar. 1, 1989), consists of the Secretariat of State, nine congregations (governing agencies), three tribunals (judicial agencies), 12 councils (promotional agencies) and three offices (specialized service agencies). All have equal juridical status with authority granted by the Pope.

SECRETARIAT OF STATE

The Secretariat of State provides the pope with the closest possible assistance in the care of the universal Church. It consists of two sections:

• The Section for General Affairs assists the Pope in expediting daily business of the Holy See. It coordinates curial operations; prepares drafts of documents entrusted to it by the pope; has supervisory duties over the *Acta Apostolicae Sedis, Annuario Pontificio,* the Vatican Press Office and the Central Statistics Office.

• The Section for Relations with States (formerly the Council for Public Affairs of the Church, a separate body) which handles diplomatic and other relations with civil governments. Attached to it is a Council of Cardinals and Bishops.

OFFICIALS: Cardinal Angelo Sodano, Secretary of State; Most Rev. Giovanni Battista Re, Deputy for General Affairs; Most Rev. Jean Louis Tauran, Secretary for Relations with States.

ADDRESS: Palazzo Apostolico Vaticano, Vatican City.

BACKGROUND: Evolved gradually from

secretarial offices (dating back to the 15th century) and the Congregation for Extraordinary Ecclesiastical Affairs (dating back to 1793; restructured as the Council for the Public Affairs of the Church by Paul VI in 1967). John Paul II gave it its present form in his June 28, 1988, reform of the Curia.

CONGREGATIONS

Congregation for the Doctrine of the Faith: Has responsibility to safeguard the doctrine of faith and morals. Accordingly, it examines doctrinal questions; promotes studies thereon; evaluates theological opinions and, when necessary and after prior consultation with concerned bishops, reproves those regarded as opposed to principles of the faith; examines books on doctrinal matters and can reprove such works, if the contents so warrant, after giving authors the opportunity to defend themselves. It examines matters pertaining to the Privilege of Faith (Petrine Privilege) in marriage cases, and safeguards the dignity of the sacrament of penance. Attached to the congregation are the Pontifical Biblical Commission and the Theological Commission

OFFICIALS: Cardinal Joseph Ratzinger, prefect; Most Rev. Alberto Bovone, secretary.

ADDRESS: Piazza del S. Uffizio 11, 00193 Rome, Italy.

BACKGROUND: At the beginning of the 13th century, legates of Innocent III were commissioned as the Holy Office of the Inquisition to combat heresy; the same task was entrusted to the Dominican Order by Gregory IX in 1231 and to the Friars Minor by Innocent IV from 1243 to 1254. On July 21, 1542 (apostolic constitution *Licet*), Paul III instituted a permanent congregation of cardinals with supreme and universal competence over matters concerning heretics and those suspected of heresy. Pius IV, St. Pius V and Sixtus V further defined the work of the congregation. St. Pius X changed its name to the Congregation of the Holy Office. Paul VI (motu proprio *Integrae Servandae,* Dec. 7, 1965), began reorganization of the Curia with this body, to which he gave the new title, Congregation for the Doctrine of the Faith. Its orientation is not merely negative, in the condemnation of error, but positive, in the promotion of orthodox doctrine.

Congregation for the Oriental Churches: Has competence in matters concerning the persons and discipline of Eastern Catholic Churches. It has jurisdiction over territories in which the majority of Christians belong to Eastern Churches (i.e., Egypt, the Sinai Peninsula, Eritrea, Northern Ethiopia, Southern Albania, Bulgaria, Cyprus, Greece, Iran, Iraq, Lebanon, Palestine, Syria, Jordan, Turkey, Afghanistan); also, over minority communities of Eastern Church members no matter where they live.

OFFICIALS: Cardinal Achille Silvestrini, prefect; Most Rev. Miroslav Stefan Marusyn, secretary. Members include all patriarchs of the Eastern Catholic Churches and major archbishops.

ADDRESS: Palazzo del Bramante, Via della Conciliazione 34, 00193 Rome, Italy.

BACKGROUND: Established by Pius IX Jan. 6, 1862 (apostolic constitution *Romani Pontifices*), and united with the Congregation for the Propagation of the Faith. The congregation was made autonomous by Benedict XV May 1, 1917 (motu proprio *Dei Providentis*), and given wider authority by Pius XI Mar. 25, 1938 (motu proprio *Sancta Dei Ecclesia*).

Congregation for Bishops: Has functions related in one way or another to bishops and the jurisdictions in which they serve. It supervises the Pontifical Commission for Latin America. A central coordinating office for Military Vicars was established Feb. 2, 1985.

OFFICIALS: Cardinal Bernardin Gantin, prefect; Most Rev. Justin Rigali, secretary.

ADDRESS: Piazza Pio XII 10, 00193 Rome, Italy.

BACKGROUND: Established by Sixtus V Jan. 22, 1588 (apostolic constitution *Immensa*); given an extension of powers by St. Pius X June 20, 1908, and Pius XII Aug. 1, 1952 (apostolic constitution *Exsul Familia*); given present title (was known as Consistorial Congregation) by Paul VI (Aug. 15, 1967); competencies redefined by John Paul II, June 28, 1988.

Congregation for Divine Worship and the Discipline of the Sacraments: Supervises everything pertaining to the promotion and regulation of the liturgy, primarily the sacraments, without prejudice to the competencies of the Congregation for the Doctrine of the Faith. Attached to the congregation are special commissions treating causes of nullity of sacred ordinations and dispensations from obligations of sacred ordination of deacons and priests.

OFFICIALS: Cardinal Antonio Maria Javierre Ortas, prefect; Most Rev. Geraldo Majella Agnelo, secretary.

ADDRESS: Piazza Pio XII 10, 00193 Rome, Italy.

BACKGROUND: Originally two separate congregations: the Congregation for Divine Worship (instituted by Paul VI, May 8, 1969) and the Congregation for the Discipline of the Sacraments (established by St. Pius X, June 29, 1908, to replace the Congregation of Rites instituted by Pope Sixtus V in 1588). They were united by Paul VI, July 11, 1975, as the Congregation for the Sacraments and Divine Worship; reestablished as separate congregations by John Paul II in an autograph letter of Apr. 5, 1984, and reunited anew by the same Pope, June 28, 1988 (apostolic constitution *Pastor Bonus*) as the Congregation for Divine Worship and the Discipline of the Sacraments.

Congregation for the Causes of Saints: Handles matters connected with beatification and canonization causes (in accordance with revised procedures decreed in 1983), and the preservation of relics.

OFFICIALS: Cardinal Angelo Felici, prefect; Most Rev. Edward Nowak, secretary.

ADDRESS: Piazza Pio XII 10, 00193 Rome, Italy.

BACKGROUND: Established by Sixtus V in 1588 as the Congregation of Rites; affected by legislation of Pius XI in 1930; title changed and functions defined by Paul VI, 1969 (apostolic constitution *Sacra Rituum Congregatio*). It was restructured and canonization procedures were revised by John Paul II in 1983 (apostolic constitution *Divinus Perfectionis Magister*).

Congregation for the Clergy: Has three offices with competencies concerning the life, discipline, rights and duties of the clergy; the preaching of the Word, catechetics, norms for religious education of children and adults; preservation and administration of the temporal goods of the Church. Attached to the congregation are the International Council for Catechetics (1973, by Paul VI) and the Pontifical Commission for the Preservation of the Artistic and Historic Patrimony of the Church (1988, by John Paul II).

OFFICIALS: Cardinal Jose T. Sanchez, prefect; Most Rev. Crescenzio Sepe, secretary.

ADDRESS: Piazza Pio XII 3, 00193 Rome, Italy.

BACKGROUND: Established by Pius IV Aug. 2, 1564 (apostolic constitution *Alias Nos*), under the title, Congregation of the Cardinals Interpreters of the Council of Trent; affected by legislation of Gregory XIII and Sixtus V; known as Congregation of the Council until Aug. 15, 1967, when Paul VI renamed it the Congregation for the Clergy and redefined its competency; John Paul II gave it added responsibilities June 28, 1988.

Congregation for Institutes of Consecrated Life and Societies of Apostolic Life: Has competence over institutes of Religious, societies of the apostolic life, third (secular) orders and secular institutes. With two sections, the congregation has authority in matters related to the establishment, general direction and suppression of the various institutes; general discipline in line with their rules and constitutions; the movement toward renewal and adaptation of institutes in contemporary circumstances; the setting up and encouragement of councils and conferences of major religious superiors for intercommunication and other purposes.

OFFICIALS: Cardinal Eduardo Martinez Somalo, prefect; Most. Rev. Francisco Javier Errazuriz Ossa, secretary.

ADDRESS: Piazza Pio XII 3, 00193 Rome, Italy.

BACKGROUND: Founded by Sixtus V May 27, 1586, with the title, Congregation for Consultations of Regulars; confirmed by the apostolic constitution *Immensa* Jan. 22, 1588; made part of the Congregation for Consultations of Bishops and other Prelates in 1601; made autonomous by St. Pius X in 1908 as Congregation of Religious; title changed to Congregation for Religious and Secular Institutes by Paul VI in 1967; given present title by John Paul II, June 28, 1988.

Congregation for Catholic Education (for Seminaries and Institutes of Study): Has supervisory competence over institutions and works of Catholic education. It carries on its work through three offices. One office handles matters connected with the direction, discipline and temporal administration of seminaries, and with the education of diocesan clergy, religious and members of secular institutes. A second office oversees Catholic universities, faculties of study and other institutions of higher learning inasmuch as they depend on the authority of the Church; encourages cooperation and mutual assistance among Catholic institutions, and the establishment of Catholic hospices and centers on campuses of non-Catholic institutions. A third office is concerned in various ways with all Catholic schools below the college-university level, with general questions concerning education and studies, and with the cooperation of conferences of bishops and civil authorities in educational matters. The congregation supervises Pontifical Works for Priestly Vocations.

OFFICIALS: Cardinal Pio Laghi, prefect; Most Rev. Jose Saraiva Martins, C.M.F., secretary.

ADDRESS: Piazza Pio XII 3, 00193 Rome, Italy.

BACKGROUND: The title (Congregation of Seminaries and Universities) and functions of the congregation were defined by Benedict XV Nov. 4, 1915; Pius XI, in 1931 and 1932, and Pius XII, in 1941 and 1949, extended its functions; Paul VI changed its title to Congregation for Catholic Education in 1967; given its present title by Pope John Paul II, June 28, 1988. Its work had previously been carried on by two other congregations erected by Sixtus V in 1588 and Leo XII in 1824.

Congregation for the Evangelization of Peoples: Directs and coordinates missionary work throughout the world. Accordingly, it has competence over those matters which concern all the missions established for the spread of Christ's kingdom without prejudice to the competence of other congregations. These include: fostering missionary vocations; assigning missionaries to fields of work; establishing ecclesiastical jurisdictions and proposing candidates to serve them as bishops and in other capacities; encouraging the recruitment and development of indigenous clergy; mobilizing spiritual and financial support for missionary activity.

To promote missionary cooperation, the congregation has a Supreme Council for the Direction of Pontifical Missionary Works composed of the Missionary Union of the Clergy and Religious, the Society for the Propagation of the Faith, the Society of St. Peter the Apostle for Native Clergy, the Society of the Holy Childhood, and the International Center of Missionary Animation.

OFFICIALS: Cardinal Jozef Tomko, prefect; Most Rev. Giuseppe Uhac, secretary.

ADDRESS: Piazza di Spagna 48, 00187 Rome, Italy.

BACKGROUND: Originated as a commission of cardinals by St. Pius V and Gregory XII for missions in East and West Indies, Italo-Greeks and for ecclesiastical affairs in Protestant territories of Europe; Clement VIII instituted a Congregation of the Propagation of the Faith in 1599 which ceased to exist after several years. Erected as a stable congregation by Gregory XV June 22, 1622 (apostolic constitution *Inscrutabili Divinae);* its functions were redefined by John Paul II, June 28, 1988.

Inter-Agency Curia Commissions

In accordance with provisions of the apostolic constitution *Pastor Bonus,* John Paul II established the following permanent commissions, to handle matters when more than one agency of the Curia is involved in activities:

• The Interdepartmental Standing Commission for matters concerning appointments to local Churches and the setting up and alteration of them and their constitution (Mar. 22, 1989). Members include officials of the Secretariat of State and Congregation for Bishops. President, Cardinal Angelo Sodano, Secretary of State.

• The Interdepartmental Standing Commission for matters concerning members, individually or as a community, of Institutes of Consecrated Life founded or working in mission territories (Mar. 22,

1989). Members include officials of the Congregations for the Evangelization of Peoples and for Institutes of Consecrated Life and Societies of Apostolic Life. President: Cardinal Jozef Tomko, prefect of the Congregation for the Evangelization of Peoples.

• The Interdepartmental Standing Commission for the formation of candidates for Sacred Orders (Mar. 22, 1989). Members include officials of the Congregations for Catholic Education, for Institutes of Consecrated Life and Societies of Apostolic Life, for Evangelization of Peoples, for Oriental Churches. President: Cardinal Pio Laghi, prefect of the Congregation for Catholic Education.

• The Interdepartmental Permanent Commission, as part of Congregation for Catholic Education, entrusted with the task of promoting a more equitable distribution of priests throughout the world (July 20, 1991). Members include secretaries of congregations for Evangelization of Peoples, for the Clergy, Catholic Education, for the Institutes of Consecrated Life and Societies of Apostolic Life; and vice-president of Commission for Latin America. President, Cardinal Pio Laghi, prefect of the Congregation for Catholic Education.

• The Permanent Interdepartmental Commission for the Church in Eastern Europe (Jan. 15, 1993), replacing the Pontifical Commission for Russia which was terminated. The commission is concerned with both Latin and Eastern-rite churches in territories of the former Soviet Union and other nations affected by the historical circumstances resulting from atheistic communism. It is responsible for promoting the apostolic mission of the Church and fostering ecumenical dialogue with the Orthodox and other Churches of the Eastern tradition. Members, under presidency of Cardinal Secretary of State, include the secretary and undersecretary of the Section for Relations with States and secretaries of Congregations for the Oriental Churches, for Institutes of Consecrated Life and Societies of Apostolic Life, secretary of the Pontifical Council for Promoting Christian Unity. President, Cardinal Angelo Sodano.

TRIBUNALS

Apostolic Penitentiary: Has jurisdiction for the internal forum only (sacramental and non-sacramental). It issues decisions on questions of conscience; grants absolutions, dispensations, commutations, sanations and condonations; has charge of non-doctrinal matters pertaining to indulgences.

OFFICIALS: Cardinal William Wakefield Baum, major penitentiary; Msgr. Luigi de Magistris, regent.

ADDRESS: Piazza della Cancelleria 1, 00186 Rome, Italy.

BACKGROUND: Origin dates back to the 12th century; affected by the legislation of many popes; radically reorganized by St. Pius V in 1569; jurisdiction limited to the internal forum by St. Pius X; Benedict XV annexed the Office of Indulgences to it Mar. 25, 1917.

Apostolic Signatura: The principal concerns of this supreme court of the Church are to resolve questions concerning juridical procedure and to supervise the observance of laws and rights at the highest level. It decides the jurisdictional competence of lower courts and has jurisdiction in cases involving personnel and decisions of the Rota. It is the supreme court of the State of Vatican City.

OFFICIAL: Most Rev. Gilberto Agustoni, pro-prefect; Most Rev. Zenon Grocholewski, secretary.

ADDRESS: Piazza della Cancelleria 1, 00186 Rome, Italy.

BACKGROUND: A permanent office of the Signatura has existed since the time of Eugene IV in the 15th century; affected by the legislation of many popes; reorganized by St. Pius X in 1908 and made the supreme tribunal of the Church.

Roman Rota: The ordinary court of appeal for cases appealed to the Holy See. It is best known for its competence and decisions in cases involving the validity of marriage.

OFFICIAL: Most Rev. Ernesto Fiore, dean.

ADDRESS: Piazza della Cancelleria 1, 00186 Rome, Italy.

BACKGROUND: Originated in the Apostolic Chancery; affected by the legislation of many popes; reorganized by St. Pius X in 1908; further revised by Pius XI in 1934; new norms approved and promulgated by John Paul II in 1982 and 1987.

COUNCILS

Pontifical Council for the Laity: Its competence covers the apostolate of the laity and their participation in the life and mission of the Church. Members are mostly lay people from different parts of the world and involved in different apostolates.

OFFICIALS: Cardinal Eduardo Francisco Pironio, president; Most Rev. Paul Josef Cordes, vice-president; Prof. Guzman Carriquiry, undersecretary.

ADDRESS: Piazza S. Calisto 16, 00153 Rome, Italy.

BACKGROUND: Established on an experimental basis by Paul VI Jan. 6, 1967; given permanent status Dec. 10, 1976 (motu proprio *Apostolatus Peragendi*).

Pontifical Council for Promoting Christian Unity: Handles relations with members of other Christian ecclesial communities; deals with the correct interpretation and execution of the principles of ecumenism; initiates or promotes Catholic ecumenical groups and coordinates on national and international levels the efforts of those promoting Christian unity; undertakes dialogue regarding ecumenical questions and activities with churches and ecclesial communities separated from the Apostolic See; sends Catholic observer-representatives to Christian gatherings, and invites to Catholic gatherings observers of other churches; orders into execution conciliar decrees dealing with ecumenical affairs. The Commission for Religious Relations with Jews is attached to the secretariat.

OFFICIALS: Cardinal Edward I. Cassidy, president; Cardinal Johannes Willebrands, president emeritus; Most Rev. Pierre Duprey, M. Afr., secretary.

ADDRESS: Via dell' Erba 1, 00193 Rome, Italy.

BACKGROUND: Established by John XXIII June 5, 1960, as a preparatory secretariat of the Second Vatican Council; raised to commission status during the first session of the council in the fall of 1962; status as a secretariat confirmed and functions defined by Paul VI in 1966 and 1967; made a pontifical council by John Paul II, June 28, 1988.

Pontifical Council for the Family: Is concerned with promoting the pastoral care of families so they may carry out their educative, evangelizing and apostolic mission and make their influence felt in areas such as defense of human life and responsible procreation according to the teachings of the Church. Members, chosen by the Pope, are married couples and men and women from all parts of the world and representing different cultures. They meet in general assembly at least once a year.

OFFICIALS: Cardinal Alfonso Lopez Trujillo, president; Most Rev. Elio Sgreccia, secretary.

ADDRESS: Piazza S. Calisto 16, 00153 Rome, Italy.

BACKGROUND: Instituted by John Paul II May 9, 1981, replacing the Committee for the Family established by Paul VI Jan. 11, 1973.

Pontifical Council for Justice and Peace: Its primary competence is to promote justice and peace in the world according to the Gospels and social teaching of the Church.

OFFICIALS: Cardinal Roger Etchegaray, president; Most Rev. Jorge Maria Mejia, vice-president; Msgr. Diarmuid Martin, undersecretary.

ADDRESS: Piazza S. Calisto 16, 00153 Rome, Italy.

BACKGROUND: Instituted by Paul VI Jan. 6, 1967, on an experimental basis; reconstituted and made a permanent commission Dec. 10, 1976; its competence was redefined and it was made a pontifical council June 28, 1988, by John Paul II.

Pontifical Council "Cor Unum": Its principal aims are to provide informational and coordinating services for Catholic aid and human development organizations and projects on a worldwide scale.

OFFICIALS: Cardinal Roger Etchegaray, president; Rev. Ivan Marin-Lopez, secretary.

ADDRESS: Piazza S. Calisto 16, 00153 Rome, Italy.

BACKGROUND: Instituted by Paul VI July 15, 1971.

Pontifical Council for Pastoral Care of Migrants and Itinerant Peoples: Is concerned with pastoral assistance to migrants, nomads, tourists, sea and air travelers.

OFFICIALS: Most Rev. Giovanni Cheli, president; Very Rev. Silvano Tomasi, C.S., secretary.

ADDRESS: Piazza S. Calisto 16, 00153 Rome, Italy.

BACKGROUND: Instituted by Paul VI and placed under general supervision of Congregation for Bishops, Mar. 19, 1970; made autonomous as a pontifical council and renamed by John Paul II, June 28, 1988.

Pontifical Council for Pastoral Assistance to Health Care Workers: Its functions are to stimulate and foster the work of formation, study and action carried out by various international Catholic organizations in the health care field.

OFFICIALS: Cardinal Fiorenzo Angelini, president; Very Rev. Jose Luis Redrado Marchite, O.H., secretary.

ADDRESS: Via della Conciliazione 3, 00193 Rome, Italy.

BACKGROUND: Established in 1985 as a commission by John Paul II; made a council June 28, 1988.

Pontifical Council for the Interpretation of Legislative Texts: Primary function is the authentic interpretation of the universal laws of the Church.

OFFICIALS: Most Rev. Vincenzo Fagiolo, president; Most Rev. Julian Herranz Casado, secretary.

ADDRESS: Piazza Pio XII 10, 00193 Rome, Italy.

BACKGROUND: Established by John Paul II, Jan. 2, 1984, as the Pontifical Commission for the Authentic Interpretation of the Code of Canon Law; name changed and given additional functions June 28, 1988.

Pontifical Council for Interreligious Dialogue: Its function is to promote studies and dialogue for the purpose of increasing mutual understanding and respect between Christians and non-Christians. The Commission for Religious Relations with Muslims is attached to the council.

OFFICIALS: Cardinal Francis Arinze, president; Most Rev. Michael Louis Fitzgerald, M. Afr., secretary.

ADDRESS: Via dell' Erba 1, 00193 Rome, Italy.

BACKGROUND: Established by Paul VI May 19, 1964, as the Secretariat for Non-Christians; given present title and functions by John Paul II, June 28, 1988.

Pontifical Council for Dialogue with Non-Believers: Merged with Pontifical Council for Culture, 1993. See below.

Pontifical Council for Culture: Its functions are to foster the Church's and the Holy See's relations with the world of culture and to establish dialogue with those who do not believe in God or who profess no religion provided these are open to sincere cooperation. It consists of two sections: (1) faith and culture; (2) dialogue with cultures.

OFFICIALS: Cardinal Paul Poupard, president; Msgr. Franc Rodé, secretary.

ADDRESS: 00120 Vatican City.

BACKGROUND: Established in 1982 by John Paul II to facilitate contacts between the saving message of the Gospel and the plurality of cultures. In a Motu Proprio dated Mar. 25, 1993, the Pope united the Pontifical Council for Culture and the Council for Dialogue with Non-Believers (established in 1965 by Paul VI) under the title Pontifical Council for Culture with expanded functions.

Pontifical Council for Social Communications: Engaged in matters pertaining to instruments of social communication so that through them the message of salvation and human progress is fostered and carried forward in civil culture and mores.

OFFICIALS: Most Rev. John P. Foley, president; Msgr. Pierfranco Pastore, secretary; Mr. Hans-Peter Rothlin, undersecretary; Cardinal Andrzej M. Deskur, president emeritus.

ADDRESS: Palazzo S. Carlo, 00120 Vatican City.

BACKGROUND: Instituted on an experimental basis by Pius XII in 1948; reorganized three times in the 1950s; made permanent commission by John XXIII Feb. 22, 1959; established as council and functions restated by John Paul II June 28, 1988.

OFFICES

Apostolic Chamber: Administers the temporal goods and rights of the Holy See between the death of one pope and the election of another, in accordance with special laws.

OFFICIALS: Cardinal Eduardo Martinez Somalo, chamberlain of the Holy Roman Church; Most Rev. Ettore Cunial, vice-chamberlain.

ADDRESS: Palazzo Apostolico, 00120 Vatican City.

BACKGROUND: Originated in the 11th century; reorganized by Pius XI in 1934; functions redefined (especially of camerlengo) by subsequent legislation in 1945, 1962 and 1975.

Prefecture for the Economic Affairs of the Holy See: A financial office which coordinates and supervises administration of the temporalities of the Holy See.

OFFICIALS: Cardinal Edmund C. Szoka, president; Msgr. Luigi Sposito, secretary.

ADDRESS: Largo del Colonnato 3, 00193 Rome, Italy.

BACKGROUND: Established by Paul VI Aug. 15, 1967; functions redefined by John Paul II, June 28, 1988..

Administration of the Patrimony of the Apostolic See: Handles the estate of the Apostolic See under the direction of papal delegates acting with ordinary or extraordinary authorization.

OFFICIALS: Cardinal Rosalio Jose Castillo Lara, S.D.B., president; Most Rev. Giovanni Lajolo, secretary.

ADDRESS: Palazzo Apostolico, 00120 Vatican City.

BACKGROUND: Some of its functions date back to 1878; established by Paul VI Aug. 15, 1967.

Other Curia Agencies

Prefecture of the Papal Household: Oversees the papal chapel — which is at the service of the pope in his capacity as spiritual head of the Church — and the pontifical family — which is at the service of the pope as a sovereign. It arranges papal audiences, has charge of preparing non-liturgical elements of papal ceremonies, makes all necessary arrangements for papal visits and trips outside the Vatican, and settles questions of protocol connected with papal audiences and other formalities.

OFFICIAL: Most Rev. Dino Monduzzi, prefect.

BACKGROUND: Established by Paul VI Aug. 15, 1967, under the title, Prefecture of the Apostolic Palace; it supplanted the Sacred Congregation for Ceremonies founded by Sixtus V Jan. 22, 1588. The office was updated and reorganized under the present title by Paul VI, Mar. 28, 1968.

Office for Liturgical Celebrations of the Supreme Pontiff: Prepares everything necessary for liturgical and other sacred celebrations by the Pope or in his name; directs everything in accordance with prescriptions of liturgical law.

MASTER OF CEREMONIES: Msgr. Piero Marini.

ADDRESS: Apostolico Vaticano, 00120 Vatican City.

BACKGROUND: Evolved gradually from the early office of Apostolic Master of Ceremonies; affected by legislation of Pope Paul IV in 1563 and Benedict XV in 1917; restructured by Paul VI in 1967; given its present title (formerly known as

Prefecture of Pontifical Ceremonies) and constituted as an autonomous agency of the Roman Curia by John Paul II, June 28, 1988.

Internationalization

As of July 21, 1993, principal officials of the Roman Curia (cardinals unless indicated otherwise) were from the following countries: Italy (Angelini, Felici, Innocenti, Laghi, Noè, Silvestrini, Sodano; Abps. Bovone, Cheli, Cunial, Fagiolo, Fiore, Lajolo, Re, Sepe; Bps. Marchisano, Monduzzi, Sgreccia); France (Etchegaray, Poupard, Abp. Tauran, Bp. Duprey); United States (Baum, Szoka, Abps. Foley, Rigali); Argentina (Pironio, Bp. Mejia); Germany (Ratzinger, Bp. Cordes); Poland (Abps. Grocholewski, Nowak); Spain (Javierre Ortas, Martinez Somalo); Australia (Cassidy); Austria (Bp. Wagner); Belgium (Abp. Schotte); Benin (Gantin); Brazil (Abp. Agnelo); Canada (Gagnon); Chile (Abp. Errazuriz Ossa); Colombia (Lopez Trujillo); Croatia (Abp. Uhac); England (Bp. Fitzgerald); Hungary (Abp. Kada); Nigeria (Arinze); Philippines (Sanchez); Portugal (Abp. Saraiva Martins); Slovak Republic (Tomko); Switzerland (Abp. Agustoni); Ukraine (Abp. Marusyn); Venezuela (Castillo Lara).

COMMISSIONS AND COMMITTEES

Listed below are non-curial institutes which assist in the work of the Holy See. Some are attached to curial agencies, as indicated. Other institutes are listed elsewhere in the Almanac; see Index.

Latin America, Commission: Instituted by Pius XII Apr. 19, 1958; attached to the Congregation for Bishops July, 1969; restructured and functions redefined by John Paul II in 1988. Cardinal Bernardin Gantin, president.

International Eucharistic Congresses, Pontifical Committee: Instituted, 1879, by Pope Leo XIII; established as a pontifical committee with new statutes by John Paul II, Feb. 11, 1986. Cardinal Edouard Gagnon, president.

Central Statistics Office: Established by Paul VI Aug. 15, 1967; attached to the Secretariat of State. Compiles, systematizes and analyzes information on the status and condition of the Church.

Fabric of St. Peter: Administration, care and preservation of Vatican Basilica. Cardinal Virgilio Noè, Archpriest of the Patriarchal Vatican Basilica, president.

Office of Papal Charities: Distributes alms and aid to those in need in the name of the Pope. Most Rev. Oscar Rizzato, almoner.

Roman Curia, Disciplinary Commission: Most Rev. Vincenzo Fagiolo, president.

Council of Cardinals for Study of Organizational and Economic Problems of the Holy See: Council established in 1981 by Pope John Paul II; composed of 15 cardinals; 14 were residential archbishops from countries outside of Italy (including Cardinals O'Connor and Mahony from the U.S.).

Theological Commission: Instituted by Paul VI Apr. 11, 1969, as an advisory adjunct of no more than 30 theologians to the Congregation for the Doctrine of the Faith; definitive statutes promulgated by John Paul II, Aug. 6, 1982. Cardinal Joseph Ratzinger, president.

Biblical Commission: Instituted by Leo XIII Oct. 30, 1902; completely restructured by Paul VI June 27, 1971; attached to the Congregation for the Doctrine of the Faith. Cardinal Joseph Ratzinger, president.

"Ecclesia Dei," Pontifical Commission: Established by John Paul II, July 2, 1988, to facilitate the return to full ecclesial communion of priests, seminarians and religious who belonged to the fraternity founded by Marcel Lefebvre. Cardinal Antonio Innocenti, president.

Revision and Emendation of the Vulgate, Pontifical Commission: Established in 1984 by John Paul II to replace the Abbey of St. Jerome instituted by Pius XI in 1933. Rev. Jean Mallet, O.S.B., director.

Cultural Patrimony of the Church, Pontifical Commission: Established by John Paul II, June 28, 1988, as Pontifical Commission for Preserving the Church's Patrimony of Art and History and attached to the Congregation for the Clergy; made autonomous and given present title Mar. 25, 1993. Most Rev. Francesco Marchisano, president.

Sacred Archeology, Commission: Instituted by Pius IX Jan, 6, 1852. Most Rev. Francesco Marchisano, president.

Historical Sciences, Pontifical Committee: Instituted by Pius XII Apr. 7, 1954, as a continuation of a commission dating from 1883. Msgr. Victor Saxer, president.

Vatican II Archives: Preserves the acts and other documents of the Second Vatican Council.

Sanctuaries of Pompei, Loreto and Bari, Cardinalatial Commission: Originated by Leo XIII for Sanctuary of Pompei, Loreto placed under commission in 1965, St. Nicholas of Bari, 1980; under supervision of the Congregation for the Clergy. Cardinal Opilio Rossi, president.

Religious Relations with Jews, Commission: Instituted by Paul VI, Oct. 22, 1974, to promote and foster relations of a religious nature between Jews and Christians; attached to the Council for Promoting Christian Unity; Cardinal Edward I. Cassidy, president.

Religious Relations with Muslims, Commission: Instituted by Paul VI, Oct. 22, 1974, to promote, regulate and interpret relations between Catholics and Muslims; attached to the Council for Interreligious Dialogue. Cardinal Francis Arinze, president.

Protection of the Historical and Artistic Monuments of the Holy See, Commission: Instituted by Pius XI in 1923, reorganized by Paul VI in 1963, Cardinal Virgilio Noè, president.

Preservation of the Faith, Erection of New Churches in Rome: Instituted by Pius XI Aug. 5, 1930, to replace a commission dating from 1902. Cardinal Camillo Ruini, president.

Institute for Works of Religion: Instituted by Pius XII June 27, 1942, to bank and administer funds for works of religion; replaced an earlier administration established by Leo XIII in 1887; reorganized by John Paul II (chirograph of Mar. 1, 1990).

Labor Office of the Apostolic See (ULSA - Ufficio del Lavoro della Sede Apostolica): Has competence in regard to those who work for the Apostolic See; charged with settling labor issues. OFFICIAL: Most Rev. Jan Schotte, president.

BACKGROUND: Instituted by John Paul II (motu proprio dated Jan. 1, 1989, and effective Mar. 1, 1989) in accordance with provisions he set down in the apostolic constitution *Pastor Bonus,* June 28, 1988 and a chirograph of June 14, 1991.

Catechism Commission: Established by John Paul II in April, 1993, to review questions about the *Catechism of the Catholic Church* and to promote its use. Cardinal Joseph Ratzinger is president.

COLLEGE OF CARDINALS

Cardinals are chosen by the pope to serve as his principal assistants and advisers in the central administration of church affairs. Collectively, they form the College of Cardinals. Provisions regarding their selection, rank, roles and prerogatives are detailed in Canons 349 to 359 of the Code of Canon Law.

History of the College

The College of Cardinals was constituted in its present form and categories of membership in the 12th century. Before that time the pope had a body of advisers selected from among the bishops of dioceses neighboring Rome, priests and deacons of Rome. The college was given definite form in 1150, and in 1179 the selection of cardinals was reserved exclusively to the pope. Sixtus V fixed the number at 70, in 1586. John XXIII set aside this rule when he increased membership at the 1959 and subsequent consistories. The number was subsequently raised to 145 by Paul VI in 1973 and to 152 by John Paul II in 1985. The

number of cardinals entitled to participate in papal elections was limited to 120.

In 1567 the title of cardinal was reserved to members of the college; previously it had been used by priests attached to parish churches of Rome and by the leading clergy of other notable churches. The Code of Canon Law promulgated in 1918 decreed that all cardinals must be priests. Previously there had been cardinals who were not priests (e.g., Cardinal Giacomo Antonelli, d. 1876, Secretary of State to Pius IX, was a deacon). John XXIII provided in the motu proprio *Cum Gravissima* Apr. 15, 1962, that cardinals would henceforth be bishops; this provision is included in the revised Code of Canon Law.

Age Limits

Pope Paul VI placed age limits on the functions of cardinals in the apostolic letter *Ingravescentem Aetatem,* dated Nov. 21, 1970, and effective as of Jan. 1, 1971. At 80, they cease to be members of curial departments and offices, and become ineligible to take part in papal elections. They retain membership in the College of Cardinals, however, with relevant rights and privileges.

Three Categories

All cardinals except Eastern patriarchs are aggregated to the clergy of Rome. This aggregation is signified by the assignment to each cardinal, except the patriarchs, of a titular church in Rome.

The three categories of members of the college are cardinal bishops, cardinal priests and cardinal deacons.

Cardinal bishops include the six titular bishops of the suburbicarian sees and Eastern patriarchs.

First in rank are the titular bishops of the suburbicarian sees, neighboring Rome: Ostia, Palestrina, Porto-Santa Rufina, Albano, Velletri-Segni, Frascati, Sabina-Poggio Mirteto. The dean of the college holds the title of the See of Ostia as well as his other suburbicarian see. These cardinal bishops are engaged in full-time service in the central administration of church affairs in departments of the Roman Curia.

Full recognition is given in the revised Code of Canon Law to the position of Eastern patriarchs as the heads of sees of apostolic origin with ancient liturgies. They are assigned rank among the cardinals in order of seniority, following the suburbicarian titleholders.

Cardinal priests, who were formerly in charge of leading churches in Rome, are bishops whose dioceses are outside Rome.

Cardinal deacons, who were formerly chosen according to regional divisions of Rome, are titular bishops assigned to full-time service in the Roman Curia.

The **dean** and **sub-dean** of the college are elected by the cardinal bishops — subject to approval by the pope — from among their number. The dean, or the sub-dean in his absence, presides over the college as the first among equals. Cardinals Bernardin Gantin and Agostino Casaroli were elected dean and sub-dean, respectively, June 4, 1993 (papal approval June 5, 1993).

Selection and Duties

Cardinals are selected by the pope and are inducted into the college in appropriate ceremonies.

Cardinals under the age of 80: elect the pope when the Holy See becomes vacant (see Index: Papal Election); and are major administrators of church affairs, serving in one or more departments of the Roman Curia. Cardinals in charge of agencies of the Roman Curia and Vatican City are asked to submit their resignation from office to the pope on reaching the age of 75. All cardinals enjoy a number of special rights and privileges. Their title, while symbolic of high honor, does not signify any extension of the powers of holy orders. They are called princes of the Church.

A **cardinal in pectore (petto)** is one whose selection has been made by the pope but whose name has not been disclosed; he has no title, rights or duties until such disclosure is made, at which time he takes precedence from the time of the secret selection.

BIOGRAPHIES OF CARDINALS

Biographies of the cardinals, as of Aug. 15, 1993, are given below in alphabetical order. For historical notes, order of seniority and geographical distribution of cardinals, see separate entries.

An asterisk indicates cardinals ineligible to take part in papal elections.

Angelini, Fiorenzo: b. Aug. 1, 1916, Rome, Italy; ord. priest Feb. 3, 1940; master of pontifical ceremonies, 1947-54; ord. bishop (titular see of Messene) July 29, 1956, and head of Rome Vicariate's section for apostolate to health care workers; archbishop, 1985, and president of newly established Curia agency for health care workers; cardinal June 28, 1991, deacon, Holy Spirit (in Sassio). President of Pontifical Council for Pastoral Assistance to Health Care Workers, 1989. Curial membership:

Evangelization of Peoples, Institutes of Consecrated Life and Societies of Apostolic Life (congregations); Family (council); Latin America (commission).

Aponte Martinez, Luis: b. Aug. 4, 1922, Lajas, Puerto Rico; ord. priest Apr. 10, 1950; parish priest at Ponce; ord. titular bishop of Lares and auxiliary of Ponce, Oct. 12, 1960; bishop of Ponce, 1963-64; archbishop of San Juan, Nov. 4, 1964; cardinal Mar. 5, 1973; titular church, St. Mary Mother of Providence (in Monteverde). Archbishop of San Juan. Curial membership:

Causes of Saints (congregation).

Aramburu,* Juan Carlos: b. Feb. 11, 1912, Reduccion, Argentina; ord. priest in Rome, Oct. 28, 1934; ord. titular bishop of Plataea and auxiliary of Tucuman, Argentina, Dec. 15, 1946; bishop, 1953, and first archbishop, 1957, of Tucuman; titular archbishop of Torri di Bizacena and coadjutor archbishop of Buenos Aires, June 14, 1967; archbishop of Buenos Aires, Apr. 22, 1975 (resigned July 10, 1990); cardinal May 24, 1976; titular church, St. John Baptist of the Florentines. Archbishop emeritus of Buenos Aires.

Arinze, Francis: b. Nov. 1, 1932, Eziowelle, Nigeria; ord. priest Nov. 23, 1958; ord. titular bishop of Fissiana and auxiliary of Onitsha, Aug. 29, 1965; archbishop of Onitsha, 1967-84; pro-president of Secretariat for Non-Christians (now the Council for Interreligious Dialogue), 1984; cardinal May 25, 1985; deacon, St. John (della Pigna). President of Council for Interreligious Dialogue, 1985. Curial membership:

Oriental Churches, Evangelization of Peoples, Causes of Saints (congregations); Laity, Christian Unity, Culture (councils); International Eucharistic Congresses (committee).

Arns, Paulo Evaristo, O.F.M.: b. Sept. 14, 1921, Forquilhinha, Brazil; ord. priest Nov. 30, 1945; held various teaching posts; director of *Sponsa Christi*, monthly review for religious, and of the Franciscan publication center in Brazil; ord. titular bishop of Respetta and auxiliary of Sao Paulo, July 3, 1966;

archbishop of Sao Paulo, Oct. 22, 1970; cardinal Mar. 5, 1973; titular church, St. Anthony of Padua (in Via Tuscolana). Archbishop of Sao Paulo. Curial membership:
Divine Worship and Sacraments (congregation).

Bafile,* Corrado: b. July 4, 1903, L'Aquila, Italy; practiced law in Rome for six years before beginning studies for priesthood; ord. priest Apr. 11, 1936; served in Vatican secretariat of state, 1939-59; ord. titular archbishop of Antiochia in Pisidia, Mar. 19, 1960; apostolic nuncio to Germany, 1960-75; pro-prefect of Congregation for Causes of Saints, July 18, 1975; cardinal May 24, 1976; deacon, S. Maria (in Portico); transferred to order of cardinal priosto, June 22, 1987; prefect of Congregation for Causes of Saints, 1976-80.

Ballestrero, Anastasio Alberto, O.C.D.: b. Oct. 3, 1913, Genoa, Italy; professed in Order of Discalced Carmelites, 1929; ord. priest June 6, 1936; provincial, 1942-48, and superior general, 1955-67, of Carmelites; author of many books on Christian life; ord. archbishop of Bari, Feb. 2, 1974; archbishop of Turin, Aug. 1, 1977 (resigned Jan. 31, 1989); cardinal June 30, 1979; titular church, S. Maria (sopra Minerva). Archbishop emeritus of Turin. Curial membership:
Institutes of Consecrated Life and Societies of Apostolic Life (congregation).

Baum, William Wakefield: b. Nov. 21, 1926, Dallas, Tex.; moved to Kansas City, Mo., at an early age; ord. priest (Kansas City-St. Joseph diocese) May 12, 1951; executive director of U.S. bishops commission for ecumenical and interreligious affairs, 1964-69; attended Second Vatican Council as *peritus* (expert adviser); ord. bishop of Springfield-Cape Girardeau, Mo., Apr. 6, 1970; archbishop of Washington, D.C., 1973-80; cardinal May 24, 1976; titular church, Holy Cross (on the Via Flaminia); prefect of Congregation for Catholic Education (Seminaries and Institutes of Study), 1980-90. Major Penitentiary, 1990. Curial membership:
Secretariat of State (second section); Doctrine of the Faith, Bishops, Oriental Churches, Institutes of Consecrated Life and Societies of Apostolic Life, Evangelization of Peoples (congregations); Patrimony of Holy See (office).

Bernardin, Joseph L.: b. Apr. 2, 1928, Columbia, S.C.; ord. priest (Charleston diocese) Apr. 26, 1952; ord. titular bishop of Lugura and auxiliary bishop of Atlanta, Ga., Apr. 26, 1966; general secretary, 1968-72, and president, 1974-77, of NCCB/USCC; archbishop of Cincinnati, 1972-82; archbishop of Chicago, July 10, 1982, installed Aug. 25, 1982; cardinal Feb. 2, 1983; titular church, Jesus the Divine Worker. Archbishop of Chicago. Curial membership:
Divine Worship and Sacraments (congregation); Christian Unity (council).

Bertoli,* Paolo: b. Feb.1, 1908, Poggio Garfagnana, Italy; ord. priest Aug. 15, 1930; entered diplomatic service of the Holy See, serving in nunciatures in Yugoslavia, France, Haiti and Switzerland; ord. titular archbishop of Nicomedia, May 11, 1952; apostolic delegate to Turkey (1952-53), nuncio to Colombia (1953-59), Lebanon (1959-60), France (1960-69); cardinal Apr. 28, 1969; prefect of

Congregation for Causes of Saints, 1969-73; entered order of cardinal bishops as titular bishop of Frascati, June 30, 1979; Chamberlain (Camerlengo) of Holy Roman Church, 1979-85.

Bevilacqua, Anthony Joseph: b. June 17, 1923, Brooklyn N.Y.; educ. Cathedral College (Brooklyn, N.Y.), Immaculate Conception Seminary (Huntington, N.Y.), Gregorian Univ. (Rome), Columbia Univ. and St. John's Univ. (New York); ord. priest (Brooklyn diocese) June 11, 1949; ord. titular bishop of Aquae Albae in Byzacena and auxiliary bishop of Brooklyn, Nov. 24, 1980; bishop of Pittsburgh Oct. 7, 1983, installed Dec. 11, 1983; archbishop of Philadelphia, Feb. 11, 1988; cardinal June 28, 1991; titular church, Most Holy Redeemer and St. Alphonsus (on Via Merulana). Archbishop of Philadelphia. Curial membership:
Causes of Saints (congregation); "Cor Unum," Migrants and Travelers (councils).

Biffi, Giacomo: b. June 13, 1928, Milan, Italy; ord. priest Dec. 23, 1950; ord. titular bishop of Fidene and auxiliary of Milan, Jan. 11, 1976; archbishop of Bologna, Apr. 19, 1984; cardinal May 25, 1985; titular church, Sts. John the Evangelist and Petronio. Archbishop of Bologna. Curial membership:
Divine Worship and Sacraments, Clergy (congregations).

Canestri, Giovanni: b. Sept. 30, 1918, Castelspina, Italy; ord. priest Apr. 12, 1941; spiritual director of Rome's seminary, 1959; ord. titular bishop of Tenedo and auxiliary to the cardinal vicar of Rome, July 30, 1961; bishop of Tortona, 1971-75; titular bishop of Monterano (personal title of archbishop) and vice regent of Rome, 1975-84; archbishop of Cagliari, 1984-87; archbishop of Genoa, July 6, 1987; cardinal June 28, 1988; titular church, St. Andrew of the Valley. Archbishop of Genoa. Curial membership:
Divine Worship and Sacraments, Clergy (congregations); Patrimony of the Holy See (office).

Caprio, Giuseppe: b. Nov. 15, 1914, Lapio, Italy; ord. priest Dec. 17, 1938; served in diplomatic missions in China (1947-51, when Vatican diplomats were expelled by communists), Belgium (1951-54), and South Vietnam (1954-56); internuncio in China with residence at Taiwan, 1959-67; ord. titular archbishop of Apollonia, Dec. 17, 1961; pro-nuncio in India, 1967-69; secretary, 1969-77, and president, 1979-81, of Administration of Patrimony of Holy See; substitute secretary of state, 1977-79; cardinal deacon June 30, 1979; transferred to order of cardinal priests, November, 1990; titular church, St. Mary of Victory; president of Prefecture of Economic Affairs of the Holy See, 1981-90. Curial membership:
Secretariat of State (second section); Bishops, Oriental Churches, Causes of Saints, Evangelization of Peoples (congregations).

Carberry,* John J.: b. July 31, 1904, Brooklyn, N.Y.; ord. priest (Brooklyn diocese) July 28, 1929; ord. titular bishop of Elis and coadjutor bishop of Lafayette, Ind., July 25, 1956; bishop of Lafayette, Nov. 20, 1957; bishop of Columbus, Ohio, Jan. 6, 1965; archbishop of St. Louis, Mo., 1968-79; cardinal Apr. 28, 1969; titular church, St. John Baptist de Rossi (Via Latina). Archbishop emeritus of St. Louis.

Carpino,* Francesco: b. May 18, 1905, Palazzolo Acreide, Italy; ord. priest Aug. 14, 1927; ord. titular archbishop of Nicomedia and coadjutor archbishop of Monreale, Apr. 8, 1951; archbishop of Monreale, 1951-61; titular archbishop of Sardica, Jan. 19, 1961; assessor of Consistorial Congregation, 1961; pro-prefect of Congregation of the Council, Apr. 7, 1967; cardinal June 26, 1967; archbishop of Palermo, 1967-70; entered order of cardinal bishops as titular bishop of Albano, Jan. 27, 1978.

Carter,* Gerald Emmett: b. Mar. 1, 1912, Montreal, Canada; ord. priest May 22, 1937; engaged in pastoral and teaching ministry in Montreal; founder and president of St. Joseph Teachers' College and co-founder and director of Thomas More Institute for adult education; ord. titular bishop of Altiburo and auxiliary bishop of London, Ont., Feb. 2, 1962; bishop of London, Ont., 1964-78; vice president, 1971-73, and president, 1975-77, of Canadian Conference of Catholic Bishops; archbishop of Toronto, 1978-90; cardinal June 30, 1979; titular church, St. Mary (in Traspontina). Archbishop emeritus of Toronto.

Casaroli, Agostino: b. Nov. 24, 1914, Castel San Giovanni, Italy; ord. priest May 27, 1937; entered service of Vatican secretariat of state, 1940; under-secretary, 1961-67, of the Congregation for Extraordinary Ecclesiastical Affairs, and secretary, 1967-79, of its successor the Council for Public Affairs of the Church; ord. titular archbishop of Cartagina, July 16, 1967; chief negotiator for the Vatican with East European communist governments; missions included visits to Hungary, Yugoslavia, Poland, Czechoslovakia, Bulgaria; headed Vatican delegations to several UN conferences and the Helsinki Conference (1975); Pro-Secretary of State and Pro-Prefect of Council for Public Affairs of the Church, Apr. 28, 1979; cardinal June 30, 1979; titular church, the Twelve Apostles; president, 1981-84, of Administration of Patrimony of Holy See and Pontifical Commission for Vatican City; entered order of cardinal bishops as titular bishop of Porto-Santa Rufina, May 25, 1985. Secretary of State, 1979-90. Sub-dean of the college of cardinals, 1993. Curial membership:

Doctrine of the Faith, Bishops (congregations); Interpretation of Legislative Texts (council); Institute for Works of Religion (commission).

Casoria,* Giuseppe: b. Oct. 1, 1908, Acerra, Italy; ord. priest Dec. 21, 1930; jurist; Roman Curia official from 1937; under-secretary, 1959-69, and secretary, 1969-73, of Congregation for Sacraments and Divine Worship; secretary of Congregation for Causes of Saints, 1973-81; ord. titular bishop of Vescovia with personal title of archbishop, Feb. 13, 1972; pro-prefect of Congregation for Sacraments and Divine Worship, 1981-83; cardinal deacon Feb. 2, 1983; transferred to order of cardinal priests Apr. 5, 1993; titular church, St. Joseph on Via Trionfale. Prefect of Congregation for Sacraments and Divine Worship, 1983-84.

Cassidy, Edward I.: b. July 5, 1924, Sydney, Australia; ord. priest July 23, 1949; entered Vatican diplomatic service in 1955; served in nunciatures in India, Ireland, El Salvador and Argentina; ord. titular archbishop of Amantia, Nov. 15, 1970; pro-nuncio to Republic of China (Taiwan), 1970-79 and pro-nuncio to Bangladesh and apostolic delegate in Burma, 1973-79; pro-nuncio to Lesotho and apostolic delegate to southern Africa, 1979-84; pro-nuncio to the Netherlands, 1984-88; substitute of the Secretary of State for General Affairs, 1988-89; president of Pontifical Council for Promoting Christian Unity, 1989; cardinal June 28, 1991; deacon, St. Mary (in via Lata). President of Pontifical Council for Promoting Christian Unity. Curial membership:

Secretariat of State (second section); Doctrine of the Faith, Bishops, Oriental Churches (congregations); Health Care Workers, Interreligious Dialogue (councils); Patrimony of the Holy See (office); Latin America (commission).

Castillo Lara, Rosalio Jose, S.D.B.: b. Sept. 4, 1922, San Casimiro, Venezuela; ord. priest Sept. 4, 1949; ord. titular bishop of Precausa, May 24, 1973; coadjutor bishop of Trujillo, 1973-76; archbishop May 26, 1982; secretary, 1975-82, and pro-president, 1982-84, of Pontifical Commission for Revision of Code of Canon Law; pro-president of Commission for Authentic Interpretation of Code of Canon Law, 1984-85; cardinal May 25, 1985; deacon, Our Lady of Coromoto (in St. John of God); president of Pontifical Council for the Interpretation of Legislative Texts, 1985-90, and of Disciplinary Commission of Roman Curia, 1981-91. President of Administration of the Patrimony of the Holy See, 1989, and the Pontifical Commission for the State of Vatican City, 1990. Curial membership:

Secretariat of State (second section); Bishops, Catholic Education, Institutes of Consecrated Life and Societies of Apostolic Life (congregations); Apostolic Signatura (tribunal); Christian Unity (council); Institute for Works of Religion (commission).

Cé, Marco: b. July 8, 1925, Izano, Italy; ord. priest Mar. 27, 1948; taught sacred scripture and dogmatic theology at seminary in his home diocese of Crema; rector of seminary, 1957; presided over diocesan liturgical commission, preached youth retreats; ord. titular bishop of Vulturia, May 17, 1970; auxiliary bishop of Bologna, 1970-76; general ecclesiastical assistant of Italian Catholic Action, 1976-78; patriarch of Venice, Dec. 7, 1978; cardinal June 30, 1979; titular church, St. Mark. Patriarch of Venice. Curial membership:

Divine Worship and Sacraments (congregation).

Ciappi,* Mario Luigi, O.P.: b. Oct. 6, 1909, Florence, Italy; ord. priest Mar. 26, 1932; papal theologian from 1955, serving Pius XII, John XXIII and Paul VI; ord. titular bishop of Misenum June 18, 1977; cardinal deacon June 27, 1977; transferred to order of cardinal priests, June 22, 1987; titular church, Sacred Heart of the Agonized Jesus.

Clancy, Edward Bede: b. Dec. 13, 1923, Lithgow, New South Wales, Australia; ord. priest July 23, 1949; ord. titular bishop of Ard Carna and auxiliary of Sydney, Jan. 19, 1974; archbishop of Canberra, 1978-83; archbishop of Sydney, Feb. 12, 1983; cardinal June 28, 1988; titular church, Holy Mary of Vallicella. Archbishop of Sydney. Curial membership:

Secretariat of State (second section); Bishops (congregation); Social Communications (council).

Coffy, Robert: b. Oct. 24, 1920, Le Biot, France; ord. priest. Oct. 28, 1944; theologian; held chair in Dogmatic Theology at major seminary in Annecy; author of numerous works; ord. bishop of Gap, Apr. 23, 1967; archbishop of Albi, 1974-85; archbishop of Marseilles, Apr. 13, 1985; cardinal June 28, 1991; titular church, St. Louis Grignon de Montfort. Archbishop of Marseilles. Curial membership: Doctrine of the Faith (congregation); Interreligious Dialogue (council).

Cordeiro, Joseph: b. Jan. 19, 1918, Bombay, India; ord. priest Aug. 24, 1946; served in educational and other diocesan posts at Karachi, Pakistan; ord. archbishop of Karachi, Aug. 24, 1958, the first native-born prelate in that see; cardinal Mar 5, 1973; titular church, St. Andrew Apostle. Archbishop of Karachi. Curial membership: Institutes of Consecrated Life and Societies of Apostolic Life, Evangelization of Peoples (congregations); Interreligious Dialogue (council).

Corripio Ahumada, Ernesto: b. June 29, 1919, Tampico, Mexico; ord. priest Oct. 25, 1942, in Rome, where he remained until almost the end of World War II; taught and held various positions in local seminary of Tampico, 1945-50; ord. titular bishop of Zapara and auxiliary bishop of Tampico, Mar. 19, 1953; bishop of Tampico, 1956-67; archbishop of Antequera, 1967-76; archbishop of Puebla de los Angeles, 1976-77; archbishop of Mexico City and primate of Mexico, July 19, 1977; cardinal June 30, 1979; titular church, Mary Immaculate al Tiburtino. Archbishop of Mexico City. Curial membership: Divine Worship and Sacraments, Clergy, Catholic Education (congregations); Economic Affairs of the Holy See (office).

Daly, Cahal Brendan: b. Oct. 1, 1917, Loughguile, Northern Ireland; ord. priest June 22, 1941; earned advanced degrees in philosophy and theology; 30 years of priestly life dedicated to teaching; attended Second Vatican Council as a theological adviser to members of Irish hierarchy; outspoken critic of violence in Northern Ireland; ord. bishop of Ardagh, July 16, 1967; bishop of Down and Connor, 1982-90; archbishop of Armagh and primate of All Ireland, Nov. 6, 1990; cardinal June 28, 1991; titular church, St. Patrick. Archbishop of Armagh and Primate of All Ireland. Curial membership: Evangelization of Peoples, Clergy (congregations); Christian Unity (council).

Danneels, Godfried: b. June 4, 1933, Kanegem, Belgium; ord. priest Aug. 17, 1957; professor of liturgy and sacramental theology at Catholic University of Louvain, 1969-77; ord. bishop of Antwerp Dec. 18, 1977; app. archbishop of Mechelen-Brussel, Dec. 19, 1979; installed Jan. 4, 1980; cardinal Feb. 2, 1983; titular church, St. Anastasia. Archbishop of Mechelen-Brussel, military ordinary of Belgium. Curial membership: Secretariat of State (second section); Doctrine of the Faith, Bishops, Divine Worship and Sacraments, Evangelization of Peoples, Catholic Education (congregations).

Darmojuwono, Justin: b. Nov. 2, 1914, Godean, Indonesia; ord. priest May 25, 1947; ord. archbishop of Semarang, Apr. 6, 1964 (resigned July 3, 1981, for health reasons); cardinal June 26, 1967; titular church, Most Holy Names of Jesus and Mary. Archbishop emeritus of Semarang.

Decourtray, Albert: b. Apr. 9, 1923, Wattignies, France; ord. priest June 29, 1947; ord. titular bishop of Ippona Zarito and auxiliary of Dijon, July 3, 1971; bishop of Dijon, 1974-81; archbishop of Lyon, Oct. 29, 1981; prelate of Mission of France, 1982-88; cardinal May 25, 1985; titular church, Most Holy Trinity (al Monte Pincio). Archbishop of Lyon. Curial membership: Christian Unity, Dialogue with Non-Believers (councils).

Deskur, Andrzej Maria: b. Feb. 29, 1924, Sancygniow, Poland; ord. priest Aug. 20, 1950, in France; assigned to Vatican secretariat of state, 1952; undersecretary and later secretary of Pontifical Commission for Film, Radio and TV (Social Communications), 1954-73; ord. titular bishop of Tene, June 30, 1974; archbishop, 1980; president of Pontifical Commission for Social Communications, 1974-84; cardinal May 25, 1985; deacon, St. Cesario (in Palatio). President emeritus of Council for Social Communications. Curial membership: Causes of Saints (congregation); Health Care Workers (council); State of Vatican City (commission).

Dezza,* Paolo, S.J.: b. Dec. 13, 1901, Parma, Italy; entered Society of Jesus in 1918; ord. priest, Mar. 25, 1928; made solemn profession as Jesuit, 1935; served as rector of Pontifical Gregorian University; delegated as head of Society of Jesus by John Paul II October, 1981, until the election of the new superior general; cardinal June 28, 1991, with permission to decline episcopal ordination; deacon, St. Ignatius of Loyola (a Campo Marzio). Rector emeritus of the Gregorian University.

do Nascimento, Alexandre: b. Mar. 1, 1925, Malanje, Angola; ord. priest Dec. 20, 1952, in Rome; professor of dogmatic theology in major seminary of Luanda, Angola; editor of *O Apostolada,* Catholic newspaper; forced into exile in Lisbon, Portugal, 1961-71; returned to Angola, 1971; active with student and refugee groups; professor at Pius XII Institute of Social Sciences; ord. bishop of Malanje, Aug. 31, 1975; archbishop of Lubango and apostolic administrator of Onjiva, 1977-86; held hostage by Angolan guerrillas, Oct. 15 to Nov. 16, 1982; cardinal Feb. 2, 1983; titular church, St. Mark in Agro Laurentino. Archbishop of Luanda, 1986. Curial membership: Evangelization of Peoples (congregation).

Duval,* Leon-Etienne: b. Nov. 9, 1903, Chenex, France; ord. priest Dec. 18, 1926; ord. bishop of Constantine, Algeria, Feb. 11, 1947; archbishop of Algiers, Feb. 3, 1954 (resigned 1988); cardinal Feb. 22, 1965; titular church, St. Balbina. Archbishop emeritus of Algiers.

Ekandem, Dominic Ignatius: b. 1917, Obio Ibiono, Nigeria; ord. priest Dec. 7, 1947; ord. titular bishop of Gerapoli di Isauri and auxiliary bishop of Calabar, Feb. 7, 1954, the first Nigerian to become a bishop; first bishop of Ikot Ekpene, 1963-89; cardinal May 24, 1976; titular church, San Marcello. First bishop of Abuja, with personal title of archbishop, 1989-1992. Archbishop-Bishop emeritus of Abuja.

Enrique y Tarancon,* Vicente: b. May 14, 1907,
Burriana, Spain; ord. priest Nov. 1, 1929; ord.
bishop of Solsona, Mar. 24, 1946; archbishop of
Oviedo, Apr. 12, 1964; archbishop of Toledo, 1969-
71; cardinal Apr. 28, 1969; titular church, St. John
Chrysostom; archbishop of Madrid, 1971-83.
Archbishop emeritus of Madrid.

Etchegaray, Roger: b. Sept. 25, 1922, Espelette,
France; ord. priest July 13, 1947; deputy director,
1961-66, and secretary general, 1966-70, of French
Episcopal Conference; ord. titular bishop of
Gemelle di Numidia and auxiliary of Paris, May 27,
1969; archbishop of Marseilles, 1970-84; prelate of
Mission de France, 1975-82; president of French
Episcopal Conference, 1979-81; cardinal June 30,
1979; titular church, St. Leo I. President, 1984, of
Councils for Justice and Peace and *Cor Unum.*
Curial membership:
Oriental Churches, Evangelization of Peoples,
Catholic Education (congregations); Apostolic Sig-
natura (tribunal); Laity, Christian Unity, Social
Communications, Interreligious Dialogue (coun-
cils); Patrimony of the Holy See (office).

Etsou-Nzabi-Bamungwabi, Frédéric, C.I.C.M.:
b. Dec. 3, 1930, Mazalonga, Zaire; ord. priest July
13, 1958; educ. Catholic Institute of Paris (degree in
sociology) and "Lumen Vitae" in Belgium (degree
in pastoral theology); ord. titular bishop of Menefes-
si and coadjutor archbishop of Mbandaka-Bikora,
Nov. 7, 1976; archbishop of Mbandaka-Bikora,
1977-1990; archbishop of Kinshasa, July 7, 1990;
cardinal June 28, 1991; titular church, St. Lucy (a
Piazza d'Armi). Archbishop of Kinshasa. Curial
membership:
Evangelization of Peoples (congregation); Family
(council).

Falcao, Jose Freire: b. Oct. 23, 1925, Erere,
Brazil; ord. priest June 19, 1949; ord. titular bishop
of Vardimissa and coadjutor of Limoeiro do Norte,
June 17, 1967; bishop of Limoeiro do Norte, Aug.
19, 1967; archbishop of Teresina, Nov. 25, 1971;
archbishop of Brasilia, Feb. 15, 1984; cardinal June
28, 1988; titular church, St. Luke (Via Prenestina).
Archbishop of Brasilia. Curial membership:
Christian Unity, Health Care Workers (councils);
Latin America (commission).

Felici, Angelo: b. July 26, 1919, Segni, Italy; ord.
priest Apr. 4, 1942; in Vatican diplomatic service
from 1945; ord. titular bishop of Cesariana, with
personal title of archbishop, Sept. 24, 1967; nuncio
to Netherlands, 1967-76, Portugal, 1976-79, France,
1979-88; cardinal June 28, 1988; deacon, Sts. Blaise
and Charles in Catinari. Prefect of Congregation for
Causes of Saints, 1988. Curial membership:
Secretariat of State (second section); Oriental
Churches, Bishops, Evangelization of Peoples, Clergy (congregations); Christian Unity (council).

Fresno Larrain, Juan Francisco: b. July 26,
1914, Santiago, Chile; ord. priest Dec. 18, 1937;
ord. bishop of Copiapo, Aug. 15, 1958; archbishop
of La Serena, 1967-83; archbishop of Santiago, May
3, 1983 (resigned Mar. 30, l990); cardinal May 25,
1985; titular church, St. Mary Immaculate of Lourdes
(a Boccea). Archbishop emeritus of Santiago. Curial
membership:
Catholic Education (congregation).

Gagnon, Edouard, P.S.S.: b. Jan. 15, 1918, Port
Daniel, Que., Canada; ord. priest Aug. 15, 1940;
ord. bishop of St. Paul in Alberta Mar. 25, 1969
(resigned May 3, 1972); rector of Canadian College
in Rome, 1972-77; vice president-secretary of
Vatican Committee for the Family, 1973-80; titular
archbishop of Giustiniana Prima, July 7, 1983; pro-
president of Pontifical Council for the Family, 1983;
cardinal May 25, 1985; deacon, St. Elena (fuori
Porta Prenestina); president of Pontifical Council for
the Family, 1985-90. President of Pontifical Committee for International Eucharistic Congresses,
1991. Curial membership:
Divine Worship and Sacraments, Causes of Saints
(congregations); Apostolic Signatura (tribunal).

Gantin, Bernardin: b. May 8, 1922, Toffo,
Dahomey (now Benin): ord. priest Jan. 14, 1951;
ord. titular bishop of Tipasa di Mauritania and
auxiliary bishop of Cotonou, Feb. 3, 1957;
archbishop of Cotonou, 1960-71; associate secretary
(1971-73) and secretary (1973-75) of Congregation
for Evangelization of Peoples; vice-president (1975)
and president (1976-84) of Pontifical Commission
for Justice and Peace; cardinal deacon June 27,
1977; transferred to order of priests June 25, 1984;
titular church, Sacred Heart of Christ the King;
titular bishop of suburbicarian see Palestrina Sept
29, 1986, when he entered the order of cardinal
bishops, and of Ostia June 5, 1993, when he became
dean of the college of cardinals. Prefect of Congregation for Bishops, 1984; president of commission for Latin America, 1984; dean of college of
cardinals, 1993. Curial membership:
Secretariat of State (second section); Doctrine of
the Faith, Divine Worship and Sacraments, Causes
of Saints, Evangelization of Peoples, Oriental Churches, Institutes of Consecrated Life and Societies of
Apostolic Life, Catholic Education (congregations);
Apostolic Signatura (tribunal); Interreligious
Dialogue, Interpretation of Legislative Texts, Social
Communications (councils); Pompeii and Loreto,
Institute for Works of Religion (commissions).

Garrone,* Gabriel-Marie: b. Oct. 12, 1901, Aix-
les-Bains, France; ord. priest Apr. 11, 1925; captain
during World War II, cited for bravery, taken
prisoner; rector of major seminary of Chambery,
1947; ord. titular archbishop of Lemno and coadjutor of Toulouse, June 24, 1947; archbishop of
Toulouse, 1956-66; titular archbishop of Torri di
Numidia and pro-prefect of Congregation of Seminaries and Universities, Mar. 24, 1966; cardinal
June 26, 1967; titular church, St. Sabina; prefect of
Congregation for Catholic Education, 1968-80.

Giordano, Michele: b. Sept. 26, 1930, S. Arcan-
gelo, Italy; ord. priest July 5, 1953; ord. titular
bishop of Lari Castello and auxiliary of Matera, Feb.
5, 1972; archbishop of Matera and Irsina, 1974-87;
archbishop of Naples, May 9, 1987; cardinal June
28, 1988; titular church, St. Joachim. Archbishop of
Naples. Curial membership:
Secretariat of State (second section); Bishops,
Evangelization of Peoples, Clergy (congregations);
Health Care Workers (council).

Glemp, Jozef: b. Dec. 18, 1929, Inowroclaw,
Poland; assigned to forced labor on German farm in
Rycerzow during Nazi occupation; ord. priest May

25, 1956; studied in Rome, 1958-64; received degree in Roman and canon law from Pontifical Lateran University; secretary of primatial major seminary at Gniezno on his return to Poland, 1964; spokesman for secretariat of primate of Poland and chaplain of primate for archdiocese of Gniezno, 1967; ord. bishop of Warmia, Apr. 21, 1979; archbishop of Gniezno, 1981-92, with title of archbishop of Warsaw and primate of Poland; cardinal Feb. 2, 1983; titular church, St. Mary in Trastevere. Archbishop of Warsaw (Mar. 25, 1992), primate of Poland, ordinary for Eastern-rite faithful in Poland who do not have ordinaries of their own rites. Curial membership:

Oriental Churches (congregation), Culture (council).

Gong (Kung) Pin-mei,* Ignatius: b. Aug. 2, 1901, P'ou-tong, China; ord. priest May 28, 1930; worked in schools and as a missionary; ord. bishop of Soochow Oct. 7, 1949; bishop of Shanghai July 15, 1950; imprisoned by Chinese communists in 1955 and sentenced to life imprisonment in 1960; paroled in 1985 after 30 years; pardoned and political rights restored Jan. 5, 1988, but was not permitted to function as a bishop; came to the United States in 1988; cardinal June 30, 1979 "in pectore"; name revealed and formally invested at June 28, 1991, public consistory; titular church, St. Sixtus. Bishop of Shanghai and apostolic administrator of Soochow. (Resides in U.S.)

Gonzalez Martin, Marcelo: b. Jan. 16, 1918, Villanuba, Spain; ord. priest June 29, 1941; taught theology and sociology at Valladolid diocesan seminary; founded organization for construction of houses for poor; ord. bishop of Astorga, Mar. 5, 1961; titular archbishop of Case Mediane and coadjutor of Barcelona, Feb. 21, 1966; archbishop of Barcelona, 1967-71; archbishop of Toledo, Dec. 3, 1971; cardinal Mar. 5, 1973; titular church, St. Augustine. Archbishop of Toledo. Curial membership:

Clergy (congregation).

Gouyon,* Paul: b. Oct. 24, 1910, Bordeaux, France; ord. priest Mar. 13, 1937; ord. bishop of Bayonne, Oct. 7, 1957; titular archbishop of Pessinonte and coadjutor archbishop of Rennes, Sept. 6, 1963; archbishop of Rennes, Sept. 4, 1964 (resigned Oct. 15, 1985); cardinal Apr. 28, 1969; titular church, Nativity of Our Lord Jesus Christ (Via Gallia). Archbishop emeritus of Rennes.

Gregoire,* Paul: b. Oct. 24, 1911, Verdun, Que., Canada; ord. priest May 22, 1937; ord. titular bishop of Curubi and auxiliary of Montreal, Dec. 27, 1961; archbishop of Montreal, Apr. 20, 1968 (retired Mar. 17, 1990); cardinal June 28, 1988; titular church, Our Lady of the Blessed Sacrament and the Holy Canadian Martyrs. Archbishop emeritus of Montreal.

Groër, Hans Hermann, O.S.B.: b. Oct. 13, 1919, Vienna, Austria; ord. priest Apr. 12, 1942; ord. archbishop of Vienna, Sept. 14, 1986; cardinal June 28, 1988; titular church, Sts. Joachim and Anne al Tuscolano. Archbishop of Vienna and ordinary of Byzantine-rite faithful living in Austria. Curial membership:

Oriental Churches, Divine Worship and Sacraments, Institutes of Consecrated Life and Societies of Apostolic Life, Catholic Education (congregations).

Gulbinowicz, Henryk Roman: b. Oct. 17, 1928, Szukiszki, Poland; ord. priest June 18, 1960; ord. titular bishop of Acci and apostolic administrator of Polish territory in Lithuanian archdiocese of Vilnius (Vilna), Feb. 8, 1970; archbishop of Wroclaw, Poland, Jan. 3, 1976; cardinal May 25, 1985; titular church, Immaculate Conception of Mary (a Grottarosa). Archbishop of Wroclaw. Curial membership:

Oriental Churches, Clergy (congregations).

Hamer, Jean Jerome, O.P.: b. June 1, 1916, Brussels, Belgium; ord. priest Aug. 3, 1941; taught dogmatic and fundamental theology and ecclesiology in France and Rome, 1944-62; author of several works; secretary of Christian Unity Secretariat, 1969-73; ord. titular bishop of Lorium with personal title of archbishop June 29, 1973; secretary of Congregation for Doctrine of the Faith, 1973-84; pro-prefect of Congregation for Religious and Secular Institutes, 1984; cardinal May 25, 1985; deacon, St. Saba. Prefect of Congregation for Institutes of Consecrated Life and Societies of Apostolic Life, 1985-92. Curial membership:

Secretariat of State (second section); Doctrine of the Faith, Bishops, Divine Worship and Sacraments, Evangelization of Peoples, Catholic Education (congregations); Interpretation of Legislative Texts (council).

Hickey, James A.: b. Oct. 11, 1920, Midland, Mich.; ord. priest (Saginaw diocese) June 15, 1946; ord. titular bishop of Taraqua and auxiliary of Saginaw, Apr. 14, 1967; rector of North American College, Rome, 1969-74; bishop of Cleveland, 1974-80; app. archbishop of Washington, D.C., installed Aug. 5, 1980; cardinal June 28, 1988; titular church, St. Mary Mother of the Redeemer. Archbishop of Washington, D.C. Curial membership:

Causes of Saints, Institutes of Consecrated Life and Societies of Apostolic Life, Catholic Education, Clergy (congregations); Family (council).

Hume, George Basil, O.S.B.: b. Mar. 2, 1923, Newcastle-upon-Tyne, England; began monastic studies at Benedictine Abbey of St. Laurence at Ampleforth, 1941; made solemn perpetual vows as Benedictine, 1945; ord. priest July 23, 1950; abbot of Ampleforth, 1963-76; ord. archbishop of Westminster, Mar. 25, 1976; cardinal May 24, 1976; titular church, St. Silvestro (in Capite). Archbishop of Westminster. Curial membership:

Divine Worship and Sacraments, Institutes of Consecrated Life and Societies of Apostolic Life (congregations); Christian Unity, Health Care Workers (councils).

Innocenti, Antonio: b. Aug. 23, 1915, Poppi, Italy; ord. priest July 17, 1938; held curial and diplomatic positions; ord. titular bishop of Eclano with personal title of archbishop, Feb. 18, 1968; nuncio to Paraguay, 1967-73; secretary of Congregation for Causes of Saints, 1973-75; secretary of Congregation for Sacraments and Divine Worship, 1975-80; nuncio to Spain, 1980-85; cardinal May 25, 1985; deacon, St. Marie (in Aquiro); prefect of

Congregation for the Clergy, 1986-91; president of Pontifical Commission for Preservation of Artistic Patrimony of the Church, 1988-91. President of Pontifical Commission "Ecclesia Dei," 1991. Curial membership: Secretariat of State (second section); Bishops, Doctrine of the Faith, Divine Worship and Sacraments, Evangelization of Peoples, Causes of Saints, Catholic Education (congregations); Interpretation of Legislative Texts (council); State of Vatican City (commission).

Javierre Ortas, Antonio Maria, S.D.B.: b. Feb. 21, 1921, Sietamo, Spain; ord. priest Apr. 24, 1949; leading European writer on ecumenism; ord. titular bishop of Meta with personal title of archbishop, June 29, 1976; Secretary of Congregation for Catholic Education, 1976-88; cardinal June 28, 1988; deacon, St. Mary Liberator (a Monte Testaccio). Librarian and Archivist of the Holy Roman Church, 1988-92. Prefect of Congregation for Divine Worship and the Sacraments, 1992. Curial membership: Doctrine of the Faith, Catholic Education (congregations); Apostolic Signatura (tribunal); Laity, Christian Unity, Interpretation of Legislative Texts (councils).

Jubany Arnau,* Narciso: b. Aug. 12, 1913, Santa Coloma de Farnes, Spain; ord. priest July 30, 1939; professor of law at Barcelona seminary; served on ecclesiastical tribunal; ord. titular bishop of Ortosia and auxiliary of Barcelona, Jan. 22, 1956; bishop of Gerona, 1964-71; archbishop of Barcelona, Dec. 3, 1971 (retired Mar. 23, 1990); cardinal Mar. 5, 1973; titular church, San Lorenzo (in Damaso). Archbishop emeritus of Barcelona. Curial membership: Divine Worship and Sacraments, Institutes of Consecrated Life and Societies of Apostolic Life (congregations).

Khoraiche,* Antoine Pierre: b. Sept. 20, 1907, Ain-Ebel, Lebanon; ord. priest Apr. 12, 1930; ord. titular bishop of Tarsus and auxiliary bishop of Sidon of the Maronites, Oct. 15, 1950; bishop of Sidon, Nov. 25, 1957; elected patriarch of Antioch for Maronites, Feb. 3, 1975, granted ecclesial communion by Paul VI, Feb. 15, 1975 (resigned Apr. 3, 1986); advocate of reconciliation among various Lebanese ethnic and religious groups and withdrawal of foreign troops from country; cardinal Feb. 2, 1983. Patriarch emeritus of Antioch for Maronites.

Kim, Stephan Sou Hwan: b. May 8, 1922, Tae Gu, Korea; ord. priest Sept. 15, 1951; ord. bishop of Masan, May 31, 1966; archbishop of Seoul, Apr. 9, 1968; cardinal Apr. 28, 1969; titular church, St. Felix of Cantalice (Centocelle). Archbishop of Seoul, apostolic administrator of Pyeong Yang. Curial membership: Evangelization of Peoples (congregation); Inter-religious Dialogue, Dialogue with Non-Believers (councils).

Kitbunchu, Michael Michai: b. Jan. 25, 1929, Samphran, Thailand; ord. priest Dec. 20, 1959, in Rome; rector of metropolitan seminary in Bangkok, 1965-72; ord. archbishop of Bangkok, June 3, 1973; cardinal Feb. 2, 1983, the first from Thailand; titular church, St. Laurence in Panisperna. Archbishop of Bangkok. Curial membership: Evangelization of Peoples (congregation).

Koenig,* Franz: b. Aug. 3, 1905, Rabenstein, Lower Austria; ord. priest Oct. 29, 1933; ord. titular bishop of Livias and coadjutor bishop of Sankt Poelten, Aug. 31, 1952; archbishop of Vienna, May 10, 1956 (resigned Sept. 16, 1985); cardinal Dec. 15, 1958; titular church, St. Eusebius; president of Secretariat (now Council) for Dialogue with Non-Believers, 1965-80. Archbishop emeritus of Vienna.

Korec, Jan Chryzostom, S.J.: b. Jan. 22, 1924, Bosany, Slovakia; entered Society of Jesus in 1939; ord. priest Oct. 1, 1950; ord. bishop secretly Aug. 24, 1951; sentenced to 12 years in prison in 1960 for helping seminarians with their study and ordaining priests; paroled in 1968; appointed bishop of Nitra Feb. 6, 1990; cardinal June 28, 1991; titular church, Sts. Fabian and Venantius (a Villa Forelli). Bishop of Nitra. Curial membership: Institutes of Consecrated Life and Societies of Apostolic Life (congregation); Culture (council).

Krol,* John Joseph: b. Oct. 26, 1910, Cleveland, Ohio; ord. priest (Cleveland diocese) Feb. 20, 1937; ord. titular bishop of Cadi and auxiliary bishop of Cleveland, Sept. 2, 1953; archbishop of Philadelphia, Feb. 11, 1961, installed Mar. 22, 1961 (resigned Feb. 11, 1988); cardinal June 26, 1967; titular church, St. Mary (della Merced) and St. Adrian Martyr; vice-president, 1966-72, and president, 1972-74, of NCCB/USCC. Archbishop emeritus of Philadelphia.

Kuharic, Franjo: b. Apr. 15, 1919, Pribic, Croatia; ord. priest July 15, 1945; ord. titular bishop of Meta and auxiliary bishop of Zagreb, May 3, 1964; apostolic administrator of archdiocese of Zagreb, 1968-70; archbishop of Zagreb, June 16, 1970; cardinal Feb. 2, 1983; titular church, St. Jerome of the Croats. Archbishop of Zagreb. Curial membership: Divine Worship and Sacraments, Clergy (congregations); Dialogue with Non-Believers (council).

Laghi, Pio: b. May 21, 1922, Castiglione, Italy; ord. priest Apr. 20, 1946; entered diplomatic service of the Holy See in 1952; served in Nicaragua, the U.S. (as secretary of the apostolic delegation, 1954-61) and India; recalled to Rome and served on Council for Public Affairs of the Church; ord. titular archbishop of Mauriana June 22, 1969; apostolic delegate to Jerusalem and Palestine, 1969-74; nuncio to Argentina, 1974-80; apostolic delegate, 1980-84, and first pro-nuncio, 1984-90 to the U.S.; pro-prefect of Congregation for Catholc Education, 1990-91; cardinal June 28, 1991; deacon, St. Mary Auxiliatrix (in Via Tuscolana). Prefect of Congregation for Catholic Education, 1991. Grand chancellor of Pontifical Gregorian University. Curial membership: Secretariat of State (second section); Bishops, Oriental Churches, Evangelization of Peoples, Clergy (congregations); Interpretation of Legislative Texts (council).

Landazuri Ricketts, Juan, O.F.M: b. Dec. 19, 1913, Arequipa, Peru; entered Franciscans, 1933; ord. priest May 16, 1939; ord. titular archbishop of Roina and coadjutor archbishop of Lima, Aug. 24,

1952; archbishop of Lima, May 2, 1955 (resigned Dec. 30, 1989); cardinal Mar. 19, 1962; titular church, St. Mary (in Aracoeli). Archbishop emeritus of Lima. Curial membership:
Institutes of Consecrated Life and Societies of Apostolic Life (congregation).
Law, Bernard F.: b. Nov. 4, 1931, Torreon, Mexico, the son of U.S. Air Force colonel; ord. priest (Jackson diocese) May 21, 1961; editor of Natchez-Jackson, Miss., diocesan paper, 1963-68; director of NCCB Committee on Ecumenical and Interreligious Affairs, 1968-71; ord. bishop of Springfield-Cape Girardeau, Mo., Dec. 5, 1973; archbishop of Boston, Jan. 11, 1984; cardinal May 25, 1985; titular church, St. Susanna. Archbishop of Boston. Curial membership:
Oriental Churches; Institutes of Consecrated Life and Societies of Apostolic Life, Evangelization of Peoples (congregations); Culture, Migrants and Travelers (councils).
Lebrun Moratinos, Jose Ali: b. Mar. 19, 1919, Puerto Cabello, Venezuela; ord. priest Dec. 19, 1943; ord. titular bishop of Arado and auxiliary bishop of Maracaibo, Sept. 2, 1956; first bishop of Maracay, 1958-62; bishop of Valencia, 1962-72; titular archbishop of Voncario and coadjutor archbishop of Caracas, Sept. 16, 1972; archbishop of Caracas, May 24, 1980; cardinal Feb. 2, 1983; titular church, St. Pancratius. Archbishop of Caracas. Curial membership:
Secretariat of State (second section); Bishops, Catholic Education (congregations).
Lopez Rodriguez, Nicolas de Jesus: b. Oct. 31, 1936, Barranca, Dominican Republic; ord. priest Mar. 18, 1961; sent to Rome for advanced studies at the Angelicum and Gregorian Univ.; served in various diocesan offices after returning to his home diocese of La Vega; ord. first bishop of San Francisco de Macoris Feb. 25, 1978; archbishop of Santo Domingo, Nov. 15, 1981; cardinal June 28, 1991; titular church, St. Pius X (alla Balduina). Archbishop of Santo Domingo and Military Ordinary for Dominican Republic. Curial membership:
Clergy, Institutes of Consecrated Life and Societies of Apostolic Life (congregations); Social Communications (council); Latin America (commission).
Lopez Trujillo, Alfonso: b. Nov. 8, 1935, Villahermosa, Colombia; ord. priest Nov. 13, 1960, in Rome; returned to Colombia, 1963; taught at major seminary; was pastoral coordinator for 1968 International Eucharistic Congress in Bogota; vicar general of Bogota, 1970-72; ord. titular bishop of Boseta (with personal title of archbishop), Mar. 25, 1971; auxiliary bishop of Bogota, 1971-72; secretary-general of CELAM, 1972-78; helped organize 1979 Puebla Conference in which Pope John Paul II participated; app. coadjutor archbishop of Medellin, 1978; archbishop of Medellin, June 2, 1979 (resigned Jan 9, 1991); president of CELAM, 1979-83; cardinal Feb. 2, 1983; titular church, St. Prisca. Archbishop emeritus of Medellin. President of the Pontifical Council for the Family, 1990. Curial membership:
Doctrine of the Faith, Bishops, Evangelization of Peoples (congregations); Migrants and Travelers

(council); Latin America, State of Vatican City (commissions).
Lorscheider, Aloisio, O.F.M.: b. Oct. 8, 1924, Estrela, Brazil; received in Franciscan Order, Feb. 1, 1942; ord. priest Aug. 22, 1948; professor of theology at the Antonianum, Rome, and director of Franciscan international house of studies; ord. bishop of Santo Angelo, Brazil, May 20, 1962; archbishop of Fortaleza, Mar. 26, 1973; president of CELAM, 1975-79; cardinal May 24, 1976; titular church, S. Pietro (in Montorio). Archbishop of Fortaleza. Curial membership:
Institutes of Consecrated Life and Societies of Apostolic Life (congregation).
Lourdusamy, D. Simon: b. Feb. 5, 1924, Kalleri, India; ord. priest Dec. 21, 1951; ord. titular bishop of Sozusa and auxiliary of Bangalore, Aug. 22, 1962; titular archbishop of Filippi and coadjutor archbishop of Bangalore, Nov. 9, 1964; archbishop of Bangalore, 1968-71; associate secretary, 1971-73, and secretary, 1973-85, of Congregation for Evangelization of Peoples; cardinal May 25, 1985; deacon, St. Mary of Grace; prefect of Congregation for Oriental Churches, 1985-91. Protodeacon, 1993. Curial membership:
Doctrine of the Faith, Evangelization of Peoples, Causes of Saints, Catholic Education (congregations); Apostolic Signatura (tribunal); Christian Unity, Interreligious Dialogue, Family, Interpretation of Legislative Texts (councils); International Eucharistic Congresses (commission).
Lubachivsky, Myroslav Ivan: b. June 24, 1914, Dolyna, Ukraine; ord. priest Sept. 21, 1938; began pastoral work in U.S., 1947; became U.S. citizen, 1952; ord. archbishop of Ukrainian-rite archeparchy of Philadelphia, Nov. 12, 1979; coadjutor archbishop of Lviv of the Ukrainians, Mar. 27, 1980; archbishop of Lviv and major archbishop of Ukrainians, Sept. 7, 1984; cardinal May 25, 1985; titular church, St. Sofia (a Via Boccea). Major Archbishop of Lviv of the Ukrainians. Curial membership:
Oriental Churches (congregation).
Lustiger, Jean-Marie: b. Sept. 17, 1926, Paris, France, of Polish-Jewish parents who emigrated to France after World War I; taken in by Catholic family in Orleans when his parents were deported during Nazi occupation (his mother died in 1943 at Auschwitz); convert to Catholicism, baptized Aug. 25, 1940; active in Young Christian Students during university days; ord. priest Apr. 17, 1954; ord. bishop of Orleans, Dec. 8, 1979; archbishop of Paris, Jan. 31, 1981; cardinal Feb. 2, 1983; titular church, Sts. Marcellinus and Peter. Archbishop of Paris, ordinary for Eastern-Rite faithful in France without ordinaries of their own. Curial membership:
Secretariat of State (second section); Divine Worship and Sacraments, Bishops, Oriental Churches, Institutes of Consecrated Life and Societies of Apostolic Life (congregations); Culture (council).
McCann,* Owen: b. June 29, 1907, Woodstock, South Africa; ord. priest Dec. 21, 1935; ord. titular bishop of Stettorio and vicar apostolic of Cape Town, May 18, 1950; first archbishop of Cape Town, Jan. 11, 1951 (retired Oct. 20, 1984); opponent of apartheid policy; cardinal Feb. 22, 1965;

titular church, St. Praxedes. Archbishop emeritus of Cape Town.

Macharski, Franciszek: b. May 20, 1927, Cracow, Poland; ord. priest Apr. 2, 1950; engaged in pastoral work, 1950-56; continued theological studies in Fribourg, Switzerland, 1956-60; taught pastoral theology at the Faculty of Theology in Cracow; app. rector of archdiocesan seminary at Cracow, 1970; ord. archbishop of Cracow, Jan. 6, 1979, by Pope John Paul II; cardinal June 30, 1979; titular church, St. John at the Latin Gate. Archbishop of Cracow. Curial membership:
Secretariat of State (second section); Bishops, Clergy, Institutes of Consecrated Life and Societies of Apostolic Life, Catholic Education (congregations).

Mahony, Roger M.: b. Feb. 27, 1936, Hollywood, Calif.; educ. St. John's Seminary (Camarillo, Calif.), National Catholic School of Social Service (Catholic Univ., Washington D.C.); ord. priest (Fresno diocese) May 1, 1962; ord. titular bishop of Tamascani and auxiliary bishop of Fresno, Mar. 19,1975; bishop of Stockton, installed Apr. 25, 1980; archbishop of Los Angeles, July 16, 1985, installed Sept. 5, 1985; cardinal June 28, 1991; titular church, Four Crowned Saints. Archbishop of Los Angeles. Curial membership:
Justice and Peace, Social Communications (councils).

Margeot, Jean: b. Feb. 3, 1916, Quatre-Bornes, Mauritius; ord. priest Dec. 17, 1938; ord. bishop of Port Louis, May 4, 1969; cardinal June 28, 1988; titular church, St. Gabriel the Archangel all'Acqua Traversa. Bishop emeritus of Port Louis (resigned Feb. 15, 1993). Curial membership:
Evangelization of Peoples (congregation); Family, Migrants and Travelers (councils).

Martinez Somalo, Eduardo: b. Mar. 31, 1927, Baños de Rio Tobia, Spain; ord. priest Mar. 19, 1950; ord. titular bishop of Tagora with personal title of archbishop, Dec. 13, 1975; in secretariat of state from 1956; substitute (assistant) secretary of state, 1979-88; cardinal June 28, 1988; deacon, Most Holy Name of Jesus; prefect of Congregation for Divine Worship and Sacraments, 1988-92. Prefect of Congregation for Institutes of Consecrated Life and Societies of Apostolic Life, 1992; Chamberlain (Camerlengo) of the Holy Roman Church, Apr. 5, 1993. Curial membership:
Secretariat of State (second section); Bishops, Causes of Saints, Evangelization of Peoples, Clergy (congregations); Interpretation of Legislative Texts (council); Latin America, Institute for Works of Religion (commissions).

Martini, Carlo Maria, S.J.: b. Feb. 15, 1927, Turin, Italy; entered Jesuits Sept. 25, 1944; ord. priest July 13, 1952; biblical scholar; seminary professor, Chieri, Italy, 1958-61; professor and later rector, 1969-78, of Pontifical Biblical Institute; rector of Pontifical Gregorian University, 1978-79; author of theological, biblical and spiritual works; ord. archbishop of Milan, Jan. 6, 1980, by Pope John Paul II; cardinal Feb. 2, 1983; titular church, St. Cecilia. Archbishop of Milan. Curial membership:
Secretariat of State (second section); Doctrine of the Faith, Bishops, Divine Worship and Sacraments, Institutes of Consecrated Life and Societies of Apostolic Life, Catholic Education (congregations); Culture (council).

Marty,* Francois: b. May 18, 1904, Pachins, France; ord. priest June 28, 1930; ord. bishop of Saint-Flour, May 1, 1952; titular archbishop of Emesa and coadjutor archbishop of Rheims, Dec. 14, 1959; archbishop of Rheims, May 9, 1960; archbishop of Paris, 1968-81; cardinal Apr. 28, 1969; titular church, St. Louis of France. Archbishop emeritus of Paris.

Mayer,* Paul Augustin, O.S.B.: b. May 23, 1911, Altötting, West Germany; ord. priest Aug. 25, 1935; rector of St. Anselm's Univ., Rome, 1949-66; secretary of Congregation for Religious and Secular Institutes, 1972-84; ord. titular bishop of Satriano with personal title of archbishop, Feb. 13, 1972; pro-prefect of Congregations for Sacraments and Divine Worship, 1984; cardinal May 25, 1985; deacon, St. Anselm. Prefect of Congregation for Divine Worship and Sacraments, 1985-88; president of Pontifical Commission "Ecclesia Dei," 1988-91.

Meisner, Joachim: b. Dec. 25, 1933, Breslau, Silesia, Germany (present-day Wroclaw, Poland); ord. priest Dec. 22, 1962; regional director of Caritas; ord. titular bishop of Vina and auxiliary of apostolic administration of Erfurt-Meiningen, E. Germany, May 17, 1975; bishop of Berlin, 1980-88; cardinal Feb. 2, 1983; titular church, St. Prudenziana. Archbishop of Cologne, Dec. 20, 1988. Curial membership:
Divine Worship and Sacraments, Clergy (congregations); Culture (council); Economic Affairs of Holy See (office).

Munoz Vega,* Pablo, S.J.: b. May 23, 1903, Mira, Ecuador; ord. priest Apr. 15, 1933; ord. titular bishop of Ceramo and auxiliary bishop of Quito, Mar. 19, 1964; archbishop of Quito, 1967-85; cardinal Apr. 28, 1969; titular church, St. Robert Bellarmine. Archbishop emeritus of Quito.

Neves, Lucas Moreira, O.P.: b. Sept. 16, 1925, Sao Joao del Rei, Brazil; ord. priest July 9, 1950; ord. titular bishop of Feradi maggiore and auxiliary of Sao Paulo, Aug. 26, 1967; assigned to Vatican, 1974; vice president of Pontifical Commission for Laity, 1974-79; archbishop Oct. 15, 1979; secretary of Congregation for Bishops, 1979-87; assigned titular see of Vescovia, Jan. 3, 1987; archbishop of Sao Salvador da Bahia, July 9, 1987; cardinal June 28, 1988; titular church, Sts. Boniface and Alexius. Archbishop of Sao Salvador da Bahia. Curial membership:
Secretariat of State (second section); Doctrine of the Faith, Bishops (congregations); Family, Culture (councils); Latin America (commission).

Noè, Virgilio: b. Mar. 30, 1922, Zelata di Bereguardo, Italy; ord. priest Oct. 1, 1944; master of pontifical ceremonies and undersecretary of Congregation for Sacraments and Divine Worship, 1970-82; ord. titular bishop of Voncario with personal title of archbishop, Mar. 6, 1982; coadjutor Archpriest of St. Peter's Basilica, 1989; vicar general of Vatican City State, Jan. 14, 1991; cardinal June 28, 1991; deacon, St. John Bosco (in Via Tuscolana). Archpriest of St. Peter's Basilica, Vicar General of Vatican City State and President of the Fabric of St. Peter, 1991. Curial membership:

Divine Worship and Sacraments, Causes of Saints (congregations).

Obando Bravo, Miguel, S.D.B.: b. Feb. 2, 1926, La Libertad, Nicaragua; ord. priest Aug. 10, 1958; ord. titular bishop of Puzia di Bizacena and auxiliary of Matagalpa, Mar. 31, 1968; archbishop of Managua, Feb. 16, 1970; cardinal May 25, 1985; titular church, St. John the Evangelist (a Spinaceta). Archbishop of Managua. Curial membership: Clergy (congregation); Latin America (commission).

O'Connor, John J.: b. Jan. 15, 1920, Philadelphia, Pa.; ord. priest (Philadelphia archdiocese) Dec. 15, 1945; joined U.S. Navy and Marine Corps as a chaplain, 1952; overseas posts included service in South Korea and Vietnam; U.S. Navy chief of chaplains, 1975; retired from Navy June 1, 1979, with rank of rear admiral; ord. titular bishop of Curzola and auxiliary of military vicariate, May 27, 1979; bishop of Scranton, May 6, 1983; archbishop of New York, Jan. 26, 1984; cardinal May 25, 1985; titular church, Sts. John and Paul. Archbishop of New York. Curial membership: Secretariat of State (second section); Bishops, Oriental Churches, Evangelization of Peoples (congregations); Family, Social Communications, Health Care Workers, Migrants and Travelers (councils); Institute for Works of Religion (commission).

Oddi,* Silvio: b. Nov. 14, 1910, Morfasso, Italy; ord. priest May 21, 1933; ord. titular archbishop of Mesembria, Sept. 27, 1953; served in Vatican diplomatic corps, 1953-69; apostolic delegate to Jerusalem, Palestine, Jordan and Cyprus, internuncio to the United Arab Republic, and nuncio to Belgium and Luxembourg; cardinal Apr. 28, 1969; titular church, St. Agatha of the Goths. Pontifical legate for Patriarchal Basilica of St. Francis of Assisi; prefect of Sacred Congregation for the Clergy, 1979-86.

Otunga, Maurice Michael: b. January, 1923, Chebukwa, Kenya; son of pagan tribal chief; baptized 1935, at age of 12; ord. priest Oct. 3, 1950, at Rome; taught at Kisumu major seminary for three years; attaché in apostolic delegation at Mombasa, 1953-56; ord. titular bishop of Tacape and auxiliary of Kisumu, Feb. 25, 1957; bishop of Kisii, 1960-69; titular archbishop of Bomarzo and coadjutor of Nairobi, Nov. 15, 1969; archbishop of Nairobi, Oct. 24, 1971; cardinal Mar. 5, 1973; titular church, St. Gregory Barbarigo. Archbishop of Nairobi, military ordinary of Kenya, 1981. Curial membership: Institutes of Consecrated Life and Societies of Apostolic Life, Evangelization of Peoples, Catholic Education (congregations).

Padiyara, Anthony: b. Feb. 11, 1921, Manimala, India; raised in Syro-Malabar family; ord. priest for Latin Rite diocese of Coimbatore, Dec. 19, 1945; first bishop of Ootacamund (Latin Rite), Oct. 16, 1955; app. archbishop of Changanacherry (Syro-Malabar rite), June 14, 1970, at which time he returned to the Syro-Malabar rite; archbishop of Ernakulam (Syro-Malabar rite), Apr. 23, 1985; cardinal June 28, 1988; titular church, St. Mary Queen of Peace (Monte Verde). First Major Archbishop of Major Archbishopric of Ernakulam-Angamaly of

Syro-Malabar rite (erected Jan. 29, 1993); enthroned May 20, 1993. Curial membership: Oriental Churches (congregation); Christian Unity, Interpretation of Legislative Texts (councils).

Palazzini,* Pietro: b. May 19, 1912, Piobbico, Pesaro, Italy; ord. priest Dec. 6, 1934; assistant vice-rector of Pontifical Major Roman Seminary and vice-rector and bursar of Pontifical Roman Seminary for Juridical Studies; professor of moral theology at Lateran University; held various offices in Roman Curia; secretary of Congregation of Council (now Clergy), 1958-73; ord. titular archbishop of Caesarea in Cappadocia, Sept. 21, 1962; author of numerous works on moral theology and law; cardinal Mar. 5, 1973; titular church, St. Jerome. Prefect of Congregation for Causes of Saints, 1980-88.

Pappalardo, Salvatore: b. Sept. 23, 1918, Villafranca Sicula, Sicily; ord. priest Apr. 12, 1941; entered diplomatic service of secretariat of state, 1947; ord. titular archbishop of Miletus, Jan. 16, 1966; pro-nuncio in Indonesia, 1966-69; president of Pontifical Ecclesiastical Academy, 1969-70; archbishop of Palermo, Oct. 17, 1970; cardinal Mar. 5, 1973; titular church, St. Mary Odigitria of the Sicilians. Archbishop of Palermo. Curial membership: Oriental Churches, Clergy (congregations).

Paskai, Laszlo, O.F.M.: b. May 8, 1927, Szeged, Hungary; ord. priest Mar. 3, 1951; ord. titular bishop of Bavagaliana and apostolic administrator of Veszprem, Apr. 5, 1978; bishop of Veszprem Mar. 31, 1979; coadjutor archbishop of Kalocsa, Apr. 5, 1982; archbishop of Esztergom, Mar. 3, 1987; cardinal June 28, 1988; titular church, St. Theresa (al Corso d'Italia). Archbishop of Esztergom. Curial membership: Oriental Churches, Institutes of Consecrated Life and Societies of Apostolic Life (congregations); Justice and Peace, Interpretation of Legislative Texts (councils).

Pavan,* Pietro: b. Aug. 30, 1903, Treviso, Italy; ord. priest July 8, 1928, expert at Vatican Council II; rector of Lateran University, 1969-74; chief contributor to drafting of encyclicals *Mater et Magistra* and *Pacem in Terris;* cardinal May 25, 1985, without episcopal ordination; deacon, St. Francis of Paola (ai Monti).

Pimenta, Simon Ignatius: b. Mar. 1, 1920, Marol, India; ord. priest Dec. 21, 1949; ord. titular bishop of Bocconia and auxiliary of Bombay, June 29, 1971; coadjutor archbishop of Bombay, Feb. 26, 1977; archbishop of Bombay, Sept. 11, 1978; cardinal June 28, 1988; titular church, Mary, Queen of the World (a Torre Spaccata). Archbishop of Bombay. Curial membership: Evangelization of Peoples (congregation); Christian Unity, Interreligious Dialogue (councils).

Piovanelli, Silvano: b. Feb. 21, 1924, Ronta di Mugello, Italy; ord. priest July 13, 1947; ord. titular bishop of Tubune di Mauretania and auxiliary of Florence, June 24, 1982; archbishop of Florence, Mar. 18, 1983; cardinal May 25, 1985; titular church, St. Mary of Graces (Via Trionfale). Archbishop of Florence. Curial membership: Catholic Education (congregation); Dialogue with Non-Believers (council).

Pironio, Eduardo: b. Dec. 3, 1920, Nueve de Julio, Argentina; ord. priest Dec. 5, 1943; taught theology at Pius XII Seminary of Mercedes diocese, 1944-59; vicar general of diocese 1958-60; attended Second Vatican Council as *peritus*; ord. titular bishop of Ceciri, May 31, 1964; apostolic administrator of diocese of Avellaneda, 1967-72; secretary general, 1967-72, and president, 1973-75, of CELAM; bishop of Mar del Plata, 1972-75; titular archbishop of Thiges and pro-prefect of Congregation for Religious and Secular Institutes, Sept. 20, 1975; cardinal deacon May 24, 1976; titular church, Sts. Cosmas and Damian; transferred to order of cardinal priests, June 22, 1987. Prefect of the Congregation for Religious and Secular Institutes, 1976-84. President of Pontifical Council for the Laity, 1984. Curial membership:
Secretariat of State (second section); Bishops, Causes of Saints, Catholic Education, Oriental Churches (congregations); Interpretation of Legislative Texts (council).

Poletti, Ugo: b. Apr. 19, 1914, Omegna, Italy; ord. priest June 29, 1938; served in various diocesan offices at Novara; ord. titular bishop of Medeli and auxiliary of Novaro, Sept. 14, 1958; president of Pontifical Mission Aid Society for Italy, 1964-67; archbishop of Spoleto, 1967-69; titular archbishop of Cittanova, 1969; served as second viceregent of Rome, 1969-72; pro-vicar general of Rome, 1972; cardinal Mar. 5, 1973; titular church, Sts. Ambrose and Charles. Vicar general of Rome, 1973-91. Archbishop of Patriarchal Liberian Basilica of St. Mary Major, 1991. Curial membership:
Secretariat of State (second section); Bishops, Divine Worship and Sacraments, Oriental Churches, Institutes of Consecrated Life and Societies of Apostolic Life (congregations).

Poupard, Paul: b. Aug. 30, 1930, Bouzille, France; ord. priest Dec. 18, 1954; scholar; author of a number of works; ord. titular bishop of Usula and auxiliary of Paris, Apr. 6, 1979; archbishop and pro-president of the Secretariat for Non-Believers, 1980; cardinal May 25, 1985; deacon, St. Eugene; president of Pontifical Councils for Dialogue with Non-Believers (1985-93) and Culture (1988-93). President of restructured Pontifical Council for Culture, 1993. Curial membership:
Divine Worship and Sacraments, Evangelization of Peoples, Catholic Education (congregations); Interreligious Dialogue (council).

Primatesta, Raul Francisco: b. Apr. 14, 1919, Capilla del Senor, Argentina; ord. priest Oct. 25, 1942, at Rome; taught at minor and major seminaries of La Plata; contributed to several theology reviews; ord. titular bishop of Tanais and auxiliary of La Plata, Aug. 15, 1957; bishop of San Rafael, 1961-65; archbishop of Cordoba, Feb. 16, 1965; cardinal Mar. 5, 1973; titular church, St. Mary Sorrowful Virgin. Archbishop of Cordoba, Argentina. Curial membership:
Clergy, Institutes of Consecrated Life and Societies of Apostolic Life (congregations).

Quarracino, Antonio: b. Aug. 8, 1923, Pollica, Italy; moved to Argentina when he was a child; ord. priest Dec. 22, 1945; ord. bishop of Nueve de Julio Apr. 8, 1962; bishop of Avellaneda, 1968-85;

archbishop of La Plata, 1985-90; archbishop of Buenos Aires, July 10, 1990; cardinal June 28, 1991; titular church, St. Mary of Health (a Primavalle). Archbishop of Buenos Aires, ordinary for Eastern-rite faithful in Argentina without ordinaries of their proper rite. Curial membership:
Bishops (congregation); Christian Unity, Health Care Workers (councils).

Ratzinger, Joseph: b. Apr. 16, 1927, Marktl am Inn, Germany; ord. priest June 29, 1951; professor of dogmatic theology at University of Regensburg, 1969-77; member of International Theological Commission, 1969-80; ord. archbishop of Munich-Freising, May 28, 1977 (resigned Feb. 15, 1982); cardinal June 27, 1977; titular church, St. Mary of Consolation (in Tiburtina); transferred to order of cardinal bishops as titular bishop of suburbicarian see of Velletri-Segni, Apr. 5, 1993. Prefect of Congregation for Doctrine of the Faith, 1981; president of Biblical and Theological Commissions. Curial membership:
Secretariat of State (second secton); Bishops, Divine Worship and Sacraments, Oriental Churches, Evangelization of Peoples, Catholic Education (congregations); Christian Unity, Culture (councils); Latin America (commission).

Razafimahatratra, Victor, S.J.: b. Sept. 8, 1921, Ambanitsilena-Ranomasina, Madagascar; entered Society of Jesus, 1945; ord. priest July 28, 1956; rector of Fianarantsoa Minor Seminary, 1960-63; Superior of Jesuit residence at Ambositra, 1963-69; rector of Antananarivo Major Seminary, 1969-71; ord. bishop of Farafangana, Apr. 18, 1971; archbishop of Tananarive (now Antananarivo), Apr. 10, 1976; cardinal May 24, 1976; titular church, Holy Cross in Jerusalem. Archbishop of Antananarivo. Curial membership:
Evangelization of Peoples (congregation).

Revollo Bravo, Mario: b. June 15, 1919, Genoa, Italy; ord. priest (Bogota, Colombia, diocese) Oct. 31, 1943; ord. titular bishop of Tinisa di Numidia and auxiliary of Bogota, Colombia, Dec. 2, 1973; archbishop of Nueva Pamplona, Feb. 28, 1978; archbishop of Bogota, July 25, 1984; cardinal June 28, 1988; titular church, St. Bartholomew (all' Isolo). Archbishop of Bogota. Curial membership:
Divine Worship and Sacraments (congregation); Latin America (council).

Ribeiro, Antonio: b. May 21, 1928, Gandarela de Basto, Portugal; ord. priest July 5, 1953; professor of fundamental theology at major seminary at Braga; ord. titular bishop of Tigillava and auxiliary of Braga, Sept. 17, 1967; patriarch of Lisbon, May 10, 1971; cardinal Mar. 5, 1973; titular church, St. Anthony of Padua (in Rome). Patriarch of Lisbon, military vicar. Curial membership:
Clergy (congregation); Culture (council).

Righi-Lambertini,* Egano: b. Feb. 22, 1906, Casalecchio di Reno, Italy; ord. priest May 25, 1929; entered service of secretariat of state, 1939; served in diplomatic missions in France (1949-54), Costa Rica (1955), England (1955-57); first apostolic delegate to Korea, 1957-60; ord. titular archbishop of Doclea, Oct. 28, 1960; apostolic nuncio in Lebanon, 1960-63, Chile, 1963-67, Italy, 1967-69; France, 1969-79; while nuncio in France he also served as special envoy at the Council of Europe, 1974-79; cardinal deacon June 30, 1979; transferred to order of cardinal priests, Nov. 26, 1990; titular church, Saint Mary (in Via).

Rossi,* **Agnelo:** b. May 4, 1913, Joaquim Egidio, Bra-zil; ord. priest Mar. 27, 1937; ord. bishop of Barra do Pirai, Apr. 15, 1956; archbishop of Ribeirao Preto, 1962-64; archbishop of Sao Paulo, 1964-70; cardinal Feb. 22, 1965; titular church, Mother of God; titular bishop of suburbicarian see of Sabina-Poggio Mirteto June 25, 1984, when he entered the order of cardinal bishops, and of Ostia, Dec. 19, 1986, when he became dean of the college of cardinals; prefect of Congregation for Evangelization of Peoples, 1970-84; president of Administration of Patrimony of the Holy See, 1984-89; Dean of the College of Cardinals, 1986-93, when he reached the age of 80 and asked to be relieved of the office as dean so he could return to his native Brazil. The Pope granted his request May 31, 1993. As a cardinal bishop he retains title to the suburbicarian see of Sabina-Poggia Mirteto.

Rossi,* **Opilio:** b. May 14, 1910, New York, N.Y.; holds Italian citizenship; ord. priest for diocese of Piacenza (now Piacenza-Bobbio), Italy, Mar. 11, 1933; served in nunciatures in Belgium, The Netherlands and Germany, 1938-53; ord. titular archbishop of Ancyra, Dec. 27, 1953; nuncio in Ecuador, 1953-59, Chile, 1959-61, Austria, 1961-76; cardinal deacon May 24, 1976; transferred to order of cardinal priests, June 22, 1987; titular church, St. Lawrence (in Lucina); president of Pontifical Committee for International Eucharistic Congresses, 1983-90. President of Commission for the Sanctuaries of Pompeii, Loreto and Bari, 1984.

Rugambwa,* **Laurean:** b. July 12, 1912, Bukongo, Tanzania; ord. priest Dec. 12, 1943; ord. titular bishop of Febiano and vicar apostolic of Lower Kagera, Feb. 10, 1952; bishop of Rutabo, Mar. 25, 1953; cardinal Mar. 28, 1960; titular church, St. Francis of Assisi (a Ripa Grande); bishop of Bukoba, 1960-68. Archbishop of Dar-es-Salaam, 1968-92. Archbishop emeritus of Dar-es-Salaam.

Ruini, Camillo: b. Feb. 19, 1931, Sassuolo, Italy; ord. priest Dec. 8, 1954; taught at seminaries in central Italy; ord. titular bishop of Nepti and auxiliary bishop of Reggio Emilia and Guastella, June 29, 1983; secretary general of Italian Bishops' Conference, 1986-91; archbishop Jan. 17, 1991; pro-vicar general of the Pope for the Rome diocese; pro-Archpriest of Patriarchal Lateran Archbasilica; cardinal June 28, 1991; titular church, St. Agnes outside the Wall. Vicar General of the Pope for the Diocese of Rome and Archpriest of Patriarchal Lateran Basilica, July, 1991. Grand Chancellor of Pontifical Lateran University. President of the *Peregrinatio ad Petri Sedem*, Dec. 29, 1992. Curial membership: Bishops (congregation).

Sabattani,* **Aurelio:** b. Oct. 18, 1912, Casal Fiumanese, Italy; ord. priest July 26, 1935; jurist; served in various assignments in his native diocese of Imola as a judge and later an official of the regional ecclesiastical tribunal of Bologna; called to Rome in 1955 as prelate auditor of the Roman Rota; ord. titular archbishop of Justinian Prima, July 25, 1965; prelate of Loreto, 1965-71; secretary of Supreme Tribunal of Apostolic Signatura and con-

sultor of Secretariat of State, 1971; pro-prefect of Apostolic Signatura, 1982-83; cardinal deacon Feb. 2, 1983; transferred to order of cardinal priests Apr. 5, 1993; titular church, St. Apollinaris; prefect of Apostolic Signatura, 1983-88; archpriest of Patriarchal Vatican Basilica and president of the Fabric of St. Peter, 1983-91; former vicar general of the Pope for Vatican City.

Saldarini, Giovanni: b. Dec. 11, 1924, Cantu, Italy; ord. priest May 31, 1947; respected scripture scholar; taught scripture at Milan archdiocesan seminary, 1952-67; ord. titular bishop of Guadiaba and auxiliary bishop of Milan, Dec. 7, 1984; archbishop of Turin Jan. 31, 1989; cardinal June 28, 1991; titular church, Sacred Heart of Jesus (a Castro Pretorio). Archbishop of Turin. Curial membership: Clergy (congregation); Laity (council).

Sales, Eugenio de Araujo: b. Nov. 8, 1920, Acari, Brazil; ord. priest Nov. 21, 1943; ord. titular bishop of Tibica and auxiliary bishop of Natal, Aug. 15, 1954; archbishop of Sao Salvador, 1968-71; cardinal Apr. 28, 1969; titular church, St. Gregory VII. Archbishop of Rio de Janeiro (1971), ordinary for Eastern Rite Catholics in Brazil without ordinaries of their own rites. Curial membership: Secretariat of State (second section); Bishops, Oriental Churches, Divine Worship and Sacraments, Clergy, Evangelization of Peoples, Catholic Education (congregations); Social Communications, Culture (councils); Economic Affairs of the Holy See (office).

Sanchez, Jose T.: b. Mar. 17, 1920, Pandan, Philippines; ord. priest May 12, 1946; ord. titular bishop of Lesvi and coadjutor bishop of Lucena, May 12, 1968; bishop of Lucena, 1976-82; archbishop of Nueva Segovia Jan. 12, 1982 (resigned Mar. 22, 1986); secretary of Congregation for Evangelization of Peoples, 1985-91; cardinal June 28, 1991; deacon, St. Pius V (a Villa Carpegna); president of Commission for Preservation of Artistic and Historic Patrimony of the Holy See, 1991-93. Prefect of Congregation for the Clergy, 1991. Curial membership: Secretariat of State (second section); Bishops, Evangelization of Peoples, Catholic Education (congregations); Interpretation of Legislative Texts (council); International Eucharistic Congresses (committee); Latin America, Sanctuaries of Pompeii, Loreto and Bari (commissions).

Santos, Alexandre Jose Maria dos, O.F.M.: b. Mar. 18, 1924, Zavala, Mozambique; ord. priest July 25, 1953; first Mozambican black priest; ord. archbishop of Maputo, Mar. 9, 1975; cardinal June 28, 1988; titular church, St. Frumentius (ai Prati Fiscali). Archbishop of Maputo. Curial membership: Evangelization of Peoples (congregation); Culture (council).

Satowaki,* **Joseph Asajiro:** b. Feb. 1, 1904, Shittsu, Japan; ord. priest Dec. 17, 1932; served in various pastoral capacities in Nagasaki archdiocese after his ordination; apostolic administrator of Taiwan (then a Japanese possession), 1941-45; director of Nagasaki minor seminary, 1945-57; vicar general of Nagasaki, 1945; ord. first bishop of Kagoshima, May 3, 1955; archbishop of Nagasaki, Dec. 19, 1968 (resigned Feb. 8, 1990); cardinal June

30, 1979; titular church, St. Mary of Peace. Archbishop emeritus of Nagasaki.

Scherer,* Alfred Vicente: b. Feb. 5, 1903, Bom Principio, Brazil; ord. priest Apr. 3, 1926; ord. archbishop of Porto Alegre, Feb. 23, 1947 (retired Aug. 29, 1981); cardinal Apr. 28, 1969; titular church, Our Lady of La Salette. Archbishop emeritus of Porto Alegre, Brazil.

Schwery, Henri: b. June 14, 1932, Saint-Leonard, Switzerland; ord. priest July 7, 1957; director of minor seminary and later rector of the College in Sion; ord. bishop of Sion, Sept. 17, 1977; cardinal June 28, 1991; titular church, Protomartyrs (a via Aurelia Antica). Bishop of Sion. Curial membership: Divine Worship and Sacraments, Clergy (congregations).

Sensi,* Giuseppe Maria: b. May 27, 1907, Cosenza, Italy; ord. priest Dec. 21, 1929; entered Vatican diplomatic service; served in nunciatures in Hungary, Switzerland, Belgium and Czechoslovakia, 1934-49; ord. titular archbishop of Sardes, July 24, 1955; apostolic nuncio to Costa Rica, 1955; apostolic delegate to Jerusalem, 1956-62; nuncio to Ireland, 1962-67, and Portugal, 1967-76; cardinal deacon May 24, 1976; transferred to order of cardinal priests, June 22, 1987; titular church, Queen of Apostles.

Silva Henriquez,* Raul, S.D.B.: b. Sept. 27, 1907, Talca, Chile; ord. priest July 3, 1938; ord. bishop of Valparaiso, Nov. 29, 1959; archbishop of Santiago de Chile, 1961-83; cardinal Mar. 19, 1962; titular church, St. Bernard (alle Terme). Archbishop emeritus of Santiago de Chile.

Silvestrini, Achille: b. Oct. 25, 1923, Brisighella, Italy; ord. priest July 13, 1946; official in Secretariat of State from 1953; ord. titular bishop of Novaliciana with personal title of archbishop, May 27, 1979; undersecretary, 1973-79, and secretary, 1979-88, of the Council for Public Affairs of the Church (now the second section of the Secretariat of State); cardinal June 28, 1988; deacon, St. Benedict Outside St. Paul's Gate; prefect of Apostolic Signatura, 1988-91. Prefect of Congregation for Oriental Churches, 1991. Curial membership: Secretariat of State (second section); Bishops, Causes of Saints, Evangelization of Peoples (congregations); Christian Unity, Interpretation of Legislative Texts Interreligious Dialogue (councils).

Simonis, Adrianus J.: b. Nov. 26, 1931, Lisse, Netherlands; ord. priest June 15, 1957; ord. bishop of Rotterdam, Mar. 20, 1971; coadjutor archbishop of Utrecht, June 27, 1983; archbishop of Utrecht, Dec. 3, 1983; cardinal May 25, 1985; titular church, St. Clement. Archbishop of Utrecht. Curial membership: Christian Unity (council).

Sin, Jaime L.: b. Aug. 31, 1928, New Washington, Philippines; ord. priest Apr. 3, 1954; diocesan missionary in Capiz, 1954-57; app. first rector of the St. Pius X Seminary, Roxas City, 1957; ord. titular bishop of Obba and auxiliary bishop of Jaro, Mar. 18, 1967; apostolic administrator of archdiocese of Jaro, June 20, 1970; titular archbishop of Massa Lubrense and coadjutor archbishop of Jaro, Jan. 15, 1972; archbishop of Jaro, 1972-74; archbishop of Manila, Jan. 21, 1974;

cardinal May 24, 1976; titular church, S. Maria (ai Monti). Archbishop of Manila. Curial membership: Divine Worship and Sacraments, Clergy, Catholic Education (congregations); Social Communications (council); Economic Affairs (office).

Sladkevicius, Vincentas: b. Aug. 20, 1920, Zasliai, Lithuania; ord. priest Mar. 25, 1944; ord. titular bishop of Abora and auxiliary of Kaisiadorys, Dec. 25, 1957, but was not permitted to exercise his office; under house arrest 1959-82; apostolic administrator of Kaisiadorys, 1982-89; cardinal June 28, 1988; titular church, Holy Spirit (alla Ferratella). Archbishop of Kaunas (Mar. 10, 1989). Curial membership: Divine Worship and Sacraments, Catholic Education (congregations); Justice and Peace, Dialogue with Non-Believers (councils).

Sodano, Angelo: b. Nov. 23, 1927, Isola d'Asti, Italy; ord. priest Sept. 23, 1950; entered diplomatic service of the Holy See in 1959; served in Ecuador and Uruguay; ord titular archbishop of Nova di Cesare, Jan. 15, 1978; nuncio to Chile, 1978-88; secretary of the Council for Relations with States, 1988-90; pro-Secretary of State, 1990 (Dec. 1)- 1991; cardinal June 28, 1991; titular church, S. Maria Nuova. Secretary of State, June 29, 1991. Curial membership: Doctrine of the Faith, Bishops, Oriental Churches (congregations).

Sterzinsky, Georg Maximilian: b. Feb. 9, 1936, Warlack, Germany; ord. priest June 29, 1960; vicar general to the apostolic administrator of Erfurt-Meiningen, 1981-89; ord. bishop of Berlin, Sept. 9, 1989; cardinal June 28, 1991; titular church, St. Joseph (all'Aurelio). Bishop of Berlin. Curial membership: Catholic Education (congregation); Dialogue with Non-Believers (council).

Stickler,* Alfons, S.D.B.: b. Aug. 23, 1910, Neunkirchen, Austria; ord. priest Mar. 27, 1937; director of the Vatican Library, 1971; ord. titular bishop of Bolsena, Nov. 1, 1983, with personal title of archbishop; Pro-Librarian and Pro-Archivist, 1984; cardinal May 25, 1985; deacon, St. George (in Velabro). Librarian and Archivist of the Holy Roman Church, 1985-88.

Suenens,* Leo Josef: b. July 16, 1904, Brussels, Belgium; ord. priest Sept. 4, 1927; ord. titular bishop of Isinda, Dec. 16, 1945; auxiliary bishop of Mechelen, 1945-61; archbishop of Mechelen-Brussels, 1961-79; cardinal Mar. 19, 1962; titular church, St. Peter in Chains. Archbishop emeritus of Mechelen-Brussels.

Suquia Goicoechea, Angel: b. Oct. 2, 1916, Zaldivia, Spain; ord. priest July 7, 1940; ord. bishop of Almeria, July 16, 1966; bishop of Malaga, 1969-73; archbishop of Santiago de Compostela, 1973-83; archbishop of Madrid, Apr. 12, 1983; cardinal May 25, 1985; titular church, Great Mother of God. Archbishop of Madrid (metropolitan archbishop, 1991, when Madrid was made metropolitan see). Curial membership: Secretariat of State (second section); Bishops, Catholic Education, Evangelization of Peoples (congregations).

Szoka, Edmund C.: b. Sept. 14, 1927, Grand Rapids, Mich.; educ. Sacred Heart Seminary

(Detroit, Mich.), St. John's Provincial Seminary (Plymouth, Mich.), Lateran Univ. (Rome); ord. priest (Marquette diocese), June 5, 1954; ord. first bishop of Gaylord, Mich., July 20, 1971; archbishop of Detroit, 1981-90; cardinal June 28, 1988; titular church, Sts. Andrew and Gregory (al Monte Celio). President of Prefecture for Economic Affairs of the Holy See, 1990. Curial membership:
Secretariat of State (second section); Causes of Saints, Bishops, Evangelization of Peoples, Clergy, Institutes of Consecrated Life and Societies of Apostolic Life (congregations).

Taofinu'u, Pio, S.M.: b. Dec. 9, 1923, Falealupo, W. Samoa; ord. priest Dec. 8, 1954; joined Society of Mary, 1955, ord. bishop of Apia (Samoa and Tokelau), May 29, 1968, the first Polynesian bishop; cardinal Mar. 5, 1973; titular church, St. Humphrey. Archbishop of Samoa-Apia and Tokelau (Sept. 10, 1982). Curial membership:
Causes of Saints (congregation).

Thiandoum, Hyacinthe: b. Feb. 2, 1921, Poponguine, Senegal; ord. priest Apr. 18, 1949; studied at Gregorian University, Rome, 1951-53; returned to Senegal, 1953; ord. archbishop of Dakar, May 20, 1962; cardinal May 24, 1976; titular church, S. Maria (del Popolo). Archbishop of Dakar. Curial membership:
Clergy, Institutes of Consecrated Life and Societies of Apostolic Life, Evangelization of Peoples (congregations); Social Communications, Culture (councils).

Todea,* Alexandru: b. June 5, 1912, Teleac, Romania; ord. priest in the Byzantine Romanian rite Mar. 25, 1939; ord. bishop secretly (titular see of Cesarololi), Nov. 19, 1950, by Archbishop Gerald P. O'Hara, Vatican representative to Romania; arrested, 1951, and sentenced to life imprisonment; granted amnesty in 1964; archbishop of Fagaras and Alba Julia, Mar. 14, 1990; cardinal June 28, 1991; titular church, St. Athanasius. Archbishop of Fagaras and Alba Julia of the Romanians.

Tomko, Jozef: b. Mar. 11, 1924, Udavske, Slovakia; ord. priest Mar. 12, 1949; ord. titular archbishop of Doclea, Sept, 15, 1979; secretary-general of the Synod of Bishops, 1979-85; cardinal May 25, 1985; deacon, Jesus the Good Shepherd (alla Montagnola). Prefect of the Congregation for the Evangelization of Peoples, 1985; Grand Chancellor of Pontifical Urban University. Curial membership:
Secretariat of State (second section); Doctrine of the Faith, Divine Worship and Sacraments, Bishops, Clergy, Institutes of Consecrated Life and Societies of Apostolic Life, Catholic Education (congregations); Christian Unity, Interreligious Dialogue, Culture, Interpretation of Legislative Texts (councils); Latin America, State of Vatican City (commissions).

Tumi, Christian Wiyghan: b. Oct. 15, 1930, Kikaikelaki, Cameroon; ord. priest Apr. 17, 1966; ord. bishop of Yagoua, Jan. 6, 1980; coadjutor archbishop of Garoua, Nov. 19, 1982; archbishop of Garoua, 1984-91; cardinal June 28, 1988; titular church, Martyrs of Uganda (a Poggio Ameno). Archbishop of Douala, Aug. 31, 1991. Curial membership:
Evangelization of Peoples (congregation); Interreligious Dialogue, Culture (councils).

Tzadua, Paulos: b. Aug. 25, 1921, Addifini, Ethiopia; ord. priest Mar. 12, 1944; ord. titular bishop of Abila di Palestina and auxiliary of Addis Ababa, May 20, 1973; archbishop of Addis Ababa, Feb. 24, 1977; cardinal May 25, 1985; titular church, Most Holy Name of Mary (a Via Latina). Archbishop of Addis Ababa. Curial membership:
Oriental Churches (congregation); Interpretation of Legislative Texts (council).

Ursi,* Corrado: b. July 26, 1908, Andria, Italy; ord. priest July 25, 1931; vice-rector and later rector of the Pontifical Regional Seminary of Molfetta, 1931-51; ord. bishop of Nardo, Sept. 30, 1951; archbishop of Acerenza, Nov. 30, 1961; archbishop of Naples, May 23, 1966 (resigned May 9, 1987); cardinal June 26, 1967; titular church, St. Callistus. Archbishop emeritus of Naples.

Vachon,* Louis-Albert: b. Feb. 4, 1912, Saint-Frederic-de-Beauce, Que., Canada; ord. priest June 11, 1938; ord. titular bishop of Mesarfelta and auxiliary of Quebec, May 14, 1977; archbishop of Quebec, Mar. 20, 1981 (resigned Mar. 17, 1990); cardinal May 25, 1985; titular church, St. Paul of the Cross (a Corviale). Archbishop emeritus of Quebec.

Vidal, Ricardo J.: b. Feb. 6, 1931, Mogpoc, Philippines; ord. priest Mar. 17, 1956; ord. titular bishop of Claterna and coadjutor of Melalos, Nov. 30, 1971; archbishop of Lipa, 1973-81; coadjutor archbishop of Cebu, Apr. 13, 1981; archbishop of Cebu, Aug. 24, 1982; cardinal May 25, 1985; titular church, Sts. Peter and Paul (in Via Ostiensi). Archbishop of Cebu. Curial membership:
Evangelizaton of Peoples (congregation); Health Care Workers (council).

Wetter, Friedrich: b. Feb. 20, 1928, Landau, West Germany; ord. priest Oct. 10, 1953; ord. bishop of Speyer, June 29, 1968; archbishop of Munich and Freising, Oct. 28, 1982; cardinal May 25, 1985; titular church, St. Stephen (al Monte Celio). Archbishop of Munich and Freising. Curial membership:
Evangelization of Peoples, Catholic Education (congregations).

Willebrands,* Johannes: b. Sept. 4, 1909, Bovenkarspel, The Netherlands; ord. priest May 26, 1934; ord. titular bishop of Mauriana, June 28, 1964; secretary of Secretariat for Christian Unity, 1960-69; cardinal Apr. 28, 1969; titular church, St. Sebastian (alle Catacombe); archbishop of Utrecht, 1975-83; president of Council for Christian Unity, 1969-89. President emeritus of the Council for Promoting Christian Unity; Camerlengo of the College of Cardinals, 1988.

Williams, Thomas Stafford: b. Mar. 20, 1930, Wellington, New Zealand; ord. priest Dec. 20, 1959, in Rome; studied in Ireland after ordination, receiving degree in social sciences; served in various pastoral assignments on his return to New Zealand; missionary in Western Samoa to 1976; ord. archbishop of Wellington, New Zealand, Dec. 20, 1979; cardinal Feb. 2, 1983; titular church, Jesus the Divine Teacher (at Pineda Sacchetti). Archbishop of Wellington. Curial membership:
Evangelization of Peoples (congregation).

Wu Cheng-Chung, John Baptist: b. Mar. 26, 1925, Shui-Tsai, mainland China; ord. priest (for

Hsinchu, Taiwan, diocese) July 6, 1952; ord. bishop of Hong Kong, July 25, 1975; cardinal June 28, 1988; titular church, Blessed Virgin Mary of Mount Carmel (a Mostacciano). Bishop of Hong Kong. Curial membership:
Evangelization of Peoples (congregation); Interreligious Dialogue, Culture (councils).
Yago, Bernard: b. July, 1916, Pass, Ivory Coast (now Côte d'Ivoire); ord. priest May 1, 1947; ord. archbishop of Abidjan, May 8, 1960, by Pope John XXIII in St. Peter's Basilica, becoming the first native member of the hierarchy of Côte d'Ivoire; cardinal Feb. 2, 1983; titular church, St. Chrysogonus. Archbishop of Abidjan. Curial membership:
Evangelization of Peoples (congregation); Christian Unity (council).
Zoungrana, Paul, M. Afr.: b. Sept 3, 1917, Ouagadougou, Upper Volta (now Burkina Faso); ord. priest May 2, 1942; ord. archbishop of Ouagadougou at St. Peter's Basilica by John XXIII, May 8, 1960; cardinal Feb. 22, 1965; titular church, St. Camillus de Lellis. Archbishop of Ouagadougou. Curial membership:
Divine Worship and Sacraments, Institutes of Consecrated Life and Societies of Apostolic Life, Evangelization of Peoples (congregation); Health Care Workers (council).

CATEGORIES OF CARDINALS
(As of Aug 15, 1993.)
Information below includes categories of cardinals and dates of consistories at which they were created. Seniority or precedence usually depends on order of elevation.

Five of these 148 cardinals were named by John XXIII (consistories of Dec. 15, 1958, Mar. 28, 1960, and Mar. 19, 1962); 47 by Paul VI (consistories of Feb. 22, 1965, June 26, 1967, Apr. 28, 1969, Mar. 5, 1973, May 24, 1976, and June 27, 1977); 96 by John Paul II (consistories of June 30, 1979, Feb. 2, 1983, May 25, 1985, June 28, 1988, June 28, 1991).

Order of Bishops
Titular Bishops of Suburbicarian Sees: Agnelo Rossi (Feb. 22, 1965); Francesco Carpino (June 26, 1967); Paolo Bertoli (Apr. 28, 1969); Bernardin Gantin, dean (June 27, 1977); Agostino Casaroli, sub-dean (June 30, 1979); Joseph Ratzinger (June 27, 1977).
Eastern Rite Patriarch: Antoine Pierre Khoraiche (Feb. 2, 1983).

Order of Priests
1958 (Dec. 15): Franz Koenig.
1960 (Mar. 28): Laurean Rugambwa.
1962 (Mar. 19): Juan Landazuri Ricketts, O.F.M., Raul Silva Henriquez, S.D.B., Leo Josef Suenens.
1965 (Feb. 22): Owen McCann, Leon-Etienne Duval, Paul Zoungrana.
1967 (June 26): Gabriel Garrone, John J. Krol, Corrado Ursi, Justin Darmojuwono.
1969 (Apr. 28): Alfredo Vicente Scherer, Silvio Oddi, Francois Marty, Paul Gouyon, Vicente Enrique y Tarancon, Pablo Muñoz Vega, S.J.; John J. Carberry, Stephan Sou Hwan Kim, Eugenio de Araujo Sales, Johannes Willebrands.

1973 (Mar. 5): Antonio Ribeiro, Joseph Cordeiro, Pietro Palazzini, Luis Aponte Martinez, Raul Francisco Primatesta, Salvatore Pappalardo, Marcelo Gonzalez Martin, Ugo Poletti, Maurice Otunga, Paulo Evaristo Arns, Narciso Jubany Arnau, Pio Taofinu'u.
1976 (May 24): Opilio Rossi, Giuseppe Maria Sensi, Juan Carlos Aramburu, Corrado Bafile, Hyacinthe Thiandoum, Jaime L. Sin, William W. Baum, Aloisio Lorscheider, Eduardo Pironio, George Basil Hume, O.S.B., Victor Razafimahatratra, Dominic Ekandem.
1977 (June 27): Mario Luigi Ciappi.
1979 (June 30): Giuseppe Caprio, Marco Cé, Egano Righi-Lambertini, Ernesto Corripio Ahumada, Joseph Asajiro Satowaki, Roger Etchegaray, Anastasio Alberto Ballestrero, O.C.D., Gerald Emmett Carter, Franciszek Macharski, Ignatius Gong (Kung) Pin-mei.
1983 (Feb. 2): Bernard Yago, Franjo Kuharic, Jose Ali Lebrun Moratinos, Joseph L. Bernardin, Michael Michai Kitbunchu, Alexandre do Nascimento, Alfonso Lopez Trujillo, Godfried Danneels, Thomas Stafford Williams, Carlo Maria Martini, Jean-Marie Lustiger, Jozef Glemp, Joachim Meisner, Aurelio Sabattani, Giuseppe Casoria.
1985 (May 25): Juan Francisco Fresno Larrain, Miguel Obando Bravo, Angel Suquia Goicoechea, Ricardo Vidal, Henryk Roman Gulbinowicz, Paulus Tzadua, Myroslav Ivan Lubachivsky, Louis-Albert Vachon, Albert Decourtray, Friedrich Wetter, Silvano Piovanelli, Adrianus J. Simonis, Bernard F. Law, John J. O'Connor, Giacomo Biffi.
1988 (June 28): Paul Gregoire, Anthony Padiyara, Jose Freire Falcao, Michele Giordano, Alexandre Jose Maria dos Santos, O.F.M., Giovanni Canestri, Simon Ignatius Pimenta, Mario Revollo Bravo, Edward Bede Clancy, Lucas Moreira Neves, O.P., James Aloysius Hickey, Edmund C. Szoka, Laszlo Paskai, O.F.M., Christian Wiyghan Tumi, Hans Hermann Groër, O.S.B., Vincentas Sladkevicius, Jean Margeot, John Baptist Wu Cheng-Chung.
1991 (June 28): Angelo Sodano, Alexandru Todea, Robert Coffy, Frédéric Etsou-Nzabi-Bamungwabi, Nicolas de Jesus Lopez Rodriguez, Antonio Quarracino, Roger Mahony, Anthony J. Bevilacqua, Giovanni Saldarini, Cahal Brendan Daly, Camillo Ruini, Jan Chryzostom Korec, Henri Schwery, Georg Sterzinsky.

Order of Deacons
1985 (May 25): Simon D. Lourdusamy, Francis A. Arinze, Antonio Innocenti, Paul Augustin Mayer, Jean Jerome Hamer, Jozef Tomko, Andrzej Maria Deskur, Paul Poupard, Rosalio Jose Castillo Lara, Edouard Gagnon, Alfons Stickler, S.D.B., Pietro Pavan.
1988 (June 28): Eduardo Martinez Somalo, Achille Silvestrini, Angelo Felici, Antonio Maria Javierre Ortas, S.D.B.
1991 (June 28): Guido Del Mestri, Pio Laghi, Edward I. Cassidy, Jose T. Sanchez, Virgilio Noè, Fiorenzo Angelini, Paolo Dezza, S.J.

DISTRIBUTION OF CARDINALS
As of Aug. 15, 1993, there were 148 cardinals from more than 60 countries or areas. Listed below are areas, countries, number and last names.

Europe — 75

Italy (34): Angelini, Bafile, Ballestrero, Bertoli, Biffi, Canestri, Caprio, Carpino, Casaroli, Casoria, Cé, Ciappi, Dezza, Felici, Giordano, Innocenti, Laghi, Martini, Noè, Oddi, Palazzini, Pappalardo, Pavan, Piovanelli, Poletti, Righi-Lambertini, Rossi (Opilio), Ruini, Sabattani, Saldarini, Silvestrini, Sensi, Sodano, Ursi.

France (8): Coffy, Decourtray, Etchegaray, Garrone, Gouyon, Lustiger, Marty, Poupard.

Spain (6): Enrique y Tarancon, Gonzalez Martin, Javierre Ortas, Jubany Arnau, Martinez Somalo, Suquia Goicoechea.

Germany (5): Mayer, Meisner, Ratzinger, Sterzinsky, Wetter.

Poland (4): Deskur, Glemp, Gulbinowicz, Macharski.

Belgium (3): Danneels, Hamer, Suenens.

Austria (3): Groer, Koenig, Stickler.

Slovak Republic (2): Korec, Tomko.

Netherlands (2): Simonis, Willebrands.

One from each of the following countries: Croatia, Kuharic; England, Hume; Hungary, Paskai; Ireland, Daly; Lithuania, Sladkevicius; Portugal, Ribeiro; Romania, Todea; Switzerland, Schwery.

Asia — 14

India (3): Lourdusamy, Padiyara, Pimenta.

Philippines (3): Sanchez, Sin, Vidal.

One from each of the following countries: China, Gong (Kung) Pin-mei (exiled); Hong Kong, Wu Cheng-Chung; Indonesia, Darmojuwono; Japan, Satowaki; Korea, Kim; Lebanon, Khoraiche; Pakistan, Cordeiro; Thailand, Kitbunchu.

Oceania — 4

Australia (2): Cassidy, Clancy. One each from: New Zealand, Williams; Pacific Islands (Samoa), Taofinu'u.

Africa — 17

Nigeria (2): Arinze, Ekandem.

One from each of the following countries: Algeria, Duval; Angola, do Nascimento; Benin, Gantin; Burkina Faso, Zoungrana; Cameroon, Tumi; Ethiopia, Tzadua; Ivory Coast, Yago; Kenya, Otunga; Madagascar, Razafimahatratra; Mauritius, Margeot; Mozambique, Santos; Senegal, Thiandoum; South Africa, McCann; Tanzania, Rugambwa; Zaire, Etsou-Nzabi-Bamungwabi.

North America — 17

United States (11): Baum, Bernardin, Bevilacqua, Carberry, Hickey, Krol, Law, Lubachivsky (major archbishop of Lviv, Ukraine), Mahony, O'Connor, Szoka.

Canada (4): Carter, Gagnon, Gregoire, Vachon.

Mexico (1): Corripio Ahumada.

Puerto Rico (1): Aponte Martinez.

Central and South America — 21

Brazil (7): Arns, Falcao, Lorscheider, Neves, Rossi (Agnelo), Sales, Scherer.

Argentina (4): Aramburu, Pironio, Primatesta, Quarrachino.

Chile (2): Fresno Larrain, Silva Henriquez.

Colombia (2): Lopez Trujillo, Revollo Bravo.

Venezuela (2): Castillo Lara, Lebrun Moratinos.

One from each of the following countries: Dominican Republic, Lopez Rodriquez; Ecuador, Munoz Vega, S.J.; Nicaragua, Obando Bravo; Peru, Landazuri Ricketts.

INELIGIBLE TO VOTE

As of Aug. 15, 1993, 41 of the 148 cardinals were ineligible to take part in a papal election in line with the apostolic letter *Ingravescentem Aetatem* effective Jan. 1, 1971, which limited the functions of cardinals after completion of their 80th year.

Cardinals affected were: Aramburu, Bafile, Bertoli, Carberry, Carpino, Carter, Casoria, Ciappi, Dezza, Duval, Enrique y Tarancon, Garrone, Gong Pin-Mei, Gouyon, Gregoire, Jubany Arnau, Khoraiche, Koenig, Krol, McCann, Marty, Mayer, Munoz Vega, Oddi, Palazzini, Pavan, Righi-Lambertini, Rossi (Agnelo), Rossi (Opilio), Rugambwa, Sabattani, Satowaki, Scherer, Sensi, Silva Henriquez, S.D.B., Stickler, S.D.B., Suenens, Todea, Ursi, Vachon, Willebrands.

Other cardinals completing their 80th year in 1993: Anastasio Alberto Ballestrero, Oct. 3; Juan Landazuri Ricketts, Dec. 19.

Cardinals completing their 80th year in 1994: Ugo Poletti, Apr. 19; Myroslav Lubachivsky, June 24; Juan Francisco Fresno Larrain, July 26; Justin Darmojuwono, Nov. 2; Giuseppe Caprio, Nov. 15; Agostino Casaroli, Nov. 24.

CARDINALS OF U.S.

As of Aug. 15, 1993, U.S. cardinals according to years of elevation (for biographies, see Index under individual name).

1967: John J. Krol (archbishop emeritus of Philadelphia); **1969:** John J. Carberry (archbishop emeritus of St. Louis); **1976:** William W. Baum (major penitentiary); **1983:** Joseph L. Bernardin (archbishop of Chicago); **1985:** Myroslav Lubachivsky (U.S. citizen; major archbishop of Lviv of the Ukrainians), Bernard F. Law (archbishop of Boston), John J. O'Connor (archbishop of New York); **1988:** James A. Hickey (archbishop of Washington), Edmund C. Szoka (president of Prefecture for Economic Affairs of the Holy See); **1991:** Roger M. Mahony (archbishop of Los Angeles), Anthony J. Bevilacqua (archbishop of Philadelphia).

U.S. cardinals of the past, according to year of elevation. (For biographical data, see Index: Bishops, U.S., of the Past.)

1875: John McCloskey; **1886:** James Gibbons; **1911:** John Farley, William O'Connell; **1921:** Dennis Dougherty; **1924:** Patrick Hayes, George Mundelein; **1946:** John Glennon, Edward Mooney, Francis Spellman, Samuel Stritch; **1953:** James F. McIntyre; **1958:** John O'Hara, C.S.C., Richard Cushing; **1959:** Albert Meyer, Aloysius Muench; **1961:** Joseph Ritter; **1965:** Lawrence J. Shehan; **1967:** Francis Brennan, John P. Cody, Patrick A. O'Boyle; **1969:** John J. Wright, Terence J. Cooke, John F. Dearden; **1973:** Humbertus S. Medeiros, Timothy Manning.

Prelates who became cardinals after returning to their native countries: John Lefebvre de Chevrus, first bishop of Boston (1808-23) and apostolic administrator of New York (1810-15), elevated to cardinalate, 1836, in France. Ignatius Persico, O.F.M.

Cap., bishop of Savannah (1870-72), elevated to cardinalate, 1893, in Italy. Diomede Falconio, O.F.M., ord. priest Buffalo, N.Y.; missionary in U.S.; apostolic delegate to the U.S. (1902-11), elevated to cardinalate, 1911, in Italy.

REPRESENTATIVES OF THE HOLY SEE

Papal representatives and their functions were the subject of a document entitled *Sollicitudo Omnium Ecclesiarum* which Pope Paul VI issued on his own initiative under the date of June 24, 1969.

Delegates and Nuncios

Papal representatives "receive from the Roman Pontiff the charge of representing him in a fixed way in the various nations or regions of the world.

"When their legation is only to local churches, they are known as apostolic delegates. When to this legation, of a religious and ecclesial nature, there is added diplomatic legation to states and governments, they receive the title of nuncio, pro-nuncio, and internuncio."

An apostolic nuncio has the diplomatic rank of ambassador extraordinary and plenipotentiary. Traditionally, because the Vatican diplomatic service has the longest uninterrupted history in the world, a nuncio has precedence among diplomats in the country to which he is accredited and serves as dean of the diplomatic corps on state occasions. Since 1965 pro-nuncios, also of ambassadorial rank, have been assigned to countries in which this prerogative is not recognized.

Other Representatives

Other representatives, who are covered in the Almanac article, Vatican Representatives to International Organizations, are clerics and lay persons "who form . . . part of a pontifical mission attached to international organizations or take part in conferences and congresses." They are variously called delegates or observers.

Service and Liaison

Representatives, while carrying out their general and special duties, are bound to respect the autonomy of local churches and bishops. Their service and liaison responsibilities include the following:

● Nomination of Bishops: To play a key role in compiling, with the advice of ecclesiastics and lay persons, and submitting lists of names of likely candidates to the Holy See with their own recommendations.

● Bishops: To aid and counsel local bishops without interfering in the affairs of their jurisdictions.

● Episcopal Conferences: To maintain close relations with them and to assist them in every possible way. (Papal representatives do not belong to these conferences.)

● Religious Communities of Pontifical Rank: To advise and assist major superiors for the purpose of promoting and consolidating conferences of men and women religious and to coordinate their apostolic activities.

● Church-State Relations: The thrust in this area is toward the development of sound relations with civil governments and collaboration in work for peace and the total good of the whole human family.

The mission of a papal representative begins with appointment and assignment by the pope and continues until termination of his mandate. He acts "under the guidance and according to the instructions of the cardinal secretary of state to whom he is directly responsible for the execution of the mandate entrusted to him by the Supreme Pontiff." Normally representatives are required to retire at the age of 75.

NUNCIOS AND DELEGATES

(Sources: *Annuario Pontificio, L'Osservatore Romano, Acta Apostolicae Sedis*, Catholic News Service.)

Data, as of August, 1993: country, rank of legation (corresponding to rank of legate unless otherwise noted), name of legate (archbishop unless otherwise noted) as available. An asterisk indicates a nuncio who is not presently dean of the diplomatic corps.

Delegate for Papal Representatives: Archbishop Francesco Monterisi, titular Archbishop of Alba Marittima. The post was established in 1973 to coordinate papal diplomatic efforts throughout the world. The office entails responsibility for "following more closely through timely visits the activities of papal representatives . . . and encouraging their rapport with the central offices" of the Secretariat of State.

Africa, Southern (Botswana, South Africa, Namibia): Pretoria, South Africa, Apostolic Delegation; Ambrose De Paoli (also Pro-Nuncio to Lesotho).

Albania: Tirana, Nunciature; Ivan Dias*.

Algeria: Algiers, Nunciature; Edmond Farhat, Pro-Nuncio (He is also Pro-Nuncio to Tunisia and Apostolic Delegate to Libya.)

Angola: Luanda, Apostolic Delegation; Felix del Blanco Prieto (also Pro-Nuncio to Sao Tome and Principe).

Antigua and Barbuda: Nunciature; Eugenio Sbarbaro, Pro-Nuncio (resides in Port of Spain, Trinidad).

Antilles: Apostolic Delegation; Eugenio Sbarbaro (resides in Port of Spain, Trinidad).

Arabian Peninsula: Apostolic Delegation; Pablo Puente (also nuncio in Kuwait and Lebanon).

Argentina: Buenos Aires, Nunciature; Ubaldo Calabresi.

Armenia: Diplomatic relations established May 23, 1992.

Australia: Canberra, Nunciature; Franco Brambilla, Pro-Nuncio.

Austria: Vienna, Nunciature; Donato Squicciarini.

Azerbaijan: Diplomatic relations established May 23, 1992.

Bahamas: Nunciature; Eugenio Sbarbaro, Pro-Nuncio (resides in Port of Spain, Trinidad).

Bangladesh: Dhaka, Nunciature; Adriano Bernardini*.

Barbados: Nunciature; Eugenio Sbarbaro, Pro-Nuncio (resides in Port of Spain, Trinidad).

Belarus: Minsk, Nunciature; Gabriel Montalvo (also Pro-Nuncio to Federal Republic of Yugoslavia and president of Pontifical Ecclesiastical Academy).

Belgium: Brussels, Nunciature; Giovanni Moretti (also Nuncio to Luxembourg and European Community).

Belize: Nunciature; Eugenio Sbarbaro, Pro-Nuncio (resides in Port of Spain, Trinidad).

Benin (formerly Dahomey): Nunciature; Andre Dupuy (resides in Accra, Ghana).

Bolivia: La Paz, Nunciature; Giovanni Tonucci.

Bosnia-Herzegovina: Nunciature; Francesco Monterisi. (He is also delegate for Papal Representatives.)

Botswana: See Africa, Southern.

Brazil: Brasilia, Nunciature; Alfio Rapisarda.

Brunei: See Malaysia and Brunei.

Bulgaria: Sofia, Nunciature (reestablished, 1990); Mario Rizzi*.

Burkina Faso: Ouagadougou, Nunciature; Janusz Bolonek, Pro-Nuncio (resides in Abidjan, Côte d'-Ivoire).

Burma: See Myanmar.

Burundi: Bujumbura, Nunciature; Rino Passigato, Pro-Nuncio.

Cameroon: Yaounde, Nunciature; Santos Abril y Castelló, Pro-Nuncio (also Pro-Nuncio to Gabon and Equatorial Guinea).

Canada: Ottawa, Nunciature; Carlo Curis, Pro-Nuncio.

Cape Verde, Republic of: Nunciature; Antonio Maria Veglio, Pro-Nuncio (resides in Dakar, Senegal).

Central African Republic: Bangui, Nunciature; Diego Causero* (also Nuncio* to Congo and Chad).

Chad: Nunciature; Diego Causero* (resides in Bangui, Central African Republic).

Chile: Santiago, Nunciature; Piero Biggio.

China: Taipei (Taiwan), Nunciature.

Colombia: Bogota, Nunciature; Paolo Romeo.

Comoros: See Madagascar.

Congo: Brazzaville, Nunciature; Nuncio* (also nuncio* to Central African Republic and Chad).

Costa Rica: San Jose, Nunciature; Giacinto Berloco.

Côte d'Ivoire (Ivory Coast): Abidjan, Nunciature; Janusz Bolonek (also pro-nuncio to Niger and Burkina Faso).

Croatia: Zagreb, Nunciature; Giulio Einaudi.

Cuba: Havana, Nunciature; Benjamin Stella*.

Cyprus: Nicosia, Nunciature; Andrea Cordero Lanza di Montezemolo, Pro-Nuncio (also Apostolic Delegate to Jerusalem).

Czech Republic: Prague, Nunciature; Giovanni Coppa.

Denmark: Copenhagen, Nunciature; Giovanni Ceirano* (also Nuncio* to Finland, Iceland, Norway and Sweden).

Djibouti: Apostolic Delegation; Patrick Coveney (resides in Addis Ababa, Ethiopia).

Dominica: Nunciature; Eugenio Sbarbaro, Pro-Nuncio (resides in Port-of-Spain, Trinidad).

Dominican Republic: Santo Domingo, Nunciature; Fortunato Baldelli (also Apostolic Delegate to Puerto Rico).

Ecuador: Quito, Nunciature; Francesco Canalini.

Egypt: Cairo, Nunciature; Antonio Magnoni, Pro-Nuncio.

El Salvador: San Salvador, Nunciature; Manuel Monteiro de Castro.

Equatorial Guinea: Santa Isabel, Nunciature; Santos Abril y Castelló, Pro-Nuncio (resides in Yaounde, Cameroon).

Estonia: Nunciature; Justo Mullor Garcia* (resides in Vilna, Lithuania).

Ethiopia: Addis Ababa, Nunciature; Patrick Coveney, Pro-Nuncio.

Fiji: Nunciature; Thomas A. White, Pro-Nuncio (resides in New Zealand).

Finland: Helsinki, Nunciature; Giovanni Ceirano* (resides in Denmark).

France: Paris, Nunciature; Lorenzo Antonetti.

Gabon: Libreville, Nunciature; Santos Abril y Castelló, Pro-Nuncio (resides in Yaounde, Cameroon).

Gambia: Nunciature; Luigi Travaglino, Pro-Nuncio (resides in Freetown, Sierra Leone).

Georgia: Diplomatic relations established May 23, 1992.

Germany: Bonn, Nunciature; Lajos Kada.

Ghana: Accra, Nunciature; Andre Dupuy (also Nuncio to Benin and Togo).

Great Britain: London, Nunciature; Luigi Barbarito, Pro-Nuncio (also papal representative to Gibraltar).

Greece: Athens, Nunciature; Luciano Storero, Pro-Nuncio.

Grenada: Nunciature; Eugenio Sbarbaro, Pro-Nuncio (resides in Port of Spain, Trinidad).

Guatemala: Guatemala City, Nunciature; Giovanni Battista Morandini.

Guinea: Conakry, Nunciature; Luigi Travaglino, Pro-Nuncio (resides in Freetown, Sierra Leone).

Guinea-Bissau: Nunciature; Antonio Maria Veglio, Pro-Nuncio (resides at Dakar, Senegal).

Haiti: Port-au-Prince, Nunciature; Lorenzo Baldisseri.

Honduras: Tegucigalpa, Nunciature; Luigi Conti.

Hungary: Budapest, Nunciature; Angelo Acerbi.

Iceland: Nunciature; Giovanni Ceirano* (resides in Denmark).

India: New Delhi, Nunciature; Giorgio Zur, Pro-Nuncio (also Pro-Nuncio to Nepal).

Indonesia: Jakarta, Nunciature; Pietro Sambi, Pro-Nuncio.

Iran: Teheran, Nunciature; Romeo Panciroli, M.C.C.I., Pro-Nuncio.

Iraq: Baghdad, Nunciature; Marian Oles, Pro-Nuncio.

Ireland: Dublin, Nunciature; Emanuele Gerada.

Italy: Rome, Nunciature; Carlo Furno.

Ivory Coast: See Côte d'Ivoire.

Jamaica: Nunciature; Eugenio Sbarbaro, Pro-Nuncio (resides in Port of Spain, Trinidad).

Japan: Tokyo, Nunciature; William A. Carew, Pro-Nuncio.

Jerusalem, Palestine, Jordan, Israel: Jerusalem,

Apostolic Delegation; Andrea Cordero Lanza di Montezemolo (also Pro-Nuncio to Cyprus).

Kazakhstan: Diplomatic relations established Oct. 17, 1992.

Kenya: Nairobi, Nunciature; Clemente Faccani, Pro-Nuncio (also Pro-Nuncio to Seychelles).

Korea: Seoul, Nunciature; Giovanni Bulaitis, Pro-Nuncio.

Kuwait: Al Kuwait, Nunciature; Pablo Puente (also nuncio to Lebanon and apostolic delegate to Arabian Peninsula).

Kyrgyzstan: Diplomatic relations established Aug. 27, 1992.

Laos: Apostolic Delegation; Luigi Bressan, (resides in Bangkok, Thailand).

Latvia: Nunciature; Justo Mullor Garcia* (resides in Vilna, Lithuania).

Lebanon: Beirut, Nunciature; Pablo Puente (also nuncio to Kuwait and apostolic delegate to Arabian Peninsula).

Lesotho: Maseru, Nunciature; Ambrose De Paoli, Pro-Nuncio (resides in Pretoria, S. Africa).

Liberia: Monrovia, Nunciature; Luigi Travaglino, Pro-Nuncio (resides in Freetown, Sierra Leone).

Libya: Apostolic Delegation; Edmond Farhat (resides in Algiers, Algeria).

Liechtenstein: Nunciature; Karl-Josef Rauber (resides in Bern, Switzerland).

Lithuania: Vilnius, Nunciature; Justo Mullor Garcia.

Luxembourg: Nunciature; Giovanni Moretti (resides in Brussels, Belgium).

Madagascar: Antananarivo, Nunciature; Blasco Francisco Collaco, Pro-Nuncio (also Pro-Nuncio to Mauritius and Apostolic Delegate to Comoros and Reunion).

Malawi: Lilongwe, Nunciature; Giuseppe Leanza, Pro-Nuncio (resides in Zambia).

Malaysia and Brunei: Apostolic Delegation; Luigi Bressan (resides in Bangkok, Thailand).

Mali: Nunciature; Antonio Maria Veglio, Pro-Nuncio (resides in Dakar, Senegal).

Malta: La Valletta, Nunciature; Pier Luigi Celata (also nuncio to San Marino and Slovenia).

Mauritania: Nouakchott, Apostolic Delegation; Antonio Maria Veglio (resides in Dakar, Senegal).

Mauritius: Port Louis, Nunciature; Blasco Francisco Collaco, Pro-Nuncio (resides in Antananarivo, Madagascar).

Mexico: Mexico City, Nunciature; Girolamo Prigione* (diplomatic relations established 1992).

Moldava: Diplomatic relations established May 23, 1992.

Mongolia: Nunciature; Giovanni Bulaitis* (resides in Seoul, Korea).

Morocco: Rabat, Nunciature; Domenico De Luca.

Mozambique: Maputo, Apostolic Delegation; . . . . . (also Pro-Nuncio to Zimbabwe).

Myanmar (formerly Burma): Apostolic Delegation; Luigi Bressan (resides in Bangkok, Thailand).

Namibia: See Africa, Southern.

Nauru: Nunciature; Thomas A. White* (resides in New Zealand).

Nepal: Nunciature; Giorgio Zur, Pro-Nuncio (resides in New Delhi, India).

Netherlands: The Hague, Nunciature; Henri Lemaitre*.

New Zealand: Wellington, Nunciature; Thomas A. White, Pro-Nuncio. (He is also Pro-Nuncio to Fiji, nuncio* to Nauru and Apostolic Delegate to Pacific Islands).

Nicaragua: Managua, Nunciature; Paolo Giglio.

Niger: Niamey, Nunciature; Janusz Bolonek, Pro-Nuncio (resides in Abidjan, Côte d'Ivoire.)

Nigeria: Lagos, Nunciature; Carlo M. Vigano, Pro-Nuncio.

Norway: Nunciature; Giovanni Ceirano* (resides in Denmark).

Pacific Islands: Apostolic Delegation; Thomas A. White (resides in New Zealand).

Pakistan: Islamabad, Nunciature; Renzo Fratini, Pro-Nuncio.

Panama: Panama, Nunciature; Osvaldo Padilla.

Papua New Guinea: Port Moresby; Nunciature; Ramiro Moliner Ingles* (also Nuncio* to Solomon Islands).

Paraguay: Asuncion, Nunciature; Jose Sebastian Laboa.

Peru: Lima, Nunciature; Luigi Dossena.

Philippines: Manila, Nunciature; Gian Vincenzo Moreni.

Poland: Warsaw; Nunciature; Jozef Kowalczyk.

Portugal: Lisbon, Nunciature; Edoardo Rovida.

Puerto Rico: See Dominican Republic.

Reunion: See Madagascar.

Romania: Bucharest, Nunciature. John Bukovsky, S.V.D.* (Diplomatic relations reestablished in 1990.)

Russia (Federation of): Moscow; Francesco Colasuonno, Apostolic Nuncio; appointed Representative of the Holy See to Russian Federation Mar. 15, 1990.

Rwanda: Kigali, Nunciature. Giuseppe Bertello*.

Saint Lucia: Nunciature; Eugenio Sbarbaro, Pro-Nuncio (resides in Port of Spain, Trinidad).

Saint Vincent and the Grenadines: Kingstown, Saint Vincent, Nunciature; Eugenio Sbarbaro, Pro-Nuncio (resides in Port of Spain, Trinidad).

San Marino: Nunciature; Pier Luigi Celata.

Sao Tome and Principe: Nunciature; Felix del Blanco Prieto, Pro-Nuncio (also apostolic delegate to Angola, where he resides).

Senegal: Dakar, Nunciature; Antonio Maria Veglio, Pro-Nuncio (also Pro-Nuncio to Cape Verde, Guinea-Bissau and Mali; Apostolic Delegate to Mauritania.)

Seychelles Islands: Nunciature; Clemente Faccani, Pro-Nuncio (resides in Nairobi, Kenya).

Sierra Leone: Freetown, Apostolic Delegation; Luigi Travaglino (also Pro-Nuncio to Gambia, Guinea and Liberia).

Singapore: Nunciature; Luigi Bressan, Pro-Nuncio. (He is also pro-nuncio to Thailand and apostolic delegate to Laos, Malaysia and Brunei, and Myanmar.)

Slovak Republic: Nunciature; Giovanni Coppa.

Slovenia: Ljubljana, Nunciature; Pier Luigi Celata.

Solomon Islands: Nunciature; Ramiro Moliner* (resides in Port Moresby, Papua New Guinea).

Somalia: Apostolic Delegation (est. 1992); Erwin Josef Ender (resides in Sudan).

South Africa: See Africa, Southern.

Spain: Madrid, Nunciature; Mario Tagliaferri.

Sri Lanka: Colombo, Nunciature; Francois Bacque, Pro-Nuncio.

Sudan: Khartoum, Nunciature; Erwin Josef Ender, Pro-Nuncio (also Apostolic Delegate to Somalia).

Swaziland: Nunciature; Ambrose De Paoli (also apostolic delegate to southern Africa).

Sweden: Nunciature; Giovanni Ceirano* (resides in Denmark).

Switzerland: Bern, Nunciature; Karl-Josef Rauber (also nuncio to Liechtenstein).

Syria (Syrian Arab Republic): Damascus, Nunciature; Pier Giacomo De Nicola.

Tanzania: Dar-es-Salaam, Nunciature; Agostino Marchetto, Pro-Nuncio.

Thailand: Bangkok, Nunciature; Luigi Bressan, Pro-Nuncio (also Pro-Nuncio to Singapore and Apostolic Delegate to Laos, Malaysia and Brunei, Myanmar).

Togo: Lome, Nunciature; Andre Dupuy (resides in Accra, Ghana).

Trinidad and Tobago: Port of Spain, Trinidad, Nunciature; Eugenio Sbarbaro, Pro-Nuncio (also Pro-Nuncio to Antigua and Barbuda, Bahamas, Barbados, Belize, Dominica, Grenada, Jamaica, Saint Lucia, Saint Vincent and the Grenadines and Apostolic Delegate to Antilles).

Tunisia: Tunis, Nunciature; Edmond Farhat, Pro-Nuncio (resides in Algiers, Algeria).

Turkey: Ankara, Nunciature; Sergio Sebastiani, Pro-Nuncio.

Ukraine: Kiev, Nunciature; Antonio Franco*.

Uganda: Kampala, Nunciature; Luiz Robles Diaz, Pro-Nuncio.

United States of America: Washington, D.C., Nunciature; Agostino Cacciavillan, Pro-Nuncio.

Uruguay: Montevideo, Nunciature; Francesco De Nittis.

Uzbekistan: Nunciature. Diplomatic relations established Oct. 17, 1992.

Venezuela: Caracas, Nunciature; Oriano Quilici.

Vietnam and Cambodia: Apostolic Delegation.

Yugoslavia: Belgrade, Nunciature; Gabriel Montalvo, pro-nuncio.

Zaire: Kinshasa-Gombe, Nunciature; Faustino Sainz Muñoz*.

Zambia: Lusaka, Nunciature; Giuseppe Leanza, Pro-Nuncio (also Pro-Nuncio to Malawi).

Zimbabwe: Harare, Nunciature; . . . . , Pro-Nuncio (is also Apostolic Delegate to Mozambique).

European Community: Brussels, Belgium, Nunciature; Giovanni Moretti, Nuncio.

Pro-Nuncio to U.S.

The representative of the Pope to the Church in the United States is Archbishop Agostino Cacciavillan. Archbishop Cacciavillan was born Aug. 14, 1926, in Novale, Italy. Ordained to the priesthood June 26, 1949, he entered the Vatican diplomatic service in 1959. He was ordained archbishop (titular see of Amiternum) Feb. 28, 1976, and served as pro-nuncio to Kenya and apostolic delegate to the Seychel-

les (1976-81) and pro-nuncio to India and Nepal (1981-90). He was appointed pro-nuncio to the United States and permanent observer to the Organization of American States, June 13, 1990. He succeeded Archbishop Pio Laghi who served as first pro-nuncio from 1984-90 (see Index, U.S.-Vatican Relations).

The U.S. Apostolic Nunciature is located at 3339 Massachusetts Ave. N.W., Washington, D.C. 20008. From 1893 to 1984, papal representatives to the Church in the U.S. were apostolic delegates (all archbishops): Francesco Satolli (1893-96), Sebastiano Martinelli, O.S.A. (1896-1902), Diomede Falconio, O.F.M. (1902-11), Giovanni Bonzano (1911-22), Pietro Fumasoni Biondi (1922-33), Amleto Cicognani (1933-58), Egidio Vagnozzi (1958-67), Luigi Raimondi (1967-73), Jean Jadot (1973-80), Pio Laghi (apostolic delegate, 1980-84; first pro-nuncio, 1984-90).

DIPLOMATS AT VATICAN

(Sources: *Annuario Pontificio, L'Osservatore Romano, Acta Apostolicae Sedis*).

Listed below are countries maintaining diplomatic relations with the Vatican, dates of establishment (in some cases) and names of Ambassadors (as of July 31, 1993). Leaders (. . . . .) indicate the post was vacant.

The dean of the diplomatic corps at the Vatican is Ambassador Joseph Amichia, representative of Côte d'Ivoire (Ivory Coast) from 1971. He became dean in 1983.

Albania (1991): Willy Gjon Kamsi.

Algeria (1972): . . . . .

Antigua and Barbuda (1986): . . . . .

Argentina (1992): Francisco Eduardo Trusso.

Armenia (1992): . . . . .

Australia (1973): Terence Barry McCarthy.

Austria: Georg Hohenberg.

Azerbaijan (1992): . . . . .

Bahamas (1979): . . . . .

Bangladesh (1972): Mufleh R. Osmany.

Barbados (1979): . . . . .

Belarus (1992): . . . . .

Belgium (1835): Henri Beyens.

Belize (1983): Robert Anthony Leslie.

Benin (formerly Dahomey) (1971): Edmond Cakpo-Tozo.

Bolivia: Daniel Cabezas Gomez.

Bosnia-Herzegovina (1992): . . . . .

Brazil: Gilberto Coutinho Paranhos Velloso.

Bulgaria (1990): Kiril Kirilov Maritchkov.

Burkina Faso (1973): . . . . .

Burundi (1963): . . . . .

Cameroon (1966): Jean Melaga.

Canada (1969): Theodore Jean Arcand.

Cape Verde (1976): Alfredo Goncalves Teixeira.

Central African Republic (1975): . . . . .

Chad (1988): . . . . .

Chile: Sergio Ossa Pretot.

China, Republic of (Taiwan) (1966): Edward Tsu-Yu Wu.

Colombia: Hernando Duran Dussan.

Congo (1977): Jean-Marie Ewengue.

Costa Rica: Manuel Antonio Hernandez Gutierrez.

Côte d'Ivoire (Ivory Coast) (1971): Joseph Amichia.

Croatia (1992): Ive Livljanic.
Cuba: Hermes Herrera Hernandez.
Cyprus (1973): Frixos Colotas.
Czech Republic (1929-50, reestablished, 1990, with Czech and Slovak Federative Republic; reaffirmed, 1993): Frantisek X. Halas.
Denmark (1982): Alf Cornelius Jonsson.
Dominica (1981): . . . . .
Dominican Republic: Ramon Arturo Caceres Rodriguez.
Ecuador: Galo Alberto Leoro Franco.
Egypt (1966): Ismail Azmy El Kattan.
El Salvador: Roberto Jose Siman Jacir.
Equatorial Guinea (1981): . . . . .
Estonia (1991): . . . . .
Ethiopia (1969): Iyassu Mengesha.
Fiji (1978): Epeli Nailaitikau.
Finland (1966): Henri Söderholm.
France: Rene Ala.
Gabon (1967): Jean-Claude Labouba.
Gambia, The (1978): Mohammadou N. Bobb.
Georgia (1992): . . . . .
Germany: Hans Joachim Hallier.
Ghana (1976): Mrs. Therese Striggner Scott.
Great Britain (1982): Andrew Eustace Palmer.
Greece (1980): Georges Christoyannis.
Grenada (1979): . . . . .
Guatemala: Mario Alfonso de la Cerda Bustamente.
Guinea (1986): Jean Delacroix Camara.
Guinea-Bissau (1986): . . . . .
Haiti: . . . . .
Honduras: Alejandro Emilio Valladares Lanza.
Hungary (1990): Sandor Keresztes.
Iceland (1976): Niels P. Sigurdsson.
India: Madhaw Keshav Mangalmurti.
Indonesia (1965): Achid Sjarif Achjadi.
Iran (1966): Mohammad Masjed Jame'i.
Iraq (1966): Wissam Chawkat Al-Zahawi.
Ireland: Gearoid P. O'Broin.
Italy: Giuseppe Baldocci.
Ivory Coast: See Côte d'Ivoire.
Jamaica (1979): Peter Carlisle Black.
Japan (1966): Masami Tanida.
Kazakhstan (1992): . . . . .
Kenya (1965): . . . . .
Korea (1966): Noh Young Park.
Kuwait (1969): Tarek Razzouqi.
Kyrgyzstan (1992): . . . . .
Latvia (1991): . . . . .
Lebanon (1966): Antoine Jemha.
Lesotho (1967): Reginald Mokheseng Tekateka.
Liberia (1966): . . . . .
Liechtenstein (1985): Nikolaus de Liechtenstein.
Lithuania: Kazys Lozoraitis.
Luxembourg (1955): Jean Wagner.
Madagascar (1967): Samuel Lahady..
Malawi (1966): Ronald Norman Levi Nkomba.
Mali (1979): . . , . .
Malta (1965): Alexander Cachia Zammit.
Mauritius: Bobooran Mahadoo.
Mexico (personal representative, 1990; diplomatic relations, 1992): Enrique Olivares Santana.
Moldava (1992): . . . . .
Monaco: Cesar Charles Solamito.

Mongolia (1992): . . . . .
Morocco: . . . . .
Nauru (1992): . . . . .
Nepal (1983): Gopal Prased Sharma.
Netherlands (1967): Roland Hugo van Limburg Stirum.
New Zealand (1973): Christopher David Beeby.
Nicaragua: Francisco José Fiallos Navarro.
Niger (1971): . . . . .
Nigeria (1976): Yaro Yusuf Mamman.
Norway (1982): Roald Knoph.
Order of Malta (see Index): Christophe de Kallay.
Pakistan (1965): . . . . .
Panama: Jorge A. Fernandez.
Papua New Guinea (1977): Peter Donigi.
Paraguay: Luis Angel Casati Ferro.
Peru: Luis Solari Tudela.
Philippines (1951): Oscar S. Villadolid.
Poland (1989): Henryk Kupiszewski.
Portugal: Antonio Augusto de Medeiros.
Romania (1920; broken off, 1948; reestablished, 1990): Gheorghe Gheorghiu.
Rwanda (1964): Francois Ngarukyintwali.
Saint Lucia (1984): Desmond Arthur McNamara.
Saint Vincent and the Grenadines (1990): . . . . .
San Marino (1986): Giovanni Galassi.
Sao Tome and Principe (1984): . . . . .
Senegal (1966): Andre J. Coulbary.
Seychelles (1984): . . . . .
Singapore (1981): . . . . .
Slovak Republic (1993; when it became independent republic): . . . . .
Slovenia (1992): Stefano Falez.
Solomon Islands (1984): . . . . .
Spain: Pedro Lopez Aguirrenbengoa.
Sri Lanka (1975): Warnasena Resaputran.
Sudan (1972): Awad El Karim Fadlalla Ali.
Swaziland (1992): . . . . .
Sweden (1982): Tom Tscherning.
Switzerland (1992): Jeno C.A. Staehlin, Ambassador with special mission to Holy See.
Syria (Arab Republic) (1966): Hunain Hatem.
Tanzania (1968): James L. Kateka.
Thailand (1969): Sinthu Sorasongkram.
Togo (1981): . . . . .
Trinidad and Tobago (1978): Lingsten Lloyd Cumberbatch.
Tunisia (1972): Hamed El Abed.
Turkey (1966): Omer Engin Lutem.
Uganda (1966): Mrs. Freda Lule Blick.
Ukraine (1992): . . . . .
United States (1984): Raymond L. Flynn.
Uruguay: Jorge Silva Cencio.
Uzbekistan (1992): . . . . .
Venezuela: Edelberto Moreno Peña.
Yugoslavia: . . . . .
Zaire (1963): Atembina-te-Bombo.
Zambia (1965): Edward M.Lubinda.
Zimbabwe (1980): Kotsho Lloyd Dube.

Personal Representatives

Russia (Federation of) (1989): Jurij Evghenievic Karlow.
United Nations (Center of Information of UN at the Holy See): Vincent Piola, Director.

U.S. — VATICAN RELATIONS

The United States and the Vatican announced Jan. 10, 1984, the establishment of full diplomatic relations, thus ending a gap of 117 years in their relations. The announcement followed action by the Congress in November, 1983, to end a prohibition on diplomatic relations enacted in 1867.

William A. Wilson, President Reagan's personal representative to the Vatican from 1981, was confirmed as the U.S. ambassador by the Senate, Mar. 7, 1984. He presented his credentials to Pope John Paul II, Apr. 9, 1984, and served until May 1986, when he resigned. He was succeeded by Frank Shakespeare, 1986-89, and Thomas P. Melady, 1989-93. Raymond L. Flynn, Mayor of Boston, was appointed by President Bill Clinton and confirmed by the Senate in July, 1993.

Archbishop Pio Laghi, apostolic delegate to the U.S. since 1980, was named first pro-nuncio by the Pope on Mar. 26, 1984. He served until 1990, when he was named prefect of the Congregation for Catholic Education. Archbishop Agostino Cacciavillan was appointed pro-nuncio June 13, 1990.

Nature of Relations

The nature of relations was described in nearly identical statements by John Hughes, a State Department spokesman, and the Vatican.

Hughes said: "The United States of America and the Holy See, in the desire to further promote the existing mutual friendly relations, have decided by common agreement to establish diplomatic relations between them at the level of embassy on the part of the United States of America, and nunciature on the part of the Holy See, as of today, Jan. 10, 1984."

The Vatican statement said: "The Holy See and the United States of America, desiring to develop the mutual friendly relations already existing, have decided by common accord to establish diplomatic relations at the level of apostolic nunciature on the side of the Holy See and of embassy on the side of the United States beginning today, Jan. 10, 1984."

The establishment of relations was criticized as a violation of the separation-of-church-and-state principle by spokesmen for the National Council of Churches, the National Association of Evangelicals, the Baptist Joint Committee on Public Affairs, Seventh Day Adventists, Americans United for Separation of Church and State, and the American Jewish Congress.

Legal Challenge Dismissed

U.S. District Judge John P. Fullam, ruling May 7, 1985, in Philadelphia, dismissed a legal challenge to U.S.-Vatican relations brought by Americans United for Separation of Church and State. He stated that Americans United and its allies in the challenge lacked legal standing to sue, and that the courts did not have jurisdiction to intervene in foreign policy decisions of the executive branch of the U.S. government. Parties to the suit brought by Americans United were the National Association of Laity, the National Coalition of American Nuns and several Protestant church organizations.

Bishop James W. Malone, president of the U.S. Catholic Conference, said in a statement: "This matter has been discussed at length for many years. It is not a religious issue but a public policy question which, happily, has now been settled in this context."

Russell Shaw, a conference spokesman, said the decision to send an ambassador to the Vatican was not a church-state issue and "confers no special privilege or status on the Church."

Earlier Relations

Official relations for trade and diplomatic purposes were maintained by the United States and the Papal States while the latter had the character of and acted like other sovereign powers in the international community.

Consular relations developed in the wake of an announcement, made by the papal nuncio in Paris to the American mission there Dec. 15, 1784, that the Papal States had agreed to open several Mediterranean ports to U.S. shipping.

U.S. consular representation in the Papal States began with the appointment of John B. Sartori, a native of Rome, in June, 1797. Sartori's successors as consuls were: Felix Cicognani, also a Roman, and Americans George W. Greene, Nicholas Browne, William C. Sanders, Daniel LeRoy, Horatio V. Glentworth, W.J. Stillman, Edwin C. Cushman, David M. Armstrong.

Consular officials of the Papal States who served in the U.S. were: Count Ferdinand Lucchesi, 1826 to 1829, who resided in Washington; John B. Sartori, 1829 to 1841, who resided in Trenton, N.J.; Daniel J. Desmond, 1841 to 1850, who resided in Philadelphia; Louis B. Binsse, 1850 to 1895, who resided in New York.

U.S. recognition of the consul of the Papal States did not cease when the states were absorbed into the Kingdom of Italy in 1871, despite pressure from Baron Blanc, the Italian minister. Binsse held the title until his death Mar. 28, 1895. No one was appointed to succeed him.

Diplomatic Relations

The U.S. Senate approved a recommendation, made by President James K. Polk in December, 1847, for the establishment of a diplomatic post in the Papal States. Jacob L. Martin, the first charge d'affaires, arrived in Rome Aug. 2, 1848, and presented his credentials to Pius IX Aug. 19. Martin, who died within a month, was succeeded by Lewis Cass, Jr. Cass became minister resident in 1854 and served in that capacity until his retirement in 1858.

John P. Stockton, who later became a U.S. Senator from New Jersey, was minister resident from 1858 to 1861. Rufus King was named to succeed him but, instead, accepted a commission as a brigadier general in the Army. Alexander W. Randall of Wisconsin took the appointment. He was succeeded in August, 1862, by Richard M. Blatchford who served until the following year. King was again nominated minister resident and served in that capacity until 1867 when the ministry was ended because of objections from some quarters in the U.S. and failure to appropriate funds for its continuation. J. C. Hooker, a secretary, remained in the Papal States until the end of March, 1868, closing the ministry and performing functions of courtesy.

Personal Envoys

Myron C. Taylor was appointed by President Franklin D. Roosevelt in 1939 to serve as his personal representative to Pope Pius XII and continued serving in that capacity during the presidency of Harry S. Truman until 1951. Henry Cabot Lodge was named to the post by President Richard M. Nixon in 1970, served also during the presidency of Gerald Ford, and represented President Carter at the canonization of St. John Neumann in 1977.

Miami attorney David Walters served as the personal envoy of President Jimmy Carter to the Pope from July, 1977, until his resignation Aug. 16, 1978. He was succeeded by Robert F. Wagner who served from October, 1978, to the end of the Carter presidency in January, 1981. William A. Wilson, appointed by President Ronald Reagan in February, 1981, served as his personal envoy until 1984 when he was named ambassador to the Vatican.

None of the personal envoys had diplomatic status. President Harry S. Truman nominated Gen. Mark Clark to be ambassador to the Vatican in 1951, but withdrew the nomination at Clark's request because of controversy over the appointment.

None of Truman's three immediate successors — Dwight D. Eisenhower, John F. Kennedy and Lyndon B. Johnson — had a personal representative to the Pope.

VATICAN CITY

The State of Vatican City (Stato della Citta del Vaticano) is the territorial seat of the papacy. The smallest sovereign state in the world, it is situated within the city of Rome, embraces an area of 108.7 acres, and includes within its limits the Vatican Palace, museums, art galleries, gardens, libraries, radio station, post office, bank, astronomical observatory, offices, apartments, service facilities, St. Peter's Basilica, and neighboring buildings between the Basilica and Viale Vaticano. The extraterritorial rights of Vatican City extend to more than 10 buildings in Rome, including the major basilicas and office buildings of various congregations of the Roman Curia, and to the papal villas at Castel Gandolfo 15 miles southeast of the City of Rome. Castel Gandolfo is the summer residence of the Holy Father.

The government of Vatican City is in the hands of the reigning pope, who has full executive, legislative and judicial power. The administration of affairs, however, is handled by the Pontifical Commission for the State of Vatican City. The legal system is based on Canon Law; in cases where this code does not obtain, the laws of the City of Rome apply. The City is an absolutely neutral state and enjoys all the rights and privileges of a sovereign power. The Secretariat of State (Papal Secretariat) maintains diplomatic relations with other nations. The citizens of Vatican City, and they alone, owe allegiance to the pope as a temporal head of state.

Cardinals of the Roman Curia residing outside Vatican City enjoy the privileges of extraterritoriality.

The normal population is approximately 1,000. While the greater percentage is made up of priests and religious, there are several hundred lay persons living in Vatican City. They are housed in their own apartments in the City and are engaged in secretarial, domestic, trade and service occupations. About 3,400 lay persons are employed by the Vatican.

Services of honor and order are performed by the Swiss Guards, who have been charged with responsibility for the personal safety of popes since 1506. Additional police and ceremonial functions are under the supervision of a special office. These functions were formerly handled by the Papal Gendarmes, the Palatine Guard of Honor, and the Guard of Honor of the Pope (Pontifical Noble Guard) which Pope Paul VI disbanded Sept. 14, 1970.

The **Basilica of St. Peter,** built between 1506 and 1626, is the largest church in Christendom (with the exception of the Basilica of Our Lady Queen of Peace in Ivory Coast) and the site of most papal ceremonies. The pope's own patriarchal basilica, however, is **St. John Lateran,** whose origins date back to 324.

St. Ann's, staffed by Augustinian Fathers, is the parish church of Vatican City. Its pastor is appointed by the pope following the recommendation of the prior general of the Augustinians and the archpriest of the Vatican Basilica.

Pastoral care in Vatican City State, which is separate from the diocese of Rome, is entrusted to the archpriest of St. Peter's Basilica, who is also vicar general for Vatican City and the papal villas at Castel Gandolf (chirograph of Pope John Paul II, Jan. 14, 1991). Cardinal Virgilio Noe was appointed to the posts, July 1, 1991.

The **Vatican Library,** one of five in the City, has among its holdings 70,000 manuscripts, 770,000 printed books, and 7,500 incunabula. The **Vatican Secret Archives,** opened to scholars by Leo XIII in 1881, contain central church documents dating back to the time of Innocent III (1198-1216). Abp. Luigi Poggi was named pro-librarian and pro-archivist, Apr. 9, 1992.

The independent temporal power of the pope, which is limited to the confines of Vatican City and small areas outside, was for many centuries more extensive than it is now. As late as the nineteenth century, the pope ruled 16,000 square miles of Papal States across the middle of Italy, with a population of over 3,000,000. In 1870 forces of the Kingdom of Italy occupied these lands which, with the exception of the small areas surrounding the Vatican and Lateran in Rome and the Villas of Castel Gandolfo, became part of the Kingdom by the Italian law of May 13, 1871.

The **Roman Question,** occasioned by this seizure

and the voluntary confinement of the pope to the Vatican, was settled with ratification of the Lateran Agreement June 7, 1929, by the Italian government and Vatican City. The agreement recognized Catholicism as the religion of Italy and provided, among other things, a financial indemnity to the Vatican in return for the former Papal States; it became Article 7 of the Italian Constitution Mar. 26, 1947.

The Lateran Agreement was superseded by a new concordat given final approval by the Italian Chamber of Deputies Mar. 20 and formally ratified June 3, 1985.

Papal Flag

The papal flag consists of two equal vertical stripes of yellow and white, charged with the insignia of the papacy on the white stripe — a triple crown or tiara over two crossed keys, one of gold and one of silver, tied with a red cord and two tassels. The divisions of the crown represent the teaching, sanctifying and ruling offices of the pope. The keys symbolize his jurisdictional authority.

The papal flag is a national flag inasmuch as it is the standard of the Supreme Pontiff as the sovereign of the state of Vatican City. It is also universally accepted by the faithful as a symbol of the supreme spiritual authority of the Holy Father.

Vatican Radio

The declared purpose of Vatican Radio Station HVJ is "that the voice of the Supreme Pastor may be heard throughout the world by means of the ether waves, for the glory of Christ and the salvation of souls." Designed by Guglielmo Marconi, the inventor of radio, and supervised by him until his death, the station was inaugurated by Pope Pius XI in 1931. The original purpose has been extended to a wide variety of programming.

Vatican Radio operates on international wave lengths, transmits programs in 37 languages, and serves as a channel of communication between the Vatican, church officials and listeners in general in many parts of the world. The station broadcasts about 361 hours and 30 minutes a week throughout the world. The daily English-language program for North America is broadcast on 6095, 7305, 9605 kilohertz.

The staff of 415 broadcasters and technicians includes 35 Jesuits. Studios and offices are at Palazzo Pio, Piazza Pia, 3, 00193 Rome. The transmitters are situated at Santa Maria di Galeria, a short distance north of Rome.

1993 Vatican Stamps and Coins

The Vatican Philatelic and Numismatic Office scheduled the following issues of stamps and coins in 1993. (Issue dates are given where available.)

Stamps: Series of definitive stamps dedicated to the art treasures of Vatican City; issued Mar. 23, 1993, in ten values (200, 300, 350, 500, 600, 700, 850, 1,000, 2,000 and 3,000 lire), bearing different illustrations.

Series commemorating the 600th anniversary of the death of St. John Nepomucene (1393).

Series celebrating the Ascension of Our Lord; issued May 22, 1993, in three values (200, 750 and 3,000 lire).

Series commemorating the 45th International Eucharistic Congress (June 7-13, Seville, Spain); issued May 22, 1993, in four values (500, 700, 1,500 and 2,500 lire), bearing different illustrations.

Series dedicated to Europe CEPT with the theme: Contemporary Art.

Series commemorating the 450th anniversary of the death of the painter Hans Holbein the Younger.

Series on travels of Pope Paul II in 1992.

Aerogram, issued June 7, 1993, commemorating the 25th anniversary of the encyclical *Humanae Vitae.*

Series of illustrated postcards.

An extraordinary series celebrating the Jan. 9-10 prayer encounter at Assisi for peace in Europe; issued Jan 9, 1993. (The Pope directed that proceeds from the sale of this series be used for works of charity especially for the people of Bosnia-Herzegovina.)

Coins: Series for fourteenth year (1992) of the Pontificate of John Paul II; issued Feb. 26, 1993, in seven values (10, 20, 50, 100, 200, 500 and 1,000 lire).

Silver coin (500 lire) commemorating the 30th anniversary of the encyclical letter *Pacem in terris*; issued June, 1993.

Papal Audiences

General audiences are scheduled weekly, on Wednesday.

In Vatican City, they are held in the Audience Hall on the south side of St. Peter's Basilica or, weather permitting, in St. Peter's Square. The hall, which was opened in 1971, has a seating capacity of 6,800 and a total capacity of 12,000.

Audiences have been held during the summer at Castel Gandolfo when the pope is there on a working vacation.

General audiences last from about 60 to 90 minutes, during which the pope gives a talk and his blessing. A résumé of the talk, which is usually in Italian, is given in several languages.

Arrangements for papal audiences are handled by an office of the Prefecture of the Apostolic Household.

American visitors can obtain passes for general audiences by applying to the Bishops' Office for United States Visitors to the Vatican, Casa Santa Maria, Via dell'Umilita, 30, 00187 Rome. Private and group audiences are reserved for dignitaries of various categories and for special occasions.

Publications

Acta Apostolicae Sedis: The only "official commentary" of the Holy See, was established in 1908 for the publication of activities of the Holy See, laws, decrees and acts of congregations and tribunals of the Roman Curia. The first edition was published in January, 1909.

St. Pius X made *AAS* an official organ in 1908. Laws promulgated for the Church ordinarily take effect three months after the date of their publication in this commentary.

The publication, mostly in Latin, is printed by the Vatican Press.

The immediate predecessor of this organ was *Acta Sanctae Sedis*, founded in 1865 and given official status by the Congregation for the Propagation of the Faith in 1904.

Annuario Pontificio: The yearbook of the Holy See. It is edited by the Central Statistics Office of the Church and is printed in Italian, with some portions in other languages, by the Vatican Polyglot Press. It covers the worldwide organization of the Church, lists members of the hierarchy, and includes a wide range of statistical information.

The publication of a statistical yearbook of the Holy See dates back to 1716, when a volume called *Notizie* appeared. Publication under the present title began in 1860, was suspended in 1870, and resumed again in 1872 under the title *Catholic Hierarchy*. This volume was printed privately at first, but has been issued by the Vatican Press since 1885. The title *Annuario Pontificio* was restored in 1912, and the yearbook was called an "official publication" until 1924.

L'Osservatore Romano: The daily newspaper of the Holy See. It began publication July 1, 1861, as an independent enterprise under the ownership and direction of four Catholic laymen headed by Marcantonio Pacelli, vice minister of the interior under Pope Pius IX and a grandfather of the late Pius XII. Leo XIII bought the publication in 1890, making it the "pope's" own newspaper.

The only official material in *L'Osservatore Romano* is that which appears under the heading, "Nostre Informazioni." This includes notices of appointments by the Holy See, the texts of papal encyclicals and addresses by the Holy Father and others, various types of documents, accounts of decisions and rulings of administrative bodies, and similar items. Additional material includes news and comment on developments in the Church and the world. Italian is the language most used.

The editorial board is directed by Prof. Mario Agnes. A staff of about 15 reporters covers Rome news sources. A corps of correspondents provides foreign coverage.

A weekly roundup edition in English was inaugurated in 1968 (Rev. Robert J. Dempsey, on leave from Chicago archdiocese, is editor). Other weekly editions are printed in French (1949), Spanish (1969), Portuguese (1970) and German (1971). The Polish edition (1980) is published monthly. *L'Osservatore della Domenica* is published weekly as a supplement to the Sunday issue of the daily edition.

Vatican Press Office: The establishment of a single Vatican Press Office was announced Feb. 29, 1968, to replace service agencies formerly operated by *L'Osservatore Romano* and an office created for press coverage of the Second Vatican Council. New directives for the office were issued in 1986. Joaquin Navarro-Valls is the director.

Vatican Information Service (VIS): Established Mar. 28, 1990, within the framework but distinct from the Vatican Press Office. Furnishes information, in English and Spanish, on pastoral and magisterial activity of the Pope through use of electronic mail and fax. Available Monday through Friday throughout the year, except the month of August.

Vatican Television Center: *Centro Televisivo Vaticano* (CTV) was instituted by John Paul II Oct. 23, 1983, with the rescript, *Ex Audentia*. Dr. Emilio Rossi is president of the administrative council.

Vatican Press: The official printing plant of the Vatican. The Vatican press was conceived by Marcellus II and Pius IV but was actually founded by Sixtus V on Apr. 27, 1587, to print the Vulgate and the writings of the Fathers of the Church and other authors. A Polyglot Press was established in 1626 by the Congregation for the Propagation of the Faith to serve the needs of the Oriental Church. St. Pius X merged both presses under the title Vatican Polyglot Press. It was renamed Vatican Press July 1, 1991, by John Paul II following restructuring. The plant has facilities for the printing of a wide variety of material in about 30 languages.

Vatican Publishing House (Libreria Editrice Vaticano): Along with the Vatican Press there always existed an office to assist in the circulation of the liturgical and juridical publications of the Apostolic See, the Congregations and later the *Acta Apostolicae Sedis*. In 1926, with the expansion of publishing activities and following the promulgation of the 1917 Code, the office was made an independent entity. An administrative council and editorial commission were instituted in 1983; in 1988 *Pastor Bonus* listed it among institutes joined to the Holy See; new statutes were approved by the Secretariat of State July 1, 1991.

Activities of the Holy See: An annual documentary volume covering the activities of the pope — his daily work, general and special audiences, discourses and messages on special occasions, visits outside the Vatican, missionary and charitable endeavors, meetings with diplomats, heads of state and others — and activities of the congregations, commissions, tribunals and offices of the Roman Curia.

Statistical Yearbook of the Church: Issued by the Central Statistics Office of the Church, it contains principal data concerning the presence and work of the Church in the world. The first issue was published in 1972 under the title *Collection of Statistical Tables, 1969*. It is printed in corresponding columns of Italian and Latin. Some of the introductory material is printed in other languages.

VATICAN REPRESENTATIVES

(Sources: *Annuario Pontificio;* Catholic News Service.)

The Vatican has representatives to or is a regular member of a number of quasi-governmental and international organizations. Most Rev. Ernesto Gallina was appointed delegate to International Governmental Organizations Jan. 12, 1991.

Governmental Organizations: United Nations (Abp. Renato Raffaele Martino, permanent observer); UN Office in Geneva and Specialized Institutes (Abp. Paul Fouad Tabet, permanent observer); International Atomic Energy Agency (Abp. Donato Squicciarini, permanent representative); UN Office at Vienna and UN Organization for Industrial Development (Abp. Donato

Squicciarini, permanent observer); UN Food and Agriculture Organization (Abp. Alois Wagner, permanent observer); UN Educational, Scientific and Cultural Organization (Msgr. Lorenzo Frana, permanent observer); Council of Europe (Msgr. Celestino Migliore, special representative with function of permanent observer); Council for Cultural Cooperation of the Council of Europe (Msgr. Celestino Migliore, delegate); Organization of American States (Abp. Agostino Cacciavillan, permanent observer, with personal title of Apostolic Nuncio); International Institute for the Unification of Private Law (Prof. Pio Ciprotti, delegate); International Committee of Military Medicine and Pharmacy (Adolphe Vander Perre, delegate), World Organization of Tourism (Rev. Pietro Fanto, permanent observer).

Universal Postal Union; International Telecommunications Union; International Council on Grain; World Organization of Intellectual Property; International Union for the Protection of Industrial Property; International Organization of Telecommunication via Satellite (Intelsat); European Conference of Postal and Telecommunication Administration (CEPT); European Organization of Telecommunication via Satellite (EUTELSAT).

Non-Governmental Organizations: International Committee of Historical Sciences (Msgr. Victor Saxer); International Committee of Paleography; International Committee of the History of Art (Prof. Carlo Pietrangeli, delegate); International Committee of Anthropological and Ethnological Sciences; International Committee for the Neutrality of Medicine (Rev. Michel Riquet, S.J., permanent observer); International Center of Study for the Preservation and Restoration of Cultural Goods (Prof. Carlo Pietrangeli, permanent observer); International Council of Monuments and Sites (Prof. Carlo Pietrangeli, delegate); International Alliance on Tourism; International Astronomical Union; International Institute of Administrative Sciences; International Technical Committee for Prevention and Extinction of Fires; World Medical Association; International Archives Council.

AMERICAN CHURCH

The Church of Santa Susanna was designated as the national church for Americans in Rome by Pope Benedict XV Jan. 10, 1922, and entrusted to the Paulist Fathers who have served there continously since then except for several years during World War II.

ISRAELI-ARAB ACCORD

Israeli Foreign Minister Shimon Peres and Mahmoud Abbas, foreign policy aide for the Palestine Liberation Organization, signed Sept. 13 a Declaration of Principles on Palestinian Self-Government. The signing took place in Washington on the White House lawn before a gathering of nearly 3,000 people, including President Clinton and former Presidents Jimmy Carter and George Bush. After the signing, two principal attendants — Israeli Prime Minister Itzhak Rabin and Yasir Arafat, chairman of the Palestine Liberation Organization — sealed the agreement, as it were,with a symbolic handshake. The declaration, to be implemented over a five-year period, guarantees Palestinian assurance of the security of Israel and provides initially for Palestinian self-government in the Gaza Strip and the West Bank.

● Several days before the signing, Pope John Paul told U.S. Ambassador Raymond Flynn that developments leading to the accord were "historic." Negotiations had taken place over a period of several months in Norway, removed from the glare of publicity.

● Archbishop John R. Roach, chairman of the bishops' International Policy Committee, said the prelates "applaud the courage, the imagination and the spirit of compromise shown in negotiating this major advance toward peace in the Holy Land."

● Latin-rite Patriarch Michel Sabbah of Jerusalem said the agreement represents the birth of "a new era and a new hope" in a land torn by conflict for decades. For peace to take hold, he said, leaders on both sides must educate their people away from violence toward a "total conversion of hearts."

● Vatican Radio commented Sept. 10: "The miracle continues. . . . The enemies of yesterday, Israelis and Palestinians, are making a fundamental gesture together — ceasing to believe that their own life postulates the elimination of the other, accepting that the other exists and recognizing the reasons for it."

Eight days after the signing of the Declaration of Principles, Pope John Paul met at Castel Gandolfo with Yisrael Meir Lau, Chief Rabbi of Israel's Ashkenazi Jews. The meeting, the first between a pope and a chief rabbi since 1948, was interpreted as a sign of moral support for the Israeli-Palestinian accord and as a possible step toward the establishment of Vatican-Israeli diplomatic relations. A Vatican statement said the meeting took place at a "delicate and important time for peace in the Holy Land and the Middle East, after long and painful conflicts."

BOSNIA-HERZEGOVINA PEACE PLAN

Bishops in beleaguered Bosnia-Herzegovina said Sept. 1 that they supported efforts to restructure the republic into three ethnically-based states, but cautioned that such a move carried the risk of a new "ethnic cleansing." They saw worrisome signs that "the projected definition of the republic's boundaries could lead to a violent return of ethnic conflict and ethnic cleansing, which is contrary to divine law and human rights." In particular, they said they could "never accept" the disappearance of the Catholic Church in areas of Bosnia-Herzegovina.

DOCTRINE OF THE CATHOLIC CHURCH

Following are excerpts from the first two chapters of the "Dogmatic Constitution on the Church" promulgated by the Second Vatican Council. They describe the relation of the Catholic Church to the Kingdom of God, the nature and foundation of the Church, the People of God, the necessity of membership and participation in the Church for salvation. Additional subjects in the constitution are treated in other Almanac entries.

I. MYSTERY OF THE CHURCH

By her relationship with Christ, the Church is a kind of sacrament or sign of intimate union with God, and of the unity of all mankind (No. 1).

He (the eternal Father) planned to assemble in the holy Church all those who would believe in Christ. Already from the beginning of the world the foreshadowing of the Church took place. She was prepared for in a remarkable way throughout the history of the people of Israel and by means of the Old Covenant. Established in the present era of time, the Church was made manifest by the outpouring of the Spirit. At the end of time she will achieve her glorious fulfillment. Then . . . all just men from the time of Adam, "from Abel, the just one, to the last of the elect," will be gathered together with the Father in the universal Church (No. 2).

When the work which the Father had given the Son to do on earth (cf. Jn. 17:4) was accomplished, the Holy Spirit was sent on the day of Pentecost in order that he might forever sanctify the Church, and thus all believers would have access to the Father through Christ in the one Spirit (cf. Eph. 2:18).

The Spirit dwells in the Church and in the hearts of the faithful as in a temple (cf. 1 Cor. 3:16; 6:19). . . . The Spirit guides the Church into the fullness of truth (cf. Jn. 16:13) and gives her a unity of fellowship and service. He furnishes and directs her with various gifts, both hierarchical and charismatic, and adorns her with the fruits of His grace (cf. Eph. 4:11-12; 1 Cor. 12:4; Gal. 5:22). By the power of the Gospel he makes the Church grow, perpetually renews her, and leads her to perfect union with her Spouse (No. 4).

Foundation of the Church

The mystery of the holy Church is manifest in her very foundation, for the Lord Jesus inaugurated her by preaching the Good News, that is, the coming of God's Kingdom, which, for centuries, had been promised in the Scriptures. . . . In Christ's word, in his works, and in his presence this Kingdom reveals itself to men.

The miracles of Jesus also confirm that the Kingdom has already arrived on earth.

Before all things, however, the Kingdom is clearly visible in the very Person of Christ, Son of God and Son of Man.

When Jesus rose up again after suffering death on the cross for mankind, he manifested that he had been appointed Lord, Messiah, and Priest forever (cf. Acts 2:36; Heb. 5:6; 7:17-21), and he poured out on his disciples the Spirit promised by the Father (cf. Acts 2:33). The Church, consequently, equipped with the gifts of her Founder and faithfully guarding his precepts . . . receives the mission to proclaim and to establish among all peoples the Kingdom of Christ and of God. She becomes on earth the initial budding forth of that Kingdom. While she slowly grows, the Church strains toward the consummation of the Kingdom and, with all her strength, hopes and desires to be united in glory with her King (No. 5).

Figures of the Church

In the Old Testament the revelation of the Kingdom had often been conveyed by figures of speech. In the same way the inner nature of the Church was now to be made known to us through various images.

The Church is a sheepfold . . . a flock . . . a tract of land to be cultivated, the field of God . . . his choice vineyard . . . the true vine is Christ . . . the edifice of God . . . the house of God . . . the holy temple (whose members are) . . . living stones . . . this holy city . . . a bride . . . our Mother . . . the spotless spouse of the spotless Lamb . . . an exile (No. 6).

In the human nature which he united to himself, the Son of God redeemed man and transformed him into a new creation (cf. Gal. 6:15; 2 Cor. 5:17) by overcoming death through his own death and resurrection. By communicating his Spirit to his brothers, called together from all peoples, Christ made them mystically into his own body.

In that body, the life of Christ is poured into the believers, who, through the sacraments, are united in a hidden and real way to Christ who suffered and was glorified. Through baptism we are formed in the likeness of Christ.

Truly partaking of the body of the Lord in the breaking of the eucharistic bread, we are taken up into communion with him and with one another (No. 7).

One Body in Christ

As all the members of the human body, though they are many, form one body, so also are the faithful in Christ (cf. 1 Cor. 12:12). Also, in the building up of Christ's body there is a flourishing variety of members and functions. There is only one Spirit who . . . distributes his different gifts for the welfare of the Church (cf. 1 Cor. 12:1-11). Among these gifts stands out the grace given to the apostles. To their authority, the Spirit himself subjected even those who were endowed with charisms (cf. 1 Cor. 14).

The head of this body is Christ (No. 7).

Mystical Body of Christ

Christ, the one Mediator, established and ceaselessly sustains here on earth his holy Church, the community of faith, hope, and charity, as a visible structure. Through her he communicates truth and grace to all. But the society furnished with hierarchical agencies and the Mystical Body of Christ are not to be considered as two realities, nor are the visible assembly and the spiritual community, nor the earthly Church and the Church enriched with heavenly things. Rather they form one interlocked reality which is comprised of a divine and a human element. For this reason ... this reality is compared to the mystery of the incarnate Word. Just as the assumed nature inseparably united to the divine Word serves him as a living instrument of salvation, so, in a similar way, does the communal structure of the Church serve Christ's Spirit, who vivifies it by way of building up the body (cf. Eph. 4:16).

This is the unique Church of Christ which in the Creed we avow as one, holy, catholic, and apostolic. After his Resurrection our Savior handed her over to Peter to be shepherded (Jn. 21:17), commissioning him and the other apostles to propagate and govern her (cf. Mt. 28:18, ff.). Her he erected for all ages as "the pillar and mainstay of the truth" (1 Tm. 3:15). This Church, constituted and organized in the world as a society, subsists in the Catholic Church, which is governed by the successor of Peter and by the bishops in union with that successor, although many elements of sanctification and of truth can be found outside of her visible structure. These elements, however, as gifts properly belonging to the Church of Christ, possess an inner dynamism toward Catholic unity.

The Church, embracing sinners in her bosom, is at the same time holy and always in need of being purified, and incessantly pursues the path of penance and renewal.

The Church, "like a pilgrim in a foreign land, presses forward ..." announcing the cross and death of the Lord until he comes (cf. 1 Cor. 11:26) (No. 8).

II. THE PEOPLE OF GOD

At all times and among every people, God has given welcome to whosoever fears him and does what is right (cf. Acts 10:35). It has pleased God, however, to make men holy and save them not merely as individuals without any mutual bonds, but by making them into a single people, a people which acknowledges him in truth and serves him in holiness. He therefore chose the race of Israel as a people unto himself. With it he set up a covenant. Step by step he taught this people by manifesting in its history both himself and the decree of his will, and by making it holy unto himself. All these things, however, were done by way of preparation and as a figure of that new and perfect covenant which was to be ratified in Christ.

Christ instituted this New Covenant, that is to say, the New Testament, in his blood (cf. 1 Cor. 11:25), by calling together a people made up of Jew and Gentile, making them one, not according to the flesh but in the Spirit.

This was to be the new People of God ... reborn ... through the Word of the living God (cf. 1 Pt. 1:23) ... from water and the Holy Spirit (cf. Jn. 3:5-6) ... "a chosen race, a royal priesthood, a holy nation, a purchased people. ... You who in times past were not a people, but are now the People of God" (1 Pt. 2:9-10).

That messianic people has for its head Christ. ... Its law is the new commandment to love as Christ loved us (cf. Jn. 13:34). Its goal is the Kingdom of God, which has been begun by God himself on earth, and which is to be further extended until it is brought to perfection by him at the end of time.

This messianic people, although it does not actually include all men, and may more than once look like a small flock, is nonetheless a lasting and sure seed of unity, hope, and salvation for the whole human race. Established by Christ as a fellowship of life, charity, and truth, it is also used by him as an instrument for the redemption of all, and is sent forth into the whole world as the light of the world and the salt of the earth (cf. Mt. 5:13-16).

Israel according to the flesh ... was already called the Church of God (Neh. 13:1; cf. Nm. 20:4; Dt. 23:1, ff.). Likewise the new Israel ... is also called the Church of Christ (cf. Mt. 16:18). For he has bought it for himself with his blood (cf. Acts 20:28), has filled it with his Spirit, and provided it with those means which befit it as a visible and social unity. God has gathered together as one all those who in faith look upon Jesus as the author of salvation and the source of unity and peace, and has established them as the Church, that for each and all she may be the visible sacrament of this saving unity (No. 9).

Priesthood

The baptized, by regeneration and the anointing of the Holy Spirit, are consecrated into ... a holy priesthood.

[All members of the Church participate in the priesthood of Christ, through the common priesthood of the faithful. See Priesthood of the Laity.]

Though they differ from one another in essence and not only in degree, the common priesthood of the faithful and the ministerial or hierarchical priesthood are nonetheless interrelated. Each of them in its own special way is a participation in the one priesthood of Christ (No. 10).

It is through the sacraments and the exercise of the virtues that the sacred nature and organic structure of the priestly community is brought into operation (No. 11). (See Role of the Sacraments.)

Prophetic Office

The holy People of God shares also in Christ's prophetic office. It spreads abroad a living witness to him, especially by means of a life of faith and charity and by offering to God a sacrifice of praise. ... The body of the faithful as a whole, anointed as they are by the Holy One (cf. Jn. 2:20, 27), cannot err in matters of belief. Thanks to a supernatural sense of faith which characterizes the People as a whole, it manifests this unerring quality when, "from the bishops down to the last member of the laity," it shows universal agreement in matters of faith and morals.

God's People accepts not the word of men but the very Word of God (cf. 1 Thes. 2:13). It clings without fail to the faith once delivered to the saints (cf. Jude 3), penetrates it more deeply by accurate insights, and applies it more thoroughly to life. All this it does under the lead of a sacred teaching authority to which it loyally defers.

It is not only through the sacraments and Church ministries that the same Holy Spirit sanctifies and leads the People of God. ... He distributes special graces among the faithful of every rank. By these gifts he makes them fit and ready to undertake the various tasks or offices advantageous for the renewal and upbuilding of the Church. ... These charismatic gifts ... are to be received with thanksgiving and consolation, for they are exceedingly suitable and useful for the needs of the Church.

Judgment as to their genuineness and proper use belongs to those who preside over the Church, and to whose special competence it belongs ... to test all things and hold fast to that which is good (cf. 1 Thes. 5:12; 19-21) (No. 12).

All Are Called

All men are called to belong to the new People of God. Wherefore this People, while remaining one and unique, is to be spread throughout the whole world and must exist in all ages, so that the purpose of God's will may be fulfilled. In the beginning God made human nature one. After his children were scattered, he decreed that they should at length be united again (cf. Jn. 11:52). It was for this reason that God sent his Son ... that he might be Teacher, King, and Priest of all, the Head of the new and universal People of the sons of God. For this God finally sent his Son's Spirit as Lord and Lifegiver. He it is who, on behalf of the whole Church and each and every one of those who believe, is the principle of their coming together and remaining together in the teaching of the apostles and in fellowship, in the breaking of bread and in prayers (cf. Acts 2:42) (No. 13).

One People of God

It follows that among all the nations of earth there is but one People of God, which takes its citizens from every race, making them citizens of a Kingdom which is of a heavenly and not an earthly nature. For all the faithful scattered throughout the world are in communion with each other in the Holy Spirit. ... the Church or People of God ... foster(s) and take(s) to herself, insofar as they are good, the ability, resources and customs of each people. Taking them to herself, she purifies, strengthens, and ennobles them ... This characteristic of universality which adorns the People of God is a gift from the Lord himself. By reason of it, the Catholic Church strives energetically and constantly to bring all humanity with all its riches back to Christ its Head in the unity of his Spirit.

In virtue of this catholicity each individual part of the Church contributes through its special gifts to the good of the other parts and of the whole Church. Thus through the common sharing of gifts ... the whole and each of the parts receive increase.

All men are called to be part of this catholic unity of the People of God. ... And there belong to it or are related to it in various ways, the Catholic faithful as well as all who believe in Christ, and indeed the whole of mankind. For all men are called to salvation by the grace of God (No. 13).

The Catholic Church

This sacred Synod turns its attention first to the Catholic faithful. Basing itself upon sacred Scripture and tradition, it teaches that the Church ... is necessary for salvation. For Christ, made present to us in his Body, which is the Church, is the one Mediator

and the unique Way of salvation. In explicit terms he himself affirmed the necessity of faith and baptism (cf. Mk. 16:16; Jn. 3:5) and thereby affirmed also the necessity of the Church, for through baptism as through a door men enter the Church. Whosoever, therefore, knowing that the Catholic Church was made necessary by God through Jesus Christ, would refuse to enter her or to remain in her could not be saved.

They are fully incorporated into the society of the Church who, possessing the Spirit of Christ, accept her entire system and all the means of salvation given to her, and through union with her visible structure are joined to Christ, who rules her through the Supreme Pontiff and the bishops. This joining is effected by the bonds of professed faith, of the sacraments, of ecclesiastical government, and of communion. He is not saved, however, who, though he is part of the body of the Church, does not persevere in charity. He remains indeed in the bosom of the Church, but ... only in a "bodily" manner and not "in his heart."

Catechumens who, moved by the Holy Spirit, seek with explicit intention to be incorporated into the Church, are by that very intention joined to her. ... Mother Church already embraces them as her own (No. 14).

Other Christians, The Unbaptized

The Church recognizes that in many ways she is linked with those who, being baptized, are honored with the name of Christian, though they do not profess the faith in its entirety or do not preserve unity of communion with the successor of Peter.

We can say that in some real way they are joined with us in the Holy Spirit, for to them also he gives his gifts and graces, and is thereby operative among them with his sanctifying power (No. 15).

Finally, those who have not yet received the Gospel are related in various ways to the People of God. In the first place there is the people to whom the covenants and the promises were given and from whom Christ was born according to the flesh (cf. Rom. 9:4-5). On account of their fathers, this people remains most dear to God, for God does not repent of the gifts he makes nor of the calls he issues (cf. Rom. 11:28-29).

But the plan of salvation also includes those who acknowledge the Creator. In the first place among these are the Moslems. ... Nor is God himself far distant from those who in shadows and images seek the unknown God.

Those also can attain to everlasting salvation who through no fault of their own do not know the Gospel of Christ or his Church, yet sincerely seek God and, moved by grace, strive by their deeds to do his will as it is known to them through the dictates of conscience. Nor does divine Providence deny the help necessary for salvation to those who, without blame on their part, have not yet arrived at an explicit knowledge of God, but who strive to live a good life, thanks to his grace. Whatever goodness or truth is found among them is looked upon by the Church as a preparation for the Gospel. She regards such qualities as given by him who enlightens all men so that they may finally have life. (No. 16).

THE POPE, TEACHING AUTHORITY, COLLEGIALITY

The Roman Pontiff — the successor of St. Peter as the Vicar of Christ and head of the Church on earth — has full and supreme authority over the universal Church in matters pertaining to faith and morals (teaching authority), discipline and government (jurisdictional authority).

The primacy of the pope is real and supreme power. It is not merely a prerogative of honor — that is, of his being regarded as the first among equals. Neither does primacy imply that the pope is just the presiding officer of the collective body of bishops. The pope is the head of the Church.

Catholic belief in the primacy of the pope was stated in detail in the dogmatic constitution on the Church, *Pastor Aeternus,* approved in 1870 by the fourth session of the First Vatican Council. Some elaboration of the doctrine was made in the *Dogmatic Constitution on the Church* which was approved and promulgated by the Second Vatican Council Nov. 21, 1964. The entire body of teaching on the subject is based on Scripture and tradition and the centuries-long experience of the Church.

Infallibility

The essential points of doctrine concerning infallibility in the Church and the infallibility of the pope were stated by the Second Vatican Council in the "Dogmatic Constitution on the Church," as follows:

"This infallibility with which the divine Redeemer willed his Church to be endowed in defining a doctrine of faith and morals extends as far as extends the deposit of divine revelation, which must be religiously guarded and faithfully expounded. This is the infallibility which the Roman Pontiff, the head of the college of bishops, enjoys in virtue of his office, when, as the supreme shepherd and teacher of all the faithful who confirms his brethren in their faith (cf. Lk. 22:32), he proclaims by a definitive act some doctrine of faith or morals. Therefore his definitions, of themselves, and not from the consent of the Church, are justly styled irreformable, for they are pronounced with the assistance of the Holy Spirit, an assistance promised to him in blessed Peter. Therefore they need no approval of others, nor do they allow an appeal to any other judgment. For then the Roman Pontiff is not pronouncing judgment as a private person. Rather, as the supreme teacher of the universal Church, as one in whom the charism of the infallibility of the Church herself is individually present, he is expounding or defending a doctrine of Catholic faith.

"The infallibility promised to the Church resides also in the body of bishops when that body exercises supreme teaching authority with the successor of Peter. To the resultant definitions the assent of the Church can never be wanting, on account of the activity of that same Holy Spirit, whereby the whole flock of Christ is preserved and progresses in unity of faith.

"But when either the Roman Pontiff or the body of bishops together with him defines a judgment, they pronounce it in accord with revelation itself. All are obliged to maintain and be ruled by this revelation, which, as written or preserved by tradition, is transmitted in its entirety through the legitimate succession of bishops and especially through the care of the Roman Pontiff himself.

"Under the guiding light of the Spirit of truth, revelation is thus religiously preserved and faithfully expounded in the Church. The Roman Pontiff and the bishops, in view of their office and of the importance of the matter, strive painstakingly and by appropriate means to inquire properly into that revelation and to give apt expression to its contents. But they do not allow that there could be any new public revelation pertaining to the divine deposit of faith" (No. 25).

Authentic Teaching

The pope rarely speaks *ex cathedra* — that is, "from the chair" of St. Peter, for the purpose of making an infallible pronouncement. More often and in various ways he states authentic teaching in line with Scripture, tradition, the living experience of the Church, and the whole analogy of faith. Of such teaching, the Second Vatican Council said in its *Dogmatic Constitution on the Church* (No. 25):

"Religious submission of will and of mind must be shown in a special way to the authentic teaching authority of the Roman Pontiff, even when he is not speaking *ex cathedra.* That is, it must be shown in such a way that his supreme magisterium is acknowledged with reverence, the judgments made by him are sincerely adhered to, according to his manifest mind and will. His mind and will in the matter may be known chiefly either from the character of the documents, from his frequent repetition of the same doctrine, or from his manner of speaking."

With respect to bishops, the constitution states: "They are authentic teachers, that is, teachers endowed with the authority of Christ, who preach to the people committed to them the faith they must believe and put into practice. By the light of the Holy Spirit, they make that faith clear, bringing forth from the treasury of revelation new things and old (cf. Mt. 13:52), making faith bear fruit and vigilantly warding off any errors which threaten their flock (cf. 2 Tm. 4:1-4).

"Bishops, teaching in communion with the Roman Pontiff, are to be respected by all as witnesses to divine and Catholic truth. In matters of faith and morals, the bishops speak in the name of Christ and the faithful are to accept their teaching and adhere to it with a religious assent of soul."

Magisterium — Teaching Authority

Responsibility for teaching doctrine and judging orthodoxy belongs to the official teaching authority of the Church.

This authority is personalized in the pope, the successor of St. Peter as head of the Church, and in the bishops together and in union with the pope, as it was originally committed to Peter and to the whole college of apostles under his leadership. They are the official teachers of the Church.

Others have auxiliary relationships with the magisterium: theologians, in the study and clarification of doctrine; teachers — priests, religious, lay persons — who cooperate with the pope and bishops in spreading knowledge of religious truth; the faithful, who by their sense of faith and personal witness contribute to the development of doctrine and the establishment of its relevance to life in the Church and the world.

The magisterium, Pope Paul VI noted in an address at a general audience Jan. 11, 1967, "is a subordinate and faithful echo and secure interpreter of the divine word." It does not reveal new truths, "nor is it superior to sacred Scripture." Its competence extends to the limits of divine revelation manifested in Scripture and tradition and the living experience of the Church, with respect to matters of faith and morals and related subjects. Official teaching in these areas is infallible when it is formally defined, for belief and acceptance by all members of the Church, by the pope, acting in the capacity of supreme shepherd of the flock of Christ; also, when doctrine is proposed and taught with moral unanimity of bishops with the pope in a solemn collegial manner, as in an ecumenical council, and/or in the ordinary course of events. Even when not infallibly defined, official teaching in the areas of faith and morals is authoritative and requires religious assent.

The teachings of the magisterium have been documented in creeds, formulas of faith, decrees and enactments of ecumenical and particular councils, various kinds of doctrinal statements, encyclical letters and other teaching instruments. They have also been incorporated into the liturgy, with the result that the law of prayer is said to be a law of belief.

Collegiality

The bishops of the Church, in union with the pope, have supreme teaching and pastoral authority over the whole Church in addition to the authority of office they have for their own dioceses.

This collegial authority is exercised in a solemn manner in an ecumenical council and can be exercised in other ways as well, "provided that the head of the college calls them to collegiate action, or at least so approves or freely accepts the united action of the dispersed bishops that it is made a true collegiate act."

This doctrine is grounded on the fact that: "Just as, by the Lord's will, St. Peter and the other apostles constituted one apostolic college, so in a similar way the Roman Pontiff as the successor of Peter, and the bishops as the successors of the apostles are joined together."

Doctrine on collegiality was stated by the Second Vatican Council in the *Dogmatic Constitution on the Church* (Nos. 22 and 23).

REVELATION

Following are excerpts from the "Dogmatic Constitution on Divine Revelation" promulgated by the Second Vatican Council. They describe the nature and process of divine revelation, inspiration and interpretation of Scripture, the Old and New Testaments, and the role of Scripture in the life of the Church.

I. REVELATION ITSELF

God chose to reveal himself and to make known to us the hidden purpose of his will (cf. Eph. 1:9) by which through Christ, the Word made flesh, man has access to the Father in the Holy Spirit and comes to share in the divine nature (cf. Eph. 2:18; 2 Pt. 1:4). Through this revelation, therefore, the invisible God (cf. Col. 1:15; 1 Tm. 1:17) ... speaks to men as friends (cf. Ex. 33:11; Jn. 15:14-15) and lives among them (cf. Bar. 3:38) so that he may invite and take them into fellowship with himself. This plan of revelation is realized by deeds and words having an inner unity: the deeds wrought by God in the history of salvation manifest and confirm the teaching and realities signified by the words, while the words proclaim the deeds and clarify the mystery contained in them. By this revelation then, the deepest truth about God and the salvation of man is made clear to us in Christ, who is the Mediator and at the same time the fullness of all revelation (No. 2).

God ... from the start manifested himself to our first parents. Then after their fall his promise of redemption aroused in them the hope of being saved (cf. Gn. 3:15), and from that time on he ceaselessly kept the human race in his care, in order to give eternal life to those who perseveringly do good in search of salvation (cf. Rom. 2:6-7). ... He called Abraham in order to make of him a great nation (cf. Gn. 12:2). Through the patriarchs, and after them through Moses and the prophets, he taught this nation to acknowledge himself as the one living and true God ... and to wait for the Savior promised by him. In this manner he prepared the way for the Gospel down through the centuries (No. 3).

Revelation in Christ

Then, after speaking in many places and varied ways through the prophets, God "last of all in these days has spoken to us by his Son" (Heb. 1:1-2). ... Jesus perfected revelation by fulfilling it through his whole work of making himself present and manifesting himself: through his words and deeds, his signs and wonders, but especially through his death and glorious resurrection from the dead and final sending of the Spirit of truth. Moreover, he confirmed with divine testimony what revelation proclaimed: that God is with us to free us from the darkness of sin and death, and to raise us up to life eternal.

The Christian dispensation, therefore, as the new and definitive covenant, will never pass away, and we now await no further new public revelation before the glorious manifestation of our Lord Jesus Christ (cf. 1 Tm. 6:14; Ti. 2:13) (No. 4).

II. TRANSMISSION OF REVELATION

God has seen to it that what he had revealed for the salvation of all nations would abide perpetually in its full integrity and be handed on to all generations. Therefore Christ the Lord, in whom the full revelation of the supreme God is brought to completion (cf. 2 Cor. 1:20; 3:16; 4:6), commissioned the apostles to preach to all men that Gospel which is the source of all saving truth and moral teaching, and thus to impart to them divine gifts. This Gospel had been promised in former times through the prophets, and Christ himself fulfilled it and promulgated it with his own lips. This commission was faithfully fulfilled by the apostles who, by their oral preaching, by example, and by ordinances, handed on what they had received from ... Christ ... or what they had learned through the prompting of the Holy Spirit. The commission was fulfilled, too, by those apostles and apostolic men who under the inspiration of the same Holy Spirit committed the message of salvation to writing (No. 7).

Tradition

But in order to keep the Gospel forever whole and alive within the Church, the apostles left bishops as their successors, "handing over their own teaching role" to them. This sacred tradition, therefore, and sacred Scripture of both the Old and the New Testament are like a mirror in which the pilgrim Church on earth looks at God (No. 7).

The apostolic preaching, which is expressed in a special way in the inspired books, was to be preserved by a continuous succession of preachers until the end of time. Therefore the apostles, handing on what they themselves had received, warn the faithful to hold fast to the traditions which they have learned. ... Now what was handed on by the apostles includes everything which contributes to the holiness of life, and the increase in faith of the People of God; and so the Church, in her teaching, life, and worship, perpetuates and hands on to all generations all that she herself is, all that she believes (No. 8).

Development of Doctrine

This tradition which comes from the apostles develops in the Church with the help of the Holy Spirit. For there is a growth in the understanding of the realities and the words which have been handed down. This happens through the contemplation and study made by believers ... through the intimate understanding of spiritual things they experience, and through the preaching of those who have received through episcopal succession the sure gift of truth. For, as the centuries succeed one another, the Church constantly moves forward toward the fullness of divine truth until the words of God reach their complete fulfillment in her.

The words of the holy Fathers witness to the living presence of this tradition, whose wealth is poured into the practice and life of the believing and praying Church. Through the same tradition the Church's full canon of the sacred books is known, and the sacred writings themselves are more profoundly understood and unceasingly made active in her; ... and the Holy Spirit, through whom the living voice of the Gospel resounds in the Church, and through her, in the world, leads unto all truth those who believe and makes the word of Christ dwell abundantly in them (cf. Col. 3:16) (No. 8).

Tradition and Scripture

Hence there exist a close connection and communication between sacred tradition and sacred Scripture. For both of them, flowing from the same divine wellspring, in a certain way merge into a unity and tend toward the same end. For sacred Scripture is the word of God inasmuch as it is consigned to writing under the inspiration of the divine Spirit. To the successors of the apostles, sacred tradition hands on in its full purity God's word, which was entrusted to the apostles by Christ the Lord and the Holy Spirit. Thus, led by the light of the Spirit of truth, these successors can in their preaching preserve this word of God faithfully, explain it, and make it more widely known. Consequently, it is not from sacred Scripture alone that the Church draws her certainty about every thing which has been revealed. Therefore both sacred tradition and sacred Scripture are to be accepted and venerated with the same sense of devotion and reverence (No. 9).

Sacred tradition and sacred Scripture form one sacred deposit of the word of God, which is committed to the Church (No. 10).

Teaching Authority of Church

The task of authentically interpreting the word of God, whether written or handed on, has been entrusted exclusively to the living teaching office of the Church, whose authority is exercised in the name of Jesus Christ. This teaching office is not above the word of God, but serves it, teaching only what has been handed on ... it draws from this one deposit of faith everything which it presents for belief as divinely revealed.

It is clear, therefore, that sacred tradition, sacred Scripture, and the teaching authority of the Church ... are so linked and joined together that one cannot stand without the others, and that all together and each in its own way under the action of the one Holy Spirit contribute effectively to the salvation of souls (No. 10).

III. INSPIRATION, INTERPRETATION

Those ... revealed realities ... contained and presented in sacred Scripture have been committed to writing under the inspiration of the Holy Spirit. Holy Mother Church, relying on the belief of the apostles, holds that the books of both the Old and New Testament in their entirety, with all their parts, are sacred and canonical because, having been written under the inspiration of the Holy Spirit (cf. Jn. 20:31; 2 Tm. 3:16; 2 Pt. 1:19-21; 3:15-16) they have God as their author and have been handed on as such to the Church herself. In composing the sacred books, God chose men and, while employed by him, they made use of their powers and abilities, so that, with him acting in them and through them, they, as true authors, consigned to writing everything and only those things which he wanted (No. 11).

Inerrancy

Therefore, since everything asserted by the inspired authors or sacred writers must be held to be asserted by the Holy Spirit, it follows that the books of Scripture must be acknowledged as teaching firmly, faithfully, and without error that truth which God wanted put into the sacred writings for the sake of our salvation. Therefore "all Scripture is inspired by God and useful for teaching, for reproving, for correcting, for instruction in justice; that the man of God may be perfect, equipped for every good work" (2 Tm. 3:16-17) (No. 11).

Literary Forms

However, since God speaks in sacred Scripture through men in human fashion, the interpreter of sacred Scripture, in order to see clearly what God wanted to communicate to us, should carefully investigate what meaning the sacred writers really intended, and what God wanted to mainfest by means of their words.

The interpreter must investigate what meaning the sacred writer intended to express and actually expressed in particular circumstances as he used contemporary literary forms in accordance with the situation of his own time and culture. For the correct understanding of what the sacred author wanted to assert, due attention must be paid to the customary and characteristic styles of perceiving, speaking, and narrating which prevailed at the time of the sacred writer, and to the customs men normally followed at that period in their everyday dealings with one another (No. 12).

Analogy of Faith

No less serious attention must be given to the content and unity of the whole of Scripture, if the meaning of the sacred texts is to be correctly brought to light. The living tradition of the whole Church must be taken into account along with the harmony which exists between elements of the faith. . . . All of what has been said about the way of interpreting Scripture is subject finally to the judgment of the Church, which carries out the divine commission and ministry of guarding and interpreting the word of God (No. 12).

IV. THE OLD TESTAMENT

In carefully planning and preparing the salvation of the whole human race, the God of supreme love, by a special dispensation, chose for himself a people to whom he might entrust his promises. First he entered into a covenant with Abraham (cf. Gn. 15:18) and, through Moses, with the people of Israel (cf. Ex. 24:8). To this people which he had acquired for himself, he so manifested himself through words and deeds as the one true and living God that Israel came to know by experience the ways of God with men. . . . The plan of salvation, foretold by the sacred authors, recounted and explained by them, is found as the true word of God in the books of the Old Testament: these books, therefore, written under divine inspiration, remain permanently valuable (No. 14).

Principal Purpose

The principal purpose to which the plan of the Old Covenant was directed was to prepare for the coming both of Christ, the universal Redeemer, and of the messianic Kingdom. . . . Now the books of the Old Testament, in accordance with the state of mankind before the time of salvation established by

Christ, reveal to all men the knowledge of God and of man and the ways in which God . . . deals with men. These books . . . show us true divine pedagogy (No. 15).

The books of the Old Testament with all their parts, caught up into the proclamation of the Gospel, acquire and show forth their full meaning in the New Testament (cf. Mt. 5:17; Lk. 24:27; Rom. 16:25-26; 2 Cor. 3:14-16) and in turn shed light on it and explain it (No. 16).

V. THE NEW TESTAMENT

The word of God . . . is set forth and shows its power in a most excellent way in the writings of the New Testament. For when the fullness of time arrived (cf. Gal. 4:4), the Word was made flesh and dwelt among us in the fullness of grace and truth (cf. Jn. 12:32). . . . This mystery had not been manifested to other generations as it was now revealed to his holy apostles and prophets in the Holy Spirit (cf. Eph. 3:4-6), so that they might preach the Gospel, stir up faith in Jesus, Christ and Lord, and gather the Church together. To these realities, the writings of the New Testament stand as a perpetual and divine witness (No. 17).

The Gospels and Other Writings

The Gospels have a special preeminence . . . for they are the principal witness of the life and teaching of the incarnate Word, our Savior.

The Church has always and everywhere held and continues to hold that the four Gospels are of apostolic origin. For what the apostles preached . . . afterwards they themselves and apostolic men, under the inspiration of the divine Spirit, handed on to us in writing: the foundation of faith, namely, the fourfold Gospel, according to Matthew, Mark, Luke, and John (No. 18).

The four Gospels, . . . whose historical character the Church unhesitatingly asserts, faithfully hand on what Jesus Christ, while living among men, really did and taught for their eternal salvation until the day he was taken up into heaven (see Acts 1:1-2). Indeed, after the ascension of the Lord the apostles handed on to their hearers what he had said and done. . . . The sacred authors wrote the four Gospels, selecting some things from the many which had been handed on by word of mouth or in writing, reducing some of them to a synthesis, explicating some things in view of the situation of their churches, and preserving the form of proclamation but always in such fashion that they told us the honest truth about Jesus. For their intention in writing was that . . . we might know "the truth" concerning those matters about which we have been instructed (cf. Lk. 1:2-4) (No. 19).

Besides the four Gospels, the canon of the New Testament also contains the Epistles of St. Paul and other apostolic writings, composed under the inspiration of the Holy Spirit. In these writings . . . those matters which concern Christ the Lord are confirmed, his true teaching is more and more fully stated, the saving power of the divine work of Christ is preached, the story is told of the beginnings of the Church and her marvelous growth, and her glorious fulfillment is foretold (No. 20).

VI. SCRIPTURE IN CHURCH LIFE

The Church has always venerated the divine Scriptures just as she venerates the body of the Lord. . . . She has always regarded the Scriptures together with sacred tradition as the supreme rule of faith, and will ever do so. For, inspired by God and committed once and for all to writing, they impart the word of God himself without change, and make the voice of the Holy Spirit resound in the words of the prophets and apostles. Therefore, like the Christian religion itself, all the preaching of the Church must be nourished and ruled by sacred Scripture (No. 21).

Easy access to sacred Scripture should be provided for all the Christian faithful. That is why the Church from the very beginning accepted as her own that very ancient Greek translation of the Old Testament which is named after seventy men (the Septuagint); and she has always given a place of honor to other translations, Eastern and Latin, especially the one known as the Vulgate. But since the word of God should be available at all times, the Church with maternal concern sees to it that suitable and correct translations are made into different languages, especially from the original texts of the sacred books. And if, given the opportunity and the approval of Church authority, these translations are produced in cooperation with the separated brethren as well, all Christians will be able to use them (No. 22).

Biblical Studies, Theology

The constitution encouraged the development and progress of biblical studies "under the watchful care of the sacred teaching office of the Church."

It noted also. "Sacred theology rests on the written word of God, together with sacred tradition, as its primary and perpetual foundation," and that "the study of the sacred page is, as it were, the soul of sacred theology" (Nos. 23, 24).

THE BIBLE

The Canon of the Bible is the Church's official list of sacred writings. These works, written by men under the inspiration of the Holy Spirit, contain divine revelation and, in conjunction with the tradition and teaching authority of the Church, constitute the rule of Catholic faith. The Canon was fixed and determined by the tradition and teaching authority of the Church.

The Catholic Canon

The Old Testament Canon of 46 books is as follows.

● **The Pentateuch, the** first five books: Genesis (Gn.), Exodus (Ex.), Leviticus (Lv.), Numbers (Nm.), Deuteronomy (Dt.).

● **Historical Books:** Joshua (Jos.), Judges (Jgs.), Ruth (Ru.) 1 and 2 Samuel (Sm.), 1 and 2 Kings (Kgs.), 1 and 2 Chronicles (Chr.), Ezra (Ezr.), Nehemiah (Neh.), Tobit (Tb.), Judith (Jdt.), Esther (Est.), 1 and 2 Maccabees (Mc.).

● **Wisdom Books:** Job (Jb.), Psalms (Ps.), Proverbs (Prv.), Ecclesiastes (Eccl.), Song of Songs (Song), Wisdom (Wis.), Sirach (Sir.).

● **The Prophets:** Isaiah (Is.), Jeremiah (Jer.), Lamentations (Lam.), Baruch (Bar.), Ezechiel (Ez.), Daniel (Dn.), Hosea (Hos.), Joel (Jl.), Amos (Am.), Obadiah (Ob.), Jonah (Jon.), Micah (Mi.), Nahum (Na.), Habakkuk (Hb.), Zephaniah (Zep.), Haggai (Hg.), Zechariah (Zec.) Malachi (Mal.).

The New Testament Canon of 27 books is as follows.

● **The Gospels** of Matthew (Mt.), Mark (Mk.), Luke (Lk.), John (Jn.)

● **The Acts of the Apostles** (Acts).

● **The Pauline Letters** — Romans (Rom.), 1 and 2 Corinthians (Cor.), Galatians (Gal.), Ephesians (Eph.), Philippians (Phil.), Colossians (Col.), 1 and 2 Thessalonians (Thes.) 1 and 2 Timothy (Tm.), Titus (Ti.), Philemon (Phlm.), Hebrews (Heb.).

● **The Catholic Letters** — James (Jas.), 1 and 2 Peter (Pt.), 1, 2 and 3 John (Jn.), Jude (Jude).

● Revelation (Rv.).

Developments

The Canon of the Old Testament was firm by the fifth century despite some questioning by scholars. It was stated by a council held at Rome in 382, by African councils held in Hippo in 393 and in Carthage in 397 and 419, and by Innocent I in 405.

All of the New Testament books were generally known and most of them were acknowledged as inspired by the end of the second century. The Muratorian Fragment, dating from about 200, listed most of the books recognized as canonical in later decrees. Prior to the end of the fourth century, however, there was controversy over the inspired character of several works — the Letter to the Hebrews, James, Jude, 2 Peter, 2 and 3 John and Revelation. Controversy ended in the fourth century and these books, along with those about which there was no dispute, were enumerated in the canon stated by the councils of Hippo and Carthage and affirmed by Innocent I in 405.

The Canon of the Bible was solemnly defined by the Council of Trent in the dogmatic decree *De Canonicis Scripturis,* Apr. 8, 1546.

Hebrew and Other Canons

The Hebrew Canon of sacred writings was fixed by tradition and the consensus of rabbis, probably by about 100 A.D. by the Synod or Council of Jamnia and certainly by the end of the second or early in the third century. It consists of the following works in three categories.

● **The Law** (Torah), the five books of Moses: Genesis, Exodus, Leviticus, Numbers, Deuteronomy.

● **The Prophets:** former prophets — Joshua, Judges, 1 and 2 Samuel, 1 and 2 Kings; latter prophets — Isaiah, Jeremiah, Ezekiel, and 12 minor prophets (Hosea, Joel, Amos, Obadiah, Jonah, Micah, Nahum, Habakkuk, Zephaniah, Haggai, Zechariah, Malachi).

● **The Writings:** 1 and 2 Chronicles, Ezra, Nehemiah, Job, Psalms, Proverbs, Ecclesiastes, Song of Songs, Ruth, Esther, Daniel.

This Canon, embodying the tradition and practice

of the Palestine community, did not include a number of works contained in the Alexandrian version of sacred writings translated into Greek between 250 and 100 B.C. and in use by Greek-speaking Jews of the Dispersion (outside Palestine). The rejected works, called apocrypha and not regarded as sacred, are: Tobit, Judith, Wisdom, Sirach, Baruch, 1 and 2 Maccabees, the last six chapters of Esther and three passages of Daniel (3:24-90; 13; 14). These books have also been rejected from the Protestant Canon, although they are included in bibles under the heading, Apocrypha.

The aforementioned books are held to be inspired and sacred by the Catholic Church. In Catholic usage, they are called deuterocanonical because they were under discussion for some time before questions about their canonicity were settled. Books regarded as canonical with little or no debate were called protocanonical. The status of both categories of books is the same in the Catholic Bible.

The Protestant Canon of the Old Testament is the same as the Hebrew.

The Old Testament Canon of some separated Eastern churches differs from the Catholic Canon.

Christians are in agreement on the Canon of the New Testament.

Languages

Hebrew, Aramaic and Greek were the original languages of the Bible. Most of the Old Testament books were written in Hebrew. Portions of Daniel, Ezra, Jeremiah, Esther, and probably the books of Tobit and Judith were written in Aramaic. The Book of Wisdom, 2 Maccabees and all the books of the New Testament were written in Greek.

Manuscripts and Versions

The original writings of the inspired authors have been lost. The Bible has been transmitted through ancient copies called manuscripts and through translations or versions.

Authoritative Greek manuscripts include the Sinaitic and Vatican manuscripts of the fourth century and the Alexandrine of the fifth century A.D. The Septuagint and Vulgate translations are in a class by themselves.

The Septuagint version, a Greek translation of the Old Testament for Greek-speaking Jews, was begun about 250 and completed about 100 B.C. The work of several Jewish translators at Alexandria, it differed from the Hebrew Bible in the arrangement of books and included several, later called deuterocanonical, which were not acknowledged as sacred by the community in Palestine.

The Vulgate was a Latin version of the Old and New Testaments produced from the original languages by St. Jerome from about 383 to 404. It became the most widely used Latin text for centuries and was regarded as basic long before the Council of Trent designated it as authentic and suitable for use in public reading, controversy, preaching and teaching. Because of its authoritative character, it became the basis for many translations into other languages. A critical revision was completed by a pontifical commission in 1977.

Hebrew and Aramaic manuscripts of great antiquity and value have figured more significantly than before in recent scriptural work by Catholic scholars, especially since their use was strongly encouraged, if not mandated, in 1943 by Pius XII in the encyclical *Divino Afflante Spiritu.*

The English translation of the Bible in general use among Catholics until well into the 20th century was the *Douay-Rheims,* so called because of the places where it was prepared and published, the New Testament at Rheims in 1582 and the Old Testament at Douay in 1609. The translation was made from the Vulgate text. As revised and issued by Bishop Richard Challoner in 1749 and 1750, it became the standard Catholic English version for about 200 years.

A revision of the Challoner New Testament, made on the basis of the Vulgate text by scholars of the Catholic Biblical Association of America, was published in 1941 in the United States under the sponsorship of the Episcopal Committee of the Confraternity of Christian Doctrine.

New American Bible

A new translation of the entire Bible, the first ever made directly into English from the original languages under Catholic auspices, was projected in 1944 and completed in the fall of 1970 with publication of the *New American Bible.* The Episcopal Committee of the Confraternity of Christian Doctrine sponsored the NAB. The translators were members of the Catholic Biblical Association of America and several fellow scholars of other faiths. The typical edition was produced by St. Anthony Guild Press, Paterson, N.J.

The *Jerusalem Bible,* published by Doubleday & Co., Inc., is an English translation of a French version based on the original languages.

Biblical translations approved for liturgical use by the National Conference of Catholic Bishops are the *New American Bible,* the *Revised Standard Version-Catholic Edition,* the *Jerusalem Bible* (1968), the *Grail Psalter* (1967) and the *New Revised Standard Version* (1992).

The Protestant counterpart of the *Douay-Rheims Bible* was the *King James Bible,* called the *Authorized Version* in England. Originally published in 1611, it was in general use for more than three centuries. Its modern revisions include the *English Revised Version,* published between 1881 and 1885; the *American Revised Version,* 1901, and revisions of the New Testament (1946) and the Old Testament (1952) published in 1957 in the United States as the *Revised Standard Version.* Another revision, a translation in the language of the present day made from Greek and Hebrew sources, is the *New English Bible,* published Mar. 16, 1970. Its New Testament portion was originally published in 1961.

Biblical Federation

In November, 1966, Pope Paul VI commissioned the Secretariat for Promoting Christian Unity to start work for the widest possible distribution of the Bible and to coordinate endeavors toward the production of Catholic-Protestant Bibles in all languages.

The World Catholic Federation for the Biblical Apostolate, established in 1969, sponsors a program designed to create greater awareness among Catholics of the Bible and its use in everyday life.

The U. S. Center for the Catholic Biblical Apostolate is related to the Secretariat for Pastoral Research and Practices, National Conference of Catholic Bishops, 3211 Fourth St. N.E., Washington, DC 20017.

APOCRYPHA

In Catholic usage, Apocrypha are books which have some resemblance to the canonical books in subject matter and title but which have not been recognized as canonical by the Church. They are characterized by a false claim to divine authority; extravagant accounts of events and miracles alleged to be supplemental revelation; material favoring heresy (especially in "New Testament" apocrypha); minimal, if any, historical value. Among examples of this type of literature itemized by J. McKenzie, S.J., in *Dictionary of the Bible* are: *the Books of Adam and Eve, Martyrdom of Isaiah, Testament of the Patriarchs, Assumption of Moses, Sibylline Oracles; Gospel of James, Gospel of Thomas, Arabic Gospel of the Infancy, History of Joseph the Carpenter; Acts of John, Acts of Paul, Acts of Peter, Acts of Andrew,* and numerous epistles.

Books of this type are called pseudepigrapha by Protestants.

In Protestant usage, some books of the Catholic Bible (deuterocanonical) are called apocrypha because their inspired character is rejected.

DEAD SEA SCROLLS

The Qumran Scrolls, popularly called the Dead Sea Scrolls, are a collection of manuscripts, all but one of them in Hebrew, found since 1947 in caves in the Desert of Juda west of the Dead Sea.

Among the findings were a complete text of Isaiah dating from the second century, B.C., more or less extensive fragments of other Old Testament texts (including the deuterocanonical Tobit), and a commentary on Habakkuk. Until the discovery of these materials, the oldest known Hebrew manuscripts were from the 10th century, A.D.

Also found were messianic and apocalyptic texts, and other writings describing the beliefs and practices of the Essenes, a rigoristic Jewish sect.

The scrolls, dating from about the first century before and after Christ, are important sources of information about Hebrew literature, Jewish history during the period between the Old and New Testaments, and the history of Old Testament texts. They established the fact that the Hebrew text of the Old Testament was fixed before the beginning of the Christian era and have had definite effects in recent critical studies and translations of the Old Testament. Together with other scrolls found at Masada, they are still the subject of intensive study.

BOOKS OF THE BIBLE

OLD TESTAMENT
(Dates are before Christ.)

Pentateuch

The Pentateuch is the collective title of the first five books of the Bible. Substantially, they identify the Israelites as Yahweh's Chosen People, cover their history from Egypt to the threshold of the Promised Land, contain the Mosaic Law and Covenant, and disclose the promise of salvation to come. Principal themes concern the divine promise of salvation, Yahweh's fidelity and the Covenant. Work on the composition of the Pentateuch was completed in the sixth century.

Genesis: The book of origins, according to its title in the Septuagint. In two parts, covers: religious prehistory, including accounts of the origin of the world and man, the original state of innocence and the fall, the promise of salvation, patriarchs before and after the Deluge, the Tower of Babel narrative, genealogies (first 11 chapters); the Covenant with Abraham and patriarchal history from Abraham to Joseph (balance of the 50 chapters). Significant are the themes of Yahweh's universal sovereignty and mercy.

Exodus: Named with the Greek word for departure, is a religious epic which describes the oppression of the 12 tribes in Egypt and their departure, liberation or passover therefrom under the leadership of Moses; Yahweh's establishment of the Covenant with them, making them his Chosen People, through the mediation of Moses at Mt. Sinai; instructions concerning the tabernacle, the sanctuary and Ark of the Covenant; the institution of the priesthood. The book is significant because of its theology of liberation and redemption. In Christian interpretation, the Exodus is a figure of baptism.

Leviticus: Mainly legislative in theme and purpose, contains laws regarding sacrifices, ceremonies of ordination and the priesthood of Aaron, legal purity, the holiness code, atonement, the redemption of offerings and other subjects. Summarily, Levitical laws provided directives for all aspects of religious observance and for the manner in which the Israelites were to conduct themselves with respect to Yahweh and each other. Leviticus was the liturgical handbook of the priesthood.

Numbers: Taking its name from censuses recounted at the beginning and near the end, is a continuation of Exodus. It combines narrative of the Israelites' desert pilgrimage from Sinai to the border of Canaan with laws related to and expansive of those in Leviticus.

Deuteronomy: The concluding book of the Pentateuch, recapitulates, in the form of a testament of Moses, the Law and much of the desert history of the Israelites; enjoins fidelity to the Law as the key to good or bad fortune for the people; gives an account of the commissioning of Joshua as the successor of Moses. Notable themes concern the election of Israel by Yahweh, observance of the Law, prohibitions against the worship of foreign gods, worship of and confidence in Yahweh, the power of Yahweh in nature. The Deuteronomic Code or motif, embodying all of these elements, was the norm for interpreting Israelite history.

Joshua, Judges, Ruth

Joshua: Records the fulfillment of Yahweh's promise to the Israelites in their conquest, occupation and division of Canaan under the leadership of Joshua. It also contains an account of the return of Transjordanian Israelites and of a renewal of the Covenant. It was redacted in final form probably in the sixth century or later.

Judges: Records the actions of charismatic leaders, called judges, of the tribes of Israel between the death of Joshua and the time of Samuel, and a crisis of idolatry among the people. The basic themes are sin and punishment, repentance and deliverance; its purpose was in line with the Deuteronomic motif, that the fortunes of the Israelites were related to their observance or non-observance of the Law and the Covenant. It was redacted in final form probably in the sixth century.

Ruth: Named for the Gentile (Moabite) woman who, through marriage with Boaz, became an Israelite and an ancestress of David (her son, Obed, became his grandfather). Themes are filial piety, faith and trust in Yahweh, the universality of messianic salvation. Dates ranging from c. 950 to the seventh century have been assigned to the origin of the book, whose author is unknown.

Historical Books

These books, while they contain a great deal of factual material, are unique in their preoccupation with presenting and interpreting it, in the Deuteronomic manner, in primary relation to the Covenant on which the nation of Israel was founded and in accordance with which community and personal life were judged.

The books are: Samuel 1 and 2, from the end of Judges (c. 1020) to the end of David's reign (c. 961); Kings 1 and 2, from the last days of David to the start of the Babylonian Exile and the destruction of the Temple (587); Chronicles 1 and 2, from the reign of Saul (c. 1020-1000) to the return of the people from the Exile (538); Ezra and Nehemiah, covering the reorganization of the Jewish community after the Exile (458-397); Maccabees 1 and 2, recounting the struggle against attempted suppression of Judaism (168-142).

Three of the books listed below — Tobit, Judith and Esther — are categorized as religious novels.

Samuel 1 and 2: A single work in concept and contents, containing episodic history of the last two Judges, Eli and Samuel, the establishment and rule of the monarchy under Saul and David, and the political consequences of David's rule. The royal messianic dynasty of David was the subject of Nathan's oracle in 2 Sm. 7. The books were edited in final form probably late in the seventh century or during the Exile.

Kings 1 and 2: Cover the last days of David and the career of Solomon, including the building of the Temple and the history of the kingdom during his reign; stories of the prophets Elijah and Elisha; the history of the divided kingdom to the fall of Israel in the North (721) and the fall of Judah in the South (587), the destruction of Jerusalem and the Temple. They reflect the Deuteronomic motif in attributing the downfall of the people to corruption of belief

and practice in public and private life. They were completed probably in the sixth century.

Chronicles 1 and 2: A collection of historical traditions interpreted in such a way as to present an ideal picture of one people governed by divine law and united in one Temple worship of the one true God. Contents include genealogical tables from Adam to David, the careers of David and Solomon, coverage of the kingdom of Judah to the Exile, and the decree of Cyrus permitting the return of the people and rebuilding of Jerusalem. Both are related to and were written about 400 by the same author, the Chronicler, who composed Ezra and Nehemiah.

Ezra and Nehemiah: A running account of the return of the people to their homeland after the Exile and of practical efforts, under the leadership of Ezra and Nehemiah, to restore and reorganize the religious and political community on the basis of Israelite traditions, divine worship and observance of the Law. Events of great significance were the building of the second Temple, the building of a wall around Jerusalem and the proclamation of the Law by Ezra. This restored community was the start of Judaism. Both are related to and were written about 400 by the same author, the Chronicler, who composed Chronicles 1 and 2.

Tobit: Written in the literary form of a novel and having greater resemblance to wisdom than to historical literature, narrates the personal history of Tobit, a devout and charitable Jew in exile, and persons connected with him, viz., his son Tobiah, his kinsman Raguel and Raguel's daughter Sarah. Its purpose was to teach people how to be good Jews. One of its principal themes is patience under trial, with trust in divine Providence which is symbolized by the presence and action of the angel Raphael. It was written about 200.

Judith: Recounts, in the literary form of a historical novel or romance, the preservation of the Israelites from conquest and ruin through the action of Judith. The essential themes are trust in God for deliverance from danger and emphasis on observance of the Law. It was written probably during the Maccabean period.

Esther: Relates, in the literary form of a historical novel or romance, the manner in which Jews in Persia were saved from annihilation through the central role played by Esther, the Jewish wife of Ahasuerus; a fact commemorated by the Jewish feast of Purim. Like Judith, it has trust in divine Providence as its theme and indicates that God's saving will is sometimes realized by persons acting in unlikely ways. It may have been written near the end of the fourth century.

Maccabees 1 and 2: While related to some extent because of common subject matter, are quite different from each other.

The first book recounts the background and events of the 40-year (175-135) struggle for religious and political freedom led by Judas Maccabaeus and his brothers against the Hellenist Seleucid kings and some Hellenophiles among the Jews. Victory was symbolized by the rededication of the Temple. Against the background of opposition between Jews and Gentiles, the author equated the survival of belief in the one true God with survival of the

Jewish people, thus identifying religion with patriotism. It was written probably near the year 100.

The second book supplements the first to some extent, covering and giving a theological interpretation to events from 180 to 162. It explains the feast of the Dedication of the Temple, a key event in the survival of Judaism which is commemorated in the feast of Hanukkah; stresses the primacy of God's action in the struggle for survival; and indicates belief in an afterlife and the resurrection of the body. It was completed probably about 124.

Wisdom Books

With the exceptions of Psalms and the Song of Songs, the titles listed under this heading are called wisdom books because their purpose was to formulate the fruits of human experience in the context of meditation on sacred Scripture and to present them as an aid toward understanding the problems of life. Hebrew wisdom literature was distinctive from pagan literature of the same type, but it had limitations; these were overcome in the New Testament, which added the dimensions of the New Covenant to those of the Old. Solomon was regarded as the archtype of the wise man.

Job: A dramatic, didactic poem consisting mainly of several dialogues between Job and his friends concerning the mystery involved in the coexistence of the just God, evil and the suffering of the just. It describes an innocent man's experience of suffering and conveys the truth that faith in and submission to God rather than complete understanding, which is impossible, make the experience bearable; also, that the justice of God cannot be defended by affirming that it is realized in this world. Of unknown authorship, it was composed between the seventh and fifth centuries.

Psalms: A collection of 150 religious songs or lyrics reflecting Israelite belief and piety dating from the time of the monarchy to the post-Exilic period, a span of well over 500 years. The psalms, which are a compendium of Old Testament theology, were used in the temple liturgy and for other occasions. They were of several types suitable for the king, hymns, lamentations, expressions of confidence and thanksgiving, prophecy, historical meditation and reflection, and the statement of wisdom. About one-half of them are attributed to David; many were composed by unknown authors.

Proverbs: The oldest book of the wisdom type in the Bible, consisting of collections of sayings attributed to Solomon and other persons regarding a wide variety of subjects including wisdom and its nature, rules of conduct, duties with respect to one's neighbor, the conduct of daily affairs. It reveals many details of Hebrew life. Its nucleus dates from the period before the Exile. The extant form of the book dates probably from the end of the fifth century.

Ecclesiastes: A treatise about many subjects whose unifying theme is the vanity of strictly human efforts and accomplishments with respect to the achievement of lasting happiness; the only things which are not vain are fear of the Lord and observance of his commandments. The pessimistic tone of the book is due to the absence of a concept of afterlife. It was written by an unknown author probably in the third century.

Song of Songs: A collection of love lyrics reflecting various themes, including the love of God for Israel and the celebration of ideal love and fidelity between man and woman. It was written by an unknown author after the Exile.

Wisdom: Deals with many subjects including the reward of justice; praise of wisdom, a gift of Yahweh proceeding from belief in him and the practice of his Law; the part played by him in the history of his people, especially in their liberation from Egypt; the folly and shame of idolatry. Its contents are taken from the whole sacred literature of the Jews and represent a distillation of its wisdom based on the law, beliefs and traditions of Israel. The last of the Old Testament books, it was written in the early part of the first century before Christ by a member of the Jewish community at Alexandria.

Sirach: Resembling Proverbs, is a collection of sayings handed on by a grandfather to his grandson. It contains a variety of moral instruction and eulogies of patriarchs and other figures in Israelite history. Its moral maxims apply to individuals, the family and community, relations with God, friendship, education, wealth, the Law, divine worship. Its theme is that true wisdom consists in the Law. (It was formerly called Ecclesiasticus, the Church Book, because of its extensive use by the Church for moral instruction.) It was written in Hebrew between 200 and 175, during a period of strong hellenistic influence, and was translated into Greek after 132.

The Prophets

These books and the prophecies they contain "express judgments of the people's moral conduct, on the basis of the Mosaic alliance between God and Israel. They teach sublime truths and lofty morals. They contain exhortations, threats, announcements of punishment, promises of deliverance. ... In the affairs of men, their prime concern is the interests of God, especially in what pertains to the Chosen People through whom the Messiah is to come; hence their denunciations of idolatry and of that externalism in worship which exclude the interior spirit of religion. They are concerned also with the universal nature of the moral law, with personal responsibility, with the person and office of the Messiah, and with the conduct of foreign nations" (*The Holy Bible,* Prophetic Books, CCD Edition, 1961; Preface). There are four major (Isaiah, Jeremiah, Ezekiel, Daniel) and 12 minor prophets (distinguished by the length of books), Lamentations and Baruch. Earlier prophets, mentioned in historical books, include Samuel, Gad, Nathan, Elijah and Elisha.

Before the Exile, prophets were the intermediaries through whom God communicated revelation to the people. Afterwards, prophecy lapsed and the written word of the Law served this purpose.

Isaiah: Named for the greatest of the prophets whose career spanned the reigns of three Hebrew kings from 742 to the beginning of the seventh century, in a period of moral breakdown in Judah and threats of invasion by foreign enemies. It is an anthology of poems and oracles credited to him and a number of followers deeply influenced by him. Of special importance are the prophecies concerning Immanuel (6 to 12), including the prophecy of the virgin birth (7:14). Chapters 40 to 55, called Deutero-Isaiah, are attributed to an anonymous poet toward the end of the Exile; this portion contains the Songs of the Servant. The concluding part of the book (56-66) contains oracles by later disciples. One of many themes in Isaiah concerned the saving mission of the remnant of Israel in the divine plan of salvation.

Jeremiah: Combines history, biography and prophecy in a setting of crisis caused by internal and external factors, viz., idolatry and general infidelity to the Law among the Israelites and external threats from the Assyrians, Egyptians and Babylonians. Jeremiah prophesied the promise of a new covenant as well as the destruction of Jerusalem and the Temple. His career began in 626 and ended some years after the beginning of the Exile. The book, the longest in the Bible, was edited in final form after the Exile.

Lamentations: A collection of five laments or elegies over the fall of Jerusalem and the fate of the people in Exile, written by an unknown eyewitness. They convey the message that Yahweh struck the people because of their sins and reflect confidence in his love and power to restore his converted people.

Baruch: Against the background of the already begun Exile, it consists of an introduction and several parts: an exile's prayer of confession and petition for forgiveness and the restoration of Israel; a poem praising wisdom and the Law of Moses; a lament in which Jerusalem, personified, bewails the fate of her people and consoles them with the hope of blessings to come; and a polemic against idolatry. Although ascribed to Baruch, Jeremiah's secretary, it was written by several authors probably in the second century.

Ezekiel: Named for the priest-prophet who prophesied in Babylon from 593 to 571, during the first phase of the Exile. To prepare his fellow early exiles for the impending fall of Jerusalem, he reproached the Israelites for past sins and predicted woes to come upon them. After the destruction of the city, the burden of his message was hope and promise of restoration. Ezekiel had great influence on the religion of Israel after the Exile.

Daniel: The protagonist is a young Jew, taken early to Babylon where he lived until about 538, who figured in a series of edifying stories which originated in Israelite tradition. The stories, whose characters are not purely legendary but rest on historical tradition, recount the trials and triumphs of Daniel and his three companions, and other episodes including those concerning Susannah, Bel, and the Dragon. The book is more apocalyptic than prophetic: it envisions Israel in glory to come and conveys the message that men of faith can resist temptation and overcome adversity. It states the prophetic themes of right conduct, divine control of men and events, and the final triumph of the kingdom. It was written by an unknown author in the 160's to give moral support to Jews

during the persecutions of the Maccabean period.

Hosea: Consists of a prophetic parallel between Hosea's marriage and Yahweh's relations with his people. As the prophet was married to a faithless wife whom he would not give up, Yahweh was bound in Covenant with an idolatrous and unjust Israel whom he would not desert but would chastise for purification. Hosea belonged to the Northern Kingdom of Israel and began his career about the middle of the eighth century. He inaugurated the tradition of describing Yahweh's relation to Israel in terms of marriage.

Joel: Is apocalyptic and eschatological regarding divine judgment, the Day of the Lord, which is symbolized by a ravaging invasion of locusts, the judgment of the nations in the Valley of Josaphat and the outpouring of the Spirit in the messianic era to come. Its message is that God will vindicate and save Israel, in view of the prayer and repentance of the people, and will punish their enemies. It was composed about 400.

Amos: Consists of an indictment against foreign enemies of Israel; a strong denunciation of the people of Israel, whose infidelity, idolatry and injustice made them subject to divine judgment and punishment; and a messianic oracle regarding Israel's restoration. Amos prophesied in the Northern Kingdom of Israel, at Bethel, in the first half of the eighth century; chronologically, he was the first of the canonical prophets.

Obadiah: A 21-verse prophecy, the shortest and one of the sternest in the Bible, against the Edomites, invaders of southern Judah and enemies of those returning from the Exile to their homeland. It was probably composed in the fifth century.

Jonah: A parable of divine mercy with the theme that Yahweh wills the salvation of all, not just a few, men who respond to his call. Its protagonist is a disobedient prophet; forced by circumstances beyond his control to preach penance among Gentiles, he is highly successful in his mission but baffled by the divine concern for those who do not belong to the Chosen People. It was written after the Exile, probably in the fifth century.

Micah: Attacks the injustice and corruption of priests, false prophets, officials and people; announces judgment and punishment to come; foretells the restoration of Israel; refers to the saving remnant of Israel. Micah was a contemporary of Isaiah.

Nahum: Concerns the destruction of Nineveh in 612 and the overthrow of the Assyrian Empire by the Babylonians.

Habakkuk: Dating from about 605-597, concerns sufferings to be inflicted by oppressors on the people of Judah because of their infidelity to the Lord. It also sounds a note of confidence in the Lord, the Savior, and declares that the just will not perish.

Zephaniah: Exercising his ministry in the second half of the seventh century, during a time of widespread idolatry, superstition and religious degradation, he prophesied impending judgment and punishment for Jerusalem and its people. He prophesied too that a holy remnant of the people (*anawim,* mentioned also by Amos) would be spared. Zephaniah was a forerunner of Jeremiah.

Haggai: One of the first prophets after the Exile, Haggai in 520 encouraged the returning exiles to reestablish their community and to complete the second Temple (dedicated in 515), for which he envisioned greater glory, in a messianic sense, than that enjoyed by the original Temple of Solomon.

Zechariah: A contemporary of Haggai, he prophesied in the same vein. A second part of the book, called Deutero-Zechariah and composed by one or more unknown authors, relates a vision of the coming of the Prince of Peace, the Messiah of the Poor.

Malachi: Written by an anonymous author, presents a picture of life in the post-Exilic community between 516 and the initiation of reforms by Ezra and Nehemiah about 432. Blame for the troubles of the community is placed mainly on priests for failure to carry out ritual worship and to instruct the people in the proper manner; other factors were religious indifference and the influence of doubters who were scandalized at the prosperity of the wicked. The vision of a universal sacrifice to be offered to Yahweh (1:11) is interpreted in Catholic theology as a prophecy of the sacrifice of the Mass. Malachi was the last of the minor prophets.

OLD TESTAMENT DATES

c. 1800 — c. 1600: Period of the patriarchs (Abraham, Isaac, Jacob).

c. 1600: Israelites in Egypt.

c. 1250: Exodus of Israelites from Egypt.

c. 1210: Entrance of Israelites into Canaan.

c. 1210 — c. 1020: Period of the Judges.

c. 1020 — c. 1000: Reign of Saul, first king.

c. 1000 — c. 961: Reign of David.

c. 961 — 922: Reign of Solomon. Temple built during his reign.

922: Division of the Kingdom into Israel (North) and Judah (South).

721: Conquest of Israel by Assyrians.

587-538: Conquest of Judah by Babylonians. Babylonian Captivity and Exile. Destruction of Jerusalem and the Temple, 587. Captivity ended with the return of exiles, following the decree of Cyrus permitting the rebuilding of Jerusalem.

515: Dedication of the Second Temple.

458-397: Restoration and reform of the Jewish religious and political community; building of the Jerusalem wall, 439. Leaders in the movement were Ezra and Nehemiah.

168-142: Period of the Maccabees; war against Syrians.

142: Independence granted to Jews by Demetrius II of Syria.

135-37: Period of the Hasmonean dynasty.

63: Beginning of Roman rule.

37-4: Period of Herod the Great.

NEW TESTAMENT BOOKS

Gospels

The term Gospel is derived from the Anglo-Saxon *god-spell* and the Greek *euangelion,* meaning good news, good tidings. In Christian use, it means the good news of salvation proclaimed by Christ and the Church, and handed on in written form in the Gospels of Matthew, Mark, Luke and John.

The initial proclamation of the coming of the kingdom of God was made by Jesus in and through his Person, teachings and actions, and especially through his Passion, death and resurrection. This proclamation became the center of Christian faith and the core of the oral Gospel tradition with which the Church spread the good news by apostolic preaching for some 30 years before it was committed to writing by the Evangelists.

Nature of the Gospels

The historical truth of the Gospels was the subject of an instruction issued by the Pontifical Commission for Biblical Studies Apr. 21, 1964.

● The sacred writers selected from the material at their disposal (the oral Gospel tradition, some written collections of sayings and deeds of Jesus, eyewitness accounts) those things which were particularly suitable to the various conditions (liturgical, catechetical, missionary) of the faithful and the aims they had in mind, and they narrated these things in such a way as to correspond with those circumstances and their aims.

● The life and teaching of Jesus were not simply reported in a biographical manner for the purpose of preserving their memory but were "preached" so as to offer the Church the basis of doctrine concerning faith and morals.

● In their works, the Evangelists presented the true sayings of Jesus and the events of his life in the light of the better understanding they had following their enlightenment by the Holy Spirit. They did not transform Christ into a "mythical" Person, nor did they distort his teaching. Passion narratives are the core of all the Gospels, covering the suffering, death and resurrection of Jesus as central events in bringing about and establishing the New Covenant. Leading up to them are accounts of the mission of John the Baptizer and the ministry of Jesus, especially in Galilee and finally in Jerusalem before the Passion. The infancy of Jesus is covered by Luke and Matthew with narratives inspired in part by appropriate Old Testament citations.

Matthew, Mark and Luke, while different in various respects, have so many similarities that they are called Synoptic; their relationships are the subject of the Synoptic Problem.

Matthew: Written probably between 80 and 100 for Jewish Christians with clear reference to Jewish background and identification of Jesus as the divine Messiah, the fulfillment of the Old Testament. Distinctive are the use of Old Testament citations regarding the Person, activity and teaching of Jesus, and the presentation of doctrine in sermons and discourses.

Mark: The first of the Gospels, dating from about 70. Written for Gentile Christians, it is noted for the realism and wealth of concrete details with which it reveals Jesus as Son of God and Savior more by his actions and miracles than by his discourses. Theologically, it is less refined than the other Gospels.

Luke: Written about 75 for Gentile Christians. It is noted for the universality of its address, the insight it provides into the Christian way of life, the place it gives to women, the manner in which it emphasizes Jesus' friendship with sinners and compassion for the suffering.

John: Edited and arranged in final form probably between 90 and 100, is the most sublime and theological of the Gospels, and is different from the Synoptics in plan and treatment. Combining accounts of signs with longer discourses and reflections, it progressively reveals the Person and mission of Jesus — as Word, Way, Truth, Life, Light — in line with the purpose, "to help you believe that Jesus is the Messiah, the Son of God, so that through this faith you may have life in his name" (Jn. 20:31). There are questions about the authorship but no doubt about the Johannine authority and tradition behind the Gospel.

Acts of the Apostles

Acts of the Apostles: Written by Luke about 75 as a supplement to his Gospel. It describes the origin and spread of Christian communities through the action of the Holy Spirit from the resurrection of Christ to the time when Paul was placed in custody in Rome in the early 60s.

Letters (Epistles)

These letters, many of which antedated the Gospels, were written in response to existential needs of the early Christian communities for doctrinal and moral instruction, disciplinary action, practical advice, and exhortation to true Christian living.

Pauline Letters

These letters, which comprise approximately one-fourth of the New Testament, are primary and monumental sources of the development of Christian theology. Several of them may not have had Paul as their actual author, but evidence of the Pauline tradition behind them is strong. The letters to the Colossians, Philippians, Ephesians and Philemon have been called the "Captivity Letters" because of a tradition that they were written while Paul was under house arrest or another form of detention.

Romans: Written about 57 probably from Corinth on the central significance of Christ and faith in him for salvation, and the relationship of Christianity to Judaism; the condition of mankind without Christ; justification and the Christian life; duties of Christians.

Corinthians 1: Written near the beginning of 57 from Ephesus to counteract factionalism and disorders, it covers community dissensions, moral irregularities, marriage and celibacy, conduct at religious gatherings, the Eucharist, spiritual gifts (charisms) and their function in the Church, charity, the resurrection of the body.

Corinthians 2: Written later in the same year as 1 Cor., concerning Paul's defense of his apostolic ministry, and an appeal for a collection to aid poor Christians in Jerusalem.

Galatians: Written probably between 54 and 55 to counteract Judaizing opinions and efforts to undermine his authority, it asserts the divine origin of Paul's authority and doctrine, states that justification is not through Mosaic Law but through faith in Christ, insists on the practice of evangelical virtues, especially charity.

Ephesians: Written probably between 61 and 63, mainly on the Church as the Mystical Body of Christ.

Philippians: Written between 56 and 57 or 61 and 63 to warn the Philippians against enemies of their faith, to urge them to be faithful to their vocation and unity of belief, and to thank them for their kindness to him while he was being held in detention.

Colossians: Written probably while he was under house arrest in Rome from 61 to 63, to counteract the influence of self-appointed teachers who were watering down doctrine concerning Christ. It includes two highly important Christological passages, a warning against false teachers, and an instruction on the ideal Christian life.

Thessalonians 1 and 2: Written within a short time of each other probably in 51 from Corinth, mainly on doctrine concerning the Parousia, the second coming of Christ.

Timothy 1 and 2, Titus: Written between 65 and 67, or perhaps in the 70's, giving pastoral counsels to Timothy and Titus who were in charge of churches in Ephesus and Crete, respectively. 1 Tm. emphasizes pastoral responsibility for preserving unity of doctrine; 2 Tm. describes Paul's imprisonment in Rome.

Philemon: A private letter written between 61 and 63 to a wealthy Colossian concerning a slave, Onesimus, who had escaped from him; Paul appealed for kind treatment of the man.

Hebrews: Dating from sometime between 70 and 96, a complex theological treatise on Christology, the priesthood and sacrifice of Christ, the New Covenant, and the pattern for Christian living. Critical opinion is divided as to whether it was addressed to Judaeo or Gentile Christians.

Catholic Letters, Revelation

These seven letters have been called "catholic" because it was thought for some time, not altogether correctly, that they were not addressed to particular communities.

James: Written sometime before 62 in the spirit of Hebrew wisdom literature and the moralism of Tobit. An exhortation to practical Christian living, it is also noteworthy for the doctrine it states on good works and its citation regarding anointing of the sick.

Peter 1 and 2: The first letter may have been written between 64 and 67 or between 90 and 95; the second may date from 100 to 125. Addressed to Christians in Asia Minor, both are exhortations to perseverance in the life of faith despite trials and difficulties arising from pagan influences, isolation from other Christians and false teaching.

John 1: Written sometime in the 90s and addressed to Asian churches, its message is that God is made known to us in the Son and that fellowship with the Father is attained by living in the light, justice and love of the Son.

John 2: Written sometime in the 90s and addressed to a church in Asia, it commends the people for standing firm in the faith and urges them to perseverance.

John 3: Written sometime in the 90s, it appears to represent an effort to settle a jurisdictional dispute in one of the churches.

Jude: Written probably about 80, it is a brief treatise against erroneous teachings and practices

opposed to law, authority and true Christian freedom.

Revelation: Written in the 90s along the lines of Johannine thought, it is a symbolic and apocalyptic treatment of things to come and of the struggle between the Church and evil combined with warning but hope and assurance to the Church regarding the coming of the Lord in glory.

INTERPRETATION OF THE BIBLE

According to the *Constitution on Revelation* issued by the Second Vatican Council, "the interpreter of Sacred Scripture, in order to see clearly what God wanted to communicate to us, should carefully investigate what meaning the sacred writers really intended, and what God wanted to manifest by means of their words" (No. 12).

Hermeneutics, Exegesis

This careful investigation proceeds in accordance with the rules of hermeneutics, the normative science of biblical interpretation and explanation. Hermeneutics in practice is called exegesis.

The principles of hermeneutics are derived from various disciplines and many factors which have to be considered in explaining the Bible and its parts. These include: the original languages and languages of translation of the sacred texts, through philology and linguistics; the quality of texts, through textual criticism; literary forms and genres, through literary and form criticism; cultural, historical, geographical and other conditions which influenced the writers, through related studies; facts and truths of salvation history; the truths and analogy of faith.

Distinctive to biblical hermeneutics, which differs in important respects from literary interpretation in general, is the premise that the Bible, though written by human authors, is the work of divine inspiration in which God reveals his plan for the salvation of men through historical events and persons, and especially through the Person and mission of Christ.

Textual, Form Criticism

Textual criticism is the study of biblical texts, which have been transmitted in copies several times removed from the original manuscripts, for the purpose of establishing the real state of the original texts. This purpose is served by comparison of existing copies; by application to the texts of the disciplines of philology and linguistics; by examination of related works of antiquity; by study of biblical citations in works of the Fathers of the Church and other authors; and by other means of literary study.

Since about 1920, the sayings of Christ have been a particular object of New Testament study, the purpose being to analyze the forms of expression used by the Evangelists in order to ascertain the words actually spoken by him.

Literary Criticism

Literary criticism aims to determine the origin and kinds of literary composition, called forms or genres, employed by the inspired authors. Such determinations are necessary for decision regarding the nature and purpose and, consequently, the meaning

of biblical passages. Underlying these studies is the principle that the manner of writing was conditioned by the intention of the authors, the meaning they wanted to convey, and the then-contemporary literary style, mode or medium best adapted to carry their message — e.g., true history, quasi-historical narrative, poems, prayers, hymns, psalms, aphorisms, allegories, discourses. Understanding these media is necessary for the valid interpretation of their message.

Literal Sense

The key to all valid interpretation is the literal sense of biblical passages. Regarding this matter and the relevance to it of the studies and procedures described above, Pius XII wrote the following in the encyclical *Divino Afflante Spiritu*.

"What the literal sense of a passage is, is not always as obvious in the speeches and writings of ancient authors of the East as it is in the works of our own time. For what they wished to express is not to be determined by the rules of grammar and philology alone nor solely by the context; the interpreter must, as it were, go back wholly in spirit to those remote centuries of the East and with the aid of history, archeology, ethnology, and other sciences accurately determine what modes of writing, so to speak, the authors of that ancient period would be likely to use and in fact did use. ... In explaining the Sacred Scripture and in demonstrating and proving its immunity from all error (the Catholic interpreter) should make a prudent use of this means, determine to what extent the manner of expression or literary mode adopted by the sacred writer may lead to a correct and genuine interpretation; and let him be convinced that this part of his office cannot be neglected without serious detriment to Catholic exegesis."

The literal sense of the Bible is the meaning in the mind of and intended by the inspired writer of a book or passage of the Bible. This is determined by the application to texts of the rules of hermeneutics. It is not to be confused with word-for-word literalism.

Typical Sense

The typical sense is the meaning which a passage has not only in itself but also in reference to something else of which it is a type or foreshadowing. A clear example is the account of the Exodus of the Israelites: in its literal sense, it narrates the liberation of the Israelites from death and oppression in Egypt; in its typical sense, it foreshadowed the liberation of men from sin through the redemptive death and resurrection of Christ. The typical sense of this and other passages emerged in the working out of God's plan of salvation history. It did not have to be in the mind of the author of the original passage.

Accommodated Senses

Accommodated, allegorical and consequent senses are figurative and adaptive meanings given to books and passages of the Bible for moral and other purposes. Such interpretations involve the danger of stretching the literal sense beyond proper proportions. Hermeneutical principles require that interpretations like these respect the integrity of the literal sense of the passages in question.

In the Catholic view, the final word on questions of biblical interpretation belongs to the teaching authority of the Church. In other views, generally derived from basic principles stated by Martin Luther, John Calvin and other reformers, the primacy belongs to individual judgment acting in response to the inner testimony of the Holy Spirit, the edifying nature of biblical subject matter, the sublimity and simplicity of the message of salvation, the intensity with which Christ is proclaimed.

Biblical Studies

The first center for biblical studies, in some strict sense of the term, was the School of Alexandria, founded in the latter half of the second century. It was noted for allegorical exegesis. Literal interpretation was a hallmark of the School of Antioch.

St. Jerome, who produced the Vulgate, and St. Augustine, author of numerous commentaries, were the most important figures in biblical studies during the patristic period. By the time of the latter's death, the Old and New Testament canons had been stabilized. For some centuries afterwards, there was little or no progress in scriptural studies, although commentaries were written, collections were made of scriptural excerpts from the writings of the Fathers of the Church, and the systematic reading of Scripture became established as a feature of monastic life.

Advances were made in the 12th and 13th centuries with the introduction of new principles and methods of scriptural analysis stemming from renewed interest in Hebraic studies and the application of dialectics.

By the time of the Reformation, the Bible had become the first book set in movable type, and more than 100 vernacular editions were in use throughout Europe.

The Council of Trent

In the wake of the Reformation, the Council of Trent formally defined the Canon of the Bible; it

also reasserted the authoritative role of tradition and the teaching authority of the Church as well as Scripture with respect to the rule of faith. In the heated atmosphere of the 16th and 17th centuries, the Bible was turned into a polemical weapon; Protestants used it to defend their doctrines, and Catholics countered with citations in support of the dogmas of the Church. One result of this state of affairs was a lack of substantial progress in biblical studies during the period.

Rationalists from the 18th century on and later Modernists denied the reality of the supernatural and doctrine concerning inspiration of the Bible, which they generally regarded as a strictly human production expressive of the religious sense and experience of mankind. In their hands, the tools of positive critical research became weapons for biblical subversion. The defensive Catholic reaction to their work had the temporary effect of alienating scholars of the Church from solid advances in archeology, philology, history, textual and literary criticism.

Catholic Developments

Major influences in bringing about a change in Catholic attitude toward use of these disciplines in biblical studies were two papal encyclicals and two institutes of special study, the Ecole Biblique, founded in Jerusalem in 1890, and the Pontifical Biblical Institute established in Rome in 1909. The encyclical *Providentissimus Deus,* issued by Leo XIII in 1893, marked an important breakthrough; in addition to defending the concept of divine inspiration and the formal inspiration of the Scriptures, it encouraged the study of allied and ancillary sciences and techniques for a more fruitful understanding of the sacred writings. The encyclical *Divino Afflante Spiritu,* 50 years later, gave encouragement for the use of various forms of criticism as tools of biblical research. The documents encouraged the work of scholars and stimulated wide communication of the fruits of their study.

Great changes in the climate and direction of biblical studies have occurred in recent years. One of them has been an increase in cooperative effort among Catholic, Protestant, Orthodox and Jewish scholars. Their common investigation of the Dead Sea Scrolls is well known. Also productive has been the collaboration of Catholics and Protestants in turning out various editions of the Bible.

The development and results of biblical studies in this century have directly and significantly affected all phases of the contemporary renewal movement in the Church. Their influence on theology, liturgy, catechetics, and preaching indicate the importance of their function in the life of the Church.

APOSTLES AND EVANGELISTS

The Apostles were the men selected, trained and commissioned by Christ to preach the Gospel, to baptize, to establish, direct and care for his Church as servants of God and stewards of his mysteries. They were the first bishops of the Church.

St. Matthew's Gospel lists the Apostles in this order: Peter, Andrew, James the Greater, John, Philip, Bartholomew, Thomas, Matthew, James the

Less, Jude, Simon and Judas Iscariot. Matthias was elected to fill the place of Judas. Paul became an Apostle by a special call from Christ. Barnabas was called an Apostle.

Two of the Evangelists, John and Matthew, were Apostles. The other two, Luke and Mark, were closely associated with the apostolic college.

Andrew: Born in Bethsaida, brother of Peter, disciple of John the Baptist, a fisherman, the first Apostle called; according to legend, preached the Gospel in northern Greece, Epirus and Scythia, and was martyred at Patras about 70; in art, is represented with an x-shaped cross, called St. Andrew's Cross; is honored as the patron of Russia and Scotland; Nov. 30.

Barnabas: Originally called Joseph but named Barnabas by the Apostles, among whom he is ranked because of his collaboration with Paul; a Jew of the Diaspora, born in Cyprus; a cousin of Mark and member of the Christian community at Jerusalem, influenced the Apostles to accept Paul, with whom he became a pioneer missionary outside Palestine and Syria, to Antioch, Cyprus and southern Asia Minor; legend says he was martyred in Cyprus during the Neronian persecution; June 11.

Bartholomew (Nathaniel): A friend of Philip; according to various traditions, preached the Gospel in Ethiopia, India, Persia and Armenia, where he was martyred by being flayed and beheaded; in art, is depicted holding a knife, an instrument of his death; Aug. 24 (Roman Rite), Aug. 25 (Byzantine Rite).

James the Greater: A Galilean, son of Zebedee, brother of John (with whom he was called a "Son of Thunder"), a fisherman; with Peter and John, witnessed the raising of Jairus' daughter to life, the transfiguration, the agony of Jesus in the Garden of Gethsemani; first of the Apostles to die, by the sword in 44 during the rule of Herod Agrippa; there is doubt about a journey legend says he made to Spain and also about the authenticity of relics said to be his at Santiago de Compostela; in art, is depicted carrying a pilgrim's bell; July 25 (Roman Rite), Apr. 30 (Byzantine Rite).

James the Less: Son of Alphaeus, called "Less" because he was younger in age or shorter in stature than James the Greater; one of the Catholic Epistles bears his name; was stoned to death in 62 or thrown from the top of the temple in Jerusalem and clubbed to death in 66; in art, is depicted with a club or heavy staff; May 3 (Roman Rite), Oct. 9 (Byzantine Rite).

John: A Galilean, son of Zebedee, brother of James the Greater (with whom he was called a "Son of Thunder"), a fisherman, probably a disciple of John the Baptist, one of the Evangelists, called the "Beloved Disciple"; with Peter and James the Greater, witnessed the raising of Jairus' daughter to life, the transfiguration, the agony of Jesus in the Garden of Gethsemani; Mary was commended to his special care by Christ; the fourth Gospel, three Catholic Epistles and Revelation bear his name; according to various accounts, lived at Ephesus in Asia Minor for some time and died a natural death about 100; in art, is represented by an eagle, symbolic of the sublimity of the contents of his Gospel; Dec. 27 (Roman Rite), May 8 (Byzantine Rite).

Jude Thaddeus: One of the Catholic Epistles, the shortest, bears his name; various traditions say he preached the Gospel in Mesopotamia, Persia and elsewhere, and was martyred; in art, is depicted with a halberd, the instrument of his death; Oct. 28 (Roman Rite), June 19 (Byzantine Rite).

Luke: A Greek convert to the Christian community, called "our most dear physician" by Paul, of whom he was a missionary companion; author of the third Gospel and Acts of the Apostles; the place — Achaia, Bithynia, Egypt — and circumstances of his death are not certain; in art, is depicted as a man, a writer, or an ox (because his Gospel starts at the scene of temple sacrifice); Oct. 18.

Mark: A cousin of Barnabas and member of the first Christian community at Jerusalem; a missionary companion of Paul and Barnabas, then of Peter; author of the Gospel which bears his name; according to legend, founded the Church at Alexandria, was bishop there and was martyred in the streets of the city; in art, is depicted with his Gospel and a winged lion, symbolic of the voice of John the Baptist crying in the wilderness, at the beginning of his Gospel; Apr. 25.

Matthew: A Galilean, called Levi by Luke and John and the son of Alphaeus by Mark, a tax collector, one of the Evangelists; according to various accounts, preached the Gospel in Judea, Ethiopia, Persia and Parthia, and was martyred; in art, is depicted with a spear, the instrument of his death, and as a winged man in his role as Evangelist; Sept. 21 (Roman Rite), Nov. 16 (Byzantine Rite).

Matthias: A disciple of Jesus whom the faithful 11 Apostles chose to replace Judas before the Resurrection; uncertain traditions report that he preached the Gospel in Palestine, Cappadocia or Ethiopia; in art, is represented with a cross and a halberd, the instruments of his death as a martyr; May 14 (Roman Rite), Aug. 9 (Byzantine Rite).

Paul: Born at Tarsus, of the tribe of Benjamin, a Roman citizen; participated in the persecution of Christians until the time of his miraculous conversion on the way to Damascus; called by Christ, who revealed himself to him in a special way; became the Apostle of the Gentiles, among whom he did most of his preaching in the course of three major missionary journeys through areas north of Palestine, Cyprus, Asia Minor and Greece; 14 epistles bear his name; two years of imprisonment at Rome, following initial arrest in Jerusalem and confinement at Caesarea, ended with martyrdom, by beheading, outside the walls of the city in 64 or 67 during the Neronian persecution; in art, is depicted in various ways with St. Peter, with a sword, in the scene of his conversion; June 29 (with St. Peter), Jan. 25 (Conversion).

Peter: Simon, son of Jona, born in Bethsaida, brother of Andrew, a fisherman; called Cephas or Peter by Christ who made him the chief of the Apostles and head of the Church as his vicar; named first in the listings of Apostles in the Synoptic Gospels and the Acts of the Apostles; with James the Greater and John, witnessed the raising of Jairus' daughter to life, the transfiguration, the agony of Jesus in the Garden of Gethsemani; was the first to preach the Gospel in and around Jerusalem and was the leader of the first Christian community there; established a local church in Antioch; presided over the Council of Jerusalem in 51; wrote two Catholic Epistles to the Christians in Asia Minor; established his see in Rome where he spent his last years and was martyred by crucifixion in 64 or 65 during the Neronian persecution; in art, is depicted carrying two keys, symbolic of his primacy in the Church; June 29 (with St. Paul), Feb. 22 (Chair of Peter).

Philip: Born in Bethsaida; according to legend, preached the Gospel in Phrygia where he suffered martyrdom by crucifixion; May 3 (Roman Rite), Nov. 14 (Byzantine Rite).

Simon: Called the Cananean or the Zealot; according to legend, preached in various places in the Middle East and suffered martyrdom by being sawed in two; in art, is depicted with a saw, the instrument of his death, or a book, symbolic of his zeal for the Law; Oct. 28 (Roman Rite), May 10 (Byzantine Rite).

Thomas (Didymus): Notable for his initial incredulity regarding the Resurrection and his subsequent forthright confession of the divinity of Christ risen from the dead; according to legend, preached the Gospel in places from the Caspian Sea to the Persian Gulf and eventually reached India where he was martyred near Madras; Thomas Christians trace their origin to him; in art, is depicted kneeling before the risen Christ, or with a carpenter's rule and square; feast, July 3 (Roman Rite), Oct. 6 (Byzantine Rite).

Judas

The Gospels record only a few facts about Judas, the Apostle who betrayed Christ.

The only non-Galilean among the Apostles, he was from Carioth, a town in southern Judah. He was keeper of the purse in the apostolic band. He was called a petty thief by John. He voiced dismay at the waste of money, which he said might have been spent for the poor, in connection with the anointing incident at Bethany. He took the initiative in arranging the betrayal of Christ. Afterwards, he confessed that he had betrayed an innocent man and cast into the Temple the money he had received for that action. Of his death, Matthew says that he hanged himself; the Acts of the Apostles states that he swelled up and burst open; both reports deal more with the meaning than the manner of his death — the misery of the death of a sinner.

The consensus of speculation over the reason why Judas acted as he did in betraying Christ focuses on disillusionment and unwillingness to accept the concept of a suffering Messiah and personal suffering of his own as an Apostle.

APOSTOLIC FATHERS, FATHERS, DOCTORS OF THE CHURCH

The writers listed below were outstanding and authoritative witnesses to authentic Christian belief and practice, and played significant roles in giving them expression.

Apostolic Fathers

The Apostolic Fathers were Christian writers of the first and second centuries whose writings echo genuine apostolic teaching. Chief in importance are: St. Clement (d.c. 97), bishop of Rome and third successor of St. Peter in the papacy; St. Ignatius (50-c. 107), bishop of Antioch and second successor of St. Peter in that see, reputed to be a disciple of St. John; St. Polycarp (69-155), bishop of Smyrna and a disciple of St. John. The authors of the *Didache* and the *Epistle of Barnabas* are also numbered among the Apostolic Fathers.

Other early ecclesiastical writers included: St. Justin, martyr (100-165), of Asia Minor and Rome, a layman and apologist; St. Irenaeus (130-202), bishop of Lyons, who opposed Gnosticism; and St. Cyprian (210-258), bishop of Carthage, who opposed Novatianism.

Fathers and Doctors

The Fathers of the Church were theologians and writers of the first eight centuries who were outstanding for sanctity and learning. They were such authoritative witnesses to the belief and teaching of the Church that their unanimous acceptance of doctrines as divinely revealed has been regarded as evidence that such doctrines were so received by the Church in line with apostolic tradition and Sacred Scripture. Their unanimous rejection of doctrines branded them as heretical. Their writings, however, were not necessarily free of error in all respects.

The greatest of these Fathers were: Sts. Ambrose, Augustine, Jerome and Gregory the Great in the West; Sts. John Chrysostom, Basil the Great, Gregory of Nazianzen and Athanasius in the East.

The Doctors of the Church were ecclesiastical writers of eminent learning and sanctity who have been given this title because of the great advantage the Church has derived from their work. Their writings, however, were not necessarily free of error in all respects.

Albert the Great, St. (c. 1200-1280): Born in Swabia, Germany; Dominican; bishop of Regensburg (1260-1262); wrote extensively on logic, natural sciences, ethics, metaphysics, Scripture, systematic theology; contributed to development of Scholasticism; teacher of St. Thomas Aquinas; canonized and proclaimed doctor, 1931; named patron of natural scientists, 1941; called Doctor Universalis, Doctor Expertus; Nov. 15.

Alphonsus Liguori, St. (1696-1787): Born near Naples, Italy; bishop of Saint Agatha of the Goths (1762-1775); founder of the Redemptorists; in addition to his principal work, *Theologiae Moralis,* wrote on prayer, the spiritual life and doctrinal subjects in response to controversy; canonized, 1839; proclaimed doctor, 1871; named patron of confessors and moralists, 1950; Aug. 1.

Ambrose, St. (c. 340-397): Born in Trier, Germany; bishop of Milan (374-397); one of the strongest opponents of Arianism in the West; his homilies and other writings — on faith, the Holy Spirit, the Incarnation, the sacraments and other subjects — were pastoral and practical; influenced the development of a liturgy at Milan which was named for him; Father and Doctor of the Church; Dec. 7.

Anselm, St. (1033-1109): Born in Aosta, Piedmont, Italy; Benedictine; archbishop of Canterbury (1093-1109); in addition to his principal work, *Cur Deus Homo,* on the atonement and reconciliation of man with God through Christ, wrote about the existence and attributes of God and defended the *Filioque* explanation of the procession of the Holy Spirit from the Father and the Son; proclaimed doctor, 1720; called Father of Scholasticism; Apr. 21.

Anthony of Padua, St. (1195-1231): Born in Lisbon, Portugal; first theologian of the Franciscan Order; preacher; canonized, 1232; proclaimed doctor, 1946; called Evangelical Doctor; June 13.

Athanasius, St. (c. 297-373): Born in Alexandria, Egypt; bishop of Alexandria (328-373); participant in the Council of Nicaea I while still a deacon; dominant opponent of Arians whose errors regarding Christ he refuted in *Apology against the Arians, Discourses against the Arians* and other works; Father and Doctor of the Church; called Father of Orthodoxy; May 2.

Augustine, St. (354-430): Born in Tagaste, North Africa; bishop of Hippo (395-430) after conversion from Manichaeism; works include the autobiographical and mystical *Confessions, City of God,* treatises on the Trinity, grace, passages of the Bible and doctrines called into question and denied by Manichaeans, Pelagians and Donatists; had strong and lasting influence on Christian theology and philosophy; Father and Doctor of the Church; called Doctor of Grace; Aug. 28.

Basil the Great, St. (c. 329-379): Born in Caesarea, Cappadocia, Asia Minor; bishop of Caesarea (370-379); wrote three books *Contra Eunomium* in refutation of Arian errors, a treatise on the Holy Spirit, many homilies and several rules for monastic life, on which he had lasting influence; Father and Doctor of the Church; called Father of Monasticism in the East; Jan. 2.

Bede the Venerable, St. (c. 673-735): Born in Northumberland, England; Benedictine; in addition to his principal work, *Ecclesiastical History of the English Nation* (covering the period 597-731), wrote scriptural commentaries; regarded as probably the most learned man in Western Europe of his time; called Father of English History; May 25.

Bernard of Clairvaux, St. (c. 1090-1153): Born near Dijon, France; abbot; monastic reformer, called the second founder of the Cistercian Order; mystical theologian with great influence on devotional life; opponent of the rationalism brought forward by Abelard and others; canonized, 1174; proclaimed doctor, 1830; called Mellifluous Doctor because of his eloquence; Aug. 20.

Bonaventure, St. (c. 1217-1274): Born near Viterbo, Italy; Franciscan; bishop of Albano (1273-1274); cardinal; wrote *Itinerarium Mentis in Deum, De Reductione Artium ad Theologiam, Breviloquium,* scriptural commentaries, additional mystical works affecting devotional life and a life of St. Francis of Assisi; canonized, 1482; proclaimed doctor, 1588; called Seraphic Doctor; July 15.

Catherine of Siena, St. (c. 1347-1380): Born in Siena, Italy; member of the Third Order of St. Dominic; mystic; authored a long series of letters, mainly concerning spiritual instruction and encouragement, to associates, and *Dialogue,* a spiritual testament in four treatises; was active in support of a crusade against the Turks and efforts to end war between papal forces and the Florentine allies; had great influence in inducing Gregory XI to return

himself and the Curia to Rome in 1377, to end the Avignon period of the papacy; canonized, 1461; proclaimed the second woman doctor, Oct. 4, 1970; Apr. 29.

Cyril of Alexandria, St. (c. 376-444): Born in Egypt; bishop of Alexandria (412-444); wrote treatises on the Trinity, the Incarnation and other subjects, mostly in refutation of Nestorian errors; made key contributions to the development of Christology; presided at the Council of Ephesus, 431; proclaimed doctor, 1882; June 27.

Cyril of Jerusalem, St. (c. 315-386): Bishop of Jerusalem from 350; vigorous opponent of Arianism; principal work, *Catecheses,* a pre baptismal explanation of the creed of Jerusalem; proclaimed doctor, 1882; Mar. 18.

Ephraem, St. (c. 306-373): Born in Nisibis, Mesopotamia; counteracted the spread of Gnostic and Arian errors with poems and hymns of his own composition; wrote also on the Eucharist and Mary; proclaimed doctor, 1920; called Deacon of Edessa and Harp of the Holy Spirit; June 9.

Francis de Sales, St. (1567-1622): Born in Savoy; bishop of Geneva (1602-1622); spiritual writer with strong influence on devotional life through treatises such as *Introduction to a Devout Life,* and *The Love of God;* canonized, 1665; proclaimed doctor, 1877; patron of Catholic writers and the Catholic press; Jan. 24.

Gregory Nazianzen, St. (c. 330-c. 390): Born in Arianzus, Cappadocia, Asia Minor; bishop of Constantinople (381-390); vigorous opponent of Arianism; in addition to five theological discourses on the Nicene Creed and the Trinity for which he is best known, wrote letters and poetry; Father and Doctor of the Church; called the Christian Demosthenes because of his eloquence and, in the Eastern Church, The Theologian; Jan. 2.

Gregory I, the Great, St. (c. 540-604): Born in Rome; pope (590-604): wrote many scriptural commentaries, a compendium of theology in the *Book of Morals* based on Job, *Dialogues* concerning the lives of saints, the immortality of the soul, death, purgatory, heaven and hell, and 14 books of letters; enforced papal supremacy and established the position of the pope vis-a-vis the emperor; worked for clerical and monastic reform and the observance of clerical celibacy; Father and Doctor of the Church; Sept. 3.

Hilary of Poitiers, St. (c. 315-368): Born in Poitiers, France; bishop of Poitiers (c. 353-368); wrote *De Synodis,* with the Arian controversy in mind, and *De Trinitate,* the first lengthy study of the doctrine in Latin; introduced Eastern theology to the West; contributed to the development of hymnology; proclaimed doctor, 1851; called the Athanasius of the West because of his vigorous defense of the divinity of Christ against Arians; Jan. 13.

Isidore of Seville, St. (c. 560-636): Born in Cartagena, Spain; bishop of Seville (c. 600-636); in addition to his principal work, *Etymologiae,* an encyclopedia of the knowledge of his day, wrote on theological and historical subjects; regarded as the most learned man of his time; proclaimed doctor, 1722; Apr. 4.

Jerome, St. (c. 343-420): Born in Stridon, Dalmatia; translated the Old Testament from Hebrew into Latin and revised the existing Latin translation of the New Testament to produce the Vulgate version of the Bible; wrote scriptural commentaries and treatises on matters of controversy; regarded as Father and Doctor of the Church from the eighth century; called Father of Biblical Science; Sept. 30.

John Chrysostom, St. (c. 347-407): Born in Antioch, Asia Minor; archbishop of Constantinople (398-407); wrote homilies, scriptural commentaries and letters of wide influence in addition to a classical treatise on the priesthood; proclaimed doctor by the Council of Chalcedon, 451; called the greatest of the Greek Fathers; named patron of preachers, 1909; called Golden-Mouthed because of his eloquence; Sept. 13.

John Damascene, St. (c. 675-c. 749): Born in Damascus, Syria; monk; wrote *Fountain of Wisdom,* a three-part work including a history of heresies and an exposition of the Christian faith, three *Discourses against the Iconoclasts,* homilies on Mary, biblical commentaries and treatises on moral subjects; proclaimed doctor, 1890; called Golden Speaker because of his eloquence; Dec. 4.

John of the Cross, St. (1542-1591): Born in Old Castile, Spain; Carmelite; founder of Discalced Carmelites; one of the greatest mystical theologians, wrote *The Ascent of Mt. Carmel — The Dark Night, The Spiritual Canticle, The Living Flame of Love;* canonized, 1726; proclaimed doctor, 1926; called Doctor of Mystical Theology; Dec. 14.

Lawrence of Brindisi, St. (1559-1619): Born in Brindisi, Italy; Franciscan (Capuchin); vigorous preacher of strong influence in the post-Reformation period; 15 tomes of collected works include scriptural commentaries, sermons, homilies and doctrinal writings; canonized, 1881; proclaimed doctor, 1959; July 21.

Leo I, the Great, St. (c. 400-461): Born in Tuscany, Italy; pope (440-461); wrote the *Tome of Leo,* to explain doctrine concerning the two natures and one Person of Christ, against the background of the Nestorian and Monophysite heresies; other works included sermons, letters and writings against the errors of Manichaeism and Pelagianism; was instrumental in dissuading Attila from sacking Rome in 452; proclaimed doctor, 1574; Nov. 10.

Peter Canisius, St. (1521-1597): Born in Nijmegen, Holland; Jesuit; wrote popular expositions of the Catholic faith in several catechisms which were widely circulated in 20 editions in his lifetime alone; was one of the moving figures in the Counter-Reformation period, especially in southern and western Germany; canonized and proclaimed doctor, 1925; Dec. 21.

Peter Chrysologus, St. (c. 400-450): Born in Imola, Italy; served as archbishop of Ravenna (c. 433-450); his sermons and writings, many of which were designed to counteract Monophysitism, were pastoral and practical; proclaimed doctor, 1729; July 30.

Peter Damian, St. (1007-1072): Born in Ravenna, Italy; Benedictine; cardinal; his writings and sermons, many of which concerned ecclesiastical and clerical reform, were pastoral and practical; proclaimed doctor, 1828; Feb. 21.

Robert Bellarmine, St. (1542-1621): Born in Tuscany, Italy; Jesuit; archbishop of Capua (1602-1605); wrote *Controversies,* a three-volume exposition of doctrine under attack during and after the Reformation, two catechisms and the spiritual work, *The Art of Dying Well;* was an authority on ecclesiology and Church-state relations; canonized, 1930; proclaimed doctor, 1931; Sept. 17.

Teresa of Jesus (Avila), St. (1515-1582): Born in Avila, Spain; entered the Carmelite Order, 1535; in the early 1560s, initiated a primitive Carmelite, discalced-Alcantarine reform which greatly influenced men and women religious, especially in Spain; wrote extensively on spiritual and mystical subjects; principal works included her *Autobiography, Way of Perfection, The Interior Castle, Meditations on the Canticle, The Foundations, Visitation of the Discalced Nuns;* canonized, 1622; proclaimed first woman doctor, Sept. 27, 1970; Oct. 15.

Thomas Aquinas, St. (1225-1274): Born near Naples, Italy; Dominican; teacher and writer on virtually the whole range of philosophy and theology; principal works were *Summa contra Gentiles,* a manual and systematic defense of Christian doctrine, and *Summa Theologiae,* a new (at that time) exposition of theology on philosophical principles; canonized, 1323; proclaimed doctor, 1567; called Doctor Communis, Doctor Angelicus, the Great Synthesizer because of the way in which he related faith and reason, theology and philosophy (especially that of Aristotle), and systematized the presentation of Christian doctrine; named patron of Catholic schools and education, 1880; Jan. 28.

CREEDS

Creeds are formal and official statements of Christian doctrine. As summaries of the principal truths of faith, they are standards of orthodoxy and are useful for instructional purposes, for actual profession of the faith and for expression of the faith in the liturgy.

Apostles' Creed

The classical creeds are the Apostles' Creed and the Creed of Nicaea-Constantinople. Two others are the Athanasian Creed and the Creed of Pius IV.

Text: I believe in God, the Father almighty, Creator of heaven and earth.

And in Jesus Christ, his only Son, our Lord; who was conceived by the Holy Spirit, born of the Virgin Mary, suffered under Pontius Pilate, was crucified, died, and was buried. He descended into hell; the third day he rose again from the dead; he ascended into heaven, sits at the right hand of God, the Father almighty; from thence he shall come to judge the living and the dead.

I believe in the Holy Spirit, the holy Catholic Church, the communion of saints, the forgiveness of sins, the resurrection of the body, and life everlasting. Amen.

Background: The Apostles' Creed reflects the

teaching of the Apostles but is not of apostolic origin. It probably originated in the second century as a rudimentary formula of faith professed by catechumens before the reception of baptism. Baptismal creeds in fourth-century use at Rome and elsewhere in the West closely resembled the present text, which was quoted in a handbook of Christian doctrine written between 710 and 724. This text was in wide use throughout the West by the ninth century. The Apostles' Creed is common to all Christian confessional churches in the West, but is not used in Eastern Churches.

Nicene Creed

The following translation of the Latin text of the creed was prepared by the International Committee on English in the Liturgy.

Text: We believe in one God, the Father, the Almighty, maker of heaven and earth, of all that is seen and unseen.

We believe in one Lord, Jesus Christ, the only Son of God, eternally begotten of the Father, God from God, Light from Light, true God from true God, begotten, not made, one in Being with the Father. Through him all things were made. For us men and for our salvation he came down from heaven: by the power of the Holy Spirit he was born of the Virgin Mary, and became man. For our sake he was crucified under Pontius Pilate; he suffered, died, and was buried. On the third day he rose again in fulfillment of the Scriptures; he ascended into heaven and is seated at the right hand of the Father. He will come again in glory to judge the living and the dead, and his kingdom will have no end.

We believe in the Holy Spirit, the Lord, the giver of life, who proceeds from the Father and the Son. With the Father and the Son he is worshiped and glorified. He has spoken through the prophets.

We believe in one holy catholic and apostolic Church. We acknowledge one baptism for the forgiveness of sins. We look for the resurrection of the dead, and the life of the world to come. Amen.

Background: The Nicene Creed (Creed of Nicaea-Constantinople) consists of elements of doctrine contained in an early baptismal creed of Jerusalem and enactments of the Council of Nicaea (325) and the Council of Constantinople (381). Its strong trinitarian content reflects the doctrinal errors, especially of Arianism, it served to counteract. Theologically, it is much more sophisticated than the Apostles' Creed. Since late in the fifth century, the Nicene Creed has been the only creed in liturgical use in the Eastern Churches. The Western Church adopted it for liturgical use by the end of the eighth century.

The Athanasian Creed

The Athanasian Creed, which has a unique structure, is a two-part summary of doctrine concerning the Trinity and the Incarnation-Redemption bracketed at the beginning and end with the statement that belief in the cited truths is necessary for salvation; it also contains a number of anathemas or condemnatory clauses regarding doctrinal errors. Although attributed to St. Athanasius, it was probably written after his death, between 381 and 428, and may have been authored by St. Ambrose. It is not accepted in the East; in the West, it formerly had place in the Roman-Rite Liturgy of the Hours and in the liturgy for the Solemnity of the Holy Trinity.

Creed of Pius IV

The Creed of Pius IV, also called the Profession of Faith of the Council of Trent, was promulgated in the bull *Injunctum Nobis*, Nov. 13, 1564. It is a summary of doctrine defined by the council concerning: Scripture and tradition, original sin and justification, the Mass and sacraments, veneration of the saints, indulgences, the primacy of the See of Rome. It was slightly modified in 1887 to include doctrinal formulations of the First Vatican Council.

MORAL OBLIGATIONS

The basic norm of Christian morality is life in Christ. This involves, among other things, the observance of the Ten Commandments, their fulfillment in the twofold law of love of God and neighbor, the implications of the Sermon on the Mount and the whole New Testament, and membership in the Church established by Christ.

THE TEN COMMANDMENTS

The Ten Commandments, the Decalogue, were given by God through Moses to his Chosen People for the guidance of their moral conduct in accord with the demands of the Covenant he established with them as a divine gift.

In the traditional Catholic enumeration and according to Dt. 5:6-21, the Commandments are:

1. "I, the Lord, am your God ... You shall not have other gods besides me. You shall not carve idols ...."

2. "You shall not take the name of the Lord, your God, in vain ...."

3. "Take care to keep holy the Sabbath day ...."

4. "Honor your father and your mother ...."

5. "You shall not kill."

6. "You shall not commit adultery."

7. "You shall not steal."

8. "You shall not bear dishonest witness against your neighbor."

9. "You shall not covet your neighbor's wife."

10. "You shall not desire your neighbor's house or field, nor his male or female slave, nor his ox or ass, nor anything that belongs to him (summarily, his goods)."

Another version of the Commandments, substantially the same, is given in Ex. 20:1-17.

The traditional enumeration of the Commandments in Protestant usage differs from the above. Thus: two commandments are made of the first, as above; the third and fourth are equivalent to the second and third, as above, and so on; and the 10th includes the ninth and 10th, as above.

Love of God and Neighbor
The first three of the commandments deal directly with man's relations with God, viz.: acknowledgment of one true God and the rejection of false gods and idols; honor due to God and his name; observance of the Sabbath as the Lord's day.

The rest cover interpersonal relationships, viz.: the obedience due to parents and, logically, to other persons in authority, and the obligations of parents to children and of persons in authority to those under their care; respect for life and physical integrity; fidelity in marriage, and chastity; justice and rights; truth; internal respect for faithfulness in marriage, chastity, and the goods of others.

Perfection in Christian Life
The moral obligations of the Ten Commandments are complemented by others flowing from the twofold law of love, the whole substance and pattern of Christ's teaching, and everything implied in full and active membership and participation in the community of salvation formed by Christ in his Church. Some of these matters are covered in other sections of the Almanac under appropriate headings.

Precepts of the Church
This text of the Precepts of the Church is from *Basic Teachings for Catholic Religious Education,* copyrighted by the National Conference of Catholic Bishops and circulated by the CNS Documentary Services, *Origins* (Vol. 2, No. 31).

From time to time the Church has listed certain specific duties of Catholics. Some duties expected of Catholic Christians today include the following. (Those traditionally mentioned as precepts of the Church are marked with an asterisk.)

1. To keep holy the day of the Lord's resurrection: to worship God by participating in Mass every Sunday and holy day of obligation:* to avoid those activities that would hinder renewal of soul and body, e.g., needless work and business activities, unnecessary shopping, etc.

2. To lead a sacramental life: to receive Holy Communion frequently and the sacrament of penance regularly — minimally, to receive the sacrament of penance at least once a year (annual confession is obligatory only if serious sin is involved)* — minimally, to receive Holy Communion at least once a year between the first Sunday of Lent and Trinity Sunday.*

3. To study Catholic teaching in preparation for the sacrament of confirmation, to be confirmed, and then to continue to study and advance the cause of Christ.

4. To observe the marriage laws of the Church:* to give religious training (by example and word) to one's children; to use parish schools and religious education programs.

5. To strengthen and support the Church:* one's own parish community and parish priests; the worldwide Church and the Holy Father.

6. To do penance, including abstaining from meat and fasting from food on the appointed days.*

7. To join in the missionary spirit and apostolate of the Church.

SOCIAL DOCTRINE

Since the end of the last century, Catholic social doctrine has been formulated in a progressive manner in a number of authoritative documents.

Outstanding examples are the encyclicals: *Rerum Novarum* ("On Capital and Labor") issued by Leo XIII in 1891; *Quadragesimo Anno* ("On Reconstruction of the Social Order") by Pius XI in 1931; *Mater et Magistra* ("Christianity and Social Progress") and *Pacem in Terris* ("Peace on Earth"), by John XXIII in 1961 and 1963, respectively; *Populorum Progressio* ("Development of Peoples"), by Paul VI in 1967; *Laborem Exercens* ("On Human Work"), *Sollicitudo Rei Socialis* ("On Social Concerns") and *Centesimus Annus* ("The 100th Year") by John Paul II in 1981, 1987 and 1991, respectively. Pius XII, among other accomplishments of ideological importance in the social field, made a distinctive contribution with his formulation of a plan for world peace and order in Christmas messages from 1939 to 1941, and in other documents.

Of particular significance are the "Pastoral Constitution on the Church in the Modern World" (*Gaudium et Spes*) issued by the Second Vatican Council and Pope John Paul's encyclical letter, "The 100th Year."

These documents represent the most serious attempts in modern times to systematize the social implications of divine revelation as well as the socially relevant writings of the Fathers and Doctors of the Church. Their contents are theological penetrations into social life, with particular reference to human rights, the needs of the poor and those in underdeveloped countries, and humane conditions of life, freedom, justice and peace. In some respects, they read like juridical documents; essentially, however, they are Gospel-oriented and pastoral in intention.

Following are brief descriptions of the nature of social teaching, the contents of the pastoral constitution, and extensive excerpts from *Centesimus Annus.*

Nature of the Doctrine
Pope John XXIII, writing in *Christianity and Social Progress,* made the following statement about the nature and scope of the doctrine stated in the encyclicals in particular and related writings in general.

"What the Catholic Church teaches and declares regarding the social life and relationships of men is beyond question for all time valid.

"The cardinal point of this teaching is that individual men are necessarily the foundation, cause, and end of all social institutions . . . insofar as they are social by nature, and raised to an order of existence that transcends and subdues nature.

"Beginning with this very basic principle whereby the dignity of the human person is affirmed and defended, Holy Church — especially during the last century and with the assistance of learned priests and laymen, specialists in the field — has arrived at clear social teachings whereby the mutual relationships of men are ordered. Taking general norms into account, these principles are in accord with the nature of things and the changed conditions of man's social life, or with the special genius of our day. Moreover, these norms can be approved by all."

THE CHURCH IN THE WORLD

Even more Gospel-oriented and pastoral in a distinctive way is the *Pastoral Constitution on the Church in the Modern World* promulgated by the Second Vatican Council in 1965.

Its purpose is to search out the signs of God's presence and meaning in and through the events of this time in human history. Accordingly, it deals with the situation of men in present circumstances of profound change, challenge and crisis on all levels of life.

The first part of the constitution develops the theme of the Church and man's calling, and focuses attention on the dignity of the human person, the problem of atheism, the community of mankind, man's activity throughout the world, and the serving and saving role of the Church in the world. This portion of the document, it has been said, represents the first presentation by the Church in an official text of an organized Christian view of man and society.

The second part of the document considers several problems of special urgency: fostering the nobility of marriage and the family (see Marriage Doctrine), the proper development of culture, socio-economic life, the life of the political community, the fostering of peace (see Peace and War), and the promotion of a community of nations.

In conclusion, the constitution calls for action to implement doctrine regarding the role and work of the Church for the total good of mankind.

CENTESIMUS ANNUS: ENCYCLICAL LETTER

"The 100th Year" is the title of Pope John Paul's ninth encyclical letter, commemorating the 100th anniversary of Pope Leo XIII's encyclical *Rerum Novarum* ("On Capital and Labor"). *Centesimus Annus*, dated May 1, 1991, was made public the following day. Its publication was one of the principal events of the year dedicated to commemoration and study of the social teaching of the Church.

Following are excerpts (in quotations) from the text circulated by the CNS Documentary Service, Origins, May 16, 1991 (Vol. 21, No. 1). Subheads have been added. Quotations indicated by single quotation marks are from other encyclicals, documents of the Second Vatican Council and other authoritative sources.

INTRODUCTION

3. "The present encyclical seeks to show the fruitfulness of the principles enunciated by Leo XIII, which belong to the Church's doctrinal patrimony and as such involve the exercise of her teaching authority. But pastoral solicitude also prompts me to propose an analysis of some events of recent history. ... Such an analysis is not meant to pass definitive judgments, since this does not fall per se within the magisterium's specific domain."

CHAPTER 1

Characteristics of Rerum Novarum

5. "The 'new things' to which the Pope devoted his attention were anything but positive. The first paragraph of the encyclical describes in strong terms the 'new things' (*rerum novarum*) which gave it its name: 'That the spirit of revolutionary change which has long been disturbing the nations of the world should have passed beyond the sphere of politics and made its influence felt in the related sphere of practical economics is not surprising. Progress in industry, the development of new trades, the changing relationship between employers and workers, the enormous wealth of a few as opposed to the poverty of the many, the increasing self-reliance of the workers and their closer association with each other,

as well as a notable decline in morality: All these elements have led to the conflict now taking place.'"

"The Pope and the Church with him were confronted, as was the civil community, by a society which was torn by a conflict all the more harsh and inhumane because it knew no rule or regulation. It was the conflict between capital and labor or — as the encyclical puts it — the worker question."

Conditions for Justice

"What was essential to the encyclical was precisely its proclamation of the fundamental conditions for justice in the economic and social situation of the time."

"To teach and to spread her social doctrine pertains to the Church's evangelizing mission and is an essential part of the Christian message, since this doctrine points out the direct consequences of that message in the life of society and situates daily work and struggles for justice in the context of bearing witness to Christ the Savior. This doctrine is likewise a source of unity and peace in dealing with the conflicts which inevitably arise in social and economic life."

"We need to repeat that there can be no genuine solution of the 'social question' apart from the Gospel, and that the 'new things' can find in the Gospel the context for their correct understanding and the proper moral perspective for judgment on them."

Fundamental Rights

6. "Pope Leo XIII affirmed the fundamental rights of workers. Indeed, the key to reading the encyclical is the dignity of the worker as such and, for the same reason, the dignity of work."

7. to 9. The encyclical stated the important principle of the right to "private property," duly qualified by the "complementary" principle of "the universal destination of the earth's goods" for the good of all.

Also affirmed were the natural right to form private associations, the right to the limitation of working hours, the right to legitimate rest, and the right of children and women to be treated differently with regard to the type and duration of work, the right to a just wage (which should be sufficient to enable a worker to support himself, his wife and his children), and the right to religious freedom.

11. "Pope Leo's encyclical . . . is an encyclical on the poor and on the terrible conditions to which the new and often violent process of industrialization had reduced great multitudes of people."

The Guiding Principle

"The main thread and in a certain sense the guiding principle of Pope Leo's encyclical and of all of the Church's social doctrine is a correct view of the human person and of his unique value, inasmuch as 'man . . . is the only creature on earth which God willed for itself.' God has imprinted his own image and likeness on man, conferring upon him an incomparable dignity, as the encyclical frequently insists. In effect, beyond the rights which man acquires by his own work, there exist rights which do not correspond to any work he performs but which flow from his essential dignity as a person."

CHAPTER 2

Toward the 'New Things' of Today

12. "Pope Leo foresaw the negative consequences — political, social and economic — of the social order proposed by 'socialism.' "

13. He defined the nature of the socialism of his day as "the suppression of private property," and said "its fundamental error is anthropological in nature." It "considers the individual person simply as an element, a molecule within the social organism, so that the good of the individual is completely subordinated to the functioning of the socio-economic organism. . . . Man is thus reduced to a series of social relationships."

However, "according to *Rerum Novarum* and the whole social doctrine of the Church, the social nature of man is not completely fulfilled in the state, but is realized in various intermediary groups, beginning with the family and including economic, social, political and cultural groups which stem from human nature itself and have their own autonomy, always with a view to the common good."

Atheism's Mistaken Concept

"The first cause of the mistaken concept of the nature of the person is "atheism. . . . The denial of God deprives the person of his foundation and consequently leads to a reorganization of the social order without reference to the person's dignity and responsibility."

14. Consequences of socialism, atheism and related errors are class struggle, militarism, war, subjection of people to the state, and a whole range of political, social and economic evils.

CHAPTER 3

The Year 1989

22. *Centesimus Annus* notes that "unexpected and promising" events of recent years have produced notable changes in countries in Eastern and Central Europe, as also in nations of Latin America, Asia and Africa. Contributing to these developments was

the Church's commitment to human rights. Coupled with the developments was hope for progressive change and for the solution of problems through the exercise of dialogue and negotiation.

23. Among factors involved in the fall of oppressive regimes were the violation of workers' rights (called decisive), peaceful protest through dialogue and negotiation as opposed to Marxist violence, and witness to the truth about conditions, etc.

24. Another factor was the inefficiency of the (Marxist) economic system. The inefficiency was not so much technological as a consequence of violations of human rights to private initiative, ownership of property and economic freedom. A related factor was the failure of oppressive regimes to realize the importance of culture for the understanding of people.

Spiritual Void

The true cause of the fall of oppressive regimes was the spiritual void brought about by atheism; because of this void, people were cast adrift without any sense of direction. Another cause was the witness of the faithful to truth.

25. to 27. Events of 1989, which had effects not only in Eastern and Central Europe but also in Third World and other countries, were an example of the success achievable by a willingness to negotiate and of the success of the Gospel spirit to stand for moral principles, come what may.

Need for Reconciliation and Rebuilding

28. "The radical reordering of economic systems, hitherto collectivized, entails problems and sacrifices. . . . It is right that in the present difficulties the formerly communist countries should be aided by the united effort of other nations. Obviously they themselves must be the primary agents of their own development, but they must also be given a reasonable opportunity to accomplish this goal, something that cannot happen without the help of other countries." Such help, however, should not lead to neglect of the Third World or abandonment of the poor. Special effort must be made to mobilize resources necessary for development in the Third World.

29. "Development must not be understood solely in economic terms, but in a way that is fully human. . . . The apex of development is the exercise of the right and duty to seek God, to know him and to live in accordance with that knowledge."

CHAPTER 4

Private Property and the Universal Destination of Material Goods

30. "In *Rerum Novarum*, Leo XIII strongly affirmed the natural character of the right to private property. . . . This right, which is fundamental for the autonomy and development of the person, has always been defended by the Church up to our own day. At the same time, the Church teaches that the possession of material goods is not an absolute right and that its limits are inscribed in its very nature as a human right.

"While the Pope proclaimed the right to private

ownership, he affirmed with equal clarity that the 'use' of goods, while marked by freedom, is subordinated to their original common destination" for the common good.

"Of its nature, private property has a social function which is based on the law of the common purpose of goods."

Origin of Material Goods

31. "The question can be raised concerning the origin of the material goods which sustain human life, satisfy people's needs and are an object of their rights.

"The original source of all that is good is the very act of God, who created both the earth and man, and who gave the earth to man so that he might have dominion over it by his work and enjoy its fruits (Gn. 1:28). God gave the earth to the whole human race for the sustenance of all its members, without excluding or favoring anyone. This is the foundation of the universal destination of the earth's goods. The earth, by reason of its fruitfulness and its capacity to satisfy human needs, is God's first gift for the sustenance of human life. But the earth does not yield its fruits without a particular human response to God's gift, that is to say, without work. It is through work that man, using his intelligence and exercising his freedom, succeeds in dominating the earth and making it a fitting home. In this way, he makes part of the earth his own, precisely the part which he has acquired through work; this is the origin of individual property. Obviously, he also has the responsibility not to hinder others from having their own part of God's gift; indeed, he must cooperate with others so that together all can dominate the earth."

Work and the Land

"In history, these two factors — work and the land — are to be found at the beginning of every human society. However, they do not always stand in the same relationship to each other. At one time the natural fruitfulness of the earth appeared to be, and was in fact, the primary factor of wealth, while work was, as it were, the help and support for this fruitfulness. In our time, the role of human work is becoming increasingly important as the productive factor both of non-material and of material wealth. Moreover, it is becoming clearer how a person's work is naturally interrelated with the work of others. More than ever, work is work with others and work for others: it is a matter of doing something for someone else. Work becomes ever more fruitful and productive to the extent that people become more knowledgeable of the productive potentialities of the earth and more profoundly cognizant of the needs of those for whom their work is done."

Ownership of Know-How

32. "In our time, in particular, there exists another form of ownership which is becoming no less important than land: the possession of know-how, technology and skill. The wealth of the industrialized nations is based much more on this kind of ownership than on natural resources."

"Today the decisive factor (in production) is increasingly man himself, that is, his knowledge, especially his scientific knowledge, his capacity for interrelated and compact organization, as well as his ability to perceive the needs of others and to satisfy them."

The Free Market

34. "It would appear that, on the level of individual nations and of international relations, the free market is the most efficient instrument for utilizing resources and effectively responding to needs." But this is true only for those needs which are "solvent," insofar as they are endowed with purchasing power, and for those resources which are "marketable," insofar as they are capable of obtaining a satisfactory price. But there are many human needs which find no place on the market. It is a strict duty of justice and truth not to allow fundamental human needs to remain unsatisfied, and not allow those burdened by such needs to perish. It is also necessary to help these needy people to acquire expertise, to enter the circle of exchange, and to develop their skills in order to make the best use of their capacities and resources. Even prior to the logic of a fair exchange of goods and the forms of justice appropriate to it, there exists something which is due to man because he is man, by reason of his lofty dignity. Inseparable from that required "something" is the possibility to survive and, at the same time, to make "an active contribution to the common good of humanity."

35. "Trade unions and other workers' organizations defend workers' rights and protect their interests as persons, while fulfilling a vital cultural role, so as to enable workers to participate more fully and honorably in the life of their nation and to assist them along the path of development."

A Society of Free Work

"In this sense, it is right to speak of a struggle against an economic system, if the latter is understood as a method of upholding the absolute predominance of capital, the possession of the means of production and of the land, in contrast to the free and personal nature of human work. In the struggle against such a system, what is being proposed as an alternative is not the socialist system, which in fact turns out to be state capitalism, but rather a society of free work, of enterprise and of participation. Such a society is not directed against the market, but demands that the market be appropriately controlled by the forces of society and by the state, so as to guarantee that the basic needs of the whole of society are satisfied."

Legitimacy of Profit

"The church acknowledges the legitimate role of profit as an indication that a business is functioning well. When a firm makes a profit, this means that productive factors have been properly employed and corresponding human needs have been duly satisfied. But profitability is not the only indicator of a firm's condition. It is possible for the financial accounts to be in order, and yet for the people — who make up the firm's most valuable asset — to be humiliated and their dignity offended. Besides being morally inadmissible, this will eventually have negative repercussions on the firm's economic efficiency. In fact, the purpose of a business firm is not simply to make a profit, but is to be found in its very existence as a community of persons who in various ways are endeavoring to satisfy their basic needs, and who form a particular group at the service of the whole of society. Profit is a regulator of the life of a business, but it is not the only one; other human and moral factors must also be considered which, in the long term, are at least equally important for the life of a business."

Stronger Nations Must Help

"It is unacceptable to say that the defeat of so-called 'real socialism' leaves capitalism as the only model of economic organization. It is necessary to break down the barriers and monopolies which leave so many countries on the margins of development, and to provide all individuals and nations with the basic conditions which will enable them to share in development. This goal calls for programmed and responsible efforts on the part of the entire international community. Stronger nations must offer weaker ones opportunities for taking their place in international life, and the latter must learn how to use these opportunities by making the necessary efforts and sacrifices, and by ensuring political and economic stability, the certainty of better prospects for the future, the improvement of workers' skills, and the training of competent business leaders who are conscious of their responsibilities."

Third World Debt

"At present, the positive efforts which have been made along these lines are being affected by the still largely unsolved problem of the foreign debt of the poorer countries. The principle that debts must be paid is certainly just. However, it is not right to demand or expect payment when the effect would be the imposition of political choices leading to hunger and despair for entire peoples. It cannot be expected that the debts which have been contracted should be paid at the price of unbearable sacrifices. In such cases it is necessary to find — as in fact is partly happening — ways to lighten, defer or even cancel the debt, compatible with the fundamental right of peoples to subsistence and progress."

Consumerism

36. "A given culture reveals its overall understanding of life through the choices it makes in production and consumption. It is here that the phenomenon of consumerism arises. In singling out new needs and new means to meet them, one must be guided by a comprehensive picture of man which respects all the dimensions of his being and which subordinates his material and instinctive dimensions to his interior and spiritual ones. If, on the contrary, a direct appeal is made to his instincts — while ignoring in various ways the reality of the person as intelligent and free —then consumer attitudes and lifestyles can be created which are objectively improper and often damaging to his physical and spiritual health. Of itself, an economic system does not possess criteria for correctly distinguishing new and higher forms of satisfying human needs from artificial new needs which hinder the formation of a mature personality. Thus, a great deal of educational and cultural work is urgently needed, including the education of consumers in the responsible use of their power of choice, the formation of a strong sense of responsibility among producers and among people in the mass media in particular, as well as the necessary intervention by public authorities."

"It is not wrong to want to live better; what is wrong is a style of life which is presumed to be better when it is directed toward 'having' rather than 'being,' and which wants to have more, not in order to be more but in order to spend life in enjoyment as an end in itself."

Ecological Considerations

37. "Equally worrying is the ecological question which accompanies the problem of consumerism and which is closely connected to it."

38. "In addition to the irrational destruction of the natural environment. we must also mention the more serious destruction of the human environment. . . . Not only has God given the earth to man, who must use it with respect for the original good purpose for which it was given to him, but man too is God's gift to man. He must therefore respect the natural and moral structure with which he has been endowed. In this context, mention should be made of the serious problems of modern urbanization, of the need for urban planning which is concerned with how people are to live, and of the attention which should be given to a 'social ecology' of work.

"Man receives from God his essential dignity and with it the capacity to transcend every social order so as to move toward truth and goodness. But he is also conditioned by the social structure in which he lives, by the education he has received and by his environment. These elements can either help or hinder his living in accordance with the truth. The decisions which create a human environment can give rise to specific structures of sin which impede the full realization of those who are in any way oppressed by them. To destroy such structures and replace them with more authentic forms of living in community is a task which demands courage and patience."

The Family and Human Ecology

39. "The first and fundamental structure for 'human ecology' is the family, in which man receives his first formative ideas about truth and goodness, and learns what it means to love and to be loved, and thus what it actually means to be a person. Here we mean the family founded on marriage, in which the mutual gift of self by husband and wife creates an environment in which children can be born and develop their potentialities, become aware of their dignity and prepare to face their unique and individual destiny." "It is necessary to go back to seeing the family as the sanctuary of life. The family is indeed sacred: it is the place in which life — the gift of God — can be properly welcomed and protected against the many attacks to which it is ex-

posed, and can develop in accordance with what constitutes authentic human growth. In the face of the so-called culture of death, the family is the heart of the culture of life."

Abortion

"Human ingenuity seems to be directed more toward limiting, suppressing or destroying the sources of life — including recourse to abortion, which unfortunately is so widespread in the world — than toward defending and opening up the possibilities of life. The encyclical *Sollicitudo Rei Socialis* denounced systematic anti-childbearing campaigns which, on the basis of a distorted view of the demographic problem and in a climate of 'absolute lack of respect for the freedom of choice of the parties involved,' often subject them 'to intolerable pressures . . . in order to force them to submit to this new form of oppression.' These policies are extending their field of action by the use of new techniques, to the point of poisoning the lives of millions of defenseless human beings, as if in a form of 'chemical warfare.' "

Economic Freedom Not Autonomous

"These criticisms are directed not so much against an economic system as against an ethical and cultural system. The economy in fact is only one aspect and one dimension of the whole of human activity. If economic life is absolutized, if the production and consumption of goods become the center of social life and society's only value, not subject to any other value, the reason is to be found not so much in the economic system itself as in the fact that the entire socio-cultural system, by ignoring the ethical and religious dimension, has been weakened, and ends by limiting itself to the production of goods and services alone.

"All of this can be summed up by repeating once more that economic freedom is only one element of human freedom. When it becomes autonomous, when man is seen more as a producer or consumer of goods than as a subject who produces and consumes in order to live, then economic freedom loses its necessary relationship to the human person and ends up by alienating and oppressing him."

41. "Obedience to the truth about God and man is the first condition of freedom, making it possible for a person to order his needs and desires and to choose the means of satisfying them according to a correct scale of values, so that the ownership of things may become an occasion of growth for him."

Capitalism

42. "Can it perhaps be said that, after the failure of communism, capitalism is the victorious social system, and that capitalism should be the goal of the countries now making efforts to rebuild their economy and society? Is this the model which ought to be proposed to the countries of the Third World which are searching for the path to true economic and civil progress?

"The answer is obviously complex. If by *capitalism* is meant an economic system which recognizes the fundamental and positive role of business, the market, private property and the result-

ing responsibility for the means of production, as well as free human creativity in the economic sector, then the answer is certainly in the affirmative, even though it would perhaps be more appropriate to speak of a *business economy, market economy* or simply *free economy*. But if by *capitalism* is meant a system in which freedom in the economic sector is not circumscribed within a strong juridical framework which places it at the service of human freedom in its totality, and which sees it as a particular aspect of that freedom, the core of which is ethical and religious, then the reply is certainly negative."

Marginalization Remains

"The Marxist solution has failed, but the realities of marginalization and exploitation remain in the world, especially the Third World, as does the reality of human alienation, especially in the more advanced countries. Against these phenomena the Church strongly raises her voice. Vast multitudes are still living in conditions of great material and moral poverty. The collapse of the communist system in so many countries certainly removes an obstacle to facing these problems in an appropriate and realistic way, but it is not enough to bring about their solution. Indeed, there is a risk that a radical capitalistic ideology could spread which refuses even to consider these problems, in the a priori belief that any attempt to solve them is doomed to failure, and which blindly entrusts their solution to the free development of market forces."

Orientation of Church Teaching

43. "The Church has no models to present; models that are real and truly effective can only arise within the framework of different historical situations, through the efforts of all those who responsibly confront concrete problems in all their social, economic, political and cultural aspects, as these interact with one another. For such a task the church offers her social teaching as an indispensable and ideal orientation, a teaching which, as already mentioned, recognizes the positive value of the market and of enterprise, but which at the same time points out that these need to be oriented toward the common good. This teaching also recognizes the legitimacy of workers' efforts to obtain full respect for their dignity and to gain broader areas of participation in the life of industrial enterprises so that, while cooperating with others and under the direction of others, they can in a certain sense 'work for themselves' through the exercise of their intelligence and freedom.

"The integral development of the human person through work does not impede but rather promotes the greater productivity and efficiency of work itself, even though it may weaken consolidated power structures. A business cannot be considered only as a 'society of capital goods'; it is also a 'society of persons' in which people participate in different ways and with specific responsibilities, whether they supply the necessary capital for the company's activities or take part in such activities through their labor. To achieve these goals there is still need for a broad associated workers' movement, directed toward the liberation and promotion of the whole person."

Private Property and Work

"In the light of today's 'new things,' we have reread the relationship between individual or private property and the universal destination of material wealth. Man fulfills himself by using his intelligence and freedom. In so doing he utilizes the things of this world as objects and instruments and makes them his own. The foundation of the right to private initiative and ownership is to be found in this activity. By means of his work man commits himself, not only for his own sake but also for others and with others. Each person collaborates in the work of others and for their good. Man works in order to provide for the needs of his family, his community, his nation and ultimately all humanity. Moreover, he collaborates in·the work of his fellow employees, as well as in the work of suppliers and in the customers' use of goods, in a progressively expanding chain of solidarity. Ownership of the means of production, whether in industry or agriculture, is just and legitimate if it serves useful work. It becomes illegitimate, however, when it is not utilized or when it serves to impede the work of others, in an effort to gain a profit which is not the result of the overall expansion of work and the wealth of society, but rather is the result of curbing them or of illicit exploitation, speculation or the breaking of solidarity among working people. Ownership of this kind has no justification, and represents an abuse in the sight of God and man.

"The obligation to earn one's bread by the sweat of one's brow also presumes the right to do so. A society in which this right is systematically denied, in which economic policies do not allow workers to reach satisfactory levels of employment, cannot be justified from an ethical point of view, nor can that society attain social peace. Just as the person fully realizes himself in the free gift of self, so too ownership morally justifies itself in the creation, at the proper time and in the proper way, of opportunities for work and human growth for all."

CHAPTER 5

State and Culture

44. "Pope Leo XIII was aware of the need for a sound theory of the state in order to ensure the normal development of man's spiritual and temporal activities, both of which are indispensable. For this reason, in one passage of *Rerum Novarum* he presents the organization of society according to the three powers — legislative, executive and judicial — something which at the time represented a novelty in church teaching. Such an ordering reflects a realistic vision of man's social nature, which calls for legislation capable of protecting the freedom of all. To that end, it is preferable that each power be balanced by other powers and by other spheres of responsibility which keep it within proper bounds. This is the principle of the 'rule of law,' in which the law is sovereign, and not the arbitrary will of individuals."

46. "The Church values the democratic system inasmuch as it ensures the participation of citizens in making political choices, guarantees to the governed the possibility both of electing and holding accountable those who govern them, and of replacing them through peaceful means when appropriate. Thus, she cannot encourage the formation of narrow ruling groups which usurp the power of the state for individual interests or for ideological ends."

Authentic Democracy

"Authentic democracy is possible only in a state ruled by law, and on the basis of a correct conception of the human person. It requires that the necessary conditions be present for the advancement both of the individual through education and formation in true ideals, and of the 'subjectivity' of society through the creation of structures of participation and shared responsibility. Nowadays there is a tendency to claim that agnosticism and skeptical relativism are the philosophy and the basic attitude which correspond to democratic forms of political life. Those who are convinced that they know the truth and firmly adhere to it are considered unreliable from a democratic point of view, since they do not accept that truth is determined by the majority, or that it is subject to variation according to different political trends. It must be observed in this regard that if there is no ultimate truth to guide and direct political activity, then ideas and convictions can easily be manipulated for reasons of power. As history demonstrates, a democracy without values easily turns into open or thinly disguised totalitarianism.

"Nor does the Church close her eyes to the danger of fanaticism or fundamentalism among those who, in the name of an ideology which purports to be scientific or religious, claim the right to impose on others their own concept of what is true and good. Christian truth is not of this kind. Since it is not an ideology, the Christian faith does not presume to imprison changing socio-political realities in a rigid schema, and it recognizes that human life is realized in history in conditions that are diverse and imperfect. Furthermore, in constantly reaffirming the transcendent dignity of the person, the Church's method is always that of respect for freedom.

"But freedom attains its full development only by accepting the truth. In a world without truth, freedom loses its foundation and man is exposed to the violence of passion and to manipulation, both open and hidden. The Christian upholds freedom and serves it."

Rights To Be Recognized

47. "Following the collapse of communist totalitarianism and of many other totalitarian and 'national security' regimes, today we are witnessing a predominance, not without signs of opposition, of the democratic ideal, together with lively attention to and concern for human rights. But for this very reason it is necessary for peoples in the process of reforming their systems to give democracy an authentic and solid foundation through the explicit recognition of those rights. Among the most important of these rights, mention must be made of the right to life, an integral part of which is the right of the child to develop in the mother's womb from the moment of conception; the right to live in a united family and in a moral environment conducive to the growth of the child's personality; the right to develop one's intelligence and freedom in seeking and knowing the truth; the right to share in the work which makes wise use of the earth's material resources, and to derive from that work the

means to support oneself and one's dependents; and the right freely to establish a family, to have and to rear children through the responsible exercise of one's sexuality. In a certain sense, the source and synthesis of these rights is religious freedom, understood as the right to live in the truth of one's faith and in conformity with one's transcendent dignity as a person."

Violations of Rights

"Even in countries with democratic forms of government, these rights are not always fully respected. Here we are referring not only to the scandal of abortion, but also to different aspects of a crisis within democracies themselves, which seem at times to have lost the ability to make decisions aimed at the common good. Certain demands which arise within society are sometimes not examined in accordance with criteria of justice and morality, but rather on the basis of the electoral or financial power of the groups promoting them. With time, such distortions of political conduct create distrust and apathy, with a subsequent decline in the political participation and civic spirit of the general population, which feels abused and disillusioned. As a result, there is a growing inability to situate particular interests within the framework of a coherent vision of the common good. The latter is not simply the sum total of particular interests; rather, it involves an assessment and integration of those interests on the basis of a balanced hierarchy of values; ultimately, it demands a correct understanding of the dignity and the rights of the person.

"The Church respects the legitimate autonomy of the democratic order and is not entitled to express preferences for this or that institutional or constitutional solution. Her contribution to the political order is precisely her vision of the dignity of the person revealed in all its fullness in the mystery of the Incarnate Word."

The State and the Economic Sector

48. "These general observations also apply to the role of the state in the economic sector. Economic activity, especially the activity of a market economy, cannot be conducted in an institutional, juridical or political vacuum. On the contrary, it presupposes sure guarantees of individual freedom and private property, as well as a stable currency and efficient public services. Hence the principal task of the state is to guarantee this security, so that those who work and produce can enjoy the fruits of their labors and thus feel encouraged to work efficiently and honestly. The absence of stability, together with the corruption of public officials and the spread of improper sources of growing rich and of easy profits deriving from illegal or purely speculative activities, constitutes one of the chief obstacles to development and to the economic order."

State Oversight

"Another task of the state is that of overseeing and directing the exercise of human rights in the economic sector. However, primary responsibility in this area belongs not to the state but to individuals and to the various groups and associations which make up society. The state could not directly ensure the right to work for all its citizens unless it controlled every aspect of economic life and restricted the free initiative of individuals. This does not mean, however, that the state has no competence in this domain, as was claimed by those who argued against any rules in the economic sphere. Rather, the state has a duty to sustain business activities by creating conditions which will ensure job opportunities, by stimulating those activities where they are lacking or by supporting them in moments of crisis.

"The state has the further right to intervene when particular monopolies create delays or obstacles to development. In addition to the tasks of harmonizing and guiding development, in exceptional circumstances the state can also exercise a substitute function, when social sectors or business systems are too weak or are just getting under way, and are not equal to the task at hand. Such supplementary interventions, which are justified by urgent reasons touching the common good, must be as brief as possible, so as to avoid removing permanently from society and business systems the functions which are properly theirs, and so as to avoid enlarging excessively the sphere of state intervention to the detriment of both economic and civil freedom."

The Welfare State

"In recent years the range of such intervention has vastly expanded, to the point of creating a new type of state, the so-called 'welfare state.' This has happened in some countries in order to respond better to many needs and demands, by remedying forms of poverty and deprivation unworthy of the human person."

However, excesses and abuses, especially in recent years, have provoked very harsh criticisms of the welfare state, dubbed the 'social assistance state.' Malfunctions and defects in the social assistance state are the result of an inadequate understanding of the tasks proper to the state. Here again the principle of subsidiarity must be respected; a community of a higher order should not interfere in the internal life of a community of a lower order, depriving the latter of its functions, but rather should support it in case of need and help to coordinate its activity with the activities of the rest of society, always with a view to the common good.

"By intervening directly and depriving society of its responsibility, the social assistance state leads to a loss of human energies and an inordinate increase of public agencies, which are dominated more by bureaucratic ways of thinking than by concern for serving their clients, and which are accompanied by an enormous increase in spending. In fact, it would appear that needs are best understood and satisfied by people who are closest to them and who act as neighbors to those in need."

Church Concern for the Needy

49. "Faithful to the mission received from Christ her founder, the Church has always been present and active among the needy, offering them material assistance in ways that neither humiliate nor reduce

them to mere objects of assistance, but which help them to escape their precarious situation by promoting their dignity as persons. With heartfelt gratitude to God, it must be pointed out that active charity has never ceased to be practiced in the Church; indeed, today it is showing a manifold and gratifying increase. In this regard, special mention must be made of volunteer work, which the Church favors and promotes by urging everyone to cooperate in supporting and encouraging its undertakings.

"In order to overcome today's widespread individualistic mentality, what is required is a concrete commitment to solidarity and charity, beginning in the family with the mutual support of husband and wife and the care which the different generations give to one another. . . . It is urgent to promote not only family policies, but also those social policies which have the family as their principal object."

52. "Another name for peace is development. Just as there is a collective responsibility for avoiding war, so too there is a collective responsibility for promoting development. Just as within individual societies it is possible and right to organize a solid economy which will direct the functioning of the market to the common good, so too there is a similar need for adequate interventions on the international level."

CHAPTER 6

Man is the Way of the Church

54. "Today, the Church's social doctrine focuses especially on man as he is involved in a complex network of relationships within modern societies. The human sciences and philosophy are helpful for interpreting man's central place within society and for enabling him to understand himself better as a 'social being.' However, man's true identity is only fully revealed to him through faith, and it is precisely from faith that the Church's social teaching begins. While drawing upon all the contributions made by the sciences and philosophy, her social teaching is aimed at helping man on the path of salvation."

"Given in Rome, at St. Peter's, on May 1, the memorial of St. Joseph the Worker, in the year 1991, the 13th of my pontificate."

STATEMENTS BY U.S. BISHOPS

Following are brief excerpts from two outstanding social documents issued by the National Conference of Catholic Bishops and the U.S. Catholic Conference: "The Challenge of Peace: God's Promise and Our Response," approved May 3, 1983; and "Economic Justice for All: Social Teaching and the U.S. Economy," approved Nov. 13, 1986. (See pp. 206-209, Catholic Almanac, 1992.)

WAR AND PEACE

1. Catholic teaching begins in every case with a presumption against war and for peaceful settlement of disputes. In exceptional cases, determined by the moral principles of the just-war tradition, some uses of force are permitted.

2. Every nation has a right and duty to defend itself against unjust aggression.

3. Offensive war of any kind is not morally justifiable.

4. It is never permitted to direct nuclear or conventional weapons to "the indiscriminate destruction of whole cities or vast areas with their populations."

Acceptable Conditions

1. We support immediate, bilateral, verifiable agreements to halt the testing, production and deployment of new nuclear weapons systems. This recommendation is not to be identified with any specific political initiative.

2. We support efforts to achieve deep cuts in the arsenals of both superpowers; efforts should concentrate first on systems which threaten the retaliatory forces of either major power.

3. We support early and successful conclusion of negotiations of a comprehensive test ban treaty.

4. We urge new efforts to prevent the spread of nuclear weapons in the world, and to control the conventional arms race, particularly the conventional arms trade.

ECONOMIC PRINCIPLES

• Every economic decision and institution must be judged in light of whether it protects or undermines the dignity of the human person.

• Human dignity can be realized and protected only in community.

• All people have a right to participate in the economic life of society.

• All members of society have a special obligation to the poor and vulnerable.

• Human rights are the minimum conditions for life in community.

• Society as a whole, acting through public and private institutions, has the moral responsibility to enhance human dignity and protect human rights.

These six moral principles are not the only ones presented in the pastoral letter, but they give an overview of the moral vision that we are trying to share. This vision of economic life cannot exist in a vacuum; it must be translated into concrete measures. Our pastoral letter spells out some specific applications of Catholic moral principles.

• We call for a new national commitment to full employment.

• We say it is a social and moral scandal that one of every seven Americans is poor, and we call for concerted efforts to eradicate poverty.

• The fulfillment of the basic needs of the poor is of the highest priority.

• We urge that all economic policies be evaluated in light of their impact on the life and stability of the family.

• We support measures to halt the loss of family farms and to resist the growing concentration in the ownership of agricultural resources.

• We specify ways in which the United States can do far more to relieve the plight of poor nations and assist in their development.

The nature and purpose of the liturgy, along with norms for its revision, were the subject matter of the *Constitution on the Sacred Liturgy* promulgated by the Second Vatican Council. The principles and guidelines stated in this document, the first issued by the Council, are summarized here and/or are incorporated in other Almanac entries on liturgical subjects.

Nature and Purpose of Liturgy

The paragraphs under this and the following subhead are quoted directly from the "Constitution on the Sacred Liturgy."

"It is through the liturgy, especially the divine Eucharistic Sacrifice, that 'the work of our redemption is exercised.' The liturgy is thus the outstanding means by which the faithful can express in their lives, and manifest to others, the mystery of Christ and the real nature of the true Church . . ." (No. 2).

"The liturgy is considered as an exercise of the priestly office of Jesus Christ. In the liturgy the sanctification of man is manifested by signs perceptible to the senses, and is effected in a way which is proper to each of these signs; in the liturgy full public worship is performed by the Mystical Body of Jesus Christ, that is, by the Head and his members.

"From this it follows that every liturgical celebration, because it is an action of Christ the priest and of his Body the Church, is a sacred action surpassing all others. No other action of the Church can match its claim to efficacy, nor equal the degree of it" (No. 7).

"The liturgy is the summit toward which the activity of the Church is directed; at the same time it is the fountain from which all her power flows. For the goal of apostolic works is that all who are made sons of God by faith and baptism should come together to praise God in the midst of his Church, to take part in her sacrifice, and to eat the Lord's Supper.

". . . From the liturgy, therefore, and especially from the Eucharist, as from a fountain, grace is channeled into us; and the sanctification of men in Christ and the glorification of God, to which all other activities of the Church are directed as toward their goal, are most powerfully achieved" (No. 10).

Full Participation

"Mother Church earnestly desires that all the faithful be led to that full, conscious, and active participation in liturgical celebrations which is demanded by the very nature of the liturgy. Such participation by the Christian people as 'a chosen race, a royal priesthood, a holy nation, a purchased people' (1 Pt. 2:9; cf. 2:4-5), is their right and duty by reason of their baptism.

"In the restoration and promotion of the sacred liturgy, this full and active participation by all the people is the aim to be considered before all else; for it is the primary and indispensable source from which the faithful are to derive the true Christian spirit . . ." (No. 14).

"In order that the Christian people may more securely derive an abundance of graces from the sacred liturgy, holy Mother Church desires to undertake with great care a general restoration of the liturgy itself. For the liturgy is made up of unchangeable elements divinely instituted, and elements subject to change. The latter not only may but ought to be changed with the passing of time if features have by chance crept in which are less harmonious with the intimate nature of the liturgy, or if existing elements have grown less functional.

"In this restoration, both texts and rites should be drawn up so that they express more clearly the holy things which they signify. Christian people, as far as possible, should be able to understand them with ease and to take part in them fully, actively, and as befits a community . . ." (No. 21).

Norms

Norms regarding the reforms concern the greater use of Scripture; emphasis on the importance of the sermon or homily on biblical and liturgical subjects; use of vernacular languages for prayers of the Mass and for administration of the sacraments; provision for adaptation of rites to cultural patterns.

Approval for reforms of various kinds — in liturgical texts, rites, etc. — depends on the Holy See, regional conferences of bishops and individual bishops, according to provisions of law. No priest has authority to initiate reforms on his own. Reforms may not be introduced just for the sake of innovation, and any that are introduced in the light of present-day circumstances should embody sound tradition.

To assure the desired effect of liturgical reforms, training and instruction are necessary for the clergy, religious and the laity. The functions of diocesan and regional commissions for liturgy, music and art are to set standards and provide leadership for instruction and practical programs in their respective fields.

Most of the constitution's provisions regarding liturgical reforms have to do with the Roman Rite. The document clearly respects the equal dignity of all rites, leaving to the Eastern Churches control over their ancient liturgies.

(For coverage of the **Mystery of the Eucharist,** see The Mass; **Other Sacraments,** see separate entries.)

Sacramentals

Sacramentals, instituted by the Church, "are sacred signs which bear a resemblance to the sacraments: they signify effects, particularly of a spiritual kind, which are obtained through the Church's intercession. By them men are disposed to receive the chief effect of the sacraments, and various occasions in life are rendered holy" (No. 60).

"Thus, for well-disposed members of the faithful, the liturgy of the sacraments and sacramentals sanctifies almost every event in their lives; they are given access to the stream of divine grace which flows from the paschal mystery of the passion, death, and resurrection of Christ, the fountain from which all sacraments and sacramentals draw their power. There is hardly any proper use of material things which cannot thus be directed toward the sanctification of men and the praise of God" (No. 61).

Some common sacramentals are priestly blessings,

blessed palm, candles, holy water, medals, scapulars, prayers and ceremonies of the Roman Ritual.

Liturgy of the Hours

The Liturgy of the Hours (Divine Office) is the public prayer of the Church for praising God and sanctifying the day. Its daily celebration is required as a sacred obligation by men in holy orders and by men and women religious who have professed solemn vows. Its celebration by others is highly commended and is to be encouraged in the community of the faithful.

"By tradition going back to early Christian times, the Divine Office is arranged so that the whole course of the day and night is made holy by the praises of God. Therefore, when this wonderful song of praise is worthily rendered by priests and others who are deputed for this purpose by Church ordinance, or by the faithful praying together with the priest in an approved form, then it is truly the voice of the bride addressing her bridegroom; it is the very prayer which Christ himself, together with his Body, addresses to the Father" (No. 84).

"Hence all who perform this service are not only fulfilling a duty of the Church, but also are sharing in the greatest honor accorded to Christ's spouse, for by offering these praises to God they are standing before God's throne in the name of the Church their Mother" (No. 85).

The Liturgy of the Hours, revised since 1965, was the subject of Pope Paul VI's apostolic constitution *Laudis Canticum,* dated Nov. 1, 1970. The master Latin text was published in 1971; its four volumes have been published in authorized English translation since May, 1975.

One-volume, partial editions of the Liturgy of the Hours containing Morning and Evening Prayer and other elements, have been published in approved English translation.

The revised Liturgy of the Hours consists of:

● Office of Readings, for reflection on the word of God. The principal parts are three psalms, biblical and non-biblical readings.

● Morning and Evening Prayer, called the "hinges" of the Liturgy of the Hours. The principal parts are a hymn, two psalms, an Old or New Testament canticle, a brief biblical reading, Zechariah's canticle (the *Benedictus,* morning) or Mary's canticle (the *Magnificat,* evening), responsories, intercessions and a concluding prayer.

● Daytime Prayer. The principal parts are a hymn, three psalms, a brief biblical reading and one of three concluding prayers corresponding to the time at which the prayer is offered (midmorning, midday, midafternoon).

● Night Prayer: The principal parts are one or two psalms, a brief biblical reading, Simeon's canticle *(Nunc Dimittis),* a concluding prayer and an antiphon in honor of Mary.

In the revised Liturgy of the Hours, the hours are shorter than they had been, with greater textual variety, meditation aids, and provision for intervals of silence and meditation. The psalms are distributed over a four-week period instead of a week; some psalms, entirely or in part, are not included. Additional canticles from the Old and New Testaments are assigned for Morning and Evening Prayer. Additional scriptural texts have been added and variously arranged for greater internal unity, correspondence to readings at Mass, and relevance to events and themes of salvation history. Readings include some of the best material from the Fathers of the Church and other authors, and improved selections on the lives of the saints.

The book used for recitation of the Office is the **Breviary.**

For coverage of the **Liturgical Year,** see Church Calendar.

Sacred Music

"The musical tradition of the universal Church is a treasure of immeasurable value, greater even than that of any other art. The main reason for this preeminence is that, as sacred melody united to words, it forms a necessary or integral part of the solemn liturgy.

"... Sacred music increases in holiness to the degree that it is intimately linked with liturgical action, winningly expresses prayerfulness, promotes solidarity, and enriches sacred rites with heightened solemnity. The Church indeed approves of all forms of true art, and admits them into divine worship when they show appropriate qualities" (No. 112).

The constitution decreed:

● Vernacular languages for the people's parts of the liturgy, as well as Latin, may be used.

● Participation in sacred song by the whole body of the faithful, and not just by choirs, is to be encouraged and brought about.

● Provisions should be made for proper musical training for clergy, religious and lay persons.

● While Gregorian Chant has a unique dignity and relationship to the Latin liturgy, other kinds of music are acceptable.

● Native musical traditions should be used, especially in mission areas.

● Various instruments compatible with the dignity of worship may be used.

Gregorian Chant: A form and style of chant called Gregorian was the basis and most highly regarded standard of liturgical music for centuries. It originated probably during the formative period of the Roman liturgy and developed in conjunction with Gallican and other forms of chant. Gregory the Great's connection with it is not clear, although it is known that he had great concern for and interest in church music. The earliest extant written versions of Gregorian Chant date from the ninth century. A thousand years later, the Benedictines of Solesmes, France, initiated a revival of chant which gave impetus to the modern liturgical movement.

Sacred Art and Furnishings

"Very rightly the fine arts are considered to rank among the noblest expressions of human genius. This judgment applies especially to religious art and to its highest achievement, which is sacred art. By their very nature both of the latter are related to God's boundless beauty, for this is the reality which these human efforts are trying to express in some way. To the extent that these works aim exclusively at turning men's thoughts to God persuasively and devoutly, they are dedicated to God and to the cause of his greater honor and glory" (No. 122).

The objective of sacred art is "that all things set apart for use in divine worship should be truly worthy, becoming, and beautiful, signs and symbols of heavenly realities. ... The Church has ... always reserved to herself the right to pass judgment upon the arts, deciding which of the works of artists are in accordance with faith, piety, and cherished traditional laws, and thereby suited to sacred purposes.

". . . Sacred furnishings should worthily and beautifully serve the dignity of worship . . ." (No. 122).

According to the constitution:

● Contemporary art, as well as that of the past, shall "be given free scope in the Church, provided that it adorns the sacred buildings and holy rites with due honor and reverence . . ." (No. 123).

● Noble beauty, not sumptuous display, should be sought in art, sacred vestments and ornaments.

● "Let bishops carefully exclude from the house of God and from other sacred places those works of artists which are repugnant to faith, morals, and Christian piety, and which offend true religious sense either by their distortion of forms or by lack of artistic worth, by mediocrity or by pretense.

● "When churches are to be built, let great care be taken that they be suitable for the celebration of liturgical services and for the active participation of the faithful" (No. 124).

● "The practice of placing sacred images in churches so that they may be venerated by the faithful is to be firmly maintained. Nevertheless, their number should be moderate and their relative location should reflect right order. Otherwise they may create confusion among the Christian people and promote a faulty sense of devotion" (No. 125).

● Artists should be trained and inspired in the spirit and for the purposes of the liturgy.

● The norms of sacred art should be revised. "These laws refer especially to the worthy and well-planned construction of sacred buildings, the shape and construction of altars, the nobility, location, and security of the Eucharistic tabernacle, the suitability and dignity of the baptistery, the proper use of sacred images, embellishments, and vestments . . ." (No. 128).

RITES

Rites are the forms and ceremonial observances of liturgical worship coupled with the total expression of the theological, spiritual and disciplinary heritages of particular churches of the East and the West.

Different rites have evolved in the course of church history, giving to liturgical worship and church life in general forms and usages peculiar and proper to the nature of worship and the culture of the faithful in various circumstances of time and place. Thus, there has been development since apostolic times in the prayers and ceremonies of the Mass, in the celebration of the sacraments, sacramentals and the Liturgy of the Hours, and in observances of the liturgical calendar. The principal sources of rites in present use were practices within the patriarchates of Rome (for the West) and Antioch, Alexandria and Constantinople (for the East). Rites are identified as Eastern or Western on the basis of their geographical area of origin in the Roman Empire.

Eastern and Roman

Eastern rites are proper to Eastern Catholic Churches (see separate entry). The principal rites are Byzantine, Alexandrian, Antiochene, Armenian and Chaldean.

The Latin or Roman rite prevails in the Western Church. It was derived from Roman practices and the use of Latin from the third century onward, and has been the rite in general use in the West since the eighth century. Other rites in limited use in the Western Church have been the Ambrosian (in the Archdiocese of Milan), the Mozarabic (in the Archdiocese of Toledo), the Lyonnais, the Braga, and rites peculiar to some religious orders like the Dominicans, Carmelites and Carthusians.

The purpose of the revision of rites in progress since the Second Vatican Council is to renew them, not to eliminate the rites of particular churches or to reduce all rites to uniformity. The Council reaffirmed the equal dignity and preservation of rites as follows.

"It is the mind of the Catholic Church that each individual church or rite retain its traditions whole and entire, while adjusting its way of life to various needs of time and place. Such individual churches, whether of the East or the West, although they differ somewhat among themselves in what are called rites (that is, in liturgy, ecclesiastical discipline and spiritual heritage), are, nevertheless, equally entrusted to the pastoral guidance of the Roman Pontiff, the divinely appointed successor of St. Peter in supreme government over the universal Church. They are, consequently, of equal dignity, so that none of them is superior to the others by reason of rite."

Determination of Rite

Determination of a person's rite is regulated by church law. Through baptism, a child becomes a member of the rite of his or her parents. If the parents are of different rites, the child's rite is decided by mutual consent of the parents; if there is lack of mutual consent, the child is baptized in the rite of the father. A candidate for baptism over the age of 14 can choose to be baptized in any approved rite. Catholics baptized in one rite may receive the sacraments in any of the approved ritual churches; they may transfer to another rite only with the permission of the Holy See and in accordance with other provisions of the Code of Canon Law.

MASS, EUCHARISTIC SACRIFICE AND BANQUET

Declarations of Vatican II

The Second Vatican Council made the following declarations among others with respect to the Mass.

"At the Last Supper, on the night when he was betrayed, our Savior instituted the Eucharistic Sacrifice of his Body and Blood. He did this in order to perpetuate the Sacrifice of the Cross throughout the centuries until he should come again, and so to entrust to his beloved spouse, the Church, a memorial of his death and resurrection: a sacrament of love, a sign of unity, a bond of charity, a paschal banquet in which Christ is consumed, the mind is filled with grace, and a pledge of future glory is given to us" (*Constitution on the Sacred Liturgy*, No. 47).

"... As often as the Sacrifice of the Cross in which 'Christ, our Passover, has been sacrificed' (1 Cor. 5:7) is celebrated on an altar, the work of our redemption is carried on. At the same time, in the sacrament of the Eucharistic bread the unity of all believers who form one body in Christ (cf. 1 Cor. 10:17) is both expressed and brought about. All men are called to this union with Christ ..." (*Dogmatic Constitution on the Church*, No. 3).

"... The ministerial priest, by the sacred power he enjoys, molds and rules the priestly people. Acting in the person of Christ, he brings about the Eucharistic Sacrifice, and offers it to God in the name of all the people. For their part, the faithful join in the offering of the Eucharist by virtue of their royal priesthood ..." (*Ibid.*, No. 10).

Declarations of Trent

Among its decrees on the Holy Eucharist, the Council of Trent stated the following points of doctrine on the Mass.

1. There is in the Catholic Church a true sacrifice, the Mass instituted by Jesus Christ. It is the sacrifice of his Body and Blood, Soul and Divinity, himself, under the appearances of bread and wine.

2. This Sacrifice is identical with the Sacrifice of the Cross, inasmuch as Christ is the Priest and Victim in both. A difference lies in the manner of offering, which was bloody upon the Cross and is bloodless on the altar.

3. The Mass is a propitiatory Sacrifice, atoning for the sins of the living and dead for whom it is offered.

4. The efficacy of the Mass is derived from the Sacrifice of the Cross, whose superabundant merits it applies to men.

5. Although the Mass is offered to God alone, it may be celebrated in honor and memory of the saints.

6. Christ instituted the Mass at the Last Supper.

7. Christ ordained the Apostles priests, giving them power and the command to consecrate his Body and Blood to perpetuate and renew the Sacrifice.

ORDER OF MASS

The Mass consists of two principal divisions called the **Liturgy of the Word**, which features the proclamation of the Word of God, and the **Eucharistic Liturgy**, which focuses on the central act of sacrifice in the Consecration and on the Eucharistic Banquet in Holy Communion. (Formerly, these divisions were called, respectively, the **Mass of the Catechumens** and the **Mass of the Faithful**.) In addition to these principal divisions, there are ancillary introductory and concluding rites.

The following description covers the Mass as celebrated with participation by the people. This Order of the Mass was approved by Pope Paul VI in the apostolic constitution *Missale Romanum* dated Apr. 3, 1969, and promulgated in a decree issued Apr. 6, 1969, by the Congregation for Divine Worship. The assigned effective date was Nov. 30, 1969.

Introductory Rites

Entrance: The introductory rites begin with the singing or recitation of an entrance song consisting of one or more scriptural verses stating the theme of the mystery, season or feast commemorated in the Mass.

Greeting: The priest and people make the Sign of the Cross together. The priest then greets them in one of several alternative ways and they reply in a corresponding manner.

Introductory Remarks: At this point, the priest or another of the ministers may introduce the theme of the Mass.

Penitential Rite: The priest and people together acknowledge their sins as a preliminary step toward worthy celebration of the sacred mysteries.

This rite includes a brief examination of conscience, a general confession of sin and plea for divine mercy in one of several ways, and a prayer for forgiveness by the priest.

Glory to God: A doxology, a hymn of praise to God, sung or said on festive occasions.

Opening Prayer: A prayer of petition offered by the priest on behalf of the worshipping community.

I. Liturgy of the Word

Readings: The featured elements of this liturgy are readings of passages from the Bible. If three readings are in order, the first is usually from the Old Testament, the second from the New Testament (Letters, Acts, Revelation), and the third from one of the Gospels; the final reading is always a selection from a Gospel. The first reading(s) is (are) concluded with the formula, "The Word of Lord" (effective Feb. 28, 1993; optional before that date), to which the people respond, "Thanks be to God." The Gospel reading is concluded with the formula, "The Gospel of the Lord," (effective as above), to which the people respond, "Praise to you, Lord Jesus Christ." Between the readings, psalm verses are sung or recited. A Gospel acclamation is either sung or omitted.

Homily: An explanation, pertinent to the mystery being celebrated and the special needs of the listeners, of some point in either the readings from sacred Scripture or in another text from the Ordinary or Proper parts of the Mass; it is a proclamation of the Good News for a response of faith.

Creed: The Nicene profession of faith, by priest and people, on certain occasions.

Prayer of the Faithful: Litany-type prayers of petition, with participation by the people. Called general intercessions, they concern needs of the Church, the salvation of the world, public authorities, persons in need, the local community.

II. Eucharistic Liturgy

Presentation of Gifts: Presentation to the priest of the gifts of bread and wine, principally, by participating members of the congregation.

Offering of and Prayer over the Gifts: Consists of the prayers and ceremonies with which the priest offers bread and wine as the elements of the sacrifice to take place during the Eucharistic Prayer and of the Lord's Supper to be shared in Holy Communion.

Washing of Hands: After offering the bread and wine, the priest cleanses his fingers with water in a brief ceremony of purification.

Pray, Brothers and Sisters: Prayer that the sacrifice to take place will be acceptable to God. The first part of the prayer is said by the priest; the second, by the people.

Prayer over the Gifts: A prayer of petition offered by the priest on behalf of the worshipping community.

Eucharistic Prayer

Preface: A hymn of praise, introducing the Eucharistic Prayer or Canon, sung or said by the priest following responses by the people. The Order of the Mass contains a variety of prefaces, for use on different occasions.

Holy, Holy, Holy; Blessed is He: Divine praises sung or said by the priest and people.

Eucharistic Prayer (Canon): Its central portion is the Consecration, when the essential act of sacrificial offering takes place with the changing of bread and wine into the Body and Blood of Christ. The various parts of the prayer, which are said by the celebrant only, commemorate principal mysteries of salvation history and include petitions for the Church, the living and dead, and remembrances of saints. There are four Eucharistic Prayers, for use on various occasions and at the option of the priest. (Additional Eucharistic Prayers for Masses with children and for reconciliation were approved in 1975.)

Doxology: A formula of divine praise sung or said by the priest while he holds aloft the chalice containing the consecrated wine in one hand and the paten containing the consecrated host in the other.

Communion Rite

Lord's Prayer: Sung or said by the priest and people.

Prayer for Deliverance from evil: Called an **embolism** because it is a development of the final petition of the Lord's Prayer; said by the priest. It concludes with a memorial of the return of the Lord to which the people respond, "For the kingdom, the power, and the glory are yours, now and forever."

Prayer for Peace: Said by the priest, with corresponding responses by the people. The priest can, in accord with local custom, bid the people to exchange a greeting of peace with each other.

Lamb of God (*Agnus Dei*): A prayer for divine mercy sung or said while the priest breaks the consecrated host and places a piece of it into the consecrated wine in the chalice.

Communion: The priest, after saying a preparatory prayer, administers Holy Communion to himself and then to the people, thus completing the sacrifice-banquet of the Mass. (This completion is realized even if the celebrant alone receives the Eucharist.) On giving the Eucharist to the people, the priest says, "The Body of Christ," to each recipient; the customary response is "Amen." If the

Eucharist is administered under the forms of bread and wine (by intinction), the priest says, "The Body and Blood of Christ."

Communion Song: Scriptural verses or a suitable hymn sung or said during the distribution of Holy Communion. After Holy Communion is received, some moments may be spent in silent meditation or in the chanting of a psalm or hymn of praise.

Prayer after Communion: A prayer of petition offered by the priest on behalf of the worshipping community.

Concluding Rite

Announcements: Brief announcements to the people are in order at this time.

Dismissal: Consists of a final greeting by the priest, a blessing, and a formula of dismissal. This rite is omitted if another liturgical action immediately follows the Mass; e.g., a procession, the blessing of the body during a funeral rite.

Some parts of the Mass are changeable with the liturgical season or feast, and are called the **proper** of the Mass. Other parts are said to be **common** because they always remain the same.

Additional Mass Notes

Catholics are seriously obliged to attend Mass in a worthy manner on Sundays and holy days of obligation. Failure to do so without a proportionately serious reason is gravely wrong.

It is the custom for priests to celebrate Mass daily whenever possible. To satisfy the needs of the faithful on Sundays and holy days of obligation, they are authorized to say Mass twice (**bination**) or even three times (**trination**). Bination is also permissible on weekdays to satisfy the needs of the faithful. On Christmas every priest may say three Masses.

The **fruits of the Mass,** which in itself is of infinite value, are: **general,** for all the faithful; **special (ministerial),** for the intentions or persons specifically intended by the celebrant; **most special (personal),** for the celebrant himself. On Sundays and certain other days pastors are obliged to offer Mass for their parishioners, or to have another priest do so. If a priest accepts a stipend or offering for a Mass, he is obliged in justice to apply the Mass for the intention of the donor. Mass may be applied for the living and the dead, or for any good intention.

Mass can be celebrated in several ways: e.g., with people present, without their presence (privately), with two or more priests as co-celebrants (concelebration), with greater or less solemnity.

Some of the various types of Masses are: **for the dead** (Funeral Mass or Mass of Christian Burial, Mass for the Dead — formerly called Requiem Mass); **ritual,** in connection with celebration of the sacraments, religious profession, etc.; **nuptial,** for married couples, with or after the wedding ceremony; **votive,** to honor a Person of the Trinity, a saint, or for some special intention. **Gregorian Masses** are a series of 30 Masses celebrated on 30 consecutive days for a deceased person.

On Good Friday instead of Mass, there is a celebration of the Lord's Passion consisting of a Liturgy of the Word, Veneration of the Cross and Holy Communion.

Places, Altars for Mass

The ordinary place for celebrating the Eucharist is a church or other sacred place, at a fixed or movable altar.

The altar is a table at which the Eucharistic Sacrifice is celebrated.

A fixed altar is attached to the floor of the church. It should be of stone, preferably, and should be consecrated. The Code of Canon Law orders observance of the custom of placing under a fixed altar relics of martyrs or other saints.

A movable altar can be made of any solid and suitable material, and should be blessed or consecrated.

Outside of a sacred place, Mass may be celebrated in an appropriate place at a suitable table covered with a linen cloth and corporal. An altar stone containing the relics of saints, which was formerly prescribed, is not required by regulations in effect since the promulgation Apr. 6, 1969, of *Institutio Generalis Missalis Romani.*

LITURGICAL VESTMENTS

In the early years of the Church, vestments worn by the ministers at liturgical functions were the same as the garments in ordinary popular use. They became distinctive when their form was not altered to correspond with later variations in popular style. Liturgical vestments are symbolic of the sacred ministry and add appropriate decorum to divine worship.

Mass Vestments

Alb: A body-length tunic of white fabric; a vestment common to all ministers of divine worship.

Amice: A rectangular piece of white cloth worn about the neck, tucked into the collar and falling over the shoulders; prescribed for use when the alb does not completely cover the ordinary clothing at the neck.

Chasuble: Originally, a large mantle or cloak covering the body, it is the outer vestment of a priest celebrating Mass or carrying out other sacred actions connected with the Mass.

Cincture: A cord which serves the purpose of a belt, holding the alb close to the body.

Dalmatic: The outer vestment worn by a deacon in place of a chasuble.

Stole: A long, band-like vestment worn by a priest about the neck and falling to about the knees. A deacon wears a stole over the left shoulder, crossed and fastened at his right side.

The material, form and ornamentation of the aforementioned and other vestments are subject to variation and adaptation, according to norms and decisions of the Holy See and concerned conferences of bishops. The overriding norm is that they should be appropriate for use in divine worship. The customary ornamented vestments are the chasuble, dalmatic and stole.

The minimal vestments required for a priest celebrating Mass are the alb, stole and chasuble.

Chasuble-Alb: A vestment combining the features of the chasuble and alb; for use with a stole by concelebrants and, by way of exception, by celebrants in certain circumstances.

Liturgical Colors

The colors of outer vestments vary with liturgical seasons, feasts and other circumstances. The colors and their use are:

Green: For the season of Ordinary Time; symbolic of hope and the vitality of the life of faith.

Violet (Purple): For Advent and Lent; may also be used in Masses for the dead; symbolic of penance. (See below, Violet for Advent.)

Red: For the Sunday of the Passion, Good Friday, Pentecost; feasts of the Passion of Our Lord, the Apostles and Evangelists, martyrs; symbolic of the supreme sacrifice of life for the love of God.

Rose: May be used in place of purple on the Third Sunday of Advent (formerly called Gaudete Sunday) and the Fourth Sunday of Lent (formerly called Laetare Sunday); symbolic of anticipatory joy during a time of penance.

White: For the seasons of Christmas and Easter; feasts and commemorations of Our Lord, except those of the Passion; feasts and commemorations of the Blessed Virgin Mary, angels, saints who are not martyrs, All Saints (Nov. 1), St. John the Baptist (June 24), St. John the Evangelist (Dec. 27), the Chair of St. Peter (Feb. 22), the Conversion of St. Paul (Jan. 25). White, symbolic of purity and integrity of the life of faith, may generally be substituted for other colors, and can be used for funeral and other Masses for the dead.

Options are provided regarding the color of vestments used in offices and Masses for the dead. The newsletter of the U.S. Bishops' Committee on the Liturgy, in line with No. 308 of the General Instruction of the Roman Missal, announced in July, 1970: "In the dioceses of the United States, white vestments may be used, in addition to violet (purple) and black, in offices and Masses for the dead."

On more solemn occasions, better than ordinary vestments may be used, even though their color (e.g., gold) does not match the requirements of the day.

Violet for Advent: Violet is the official liturgical color for the season of Advent, according to the September, 1988, edition of the newsletter of the U.S. Bishops' Committee on the Liturgy. Blue was being proposed in order to distinguish between the Advent season and the specifically penitential season of Lent. The newsletter said, however, that "the same effect can be achieved by following the official color sequence of the Church, which requires the use of violet for Advent and Lent, while taking advantage of the varying shades which exist for violet. ... Light blue vestments are not authorized for use in the United States."

Considerable freedom is permitted in the choice of colors of vestments worn for votive Masses.

Other Vestments

Cappa Magna: Flowing vestment with a train, worn by bishops and cardinals.

Cassock: A non-liturgical, full-length, close-fitting robe for use by priests and other clerics under liturgical vestments and in ordinary use; usually black for priests, purple for bishops and other prelates, red for cardinals, white for the pope. In place of a cassock, priests belonging to religious institutes wear the habit proper to their institute.

Cope: A mantle-like vestment open in front and fastened across the chest; worn by sacred ministers in processions and other ceremonies, as prescribed by appropriate directives.

Habit: The ordinary (non-liturgical) garb of members of religious institutes, analogous to the cassock of diocesan priests; the form of habits varies from institute to institute.

Humeral Veil: A rectangular vestment worn about the shoulders by a deacon or priest in Eucharistic processions and for other prescribed liturgical ceremonies.

Mitre: A headdress worn at some liturgical functions by bishops, abbots and, in certain cases, other ecclesiastics.

Pallium: A circular band of white wool about two inches wide, with front and back pendants, marked with six crosses, worn about the neck. It is a symbol of the fullness of the episcopal office. Pope Paul VI, in a document issued July 20, 1978, on his own initiative and entitled *Inter Eximia Episcopalis,* restricted its use to the pope and archbishops of metropolitan sees. In 1984, Pope John Paul II decreed that the pallium would ordinarily be conferred by the pope on the solemnity of Sts. Peter and Paul, June 29. The pallium is made from the wool of lambs blessed by the pope on the feast of St. Agnes (Jan. 21).

Rochet: A knee-length, white linen-lace garment of prelates worn under outer vestments.

Surplice: a loose, flowing vestment of white fabric with wide sleeves. For some functions, it is interchangeable with an alb.

Zucchetto: A skullcap worn by bishops and other prelates.

SACRED VESSELS, LINENS

Vessels

Paten and Chalice: The principal sacred vessels required for the celebration of Mass are the paten (plate) and chalice cup) in which bread and wine, respectively, are offered, consecrated and consumed. Both should be made of solid and noble material which is not easily breakable or corruptible. Gold coating is required of the interior parts of sacred vessels subject to rust. The cup of a chalice should be made of non-absorbent material.

Vessels for containing consecrated hosts (see below) can be made of material other than solid and noble metal — e.g., ivory, more durable woods — provided the substitute material is locally regarded as noble or rather precious and is suitable for sacred use.

Sacred vessels should be blessed, according to prescribed requirements.

Vessels, in addition to the paten, for containing consecrated hosts are:

Ciborium: Used to hold hosts for distribution to the faithful and for reservation in the tabernacle.

Luna, Lunula, Lunette: A small receptacle which holds the sacred host in an upright position in the monstrance.

Monstrance, Ostensorium: A portable receptacle so made that the sacred host, when enclosed therein, may be clearly seen, as at Benediction or during extended exposition of the Blessed Sacrament.

Pyx: A watch-shaped vessel used in carrying the Eucharist to the sick.

Linens

Altar Cloth: A white cloth, usually of linen, covering the table of an altar. One cloth is sufficient. Three were used according to former requirements.

Burse: A square, stiff flat case, open at one end, in which the folded corporal can be placed; the outside is covered with material of the same kind and color as the outer vestments of the celebrant.

Corporal: A square piece of white linen spread on the altar cloth, on which rest the vessels holding the Sacred Species — the consecrated host(s) and wine — during the Eucharistic Liturgy. The corporal is similarly used whenever the Blessed Sacrament is removed from the tabernacle; e.g., during Benediction the vessel containing the Blessed Sacrament rests on a corporal.

Finger Towel: A white rectangular napkin used by the priest to dry his fingers after cleansing them following the offering of gifts at Mass.

Pall: A square piece of stiff material, usually covered with linen, which can be used to cover the chalice at Mass.

Purificator: A white rectangular napkin used for cleansing sacred vessels after the reception of Communion at Mass.

Veil: The chalice intended for use at Mass can be covered with a veil made of the same material as the outer vestments of the celebrant.

THE CHURCH BUILDING

A church is a building set aside and dedicated for purposes of divine worship, the place of assembly for a worshipping community.

A Catholic church is the ordinary place in which the faithful assemble for participation in the Eucharistic Liturgy and other forms of divine worship.

In the early years of Christianity, the first places of assembly for the Eucharistic Liturgy were private homes (Acts 2:46; Rom. 16:5; 1 Cor. 16:5; Col. 4:15) and, sometimes, catacombs. Church building began in the latter half of the second century during lulls in persecution and became widespread after enactment of the Edict of Milan in 313, when it finally became possible for the Church to emerge completely from the underground. The oldest and basic norms regarding church buildings date from about that time.

The essential principle underlying all norms for church building was reformulated by the Second Vatican Council, as follows: "When churches are to be built, let great care be taken that they be suitable for the celebration of liturgical services and for the active participation of the faithful" *(Constitution on the Sacred Liturgy,* No. 124).

This principle was subsequently elaborated in detail by the Congregation for Divine Worship in a document entitled *Institutio Generalis Missalis Romani,* which was approved by Paul VI Apr. 3 and promulgated by a decree of the congregation dated Apr. 6, 1969. Coverage of the following items reflects the norms stated in Chapter V of this document.

Main Features

Sanctuary: The part of the church where the altar of sacrifice is located, the place where the ministers of the liturgy lead the people in prayer, proclaim the word of God and celebrate the Eucharist. It is set off from the body of the church by a distinctive structural feature — e.g., elevation above the main floor — or by ornamentation. (The traditional communion rail, removed in recent years in many churches, served this purpose of demarcation.) The customary location of the sanctuary is at the front of the church; it may, however, be centrally located.

Altar: The main altar of sacrifice and table of the Lord is the focal feature of the sanctuary and entire church. It stands by itself, so that the ministers can move about it freely, and is so situated that they face the people during the liturgical action. In addition to this main altar, there may also be others; in new churches, these are ideally situated in side chapels or alcoves removed to some degree from the body of the church.

Adornment of the Altar: The altar table is covered with a suitable linen cloth. Required candelabra and a cross are placed upon or near the altar in plain sight of the people and are so arranged that they do not obscure their view of the liturgical action.

Seats of the Ministers: The seats of the ministers should be so arranged that they are part of the seating arrangement of the worshiping congregation and suitably placed for the performance of ministerial functions. The seat of the celebrant or chief concelebrant should be in a presiding position.

Ambo, Pulpit, Lectern: The stand at which scriptural lessons and psalm responses are read, the word of God preached, and the prayer of the faithful offered. It is so placed that the ministers can be easily seen and heard by the people.

Places for the People: Seats and kneeling benches (pews) and other accommodations for the people are so arranged that they can participate in the most appropriate way in the liturgical action and have freedom of movement for the reception of Holy Communion. Reserved seats are out of order.

Place for the Choir: Where it is located depends on the most suitable arrangement for maintaining the unity of the choir with the congregation and for providing its members maximum opportunity for carrying out their proper function and participating fully in the Mass.

Tabernacle: The best place for reserving the Blessed Sacrament is in a chapel suitable for the private devotion of the people. If this is not possible, reservation should be at a side altar or other appropriately adorned place. In either case, the Blessed Sacrament should be kept in a tabernacle, i.e., a safe-like, secure receptacle.

Statues: Images of the Lord, the Blessed Virgin Mary and the saints are legitimately proposed for the veneration of the faithful in churches. Their number and arrangement, however, should be ordered in such a way that they do not distract the people from the central celebration of the Eucharistic Liturgy. There should be only one statue of one and the same saint in a church.

General Adornment and Arrangement of Churches: Churches should be so adorned and fitted out that they serve the direct requirements of divine worship and the needs and reasonable convenience of the people.

Other Items

Ambry: A box containing the holy oils, attached to the wall of the sanctuary in some churches.

Baptistery: The place for administering baptism. Some churches have baptisteries adjoining or near the entrance, a position symbolizing the fact that persons are initiated in the Church and incorporated in Christ through this sacrament. Contemporary liturgical practice favors placement of the baptistery near the sanctuary and altar, or the use of a portable font in the same position, to emphasize the relationship of baptism to the Eucharist, the celebration in sacrifice and banquet of the death and resurrection of Christ.

Candles: Used more for symbolical than illuminative purposes, they represent Christ, the light and life of grace, at liturgical functions. They are made of beeswax. (See Index: Paschal Candle.)

Confessional, Reconciliation Room: A booth-like structure for the hearing of confessions, with separate compartments for the priest and penitents and a grating or screen between them. The use of confessionals became general in the Roman Rite after the Council of Trent. Since the Second Vatican Council, there has been a trend in the U.S. to replace or supplement confessionals with small reconciliation rooms so arranged that priest and penitent can converse face-to-face.

Crucifix: A cross bearing the figure of the body of Christ, representative of the Sacrifice of the Cross.

Cruets: Vessels containing the wine and water used at Mass. They are placed on a credence table in the sanctuary.

Holy Water Fonts: Receptacles containing holy water, usually at church entrances, for the use of the faithful.

Sanctuary Lamp: A lamp which is kept burning continuously before a tabernacle in which the Blessed Sacrament is reserved, as a sign of the Real Presence of Christ.

LITURGICAL DEVELOPMENTS

The principal developments covered in this article are enactments of the Holy See and actions related to their implementation in the United States.

Modern Movement

Origins of the modern movement for renewal in the liturgy date back to the 19th century. The key contributing factor was a revival of liturgical and scriptural studies. Of special significance was the work of the Benedictine monks of Solesmes, France, who aroused great interest in the liturgy through the restoration of Gregorian Chant. St. Pius X approved their work in a motu proprio of 1903 and gave additional encouragement to liturgical study and development.

St. Pius X did more than any other single pope to

promote early first Communion and the practice of frequent Communion, started the research behind a revised breviary, and appointed a group to investigate possible revisions in the Mass.

The movement attracted some attention in the 1920s and 30s but made little progress.

Significant pioneering developments in the U.S. during the 20s, however, were the establishment of the Liturgical Press, the beginning of publication of *Orate Fratres* (now *Worship*), and the inauguration of the League of the Divine Office by the Benedictines at St. John's Abbey, Collegeville, Minn. Later events of influence were the establishment of the Pius X School of Liturgical Music at Manhattanville College of the Sacred Heart and the organization of a summer school of liturgical music at Mary Manse College by the Gregorian Institute of America. The turning point toward real renewal was reached during and after World War II.

Pius XII gave it impetus and direction, principally through the background teaching in his encyclicals on the *Mystical Body* (1943), *Sacred Liturgy* (1947), and *On Sacred Music* (1955), and by means of specific measures affecting the liturgy itself. His work was continued during the pontificates of his successors. The Second Vatican Council, in virtue of its *Constitution on the Sacred Liturgy*, inaugurated changes of the greatest significance.

Before and After Vatican II

The most significant liturgical changes made in the years immediately preceding the Second Vatican Council were the following:

(1) Revision of the Rites of Holy Week, for universal observance from 1956.

(2) Modification of the Eucharistic fast and permission for afternoon and evening Mass, in effect from 1953 and extended in 1957.

(3) The Dialogue Mass, introduced in 1958.

(4) Use of popular languages in administration of the sacraments.

(5) Calendar-missal-breviary reform, in effect from Jan. 1, 1961.

(6) Seven-step administration of baptism for adults, approved in 1962.

The *Constitution on the Sacred Liturgy* approved (2,174 to 4) and promulgated by the Second Vatican Council Dec. 4, 1963, marked the beginning of a profound renewal in the Church's corporate worship. Implementation of some of its measures was ordered by Paul VI Jan. 25, 1964, in the motu proprio *Sacram Liturgiam*. On Feb. 29, a special commission, the Consilium for Implementing the Constitution on the Sacred Liturgy, was formed to supervise the execution of the entire program of liturgical reform. Implementation of the program on local and regional levels was left to bishops acting through their own liturgical commissions and in concert with their fellow bishops in national conferences.

Liturgical reform in the United States has been carried out under the direction of the Liturgy Committee, National Conference of Catholic Bishops. Its secretariat, established early in 1965, is located at 3211 Fourth St. N.E., Washington, D.C. 20017.

Stages of Development

Liturgical development after the Second Vatican Council proceeded in several stages. It started with the formulation of guidelines and directives, and with the translation into vernacular languages of virtually unchanged Latin ritual texts. Then came structural changes in the Mass, the sacraments, the calendar, the Divine Office and other phases of the liturgy. These revisions were just about completed with the publication of a new order for the sacrament of penance in February, 1974. A continuing phase of development, in progress from the beginning, involves efforts to deepen the liturgical sense of the faithful, to increase their participation in worship and to relate it to full Christian life.

Texts and Translations

The master texts of all documents on liturgical reform are in Latin. Effective dates of their implementation have depended on the completion and approval of appropriate translations into vernacular languages. English translations were made by the International Committee for English in the Liturgy.

The principal features of liturgical changes and the effective dates of their introduction in the United States are covered below under topical headings. (For expanded coverage of various items, especially the sacraments, see additional entries.)

The Mass

A new Order of the Mass, supplanting the one authorized by the Council of Trent in the 16th century, was introduced in the U.S. Mar. 22, 1970. It had been approved by Paul VI in the apostolic constitution *Missale Romanum,* dated Apr. 3, 1969.

Preliminary and related to it were the following developments.

Mass in English: Introduced Nov. 29, 1964. In the same year, Psalm 42 was eliminated from the prayers at the foot of the altar.

Incidental Changes: The last Gospel (prologue of John) and vernacular prayers following Mass were eliminated Mar. 7, 1965. At the same time, provision was made for the celebrant to say aloud some prayers formerly said silently.

Rubrics: An instruction entitled *Tres Abhinc Annos,* dated May 4 and effective June 29, 1967, simplified directives for the celebration of Mass, approved the practice of saying the canon aloud, altered the Communion and dismissal rites, permitted purple instead of black vestments in Masses for the dead, discontinued wearing of the maniple, and approved in principle the use of vernacular languages for the canon, ordination rites, and lessons of the Divine Office when read in choir.

Eucharistic Prayers (Canons): Three additional Eucharistic prayers authorized May 23, 1968, were approved for use in vernacular translation the following Aug. 15. They have the same basic structure as the traditional Roman Canon, whose use in English was introduced Oct. 22, 1967.

The customary Roman Canon, which dates at least from the beginning of the fifth century and has remained substantially unchanged since the seventh century, is the first in the order of listing of the Eucharistic prayers. It can be used at any time, but is the one of choice for most Sundays, some special feasts like Easter and Pentecost, and for feasts of the Apostles and other saints who are commemorated in the canon. Any preface can be used with it.

The second Eucharistic prayer, the shortest and simplest of all, is best suited for use on weekdays and various special circumstances. It has a preface of its own, but others may be used with it. This canon bears a close resemblance to the one framed by St. Hippolytus about 215.

The third Eucharistic prayer is suitable for use on Sundays and feasts as an alternative to the Roman Canon. It can be used with any preface and has a special formula for remembrance of the dead.

The fourth Eucharistic prayer, the most sophisticated of them all, presents a broad synthesis of salvation history. Based on the Eastern tradition of Antioch, it is best suited for use at Masses attended by persons versed in Sacred Scripture. It has an unchangeable preface.

Five additional Eucharistic prayers — three for Masses with children and two for Masses of reconciliation — were approved in 1974 and 1975, respectively, by the Congregation for the Sacraments and Divine Worship.

Lectionary: A new compilation of scriptural readings and psalm responsories for Mass was published in 1969. The *Lectionary* contains a three-year cycle of readings for Sundays and solemn feasts, a two-year weekday cycle, and a one-year cycle for the feasts of saints, in addition to readings for a variety of votive Masses, ritual Masses and Masses for various needs. There are also responsorial psalms to follow the first readings and gospel or alleluia versicles.

A second edition of the *Lectionary,* substantially the same as the first, was published in 1981. New features included an expanded introduction, extensive scriptural references and additional readings for a number of solemnities and feasts.

Sacramentary (Missal): The Vatican Polyglot Press began distribution in June, 1970, of the Latin text of a new *Roman Missal,* the first revision published in 400 years. The English translation was authorized for optional use beginning July 1, 1974; the mandatory date for use was Dec. 1, 1974.

The Missal is the celebrant's book of prayers and sacramental formulas and does not include the readings of the Mass, such as the Gospel and the Epistle. It contains the texts of entrance songs, prefaces and other prayers of the Mass. The number of prefaces is four times greater than it had been. There are 10 commons (or sets of Mass prayers) of martyrs, two of doctors of the Church, and a dozen for saints or groups of saints of various kinds, such as religious, educators and mothers of families. There are Masses during which certain sacraments are administered and others for religious profession, the Church, the pope, priests, Christian unity, the evangelization of nations, persecuted Christians and other intentions.

Study of the Mass: The Bishops' Committee on the Liturgy, following approval by the National Conference of Catholic Bishops in May, 1979, began a study of the function and position of some elements of the Mass, including the Gloria, the sign of peace, the penitential rite and the readings.

Several phases of the study have been completed, and work is still under way toward completion of the project.

Mass for Special Groups: Reasons and norms for the celebration of Mass at special gatherings of the faithful were the subject of an instruction issued May 15, 1969. Two years earlier, the U.S. Bishops' Liturgy Committee went on record in support of the celebration of Mass in private homes under appropriate conditions.

Sunday Mass on Saturday: The Congregation for the Clergy, under date of Jan. 10, 1970, granted the request that the faithful, where bishops consider it pastorally necessary or useful, may satisfy the precept of participating in Mass in the late afternoon or evening hours of Saturdays and the days before holy days of obligation. This provision is stated in Canon 1248 of the Code of Canon Law.

Bination and Trination: Canon 905 of the Code of Canon Law provides that local ordinaries may permit priests to celebrate Mass twice a day (bination), for a just cause; in cases of pastoral need, they may permit priests to celebrate Mass three times a day (trination) on Sundays and holy days of obligation. ·

Mass in Latin: According to notices issued by the Congregation for Divine Worship June 1, 1971, and Oct. 28, 1974: (1) Bishops may permit the celebration of Mass in Latin for mixed-language groups. (2) Bishops may permit the celebration of one or two Masses in Latin on weekdays or Sundays in any church, irrespective of mixed-language groups involved (1971). (3) Priests may celebrate Mass in Latin when people are not present. (4) The approved revised Order of the Mass is to be used in Latin as well as vernacular languages. (5) By way of exception, bishops may permit older and handicapped priests to use the Council of Trent's Order of the Mass in private celebration of the holy Sacrifice. (See Permission for Tridentine Mass.)

Mass Obligation Waived: The Congregation for Bishops approved July 4, 1992, a resolution of the U.S. bishops to waive the Mass attendance obligation for the holy days of Mary, the Mother of God (Jan. 1), the Assumption of Mary (Aug. 15) and All Saints (Nov. 1) when these solemnities fall on Saturday or Monday.

Inter-Ritual Concelebration: The Apostolic Delegation (now Nunciature) in Washington, D.C., announced in June, 1971, that it had received authorization to permit priests of Roman and Eastern rites to celebrate Mass together in the rite of the host church. It was understood that the inter-ritual concelebrations would always be "a manifestation of the unity of the Church and of communion among particular churches."

Ordo of the Sung Mass: In a decree dated June 24 and made public Aug. 24, 1972, the Congregation for Divine Worship issued a new *Ordo of the Sung Mass* — containing Gregorian chants in Latin — to replace the *Graduale Romanum.*

Mass for Children: Late in 1973, the Congregation for Divine Worship issued special guidelines for children's Masses, providing accommodations to the mentality and spiritual growth of pre-adolescents while retaining the principal parts and structures of the Mass. The *Directory for Masses with Children* was approved by Paul VI Oct. 22 and was dated Nov. 1, 1973. Three Eucharistic prayers for Masses with children were approved by the congregation in 1974; English versions were approved June 5, 1975. Their use, authorized originally for a limited period of experimentation, was extended indefinitely Dec. 15, 1980.

Lectionary for Children: A lectionary for Masses with children, with an announced publication date of Sept., 1993, was authorized for use by choice beginning Nov. 28, 1993.

Sacraments

The general use of English in administration of the sacraments was approved for the U.S. Sept. 14, 1964. Structural changes of the rites were subsequently made and introduced in the U.S. as follows.

Pastoral Care of the Sick: Revised rites, covering also administration of the Eucharist to sick persons, were approved Nov. 30, 1972, and published Jan. 18, 1973. The effective date for use of the provisional English prayer formula was Dec. 1, 1974. The mandatory effective date for use of the ritual, *Pastoral Care of the Sick* in English, was Nov. 27, 1983.

Baptism: New rites for the baptism of infants, approved Mar. 19, 1969, were introduced June 1, 1970.

Rite of Christian Initiation of Adults: Revised rites were issued Jan. 6, 1972, for the Christian initiation of adults — affecting preparation for and reception of baptism, the Eucharist and confirmation; also, for the reception of already baptized adults into full communion with the Church. These rites, which were introduced in the U.S. on the completion of English translation, nullified a seven-step baptismal process approved in 1962. On Mar. 8, 1988, the National Conference of Catholic Bishops was notified that the Congregation for Divine Worship had approved the final English translation of the Rite of Christian Initiation of Adults. The mandatory date for putting the rite into effect was Sept. 1, 1988.

Confirmation: Revised rites, issued Aug. 15, 1971, became mandatory in the U.S. Jan. 1, 1973. The use of a stole by persons being confirmed should be avoided, according to an item in the December, 1984, edition of the *Newsletter* of the Bishops' Committee on the Liturgy. The item said: "The distinction between the universal priesthood of all the baptized and the ministerial priesthood of the ordained is blurred when the distinctive garb (the stole) of ordained ministers is used in this manner."

A norm regarding the proper age for confirmation was approved by the U.S. bishops in June, 1993. Ratification of the norm by the Holy See was pending at the time of writing. The norm reads: "In accord with prescriptions of canon 891, the National Conference of Catholic Bishops hereby decrees that the sacrament of confirmation in the Latin rite shall be conferred between the age of discretion, which is about the age of seven, and 18 years of age, within the limits determined by the diocesan bishop and with regard for the legitimate exceptions given in canon 891, namely, when there is danger of death or where, in the judgment of the minister, grave cause urges otherwise."

Special Ministers of the Eucharist: The designation of lay men and women to serve as special ministers of the Eucharist was authorized by Paul VI in an "Instruction on Facilitating Communion in Particular Circumstances" *(Immensae Caritatis)*, dated Jan. 29 and published by the Congregation for Divine Worship Mar. 29, 1973. Provisions concerning them are contained in Canons 230 and 910 of the Code of Canon Law.

Qualified lay persons may serve as special ministers for specific occasions or for extended periods in the absence of a sufficient number of priests and deacons to provide reasonable and appropriate service in the distribution of Holy Communion, during Mass and outside of Mass (to the sick and shut-ins). Appointments of ministers are made by priests with the approval of the appropriate bishop.

The Newsletter of the U.S. Bishops' Committee on the Liturgy stated in its February, 1988, edition: "When ordinary ministers (bishops, priests, deacons) are present during a Eucharistic celebration, whether they are participating in it or not, and are not prevented from doing so, they are to assist in the distribution of Communion. Accordingly, if the ordinary ministers are in sufficient number, special ministers of the Eucharist are not allowed to distribute Communion at that Eucharistic celebration." Pope John Paul approved this decision and ordered it published June 15, 1987.

Holy Orders: Revised ordination rites for deacons, priests and bishops, validated by prior experimental use, were approved in 1970. The sacrament of holy orders underwent further revision in 1972 with the elimination of the Church-instituted orders of porter, reader, exorcist, acolyte and subdeacon, and of the tonsure ceremony symbolic of entrance into the clerical state. The former minor orders of reader and acolyte were changed from orders to ministries.

Matrimony: A revised rite for the celebration of marriage was promulgated by the Congregation for Divine Worship and the Discipline of the Sacraments Mar. 19, 1969, and went into effect June 1, 1970. A second typical edition of the order of celebration, with revisions in accord with provisions of the Code of Canon Law promulgated in 1983, was approved and published in 1990 (*Notitiae*, Vol. 26, No.6). The date for implementation was reported to be dependent on the completion of required translations and appropriate formalities.

Penance: Ritual revision of the sacraments was completed with the approval by Paul VI Dec. 2, 1973, of new directives for the sacrament of penance or reconciliation. The U.S. Bishops' Committee on the Liturgy set Feb. 27, 1977, as the mandatory date for use of the new rite. The committee also declared that it could be used from Mar. 7, 1976, after adequate preparation of priests and people. Earlier, authorization was given by the Holy See in 1968 for the omission of any reference to excommunication or other censures in the formula of absolution unless there was some indication that a censure had actually been incurred by a penitent.

Additional Developments

Music: An instruction on Music in the Liturgy, dated Mar. 5 and effective May 14, 1967, encouraged congregational singing during liturgical celebrations and attempted to clarify the role of choirs and trained singers. More significantly, the instruction indicated that a major development under way in the liturgy was a gradual erasure of the distinctive lines traditionally drawn between the sung liturgy and the spoken liturgy, between what had been called the high Mass and the low Mass.

In the same year, the U.S. Bishops' Liturgy Committee approved the use of contemporary music, as well as guitars and other suitable instruments, in the liturgy. The Holy See authorized in 1968 the use of musical instruments other than the organ in liturgical services, "provided they are played in a manner suitable to worship."

Calendar: A revised liturgical calendar approved by Paul VI Feb. 14 and made public May 9, 1969, went into effect in the U.S. in 1972. Since that time, memorials and feasts of beatified persons and saints have been added.

Communion in Hand: Since 1969, the Holy See has approved the practice of in-hand reception of the Eucharist in regions and countries where it had the approval of the appropriate episcopal conferences. The first grant of approval was to Belgium, in May, 1969. Approval was granted the United States in June, 1977.

Liturgy of the Hours: The background, contents, scope and purposes of the revised Divine Office, called the Liturgy of the Hours, were described by Paul VI in the apostolic constitution *Laudis Canticum,* dated Nov. 1, 1970. A provisional English version, incorporating basic features of the master Latin text, was published in 1971. The four complete volumes of the Hours in English have been published since May, 1975. One-volume, partial editions have also been published in approved form. Nov. 27, 1977, was set by the Congregation for Divine Worship and the National Conference of Catholic Bishops as the effective date for exclusive use in liturgical worship of the translation of the Latin text of the Liturgy of the Hours approved by the International Committee on English in the Liturgy.

Holy Week: The English version of revised Holy Week rites went into effect in 1971. They introduced concelebration of Mass, placed new emphasis on commemorating the institution of the priesthood on Holy Thursday and modified Good Friday prayers for other Christians, Jews and other non-Christians.

In another action, the Congregation for Divine Worship released Feb. 20, 1988, a "Circular Letter concerning the Preparation and Celebration of the Easter Feasts." It called the feasts the "summit of the whole liturgical year," and criticized practices which dilute or change appropriate norms for their celebration. Singled out for blame for the abuse or ignorance of norms was the "inadequate formation given to the clergy and the faithful regarding the paschal mystery as the center of the liturgical year and of Christian life." The document set out the appropriate norms for the Lenten season, Holy Week, the Easter Triduum, Easter and the weeks following. It was particularly insistent on the proper celebration of the Easter Vigil, to take place after nightfall on Saturday and before dawn on Sunday.

Oils: The Congregation for Divine Worship issued a directive in 1971 permitting the use of other oils — from plants, seeds or coconuts — instead of the traditional olive oil in administering some of the sacraments. The directive also provided that oils could be blessed at other times than at the usual Mass of Chrism on Holy Thursday, and authorized bishops' conferences to permit priests to bless oils in cases of necessity.

Dancing and Worship: Dancing and worship was the subject of an essay which appeared in a 1975 edition of *Notitiae* (11, pp. 202-205), the official journal of the Congregation for the Sacraments and Divine Worship. The article was called a "qualified and authoritative sketch," and should be considered "an authoritative point of reference for every discussion of the matter."

The principal points of the essay were:

● "The dance has never been made an integral part of the official worship of the Latin Church."

● "If the proposal of the religious dance in the West is really to be made welcome, care will have to be taken that in its regard a place be found outside of the liturgy, in assembly areas which are not strictly liturgical. Moreover, the priests must always be excluded from the dance."

Mass for Deceased Non-Catholic Christians: The Congregation for the Doctrine of the Faith released a decree June 11, 1976, authorizing the celebration of public Mass for deceased non-Catholic Christians under certain conditions: "(1) The public celebration of the Masses must be explicitly requested by the relatives, friends, or subjects of the deceased person for a genuine religious motive. (2) In the Ordinary's judgment, there must be no scandal for the faithful."

Environment and Art in Catholic Worship: A booklet with this title was issued by the U.S. Bishops' Committee on the Liturgy in March, 1978.

Doxology: The bishops' committee called attention in August, 1978, to the directive that the Doxology concluding the Eucharistic Prayer is said or sung by the celebrant (concelebrants) alone, to which the people respond, "Amen."

Churches, Altars, Chalices: The Newsletter of the U.S. Bishops' Committee on the Liturgy reported in November, 1978, that the Congregation for Divine Worship had given provisional approval of a new English translation for the rite of dedicating churches and altars, and of a new form for the blessing of chalices.

Eucharistic Worship: This was the subject of two documents issued in 1980. *Dominicae Coenae* was a letter addressed by Pope John Paul to bishops throughout the world in connection with the celebration of Holy Thursday; it was dated Feb. 24 and released Mar.18. It was more doctrinal in content than the "Instruction on Certain Norms concerning Worship of the Eucharistic Mystery" (*Inaestimabile Donum,* "The Priceless Gift"), which was approved by the Pope Apr. 17 and published by the Congregation for the Sacraments and Divine Worship May 23. Its stated purpose was to reaffirm and clarify teaching on liturgical renewal contained in enactments of the Second Vatican Council and in several related implementing documents.

Tridentine Mass: The celebration of Mass according to the 1962 typical (master) edition of the Roman Missal — the so-called Tridentine Mass — was authorized by Pope John Paul under certain conditions. So stated a letter from the Congregation for Divine Worship, dated Oct. 3, 1984. The letter said the Pope wished to be responsive to priests and faithful who remained attached to the so-called Tridentine rite. The principal condition for the celebration was: "There must be unequivocal, even public, evidence that the priest and people petitioning have no ties with those who impugn the lawfulness and doctrinal soundness of the Roman Missal promulgated in 1970 by Pope Paul VI." (This, in particular, with reference to the followers of dissident Archbishop Marcel Lefebvre.)

Six guidelines for celebration of the Tridentine Mass were contained in the letter regarding its "wide and generous" use, for two purposes: to win back Lefebvre followers and to clear up misunderstandings about liberal permission for use of the Tridentine rite. The letter, from the Pontifical Commission Ecclesia Dei, said in part:

● The Tridentine Mass can be celebrated in a parish church, so long as it provides a pastoral service and is harmoniously integrated into the parish liturgical schedule.

● When requested, the Mass should be offered on a regular Sunday and holyday basis, "at a central location, at a convenient time" for a trial period of several months, with "adjustment" later if needed.

● Celebrants of the Mass should make it clear that they acknowledge the validity of the postconciliar liturgy.

● Although the commission has the authority to grant use of the Tridentine rite to all groups that request it, the commission "would much prefer that such faculties be granted by the Ordinary himself so that ecclesial communion can be strengthened."

● While the new Lectionary in the vernacular can be used in the Tridentine Mass, as suggested by the Second Vatican Council, it should not be "imposed on congregations that decidedly wish to maintain the former liturgical tradition in its integrity."

● Older and retired priests who have asked permission to celebrate Mass according to the Tridentine rite should be given the chance to do so for groups that request it.

Spanish: In accord with decrees of the Congregation for Divine Worship, Spanish was approved as a liturgical language in the U.S. (Jan. 19, 1985). The *texto unico* of the Ordinary of the Mass became mandatory in the U.S. Dec. 3, 1989. Spanish translations of Proper-of-the-Mass texts proper to U.S. dioceses were approved Mar. 12, 1990. An approved Spanish version of the Rite for the Christian Initiation of Adults was published in 1991.

Funeral Rites: A revised Order of Christian Funerals became mandatory in the U.S. Nov. 2, 1989.

Popular Piety and Liturgy: The relation of popular piety to the liturgy was the subject of remarks by Pope John Paul at a meeting with a group of Italian bishops Apr. 24, 1986. He said, in part:

"An authentic liturgical ministry will never be able to neglect the riches of popular piety, the values proper to the culture of a people, so that such riches might be illuminated, purified and introduced into the liturgy as an offering of the people."

Extended Eucharistic Exposition: In response to queries, the Secretariat of the U.S. Bishops' Committee on the Liturgy issued an advisory stating that liturgical law permits and encourages in parish churches:

● a. exposition of the Blessed Sacrament for an extended period of time once a year, with consent of the local Ordinary and only if suitable numbers of the faithful are expected to be present;

● b. exposition ordered by the local Ordinary, for a grave and general necessity, for a more extended period of supplication when the faithful assemble in large numbers.

With regard to perpetual exposition, this form is generally permitted only in the case of those religious communities of men or women who have the general practice of perpetual Eucharistic adoration or adoration over extended periods of time.

The Secretariat's advisory appeared in the June-July, 1986, edition of the Newsletter of the Bishops' Committee on the Liturgy.

Native American Languages: The Newsletter of the U.S. Bishops' Committee on the Liturgy reported in December, 1986, and May, 1987, respectively, that the Congregation for Divine Worship had authorized Mass translations in Navajo and Choctaw. Lakota was approved as a liturgical language in 1989.

Communion Guidelines: The U.S. Bishops' Committee on the Liturgy, in the December, 1986, Newsletter, reported that advisories were to be included in missalettes noting that: (1) The Eucharist is to be received by Catholics only, except in certain specific cases. (2) To receive Communion worthily, a person must be in the state of grace (i.e., free of serious sin) and observe the eucharistic fast (see separate entry).

Unauthorized Eucharistic Prayers: The May, 1987, Newsletter of the U.S. Bishops' Committee on the Liturgy restated the standing prohibition against the use of any Eucharistic Prayers other than those contained in the *Sacramentary*. Specifically, the article referred to the 25 unauthorized prayers in a volume entitled *Spoken Visions*.

Homilist: According to the Pontifical Commission for the Authentic Interpretation of Canon Law, the diocesan bishop cannot dispense from the requirement of Canon 767, par. 1, that the homily in the liturgy be reserved to a priest or deacon. Pope John Paul approved this decision and ordered it published June 20, 1987.

Concerts in Churches: In a letter released Dec. 5, 1987, the Congregation for Divine Worship declared that churches might be used on a limited basis for concerts of sacred or religious music but not for concerts featuring secular music.

Blessings: A revised *Book of Blessings* was ordered into use beginning Dec. 3, 1989.

SACRAMENTS

The sacraments are actions of Christ and his Church (itself a kind of sacrament) which signify grace, cause it in the act of signifying it, and confer it upon persons properly disposed to receive it. They perpetuate the redemptive activity of Christ, making it present and effective. They infallibly communicate the fruit of that activity — namely grace — to responsive persons with faith. Sacramental actions consist of the union of sensible signs (matter of the sacraments) with the words of the minister (form of the sacraments).

Christ himself instituted the seven sacraments of the New Law by determining their essence and the efficacy of their signs to produce the grace they signify.

Christ is the principal priest or minister of every sacrament; human agents — an ordained priest, baptized persons contracting marriage with each other, any person conferring emergency baptism in a proper manner — are secondary ministers. Sacraments have efficacy from Christ, not from the personal dispositions of their human ministers.

Each sacrament confers sanctifying grace for the special purpose of the sacrament; this is, accordingly, called sacramental grace. It involves a right to actual graces corresponding to the purposes of the respective sacraments.

Baptism, confirmation and the Eucharist are sacraments of initiation; penance (reconciliation) and anointing of the sick, sacraments of healing; order and matrimony, sacraments for service.

While sacraments infallibly produce the grace they signify, recipients benefit from them in proportion to their personal dispositions. One of these is the intention to receive sacraments as sacred signs of God's saving and grace-giving action. The state of grace is also necessary for fruitful reception of the Holy Eucharist, confirmation, matrimony, holy orders and anointing of the sick. Baptism is the sacrament in which grace is given in the first instance and original sin is remitted. Penance is the secondary sacrament of reconciliation, in which persons guilty of serious sin after baptism are reconciled with God and the Church, and in which persons already in the state of grace are strengthened in that state.

Role of Sacraments

The Second Vatican Council prefaced a description of the role of the sacraments with the following statement concerning participation by all the faithful in the priesthood of Christ and the exercise of that priesthood by receiving the sacraments (*Dogmatic Constitution on the Church,* Nos. 10 and 11).

"The baptized by regeneration and the anointing of the Holy Spirit are consecrated into a spiritual house and a holy priesthood. Thus through all those works befitting Christian men they can offer spiritual sacrifice and proclaim the power of him who has called them out of darkness into his marvelous light (cf. 1 Pt. 2:4-10)."

"Though they differ from one another in essence and not only in degree, the common priesthood of the faithful and the ministerial or hierarchical priesthood (of those ordained to holy orders) are nonetheless interrelated. Each of them in its own special way is a participation in the one priesthood of Christ. The ministerial priest, by the sacred power he enjoys, molds and rules the priestly people. Acting in the Person of Christ, he brings about the Eucharistic Sacrifice, and offers it to God in the name of all the people. For their part, the faithful join in the offering of the Eucharist by virtue of their royal priesthood. They likewise exercise that priesthood by receiving the sacraments, by prayer and thanksgiving, by the witness of a holy life, and by self-denial and active charity."

"It is through the sacraments and the exercise of the virtues that the sacred nature and organic structure of the priestly community is brought into operation."

Baptism: "Incorporated into the Church through baptism, the faithful are consecrated by the baptismal character to the exercise of the cult of the Christian religion. Reborn as sons of God, they must confess before men the faith which they have received from God through the Church."

Confirmation: "Bound more intimately to the Church by the sacrament of confirmation, they are endowed by the Holy Spirit with special strength. Hence they are more strictly obliged to spread and defend the faith both by word and by deed as true witnesses of Christ."

Eucharist: "Taking part in the Eucharistic Sacrifice, which is the fount and apex of the whole Christian life, they offer the divine Victim to God, and offer themselves along with It. Thus, both by the act of oblation and through holy Communion, all perform their proper part in this liturgical service, not, indeed. all in the same way but each in that way which is appropriate to himself. Strengthened anew at the holy table by the Body of Christ, they manifest in a practical way that unity of God's People which is suitably signified and wondrously brought about by this most awesome sacrament."

Penance: "Those who approach the sacrament of penance obtain pardon from the mercy of God for offenses committed against him. They are at the same time reconciled with the Church, which they have wounded by their sins, and which by charity, example, and prayer seeks their conversion."

Anointing of the Sick: "By the sacred anointing of the sick and the prayer of her priests, the whole Church commends those who are ill to the suffering and glorified Lord, asking that he may lighten their suffering and save them (cf. Jas. 5:14-16). She exhorts them, moreover, to contribute to the welfare of the whole People of God by associating themselves freely with the passion and death of Christ (cf. Rom. 8:17; Col. 1:24; 2 Tm. 2:11-12; 1 Pt. 4:13)."

Order: "Those of the faithful who are consecrated by holy orders are appointed to feed the Church in Christ's name with the Word and the grace of God."

Matrimony: "Christian spouses, in virtue of the sacrament of matrimony, signify and partake of the mystery of that unity and fruitful love which exists between Christ and his Church (cf. Eph. 5:32). The spouses thereby help each other to attain to holiness in their married life and by the rearing and education of their children. And so, in their state and way of life, they have their own special gift among the People of God (cf. 1 Cor. 7:7).

"For from the wedlock of Christians there comes the family, in which new citizens of human society are born. By the grace of the Holy Spirit received in baptism these are made children of God, thus perpetuating the People of God through the centuries. The family is, so to speak, the domestic Church. In it parents should, by their word and example, be the first preachers of the faith to their children. They should encourage them in the vocation which is proper to each of them, fostering with special care any religious vocation."

"Fortified by so many and such powerful means of salvation, all the faithful, whatever their condition or state, are called by the Lord, each in his own way, to that perfect holiness whereby the Father himself is perfect."

Baptism

Baptism is the sacrament of spiritual regeneration by which a person is incorporated in Christ and made a member of his Mystical Body, given grace, and cleansed of original sin. Actual sins and the punishment due for them are remitted also if the person baptized was guilty of such sins (e.g., in the case of a person baptized after reaching the age of reason). The theological virtues of faith, hope and charity are given with grace. The sacrament confers a character on the soul and can be received only once.

The matter is the pouring of water. The form is: "I baptize you in the name of the Father and of the Son and of the Holy Spirit."

The minister of solemn baptism is a bishop, priest or deacon, but in case of emergency anyone, including a non-Catholic, can validly baptize. The minister pours water on the forehead of the person being baptized and says the words of the form while the water is flowing. The water used in solemn baptism is blessed during the rite.

Baptism is conferred in the Roman Rite by immersion or infusion (pouring of water), depending on the directive of the appropriate conference of bishops, according to the Code of Canon Law. The Church recognizes as valid baptisms properly performed by non-Catholic ministers. The baptism of infants has always been considered valid and the general practice of infant baptism was well established by the fifth century. Baptism is conferred conditionally when there is doubt about the validity of a previous baptism.

Baptism is necessary for salvation. If a person cannot receive the baptism of water described above, this can be supplied by baptism of blood (martyrdom suffered for the Catholic faith or some Christian virtue) or by baptism of desire (perfect contrition joined with at least the implicit intention of doing whatever God wills that people should do for salvation).

A sponsor is required for the person being baptized. (See Godparents, below).

A person must be validly baptized before he or she can receive any of the other sacraments.

Christian Initiation of Infants: Infants should be solemnly baptized as soon after birth as conveniently possible. In danger of death, anyone may baptize an infant. If the child survives, the ceremonies of solemn baptism should be supplied.

The sacrament is ordinarily conferred by a priest or deacon of the parents' parish.

Catholics 16 years of age and over who have received the sacraments of confirmation and the Eucharist and are practicing their faith are eligible to be sponsors or godparents. Only one is required. Two, one of each sex, are permitted. A non-Catholic Christian cannot be a godparent for a Catholic child, but may serve as a witness to the baptism. A Catholic may not be a godparent for a child baptized in a non-Catholic religion, but may be a witness.

The role of godparents in baptismal ceremonies is secondary to the role of the parents. They serve as representatives of the community of faith and with the parents request baptism for the child and perform other ritual functions. Their function after baptism is to serve as proxies for the parents if the parents should be unable or fail to provide for the religious training of the child.

At baptism every child should be given a name with Christian significance, usually the name of a saint, to symbolize newness of life in Christ.

Christian Initiation of Adults: According to the *Ordo Initiationis Christianae Adultorum* ("Rite of the Christian Initiation of Adults") issued by the Congregation for Divine Worship under date of Jan. 6, 1972, and put into effect in revised form Sept. 1, 1988, adults are prepared for baptism and reception into the Church in several stages:

• An initial period of inquiry, instruction and evangelization.

• The catechumenate, a period of at least a year of formal instruction and progressive formation in and familiarity with Christian life. It starts with a statement of purpose and includes a rite of election.

• Immediate preparation, called a period of purification and enlightenment, from the beginning of Lent to reception of the sacraments of initiation — baptism, confirmation, Holy Eucharist — during ceremonies of the Easter Vigil. The period is marked by scrutinies, formal giving of the creed and the Lord's Prayer, the choice of a Christian name, and a final statement of intention.

• A mystagogic phase whose objective is greater familiarity with Christian life in the Church through observances of the Easter season and association with the community of the faithful, and through extended formation for about a year.

National Statutes for the Catechumenate were approved by the National Conference of Catholic Bishops Nov. 11, 1986, and were subsequently ratified by the Vatican.

The priest who baptizes a catechumen can also administer the sacrament of confirmation.

A sponsor is required for the person being baptized.

The *Ordo* also provides a simple rite of initiation for adults in danger of death and for cases in which all stages of the initiation process are not necessary, and guidelines for: (1) the preparation of adults for the sacraments of confirmation and Holy Eucharist in cases where they have been baptized but have not received further formation in the Christian life; (2) for the formation and initiation of children of catechetical age.

The Church recognizes the right of anyone over the age of seven to request baptism and to receive the sacrament after completing a course of instruction and giving evidence of good will. Practically, in the case of minors in a non-Catholic family or environment, the Church accepts them when other circumstances favor their ability to practice the faith — e.g., well-disposed family situation, the presence of another or several Catholics in the family. Those who are not in such favorable circumstances are prudently advised to defer reception of the sacrament until they attain the maturity necessary for independent practice of the faith.

Reception of Baptized Christians: Procedure for the reception of already baptized Christians into full communion with the Catholic Church is distinguished from the catechumenate, since they have received some Christian formation. Instruction and formation are provided as necessary, however; and conditional baptism is administered if there is reasonable doubt about the validity of the person's previous baptism.

In the rite of reception, the person is invited to join the community of the Church in professing the Nicene Creed and is asked to state: "I believe and profess all that the holy Catholic Church believes, teaches, and proclaims as revealed by God." The priest places his hand on the head of the person, states the formula of admission to full communion, confirms (in the absence of a bishop), gives a sign of peace, and administers Holy Communion during a Eucharistic Liturgy.

Confirmation

Confirmation is the sacrament by which a baptized person, through anointing with chrism and the imposition of hands, is endowed with the fullness of baptismal grace; is united more intimately to the Church; is enriched with the special power of the Holy Spirit; is committed to be an authentic witness to Christ in word and action. The sacrament confers a character on the soul and can be received only once.

According to the apostolic constitution *Divinae Consortium Naturae* dated Aug. 15, 1971, in conjunction with the *Ordo Confirmationis* ("Rite of Confirmation"): "The sacrament of confirmation is conferred through the anointing with chrism on the forehead, which is done by the imposition of the hand (matter of the sacrament), and through the words: 'N . . ., receive the seal of the Holy Spirit, the Gift of the Father' " (form of the sacrament). On May 5, 1975, bishops' conferences in English-speaking countries were informed by the Congregation for Divine Worship that Pope Paul had approved this English version of the form of the sacrament: "Be sealed with the gift of the Holy Spirit."

The ordinary minister of confirmation in the Roman Rite is a bishop. Priests may be delegated for the purpose. A pastor can confirm a parishioner in danger of death, and a priest can confirm in ceremonies of Christian initiation and at the reception of a baptized Christian into union with the Church.

Ideally, the sacrament is conferred during the Eucharistic Liturgy. Elements of the rite include renewal of the promises of baptism, which confirmation ratifies and completes, and the laying on of hands by the confirming bishop and priests participating in the ceremony.

"The entire rite," according to the *Ordo;* "has a twofold meaning. The laying of hands upon the candidates, done by the bishop and the concelebrating priests, expresses the biblical gesture by which the gift of the Holy Spirit is invoked . . . . The anointing with chrism and the accompanying words clearly signify the effect of the Holy Spirit. Signed with the perfumed oil by the bishop's hand, the baptized person receives the indelible character, the seal of the Lord, together with the Spirit who is given and who conforms the person more perfectly to Christ and gives him the grace of spreading the Lord's presence among men."

A sponsor is required for the person being confirmed. Eligible is any Catholic 16 years of age or older who has received the sacraments of confirmation and the Eucharist and is practicing the faith. The baptismal sponsor, preferably, can also be the sponsor for confirmation. Parents may present their children for confirmation but cannot be sponsors.

In the Roman Rite, it has been customary for children to receive confirmation within a reasonable time after first Communion and confession. There is a developing trend, however, to defer confirmation until later when its significance for mature Christian living becomes more evident. In the Eastern Rites, confirmation is administered at the same time as baptism.

Eucharist

The Holy Eucharist is a sacrifice (see The Mass) and the sacrament in which Christ is present and is received under the appearances of bread and wine.

The matter is bread of wheat, unleavened in the Roman Rite and leavened in the Eastern Rites, and wine of grape. The form consists of the words of consecration said by the priest at Mass: "This is my body . . . . This is the cup of my blood" (according to the traditional usage of the Roman Rite).

Only a priest can consecrate bread and wine so they become the body and blood of Christ. After consecration, however, the Eucharist can be administered by deacons and, for various reasons, by religious and lay persons.

Priests celebrating Mass receive the Eucharist under the species of bread and wine. In the Roman Rite, others receive under the species of bread only, i.e., the consecrated host, or in some circumstances they may receive under the species of both bread and wine. In Eastern-Rite practice, the faithful generally receive a piece of consecrated leavened bread which has been dipped into consecrated wine (i.e., by intinction).

Conditions for receiving the Eucharist, commonly called Holy Communion, are the state of grace, the right intention and observance of the Eucharistic fast.

The faithful of Roman Rite are required by a precept of the Church to receive the Eucharist at least once a year, ordinarily during the Easter time.

(See Eucharistic Fast, Mass, Transubstantiation, Viaticum.)

First Communion and Confession: Children are to be prepared for and given opportunity for receiving both sacraments (Eucharist and reconciliation, or penance) on reaching the age of discretion, at which time they become subject to general norms concerning confession and Communion. This, together with a stated preference for first confession before first Communion, was the central theme of a document entitled *Sanctus Pontifex* and published May 24, 1973, by the Congregation for the Discipline of the Sacraments and the Congregation for the Clergy, with the approval of Pope Paul VI.

What the document prescribed was the observance of practices ordered by St. Pius X in the decree *Quam Singulari* of Aug. 8, 1910. Its purpose was to counteract pastoral and catechetical experiments virtually denying children the opportunity of receiving both sacraments at the same time. Termination of such experiments was ordered by the end of the 1972-73 school year.

At the time the document was issued, two- or three-year experiments of this kind — routinely deferring reception of the sacrament of penance until after the first reception of Holy Communion — were in effect in more than half of the dioceses of the U.S. They have remained in effect in many places, despite the advisory from the Vatican.

One reason stated in support of such experiments is the view that children are not capable of serious sin at the age of seven or eight, when Communion is generally received for the first time, and therefore prior reception of the sacrament of penance is not necessary. Another reason is the purpose of making the distinctive nature of the two sacraments clearer to children.

The Vatican view reflected convictions that the principle and practice of devotional reception of penance are as valid for children as they are for adults, and that sound catechetical programs can avoid misconceptions about the two sacraments.

A second letter on the same subject and in the same vein was released May 19, 1977, by the aforementioned congregations. It was issued in response to the question:

" 'Whether it is allowed after the declaration of May 24, 1973, to continue to have, as a general rule, the reception of first Communion precede the reception of the sacrament of penance in those parishes in which this practice developed in the past few years.'

"The Sacred Congregations for the Sacraments and Divine Worship and for the Clergy, with the approval of the Supreme Pontiff, reply: Negative, and according to the mind of the declaration.

"The mind of the declaration is that one year after the promulgation of the same declaration, all experiments of receiving first Communion without the sacrament of penance should cease so that the discipline of the Church might be restored, in the spirit of the decree, *Quam Singulari*."

The two letters from the Vatican congregations have not produced uniformity of practice in this country. Simultaneous preparation for both sacraments is provided in some dioceses where a child has the option of receiving either sacrament first, with the counsel of parents, priests and teachers. Programs in other dioceses are geared first to recep-

tion of Communion and later to reception of the sacrament of reconciliation.

Commentators on the letters note that: they are disciplinary rather than doctrinal in content; they are subject to pastoral interpretation by bishops; they cannot be interpreted to mean that a person who is not guilty of serious sin must be required to receive the sacrament of penance before (even first) Communion.

Canon 914 of the Code of Canon Law states that sacramental confession should precede first Communion.

Holy Communion under the Forms of Bread and Wine (by separate taking of the consecrated bread and wine or by intinction, the reception of the host dipped in the wine): Such reception is permitted under conditions stated in instructions issued by the Congregation for Divine Worship (May 25, 1967; June 29, 1970), the *General Instruction on the Roman Missal* (No. 242), and directives of bishops' conferences and individual bishops.

Accordingly, Communion can be administered in this way to: persons being baptized, received into communion with the Church, confirmed, receiving anointing of the sick; couples at their wedding or jubilee; religious at profession or renewal of profession; lay persons receiving an ecclesiastical assignment (e.g., lay missionaries); participants at concelebrated Masses, retreats, pastoral commission meetings, daily Masses and, in the U.S., Masses on Sundays and holy days of obligation.

A communicant has the option of receiving the Eucharist under the form of bread alone or under the forms of bread and wine.

Holy Communion More Than Once a Day: A person who has already received the Eucharist may receive it (only) once again on the same day only during a Eucharistic celebration in which the person participates. A person in danger of death who has already received the Eucharist once or twice is urged to receive Communion again as Viaticum. Pope John Paul approved this decision, in accord with Canon 917, and ordered it published July 11, 1984.

Holy Communion and Eucharistic Devotion outside of Mass: These were the subjects of an instruction *(De Sacra Communione et de Cultu Mysterii Eucharistici extra Missam)* dated June 21 and made public Oct. 18, 1973, by the Congregation for Divine Worship.

Holy Communion can be given outside of Mass to persons unable for a reasonable cause to receive it during Mass on a given day. The ceremonial rite is modeled on the structure of the Mass, consisting of a penitential act, a scriptural reading, the Lord's Prayer, a sign or gesture of peace, giving of the Eucharist, prayer and final blessing. Viaticum and Communion to the sick can be given by extraordinary ministers (authorized lay persons) with appropriate rites.

Forms of devotion outside of Mass are exposition of the Blessed Sacrament (by men or women religious, especially, or lay persons in the absence of a priest; but only a priest can give the blessing), processions and congresses with appropriate rites.

Intercommunion: Church policy on intercommunion was stated in an "Instruction on the Admission of Other Christians to the Eucharist," dated June 1 and made public July 8, 1972, against the background of the *Decree on Ecumenism* approved by the Second Vatican Council, and the *Directory on Ecumenism* issued by the Secretariat for Promoting Christian Unity in 1967, 1970 and 1993.

Basic principles related to intercommunion are:

• "There is an indissoluble link between the mystery of the Church and the mystery of the Eucharist, or between ecclesial and Eucharistic communion; the celebration of the Eucharist of itself signifies the fullness of profession of faith and ecclesial communion" (1972 Instruction).

• "Eucharistic communion practiced by those who are not in full ecclesial communion with each other cannot be the expression of that full unity which the Eucharist of its nature signifies and which in this case does not exist; for this reason such communion cannot be regarded as a means to be used to lead to full ecclesial communion" (1972 Instruction).

• The question of reciprocity "arises only with those churches which have preserved the substance of the Eucharist, the sacrament of orders and apostolic succession" (1967 Directory).

• "A Catholic cannot ask for the Eucharist except from a minister who has been validly ordained" (1967 Directory).

The policy distinguishes between separated Eastern Christians and other Christians.

With Separated Eastern Christians (e.g., Orthodox): These may be given the Eucharist (as well as penance and anointing of the sick) at their request. Catholics may receive these same sacraments from priests of separated Eastern churches if they experience genuine spiritual necessity, seek spiritual benefit, and access to a Catholic priest is morally or physically impossible. This policy (of reciprocity) derives from the facts that the separated Eastern churches have apostolic succession through their bishops, valid priests, and sacramental beliefs and practices in accord with those of the Catholic Church.

With Other Christians (e.g., members of Reformation-related churches, others): Admission to the Eucharist in the Catholic Church, according to the *Directory on Ecumenism,* "is confined to particular cases of those Christians who have a faith in the sacrament in conformity with that of the Church, who experience a serious spiritual need for the Eucharistic sustenance, who for a prolonged period are unable to have recourse to a minister of their own community and who ask for the sacrament of their own accord; all this provided that they have proper dispositions and lead lives worthy of a Christian." The spiritual need is defined as "a need for an increase in spiritual life and a need for a deeper involvement in the mystery of the Church and its unity."

Circumstances under which Communion may be given to other properly disposed Christians are danger of death, imprisonment, persecution, grave spiritual necessity coupled with no chance of recourse to a minister of their own community.

Catholics cannot ask for the Eucharist from ministers of other Christian churches who have not been validly ordained to the priesthood.

Penance

Penance is the sacrament by which sins committed after baptism are forgiven and a person is reconciled with God and the Church.

Individual and integral confession and absolution are the only ordinary means for the forgiveness of serious sin and for reconciliation with God and the Church.

(Other than ordinary means are perfect contrition and general absolution without prior confession, both of which require the intention of subsequent confession and absolution.)

A revised ritual for the sacrament — *Ordo Paenitentiae,* published by the Congregation of Divine Worship Feb. 7, 1974, and made mandatory in the U.S. from the first Sunday of Lent, 1977 — reiterates standard doctrine concerning the sacrament; emphasizes the social (communal and ecclesial) aspects of sin and conversion, with due regard for personal aspects and individual reception of the sacrament; prescribes three forms for celebration of the sacrament; and presents models for community penitential services.

The basic elements of the sacrament are sorrow for sin because of a supernatural motive, confession (of previously unconfessed mortal or grave sins, required; of venial sins also, but not of necessity), and reparation (by means of prayer or other act enjoined by the confessor), all of which comprise the matter of the sacrament; and absolution, which is the form of the sacrament.

The traditional words of absolution — "I absolve you from your sins in the name of the Father, and of the Son, and of the Holy Spirit" — remain unchanged at the conclusion of a petition in the new rite that God may grant pardon and peace through the ministry of the Church.

The minister of the sacrament is an authorized priest — i.e., one who, besides having the power of orders to forgive sins, also has faculties of jurisdiction granted by an ecclesiastical superior and/or by canon law.

The sacrament can be celebrated in three ways.

• For individuals: The traditional manner remains acceptable but is enriched with additional elements including: reception of the penitent and making of the Sign of the Cross; an exhortation by the confessor to trust in God; a reading from Scripture; confession of sins; manifestation of repentance; petition for God's forgiveness through the ministry of the Church and the absolution of the priest; praise of God's mercy, and dismissal in peace. Some of these elements are optional.

• For several penitents, in the course of a community celebration including a Liturgy of the Word of God and prayers, individual confession and absolution, and an act of thanksgiving.

• For several penitents, in the course of a community celebration, with general confession and general absolution. In extraordinary cases, reconciliation may be attained by general absolution without prior individual confession as, for example, under these circumstances: (1) danger of death, when there is neither time nor priests available for hearing confessions; (2) grave necessity of a number of penitents who, because of a shortage of confessors, would be deprived of sacramental grace or Communion for a lengthy period of time through no fault of their own. Persons receiving general absolution are obliged to be properly disposed and resolved to make an individual confession of the grave sins from which they have been absolved; this confession should be made as soon as the opportunity to confess presents itself and before any second reception of general absolution.

Norms regarding general absolution, issued by the Congregation for the Doctrine of the Faith in 1972, are not intended to provide a basis for convoking large gatherings of the faithful for the purpose of imparting general absolution, in the absence of extraordinary circumstances. Judgment about circumstances that warrant general absolution belongs principally to the bishop of the place, with due regard for related decisions of appropriate episcopal conferences.

Communal celebrations of the sacrament are not held in connection with Mass.

The place of individual confession, as determined by episcopal conferences in accordance with given norms, can be the traditional confessional or another appropriate setting.

A precept of the Church obliges the faithful guilty of grave sin to confess at least once a year.

The Church favors more frequent reception of the sacrament not only for the reconciliation of persons guilty of serious sins but also for reasons of devotion. Devotional confession — in which venial sins or previously forgiven sins are confessed — serves the purpose of confirming persons in penance and conversion.

Penitential Celebrations: Communal penitential celebrations are designed to emphasize the social dimensions of Christian life — the community aspects and significance of penance and reconciliation.

Elements of such celebrations are community prayer, hymns and songs, scriptural and other readings, examination of conscience, general confession and expression of sorrow for sin, acts of penance and reconciliation, and a form of non-sacramental absolution resembling the one in the penitential rite of the Mass.

If the sacrament is celebrated during the service, there must be individual confession and absolution of sin.

(See Absolution, Confession, Confessional, Confessor, Contrition, Faculties, Forgiveness of Sin, Power of the Keys, Seal of Confession, Sin.)

Anointing of the Sick

This sacrament, promulgated by St. James the Apostle (Jas. 5:13-15), can be administered to the faithful after reaching the age of reason who begin to be in danger because of illness or old age. By the anointing with blessed oil and the prayer of a priest, the sacrament confers on the person comforting grace; the remission of venial sins and inculpably unconfessed mortal sins, together with at least some of the temporal punishment due for sins; and, sometimes, results in an improved state of health.

The matter of this sacrament is the anointing with blessed oil (of the sick — olive oil, or vegetable oil if necessary) of the forehead and hands; in cases of necessity, a single anointing of another portion of the body suffices. The form is: "Through this holy anointing and his most loving mercy, may the Lord assist you by the grace of the Holy Spirit so that,

when you have been freed from your sins, he may save you and in his goodness raise you up."

Anointing of the sick, formerly called extreme unction, may be received more than once, e.g., in new or continuing stages of serious illness. Ideally, the sacrament should be administered while the recipient is conscious and in conjunction with the sacraments of penance and the Eucharist. It should be administered in cases of doubt as to whether the person has reached the age of reason, is dangerously ill or dead.

The sacrament can be administered during a communal celebration in some circumstances, as in a home for the aged.

Matrimony

Coverage of the sacrament of matrimony is given in the articles: Marriage Doctrine, *Humanae Vitae,* Marriage Laws, Pastoral Ministry for Divorced and Remarried.

Order

Order is the sacrament by which the mission given by Christ to the Apostles continues to be exercised in the Church until the end of time; it is the sacrament of apostolic mission.It has

three grades: episcopacy, priesthood and diaconate. The sacrament confers a character on the soul and can be received only once. The minister of the sacrament is a bishop.

Order, like matrimony but in a different way, is a social sacrament. As the Second Vatican Council declared in the *Dogmatic Constitution on the Church:*

"For the nurturing and constant growth of the People of God, Christ the Lord instituted in his Church a variety of ministries, which work for the good of the whole body. For those ministers who are endowed with sacred power are servants of their brethren, so that all who are of the People of God, and therefore enjoy a true Christian dignity, can work toward a common goal freely and in an orderly way, and arrive at salvation" (No. 18).

Bishop: The fullness of the priesthood belongs to those who have received the order of bishop. Bishops, in hierarchical union with the pope and their fellow bishops, are the successors of the Apostles as pastors of the Church: they have individual responsibility for the care of the local churches they serve and collegial responsibility for the care of the universal Church (see Collegiality). In the ordination or consecration of bishops, the essential form is the imposition of hands by the consecrator(s) and the assigned prayer in the preface of the rite of ordination.

"With their helpers, the priests and deacons, bishops have ... taken up the service of the community presiding in place of God over the flock whose shepherds they are, as teachers of doctrine, priests of sacred worship, and officers of good order" (No. 20).

Priests: A priest is an ordained minister with the power to celebrate Mass, administer the sacraments, preach and teach the word of God, impart blessings, and perform additional pastoral functions, according to the mandate of his ecclesiastical superior.

Concerning priests, the Second Vatican Council stated in the *Dogmatic Constitution on the Church* (No. 28):

"The divinely established ecclesiastical ministry is exercised on different levels by those who from antiquity have been called bishops, priests, and deacons. Although priests do not possess the highest degree of the priesthood, and although they are dependent on the bishops in the exercise of their power, they are nevertheless united with the bishops in sacerdotal dignity. By the power of the sacrament of orders, and in the image of Christ the eternal High Priest (Hb. 5:1-10; 7:24; 9:11-28), they are consecrated to preach the Gospel, shepherd the faithful, and celebrate divine worship as true priests of the New Testament. . . .

"Priests, prudent cooperators with the episcopal order as well as its aides and instruments, are called to serve the People of God. They constitute one priesthood with their bishop, although that priesthood is comprised of different functions."

In the ordination of a priest of Roman Rite, the essential matter is the imposition of hands on the heads of those being ordained by the ordaining bishop. The essential form is the accompanying prayer in the preface of the ordination ceremony. Other elements in the rite are the presentation of the implements of sacrifice — the chalice containing the wine and the paten containing a host — with accompanying prayers.

Deacon: There are two kinds of deacons: those who receive the order and remain in it permanently, and those who receive the order while advancing to priesthood. The following quotation — from Vatican II's *Dogmatic Constitution on the Church* (No. 29) —describes the nature and role of the diaconate, with emphasis on the permanent diaconate.

"At a lower level of the hierarchy are deacons, upon whom hands are imposed 'not unto the priesthood, but unto a ministry of service.' For strengthened by sacramental grace, in communion with the bishop and his group of priests, they serve the People of God in the ministry of the liturgy, of the word, and of charity. It is the duty of the deacon, to the extent that he has been authorized by competent authority, to administer baptism solemnly, to be custodian and dispenser of the Eucharist, to assist at and bless marriages in the name of the Church, to bring Viaticum to the dying, to read the sacred Scripture to the faithful, to instruct and exhort the people, to preside at the worship and prayer of the faithful, to administer sacramentals, and to officiate at funeral and burial services. (Deacons are) dedicated to duties of charity and administration."

"The diaconate can in the future be restored as a proper and permanent rank of the hierarchy. It pertains to the competent territorial bodies of bishops, of one kind or another, to decide, with the approval of the Supreme Pontiff, whether and where it is opportune for such deacons to be appointed for the care of souls. With the consent of the Roman Pontiff, this diaconate will be able to be conferred upon men of more mature age, even upon those living in the married state. It may also be conferred upon suitable young men. For them, however, the law of celibacy must remain intact" (No. 29).

The Apostles ordained the first seven deacons (Acts 6:1-6): Stephen, Philip, Prochorus, Nicanor, Timon, Parmenas, Nicholas.

Other Ministries: The Church later assigned ministerial duties to men in several other orders, as:

Subdeacon, with specific duties in liturgical worship, especially at Mass. The order, whose first extant mention dates from about the middle of the third century, was regarded as minor until the 13th century; afterwards, it was called a major order in the West but not in the East.

Acolyte, to serve in minor capacities in liturgical worship; a function now performed by Mass servers.

Exorcist, to perform services of exorcism for expelling evil spirits; a function which came to be reserved to specially delegated priests.

Lector, to read scriptural and other passages during liturgical worship; a function now generally performed by lay persons.

Porter, to guard the entrance to an assembly of Christians and to ward off undesirables who tried to gain admittance; an order of early origin and utility but of present insignificance.

Long after it became evident that these positions and functions had fallen into general disuse or did not require clerical ordination, the Holy See started a revision of the orders in 1971. By an indult of Oct. 5, the bishops of the United States were permitted to omit ordaining porters and exorcists. Another indult, dated three days later, permitted the use of revised rites for ordaining acolytes and lectors.

To complete the revision, Pope Paul VI abolished Sept. 14, 1972, the orders of porter, exorcist and subdeacon; decreed that laymen, as well as candidates for the diaconate and priesthood, can be installed (rather than ordained) in the ministries (rather than orders) of acolyte and lector; reconfirmed the suppression of tonsure and its replacement with a service of dedication to God and the Church; and stated that a man enters the clerical state on ordination to the diaconate.

PERMANENT DIACONATE

Restoration of the permanent diaconate in the Roman rite — making it possible for men to become deacons permanently, without going on to the priesthood — was promulgated by Pope Paul VI June 18, 1967, in a document entitled *Sacrum Diaconatus Ordinem* ("Sacred Order of the Diaconate").

The Pope's action implemented the desire expressed by the Second Vatican Council for reestablishment of the diaconate as an independent order in its own right not only to supply ministers for carrying on the work of the Church but also to complete the hierarchical structure of the Church of Roman rite.

Permanent deacons have been traditional in the Eastern Church. The Western Church, however, since the fourth or fifth century, generally followed the practice of conferring the diaconate only as a sacred order preliminary to the priesthood, and of restricting the ministry of deacons to liturgical functions.

The Pope's document, issued on his own initiative, provided:

• Qualified unmarried men 25 years of age or

older may be ordained permanent deacons. They cannot marry after ordination.

• Qualified married men 35 years of age or older may be ordained permanent deacons. The consent of the wife of a prospective deacon is required. A married deacon cannot remarry after the death of his wife.

• Preparation for the diaconate includes a course of study and formation over a period of at least three years.

• Candidates who are not Religious must be affiliated with a diocese. Reestablishment of the permanent diaconate among Religious is reserved to the Holy See.

• Deacons will practice their ministry under the direction of a bishop and with the priests with whom they will be associated. (For functions, see also the description of deacon, under Holy Orders.)

Restoration of the permanent diaconate in the United States was approved by the Holy See in October, 1968. Shortly afterwards the U.S. bishops established a committee for the permanent diaconate, which is chaired by Bishop Dale J. Melczek, apostolic administrator of Gary. The committee operates through a secretariat, with offices at 3211 Fourth St. N. E., Washington, D.C. 20017. Samuel M. Taub, permanent deacon, is executive director.

Status and Functions

Reports filed by diocesan program directors indicate that, as of Jan. 1, 1993, there were in the U.S. 10,840 permanent deacons (456 more than in 1991) and nearly 2,000 candidates. Hispanic deacons comprised 13 percent of the total; African-Americans, 3 percent. Thirty-one dioceses had 100 or more deacons.

Of the total number of deacons, 92 percent are married; 16 percent are salaried by contract. Forty-four deacons are serving as administrators of parishes or missions. There are 38 deacons in religious institutes; 131 deacons have been ordained for the Eastern Rites. In 67 dioceses a deacon is the director of the diaconate; nearly 600 deacons are reported either "inactive/retired" or "not functioning."

Training programs of spiritual, theological and pastoral formation are based on guidelines emanating from the National Conference of Catholic Bishops.

Deacons have various functions, depending on the nature of their assignments. Liturgically, they can officiate at baptisms, weddings, wake services and funerals, can preach and distribute Holy Communion. Some are engaged in religious education work. All are intended to carry out works of charity and pastoral service of one kind or another.

The majority of permanent deacons, 92 per cent of whom are married, continue in their secular work. Their ministry of service is developing in three dimensions: of liturgy, of the word, and of charity. Depending on the individual deacon's abilities and preference, he is assigned by his bishop to either a parochial ministry or to one particular field of service. The latter is the most challenging ministry to develop. Deacons are active in a variety of ministries including those to prison inmates and their families, the sick in hospitals, nursing homes and homes for the aged, alienated youth, the elderly and the poor, and in various areas of legal service to the indigent, of education and campus ministry. The possibilities for diaconal ministry are under realistic assessment in a number of dioceses.

National Association of Permanent Diaconate Directors: Membership organization of directors, vicars and other staff personnel of permanent diaconate programs. Established in 1977 to promote effective communication and facilitate the exchange of information and resources of members; to develop professional expertise and promote research, training and self evaluation; to foster accountability and seek ways to promote means of implementing solutions to problems. NAPDD is governed by an executive board of elected officers. President for the 1993-94 term, Ann Healey of Fort Worth. Executive director, Deacon John Pistone. Office, 1337 W. Ohio St., Chicago, Ill. 60622.

MARRIAGE DOCTRINE

The following excerpts, stating key points of doctrine on marriage, are from the *Pastoral Constitution on the Church in the Modern World* (Nos. 48 to 51) promulgated by the Second Vatican Council.

Conjugal Covenant

The intimate partnership of married life and love has been established by the Creator and qualified by his laws. It is rooted in the conjugal covenant of irrevocable personal consent.

God himself is the author of matrimony, endowed as it is with various benefits and purposes. All of these have a very decisive bearing on the continuation of the human race, on the personal development and eternal destiny of the individual members of a family, and on the dignity, stability, peace, and prosperity of the family itself and of human society as a whole. By their very nature, the institution of matrimony itself and conjugal love are ordained for the procreation and education of children, and find in them their ultimate crown.

Thus a man and a woman ... render mutual help and service to each other through an intimate union of their persons and of their actions. Through this union they experience the meaning of their oneness and attain to it with growing perfection day by day. As a mutual gift of two persons, this intimate union, as well as the good of the children, imposes total fidelity on the spouses and argues for an unbreakable oneness between them (No. 48).

Sacrament of Matrimony

Christ the Lord abundantly blessed this many-faceted love. ... The Savior of men and the Spouse of the Church comes into the lives of married Christians through the sacrament of matrimony. He abides with them thereafter so that, just as he loved the Church and handed himself over on her behalf, the spouses may love each other with perpetual fidelity through mutual self-bestowal.

Graced with the dignity and office of fatherhood and motherhood, parents will energetically acquit themselves of a duty which devolves primarily on them; namely, education, and especially religious education.

The Christian family, which springs from marriage as a reflection of the loving covenant uniting Christ with the Church, and as a participation in that covenant, will manifest to all men the Savior's living presence in the world, and the genuine nature of the Church (No. 48).

Conjugal Love

The biblical Word of God several times urges the betrothed and the married to nourish and develop their wedlock by pure conjugal love and undivided affection.

This love is an eminently human one since it is directed from one person to another through an affection of the will. It involves the good of the whole person. Therefore it can enrich the expressions of body and mind with a unique dignity, ennobling these expressions as special ingredients and signs of the friendship distinctive of marriage. This love the Lord has judged worthy of special gifts, healing, perfecting, and exalting gifts of grace and of charity.

Such love, merging the human with the divine, leads the spouses to a free and mutual gift of themselves, a gift proving itself by gentle affection and by deed. Such love pervades the whole of their lives. Indeed, by its generous activity it grows better and grows greater. Therefore it far excels mere erotic inclination, which, selfishly pursued, soon enough fades wretchedly away.

This love is uniquely expressed and perfected through the marital act. The actions within marriage by which the couple are united intimately and chastely are noble and worthy ones. Expressed in a manner which is truly human, these actions signify and promote that mutual self-giving by which spouses enrich each other with a joyful and a thankful will.

Sealed by mutual faithfulness and hallowed above all by Christ's sacrament, this love remains steadfastly true in body and in mind, in bright days or dark. It will never be profaned by adultery or divorce. Firmly established by the Lord, the unity of marriage will radiate from the equal personal dignity of wife and husband, a dignity acknowledged by mutual and total love.

The steady fulfillment of the duties of this Christian vocation demands notable virtue. For this reason, strengthened by grace for holiness of life, the couple will painstakingly cultivate and pray for constancy of love, largeheartedness, and the spirit of sacrifice (No. 49).

Fruitfulness of Marriage

Marriage and conjugal love are by their nature ordained toward the begetting and educating of children. Children are really the supreme gift of marriage and contribute very substantially to the welfare of their parents. . . . God himself . . . wished to share with man a certain special participation in his own creative work. Thus he blessed male and female, saying: "Increase and multiply" (Gn. 1:28).

Hence, while not making the other purposes of matrimony of less account, the true practice of conjugal love, and the whole meaning of the family life which results from it, have this aim: that the couple be ready with stout hearts to cooperate with the love of the Creator and the Savior, who through them will enlarge and enrich his own family day by day.

Parents should regard as their proper mission the task of transmitting human life and educating those to whom it has been transmitted. They should realize that they are thereby cooperators with the love of God the Creator, and are, so to speak, the interpreters of that love. Thus they will fulfill their task with human and Christian responsibility (No. 50).

Norms of Judgment

They will thoughtfully take into account both their own welfare and that of their children, those already born and those who may be foreseen. For this accounting they will reckon with both the material and the spiritual conditions of the times as well as of their state in life. Finally, they will consult the interests of the family group, of temporal society, and of the Church herself.

The parents themselves should ultimately make this judgment in the sight of God. But in their manner of acting, spouses should be aware that they cannot proceed arbitrarily. They must always be governed according to a conscience dutifully conformed to the divine law itself, and should be submissive toward the Church's teaching office, which authentically interprets that law in the light of the Gospel. That divine law reveals and protects the integral meaning of conjugal love, and impels it toward a truly human fulfillment.

Marriage, to be sure, is not instituted solely for procreation. Rather, its very nature as an unbreakable compact between persons, and the welfare of the children, both demand that the mutual love of the spouses, too, be embodied in a rightly ordered manner, that it grow and ripen. Therefore, marriage persists as a whole manner and communion of life, and maintains its value and indissolubility, even when offspring are lacking — despite, rather often, the very intense desire of the couple (No. 50).

Love and Life

This Council realizes that certain modern conditions often keep couples from arranging their married lives harmoniously, and that they find themselves in circumstances where at least temporarily the size of their families should not be increased. As a result, the faithful exercise of love and the full intimacy of their lives are hard to maintain. But where the intimacy of married life is broken off, it is not rare for its faithfulness to be imperiled and its quality of fruitfulness ruined. For then the upbringing of the children and the courage to accept new ones are both endangered.

To these problems there are those who presume to offer dishonorable solutions. Indeed, they do not recoil from the taking of life. But the Church issues the reminder that a true contradiction cannot exist between the divine laws pertaining to the transmission of life and those pertaining to the fostering of authentic conjugal love.

Church Teaching

For God, the Lord of Life, has conferred on men the surpassing ministry of safeguarding life — a ministry which must be fulfilled in a manner which is worthy of men. Therefore from the moment of its conception life must be guarded with the greatest care, while abortion and infanticide are unspeakable crimes. The sexual characteristics of man and the human faculty of reproduction wonderfully exceed the dispositions of lower forms of life. Hence the acts themselves which are proper to conjugal love and which are exercised in accord with genuine human dignity must be honored with great reverence (No. 51).

Therefore when there is question of harmonizing conjugal love with the responsible transmission of life, the moral aspect of any procedure does not depend solely on the sincere intentions or on an evaluation of motives. It must be determined by ob-

jective standards. These, based on the nature of the human person and his acts, preserve the full sense of mutual self-giving and human procreation in the context of true love. Such a goal cannot be achieved unless the virtue of conjugal chastity is sincerely practiced. Relying on these principles, sons of the Church may not undertake methods of regulating procreation which are found blameworthy by the teaching authority of the Church in its unfolding of the divine law.

Everyone should be persuaded that human life and the task of transmitting it are not realities bound up with this world alone. Hence they cannot be measured or perceived only in terms of it, but always have a bearing on the eternal destiny of men (No. 51).

HUMANAE VITAE

Marriage doctrine and morality were the subjects of the encylical *Humanae Vitae* ("Of Human Life" issued by Pope Paul VI, July 29, 1968. Following are a number of key excerpts from the document which was framed in the pattern of traditional teaching and statements by the Second Vatican Council.

Each and every marriage act ("quilibet matrimonii usus") must remain open to the transmission of life (No. 11).

Indeed, by its intimate structure, the conjugal act, while most closely uniting husband and wife, capacitates them for the generation of new lives according to laws inscribed in the very being of man and of woman. By safeguarding both these essential aspects, the unitive and the procreative, the conjugal act preserves in its fullness the sense of true mutual love and its ordination toward man's most high calling to parenthood (No. 12).

It is, in fact, justly observed that a conjugal act imposed upon one's partner without regard for his or her condition and lawful desires is not a true act of love, and therefore denies an exigency of right moral order in the relationships between husband and wife. Hence, one who reflects well must also recognize that a reciprocal act of love which jeopardizes the responsibility to transmit life — which God the Creator, according to particular laws, inserted therein — is in contradiction with the design constitutive of marriage and with the will of the Author of life. To use this divine gift, destroying, even if only partially, its meaning and its purpose, is to contradict the nature both of man and of woman and of their most intimate relationship, and therefore it is to contradict also the plan of God and his will (No. 13).

Forbidden Actions

The direct interruption of the generative process already begun, and, above all, directly willed and procured abortion, even if for therapeutic reasons, are to be absolutely excluded as licit means of regulating birth.

Equally to be excluded ... is direct sterilization, whether perpetual or temporary, whether of the man or of the woman. Similarly excluded is every action which, either in anticipation of the conjugal act, or in its accomplishment, or in the development of its

natural consequences, proposes, whether as an end or as a means, to render procreation impossible.

To justify conjugal acts made intentionally infecund, one cannot invoke as valid reasons the lesser evil, or the fact that such acts would constitute a whole together with the fecund acts already performed or to follow later and hence would share in one and the same moral goodness. In truth, if it is sometimes licit to tolerate a lesser evil in order to avoid a greater evil or to promote a greater good, it is not licit, even for the gravest reasons, to do evil so that good may follow therefrom; that is, to make into the object of a positive act of the will something which is intrinsically disorder, and hence unworthy of the human person, even when the intention is to safeguard or promote individual, family or social well-being.

Consequently, it is an error to think that a conjugal act which is deliberately made infecund, and so is intrinsically dishonest, could be made honest and right by the ensemble of a fecund conjugal life (No. 14).

If, then, there are serious motives to space out births, which derive from the physical or psychological conditions of husband and wife, or from external conditions, the Church teaches that it is then licit to take into account the natural rhythms immanent in the generative functions, for the use of marriage in the infecund periods only, and in this way to regulate birth without offending earlier stated principles (No. 16).

Pastoral Concerns

We do not at all intend to hide the sometimes serious difficulties inherent in the life of Christian married persons; for them, as for everyone else, "the gate is narrow and the way is hard that leads to life." But the hope of that life must illuminate their way, as with courage they strive to live with wisdom, justice and piety in this present time, knowing that the figure of this world passes away.

Let married couples then, face up to the efforts needed, supported by the faith and hope which "do not disappoint ... because God's love has been poured into our hearts through the Holy Spirit, who has been given to us." Let them implore divine assistance by persevering prayer; above all, let them draw from the source of grace and charity in the Eucharist. And, if sin should still keep its hold over them, let them not be discouraged but rather have recourse with humble perseverance to the mercy of God, which is poured forth in the sacrament of penance (No. 25).

25TH ANNIVERSARY

Following is the conclusion of a statement issued by the U.S. Bishops' Committee for Pro-Life Activities on the occasion of the 25th anniversary of the publication July 25, 1968, of Pope Paul VI's encyclical letter, *Of Human Life.*

The text of the statement was circulated by the CNS Documentary Service, Origins, Aug. 12, 1993 (Vol. 23, No. 10).

Humanae Vitae represents a call to celebrate and reverence God's vision of human sexuality. It reminds us that we are stewards of God's gifts of marital love and procreation. It sounded a prophetic message for people to live chastely, to welcome children and protect families, and never to treat human life as a commodity. Ultimately, it challenged the people of God to grow in Christian maturity.

Realizing that 25 years represents the coming of a new generation, it is our hope that the new genera-tion might read *Humanae Vitae* and hear its gentle and loving message. In the face of a society that has lost sight of the profound meaning of marital intimacy, a society that has separated sexuality from married love and intimacy from procreation, it is important to call everyone to listen once again to the wisdom of *Humanae Vitae* and to make the Church's teaching the foundation for a renewed understanding of marriage and family life.

Recalling the teachings expressed in *Humanae Vitae,* we renew our commitment to respect for human life. We rededicate ourselves to increase our efforts to expand Christian education, pastoral programs for engaged and married couples, and natural family planning services. We will work to dispel confusions of our age and strive to help our brothers and sisters respect the "laws written by God in our very nature, laws which we "must observe with intelligence and love" (*Humanae Vitae*, 31).

In our pastoral efforts and in support of the Church's consistent teaching as presented in *Humanae Vitae,* on this 25th anniversary we pledge ourselves to "work ardently and incessantly for the safeguarding and holiness of marriage, so that it may always be lived in its entire human and Christian fullness" (*Humanae Vitae*, 30).

MARRIAGE LAWS

The Catholic Church claims jurisdiction over its members in matters pertaining to marriage. which is a sacrament. Church legislation on the subject is stated principally in 111 canons of the Code of Canon Law.

Marriage laws of the Church provide juridical norms in support of the marriage covenant. In 10 chapters, the revised Code covers: pastoral directives for preparing men and women for marriage; impediments in general and in particular; matrimonial consent; form for the celebration of marriage; mixed marriages; secret celebration of marriage; effects of marriage; separation of spouses, and convalidation of marriage.

Catholics are bound by all marriage laws of the Church. Non-Catholics, whether baptized or not, are not considered bound by these ecclesiastical laws except in cases of marriage with a Catholic. Certain natural laws, in the Catholic view, bind all men and women, irrespective of their religious beliefs; accordingly, marriage is prohibited before the time of puberty, without knowledge and free mutual consent, in the case of an already existing valid marriage bond, in the case of antecedent and perpetual impotence.

Formalities

These include, in addition to arrangements for the time and place of the marriage ceremony, doctrinal and moral instruction concerning marriage and the recording of data which verifies in documentary form the eligibility and freedom of the persons to marry. Records of this kind, which are confidential, are preserved in the archives of the church where the marriage takes place.

Premarital instructions are the subject matter of Pre-Cana Conferences.

Marital Consent

Matrimonial consent can be invalidated by an essential defect, substantial error, the strong influence of force and fear, the presence of a condition or intention against the nature of marriage.

Form of Marriage

A Catholic is required, for validity and lawfulness, to contract marriage — with another Catholic or with a non-Catholic — in the presence of a competent priest or deacon and two witnesses.

There are two exceptions to this law. A Roman Rite Catholic (since Mar. 25, 1967) or an Eastern Rite Catholic (since Nov. 21, 1964) can contract marriage validly in the presence of a priest of a separated Eastern Rite Church, provided other requirements of law are complied with. With permission of the competent Roman-Rite or Eastern-Rite bishop, this form of marriage is lawful, as well as valid. (See Eastern Rite Laws, below.)

With these two exceptions, and aside from cases covered by special permission, the Church does not regard as valid any marriages involving Catholics which take place before non-Catholic ministers of religion or civil officials.

(An excommunication formerly in force against Catholics who celebrated marriage before a non-Catholic minister was abrogated in a decree issued by the Sacred Congregation for the Doctrine of the Faith on Mar. 18, 1966.)

The ordinary place of marriage is the parish of either Catholic party or of the Catholic party in case of a mixed marriage.

Church law regarding the form of marriage does not affect non-Catholics in marriages among themselves. The Church recognizes as valid the marriages of non-Catholics before ministers of religion and civil officials, unless they are rendered null and void on other grounds.

The canonical form is not to be observed in the case of a marriage between a non-Catholic and a baptized Catholic who has left the Church by a formal act.

Impediments

Diriment Impediments to marriage are factors which render a marriage invalid.

• age, which obtains before completion of the 14th year for a woman and the 16th year for a man;

• impotency, if it is antecedent to the marriage and permanent (this differs from sterility, which is not an impediment);

• the bond of an existing valid marriage;

• disparity of worship, which obtains when one party is a Catholic and the other party is unbaptized;

• sacred orders;

• religious profession of the perpetual vow of chastity;

• abduction, which impedes the freedom of the person abducted;

• crime, variously involving elements of adultery, promise or attempt to marry, conspiracy to murder a husband or wife;

• blood relationship in the direct line (father-daughter, mother-son, etc.) and to the fourth degree inclusive of the collateral line (brother-sister, first cousins);

• affinity, or relationship resulting from a valid marriage, in any degree of the direct line;

• public honesty, arising from an invalid marriage or from public or notorious concubinage; it renders either party incapable of marrying blood relatives of the other in the first degree of the direct line.

• legal relationship arising from adoption; it renders either party incapable of marrying relatives of the other in the direct line or in the second degree of the collateral line.

Dispensations from Impediments: Persons hindered by impediments cannot marry unless they are dispensed therefrom in view of reasons recognized in canon law. Local bishops can dispense from the impediments most often encountered (e.g., disparity of worship) as well as others.

Decision regarding some dispensations is reserved to the Holy See.

Separation

A valid and consummated marriage of baptized persons cannot be dissolved by any human authority or any cause other than the death of one of the persons.

In other circumstances:

• 1. A valid but unconsummated marriage of baptized persons, or of a baptized and an unbaptized person, can be dissolved:

a. by the solemn religious profession of one of the persons, made with permission of the pope. In such a case, the bond is dissolved at the time of profession, and the other person is free to marry again.

b. by dispensation from the pope, requested for a grave reason by one or both of the persons. If the dispensation is granted, both persons are free to marry again.

Dispensations in these cases are granted for reasons connected with the spiritual welfare of the concerned persons.

• 2. A legitimate marriage, even consummated, of unbaptized persons can be dissolved in favor of one of them who subsequently receives the sacrament of baptism. This is the Pauline Privilege, so called because it was promulgated by St. Paul (1 Cor. 7:12-15) as a means of protecting the faith of converts. Requisites for granting the privilege are:

a. marriage prior to the baptism of either person;

b. reception of baptism by one person;

c. refusal of the unbaptized person to live in peace with the baptized person and without interfering with his or her freedom to practice the Christian faith. The privilege does not apply if the unbaptized person agrees to these conditions.

• 3. A legitimate and consummated marriage of a baptized and an unbaptized person can be dissolved by the pope in virtue of the Privilege of Faith, also called the Petrine Privilege.

Civil Divorce

Because of the unity and the indissolubility of marriage, the Church denies that civil divorce can break the bond of a valid marriage, whether the marriage involves two Catholics, a Catholic and a non-Catholic, or non-Catholics with each other.

In view of serious circumstances of marital distress, the Church permits an innocent and aggrieved party, whether wife or husband, to seek and obtain a civil divorce for the purpose of acquiring title and right to the civil effects of divorce, such as separate habitation and maintenance, and the custody of children. Permission for this kind of action should be obtained from proper church authority. The divorce, if obtained, does not break the bond of a valid marriage.

Under other circumstances — as would obtain if a marriage was invalid (see Annulment, below) — civil divorce is permitted for civil effects and as a civil ratification of the fact that the marriage bond really does not exist.

Annulment

This is a decision by a competent church authority — e.g., a bishop, a diocesan marriage tribunal, the Roman Rota — that an apparently valid marriage was actually invalid from the beginning because of the unknown or concealed existence, from the beginning, of a diriment impediment, an essential defect in consent, radical incapability for marriage, or a condition placed by one or both of the parties against the very nature of marriage.

Eastern Rite Laws

Marriage laws of the Eastern Church differ in several respects from the legislation of the Roman Rite. The regulations in effect since May 2, 1949, were contained in the motu proprio *Crebre Allatae* issued by Pius XII the previous February.

According to both the Roman Code of Canon Law and the Oriental Code, marriages between Roman Rite Catholics and Eastern Rite Catholics ordinarily take place in the rite of the groom and have canonical effects in that rite.

Regarding the form for the celebration of marriages between Eastern Catholics and baptized Eastern non-Catholics, the Second Vatican Council declared:

"By way of preventing invalid marriages between

Eastern Catholics and baptized Eastern non-Catholics, and in the interests of the permanence and sanctity of marriage and of domestic harmony, this sacred Synod decrees that the canonical 'form' for the celebration of such marriages obliges only for lawfulness. For their validity, the presence of a sacred minister suffices, as long as the other requirements of law are honored" *(Decree on Eastern Catholic Churches,* No. 18).

Marriages taking place in this manner are lawful, as well as valid, with permission of a competent Eastern Rite bishop.

The Rota

The Roman Rota is the ordinary court of appeal for marriage, and some other cases, which are appealed to the Holy See from lower church courts. Appeals are made to the Rota if decisions by diocesan and archdiocesan courts fail to settle the matter in dispute.

MIXED MARRIAGES

"Mixed Marriages" *(Matrimonia Mixta)* was the subject of: (1) a letter issued under this title by Pope Paul VI Mar. 31, 1970, and (2) a statement, *Implementation of the Apostolic Letter on Mixed Marriages,* approved by the National Conference of Catholic Bishops Nov. 16, 1970.

One of the key points in the bishops' statement referred to the need for mutual pastoral care by ministers of different faiths for the sacredness of marriage and for appropriate preparation and continuing support of parties to a mixed marriage.

Pastoral experience, which the Catholic Church shares with other religious bodies, confirms the fact that marriages of persons of different beliefs involve special problems related to the continuing religious practice of the concerned persons and to the religious education and formation of their children.

Pastoral measures to minimize these problems include instruction of a non-Catholic party in essentials of the Catholic faith for purposes of understanding. Desirably, some instruction should also be given the Catholic party regarding his or her partner's beliefs.

Requirements

The Catholic party to a mixed marriage is required to declare his (her) intention of continuing practice of the Catholic faith and to promise to do all in his (her) power to share his (her) faith with children born of the marriage by having them baptized and raised as Catholics. No declarations or promises are required of the non-Catholic party, but he (she) must be informed of the declaration and promise made by the Catholic.

Notice of the Catholic's declaration and promise is an essential part of the application made to a bishop for (1) permission to marry a baptized non-Catholic, or (2) a dispensation to marry an unbaptized non-Catholic.

A mixed marriage can take place with a Nuptial Mass. (The bishops' statement added this caution: "To the extent that Eucharistic sharing is not permitted by the general discipline of the Church, this is to be considered when plans are being made to have the mixed marriage at Mass or not.")

The ordinary minister at a mixed marriage is an authorized priest or deacon, and the ordinary place is the parish church of the Catholic party. A non-Catholic minister may not only attend the marriage ceremony but may also address, pray with and bless the couple.

For appropriate pastoral reasons, a bishop can grant a dispensation from the Catholic form of marriage and can permit the marriage to take place in a non-Catholic church with a non-Catholic minister as the officiating minister. A priest may not only attend such a ceremony but may also address, pray with and bless the couple.

"It is not permitted," however, the bishops' statement declared, "to have two religious services or to have a single service in which both the Catholic marriage ritual and a non-Catholic marriage ritual are celebrated jointly or successively."

PASTORAL MINISTRY FOR DIVORCED AND REMARRIED

Ministry to divorced and remarried Catholics is a difficult field of pastoral endeavor, situated as it is in circumstances tantamount to the horns of a dilemma.

At Issue

On the one side is firm church teaching on the permanence of marriage and norms against reception of the Eucharist and full participation in the life of the Church by Catholics in irregular unions.

On the other side are men and women with broken unions followed by second and perhaps happier attempts at marriage which the Church does not recognize as valid and which may not be capable of being validated because of the existence of an earlier marriage bond.

Factors involved in these circumstances are those of the Church, upholding its doctrine and practice regarding the permanence of marriage, and those of many men and women in irregular second marriages who desire full participation in the life of the Church.

Sacramental participation is not possible for those whose first marriage was valid, although there is no bar to their attendance at Mass, to sharing in other activities of the Church, or to their efforts to have children baptized and raised in the Catholic faith.

An exception to this rule is the condition of a divorced and remarried couple living in a brother-sister relationship.

There is no ban against sacramental participation by separated or divorced persons who have not attempted a second marriage, provided the usual conditions for reception of the sacraments are in order.

Unverified estimates of the number of U.S. Catholics who are divorced and remarried vary between six and eight million.

Tribunal Action

What can the Church do for them and with them in pastoral ministry, is an old question charged with new urgency because of the rising number of divorced and remarried Catholics.

One way to help is through the agency of marriage tribunals charged with responsibility for investigating and settling questions concerning the validity or invalidity of a prior marriage. There are reasons in canon law justifying the Church in declaring a particular marriage null and void from the beginning, despite the short- or long-term existence of an apparently valid union.

Decrees of nullity (annulments) are not new in the history of the Church. If such a decree is issued, a man or woman is free to validate a second marriage and live in complete union with the Church.

The 1991 *Statistical Yearbook of the Church,* reported that in 1991 U.S. tribunals issued 63,933 annulments (in ordinary and documentary processes). The canonical reasons were: invalid consent (42,617), impotence (195), other impediments (2,442), defect of form (18,679). Worldwide, 80,711 decrees or declarations of nullity were issued in 1991.

Reasons behind Decrees

Pastoral experience reveals that some married persons, a short or long time after contracting an apparently valid marriage, exhibit signs that point back to the existence, at the time of marriage, of latent and serious personal deficiencies which made them incapable of valid consent and sacramental commitment.

Such deficiencies might include gross immaturity and those affecting in a serious way the capacity to love, to have a true interpersonal and conjugal relationship, to fulfill marital obligations, to accept the faith aspect of marriage.

Psychological and behavioral factors like these have been given greater attention by tribunals in recent years and have provided grounds for numerous decrees of nullity.

Decisions of this type do not indicate any softening of the Church's attitude regarding the permanence of marriage. They affirm, rather, that some persons who have married were really not capable of doing so.

Serious deficiencies in the capacity for real interpersonal relationship in marriage were the reasons behind a landmark decree of nullity issued in 1973 by the Roman Rota, the Vatican high court of appeals in marriage cases. Pope John Paul referred to such deficiencies — the "grave lack of discretionary judgment," incapability of assuming "essential matrimonial rights and obligations," for example — in an address Jan. 26, 1984, to personnel of the Rota.

The tribunal way to a decree of nullity regarding a previous marriage, however, is not open to many persons in second marriages — because grounds are either lacking or, if present, cannot be verified in tribunal process.

Unacceptable Solution

One unacceptable solution of the problem, called "good conscience procedure," involves administration of the sacraments of penance and the Eucharist to divorced and remarried Catholics unable to obtain a decree of nullity for a first marriage who are living in a subsequent marriage "in good faith."

This procedure, despite the fact that it has no standing or recognition in church law, is being advocated and practiced by some priests and remarried Catholics.

COMPASSIONATE RESPONSE TO AIDS VICTIMS

The church response to the AIDS crisis must include education of the entire community and compassionate assistance to the victims, said a statement issued in June, 1993, by the Catholic AIDS Ministry of the Archdiocese of Seattle.

"Every illness and human crisis calls for a Christian response, said an introductory note to the 16-page "pastoral statement of solidarity with members of our community touched by HIV/AIDS."

"Charity and humility call us to avoid being judgmental when dealing with people who are ill and instead find ways to care for them and to respond to them and their loved ones with the understanding and compassion of Christ," it said.

"It is imperative that we all raise our level of HIV/AIDS consciousness and knowledge and be able to make it clear to infected persons that we will not reject those among us who are ill," it added.

Recommendations

The statement recommended the appointment of a staff person or AIDS advocacy committee in each parish to coordinate such activities as support groups, information gathering on available community services, regular pastoral visits, opportunities for prayer and the sacraments, funeral services and grief support, education of all parish groups and recruitment of volunteers for AIDS service agencies.

On a one-to-one basis, the document made these recommendations:

● "Don't avoid an infected person. In whatever way you can, try to be their for them."

● "Allow the person to express emotions."

● "With sensitivity to a person's physical limitations, invite the person to do things together."

● Offer a "silent presence" for those who might not want to talk, and provide "opportunities for group sharing and prayer in the church setting" for family members, loved ones, friends and AIDS caregivers.

● Provide opportunities for celebration of the sacraments of anointing of the sick, penance and Communion. "Regular sharing of Scriptures and Communion are frequently key moments of preparation to live what is left of life and to be ready to meet the Lord in dying," the document said.

In the United States in the period between the early 1980s when HIV/AIDS was discovered and January, 1993, 242,146 AIDS cases were reported, and 158,243 persons died; it was estimated that a million persons were infected with HIV.

THE CHURCH CALENDAR

The calendar of the Roman Church consists of an arrangement throughout the year of a series of liturgical seasons, commemorations of divine mysteries and commemorations of saints for purposes of worship.

The purposes of this calendar were outlined in the *Constitution on the Sacred Liturgy* (Nos. 102-105) promulgated by the Second Vatican Council.

Within the cycle of a year . . . (the Church) unfolds the whole mystery of Christ, not only from his incarnation and birth until his ascension, but also as reflected in the day of Pentecost, and the expectation of a blessed, hoped-for return of the Lord.

Recalling thus the mysteries of redemption, the Church opens to the faithful the riches of her Lord's powers and merits, so that these are in some way made present at all times, and the faithful are enabled to lay hold of them and become filled with saving grace (No. 102).

In celebrating this annual cycle of Christ's mysteries, holy Church honors with special love the Blessed Mary, Mother of God (No. 103).

The Church has also included in the annual cycle days devoted to the memory of the martyrs and the other saints . . . (who) sing God's perfect praise in heaven and offer prayers for us. By celebrating the passage of these saints from earth to heaven the Church proclaims the paschal mystery as achieved in the saints who have suffered and been glorified with Christ; she proposes them to the faithful as examples who draw all to the Father through Christ, and through their merits she pleads for God's favors (No. 104).

In the various seasons of the year and according to her traditional discipline, the Church completes the formation of the faithful by means of pious practices for soul and body, by instruction, prayer, and works of penance and mercy (No. 105).

THE ROMAN CALENDAR

Norms for a revised calendar for the Western Church as decreed by the Second Vatican Council were approved by Paul VI in the *motu proprio Mysterii Paschalis* dated Feb. 14, 1969. The revised calendar was promulgated a month later by a decree of the Congregation for Divine Worship and went into effect Jan. 1, 1970, with provisional modifications. Full implementation of all its parts was delayed in 1970 and 1971, pending the completion of work on related liturgical texts. The U.S. bishops ordered the calendar into effect for 1972.

The Seasons

Advent: The liturgical year begins with the first Sunday of Advent, which introduces a season of four weeks or slightly less duration with the theme of expectation of the coming of Christ. During the first two weeks, the final coming of Christ as Lord and Judge at the end of the world is the focus of attention. From Dec. 17 to 24, the emphasis shifts to anticipation of the celebration of his Nativity on the solemnity of Christmas.

Advent has four Sundays. Since the 10th century, the first Sunday has marked the beginning of the liturgical year in the Western Church. In the Middle Ages, a kind of pre-Christmas fast was in vogue during the season.

Christmas Season: The Christmas season begins with the vigil of Christmas and lasts until the Sunday after January 6, inclusive.

The period between the end of the Christmas season and the beginning of Lent belongs to the Ordinary Time of the year. Of variable length, the pre-Lenten phase of this season includes what were formerly called the Sundays after Epiphany and the suppressed Sundays of Septuagesima, Sexagesima and Quinquagesima.

Lent: The penitential season of Lent begins on Ash Wednesday, which occurs between Feb. 4 and Mar. 11, depending on the date of Easter, and lasts until the Mass of the Lord's Supper (Holy Thursday). It has six Sundays. The sixth Sunday marks the beginning of Holy Week and is known as Passion (formerly called Palm) Sunday.

The origin of Lenten observances dates back to the fourth century or earlier.

Easter Triduum: The Easter Triduum begins with evening Mass of the Lord's Supper and ends with Evening Prayer on Easter Sunday.

Easter Season: The Easter season whose theme is resurrection from sin to the life of grace, lasts for 50 days, from Easter to Pentecost. Easter, the Sunday after the first full moon following the vernal equinox, occurs between Mar. 22 and Apr. 25. The terminal phase of the Easter season, between the solemnities of the Ascension of the Lord and Pentecost, stresses anticipation of the coming and action of the Holy Spirit.

Ordinary Time: The season of Ordinary Time begins on Monday (or Tuesday if the feast of the Baptism of the Lord is celebrated on that Monday) after the Sunday following January 6 and continues until the day before Ash Wednesday, inclusive. It begins again on the Monday after Pentecost and ends on the Saturday before the first Sunday of Advent. It consists of 33 or 34 weeks. The last Sunday is celebrated as the Solemnity of Christ the King. The overall purpose of the season is to elaborate the themes of salvation history.

The various liturgical seasons are characterized in part by the scriptural readings and Mass prayers assigned to each of them. During Advent, for example, the readings are messianic; during the Easter season, from the Acts of the Apostles, chronicling the Resurrection and the original proclamation of Christ by the Apostles, and from the Gospel of John; during Lent, baptismal and penitential passages. Mass prayers reflect the meaning and purpose of the various seasons.

Commemorations of Saints

The commemorations of saints are celebrated concurrently with the liturgical seasons and feasts of our Lord. Their purpose is to illustrate the paschal mysteries as reflected in the lives of saints, to honor them as heroes of holiness, and to appeal for their intercession.

In line with revised regulations, some former feasts were either abolished or relegated to observance in particular places by local option for one of two reasons: (1) lack of sufficient historical evidence for observance of the feasts; (2) lack of universal significance.

The commemoration of a saint, as a general rule, is observed on the day of death (*dies natalis,* day of birth to glory with God in heaven). Exceptions to this rule include the feasts of St. John the Baptist, who is honored on the day of his birth; Sts. Basil the Great and Gregory Nazianzen, and the brother Saints, Cyril and Methodius, who are commemorated in joint feasts. Application of this general rule in the revised calendar resulted in date changes of some observances.

Sundays and Other Holy Days

Sunday is the original Christian feast day and holy day of obligation because of the unusually significant events of salvation history which took place and are commemorated on the first day of the week — viz., the Resurrection of Christ, the key event of his life and the fundamental fact of Christianity; and the descent of the Holy Spirit upon the Apostles on Pentecost, the birthday of the Church. The transfer of observance of the Lord's Day from the Sabbath to Sunday was made in apostolic times. The Mass and Liturgy of the Hours (Divine Office) of each Sunday reflect the themes and set the tones of the various liturgical seasons.

Holy days of obligation are special occasions on which Catholics who have reached the age of reason are seriously obliged, as on Sundays, to assist at Mass: they are also to refrain from work and involvement with business which impede participation in divine worship and the enjoyment of appropriate rest and relaxation.

The holy days of obligation observed in the United States are: Christmas, the Nativity of Jesus, Dec. 25; Solemnity of Mary the Mother of God, Jan. 1; Ascension of the Lord; Assumption of Blessed Mary the Virgin, Aug. 15; All Saints' Day, Nov. 1; Immaculate Conception of Blessed Mary the Virgin, Dec. 8.

Effective Jan. 1, 1993, in the United States, the precept to attend Mass is abrogated whenever the Solemnity of Mary (Jan. 1), the Assumption (Aug. 15), or All Saints (Nov. 1) falls on a Saturday or Monday (December 13, 1991, decree of the National Conference of Catholic Bishops approved and confirmed by the Apostolic See July 4, 1992).

In addition to these, there are four other holy days of obligation prescribed in the general law of the Church which are not so observed in the U.S.: Epiphany, Jan. 6; St. Joseph, Mar. 19; Corpus Christi; Sts. Peter and Paul, June 29. The solemnities of Epiphany and Corpus Christi are transferred to a Sunday in countries where they are not observed as holy days of obligation.

Solemnities, Feasts, Memorials

Categories of observances according to dignity and manner of observance are: solemnities, principal days in the calendar (observance begins with Evening Prayer I of the preceding day; some have their own vigil Mass); feasts (celebrated within the limits of the natural day); obligatory memorials (celebrated throughout the Church); optional memorials (observable by choice).

Fixed observances are those which are regularly celebrated on the same calendar day each year.

Movable observances are those which are not observed on the same calendar day each year. Ex-

amples of these are Easter (the first Sunday after the first full moon following the vernal equinox), Ascension (40 days after Easter), Pentecost (50 days after Easter), Trinity Sunday (first after Pentecost), Christ the King (last Sunday of the liturgical year).

Weekdays, Days of Prayer

Weekdays are those on which no proper feast or vigil is celebrated in the Mass or Liturgy of the Hours (Divine Office). On such days, the Mass may be that of the preceding Sunday, which expresses the liturgical spirit of the season, an optional memorial, a votive Mass, or a Mass for the dead. Weekdays of Advent and Lent are in a special category of their own.

Days of Prayer: Dioceses, at times to be designated by local bishops, should observe "days or periods of prayer for the fruits of the earth, prayer for human rights and equality, prayer for world justice and peace, and penitential observance outside of Lent." So stated the *Instruction on Particular Calendars* (No. 331) issued by the Congregation for the Sacraments and Divine Worship June 24, 1970.

These days are contemporary equivalents of what were formerly called ember and rogation days.

Ember days originated at Rome about the fifth century, probably as Christian replacements for seasonal festivals of agrarian cults. They were observances of penance, thanksgiving, and petition for divine blessing on the various seasons; they also were occasions of special prayer for clergy to be ordained. These days were observed four times a year.

Rogation days originated in France about the fifth century. They were penitential in character and also occasions of prayer for a bountiful harvest and protection against evil.

Days and Times of Penance

Fridays throughout the year and the season of Lent are penitential times.

● Abstinence: Catholics in the United States, from the age of 14 throughout life, are obliged to abstain from meat on Ash Wednesday, the Fridays of Lent and Good Friday. The law forbids the use of meat, but not of eggs, the products of milk or condiments made of animal fat. Permissible are soup flavored with meat, meat gravy and sauces. The obligation to abstain from meat is not in force on days celebrated as solemnities (e.g., Christmas, Sacred Heart).

● Fasting: Catholics in the United States, from the day after their 18th birthday to the day after their 59th birthday, are also obliged to fast on Ash Wednesday and Good Friday. The law allows only one full meal a day, but does not prohibit the taking of some food in the morning and evening, observing — as far as quantity and quality are concerned — approved local custom. The order of meals is optional; i.e., the full meal may be taken in the evening instead of at midday. Also: (1) The combined quantity of food taken at the two lighter meals should not exceed the quantity taken at the full meal. (2) The drinking of ordinary liquids does not break the fast.

● Obligation: There is a general obligation to do penance for sins committed and for the remission of punishment due because of sin. Substantial observance of fasting and abstinence, prescribed for the community of the Church, is a matter of serious obligation; it allows, however, for alternate ways of doing penance (e.g., works of charity, prayer and prayer-related practices, alsmgiving).

Readings at Mass

The texts of scriptural readings for Mass on Sundays, holy days and some other days are indicated under the respective dates. The second (B) cycle is prescribed for Sunday Masses in the 1994 liturgical year (Nov. 28, 1993, to Nov. 26, 1994). The third (C) cycle is prescribed for the 1995 liturgical year which begins with the first Sunday of Advent, Nov. 27, 1994. Weekday cycles of readings are the second and first, respectively, for liturgical years 1994 and 1995.

Monthly Prayer Intentions

Intentions chosen and recommended by Pope John Paul II to the prayers of the faithful and circulated by the Apostleship of Prayer are given for each month of the calendar. He has expressed his desire that all Catholics make these intentions their own "in the certainty of being united with the Holy Father and praying according to his intentions and desires." These intentions represent the worldwide needs of the Church as seen through the eyes of the Holy Father.

Celebrations in U.S. Particular Calendar

The General Norms for the Liturgical Year and the Calendar, issued in 1969 and published along with the General Roman Calendar for the Universal Church, noted that the calendar consists of the General Roman Calendar used by the entire Church and of particular calendars used in particular churches (nations or dioceses) or in families of religious. Particular calendars must be drawn up by appropriate episcopal conferences and approved by the Apostolic See.

The particular calendar for the U.S. contains the following celebrations (as of December, 1992). **January:** 4, Elizabeth Ann Seton; 5, John Neumann; 6, Bl. Andre Bessette. **March:** 3, Bl. Katharine Drexel. **May:** 15, Isidore the Farmer. **July:** 1, Bl. Junipero Serra; 4, Independence Day; 14, Bl. Kateri Tekakwitha. **August:** 18, Jane Frances de Chantal. **September:** 9, Peter Claver. **October:** 6, Bl. Marie Rose Durocher; 19, Isaac Jogues and John de Brebeuf and Companions; 20, Paul of the Cross. **November:** 13, Frances Xavier Cabrini; 18, Rose Philippine Duchesne; 23, Bl. Miguel Agustín Pro; Fourth Thursday, Thanksgiving Day. **December:** 9, Bl Juan Diego; 12, Our Lady of Guadalupe.

TABLE OF MOVABLE FEASTS

Year	Ash Wednesday	Easter	Ascension	Pentecost	Weeks of Ordinary Time Before Lent Week	Ends	After Pent. Week	Begins	First Sunday of Advent
1994	Feb. 16	Apr. 3	May 12	May 22	6	Feb. 15	8	May 23	Nov. 27
1995	Mar. 1	Apr. 16	May 25	June 4	8	Feb. 28	9	June 5	Dec. 3
1996	Feb. 21	Apr. 7	May 16	May 26	7	Feb. 20	8	May 27	Dec. 1
1997	Feb. 12	Mar. 30	May 8	May 18	5	Feb. 11	7	May 19	Nov. 30
1998	Feb. 25	Apr. 12	May 21	May 31	7	Feb. 24	9	June 1	Nov. 29
1999	Feb. 17	Apr. 4	May 13	May 23	6	Feb. 16	8	May 24	Nov. 28
2000	Mar. 8	Apr. 23	June 1	June 11	9	Mar. 7	10	June 12	Dec. 3
2001	Feb. 28	Apr. 15	May 24	June 3	8	Feb. 27	9	June 4	Dec. 2
2002	Feb. 13	Mar. 31	May 9	May 19	5	Feb. 12	7	May 20	Dec. 1
2003	Mar. 5	Apr. 20	May 29	June 8	8	Mar. 4	10	June 9	Nov. 30
2004	Feb. 25	Apr. 11	May 20	May 30	7	Feb. 24	9	May 31	Nov. 28
2005	Feb. 9	Mar. 27	May 5	May 15	5	Feb. 8	7	May 16	Nov. 27
2006	Mar. 1	Apr. 16	May 25	June 4	8	Feb. 28	9	June 5	Dec. 3
2007	Feb. 21	Apr. 8	May 17	May 27	7	Feb. 20	8	May 28	Dec. 2
2008	Feb. 6	Mar. 23	May 1	May 11	4	Feb. 5	6	May 12	Nov. 30
2009	Feb. 25	Apr. 12	May 21	May 31	7	Feb. 24	9	June 1	Nov. 29
2010	Feb. 17	Apr. 4	May 13	May 23	6	Feb. 16	8	May 24	Nov. 28
2011	Mar. 9	Apr. 24	June 2	June 12	9	Mar. 8	11	June 13	Nov. 27
2012	Feb. 22	Apr. 8	May 17	May 27	7	Feb. 21	8	May 28	Dec. 2
2013	Feb. 13	Mar. 31	May 9	May 19	5	Feb. 12	7	May 20	Dec. 1
2014	Mar. 5	Apr. 20	May 29	June 8	8	Mar. 8	10	June 9	Nov. 30
2015	Feb. 18	Apr. 5	May 14	May 24	6	Feb. 17	8	May 25	Nov. 29
2016	Feb. 10	Mar. 27	May 5	May 15	5	Feb. 9	7	May 16	Nov. 27
2017	Mar. 1	Apr. 16	May 25	June 4	7	Feb. 28	9	June 5	Dec. 3

JANUARY 1994

Prayer Intentions: FAMILY IN CHURCH AND SOCIETY: That families work generously for the spiritual growth of the Christian community and the whole of society (General). CHRISTIAN UNITY: That ecumenical dialogue and prayer for Christian unity be profoundly missionary (Mission).

1—Sat. **Solemnity of Mary, Mother of God. Holy day of obligation (Dispensation from Mass obligation, U.S., because holy day falls on Saturday)** (Nm. 6:22-27; Gal. 4:4-7; Lk. 2:16-21.)

2—Sun. **Epiphany of the Lord; solemnity.** (Is. 60:1-6; Eph. 3:2-3a, 5-6; Mt. 2:1-12.) [Sts. Basil the Great and Gregory Nazianzen, bishops-doctors; memorial.]

3—Mon. Weekday.

4—Tues. St. Elizabeth Ann Seton; memorial (in U.S.).

5—Wed. St. John Neumann, bishop; memorial, in U.S.

6—Thurs. Weekday. Bl. Andre Bessette, religious; optional memorial (in U.S.).

7—Fri. Weekday. St. Raymond of Penyafort, priest; optional memorial.

8—Sat. Weekday.

9—Sun. **Baptism of the Lord; feast.** (Is. 42:1-4, 6-7; Acts 10:34-38; Mk. 1:6b-11.) [Last day of Christmas Season.]

10—Mon. Weekday. (First Week of the Year.)

11—Tues. Weekday.

12—Wed. Weekday.

13—Thurs. Weekday. St. Hilary, bishop-doctor; optional memorial.

14—Fri. Weekday.

15—Sat. Weekday. BVM on Saturday; optional memorial.

16—**Second Sunday of the Year.** (1 Sm. 3:3b-10, 19; 1 Cor. 6:13c-15a, 17-20; Jn. 1:35-42.)

17—Mon. St. Anthony, abbot; memorial.

18—Tues. Weekday.

19—Wed. Weekday.

20—Thurs. Weekday. St. Fabian, pope-martyr, or St. Sebastian, martyr; optional memorials.

21—Fri. St. Agnes, virgin-martyr; memorial.

22—Sat. Weekday. St. Vincent, deacon-martyr, or BVM on Saturday; optional memorials.

23—**Third Sunday of the Year.** (Jon. 3:1-5, 10; 1 Cor. 7:29-31; Mk. 1:21-28.)

24—Mon. St. Francis de Sales, bishop-doctor; memorial.

25—Tues. Conversion of St. Paul; feast.

26—Wed. Sts. Timothy and Titus, bishops; memorial.

27—Thurs. Weekday. St. Angela Merici, virgin; optional memorial.

28—Fri. St. Thomas Aquinas, priest-doctor; memorial.

29—Sat. Weekday. BVM on Saturday; optional memorial.

30—**Fourth Sunday of the Year.** (Dt. 18:15-20; 1 Cor. 7:32-35; Mk. 1:21-28.)

31—Mon. St. John Bosco, priest; memorial.

Week of Prayer for Christian Unity, Jan. 18 to 25.

Scheduled Events: World Day of Peace, Jan. 1, on the theme, "The Family Creates the Peace of the Human Family"; Martin Luther King Day, Jan. 17; March for Life, Jan. 22, anniversary of Roe v. Wade, the pro-abortion decision of the Supreme Court; Jan. 30, beginning of Catholic Schools Week.

FEBRUARY 1994

Prayer Intentions: WORLD DAY OF THE SICK: That the World Day of the Sick help people recognize the suffering, glorious face of Christ in all who are sick (General). TERMINALLY ILL: That contagious and terminally ill in developing nations, especially AIDS victims, receive the care they need (Mission).

1—Tues. Weekday.

2—Wed. Presentation of the Lord; feast.

3—Thurs. Weekday. St. Blase, bishop-martyr, or St. Ansgar, bishop; optional memorials.

4—Fri. Weekday.

5—Sat. St. Agatha, virgin-martyr; memorial.

6—**Fifth Sunday of the Year.** (Jb. 7:1-4, 6-7; 1 Cor. 9:16-19, 22-23; Mk. 1:29-39.) [Sts. Paul Miki and Companions, martyrs; memorial].

7—Mon. Weekday.

8—Tues. Weekday. St. Jerome Emiliani; optional memorial.

9—Wed. Weekday.

10—Thurs. St. Scholastica, virgin; memorial.

11—Fri. Weekday. Our Lady of Lourdes; optional memorial.

12—Sat. Weekday. BVM on Saturday; optional memorial.

13—**Sixth Sunday of the Year.** (Lv. 13:1-2, 45-46; 1 Cor. 10:31 to 11:1; Mk. 1:40-45.)

14—Mon. Sts. Cyril, monk, and Methodius, bishop; memorial.

15—Tues. Weekday.

16—Ash Wednesday. Beginning of Lent. *Fast and abstinence.* Ashes are blessed on this day and imposed on the forehead of the faithful to remind them of their obligation to do penance for sin and to seek spiritual renewal by means of prayer, fasting, good works, and by bearing with patience and for God's purposes the trials and difficulties of everyday life.

17—Thurs. Weekday of Lent. [Seven Holy Founders of the Servite Order; optional memorial.]

18—Fri. Weekday of Lent. *Abstinence.*

19—Sat. Weekday of Lent.

20—**First Sunday of Lent.** (Gn. 9:8-15; 1 Pt. 3:18-22; Mk. 1:12-15.)

21—Mon. Weekday of Lent. [St. Peter Damien, bishop-doctor; optional memorial.]

22—Tues. Chair of Peter, apostle; feast. Weekday of Lent.

23—Wed. Weekday of Lent. [St. Polycarp, bishop-martyr; memorial.]

24—Thurs. Weekday of Lent.

25—Fri. Weekday of Lent. *Abstinence.*

26—Sat. Weekday of Lent.

27—**Second Sunday of Lent.** (Gn. 22:1-2, 9a, 10-13, 15-18; Rom. 8:31b-34; Mk. 9:2-10.)

28—Mon. Weekday of Lent.

The blessing of throats on the optional memorial of St. Blase Feb. 3 is in accord with the legend that a boy in danger of choking to death was saved through his intercession. The blessing is given with the prayer: "Through the intercession of St. Blase, bishop and martyr, may the Lord free you from ailments of the throat and every other evil."

Scheduled Event: Day of the Sick, Feb. 11.

MARCH 1994

Prayer Intentions: VICTIMS OF HUNGER AND MISERY: That all nations work together effectively to help the victims of hunger and misery (General). REFUGEES AND IMMIGRANTS: That refugees and immigrants in every country receive a fraternal welcome and adequate assistance (Mission).

1—Tues. Weekday of Lent.

2—Wed. Weekday of Lent.

3—Thurs. Weekday of Lent. [Bl. Katharine Drexel, virgin; optional memorial (in U.S.).]

4—Fri. Weekday of Lent. *Abstinence.* [St. Casimir; memorial.]

5—Sat. Weekday of Lent.

6—**Third Sunday of Lent.** (Ex. 20:1-17; 1 Cor. 1:22-25; Jn. 2:13-25.)

7—Mon. Weekday of Lent. [Sts. Perpetua and Felicity, martyrs; memorial.]

8—Tues. Weekday of Lent. [St. John of God; optional memorial.]

9—Wed. Weekday of Lent. [St. Frances of Rome; optional memorial.]

10—Thurs. Weekday of Lent.

11—Fri. Weekday of Lent. *Abstinence.*

12—Sat. Weekday of Lent.

13—**Fourth Sunday of Lent.** (2 Chr. 36:14-16, 19-23; Eph. 2:4-10; Jn. 3:14-21.)

14—Mon. Weekday of Lent.

15—Tues. Weekday of Lent.

16—Wed. Weekday of Lent.

17—Thurs. Weekday of Lent. [St. Patrick, bishop; optional memorial.]

18—Fri. Weekday of Lent. *Abstinence.* [St. Cyril of Jerusalem, bishop-doctor; optional memorial.]

19—Sat. St. Joseph; solemnity.

20—**Fifth Sunday of Lent.** (Jer. 31:31-34; Heb. 5:7-9; Jn. 12:20-33.)

21—Mon. Weekday of Lent.

22—Tues. Weekday of Lent.

23—Wed. Weekday of Lent. [St. Turibius, bishop; optional memorial.]

24—Thurs. Weekday of Lent.

25—Fri. Annunciation of the Lord; solemnity.

26—Sat. Weekday of Lent.

27—**Passion Sunday (Palm Sunday).** Procession—Mk. 11:1-10 or Jn. 12:12-16. Mass—Is. 50:4-7; Phil. 2:6-11;Mk. 14:1 to 15:47.)

28—Monday of Holy Week.

29—Tuesday of Holy Week.

30—Wednesday of Holy Week.

31—Thursday of Holy Week. Holy Thursday. The Easter Triduum begins with evening Mass of the Supper of the Lord.

Support for the needy, care for others in straitened circumstances, is an expression of the virtue of charity or love of neighbor. Such witness is powerful, not only for the relief of the unfortunate but also as a convincing sign of faith in practice. The kind of sign that made people say, as noted in the Acts of the Apostles, "See how these Christians love one another." And those of other faiths besides. Giving support to persons in need, as an expression of love for God, is an authentic and purifying penitential practice for Lent—and all times.

APRIL 1994

Prayer Intentions: PRIESTS AND SERVICE: For priests, mindful of their consecration to be authentic men of God as they give an example of fraternal service to all (General). MISSION ZEAL OF LOCAL CHURCHES: That the constant gift of the Spirit help particular Churches everywhere become courageous promoters of mission (Mission).

1—Friday of the Passion. Good Friday. *Fast and abstinence.*

2—Holy Saturday. The Easter Vigil. [St. Francis of Paola, hermit; optional memorial.]

3—**Easter Sunday.** (Acts 10:34a, 37-43; Col. 3:1-4 or 1 Cor. 5:6b-8; Jn. 20:1-9 or Mt. 28:1-10 or (evening) Lk. 24:13-35.)

4—Monday of Easter Octave. [St. Isidore of Seville, bishop-doctor; optional memorial.]

5—Tuesday of Easter Octave. [St. Vincent Ferrer, priest; optional memorial.]

6—Wednesday of Easter Octave.

7—Thursday of Easter Octave. [St. John Baptist de la Salle, priest; memorial.]

8—Friday of Easter Octave.

9—Saturday of Easter Octave.

10—**Second Sunday of Easter.** (Acts 4:32-35; 1 Jn. 5:1-6; Jn. 20:19-31.)

11—Mon. St. Stanislaus, bishop-martyr; memorial.

12—Tues. Weekday.

13—Wed. Weekday. St. Martin I, pope-martyr; optional memorial.

14—Thurs. Weekday.

15—Fri. Weekday.

16—Sat. Weekday.

17—**Third Sunday of Easter.** (Acts 3:13-15, 17-19; 1 Jn. 2:1-5a; Lk. 24:35-48.)

18—Mon. Weekday.

19—Tues. Weekday.

20—Wed. Weekday.

21—Thurs. Weekday. St. Anselm, bishop-doctor; optional memorial.

22—Fri. Weekday.

23—Sat. Weekday. St. George, martyr; optional memorial.

24—**Fourth Sunday of Easter.** (Acts. 4:8-12; 1 Jn. 3:1-2; Jn. 10:11-18.) [St. Fidelis of Sigmaringen, priest-martyr; optional memorial.]

25—Mon. St. Mark, evangelist; feast.

26—Tues. Weekday.

27—Wed. Weekday.

28—Thurs. Weekday. St. Peter Chanel, priest-martyr; optional memorial.

29—Fri. St. Catherine of Siena, virgin-doctor; memorial.

30—Sat. Weekday. St. Pius V, pope; optional memorial.

The Sacred Triduum, from Holy Thursday to the Vigil of Easter, and the week-long celebration of Easter comprise the most solemn and deeply mysterious period in the liturgical year.

Scheduled Events: Convention of the National Catholic Educational Association, Apr. 4-7; NFPC Convention, Apr. 25-29.

MAY 1994

Prayer Intentions: CHURCH UNITY: *That the bonds of unity and communion be strengthened between the laity and priests, priests and bishops, bishops and the pope (General).*
MARIAN SHRINES AND THE MISSIONS: *That popular piety nourished in pilgrims at Marian shrines inspire fervent zeal for the missions (Mission).*

1—**Fifth Sunday of Easter.** (Acts. 9:26-31; 1 Jn. 3:18-
   24; Jn. 15:1-8.) [St. Joseph the Worker; optional
   memorial.]
2—Mon. St. Athanasius, bishop-doctor; memorial.
3—Tues. Sts. Philip and James, apostles; feast.
4—Wed. Weekday.
5—Thurs. Weekday.
6—Fri. Weekday.
7—Sat. Weekday.
8—**Sixth Sunday of Easter.** (Acts 10:25-26, 34-
   35, 44-48; 1 Jn. 4:7-10; Jn. 15:9-17.)
9—Mon. Weekday.
10—Tues. Weekday.
11—Wed. Weekday.
12—**Thurs. Ascension of the Lord; solemnity.
   Holy day of obligation.** (Acts 1:1-11; Eph.
   1:17-23; Mk. 16:15-20.) [Sts. Nereus and
   Achilleus, martyrs, or St. Pancras, martyr; optional memorials.]
13—Fri. Weekday.
14—Sat. St. Matthias, apostle; feast.
15—**Seventh Sunday of Easter.** (Acts 1:15-17, 20a,
   20c-26; 1 Jn. 4:11-16; Jn. 17:11b-19.) [St. Isidore
   the Farmer; optional memorial (in U.S.)].
16—Mon. Weekday.
17—Tues. Weekday.
18—Wed. Weekday. St. John I, pope-martyr; optional memorial.
19—Thurs. Weekday.
20—Fri. Weekday. St. Bernardine of Siena, priest;
   optional memorial.
21—Sat. Weekday.
22—**Sun. Pentecost; solemnity.** (Acts 2:1-11; 1
   Cor. 12:3b-7, 12-13; Jn. 20:19-23.)
23—Mon. Weekday. (Eighth Week of the Year.)
24—Tues. Weekday.
25—Wed. Weekday. St. Bede the Venerable, priest-
   doctor, or St. Gregory VII, pope, or St. Mary
   Magdalene de Pazzi, virgin; optional memorials.
26—Thurs. St. Philip Neri, priest; memorial.
27—Fri. Weekday. St. Augustine of Canterbury,
   bishop; optional memorial.
28—Sat. Weekday. BVM on Saturday; optional
   memorial.
29—**Sun. Most Holy Trinity; solemnity.** (Dt. 4:32-
   34, 39-40; Rom. 8:14-17; Mt. 28:16-20.)
30—Mon. Weekday. (Ninth Week of the Year.)
31—Tues. Visitation of Blessed Mary the Virgin;
   feast.

*Feasts: Solemnities of the Easter Season: Ascension
of the Lord, May 12, and Pentecost, May 22.
Visitation of the Blessed Virgin Mary, May 31,
recalls Mary's readiness to help Elizabeth and
the prophetic Magnificat canticle.*

*Scheduled Events: Orthodox Easter, May 1;
Mother's Day, May 8; Annual CPA Convention,
May 26 to 28; Memorial Day, May 30.*

JUNE 1994

Prayer Intentions: SPIRITUALITY OF THE HEART
OF CHRIST: *That the spirituality of the Heart
of Christ be at the center of the formation given
to future priests, religious and lay people
(General).* BL. BAKHITA AND DIALOGUE:
*That the witness and intercession of Bl.
Josephine Bakhita foster respect and dialogue
between Christians and Muslims in Sudan and
elsewhere (Mission).*

1—Wed. St. Justin, martyr; memorial.
2—Thurs. Weekday. Sts. Marcellinus and Peter,
   martyrs; optional memorial.
3—Fri. Sts. Charles Lwanga and Companions,
   martyrs; memorial.
4—Sat. Weekday. BVM on Saturday; optional
   memorial.
5—**Sun. Corpus Christi; solemnity.** (Ex. 24:3-8;
   Heb. 9:11-15; Mk. 14:12-16, 22-26.) [St.
   Boniface, bishop-martyr; memorial.)
6—Mon. Weekday. St. Norbert, bishop; optional
   memorial. (Tenth Week of the Year.)
7—Tues. Weekday.
8—Wed. Weekday.
9—Thurs. Weekday. St. Ephraem, deacon-doctor,
   optional memorial.
10—Fri. Sacred Heart of Jesus; solemnity.
11—Sat. St. Barnabas, apostle; memorial. [Immacu-
   late Heart of Mary; optional memorial.]
12—**Eleventh Sunday of the Year.** (Ez. 17:22-24;
   2 Cor. 5:6-10; Mk. 4: 26-34.)
13—Mon. St. Anthony of Padua, priest-doctor;
   memorial.
14—Tues. Weekday.
15—Wed. Weekday.
16—Thurs. Weekday.
17—Fri. Weekday.
18—Sat. Weekday. BVM on Saturday; optional
   memorial.
19—**Twelfth Sunday of the Year.** (Jb. 38:1, 8-11;
   2 Cor. 5:14-17; Mk. 4:35-41.) [St. Romuald,
   abbot; optional memorial.]
20—Mon. Weekday.
21—Tues. St. Aloysius Gonzaga, religious; memorial.
22—Wed. Weekday. St. Paulinus of Nola, bishop,
   or Sts. John Fisher, bishop-martyr, and Thomas
   More, martyr; optional memorials.
23—Thurs. Weekday.
24—Fri. Birth of St. John the Baptist; solemnity.
25—Sat. Weekday. BVM on Saturday; optional memorial.
26—**Thirteenth Sunday of the Year.** (Wis. 1:13-
   15 and 2:23-24; 2 Cor. 8:7, 9, 13-15; Mk. 5:21-
   43.)
27—Mon. Weekday. St. Cyril of Alexandria, bishop-
   doctor; optional memorial.
28—Tues. St. Irenaeus, bishop-martyr; memorial.
29—Wed. Sts. Peter and Paul, apostles; solemnity.
30—Thurs. Weekday. First Martyrs of the Roman
   Church; optional memorial.

*Feasts: Corpus Christi, June 5; Sacred Heart, June 10;
St. Anthony of Padua, June 13; Birth of St. John
the Baptist, June 24; Sts. Peter and Paul, June 29.*

*Scheduled Events: Convention of Catholic Theologi-
cal Society of America, June 9-12; General
Meeting of the National Conference of Catholic
Bishops, June 16 to 22; Father's Day, June 19.*

JULY 1994

Prayer Intentions: DEFENSE OF HUMAN LIFE: That all people defend and promote the value of human life in all its phases and expressions (General). MISSION SPIRIT OF THE FAMILY: That Christian parents educate their children to missionary spirituality and solidarity (Mission).

1—Fri. Weekday. Bl. Junipero Serra, priest; optional memorial (in U.S.).

2—Sat. Weekday. BVM on Saturday; optional memorial.

3—**Fourteenth Sunday of the Year.** (Ez. 2:2-5; 2 Cor. 12:7-10; Mk. 6:1-6.) [St. Thomas, apostle; feast.]

4—Mon. Independence Day in U.S., optional Mass for a special occasion; St. Elizabeth of Portugal, optional memorial.

5—Tues. Weekday. St. Anthony Zaccaria, priest; optional memorial.

6—Wed. Weekday. St. Maria Goretti, virgin-martyr; optional memorial.

7—Thurs. Weekday.

8—Fri. Weekday.

9—Sat. Weekday. BVM on Saturday; optional memorial.

10—**Fifteenth Sunday of the Year.** (Am. 7:12-15; Eph. 1:3-14; Mk. 6:7-13.)

11—Mon. St. Benedict, abbot; memorial.

12—Tues. Weekday.

13—Wed. Weekday. St. Henry; optional memorial.

14—Thurs. Bl. Kateri Tekakwitha, virgin; memorial (in U.S.). Weekday. St. Camillus de Lellis, priest; optional memorial.

15—Fri. St. Bonaventure, bishop-doctor; memorial.

16—Sat. Weekday. Our Lady of Mt. Carmel; optional memorial.

17—**Sixteenth Sunday of the Year.** (Jer. 23:1-6; Eph. 2:13-18; Mk. 6:30-34.)

18—Mon. Weekday.

19—Tues. Weekday.

20—Wed. Weekday.

21—Thurs. Weekday. St. Lawrence of Brindisi, priest-doctor; optional memorial.

22—Fri. St. Mary Magdalene; memorial.

23—Sat. Weekday. St. Bridget, religious, or BVM on Saturday; optional memorials.

24—**Seventeenth Sunday of the Year.** (2 Kgs. 4:42-44; Eph. 4:1-6; Jn. 6:1-15.)

25—Mon. St. James, apostle; feast.

26—Tues. Sts. Joachim and Anne, parents of Blessed Mary the Virgin; memorial.

27—Wed. Weekday.

28—Thurs. Weekday.

29—Fri. St. Martha; memorial.

30—Sat. Weekday. St. Peter Chrysologus, bishop-doctor, or BVM on Saturday; optional memorials.

31—**Eighteenth Sunday of the Year.** (Ex. 16:2-4, 12-15; Eph. 4:17, 20-24; Jn. 6:24-35.) [St. Ignatius of Loyola, priest; memorial.]

Feasts: Blessed Junipero Serra, whose optional memorial may be observed July 1, founder of California missions; St. Thomas, apostle, July 3 (outranked by Sunday this year), pioneer evangelizer of India; St. Benedict, July 11, founder of monasticism in Western Europe, patron saint of Europe; St. Bonaventure, July 15, called the second founder of the Franciscan Order; St. Ignatius of Loyola, July 31 (outranked by Sunday this year), founder of the Society of Jesus.

Scheduled Event: Independence Day, July 4.

AUGUST 1994

Prayer Intentions: YOUTH AND THE ENVIRON-MENT: For youth, as they work to protect the natural beauty of the environment and make it a more pleasant place to live (General). MEDIA AND EVANGELIZATION: That communications media help missionary and evangelizing activities to be more direct and effective (Mission).

1—Mon. St. Alphonsus Liguori, bishop-doctor; memorial.

2—Tues. Weekday. St. Eusebius of Vercelli, bishop; optional memorial.

3—Wed. Weekday.

4—Thurs. St. John Vianney, priest; memorial.

5—Fri. Weekday. Dedication of St. Mary Major Basilica; optional memorial.

6—Sat. Transfiguration of the Lord; feast.

7—**Nineteenth Sunday of the Year.** (1 Kgs. 19:4-8; Eph. 4:30 to 5:2; Jn. 6:41-51.) [Sts. Sixtus II, pope, and Companions, martyrs, or St. Cajetan, priest; optional memorials.]

8—Mon. St. Dominic, priest; memorial.

9—Tues. Weekday.

10—Wed. St. Lawrence, deacon-martyr; feast.

11—Thurs. St. Clare, virgin; memorial.

12—Fri. Weekday.

13—Sat. Weekday. Sts. Pontian, pope, and Hippolytus, priest, martyrs, or BVM on Saturday; optional memorials.

14—**Twentieth Sunday of the Year.** (Prv. 9:1-6; Eph. 5:15-20; Jn. 6:51-58.) [St. Maximilian Kolbe, priest-martyr; memorial.]

15—**Mon. Assumption of Blessed Mary the Virgin; solemnity. Holy day of obligation (precept to attend Mass abrogated in U.S.)** (Rv. 11:19a and 12:1-6a, 10ab; 1 Cor. 15:20-26; Lk. 1:39-56.)

16—Tues. Weekday. St. Stephen of Hungary; optional memorial.

17—Wed. Weekday.

18—Thurs. Weekday. St. Jane Frances de Chantal, virgin; optional memorial (in U.S.).

19—Fri. Weekday. St. John Eudes, priest; optional memorial.

20—Sat. St. Bernard of Clairvaux, abbot-doctor; memorial.

21—**Twenty-First Sunday of the Year.** (Jos. 24:1-2a, 15-17, 18b; Eph. 5:21-32; Jn. 6:60-69.) [St. Pius X, pope; memorial.]

22—Mon. Queenship of Mary; memorial.

23—Tues. Weekday. St. Rose of Lima, virgin; optional memorial.

24—Wed. St. Bartholomew, apostle; feast.

25—Thurs. Weekday. St. Louis, or St. Joseph Calasanz, priest; optional memorials.

26—Fri. Weekday.

27—Sat. St. Monica, memorial.

28—**Twenty-Second Sunday of the Year.** (Dt. 4:1-2, 6-8; Jas. 1:17-18, 21b-22, 27; Mk. 7:1-8, 14-15, 21-23.) [St. Augustine, bishop-doctor; memorial.]

29—Mon. Beheading of St. John the Baptist; memorial.

30—Tues. Weekday.

31—Wed. Weekday.

Feasts: Assumption of Mary, Aug. 15; St. Bernard, Aug. 20, leader of monasticism; St. Augustine, Aug. 28 (outranked by Sunday), influential theologian.

SEPTEMBER 1994

Prayer Intentions: AN END TO RACISM: That the human family vigorously reject every form of racism and fear of foreigners (General).
RECONCILIATION IN AFRICA AND ASIA: That the peoples of Africa and Asia fully attain reconciliation and peace (Mission).

1—Thurs. Weekday.

2—Fri. Weekday.

3—Sat. St. Gregory the Great, pope-doctor; memorial.

4—**Twenty-Third Sunday of the Year.** (Is. 35:4-7a; Jas. 2:1-5; Mk. 7:31-37.)

5—Mon. Labor Day Votive Mass (prescribed in U.S.). Weekday.

6—Tues. Weekday.

7—Wed. Weekday.

8—Thurs. Birth of Mary; feast.

9—Fri. St. Peter Claver, priest; memorial (in U.S.). Weekday.

10—Sat. Weekday. BVM on Saturday; optional memorial.

11—**Twenty-Fourth Sunday of the Year.** (Is. 50:5-9a; Jas. 2:14-18; Mk. 8:27-35.)

12—Mon. Weekday.

13—Tues. St. John Chrysostom, bishop-doctor; memorial.

14—Wed. Triumph of the Cross; feast.

15—Thurs. Our Lady of Sorrows; memorial.

16—Fri. Sts. Cornelius, pope, and Cyprian, bishop, martyrs; memorial.

17—Sat. Weekday. St. Robert Bellarmine, bishop-doctor, or BVM on Saturday; optional memorials.

18—**Twenty-Fifth Sunday of the Year.** (Wis. 2:12, 17-20; Jas. 3:16 to 4:3; Mk. 9:30-37.)

19—Mon. St. Januarius, bishop-martyr; optional memorial.

20—Tues. Sts. Andrew Kim, priest, Paul Chong, lay apostle, and Companions, martyrs of Korea; memorial.

21—Wed. St. Matthew, apostle-evangelist; feast.

22—Thurs. Weekday.

23—Fri. Weekday.

24—Sat. Weekday. BVM on Saturday; optional memorial.

25—**Twenty-Sixth Sunday of the Year.** (Nm. 11:25-29; Jas. 5:1-6; Mk. 9:38-43, 45, 47-48.)

26—Mon. Weekday. Sts. Cosmas and Damian, martyrs; optional memorial.

27—Tues. St. Vincent de Paul, priest; memorial.

28—Wed. Weekday. St. Wenceslaus, martyr, or Sts. Lawrence Ruiz and Companions, martyrs; optional memorials.

29—Thurs. Sts. Michael, Gabriel and Raphael, archangels; feast.

30—Fri. St. Jerome, priest-doctor; memorial.

The celebration of Labor Day pinpoints the dignity of work by Christians in collaborating with the Father in making good things, with the Son in the ministering of redemption to and with others, in sharing the gifts of the Holy Spirit for the transformation of the world.

The Labor Day theme, the dignity of work, was the subject of Pope John Paul's encyclical, "Laborem Exercens."

OCTOBER 1994

Prayer Intentions: FELLOWSHIP AMONG RELIGIOUS: That fellowship and communion in institutes of consecrated life be an eloquent sign of the charity that unites Christ's followers (General). SYNOD OF BISHOPS ON RELIGIOUS LIFE: That the Synod of Bishops help religious institutes rediscover the value of missionary formation and apostolates (Mission).

1—Sat. St. Therese of the Child Jesus, virgin; memorial.

2—**Twenty-Seventh Sunday of the Year.** (Gn. 2:18-24; Heb. 2:9-11; Mk. 10:2-16.) [Guardian Angels; memorial.]

3—Mon. Weekday.

4—Tues. St. Francis of Assisi; memorial.

5—Wed. Weekday.

6—Thurs. Weekday. Bl. Marie-Rose Durocher, virgin; optional memorial (in U.S.). St. Bruno, priest; optional memorial.

7—Fri. Our Lady of the Rosary; memorial.

8—Sat. Weekday. BVM on Saturday; optional memorial.

9—**Twenty-Eighth Sunday of the Year.** (Wis. 7:7-11; Heb. 4:12-13; Mk. 10:17-30.) [Sts. Denis, bishop, and Companions, martyrs, or St. John Leonardi, priest; optional memorials.]

10—Mon. Weekday.

11—Tues. Weekday.

12—Wed. Weekday.

13—Thurs. Weekday.

14—Fri. Weekday. St. Callistus I, pope-martyr; optional memorial.

15—Sat. St. Teresa of Jesus (Avila), virgin-doctor; memorial.

16—**Twenty-Ninth Sunday of the Year.** (Is. 53:10-11; Heb. 4:14-16; Mk. 10:35-45.) [St. Hedwig, religious, or St. Margaret Mary Alacoque, virgin; optional memorials.]

17—Mon. St. Ignatius of Antioch, bishop-martyr; memorial.

18—Tues. St. Luke, evangelist; feast.

19—Wed. Sts. Isaac Jogues, John de Brebeuf, priests, and Companions, martyrs; memorial (in U.S.). Weekday. St. Paul of the Cross (general calendar); optional memorial.

20—Thurs. Weekday. St. Paul of the Cross (in U.S.); optional memorial.

21—Fri. Weekday.

22—Sat. Weekday. BVM on Saturday; optional memorial.

23—**Thirtieth Sunday of the Year.** (Jer. 31:7-9; Heb. 5:1-6; Mk. 10:46-52.) [St. John of Capistrano, priest; optional memorial.]

24—Mon. Weekday. St. Anthony Mary Claret, bishop; optional memorial.

25—Tues. Weekday.

26—Wed. Weekday.

27—Thurs. Weekday.

28—Fri. Sts. Simon and Jude, apostles; feast.

29—Sat. Weekday. BVM on Saturday; optional memorial.

30—**Thirty-First Sunday of the Year.** (Dt. 6:2-6; Heb. 7:23-28; Mk. 12:28b-34.)

31—Mon. Weekday.

Feasts: St. Therese of the Child Jesus, Oct. 1; Guardian Angels, Oct. 2; St. Francis of Assisi, Oct. 4; Our Lady of the Rosary, Oct. 7; St. Teresa of Avila, doctor of the Church, mystic, Oct. 15; St. Luke, one of the evangelists, Oct. 18; Sts. Isaac Jogues and Companions, North American martyrs, Oct. 19.

October is the Month of the Rosary.

NOVEMBER 1994

Prayer Intentions: FOR POLITICIANS: That politicians responsibly fulfil their vocation to open and generous service (General). THE GOSPEL IN ASIA: That the preaching of the Gospel encounter in Asia deep and sincere acceptance and be abundantly fruitful (Mission).

1—**Tues. All Saints; solemnity. Holy day of obligation.** (Rv. 7:2-4, 9-14; 1 Jn. 3:1-3; Mt. 5:1-12a.)
2—Wed. Commemoration of All the Faithful Departed (All Souls' Day).
3—Thurs. Weekday. St. Martin de Porres, religious, optional memorial.
4—Fri. St. Charles Borromeo, bishop; memorial.
5—Sat. Weekday. BVM on Saturday; optional memorial.
6—**Thirty-Second Sunday of the Year.** (1 Kgs. 17:10-16; Heb. 9:24-28; Mk. 12:38-44.)
7—Mon. Weekday.
8—Tues. Weekday.
9—Wed. Dedication of St. John Lateran (Archbasilica of Most Holy Savior); feast.
10—Thurs. St. Leo the Great, pope-doctor; memorial.
11—Fri. St. Martin of Tours, bishop; memorial.
12—Sat. St. Josaphat, bishop-martyr; memorial.
13—**Thirty-Third Sunday of Year.** (Dn. 12:1-3; Heb. 10:11-14, 18; Mk. 13:24-32.) [St. Frances Xavier Cabrini, virgin; memorial (in U.S.).]
14—Mon. Weekday.
15—Tues. Weekday. St. Albert the Great, bishop-doctor; optional memorial.
16—Wed. Weekday. St. Margaret of Scotland, or St. Gertrude, virgin; optional memorials.
17—Thurs. St. Elizabeth of Hungary, religious; memorial.
18—Fri. Weekday. Dedication of Basilicas of Sts. Peter and Paul or (in U.S.) St. Rose Philippine Duchesne, virgin; optional memorials.
19—Sat. Weekday. BVM on Saturday; optional memorial.
20—**Sun. Christ the King; solemnity.** (Dn. 7:13-14; Rv. 1:5-8; Jn. 18:33b-37.)
21—Mon. Presentation of Blessed Mary the Virgin; memorial. (Thirty-Fourth [Last] Week of the Year.)
22—Tues. St. Cecilia, virgin-martyr; memorial.
23—Wed. Weekday. Bl. Miguel Agustín Pro, priest-martyr; optional memorial (in U.S.); St. Clement I, pope-martyr, or St. Columban, abbot; optional memorials.
24—Thurs. Thanksgiving Day (in U.S.); optional Mass for a special occasion. St. Andrew Dung-Lac, priest, and Companions, martyrs; memorial.
25—Fri. Weekday.
26—Sat. Weekday. BVM on Saturday; optional memorial.
27—**First Sunday of Advent.** [Start of 1995 liturgical year.] (Jer. 33:14-16; 1 Thes. 3:12 to 4:2; Lk. 21:25-28, 34-36.)
28—Mon. Weekday of Advent.
29—Tues. Weekday of Advent.
30—Wed. St. Andrew, apostle; feast.

Feasts: Nov. 1, All Saints, and All Souls, Nov. 2, feasts of the communion of saints; Dedication of the Patriarchal Basilica of St. John Lateran, dating from the time of Constantine, Nov. 9; St. Frances Xavier Cabrini, first U.S. citizen saint, Nov. 13; Christ the King, Nov. 20.

DECEMBER 1994

Prayer Intentions: THE APOSTOLATE OF PRAYER: That the 150th anniversary of the Apostleship of Prayer help Christians to revitalize apostolic zeal for the new evangelization (General). SPECIAL SYNOD OF AFRICAN BISHOPS: That the special Synod of Africa strengthen communion, collaboration and a missionary spirit in the Churches of that continent. (Mission).

1—Thurs. Weekday of Advent.
2—Fri. Weekday of Advent.
3—Sat. St. Francis Xavier, priest; memorial.
4—**Second Sunday of Advent.** (Bar. 5:1-9; Phil. 1:4-6, 8-11; Lk. 3:1-6.) [St. John Damascene, priest-doctor; optional memorial.]
5—Mon. Weekday of Advent.
6—Tues. Weekday of Advent. St. Nicholas, bishop; optional memorial.
7—Wed. St. Ambrose, bishop-doctor; memorial.
8—**Thurs. Immaculate Conception of Blessed Mary the Virgin; solemnity. Holy day of obligation.** (Gn. 3:9-15, 20; Eph. 1:3-6, 11-12; Lk. 1:26-38.)
9—Fri. Weekday of Advent. Bl. Juan Diego; optional memorial (in U.S.).
10—Sat. Weekday of Advent.
11—**Third Sunday of Advent.** (Zep. 3:14-18a; Phil. 4:4-7; Lk. 3:10-18.) [St. Damasus I, pope; optional memorial.]
12—Mon. Our Lady of Guadalupe; feast (in U.S.).
13—Tues. St. Lucy, virgin-martyr; memorial.
14—Wed. St. John of the Cross, priest-doctor; memorial.
15—Thurs. Weekday of Advent.
16—Fri. Weekday of Advent.
17—Sat. Weekday of Advent.
18—**Fourth Sunday of Advent.** (Mi. 5:1-4a; Heb. 10:5-10; Lk. 1:39-45.)
19—Mon. Weekday of Advent.
20—Tues. Weekday of Advent.
21—Wed. Weekday of Advent. St. Peter Canisius, priest-doctor; optional memorial.
22—Thurs. Weekday of Advent.
23—Fri. Weekday of Advent. St. John of Kanty, priest; optional memorial.
24—Sat. Weekday of Advent.
25—**Sun. Christmas. Birth of the Lord; solemnity. Holy day of obligation.** (Vigil — Is. 62:1-5; Acts 13:16-17, 22-25; Mt. 1:1-25. Midnight—Is. 9:1-6; Ti. 2:11-14; Lk. 2:1-14. At Dawn — Is. 62:11-12; Ti. 3:4-7; Lk. 2:15-20. During the Day — Is. 57:7-10; Heb. 1:1-6; Jn. 1:1-18.)
26—Mon. St. Stephen, first martyr; feast.
27—Tues. St. John, apostle-evangelist; feast.
28—Wed. Holy Innocents, martyrs; feast.
29—Thurs. Fifth Day of Christmas Octave. St. Thomas Becket, bishop-martyr; optional memorial.
30—Fri. Sixth Day of Christmas Octave.
31—Sat. Seventh Day of Christmas Octave. St. Sylvester I, pope; optional memorial.

Feasts: St. Francis Xavier, patron of missions and missionaries, Dec. 3; Immaculate Conception, Dec. 8; Our Lady of Guadalupe, patroness of the Americas, Dec. 12; Birth of the Lord, Dec. 25.

HOLY DAYS AND OTHER OBSERVANCES

The following list includes the six holy days of obligation observed in the United States and additional observances of devotional and historical significance. The dignity or rank of observances is indicated by the terms: **solemnity** (highest in rank); **feast; memorial** (for universal observance); **optional memorial** (for celebration by choice).

All Saints, Nov. 1, holy day of obligation, solemnity. Commemorates all the blessed in heaven, and is intended particularly to honor the blessed who have no special feasts. The background of the feast dates to the fourth century when groups of martyrs, and later other saints, were honored on a common day in various places. In 609 or 610, the Pantheon, a pagan temple at Rome, was consecrated as a Christian church for the honor of Our Lady and the martyrs (later all saints). In 835, Gregory IV fixed Nov. 1 as the date of observance.

All Souls, Commemoration of the Faithful Departed, Nov. 2. The dead were prayed for from the earliest days of Christianity. By the sixth century it was customary in Benedictine monasteries to hold a commemoration of deceased members of the order at Pentecost. A common commemoration of all the faithful departed on the day after All Saints was instituted in 998 by St. Odilo, of the Abbey of Cluny, and an observance of this kind was accepted in Rome in the 14th century.

Annunciation of the Lord (formerly, Annunciation of the Blessed Virgin Mary), Mar. 25, solemnity. A feast of the Incarnation which commemorates the announcement by the Archangel Gabriel to the Virgin Mary that she was to become the Mother of Christ (Lk. 1:26-38), and the miraculous conception of Christ by her. The feast was instituted about 430 in the East. The Roman observance dates from the seventh century, when celebration was said to be universal.

Ascension of the Lord, movable observance held 40 days after Easter, holy day of obligation, solemnity. Commemorates the Ascension of Christ into heaven 40 days after his Resurrection from the dead (Mk. 16:19; Lk. 24:51; Acts 1:2). The feast recalls the completion of Christ's mission on earth for the salvation of all people and his entry into heaven with glorified human nature. The Ascension is a pledge of the final glorification of all who achieve salvation. Documentary evidence of the feast dates from early in the fifth century, but it was observed long before that time in connection with Pentecost and Easter.

Ash Wednesday, movable observance, six and one-half weeks before Easter. It was set as the first day of Lent by Pope St. Gregory the Great (590-604) with the extension of an earlier and shorter penitential season to a total period including 40 weekdays of fasting before Easter. It is a day of fast and abstinence. Ashes, symbolic of penance, are blessed and distributed among the faithful during the day. They are used to mark the forehead with the Sign of the Cross, with the reminder: "Remember, man, that you are dust, and unto dust you shall return," or: "Repent, and believe the Good News."

Assumption, Aug. 15, holy day of obligation, solemnity. Commemorates the taking into heaven of Mary, soul and body, at the end of her life on earth, a truth of faith that was proclaimed a dogma by Pius XII on Nov. 1, 1950. One of the oldest and most solemn feasts of Mary, it has a history dating back to at least the seventh century when its celebration was already established at Jerusalem and Rome.

Baptism of the Lord, movable, usually celebrated on the Sunday after January 6, feast. Recalls the baptism of Christ by John the Baptist (Mk. 1:9-11), an event associated with the liturgy of the Epiphany. This baptism was the occasion for Christ's manifestation of himself at the beginning of his public life.

Birth of Mary, Sept. 8, feast. This is a very old feast which originated in the East and found place in the Roman liturgy in the seventh century.

Candlemas Day, Feb. 2. See Presentation of the Lord.

Chair of Peter, Feb. 22, feast. The feast, which has been in the Roman calendar since 336, is a liturgical expression of belief in the episcopacy and hierarchy of the Church.

Christmas, Birth of Our Lord Jesus Christ, Dec. 25, holy day of obligation, solemnity. Commemorates the birth of Christ (Lk. 2:1-20). This event was originally commemorated in the East on the feast of Epiphany or Theophany. The Christmas feast itself originated in the West; by 354 it was certainly kept on Dec. 25. This date may have been set for the observance to offset pagan ceremonies held at about the same time to commemorate the birth of the sun at the winter solstice. There are texts for three Christmas Masses — at midnight, dawn and during the day.

Christ the King, movable, celebrated on the last Sunday of the liturgical year, solemnity. Commemorates the royal prerogatives of Christ and is equivalent to a declaration of his rights to the homage, service and fidelity of men in all phases of individual and social life. Pius XI instituted the feast Dec. 11, 1925.

Conversion of St. Paul, Jan. 25, feast. An observance mentioned in some calendars from the 8th and 9th centuries. Pope Innocent III (1198-1216) ordered its observance with great solemnity.

Corpus Christi, movable, celebrated on the Thursday (or Sunday, as in the U.S.) following Trinity Sunday, solemnity. Commemorates the institution of the Holy Eucharist (Mt. 26:26-28). The feast originated at Liege in 1246 and was extended throughout the Church in the West by Urban IV in 1264. St. Thomas Aquinas composed the Liturgy of the Hours for the feast.

Dedication of St. John Lateran, Nov. 9, feast. Commemorates the first public consecration of a church, that of the Basilica of the Most Holy Savior by Pope St. Sylvester Nov. 9, 324. The church, as well as the Lateran Palace, was the gift of Emperor Constantine. Since the 12th century it has been known as St. John Lateran, in honor of John the Baptist after whom the adjoining baptistery was named. It was rebuilt by Innocent X (1644-55), reconsecrated by Benedict XIII in 1726, and enlarged by Leo XIII (1878-1903). This basilica is regarded as the church of highest dignity in Rome and throughout the Roman Rite.

Dedication of St. Mary Major, Aug. 5, optional memorial. Commemorates the rebuilding and dedication by Pope Sixtus III (432-40) of a church in honor of Blessed Mary the Virgin. This is the Basilica of St. Mary Major on the Esquiline Hill in Rome. An earlier building was erected during the pontificate of Liberius (352-66); according to legend, it was located on a site covered by a miraculous fall of snow seen by a nobleman favored with a vision of Mary.

Easter, movable celebration held on the first Sunday after the full moon following the vernal equinox (between Mar. 22 and Apr. 25), solemnity with an octave. Commemorates the Resurrection of Christ from the dead (Mk. 16:1-7). The observance of this mystery, kept since the first days of the Church, extends throughout the Easter season which lasts until the feast of Pentecost, a period of 50 days. Every Sunday in the year is regarded as a "little" Easter. The date of Easter determines the dates of movable feasts, such as Ascension and Pentecost, and the number of weeks before Lent and after Pentecost.

Easter Vigil, called by St. Augustine the "Mother of All Vigils," the night before Easter. Ceremonies are all related to the Resurrection and renewal-in-grace theme of Easter: blessing of the new fire, procession with the Easter Candle, singing of the Easter Proclamation (Exsultet), Liturgy of the Word with at least three Old Testament readings, the Litany of Saints, blessing of water, baptism of converts and infants, renewal of baptismal promises, Liturgy of the Eucharist. The vigil ceremonies are held after nightfall on Saturday.

Epiphany of the Lord, Jan. 6 or (in the U.S.) a Sunday between Jan. 2 and 8, solemnity. Commemorates the manifestations of the divinity of Christ. It is one of the oldest Christian feasts, with an Eastern origin traceable to the beginning of the third century and antedating the Western feast of Christmas. Originally, it commemorated the manifestations of Christ's divinity — or Theophany — in his birth, the homage of the Magi, and baptism by John the Baptist. Later, the first two of these commemorations were transferred to Christmas when the Eastern Church adopted that feast between 380 and 430. The central feature of the Eastern observance now is the manifestation or declaration of Christ's divinity in his baptism and at the beginning of his public life. The Epiphany was adopted by the Western Church during the same period in which the Eastern Church accepted Christmas. In the Roman Rite, commemoration is made in the Mass of the homage of the wise men from the East (Mt. 2:1-12).

Good Friday, the Friday before Easter, the second day of the Easter Triduum. Liturgical elements of the observance are commemoration of the Passion and Death of Christ in the reading of the Passion (according to John), special prayers for the Church and people of all ranks, the veneration of the Cross, and a Communion service. The celebration takes place in the afternoon, preferably at 3:00 p.m.

Guardian Angels, Oct. 2, memorial. Commemorates the angels who protect people from spiritual and physical dangers and assist them in doing good. A feast in their honor celebrated in Spain in the 16th century was extended to the whole Church by Paul V in 1608. In 1670, Clement X set Oct. 2 as the date of observance. Earlier, guardian angels were honored liturgically in conjunction with the feast of St. Michael.

Holy Family, movable observance on the Sunday after Christmas, feast. Commemorates the Holy Family of Jesus, Mary and Joseph as the model of domestic society, holiness and virtue. The devotional background of the feast was very strong in the 17th century. In the 18th century, in prayers composed for a special Mass, a Canadian bishop likened the Christian family to the Holy Family. Leo XIII consecrated families to the Holy Family. In 1921, Benedict XV extended the Divine Office and Mass of the feast to the whole Church.

Holy Innocents, Dec. 28, feast. Commemorates the infants who suffered death at the hands of Herod's soldiers seeking to kill the child Jesus (Mt. 2:13-18). A feast in their honor has been observed since the fifth century.

Holy Saturday, the day before Easter. The Sacrifice of the Mass is not celebrated, and Holy Communion may be given only as Viaticum. If possible the Easter fast should be observed until the Easter Vigil.

Holy Thursday, the Thursday before Easter. Commemorates the institution of the sacraments of the Eucharist and holy orders, and the washing of the feet of the Apostles by Jesus at the Last Supper. The Mass of the Lord's Supper in the evening marks the beginning of the Easter Triduum. Following the Mass, there is a procession of the Blessed Sacrament to a place of reposition for adoration by the faithful. At an earlier Mass of Chrism, bishops bless oils (of catechumens, chrism, the sick) for use during the year. (For pastoral reasons, diocesan bishops may permit additional Masses, but these should not overshadow the principal Mass of the Lord's Supper.)

Immaculate Conception, Dec. 8, holy day of obligation, solemnity. Commemorates the fact that Mary, in view of her calling to be the Mother of Christ and in virtue of his merits, was preserved from the first moment of her conception from original sin and was filled with grace from the very beginning of her life. She was the only person so preserved from original sin. The present form of the feast dates from Dec. 8, 1854, when Pius IX defined the dogma of the Immaculate Conception. An earlier feast of the Conception, which testified to long-existing belief in this truth, was observed in the East by the eighth century, in Ireland in the ninth, and subsequently in European countries. In 1846, Mary was proclaimed patroness of the U.S. under this title.

Immaculate Heart of Mary, Saturday following the second Sunday after Pentecost, optional memorial. On May 4, 1944, Pius XII ordered this feast observed throughout the Church in order to obtain Mary's intercession for "peace among nations, freedom for the Church, the conversion of sinners, the love of purity and the practice of virtue." Two years earlier, he consecrated the entire human race to Mary under this title. Devotion to Mary under the title of her Most Pure Heart originated during the Middle Ages. It was given great impetus in the 17th century by the preaching of St. John Eudes, who was the first to celebrate a Mass and Divine Office of Mary under this title. A feast, celebrated in various places and on different dates, was authorized in 1799.

Joachim and Ann, July 26, memorial. Commemorates the parents of Mary. A joint feast, celebrated Sept. 9, originated in the East near the end of the sixth century. Devotion to Ann, introduced in the eighth century at Rome, became widespread in Europe in the 14th century; her feast was extended throughout the Latin Church in 1584. A feast of Joachim was introduced in the West in the 15th century.

John the Baptist, Birth, June 24, solemnity. The precursor of Christ, whose cousin he was, was commemorated universally in the liturgy by the fourth century. He is the only saint, except the Blessed Virgin Mary, whose birthday is observed as a feast. Another feast, on Aug. 29, commemorates his passion and death at the order of Herod (Mk. 6:14-29).

Joseph, Mar. 19, solemnity. Joseph is honored as the husband of the Blessed Virgin Mary, the patron and protector of the universal Church and workman. Devotion to him already existed in the eighth century in the East, and in the 11th in the West. Various feasts were celebrated before the 15th century when Mar. 19 was fixed for his commemoration; this feast was extended to the whole Church in 1621 by Gregory XV. In 1955, Pius XII instituted the feast of St. Joseph the Workman for observance May 1; this feast, which may be celebrated by local option, supplanted the Solemnity or Patronage of St. Joseph formerly observed on the third Wednesday after Easter. St. Joseph was proclaimed protector and patron of the universal Church in 1870 by Pius IX.

Michael, Gabriel and Raphael, Archangels, Sept. 29, feast. A feast bearing the title of Dedication of St. Michael the Archangel formerly commemorated on this date the consecration in 530 of a church near Rome in honor of Michael, the first angel given a liturgical feast. For a while, this feast was combined with a commemoration of the Guardian Angels. The separate feasts of Gabriel (Mar. 24) and Raphael (Oct. 24) were suppressed by the calendar in effect since 1970 and this joint feast of the three archangels was instituted.

Octave of Christmas, Jan. 1. See Solemnity of Mary, Mother of God.

Our Lady of Guadalupe, Dec. 12, feast (in the U.S.). Commemorates under this title the appearances of the Blessed Virgin Mary in 1531 to an Indian, Juan Diego, on Tepeyac hill outside Mexico City (see Apparitions of the Blessed Virgin Mary). The celebration, observed as a memorial in the U.S., was raised to the rank of feast at the request of the National Conference of Catholic Bishops. Approval was granted in a decree dated Jan. 8, 1988.

Our Lady of Sorrows, Sept. 15, memorial. Recalls the sorrows experienced by Mary in her association with Christ: the prophecy of Simeon (Lk. 2:34-35), the flight into Egypt (Mt. 2:13-21), the three-day separation from Jesus (Lk. 2:41-50), and

four incidents connected with the Passion: her meeting with Christ on the way to Calvary, the crucifixion, the removal of Christ's body from the cross, and his burial (Mt. 27:31-61; Mk. 15:20-47; Lk. 23:26-56; Jn. 19:17-42). A Mass and Divine Office of the feast were celebrated by the Servites, especially, in the 17th century, and in 1817 Pius VII extended the observance to the whole Church.

Our Lady of the Rosary, Oct. 7, memorial. Commemorates the Virgin Mary through recall of the mysteries of the Rosary which recapitulate events in her life and the life of Christ. The feast was instituted to commemorate a Christian victory over invading Mohammedan forces at Lepanto on Oct. 7, 1571, and was extended throughout the Church by Clement XI in 1716.

Passion Sunday (formerly called **Palm Sunday**), the Sunday before Easter. Marks the start of Holy Week by recalling the triumphal entry of Christ into Jerusalem at the beginning of the last week of his life (Mt. 21:1-9). A procession and other ceremonies commemorating this event were held in Jerusalem from very early Christian times and were adopted in Rome by the ninth century, when the blessing of palm for the occasion was introduced. Full liturgical observance includes the blessing of palm and a procession before the principal Mass of the day. The Passion, by Matthew, Mark or Luke, is read during the Mass.

Pentecost, also called **Whitsunday,** movable celebration held 50 days after Easter, solemnity. Commemorates the descent of the Holy Spirit upon the Apostles, the preaching of Peter and the other Apostles to Jews in Jerusalem, the baptism and aggregation of some 3,000 persons to the Christian community (Acts 2:1-41). It is regarded as the birthday of the Catholic Church. The original observance of the feast antedated the earliest extant documentary evidence from the third century.

Peter and Paul, June 29, solemnity. Commemorates the martyrdoms of Peter by crucifixion and Paul by beheading during the Neronian persecution. This joint commemoration of the chief Apostles dates at least from 258 at Rome.

Presentation of the Lord (formerly called Purification of the Blessed Virgin Mary, also Candlemas), Feb. 2, feast. Commemorates the presentation of Jesus in the Temple — according to prescriptions of Mosaic Law (Lv. 12:2-8; Ex. 13:2; Lk. 2:22-32) — and the purification of Mary 40 days after his birth. In the East, where the feast antedated fourth century testimony regarding its existence, it was observed primarily as a feast of Our Lord; in the West, where it was adopted later, it was regarded more as a feast of Mary until the calendar in effect since 1970. Its date was set for Feb. 2 after the celebration of Christmas was fixed for Dec. 25, late in the fourth century. The blessing of candles, probably in commemoration of Christ who was the Light to enlighten the Gentiles, became common about the 11th century and gave the feast the secondary name of Candlemas.

Queenship of Mary, Aug. 22, memorial. Commemorates the high dignity of Mary as Queen of heaven, angels and men. Universal observance of the memorial was ordered by Pius XII in the encyclical *Ad Caeli Reginam,* Oct. 11, 1954, near the close of a Marian Year observed in connection with the centenary of the proclamation of the dogma of the Immaculate Conception and four years after the proclamation of the dogma of the Assumption. The original date of the memorial was May 31.

Resurrection. See Easter.

Sacred Heart of Jesus, movable observance held on the Friday after the second Sunday after Pentecost (Corpus Christi, in the U.S.), solemnity. The object of the devotion is the divine Person of Christ, whose heart is the symbol of his love for all people — for whom he accomplished the work of Redemption. The Mass and Office on the feast were prescribed by Pius XI in 1929. Devotion to the Sacred Heart was introduced into the liturgy in the 17th century through the efforts of St. John Eudes who composed an Office and Mass for the feast. It was furthered as the result of the revelations of St. Margaret Mary Alacoque after 1675 and by the work of St. Claude La Colombiere, S.J. In 1765, Clement XIII approved a Mass and Office for the feast, and in 1856 Pius IX extended the observance throughout the Roman Rite.

Solemnity of Mary, Mother of God, Jan. 1, holy day of obligation, solemnity. The calendar in effect since 1970, in accord with Eastern tradition, reinstated the Marian character of this commemoration on the octave day of Christmas. The former feast of the Circumcision, dating at least from the first half of the sixth century, marked the initiation of Jesus (Lk. 2:21) in Judaism and by analogy focused attention on the initiation of persons in the Christian religion and their incorporation in Christ through baptism. The feast of the Solemnity supplants the former feast of the Maternity of Mary observed on Oct. 11.

Transfiguration of the Lord, Aug. 6, feast. Commemorates the revelation of his divinity by Christ to Peter, James and John on Mt. Tabor (Mt. 17:1-9).

The feast, which is very old, was extended throughout the universal Church in 1457 by Callistus III.

Trinity, Most Holy, movable observance held on the Sunday after Pentecost, solemnity. Commemorates the most sublime mystery of the Christian faith, i.e., that there are Three Divine Persons — Father, Son and Holy Spirit — in one God (Mt. 28:18-20). A votive Mass of the Most Holy Trinity dates from the seventh century; an Office was composed in the 10th century; in 1334, John XXII extended the feast to the universal Church.

Triumph of the Cross, Sept. 14, feast. Commemorates the finding of the cross on which Christ was crucified, in 326 through the efforts of St. Helena, mother of Constantine; the consecration of the Basilica of the Holy Sepulchre nearly 10 years later; and the recovery in 628 or 629 by Emperor Heraclius of a major portion of the cross which had been removed by the Persians from its place of veneration at Jerusalem. The feast originated in Jerusalem and spread through the East before being adopted in the West. General adoption followed the building at Rome of the Basilica of the Holy Cross "in Jerusalem," so called because it was the place of enshrinement of a major portion of the cross of crucifixion.

Visitation, May 31, feast. Commemorates Mary's visit to her cousin Elizabeth after the Annunciation and before the birth of John the Baptist, the precursor of Christ (Lk. 1:39-47). The feast had a medieval origin and was observed in the Franciscan Order before being extended throughout the Church by Urban VI in 1389. It is one of the feasts of the Incarnation and is notable for its recall of the Magnificat, one of the few New Testament canticles, which acknowledges the unique gifts of God to Mary because of her role in the redemptive work of Christ. The canticle is recited at Evening Prayer in the Liturgy of the Hours.

SAINTS

Biographical sketches of additional saints and blessed are under other Almanac titles. See Index, under name of saint. For Beatification and Canonization procedures, see those entries in the Glossary.

An asterisk with a feast date indicates that the saint is listed in the General Roman Calendar or the proper calendar for U.S. dioceses. For rank of observances, see listing in calendar for current year on preceding pages.

Adjutor (d. 1131): Norman knight; fought in First Crusade; monk-recluse after his return; Apr. 30.

Agatha (d. c. 250): Sicilian virgin-martyr; her intercession credited in Sicily with stilling eruptions of Mt. Etna; patron of nurses; Feb. 5*.

Agnes (d. c. 304): Roman virgin-martyr; martyred at age of 10 or 12; patron of young girls; Jan. 21*.

Aloysius Gonzaga (1568-1591): Italian Jesuit; died while nursing plague-stricken; canonized 1726; patron of youth; June 21*.

Amand (d. c. 676): Apostle of Belgium; b. France; established monasteries throughout Belgium; Feb. 6.

Andre Bessette, Bl. (Bro. Andre) (1845-1937):

Canadian Holy Cross Brother; prime mover in building of St. Joseph's Oratory, Montreal; beatified May 23, 1982; Jan. 6* (U.S.).

Andre Grasset de Saint Sauveur, Bl. (1758-1792): Canadian priest; martyred in France, Sept. 2, 1792, during the Revolution; one of a group called the Martyrs of Paris who were beatified in 1926; Sept. 2.

Andrew Bobola (1592-1657): Polish Jesuit; joined Jesuits at Vilna; worked for return of Orthodox to union with Rome; martyred; canonized 1938; May 16.

Andrew Corsini (1302-1373): Italian Carmelite; bishop of Fiesoli; mediator between quarrelsome Italian states; canonized 1629; Feb. 4.

Andrew Dung-Lac and Companions (d. 18th-19th c.): Martyrs of Vietnam. Total of 117 included 96 Vietnamese, 11 Spanish and 10 French missionaries (8 bishops; 50 priests, including Andrew Dung-Lac; 1 seminarian, 58 lay persons). Canonized June 19, 1988; inscribed in General Roman Calendar, 1989, as a memorial. Nov. 24*.

Andrew Fournet (1752-1834): French priest; co-founder with St. Jeanne Elizabeth Bichier des Anges of the Daughters of the Holy Cross of St. Andrew; canonized 1933; May 13.

Andrew Kim, Paul Chong and Companions (d. between 1839-1867): Korean martyrs (103) killed in persecutions of 1839, 1846, 1866, and 1867; among them were Andrew Kim, the first Korean priest, and Paul Chong, lay apostle; canonized May 6, 1984, during Pope John Paul II's visit to Korea; entered into General Roman Calendar, 1985, as a memorial. Sept. 20*.

Angela Merici (1474-1540): Italian secular Franciscan; foundress of Company of St. Ursula, 1535, the first teaching order of women Religious in the Church; canonized 1807; Jan. 27*.

Angelico, Bl. (Fra Angelico; John of Faesulis) (1387-1455): Dominican; Florentine painter of early Renaissance; proclaimed blessed by John Paul II, Feb. 3, 1982; patron of artists; Feb. 18.

Anne Mary Javouhey, Bl. (1779-1851): French virgin; foundress of Institute of St. Joseph of Cluny, 1812; beatified 1950; July 15.

Ansgar (801-865): Benedictine monk; b. near Amiens; archbishop of Hamburg; missionary in Denmark, Sweden, Norway and northern Germany; apostle of Scandinavia; Feb. 3.*

Anthony (c. 251-c. 354): Abbot; Egyptian hermit; patriarch of all monks; established communities for hermits which became models for monastic life, especially in the East; friend and supporter of St. Athanasius in the latter's struggle with the Arians; Jan. 17*.

Anthony Claret (1807-1870): Spanish bishop; founder of Missionary Sons of the Immaculate Heart of Mary (Claretians), 1849; archbishop of Santiago, Cuba, 1851-57; canonized 1950; Oct. 24*.

Anthony Gianelli (1789-1846): Italian bishop; as parish priest, founded the Daughters of Our Lady of the Garden, 1829; bishop of Bobbio, 1838; canonized 1951; June 7.

Anthony Zaccaria (1502-1539): Italian priest; founder of Barnabites (Clerks Regular of St. Paul), 1530; canonized 1897; July 5*.

Apollonia (d. 249): Deaconess of Alexandria; martyred during persecution of Decius; her patronage of dentists and those suffering from toothaches probably rests on tradition that her teeth were broken by her persecutors; Feb. 9.

Augustine of Canterbury (d. 604 or 605): Italian missionary; apostle of the English; sent by Pope Gregory I with 40 monks to evangelize England; arrived there 597; first archbishop of Canterbury; May 27*.

Bartolomea Capitania (1807-1833): Italian foundress with Vincenza Gerosa of the Sisters of Charity of Lovere; canonized 1950; July 26.

Beatrice da Silva Meneses (1424-1490): Foundress, b. Portugal; founded Congregation of the Immaculate Conception, 1484, in Spain; canonized 1976; Sept. 1.

Benedict Joseph Labre (1748-1783): French layman; pilgrim-beggar; noted for his piety and love of prayer before the Blessed Sacrament; canonized 1883; Apr. 16.

Benedict of Nursia (c. 480-547): Abbot; founder of monasticism in Western Europe; established monastery at Monte Cassino; proclaimed patron of Europe by Paul VI in 1964; July 11*.

Benedict the Black (il Moro) (1526-1589): Sicilian Franciscan; born a slave; joined Franciscans as lay brother; appointed guardian and novice master; canonized 1807; Apr. 3.

Bernadette Soubirous (1844-1879): French peasant girl favored with series of visions of Blessed Virgin Mary at Lourdes (see Lourdes Apparitions); joined Institute of Sisters of Notre Dame at Nevers, 1866; canonized 1933; Apr. 16.

Bernard of Montjoux (or Menthon) (d. 1081): Augustinian canon; probably born in Italy; founded Alpine hospices near the two passes named for him; patron of mountaineers; May 28.

Bernardine of Feltre, Bl. (1439-1494): Italian Franciscan preacher; a founder of *montes pietatis;* Sept. 28.

Bernardine of Siena (1380-1444): Italian Franciscan; noted preacher and missioner; spread of devotion to Holy Name is attributed to him; represented in art holding to his breast the monogram IHS; canonized 1450; May 20*.

Blase (d. c. 316): Armenian bishop; martyr; the blessing of throats on his feast day derives from tradition that he miraculously saved the life of a boy who had half-swallowed a fish bone; Feb. 3*.

Boniface (Winfrid) (d. 754): English Benedictine; bishop; martyr; apostle of Germany; established monastery at Fulda which became center of missionary work in Germany; archbishop of Mainz; martyred near Dukkum in Holland; June 5*.

Brendan (c. 489-583): Irish abbot; founded monasteries; his patronage of sailors probably rests on a legend that he made a seven-year voyage in search of a fabled paradise; called Brendan the Navigator; May 16.

Bridget (Brigid) (c. 450-525): Irish nun; founded religious community at Kildare, the first in Ireland; patron, with Sts. Patrick and Columba, of Ireland; Feb. 1.

Bridget (Birgitta) (c. 1303-1373): Swedish mystic; widow; foundress of Order of Our Savior (Brigittines); canonized 1391; patroness of Sweden; July 23*.

Bruno (1030-1101): German monk; founded Carthusians, 1084, in France; Oct. 6*.

Cabrini, Mother: See Frances Xavier Cabrini.

Cajetan (Gaetano) of Thiene (1480-1547): Italian lawyer; religious reformer; a founder of Oratory of Divine Love, forerunner of the Theatines; canonized 1671; Aug. 7*.

Callistus I (d. 222): Pope, 217-222; martyr; condemned Sabellianism and other heresies; advocated a policy of mercy toward repentant sinners; Oct. 14*.

Camillus de Lellis (1550-1614): Italian priest; founder of Camillians (Ministers of the Sick); canonized 1746; patron of the sick and of nurses; July 14*.

Casimir (1458-1484): Polish prince; grand duke of Lithuania; noted for his piety; buried at cathedral in Vilna, Lithuania; canonized 1521; patron of Poland and Lithuania; Mar. 4.*

Cassian of Tangier (d. 298): Roman martyr; an official court stenographer who declared himself a Christian; patron of stenographers; Dec. 3.

Catherine Laboure (1806-1876): French

Religious; favored with series of visions soon after she joined Sisters of Charity of St. Vincent de Paul in Paris in 1830; first Miraculous Medal (see Index) struck in 1832 in accord with one of the visions; canonized 1947; Nov. 28.

Catherine of Bologna (1413-1463): Italian Poor Clare; mystic, writer, artist; canonized 1712; patron of artists; May 9.

Cecilia (2nd-3rd century): Roman virgin-martyr; traditional patroness of musicians; Nov. 22.*

Charles Borromeo (1538-1584): Italian cardinal; nephew of Pope Pius IV; cardinal bishop of Milan; influential figure in Church reform in Italy; promoted education of clergy; canonized 1610; Nov. 4*.

Charles Lwanga and Companions (d. between 1885 and 1887): Twenty-two Martyrs of Uganda, many of them pages of King Mwanga of Uganda, who were put to death because they denounced his corrupt lifestyle; canonized 1964; first martyrs of black Africa; June 3.*

Charles of Sezze (1616-1670): Italian Franciscan lay brother who served in humble capacities; canonized 1959; Jan. 6.

Christopher (3rd cent.): Early Christian martyr inscribed in Roman calendar about 1550; feast relegated to particular calendars because of legendary nature of accounts of his life; traditional patron of travelers; July 25.

Clare (1194-1253): Foundress of Poor Clares; b. at Assisi; was joined in religious life by her sisters, Agnes and Beatrice, and eventually her widowed mother Ortolana; canonized 1255; patroness of television; Aug. 11.*

Claude La Colombiere (1641-1682): French Jesuit; spiritual director of St. Margaret Mary Alacoque; instrumental in spreading devotion to the Sacred Heart; beatified, 1929; canonized May 31, 1992; Feb. 15.

Clement Hofbauer (1751-1820): Redemptorist priest, missionary; born in Moravia; helped spread Redemptorists north of the Alps; canonized 1909; Mar. 15.

Clement I (d. c. 100): Pope, 88-97; third successor of St. Peter; wrote important letter to Church in Corinth settling disputes there; venerated as a martyr; Nov. 23*.

Columba (521-597): Irish monk; founded monasteries in Ireland; missionary in Scotland; established monastery at Iona which became the center for conversion of Picts, Scots, and Northern English; Scotland's most famous saint; patron saint of Ireland (with Sts. Patrick and Brigid); June 9.

Columban (545-615): Irish monk; scholar; founded monasteries in England and Brittany (famous abbey of Luxeuil), forced into exile because of his criticism of Frankish court; spent last years in northern Italy where he founded abbey at Bobbio; Nov. 23*.

Conrad of Parzham (1818-1894): Bavarian Capuchin lay brother; served as porter at the Marian shrine of Altotting in Upper Bavaria for 40 years; canonized 1934; Apr. 21.

Contardo Ferrini, Bl. (1859-1902): Italian secular Franciscan; model of the Catholic professor; beatified 1947; patron of universities; Oct. 20.

Cornelius (d. 253): Pope, 251-253; promoted a policy of mercy with respect to readmission of repentant Christians who had fallen away during the persecution of Decius *(lapsi);* banished from Rome during persecution of Gallus; regarded as a martyr; Sept. 16 (with Cyprian)*.

Cosmas and Damian (d. c. 303): Arabian twin brothers, physicians; martyred during Diocletian persecution; patrons of physicians; Sept. 26*.

Crispin and Crispinian (3rd cent.): Early Christian martyrs; said to have met their deaths in Gaul; patrons of shoemakers, a trade they pursued; Oct. 25.

Crispin of Viterbo (1668-1750): Capuchin brother; canonized June 20, 1982; May 21.

Cyprian (d. 258): Early ecclesiastical writer; b. Africa; bishop of Carthage, 249-258; supported Pope St. Cornelius concerning the readmission of Christians who had apostasized in time of persecution; erred in his teaching that baptism administered by heretics and schismatics was invalid; wrote *De Unitate;* Sept. 16 (with St. Cornelius)*.

Cyril and Methodius (9th century): Greek missionaries; brothers venerated as apostles of the Slavs; Cyril (d. 869) and Methodius (d. 885) began their missionary work in Moravia in 863; developed a Slavonic alphabet; used the vernacular in the liturgy, a practice that was eventually approved; declared patrons of Europe with St. Benedict, Dec. 31, 1980; Feb. 14*.

Damasus I (d. 384): Pope, 366-384; opposed Arians and Apollinarians; commissioned St. Jerome to work on Bible translation; developed Roman liturgy; Dec. 11*.

Damian: See Cosmas and Damian.

David (5th or 6th cent.): Nothing for certain known of his life; said to have founded monastery at Menevia; patron saint of Wales; Mar. 1.

Denis and Companions (d. 3rd cent.): Denis, bishop of Paris, and two companions identified by early writers as Rusticus, a priest, and Eleutherius, a deacon; martyred near Paris; Denis is popularly regarded as the apostle and a patron saint of France; Oct. 9*.

Dismas (1st cent.): Name given to repentant thief (Good Thief) to whom Jesus promised salvation (Lk. 23:40-43); regarded as patron of prisoners; Mar. 25 (observed on second Sunday of October in U.S. prison chapels).

Dominic (Dominic de Guzman) (1170-1221): Spanish priest; founded the Order of Preachers (Dominicans), 1215, in France; preached against the Albigensian heresy; a contemporary of St. Francis of Assisi; canonized 1234; Aug. 8*.

Dominic Savio (1842-1857): Italian youth; pupil of St. John Bosco; died before his 15th birthday; canonized 1954; patron of choir boys; May 6.

Duns Scotus, John (d. 1308): Scottish Franciscan; theologian; advanced theological arguments for doctrine of the Immaculate Conception; proclaimed blessed; cult solemnly confirmed by John Paul II, Mar. 20, 1993; Nov. 8.

Dunstan (c. 910-988): English monk; archbishop of Canterbury; initiated reforms in religious life; counselor to several kings; considered one of greatest Anglo-Saxon saints; patron of goldsmiths, locksmiths, jewelers (trades in which he is said to have excelled); May 17.

Dymphna (dates unknown): Nothing certain known of her life; according to legend, she was an Irish maiden murdered by her heathen father at Gheel near Antwerp, Belgium, where she had fled to escape his advances; her relics were discovered there in the 13th century; since that time cures of mental illness and epilepsy have been attributed to her intercession; patron of those suffering from mental illness; May 15.

Edith Stein, Bl. (1891-1942): German Carmelite (Teresa Benedicta of the Cross); born of Jewish parents; author and lecturer; baptized in Catholic Church, 1922; arrested with her sister Rosa in 1942 and put to death at Auschwitz; beatified 1987, by Pope John Paul II during his visit to West Germany. Aug. 10.

Edmund Campion (1540-1581): English Jesuit; convert 1573; martyred at Tyburn; canonized 1970, one of the Forty English and Welsh Martyrs; Dec. 1.

Edward the Confessor (d. 1066): King of England, 1042-66; canonized 1161; Oct. 13.

Eligius (c. 590-660): Bishop; born in Gaul; founded monasteries and convents; bishop of Noyon and Tournai; famous worker in gold and silver; Dec. 1.

Elizabeth Ann Seton (1774-1821): American foundress; convert, 1805; founded Sisters of Charity in the U.S.; beatified 1963; canonized Sept. 14, 1975; the first American-born saint; Jan. 4 (U.S.)*.

Elizabeth of Hungary (1207-1231): Became secular Franciscan after death of her husband in 1227; devoted life to poor and destitute; a patron of the Secular Franciscan Order; canonized 1235; Nov. 17*.

Elizabeth of Portugal (1271-1336): Queen of Portugal; b. Spain; retired to Poor Clare convent as a secular Franciscan after the death of her husband; canonized 1626; July 4*.

Emily de Rodat (1787-1852): French foundress of the Congregation of the Holy Family of Villefranche; canonized 1950; Sept. 19.

Emily de Vialar (1797-1856): French foundress of the Sisters of St. Joseph of the Apparition; canonized 1951; June 17.

Erasmus (Elmo) (d. 303): Life surrounded by legend; martyred during Diocletian persecution; patron of sailors; June 2.

Ethelbert (552-616): King of Kent, England; baptized by St. Augustine of Canterbury, 597; issued legal code; furthered spread of Christianity; Feb. 26.

Euphrasia Pelletier (1796-1868): French Religious; founded Sisters of the Good Shepherd at Angers, 1829; canonized 1940; Apr. 24.

Eusebius of Vercelli (283-370): Italian bishop; exiled from his see (Vercelli) for a time because of his opposition to Arianism; considered a martyr because of sufferings he endured; Aug. 2*.

Fabian (d. 250): Pope, 236-250; martyred under Decius; Jan. 20*.

Felicity: See Perpetua and Felicity.

Ferdinand III (1198-1252): King of Castile and Leon; waged successful crusade against Mohammedans in Spain; founded university at Salamanca; canonized 1671; May 30.

Fiacre (Fiachra) (d. c. 670): Irish hermit; patron of gardeners; Aug. 30.

Fidelis of Sigmaringen (Mark Rey) (1577-1622): German Capuchin; lawyer before he joined the Capuchins; missionary to Swiss Protestants; stabbed to death by peasants who were told he was agent of Austrian emperor; Apr. 24*.

Frances of Rome (1384-1440): Italian model for housewives and widows; happily married for 40 years; after death of her husband in 1436 joined community of Benedictine Oblates she had founded; canonized 1608; patron of motorists; Mar. 9*.

Frances Xavier Cabrini (Mother Cabrini) (1850-1917): American foundress; b. Italy; founded the Missionary Sisters of the Sacred Heart, 1877; settled in the U.S. 1889; became an American citizen in Seattle 1909; worked among Italian immigrants; canonized 1946, the first American citizen so honored; Nov. 13 (U.S.)*.

Francis Borgia (1510-1572): Spanish Jesuit; joined Jesuits after death of his wife in 1546; became general of the Order, 1565; Oct. 10.

Francis Caracciolo (1563-1608): Italian priest; founder with Father Augustine Adorno of the Clerks Regular Minor (Adorno Fathers); canonized 1807; June 4.

Francis Fasani (1681-1742); Italian Conventual Franciscan; model of priestly ministry, especially in service to poor and imprisoned; canonized 1986; Nov. 27.

Francis of Assisi (Giovanni di Bernardone) (1181/82-1226): Founder of the Franciscans, 1209; received stigmata 1224; canonized 1228; one of best known and best loved saints; patron of Italy, Catholic Action and ecologists; Oct. 4*.

Francis of Paola (1416-1507): Italian hermit: founder of Minim Friars; Apr. 2*.

Francis Xavier (1506-1552): Spanish Jesuit; missionary to Far East; canonized 1602; patron of foreign missions; considered one of greatest Christian missionaries; Dec. 3*.

Francis Xavier Bianchi (1743-1815): Italian Barnabite; acclaimed apostle of Naples because of his work there among the poor and abandoned; canonized 1951; Jan. 31.

Gabriel of the Sorrowful Mother (Francis Possenti) (1838-1862): Italian Passionist; died while a scholastic; canonized 1920; Feb. 27.

Gaspar (Caspar) del Bufalo (1786-1836): Italian priest; founded Missionaries of the Precious Blood, 1815; canonized 1954; Jan. 2.

Gemma Galgani (1878-1903): Italian laywoman; visionary; subject of extraordinary religious experiences; canonized 1940; Apr. 11.

Genesius (d. c. 300): Roman actor; according to legend, was converted while performing a burlesque of Christian baptism and was subsequently martyred; patron of actors; Aug. 25.

Genevieve (422-500): French nun; a patroness and protectress of Paris; events of her life not authenticated; Jan. 3.

George (d. c. 300): Martyr, probably during Diocletian persecution in Palestine; all other incidents of his life, including story of the dragon, are legendary; patron of England; Apr. 23*.

Gerard Majella (1725-1755): Italian Redemptorist lay brother; noted for supernatural occurrences in his life including bilocation and reading of consciences; canonized 1904; patron of mothers; Oct. 16.

Gertrude (1256-1302): German mystic; writer; helped spread devotion to the Sacred Heart; Nov. 16*.

Gregory VII (Hildebrand) (1020?-1085): Pope, 1075-1085; Benedictine monk; adviser to several popes; as pope, strengthened interior life of Church and fought against lay investiture; driven from Rome by Henry IV; died in exile; canonized 1584; May 25.*

Gregory Barbarigo (1626-1697): Italian cardinal; noted for his efforts to bring about reunion of separated Christians; canonized 1960; June 18.

Gregory of Nyssa (c. 335-395): Bishop; theologian; younger brother of St. Basil the Great; Mar. 9.

Gregory Thaumaturgus (c. 213-268): Bishop of Neocaesarea; missionary, famed as wonder worker; Nov. 17.

Gregory the Illuminator (257-332): Martyr; bishop; apostle and patron saint of Armenia; helped free Armenia from the Persians; Sept. 30.

Hedwig (1174-1243): Moravian noblewoman; married duke of Silesia, head of Polish royal family; fostered religious life in country; canonized 1266; Oct. 16*.

Helena (250-330): Empress; mother of Constantine the Great; associated with discovery of the True Cross; Aug. 18.

Henry (972-1024): Bavarian emperor; cooperated with Benedictine abbeys in restoration of ecclesiastical and social discipline; canonized 1146; July 13*.

Herman Joseph (1150-1241): German Premonstratensian; his visions were the subjects of artists; writer; cult approved, 1958; Apr. 7.

Hippolytus (d. c. 236): Roman priest; opposed Pope St. Callistus I in his teaching about the readmission to the Church of repentant Christians who had apostasized during time of persecution; elected antipope; exiled to Sardinia; reconciled before his martyrdom; important ecclesiastical writer; Aug. 13* (with Pontian).

Hubert (d. 727): Bishop; his patronage of hunters is based on legend that he was converted while hunting; Nov. 3.

Hugh of Cluny (the Great) (1024-1109): Abbot of Benedictine foundation at Cluny; supported popes in efforts to reform ecclesiastical abuses; canonized 1120; Apr. 29.

Ignatius of Antioch (d. c. 107): Early ecclesiastical writer; martyr; bishop of Antioch in Syria for 40 years; Oct. 17*.

Ignatius of Laconi (1701-1781): Italian Capuchin lay brother whose 60 years of religious life were spent in Franciscan simplicity; canonized 1951; May 11.

Ignatius of Loyola (1491-1556): Spanish soldier; renounced military career after recovering from wounds received at siege of Pampeluna (Pamplona) in 1521; founded Society of Jesus (Jesuits), 1534, at Paris; wrote *The Book of Spiritual Exercises;* canonized 1622; July 31*.

Irenaeus of Lyons (130-202): Early ecclesiastical writer; opposed Gnosticism; bishop of Lyons; traditionally regarded as a martyr; June 28*.

Isidore the Farmer (d. 1170): Spanish layman; farmer; canonized 1622; patron of farmers; May 15 (U.S.)*.

Jane Frances de Chantal (1572-1641): French widow; foundress, under guidance of St. Francis de Sales, of Order of the Visitation; canonized 1767; Dec. 12* (General Roman Calendar); Aug. 18* (U.S.).

Januarius (Gennaro) (d. 304): Bishop of Benevento; martyred during Diocletian persecution; fame rests on liquefaction of some of his blood preserved in a phial at Naples, an unexplained phenomenon which has occurred regularly several times each year for over 400 years; declared patron of Campania region around Naples, 1980; Sept. 19*.

Jeanne Delanoue (1666-1736): French foundress of Sisters of St. Anne of Providence, 1704; canonized 1982; Aug. 16.

Jeanne (Joan) de Lestonnac (1556-1640): French foundress; widowed in 1597; founded the Religious of Notre Dame 1607; canonized 1947; Feb. 2.

Jeanne de Valois (Jeanne of France) (1464-1505): French foundress; deformed daughter of King Louis XI; was married in 1476 to Duke Louis of Orleans who had the marriage annulled when he ascended the throne as Louis XII; Jeanne retired to life of prayer; founded contemplative Annonciades of Bourges, 1504; canonized 1950; Feb. 5.

Jeanne Elizabeth Bichier des Anges (1773-1838): French Religious; co-founder with St. Andrew Fournet of Daughters of the Cross of St. Andrew, 1807; canonized 1947; Aug. 26.

Jeanne Jugan, Bl. (1792-1879): French Religious; foundress of Little Sisters of the Poor; beatified Oct. 3, 1982; Aug. 30.

Jerome Emiliani (1481-1537): Venetian priest; founded Somascan Fathers, 1532, for care of orphans; canonized 1767; patron of orphans and abandoned children; Feb. 8*.

Joan Antida Thouret (1765-1826): French Religious; founded, 1799, congregation now known as Sisters of Charity of St. Joan Antida; canonized 1934; Aug. 24.

Joan of Arc (1412-1431): French heroine, called The Maid of Orleans, La Pucelle; led French army in 1429 against English invaders besieging Orleans; captured by Burgundians the following year; turned over to ecclesiastical court on charge of heresy, found guilty and burned at the stake; her innocence was declared in 1456; canonized 1920; patroness of France; May 30.

Joaquina de Vedruna de Mas (1783-1854): Spanish foundress; widowed in 1816; after providing for her children, founded the Carmelite Sisters of Charity; canonized 1959; Aug. 28.

John I (d. 526): Pope, 523-526; martyr; May 18*.

John Baptist de la Salle (1651-1719): French priest; founder of Brothers of the Christian Schools, 1680; canonized 1900; patron of teachers; Apr. 7*.

John Berchmans (1599-1621): Belgian Jesuit scholastic; patron of Mass servers; canonized 1888; Aug. 13.

John (Don) Bosco (1815-1888): Italian priest; founded Salesians, 1859, for education of boys and cofounded the Daughters of Mary Help of Christians for education of girls; canonized 1934; Jan. 31*.

John Capistran (1386-1456): Italian Franciscan; preacher; papal diplomat; canonized 1690; declared patron of military chaplains, Feb. 10, 1984. Oct. 23*.

John de Ribera (1532-1611): Spanish bishop and statesman; archbishop of Valencia, 1568-1611, and viceroy of that province; canonized 1960; Jan. 6.

John Eudes (1601-1680): French priest; founder of Sisters of Our Lady of Charity of Refuge, 1642, and Congregation of Jesus-Mary (Eudists), 1643; canonized 1925; Aug. 19*.

John Fisher (1469-1535): English prelate; theologian; martyr; bishop of Rochester, cardinal; refused to recognize validity of Henry VIII's marriage to Anne Boleyn; upheld supremacy of the pope; beheaded for refusing to acknowledge Henry as head of the Church; canonized 1935; June 22 (with St. Thomas More)*.

John Gualbert (d. 1073): Italian priest; founder of Benedictine congregation of Vallombrosians, 1039; canonized 1193; July 12.

John Kanty (Cantius) (1395-1473): Polish theologian; canonized 1767; Dec. 23*.

John Leonardi (1550-1609): Italian priest; worked among prisoners and the sick; founded Clerics Regular of the Mother of God; canonized 1938; Oct. 9.*

John Nepomucene (1345-1393): Bohemian priest; regarded as a martyr; canonized 1729; patron of Czechoslovakia; May 16.

John Nepomucene Neumann (1811-1860): American prelate; b. Bohemia; ordained in New York 1836; missionary among Germans near Niagara Falls before joining Redemptorists, 1840; bishop of Philadelphia, 1852; first bishop in U.S. to prescribe Forty Hours devotion in his diocese; beatified 1963; canonized June 19, 1977; Jan. 5 (U.S.)*.

John of Avila (1499-1569): Spanish priest; preacher; ascetical writer; spiritual adviser of St. Teresa of Jesus (Avila); canonized 1970; May 10.

John of Britto (1647-1693): Portuguese Jesuit; missionary in India where he was martyred; canonized 1947; Feb. 4.

John of God (1495-1550): Portuguese founder; his work among the sick poor led to foundation of Brothers Hospitallers of St. John of God, 1540, in Spain; canonized 1690; patron of sick, nurses, hospitals; Mar. 8*.

John of Matha (1160-1213): French priest; founder of the Order of Most Holy Trinity, whose original purpose was the ransom of prisoners from the Moslems; Feb. 8.

John Ogilvie (1579-1615): Scottish Jesuit; martyr; canonized 1976, the first canonized Scottish saint since 1250 (Margaret of Scotland); Mar. 10.

John Vianney (Cure of Ars) (1786-1859): French parish priest; noted confessor, spent 16 to 18 hours a day in confessional; canonized 1925; patron of parish priests; Aug. 4*.

Josaphat Kuncevyc (1584-1623): Basilian monk; b. Poland; archbishop of Polotsk, Lithuania; worked for reunion of separated Eastern Christians with Rome; martyred by mob of schismatics; canonized 1867; Nov. 12*.

Joseph Benedict Cottolengo (1786-1842): Italian priest; established Little Houses of Divine Providence (Piccola Casa) for care of orphans and the sick; canonized 1934; Apr. 30.

Joseph Cafasso (1811-1860): Italian priest; renowned confessor; promoted devotion to Blessed Sacrament; canonized 1947; June 23.

Joseph Calasanz (1556-1648): Spanish priest; founder of Piarists (Order of Pious Schools); canonized 1767; Aug. 25*.

Joseph of Cupertino (1603-1663): Italian Franciscan; noted for remarkable incidents of levitation; canonized 1767; Sept. 18.

Joseph Pignatelli (1737-1811): Spanish Jesuit; left Spain when Jesuits were banished in 1767; worked for revival of the Order; named first superior when Jesuits were reestablished in Kingdom of Naples, 1804; canonized 1954; Nov. 28.

Juan Diego, Bl. (16th cent.): Mexican Indian, convert; indigenous name according to tradition *Cuauhtlatohuac* ("The eagle who speaks"); favored with apparitions of Our Lady (see Index: Our Lady of Guadalupe) on Tepeyac hill; beatified, 1990; Dec. 9* (U.S.).

Julia Billiart (1751-1816): French foundress; founded Sisters of Notre Dame de Namur, 1804; canonized 1969; Apr. 8.

Justin de Jacobis (1800-1860): Italian Vincentian; bishop; missionary in Ethiopia; canonized 1975; July 31.

Justin Martyr (100-165): Early ecclesiastical writer; *Apologies for the Christian Religion, Dialog with the Jew Tryphon;* martyred at Rome; June 1*.

Kateri Tekakwitha, Bl. (1656-1680): "Lily of the Mohawks." Indian maiden born at Ossernenon (Auriesville), N.Y.; baptized Christian, Easter, 1676, by Jesuit missionary Father Jacques de Lambertville; lived life devoted to prayer, penitential practices and care of sick and aged in Christian village of Caughnawaga near Montreal where her relics are now enshrined; beatified June 22, 1980; July 14* (in U.S.).

Katharine Drexel, Bl. (1858-1955): Philadelphia-born heiress; devoted wealth to founding schools and missions for Indians and Blacks; foundress of Sisters of Blessed Sacrament for Indians and Colored People, 1891; beatified 1988; Mar. 3* (U.S.).

Ladislaus (1040-1095): King of Hungary; supported Pope Gregory VII against Henry IV; canonized 1192; June 27.

Lawrence (d. 258): Widely venerated martyr who suffered death, according to a long-standing but unverifiable legend, by fire on a gridiron; Aug. 10*.

Lawrence (Lorenzo) Ruiz and Companions (d. 1630s): Martyred in or near the city of Nagasaki, Japan; Lawrence Ruiz, first Filipino saint, and 15 companions (nine Japanese, four Spaniards, one Italian and one Frenchman); canonized 1987; Sept. 28*.

Leonard Murialdo (1828-1900): Italian priest; educator; founder of Pious Society of St. Joseph of Turin, 1873; canonized 1970; Mar. 30.

Leonard of Port Maurice (1676-1751): Italian Franciscan; ascetical writer; preached missions throughout Italy; canonized 1867; patron of parish missions; Nov. 26.

Leopold Mandic (1866-1942): Croatian-born

Franciscan priest, noted confessor; spent most of his priestly life in Padua, Italy; canonized, 1983, July 30.

Louis IX (1215-1270): King of France, 1226-1270; participated in Sixth Crusade; patron of Secular Franciscan Order; canonized 1297; Aug. 25*.

Louis de Montfort (1673-1716): French priest; founder of Sisters of Divine Wisdom, 1703, and Missionaries of Company of Mary, 1715; wrote *True Devotion to the Blessed Virgin;* canonized 1947; Apr. 28.

Louis Zepherin Moreau, Bl. (d. 1901): Canadian bishop; headed St. Hyacinthe, Que., diocese, 1876-1901; beatified 1987; May 24.

Louise de Marillac (1591-1660): French foundress, with St. Vincent de Paul, of the Sisters of Charity; canonized 1934; Mar. 15.

Lucy (d. 304): Sicilian maiden; martyred during Diocletian persecution; one of most widely venerated early virgin-martyrs; patron of Syracuse, Sicily; invoked by those suffering from eye diseases; Dec. 13*.

Lucy Filippini (1672-1732): Italian educator, helped improve status of women through education; considered a founder of the Religious Teachers Filippini, 1692; canonized 1930; Mar. 25.

Madeleine Sophie Barat (1779-1865): French foundress of the Society of the Sacred Heart of Jesus; canonized 1925; May 25.

Malachy (1095-1148): Irish bishop; instrumental in establishing first Cistercian house in Ireland, 1142; canonized 1190; Nov. 3 (See Index: Prophecies of St. Malachy).

Marcellinus and Peter (d.c. 304): Early Roman martyrs; June 2*.

Margaret Clitherow (1556-1586): English martyr; convert shortly after her marriage; one of Forty Martyrs of England and Wales; canonized 1970; Mar. 25.

Margaret Mary Alacoque (1647-1690): French Religious; spread devotion to Sacred Heart in accordance with revelations made to her in 1675 (see Sacred Heart); canonized 1920; Oct. 16*.

Margaret of Cortona (1247-1297): Secular Franciscan; reformed her life in 1273 following the violent death of her lover; canonized 1728; May 16.

Margaret of Hungary (1242-1270): Contemplative; daughter of King Bela IV of Hungary; lived a life of self-imposed penances; canonized 1943; Jan. 18.

Margaret of Scotland (1050-1093): Queen of Scotland; noted for solicitude for the poor and promotion of justice; canonized 1250; Nov. 16*.

Maria Goretti (1890-1902): Italian virgin-martyr; a model of purity; canonized 1950; July 6*.

Mariana Paredes of Jesus (1618-1645): South American recluse; Lily of Quito; canonized, 1950; May 28.

Marie-Leonie Paradis, Bl. (1840-1912): Canadian Religious; founded Little Sisters of the Holy Family, 1880; beatified 1984; May 4.

Marie-Rose Durocher, Bl. (1811-1849): Canadian Religious; foundress of Sisters of Holy Names of Jesus and Mary; beatified 1982; Oct. 6* (in U.S.).

Martha (1st cent.): Sister of Lazarus and Mary of Bethany; Gospel accounts record her concern for homely details; patron of cooks; July 29*.

Martin I (d. 655): Pope, 649-55; banished from Rome by emperor in 653 because of his condemnation of Monothelites; considered a martyr; Apr. 13*.

Martin of Tours (316-397): Bishop of Tours; opposed Arianism and Priscillianism; pioneer of Western monasticism, before St. Benedict; Nov. 11*.

Mary Domenica Mazzarello (1837-1881): Italian foundress, with St. John Bosco, of the Daughters of Mary Help of Christians, 1872; canonized 1951; May 14.

Mary Josepha Rossello (1811-1881): Italian-born foundress of the Daughters of Our Lady of Mercy; canonized 1949; Dec. 7.

Mary Magdalen Postel (1756-1846): French foundress of the Sisters of Christian Schools of Mercy, 1807; canonized 1925; July 16.

Mary Magdalene (1st cent.): Gospels record her as devoted follower of Christ to whom she appeared after the Resurrection; her identification with Mary of Bethany (sister of Martha and Lazarus) and the woman sinner (Lk 7:36-50) has been questioned; July 22*.

Mary Magdalene dei Pazzi (1566-1607): Italian Carmelite nun; recipient of mystical experiences; canonized 1669; May 25*.

Mary Michaela Desmaisières (1809-1865): Spanish-born foundress of the Institute of the Handmaids of the Blessed Sacrament, 1848; canonized 1934; Aug. 24.

Maximilian Kolbe (1894-1941): Polish Conventual Franciscan; prisoner at Auschwitz who heroically offered his life in place of a fellow prisoner; beatified 1971, canonized 1982; Aug. 14*.

Methodius: See Index.

Miguel Febres Cordero (1854-1910): Ecuadorean Christian Brother; educator; canonized 1984; Feb. 9.

Miguel Pro, Bl. (1891-1927): Mexican Jesuit; joined Jesuits, 1911; forced to flee because of religious persecution; ordained in Belgium, 1925; returned to Mexico, 1926, to minister to people despite government prohibition; unjustly accused of assassination plot against president; arrested and executed; beatified 1988. Nov. 23* (U.S.).

Monica (332-387): Mother of St. Augustine; model of a patient mother; her feast is observed in the Roman calendar the day before her son's; Aug. 27*.

Nereus and Achilleus (d. c. 100): Early Christian martyrs; soldiers who, according to legend, were baptized by St. Peter; May 12*.

Nicholas of Flue (1417-1487): Swiss layman; at the age of 50, with the consent of his wife and 10 children, he retreated from the world to live as a hermit; called Brother Claus by the Swiss; canonized 1947; Mar. 21.

Nicholas of Myra (4th cent.): Bishop of Myra in Asia Minor; one of most popular saints in both East and West; most of the incidents of his life are based on legend; patron of Russia; Dec. 6*.

Nicholas of Tolentino (1245-1305): Italian hermit; famed preacher; canonized 1446; Sept. 10.

Nicholas Tavelic and Companions (Deodatus of Aquitaine, Peter of Narbonne, Stephen of Cuneo) (d. 1391): Franciscan missionaries; martyred by Moslems in the Holy Land: canonized 1970; Nov. 14.

Norbert (1080-1134): German bishop; founded Canons Regular of Premontre (Premonstratensians, Norbertines), 1120; promoted reform of the clergy, devotion to Blessed Sacrament; canonized 1582; June 6*.

Odilia (d. c. 720): Benedictine abbess; according to legend she was born blind, abandoned by her family and adopted by a convent of nuns where her sight was miraculously restored; patroness of blind; Dec. 13.

Oliver Plunket (1629-1681): Irish martyr; theologian; archbishop of Armagh and primate of Ireland; beatified 1920; canonized, 1975; July 1.

Pancras (d. c. 304): Roman martyr; May 12*.

Paola Frassinetti (1809-1882): Italian Religious; foundress, 1834, of Sisters of St. Dorothy; canonized 1984; June 11.

Paschal Baylon (1540-1592): Spanish Franciscan lay brother; spent life as door-keeper in various Franciscan friaries; defended doctrine of Real Presence in Blessed Sacrament; canonized 1690; patron of all Eucharistic confraternities and congresses, 1897; May 17.

Patrick (389-461): Famous missionary of Ireland; began missionary work in Ireland about 432; organized the Church there and established it on a lasting foundation; patron of Ireland, with Sts. Bridget and Columba; Mar. 17*.

Paul Miki and Companions (d. 1597): Martyrs of Japan; Paul Miki, Jesuit, and twenty-five other priests and laymen were martyred at Nagasaki; canonized 1862, the first canonized martyrs of the Far East; Feb. 6*.

Paul of the Cross (1694-1775): Italian Religious; founder of the Passionists; canonized 1867; Oct 19* (Oct. 20, U.S.*).

Paulinus of Nola (d. 451): Bishop of Nola (Spain); writer; June 22*.

Peregrine (1260-1347): Italian Servite; invoked against cancer (he was miraculously cured of cancer of the foot after a vision); canonized 1726; May 1.

Perpetua and Felicity (d. 203): Martyrs; Perpetua was a young married woman; Felicity was a slave girl; Mar. 7*.

Peter Chanel (1803-1841): French Marist; missionary to Oceania, where he was martyred; canonized 1954; Apr. 28*.

Peter Fourier (1565-1640): French priest; cofounder with Alice LeClercq (Mother Teresa of Jesus) of the Augustinian Canonesses of Our Lady, 1598; canonized 1897; Dec. 9.

Peter Gonzalez (1190-1246): Spanish Dominican; worked among sailors; court chaplain and confessor of King St. Ferdinand of Castile; patron of sailors; Apr. 14.

Peter Julian Eymard (1811-1868): French priest; founder of the Congregation of the Blessed Sacrament (men), 1856, and Servants of the Blessed Sacrament (women), 1864; dedicated to Eucharistic apostolate; canonized 1962; Aug. 1.

Peter Nolasco (c. 1189-1258): Born in Langueduc area of present-day France; founded the Mercedarians (Order of Our Lady of Mercy), 1218, in Spain; canonized 1628; Jan. 31.

Peter of Alcantara (1499-1562): Spanish Franciscan; mystic; initiated Franciscan reform; confessor

of St. Teresa of Jesus (Avila); canonized 1669; Oct. 22 (in U.S.).

Philip Benizi (1233-1285): Italian Servite; noted preacher, peacemaker; canonized 1671; Aug. 23.

Philip Neri (1515-1595): Italian Religious; founded Congregation of the Oratory; considered a second apostle of Rome because of his mission activity there; canonized 1622; May 26*.

Philip of Jesus (1517-1597): Mexican Franciscan; martyred at Nagasaki, Japan; canonized 1862; patron of Mexico City; Feb. 6*.

Pius V (1504-1572): Pope, 1566-1572; enforced decrees of Council of Trent; organized expedition against Turks resulting in victory at Lepanto; canonized 1712; Apr. 30*.

Polycarp (2nd cent.): Bishop of Smyrna; ecclesiastical writer; martyr; Feb. 23*.

Pontian (d. c. 235): Pope, 230-235; exiled to Sardinia by the emperor; regarded as a martyr; Aug. 13 (with Hippolytus)*.

Rafaela Maria Porras y Ayllon (1850-1925): Spanish Religious; founded the Handmaids of the Sacred Heart, 1877; canonized 1977; Jan. 6.

Raymond Nonnatus (d. 1240): Spanish Mercedarian; cardinal; devoted his life to ransoming captives from the Moors; Aug. 31.

Raymond of Penyafort (1175-1275): Spanish Dominican; confessor of Gregory IX; systematized and codified canon law, in effect until 1917; master general of Dominicans, 1238; canonized 1601; Jan. 7*.

Rita of Cascia (1381-1457): Widow; cloistered Augustinian Religious of Umbria; invoked in impossible and desperate cases; May 22.

Robert Southwell (1561-1595): English Jesuit; poet; martyred at Tyburn; canonized 1970, one of the Forty English and Welsh Martyrs; Feb. 21.

Roch (1350-1379): French layman; pilgrim; devoted life to care of plague-stricken; widely venerated; invoked against pestilence; Aug. 17.

Romuald (951-1027): Italian monk; founded Camaldolese Benedictines; June 19*.

Rose of Lima (1586-1617): Peruvian Dominican tertiary; first native-born saint of the New World; canonized 1671; Aug. 23*.

Scholastica (d. c. 559): Sister of St. Benedict; regarded as first nun of the Benedictine Order; Feb. 10*.

Sebastian (3rd cent.): Roman martyr; traditionally pictured as a handsome youth with arrows; martyred; patron of athletes, archers; Jan. 20*.

Seven Holy Founders of the Servants of Mary (Buonfiglio Monaldo, Alexis Falconieri, Benedict dell'Antello, Bartholomew Amidei, Ricovero Uguccione, Gerardino Sostegni, John Buonagiunta Monetti): Florentine youths who founded Servites, 1233, in obedience to a vision; canonized 1888; Feb. 17*.

Sharbel Makhlouf (1828-1898): Lebanese Maronite monk-hermit; canonized 1977; Dec. 24.

Sixtus II and Companions (d. 258): Sixtus, pope 257-258, and four deacons, martyrs; Aug. 7*.

Stanislaus (1030-1079): Polish bishop; martyr; canonized 1253; Apr. 11*.

Stephen (d. c. 33): First Christian martyr; chosen by the Apostles as the first of the seven deacons; stoned to death; Dec. 26*.

Stephen (975-1038): King; apostle of Hungary;

welded Magyars into national unity; canonized 1083; Aug. 16*.

Sylvester I (d. 335): Pope 314-335; first ecumenical council held at Nicaea during his pontificate; Dec. 31*.

Tarcisius (d. 3rd cent.): Early martyr; according to tradition, was martyred while carrying the Blessed Sacrament to some Christians in prison; patron of first communicants; Aug. 15.

Teresa Margaret Redi (1747-1770): Italian Carmelite; lived life of prayer and austere penance; canonized 1934; Mar. 11.

Teresa of Jesus Jornet Ibars (1843-1897): Spanish Religious; founded the Little Sisters of the Abandoned Aged, 1873; canonized 1974; Aug. 26.

Therese Couderc (1805-1885): French Religious; foundress of the Religious of Our Lady of the Retreat in the Cenacle, 1827; canonized 1970; Sept. 26.

Therese of Lisieux (1873-1897): French Carmelite nun; b. Therese Martin; allowed to enter Carmel at 15, died nine years later of tuberculosis; her "little way" of spiritual perfection became widely known through her spiritual autobiography; despite her obscure life, became one of the most popular saints; canonized 1925; patron of foreign missions; Oct. 1*.

Thomas Becket (1118-1170): English martyr; archbishop of Canterbury; chancellor under Henry II; murdered for upholding rights of the Church; canonized 1173; Dec. 29*.

Thomas More (1478-1535): English martyr; statesman, chancellor under Henry VIII; author of *Utopia*; opposed Henry's divorce, refused to renounce authority of the papacy; beheaded; canonized 1935; June 22 (with St. John Fisher)*.

Thorlac (1133-1193): Icelandic bishop; instituted reforms; although his cult was never officially approved, he was declared patron of Iceland, Jan. 14, 1984; Dec. 23.

Timothy (d. c. 97): Bishop of Ephesus; disciple and companion of St. Paul; martyr; Jan. 26*.

Titus (d. c. 96): Bishop; companion of St. Paul; recipient of one of Paul's epistles; Jan. 26*.

Titus Brandsma, Bl. (1881-1942): Dutch Carmelite priest; professor, scholar, journalist; denounced Nazi persecution of Jews; arrested by Nazis, Jan. 19, 1942; executed by lethal injection at Dachau, July 26, 1942; beatified 1985; July 26.

Valentine (d. 269): Priest, physician; martyred at Rome; legendary patron of lovers; Feb. 14.

Vicenta Maria Lopez y Vicuna (1847-1896): Spanish foundress of the Daughters of Mary Immaculate for domestic service; canonized 1975; Dec. 26.

Vincent (d. 304): Spanish deacon; martyr; Jan. 22.*

Vincent de Paul (1581?-1660): French priest; founder of Congregation of the Mission (Vincentians, Lazarists) and co-founder of Sisters of Charity; declared patron of all charitable organizations and works by Leo XIII; canonized 1737; Sept. 27*.

Vincent Ferrer (1350-1418): Spanish Dominican; famed preacher; Apr. 5*.

Vincent Pallotti (1795-1850): Italian priest; founded Society of the Catholic Apostolate (Pallottines), 1835; Jan. 22.

Vincent Strambi (1745-1824): Italian Passionist; bishop; reformer; canonized 1950; Sept. 25.

Vincenza Gerosa (1784-1847): Italian co-foundress of the Sisters of Charity of Lovere; canonized 1950; June 28.

Vitus (d.c. 300): Martyr; died in Lucania, southern Italy; regarded as protector of epileptics and those suffering from St. Vitus Dance (chorea); June 15.

Walburga (d. 779): English-born Benedictine Religious; belonged to group of nuns who established convents in Germany at the invitation of St. Boniface; abbess of Heidenheim; Feb. 25.

Wenceslaus (d. 935): Duke of Bohemia; martyr; patron of Bohemia; Sept. 28*.

Zita (1218-1278): Italian maid; noted for charity to poor; patron of domestics; Apr. 27.

SAINTS—PATRONS AND INTERCESSORS

A patron is a saint who is venerated as a special intercessor before God. Most patrons have been so designated as the result of popular devotion and long-standing custom. In many cases, the fact of existing patronal devotion is clear despite historical obscurity regarding its origin. The Church has made official designation of relatively few patrons; in such cases, the dates of designation are given in parentheses in the list below. The theological background of the patronage of saints includes the dogmas of the Mystical Body of Christ and the Communion of Saints.

Listed below are patron saints of occupations and professions, and saints whose intercession is sought for special needs.

Accountants: Matthew.

Actors: Genesius.

Advertisers: Bernardine of Siena (May 20, 1960).

Alpinists: Bernard of Montjoux (or Menthon) (Aug. 20, 1923).

Altar boys: John Berchmans.

Anesthetists: Rene Goupil.

Animals: Francis of Assisi.

Archers: Sebastian.

Architects: Thomas, Apostle.

Art: Catherine of Bologna.

Artists: Luke, Catherine of Bologna, Bl. Angelico (Feb. 21, 1984).

Astronomers: Dominic.

Athletes: Sebastian.

Authors: Francis de Sales.

Aviators: Our Lady of Loreto (1920), Therese of Lisieux, Joseph of Cupertino.

Bakers: Elizabeth of Hungary, Nicholas.

Bankers: Matthew.

Barbers: Cosmas and Damian, Louis.

Barren women: Anthony of Padua, Felicity.

Basket-makers: Anthony, Abbot.

Beggars: Martin of Tours.

Blacksmiths: Dunstan.

Blind: Odilia, Raphael.

Blood banks: Januarius.

Bodily ills: Our Lady of Lourdes.

Bookbinders: Peter Celestine.

Bookkeepers: Matthew.

Booksellers: John of God.

Boy Scouts: George.

Brewers: Augustine of Hippo, Luke, Nicholas of Myra.

Bricklayers: Stephen.

Brides: Nicholas of Myra.

Brushmakers: Anthony, Abbot.

Builders: Vincent Ferrer.

Butchers: Anthony (Abbot), Luke.

Cabdrivers: Fiacre.
Cabinetmakers: Anne.
Cancer patients: Peregrine.
Canonists: Raymond of Peñafort.
Carpenters: Joseph.
Catechists: Viator, Charles Borromeo, Robert Bellarmine.
Catholic Action: Francis of Assisi (1916).
Chandlers: Ambrose, Bernard of Clairvaux.
Charitable societies: Vincent de Paul (May 12, 1885).
Children: Nicholas of Myra.
Children of Mary: Agnes, Maria Goretti.
Choirboys: Dominic Savio (June 8, 1956), Holy Innocents.
Church: Joseph (Dec. 8, 1870).
Clerics: Gabriel of the Sorrowful Mother.
Communications personnel: Bernardine.
Confessors: Alphonsus Liguori (Apr. 26, 1950), John Nepomucene.
Convulsive children: Scholastica.
Cooks: Lawrence, Martha.
Coopers: Nicholas of Myra.
Coppersmiths: Maurus.
Dairy workers: Brigid.
Deaf: Francis de Sales.
Dentists: Apollonia.
Desperate situations: Gregory of Neocaesarea, Jude Thaddeus, Rita of Cascia.
Dietitians (in hospitals): Martha.
Dyers: Maurice, Lydia.
Dying: Joseph.
Ecologists: Francis of Assisi (Nov. 29, 1979).
Editors: John Bosco.
Emigrants: Frances Xavier Cabrini (Sept. 8, 1950).
Engineers: Ferdinand III.
Epilepsy, Motor Diseases: Vitus, Willibrord.
Eucharistic congresses and societies: Paschal Baylon (Nov. 28, 1897).
Expectant mothers: Raymond Nonnatus, Gerard Majella.
Eye diseases: Lucy.
Falsely accused: Raymond Nonnatus.
Farmers: George, Isidore.
Farriers: John the Baptist.
Firemen: Florian.
Fire prevention: Catherine of Siena.
First communicants: Tarcisius.
Fishermen: Andrew.
Florists: Therese of Lisieux.
Forest workers: John Gualbert.
Foundlings: Holy Innocents.
Fullers: Anastasius the Fuller, James the Less.

Funeral directors: Joseph of Arimathea, Dismas.
Gardeners: Adelard, Tryphon, Fiacre, Phocas.
Glassworkers: Luke.
Goldsmiths: Dunstan, Anastasius.
Gravediggers: Anthony, Abbot.
Greetings: Valentine.
Grocers: Michael.
Hairdressers: Martin de Porres.
Happy meetings: Raphael.
Hatters: Severus of Ravenna, James the Less.
Headache sufferers: Teresa of Jesus (Avila).
Heart patients: John of God.
Hospital administrators: Basil the Great, Frances X. Cabrini.
Hospitals: Camillus de Lellis and John of God (June 22, 1886), Jude Thaddeus.
Housewives: Anne.
Hunters: Hubert, Eustachius.
Infantrymen: Maurice.
Innkeepers: Amand, Martha.
Invalids: Roch.
Jewelers: Eligius, Dunstan.
Journalists: Francis de Sales (Apr. 26, 1923).
Jurists: John Capistran.
Laborers: Isidore, James, John Bosco.
Lawyers: Ivo (Yves Helory), Genesius, Thomas More.
Learning: Ambrose.
Librarians: Jerome.
Lighthouse keepers: Venerius (Mar. 10, 1961).
Locksmiths: Dunstan.
Maids: Zita.
Marble workers: Clement I.
Mariners: Michael, Nicholas of Tolentino.
Medical record librarians: Raymond of Peñafort.
Medical social workers: John Regis.
Medical technicians: Albert the Great.
Mentally ill: Dymphna.
Merchants: Francis of Assisi, Nicholas of Myra.
Messengers: Gabriel.
Metal workers: Eligius.
Military chaplains: John Capistran (Feb. 10, 1984).
Millers: Arnulph, Victor.
Missions, Foreign: Francis Xavier (Mar. 25, 1904), Therese of Lisieux (Dec. 14, 1927).
Missions, Black: Peter Claver (1896, Leo XIII), Benedict the Black.
Missions, Parish: Leonard of Port Maurice (Mar. 17, 1923).
Mothers: Monica.
Motorcyclists: Our Lady of Grace.

Motorists: Christopher, Frances of Rome.
Mountaineers: Bernard of Montjoux (or Menthon).
Musicians: Gregory the Great, Cecilia, Dunstan.
Notaries: Luke, Mark.
Nurses: Camillus de Lellis and John of God (1930, Pius XI), Agatha, Raphael.
Nursing and nursing service: Elizabeth of Hungary, Catherine of Siena.
Orators: John Chrysostom (July 8, 1908).
Organ builders: Cecilia.
Orphans: Jerome Emiliani.
Painters: Luke.
Paratroopers: Michael.
Pawnbrokers: Nicholas.
Pharmacists: Cosmas and Damian, James the Greater.
Pharmacists (in hospitals): Gemma Galgani.
Philosophers: Justin.
Physicians: Pantaleon, Cosmas and Damian, Luke, Raphael.
Pilgrims: James the Greater.
Plasterers: Bartholomew.
Poets: David, Cecilia.
Poison sufferers: Benedict.
Policemen: Michael.
Poor: Lawrence, Anthony of Padua.
Poor souls: Nicholas of Tolentino.
Porters: Christopher.
Possessed: Bruno, Denis.
Postal employees: Gabriel.
Priests: Jean-Baptiste Vianney (Apr. 23, 1929).
Printers: John of God, Augustine of Hippo, Genesius.
Prisoners: Dismas, Joseph Cafasso.
Protector of crops: Ansovinus.
Public relations: Bernardine of Siena (May 20, 1960).
Public relations (of hospitals): Paul, Apostle.
Radiologists: Michael (Jan. 15, 1941).
Radio workers: Gabriel.
Retreats: Ignatius Loyola (July 25, 1922).
Rheumatism: James the Greater.
Saddlers: Crispin and Crispinian.
Sailors: Cuthbert, Brendan, Eulalia, Christopher, Peter Gonzales, Erasmus, Nicholas.
Scholars: Brigid.
Schools, Catholic: Thomas Aquinas (Aug. 4, 1880), Joseph Calasanz (Aug. 13, 1948).
Scientists: Albert (Aug. 13, 1948).
Sculptors: Four Crowned Martyrs.
Seamen: Francis of Paola.
Searchers of lost articles: Anthony of Padua.

Secretaries: Genesius.
Secular Franciscans: Louis of France, Elizabeth of Hungary.
Seminarians: Charles Borromeo.
Servants: Martha, Zita.
Shoemakers: Crispin and Crispinian.
Sick: Michael, John of God and Camillus de Lellis (June 22, 1886).
Silversmiths: Andronicus.
Singers: Gregory, Cecilia.
Skaters: Lidwina.
Skiers: Bernard of Montjoux (or Menthon).
Social workers: Louise de Marillac (Feb. 12, 1960).
Soldiers: Hadrian, George, Ignatius, Sebastian, Martin of Tours, Joan of Arc.
Speleologists: Benedict.
Stenographers: Genesius, Cassian.
Stonecutters: Clement.
Stonemasons: Stephen.
Students: Thomas Aquinas.
Surgeons: Cosmas and Damian, Luke.
Swordsmiths: Maurice.
Tailors: Homobonus.
Tanners: Crispin and Crispinian, Simon.
Tax collectors: Matthew.
Teachers: Gregory the Great, John Baptist de la Salle (May 15, 1950).
Telecommunications workers: Gabriel (Jan. 12, 1951).
Television: Clare of Assisi (Feb. 14, 1958).
Television workers: Gabriel.
Theologians: Augustine, Alphonsus Liguori.
Throat ailments: Blase.
Travelers: Anthony of Padua, Nicholas of Myra, Christopher, Raphael.
Travel hostesses: Bona (Mar. 2, 1962).
Universities: Blessed Contardo Ferrini.
Vocations: Alphonsus.
Watchmen: Peter of Alcantara.
Weavers: Paul the Hermit, Anastasius the Fuller, Anastasia.
Wine merchants: Amand.
Women in labor: Anne.
Workingmen: Joseph.
Writers: Francis de Sales (Apr. 26, 1923), Lucy.
Yachtsmen: Adjutor.
Young girls: Agnes.
Youth: Aloysius Gonzaga (1729, Benedict XIII; 1926, Pius XI), John Berchmans, Gabriel of the Sorrowful Mother.

Patron Saints of Places

Alsace: Odilia.
Americas: Our Lady of Guadalupe, Rose of Lima.
Angola: Immaculate Heart of Mary (Nov. 21, 1984).
Argentina: Our Lady of Lujan.
Armenia: Gregory Illuminator.
Asia Minor: John, Evangelist.
Australia: Our Lady Help of Christians.
Belgium: Joseph.
Bohemia: Wenceslaus, Ludmilla.
Bolivia: Our Lady of Copacabana "Virgen de la Candelaria."
Borneo: Francis Xavier.
Brazil: Nossa Senhora de Aparecida, Immaculate Conception, Peter of Alcantara.
Canada: Joseph, Anne.
Chile: James the Greater, Our Lady of Mt. Carmel.
China: Joseph.
Colombia: Peter Claver, Louis Bertran.
Corsica: Immaculate Conception.
Cuba: Our Lady of Charity.
Czechoslovakia: Wenceslaus, John Nepomucene, Procopius.
Denmark: Ansgar, Canute.
Dominican Republic: Our Lady of High Grace, Dominic.
East Indies: Thomas, Apostle.
Ecuador: Sacred Heart.
El Salvador: Our Lady of Peace (Oct. 10, 1966).
England: George.
Equatorial Guinea: Immaculate Conception (May 25, 1986).
Europe: Benedict (1964), Cyril and Methodius, co-patrons (Dec. 31, 1980).
Finland: Henry.
France: Our Lady of the Assumption, Joan of Arc, Therese (May 3, 1944).
Germany: Boniface, Michael.
Gibraltar: Blessed Virgin Mary under title, "Our Lady of Europe" (May 31, 1979).
Greece: Nicholas, Andrew.
Holland: Willibrord.
Hungary: Blessed Virgin, "Great Lady of Hungary," Stephen, King.
Iceland: Thorlac (Jan. 14, 1984).
India: Our Lady of Assumption.
Ireland: Patrick, Brigid and Columba.
Italy: Francis of Assisi, Catherine of Siena.
Japan: Peter Baptist.
Korea: Joseph and Mary, Mother of the Church.
Lesotho: Immaculate Heart of Mary.
Lithuania: Casimir, Bl. Cunegunda.
Luxembourg: Willibrord.
Malta: Paul, Our Lady of the Assumption.
Mexico: Our Lady of Guadalupe.
Monaco: Devota.

Moravia: Cyril and Methodius.
New Zealand: Our Lady Help of Christians.
Norway: Olaf.
Papua New Guinea (including northern Solomon Islands): Michael the Archangel (May 31, 1979).
Paraguay: Our Lady of Assumption (July 13, 1951).
Peru: Joseph (Mar. 19, 1957).
Philippines: Sacred Heart of Mary.
Poland: Casimir, Bl. Cunegunda, Stanislaus of Cracow, Our Lady of Czestochowa.
Portugal: Immaculate Conception, Francis Borgia, Anthony of Padua, Vincent of Saragossa, George.
Russia: Andrew, Nicholas of Myra, Therese of Lisieux.
Scandinavia: Ansgar.
Scotland: Andrew, Columba.
Silesia: Hedwig.
Slovakia: Our Lady of Sorrows.
South Africa: Our Lady of Assumption (Mar. 15, 1952).
South America: Rose of Lima.
Solomon Islands: BVM, under title Most Holy Name of Mary (Sept. 4, 1991).
Spain: James the Greater, Teresa.
Sri Lanka (Ceylon): Lawrence.
Sweden: Bridget, Eric.
Tanzania: Immaculate Conception (Dec. 8, 1964).
United States: Immaculate Conception (1846).
Uruguay: Blessed Virgin Mary under title "La Virgen de los Treinte y Tres" (Nov. 21, 1963).
Venezuela: Our Lady of Coromoto.
Wales: David.
West Indies: Gertrude.

Emblems, Portrayals of Saints

Agatha: Tongs, veil.
Agnes: Lamb.
Ambrose: Bees, dove, ox, pen.
Andrew: Transverse cross.
Anne, Mother of the Blessed Virgin: Door.
Anthony, Abbot: Bell, hog.
Anthony of Padua: Infant Jesus, bread, book, lily.
Augustine of Hippo: Dove, child, shell, pen.
Barnabas: Stones, ax, lance.
Bartholomew: Knife, flayed and holding his skin.
Benedict: Broken cup, raven, bell, crosier, bush.
Bernard of Clairvaux: Pen, bees, instruments of the Passion.
Bernardine of Siena: Tablet or sun inscribed with IHS.
Blase: Wax, taper, iron comb.

Bonaventure: Communion, ciborium, cardinal's hat.
Boniface: Oak, ax, book, fox, scourge, fountain, raven, sword.
Bridget of Sweden: Book, pilgrim's staff.
Bridget of Kildare: Cross, flame over her head, candle.
Catherine of Ricci: Ring, crown, crucifix.
Catherine of Siena: Stigmata, cross, ring, lily.
Cecilia: Organ.
Charles Borromeo: Communion, coat of arms with word *Humilitas*.
Christopher: Giant, torrent, tree, Child Jesus on his shoulders.
Clare of Assisi: Monstrance.
Cosmas and Damian: A phial, box of ointment.
Cyril of Alexandria: Blessed Virgin holding the Child Jesus, pen.
Cyril of Jerusalem: Purse, book.
Dominic: Rosary, star.
Edmund the Martyr: Arrow, sword.
Elizabeth of Hungary: Alms, flowers, bread, the poor, a pitcher.
Francis of Assisi: Wolf, birds, fish, skull, the Stigmata.
Francis Xavier: Crucifix, bell, vessel.
Genevieve: Bread, keys, herd, candle.
George: Dragon.
Gertrude: Crown, taper, lily.
Gervase and Protase: Scourge, club, sword.
Gregory I (the Great): Tiara, crosier, dove.
Helena: Cross.

Hilary: Stick, pen, child.
Ignatius of Loyola: Communion, chasuble, book, apparition of Our Lord.
Isidore: Bees, pen.
James the Greater: Pilgrim's staff, shell, key, sword.
James the Less: Square rule, halberd, club.
Jerome: Lion.
John Berchmans: Rule of St. Ignatius, cross, rosary.
John Chrysostom: Bees, dove, pen.
John of God: Alms, a heart, crown of thorns.
John the Baptist: Lamb, head on platter, skin of an animal.
John the Evangelist: Eagle, chalice, kettle, armor.
Josaphat Kuncevyc: Chalice, crown, winged deacon.
Joseph, Spouse of the Blessed Virgin: Infant Jesus, lily, rod, plane, carpenter's square.
Jude: Sword, square rule, club.
Justin Martyr: Ax, sword.
Lawrence: Cross, book of the Gospels, gridiron.
Leander of Seville: A pen.
Liborius: Pebbles, peacock.
Longinus: In arms at foot of the cross.
Louis IX of France: Crown of thorns, nails.
Lucy: Cord, eyes on a dish.
Luke: Ox, book, brush, palette.
Mark: Lion, book.
Martha: Holy water sprinkler, dragon.

Mary Magdalene: Alabaster box of ointment.
Matilda: Purse, alms.
Matthew: Winged man, purse, lance.
Matthias: Lance.
Maurus: Scales, spade, crutch.
Meinrad: Two ravens.
Michael: Scales, banner, sword, dragon.
Monica: Girdle, tears.
Nicholas: Three purses or balls, anchor or boat, child.
Patrick: Cross, harp, serpent, baptismal font, demons, shamrock.
Paul: Sword, book or scroll.
Peter: Keys, boat, cock.
Philip, Apostle: Column.
Philip Neri: Altar, chasuble, vial.
Rita of Cascia: Rose, crucifix, thorn.
Roch: Angel, dog, bread.
Rose of Lima: Crown of thorns, anchor, city.
Sebastian: Arrows, crown.
Simon Stock: Scapular.
Teresa of Jesus (Avila): Heart, arrow, book.
Therese of Lisieux: Roses entwining a crucifix.
Thomas, Apostle: Lance, ax.
Thomas Aquinas: Chalice, monstrance, dove, ox, person trampled under foot.
Vincent (Deacon): Gridiron, boat.
Vincent de Paul: Children.
Vincent Ferrer: Pulpit, cardinal's hat, trumpet, captives.

THE MOTHER OF JESUS IN CATHOLIC UNDERSTANDING

This article was written by the Rev. Eamon R. Carroll, O. Carm., retired member of the theological faculty of Loyola University, Chicago; author of Marian writings including "Understanding the Mother of Jesus" (published by M. Glazier, Wilmington, Del.; 1979).

Documents of the Second Vatican Council have provided the charter for current Catholic understanding of the Virgin Mary, Mother of Jesus. This conciliar teaching was expanded and applied in the pastoral letter, "Behold Your Mother: Woman of Faith," issued by the U.S. bishops Nov. 21, 1973. Pope Paul VI added guidelines for devotion, in the revised liturgy and with respect to the Rosary, in the letter *Marialis Cultus* ("To Honor Mary"), dated Feb. 2, 1974. Pope John Paul devoted an encyclical letter entitled *Mater Redemptoris* ("Mother of the Redeemer") to the role of Mary in the mystery of Christ, and her active and exemplary presence in the life of the Church, Mar. 25, 1987.

Conciliar Documents

The first conciliar document, the *Constitution on the Sacred Liturgy*, linked Mary with the life, death and exaltation of Jesus, stating: "In celebrating this annual cycle of Christ's mysteries, holy Church honors with special love blessed Mary, Mother of God, who is joined by an inseparable bond to the saving work of her Son. In her the Church holds up and admires the most excellent fruit of the redemption, and joyfully contemplates, as in a faultless manner, that which she herself wholly desires and hopes to be" (No. 103).

The eighth and final chapter of the *Dogmatic Constitution on the Church* is entitled "The Blessed Virgin Mary, Mother of God, in the Mystery of Christ and the Church." The seventh chapter deals with the communion of saints, the bond between the pilgrim Church on earth and the blessed joined to the risen Christ — what John deSatgé, an English Anglican, describes as the "mutual sharing and caring in Christ for one another." At the Eucharist, above all, "in union with the whole Church we honor Mary, the ever-Virgin Mother of Jesus Christ our Lord and God" (First Eucharistic Prayer; cf. *Constitution on the Church*, No. 50).

What Catholics believe about the Mother of Jesus is the basis for her place in their prayer life, both in the liturgy and particularly the Eucharist, and in other forms of piety, especially the Rosary. The Church's growth in insight about the Blessed Virgin comes about as Christians ponder the meaning of Mary in prayer as well as in study. The Church has come to know Mary's role by experience and by contemplation of her hidden holiness (*Constitution on the Church*, No. 64). The tradition about Mary has been transmitted by doctrinal teaching and also by life and worship, even as in her own life Mary treasured in her heart God's words and deeds (*Dogmatic Constitution on Divine Revelation*, No. 8).

Mary in the Bible

The possibility of consensus on the Virgin Mary in the Bible was the theme of a book published in 1978, entitled *Mary in the New Testament* (edited by R. E. Brown, J. A. Fitzmyer, J. Reumann and K. P. Donfried). Limiting their study to the New Testament and using critical techniques of interpretation, a team of 12 authors — Catholics, Lutherans, Anglicans and others — agreed on a biblical portrait of Mary the Virgin as the great gospel model of faith commitment.

One valuable insight centers on the "true kinsmen" incident (Mk. 3:31-35; Mt. 12:46-50; Lk. 8:19-21). One day while Jesus was preaching, word was sent to him that his "mother and brethren" wished to see him. In St. Mark, the oldest account, there is a sharp distinction between the circle of the hearers of Jesus, who were "inside" and counted as his "true family," and the relatives "outside," who failed to understand him. St. Mark does not clearly place Mary among the outsiders, but neither does he carefully distinguish her from the other relatives who did not esteem Jesus. St. Luke shifts the focus completely, placing the relatives, especially the Mother of Jesus, among the true followers, as he does also in the Acts of the Apostles by mentioning them in the Upper Room before Pentecost.

St. Luke is fond of speaking of the "word of God." At the Annunciation, Mary consented with the statement, "Be it done to me according to your word" (Lk. 1:26-38), and "the Word was made flesh" (Jn. 1:14). Jesus said in reply to the message about his visitors, "My mother and my brothers are those who hear the word of God and do it" (Lk. 8:21). St. Luke relates this event just after the parables of the sower and the seed and the lamp on the lampstand. Consistent with his high praise of the Virgin Mary in the infancy chapters, he regards Mary as the rich soil — she heard the word and brought forth fruit in abundance, the Holy One who is the Son of God. She is the pure light, rekindled by the coming of the Redeemer; she is the "woman clothed with the sun" (Rv. 12:1), for Jesus is the "sun of justice."

St. Luke alone saved one other mention of Mary during the public ministry of Jesus, in the story of the "enthusiastic woman" (Lk. 11:27-28). One day while Jesus was preaching, a woman cried out, "Blessed is the womb that bore you and the breasts that nursed you." He replied, "Still more blessed are those who hear the word of God and keep it." The obedient Mary, handmaid of the Lord, brought together opposed beatitudes — the anonymous woman's praise of her motherhood and Jesus'

tribute to her faith. In the opening chapter of St. Luke, Elizabeth did the same when, filled with the Holy Spirit, she returned Mary's greeting with the loud cry, "Of all women you are the most blessed, and blessed is the fruit of your womb." Continuing in praise of her young cousin's faith, she added: "Yes, blessed is she who has believed, for the things promised her by the Lord will be fulfilled" (Lk. 1:39-45).

Mary the Virgin

Both St. Luke and St. Matthew, whose infancy narratives differ so much otherwise, agree that Mary conceived Jesus virginally, that her Son had no human father. The Creed affirms that Jesus was "conceived of the Virgin Mary by the power of the Holy Spirit." St. Luke writes of the virginal conception of Jesus from the standpoint of Mary. To her question, "How can this be since I know not man?" the angel replied by appealing to God's power.

St. Matthew's viewpoint is that of Joseph, who was informed in a dream-vision that Mary's child was of no human father. God accomplishes his saving purposes without dependence on the will of the flesh and the will of man (Jn. 1:13). God shows his favor where he chooses — whether for the barren Sara, wife of Abraham, or aged Elizabeth, the wife of Zechariah, or the Virgin Mary. In the words of the promise to Abraham, repeated by Gabriel to Mary, "Nothing is impossible to God" (Lk. 1:37; Gn. 18:14).

Mary and Joseph accepted as God's will the virginal conception, an unprecedented event, the sign of God sending his Son to be the Savior. Their lives were henceforth totally dedicated to the service of Jesus.

As various forms of Christian witness developed in the Church, the conviction that Mary remains always a virgin came to be held as Catholic doctrine. The Gospels leave undecided the identity of the "brethren" of Jesus. From lived experience, in the fourth century the Church had come to see Mary's life-long virginity as part of her commitment to her Son and his mission. Such "development of doctrine" remains a point of difference between Catholics and Protestants, although the great Reformers — Luther, Calvin and later John Wesley — all held that Mary was ever-Virgin.

St. Luke and St. John on Mary

Along with the role of Mary in the childhood of Jesus, St. Luke sees her as part of the fulfillment of messianic prophecy. The Second Vatican Council spoke of "the exalted daughter of Zion in whom the times are fulfilled after the long waiting for the promise, and the new economy inaugurated when the Son of God takes on human nature from her in order to free men from sin by the mysteries of his flesh." The expectations of Israel for the Messiah reach their peak in Mary of Nazareth: "She stands out among the Lord's lowly and poor who confidently look for salvation from him" (*Constitution on the Church*, No. 55).

The Gospel of St. John introduces Mary at the opening and closing of her Son's ministry, which began with the first of his signs at Cana (Jn. 2:1-11) and ended on Calvary (Jn. 19). Both scenes deal with a "third day," both turn on the "hour," not yet come at Cana but achieved in the decisive event of Calvary. In both, Jesus addresses his Mother with the unaccustomed title, "Woman." The request of Mary at Cana is for more than wine to save the wedding feast. She stands for Israel of old, symbolized by the water pots required for religious purifications; Mary stands also for the new Israel, the Church, the bride of Christ, symbolized by the abundant choice wine of the messianic banquet. The marriage feast looks forward to the hour when Christ, the bridegroom, will lay down his life in love for his bride, the Church.

When Jesus spoke from the cross to his Mother and the beloved disciple, "Woman, behold your son," and "Behold your Mother," more was meant than that the disciple should provide for Mary's care (Jn. 19:26-27). In his farewell discourse at the Last Supper, Jesus spoke of the woman in agony because her hour had come. "But when she has borne her child, she no longer remembers her pain for joy that a man has been born into the world" (Jn. 16:21). The longing of Israel for the coming of the Messiah was sometimes compared to labor pains. The "daughter of Zion" had been promised she would become the mother of all races and all nations. The words of Jesus on Calvary announced the fulfillment of that promise; Mary stands for the "woman" who is mother Church, new Israel, new People of God.

In St. John's Gospel, it is only after his words to his Mother and the disciple that Jesus, knowing "that everything was now finished," said, "I am thirsty," and then, "Now it is finished." "Then he bowed his head and delivered over his spirit" (Jn. 19:28-29).

The giving up of the spirit means both the expiring of Jesus and the giving of the Holy Spirit to the Church. The wine Mary requested at Cana was the wine of the Spirit, to be poured out at the messianic banquet. The prayer for the wine of the Spirit is answered through the self-surrender of Jesus on the cross. The triumphant Christ "gives up his spirit," and the Church comes into being. The Acts of the Apostles describes the effects of the outpouring of the Spirit at Pentecost and afterwards. What Mary requested at Cana, what she prayed for in agony at the cross of Jesus, what she sought before Pentecost in union with the Apostles and relatives and the women — all "with one accord devoted to prayer" — is the gift of the Spirit. At Nazareth Mary conceived her Son, and God became man by the power of the Holy Spirit; in the Upper Room she prayed for the Spirit that Jesus be born again in the members of his Church (*Constitution on the Church*, No. 59).

The New Eve

To the titles of Mary already familiar from the Gospels — "the Virgin," "Favored One," "Mother of Jesus," "Mother of my Lord" (Elizabeth's greeting, meaning "Mother of the Messianic King") — the early Church added other descriptions. By the mid-second century Mary was being compared to Eve. Eve was deceived by the word of the evil angel and by disobedience brought death; Mary, the obedient Virgin, heeded the message of the good angel and by her consent brought Life to the world. The title of "New Eve" became common for Mary. By the time of St. Jerome (d. 419), it was proverbial to say, "Death through Eve, life through Mary."

Immaculate Conception

Reflecting on the Blessed Virgin, Christians pondered various aspects of her holiness. The question arose of her freedom from original sin, God's gift of grace that came to be called her Immaculate Conception (not to be confused with the virginal conception of Jesus, for Mary was the child of the father and mother recalled as Joachim and Anne). It took centuries of development before the Immaculate Conception was held to be revealed by God and defined as dogma by Pius IX in 1854. The absence of clear scriptural evidence was one delaying factor; another was lack of clarity about the meaning of original sin; and most cogent was the requirement that Mary be beneficiary of the saving work of Christ. As the English Anglican John deSatgé expresses it, "Mary, who rejoiced in her Savior, was the last person to have no need of one." The Franciscan John Duns Scotus (d. 1308) suggested that Mary was kept free of original sin by a "preservative redemption" — in anticipation of the foreseen merits of Jesus Christ — the explanation eventually recognized as revealed truth.

The Assumption

The final facet of Mary's holiness is the Assumption, her union body and soul with the risen Christ in the glory of heaven, defined as dogma by Pope Pius XII in 1950. By the sixth century the feast of the Assumption was being celebrated in the East, a development from a still earlier August 15 feast that had been known as the Memory of Mary (like the birthdays into heaven of the martyrs), as the Passing of Mary, and as the Dormition or Falling Asleep of the Mother of God. There is no compelling biblical testimony; the appeal is to the concordant faith of the Church, convinced that the promise of the resurrection of the flesh in union with the risen Savior has already been fulfilled for the Mother of the Lord, who gave him human birth in her pure body and was his loyal disciple unto the end.

Model of the Church

All beliefs about the Blessed Virgin lead to Christ. God kept her free from original sin for the sake of Jesus, that she might give herself wholeheartedly to his life and work (*Constitution on the Church*, No. 56), and in consideration of his redemptive mission. Mary's Assumption is her reunion with her Son in the power of his resurrection. The Marian privileges of the Immaculate Conception and the Assumption enrich also the self-understanding of the Church, for she is the "most excellent fruit of the redemption, the spotless model of the Church," the one in whom Christians admire God's plan for his Church. "In the most holy Virgin the Church has already reached that perfection whereby she exists without spot or wrinkle (Eph. 5:27)" (*Constitution on the Church*, No. 65).

Mary Immaculate is a sign of the love of Christ for his bride, the Church; the bridegroom purifies her by his blood to make her all-holy. The preface for the Solemnity of the Immaculate Conception (December 8) addresses the Father: "You allowed no stain of sin to touch the Virgin Mary. Full of grace, she was to be a worthy Mother of your Son, your sign of favor to the Church at its beginning, and the promise of its perfection as the bride of Christ, radiantly beautiful."

Faithful to his promise, Christ has prepared a place for his bride, the Church. In Mary, daughter of the Church, now joined to Christ body and soul in glory, the pilgrim Church sees the successful completion of its own journey. The resurrection of Jesus is the central truth; the Assumption of Mary is the living sign of the Church's call to glory, to loving union with the victorious Redeemer. The preface at Mass for August 15 reads: "Today the Virgin Mother of God was taken up into heaven to be the beginning and the pattern of the Church in its perfection, and a sign of sure hope and comfort for your pilgrim people. You would not allow decay to touch her body, for she had given birth in the glory of the Incarnation to your Son, the Lord of all life." (Cf. also *Constitution on the Church,* No. 68.)

Mother of God

In 325 the first ecumenical council, at Nicaea, proclaimed that Jesus is truly Son of God. Defenders of the faith there were the first to call Mary "Mother of God." At the third ecumenical council, Ephesus, in 431, it was solemnly established that the Virgin Mary is indeed "Mother of God," for the Son to whom she gave birth is the pre-existent Second Person of the Blessed Trinity. "Mother of God" had already been used as a popular title in some parts of the Church, and after Ephesus it was adopted in the prayers of the Mass, as is still the practice in the Catholic Church and all Eastern Churches. For example, the current third Eucharistic Prayer reads: "May he (the Holy Spirit) make us an everlasting gift to you (the Father) and enable us to share in the inheritance of your saints, with Mary, the Virgin Mother of God."

Mother of the Church

When the Church began to celebrate the Assumption of Mary, it did so in the conviction Mary did not leave the members of the Church orphans when her days on earth were ended. She continues her interest for them in union with her Son, the supreme intercessor. By the time of the Council of Ephesus in 431, authors of both the East and West — like St. Ephrem of Syria (d. 373) and St. Ambrose of Italy (d. 397) — proposed Mary as the model of Christian life, and the practice of asking her to pray for her clients on earth began to appear. The feasts of the Nativity of Mary (September 8), the Annunciation (March 25) and the Presentation of Jesus (February 2, also known as the Purification of Mary or Candlemas) have been kept from the sixth and seventh centuries.

When the words of Gabriel and Elizabeth from St. Luke's infancy narrative became part of prayer, the first part of the Hail Mary, their use led to deeper awareness of Mary's holiness as well as to counting on her heavenly help — well expressed in the second part of the Hail Mary — "Holy Mary, Mother of God, pray for us sinners now and at the hour of our death," which reached its fixed form only in the fifteenth century. Mary's place in liturgical prayer and in private prayer reflected and strengthened the sense of her continuing role as loving friend in heaven of the Church on earth. People asked Mary's prayers on their behalf, recalling Mary's own "pilgrimage of faith" and trusting in her abiding maternal care.

Greek homilists like St. John of Damascus (d. ca. 749), St. Andrew of Crete (d. 740) and St. Germanus of Constantinople (d. ca. 733) sang Mary's praises and urged confidence in her loving intercession with Christ. In the West, after the upsurge of the Carolingian times (about 800), remembered for the origin of the Saturday observance in honor of Mary, came the flowering of medieval piety, as evidenced in the writings of St. Anselm (d. 1109), St. Bernard (d. 1153) and his fellow Cistercians, and the great scholastic doctors like St. Thomas Aquinas (d. 1274) and St. Bonaventure (d. 1274). The medieval authors described Mary as Mediatrix of grace, Dispensatrix of grace, spiritual Mother. Blessed Guerric, the Cistercian abbot of Igny (France, d. 1157), emphasized the maternal role of Mary in the formation of Christ in the faithful: "Like the Church of which she is a figure, Mary is Mother of all who are born to life."

Christian Unity and Mary

At the Reformation, in reaction to abuses, the invocation of the saints was rejected as harmful to confidence in Christ, the unique Mediator. Since the sixteenth century Western Christians have been sharply divided in their understanding of the communion of saints and the legitimacy of "praying to Mary." Recent events, however, hold out hope for a meeting of minds and hearts even in this sensitive area. The Second Vatican Council offered a biblical portrait of Mary without neglecting later developments in doctrine and devotion. The council described the place of Mary in words designed to meet Protestant difficulties; e.g., the much misunderstood word, Mediatrix, was used once only and was explained as completely dependent on the unique mediatorship of Christ (*Constitution on the Church,* Nos. 67, 69).

The conciliar *Decree on Ecumenism,* issued Nov. 21, 1964, spoke of the "order" or "hierarchy of truths" among Catholic doctrines, which differ in their relationship to the foundation of the faith (No. 11). The foundation is Jesus Christ, and here all Christians share a common profession of faith. The document mentioned realistically some differences that still divide Catholics and other Christians, in this "order of truths": the meaning of the Incarnation and Redemption, the mystery and ministry of the Church, and the role of Mary in the work of salvation (No. 20). The decree also said in this context: "We rejoice to see our separated brethren looking to Christ as the source and center of ecclesiastical communion. Inspired by longing for union with Christ, they feel compelled to search for unity ever more ardently, and to bear witness to their faith among all the peoples of the earth."

The formation of the Ecumenical Society of the Blessed Virgin Mary in England in 1967, and of the American branch in 1976, is an encouraging sign. The American bishops' pastoral, *"Behold Your Mother,"* appealed to the "basic reverence" of all Christians for Mary, "a veneration deeper than doctrinal differences and theological disputes" (Nos. 101-112). Pope Paul VI's major document, *Marialis Cultus,* contains an appeal to other Christians (Nos. 32 and 33). With Christians of the East, said Pope Paul, Catholics honor the Mother of God as "hope of Christians." Catholics join with Anglicans and Protestants in common praise of God, using the Virgin's own words (Lk. 1:46-55). It may well be that the growing interest in the bonds between the Blessed Virgin and the Holy Spirit will help bring Christians together. The Spirit of unity inspired Mary's prophecy: "All generations will call me blessed, because he who is mighty has done great things for me" (Lk. 1:48-49).

APPARITIONS OF THE BLESSED VIRGIN MARY

Only seven of the best known apparitions of the Blessed Virgin Mary are described briefly below.

The sites of the following apparitions have become shrines and centers of pilgrimage. Miracles of the moral and physical orders have been reported as occurring at these places and/or in connection with related practices of prayer and penance.

Banneux, near Liege, Belgium: Mary appeared eight times between Jan. 15 and Mar. 2, 1933, to an 11-year-old peasant girl, Mariette Beco, in a garden behind the family cottage in Banneux, near Liege. She called herself the Virgin of the Poor, and has since been venerated as Our Lady of the Poor, the Sick, and the Indifferent. A small chapel was built by a spring near the site of the apparitions and was blessed Aug. 15, 1933. Approval of devotion to Our Lady of Banneux was given in 1949 by Bishop Louis J. Kerkhofs of Liege, and a statue of that title was solemnly crowned in 1956.

The **International Union of Prayer,** for devotion to the Virgin of the Poor, has approximately two million members.

Beauraing, Belgium: Mary appeared 33 times between Nov. 29, 1932, and Jan. 3, 1933, to five children in the garden of a convent school in Beauraing. A chapel, which became a pilgrimage center, was erected on the spot. Reserved approval of devotion to Our Lady of Beauraing was given Feb. 2, 1943, and final approbation July 2, 1949, by Bishop Charue of Namur (d. 1977).

The **Marian Union of Beauraing,** a prayer association for the conversion of sinners, has thousands of members throughout the world (see Pro Maria Committee).

Fatima, Portugal: Mary appeared six times between May 13 and Oct. 13, 1917, to three children (Lucia dos Santos, 10, who is now a Carmelite nun; Francisco Marto, 9, who died in 1919; and his sister Jacinta, 7, who died in 1920) in a field called Cova da Iria near Fatima, north of Lisbon. She recommended frequent recitation of the Rosary; urged works of mortification for the conversion of sinners; called for devotion to herself under the title of her Immaculate Heart; asked that the people of Russia be consecrated to her under this title, and that the faithful make a Communion of reparation on the first Saturday of each month.

The apparitions were declared worthy of belief in October, 1930, after a seven-year canonical investigation, and devotion to Our Lady of Fatima was authorized under the title of Our Lady of the Rosary. In October, 1942, Pius XII consecrated the world to Mary under the title of her Immaculate Heart. Ten years later, in the first apostolic letter addressed directly to the peoples of Russia, he consecrated them in a special manner to Mary.

Fatima, with its sanctuary and basilica, ranks with Lourdes as the greatest of modern Marian shrines. (See First Saturday Devotion.)

Guadalupe, Mexico: Mary appeared four times in 1531 to an Indian, Juan Diego (declared Blessed in 1990), on Tepeyac hill outside of Mexico City, and instructed him to tell Bishop Zumarraga of her wish that a church be built there. The bishop complied with the request about two years later after being convinced of the genuineness of the apparition by the evidence of a miraculously painted life-size figure of the Virgin on the mantle of the Indian. The mantle bearing the picture has been preserved and is enshrined in the Basilica of Our Lady of Guadalupe, which has a long history as a center of devotion and pilgrimage in Mexico. The shrine church, originally dedicated in 1709 and subsequently enlarged, has the title of basilica.

Benedict XIV, in a decree issued in 1754, authorized a Mass and Office under the title of Our Lady of Guadalupe for celebration on Dec. 12, and named Mary the patroness of New Spain. Our Lady of Guadalupe was designated patroness of Latin America by St. Pius X in 1910 and patroness of the Americas by Pius XII in 1945.

La Salette, France: Mary appeared as a sorrowing and weeping figure Sept. 19, 1846, to two peasant children, Melanie Matthieu, 15, and Maximin Giraud, 11, at La Salette in southern France. The message she confided to them, regarding the necessity of penance, was communicated to Pius IX in 1851 and has since been known as the "secret" of La Salette. Bishop de Bruillard of Grenoble declared in 1851 that the apparition was credible, and devotion to Mary under the title of Our Lady of La Salette was authorized. The devotion has been confirmed by popes since the time of Pius IX, and a Mass and office with this title were authorized in 1942. The shrine church was given the title of minor basilica in 1879.

Lourdes, France: Mary, identifying herself as the Immaculate Conception, appeared 18 times between Feb. 11 and July 16, 1858, to 14-year-old Bernadette Soubirous at the grotto of Massabielle near Lourdes in southern France. Her message concerned the necessity of prayer and penance for the conversion of peoples. Mary's request that a chapel be built at the grotto and spring was fulfilled in 1862 after four years of rigid examination established the credibility of the apparitions. Devotion under the title of Our Lady of Lourdes was authorized later, and a Feb. 11 feast commemorating the apparitions was instituted by Leo XIII. St. Pius X extended this feast throughout the Church in 1907.

The Church of Notre Dame was made a basilica in 1870, and the Church of the Rosary was built later. The underground Church of St. Pius X, with a capacity of 20,000 persons, was consecrated Mar. 25, 1958.

Our Lady of the Miraculous Medal, France: Mary appeared three times in 1830 to Catherine Laboure in the chapel of the motherhouse of the Daughters of Charity of St. Vincent de Paul, Rue de Bac, Paris. She commissioned Catherine to have made the medal of the Immaculate Conception, now known as the Miraculous Medal, and to spread devotion to her under this title. In 1832, the medal was struck according to the model revealed to Catherine.

CRITERIA OF APPARITIONS

These were the subjects of a series of articles published early in 1990 in *La Civilta Cattolica,* the influential Jesuit periodical. Father Giandomenico Mucci, the author, said the articles were not specifically written with Medjugorje in mind, but that many of the criteria could be applied to that case.

His main point in writing was to say that, in an age of mushrooming alleged private apparitions, the Church should not lose sight of its traditional process of discernment.

Discernment is necessary because of the "great dangers" to spiritual life posed by the "enthusiastic, acritical and naive acceptance of such phenomena," he said. He cited an estimate that three-fourths of private "revelations" are illusory.

Among the traditional criteria of an apparition's authenticity, he cited the following.

● While God can choose anyone, even public sinners, for visions or apparitions, they should show spiritual progress afterward. The purpose of such revelations, after all, is to help the person grow in grace.

● To aid in discernment, visionaries need spiritual directors, "a species that cannot be improvised and which today is painfully missing."

● Spiritual directors should never push seers to ask questions about people during apparitions. This is mere "childishness."

● The apparitions should "never produce any sentiment of contempt toward anyone."

● Authentic texts of the revelation must be procured, without corrections or amendments.

● "Predictions that do not come true or are continually postponed do not speak in favor of their divine origin."

● Revelations are suspect when they aim to settle theological or other disputes.

● "In giving visions and revelations, the Lord does not intend to do archeological or historical work in front of the seer."

Father Mucci said in an interview that, while he had not studied the Medjugorje events firsthand, he was skeptical of their genuineness. From the Church's point of view, he said, there were two theoretical obstacles to the alleged apparitions: first, they involve a large number of seers; second, Mary's reported messages seem unnecessarily repetitive. "All the messages I've seen from Medjugorje can be reduced to one word, conversion. One does not understand why Mary must repeat herself like that. Nor can one understand the banality of the language," he said.

He also said that the availability of the young seers — through books, interviews, television and other media — appeared to set them apart from traditional visionaries, who often hide from the public.

Father Mucci pointed out that the Vatican is not obliged to pass judgment on the authenticity of supposed apparitions, although it can do so — as it did in the case of Lourdes, for one example.

EVENTS OF MEDJUGORJE

Alleged apparitions of Mary to six young people of Medjugorje, Bosnia-Herzegovina, have been the center of interest and controversy since they were first reported in June, 1981, initially in a neighboring hillside field, subsequently in the village church of St. James and even in places far removed from Medjugorje.

Reports say the alleged visionaries have seen, heard and touched Mary during visions, and that they have variously received several or all of 10 secret messages related to world events and urging a quest for peace through prayer, penance and personal conversion. An investigative commission appointed by local Bishop Pavao Zanic of Mostar-Duvno reported in March, 1984, that the authenticity of the apparitions had not been established and that cases of reported healings had not been verified. He called the apparitions a case of "collective hallucination" exploited by local Franciscan priests at odds with him over control of a parish.

Archbishop Frane Franic of Split-Makarska, on

the other hand, said in December, 1985: "Speaking as a believer and not as a bishop, my personal conviction is that the events at Medjugorje are of supernatural inspiration." He based his conviction on the observation of spiritual benefits related to the reported events, such as the spiritual development of the six young people, the increases in Mass attendance and sacramental practice at the scene of the apparitions, and the incidence of reconciliation among people.

"Further exploration" of the events at Medjugorje on the national level, as distinguished from the earlier diocesan investigation, was announced in a communique published in the official bulletin of the Archdiocese of Zagreb, dated Jan. 29, 1987.

"On the basis of research conducted so far, one cannot affirm that supernatural apparitions are involved" at Medjugorje, declared the bishops of Yugoslavia (19 to 1), in a statement published Jan. 2, 1991.

EASTERN CATHOLIC CHURCHES

The Second Vatican Council, in its *Decree on Eastern Catholic Churches*, stated the following points regarding Eastern heritage, patriarchs, sacraments and worship.

Venerable Churches: The Catholic Church holds in high esteem the institutions of the Eastern Churches, their liturgical rites, ecclesiastical traditions, and Christian way of life. For, distinguished as they are by their venerable antiquity, they are bright with that tradition which was handed down from the Apostles through the Fathers, and which forms part of the divinely revealed and undivided heritage of the universal Church (No. 1).

That Church, Holy and Catholic, which is the Mystical Body of Christ, is made up of the faithful who are organically united in the Holy Spirit through the same faith, the same sacraments, and the same government and who, combining into various groups held together by a hierarchy, form separate Churches or rites. . . . It is the mind of the Catholic Church that each individual Church or rite retain its traditions whole and entire, while adjusting its way of life to the various needs of time and place (No. 2).

Such individual Churches, whether of the East or of the West, although they differ somewhat among themselves in what are called rites (that is, in liturgy, ecclesiastical discipline, and spiritual heritage) are, nevertheless, equally entrusted to the pastoral guidance of the Roman Pontiff, the divinely appointed successor of St. Peter in supreme government over the universal Church. They are consequently of equal dignity, so that none of them is superior to the others by reason of rite (No. 3).

Eastern Heritage: Each and every Catholic, as also the baptized . . . of every non-Catholic Church or community who enters into the fullness of Catholic communion, should everywhere retain his proper rite, cherish it, and observe it to the best of his ability (No. 4).

The Churches of the East, as much as those of the West, fully enjoy the right, and are in duty bound, to rule themselves. Each should do so according to its proper and individual procedures (No. 5).

All Eastern rite members should know and be convinced that they can and should always preserve their lawful liturgical rites and their established way of life, and that these should not be altered except by way of an appropriate and organic development (No. 6).

Patriarchs: The institution of the patriarchate has existed in the Church from the earliest times and was recognized by the first ecumenical Synods.

By the name Eastern Patriarch is meant the bishop who has jurisdiction over all bishops (including metropolitans), clergy, and people of his own territory or rite, in accordance with the norms of law and without prejudice to the primacy of the Roman Pontiff (No. 7).

Though some of the patriarchates of the Eastern Churches are of later origin than others, all are equal in patriarchal dignity. Still the honorary and lawfully established order of precedence among them is to be preserved (No. 8).

In keeping with the most ancient tradition of the Church, the Patriarchs of the Eastern Churches are to be accorded exceptional respect, since each presides over his patriarchate as father and head.

This sacred Synod, therefore, decrees that their rights and privileges should be re-established in accord with the ancient traditions of each Church and the decrees of the ecumenical Synods.

The rights and privileges in question are those which flourished when East and West were in union, though they should be somewhat adapted to modern conditions.

The Patriarchs with their synods constitute the superior authority for all affairs of the patriarchate, including the right to establish new eparchies and to nominate bishops of their rite within the territorial bounds of the patriarchate, without prejudice to the inalienable right of the Roman Pontiff to intervene in individual cases (No. 9).

What has been said of Patriarchs applies as well, under the norm of law, to major archbishops, who preside over the whole of some individual Church or rite (No. 10).

Sacraments: This sacred Ecumenical Synod endorses and lauds the ancient discipline of the sacraments existing in the Eastern Churches, as also the practices connected with their celebration and administration (No. 12).

With respect to the minister of holy chrism (confirmation), let that practice be fully restored which existed among Easterners in most ancient times. Priests, therefore, can validly confer this sacrament, provided they use chrism blessed by a Patriarch or bishop (No. 13).

In conjunction with baptism or otherwise, all Eastern-Rite priests can confer this sacrament validly on all the faithful of any rite, including the Latin; licitly, however, only if the regulations of both common and particular law are observed. Priests of the Latin rite, to the extent of the faculties they enjoy for administering this sacrament, can confer it also on the faithful of Eastern Churches, without prejudice to rite. They do so licitly if the regulations of both common and particular law are observed (No. 14).

The faithful are bound on Sundays and feast days to attend the divine liturgy or, according to the regulations or custom of their own rite, the celebration of the Divine Praises. That the faithful may be able to satisfy their obligation more easily, it is decreed that this obligation can be fulfilled from the Vespers of the vigil to the end of the Sunday or the feast day (No. 15).

Because of the everyday intermingling of the communicants of diverse Eastern Churches in the same Eastern region or territory, the faculty for hearing confession, duly and unrestrictedly granted by his proper bishop to a priest of any rite, is applicable to the entire territory of the grantor, also to the places and the faithful belonging to any other rite in the same territory, unless an Ordinary of the place explicitly decides otherwise with respect to the places pertaining to his rite (No. 16).

This sacred Synod ardently desires that where it has fallen into disuse the office of the permanent diaconate be restored. The legislative authority of each individual church should decide about the subdiaconate and the minor orders (No. 17).

By way of preventing invalid marriages between Eastern Catholics and baptized Eastern non-Catholics, and in the interests of the permanence and sanctity of marriage and of domestic harmony, this sacred Synod decrees that the canonical 'form' for the celebration of such marriages obliges only for lawfulness. For their validity, the presence of a sacred minister suffices, as long as the other requirements of law are honored (No. 18).

Worship: Henceforth, it will be the exclusive right of an ecumenical Synod or the Apostolic See to establish, transfer, or suppress feast days common to all the Eastern Churches. To establish, transfer, or suppress feast days for any of the individual Churches is within the competence not only of the Apostolic See but also of a patriarchal or archiepiscopal synod, provided due consideration is given to the entire region and to other individual Churches (No. 19).

Until such time as all Christians desirably concur on a fixed day for the celebration of Easter, and with a view meantime to promoting unity among the Christians of a given area or nation, it is left to the Patriarchs or supreme authorities of a place to reach a unanimous agreement, after ascertaining the views of all concerned, on a single Sunday for the observance of Easter (No. 20).

With respect to rules concerning sacred seasons, individual faithful dwelling outside the area or territory of their own rite may conform completely to the established custom of the place where they live. When members of a family belong to different rites, they are all permitted to observe sacred seasons according to the rules of any one of these rites (No. 21).

From ancient times the Divine Praises have been held in high esteem among all Eastern Churches. Eastern clerics and religious should celebrate these Praises as the laws and customs of their own traditions require. To the extent they can, the faithful too should follow the example of their forebears by assisting devoutly at the Divine Praises (No. 22).

RITES, JURISDICTIONS AND FAITHFUL OF EASTERN CHURCHES

Introduction

The Catholic Church originated in Palestine, whence it spread to other regions of the world where certain places became key centers of Christian life with great influence on the local churches in their respective areas. Such centers were Jerusalem, Alexandria, Antioch and Constantinople in the East, and Rome in the West. The eastern Mother Churches, with rites bearing their names, were Alexandrian, Antiochene, Armenian, Byzantine and Chaldean. The usages of these churches expressed the one faith in different ways in theology, liturgy, hierarchy and governance, tradition and culture. Hence, the different rites.

The main lines of Eastern Church patriarchal organization and usages were drawn before the Roman Empire became two empires, East (Byzantine) and West (Roman), in 292. Eastern Church members, originally within the boundaries of the Eastern Empire, eventually spread to other parts of the world where they have continued to maintain their distinctive religious identity and heritage on a par with the faithful of Roman (Latin) rite.

Most of the Eastern Churches now in communion with the Holy See were at some time in the past separated from it because of developments and events connected with the Schism of 1054.

Statistics

(Principal source: *Annuario Pontificio, 1993*.)

These statistics are for Eastern-rite jurisdictions only, and do not include Eastern-rite Catholics under the jurisdiction of Roman-rite bishops. Some of the figures reported are only approximate. Some of the jurisdictions listed were long inactive because of government suppression.

Alexandrian

Called the Liturgy of St. Mark, the Alexandrian Rite was modified by the Copts and Melkites, and contains elements of the Byzantine Rite of St. Basil and the liturgies of Sts. Mark, Cyril and Gregory of Nazianzen. The liturgy is substantially that of the Coptic Church, which is divided into two branches — the Coptic or Egyptian, and the Ethiopian or Abyssinian. The churches of this rite are:

COPTIC: Jurisdictions (located in Egypt): patriarchate of Alexandria, five dioceses; 181,413. Copts resumed communion with Rome about 1741; situated in Egypt, the Near East; liturgical languages are Coptic, Arabic.

ETHIOPIAN: Jurisdictions (located in Ethiopia): one metropolitan, two dioceses; 132,697. Ethiopians resumed communion with Rome in 1846: situated in Ethiopia, Jerusalem, Somalia; liturgical language is Geez.

Antiochene

This is the source of more derived rites than any of the other parent rites. Its origin can be traced to the Eighth Book of the *Apostolic Constitutions* and to the Liturgy of St. James of Jerusalem, which ultimately spread throughout the whole patriarchate and displaced older forms based on the *Apostolic Constitutions*. The churches of this rite are:

MALANKAR: Jurisdictions (located in India): one metropolitan, two dioceses; 295,467. Malankarese resumed communion with Rome in 1930; situated in India; liturgical languages are Syriac, Malayalam.

MARONITE: Jurisdictions (located in Lebanon, Cyprus, Egypt, Syria, U.S., Argentina, Brazil, Australia, Canada): patriarchate of Antioch, 20 archdioceses and dioceses, one patriarchal vicariate; 3,301,614. Where no special jurisdictions exist, they are under jurisdiction of local Roman-rite bishops. United to the Holy See since the time of their founder, St. Maron; have no counterparts among the separated Eastern Christians: situated throughout the world: liturgical languages are Syriac, Arabic.

SYRIAN: Jurisdictions (located in Lebanon, Iraq, Egypt and Syria): patriarchate of Antioch, one metropolitan, six archdioceses and dioceses, four patriarchal vicariates; 102,870. Syrians Resumed communion with Rome in 1781; situated in Asia, Africa, the Americas, Australia; liturgical languages are Syriac, Arabic.

Armenian

Substantially, although using a different language, this is the Greek Liturgy of St. Basil; it is considered an older form of the Byzantine Rite, and incorporates some modifications from the Antiochene Rite. The church of this rite is:

ARMENIAN, exclusively: Jurisdictions (located in Lebanon, Iran, Iraq, Egypt, Syria, Turkey, Ukraine, France, Greece, Romania, Armenia (for Eastern Europe), Argentina (eparchy and exarchate for Latin America, including Mexico), and the United States (for Canada and the U.S.): patriarchate of Cilicia, 10 archdioceses and dioceses, two patriarchal exarchates, two apostolic exarchates, three ordinariates; 146,630. Armenians resumed communion with Rome during the time of the Crusades; situated in the Near East, Europe, Africa, the Americas, Australasia; liturgical language is Classical Armenian.

Byzantine

Based on the Rite of St. James of Jerusalem and the churches of Antioch, and reformed by Sts. Basil and John Chrysostom, the Byzantine Rite is proper to the Church of Constantinople. (The city was called Byzantium before Constantine changed its name; the modern name is Istanbul.) It is now used by the majority of Eastern Catholics and by the Eastern Orthodox Church (which is not in union with Rome). It is, after the Roman, the most widely used rite. The churches of this rite are:

ALBANIAN: Jurisdiction (located in Albania): one apostolic administration. Albanians resumed communion with Rome about 1628; situated in Albania; liturgical language is Albanian.

BELARUSSIAN (formerly Byelorussian, also known as White Russian): They have an apostolic visitator. Belarussians resumed communion with Rome in the 17th century; situated in Europe, the Americas, Australia; liturgical language is Old Slavonic.

BULGARIAN: Jurisdiction (located in Bulgaria): one apostolic exarchate; 25,000. Bulgarians resumed communion with Rome about 1861; situated in Bulgaria; liturgical language is Old Slavonic.

CROATIAN: Jurisdiction (located in Croatia): one diocese; 48,800. They are under the jurisdiction of Ruthenian bishops elsewhere. Resumed communion with Rome in 1611; situated in Croatia, the Americas; liturgical language is Old Slavonic.

GREEK: Jurisdictions (located in Greece and Turkey): two exarchates; 2,350. Greeks resumed communion with Rome in 1829; situated in Greece, Asia Minor, Europe; liturgical language is Greek.

HUNGARIAN: Jurisdictions (located in Hungary): one diocese and one exarchate: 279,195. Descendants of Ruthenians who resumed communion with Rome in 1646; situated in Hungary, the rest of Europe, the Americas; liturgical languages are Greek, Hungarian, English.

ITALO-ALBANIAN: Jurisdictions (located in Italy): two dioceses, one abbacy; 61,597. Italo-Albanians were never separated from Rome; situated in Italy, Sicily, the Americas; liturgical languages are Greek, Italo-Albanian.

MELKITE (GREEK CATHOLIC-MELKITE): Jurisdictions (located in Syria, Lebanon, Jordan, Israel, U.S., Brazil, Venezuela, Canada, Australia, Mexico): patriarchate of Antioch (with patriarchal vicariates in Egypt, Sudan, Jerusalem, Iraq and Kuwait), 19 archdioceses and dioceses, one exarchate; 1,093,778. Melkites resumed communion with Rome during the time of the Crusades, but definitive reunion did not take place until early in the 18th century; situated in the Middle East, Asia, Africa, Europe, the Americas, Australia; liturgical languages are Greek, Arabic, English, Portuguese, Spanish.

ROMANIAN: Jurisdictions (located in Romania and U.S.): one archdiocese, five dioceses; 1,847,686 (includes one diocesan report dating from 1948). Romanians resumed communion with Rome in 1697; situated in Romania, the rest of Europe, the Americas; liturgical language is Modern Romanian.

RUSSIAN: Jurisdictions (located in Russia and China): two exarchates. Russians resumed communion with Rome about 1905; situated in Europe, the Americas, Australia, China; liturgical language is Old Slavonic.

RUTHENIAN, or CARPATHO-RUSSIAN (Rusin): Jurisdictions (located in Ukraine and the U.S.): one archdiocese, four dioceses; 510,255. Ruthenians resumed communion with Rome in the Union of Brest-Litovek, 1596, and the Union of Uzhorod, Apr. 24, 1646; situated in Europe, the Americas, Australia; liturgical languages are Old Slavonic, English.

SLOVAK: Jurisdictions (located in Slovakia and Canada): two dioceses; 430,000.

UKRAINIAN, or GALICIAN RUTHENIAN: Jurisdictions (located in Ukraine, Poland, the U.S., Canada, England, Australia, Germany, France, Brazil, Argentina): major archbishopric of Lviv, two metropolitans, 12 dioceses, three apostolic exarchates; 4,888,491. Ukrainians resumed communion with Rome about 1595; situated in Europe, the Americas, Australasia; liturgical languages are Old Slavonic and Ukrainian.

Chaldean

This rite, listed as separate and distinct by the Congregation for the Oriental Churches, was derived from the Antiochene Rite. The churches of this rite are:

CHALDEAN: Jurisdictions (located in Iraq, Iran, Lebanon, Egypt, Syria, Turkey, U.S.): patriarchate of Babylonia, 19 archdioceses and dioceses; 633,220 (some figures date from 1989). There is a patriarchal exarch for Jerusalem. Chaldeans, descendants of the Nestorians, resumed communion with Rome in 1692; situated throughout the Middle East, in Europe, Africa, the Americas; liturgical languages are Syriac, Arabic.

SYRO-MALABAR: Jurisdictions (located in India): major archbishopric of Ernakulam-Angamaly (1993), one archdiocese, 19 dioceses; 3,036,193. Descended from the St. Thomas Christians of India; liturgical languages are Syriac and Malayalam.

EASTERN JURISDICTIONS

For centuries Eastern Churches were identifiable with a limited number of nationality and language groups in certain countries of the Middle East, Eastern Europe, Asia and Africa. The persecution of religion in the former Soviet Union since 1917 and in communist-controlled countries for more than 40 years following World War II — in addition to decimating and destroying the Church in those places — resulted in the emigration of many Eastern-Rite Catholics from their homelands. This forced emigration, together with voluntary emigration, has led to the spread of Eastern Churches to many other countries.

Europe

(Bishop Krikor Ghabroyan, of the Armenian Eparchy of Sainte-Croix-de-Paris, France, is apostolic visitor for Armenian Catholics in Western Europe who do not have their own bishop. Bishop Youssef Ibrahim Sarraf of Cairo of the Chaldeans is apostolic visitor for Chaldeans in Europe. Bishop Joseph Khoury, an official of the Congregation for the Oriental Churches, is apostolic visitor for Maronites in Western and Northern Europe.)

ALBANIA: Byzantine Rite, apostolic administration.

ARMENIA: Armenian Rite, ordinariate (for Armenians of Eastern Europe).

AUSTRIA: Byzantine Rite, ordinariate.

BULGARIA: Byzantine Rite (Bulgarians), apostolic exarchate.

CROATIA: Byzantine Rite, eparchy.

FRANCE: Byzantine Rite (Ukrainians), apostolic exarchate.

Armenian Rite, eparchy (1986).

Ordinariate for all other Eastern-Rite Catholics.

GERMANY: Byzantine Rite (Ukrainians), apostolic exarchate.

GREAT BRITAIN: Byzantine Rite (Ukrainians), apostolic exarchate.

GREECE: Byzantine Rite, apostolic exarchate.

Armenian Rite, ordinariate.

HUNGARY: Byzantine Rite (Hungarians), eparchy, apostolic exarchate.

ITALY: Byzantine Rite (Italo-Albanians), two eparchies, one abbacy.

POLAND: Byzantine Rite (Ukrainian), eparchy.

Ordinariate for all other Eastern-Rite Catholics.

ROMANIA: Byzantine Rite (Romanians), metropolitan, four eparchies.

Armenian Rite, ordinariate.

RUSSIA: Byzantine Rite (Russians), apostolic exarchate (for Byzantine-rite Catholics in Moscow).

SLOVAKIA (Czech and Slovak Federative Republic): Byzantine Rite (Slovakians and other Byzantine-Rite Catholics), eparchy.

UKRAINE: Armenian Rite, archeparchy.

Byzantine Rite (Ruthenians), eparchy; (Ukrainians), major archbishopric, one eparchy.

Asia

CHINA: Byzantine Rite (Russians), apostolic exarchate.

CYPRUS: Antiochene Rite (Maronites), archeparchy.

INDIA: Antiochene Rite (Malankarese), metropolitan see, two eparchies.

Chaldean Rite (Syro-Malabarese), major archbishopric (1993), one metropolitan see, 19 eparchies.

IRAN: Chaldean Rite (Chaldeans), two metropolitan sees, one archeparchy, one eparchy.

Armenian Rite, eparchy.

IRAQ: Antiochene Rite (Syrians), two archeparchies.

Byzantine Rite (Greek-Melkites), patriarchal exarchate.

Chaldean Rite (Chaldeans), patriarchate, two metropolitan sees, eight archeparchies and eparchies.

Armenian Rite, archeparchy.

ISRAEL (includes Jerusalem): Antiochene Rite (Syrians), patriarchal vicariate; (Maronites), patriarchal vicariate.

Byzantine Rite (Greek-Melkites), archeparchy, patriarchal exarchate.

Chaldean Rite (Chaldeans), patriarchal exarchate.

Armenian Rite, patriarchal exarchate.

JORDAN: Byzantine Rite (Greek-Melkites), archeparchy.

KUWAIT: Byzantine Rite (Greek-Melkites), patriarchal vicariate.

LEBANON: Antiochene Rite (Maronites), patriarchate, ten archeparchies and eparchies; (Syrians), patriarchate.

Byzantine Rite (Greek-Melkites), two metropolitan and five archeparchal sees.

Chaldean Rite (Chaldeans), eparchy.

Armenian Rite, patriarchate, eparchy.

SYRIA: Antiochene Rite (Maronites), two archeparchies, one eparchy; (Syrians), two metropolitan and two archeparchal sees.

Byzantine Rite (Greek-Melkites), patriarchate, four metropolitan sees, one archeparchy.

Chaldean Rite (Chaldeans), eparchy.

Armenian Rite, archeparchy, eparchy, patriarchal exarchate.

TURKEY (Europe and Asia): Antiochene Rite (Syrians), patriarchal exarchate.

Byzantine Rite (Greeks), apostolic exarchate.

Chaldean Rite (Chaldeans), one archeparchy.

Armenian Rite, archeparchy.

Oceania

AUSTRALIA: Byzantine Rite (Ukrainians), eparchy; (Greek-Melkites), eparchy (1987).

Antiochene Rite (Maronites), eparchy.

Africa

EGYPT: Alexandrian Rite (Copts), patriarchate, five eparchies.

Antiochene Rite (Maronites), eparchy; (Syrians), eparchy.

Byzantine Rite (Greek-Melkites), patriarchal exarchate.

Chaldean Rite (Chaldeans), eparchy.

Armenian Rite, eparchy.

ETHIOPIA: Alexandrian Rite (Ethiopians), metropolitan see, two eparchies.

SUDAN: Byzantine Rite (Greek-Melkites), patriarchal vicariate.

North America

CANADA: Byzantine Rite (Ukrainians), one metropolitan, four eparchies; (Slovaks), eparchy; (Greek-Melkites), eparchy.

Armenian Rite, apostolic exarchate for Canada and the U.S. (New York is see city).

Antiochene Rite (Maronites), eparchy.

UNITED STATES: Antiochene Rite (Maronites), eparchy.

Byzantine Rite (Ukrainians), one metropolitan see, three eparchies; (Ruthenians), one metropolitan see, three eparchies; (Greek-Melkites), eparchy; (Romanians), eparchy; (Belarussians), apostolic visitator.

Armenian Rite, apostolic exarchate for Canada and U.S. (New York is see city).

Chaldean Rite, eparchy.

Other Eastern-Rite Catholics are under the jurisdiction of local Roman-Rite bishops. (See Eastern-Rite Catholics in the United States.)

MEXICO: Byzantine Rite (Greek-Melkites), eparchy.

South America

Armenian-Rite Catholics in Latin America (including Mexico and excluding Argentina) are under the jurisdiction of an apostolic exarchate (see city, Buenos Aires, Argentina).

ARGENTINA: Byzantine Rite (Ukrainians), eparchy.

Antiochene Rite (Maronites), eparchy.

Armenian Rite, eparchy.

Ordinariate for all other Eastern-Rite Catholics.

BRAZIL: Antiochene Rite (Maronites), eparchy.

Byzantine Rite (Greek-Melkites), eparchy; (Ukrainians), eparchy.

Ordinariate for all other Eastern-Rite Catholics.

VENEZUELA: Byzantine Rite (Greek-Melkites) apostolic exarchate.

SYNODS, ASSEMBLIES

These assemblies are collegial bodies which have pastoral authority over members of the Eastern Catholic Churches. (Canons 102-113, 152-153, 322 of Oriental Code of Canon Law.)

Patriarchal Synods: Copts: Stephanos II Ghattas, C.M., patriarch of Alexandria of the Copts.

Melkites: Maximos V Hakim, patriarch of Antioch of the Greek Catholics-Melkites.

Syrians: Ignace Antoine II Hayek, patriarch of Antioch of the Syrians.

Maronites: Nasrallah Pierre Sfeir, patriarch of Antioch of the Maronites.

Chaldeans: Raphael I Bidawid, patriarch of Babylonia of the Chaldeans.

Armenians: Jean Pierre XVIII Kasparian, patriarch of Cilicia of the Armenians.

Major Archiepiscopal Synods: The Synod of the Ukrainian Catholic Church (raised to major archiepiscopal status Dec. 23, 1963): Cardinal Myroslav Ivan Lubachivsky, major archbishop of Lviv of the Ukrainians, president.

The Synod of the Syro-Malabar Church (raised to major archiepiscopal status, Jan. 29, 1993): Archbishop Abraham Kattumana, pontifical delegate, president.

Assemblies, Conferences: Assembly of the Catholic Hierarchy of Egypt (Dec. 5, 1983): Stephanos II Ghattas, C.M., patriarch of Alexandria of the Copts, president.

Assembly of Catholic Patriarchs and Bishops of Lebanon: Nasrallah Pierre Sfeir, patriarch of Antioch of the Maronites, president.

Assembly of Ordinaries of the Syrian Arab Republic: Maximos V Hakim, patriarch of Antioch of the Greek Catholics-Melkites, president.

Interritual Union of the Bishops of Iraq: Raphael I Bidawid, patriarch of Babylonia of the Chaldeans, president.

Iranian Episcopal Conference (Aug. 11, 1977): Most Rev. Youhannan Semaan Issayi, metropolitan of Teheran of the Chaldeans, president.

Episcopal Conference of Turkey (Nov. 30, 1987): Hovhannes Tcholakian, archbishop of Istanbul of the Armenians, president.

EASTERN CATHOLIC CHURCHES IN U.S.

(Statistics, from the *1993 Annuario Pontificio,* unless noted otherwise, are membership figures reported by Eastern-Rite jurisdictions. Additional Eastern-Rite Catholics are included in statistics for Roman-Rite dioceses.)

Byzantine Tradition

Ukrainians: There were 144,897 reported in four jurisdictions in the U.S.: the metropolitan see of Philadelphia (1924, metropolitan 1958) and the suffragan sees of Stamford, Conn. (1956), St. Nicholas of Chicago (1961) and St. Josaphat in Parma (1983).

Ruthenians: There were 210,255 reported in four jurisdictions in the U.S.: the metropolitan see of Pittsburgh (est. 1924 at Pittsburgh; metropolitan and transferred to Munhall, 1969; transferred to Pittsburgh, 1977) and the suffragan sees of Passaic, N.J. (1963), Parma, Ohio (1969) and Van Nuys, Calif. (1981). Hungarian and Croatian Byzantine Catholics in the U.S. are also under the jurisdiction of Ruthenian-Rite bishops.

Melkites (Greek Catholics-Melkites): There were 27,000 reported under the jurisdiction of the Melkite eparchy of Newton, Mass. (established as an exarchate, 1965; eparchy, 1976).

Romanians: There were 5,200 reported in 15 Romanian Catholic Byzantine Rite parishes in the U.S., under the jurisdiction of the Romanian eparchy of St. George Martyr, Canton, Ohio (established as an exarchate, 1982; eparchy, 1987).

Belarussians: Have one parish in the U.S. — Christ the Redeemer, Chicago, Ill.

Russians: Have parishes in California (St. Andrew, El Segundo, and Our Lady of Fatima Center, San Francisco); New York (St. Michael's

Chapel of St. Patrick's Old Cathedral). They are under the jurisdiction of local Roman-Rite bishops.

Alexandrian Tradition

Copts: Have a Catholic Chapel — Resurrection, in Brooklyn, N.Y.

Antiochene Tradition

Maronites: There were 53,222 reported under the jurisdiction of the eparchy of St. Maron, Brooklyn (established at Detroit as an exarchate, 1966; eparchy, 1972; transferred to Brooklyn, 1977).

Malankarese: Have a mission in Chicago.

Armenian Tradition

An apostolic exarchate for Canada and the United States (see city, New York) was established July 3, 1981; 39,000 in both countries.

Chaldean Tradition

Chaldeans: There were 60,000 reported under the jurisdiction of the eparchy of St. Thomas Apostle of Detroit (established as an exarchate, 1982; eparchy, 1986).

Syro-Malabarese: Have mission churches in Chicago and several other cities.

BYZANTINE DIVINE LITURGY

The Divine Liturgy in all rites is based on the consecration of bread and wine by the narration-reactualization of the actions of Christ at the Last Supper. Aside from this fundamental usage, there are differences between the Roman (Latin) Rite and Eastern Rites, and among the Eastern Rites themselves. Following is a general description of the Byzantine Divine Liturgy which is in widest use in the Eastern-Rite Churches.

In the Byzantine, as in all Eastern Rites, the bread and wine are prepared at the start of the Liturgy. The priest does this in a little niche or at a table in the sanctuary. Taking a round loaf of leavened bread stamped with religious symbols, he cuts out a square host and other particles while reciting verses expressing the symbolism of the action. When the bread and wine are ready, he says a prayer of offering and incenses the oblations, the altar, the icons and the people.

Liturgy of the Catechumens: At the altar a litany for all classes of people is sung by the priest. The congregation answers, "Lord, have mercy."

The Little Entrance comes next. In procession, the priest leaves the sanctuary carrying the Book of the Gospels, and then returns. He sings prayers especially selected for the day and the feast. These are followed by the solemn singing of the prayer, "Holy God, Holy Mighty One, Holy Immortal One."

The Epistle follows. The Gospel is sung or read by the priest facing the people at the middle door of the sanctuary.

An interruption after the Liturgy of the Catechumens, formerly an instructional period for those learning the faith, is clearly marked. Catechumens, if present, are dismissed with a prayer. Following this are a prayer and litany for the faithful.

Great Entrance: The Great Entrance or solemn Offertory Procession then takes place. The priest first says a long silent prayer for himself, in preparation for the great act to come. Again he incenses the oblations, the altar, the icons and people. He goes to the table on the gospel side for the veil-covered paten and chalice. When he arrives back at the sanctuary door, he announces the intention of the Mass in the prayer: "May the Lord God remember all of you in his kingdom, now and forever."

After another litany, the congregation recites the Nicene Creed.

Consecration: The most solemn portion of the sacrifice is introduced by the preface, which is very much like the preface of the Roman Rite. At the beginning of the last phrase, the priest raises his voice to introduce the singing of the Sanctus. During the singing he reads the introduction to the words of consecration.

The words of consecration are sung aloud, and the people sing "Amen" to both consecrations. As the priest raises the Sacred Species in solemn offering, he sings: "Thine of Thine Own we offer unto Thee in behalf of all and for all."

A prayer to the Holy Spirit is followed by the commemorations, in which special mention is made of the all-holy, most blessed and glorious Lady, the Mother of God and ever-Virgin Mary. The dead are remembered and then the living.

Holy Communion: A final litany for spiritual gifts precedes the Our Father. The Sacred Body and Blood are elevated with the words, "Holy Things for the Holy." The Host is then broken and commingled with the Precious Blood. The priest recites preparatory prayers for Holy Communion, consumes the Sacred Species, and distributes Holy Communion to the people under the forms of both bread and wine. During this time a communion verse is sung by the choir or congregation.

The Liturgy closes quickly after this. The consecrated Species of bread and wine are removed to the side table to be consumed later by the priest. A prayer of thanksgiving is recited, a prayer for all the people is said in front of the icon of Christ, a blessing is invoked upon all, and the people are dismissed.

BYZANTINE CALENDAR

The Byzantine-Rite calendar has many distinctive features of its own, although it shares common elements with the Roman-Rite calendar — e.g., general purpose, commemoration of the mysteries of faith and of the saints, identical dates for some feasts. Among the distinctive things are the following.

The liturgical year begins on Sept. 1, the **Day of Indiction,** in contrast with the Latin or Roman start on the First Sunday of Advent late in November or early in December. The Advent season begins on Dec. 10.

Cycles of the Year

As in the Roman usage, the dating of feasts follows the Gregorian Calendar. Formerly, until well into this century, the Julian Calendar was used. (The Julian Calendar, which is now about 13 days late, is still used by some Eastern-Rite Churches.)

The year has several cycles, which include proper seasons, the feasts of saints, and series of New Testament readings. All of these elements of worship are contained in liturgical books of the rite.

The ecclesiastical calendar, called the **Menologion,** explains the nature of feasts, other observances and matters pertaining to the liturgy for each day of the year. In some cases, its contents include the lives of saints and the history and meaning of feasts.

The Divine Liturgy (Mass) and Divine Office for the proper of the saints, fixed feasts, and the Christmas season are contained in the **Menaion.** The **Triodion** covers the pre-Lenten season of preparation for Easter; Lent begins two days before the Ash Wednesday observance of the Roman Rite. The **Pentecostarion** contains the liturgical services from Easter to the Sunday of All Saints, the first after Pentecost. The **Evangelion** and **Apostolos** are books in which the Gospels, and Acts of the Apostles and the Epistles, respectively, are arranged according to the order of their reading in the Divine Liturgy and Divine Office throughout the year.

The cyclic progression of liturgical music throughout the year, in successive and repetitive periods of eight weeks, is governed by the **Oktoechos,** the Book of Eight Tones.

Sunday Names

Many Sundays are named after the subject of the Gospel read in the Mass of the day or after the name of a feast falling on the day — e.g., Sunday of the Publican and Pharisee, of the Prodigal Son, of the Samaritan Woman, of St. Thomas the Apostle, of the Fore-Fathers (Old Testament Patriarchs). Other Sundays are named in the same manner as in the Roman calendar — e.g., numbered Sundays of Lent and after Pentecost.

Holy Days

The calendar lists about 28 holy days. Many of the major holy days coincide with those of the Roman calendar, but the feast of the Immaculate Conception is observed on Dec. 9 instead of Dec. 8, and the feast of All Saints falls on the Sunday after Pentecost rather than on Nov. 1. Instead of a single All Souls' Day, there are five All Souls' Saturdays.

According to regulations in effect in the Byzantine-Rite (Ruthenian) Archeparchy of Pittsburgh and its suffragan sees of Passaic, Parma and Van Nuys, holy days are obligatory, solemn and simple, and attendance at the Divine Liturgy is required on five obligatory days — the feasts of the Epiphany, the Ascension, Sts. Peter and Paul, the Assumption of the Blessed Virgin Mary, and Christmas. Although attendance at the liturgy is not obligatory on 15

solemn and seven simple holy days, it is recommended.

In the Byzantine-Rite (Ukrainian) Archeparchy of Philadelphia and its suffragan sees of St. Josaphat in Parma, St. Nicholas (Chicago) and Stamford, the obligatory feasts are the Circumcision, Epiphany, Annunciation, Easter, Ascension, Pentecost, Dormition (Assumption of Mary), Immaculate Conception and Christmas.

Lent

The first day of Lent — the Monday before Ash Wednesday of the Roman Rite — and Good Friday are days of strict abstinence for persons in the age bracket of obligation. No meat, eggs, or dairy products may be eaten on these days.

All persons over the age of 14 must abstain from meat on Fridays during Lent, Holy Saturday, and the vigils of the feasts of Christmas and Epiphany; abstinence is urged, but is not obligatory, on Wednesdays of Lent. The abstinence obligation is not in force on certain "free" or "privileged" Fridays.

Synaxis

An observance without a counterpart in the Roman calendar is the synaxis. This is a commemoration, on the day following a feast, of persons involved with the occasion for the feast — e.g., Sept. 9, the day following the feast of the Nativity of the Blessed Virgin Mary, is the Synaxis of Joachim and Anna, her parents.

Holy Week

In the Byzantine Rite, Lent is liturgically concluded with the Saturday of Lazarus, the day before Palm Sunday, which commemorates the raising of Lazarus from the dead.

On the following Monday, Tuesday and Wednesday, the Liturgy of the Presanctified is prescribed.

On Holy Thursday, the Liturgy of St. Basil the Great is celebrated together with Vespers.

The Divine Liturgy is not celebrated on Good Friday.

On Holy Saturday, the Liturgy of St. Basil the Great is celebrated along with Vespers.

BYZANTINE FEATURES

Art: Named for the empire in which it developed, Byzantine art is a unique blend of imperial Roman and classic Hellenic culture with Christian inspiration. The art of the Greek Middle Ages, it reached a peak of development in the 10th or 11th century. Characteristic of its products, particularly in mosaic and painting, are majesty, dignity, refinement and grace. Its sacred paintings, called icons, are reverenced highly in all Eastern Rites.

Church Building: The classical model of Byzantine church architecture is the Church of the Holy Wisdom (Hagia Sophia), built in Constantinople in the first half of the sixth century and still standing. The square structure, extended in some cases in the form of a cross, is topped by a distinctive onion-shaped dome and surmounted by a triple-bar cross. The altar is at the eastern end of building, where the wall bellies out to form an apse. The altar and sanctuary are separated from the body of the church by a fixed or movable screen, the iconostas, to which icons or sacred pictures are attached (see below).

Clergy: The Byzantine Rite has married as well as celibate priests. In places other than the U.S., where married candidates have not been accepted for ordination since about 1929, men already married can be ordained to the diaconate and priesthood and can continue in marriage after ordination. Celibate deacons and priests cannot marry after ordination; neither can a married priest remarry after the death of his wife. Bishops must be unmarried.

Iconostas: A large screen decorated with sacred pictures or icons which separates the sanctuary from the nave of a church; its equivalent in the Roman Rite, for thus separating the sanctuary from the nave, is an altar rail.

An iconostas has three doors through which the sacred ministers enter the sanctuary during the Divine Liturgy: smaller (north and south) Deacons' Doors and a large central Royal Door.

The Deacons' Doors usually feature the icons of Sts. Gabriel and Michael; the Royal Door, the icons of the Evangelists — Matthew, Mark, Luke and John. To the right and left of the Royal Door are the icons of Christ the Teacher and of the Blessed Virgin Mary with the Infant Jesus. To the extreme right and left are the icons of the patron of the church and St. John the Baptist (or St. Nicholas of Myra).

Immediately above the Royal Door is a picture of the Last Supper. To the right are six icons depicting the major feasts of Christ, and to the left are six icons portraying the major feasts of the Blessed Virgin Mary. Above the picture of the Last Supper is a large icon of Christ the King.

Some icon screens also have pictures of the 12 Apostles and the major Old Testament prophets surmounted by a crucifixion scene.

Liturgical Language: In line with Eastern tradition, Byzantine practice has favored the use of the language of the people in the liturgy. Two great advocates of the practice were Sts. Cyril and Methodius, apostles of the Slavs, who devised the Cyrillic alphabet and pioneered the adoption of Slavonic in the liturgy.

Sacraments: Baptism is administered by immersion, and confirmation is conferred at the same time. The Eucharist is administered by intinction, i.e., by giving the communicant a piece of consecrated leavened bread which has been dipped into the consecrated wine. When giving absolution in the sacrament of penance, the priest holds his stole over the head of the penitent. Distinctive marriage ceremonies include the crowning of the bride and groom. Ceremonies for anointing the sick closely resemble those of the Roman Rite. Holy orders are conferred by a bishop.

Sign of the Cross: The sign of the cross in conjunction with a deep bow expresses reverence for the presence of Christ in the Blessed Sacrament. (See also entry in Glossary.)

VESTMENTS, APPURTENANCES

Sticharion: A long white garment of linen or silk with wide sleeves and decorated with embroidery; formerly the vestment for clerics in minor orders, acolytes, lectors, chanters, and subdeacons; symbolic of purity.

Epitrachelion: A stole with ends sewn together, having a loop through which the head is passed; its several crosses symbolize priestly duties.

Zone: A narrow clasped belt made of the same material as the epitrachelion; symbolic of the wisdom of the priest, his strength against enemies of the Church and his willingness to perform holy duties.

Epimanikia: Ornamental cuffs; the right cuff symbolizing strength, the left, patience and good will.

Phelonion: An ample cape, long in the back and sides and cut away in front; symbolic of the higher gifts of the Holy Spirit.

Antimension: A silk or linen cloth laid on the altar for the Liturgy; it may be decorated with a picture of the burial of Christ and the instruments of his passion; the relics of martyrs are sewn into the front border.

Eileton: A linen cloth which corresponds to the Roman-Rite corporal.

Poterion: A chalice or cup which holds the wine and Precious Blood.

Diskos: A shallow plate, which may be elevated on a small stand, corresponding to the Roman-Rite paten.

Asteriskos: Made of two curved bands of gold or silver which cross each other to form a double arch; a star depends from the junction, which forms a cross; it is placed over the diskos holding the consecrated bread and is covered with a veil.

Veils: Three are used, one to cover the poterion, the second to cover the diskos, and the third to cover both.

Spoon: Used in administering Holy Communion by intinction; consecrated leavened bread is dipped into consecrated wine and spooned onto the tongue of the communicant.

Lance: A metal knife used for cutting up the bread to be consecrated during the Liturgy.

SEPARATED EASTERN CHURCHES

ORTHODOX

Orthodox Churches are churches of Eastern rites which were in communion with the Holy See until the Schism of 1054. Although they withdrew from communion at that time, they retained, and still retain, essential features of the Mother Churches from which they derived: matters of faith and morals, valid orders and sacraments, liturgy, patriarchal jurisdiction and general discipline. Along with the lack of communion with the Holy See, the Orthodox Churches recognize only the first seven ecumenical councils.

Like their Catholic counterparts, Orthodox Churches are organized in jurisdictions under patriarchs. The patriarchs are the heads of approximately 15 autocephalic and several other autonomous jurisdictions organized along lines of nationality and/or language.

The Ecumenical Patriarch of Constantinople has the primacy of honor among his equal patriarchs but his actual jurisdiction is limited to his own patriarchate. As the spiritual head of worldwide Orthodoxy, he keeps the book of the Holy Canons of the Autocephalous Churches, in which recognized Orthodox Churches are registered, and has the right to call Pan-Orthodox assemblies.

Top-level relations between the Churches have improved in recent years through the efforts of Ecumenical Patriarch Athenagoras I, John XXIII, Paul VI and Patriarch Dimitrios I. Pope Paul met with Athenagoras three times before the latter's death in 1972. The most significant action of both spiritual leaders was their mutual nullification of excommunications imposed by the two Churches on each other in 1054. Development of better relations with the Orthodox has been a priority of John Paul II since the beginning of his pontificate. Both he and Orthodox Ecumenical Patriarch Bartholomeos have made known their commitment to better relations, despite contentions between Eastern Catholic and Orthodox Churches over charges of proselytism and rival property claims in places liberated from anti-religious communist control in the recent past.

The largest Orthodox body in the western hemisphere is the Greek Orthodox Archdiocese of North and South America consisting of the Archdiocese of New York, nine dioceses in the U.S., and one diocese each in Canada and South America; it is headed by Archbishop Iakovos and has an estimated membership of 1.9 million. The second largest is the Orthodox Church in America, with approximately one million members; it was given independent status by the Patriarchate of Moscow May 18, 1970, against the will of Athenagoras I who refused to register it in the book of the Holy Canons of Autocephalous Churches. An additional 650,000 or more Orthodox belong to smaller national and language jurisdictions.

Heads of orthodox jurisdictions in this hemisphere hold membership in the Standing Conference of Canonical Orthodox Bishops in the Americas.

Jurisdictions

The principal jurisdictions of the Greek, Russian and other Orthodox Churches are as follows.

Greek: Patriarchate of Constantinople, with jurisdiction in Turkey, Crete, the Dodecanese, Western Europe, the Americas, Australia.

Patriarchate of Alexandria, with jurisdiction in Egypt and the rest of Africa; there is also a native African Orthodox Church in Kenya and Uganda.

Patriarchate of Antioch (Melkites or Syrian Orthodox), with jurisdiction in Syria, Lebanon, Iraq, Australasia, the Americas; Syrian or Arabic, in place of Greek, is the liturgical language.

Patriarchate of Jerusalem, with jurisdiction in Israel and Jordan.

Churches of Greece, Cyprus and Sinai are autocephalic but maintain relations with their fellow Orthodox.

Russian: Patriarchate of Moscow with jurisdiction centered in the former Soviet Union.

Other: Patriarchate of Serbia, with jurisdiction in Yugoslavia, Western Europe, the Americas, Australasia.

Patriarchates of Rumania and Bulgaria.

Katholikate of Georgia, the Soviet Union.

Belarussians and Ukrainian Byzantines.

Churches of Albania, China, Czechoslovakia, Estonia, Finland, Hungary, Japan, Latvia, Lithuania, Poland.

Other minor communities in various places; e.g., Korea, the U.S., Carpatho-Russia.

The Division of Archives and Statistics of the Eastern Orthodox World Foundation reported a 1970 estimate of more than 200 million Orthodox Church members throughout the world. Other sources estimate the total to be approximately 125 million.

Conference of Orthodox Bishops

The Standing Conference of Canonical Orthodox Bishops in the Americas was established in 1960 to achieve cooperation among the various Orthodox jurisdictions in the Americas. Chairman, Archbishop Iakovos; Ecumenical Officer, Rev. Dr. Milton B. Efthimiou. Ecumenical office: 8-10 East 79th St., New York, N.Y. 10021.

Member churches of the conference are the: Albanian Orthodox Diocese of America (Ecumenical Patriarchate), American Carpatho-Russian Orthodox Greek Catholic Diocese in the U.S.A. (Ecumenical Patriarchate), Antiochian Orthodox Christian Archdiocese of North America, Bulgarian Eastern Orthodox Church, Greek Orthodox Archdiocese of North and South America (Ecumenical Patriarchate), Orthodox Church in America, Romanian Orthodox Missionary Archdiocese in America and Canada, Serbian Orthodox Church in the United States of America and Canada, Ukrainian Orthodox Church in the United States (Ecumenical Patriarchate), Ukrainian Orthodox Church of Canada (Ecumenical Patriarchate).

ANCIENT CHURCHES OF THE EAST

Ancient Churches of the East, which are distinct from Orthodox Churches, were the subject of an article by Gerard Daucourt published in the Feb. 16, 1987, English edition of L'Osservatore Romano. Following is an excerpt.

By Ancient Churches of the East one means: the Assyrian Oriental Church (formerly called Nestorian), the Armenian Church, the Coptic Church, the Ethiopian Church, the Syrian Church (sometimes called Syro-Jacobite) and the Syrian Church of India.

After the Council of Ephesus (431), the Assyrian Oriental Church did not maintain communion with the rest of the Christian world. For reasons as much and perhaps more political than doctrinal, it did not accept the Council's teaching (that Mary is the Mother of God, in opposition to the opinion of Nestorius; see Nestorianism. For this reason, the Assyrian Oriental Church came to be called Nestorian.) It is well known that in the 16th century a great segment of the faithful of this Church entered into communion with the See of Rome and constitutes today, among the Oriental Catholic Churches, the Chaldean Patriarchate.

The Patriarch of the Assyrian Oriental Church, His Holiness Mar Denkha IV, in the course of his visit to the Holy Father and to the Church of Rome of 7 to 9 November, 1984, requested that people stop using the term "Nestorian" to designate his Church and expressed the desire that a declaration made jointly by the Pope of Rome and himself may one day serve to express the common faith of the two Churches in Jesus Christ, Son of God incarnate, born of the Virgin Mary. The labours of Catholic historians and theologians have, moreover, already contributed to showing that such a declaration would be possible.

The other Ancient Churches of the East for a long time have been designated by the term "Monophysite Churches" (see Monophysitism). It is regrettable to find this name still employed sometimes in certain publications, since already in 1951, in the encyclical *Sempiternus Rex,* on the occasion of the 15th centenary of the Council of Chalcedon, Pius XII declared with regard to the Christians of these Churches: "They depart from the right way only in terminology, when they expound the doctrine of the Incarnation of the Lord. This may be deduced from their liturgical and theological books."

In this same encyclical, Pius XII expressed the view that the separation at the doctrinal level came about "above all, through a certain ambiguity of terminology that occurred at the beginning."

Since then, two important declarations have been arrived at in line with the ecumenical stance taken by the Church at the Second Vatican Council and the labors of the theologians (particularly in the framework of the Foundation "Pro Oriente" of Vienna). One was signed by Pope Paul VI and Coptic Patriarch Shenouda III on 10 May, 1973, and the other by Pope John Paul II and the Syrian Patriarch Ignace Zakka I Iwas, on 23 June, 1984. In both of these texts, the hierarchies of the respective Churches confess one and the same faith in the mystery of the Word Incarnate. After such declarations, it is no longer possible to speak in general terms of the "Monophysite" Churches.

The Armenian Church has communicants in the Soviet Union, the Middle and Far East, the Americas. The Coptic Church has communicants in the Middle East, the Americas, India.

Members of the Assyrian Oriental Church are scattered throughout the world.

It is estimated that there are approximately 10 million or more members of these other Eastern Churches throughout the world. For various reasons, a more accurate determination is not possible.

EASTERN ECUMENISM

The Second Vatican Council, in the *Decree on Eastern Catholic Churches,* pointed out the special role they have to play "in promoting the unity of all Christians, particularly Easterners." The document also stated in part as follows.

The Eastern Churches in communion with the Apostolic See of Rome have a special role to play in promoting the unity of all Christians, particularly Easterners, according to the principles of this sacred Synod's *Decree on Ecumenism* first of all by prayer, then by the example of their lives, by religious fidelity to ancient Eastern traditions, by greater mutual knowledge, by collaboration, and by a brotherly regard for objects and attitudes (No. 24).

If any separated Eastern Christian should, under the guidance of grace of the Holy Spirit, join himself to Catholic unity, no more should be required of him than what a simple profession of the Catholic faith demands. A valid priesthood is preserved among Eastern clerics. Hence, upon joining themselves to the unity of the Catholic Church, Eastern clerics are permitted to exercise the orders they possess, in accordance with the regulations established by the competent authority (No. 25).

Divine Law forbids any common worship (*communicatio in sacris*) which would damage the unity of the Church, or involve formal acceptance of falsehood or the danger of deviation in the faith, of scandal, or of indifferentism. At the same time, pastoral experience clearly shows that with respect to our Eastern brethren there should and can be taken into consideration various circumstances affecting individuals, wherein the unity of the Church is not jeopardized nor are intolerable risks involved, but in which salvation itself and the spiritual profit of souls are urgently at issue.

Hence, in view of special circumstances of time, place, and personage, the Catholic Church has often adopted and now adopts a milder policy, offering to all the means of salvation and an example of charity among Christians through participation in the sacraments and in other sacred functions and objects. With these considerations in mind, and "lest because of the harshness of our judgment we prove an obstacle to those seeking salvation," and in order to promote closer union with the Eastern Churches separated from us, this sacred Synod lays down the following policy:

In view of the principles recalled above, Eastern Christians who are separated in good faith from the Catholic Church, if they ask of their own accord and have the right dispositions, may be granted the sacraments of penance, the Eucharist, and the anointing of the sick. Furthermore, Catholics may ask for these same sacraments from those non-Catholic ministers whose Churches possess valid sacraments, as often as necessity or a genuine spiritual benefit recommends such a course of action, and when access to a Catholic priest is physically or morally impossible (Nos. 26, 27).

Again, in view of these very same principles, Catholics may for a just cause join with their separated Eastern brethren in sacred functions, things, and places (No. 28).

This more lenient policy with regard to common worship involving Catholics and their brethren of the separated Eastern Churches is entrusted to the care and execution of the local Ordinaries so that, by taking counsel among themselves and, if circumstances warrant, after consultation also with the Ordinaries of the separated Churches, they may govern relations between Christians by timely and effective rules and regulations.

EASTERN ECUMENICAL DEVELOPMENTS

Pledge of Cooperation: At the conclusion Jan. 25, 1993, of the Week of Prayer for Christian Unity, Pope John Paul pledged increased cooperation with Orthodox Christians, especially in Eastern Europe. He said: "It is the firm intention of the Catholic Church to make every possible effort so that, with the barriers of misunderstanding knocked down and the stumbling blocks present on the way of dialogue, the whole body of Christ before long can breathe with the 'two lungs' of the church communities of East and West totally reconciled."

Need for Trust: While Catholic-Orthodox relations remain strained on upper levels over charges of proselytism by Catholics and efforts by Catholics to reclaim property expropriated under communist rule, members of both churches on local levels were reported to be cooperating in ventures of mutual concern. They agreed, for example, that disputes had not prevented their communicants from working together to rebuild the former U.S.S.R.'s long-suppressed Christian culture and spiritual life. Paulist Father Ronald G. Roberson, a former staff member of the Pontifical Council for Promoting Christian Unity, spoke Mar. 18, 1993, about the need for mutual trust and reconciliation among Catholics and Orthodox.

Visit of Ethiopian Orthodox Patriarch: "Your presence in Rome reminds us of that long tradition of Ethiopian pilgrims who, since the Middle Ages, have come to Rome in great numbers to venerate the tomb of the Prince of the Apostles," said Pope John Paul as he welcomed Patriarch Abuna Paulos in June, 1993.

"The deep communion that exists between us," the Holy Father continued, "despite the vicissitudes of history, is rooted in the fundamental realities of our Christian faith. For we share the faith handed down from the Apostles, as also the same sacraments and the same ministry rooted in the apostolic succession.

All this should spur us on to seek new and suitable ways of fostering the rediscovery of our communion in the concrete daily life of the faithful of our two Churches.

"We must do all we can to heal the memories of misunderstanding in the past, and to promote new attitudes based on forgiveness, mutual esteem and respect."

Balamand Document: In an important step forward in Catholic-Orthodox relations, theologians from both churches approved a document intended to defuse pastoral tension over the issue of alleged proselytism by Roman Catholics. Specifically, they agreed that it was unacceptable to seek conversions from among each other's faithful. Discussions dealt with theological and practical questions posed by the existence and pastoral activity of Eastern Catholic churches following their liberation from communist oppression. The document was produced during the seventh plenary session of the International Catholic-Orthodox Commission for Theological Dialogue held June 17 to 24 in Balamand, Lebanon. Attention was focused on a working paper entitled "Uniatism, a Method of Union of the Past, and the Current Search for Full Communion," drafted at a meeting held in Ariccia in June, 1991. The new document, with its statement of principles and guidelines regarding the status and activity of Eastern-rite Catholic churches, was to be submitted to Roman Catholic and Orthodox authorities for approval and implementation.

The meeting was attended by 24 Catholics and representatives of nine autocephalous and autonomous Orthodox churches: Constantinople, Alexandria, Antioch, Moscow, Romania, Cyprus, Poland, Albania and Finland. Several Orthodox churches were not represented.

Fraternal Dialogue Is Not Proselytism: Many of the concerns that preoccupied participants in the Balamand meeting were the subjects of a document issued a year or more earlier by the Pontifical Commission for Russia, under the title, "General Principles and Practical Norms for Coordinating the Evangelizing Activity and Ecumenical Commitment of the Catholic Church in Russia and in the Other Countries of the Commonwealth of Independent States."

The document said that the churches in union with Rome in the territories of the former Soviet Union and in Eastern Europe were "in no way intended to bring the Catholic Church into competition with the Russian Orthodox Church or with other Christian churches."

The text discussed proselytism, the use of church buildings, dialogue and other aspects of ecumenism in a region where conflicts over the ownership of church buildings and charges of Catholic Church proselytism had been heard since the breakup of the Soviet Union led to the legalization of churches in union with the Holy See.

"So-called proselytism, meaning the exercise of any sort of pressure on peoples' consciences . . . is completely different from the apostolate, and it is certainly not the method used by the pastors of the Catholic Church," said the document. "The way to achieve Christian unity is certainly not proselytism but, rather, fraternal dialogue between the followers of Christ."

But, it cannot be considered proselytism when "entire communities . . . which during the years of suppression and persecution . . . were forced, in order to survive, to declare themselves Orthodox, have . . . manifested" their unity with Rome.

With practical directives, the document called for the promotion of "a good understanding with local authorities of the Orthodox Church," including respect for the difficulties the Orthodox Church itself had faced, and a willingness to make authorities of that church aware in advance of all important pastoral initiatives by Catholics.

Malabar Synod: Twenty-four bishops attended the five-day, first Synod of the Major Archbishopric of Ernakulam-Angamaly of Malabar Christians, held in May, 1993. The Syro-Malabar Church, established mainly in Kerala, India, is the second largest Oriental Catholic Church.

PROTESTANT CHURCHES

MEN, DOCTRINES, CHURCHES OF THE REFORMATION

Some of the leading figures, doctrines and churches of the Reformation are covered below. A companion article covers Major Protestant Churches in the United States.

John Wycliff (c. 1320-1384): English priest and scholar who advanced one of the leading Reformation ideas nearly 200 years before Martin Luther — that the Bible alone is the sufficient rule of faith — but had only an indirect influence on the 16th century Reformers. Supporting belief in an inward and practical religion, he denied the divinely commissioned authority of the pope and bishops of the Church; he also denied the Real Presence of Christ in the Holy Eucharist, and wrote against the sacrament of penance and the doctrine of indulgences. Nearly 20 of his propositions were condemned by Gregory XI in 1377; his writings were proscribed more extensively by the Council of Constance in 1415. His influence was strongest in Bohemia and Central Europe.

John Hus (c. 1369-1415): A Bohemian priest and preacher of reform who authored 30 propositions condemned by the Council of Constance. Excommunicated in 1411 or 1412, he was burned at the stake in 1415. His principal errors concerned the nature of the Church and the origin of papal authority. He spread some of the ideas of Wycliff but did not subscribe to his views regarding faith alone as the condition for justification and salvation, the sole sufficiency of Scripture as the rule of faith, the Real Presence of Christ in the Eucharist, and the sacramental system. In 1457 some of his followers founded the Church of the Brotherhood which later became known as the United Brethren or Moravian Church and is considered the earliest independent Protestant body.

Martin Luther (1483-1546): An Augustinian friar, priest and doctor of theology, the key figure in the Reformation. In 1517, as a special indulgence was being preached in Germany, and in view of needed reforms within the Church, he published at Wittenberg 95 theses concerning matters of Catholic belief and practice. Leo X condemned 41 statements from Luther's writings in 1520. Luther, refusing to recant, was excommunicated the following year. His teachings strongly influenced subsequent Lutheran theology; its statements of faith are found in the Book of Concord (1580).

Luther's doctrine included the following: The sin of Adam, which corrupted human nature radically (but not substantially), has affected every aspect of man's being. Justification, understood as the forgiveness of sins and the state of righteousness, is by grace for Christ's sake through faith. Faith involves not merely intellectual assent but an act of confidence by the will. Good works are indispensably necessary concomitants of faith, but do not merit salvation. Of the sacraments, Luther retained baptism, penance and the Holy Communion as effective vehicles of the grace of the Holy Spirit; he held that in the Holy Communion the consecrated bread and wine are the Body and Blood of Christ. The rule of faith is the divine revelation in the Sacred Scriptures. He rejected purgatory, indulgences and the invocation of the saints, and held that prayers for the dead have no efficacy. Lutheran tenets not in agreement with Catholic doctrine were condemned by the Council of Trent.

Anabaptism: Originated in Saxony in the first quarter of the 16th century and spread rapidly through southern Germany. Its doctrine included several key Lutheran tenets but was not regarded with favor by Luther, Calvin or Zwingli. Anabaptists believed that baptism is for adults only and that infant baptism is invalid. Their doctrine of the Inner Light, concerning the direct influence of the Holy Spirit on the believer, implied rejection of Catholic doctrine concerning the sacraments and the nature of the Church. Eighteen articles of faith were formulated in 1632 in Holland. Mennonites are Anabaptists.

Ulrich Zwingli (1484-1531): A priest who triggered the Reformation in Switzerland with a series of New Testament lectures in 1519, later disputations and by other actions. He held the Gospel to be the only basis of truth; rejected the Mass (which he suppressed in 1525 at Zurich), penance and other sacraments; denied papal primacy and doctrine concerning purgatory and the invocation of saints; rejected celibacy, monasticism and many traditional practices of piety. His symbolic view of the Eucharist, which was at odds with Catholic doctrine, caused an irreconcilable controversy with Luther and his followers. Zwingli was killed in a battle between the forces of Protestant and Catholic cantons in Switzerland.

John Calvin (1509-1564): French leader of the Reformation in Switzerland, whose key tenet was absolute predestination of some persons to heaven and others to hell. He rejected Catholic doctrine in 1533 after becoming convinced of a personal mission to reform the Church. In 1536 he published the first edition of *Institutes of the Christian Religion,* a systematic exposition of his doctrine which became the classic textbook of Reformed — as distinguished from Lutheran — theology. To Luther's principal theses — regarding Scripture as the sole rule of faith, the radical corruption of human nature, and justification by faith alone — he added absolute predestination, certitude of salvation for the elect, and the incapability of the elect to lose grace. His Eucharistic theory, which failed to mediate the Zwingli-Luther controversy, was at odds with Catholic doctrine. From 1555 until his death Calvin was the virtual dictator of Geneva, the capital of the non-Lutheran Reformation in Europe.

Arminianism: A modification of the rigid predestinationism of Calvin, set forth by Jacob Arminius (1560-1609) and formally stated in the *Remonstrance* of 1610. Arminianism influenced some Calvinist bodies.

Unitarianism: A 16th century doctrine which rejected the Trinity and the divinity of Christ in favor of a uni-personal God. It claimed scriptural support for a long time but became generally rationalistic with respect to "revealed" doctrine as well as in ethics and its world-view. One of its principal early proponents was Faustus Socinus (1539-1604), a leader of the Polish Brethren.

A variety of communions developed in England in the Reformation and post-Reformation periods.

Puritans: Extremists who sought church reform along Calvinist lines in severe simplicity. (Use of the term was generally discontinued after 1660.)

Presbyterians: Basically Calvinistic, called Presbyterian because church polity centers around assemblies of presbyters or elders. John Knox (c. 1513-1572) established the church in Scotland.

Congregationalists: Evangelical in spirit and seeking a return to forms of the primitive church, they uphold individual freedom in religious matters, do not require the acceptance of a creed as a condition for communion, and regard each congregation as autonomous. Robert Browne influenced the beginnings of Congregationalism.

Quakers: Their key belief is in internal divine illumination, the inner light of the living Christ, as the only source of truth and inspiration. George Fox (1624-1691) was one of their leaders in England. Called the Society of Friends, the Quakers are noted for their pacificism.

Baptists: So called because of their doctrine concerning baptism. They reject infant baptism and consider only baptism by immersion as valid. Leaders in the formation of the church were John Smyth (d. 1612) in England and Roger Williams (d. 1683) in America.

Methodists: A group who broke away from the Anglican Communion under the leadership of John Wesley (1703-1791), although some Anglican beliefs were retained. Doctrines include the witness of the Spirit to the individual and personal assurance of salvation. Wesleyan Methodists do not subscribe to some of the more rigid Calvinistic tenets held by other Methodists.

Universalism: A product of 18th-century liberal Protestantism in England. The doctrine is not Trinitarian and includes a tenet that all men will ultimately be saved.

ANGLICAN COMMUNION

This communion, which regards itself as the same apostolic Church as that which was established by early Christians in England, derived not from Reformation influences but from the renunciation of papal jurisdiction by Henry VIII (1491-1547). His Act of Supremacy in 1534 called Christ's Church an assembly of local churches subject to the prince, who was vested with fullness of authority and jurisdiction. In spite of Henry's denial of papal authority, this Act did not reject substantially other principal articles of faith. Notable changes, proposed and adopted for the reformation of the church, took place in the subsequent reigns of James VI and Elizabeth, with respect to such matters as Scripture as the rule of faith, the sacraments, the nature of the Mass, and the constitution of the hierarchy. There are 27 provinces in the Anglican Communion. (See Episcopal Church; Anglican Orders; Anglican-Catholic Final Report: Vatican Response.)

MAJOR PROTESTANT CHURCHES IN THE UNITED STATES

There are more than 250 Protestant church bodies in the United States.

The majority of U.S. Protestants belong to the following denominations: Baptist, Methodist, Lutheran, Presbyterian, Protestant Episcopal, United Church of Christ, the Christian Church (Disciples of Christ), Evangelicals.

See Ecumenical Dialogues, Reports and related entries for coverage of relations between the Catholic Church and other Christian churches.

Baptist Churches
(Courtesy of the Office of Communication, American Baptist Churches in the U.S.A.)

Baptist churches, comprising the largest of all American Protestant denominations, were first established by John Smyth near the beginning of the 17th century in England. The first Baptist church in America was founded at Providence by Roger Williams in 1639.

Largest of the nearly 30 Baptist bodies in the U.S. are:

The Southern Baptist Convention, 901 Commerce St., Nashville, Tenn. 37203, with 15.3 million members.

The National Baptist Convention, U.S.A., Inc., 915 Spain St., Baton Rouge, La. 70802, with 8 million members;

The National Baptist Convention of America, Inc., 1327 Pierre Ave., Shreveport, La. 71103, with 4.5 million members.

The American Baptist Churches in the U.S.A., P.O. Box 851, Valley Forge, Pa. 19482, with 1.5 million members.

The total number of U.S. Baptists is more than 29 million. The world total is 33 million.

Proper to Baptists is their doctrine on baptism. Called an "ordinance" rather than a sacrament, baptism by immersion is a sign that one has experienced and decided in favor of the salvation offered by Christ. It is administered only to persons who are able to make a responsible decision. Baptism is not administered to infants.

Baptists do not have a formal creed but generally subscribe to two professions of faith formulated in 1689 and 1832 and are in general agreement with classical Protestant theology regarding Scripture as the sole rule of faith, original sin, justification through faith in Christ, and the nature of the Church. Their local churches are autonomous.

Worship services differ in form from one congregation to another. Usual elements are the reading of Scripture, a sermon, hymns, vocal and silent prayer. The Lord's Supper, called an "ordinance," is celebrated at various intervals.

Methodist Churches
(Courtesy of Joe Hale, General Secretary of the World Methodist Council.)

John Wesley (1703-1791), an Anglican clergyman, was the founder of Methodism. In 1738, following a period of missionary work in America and strongly influenced by the Moravians, he experienced a new conversion to Christ and shortly thereafter became a leader in a religious awakening in England. By the end of the 18th century, Methodism was strongly rooted also in America.

The United Methodist Church, formed in 1968 by a merger of the Methodist Church and the Evangelical United Brethren Church, is the second largest Protestant denomination in the U.S., with more than nine million members; its principal agencies are located in New York, Evanston, Ill., Nashville, Tenn., Washington, D.C., Dayton, O., and Lake Junaluska, N.C. (World Methodist Council, P.O. Box 518. 28745). The second largest body, with more than two million communicants, is the African Methodist Episcopal Church. Four other major churches in the U.S. are the African Methodist Episcopal Zion, Christian Methodist Episcopal, Free Methodist Church and the Wesleyan Church. The total Methodist membership in the U.S. is about 15.5 million.

Worldwide, there are more than 68 autonomous Methodist/Wesleyan churches in 93 countries, with a membership of more than 29 million. All of them participate in the World Methodist Council, which gives global unity to the witness of Methodist communicants.

Methodism, although it has a base in Calvinistic theology, rejects absolute predestination and maintains that Christ offers grace freely to all men, not just to a select elite. Wesley's distinctive doctrine was the "witness of the Spirit" to the individual soul and personal assurance of salvation. He also emphasized the central themes of conversion and holiness. Methodists are in general agreement with classical Protestant theology regarding Scripture as the sole rule of faith, original sin, justification through faith in Christ, the nature of the Church, and the sacraments of baptism and the Lord's Supper. Church polity is structured along episcopal lines in America, with ministers being appointed to local churches by a bishop; churches stemming from British Methodism do not have bishops but vest appointive powers within an appropriate conference. Congregations are free to choose various forms of worship services; typical elements are readings from Scripture, sermons, hymns and prayers.

Lutheran Churches

(Courtesy of Deacon Tom Dorris, editor of Ecumenical Press Service, Box 2100, CH-1211 Geneva 2, Switzerland; and other Lutheran sources.)

The origin of Lutheranism is generally traced to Oct. 31, 1517, when Martin Luther — Augustinian friar, priest, doctor of theology — tacked "95 Theses" to the door of the castle church in Wittenberg, Germany. This call to debate on the subject of indulgences and related concerns has come to symbolize the beginning of the Reformation. Luther and his supporters intended to reform the Church they knew. Though Lutheranism has come to be visible in separate denominations and national churches, at its heart it professes itself to be a confessional movement within the one, holy, catholic and apostolic Church.

The world's 60 million Lutherans form the third largest grouping of Christians, after Roman Catholics and Orthodox. About 55 million of them belong to church bodies which make up the Lutheran World Federation, headquartered in Geneva.

There are about 8.5 million Lutherans in the United States, making them the fourth largest Christian grouping, after Roman Catholics, Baptists and Methodists. Although there are nearly 20 U.S. Lutheran church bodies, all but 100,000 Lutherans belong to either the Evangelical Lutheran Church in America (with 5.2 million members and headquarters at 8765 W. Higgins Rd., Chicago, Ill. 60631), The Lutheran Church-Missouri Synod (with 2.61 million members and headquarters at 1333 S. Kirkwood Rd., St. Louis, Mo. 63122), or the Wisconsin Evangelical Lutheran Synod (with 420,000 members and headquarters at 2929 N. Mayfair Rd., Milwaukee, Wis. 53222).

The Evangelical Lutheran Church in America and the Lutheran Church-Missouri Synod carry out some work together through inter-Lutheran agencies such as Lutheran World Relief and Lutheran Immigration and Refugee Services; both agencies have offices at 390 Park Ave. South, New York, N.Y. 10010.

The statements of faith which have shaped the confessional life of Lutheranism are found in the *Book of Concord.* This 1580 collection includes the three ancient ecumenical creeds (Apostles', Nicene and Athanasian), Luther's *Large and Small Catechisms* (1529), the *Augsburg Confession* (1530) and the *Apology* in defense of it (1531), the *Smalcald Articles* (including the "Treatise on the Power and Primacy of the Pope") (1537), and the *Formula of Concord* (1577).

The central Lutheran doctrinal proposition is that Christians "receive forgiveness of sins and become righteous before God by grace, for Christ's sake." Baptism and the Lord's Supper (Holy Communion, the Eucharist) are universally celebrated among Lutherans as sacramental means of grace. Lutherans also treasure the Word proclaimed in the reading of the Scriptures, preaching and absolution.

Generally in Lutheranism, the bishop, or a pastor (presbyter/priest) authorized by the bishop, is the minister of ordination. Much of Lutheranism continues what it understands as the historic succession of bishops (though without considering the historic episcopate essential for the church). All of Lutheranism is concerned to preserve apostolic succession in life and doctrine.

Lutheran jurisdictions corresponding to dioceses are called districts or synods in North America. There are more than 100 of them; each of them is headed by a bishop or president.

Presbyterian Churches

Presbyterians are so called because of their tradition of governing the church through a system of representative bodies composed of elders (presbyters).

Presbyterianism is a part of the Reformed Family of Churches that grew out of the theological work of John Calvin following the Lutheran Reformation, to which it is heavily indebted. Countries in which it acquired early strength and influence were Switzerland, France, Holland, Scotland and England.

Presbyterianism spread widely in this country in the latter part of the 18th century and afterwards. Presently, it has approximately 4.5 million communicants in nine bodies.

The two largest Presbyterian bodies in the country — the United Presbyterian Church in the U.S.A. and the Presbyterian Church in the United States — were reunited in June, 1983, to form the Presbyterian Church (U.S.A.), with a membership of 3 million. Its national offices are located at 100 Witherspoon St., Louisville, Ky. 40202.

These churches, now merged, are closely allied with the Reformed Church in America, the United Church of Christ, the Cumberland Presbyterian Churches and the Associate Reformed Presbyterian Church.

In Presbyterian doctrine, baptism and the Lord's Supper, viewed as seals of the covenant of grace, are regarded as sacraments. Baptism, which is not necessary for salvation, is conferred on infants and adults The Lord's Supper is celebrated as a covenant of the Sacrifice of Christ. In both sacraments, a doctrine of the real presence of Christ is considered the central theological principle.

The Church is twofold, being invisible and also visible; it consists of all of the elect and all those Christians who are united in Christ as their immediate head.

Presbyterians are in general agreement with classical Protestant theology regarding Scripture as the sole rule of faith and practice, salvation by grace, and justification through faith in Christ.

Presbyterian congregations are governed by a session composed of elders (presbyters) elected by the communicant membership. On higher levels there are presbyteries, synods and a general assembly with various degrees of authority over local bodies; all such representative bodies are composed of elected elders and ministers in approximately equal numbers. The church annually elects a moderator who presides at the General Assembly and travels throughout the church to speak to and hear from the members.

Worship services, simple and dignified, include sermons, prayer, reading of the Scriptures and hymns. The Lord's Supper is celebrated at intervals.

Doctrinal developments of the past several years included approval in May, 1967, by the General Assembly of the United Presbyterian Church of a contemporary confession of faith to supplement the historic Westminster Confession. A statement entitled "The Declaration of Faith" was approved in 1977 by the Presbyterian Church in the U.S. for teaching and liturgical use.

The reunited church adopted "A Brief Statement of Reformed Faith" in 1991 regarding urgent concerns of the church.

Episcopal Church

(Courtesy of The Episcopal Church Center, Office of Communication.)

The Episcopal Church, which includes 118 dioceses in the United States, Central and South America, and elsewhere overseas, regards itself as part of the same apostolic church which was established by early Christians in England. Established in this country during the colonial period, it became independent of the jurisdiction of the Church of England when a new constitution and Prayer Book were adopted at a general convention held in 1789. It has approximately 2.4 million members worldwide.

Offices of the presiding bishop and the executive council are located at 815 Second Ave., New York, N.Y. 10017.

The presiding bishop is chief pastor and primate; he is elected by the House of Bishops and confirmed by the House of Deputies.

The Episcopal Church, which is a part of the Anglican Communion, regards the Archbishop of Canterbury as the "First among Equals," though not under his authority.

The Anglican Communion, worldwide, has 70 million members in 31 self-governing churches.

Official statements of belief and practice are found in the Book of Common Prayer. Scripture has primary importance with respect to the rule of faith, and authority is also attached to tradition.

An episcopal system of church government prevails, but presbyters, deacons and lay persons also have an active voice in church affairs. The levels of government are the general convention, and executive council, dioceses, and local parishes. At the parish level, the congregation has the right to select its own rector, with the consent of the bishop.

Liturgical worship is according to the Book of Common Prayer as adopted in 1979, but details of ceremonial practice vary from one congregation to another.

United Church of Christ

(Courtesy of the Edith A. Guffey, Secretary of the United Church of Christ.)

The 1,605,604-member (in 1989) United Church of Christ was formed in 1957 by a union of the Congregational Christian and the Evangelical and Reformed Churches. The former was originally established by the Pilgrims and the Puritans of the Massachusetts Bay Colony, while the latter was founded in Pennsylvania in the early 1700s by settlers from Central Europe. The denomination had 6,362 congregations throughout the United States in 1988.

It considers itself "a united and uniting church" and keeps itself open to all ecumenical options.

Its headquarters are located at 700 Prospect, Cleveland, Ohio 44120.

Its statement of faith recognizes Jesus Christ as "our crucified and risen Lord (who) shared our common lot, conquering sin and death and reconciling the world to himself." It believes in the life after death, and the fact that God "judges men and nations by his righteous will declared through prophets and apostles."

The United Church further believes that Christ calls its members to share in his baptism "and eat at his table, to join him in his passion and victory." Each local church is free to adopt its own methods of worship and to formulate its own covenants and confessions of faith. Some celebrate communion weekly; others, monthly or on another periodical basis. Like other Calvinistic bodies, it believes that Christ is spiritually present in the sacrament.

The United Church is governed along congregational lines, and each local church is autonomous. However, the actions of its biennial General Synod are taken with great seriousness by congregations. Between synods, a 44-member executive council oversees the work of the church.

Christian Church (Disciples of Christ)

(Courtesy of Cathy Hinkle, Office of Communication.)
The Christian Church (Disciples of Christ) originated early in the 1800's from two movements against rigid denominationalism led by Presbyterians Thomas and Alexander Campbell in western Pennsylvania and Barton W. Stone in Kentucky. The two movements developed separately for about 25 years before being merged in 1832.

The church, which identifies itself with the Protestant mainstream, has more than one million members in more than 4,000 congregations in the U.S. and Canada. The greatest concentration of members in the U.S. is located roughly along the old frontier line, in an arc sweeping from Ohio and Kentucky through the Midwest and down into Oklahoma and Texas.

The general offices of the church are located at 222 South Downey Ave., Box 1986, Indianapolis, Ind. 46206.

The church's persistent concern for Christian unity is based on a conviction expressed in a basic document, *Declaration and Address,* dating from its founding. The document states: "The church of Christ upon earth is essentially, intentionally and constitutionally one."

The Disciples have no official doctrine or dogma. Their worship practices vary widely from more common informal services to what could almost be described as "high church" services. Membership is granted after a simple statement of belief in Jesus Christ and baptism by immersion; most congregations admit un-immersed transfers from other denominations. The Lord's Supper or Eucharist, generally called Communion, is always open to Christians of all persuasions. Lay men and women routinely preside over the Lord's Supper, which is celebrated each Sunday; they often preach and perform other pastoral functions as well. Distinction between ordained and non-ordained members is blurred somewhat because of the Disciples' emphasis on all members of the church as ministers.

The Christian Church is oriented to congregational government, and has a unique structure in which three sections of polity (general, regional and congregational) operate as equals rather than in a pyramid of authority. At the national or international level, it is governed by a general assembly which has voting representation direct from congregations and regions as well as all ordained clergy.

Evangelicalism

Evangelicalism, dating from 1735 in England (the Evangelical Revival) and after 1740 in the United States (the Great Awakening), has had and continues to have widespread influence in Protestant churches. It has been estimated that about 45 millon American Protestants — communicants of both large denominations and small bodies — are evangelicals.

The Bible is their rule of faith and religious practice. Being born again in a life-changing experience through faith in Christ is the promise of salvation. Missionary work for the spread of the Gospel is a normal and necessary activity. Additional matters of belief and practice are generally of a conservative character. Fundamentalists, numbering perhaps 4.5 million, comprise an extreme right-wing subculture of evangelicalism.They are distinguished mainly by militant biblicism, belief in the absolute inerrancy of the Bible and emphasis on the Second Coming of Christ. Fundamentalism developed early in the 20th century in reaction against liberal theology and secularizing trends in mainstream and other Protestant denominations.

The Holiness or Perfectionist wing of evangelicalism evolved from Methodist efforts to preserve, against a contrary trend, the personal-piety and inner-religion concepts of John Wesley. There are at least 30 Holiness bodies in the U.S.

Pentecostals, probably the most demonstrative of evangelicals, are noted for speaking in tongues and the stress they place on healing, prophecy and personal testimony to the practice and power of evangelical faith.

Assemblies of God

Assemblies (Churches) of God form the largest body (more than 2 million members) in the Pentecostal Movement which developed from (1) the Holiness Revival in the Methodist Church after the Civil War and (2) the Apostolic Faith Movement at the beginning of the 20th century. Members share with other Pentecostals belief in the religious experience of conversion and in the baptism by the Holy Spirit that sanctifies. Distinctive to them is the emphasis they place on the charismatic gifts of the apostolic church, healing and speaking in tongues, which are signs of the "second blessing" of the Holy Spirit. The Assemblies are strongly fundamentalist in theology; are loosely organized in various districts, with democratic procedures; are vigorously evangelistic. There is considerable freedom in expressions of the Spirit, sermons and hymns. The moral code is rigid.

Black Church Growth: Black Christians formed some of the fastest-growing denominations in the United States, according to the 1993 *Yearbook of American and Canadian Churches,* produced by the National Council of Churches of Christ in the U.S.A. and published by Abingdon Press, Nashville, Tenn. One trend article in the 1993 edition noted that in the 1980s the Church of God in Christ, an African-American pentecostal church, became "the fastest-growing major denomination in the United States and the nation's fifth largest denomination overall." The church gained an average of 200,000 members and 600 new congregations a year since 1982.

ECUMENISM

The modern ecumenical movement, which started about 1910 among Protestants and led to formation of the World Council of Churches in 1948, developed outside the mainstream of Catholic interest for many years. It has now become for Catholics as well one of the great religious facts of our time.

The magna charta of ecumenism for Catholics is a complex of several documents which include, in the first place, the *Decree on Ecumenism* promulgated by the Second Vatican Council Nov. 21, 1964. Other enactments underlying and expanding this decree are the *Dogmatic Constitution on the Church,* the *Decree on Eastern Catholic Churches,* and the *Pastoral Constitution on the Church in the Modern World.*

VATICAN II DECREE

The following excerpts from the *Decree on Ecumenism* cover the broad theological background and principles and indicate the thrust of the Church's commitment to ecumenism, under the subheads: Elements Common to Christians, Unity Lacking, What the Movement Involves, Primary Duty of Catholics.

Men who believe in Christ and have been properly baptized are brought into a certain, though imperfect, communion with the Catholic Church. Undoubtedly, the differences that exist in varying degrees between them and the Catholic Church — whether in doctrine and sometimes in discipline, or concerning the structure of the Church — do indeed create many and sometimes serious obstacles to full ecclesiastical communion. These the ecumenical movement is striving to overcome (No. 3).

Elements Common to Christians

Moreover some, even very many, of the most significant elements or endowments which together go to build up and give life to the Church herself can exist outside the visible boundaries of the Catholic Church: the written word of God; the life of grace; faith, hope, and charity, along with other interior gifts of the Holy Spirit and visible elements. All of these, which come from Christ and lead back to Him, belong by right to the one Church of Christ (No. 3).

[In a later passage, the decree singled out a number of elements which the Catholic Church and other churches have in common but not in complete agreement: confession of Christ as Lord and God and as mediator between God and man; belief in the Trinity; reverence for Scripture as the revealed word of God; baptism and the Lord's Supper; Christian life and worship; faith in action; concern with moral questions.]

The brethren divided from us also carry out many of the sacred actions of the Christian religion. Undoubtedly, in ways that vary according to the condition of each church or community, these actions can truly engender a life of grace, and can be rightly described as capable of providing access to the community of salvation.

It follows that these separated Churches and Communities, though we believe they suffer from defects already mentioned, have by no means been deprived of significance and importance in the mystery of salvation. For the Spirit of Christ has not refrained from using them as means of salvation which derive their efficacy from the very fullness of grace and truth entrusted to the Catholic Church (No. 3).

Unity Lacking

Nevertheless, our separated brethren, whether considered as individuals or as Communities and Churches, are not blessed with that unity which Jesus Christ wished to bestow on all those whom he has regenerated and vivified into one body and newness of life — that unity which the holy Scriptures and the revered tradition of the Church proclaim. For it is through Christ's Catholic Church alone, which is the all-embracing means of salvation, that the fullness of the means of salvation can be obtained. It was to the apostolic college alone, of which Peter is the head, that we believe our Lord entrusted all the blessings of the New Covenant, in order to establish on earth the one Body of Christ into which all those should be fully incorporated who already belong in any way to God's People (No. 3).

What the Movement Involves

Today, in many parts of the world, under the inspiring grace of the Holy Spirit, multiple efforts are being expended through prayer, word, and action to attain that fullness of unity which Jesus Christ desires. This sacred Synod, therefore, exhorts all the Catholic faithful to recognize the signs of the times and to participate skillfully in the work of ecumenism.

The "ecumenical movement" means those activities and enterprises which, according to various needs of the Church and opportune occasions, are started and organized for the fostering of unity among Christians. These are:

● First, every effort to eliminate words, judgments, and actions which do not respond to the condition of separated brethren with truth and fairness and so make mutual relations between them more difficult.

● Then, "dialogue" between competent experts from different Churches and Communities [scholarly ecumenism].

● In addition, these Communions cooperate more closely in whatever projects a Christian conscience demands for the common good [social ecumenism].

● They also come together for common prayer, where this is permitted [spiritual ecumenism].

● Finally, all are led to examine their own faithfulness to Christ's will for the Church and, wherever necessary, undertake with vigor the task of renewal and reform.

It is evident that the work of preparing and reconciling those individuals who wish for full Catholic communion is of its nature distinct from ecumenical action. But there is no opposition between the two, since both proceed from the wondrous providence of God (No. 4).

Primary Duty of Catholics

In ecumenical work, Catholics must assuredly be concerned for their separated brethren, praying for them, keeping them informed about the Church, making the first approaches toward them. But their primary duty is to make an honest and careful appraisal of whatever needs to be renewed and achieved in the Catholic household itself, in order that its life may bear witness more loyally and luminously to the teachings and ordinances which have been handed down from Christ through the Apostles.

Every Catholic must ... aim at Christian perfection (cf. Jas. 1:4; Rom. 12:1-2) and, each according to his station, play his part so that the Church ... may daily be more purified and renewed, against the day when Christ will present her to himself in all her glory, without spot or wrinkle (cf. Eph. 5:27).

Catholics must joyfully acknowledge and esteem the truly Christian endowments from our common heritage which are to be found among our separated brethren.

Nor should we forget that whatever is wrought by the grace of the Holy Spirit in the hearts of our separated brethren can contribute to our own edification. Whatever is truly Christian never conflicts with the genuine interests of the faith; indeed, it can always result in a more ample realization of the very mystery of Christ and the Church (No. 4).

Participation in Worship

Norms concerning participation by Catholics in the worship of other Christian Churches were sketched in this conciliar decree and elaborated in a number of other documents such as: the *Decree on Eastern Catholic Churches*, promulgated by the Second Vatican Council in 1964; *Interim Guidelines for Prayer in Common*, issued June 18, 1965, by the U.S. Bishops' Committee for Ecumenical and Interreligious Affairs; a *Directory on Ecumenism*, published in 1967 by the Vatican Secretariat for Promoting Christian Unity; additional communications from the U.S. Bishops' Committee, and numerous sets of guidelines issued locally by and for dioceses throughout the U.S.

The norms encourage common prayer services for Christian unity and other intentions. Beyond that, they draw a distinction between separated churches of the Reformation tradition and of the Anglican Communion and separated Eastern churches, in view of doctrine and practice the Catholic Church has in common with the latter concerning the apostolic succession of bishops, holy orders, liturgy, and other credal matters.

Full participation by Catholics in official Protestant liturgies is prohibited, because it implies profession of the faith expressed in the liturgy. Intercommunion by Catholics at Protestant liturgies is prohibited. Under certain conditions, Protestants may be given Holy Communion in the Catholic Church (see Intercommunion). A Catholic may stand as a witness, but not as a sponsor, in baptism, and as a witness in the marriage of separated Christians. Similarly, a Protestant may stand as a witness, but not as a sponsor, in a Catholic baptism, and as a witness in the marriage of Catholics.

Separated Eastern Churches

The principal norms regarding liturgical participation with separated Eastern Christians are included under Eastern Ecumenism.

ECUMENICAL AGENCIES

Pontifical Council

The top-level agency for Catholic ecumenical efforts is the Pontifical Council for Promoting Christian Unity (formerly the Secretariat for Promoting Christian Unity), which originated in 1960 as a preparatory commission for the Second Vatican Council. Its purposes are to provide guidance and, where necessary, coordination for ecumenical endeavor by Catholics, and to establish and maintain relations with representatives of other Christian Churches for ecumenical dialogue and action.

The council, under the direction of Cardinal Edward I. Cassidy (successor to Cardinal Johannes Willebrands), has established firm working relations with representative agencies of other churches and the World Council of Churches. It has joined in dialogue with Orthodox Churches, the Anglican Communion, the Lutheran World Federation, the World Alliance of Reformed Churches, the World Methodist Council and other religious bodies. In the past several years, staff members and representatives of the council have been involved in one way or another in nearly every significant ecumenical enterprise and meeting held throughout the world.

While the council and its counterparts in other churches have focused primary attention on theological and other related problems of Christian unity, they have also begun, and in increasing measure, to emphasize the responsibilities of the churches for greater unity of witness and effort in areas of humanitarian need.

Bishops' Committee

The U.S. Bishops' Committee for Ecumenical and Interreligious Affairs was established by the American hierarchy in 1964. Its purposes are to maintain relationships with other Christian churches and other religious communities at the national level, to advise and assist dioceses in developing and applying ecumenical policies, and to maintain liaison with corresponding Vatican offices — the Councils for Christian Unity and for Interreligious Dialogue.

This standing committee of the National Conference of Catholic Bishops is chaired by Archbishop Rembert G. Weakland of Milwaukee. Operationally, the committee is assisted by a secretariat with the Rev. John F. Hotchkin, director; Dr. Eugene J. Fisher, executive secretary for Catholic-Jewish Relations; Dr. John Borelli, Jr., executive secretary for Interreligious Relations.

The committee co-sponsors several national consultations with other churches and confessional families. These bring together Catholic representatives and their counterparts from the Episcopal Church, the Lutheran Church, the Polish National Catholic Church, the United Methodist Church, the

Orthodox Churches, the Oriental Orthodox Churches, the Alliance of Reformed Churches (North American area), the Interfaith Witness Department of the Home Mission Board of the Southern Baptist Convention. (See Ecumenical Dialogues.)

The committee relates with the National Council of Churches of Christ, through membership in the Faith and Order Commission and through observer relationship with the Commission on Regional and Local Ecumenism, and has sponsored a joint study committee investigating the possibility of Roman Catholic membership in that body.

Advisory and other services are provided by the committee to ecumenical commissions and agencies in dioceses throughout the country.

Through its Section for Catholic-Jewish Relations, the committee is in contact with several national Jewish agencies and bodies. Issues of mutual interest and shared concern are reviewed for the purpose of furthering deeper understanding between the Catholic and Jewish communities.

Through its Section for Interreligious Relations, the committee promotes activity in wider areas of dialogue with other religions, notably, with Muslims, Buddhists and Hindus.

Offices of the committee are located at 3211 Fourth St. N.E., Washington, D.C. 20017.

World Council

The World Council of Churches is a fellowship of churches which acknowledge "Jesus Christ as Lord and Savior." It is a permanent organization providing constituent members — 307 churches with some 450 million communicants in 100 countries — with opportunities for meeting, consultation and cooperative action with respect to doctrine, worship, practice, social mission, evangelism and missionary work, and other matters of mutual concern.

The WCC was formally established Aug. 23, 1948, in Amsterdam with ratification of a constitution by 147 communions. This action merged two previously existing movements — Life and Work (social mission), Faith and Order (doctrine) — which had initiated practical steps toward founding a fellowship of Christian churches at meetings held in Oxford, Edinburgh and Utrecht in 1937 and 1938. A third movement for cooperative missionary work, which originated about 1910 and, remotely, led to formation of the WCC, was incorporated into the council in 1971 under the title of the International Missionary Council (now the Commission for World Mission and Evangelism).

Additional general assemblies of the council have been held since the charter meeting of 1948: in Evanston, Ill. (1954), New Delhi, India (1961), Uppsala, Sweden (1968), Nairobi, Kenya (1975) and Vancouver, British Columbia, Canada (1983). The 1991 general assembly was held in Canberra, Australia.

Between assemblies, the council operates through a central committee which meets every 12 or 18 months, and an executive committee which meets every six months.

The council continues the work of the International Missionary Council, the Commission on Faith and Order, and the Commission on Church and Society. The work of the council is carried out through four program units: unity and renewal; mission, education and witness; justice, peace and creation; sharing and service.

Liaison between the council and the Vatican has been maintained since 1966 through a joint working group. Roman Catholic membership in the WCC is a question officially on the agenda of this body. The Joint Commission on Society, Development and Peace (SODEPAX) was an agency of the council and the Pontifical Commission for Justice and Peace from 1968 to Dec. 31, 1980, after which another working group was formed. Roman Catholics serve individually as full members of the Commission on Faith and Order and in various capacities on other program committees of the council.

WCC headquarters are located in Geneva, Switzerland. The United States Conference for the World Council of Churches at 475 Riverside Drive, Room 915, New York, N.Y. 10115, provides liaison between the U.S. churches and Geneva, a communications office for secular and church media relations, and a publications office. The WCC also maintains fraternal relations with regional, national and local councils of churches throughout the world.

The Rev. Konrad Raiser, a Lutheran from Germany, was elected general secretary, Aug. 24, 1992.

WCC presidents are: Prof. Dr. Anna Marie Aagaard, Denmark; Bishop Vinton R. Anderson, St. Louis, U.S.A.; Bishop Leslie Boseto, Munda, Western Province, Solomon Islands; Mrs. Priyanka Mendis, Idama, Moratuwa, Sri Lanka; His Beatitude Patriarch Parthenios, Alexandria, Egypt; Rev. Eunice Santana, Bayamon, Puerto Rico; His Holiness Pope Shenouda, Cairo, Egypt; Dr. Aaron Tolen, Yaounde, Cameroun.

National Council of Churches

The National Council of the Churches of Christ in the U.S.A., the largest ecumenical body in the United States, is an organization of 32 Protestant, Orthodox and Anglican church bodies with an aggregate membership of about 42 million.

The NCC, established by the churches in 1950, was structured through the merger of 12 separate cooperative agencies. Presently, through four main program units, the NCC carries on work in behalf of member churches in overseas ministries, Christian education, domestic social action, communications, disaster relief, refugee assistance, rehabilitation and development, biblical translation, regional and local ecumenism, international affairs, theological dialogue, interfaith activities, worship and evangelism, and other areas.

Policies of the NCC are determined by a general board of approximately 260 members appointed by the constituent churches. The governing board meets once a year.

NCC presidents: The Rev. Syngman Rhee (for 1992-93), Dr. Gordon L. Sommers (for 1994-95). General secretary: The Rev. Joan Brown Campbell.

NCC headquarters are located at 475 Riverside Drive, New York, N.Y. 10115.

Consultation on Church Union

(Courtesy of Rev. David W.A. Taylor, General Secretary.)

The Consultation on Church Union, officially begun in 1962, is a venture of American churches seeking a united church "truly catholic, truly evangelical, and truly reformed." The churches engaged in this process, representing 25 million Christians, are the African Methodist Episcopal Church, the African Methodist Episcopal Zion Church, the Christian Church (Disciples of Christ), the Christian Methodist Episcopal Church, the Episcopal Church, the Presbyterian Church (U.S.A); the United Church of Christ, the United Methodist Church and the International Council of Community Churches.

At a plenary assembly of COCU in December, 1988, a plan of church unity was unanimously approved for submission to member churches for their action. The plan is contained in a 102-page document entitled "Churches in Covenant Communion: The Church of Christ Uniting." It proposes the formation of a covenant communion of the churches which, while remaining institutionally autonomous, would embrace together eight elements of ecclesial communion: claiming unity in faith, commitment to seek unity with wholeness, mutual recognition of members in one baptism, mutual recognition of each other as churches, mutual recognition and reconciliation of ordained ministries, celebrating the Eucharist together, engaging together in Christ's mission, and the formation together of covenanting councils at each level (national, regional, and local).

Vivian U. Robinson, Ph.D., a lay member of the Christian Methodist Episcopal Church, was elected president in 1988. The Rev. David W.A. Taylor is General Secretary.

Offices are located at 151 Wall St., Princeton, N.J. 08540.

Graymoor Institute

The Graymoor Ecumenical and Interreligious Institute is a forum where issues that confront the Christian Churches are addressed, the spiritual dimensions of ecumenism are fostered, and information, documentation and developments within the ecumenical movement are published through *Ecumenical Trends,* a monthly journal, and *Atonement,* five times a year. Director: The Rev. Elias D. Mallon, S.A. Address: 475 Riverside Dr., Rm. 1960, New York, N.Y. 10115.

U.S. ECUMENICAL DIALOGUES

Representatives of the Bishops' Committee for Ecumenical and Interreligious Affairs, National Conference of Catholic Bishops, have met in dialogue with representatives of other churches since the 1960s, for discussion of a wide variety of subjects related to the quest for unity among Christians. Following is a list of dialogue groups and the years in which dialogue began.

Anglican-Roman Catholic Consultation, 1965; Eastern Orthodox Consultation (Theologians), 1965; Eastern Orthodox and Roman Catholic Bishops, Joint Committee, 1981; Lutheran Consultation, 1965; Oriental Orthodox Consultation (with Armenian, Coptic, Ethiopian, Indian Malabar and Syrian Orthodox Churches), 1978; Polish National-Catholic Consultation, 1984; Presbyterian/Reformed Consultation, 1965; Southern Baptist Conversations, 1969; United Methodist Consultation, 1966.

ECUMENICAL REPORTS

(Source: Rev. John F. Hotchkin, Secretariat of the Bishops' Committee for Ecumenical and Interreligious Affairs, National Conference of Catholic Bishops.)

Common Declarations of Popes, Other Prelates

The following ecumenical statements, issued by several popes and prelates of other Christian churches, carry the authority given them by their signators.

Paul VI and Orthodox Ecumenical Patriarch Athenagoras I, First Common Declaration, Dec. 7, 1965: They hoped the differences between the churches would be overcome with the help of the Holy Spirit, and that their "full communion of faith, brotherly concord and sacramental life" would be restored.

Paul VI and Anglican Archbishop Michael Ramsey of Canterbury, Mar. 24, 1966: They stated their intention "to inaugurate between the Roman Catholic Church and the Anglican Communion a serious dialogue which, founded on the Gospels and on the ancient common traditions, may lead to that unity in truth for which Christ prayed."

Paul VI and Patriarch Athenagoras I, Second Common Declaration, Oct. 27, 1967: They wished "to emphasize their conviction that the restoration of full communion (between the churches) . . . is to be found within the framework of the renewal of the Church and of Christians in fidelity to the traditions of the Fathers and to the inspirations of the Holy Spirit who remains always with the Church."

Paul VI and Vasken I, Orthodox Catholicos-Patriarch of All Armenians, May 12, 1970: They called for closer collaboration "in all domains of Christian life. . . . This collaboration must be based on the mutual recognition of the common Christian faith and the sacramental life, on the mutual respect of persons and their churches."

Paul VI and Mar Ignatius Jacob III, Syrian Orthodox Patriarch of Antioch, Oct. 27, 1971: They declared themselves to be "in agreement that there is no difference in the faith they profess concerning the mystery of the Word of God made flesh and become really man, even if over the centuries difficulties have arisen out of the different theological expressions by which this faith was expressed."

Paul VI and Shenouda III, Coptic Orthodox Pope of Alexandria, May 10, 1973: Their common declaration recalls the common elements of the Catholic and Coptic Orthodox faith in the Trinity, the divinity and humanity of Christ, the seven sacraments, the Virgin Mary, the Church founded upon the Apostles, and the Second Coming of Christ. It recognizes that the two churches "are not able to give more perfect witness to this new life in Christ because of existing divisions which have behind them centuries of difficult history" dating back to the year 451 A.D. In spite of these difficulties, they expressed "determination and confidence in the Lord to achieve the fullness and perfection of that unity which is his gift."

Paul VI and Anglican Archbishop Donald Coggan of Canterbury, Apr. 29, 1977: They stated many points on which Anglicans and Roman Catholics hold the faith in common and called for greater cooperation between Anglicans and Roman Catholics.

John Paul II and Orthodox Ecumenical Patriarch Dimitrios I, First Common Declaration, Nov. 30, 1979: "Purification of the collective memory of our churches is an important fruit of the dialogue of charity and an indispensable condition of future progress." They announced the establishment of the Catholic-Orthodox Theological Commission.

John Paul II and Anglican Archbishop Robert Runcie of Canterbury, May 29, 1982: They agreed to establish a new Anglican-Roman Catholic commission with the task of continuing work already begun toward the eventual resolution of doctrinal differences.

John Paul II and Ignatius Zakka I, Syrian Orthodox Patriarch of Antioch, June 23, 1984: They recalled and solemnly reaffirmed the common profession of faith made by their predecessors, Paul VI and Mar Ignatius Jacob III, in 1971. They said: "The confusions and the schisms that occurred between the churches . . . , they realize today, in no way affect or touch the substance of their faith, since these arose only because of differences in terminology and culture, and in the various formulae adopted by different theological schools to express the same matter. Accordingly, we find today no real basis for the sad divisions which arose between us concerning the doctrine of the Incarnation." On the pastoral level, they declared: "It is not rare . . . for our faithful to find access to a priest of their own church materially or morally impossible. Anxious to meet their needs and with their spiritual benefit in mind, we authorize them in such cases to ask for the sacraments of penance, Eucharist and anointing of the sick from lawful priests of either of our two sister churches, when they need them."

John Paul II and Orthodox Ecumenical Patriarch Dimitrios I, Second Common Declaration, Dec. 7, 1987: Dialogue conducted since 1979 indicated that the churches can already profess together as common faith about the mystery of the Church and the connection between faith and the sacraments. They also stated that, "when unity of faith is assured, a certain diversity of expressions . . . does not create obstacles to unity, but enriches the life of the Church and the understanding, always imperfect, of the revealed mystery."

John Paul II and Anglican Archbishop Robert Runcie of Canterbury, Oct. 2, 1989: They said: "We solemnly re-commit ourselves and those we represent to the restoration of visible unity and full ecclesial communion in the confidence that to seek anything less would be to betray our Lord's intention for the unity of his people."

INTERNATIONAL BILATERAL COMMISSIONS

Anglican-Roman Catholic International Commission, sponsored by the Pontifical Council for Promoting Christian Unity and the Lambeth Conference, from 1970 to 1981; succeeded by a **Second Anglican-Roman Catholic International Commission,** called into being by the Common Declaration of Pope John Paul and the Archbishop of Canterbury in 1982.

The International Theological Colloquium between Baptists and Catholics, established in 1984 by the Pontifical Council for Promoting Christian Unity and the Commission for Faith and Interchurch Cooperation of the Baptist World Alliance.

The Disciples of Christ-Roman Catholic Dialogue, organized by the Council of Christian Unity of the Christian Church (Disciples of Christ) and the U.S. Bishops' Committee for Ecumenical and Interreligious Affairs, along with participation by the Disciples' Ecumenical Consultative Council and the Unity Council; since 1977.

The Evangelical-Roman Catholic Dialogue on Mission, organized by Evangelicals and the Pontifical Council for Promoting Christian Unity; from 1977.

The Joint Lutheran-Roman Catholic Study Commission, established by the Pontifical Council for Promoting Christian Unity and the Lutheran World Federation; from 1967.

The International Catholic-Orthodox Theological Commission, established by the Holy See and 14 autocephalous Orthodox Churches, began its work at a first session held at Patmos/Rhodes in 1980. Subsequent sessions have been held at Munich (1982), Crete (1984), Bari (1987), Valamo (1988) and Freising (1990).

Pentecostal-Roman Catholic Conversations, since 1966.

The Reformed-Roman Catholic Conversations, inaugurated in 1970 by the Pontifical Council for Promoting Christian Unity and the World Alliance of Reformed Churches.

INTERFAITH STATEMENTS

The ecumenical statements listed below, and others like them, reflect the views of participants in the dialogues which produced them. They have not been formally accepted by the respective churches as formulations of doctrine or points of departure for practical changes in discipline. (For other titles, see U.S.Ecumenical Dialogues, Ecumenical Reports.)

• The "Windsor Statement" on Eucharistic doctrine, published Dec. 31, 1971, by the Anglican-Roman Catholic International Commission of theologians. (For text, see pages 132-33 of the 1973 *Catholic Almanac*.)

• The "Canterbury Statement" on ministry and ordination, published Dec. 13, 1973, by the same commission. (For excerpts, see pages 127-30 of the 1975 *Catholic Almanac*.)

• "Papal Primacy / Converging Viewpoints," published Mar. 4, 1974, by the dialogue group sanctioned by the U.S.A. National Convention of the World Lutheran Federation and the U.S. Bishops' Committee for Ecumenical and Interreligious Affairs. (For excerpts, see pages 130-31 of the 1975 *Catholic Almanac*.)

• An "Agreed Statement on the Purpose of the Church," published Oct. 31, 1975, by the Anglican-Roman Catholic Consultation in the U.S.

• "Christian Unity and Women's Ordination," published Nov. 7, 1975, by the same consultation, in which it was said that the ordination of women (approved in principle by the Anglican Communion but not by the Catholic Church) would "introduce a new element" in dialogue but would not mean the end of consultation nor the abandonment of its declared goal of full communion and organic unity.

• "Holiness and Spirituality of the Ordained Ministry," issued early in 1976 by theologians of the Catholic Church and the United Methodist Church; the first statement resulting from dialogue begun in 1966.

• "Mixed Marriages," published in the spring of 1976 by the Anglican-Roman Catholic Consultation in the U.S.

• "Bishops and Presbyters," published in July, 1976, by the Orthodox-Roman Catholic Consultation in the U.S. on the following points of common understanding: (1) Ordination in apostolic succession is required for pastoral office in the Church. (2) Presiding at the Eucharistic Celebration is a task belonging to those ordained to pastoral service. (3) The offices of bishop and presbyter are different realizations of the sacrament of order. (4) Those ordained are claimed permanently for the service of the Church.

• "The Principle of Economy," published by the body named above at the same time, concerning God's plan and activities in human history for salvation.

• "Venice Statement" on authority in the Church, published Jan. 20, 1977, by the Anglican-Roman

Catholic International Commission of theologians. (For text, see pages 145-50 of the 1978 *Catholic Almanac*.)

• "Response to the Venice Statement," issued Jan. 4, 1978, by the Anglican-Roman Catholic Consultation in the U.S.A., citing additional questions.

• "The Presence of Christ in Church and World," published early in 1978 by representatives of the Vatican Secretariat for Promoting Christian Unity and the World Alliance of Reformed Churches.

• "An Ecumenical Approach to Marriage," published in January, 1978, by representatives of the Catholic Church, the Lutheran World Federation and the World Alliance of Reformed Churches.

• "Teaching Authority and Infallibility in the Church," released in October, 1978, by the Catholic-Lutheran dialogue group in the U.S.

• "The Eucharist," reported early in 1979, in which the Roman Catholic-Lutheran Commission indicated developing convergence of views.

• "The Holy Spirit," issued Feb. 12, 1979, by the International Catholic-Methodist Commission.

• A statement on "Ministry in the Church," published in March, 1981, by the International Roman Catholic-Lutheran Joint Commission, regarding possible mutual recognition of ministries.

• The Final Report of the Anglican-Roman Catholic International Commission, released late in March, 1982, on the results of 12 years of dialogue. (See Anglican-Roman Catholic Report: Vatican Response.)

• "Justification by Faith," issued Sept. 30, 1983, by the U.S. Lutheran-Roman Catholic dialogue group, claiming a "fundamental consensus on the Gospel."

• "Images of God: Reflections on Christian Anthropology," released Dec. 22, 1983, by the Anglican-Roman Catholic Dialogue in the United States.

• "Salvation and the Church," issued Jan. 22, 1987, by the Second Anglican-Roman Catholic International Commission.

• "Faith, Sacraments and the Unity of the Church," issued by the Mixed International Commission for Theological Dialogue between the Catholic Church and the Orthodox Churches in June, 1987.

ANGLICAN-ROMAN CATHOLIC REPORT: VATICAN RESPONSE

The Vatican issued an official response Dec. 5, 1991, to the Final Report of the first Anglican-Roman Catholic International Commission. The report, the product of Catholic-Anglican dialogue from 1970 to 1981, was published in 1982. The response was developed jointly by the Congregation for the Doctrine of the Faith and the Pontifical Council for Promoting Christian Unity. It was the first official Catholic response to an agreed ecumenical statement.

The following excerpts are from the text circulated by the CNS Documentary Service, Origins, Dec. 19, 1991 (Vol. 21, No. 28). Subheads have been added.

Product of Dialogue

The report is a result of an in-depth study of certain questions of faith by partners in dialogue and witnesses to the achievement of points of conver-

gence and even of agreement which many would not have thought possible before the commission began its work. As such, it constitutes a significant milestone not only in relations between the Catholic Church and the Anglican Communion but in the ecumenical movement as a whole.

The Catholic Church judges, however, that it is not yet possible to state that substantial agreement has been reached on all the questions studied by the commission. There still remain between Anglicans and Catholics important differences regarding essential matters of Catholic doctrine.

Eucharist: With respect to Eucharistic doctrine, the members of the commission were able to achieve the most notable progress toward a consensus. Together they affirm "that the Eucharist is a sacrifice in the sacramental sense, provided that it is made clear that this is not a repetition of the historical sacrifice." Areas of agreement are also evident in respect of the real presence of Christ.

However, the faith of the Catholic Church in the Eucharist would be more clearly reflected if the following points were explicitly affirmed:

• that in the Eucharist the Church, doing what Christ commanded his Apostles to do at the Last Supper, makes present the sacrifice of Calvary;

• that the sacrifice of Christ is made present with all its effects, thus affirming the propitiatory nature of the Eucharistic Sacrifice, which can be applied also to the deceased.

Real consensus between Anglicans and Catholics (regarding reservation of the Eucharist) is lacking.

Ordination and Ministry: The distinction between the priesthood common to all the baptized and the ordained priesthood is explicitly acknowledged. The ordained ministry "is not an extension of the common Christian priesthood but belongs to another realm of the gifts of the Spirit." Ordination is described as a "sacramental act and the ordained ministry as being an essential element of the Church. ... It is only the ordained priest who presides at the Eucharist."

The Vatican statement said the Final Report would be helped if the following points were made clearer:

• that only a validly ordained priest can be the minister who, in the person of Christ, brings into being the sacrament of the Eucharist;

• that it was Christ himself who instituted the sacrament of order as the rite which confers the priesthood of the New Covenant.

Authority, Infallibility, Mary: When it comes to the question of authority in the Church, it must be noted that the Final Report makes no claim to substantial agreement.

There are still other areas that are essential to Catholic doctrine on which complete agreement or even at times convergence has eluded the Anglican-Roman Catholic Commission.

This is particularly true in respect of the Catholic dogma of papal infallibility. ... "In spite of our agreement over the need for a universal primacy in a united church, Anglicans do not accept the guaranteed possession of such a gift of divine assistance in judgment necessarily attached to the office of the Bishop of Rome by virtue of which his formal decisions can be known to be assured before their reception by the faithful."

Similarly, the commission has not been able to record any real consensus on Marian dogmas. ... "The dogmas of the Immaculate Conception and the Assumption raise a special problem for those Anglicans who do not consider that the precise definitions given by these dogmas are sufficiently supported by Scripture."

Apostolic Succession

The Catholic Church recognizes in the apostolic succession both an unbroken line of episcopal ordination from Christ through the apostles down through the centuries to the bishops of today and an uninterrupted continuity in Christian doctrine from Christ to those today who teach in union with the college of bishops and its head, the successor of Peter. ... This question lies at the very heart of the ecumenical discussion and touches vitally all the themes dealt with by ARCIC I: the reality of the Eucharist, the sacramentality of the ministerial priesthood, the nature of the Roman primacy.

There is need for further study concerning Scripture, tradition and the magisterium and their interrelationship since, according to Catholic teaching, Christ has given to his Church full authority to continue, with the uninterrupted and efficacious assistance of the Holy Spirit, "to preserve this word of God faithfully, explain it and make it more widely known."

DIRECTORY ON ECUMENISM

A new *Directory for the Application of the Principles and Norms of Ecumenism* was approved by Pope John Paul Mar. 25, 1993, and published early in June. The Pontifical Council for Promoting Christian Unity said on release of the document that revision of Directories issued in 1967 and 1970 was necessary in view of subsequent developments. These included promulgation of the *Code of Canon Law* for the Latin Church in 1983 and of the *Code of Canons of the Eastern Churches* in 1990; publication of the Catechism of the Catholic Church in 1992; additional documents and the results of theological dialogues.

The following excerpts are from the text published in the June 16, 1993, English edition of L'Osservatore Romano.

Address and Purpose

"The Directory is addressed to the pastors of the Catholic Church, but it also concerns all the faithful, who are called to pray and work for the unity of Christians, under the direction of their bishops."

"At the same time, it is hoped that the Directory will also be useful to members of churches and ecclesial communities that are not in full communion with the Catholic Church."

"The new edition of the Directory is meant to be an instrument at the service of the whole Church, and especially of those who are directly engaged in ecumenical activity in the Catholic Church. The Directory intends to motivate, enlighten and guide this activity, and in some particular cases also to give binding directives in accordance with the proper competence of the Pontifical Council for Promoting Christian Unity."

Outline

Principles and norms of the document are covered in five chapters.

"**I. The Search for Christian Unity.** The ecumenical commitment of the Catholic Church based on the doctrinal principles of the Second Vatican Council.

"**II. Organization in the Catholic Church at the Service of Christian Unity.** Persons and structures involved in promoting ecumenism at all levels, and the norms that direct their activity.

"III. Ecumenical Formation in the Catholic Church. Categories of people to be formed, those responsible for formation; the aims and methods of formation; its doctrinal and practical aspects.

"IV. Communion in Life and Spiritual Activity among the Baptized. The communion that exists with other Christians on the basis of the sacramental bond of baptism, and the norms for sharing in prayer and other spiritual activities, including, in particular cases, sacramental sharing.

"V. Ecumenical Cooperation, Dialogue and Common Witness. Principles, different forms and norms for cooperation between Christians with a view to dialogue and common witness in the world."

ECUMENICAL DEVELOPMENTS

Catholic-Lutheran Dialogue: At a Feb. 18-to-21 meeting in West Palm Beach, theologians and other representatives of the two churches agreed that their churches should formulate a process by which they might declare that some Reformation-era condemnations are no longer applicable. While the principal purpose of the meeting was to set future directions of dialogue in the U.S., they described it as a first-ever, in-depth consultation to reflect on how their national and international dialogues relate to one another and how the directions they take in the future can be most beneficial to one another. Participants recommended planning for some sort of "public affirmation of the goal of full communion" to witness the progress made in 27 years of dialogue as well as a commitment to continue the work.

Participation in Church Councils: Catholic churches in various places may participate in national or regional councils of churches, but must do so with care for their identity as part of the Church Universal, according to Cardinal Edward I. Cassidy.

The cardinal, president of the Pontifical Council for Promoting Christian Unity, said in March, 1993, that the experience of the 47 national and three regional councils with Roman Catholic membership had positive benefits and possible dangers. "Undoubtedly, membership in these bodies provides the Catholic Church with an important opportunity for cooperation and common witness," he observed. At the same time, some of the difficulties experienced by members of national councils had their source "in a lack of agreement on the aim and function" of the councils. "Part of the problem lies in the failure to understand how the Catholic Church sees itself at the local level in relation to ecumenical involvement at that level." When the local Catholic Church works with other churches and communities, it does so "within the framework of the communion of faith and discipline of the whole Catholic Church." Therefore, said the cardinal, the constitutions of national and regional councils must allow council members to express their common concerns in a way that leaves individual member churches free to dissent, especially with respect to "difficult ethical and moral questions."

Sacraments for Polish National Catholics: In response to a request from the Polish National Catholic Church, the Vatican announced in May, 1993, that its members may ask for and receive the sacraments of penance, Eucharist and anointing of the sick from Roman Catholic priests. Polish National Catholic officials said the Vatican ruling "strengthens those fraternal ties which already exist" between the churches and opens the way to increased "opportunities for pastoral care and common witness." Father John F. Hotchkin, executive director of the Secretariat for Ecumenical and Interreligious Affairs, National Conference of Catholic Bishops, said the decision could have significant impact for Polish National Catholics because it offers them access, at their request, to Mass and the sacraments in parts of the country where their own church has no priests or parishes.

Ecumenism a Priority: Calling ecumenism a priority of the Church and not just an area of specialization for interested individuals, Cardinal Edward I. Cassidy said that conversion and education are needed within the Church for all of its members to recognize the importance of Christian unity and efforts to achieve it. The president of the Pontifical Council for Promoting Christian Unity spoke May 10 at the opening of a six-day interfaith meeting attended by representatives of eight Anglican, Orthodox and Protestant churches. The cardinal focused attention on several points, including:

• the importance of ecumenical formation in seminaries and schools of theology;

• reception of the results of dialogue between Catholics and representatives of other churches, called "one of the greatest challenges facing the ecumenical movement at present";

• friendly and respectful relations between local Christian churches, without which "little real progress will be made in the theological dialogue or, indeed, in the ecumenical movement as such."

Faith and Order Conference: Twenty-six representatives of the Pontifical Council for Promoting Christian Unity attended the Fifth World Conference on Faith and Order Aug. 4 to 13, 1993, in Santiago de Compostela, Spain. The underlying theme of discussions was the future role of the Faith and Order movement and its relations to the World Council of Churches and other ecumenical bodies.

JUDAISM

Judaism is the religion of the Hebrew Bible and of contemporary Jews. Divinely revealed and with a patriarchal background (Abraham, Isaac, Jacob), it originated with the Mosaic Covenant, was identified with the Israelites, and achieved distinctive form and character as the religion of the Torah (Law, "The Teaching") from this Covenant and reforms initiated by Ezra and Nehemiah after the Babylonian Exile.

Judaism does not have a formal creed but its principal points of belief are clear. Basic is belief in one transcendent God who reveals himself through the Torah, the prophets, the life of his people and events of history. The fatherhood of God involves the brotherhood of all humanity. Religious faith and practice are equated with just living according to God's Law. Moral conviction and practice are regarded as more important than precise doctrinal formulation and profession. Formal worship, whose principal act was sacrifice from the Exodus times to 70 A.D., is by prayer, reading and meditating upon the sacred writings, and observance of the Sabbath and festivals.

Judaism has messianic expectations of the complete fulfillment of the Covenant, the coming of God's kingdom, the ingathering of his people, and final judgment and retribution for all. Views differ regarding the manner in which these expectations will be realized — through a person, the community of God's people, an evolution of historical events, an eschatological act of God himself. Individual salvation expectations also differ, depending on views about the nature of immortality, punishment and reward, and related matters.

Sacred Books

The sacred books are the 24 books of the Masoretic Hebrew Text of The Law, the Prophets and the Writings (see The Bible). Together, they contain the basic instruction or norms for just living. In some contexts, the term Law or Torah refers only to the Pentateuch (Genesis, Exodus, Leviticus, Numbers, Deuteronomy); in others, it denotes all the sacred books and/or the whole complex of written and oral tradition.

Also of great authority are two Talmuds which were composed in Palestine and Babylon in the fourth and fifth centuries A.D., respectively. They consist of the Mishna, a compilation of oral laws, and the Gemara, a collection of rabbinical commentary on the Mishna. Midrash are collections of scriptural comments and moral counsels.

Priests were the principal official ministers during the period of sacrificial and temple worship. Rabbis were, and continue to be, teachers and leaders of prayer. The synagogue is the place of community worship. The family and home are focal points of many aspects of Jewish worship and practice.

Of the various categories of Jews, Orthodox are the most conservative in adherence to strict religious traditions. Others — Reformed, Conservative, Reconstructionist — are liberal in comparison with the Orthodox. They favor greater or less modification of religious practices in accommoda-tion to contemporary culture and living conditions.

Principal events in Jewish life include the circumcision of males, according to prescriptions of the Covenant; the bar and bat mitzvah which marks the coming-of-age of boys and girls in Judaism at the age of 13; marriage; and observance of the Sabbath and festivals.

Observances of the Sabbath and festivals begin at sundown of the previous calendar day and continue until the following sundown.

Sabbath: Saturday, the weekly day of rest prescribed in the Decalogue.

Sukkoth (Tabernacles): A seven-to-nine-day festival in the month of Tishri (Sept.-Oct.), marked by some Jews with Covenant-renewal and reading of The Law. It originated as an agricultural feast at the end of the harvest and got its name from the temporary shelters used by workers in the fields.

Hanukkah (The Festival of Lights, the Feast of Consecration and of the Maccabees): Commemorates the dedication of the new altar in the Temple at Jerusalem by Judas Maccabeus in 165 B.C. The eight-day festival, during which candles in an eight-branch candelabra are lighted in succession, one each day, occurs near the winter solstice, close to Christmas time.

Pesach (Passover): A seven-day festival commemorating the liberation of the Israelites from Egypt. The narrative of the Exodus, the Haggadah, is read at ceremonial Seder meals on the first and second days of the festival, which begins on the 14th day of Nisan (Mar.-Apr.).

Shavuoth, Pentecost (Feast of Weeks): Observed 50 days after Passover. Some Jews regard it as commemorative of the anniversary of the revelation of The Law to Moses.

Purim: A joyous festival observed on the 14th day of Adar (Feb.-Mar.), commemorating the rescue of the Israelites from massacre by the Persians through the intervention of Esther. The festival is preceded by a day of fasting. A gift- and alms-giving custom became associated with it in medieval times.

Rosh Hashana (Feast of Trumpets, New Year): Observed on the first day of Tishri (Sept.-Oct.), the festival focuses attention on the ways of life and the ways of death. It is second in importance only to the most solemn observance of Yom Kippur, which is celebrated 10 days later.

Yom Kippur (Day of Atonement): The highest holy day, observed with strict fasting. It occurs 10 days after Rosh Hashana.

Yom HaShoah (Holocaust Memorial Day): Observed in the week after Passover; increasingly observed with joint Christian-Jewish services of remembrance.

CATHOLIC-JEWISH RELATIONS

The Second Vatican Council, in addition to the *Decree on Ecumenism* concerning the movement for unity among Christians, stated the mind of the Church on a similar matter in a *Declaration on the Relationship of the Church to Non-Christian Religions.* This document, as the following excerpts indicate, backgrounds the reasons and directions of the Church's regard for the Jews. (Other portions of the document refer to Hindus, Buddhists and Muslims.)

Spiritual Bond

As this sacred Synod searches into the mystery of the Church, it recalls the spiritual bond linking the people of the New Covenant with Abraham's stock.

For the Church of Christ acknowledges that, according to the mystery of God's saving design, the beginnings of her faith and her election are already found among the patriarchs, Moses, and the prophets. She professes that all who believe in

Christ, Abraham's sons according to faith (cf. Gal. 3:7), are included in the same patriarch's call, and likewise that the salvation of the Church was mystically foreshadowed by the Chosen People's exodus from the land of bondage.

The Church, therefore, cannot forget that she received the revelation of the Old Testament through the people with whom God in his inexpressible mercy deigned to establish the Ancient Covenant. Nor can she forget that she draws sustenance from the root of that good olive tree onto which have been grafted the wild olive branches of the Gentiles (cf. Rom.11:17-24). Indeed, the Church believes that by his cross Christ, our Peace, reconciled Jew and Gentile, making them both one in himself (cf. Eph. 2:14-16).

The Jews still remain most dear to God because of their fathers, for he does not repent of the gifts he makes nor of the calls he issues (cf. Rom. 11:28-29). In company with the prophets and the same Apostle (Paul), the Church awaits that day, known to God alone, on which all peoples will address the Lord in a single voice and "serve him with one accord" (Zeph. 3:9; cf. Is. 66:23; Ps. 65:4; Rom. 11:11-32).

Since the spiritual patrimony common to Christians and Jews is thus so great, this sacred Synod wishes to foster and recommend that mutual understanding and respect which is the fruit above all of biblical and theological studies, and of brotherly dialogues.

No Anti-Semitism

True, authorities of the Jews and those who followed their lead pressed for the death of Christ (cf. Jn. 19:6); still, what happened in his passion cannot be blamed upon all the Jews then living, without distinction, nor upon the Jews of today. Although the Church is the new People of God, the Jews should not be presented as repudiated or cursed by God, as if such views followed from the holy Scriptures. All should take pains, then, lest in catechetical instruction and in the preaching of God's Word they teach anything out of harmony with the truth of the Gospel and the spirit of Christ.

The Church repudiates all persecutions against any man. Moreover, mindful of her common patrimony with the Jews, and motivated by the Gospel's spiritual love and by no political considerations, she deplores the hatred, persecutions, and displays of anti-Semitism directed against the Jews at any time and from any source (No. 4).

The Church rejects, as foreign to the mind of Christ, any discrimination against men or harassment of them because of their race, color, condition of life, or religion (No. 5).

Bishops' Secretariat

The American hierarchy's first move toward implementation of the Vatican II *Declaration on the Relationship of the Church to Non-Christian Religions (Nostra Aetate)* was to establish, in 1965, a Subcommission for Catholic-Jewish Relations in the framework of its Commission for Ecumenical and Interreligious Affairs. This subcommission was reconstituted and given the title of secretariat in September, 1967. Its moderator is Cardinal John J. O'Connor of New York. The Secretariat for Catholic-Jewish Relations is located at 3211 Fourth St. N.E., Washington, D.C. 20017 and is directed by Dr. Eugene J. Fisher.

According to the key norm of a set of guidelines issued by the secretariat Mar. 16, 1967, and updated Apr. 9, 1985: "The general aim of all Catholic-Jewish meetings (and relations) is to increase our understanding both of Judaism and the Catholic faith, to eliminate sources of tension and misunderstanding, to initiate dialogue or conversations on different levels, to multiply intergroup meetings between Catholics and Jews, and to promote cooperative social action."

Vatican Guidelines

In a document issued Jan. 3, 1975, the Vatican Commission for Religious Relations with the Jews offered a number of suggestions and guidelines for implementing the Christian-Jewish portion of the Second Vatican Council's *Declaration on Relations with Non-Christian Religions.*

Among "suggestions from experience" were those concerning dialogue, liturgical links between Christian and Jewish worship, the interpretation of biblical texts, teaching and education for the purpose of increasing mutual understanding, and joint social action.

The document concluded with the statement: "On Oct. 22, 1974, the Holy Father instituted for the universal Church this Commission for Religious Relations with the Jews, joined to the Secretariat for Promoting Christian Unity. This special commission, created to encourage and foster religious relations between Jews and Catholics — and to do so in collaboration with other Christians — will be, within the limits of its competence, at the service of all interested organizations, providing information for them and helping them to pursue their task in conformity with the instructions of the Holy See."

Notes on Preaching and Catechesis

On June 24, 1985, the Vatican Commission for Religious Relations with the Jews promulgated its "Notes on the Correct Way to Present Jews and Judaism in Preaching and Catechesis in the Roman Catholic Church," with the intent of providing "a helpful frame of reference for those who are called upon in the course of their teaching assignments to speak about Jews and Judaism and who wish to do so in keeping with the current teaching of the Church in this area."

The document states emphatically that, since the relationship between the Church and the Jewish people is one "founded on the design of the God of the Covenant," Judaism does not occupy "an occasional and marginal place in catechesis," but an "essential" one that "should be organically integrated" throughout the curriculum on all levels of Catholic education.

The Notes discuss the relationship between the Hebrew Scriptures and the New Testament, focusing especially on typology, which is called "the sign of a problem unresolved." Underlined is the "eschatological dimension," that "the people of God of the Old and the New Testament are tending toward a like end in the future: the coming or return of the

Messiah." Jewish witness to God's Kingdom, the Notes declare, challenges Christians to "accept our responsibility to prepare the world for the coming of the Messiah by working together for social justice . . . and reconciliation."

The Notes emphasize the Jewishness of Jesus' teaching, correct misunderstandings concerning the portrayal of Jews in the New Testament and describe the Jewish origins of Christian liturgy. One section addresses the "spiritual fecundity" of Judaism to the present, its continuing "witness — often heroic — of its fidelity to the one God," and mandates the development of Holocaust curricula and a positive approach in Catholic education to the "religious attachment which finds its roots in biblical tradition" between the Jewish people and the Land of Israel, affirming the "existence of the State of Israel" on the basis of "the common principles of international law."

Papal Statements

(Courtesy of Dr. Eugene Fisher, associate director of the Bishops' Committee for Ecumenical and Interreligious Affairs.)

Pope John Paul, in a remarkable series of addresses beginning in 1979, has sought to promote and give shape to the development of dialogue between Catholics and Jews.

In a homily delivered June 7, 1979, at Auschwitz, which he called the "Golgotha of the Modern World," he prayed movingly for "the memory of the people whose sons and daughters were intended for total extermination."

In a key address delivered Nov. 17, 1980, to the Jewish community in Mainz, the Pope articulated his vision of the three "dimensions" of the dialogue: (1) "the meeting between the people of God of the Old Covenant . . . and the people of the New Covenant"; (2) the encounter of "mutual esteem between today's Christian churches and today's people of the Covenant concluded with Moses"; (3) the "holy duty" of witnessing to the one God in the world and "jointly to work for peace and justice."

In addressing representatives of episcopal conferences gathered in Rome from around the world, the Pope again stressed Mar. 6, 1982, the continuing validity of God's covenant with the Jewish people.

On Mar. 22, 1984, at an audience with members of the Anti-Defamation League of B'nai B'rith, the Pope commented on "the mysterious spiritual link which brings us close together, in Abraham and through Abraham, in God who chose Israel and brought forth the Church from Israel." He urged joint social action on "the great task of promoting justice and peace."

In receiving a delegation of the American Jewish Committee Feb. 14, 1985, the Holy Father confirmed that *Nostra Aetate* "remains always for us . . . a teaching which is necessary to accept not merely as something fitting, but much more as an expression of the faith, as an inspiration of the Holy Spirit, as a word of the divine wisdom."

During his historic visit to the Great Synagogue in Rome Apr. 13, 1986, the Holy Father affirmed that God's covenant with the Jewish people is "ir-revocable," and stated: "The Jewish religion is not 'extrinsic' to us, but in a certain way is 'intrinsic' to our own religion. With Judaism, therefore, we have a relationship which we do not have with any other religion."

Meeting with the Jewish community in Sydney, Australia, Nov. 26, 1986, the Holy Father termed the 20th century "the century of the Shoah" (Holocaust) and called "sinful" any "acts of discrimination or persecution against Jews."

On June 14, 1987, meeting with the Jewish community of Warsaw, the Pope called the Jewish witness to the Shoah (Holocaust) a "saving warning before all of humanity" which reveals "your particular vocation, showing you (Jews) to be still the heirs of that election to which God is faithful."

A collection of Pope John Paul's addresses, *On Jews and Judaism* 1979-1986, prepared by the NCCB Secretariat was sent to the Pope Aug. 12, 1987. In a response of Aug. 17, the Pope reiterated his Warsaw statement and added: "Before the vivid memory of the extermination (Shoah), it is not permissible for anyone to pass by with indifference. . . . The sufferings endured by the Jews are also for the Catholic Church a motive of sincere sorrow, especially when one thinks of the indifference and sometimes resentment which . . . have divided Jews and Christians."

Meeting with Jewish leaders Sept. 11, 1987, in Miami, the Pope praised the efforts in theological dialogue and educational reform implemented in the U.S. since the Second Vatican Council; affirmed the existence of the State of Israel "according to international law," and urged "common educational programs on the Holocaust so that never again will such a horror be possible. Never again!"

In an apostolic letter on the 50th anniversary of World War II (Aug. 27, 1989), the Pope stressed the uniqueness of the Jewish sufferings of the Shoah, "which will forever remain a shame for humanity."

On Aug. 14, 1991, during a visit to his home town of Wadowice, Poland, the Pope recalled with sadness the deaths of his Jewish classmates at the hands of the Nazis during World War II: "In the school of Wadowice there were Jewish believers who are no longer with us. There is no longer a synagogue near the school. . . . It is true that your people (the Jews) were on the front lines. . . . The Polish Pope has a special relationship to that period because, together with you, we lived through all that in our Fatherland."

International Liaison Committee

The International Catholic-Jewish Liaison Committee was formed in 1971 and is the official link between the Commission for Religious Relations with the Jewish People and the International Jewish Committee for Interreligious Consultations. The committee meets every 18 months to examine matters of common interest.

Topics under discussion have included: mission and witness (Venice, 1977), religious education (Madrid, 1978), religious liberty and pluralism (Regensburg, 1979), religious commitment (London, 1981), the sanctity of human life in an age of violence (Milan, 1982), youth and faith (Amsterdam, 1984), the

Vatican Notes on Preaching and Catechesis (Rome, 1985), the Holocaust (Prague, 1990), education and social action (Baltimore, Md., 1992). The 1994 meeting was scheduled to be held in Jerusalem.

The Holy See appointed Dr. Eugene Fisher a member of the Liaison Committee Apr. 1, 1984. He is the only lay person and the only American on the committee.

In 1988, the Vatican Library published "selected documents" of the Liaison Committee under the title, *Fifteen Years of Catholic-Jewish Relations.*

Pope John Paul, addressing in Rome a celebration of *Nostra Aetate* (the Second Vatican Council's "Declaration on the Relationship of the Church to Non-Christian Religions") by the Liaison Committee, stated: "What you are celebrating is nothing other than the divine mercy which is guiding Christians and Jews to mutual awareness, respect, cooperation and solidarity. . . . The universal openness of *Nostra Aetate* is anchored in and takes its orientation from a high sense of the absolute singularity of God's choice of a particular people. . . . The Church is fully aware that Sacred Scripture bears witness that the Jewish people, this community of faith and custodian of a tradition thousands of years old, is an intimate part of the mystery of revelation and of salvation."

U.S. Dialogue

The National Workshop on Christian-Jewish Relations, begun in 1973 by the NCCB Secretariat, draws more than 1,000 participants from around the world. Recent workshops have been held in Baltimore (1986), Minneapolis (1987), Charleston, S.C (1989), Chicago (1990) and Pittsburgh (1992). The 1994 meeting was scheduled to be held in Tulsa.

In October, 1987, the Bishops' Committee for Ecumenical and Interreligious Affairs began a review of twice-yearly consultations with representatives of the Synagogue Council of America. Topics of discussion have included education, human rights, respect for life, the Middle East. On June 19, 1990, the group issued a joint statement on moral values in public education.

Ongoing relationships are maintained by the NCCB Secretariat with such Jewish agencies as the American Jewish Committee, the Anti-Defamation League of B'nai B'rith, the Union of American Hebrew Congregations and the American Jewish Congress.

In June, 1988, the Bishops' Committee for Ecumenical and Interreligious Affairs published in Spanish and English *Criteria for the Evaluation of Dramatizations of the Passion,* providing for the first time Catholic guidelines for passion plays.

In January, 1989, the Bishops' Committee for the Liturgy issued guidelines for the homiletic presentation of Judaism under the title, "God's Mercy Endures Forever."

In recent years joint Holocaust memorial services of reconciliation have been held in several diocesan cathedrals on the Sunday closest to Yom HaShoah. The 1993 services were scheduled to be held on Apr. 18.

The 500th anniversary of the expulsion of Jews from Spain was commemorated Mar. 26, 1992, in Toledo, Spain, where Archbishop Ramon Torella addressed a delegation of the Central Conference of American Rabbis with a call for Catholic *teshuvah* (repentance). He said: "1492 was a time for persecution, rejection, eviction, dispossession, forced conversion, exile and even death. . . . (In) 1492 a wall was built, in a sense stronger and more impervious than the Iron Curtain, fallen to pieces not so long ago. 1992 should be a year of *teshuvah*, but also, at the same time, a year of joy. *Teshuvah*, in fact, does not destroy but liberates, thanks to the Lord's mercy and our brothers' disposition for reconciliation." This sentiment was made that of the whole Church by Cardinal Edward Cassidy, president of the Pontifical Council for Promoting Christian Unity, in his opening remarks at the 1992 meeting of the International Liaison Committee in Baltimore.

ISLAM

(Courtesy of Dr. John Borelli, executive secretary for Interreligious Relations, NCCB.)

Islam is the religion of Muhammad and those who follow his example, called Muslims or Moslems. Islam, meaning grateful surrender (to God), originated with Muhammad and the revelation he is believed to have received. Muslims acknowledge that this revelation, recorded in the Quran, is from the one God and do not view Islam as a new religion. They profess that Muhammad was the last in a long series of prophets, most of whom are named in the Hebrew Bible and the New Testament, beginning with Adam and continuing through Noah, Abraham, Moses, Jesus and down to Muhammad.

Muslims believe in the one God, Allah in Arabic, and cognate with the Hebrew Elohim and the ancient Aramaic Ekah. According to the Quran, God is one and transcendent, Creator and Sustainer of the universe, all-merciful and all-compassionate Ruler and Judge. God possesses numerous other titles, known collectively as the 99 other names of God. The profession of faith states: "There is no god but the God and Muhammad is the messenger of God."

The essential duties of Muslims are to: witness the faith by daily recitation of the profession of faith; worship five times a day facing in the direction of the holy city of Mecca; give alms; fast daily from dawn to dusk during the month of Ramadan; make a pilgrimage to Mecca once if possible.

Muslims believe in final judgment, heaven and hell. Morality and following divinely revealed moral norms are extremely important to Muslims. Some dietary regulations are in effect. On Fridays, the noon prayer is a congregational (juma) prayer which should be said in a mosque. The general themes of prayer are adoration and thanksgiving. Muslims do not have an ordained ministry.

The basis of Islamic belief is the Quran, the created word of God revealed to Muhammad through the angel Gabriel over a period of 23 years. The contents of this sacred book are complemented by the Sunna, a collection of sacred traditions from the life of the prophet Muhammad, and reinforced by Ijma, the consensus of Islamic scholars of Islamic Law (Shariah) which guarantees them against errors in matters of belief and practice.

Conciliar Statement

The attitude of the Church toward Islam was stated as follows in the Second Vatican Council's *Declaration on the Relationship of the Church to Non-Christian Religions* (No. 3).

"Upon the Muslims, too, the Church looks with esteem. They adore one God, living and enduring, merciful and all-powerful, Maker of heaven and earth and Speaker to men. They strive to submit wholeheartedly even to his inscrutable decrees, just as did Abraham, with whom the Islamic faith is pleased to associate itself. Though they do not acknowledge Jesus as God, they revere him as a prophet. They also honor Mary, his virgin mother; at times they call on her, too, with devotion. In addition they await the day of judgment when God will give each man his due after raising him up. Conse-quently, they prize the moral life, and give worship to God especially through prayer, almsgiving and fasting.

"Although in the course of the centuries many quarrels and hostilities have arisen between Christians and Muslims, this most sacred Synod urges all to forget the past and to strive sincerely for mutual understanding. On behalf of all mankind, let them make common cause of safeguarding and fostering social justice, moral values, peace and freedom."

Dialogue

Pope John Paul has met with Muslim leaders and delegations both in Rome and during his trips abroad. He has addressed large gatherings of Muslims in Morocco, Indonesia, Mali and elsewhere. The Pontifical Council for Interreligious Dialogue has held formal dialogues with Islamic organizations from time to time. In the U.S., the bishops' Secretariat for Ecumenical and Interreligious Affairs has held three annual consultations on relations with Muslims and several special dialogues related to international crises. An annual dialogue with participation of Catholics and Muslims from several U.S. cities was initiated in October, 1991.

NON-ABRAHAMIC RELIGIONS

(Courtesy of Dr. John Borelli.)

Hinduism and Buddhism — along with Confucianism, Taoism, Shinto, Native American Traditions and other religions — unlike Judaism, Christianity and Islam, are called non-Abrahamic because in them Abraham is not shared as a father in faith.

Common elements among Judaism, Christianity and Islam are more extensive than each has with any other religion. All three are scriptural religions, with Christian scripture making reference to Jewish scripture and Islamic scripture making references to the earlier two. The life of the religious community of each religion is defined through the content and use of its scripture. More common elements among the three religions can be discovered through the study of religious law, liturgy, spirituality and theology.

Two of the principal non-Abrahamic religions are Hinduism and Buddhism.

In its *Declaration on the Relationship of the Church to Non-Christian Religions,* the Second Vatican Council stated: "In Hinduism men contemplate the divine mystery and express it through an unspent fruitfulness of myths and through searching philosophical inquiry. They seek release from the anguish of our condition through ascetical practices or deep meditation or a loving, trusting flight toward God."

Catholics, especially in India, have sought good relations with Hindus and have engaged in numerous dialogues and conferences. In papal visits to India, Paul VI in 1964 and John Paul II in 1986 addressed words of respect for Indian, particularly Hindu, religious leaders. Pope John Paul said to Hindus in 1986: "Your overwhelming sense of the primacy of religion and of the greatness of the Supreme Being has been a powerful witness against a materialistic and atheistic view of life."

"Buddhism in its multiple forms acknowledges the radical insufficiency of this shifting world. It teaches a path by which men, in a devout and confident spirit, can either reach a state of absolute freedom or attain supreme enlightenment by their own efforts or by higher assistance." So stated the Second Vatican Council in its *Declaration on the Relationship of the Church to Non-Christian Religions.*

Numerous delegations of Buddhists, and leading monks have been received by the popes. At the 1986 World Day of Prayer for Peace at Assisi, the Dalai Lama, principal teacher of the Gelug lineage, was placed immediately to the Holy Father's left. Numerous dialogues and good relations beteen Catholics and Buddhists exist in nearly all countries where Buddhists are found, including the United States.

Formal dialogues in the Archdioceses of Los Angeles, San Francisco, Chicago and the Diocese of Honolulu are held from time to time. The Monastic Interreligious Dialogue, a consortium of Catholic monastics, has enjoyed rich exchanges with Buddhist monastics since 1981. In 1989, the Secretariat for Ecumenical and Interreligious Affairs, N.C.C.B., convened its first national consultation on relations with Buddhists; a second consulation was held in 1990.

Ramadan Message: Cardinal Francis Arinze greeted Muslims at the close of Ramadan in March, 1993, saying: "Genuine religion based on belief in God and the desire to do his will is not a divisive and disruptive element in society but is, rather, the firmest foundation for love of others, for justice and for a more fraternal and peaceful society."

GLOSSARY

A

Abbacy: A non-diocesan territory whose people are under the pastoral care of an abbot acting in general in the manner of a bishop.

Abbess: The female superior of a monastic community of nuns; e.g., Benedictines, Poor Clares, some others. Elected by members of the community, an abbess has general authority over her community but no sacramental jurisdiction.

Abbey: See Monastery.

Abbot: The male superior of a monastic community of men religious; e.g., Benedictines, Cistercians, some others. Elected by members of the community, an abbot has ordinary jurisdiction and general authority over his community. Eastern-Rite equivalents of an abbot are a *hegumen* and an *archimandrite.* A regular abbot is the head of an abbey or monastery. An abbot general or archabbot is the head of a congregation consisting of several monasteries. An abbot primate is the head of the modern Benedictine Confederation.

Ablution: A term derived from Latin, meaning washing or cleansing, and referring to the cleansing of the hands of a priest celebrating Mass, after the offering of gifts; and to the cleansing of the chalice with water and wine after Communion.

Abortion: Abortion is not only "the ejection of an immature fetus" from the womb, but is "also the killing of the same fetus in whatever way at whatever time from the moment of conception it may be procured." (This clarification of Canon 1398, reported in the Dec. 5, 1988, edition of *L'-Osservatore Romano,* was issued by the Pontifical Council for the Interpretation of Legislative Texts — in view of scientific developments regarding ways and means of procuring abortion.) Accidental expulsion, as in cases of miscarriage, is without moral fault. Direct abortion, in which a fetus is intentionally removed from the womb, constitutes a direct attack on an innocent human being, a violation of the Fifth Commandment. A person who procures a completed abortion is automatically excommunicated (Canon 1398 of the Code of Canon Law); also excommunicated are all persons involved in a deliberate and successful effort to bring about an abortion. Direct abortion is not justifiable for any reason, e.g.: therapeutic, for the physical and/or psychological welfare of the mother; preventive, to avoid the birth of a defective or unwanted child; social, in the interests of family and/or community. Indirect abortion, which occurs when a fetus is expelled during medical or other treatment of the mother for a reason other than procuring expulsion, is permissible under the principle of double effect for a proportionately serious reason; e.g., when a medical or surgical procedure is necessary to save the life of the mother.

Absolution, Sacramental: The act by which an authorized priest, acting as the agent of Christ and minister of the Church, grants forgiveness of sins in the sacrament of penance. The essential formula of absolution is: "I absolve you from your sins; in the name of the Father, and of the Son, and of the Holy Spirit. Amen." Priests receive the power to absolve in virtue of their ordination and the right to exercise this power in virtue of faculties of jurisdiction given them by their bishop, their religious superior, or by canon law. The faculties of jursidiction can be limited or restricted regarding certain sins and penalties or censures. In cases of necessity, and also in cases of the absence of their own confessors, Eastern- and Roman-Rite Catholics may ask for and receive sacramental absolution from an Eastern- or Roman-Rite priest. Any priest can absolve a person in danger of death; in the absence of a priest with the usual faculties, this includes a laicized priest or a priest under censure. (See additional entry under Sacraments.)

Accessory to Another's Sin: One who culpably assists another in the performance of an evil action. This may be done by counsel, command, provocation, consent, praise, flattery, concealment, participation, silence, defense of the evil done.

Adoration: The highest act and purpose of religious worship, which is directed in love and reverence to God alone in acknowledgment of his infinite perfection and goodness, and of his total dominion over creatures. Adoration, which is also called *latria,* consists of internal and external elements, private and social prayer, liturgical acts and ceremonies, and especially sacrifice.

Adultery: (1) Sexual intercourse between a married person and another to whom one is not married; a violation of the obligations of chastity and justice. The Sixth Commandment prohibition against adultery also prohibits all external sins of a sexual nature. (2) Any sin of impurity (thought, desire, word, action) involving a married person who is not one's husband or wife has the nature of adultery.

Adventists: Members of several Christian sects whose doctrines are dominated by belief in a more or less imminent second advent or coming of Christ upon earth for a glorious 1,000-year reign of righteousness. This reign, following victory by the forces of good over evil in a final Battle of Armageddon, will begin with the resurrection of the chosen and will end with the resurrection of all others and the annihilation of the wicked. Thereafter, the just will live forever in a renewed heaven and earth. A sleep of the soul takes place between the time of death and the day of judgment. There is no hell. The Bible, in fundamentalist interpretation, is regarded as the only rule of faith and practice. About six sects have developed in the course of the Adventist movement which originated with William Miller (1782-1849) in the United States. Miller, on the basis of calculations made from the Book of Daniel, predicted that the second advent of Christ would occur between 1843 and 1844. After the prophecy went unfulfilled, divisions occurred in the movement and the Seventh Day Adventists, whose actual formation dates from 1860, emerged as the largest single body. The observance of Saturday instead of Sunday as the Lord's Day dates from 1844.

Advent Wreath: A wreath of laurel, spruce, or similar foliage with four candles which are lighted successively in the weeks of Advent to symbolize the approaching celebration of the birth of Christ, the Light of the World, at Christmas. The wreath originated among German Protestants.

Agape: A Greek word, meaning love, love feast, designating the meal of fellowship eaten at some gatherings of early Christians. Although held in some places in connection with the Mass, the agape was not part of the Mass, nor was it of universal institution and observance. It was infrequently observed by the fifth century and disappeared altogether between the sixth and eighth centuries.

Age of Reason: (1) The time of life when one begins to distinguish between right and wrong, to understand an obligation and take on moral responsibility; seven years of age is the presumption in church law. (2) Historically, the 18th century period of Enlightenment in England and France, the age of the Encyclopedists and Deists. According to a basic thesis of the Enlightenment, human experience and reason are the only sources of certain knowledge of truth; consequently, faith and revelation are discounted as valid sources of knowledge, and the reality of supernatural truth is called into doubt and/or denied.

Aggiornamento: An Italian word having the general meaning of bringing up to date, renewal, revitalization, descriptive of the processes of spiritual renewal and institutional reform and change in the Church; fostered by the Second Vatican Council.

Agnosticism: A theory which holds that a person cannot have certain knowledge of immaterial reality, especially the existence of God and things pertaining to him. Immanuel Kant, one of the philosophical fathers of agnosticism, stood for the position that God, as well as the human soul, is unknowable on speculative grounds; nevertheless, he found practical imperatives for acknowledging God's existence, a view shared by many agnostics. The First Vatican Council declared that the existence of God and some of his attributes can be known with certainty by human reason, even without divine revelation. The word agnosticism was first used, in the sense given here, by T. H. Huxley in 1869.

Agnus Dei: A Latin phrase, meaning Lamb of God. (1) A title given to Christ, the Lamb (victim) of the Sacrifice of the New Law (on Calvary and in Mass). (2) A prayer said at Mass before the reception of Holy Communion. (3) A sacramental. It is a round paschal-candle fragment blessed by the pope. On one side it bears the impression of a lamb, symbolic of Christ. On the reverse side, there may be any one of a number of impressions; e.g., the figure of a saint, the name and coat of arms of the reigning pope. The *agnus dei* may have originated at Rome in the fifth century. The first definite mention of it dates from about 820.

Akathist Hymn: The most profound and famous expression of Marian devotion in churches of the Byzantine rite. It consists of 24 sections, 12 of which relate to the Gospel of the Infancy and 12 to the mysteries of the Incarnation and the virginal motherhood of Mary. In liturgical usage, it is sung in part in Byzantine churches on the first four Saturdays of Lent and in toto on the fifth Saturday; it is also recited in private devotion. It is of unknown origin prior to 626, when its popularity increased as a hymn of thanksgiving after the successful defense and liberation of Constantinople, which had been under siege by Persians and Avars. Akathist means "without sitting," indicating that the hymn is recited or sung while standing. Pope John Paul, in a decree dated May 25, 1991, granted a plenary indulgence to the faithful of any rite who recite the hymn in a church or oratory, as a family, in a religious community or in a pious association — in conjunction with the usual conditions of freedom from attachment to sin, reception of the sacraments of penance and the Eucharist, and prayers for the intention of the Pope (e.g., an Our Father, the Apostles' Creed and an aspiration). A partial indulgence can be gained for recitation of the hymn in other circumstances.

Alleluia: An exclamation of joy derived from Hebrew, "All hail to him who is, praise God," with various use in the liturgy and other expressions of worship.

Allocution: A formal type of papal address, as distinguished from an ordinary sermon or statement of views.

Alms: An act, gift or service of compassion, motivated by love of God and neighbor, for the help of persons in need; an obligation of charity, which is measurable by the ability of one person to give assistance and by the degree of another's need. Almsgiving, along with prayer and fasting, is regarded as a work of penance as well as an exercise of charity. (See Corporal and Spiritual Works of Mercy.)

Alpha and Omega: The first and last letters of the Greek alphabet, used to symbolize the eternity of God (Rv. 1:8) and the divinity and eternity of Christ, the beginning and end of all things (Rv. 21:6; 22:13). Use of the letters as a monogram of Christ originated in the fourth century or earlier.

Amen: A Hebrew word meaning truly, it is true. In the Gospels, Christ used the word to add a note of authority to his statements. In other New Testament writings, as in Hebrew usage, it was the concluding word to doxologies. As the concluding word of prayers, it expresses assent to and acceptance of God's will.

Anathema: A Greek word with the root meaning of cursed or separated and the adapted meaning of excommunication, used in church documents, especially the canons of ecumenical councils, for the condemnation of heretical doctrines and of practices opposed to proper discipline.

Anchorite: A kind of hermit living in complete isolation and devoting himself exclusively to exercises of religion and severe penance according to a rule and way of life of his own devising. In early Christian times, anchorites were the forerunners of the monastic life. The closest contemporary approach to the life of an anchorite is that of Carthusian and Camaldolese hermits.

Angels: Purely spiritual beings with intelligence and free will, whose name indicates their mission as ministers of God and ministering spirits to men. They were created before the creation of the visible universe; the devil and bad angels, who were created good, fell from glory through their own fault. In addition to these essentials of defined doctrine, it is held that angels are personal beings; they can intercede for persons; fallen angels were banished from God's glory in heaven to hell; bad angels can tempt persons to commit sin. The doctrine of guardian angels, although not explicitly defined as a matter of faith, is rooted in long-standing tradition. No authoritative declaration has ever been issued regarding choirs or various categories of angels: according to theorists, there are nine choirs, consisting of seraphim, cherubim, thrones, dominations, principalities, powers, virtues, archangels and angels. In line with scriptural usage, only three angels can be named—Michael, Raphael and Gabriel.

Angelus: A devotion which commemorates the Incarnation of Christ. It consists of three versicles, three Hail Marys and a special prayer, and recalls the announcement to Mary by the Archangel Gabriel that she was chosen to be the Mother of Christ, her acceptance of the divine will, and the Incarnation (Lk. 1:26-38). The Angelus is recited in the morning, at noon and in the evening. The practice of reciting the Hail Mary in honor of the Incarnation was introduced by the Franciscans in 1263. The *Regina Caeli*, commemorating the joy of Mary at Christ's Resurrection, replaces the Angelus during the Easter season.

Anger: Passionate displeasure arising from some kind of offense suffered at the hands of another person, frustration or other cause, combined with a tendency to strike back at the cause of the displeasure; a violation of the Fifth Commandment and one of the capital sins if the displeasure is out of proportion to the cause and or if the retaliation is unjust.

Anglican Orders: Holy orders conferred according to the rite of the Anglican Church, which Leo XIII declared null and void in the bull *Apostolicae Curae,* Sept. 13, 1896. The orders were declared null because they were conferred according to a rite that was substantially defective in form and intent, and because of a break in apostolic succession that occurred when Matthew Parker became head of the Anglican hierarchy in 1559. In making his declaration, Pope Leo cited earlier arguments against validity made by Julius III in 1553 and 1554 and by Paul IV in 1555. He also noted related directives requiring absolute ordination, according to the Catholic ritual, of convert ministers who had been ordained according to the Anglican Ordinal.

Antichrist: The man of sin, the lawless and wicked antagonist of Christ and the work of God; a mysterious figure of prophecy mentioned in the New Testament. Supported by Satan, submitting to no moral restraints, and armed with tremendous power, Antichrist will set himself up in opposition to God, work false miracles, persecute the People of God, and employ unimaginable means to lead people into error and evil during a period of widespread defection from the Christian faith before the end of time; he will be overcome by Christ. Catholic thinkers have regarded Antichrist as a person, a caricature of Christ, who will lead a final violent struggle against God and his people; they have also applied the title to personal and impersonal forces in history hostile to God and the Church. Official teaching has said little about Antichrist. In 1318, it labeled as partly heretical, sense-

less, and fanciful the assertions made by the Fraticelli about his coming; in 1415, the Council of Constance condemned the Wycliff thesis that excommunications made by the pope and other prelates were the actions of Antichrist.

Antiphon: (1) A short verse or text, generally from Scripture, recited in the Liturgy of the Hours before and after psalms and canticles. (2) Any verse sung or recited by one part of a choir or congregation in response to the other part, as in antiphonal or alternate chanting.

Apologetics: The science and art of developing and presenting the case for the reasonableness of the Christian faith, by a wide variety of means including facts of experience, history, science, philosophy. The constant objective of apologetics, as well as of the total process of pre-evangelization, is preparation for response to God in faith; its ways and means, however, are subject to change in accordance with the various needs of people and different sets of circumstances.

Apostasy: (1) The total and obstinate repudiation of the Christian faith. An apostate automatically incurs a penalty of excommunication. (2) Apostasy from orders is the unlawful withdrawal from or rejection of the obligations of the clerical state by a man who has received major orders. An apostate from orders is subject to a canonical penalty. (3) Apostasy from the religious life occurs when a Religious with perpetual vows unlawfully leaves the community with the intention of not returning, or actually remains outside the community without permission. An apostate from religious life is subject to a canonical penalty.

Apostolate: The ministry or work of an apostle. In Catholic usage, the word is an umbrella-like term covering all kinds and areas of work and endeavor for the service of God and the Church and the good of people. Thus, the apostolate of bishops is to carry on the mission of the Apostles as pastors of the People of God: of priests, to preach the word of God and to carry out the sacramental and pastoral ministry for which they are ordained; of religious, to follow and do the work of Christ in conformity with the evangelical counsels and their rule of life; of lay persons, as individuals and/or in groups, to give witness to Christ and build up the kingdom of God through practice of their faith, professional competence and the performance of good works in the concrete circumstances of daily life. Apostolic works are not limited to those done within the Church or by specifically Catholic groups, although some apostolates are officially assigned to certain persons or groups and are under the direction of church authorities. Apostolate derives from the commitment and obligation of baptism, confirmation, holy orders, matrimony, the duties of one's state in life, etc.

Apostolic Succession: Bishops of the Church, who form a collective body or college, are successors to the Apostles by ordination and divine right; as such they carry on the mission entrusted by Christ to the Apostles as guardians and teachers of the deposit of faith, principal pastors and spiritual authorities of the faithful. The doctrine of apostolic succession is based on New Testament evidence and the constant teaching of the Church, reflected as early as the end of the first century in a letter of Pope St. Clement to the Corinthians. A significant facet of the doctrine is the role of the pope as the successor of St. Peter, the vicar of Christ and head of the college of bishops. The doctrine of apostolic succession means more than continuity of apostolic faith and doctrine; its basic requisite is ordination by the laying on of hands in apostolic succession.

Archangel: An angel who carries out special missions for God in his dealings with persons. Three of them are named in the Bible: Michael, leader of the angelic host and protector of the synagogue; Raphael, guide of Tobiah and healer of his father, who is regarded as the patron of travelers; Gabriel, called the angel of the Incarnation because of his announcement to Mary that she was to be the Mother of Christ.

Archdiocese: An ecclesiastical jurisdiction headed by an archbishop. An archdiocese is usually a metropolitan see, i.e., the principal one of a group of dioceses comprising a province; the other dioceses in the province are suffragan sees.

Archives: Documentary records, and the place where they are kept, of the spiritual and temporal government and affairs of the Church, a diocese, church agencies like the departments of the Roman Curia, bodies like religious institutes, and individual parishes. The collection, cataloguing, preserving, and use of these records are governed by norms stated in canon law and particular regulations. The strictest secrecy is always in effect for confidential records concerning matters of conscience, and documents of this kind are destroyed as soon as circumstances permit.

Ark of the Covenant: The sacred chest of the Israelites in which were placed and carried the tablets of stone inscribed with the Ten Commandments, the basic moral precepts of the Old Covenant (Ex. 25: 10-22; 37:1-9). The Ark was also a symbol of God's presence. The Ark was probably destroyed with the Temple in 587 B.C.

Asceticism: The practice of self-discipline. In the spiritual life, asceticism — by personal prayer, meditation, self-denial, works of mortification, and outgoing interpersonal works — is motivated by love of God and contributes to growth in holiness.

Ashes: Religious significance has been associated with their use as symbolic of penance since Old Testament times. Thus, ashes of palm blessed on the previous Sunday of the Passion are placed on the foreheads of the faithful on Ash Wednesday to remind them to do works of penance, especially during the season of Lent, and that they are dust and unto dust will return. Ashes are a sacramental.

Aspergillum: A vessel or device used for sprinkling holy water. The ordinary type is a metallic rod with a bulbous tip which absorbs the water and discharges it at the motion of the user's hand.

Aspersory: A portable metallic vessel, similar to a pail, for carrying holy water.

Aspiration (Ejaculation): Short exclamatory prayer; e.g., My Jesus, mercy.

Atheism: Denial of the existence of God, finding expression in a system of thought (speculative atheism) or a manner of acting (practical atheism) as though there were no God. The Second Vatican Council, in its *Pastoral Constitution on the Church in the Modern World* (Nos. 19 to 21), noted that a profession of atheism may represent an explicit denial of God. the rejection of a wrong notion of God, an affirmation of man rather than of God, an extreme protest against evil. It said that such a profession might result from acceptance of such propositions as: there is no absolute truth; man can assert nothing, absolutely nothing, about God; everything can be explained by scientific reasoning alone; the whole question of God is devoid of meaning. The constitution also cited two opinions of influence in atheistic thought. One of them regards recognition of dependence on God as incompatible with human freedom and independence. The other views belief in God and religion as a kind of opiate which sedates man on earth, reconciling him to the acceptance of suffering, injustice, shortcomings, etc., because of hope for greater things after death, and thereby hindering him from seeking and working for improvement and change for the better here and now. All of these views, in one way or another, have been involved in the No-God and Death-of-God schools of thought in recent and remote history.

Atonement: The redemptive activity of Christ, who reconciled man with God through his Incarnation and entire life, and especially by his suffering and Resurrection. The word also applies to prayer and good works by which persons join themselves with and take part in Christ's work of reconciliation and reparation for sin.

Attributes of God: Perfections of God. God possesses — and is — all the perfections of being, without limitation. Because he is infinite, all of these perfections are one, perfectly united in him. Man, however, because of the limited power of understanding, views these perfections separately, as distinct characteristics — even though they are not actually distinct in God. Thus God is: almighty, eternal, holy, immortal, immense, immutable, incomprehensible, ineffable, infinite, invisible, just, loving, merciful, most high, most wise, omnipotent, omniscient, omnipresent, patient, perfect, provident, supreme, true.

Avarice (Covetousness): A disorderly and unreasonable attachment to and desire for material things; called a capital sin because it involves preoccupation with material things to the neglect of spiritual goods and obligations of justice and charity.

Ave Maria: See Hail Mary.

B

Baldachino: A canopy over an altar.

Base Ecclesial Communities: The concept and operational model of basic Christian communities — *comunidades de base* — envision relatively small communities of the faithful integrated for religious and secular life, with maximum potential for liturgical and sacramental participation, pastoral ministry, apostolic activity, and for personal and social development. Communities of this type originated mainly in Latin America; thousands of them are now contributing to the vitality of parishes and dioceses in many countries throughout the world.

Pope Paul VI, in *Evangelii Nuntiandi*, stated: The name "Ecclesial Communities" can be given only to those "that appear and develop ... within the Church, having solidarity with her life, being nourished by her teaching and united with her pastors." The name should not be attributed to those "that come together in a spirit of bitter criticism of the Church" and radically oppose the Church. Only the genuine base ecclesial communities "will be a place of evangelization for the benefit of the bigger communities, especially the individual churches ... and will be a hope for the universal Church to the extent ... that they constantly grow in missionary consciousness, fervor, commitment and zeal."

Beatification: A preliminary step toward canonization of a saint. It begins with an investigation of the candidate's life, writings and heroic practice of virtue, and, except in the case of martyrs, the certification of one miracle worked by God through his or her intercession. If the findings of the investigation so indicate, the pope decrees that the Servant of God may be called *Blessed* and may be honored locally or in a limited way in the liturgy. Additional procedures lead to canonization (see separate entry).

Beatific Vision: The intuitive, immediate and direct vision and experience of God enjoyed in the light of glory by all the blessed in heaven. The vision is a supernatural mystery.

Beatitude: A literary form of the Old and New Testaments in which blessings are promised to persons for various reasons. Beatitudes are mentioned 26 times in the Psalms, and in other books of the Old Testament. The best known beatitudes — identifying blessedness with participation in the kingdom of God and his righteousness, and descriptive of the qualities of Christian perfection — are those recounted in Mt. 5:3-11 and Lk. 6:20-22.

Benedictus: The canticle or hymn of Zechariah at the circumcision of St. John the Baptist (Lk. 1:68-79). It is an expression of praise and thanks to God for sending John as a precursor of the Messiah. The *Benedictus* is recited in the Liturgy of the Hours as part of the Morning Prayer.

Biglietto: A papal document of notification of appointment to the cardinalate.

Biretta: A stiff, square hat with three ridges on top worn by clerics in church and on other occasions.

Blasphemy: Any expression of insult or contempt with respect to God, principally, and to holy persons and things, secondarily; a violation of the honor due to God in the context of the First and Second Commandments.

Blasphemy of the Spirit: Deliberate resistance to the Holy Spirit, called the unforgivable sin (Mt. 12:31) because it makes his saving action impossible. Thus, the only unforgivable sin is the one for which a person will not seek pardon from God.

Blessing: Invocation of God's favor, by official ministers of the Church or by private individuals. Blessings are recounted in the Old and New Testaments, and are common in the Christian tradition. Many types of blessings are listed in the *Roman Ritual*. Private blessings, as well as those of an official kind, are efficacious. Blessings are imparted with the Sign of the Cross and appropriate prayer.

Boat: A small vessel used to hold incense which is to be placed in the censer.

Brief, Apostolic: A papal letter, less formal than a bull, signed for the pope by a secretary and impressed with the seal of the Fisherman's Ring. Simple apostolic letters of this kind are issued for beatifications and with respect to other matters.

Bull, Apostolic: The most solemn form of papal document, beginning with the name and title of the pope (e.g., John Paul II, Servant of the Servants of God), dealing with an important subject, and having attached to it either a leaden seal called a *bulla* or a red ink imprint of the device on the seal. Bulls are issued to confer the titles of bishops and cardinals, to promulgate canonizations, and for other purposes. A collection of bulls is called a *bullarium*.

Burial, Ecclesiastical: Interment with ecclesiastical rites, a right of the Christian faithful. The Church recommends burial of the bodies of the dead, but cremation is permissible if it does not involve reasons against church teaching. Ecclesiastical burial is in order for catechumens; for unbaptized children whose parents intended to have them baptized before death; and even — in the absence of their own ministers — for baptized non-Catholics unless it would be considered against their will.

C

Calumny: Harming the name and good reputation of a person by lies; a violation of obligations of justice and truth. Restitution is due for calumny.

Calvary: A knoll about 15 feet high just outside the western wall of Jerusalem where Christ was crucified, so called from the Latin *calvaria* (skull) which described its shape.

Canon: A Greek word meaning rule, norm, standard, measure. (1) The word designates the Canon of Sacred Scripture, which is the list of books recognized by the Church as inspired by the Holy Spirit. (2) The term also designates the canons, (Eucharistic Prayers, anaphoras) of the Mass, the core of the liturgy. (3) Certain dignitaries of the Church have the title of Canon, and some Religious are known as Canons.

Canonization: An infallible declaration by the pope that a person, who died as a martyr and/or practiced Christian virtue to a heroic degree, is now in heaven and is worthy of honor and imitation by all the faithful. Such a declaration is preceded by the process of beatification and another detailed investigation concerning the person's reputation for holiness, writings, and (except in the case of martyrs) a miracle ascribed to his or her intercession after death. The pope can dispense from some of the formalities ordinarily required in canonization procedures (equivalent canonization), as Pope John XXIII did in the canonization of St. Gregory Barbarigo on May 26, 1960. A saint is worthy of honor in liturgical worship throughout the universal Church. From its earliest years the Church has venerated saints. Public official honor always required the approval of the bishop of the place. Martyrs were the first to be honored. St. Martin of Tours, who died in 397, was an early non-martyr venerated as a saint. The earliest canonization by a pope with positive documentation was that of St. Ulrich (Uldalric) of Augsburg by John XV in 993. Alexander III reserved the process of canonization to the Holy See in 1171. In 1588 Sixtus V established the Sacred Congregation of Rites for the principal purpose of handling causes for beatification and canonization: this function is now the work of the Congregation for the Causes of Saints. The official listing of saints and blessed is contained in the *Roman Martyrology* (being revised and updated) and related decrees issued after its last publication. Butler's unofficial *Lives of the Saints* (1956) contains 2,565 entries. The Church regards all persons in heaven as saints, not just those who have been officially canonized. (See Beatification, Saints, Canonizations by Leo XIII and His Successors.)

Canon Law: The Code of Canon Law enacted and promulgated by ecclesiastical authority for the orderly and pastoral administration and government of the Church. A revised Code for the Latin rite, effective Nov. 27, 1983, consists of 1,752 canons in seven books under the titles of general norms, the people of God, the teaching mission of the Church, the sanctifying mission of the Church, temporal goods of the Church, penal law and procedural law. The antecedent of this Code was promulgated in 1917 and became effective in 1918; it consisted of 2,414 canons in five books covering general rules, ecclesiastical persons, sacred things, trials, crimes and punishments. There is a separate Code of the Canons of Eastern Churches, in effect since Oct. 1, 1991.

Canticle: A scriptural chant or prayer differing from the psalms. Three of the canticles prescribed for use in the Liturgy of the Hours are: the *Magnificat* (Lk. 1:46-55), the *Benedictus* (Lk. 1:68-79), and the *Nunc Dimittis* (Lk. 2:29-32).

Capital Punishment: Punishment for crime by means of the death penalty. The political community, which has authority to provide for the common good, has the right to defend itself and its members against unjust aggression and may in extreme cases punish with the death penalty persons found guilty before the law of serious crimes against individuals and a just social order. Such punishment is essentially vindictive. Its value as a crime deterrent is a matter of perennial debate. The prudential judgment as to whether or not there should be capital punishment belongs to the civic community. The U.S. Supreme Court, in a series of decisions dating from June 29, 1972, ruled against the constitutionality of statutes on capital punishment except in specific cases and with appropriate consideration, with respect to sentence, of mitigating circumstances of the crime. Capital punishment was the subject of a statement issued Mar. 1, 1978, by the Committee on Social Development and World Peace, U.S. Catholic Conference. The statement said, in part: "The use of the death penalty involves deep moral and religious questions as well as political and legal issues. In 1974, out of a commitment to the value and dignity of human life, the Catholic bishops of the United States declared their opposition to capital punishment. We continue to support this position, in the belief that a return to the use of the death penalty can only lead to the further erosion of respect for life in our society." Additional statements against capital punishment have been issued by Pope John Paul II, numerous bishops and other sources. More than 200 executions have taken place in the U.S. since 1976.

Capital Sins: Moral faults which, if habitual, give rise to many more sins. They are pride, covetousness, lust, anger, gluttony, envy, sloth. The opposite virtues are: humility, liberality, chastity, meekness, temperance, brotherly love, diligence.

Cardinal Virtues: The four principal moral virtues are prudence, justice, temperance and fortitude.

Catacombs: Underground Christian cemeteries in various cities of the Roman Empire and Italy, especially in the vicinity of Rome; the burial sites of many martyrs and other Christians.

Catechesis: Religious instruction and formation not only for persons preparing for baptism but also for the faithful in various stages of their spiritual development.

Catechism: A summary of Christian doctrine usually in question and answer form, used for purposes of instruction.

Catechumen: A person preparing in a program (catechumenate) of instruction and spiritual formation for baptism and reception into the Church. The Church has a special relationship with catechumens. It invites them to lead the life of the Gospel, introduces them to the celebration of the sacred rites, and grants them various prerogatives that are proper to the faithful (one of which is the right to ecclesiastical burial). (See Rite of Christian Initiation of Adults, under Baptism.)

Cathedra: A Greek word for chair, designating the chair or seat of a bishop in the principal church of his diocese, which is therefore called a cathedral (see separate entry).

Cathedraticum: The tax paid to a bishop by all churches and benefices subject to him for the support of episcopal administration and for works of charity.

Catholic: A Greek word, meaning universal, first used in the title Catholic Church in a letter written by St. Ignatius of Antioch about 107 to the Christians of Smyrna.

Celebret: A Latin word, meaning Let him celebrate, the name of a letter of recommendation issued by a bishop or other superior stating that a priest is in good standing and therefore eligible to celebrate Mass or perform other priestly functions.

Celibacy: The unmarried state of life, required in the Roman Church of candidates for holy orders and of men already ordained to holy orders, for the practice of perfect chastity and total dedication to the service of people in the ministry of the Church. Celibacy is enjoined as a condition for ordination by church discipline and law, not by dogmatic necessity. In the Roman Church, a consensus in favor of celibacy developed in the early centuries while the clergy included both celibates and men who had been married once. The first local legislation on the subject was enacted by a local council held in Elvira, Spain, about 306; it forbade bishops, priests, deacons and other ministers to have wives. Similar enactments were passed by other local councils from that time on, and by the 12th century particular laws regarded marriage by clerics in major orders to be not only unlawful but also null and void. The latter view was translated by the Second Lateran Council in 1139 into what seems to be the first written universal law making holy orders an invalidating impediment to marriage. In 1563 the Council of Trent ruled definitely on the matter and established the discipline in force in the Roman Church. Some exceptions to this discipline have been made in recent years. Several married Protestant and Episcopalian (Anglican) clergymen who became converts and were subsequently ordained to the priesthood have been permitted to continue in marriage. Married men over the age of 35 can be ordained to the permanent diaconate. Eastern Church discipline on celibacy differs from that of the Roman Church. In line with legislation enacted by the Synod of Trullo in 692 and still in force, candidates for holy orders may marry before becoming deacons and may continue in marriage thereafter, but marriage after ordination is forbidden. Eastern-Rite bishops in the U.S., however, do not ordain married candidates for the priesthood. Eastern-Rite bishops are unmarried.

Cenacle: The upper room in Jerusalem where Christ ate the Last Supper with his Apostles.

Censer: A metal vessel with a perforated cover and suspended by chains, in which incense is burned. It is used at some Masses, Benediction of the Blessed Sacrament and other liturgical functions.

Censorship of Books: An exercise of vigilance by the Church for safeguarding authentic religious teaching. Pertinent legislation in a decree issued by the Congregation for the Doctrine of the Faith Apr. 9, 1975, is embodied in the Code of Canon Law (Book III, Title IV). (1) Pre-publication clearance is required for: editions of Sacred Scripture, liturgical texts and books of private devotion, catechisms and other writings relating to catechetical instruction. Books dealing with Scripture, theology, canon law, church history and religious or moral disciplines may not be used as basic texts in educational institutions (from elementary to university levels) unless they have been published with the approval of competent church authority. (2) Pre-publication clearance is recommended for all books on the aforementioned subjects, even though they are not used as basic texts in teaching. (3) Books or other writings dealing with religion or morals may not be displayed, sold or given out in churches or oratories unless published with the approval of competent ecclesiastical authority. (4) Except for a just and reasonable cause, Catholics should not write for newspapers, magazines or periodicals which regularly and openly prove to be inimical to the Catholic religion and good morals. The approval of the local bishop is required before clerics or members of religious institutes (who also need the approval of their superior) may write for such publications. Permission to publish works of a religious character, together with the apparatus of reviewing them beforehand, falls under the authority of the bishop of the place where the writer lives or where the works are published. Clearance for publication is usually indicated by the terms *Nihil obstat* (Nothing stands in the way) issued by the censor and

Imprimatur (Let it be printed) authorized by the bishop. The clearing of works for publication does not necessarily imply approval of an author's viewpoint or his manner of handling a subject.

Censures: Sanctions inflicted by the Church on baptized Roman Catholics 18 years of age or older for committing certain serious offenses and for being or remaining obstinate therein: (1) excommunication (exclusion from the community of the faithful, barring a person from sacramental and other participation in the goods and offices of the community of the Church), (2) suspension (prohibition of a cleric to exercise orders) and (3) interdict (deprivation of the sacraments and liturgical activities). The intended purposes of censures are to correct and punish offenders; to deter persons from committing sins which, more seriously and openly than others, threaten the common good of the Church and its members; and to provide for the making of reparation for harm done to the community of the Church. Censures may be incurred automatically (*ipso facto*) on the commission of certain offenses for which fixed penalties have been laid down in church law (*latae sententiae*); or they may be inflicted by sentence of a judge (*ferendae sententiae*). Automatic excommunication is incurred for the offenses of abortion, apostasy, heresy and schism. Obstinacy in crime — also called contumacy, disregard of a penalty, defiance of church authority — is presumed by law in the commission of offenses for which automatic censures are decreed. The presence and degree of contumacy in other cases, for which judicial sentence is required, is subject to determination by a judge. Absolution can be obtained from any censure, provided the person repents and desists from obstinacy. Absolution may be reserved to the pope, the bishop of a place, or the major superior of an exempt clerical religious institute. In danger of death, any priest can absolve from all censures; in other cases, faculties to absolve from reserved censures can be exercised by competent authorities or given to other priests. The penal law of the Church is contained in Book VI of the Code of Canon Law.

Ceremonies, Master of: One who directs the proceedings of a rite or ceremony during the function.

Chamberlain (Camerlengo): (1) the Chamberlain of the Holy Roman Church is a cardinal who administers the property and revenues of the Holy See. On the death of the pope he becomes head of the College of Cardinals and summons and directs the conclave until a new pope is elected. (2) the Chamberlain of the College of Cardinals has charge of the property and revenues of the College and keeps the record of business transacted in consistories. (3) the Chamberlain of the Roman Clergy is the president of the secular clergy of Rome.

Chancellor: Notary of a diocese, who draws up written documents in the government of the diocese; takes care of, arranges and indexes diocesan archives, records of dispensations and ecclesiastical trials.

Chancery: (1) A branch of church administration that handles written documents used in the government of a diocese. (2) The administrative office of a diocese, a bishop's office.

Chapel: A building or part of another building used for divine worship; a portion of a church set aside for the celebration of Mass or for some special devotion.

Chaplain: A priest appointed for the pastoral service of any division of the armed forces, religious communities, institutions, various groups of the faithful.

Chaplet: A term, meaning little crown, applied to a rosary or, more commonly, to a small string of beads used for devotional purposes; e.g., the Infant of Prague chaplet.

Chapter: A general meeting of delegates of religious orders for elections and the handling of other important affairs of their communities.

Charismatic Renewal: A movement which originated with a handful of Duquesne University students and faculty members in the 1966-67 academic year and spread from there to Notre Dame, Michigan State University, the University of Michigan, other campuses and cities throughout the U.S., and to well over 100 other countries. Scriptural keys to the renewal are: Christ's promise to send the Holy Spirit upon the Apostles; the description, in the Acts of the Apostles, of the effects of the coming of the Holy Spirit upon the Apostles on Pentecost; St. Paul's explanation, in the Letter to the Romans and I Corinthians, of the charismatic gifts (for the good of the Church and persons) the Holy Spirit would bestow on Christians; New Testament evidence concerning the effects of charismatic gifts in and through the early Church. The personal key to the renewal is baptism of the Holy Spirit. This is not a new sacrament but the personally experienced actualization of grace already sacramentally received, principally in baptism and confirmation. The experience of baptism of the Holy Spirit is often accompanied by the reception of one or more charismatic gifts. The characteristic form of the renewal is the weekly prayer meeting, a gathering which includes periods of spontaneous prayer, singing, sharing of experience and testimony, fellowship and teaching. The International Catholic Charismatic Renewal Office is located at Palazzo della Cancelleria, 00120 Vatican City.Via Feruccio, 19, 00185, Rome, Italy. The U.S. National Service Committee has the mailing address of P.O. Box 628, Locust Grove, VA 22508.

Charisms: Gifts or graces given by God to persons for the good of others and the Church. Examples are special gifts for apostolic work, prophecy, healing, discernment of spirits, the life of evangelical poverty, here-and-now witness to faith in various circumstances of life. The Second Vatican Council made the following statement about charisms in the *Dogmatic Constitution on the Church* (No. 12): "It is not only through the sacraments and Church ministries that the same Holy Spirit sanctifies and leads the People of God and enriches it with virtues. Allotting his gifts 'to everyone according as he will' (1 Cor. 12:11), he distributes special graces among the faithful of every rank. By these gifts he makes them fit and ready to undertake the various tasks or offices advantageous for the renewal and upbuilding of the Church, according to the words of the Apostle: 'The manifestation of the Spirit is given to everyone for profit' (1 Cor. 12:7). These charismatic gifts, whether they be the most outstanding or the more simple and widely diffused, are to be received with thanksgiving and consolation, for they are exceedingly suitable and useful for the needs of the Church. "Still, extraordinary gifts are not to be rashly sought after, nor are the fruits of apostolic labor to be presumptuously expected from them. In any case, judgment as to their genuineness and proper use belongs to those who preside over the Church, and to whose special competence it belongs, not indeed to extinguish the Spirit, but to test all things and hold fast to that which is good" (cf. 1 Thes. 5:12; 19-21).

Charity: Love of God above all things for his own sake, and love of one's neighbor as oneself because and as an expression of one's love for God; the greatest of the three theological virtues. The term is sometimes also used to designate sanctifying grace.

Chastity: Properly ordered behavior with respect to sex. In marriage, the exercise of the procreative power is integrated with the norms and purposes of marriage. Outside of marriage, the rule is self-denial of the voluntary exercise and enjoyment of the procreative faculty in thought, word or action. The vow of chastity, which reinforces the virtue of chastity with the virtue of religion, is an evangelical counsel and one of the three vows professed by Religious.

Chirograph or Autograph Letter: A letter written by a pope himself, in his own handwriting.

Christ: The title of Jesus, derived from the Greek translation *Christos* of the Hebrew term *Messiah,* meaning the Anointed of God, the Savior and Deliverer of his people. Christian use of the title is a confession of belief that Jesus is the Savior.

Christianity: The sum total of things related to belief in Christ — the Christian religion, Christian churches, Christians themselves, society based on and expressive of Christian beliefs, culture reflecting Christian values.

Christians: The name first applied about the year 43 to followers of Christ at Antioch, the capital of Syria. It was used by the pagans as a contemptuous term. The word applies to persons who profess belief in the divinity and teachings of Christ and who give witness to him in life.

Christian Science: A religious doctrine consisting of Mary Baker Eddy's interpretation and formulation of the actions and teachings of Christ. Its basic tenets reflect Mrs. Eddy's ideas regarding the reality of spirit and its control and domination of what is not spirit. The basic statement of the doctrine is contained in *Science and Health, with Key to the Scriptures,* which she first published in 1875, nine years after being saved from death and healed on reading the New Testament. Mary Baker Eddy (1821-1910) established the church in 1879, and in 1892 founded at Boston the First Church of Christ, Scientist, of which all other Christian Science churches are branches. The individual churches are self-governing and self-supporting under the general supervision of a board of directors. Services consist of readings of portions of Scripture and *Science and Health.* One of the church's publications, *The Christian Science Monitor,* has a worldwide reputation as a journal of news and opinion.

Church: (1) See several entries under Church, Catholic. The universal Church is the Church spread throughout the world. The local Church is the Church in a particular locality; e.g., a diocese. The Church embraces all of its members — on earth, in heaven, in purgatory. (2) In general, any religious body. (3) A building set aside and dedicated for divine worship.

Circumcision: A ceremonial practice symbolic of initiation and participation in the covenant between God and Abraham.

Circumincession: The indwelling of each divine Person of the Holy Trinity in the others.

Clergy: Men ordained to holy orders and commissioned for sacred ministries and assigned to pastoral and other duties for the service of the people and the Church. (1) Diocesan or secular clergy are committed to pastoral ministry in parishes and in other capacities in a particular church (diocese) under the direction of their bishop, to whom they are bound by a promise of obedience. (2) Regular clergy belong to religious institutes (orders, congregations, societies — institutes of consecrated life) and are so called because they observe the rule (*regula*, in Latin) of their respective institutes. They are committed to the ways of life and apostolates of their institutes. In ordinary pastoral ministry, they are under the direction of local bishops as well as their own superiors.

Clericalism: A term generally used in a derogatory sense to mean action, influence and interference by the Church and the clergy in matters with which they allegedly should not be concerned. Anticlericalism is a reaction of antipathy, hostility, distrust and opposition to the Church and clergy arising from real and/or alleged faults of the clergy, overextension of the role of the laity, or for other reasons.

Cloister: Part of a monastery, convent or other house of religious reserved for use by members of the institute. Houses of contemplative Religious have a strict enclosure.

Code: A digest of rules or regulations, such as the Code of Canon Law.

Collegiality: A term in use especially since the Second Vatican Council to describe the authority exercised by the College of Bishops. The bishops of the Church, in union with and subordinate to the pope — who has full, supreme and universal power over the Church which he can always exercise independently — have supreme teaching and pastoral authority over the whole Church. In addition to their proper authority of office for the good of the faithful in their respective dioceses or other jurisdictions, the bishops have authority to act for the good of the universal Church. This collegial authority is exercised in a solemn manner in an ecumenical council and can also be exercised in other ways sanctioned by the pope. Doctrine on collegiality was set forth by the Second Vatican Council in the *Dogmatic Constitution on the Church.* (See separate entry.) By extension, the concept of collegiality is applied to other forms of participation and co-responsibility by members of a community.

Commissariat of the Holy Land: A special jurisdiction within the Order of Friars Minor, whose main purposes are the collecting of alms for support of the Holy Places in Palestine and staffing of the Holy Places and missions in the Middle East with priests and brothers. There are about 70 such commissariats in more than 30 countries. One of them has headquarters at Mt. St. Sepulchre, Washington, D.C. Franciscans have had custody of the Holy Places since 1342.

Communion of Faithful, Saints: The communion of all the People of God — on earth, in heavenly glory, in purgatory — with Christ and each other in faith, grace, prayer and good works.

Communism: The substantive principles of modern communism, a theory and system of economics and social organization, were stated about the middle of the 19th century by Karl Marx, author of *The Communist Manifesto* and, with Friedrich Engels, *Das Kapital.* The elements of communist ideology include: radical materialism; dialectical determinism; the inevitability of class struggle and conflict, which is to be furthered for the ultimate establishment of a worldwide, classless society; common ownership of productive and other goods; the subordination of all persons and institutions to the dictatorship of the collectivity; denial of the rights, dignity and liberty of persons; militant atheism and hostility to religion, utilitarian morality. Communism in theory and practice has been the subject of many papal documents and statements. Pius IX condemned it in 1846. Leo XIII dealt with it at length in the encyclical letters *Quod Apostolici Muneris* in 1878 and *Rerum Novarum* in 1891. Pius XI wrote on the same subject in the encyclicals *Quadragesimo Anno* in 1931 and *Divini Redemptoris* in 1937. These writings have been updated and developed in new directions by Pius XII, John XXIII, Paul VI and John Paul II.

Concelebration: The liturgical act in which several priests, led by one member of the group, offer Mass together, all consecrating the bread and wine. Concelebration has always been common in churches of Eastern Rite. In the Roman Rite, it was long restricted, taking place only at the ordination of bishops and the ordination of priests. The *Constitution on the Sacred Liturgy* issued by the Second Vatican Council set new norms for concelebration, which is now relatively common in the Roman Rite.

Concordance, Biblical: An alphabetical verbal index enabling a user knowing one or more words of a scriptural passage to locate the entire text.

Concordat: A church-state treaty with the force of law concerning matters of mutual concern — e.g., rights of the Church, arrangement of ecclesiastical jurisdictions, marriage laws, education. Approximately 150 agreements of this kind have been negotiated since the Concordat of Worms in 1122.

Concupiscence: Any tendency of the sensitive appetite. The term is most frequently used in reference to desires and tendencies for sinful sense pleasure.

Confession: Sacramental confession is the act by which a person tells or confesses his sins to a priest who is authorized to give absolution in the sacrament of penance.

Confessor: A priest who administers the sacrament of penance. The title of confessor, formerly given to a category of male saints, was suppressed with publication of the calendar reform of 1969.

Confraternity: An association whose members

practice a particular form of religious devotion and/or as engaged in some kind of apostolic work.

Conscience: Practical judgment concerning the moral goodness or sinfulness of an action (thought, word, desire). In the Catholic view, this judgment is made by reference of the action, its attendant circumstances and the intentions of the person to the requirements of moral law as expressed in the Ten Commandments, the summary law of love for God and neighbor, the life and teaching of Christ, and the authoritative teaching and practice of the Church with respect to the total demands of divine Revelation. A person is obliged: (1) to obey a certain and correct conscience; (2) to obey a certain conscience even if it is inculpably erroneous; (3) not to obey, but to correct, a conscience known to be erroneous or lax; (4) to rectify a scrupulous conscience by following the advice of a confessor and by other measures; (5) to resolve doubts of conscience before acting. It is legitimate to act for solid and probable reasons when a question of moral responsibility admits of argument (see Probabilism).

Conscience, Examination of: Self-examination to determine one's spiritual state before God, regarding one's sins and faults. It is recommended as a regular practice and is practically necessary in preparing for the sacrament of penance. The *particular examen* is a regular examination to assist in overcoming specific faults and imperfections.

Consistory: An assembly of cardinals presided over by the pope.

Constitution: (1) An apostolic or papal constitution is a document in which a pope enacts and promulgates law. (2) A formal and solemn document issued by an ecumenical council on a doctrinal or pastoral subject, with binding force in the whole Church; e.g., the four constitutions issued by the Second Vatican Council on the Church, liturgy, Revelation, and the Church in the modern world. (3) The constitutions of institutes of consecrated life and societies of apostolic life spell out details of and norms drawn from the various rules for the guidance and direction of the life and work of their members.

Consubstantiation: A theory which holds that the Body and Blood of Christ coexist with the substance of bread and wine in the Holy Eucharist. This theory, also called *impanation,* is incompatible with the doctrine of transubstantiation.

Contraception: Anything done by positive interference to prevent sexual intercourse from resulting in conception. Direct contraception is against the order of nature. Indirect contraception — as a secondary effect of medical treatment or other action having a necessary, good, non-contraceptive purpose — is permissible under the principle of the double effect. The practice of periodic continence is not contraception because it does not involve positive interference with the order of nature.

Contrition: Sorrow for sin coupled with a purpose of amendment. Contrition arising from a supernatural motive is necessary for the forgiveness of sin. (1) Perfect contrition is total sorrow for and renunciation of attachment to sin, arising from the motive of pure love of God. Perfect contrition, which implies the intention of doing all God wants done for the forgiveness of sin (including confession

in a reasonable period of time), is sufficient for the forgiveness of serious sin and the remission of all temporal punishment due for sin. (The intention to receive the sacrament of penance is implicit — even if unrealized, as in the case of some persons — in perfect contrition.) (2) Imperfect contrition or attrition is sorrow arising from a quasi-selfish supernatural motive; e.g., the fear of losing heaven, suffering the pains of hell, etc. Imperfect contrition is sufficient for the forgiveness of serious sin when joined with absolution in confession, and sufficient for the forgiveness of venial sin even outside of confession.

Contumely: Personal insult, reviling a person in his presence by accusation of moral faults, by refusal of recognition or due respect; a violation of obligations of justice and charity.

Corporal Works of Mercy: Feeding the hungry, giving drink to the thirsty, clothing the naked, visiting the imprisoned, sheltering the homeless, visiting the sick, burying the dead.

Council, Plenary: A council held for the particular churches belonging to the same episcopal conference. Such a council can be convoked to take action related to the pastoral activity and mission of the Church in the territory. The membership of such councils is fixed by canon law; their decrees, when approved by the Holy See, are binding in the territory (see Index, Plenary Councils of Baltimore).

Councils, Provincial: Meetings of the bishops of a province. The metropolitan, or ranking archbishop, of an ecclesiastical province convenes and presides over such councils in a manner prescribed by canon law to take action related to the life and mission of the Church in the province. Acts and decrees must be approved by the Holy See before being promulgated.

Counsels, Evangelical: Gospel counsels of perfection, especially voluntary poverty, perfect chastity and obedience, which were recommended by Christ to those who would devote themselves exclusively and completely to the immediate service of God. Religious (members of institutes of consecrated life) bind themselves by public vows to observe these counsels in a life of total consecration to God and service to people through various kinds of apostolic works.

Counter-Reformation: The period of approximately 100 years following the Council of Trent, which witnessed a reform within the Church to stimulate genuine Catholic life and to counteract effects of the Reformation.

Covenant: A bond of relationship between parties pledged to each other. God-initiated covenants in the Old Testament included those with Abraham, Noah, Moses, Levi, David. The Mosaic (Sinai) covenant made Israel God's Chosen People on terms of fidelity to true faith, true worship, and righteous conduct according to the Decalogue. The New Testament covenant, prefigured in the Old Testament, is the bond people have with God through Christ. All people are called to be parties to this perfect and everlasting covenant, which was mediated and ratified by Christ. The marriage covenant seals the closest possible relationship between a man and a woman.

Creation: The production by God of something

out of nothing. The biblical account of creation is contained in the first two chapters of Genesis.

Creator: God, the supreme, self-existing Being, the absolute and infinite First Cause of all things.

Creature: Everything in the realm of being is a creature, except God.

Cremation: The reduction of a human corpse to ashes by means of fire. Cremation is not in line with Catholic tradition and practice, even though it is not opposed to any article of faith. The Congregation for the Doctrine of the Faith, under date of May 8, 1963, circulated among bishops an instruction which upheld the traditional practices of Christian burial but modified anti-cremation legislation. Cremation may be permitted for serious reasons, of a private as well as public nature, provided it does not involve any contempt of the Church or of religion, or any attempt to deny, question, or belittle the doctrine of the resurrection of the body. The person may receive the last rites and be given ecclesiastical burial. A priest may say prayers for the deceased at the crematorium, but full liturgical ceremonies may not take place there. The remains must be treated with respect and placed in consecrated ground. The principal reason behind an earlier prohibition against cremation was the fact that, historically, the practice had represented an attempt to deny the doctrine of the resurrection of the body. (See Burial, Ecclesiastical.)

Crib: A devotional representation of the birth of Jesus. The custom of erecting cribs is generally attributed to St. Francis of Assisi who in 1223 obtained from Pope Honorius III permission to use a crib and figures of the Christ Child, Mary, St. Joseph, and others, to represent the mystery of the Nativity.

Crosier: The bishop's staff, symbolic of his pastoral office, responsibility and authority; used at liturgical functions.

Crypt: An underground or partly underground chamber; e.g., the lower part of a church used for worship and/or burial.

Cura Animarum: A Latin phrase, meaning care of souls, designating the pastoral ministry and responsibility of bishops and priests.

Curia: The personnel and offices through which (1) the pope administers the affairs of the universal Church, the Roman Curia (see separate entry), or (2) a bishop the affairs of a diocese, diocesan curia. The principal officials of a diocesan curia are the vicar general of the diocese, the chancellor, officials of the diocesan tribunal or court, examiners, consultors, auditors, notaries.

Custos: A religious superior who presides over a number of convents collectively called a custody. In some institutes of consecrated life a custos may be the deputy of a higher superior.

D

Deaconess: A woman officially appointed and charged by the Church to carry out service-like functions. Phoebe apparently was one (Rom. 16:1-2); a second probable reference to the office is in 1 Tm. 3:11. The office — for assistance at the baptism of women, for pastoral service to women and for works of charity — had considerable development in the third and also in the fourth century when the actual term came into use (in place of such designations as *diacona, vidua, virgo canonica*). Its importance declined subsequently with the substitution of infusion in place of immersion as the common method of baptism in the West, and with the increase of the practice of infant baptism. There is no record of the ministry of deaconess in the West after the beginning of the 11th century. The office continued, however, for a longer time in the East. The Vatican's Theological Commission, in a paper prepared in 1971, noted that there had been in the past a form of diaconal ordination for women. With a rite and purpose distinctive to women, it differed essentially from the ordination of deacons, which had sacramental effects. Several Christian churches have had revivals of the office of deaconess since the 1830s. There is a contemporary movement in support of such a revival among some Catholics.

Dean: (1) A priest with supervisory responsibility over a section of a diocese known as a deanery. The post-Vatican II counterpart of a dean is an episcopal vicar. (2) The senior or ranking member of a group.

Dean of the College of Cardinals: See Index.

Decision: A judgment or pronouncement on a cause or suit, given by a church tribunal or official with judicial authority. A decision has the force of law for concerned parties.

Declaration: (1) An ecclesiastical document which presents an interpretation of an existing law. (2) A position paper on a specific subject; e.g., the three declarations issued by the Second Vatican Council on religious freedom, non-Christian religions, and Christian education.

Decree: An edict or ordinance issued by a pope and/or by an ecumenical council, with binding force in the whole Church; by a department of the Roman Curia, with binding force for concerned parties; by a territorial body of bishops, with binding force for persons in the area; by individual bishops, with binding force for concerned parties until revocation or the death of the bishop. The nine decrees issued by the Second Vatican Council were combinations of doctrinal and pastoral statements with executive orders for action and movement toward renewal and reform in the Church.

Dedication of a Church: The ceremony whereby a church is solemnly set apart for the worship of God. The custom of dedicating churches had an antecedent in Old Testament ceremonies for the dedication of the Temple, as in the times of Solomon and the Maccabees. The earliest extant record of the dedication of a Christian church dates from early in the fourth century, when it was done simply by the celebration of Mass. Other ceremonies developed later. A church can be dedicated by a simple blessing or a solemn consecration. The rite of consecration is generally performed by a bishop.

Deism: A system of natural religion which acknowledges the existence of God but regards him as so transcendent and remote from man and the universe that divine revelation and the supernatural order of things are irrelevant and unacceptable. It developed from rationalistic principles in England in the 17th and 18th centuries, and had Voltaire, Rousseau and the Encyclopedists among its advocates in France.

Despair: Abandonment of hope for salvation arising from the conviction that God will not provide the necessary means for attaining it, that following God's way of life for salvation is impossible, or that one's sins are unforgivable; a serious sin against the Holy Spirit and the theological virtues of hope and faith, involving distrust in the mercy and goodness of God and a denial of the truths that God wills the salvation of all persons and provides sufficient grace for it. Real despair is distinguished from unreasonable fear with respect to the difficulties of attaining salvation, from morbid anxiety over the demands of divine justice, and from feelings of despair.

Detraction: Revelation of true but hidden faults of a person without sufficient and justifying reason; a violation of requirements of justice and charity, involving the obligation to make restitution when this is possible without doing more harm to the good name of the offended party. In some cases, e.g., to prevent evil, secret faults may and should be disclosed.

Devil: (1) Lucifer, Satan, chief of the fallen angels who sinned and were banished from heaven. Still possessing angelic powers, he can cause such diabolical phenomena as possession and obsession, and can tempt men to sin. (2) Any fallen angel.

Devotion: (1) Religious fervor, piety; dedication. (2) The consolation experienced at times during prayer; a reverent manner of praying.

Devotions: Pious practices of members of the Church include not only participation in various acts of the liturgy but also in other acts of worship generally called popular or private devotions. Concerning these, the Second Vatican Council said in the *Constitution on the Sacred Liturgy* (No. 13): "Popular devotions of the Christian people are warmly commended, provided they accord with the laws and norms of the Church. Such is especially the case with devotions called for by the Apostolic See. Devotions proper to the individual churches also have a special dignity. ... These devotions should be so drawn up that they harmonize with the liturgical seasons, accord with the sacred liturgy, are in some fashion derived from it, and lead the people to it, since the liturgy by its very nature far surpasses any of them." Devotions of a liturgical type are Exposition of the Blessed Sacrament, recitation of Evening Prayer and Night Prayer of the Liturgy of the Hours. Examples of paraliturgical devotion are a Bible Service or Vigil, and the Angelus, Rosary and Stations of the Cross, which have a strong scriptural basis.

Diocese: A particular church, a fully organized ecclesiastical jurisdiction under the pastoral direction of a bishop as local Ordinary.

Discalced: Of Latin derivation and meaning without shoes, the word is applied to religious orders or congregations whose members go barefoot or wear sandals.

Disciple: A term used sometimes in reference to the Apostles but more often to a larger number of followers (70 or 72) of Christ mentioned in Lk. 10:1.

Disciplina Arcani: A Latin phrase, meaning discipline of the secret and referring to a practice of the early Church, especially during the Roman persecutions, to: (1) conceal Christian truths from those who, it was feared, would misinterpret, ridicule and profane the teachings, and persecute Christians for believing them; (2) instruct catechumens in a gradual manner, withholding the teaching of certain doctrines until the catechumens proved themselves of good faith and sufficient understanding.

Dispensation: The relaxation of a law in a particular case. Laws made for the common good sometimes work undue hardship in particular cases. In such cases, where sufficient reasons are present, dispensations may be granted by proper authorities. Bishops, religious superiors and others may dispense from certain laws; the pope can dispense from all ecclesiastical laws. No one has authority to dispense from obligations of the divine law.

Divination: Attempting to foretell future or hidden things by means of things like dreams, necromancy, spiritism, examination of entrails, astrology, augury, omens, palmistry, drawing straws, dice, cards, etc. Practices like these attribute to creatural things a power which belongs to God alone and are violations of the First Commandment.

Divine Praises: Fourteen praises recited or sung at Benediction of the Blessed Sacrament in reparation for sins of sacrilege, blasphemy and profanity. Some of these praises date from the end of the 18th century: Blessed be God. / Blessed be his holy Name. / Blessed be Jesus Christ, true God and true Man. / Blessed be the Name of Jesus. / Blessed be his most Sacred Heart. / Blessed be his most Precious Blood. / Blessed be Jesus in the most holy Sacrament of the Altar. / Blessed be the Holy Spirit, the Paraclete. / Blessed be the great Mother of God, Mary most holy. / Blessed be her holy and Immaculate Conception. / Blessed be her glorious Assumption. / Blessed be the name of Mary, Virgin and Mother. / Blessed be St. Joseph, her most chaste Spouse. / Blessed be God in his Angels and in his Saints.

Double Effect Principle: Actions sometimes have two effects closely related to each other, one good and the other bad, and a difficult moral question can arise: Is it permissible to place an action from which two such results follow? It is permissible to place the action, if: the action is good in itself and is directly productive of the good effect; the circumstances are good; the intention of the person is good; the reason for placing the action is proportionately serious to the seriousness of the indirect bad effect. For example: Is it morally permissible for a pregnant woman to undergo medical or surgical treatment for a pathological condition if the indirect and secondary effect of the treatment will be the loss of the child? The reply is affirmative, for these reasons: The action, i.e., the treatment, is good in itself, cannot be deferred until a later time without very serious consequences, and is ordered directly to the cure of critically grave pathology. By means of the treatment, the woman intends to save her life, which she has a right to do. The loss of the child is not directly sought as a means for the cure of the mother but results indirectly and in a secondary manner from the placing of the action, i.e., the treatment, which is good in itself. The double effect principle does not support the principle that the end justifies the means.

Doxology: (1) The lesser doxology, or ascription of glory to the Trinity, is the Glory be to the Father. The first part dates back to the third or fourth century, and came from the form of baptism. The concluding words, As it was in the beginning, etc., are of later origin. (2) The greater doxology, Glory to God in the highest, begins with the words of angelic praise at the birth of Christ recounted in the Infancy Narrative (Lk. 2:14). It is often recited at Mass. Of early Eastern origin, it is found in the *Apostolic Constitutions* in a form much like the present. (3) The formula of praise at the end of the Eucharistic Prayer at Mass, sung or said by the celebrant while he holds aloft the paten containing the consecrated host in one hand and the chalice containing the consecrated wine in the other.

Dulia: A Greek term meaning the veneration or homage, different in nature and degree from that given to God, paid to the saints. It includes honoring the saints and seeking their intercession with God.

Duty: A moral obligation deriving from the binding force of law, the exigencies of one's state in life, and other sources.

E

Easter Controversy: A three-phase controversy over the time for the celebration of Easter. Some early Christians in the Near East, called Quartodecimans, favored the observance of Easter on the 14th day of Nisan, the spring month of the Hebrew calendar, whenever it occurred. Against this practice, Pope St. Victor I, about 190, ordered a Sunday observance of the feast. The Council of Nicaea, in line with usages of the Church at Rome and Alexandria, decreed in 325 that Easter should be observed on the first Sunday following the first full moon of spring. Uniformity of practice in the West was not achieved until several centuries later, when the British Isles, in delayed compliance with measures enacted by the Synod of Whitby in 664, accepted the Roman date of observance. Unrelated to the controversy is the fact that some Eastern Christians, in accordance with traditional calendar practices, celebrate Easter at a different time than the Roman and Eastern Churches.

Easter Duty, Season: The serious obligation binding Catholics of Roman Rite, to receive the Eucharist during the Easter season (in the U.S., from the first Sunday of Lent to and including Trinity Sunday).

Easter Water: Holy water blessed with special ceremonies and distributed on the Easter Vigil; used during Easter Week for blessing the faithful and homes.

Ecclesiology: Study of the nature, constitution, members, mission, functions, etc., of the Church.

Ecstasy: An extraordinary state of mystical experience in which a person is so absorbed in God that the activity of the exterior senses is suspended.

Ecumenism: The movement of Christians and their churches toward the unity willed by Christ. The Second Vatican Council called the movement "those activities and enterprises which, according to various needs of the Church and opportune occasions, are started and organized for the fostering of unity among Christians" (*Decree on Ecumenism*, No. 4). Spiritual ecumenism, i.e., mutual prayer for unity, is the heart of the movement. The movement also involves scholarly and pew-level efforts for the development of mutual understanding and better interfaith relations in general, and collaboration by the churches and their members in the social area. (See separate entries.)

Elevation: The raising of the host after consecration at Mass for adoration by the faithful. The custom was introduced in the Diocese of Paris about the close of the 12th century to offset an erroneous teaching of the time which held that transubstantiation of the bread did not take place until after the consecration of the wine in the chalice. The elevation of the chalice following the consecration of the wine was introduced in the 15th century.

End Justifies the Means: An unacceptable ethical principle which states that evil means may be used to produce good effects.

Envy: Sadness over another's good fortune because it is considered a loss to oneself or a detraction from one's own excellence; one of the seven capital sins, a violation of the obligations of charity.

Epikeia: A Greek word meaning reasonableness and designating a moral theory and practice, a mild interpretation of the mind of a legislator who is prudently considered not to wish positive law to bind in certain circumstances. Use of the principle is justified in practice when the lawgiver himself cannot be appealed to and when it can be prudently assumed that in particular cases, e.g., because of special hardship, he would not wish the law to be applied in a strict manner. Epikeia may not be applied with respect to acts that are intrinsically wrong or those covered by laws which automatically make them invalid.

Episcopate: (1) The office, dignity and sacramental powers bestowed upon a bishop at his ordination. (2) The body of bishops collectively.

Equivocation: (1) The use of words, phrases, or gestures having more than one meaning in order to conceal information which a questioner has no strict right to know. It is permissible to equivocate (have a broad mental reservation) in some circumstances. (2) A lie, i.e., a statement of untruth. Lying is intrinsically wrong. A lie told in joking, evident as such, is not wrong.

Eschatology: Doctrine concerning the last things: death, judgment, heaven and hell, and the final state of perfection of the people and kingdom of God at the end of time.

Eternity: The interminable, perfect possession of life in its totality without beginning or end; an attribute of God, who has no past or future but always is. Man's existence has a beginning but no end and is, accordingly, called immortal.

Ethics: Moral philosophy, the science of the morality of human acts deriving from natural law, the natural end of man, and the powers of human reason. It includes all the spheres of human activity — personal, social, economic, political, etc. Ethics is distinct from but can be related to moral theology, whose primary principles are drawn from divine revelation.

Eucharistic Congresses: Public demonstrations of faith in the Holy Eucharist. Combining liturgical services, other public ceremonies, subsidiary meetings, different kinds of instructional and inspirational elements, they are unified by central themes and serve to increase understanding of and devotion to Christ in the Eucharist, and to relate this liturgy of worship and witness to life. The first international congress developed from a proposal by Marie Marthe Tamisier of Touraine, organizing efforts of Msgr. Louis Gaston de Segur, and backing by industrialist Philibert Vrau. It was held with the approval of Pope Leo XIII at the University of Lille, France, and was attended by some 800 persons from France, Belgium, Holland, England, Spain and Switzerland. International congresses are organized by the Pontifical Committee for International Eucharistic Congresses. Participants include clergy, religious and lay persons from many countries, and representatives of national and international Catholic organizations. Forty-five international congresses were held from 1881 to 1993: Lille (1881), Avignon (1882), Liege (1883), Freiburg (1885), Toulouse (1886), Paris (1888), Antwerp (1890), Jerusalem (1893), Rheims (1894), Paray-le-Monial (1897), Brussels (1898), Lourdes (1899), Angers (1901), Namur (1902), Angouleme (1904), Rome (1905), Tournai (1906), Metz (1907), London (1908), Cologne (1909), Montreal (1910), Madrid (1911), Vienna (1912), Malta (1913), Lourdes (1914), Rome (1922), Amsterdam (1924), Chicago (1926), Sydney (1928), Carthage (1930), Dublin (1932), Buenos Aires (1934), Manila (1937), Budapest (1938), Barcelona (1952), Rio de Janeiro (1955), Munich, Germany (1960), Bombay, India (1964), Bogota, Colombia (1968), Melbourne, Australia (1973), Philadelphia (1976), Lourdes (1981), Nairobi, Kenya (1985), Seoul, South Korea (1989), Seville, Spain (1993). The 46th Congress is to be held in 1997 in Wroclaw, Poland.

Eugenics: The science of heredity and environment for the physical and mental improvement of offspring. Extreme eugenics is untenable in practice because it advocates immoral means, such as compulsory breeding of the select, sterilization of persons said to be unfit, abortion, and unacceptable methods of birth regulation.

Euthanasia: Mercy killing, the direct causing of death for the purpose of ending human suffering. Euthanasia is murder and is totally illicit, for the natural law forbids the direct taking of one's own life or that of an innocent person. The use of drugs to relieve suffering in serious cases, even when this results in a shortening of life as an indirect and secondary effect, is permissible under conditions of the double effect principle. It is also permissible for a seriously ill person to refuse to follow — or for other responsible persons to refuse to permit — extraordinary medical procedures even though the refusal might entail shortening of life. (See separate entries.)

Evangelization: Proclamation of the Gospel, the Good News of salvation in and through Christ, among those who have not yet known or received it; and efforts for the progressive development of the life of faith among those who have already received the Gospel and all that it entails. Evangelization is the primary mission of the Church, in which all members of the Church are called to participate. (See separate entries.)

Evolution: Scientific theory concerning the development of the physical universe from unorganized matter (inorganic evolution) and, especially, the development of existing forms of vegetable, animal and human life from earlier and more primitive organisms (organic evolution). Various ideas about evolution were advanced for some centuries before scientific evidence in support of the mainline theory of organic evolution, which has several formulations, was discovered and verified in the second half of the 19th century and afterwards. This evidence — from the findings of comparative anatomy and other sciences — confirmed evolution within species and cleared the way to further investigation of questions regarding the processes of its accomplishment. While a number of such questions remain open with respect to human evolution, a point of doctrine not open to question is the immediate creation of the human soul by God. For some time, theologians regarded the theory with hostility, considering it to be in opposition to the account of creation in the early chapters of Genesis and subversive of belief in such doctrines as creation, the early state of man in grace, and the fall of man from grace. This state of affairs and the tension it generated led to considerable controversy regarding an alleged conflict between religion and science. Gradually, however, the tension was diminished with the development of biblical studies from the latter part of the 19th century onwards, with clarification of the distinctive features of religious truth and scientific truth, and with the refinement of evolutionary concepts. So far as the Genesis account of creation is concerned, the Catholic view is that the writer(s) did not write as a scientist but as the communicator of religious truth in a manner adapted to the understanding of the people of his time. He used anthropomorphic language, the figure of days and other literary devices to state the salvation truths of creation, the fall of man from grace, and the promise of redemption. It was beyond the competency and purpose of the writer(s) to describe creation and related events in a scientific manner.

Excommunication: A penalty or censure by which a baptized Roman Catholic is excluded from the communion of the faithful, for committing and remaining obstinate in certain serious offenses specified in canon law; e.g. heresy, schism, apostasy, abortion. As by baptism a person is made a member of the Church in which there is a communication of spiritual goods, so by excommunication he is deprived of the same spiritual goods until he repents and receives absolution. Even though excommunicated, a person is still responsible for fulfillment of the normal obligations of a Catholic. (See Censures).

Existentialism: A philosophy with radical concern for the problems of individual existence and identity viewed in particular here-and-now patterns of thought which presuppose irrationality and absurdity in human life and the whole universe. It is preoccupied with questions about freedom, moral decision and responsibility against a background of denial of objective truth and universal norms of conduct; is characterized by prevailing anguish, dread, fear, pessimism, despair; is generally atheistic, although its modern originator, Soren Kierkegaard (d. 1855), and Gabriel Marcel (d. 1973) attempted to give it a Christian orientation. Pius XII called it "the new erroneous philosophy which, opposing itself to idealism, immanentism and pragmatism, has assumed the name of existentialism, since it concerns itself only with the existence of individual things and neglects all consideration of their immutable essences" (Encyclical *Humani Generis,* Aug. 12, 1950).

Exorcism: (1) Driving out evil spirits; a rite in which evil spirits are charged and commanded on the authority of God and with the prayer of the Church to depart from a person or to cease causing harm to a person suffering from diabolical possession or obsession. The sacramental is officially administered by a priest delegated for the purpose by the bishop of the place. Elements of the rite include the Litany of Saints; recitation of the Our Father, one or more creeds, and other prayers; specific prayers of exorcism; the reading of Gospel passages and use of the Sign of the Cross. (2) Exorcisms which do not imply the conditions of either diabolical possession or obsession form part of the ceremony of baptism and are also included in formulas for various blessings; e.g., of water.

Exposition of the Blessed Sacrament: "In churches where the Eucharist is regularly reserved, it is recommended that solemn exposition of the Blessed Sacrament for an extended period of time should take place once a year, even though the period is not strictly continuous. ... Shorter expositions of the Eucharist **(Benediction)** are to be arranged in such a way that the blessing with the Eucharist is preceded by a reasonable time for readings of the word of God, songs, prayers and a period for silent prayer." So stated Vatican directives issued in 1973.

F

Faculties: Grants of jurisdiction or authority by the law of the Church or superiors (pope, bishop, religious superior) for exercise of the powers of holy orders; e.g., priests are given faculties to hear confessions, officiate at weddings; bishops are given faculties to grant dispensations, etc.

Faith: In religion, faith has several aspects. Catholic doctrine calls faith the assent of the mind to truths revealed by God, the assent being made with the help of grace and by command of the will on account of the authority and trustworthiness of God revealing. The term faith also refers to the truths that are believed (content of faith) and to the way in which a person, in response to Christ, gives witness to and expresses belief in daily life (living faith). All of these elements, and more, are included in the following statement: " 'The obedience of faith' (Rom. 16:26; 1:5; 2 Cor. 10:5-6) must be given to God who reveals, an obedience by which man entrusts his whole self freely to God, offering 'the full submission of intellect and will to God who reveals' (First Vatican Council, *Dogmatic Constitution on the Catholic Faith,* Chap. 3), and freely assenting to the truth revealed by him. If this faith is to be shown, the grace of God and the interior help of the Holy Spirit must precede and assist, moving the heart and turning it to God, opening the eyes of the mind, and giving 'joy and ease to everyone in assenting to the truth and believing it' " (Second Council of Orange, Canon 7) (Second Vatican Council, *Constitution on Revelation,* No. 5). Faith is necessary for salvation.

Faith, Rule of: The norm or standard of religious belief. The Catholic doctrine is that belief must be professed in the divinely revealed truths in the Bible and tradition as interpreted and proposed by the infallible teaching authority of the Church.

Fast, Eucharistic: Abstinence from food and drink, except water and medicine, is required for one hour before the reception of the Eucharist. Persons who are advanced in age or suffer from infirmity or illness, together with those who care for them, can receive Holy Communion even if they have not abstained from food and drink for an hour. A priest celebrating two or three Masses on the same day can eat and drink something before the second or third Mass without regard for the hour limit.

Father: A title of priests, who are regarded as spiritual fathers because they are the ordinary ministers of baptism, by which persons are born to supernatural life, and because of their pastoral service to people.

Fear: A mental state caused by the apprehension of present or future danger. Grave fear does not necessarily remove moral responsibility for an act, but may lessen it.

First Friday: A devotion consisting of the reception of Holy Communion on the first Friday of nine consecutive months in honor of the Sacred Heart of Jesus and in reparation for sin. (See Sacred Heart, Promises.)

First Saturday: A devotion tracing its origin to the apparitions of the Blessed Virgin Mary at Fatima in 1917. Those practicing the devotion go to confession and, on the first Saturday of five consecutive months, receive Holy Communion, recite five decades of the Rosary, and meditate on the mysteries for 15 minutes.

Fisherman's Ring: A signet ring engraved with the image of St. Peter fishing from a boat, and encircled with the name of the reigning pope. It is not worn by the pope. It is used to seal briefs, and is destroyed after each pope's death.

Forgiveness of Sin: Catholics believe that sins are forgiven by God through the mediation of Christ in view of the repentance of the sinner and by means of the sacrament of penance. (See Penance, Contrition).

Fortitude: Courage to face dangers or hardships for the sake of what is good; one of the four cardinal virtues and one of the seven gifts of the Holy Spirit.

Fortune Telling: Attempting to predict the future or the occult by means of cards, palm reading, etc.; a form of divination, prohibited by the First Commandment.

Forty Hours Devotion: A Eucharistic observance consisting of solemn exposition of the Blessed Sacrament coupled with special Masses and forms of prayer, for the purposes of making reparation for sin and praying for God's blessings of grace and peace. The devotion was instituted in 1534 in Milan. St. John Neumann of Philadelphia was the first bishop in the U.S. to prescribe its observance in his diocese. For many years in this country, the observance was held annually on a rotating basis in all parishes of a diocese. Simplified and abbreviated Eucharistic observances have taken the place of the devotion in some places.

Forum: The sphere in which ecclesiastical authority or jurisdiction is exercised. (1) External: Authority is exercised in the external forum to deal with matters affecting the public welfare of the Church and its members. Those who have such authority because of their office (e.g., diocesan bishops) are called ordinaries. (?) Internal: Authority is exercised in the internal forum to deal with matters affecting the private spiritual good of individuals. The sacramental forum is the sphere in which the sacrament of penance is administered; other exercises of jurisdiction in the internal forum take place in the non-sacramental forum.

Franciscan Crown: A seven-decade rosary used to commemorate the seven Joys of the Blessed Virgin: the Annunciation, the Visitation, the Nativity of Our Lord, the Adoration of the Magi, the Finding of the Child Jesus in the Temple, the Apparition of the Risen Christ to his Mother, the Assumption and Coronation of the Blessed Virgin. Introduced in 1422, the Crown originally consisted only of seven Our Fathers and 70 Hail Marys. Two Hail Marys were added to complete the number 72 (thought to be the number of years of Mary's life), and one Our Father, Hail Mary and Glory be to the Father are said for the intention of the pope.

Freedom, Religious: The Second Vatican Council declared that the right to religious freedom in civil society "means that all men are to be immune from coercion on the part of individuals or of social groups and of any human power, in such wise that in matters religious no one is to be forced to act in a manner contrary to his own beliefs. Nor is anyone to be restrained from acting in accordance with his own beliefs, whether privately or publicly, whether alone or in association with others, within due limits" of requirements for the common good. The foundation of this right in civil society is the "very dignity of the human person" (*Declaration on Religious Freedom,* No. 2). The conciliar statement did not deal with the subject of freedom within the Church. It noted the responsibility of the faithful "carefully to attend to the sacred and certain doctrine of the Church" (No. 14).

Freemasons: A fraternal order which originated in London in 1717 with the formation of the first Grand Lodge of Freemasons. From England, the order spread to Europe and elsewhere. Its principles and basic rituals embody a naturalistic religion, active participation in which is incompatible with Christian faith and practice. Grand Orient Freemasonry, developed in Latin countries, is atheistic, irreligious and anticlerical. In some places, Freemasonry has been regarded as subversive of the state; in Catholic quarters, it has been considered hostile to the Church and its doctrine. In the United States, Freemasonry has been widely regarded as a fraternal and philanthropic order. For serious doctrinal and pastoral reasons, Catholics were forbidden to join the Freemasons under penalty of excommunication, according to church law before 1983. Eight different popes in 17 different pronouncements, and at least six different local councils, condemned Freemasonry. The first condemnation was made by Clement XII in 1738. Eastern Orthodox and many Protestant bodies have also opposed the order. In the U.S., there was some easing of the ban against Masonic membership by Catholics in view of a letter written in 1974 by Cardinal Franjo Seper, prefect of the Congregation for the Doctrine of the Faith. The letter was interpreted to mean that Catholics might join Masonic lodges which were not anti-Catholic. This was called erroneous in a declaration issued by the Doctrinal Congregation Feb. 17, 1981. The prohibition against Masonic membership was restated in a declaration issued by the Doctrinal Congregation Nov. 26, 1983, with the approval of Pope John Paul II, as follows. "The Church's negative position on Masonic associations . . . remains unaltered, since their principles have always been regarded as irreconcilable with the Church's doctrine. Hence, joining them remains prohibited by the Church. Catholics enrolled in Masonic associations are involved in serious sin and may not approach Holy Communion. Local ecclesiastical authorities do not have the faculty to pronounce a judgment on the nature of Masonic associations which might include a diminution of the above-mentioned judgment." This latest declaration, like the revised Code of Canon Law, does not include a penalty of excommunication for Catholics who join the Masons. Local bishops are not authorized to grant dispensations from the prohibition. The foregoing strictures against Masonic membership by Catholics were reiterated in a report by the Committee for Pastoral Research and Practice, National Conference of Catholic Bishops, released through Catholic News Service June 7, 1985.

Free Will: The faculty or capability of making a reasonable choice among several alternatives. Freedom of will underlies the possibility and fact of moral responsibility.

Friar: Term applied to members of mendicant orders to distinguish them from members of monastic orders. (See Mendicants.)

Fruits of the Holy Spirit: Charity, joy, peace, patience, benignity, goodness, longanimity, mildness, faith, modesty, continence, chastity.

G

Gambling: The backing of an issue with a sum of money or other valuables, which is permissible if the object is honest, if the two parties have the free disposal of their stakes without prejudice to the rights of others, if the terms are thoroughly understood by both parties, and if the outcome is not known beforehand. Gambling often falls into disrepute and may be forbidden by civil law, as well as by divine law, because of cheating, fraud and other accompanying evils.

Gehenna: Greek form of a Jewish name, *Gehinnom,* for a valley near Jerusalem, the site of Moloch worship; used as a synonym for hell.

Genuflection: Bending of the knee, a natural sign of adoration or reverence, as when persons genuflect with the right knee in passing before the tabernacle to acknowledge the Eucharistic presence of Christ.

Gethsemani: A Hebrew word meaning oil press, designating the place on the Mount of Olives where Christ prayed and suffered in agony the night before he died.

Gifts of the Holy Spirit: Supernatural habits disposing a person to respond promptly to the inspiration of grace; promised by Christ and communicated through the Holy Spirit, especially in the sacrament of confirmation. They are: wisdom, understanding, counsel, fortitude, knowledge, piety, fear of the Lord.

Gluttony: An unreasonable appetite for food and drink; one of the seven capital sins.

God: The infinitely perfect Supreme Being, uncaused and absolutely self-sufficient, eternal, the Creator and final end of all things. The one God subsists in three equal Persons, the Father and the Son and the Holy Spirit. God, although transcendent and distinct from the universe, is present and active in the world in realization of his plan for the salvation of human beings, principally through Revelation, the operations of the Holy Spirit, the life and ministry of Christ, and the continuation of Christ's ministry in the Church. The existence of God is an article of faith, clearly communicated in divine Revelation. Even without this Revelation, however, the Church teaches, in a declaration by the First Vatican Council, that human beings can acquire certain knowledge of the existence of God and some of his attributes. This can be done on the bases of principles of reason and reflection on human experience. Non-revealed arguments or demonstrations for the existence of God have been developed from the principle of causality; the contingency of human beings and the universe; the existence of design, change and movement in the universe; human awareness of moral responsibility; widespread human testimony to the existence of God.

Grace: A free gift of God to persons (and angels), grace is a created sharing or participation in the life of God. It is given to persons through the merits of Christ and is communicated by the Holy Spirit. It is necessary for salvation. The principal means of grace are the sacraments (especially the Eucharist), prayer and good works. (1) Sanctifying or habitual grace makes persons holy and pleasing to God, adopted children of God, members of Christ, temples of the Holy Spirit, heirs of heaven capable of supernaturally meritorious acts. With grace, God gives persons the supernatural virtues and gifts of the Holy Spirit. The sacraments of baptism and penance were instituted to give grace to those who do not have it; the other sacraments, to increase it in those already in the state of grace. The means for growth in holiness, or the increase of grace, are prayer, the sacraments, and good works. Sanctifying grace is lost by the commission of serious sin. Each sacrament confers sanctifying grace for the special purpose of the sacrament; in this context, grace is called sacramental grace. (2) Actual grace is a supernatural help of God which enlightens and strengthens a person to do good and to avoid evil. It is not a permanent quality, like sanctifying grace. It is necessary for the performance of supernatural acts. It can be resisted and refused. Persons in the state of serious sin are given actual grace to lead them to repentance.

Grace at Meals: Prayers said before meals, asking a blessing of God, and after meals, giving thanks to God. In addition to traditional prayers for these purposes, many variations suitable for different occasions are possible, at personal option.

H

Habit: (1) A disposition to do things easily, given with grace (and therefore supernatural) and/or acquired by repetition of similar acts. (2) The garb worn by Religious.

Hagiography: Writings or documents about saints and other holy persons.

Hail Mary: A prayer addressed to the Blessed Virgin Mary; also called the *Ave Maria* (Latin equivalent of Hail Mary) and the Angelic Salutation. In three parts, it consists of the words addressed to Mary by the Archangel Gabriel on the occasion of the Annunciation, in the Infancy Narrative (Hail full of grace, the Lord is with you, blessed are you among women.); the words addressed to Mary by her cousin Elizabeth on the occasion of the Visitation (Blessed is the fruit of your womb.); a concluding petition (Holy Mary, Mother of God, pray for us sinners now and at the hour of our death. Amen.). The first two salutations were joined in Eastern Rite formulas by the sixth century, and were similarly used at Rome in the seventh century. Insertion of the name of Jesus at the conclusion of the salutations was probably made by Urban IV about 1262. The present form of the petition was incorporated into the breviary in 1514.

Heaven: The state of those who, having achieved salvation, are in glory with God and enjoy the beatific vision. The phrase, kingdom of heaven, refers to the order or kingdom of God, grace, salvation.

Hell: The state of punishment of the damned — i.e., those who die in mortal sin, in a condition of self-alienation from God and of opposition to the divine plan of salvation. The punishment of hell begins immediately after death and lasts forever.

Heresy: The obstinate post-baptismal denial or doubt by a Catholic of any truth which must be believed as a matter of divine and Catholic faith (Canon 751, of the Code of Canon Law). Formal heresy involves deliberate resistance to the authority of God who communicates revelation through Scripture and tradition and the teaching authority of the Church. Heretics automatically incur the penalty of excommunication (Canon 1364 of the Code of Canon Law). Heresies have been significant not only as disruptions of unity of faith but also as occasions for the clarification and development of doctrine. Heresies from the beginning of the Church to the 13th century are described in Dates and Events in Church History.

Hermit: See Anchorite.

Heroic Act of Charity: The completely unselfish offering to God of one's good works and merits for the benefit of the souls in purgatory rather than for oneself. Thus a person may offer to God for the souls in purgatory all the good works he performs during life, all the indulgences he gains, and all the prayers and indulgences that will be offered for him after his death. The act is revocable at will, and is not a vow. Its actual ratification depends on the will of God.

Heterodoxy: False doctrine, teaching or belief; a departure from truth.

Holy See: (1) The diocese of the pope, Rome. (2) The pope himself and/or the various officials and bodies of the Church's central administration at Vatican City — the Roman Curia — which act in the name and by authority of the pope.

Holy Spirit: God the Holy Spirit, third Person of the Holy Trinity, who proceeds from the Father and the Son and with whom he is equal in every respect; inspirer of the prophets and writers of sacred Scripture; promised by Christ to the Apostles as their advocate and strengthener; appeared in the form of a dove at the baptism of Christ and as tongues of fire at his descent upon the Apostles; soul of the Church and guarantor, by his abiding presence and action, of truth in doctrine; communicator of grace to human beings, for which reason he is called the sanctifier.

Holy Water: Water blessed by the Church and used as a sacramental, a practice which originated in apostolic times.

Holy Year: A year during which the pope grants the plenary Jubilee Indulgence to the faithful who fulfill certain conditions. For those who make a pilgrimage to Rome during the year, the conditions are reception of the sacraments of penance and the Eucharist, visits and prayer for the intention of the pope in the basilicas of St. Peter, St. John Lateran, St. Paul and St. Mary Major. For those who do not make a pilgrimage to Rome, the conditions are reception of the sacraments and prayer for the pope during a visit or community celebration in a church designated by the bishop of the locality. Holy Year observances have biblical counterparts in the Years of Jubilee observed at 50-year intervals by the pre-exilic Israelites (Lv. 25:25-54) — when debts were pardoned and slaves freed (Lv. 25:25-54) — and in sabbatical years observed from the end of the Exile to 70 A.D. — in which debts to fellow Jews were remitted. The practice of Christians from early times to go on pilgrimage to the Holy Land, the shrines of martyrs and the tombs of the Apostles in Rome influenced the institution of Holy Years. There was also a prevailing belief among the people that every 100th year was a year of "Great Pardon." Accordingly, even before Boniface VIII formally proclaimed the first Holy Year Feb. 22, 1300, scores of thousands of pilgrims were already on the way to or in Rome. Medieval popes embodied in the observance of Holy Years the practice of good works (reception of the sacraments of penance and the Eucharist, pilgrimages and/or visits to the tombs of the Apostles, and related actions) and spiritual benefits (particularly, special indulgences for the souls in purgatory). These and related practices, with suitable changes for celebrations in local churches, remain staple features of Holy Year observances. The first three Holy Years were observed in 1300, 1350 and 1390. Subsequent ones were celebrated at 25-year intervals except in 1800 and 1850 when, respectively, the French invasion of Italy and political turmoil made observance impossible. Pope Paul II (1464-1471) set the 25-year timetable. In 1500, Pope Alexander VI prescribed the start and finish ceremonies — the opening and closing of the Holy Doors in the major basilicas on successive Christmas Eves. All but a few of the earlier Holy Years were classified as ordinary. Several — like those of 1933 and 1983-84 to commemorate the 1900th and 1950th anniversaries of the death and resurrection of Christ — were in the extraordinary category.

Homosexuality: The condition of a person whose sexual orientation is toward persons of the same rather than the opposite sex. The condition, is not sinful in itself. Homosexual acts are seriously sinful in themselves; subjective responsibility for such acts, however, may be conditioned and diminished by compulsion and related factors.

Hope: One of the three theological virtues, by which one firmly trusts that God wills his salvation and will give him the means to attain it.

Hosanna: A Hebrew word, meaning O Lord, save, we pray.

Host, The Sacred: The bread under whose appearances Christ is and remains present in a unique manner after the consecration which takes place during Mass. (See Transubstantiation.)

Humanism: A world view centered on man, to the exclusion of anything supernatural; related to secularism.

Humility: A virtue which induces a person to evaluate himself or herself at his or her true worth, to recognize his or her dependence on God, and to give glory to God for the good he or she has and can do.

Hyperdulia: The special veneration accorded the Blessed Virgin Mary because of her unique role in the mystery of Redemption, her exceptional gifts of grace from God, and her pre-eminence among the saints. Hyperdulia is not adoration; only God is adored.

Hypnosis: A mental state resembling sleep, induced by suggestion, in which the subject does the bidding of the hypnotist. Hypnotism is permissible under certain conditions: the existence of a serious reason, e.g., for anesthetic or therapeutic purposes, and the competence and integrity of the hypnotist. Hypnotism may not be practiced for the sake of amusement. Experiments indicate that, contrary to popular opinion, hypnotized subjects may be induced to perform immoral acts which, normally, they would not do.

Hypostatic Union: The union of the human and divine natures in the one divine Person of Christ.

I

Icons: Byzantine-style paintings or representations of Christ, the Blessed Virgin and other saints, venerated in the Eastern Churches where they take the place of statues.

Idolatry: Worship of any but the true God; a violation of the First Commandment.

IHS — In Greek, the first three letters of the name of Jesus — Iota, Eta, Sigma.

Immortality: The survival and continuing existence of the human soul after death.

Impurity: Unlawful indulgence in sexual pleasure. (See Chastity.)

Incardination: The affiliation of a priest to his diocese. Every secular priest must belong to a certain diocese. Similarly, every priest of a religious community must belong to some jurisdiction of his community; this affiliation, however, is not called incardination.

Incarnation: (1) The coming-into-flesh or taking of human nature by the Second Person of the Trinity. He became human as the Son of Mary, being miraculously conceived by the power of the Holy Spirit, without ceasing to be divine. His divine Person hypostatically unites his divine and human natures. (2) The supernatural mystery coextensive with Christ from the moment of his human conception and continuing through his life on earth; his sufferings and death; his resurrection from the dead and ascension to glory with the Father; his sending, with the Father, of the Holy Spirit upon the Apostles and the Church; and his unending mediation with the Father for the salvation of human beings.

Incense: A granulated substance which, when burnt, emits an aromatic smoke. It symbolizes the zeal with which the faithful should be consumed, the good odor of Christian virtue, the ascent of prayer to God.

Incest: Sexual intercourse with relatives by blood or marriage; a sin of impurity and also a grave violation of the natural reverence due to relatives. Other sins of impurity (desire, etc.) concerning relatives have the nature of incest.

Inculturation: This was one of the subjects of an address delivered by Pope John Paul II Feb. 15, 1982, at a meeting in Lagos with the bishops of Nigeria. "An important aspect of your own evangelizing role is the whole dimension of the inculturation of the Gospel into the lives of your people. . . . The Church truly respects the culture of each people. In offering the Gospel message, the Church does not intend to destroy or to abolish what is good and beautiful. In fact, she recognizes many cultural values and, through the power of the Gospel, purifies and takes into Christian worship certain elements of a people's customs. The Church comes to bring Christ; she does not come to bring the culture of another race. Evangelization aims at penetrating and elevating culture by the power of the Gospel. . . . It is through the Providence of God that the divine message is made incarnate and is communicated through the culture of each people. It is forever true that the path of culture is the path of man, and it is on this path that man encounters the one who embodies the values of all cultures and fully reveals the man of each culture to himself. The Gospel of Christ, the Incarnate Word, finds its home along the path of culture, and from this path it continues to offer its message of salvation and eternal life."

Index of Prohibited Books: A list of books which Catholics were formerly forbidden to read, possess or sell, under penalty of excommunication. The books were banned by the Holy See after publication because their treatment of matters of faith and morals and related subjects were judged to be erroneous or serious occasions of doctrinal error.

Some books were listed in the Index by name; others were covered under general norms. The Congregation for the Doctrine of the Faith declared June 14, 1966, that the Index and its related penalties of excommunication no longer had the force of law in the Church. Persons are still obliged, however, to take normal precautions against occasions of doctrinal error.

Indifferentism: A theory that any one religion is as true and good — or false — as any other religion, and that it makes no difference, objectively, what religion one professes, if any. The theory is completely subjective, finding its justification entirely in personal choice without reference to or respect for objective validity. It is also self-contradictory, since it regards as equally acceptable — or unacceptable — the beliefs of all religions, which in fact are not only not all the same but are in some cases opposed to each other.

Indulgence: According to *The Doctrine and Practice of Indulgences,* an apostolic constitution issued by Paul VI Jan. 1, 1967, an indulgence is the remission before God of the temporal punishment due for sins already forgiven as far as their guilt is concerned, which a follower of Christ — with the proper dispositions and under certain determined conditions — acquires through the intervention of the Church. The Church grants indulgences in accordance with doctrine concerning the superabundant merits of Christ and the saints, the Power of the Keys, and the sharing of spiritual goods in the communion of saints. An indulgence is partial or plenary, depending on whether it does away with either part or all of the temporal punishment due for sin. Both types of indulgences can always be applied to the dead by way of suffrage; the actual disposition of indulgences applied to the dead rests with God. (1) Partial indulgence: Properly disposed faithful who perform an action to which a partial indulgence is attached obtain, in addition to the remission of temporal punishment acquired by the action itself, an equal remission of punishment through the intervention of the Church. (This grant was formerly designated in terms of days and years.) The proper dispositions for gaining a partial indulgence are sorrow for sin and freedom from serious sin, performance of the required good work, and the intention (which can be general or immediate) to gain the indulgence. In addition to customary prayers and other good works to which partial indulgences are attached, there are general grants of partial indulgences to the faithful who: (a) with some kind of prayer, raise their minds to God with humble confidence while carrying out their duties and bearing the difficulties of everyday life; (b) motivated by the spirit of faith and compassion, give of themselves or their goods for the service of persons in need; (c) in a spirit of penance, spontaneously refrain from the enjoyment of things which are lawful and pleasing to them. (2) Plenary indulgence: To gain a plenary indulgence, it is necessary for a person to be free of all attachment to sin, to perform the work to which the indulgence is attached, and to fulfill the three conditions of sacramental confession, Eucharistic Communion, and prayer for the intention of the pope. The three conditions may be fulfilled several days before or after the performance of the prescribed work, but it is fitting that Communion be received and prayers for the intentions of the pope be offered on the same day the work is performed. The condition of praying for the pope's intention is fully satisfied by praying one Our Father and one Hail Mary, and sometimes the Creed, but persons are free to choose other prayers. Four of the several devotional practices for which a plenary indulgence is granted are: (a) adoration of the Blessed Sacrament for at least one-half hour; (b) devout reading of sacred Scripture for at least one-half hour; (c) the Way of the Cross; (d) recitation of the Rosary in a church, public oratory or private chapel, or in a family group, a religious community or pious association. Only one plenary indulgence can be gained in a single day. The Apostolic Penitentiary issued a decree Dec. 14, 1985, granting diocesan bishops the right to impart — three times a year on solemn feasts of their choice — the papal blessing with a plenary indulgence to those who cannot be physically present but who follow the sacred rites at which the blessing is imparted by radio or television transmission. In July, 1986, publication was announced of a new and simplified *Enchiridion Indulgentiarum*, in accord with provisions of the revised Code of Canon Law.

Indult: A favor or privilege granted by competent ecclesiastical authority, giving permission to do something not allowed by the common law of the Church.

Infant Jesus of Prague: An 18-inch-high wooden statue of the Child Jesus which has figured in a form of devotion to the Holy Childhood and Kingship of Christ since the 17th century. Of uncertain origin, the statue was presented by Princess Polixena to the Carmelites of Our Lady of Victory Church, Prague, in 1628.

Infused Virtues: The theological virtues of faith, hope, and charity; principles or capabilities of supernatural action, they are given with sanctifying grace by God rather than acquired by repeated acts of a person. They can be increased by practice; they are lost by contrary acts. Natural-acquired moral virtues, like the cardinal virtues of prudence, justice, temperance, and fortitude, can be considered infused in a person whose state of grace gives them supernatural orientation.

Inquisition: A tribunal for dealing with heretics, authorized by Gregory IX in 1231 to search them out, hear and judge them, sentence them to various forms of punishment, and in some cases to hand them over to civil authorities for punishment. The Inquisition was a creature of its time when crimes against faith, which threatened the good of the Christian community, were regarded also as crimes against the state, and when heretical doctrines of such extremists as the Cathari and Albigensians threatened the very fabric of society. The institution, which was responsible for many excesses, was most active in the second half of the 13th century.

Inquisition, Spanish: An institution peculiar to Spain and the colonies in Spanish America. In 1478, at the urging of King Ferdinand, Pope Sixtus IV approved the establishment of the Inquisition for trying charges of heresy brought against Jewish

(Marranos) and Moorish (Moriscos) converts. It acquired jurisdiction over other cases as well, however, and fell into disrepute because of irregularities in its functions, cruelty in its sentences, and the manner in which it served the interests of the Spanish crown more than the accused persons and the good of the Church. Protests by the Holy See failed to curb excesses of the Inquisition, which lingered in Spanish history until early in the 19th century.

I N R I: The first letters of words in the Latin inscription atop the cross on which Christ was crucified: (I)esus (N)azaraenus, (R)ex (J)udaeorum — Jesus of Nazareth, King of the Jews.

Insemination, Artificial: The implanting of human semen by some means other than consummation of natural marital intercourse. In view of the principle that procreation should result only from marital intercourse, donor insemination is not permissible.

In Sin: The condition of a person called spiritually dead because he or she does not possess sanctifying grace, the principle of supernatural life, action and merit. Such grace can be regained through repentance.

Instruction: A document containing doctrinal explanations, directive norms, rules, recommendations, admonitions, issued by the pope, a department of the Roman Curia or other competent authority in the Church. To the extent that they so prescribe, instructions have the force of law.

Intercommunion, Eucharistic Sharing: The common celebration and reception of the Eucharist by members of different Christian churches; a pivotal issue in ecumenical theory and practice. Catholic participation and intercommunion in the Eucharistic liturgy of another church without a valid priesthood and with a variant Eucharistic belief is out of order. Under certain conditions, other Christians may receive the Eucharist in the Catholic Church (see additional Intercommunion entry). Intercommunion is acceptable to some Protestant churches and unacceptable to others.

Interdict: A censure imposed on persons for certain violations of church law. Interdicted persons may not take part in certain liturgical services, administer or receive certain sacraments.

Interregnum: The period of time between the death of a pope and the election of his successor. Another term applied to the period is *Sede vacante*, meaning the See (of Rome) being vacant. The main concerns during an interregnum are matters connected with the death and burial of the pope, the election of his successor, and the maintenance of ordinary routine for the proper functioning of the Roman Curia and the Diocese of Rome. Interregnum procedures follow norms contained in the apostolic constitution *Romano Pontifici Eligendo* issued by Paul VI Oct. 1, 1975. "During the vacancy of the Apostolic See," the constitution states, "the government of the Church is entrusted to the College of Cardinals for the sole dispatch of ordinary business and of matters which cannot be postponed, and for the preparation of everything necessary for the election of the new pope." The general congregation of the whole college, presided over by the dean, sub-dean or senior cardinal, has responsibility for major decisions during an interregnum. Other decisions of a routine nature are left to a particular congregation consisting of the chamberlain of the Holy Roman Church and three assistant cardinals. The chamberlain of the Holy Roman Church and the dean of the college are the key officials, with directive responsibilities before and during the electoral conclave. The chamberlain is in general charge of ordinary administration. He — or the dean prior to a chamberlain's election by the cardinals — certifies the death of the pope; orders the destruction of the Fisherman's Ring and personal seals of the pope; and sets in motion procedures, carried out in collaboration with the dean, for informing the world about the pope's death, for funeral preparations, and for summoning and supervising the conclave for the election of a new pope. Cardinals in charge of departments of the Roman Curia relinquish their offices at the death of the pope. Remaining in office, however, are the vicar of Rome, for ordinary jurisdiction over the diocese, and the major penitentiary. Papal representatives, such as nuncios and apostolic delegates, remain in office. The congregations, offices and tribunals of the Curia retain ordinary jurisdiction for routine affairs but may not initiate new business during an interregnum. If the pope should die during sessions of an ecumenical council or the Synod of Bishops, they would automatically be suspended. The deceased pope is buried in St. Peter's Basilica, following prescribed ceremonies and traditional customs during a mourning period of nine days. The conclave for the election of a new pope begins no sooner than 15 and no later than 20 days after the death of his predecessor. On the election of the new pope, the interregnum comes to an end.

Intinction: A method of administering Holy Communion under the dual appearances of bread and wine, in which the consecrated host is dipped in the consecrated wine before being given to the communicant. The administering of Holy Communion in this manner, which has been traditional in Eastern-Rite liturgies, was authorized in the Roman Rite for various occasions by the *Constitution on the Sacred Liturgy* promulgated by the Second Vatican Council.

Irenicism: Peace-seeking, conciliation, as opposed to polemics; an important element in ecumenism, provided it furthers pursuit of the Christian unity willed by Christ without degenerating into a peace-at-any-price disregard for religious truth.

Irregularity: A permanent impediment to the lawful reception or exercise of holy orders. The Church instituted irregularities — which include apostasy, heresy, homicide, attempted suicide — out of reverence for the dignity of the sacraments.

Itinerarium: Prayers for a spiritually profitable journey.

J

Jansenism: Opinions developed and proposed by Cornelius Jansenius (1585-1638). He held that: human nature was radically and intrinsically corrupted by original sin; some men are predestined to heaven and others to hell; Christ died only for those predestined to heaven; for those who are predestined, the operations of grace are irresistible. Jansenism also advocated an extremely rigorous code of morals and asceticism. The errors were proscribed by Urban VIII in 1642, by Innocent X in 1653, by Clement XI in 1713, and by other popes. Despite these condemnations, the rigoristic spirit of Jansenism lingered for a long time afterwards, particularly in France.

Jehovah's Witnesses: The Witnesses, together with the Watchtower and Bible Tract Society, trace their beginnings to a Bible class organized by Charles Taze Russell in 1872 at Allegheny, Pa. They take their name from a passage in Isaiah (43:12): " 'You are my witnesses,' says Jehovah." They are generally fundamentalist and revivalist with respect to the Bible, and believe that Christ is God's Son but is inferior to God. They place great emphasis on the Battle of Armageddon (as a decisive confrontation of good and evil) that is depicted vividly in Revelation, believing that God will then destroy the existing system of things and that, with the establishment of Jehovah's Kingdom, a small band of 144,000 spiritual sons of God will go to heaven, rule with Christ, and share in some way their happiness with some others. Each Witness is considered by the society to be an ordained minister charged with the duty of spreading the message of Jehovah, which is accomplished through publications, house-to-house visitations, and other methods. The Witnesses refuse to salute the flag of any nation, regarding this as a form of idolatry, or to sanction blood transfusions even for the saving of life. There are approximately one million Witnesses in more than 22,000 congregations in some 80 countries. The freedom and activities of Witnesses are restricted in some places.

Jesus: The name of Jesus, meaning Savior in Christian usage, derived from the Aramaic and Hebrew *Yeshua* and *Joshua*, meaning *Yahweh* is salvation.

Jesus Prayer: A form of prayer dating back to the fifth century, "Lord Jesus Christ, Son of God, have mercy on me (a sinner)."

Judgment: (1) Last or final judgment: Final judgment by Christ, at the end of the world and the general resurrection. (2) Particular judgment: The judgment that takes place immediately after a person's death, followed by entrance into heaven, hell or purgatory.

Jurisdiction: Right, power, authority to rule. Jurisdiction in the Church is of divine institution; has pastoral service for its purpose; includes legislative, judicial and executive authority; can be exercised only by persons with the power of orders. (1) Ordinary jurisdiction is attached to ecclesiastical offices by law; the officeholders, called Ordinaries, have authority over those who are subject to them. (2) Delegated jurisdiction is that which is granted to persons rather than attached to offices. Its extent depends on the terms of the delegation.

Justice: One of the four cardinal virtues by which a person gives to others what is due to them as a matter of right. (See Cardinal Virtues.)

Justification: The act by which God makes a person just, and the consequent change in the spiritual status of a person, from sin to grace; the remission of sin and the infusion of sanctifying grace through the merits of Christ and the action of the Holy Spirit.

K

Kerygma: Proclaiming the word of God, in the manner of the Apostles, as here and now effective for salvation. This method of preaching or instruction, centered on Christ and geared to the facts and themes of salvation history, is designed to dispose people to faith in Christ and or to intensify the experience and practice of that faith in those who have it.

Keys, Power of the: Spiritual authority and jurisdiction in the Church, symbolized by the keys of the kingdom of heaven. Christ promised the keys to St. Peter, as head-to-be of the Church (Mt. 16:19), and commissioned him with full pastoral responsibility to feed his lambs and sheep (Jn. 21:15-17), The pope, as the successor of St. Peter, has this power in a primary and supreme manner. The bishops of the Church also have the power, in union with and subordinate to the pope. Priests share in it through holy orders and the delegation of authority. Examples of the application of the Power of the Keys are the exercise of teaching and pastoral authority by the pope and bishops, the absolving of sins in the sacrament of penance, the granting of indulgences, the imposing of spiritual penalties on persons who commit certain serious sins.

L

Laicization: The process by which a man ordained to holy orders is relieved of the obligations of orders and the ministry and is returned to the status of a lay person.

Languages of the Church: The first language in church use, for divine worship and the conduct of ecclesiastical affairs, was Aramaic, the language of the first Christians in and around Jerusalem. As the Church spread westward, Greek was adopted and prevailed until the third century when it was supplanted by Latin for official use in the West. According to traditions established very early in churches of the Eastern Rites, many different languages were adopted for use in divine worship and for the conduct of ecclesiastical affairs. The practice was, and still is, to use the vernacular or a language closely related to the common tongue of the people. In the Western Church, Latin prevailed as the general official language until the promulgation on Dec. 4, 1963, of the *Constitution on the Sacred Liturgy* by the second session of the Second Vatican Council. Since that time, vernacular languages have come into use in the Mass, administration of the sacraments, and the Liturgy of the Hours. The change was introduced in order to make the prayers and ceremonies of divine worship more informative and meaningful to all. Latin, however, remains the official language for documents of the Holy See, administrative and procedural matters.

Law: An ordinance or rule governing the activity of things. (1) Natural law: Moral norms corresponding to man's nature by which he orders his conduct toward God, neighbor, society and himself. This law, which is rooted in human nature, is of divine origin, can be known by the use of reason, and binds all persons having the use of reason. The Ten Commandments are declarations and amplifications of natural law. The primary precepts of natural law, to do good and to avoid evil, are universally recog-

nized, despite differences with respect to understanding and application resulting from different philosophies of good and evil. (2) Divine positive law: That which has been revealed by God. Among its essentials are the twin precepts of love of God and love of neighbor, and the Ten Commandments. (3) Ecclesiastical law: That which is established by the Church for the spiritual welfare of the faithful and the orderly conduct of ecclesiastical affairs. (See Canon Law.) (4) Civil law: That which is established by a socio-political community for the common good.

Liberalism: A multiphased trend of thought and movement favoring liberty, independence and progress in moral, intellectual, religious, social, economic and political life. Traceable to the Renaissance, it developed through the Enlightenment, the rationalism of the 19th century, and modernist-and existentialist-related theories of the 20th century. Evaluations of various kinds of liberalism depend on the validity of their underlying principles. Extremist positions — regarding subjectivism, libertinarianism, naturalist denials of the supernatural, and the alienation of individuals and society from God and the Church were condemned by Gregory XVI in the 1830s, Pius IX in 1864, Leo XIII in 1899, and St. Pius X in 1907. There is, however, nothing objectionable about forms of liberalism patterned according to sound principles of Christian doctrine.

Liberation Theology: Deals with the relevance of Christian faith and salvation — and, therefore, of the mission of the Church — to efforts for the promotion of human rights, social justice and human development. It originated in the religious, social, political and economic environment of Latin America, with its contemporary need for a theory and corresponding action by the Church, in the pattern of its overall mission, for human rights and integral personal and social development. Some versions of liberation theology are at variance with the body of church teaching because of their ideological concept of Christ as liberator, and also because they play down the primary spiritual nature and mission of the Church. Instructions from the Congregation for the Doctrine of the Faith — "On Certain Aspects of the Theology of Liberation" (Sept. 3, 1984) and "On Christian Freedom and Liberation" (Apr. 5, 1986) — contain warnings against translating sociology into theology and advocating violence in social activism.

Life in Outer Space: Whether rational life exists on other bodies in the universe besides earth, is a question for scientific investigation to settle. The possibility can be granted, without prejudice to the body of revealed truth.

Limbo: The limbo of the fathers was the state of rest and natural happiness after death enjoyed by the just of pre-Christian times until they were admitted to heaven following the Ascension of Christ. Belief in this matter is stated in the Apostles' Creed. The existence of a limbo for unbaptized persons of infant status — a state of rest and natural happiness — has never been formally defined.

Litany: A prayer in the form of responsive petition; e.g., St. Joseph, pray for us, etc. Examples are the litanies of Loreto (Litany of the Blessed Mother), the Holy Name, All Saints, the Sacred Heart, the Precious Blood, St. Joseph, Litany for the Dying.

Loreto, House of: A Marian shrine in Loreto, Italy, consisting of the home of the Holy Family which, according to an old tradition, was transported in a miraculous manner from Nazareth to Dalmatia and finally to Loreto between 1291 and 1294. Investigations conducted shortly after the appearance of the structure in Loreto revealed that its dimensions matched those of the house of the Holy Family missing from its place of enshrinement in a basilica at Nazareth. Among the many popes who regarded it with high honor was John XXIII, who went there on pilgrimage Oct. 4, 1962. The house of the Holy Family is enshrined in the Basilica of Our Lady.

Lust: A disorderly desire for sexual pleasure; one of the seven capital sins.

M

Magi: In the Infancy Narrative of St. Matthew's Gospel (2:1-12), three wise men from the East whose visit and homage to the Child Jesus at Bethlehem indicated Christ's manifestation of himself to non-Jewish people. The narrative teaches the universality of salvation. The traditional names of the Magi are Caspar, Melchior and Balthasar.

Magnificat: The canticle or hymn of the Virgin Mary on the occasion of her visitation to her cousin Elizabeth (Lk. 1:46-55). It is an expression of praise, thanksgiving and acknowledgment of the great blessings given by God to Mary, the Mother of the Second Person of the Blessed Trinity made Man. The Magnificat is recited in the Liturgy of the Hours as part of the Evening Prayer.

Martyr: A Greek word, meaning witness, denoting one who voluntarily suffered death for the faith or some Christian virtue.

Martyrology: A catalogue of martyrs and other saints, arranged according to the calendar. The *Roman Martyrology* contains the official list of saints venerated by the Church. Additions to the list are made in beatification and canonization decrees of the Congregation for the Causes of Saints.

Mass for the People: On Sundays and certain feasts throughout the year pastors are required to offer Mass for the faithful entrusted to their care. If they cannot offer the Mass on these days, they must do so at a later date or provide that another priest offer the Mass.

Materialism: Theory which holds that matter is the only reality, and everything in existence is merely a manifestation of matter; there is no such thing as spirit, and the supernatural does not exist. Materialism is incompatible with Christian doctrine.

Meditation: Mental, as distinguished from vocal, prayer, in which thought, affections, and resolutions of the will predominate. There is a meditative element to all forms of prayer, which always involves the raising of the heart and mind to God.

Mendicants: A term derived from Latin and meaning beggars, applied to members of religious orders without property rights; the members, accordingly, worked or begged for their support. The original mendicants were Franciscans and Dominicans in the early 13th century; later, the Carmelites, Augustinians, Servites and others were given the mendicant title and privileges, with respect to exemption from episcopal jurisdiction and wide faculties for preaching and administering the sacrament of penance. The practice of begging is limited at the present time, although it is still allowed with the permission of competent superiors and bishops. Mendicants are supported by free will offerings and income received for spiritual services and other work.

Mercy, Divine: The love and goodness of God, manifested particularly in a time of need.

Merit: In religion, the right to a supernatural reward for good works freely done for a supernatural motive by a person in the state of and with the assistance of grace. The right to such reward is from God, who binds himself to give it. Accordingly, good works, as described above, are meritorious for salvation.

Metempsychosis: Theory of the passage or migration of the human soul after death from one body to another for the purpose of purification from guilt. The theory denies the unity of the soul and human personality, and the doctrine of individual moral responsibility.

Millennium: A thousand-year reign of Christ and the just upon earth before the end of the world. This belief of the Millenarians, Chiliasts, and some sects of modern times is based on an erroneous interpretation of Rv. 20.

Miracles: Observable events or effects in the physical or moral order of things, with reference to salvation, which cannot be explained by the ordinary operation of laws of nature and which, therefore, are attributed to the direct action of God. They make known, in an unusual way, the concern and intervention of God in human affairs for the salvation of men. The most striking examples are the miracles worked by Christ. Numbering about 35, they included his own Resurrection; the raising of three persons to life (Lazarus, the daughter of Jairus, the son of the widow of Naim); the healing of blind, leprous and other persons; nature miracles; and prophecies, or miracles of the intellectual order. The foregoing notion of miracles, which is based on the concept of a fixed order of nature, was not known by the writers of Sacred Scripture. In the Old Testament, particularly, they called some things miraculous which, according to the definition in contemporary use, may or may not have been miracles. Essentially, however, the occurrences so designated were regarded as exceptional manifestations of God's care and concern for the salvation of his people. The miracles of Christ were miracles in the full sense of the term. The Church believes it is reasonable to accept miracles as manifestations of divine power for purposes of salvation. God, who created the laws of nature, is their master; hence, without disturbing the ordinary course of things, he can — and has in the course of history before and after Christ — occasionally set aside these laws and has also produced effects beyond their power of operation. The Church does not regard as miraculous just anything which does not admit of easy explanation; on the contrary, miracles are acknowledged only when the events have a bearing on the order of grace and every possible natural explanation has been tried and found wanting. (The transubstantiation — i.e., the conversion of the whole substance of bread and wine, their sensible appearances alone remaining, into the Body and Blood of Christ in the act of Consecration at Mass — is not an observable event. Traditionally, however, it has been called a miracle.)

Missal: A liturgical book of Roman Rite also called the *Sacramentary,* containing the celebrant's prayers of the Mass, along with general instructions and ceremonial directives. The Latin text of the new *Roman Missal,* replacing the one authorized by the Council of Trent in the 16th century, was published by the Vatican Polyglot Press in 1970. Its use in English was made mandatory in the U.S. from Dec. 1, 1974. Readings and scriptural responsories formerly in the missal are contained in the *Lectionary.*

Missiology: Study of the missionary nature, constitution and activity of the Church in all aspects: theological reasons for missionary activity, laws and instructions of the Holy See, history of the missions, social and cultural background, methods, norms for carrying on missionary work.

Mission: (1) Strictly, it means being sent to perform a certain work, such as the mission of Christ to redeem mankind, the mission of the Apostles and the Church and its members to perpetuate the prophetic, priestly and royal mission of Christ. (2) A place where: the Gospel has not been proclaimed; the Church has not been firmly established; the Church, although established, is weak. (3) An ecclesiastical territory with the simplest kind of canonical organization, under the jurisdiction of the Congregation for the Evangelization of Peoples. (4) A church or chapel without a resident priest. (5) A special course of sermons and spiritual exercises conducted in parishes for the purpose of renewing and deepening the spiritual life of the faithful and for the conversion of lapsed Catholics.

Modernism: The "synthesis of all heresies," which appeared near the beginning of the 20th century. It undermines the objective validity of religious beliefs and practices which, it contends, are products of the subconscious developed by mankind under the stimulus of a religious sense. It holds that the existence of a personal God cannot be demonstrated, the Bible is not inspired, Christ is not divine, nor did he establish the Church or institute the sacraments. A special danger lies in modernism, which is still influential, because it uses Catholic terms with perverted meanings. St. Pius X condemned 65 propositions of modernism in 1907 in the decree *Lamentabili* and issued the encyclical *Pascendi* to explain and analyze its errors.

Monastery: The dwelling place, as well as the community thereof, of monks belonging to the Benedictine and Benedictine-related orders like the Cistercians and Carthusians; also, the Augustinians and Canons Regular. Distinctive of monasteries are: their separation from the world; the enclosure or cloister; the permanence or stability of attachment characteristic of their members; autonomous government in accordance with a monastic rule, like that of St. Benedict in the West or of St. Basil in the East; the special dedication of its members to the community celebration of the liturgy as well as to work that is suitable to the surrounding area and the needs of its people. Monastic superiors of men have such titles as abbot and prior; of women, abbess and prioress. In most essentials, an abbey is the same as a monastery.

Monk: A member of a monastic order — e.g., the Benedictines, the Benedictine-related Cistercians and Carthusians, and the Basilians, who bind themselves by religious profession to stable attachment to a monastery, the contemplative life and the work of their community. In popular use, the title is wrongly applied to many men religious who really are not monks.

Monotheism: Belief in and worship of one God.

Morality: Conformity or difformity of behavior to standards of right conduct. (See Moral Obligations, Commandments of God, Precepts of the Church, Conscience, Law.)

Mormons: Members of the Church of Jesus Christ of Latter-Day Saints. The church was established by Joseph Smith (1805-1844) at Fayette, N.Y., three years after he said he had received from an angel golden tablets containing the *Book of the Prophet Mormon.* This book, the Bible, *Doctrine and Covenants,* and *The Pearl of Great Price,* are the basic doctrinal texts of the church. Characteristic of the Mormons are strong belief in the revelations of their leaders, among whom was Brigham Young; a strong community of religious-secular concern; a dual secular and spiritual priesthood, and vigorous missionary activity. The headquarters of the church are located at Salt Lake City, Utah, where the Mormons first settled in 1847.

Mortification: Acts of self-discipline, including prayer, hardship, austerities and penances undertaken for the sake of progress in virtue.

Motu Proprio: A Latin phrase designating a document issued by a pope on his own initiative. Documents of this kind often concern administrative matters.

Mysteries of Faith: Supernatural truths whose existence cannot be known without revelation by God and whose intrinsic truth, while not contrary to reason, can never be wholly understood even after revelation. These mysteries are above reason, not against reason. Among them are the divine mysteries of the Trinity, Incarnation and Eucharist. Some mysteries — e.g., concerning God's attributes — can be known by reason without revelation, although they cannot be fully understood.

N

Necromancy: Supposed communication with the dead; a form of divination.

Non-Expedit: A Latin expression. It is not expedient (fitting, proper), used to state a prohibition or refusal of permission.

Novena: A term designating public or private devotional practices over a period of nine consecutive days; or, by extension, over a period of nine weeks, in which one day a week is set aside for the devotions.

Novice: A man or woman preparing, in a formal

period of trial and formation called a novitiate, for membership in an institute of consecrated life. The novitiate lasts a minimum of 12 and a maximum of 24 months; at its conclusion, the novice professes temporary vows of poverty, chastity and obedience. Norms require that certain periods of time be spent in the house of novitiate: the first three months, one solid period of six months, the final month before the profession of temporary commitment. Periods of apostolic work are also required, to acquaint the novice with the apostolate(s) of the institute. A novice is not bound by the obligations of the professed members of the institute, is free to leave at any time, and may be discharged at the discretion of competent superiors. The immediate superior of a novice is a director of formation.

Nun: (1) Strictly, a member of a religious order of women with solemn vows (moniales). (2) In general, all women religious, even those in simple vows who are more properly called sisters.

Nunc Dimittis: The canticle or hymn of Simeon at the sight of Jesus at the Temple on the occasion of his presentation (Lk. 2:29-32). It is an expression of joy and thanksgiving for the blessing of having lived to see the Messiah. It is prescribed for use in the Night Prayer of the Liturgy of the Hours.

O

Oath: Calling upon God to witness the truth of a statement. Violating an oath, e.g., by perjury in court, or taking an oath without sufficient reason, is a violation of the honor due to God.

Obedience: Submission to one in authority. General obligations of obedience fall under the Fourth Commandment. The vow of obedience professed by religious is one of the evangelical counsels.

Obsession, Diabolical: The extraordinary state of one who is seriously molested by evil spirits in an external manner. Obsession is more than just temptation.

Occultism: Practices involving ceremonies, rituals, chants, incantations, other cult-related activities intended to affect the course of nature, the lives of practitioners and others, through esoteric powers of magic, diabolical or other forces; one of many forms of superstition.

Octave: A period of eight days given over to the celebration of a major feast such as Easter.

Oils, Holy: The oils consecrated by bishops on Holy Thursday or another suitable day, and by priests under certain conditions for use in certain sacraments and consecrations. (1) The oil of catechumens (olive or vegetable oil), used at baptism; also, poured with chrism into the baptismal water blessed in Easter Vigil ceremonies. (2) Chrism (olive or vegetable oil mixed with balm), used at baptism, in confirmation, at the ordination of a priest and bishop, in the dedication of churches and altars. (3) Oil of the sick (olive or vegetable oil) used in anointing the sick.

Old Catholics: Several sects, including: (1) the Church of Utrecht, which severed relations with Rome in 1724; (2) the National Polish Church in the U.S., which had its origin near the end of the 19th century; (3) German, Austrian and Swiss Old Catholics, who broke away from union with Rome following the First Vatican Council in 1870 because they objected to the dogma of papal infallibility. The formation of the Old Catholic communion of Germans, Austrians and Swiss began in 1870 at a public meeting held in Nuremberg under the leadership of A. Dollinger. Four years later episcopal succession was established with the ordination of an Old Catholic German bishop by a prelate of the Church of Utrecht. In line with the "Declaration of Utrecht" of 1889, they accept the first seven ecumenical councils and doctrine formulated before 1054, but reject communion with the pope and a number of other Catholic doctrines and practices. They have a valid priesthood and valid sacraments. *The Oxford Dictionary of the Christian Church* notes that they have recognized Anglican ordinations since 1925, that they have had full communion with the Church of England since 1932, and that their bishops, using their own formula, have taken part in the ordination of Anglican bishops. This communion does not recognize the "Old Catholic" status of several smaller sects calling themselves such. In turn, connection with it is disavowed by the Old Roman Catholic Church headquartered in Chicago, which contends that it has abandoned the traditions of the Church of Utrecht. The United States is the only English-speaking country with Old Catholic communities.

Opus Dei: Opus Dei was founded in 1928 in Madrid by Msgr. Josemaria Escriva (beatified in 1992) with the aim of spreading throughout all sectors of society a profound awareness of the universal call to holiness and apostolate (of Christian witness and action) in the ordinary circumstances of life, and, more specifically, through one's professional work. On Nov. 28, 1982, Pope John Paul II established Opus Dei as a personal prelature with the full title, Prelature of the Holy Cross and Opus Dei. The 1993 edition of *Annuario Pontificio* reported that the prelature had 1,459 priests (40 newly ordained) and 348 major seminarians. Also, there were 76,934 lay persons — men and women, married and single, of every class and social condition — of about 80 nationalities. In the United States, members of Opus Dei, along with cooperators and friends, conduct apostolic works corporately in major cities in the East and Midwest, Texas and on the West Coast. Elsewhere, corporate works include universities, vocational institutes, training schools for farmers and numerous other apostolic initiatives. An information office is located at 330 Riverside Dr., New York, NY 10025.

Oratory: A chapel.

Ordinariate: An ecclesiastical jurisdiction for special purposes and people. Examples are military ordinariates for armed services personnel (in accord with provisions of the apostolic constitution *Spirituali militum curae*, Apr. 21, 1986) and Eastern-Rite ordinariates in places where Eastern-Rite dioceses do not exist.

Ordination: The consecration of sacred ministers for divine worship and the service of people in things pertaining to God. The power of ordination comes from Christ and the Church, and must be conferred by a minister capable of communicating it.

Organ Transplants: The transplanting of organs from one person to another is permissible provided it is done with the consent of the concerned parties and does not result in the death or essential mutilation of the donor. Advances in methods and technology have increased the range of transplant possibilities in recent years.

Original Sin: The sin of Adam (Gn. 2:8—3:24), personal to him and passed on to all persons as a state of privation of grace. Despite this privation and the related wounding of human nature and weakening of natural powers, original sin leaves unchanged all that man himself is by nature. The scriptural basis of the doctrine was stated especially by St. Paul in 1 Cor. 15:21ff., and Romans 5:12-21. Original sin is remitted by baptism and incorporation in Christ, through whom grace is given to persons. Pope John Paul, while describing original sin during a general audience Oct. 1, 1986, called it "the absence of sanctifying grace in nature which has been diverted from its supernatural end."

O Salutaris Hostia: The first three Latin words, O Saving Victim, of a Benediction hymn.

Ostpolitik: Policy adopted by Pope Paul VI in an attempt to improve the situation of Eastern European Catholics through diplomatic negotiations with their governments.

Oxford Movement: A movement in the Church of England from 1833 to about 1845 which had for its objective a threefold defense of the church as a divine institution, the apostolic succession of its bishops, and the Book of Common Prayer as the rule of faith. The movement took its name from Oxford University and involved a number of intellectuals who authored a series of influential *Tracts for Our Times.* Some of its leading figures — e.g., F. W. Faber, John Henry Newman and Henry Edward Manning — became converts to the Catholic Church. In the Church of England, the movement affected the liturgy, historical and theological scholarship, the status of the ministry, and other areas of ecclesiastical life.

P

Paganism: A term referring to non-revealed religions, i.e., religions other than Christianity, Judaism and Mohammedanism.

Palms: Blessed palms are a sacramental. They are blessed and distributed on the Sunday of the Passion in commemoration of the triumphant entrance of Christ into Jerusalem. Ashes of the burnt palms are used on Ash Wednesday.

Pange Lingua: First Latin words, Sing, my tongue, of a hymn in honor of the Holy Eucharist, used particularly on Holy Thursday and in Eucharistic processions.

Pantheism: Theory that all things are part of God, divine, in the sense that God realizes himself as the ultimate reality of matter or spirit through being and/or becoming all things that have been, are, and will be. The theory leads to hopeless confusion of the Creator and the created realm of being, identifies evil with good, and involves many inherent contradictions.

Papal Election: The pope is elected by members of the College of Cardinals in a secret conclave or meeting convened ordinarily in secluded quarters of the Vatican Palace between 15 and 20 days after the death of his predecessor. Cardinals under the age of 80, totaling no more than 120, are eligible to participate in a papal election. Following are some of the principal regulations decreed by Paul VI Oct. 1, 1975, in the apostolic constitution *Romano Pontifici Eligendo.* The ordinary manner of election is by scrutiny, with two votes each morning and afternoon in the Sistine Chapel until one of the candidates receives a two-thirds majority. Alternative methods, which can be adopted by unanimous agreement of the cardinals in difficult cases, are provided for: (1) by delegation, in which the cardinals designate a limited number (nine to 15) to make the choice; (2) by changing the majority rule from two-thirds vote to an absolute majority plus one; (3) by limiting final choice, if the procedure in force becomes protracted, to one between the two candidates who received the largest numbers of votes, but not a required majority, in the most recent balloting. An unusual manner of election is by acclamation or inspiration — that is, by spontaneous, unanimous choice without any need for normal voting procedure. The elected candidate is asked by the dean of the college if he accepts the election. If he does so and is already a bishop, he immediately becomes the bishop of Rome and pope, and signifies the name by which he will be called. The cardinals then pledge their obedience to him before the senior cardinal deacon proclaims his election to the world from the main balcony of the Vatican and the new pope imparts his blessing *Urbi et Orbi* (to the City and the World). If the candidate is not a bishop, he is so ordained before receiving the pledge of obedience and being proclaimed pope. The subsequent installation of the pope is a ceremonial recognition of the fact of his election. The pope is elected for life. If one should resign, a new pope would be elected in accordance with the foregoing regulations. Rigid rules govern the conclave — its personnel, freedom from internal and external influence and interference, absolute secrecy (with a ban on recording devices and a prohibition against any disclosures). Ordinarily, the first indication that a new pope has been elected is a plume of white smoke rising from the Vatican on burning of the last ballots. Early methods of electing a pope — with various degrees of participation by the clergy and people of Rome and others — were set aside by Pope Nicholas II, who decreed in 1059 that cardinal bishops would be the electors. Further modification of the process was decreed by the Lateran Council in 1179 (that election would take place by a two-thirds majority vote of the cardinals) and by Pope Gregory X in 1274 (regarding a secluded conclave arrangement for elections).

Paraclete: A title of the Holy Spirit meaning, in Greek, Advocate, Consoler.

Parental Duties: All duties related to the obligation of parents to provide for the welfare of their children. These obligations fall under the Fourth Commandment.

Parish: A community of the faithful served by a pastor charged with responsibility for providing them with full pastoral service. Most parishes are territorial, embracing all of the faithful in a certain area of a diocese: some are personal or national, for certain classes of people, without strict regard for their places of residence.

Parousia: The coming, or saving presence, of Christ which will mark the completion of salvation history and the coming to perfection of God's kingdom at the end of the world.

Paschal Candle: A large candle, symbolic of the risen Christ, blessed and lighted on the Easter Vigil and placed at the altar until Pentecost. It is ornamented with five large grains of incense, representing the wounds of Christ, inserted in the form of a cross; the Greek letters Alpha and Omega, symbolizing Christ the beginning and end of all things, at the top and bottom of the shaft of the cross; and the figures of the current year of salvation in the quadrants formed by the cross.

Paschal Precept: Church law requiring reception of the Eucharist in the Easter season (see separate entry) unless, for a just cause, once-a-year reception takes place at another time.

Passion of Christ: Sufferings of Christ, recorded in the four Gospels.

Pastor: An ordained minister charged with responsibility for the doctrinal, sacramental and related service of people committed to his care; e.g., a bishop for the people in his diocese, a priest for the people of his parish.

Pater Noster: The initial Latin words, Our Father, of the Lord's Prayer.

Peace, Sign of: A gesture of greeting — e.g., a handshake — exchanged by the ministers and participants at Mass.

Pectoral Cross: A cross worn on a chain about the neck and over the breast by bishops and abbots as a mark of their office.

Penance or Penitence: (1) The spiritual change or conversion of mind and heart by which a person turns away from sin, and all that it implies, toward God, through a personal renewal under the influence of the Holy Spirit. In the apostolic constitution *Paenitemini*, Pope Paul VI called it "a religious, personal act which has as its aim love and surrender to God." Penance involves sorrow and contrition for sin, together with other internal and external acts of atonement. It serves the purposes of reestablishing in one's life the order of God's love and commandments, and of making satisfaction to God for sin. A divine precept states the necessity of penance for salvation: "Unless you do penance, you shall all likewise perish" (Lk. 13:3) ... "Be converted and believe in the Gospel" (Mk. 1:15). In the penitential discipline of the Church, the various works of penance have been classified under the headings of prayer (interior), fasting and almsgiving (exterior). The Church has established minimum requirements for the common and social observance of the divine precept by Catholics — e.g., by requiring them to fast and/or abstain on certain days of the year. These observances, however, do not exhaust all the demands of the divine precept, whose fulfillment is a matter of personal responsibility; nor do they have any real value unless they proceed from the internal spirit and purpose of penance. Related to works of penance for sins actually committed are works of mortification. The purpose of the latter is to develop

— through prayer, fasting, renunciations and similar actions —self-control and detachment from things which could otherwise become occasions of sin. (2) Penance is a virtue disposing a person to turn to God in sorrow for sin and to carry out works of amendment and atonement. (3) The sacrament of penance and sacramental penance.

Perjury: Taking a false oath, lying under oath, a violation of the honor due to God.

Persecution, Religious: A campaign waged against a church or other religious body by persons and governments intent on its destruction. The best known campaigns of this type against the Christian Church were the Roman persecutions which occured intermittently from about 54 to the promulgation of the Edict of Milan in 313, The most extensive persecutions took place during the reigns of Nero, the first major Roman persecutor, Domitian, Trajan, Marcus Aurelius, and Diocletian. Besides the Roman persecutions, the Catholic Church has been subject to many others, including those of the 20th century in Communist-controlled countries.

Personal Prelature: A special-purpose jurisdiction — for particular pastoral and missionary work, etc. — consisting of secular priests and deacons and open to lay persons willing to dedicate themselves to its apostolic works. The prelate in charge is an Ordinary, with the authority of office; he can establish a national or international seminary, incardinate its students and promote them to holy orders under the title of service to the prelature. The prelature is constituted and governed according to statutes laid down by the Holy See. Statutes define its relationship and mode of operation with the bishops of territories in which members live and work. Opus Dei is a personal prelature.

Peter's Pence: A collection made each year among Catholics for the maintenance of the pope and his works of charity. It was originally a tax of a penny on each house, and was collected on St. Peter's day, whence the name. It originated in England in the eighth century.

Petition: One of the four purposes of prayer. In prayers of petition, persons ask of God the blessings they and others need.

Pharisees: Influential class among the Jews, referred to in the Gospels, noted for their self-righteousness, legalism, strict interpretation of the Law, acceptance of the traditions of the elders as well as the Law of Moses, and beliefs regarding angels and spirits, the resurrection of the dead and judgment. Most of them were laymen, and they were closely allied with the Scribes; their opposite numbers were the Sadducees. The Pharisaic and rabbinical traditions had a lasting influence on Judaism following the destruction of Jerusalem in 70 A.D.

Pious Fund: Property and money originally accumulated by the Jesuits to finance their missionary work in Lower California. When the Jesuits were expelled from the territory in 1767, the fund was appropriated by the Spanish Crown and used to support Dominican and Franciscan missionary work in Upper and Lower California. In 1842 the Mexican government took over administration of the fund, incorporated most of the revenue into the national treasury, and agreed to pay the Church interest of six per cent a year on the capital so incorporated. From 1848 to 1967 the fund was the subject of lengthy negotiations between the U.S. and Mexican governments because of the latter's failure to make payments as agreed. A lump-sum settlement was made in 1967 with payment by Mexico to the U.S. government of more than $700,000, to be turned over to the Archdiocese of San Francisco.

Polytheism: Belief in and worship of many gods or divinities, especially prevalent in pre-Christian religions.

Poor Box: Alms-box; found in churches from the earliest days of Christianity.

Pope Joan: Alleged name of a woman falsely said to have been pope from 855-858, the years of the reign of Benedict III. The myth was not heard of before the 13th century.

Portiuncula: (1) Meaning little portion (of land), the Portiuncula was the chapel of Our Lady of the Angels near Assisi, Italy, which the Benedictines gave to St. Francis early in the 13th century. He repaired the chapel and made it the first church of the Franciscan Order. It is now enshrined in the Basilica of St. Mary of the Angels in Assisi. (2) The plenary Portiuncula Indulgence, or Pardon of Assisi, was authorized by Honorius III. Originally, it could be gained for the souls in purgatory only in the chapel of Our Lady of the Angels; by later concessions, it could be gained also in other Franciscan and parish churches. The Portiuncula Indulgence (applicable also to the souls in purgatory) can ordinarily be gained from noon of Aug. 1 to midnight of Aug. 2. The conditions are, in addition to freedom from attachment to sin: reception of the sacraments of penance and the Eucharist on or near the day and a half; a visit to a parish church within the day and a half, during which the Our Father, the Creed and an aspiration are offered for the intentions of the pope.

Possession, Diabolical: The extraordinary state of a person who is tormented from within by evil spirits who exercise strong influence over his powers of mind and body.

Postulant: One of several names used to designate a candidate for membership in a religious institute during the period before novitiate.

Poverty: (1) The quality or state of being poor, in actual destitution and need, or being poor in spirit. In the latter sense, poverty means the state of mind and disposition of persons who regard material things in proper perspective as gifts of God for the support of life and its reasonable enrichment, and for the service of others in need. It means freedom from unreasonable attachment to material things as ends in themselves, even though they may be possessed in small or large measure. (2) One of the evangelical counsels professed as a public vow by members of an institute of consecrated life. It involves the voluntary renunciation of rights of ownership and of independent use and disposal of material goods; or, the right of independent use and disposal, but not of the radical right of ownership. Religious institutes provide their members with necessary and useful goods and services from common resources. The manner in which goods are received and/or handled by religious is determined by poverty of spirit and the rule and constitutions of their institute.

Pragmatism: Theory that the truth of ideas, concepts and values depends on their utility or capacity to serve a useful purpose rather than on their conformity with objective standards; also called utilitarianism.

Prayer: The raising of the mind and heart to God in adoration, thanksgiving, reparation and petition. Prayer, which is always mental because it involves thought and love of God, may be vocal, meditative, private and personal, social, and official. The official prayer of the Church as a worshipping community is called the liturgy.

Precepts: Commands or orders given to individuals or communities in particular cases; they establish law for concerned parties. Preceptive documents are issued by the pope, departments of the Roman Curia and other competent authority in the Church.

Presence of God: A devotional practice of increasing one's awareness of the presence and action of God in daily life.

Presumption: A violation of the theological virtue of hope, by which a person striving for salvation either relies too much on his own capabilities or expects God to do things which he cannot do, in keeping with his divine attributes, or does not will to do, according to his divine plan. Presumption is the opposite of despair.

Preternatural Gifts: Exceptional gifts, beyond the exigencies and powers of human nature, enjoyed by Adam in the state of original justice: immunity from suffering and death, superior knowledge, integrity or perfect control of the passions. These gifts were lost as the result of original sin; their loss, however, implied no impairment of the integrity of human nature.

Pride: Unreasonable self-esteem; one of the seven capital sins.

Prie-Dieu: A French phrase, meaning pray God, designating a kneeler or bench suitable for kneeling while at prayer.

Priesthood of the Laity: Lay persons share in the priesthood of Christ in virtue of the sacraments of baptism and confirmation. They are not only joined with Christ for a life of union with him but are also deputed by him for participation in his mission, now carried on by the Church, of worship, teaching, witness and apostolic works. St. Peter called Christians "a royal priesthood" (1 Pt. 2:9) in this connection. St. Thomas Aquinas declared: "The sacramental characters (of baptism and confirmation) are nothing else than certain sharings of the priesthood of Christ, derived from Christ himself." The priesthood of the laity differs from the official ministerial priesthood of ordained priests and bishops — who have the power of holy orders for celebrating the Eucharist, administering the other sacraments, and providing pastoral care. The ministerial priesthood, by divine commission, serves the universal priesthood. (See Role of Sacraments.)

Primary Option: The life-choice of a person for or against God which shapes the basic orientation of moral conduct. A primary option for God does not preclude the possibility of serious sin.

Prior: A superior or an assistant to an abbot in a monastery.

Privilege: A favor, an exemption from the obligation of a law. Privileges of various kinds, with respect to ecclesiastical laws, are granted by the pope, departments of the Roman Curia and other competent authority in the Church.

Probabilism: A moral system for use in cases of conscience which involve the obligation of doubtful laws. There is a general principle that a doubtful law does not bind. Probabilism, therefore, teaches that it is permissible to follow an opinion favoring liberty, provided the opinion is certainly and solidly probable. Probabilism may not be invoked when there is question of: a certain law or the certain obligation of a law; the certain right of another party; the validity of an action; something which is necessary for salvation.

Pro-Cathedral: A church used as a cathedral.

Promoter of the Faith: An official of the Congregation for the Causes of Saints, whose role in beatification and canonization procedures is to establish beyond reasonable doubt the validity of evidence regarding the holiness of prospective saints and miracles attributed to their intercession.

Prophecies of St. Malachy: These so-called prophecies, listing the designations of 102 popes and 10 antipopes, bear the name they have because they have been falsely attributed to St. Malachy, bishop of Armagh, who died in 1148. Actually, they are forgeries by an unknown author and came to light only in the last decade of the 16th century. The first 75 prophecies cover the 65 popes and 10 antipopes from Celestine II (1143-1144) to Gregory XIV (1590-91), and are exact with respect to names, coats of arms, birthplaces, and other identifying characteristics. This portion of the work, far from being prophetic, is the result of historical knowledge or hindsight. The 37 designations following that of Gregory are vague, fanciful, and subject to wide interpretation. According to the prophecies, John Paul II, from the Labor of the Sun, will have only two successors before the end of the world.

Prophecy: (1) The communication of divine revelation by inspired intermediaries, called prophets, between God and his people. Old Testament prophecy was unique in its origin and because of its ethical and religious content, which included disclosure of the saving will of Yahweh for the people, moral censures and warnings of divine punishment because of sin and violations of the Law and Covenant, in the form of promises, admonitions, reproaches and threats. Although Moses and other earlier figures are called prophets, the period of prophecy is generally dated from the early years of the monarchy to about 100 years after the Babylonian Exile. From that time on the written Law and its interpreters supplanted the prophets as guides of the people. Old Testament prophets are cited in the New Testament, with awareness that God spoke through them and that some of their oracles were fulfilled in Christ. John the Baptist is the outstanding prophetic figure in the New Testament. Christ never claimed the title of prophet for himself, although some people thought he was one. There were prophets in the early Church, and St.

Paul mentioned the charism of prophecy in 1 Cor. 14:1-5. Prophecy disappeared after New Testament times. Revelation is classified as the prophetic book of the New Testament. (2) In contemporary non-scriptural usage, the term is applied to the witness given by persons to the relevance of their beliefs in everyday life and action.

Province: (1) A territory comprising one archdiocese called the metropolitan see and one or more dioceses called suffragan sees. The head of the archdiocese, an archbishop, has metropolitan rights and responsibilities over the province. (2) A division of a religious order under the jurisdiction of a provincial superior.

Prudence: Practical wisdom and judgment regarding the choice and use of the best ways and means of doing good; one of the four cardinal virtues.

Punishment Due for Sin: The punishment which is a consequence of sin. It is of two kinds: (1) Eternal punishment is the punishment of hell, to which one becomes subject by the commission of mortal sin. Such punishment is remitted when mortal sin is forgiven. (2) Temporal punishment is a consequence of venial sin and/or forgiven mortal sin; it is not everlasting and may be remitted in this life by means of penance. Temporal punishment unremitted during this life is remitted by suffering in purgatory.

Purgatory: The state or condition of purification in which those who have died in the state of grace, but with some attachment to sin, suffer for a time before they are admitted to the glory and happiness of heaven. In this state and period of passive suffering, they are purified of unrepented venial sins, satisfy the demands of divine justice for temporal punishment due for sins, and are thus converted to a state of worthiness of the beatific vision.

R

Racism: A theory which holds that any one or several of the different races of the human family are inherently superior or inferior to any one or several of the others. The teaching denies the essential unity of the human race, the equality and dignity of all persons because of their common possession of the same human nature, and the participation of all in the divine plan of redemption. It is radically opposed to the virtue of justice and the precept of love of neighbor. Differences of superiority and inferiority which do exist are the result of accidental factors operating in a wide variety of circumstances, and are in no way due to essential defects in any one or several of the branches of the one human race. The theory of racism, together with practices related to it, is incompatible with Christian doctrine.

Rash Judgment: Attributing faults to another without sufficient reason; a violation of the obligations of justice and charity.

Rationalism: A theory which makes the mind the measure and arbiter of all things, including religious truth. A product of the Enlightenment, it rejects the supernatural, divine revelation, and authoritative teaching by any church.

Recollection: Meditation, attitude of concentration or awareness of spiritual matters and things pertaining to salvation and the accomplishment of God's will.

Relativism: Theory which holds that all truth, including religious truth, is relative, i.e., not absolute, certain or unchanging; a product of agnosticism, indifferentism, and an unwarranted extension of the notion of truth in positive science. Relativism is based on the tenet that certain knowledge of any and all truth is impossible. Therefore, no religion, philosophy or science can be said to possess the real truth; consequently, all religions, philosophies and sciences may be considered to have as much or as little of truth as any of the others.

Relics: The physical remains and effects of saints, which are considered worthy of veneration inasmuch as they are representative of persons in glory with God. Catholic doctrine proscribes the view that relics are not worthy of veneration. In line with norms laid down by the Council of Trent and subsequent enactments, discipline concerning relics is subject to control by the Congregations for the Causes of Saints and for Divine Worship and the Discipline of the Sacraments.

Religion: The adoration and service of God as expressed in divine worship and in daily life. Religion is concerned with all of the relations existing between God and human beings, and between humans themselves because of the central significance of God. Objectively considered, religion consists of a body of truth which is believed, a code of morality for the guidance of conduct, and a form of divine worship. Subjectively, it is a person's total response, theoretically and practically, to the demands of faith; it is living faith, personal engagement, self-commitment to God. Thus, by creed, code and cult, a person orders and directs his or her life in reference to God and, through what the love and service of God implies, to all people and all things.

Reliquary: A vessel for the preservation and exposition of a relic; sometimes made like a small monstrance.

Reparation: The making of amends to God for sin committed; one of the four ends of prayer and the purpose of penance.

Rescript: A written reply by an ecclesiastical superior regarding a question or request; its provisions bind concerned parties only. Papal dispensations are issued in the form of rescripts.

Reserved Case: A sin or censure, absolution from which is reserved to religious superiors, bishops, the pope, or confessors having special faculties. Reservations are made because of the serious nature and social effects of certain sins and censures.

Restitution: An act of reparation for an injury done to another. The injury may be caused by taking and/or retaining what belongs to another or by damaging either the property or reputation of another. The intention of making restitution, usually in kind, is required as a condition for the forgiveness of sins of injustice, even though actual restitution is not possible.

Ring: In the Church a ring is worn as part of the insignia of bishops, abbots, et al.; by sisters to denote their consecration to God and the Church. The wedding ring symbolizes the love and union of husband and wife.

Ritual: A book of prayers and ceremonies used in the administration of the sacraments and other ceremonial functions. In the Roman Rite, the standard book of this kind is the Roman Ritual.

Rogito: The official notarial act or document testifying to the burial of a pope.

Rosary: A form of mental and vocal prayer centered on mysteries or events in the lives of Jesus and Mary. Its essential elements are meditation on the mysteries and the recitation of a number of decades of Hail Marys, each beginning with the Lord's Prayer. Introductory prayers may include the Apostles' Creed, an initial Our Father, three Hail Marys and a Glory be to the Father; each decade is customarily concluded with a Glory be to the Father; at the end, it is customary to say the Hail, Holy Queen and a prayer from the liturgy for the feast of the Blessed Virgin Mary of the Rosary. The **Mysteries of the Rosary,** which are the subject of meditation, are: (1) Joyful — the Annunciation to Mary that she was to be the Mother of Christ, her visit to Elizabeth, the birth of Jesus, the presentation of Jesus in the Temple, the finding of Jesus in the Temple. (2) Sorrowful — Christ's agony in the Garden of Gethsemani, scourging at the pillar, crowning with thorns, carrying of the Cross to Calvary, and crucifixion. (3) Glorious — the Resurrection and Ascension of Christ, the descent of the Holy Spirit upon the Apostles, Mary's Assumption into heaven and her crowning as Queen of angels and men. The complete Rosary, called the Dominican Rosary, consists of 15 decades. In customary practice, only five decades are usually said at one time. Rosary beads are used to aid in counting the prayers without distraction. The Rosary originated through the coalescence of popular devotions to Jesus and Mary from the 12th century onward. Its present form dates from about the 15th century. Carthusians contributed greatly toward its development; Dominicans have been its greatest promoters.

S

Sabbath: The seventh day of the week, observed by Jews and Sabbatarians as the day for rest and religious observance.

Sacramentary: One of the first liturgical books, containing the celebrant's part of the Mass and rites for administration of the sacraments. The earliest book of this kind, the Leonine Sacramentary, dates from the middle or end of the sixth century. The *Sacramentary* in current use is the same as the *Roman Missal.*

Sacrarium: A basin with a drain leading directly into the ground; standard equipment of a sacristy.

Sacred Heart, Enthronement: An acknowledgment of the sovereignty of Jesus Christ over the Christian family, expressed by the installation of an image or picture of the Sacred Heart in a place of honor in the home, accompanied by an act of consecration.

Sacred Heart, Promises: Twelve promises to persons having devotion to the Sacred Heart of Jesus, which were communicated by Christ to St. Margaret Mary Alacoque in a private revelation in 1675: (1) I will give them all the graces necessary in their state in life. (2) I will establish peace in their homes. (3) I will comfort them in all their afflictions. (4) I will be their secure refuge during life and, above all, in death. (5) I will bestow abundant blessing upon all their undertakings. (6) Sinners shall find in my Heart the source and the infinite ocean of mercy. (7) By devotion to my Heart tepid souls shall grow fervent. (8) Fervent souls shall quickly mount to high perfection. (9) I will bless every place where a picture of my Heart shall be set up and honored. (10) I will give to priests the gift of touching the most hardened hearts. (11) Those who promote this devotion shall have their names written in my Heart, never to be blotted out. (12) I will grant the grace of final penitence to those who communicate (receive Holy Communion) on the first Friday of nine consecutive months.

Sacrilege: Violation of and irreverence toward a person, place or thing that is sacred because of public dedication to God; a sin against the virtue of religion. Personal sacrilege is violence of some kind against a cleric or religious, or a violation of chastity with a cleric or religious. Local sacrilege is the desecration of sacred places. Real sacrilege is irreverence with respect to sacred things, such as the sacraments and sacred vessels.

Sacristy: A utility room where vestments, church furnishings and sacred vessels are kept and where the clergy vest for sacred functions.

Sadducees: The predominantly priestly party among the Jews in the time of Christ, noted for extreme conservatism, acceptance only of the Law of Moses, and rejection of the traditions of the elders. Their opposite numbers were the Pharisees.

Saints, Cult of: The veneration, called dulia, of holy persons who have died and are in glory with God in heaven; it includes honoring them and petitioning them for their intercession with God. Liturgical veneration is given only to saints officially recognized by the Church; private veneration may be given to anyone thought to be in heaven. The veneration of saints is essentially different from the adoration given to God alone; by its very nature, however, it terminates in the worship of God. According to the Second Vatican Council's *Dogmatic Constitution on the Church* (No. 50): "It is supremely fitting ... that we love those friends and fellow heirs of Jesus Christ, who are also our brothers and extraordinary benefactors, that we render due thanks to God for them and 'suppliantly invoke them and have recourse to their prayers, their power and help in obtaining benefits from God through his Son, Jesus Christ, our Lord, who is our sole Redeemer and Savior.' For by its very nature every genuine testimony of love which we show to those in heaven tends toward and terminates in Christ, who is the 'crown of all saints.' Through him it tends toward and terminates in God, who is wonderful in his saints and is magnified in them."

Salvation: The liberation of persons from sin and its effects, reconciliation with God in and through Christ, the attainment of union with God forever in the glory of heaven as the supreme purpose of life and as the God-given reward for fulfillment of his will on earth. Salvation-in-process begins and continues in this life through union with Christ in faith professed and in action; its final term is union with God and the whole community of the saved in the ultimate perfection of God's kingdom. The Church teaches that: God wills the salvation of all men; men are saved in and through Christ; membership in the Church established by Christ, known and understood as the community of salvation, is necessary for salvation; men with this knowledge and understanding who deliberately reject this Church, cannot be saved. The Catholic Church is the Church founded by Christ. (See below, Salvation outside the Church.)

Salvation History: The facts and the record of God's relations with human beings, in the past, present and future, for the purpose of leading them to live in accordance with his will for the eventual attainment after death of salvation, or everlasting happiness with him in heaven. The essentials of salvation history are: God's love for all human beings and will for their salvation; his intervention and action in the world to express this love and bring about their salvation; the revelation he made of himself and the covenant he established with the Israelites in the Old Testament; the perfecting of this revelation and the new covenant of grace through Christ in the New Testament; the continuing action-for-salvation carried on in and through the Church; the communication of saving grace to people through the merits of Christ and the operations of the Holy Spirit in the here-and-now circumstances of daily life and with the cooperation of people themselves.

Salvation outside the Church: The Second Vatican Council covered this subject summarily in the following manner: "Those also can attain to everlasting salvation who through no fault of their own do not know the Gospel of Christ or his Church, yet sincerely seek God and, moved by grace, strive by their deeds to do his will as it is known to them through the dictates of conscience. Nor does divine Providence deny the help necessary for salvation to those who, without blame on their part, have not yet arrived at an explicit knowledge of God, but who strive to live a good life, thanks to his grace. Whatever good or truth is found among them is looked upon by the Church as a preparation for the Gospel. She regards such qualities as given by him who enlightens all men so that they may finally have life" *(Dogmatic Constitution on the Church,* No. 16).

Satanism: Worship of the devil, a blasphemous inversion of the order of worship which is due to God alone.

Scandal: Conduct which is the occasion of sin to another person.

Scapular: (1) A part of the habit of some religious orders like the Benedictines and Dominicans; a nearly shoulder-wide strip of cloth worn over the tunic and reaching almost to the feet in front and behind. Originally a kind of apron, it came to symbolize the cross and yoke of Christ. (2) Scapulars worn by lay persons as a sign of association with religious orders and for devotional purposes are an adaptation of monastic scapulars. Approved by the Church as sacramentals, they consist of two small squares of woolen cloth joined by strings and are worn about the neck. They are given for wearing in a ceremony of investiture or enrollment. There are nearly 20 scapulars for devotional use: the five principal ones are generally understood to include those of Our Lady of Mt. Carmel (the brown Carmelite Scapular), the Holy Trinity, Our Lady of the Seven

Dolors, the Passion, the Immaculate Conception.

Scapular Medal: A medallion with a representation of the Sacred Heart on one side and of the Blessed Virgin Mary on the other. Authorized by St. Pius X in 1910, it may be worn or carried in place of a scapular by persons already invested with a scapular.

Scapular Promise: According to a legend of the Carmelite Order, the Blessed Virgin Mary appeared to St. Simon Stock in 1251 at Cambridge and declared that wearers of the brown Carmelite Scapular would be saved from hell and taken to heaven by her on the first Saturday after death. The validity of the legend has never been the subject of official decision by the Church. Essentially, it expresses belief in the intercession of Mary and the efficacy of sacramentals in the context of truly Christian life.

Schism: Derived from a Greek word meaning separation, the term designates formal and obstinate refusal by a baptized Catholic, called a *schismatic*, to be in communion with the pope and the Church. The canonical penalty is excommunication. One of the most disastrous schisms in history resulted in the definitive separation of the Church in the East from union with Rome about 1054.

Scholasticism: The term usually applied to the Catholic theology and philosophy which developed in the Middle Ages.

Scribes: Hebrew intellectuals noted for their knowledge of the Law of Moses, influential from the time of the Exile to about 70 A.D. Many of them were Pharisees. They were the antecedents of rabbis and their traditions, as well as those of the Pharisees, had a lasting influence on Judaism following the destruction of Jerusalem in 70 A.D.

Scruple: A morbid, unreasonable fear and anxiety that one's actions are sinful when they are not, or more seriously sinful than they actually are. Compulsive scrupulosity is quite different from the transient scrupulosity of persons of tender or highly sensitive conscience, or of persons with faulty moral judgment.

Seal of Confession: The obligation of secrecy which must be observed regarding knowledge of things learned in connection with the confession of sin in the sacrament of penance. The seal covers matters whose revelation would make the sacrament burdensome. Confessors are prohibited, under penalty of excommunication, from making any direct revelation of confessional matter; this prohibition holds, outside of confession, even with respect to the person who made the confession unless the person releases the priest from the obligation. Persons other than confessors are obliged to maintain secrecy, but not under penalty of excommunication. General, non-specific discussion of confessional matter does not violate the seal.

Secularism: A school of thought, a spirit and manner of action which ignores and/or repudiates the validity or influence of supernatural religion with respect to individual and social life. In describing secularism in their annual statement in 1947, the bishops of the United States said in part: ". . . There are many men — and their number is daily increasing — who in practice live their lives without recognizing that this is God's world. For the most part they do not deny God. On formal occasions they may even mention his name. Not all of them would subscribe to the statement that all moral values derive from merely human conventions. But they fail to bring an awareness of their responsibility to God into their thought and action as individuals and members of society. This, in essence, is what we mean by secularism."

See: Another name for diocese or archdiocese.

Seminary: A house of study and formation for men, called seminarians, preparing for the priesthood. Traditional seminaries date from the Council of Trent in the middle of the 16th century; before that time, candidates for the priesthood were variously trained in monastic schools, universities under church auspices, and in less formal ways. At the present time, seminaries are undergoing considerable change for the improvement of academic and formation programs and procedures.

Sermon on the Mount: A compilation of sayings of Our Lord in the form of an extended discourse in Matthew's Gospel (5:1 to 7:27) and, in a shorter discourse, in Luke (6:17-49). The passage in Matthew, called the "Constitution of the New Law," summarizes the living spirit of believers in Christ and members of the kingdom of God. Beginning with the Beatitudes and including the Lord's Prayer, it covers the perfect justice of the New Law, the fulfillment of the Old Law in the New Law of Christ, and the integrity of internal attitude and external conduct with respect to love of God and neighbor, justice, chastity, truth, trust and confidence in God.

Seven Last Words of Christ: Words of Christ on the Cross. (1) "Father, forgive them; for they do not know what they are doing." (2) To the penitent thief: "I assure you: today you will be with me in Paradise." (3) To Mary and his Apostle John: "Woman, there is your son . . . There is your mother." (4) "My God, my God, why have you forsaken me?" (5) "I am thirsty." (6) "Now it is finished." (7) "Father, into your hands I commend my spirit."

Shrine, Crowned: A shrine approved by the Holy See as a place of pilgrimage. The approval permits public devotion at the shrine and implies that at least one miracle has resulted from devotion at the shrine. Among the best known crowned shrines are those of the Virgin Mary at Lourdes and Fatima. Shrines with statues crowned by Pope John Paul in 1985 in South America were those of Our Lady of Coromoto, patroness of Venezuela, in Caracas, and Our Lady of Carmen of Paucartambo in Cuzco, Peru.

Shroud of Turin: A strip of brownish linen cloth, 14 feet, three inches in length and three feet, seven inches in width, bearing the front and back imprint of a human body. A tradition dating from the seventh century, which has not been verified beyond doubt, claims that the shroud is the fine linen in which the body of Christ was wrapped for burial. The early history of the shroud is obscure. It was enshrined at Lirey, France, in 1354 and was transferred in 1578 to Turin, Italy, where it has been kept in the cathedral down to the present time. Scientific investigation, which began in 1898, seems to indicate that the markings on the shroud are those of a human body. The shroud, for the first time since 1933, was placed on public view from Aug. 27 to Oct. 8, 1978, and was seen by an estimated 3.3 million people. Scientists conducted intensive studies of it thereafter, finally determining that the material of the shroud dated from between 1260 and 1390. The shroud, which had been the possession of the House of Savoy, was willed to Pope John Paul II in 1983.

Sick Calls: When a person is confined at home by illness or other cause and is unable to go to church for reception of the sacraments, a parish priest should be informed and arrangements made for him to visit the person at home. Such visitations are common in pastoral practice, both for special needs and for providing persons with regular opportunities for receiving the sacraments. If a priest cannot make the visitation, arrangements can be made for a deacon or Eucharistic minister to bring Holy Communion to the homebound or bedridden person.

Sign of the Cross: A sign, ceremonial gesture or movement in the form of a cross by which a person confesses faith in the Holy Trinity and Christ, and intercedes for the blessing of himself or herself, other persons and things. In Roman-Rite practice, a person making the sign touches the fingers of the right hand to forehead, below the breast, left shoulder and right shoulder while saying: "In the name of the Father, and of the Son, and of the Holy Spirit." The sign is also made with the thumb on the forehead, the lips, and the breast. For the blessing of persons and objects, a large sign of the cross is made by movement of the right hand. In Eastern-Rite practice, the sign is made with the thumb and first two fingers of the right hand joined together and touching the forehead, below the breast, the right shoulder and the left shoulder; the formula generally used is the doxology, "O Holy God, O Holy Strong One, O Immortal One." The Eastern manner of making the sign was general until the first half of the 13th century; by the 17th century, Western practice involved the whole right hand and the reversal of direction from shoulder to shoulder.

Signs of the Times: Contemporary events, trends and features in culture and society, the needs and aspirations of people, all the factors that form the context in and through which the Church has to carry on its saving mission. The Second Vatican Council spoke on numerous occasions about these signs and the relationship between them and a kind of manifestation of God's will, positive or negative, and about subjecting them to judgment and action corresponding to the demands of divine revelation through Scripture, Christ, and the experience, tradition and teaching authority of the Church.

Simony: The deliberate intention and act of selling and/or buying spiritual goods or material things so connected with the spiritual that they cannot be separated therefrom; a violation of the virtue of religion, and a sacrilege, because it wrongfully puts a material price on spiritual things, which cannot be either sold or bought. In church law, actual sale or purchase is subject to censure in some cases. The term is derived from the name of Simon Magus, who attempted to buy from Sts. Peter and John the power to confirm people in the Holy Spirit (Acts 8:4-24).

Sin: (1) Actual sin is rejection of God manifested by free and deliberate violation of his law by thought, word or action. (a) Mortal sin — involving serious matter, sufficient reflection and full consent

— results in total alienation from God, making a person dead to sanctifying grace, incapable of performing meritorious supernatural acts and subject to everlasting punishment. (b) Venial sin — involving less serious matter, reflection and consent — does not have such serious consequences. (2) Original sin is the sin of Adam, with consequences for all human beings. (See separate entry.)

Sins against the Holy Spirit: Despair of salvation, presumption of God's mercy, impugning the known truths of faith, envy at another's spiritual good, obstinacy in sin, final impenitence. Those guilty of such sins stubbornly resist the influence of grace and, as long as they do so, cannot be forgiven.

Sins, Occasions of: Circumstances (persons, places, things, etc.) which easily lead to sin. There is an obligation to avoid voluntary proximate occasions of sin, and to take precautions against the dangers of unavoidable occasions.

Sins That Cry to Heaven for Vengeance: Willful murder, sins against nature, oppression of the poor, widows and orphans, defrauding laborers of their wages.

Sister: Any woman religious, in popular speech; strictly, the title applies only to women religious belonging to institutes whose members never professed solemn vows. Most of the institutes whose members are properly called Sisters were established during and since the 19th century. Women religious with solemn vows, or belonging to institutes whose members formerly professed solemn vows, are properly called nuns.

Sisterhood: A generic term referring to the whole institution of the life of women religious in the Church, or to a particular institute of women religious.

Situation Ethics: A subjective, individualistic ethical theory which denies the binding force of ethical principles as universal laws and preceptive norms of moral conduct, and proposes that morality is determined only by situational conditions and considerations and the intention of the person. In an instruction issued on the subject in May, 1956, the Congregation for the Holy Office (now the Congregation for the Doctrine of the Faith) said: "It ignores the principles of objective ethics. This 'New Morality,' it is claimed, is not only the equal of objective morality, but is superior to it. The authors who follow this system state that the ultimate determining norm for activity is not the objective order as determined by the natural law and known with certainty from this law. It is instead some internal judgment and illumination of the mind of every individual by which the mind comes to know what is to be done in a concrete situation. This ultimate decision of man is, therefore, not the application of the objective law to a particular case after the particular circumstances of a 'situation' have been considered and weighed according to the rules of prudence, as the more important authors of objective ethics teach; but it is, according to them, immediate, internal illumination and judgment. With regard to its objective truth and correctness, this judgment, at least in many things, is not ultimately measured, is not to be measured or is not measurable by any objective norm found outside man and independent of his subjective persuasion, but it is fully sufficient in itself. . . . Much that is stated in this system of 'Situation Ethics' is contrary to the truth of reality and to the dictate of sound reason. It gives evidence of relativism and modernism, and deviates far from the Catholic teaching handed down through the ages."

Slander: Attributing to a person faults which he or she does not have; a violation of the obligations of justice and charity, for which restitution is due.

Sloth: One of the seven capital sins; spiritual laziness, involving distaste and disgust for spiritual things; spiritual boredom, which saps the vigor of spiritual life. Physical laziness is a counterpart of spiritual sloth.

Sorcery: A kind of black magic in which evil is invoked by means of diabolical intervention; a violation of the virtue of religion.

Soteriology: The division of theology which treats of the mission and work of Christ as Redeemer.

Species, Sacred: The appearances of bread and wine (color, taste, smell, etc.) which remain after the substance has been changed at the Consecration of the Mass into the Body and Blood of Christ. (See Transubstantiation.)

Spiritism: Attempts to communicate with spirits and departed souls by means of seances, table tapping, ouija boards, and other methods; a violation of the virtue of religion. Spiritualistic practices are noted for fakery.

Spiritual Works of Mercy: Works of spiritual assistance, motivated by love of God and neighbor, to persons in need: counseling the doubtful, instructing the ignorant, admonishing sinners, comforting the afflicted, forgiving offenses, bearing wrongs patiently, praying for the living and the dead.

Stational Churches, Days: Churches, especially in Rome, where the clergy and lay people were accustomed to gather with their bishop on certain days for the celebration of the liturgy. The 25 early titular or parish churches of Rome, plus other churches, each had their turn as the site of divine worship in practices which may have started in the third century. The observances were rather well developed toward the latter part of the fourth century, and by the fifth they included a Mass concelebrated by the pope and attendant priests. On some occasions, the stational liturgy was preceded by a procession from another church called a collecta. There were 42 Roman stational churches in the eighth century, and 89 stational services were scheduled annually in connection with the liturgical seasons. Stational observances fell into disuse toward the end of the Middle Ages. Some revival was begun by John XXIII in 1959 and continued by Paul VI and John Paul II.

Stations (Way) of the Cross: A form of devotion commemorating the Passion and death of Christ, consisting of a series of meditations (stations): (1) his condemnation to death, (2) taking up of the cross, (3) the first fall on the way to Calvary, (4) meeting his Mother, (5) being assisted by Simon of Cyrene and (6) by the woman Veronica who wiped his face, (7) the second fall, (8) meeting the women of Jerusalem, (9) the third fall, (10) being stripped and (11) nailed to the cross, (12) his death, (13) the removal of his body from the cross and (14) his burial. Depictions of these scenes are mounted in most churches, chapels and in some other places, beneath small crosses. A person making the Way of the Cross passes before these stations, or stopping points, pausing at each for meditation. If the stations are made by a group of people, only the leader has to pass from station to station. A plenary indulgence is granted to the faithful who make the stations, under the usual conditions: freedom from all attachment to sin, reception of the sacraments of penance and the Eucharist, and prayers for the intentions of the pope. Those who are impeded from making the stations in the usual manner can gain the same indulgence if, along with the aforementioned conditions, they spend at least a half hour in spiritual reading and meditation on the passion and death of Christ. The stations originated remotely from the practice of Holy Land pilgrims who visited the actual scenes of incidents in the Passion of Christ. Representations elsewhere of at least some of these scenes were known as early as the fifth century. Later, the stations evolved in connection with and as a consequence of strong devotion to the Passion in the 12th and 13th centuries. Franciscans, who were given custody of the Holy Places in 1342, promoted the devotion widely; one of them, St. Leonard of Port Maurice, became known as the greatest preacher of the Way of the Cross in the 18th century. The general features of the devotion were fixed by Clement XII in 1731. On Good Friday, 1991, Pope John Paul made the stations in a manner different from the usual way, using stations based entirely on Gospel texts: (1) Jesus in the Garden of Olives, (2) Jesus is betrayed by Judas and arrested, (3) Jesus is condemned by the Sanhedrin, (4) Jesus is denied by Peter, (5) Jesus is condemned by Pilate, (6) Jesus is scourged and crowned with thorns, (7) Jesus is made to carry his cross, (8) Simon of Cyrene helps Jesus carry his cross, (9) Jesus meets the women of Jerusalem, (10) Jesus is crucified, (11) Jesus promises the Kingdom to the repentant thief, (12) On the cross Jesus speaks to his mother and his beloved disciple John, (13) Jesus dies on the cross, (14) Jesus is laid in the tomb.

Statutes: Virtually the same as decrees (see separate entry), they almost always designate laws of a particular council or synod rather than pontifical laws.

Stigmata: Marks of the wounds suffered by Christ in his crucifixion, in hands and feet by nails, and side by the piercing of a lance. Some persons, called stigmatists, have been reported as recipients or sufferers of marks like these. The Church, however, has never issued any infallible declaration about their possession by anyone, even in the case of St. Francis of Assisi whose stigmata seem to be the best substantiated and may be commemorated in the Roman-Rite liturgy. Ninety percent of some 300 reputed stigmatists have been women. Judgment regarding the presence, significance, and manner of causation of stigmata would depend, among other things, on irrefutable experimental evidence.

Stipend, Mass: An offering given to a priest for applying the fruits of the Mass according to the intention of the donor. The offering is a contribution to the support of the priest. The disposition of the fruits of the sacrifice, in line with doctrine concerning the Mass in particular and prayer in general, is subject to the will of God. In the early Christian centuries, when Mass was not offered for the intentions of particular persons, the participants made offerings of bread and wine for the sacrifice and their own Holy Communion, and of other things useful for the support of the clergy and the poor. Some offerings may have been made as early as the fourth century for the celebration of Mass for particular intentions, and there are indications of the existence of this practice from the sixth century when private Masses began to be offered. The earliest certain proof of stipend practice, however, dates from the eighth century. By the 11th century, along with private Mass, it was established custom. Mass offerings and intentions were the subjects of a decree approved by John Paul II and made public Mar. 22, 1991. (1) Normally, no more than one offering should be accepted for a Mass; the Mass should be offered in accord with the donor's intention; the priest who accepts the offering should celebrate the Mass himself or have another priest do so. (2) Several Mass intentions, for which offerings have been made, can be combined for a "collective" application of a single Mass only if the previous and explicit consent of the donors is obtained. Such Masses are an exception to the general rule.

Stole Fee: An offering given on certain occasions; e.g., at a baptism, wedding, funeral, for the support of the clergy who administer the sacraments and perform other sacred rites.

Stoup: A vessel used to contain holy water.

Suffragan See: Any diocese, except the archdiocese, within a province.

Suicide: The taking of one's own life; a violation of God's dominion over human life. Ecclesiastical burial is denied to persons while in full possession of their faculties; it is permitted in cases of doubt.

Superrogation: Good and various actions which go beyond the obligations of duty and the requirements enjoined by God's law as necessary for salvation. Examples of these works are the profession and observance of the evangelical counsels of poverty, chastity, and obedience, and efforts to practice charity to the highest degree.

Supernatural: Above the natural; that which exceeds and is not due or owed to the essence, exigencies, requirements, powers and merits of created nature. While human beings have no claim on supernatural things and do not need them in order to exist and act on a natural level, they do need them in order to exist and act in the higher order or economy of grace established by God for their salvation. God has freely given them certain things which are beyond the powers and rights of their human nature. Examples of the supernatural are: grace, a kind of participation by human beings in the divine life, by which they become capable of performing acts meritorious for salvation; divine revelation by which God manifests himself to them and makes known truth that is inaccessible to human reason alone; faith, by which they believe divine truth because of the authority of God who reveals it through Sacred Scripture and tradition and the teaching of his Church.

Superstition: A violation of the virtue of religion, by which God is worshipped in an unworthy manner or creatures are given honor which belongs to God alone. False, vain, or futile worship involves ele-ments which are incompatible with the honor and respect due to God, such as error, deception, and bizarre practices. Examples are: false and exaggerated devotions, chain prayers and allegedly unfailing prayers, the mixing of unbecoming practices in worship. The second kind of superstition attributes to persons and things powers and honor which belong to God alone. Examples are: idolatry, divination, magic, spiritism, necromancy.

Suspension: A censure by which a cleric is forbidden to exercise some or all of his powers of orders and jurisdiction, or to accept the financial support of his benefices.

Swearing: Taking an oath; calling upon God to witness the truth of a statement; a legitimate thing to do for serious reasons and under proper circumstances, as in a court of law. To swear without sufficient reason is to dishonor God's name; to swear falsely in a court of law is perjury.

Swedenborgianism: A doctrine developed in and from the writings of Emmanuel Swedenborg (1688-1772), who claimed that during a number of visions he had in 1745 Christ taught him the spiritual sense of Sacred Scripture and commissioned him to communicate it to others. He held that, just as Christianity succeeded Judaism, so his teaching supplemented Christianity. He rejected belief in the Trinity, original sin, the Resurrection, and all the sacraments except baptism and the Eucharist. His followers are members of the Church of the New Jerusalem or of the New Church.

Syllabus, The: (1) When not qualified, the term refers to the list of 80 errors accompanying Pope Pius IX's encyclical *Quanta Cura*, issued in 1864. (2) The *Syllabus* of St. Pius X in the decree *Lamentabili*, issued by the Holy Office July 4, 1907, condemning 65 heretical propositions of modernism. This schedule of errors was followed shortly by that pope's encyclical *Pascendi*, the principal ecclesiastical document against modernism, issued Sept. 8, 1907.

Synod, Diocesan: Meeting of representative persons of a diocese — priests, religious, lay persons — with the bishop, called by him for the purpose of considering and taking action on matters affecting the life and mission of the Church in the diocese. Persons taking part in a synod have consultative status; the bishop alone is the legislator, with power to authorize synodal decrees. According to canon law, every diocese should have a synod every 10 years.

T

Te Deum: The opening Latin words, Thee, God, of a hymn of praise and thanksgiving prescribed for use in the Office of Readings of the Liturgy of the Hours on many Sundays, solemnities and feasts.

Temperance: Moderation, one of the four cardinal virtues.

Temptation: Any enticement to sin, from any source: the strivings of one's own faculties, the action of the devil, other persons, circumstances of life, etc. Temptation itself is not sin. Temptation can be avoided and overcome with the use of prudence and the help of grace.

Thanksgiving: An expression of gratitude to God for his goodness and the blessings he grants; one of the four ends of prayer.

Theism: A philosophy which admits the existence of God and the possibility of divine revelation; it is generally monotheistic and acknowledges God as transcendent and also active in the world. Because it is a philosophy rather than a system of theology derived from revelation, it does not include specifically Christian doctrines, like those concerning the Trinity, the Incarnation and Redemption.

Theological Virtues: The virtues which have God for their direct object: faith, or belief in God's infallible teaching; hope, or confidence in divine assistance; charity, or love of God. They are given to a person with grace in the first instance, through baptism and incorporation in Christ.

Theology: Knowledge of God and religion, deriving from and based on the data of divine Revelation, organized and systematized according to some kind of scientific method. It involves systematic study and presentation of the truths of divine Revelation in Sacred Scripture, tradition, and the teaching of the Church. The Second Vatican Council made the following declaration about theology and its relation to divine Revelation: "Sacred theology rests on the written word of God, together with sacred tradition, as its primary and perpetual foundation. By scrutinizing in the light of faith all truth stored up in the mystery of Christ, theology is most powerfully strengthened and constantly rejuvenated by that word. For the sacred Scriptures contain the word of God and, since they are inspired, really are the word of God; and so the study of the sacred page is, as it were, the soul of sacred theology" *(Constitution on Revelation.* No. 24). Theology has been divided under various subject headings. Some of the major fields have been: dogma (systematic theology), moral, pastoral, ascetics (the practice of virtue and means of attaining holiness and perfection), mysticism (higher states of religious experience). Other subject headings include ecumenism (Christian unity, interfaith relations), ecclesiology (the nature and constitution of the Church), Mariology (doctrine concerning the Blessed Virgin Mary), the sacraments, etc.

Tithing: Contribution of a portion of one's income, originally one-tenth, for purposes of religion and charity. The practice is mentioned 46 times in the Bible. In early Christian times, tithing was adopted in continuance of Old Testament practices of the Jewish people, and the earliest positive church legislation on the subject was enacted in 567. Catholics are bound in conscience to contribute to the support of their church, but the manner in which they do so is not fixed by law. Tithing, which amounts to a pledged contribution of a portion of one's income, has aroused new attention in recent years in the United States.

Titular Sees: Dioceses where the Church once flourished but which later were overrun by pagans or Muslims and now exist only in name or title. Bishops without a territorial or residential diocese of their own; e.g., auxiliary bishops, are given titular sees.

Transfinalization, Transignification: Terms coined to express the sign value of consecrated bread and wine with respect to the presence and action of Christ in the Eucharistic sacrifice and the spiritually vivifying purpose of the Eucharistic banquet in Holy Communion. The theory behind the terms has strong undertones of existential and "sign" philosophy, and has been criticized for its openness to interpretations at variance with the doctrine of transubstantiation and the abiding presence of Christ under the appearances of bread and wine after the sacrifice of the Mass and Communion have been completed. The terms, if used as substitutes for transubstantiation, are unacceptable; if they presuppose transubstantiation, they are acceptable as clarifications of its meaning.

Transubstantiation: "The way Christ is made present in this sacrament (Holy Eucharist) is none other than by the change of the whole substance of the bread into his Body, and of the whole substance of the wine into his Blood (in the Consecration at Mass) . . . this unique and wonderful change the Catholic Church rightly calls transubstantiation" (encyclical *Mysterium Fidei* of Paul VI, Sept. 3, 1965). The first official use of the term was made by the Fourth Council of the Lateran in 1215. Authoritative teaching on the subject was issued by the Council of Trent.

Treasury of the Church: The superabundant merits of Christ and the saints from which the Church draws to confer spiritual benefits, such as indulgences.

Triduum: A three-day series of public or private devotions.

U-Z

Usury: Excessive interest charged for the loan and use of money; a violation of justice.

Veronica: A word resulting from the combination of a Latin word for true, *vera*, and a Greek word for image, *eikon*, designating a likeness of the face of Christ or the name of a woman said to have given him a cloth on which he caused an imprint of his face to appear. The veneration at Rome of a likeness depicted on cloth dates from about the end of the 10th century; it figured in a popular devotion during the Middle Ages, and in the Holy Face devotion practiced since the 19th century. A faint, indiscernible likeness said to be of this kind is preserved in St. Peter's Basilica. The origin of the likeness is uncertain, and the identity of the woman is unknown. Before the 14th century, there were no known artistic representations of an incident concerning a woman who wiped the face of Christ with a piece of cloth while he was carrying the Cross to Calvary.

Viaticum: Holy Communion given to those in danger of death. The word, derived from Latin, means provision for a journey through death to life hereafter.

Vicar General: A priest or bishop appointed by the bishop of a diocese to serve as his deputy, with ordinary executive power, in the administration of the diocese.

Virginity: Observance of perpetual sexual abstinence. The state of virginity, which is embraced for the love of God by religious with a public vow or by others with a private vow, was singled out for high praise by Christ (Mt. 19:10-12) and has always been so regarded by the Church. In the encyclical *Sacra Virginitas*, Pius XII stated: "Holy virginity and that perfect chastity which is consecrated to the service of God is without doubt among the most perfect treasures which the founder of the Church has left in heritage to the society which he established." Paul VI approved in 1970 a rite in which women can consecrate their virginity "to Christ and their brethren" without becoming members of a religious institute. The *Ordo Consecrationis Virginum,* a revision of a rite promulgated by Clement VII in 1596, is traceable to the Roman liturgy of about 500.

Virtue: A habit or established capability for performing good actions. Virtues are *natural* (acquired and increased by repeating good acts) and/or *supernatural* (given with grace by God).

Vocation: A call to a way of life. Generally, the term applies to the common call of all persons, from God, to holiness and salvation. Specifically, it refers to particular states of life, each called a vocation, in which response is made to this universal call; viz., marriage, the religious life and/or priesthood, the single state freely chosen or accepted for the accomplishment of God's will. The term also applies to the various occupations in which persons make a living. The Church supports the freedom of each individual in choosing a particular vocation, and reserves the right to pass on the acceptability of candidates for the priesthood and religious life. Signs or indicators of particular vocations are many, including a person's talents and interests, circumstances and obligations, invitations of grace and willingness to respond thereto.

Vow: A promise made to God with sufficient knowledge and freedom, which has as its object a moral good that is possible and better than its voluntary omission. A person who professes a vow binds himself or herself by the virtue of religion to fulfill the promise. The best known examples of vows are those of poverty, chastity and obedience professed by religious (see Evangelical Counsels, individual entries). Public vows are made before a competent person, acting as an agent of the Church, who accepts the profession in the name of the Church, thereby giving public recognition to the person's dedication and consecration to God and divine worship. Vows of this kind are either solemn, rendering all contrary acts invalid as well as unlawful; or simple, rendering contrary acts unlawful. Solemn vows are for life; simple vows are for a definite period of time or for life. Vows professed without public recognition by the Church are called private vows. The Church, which has authority to accept and give public recognition to vows, also has authority to dispense persons from their obligations for serious reasons.

Week of Prayer for Christian Unity: Eight days of prayer, from Jan. 18 to 25, for the union of all persons in the Church established by Christ. On the initiative of Father Paul James Francis Wattson, S.A., of Graymoor, N.Y., it originated in 1908 as the Chair of Unity Octave. In recent years, its observance on an interfath basis has increased greatly.

Witness, Christian: Practical testimony or evidence given by Christians of their faith in all circumstances of life — by prayer and general conduct, through good example and good works, etc.; being and acting in accordance with Christian belief; actual practice of the Christian faith.

CATHOLIC CONTRIBUTION TO CONFERENCE

The contribution of Catholic delegates to the Fifth World Conference on Faith and Order was certainly evident, according to the director of the Faith and Order Commission. The Rev. Gunther Gassman, a German Lutheran, said sacramental and theological emphases in conference documents were stronger than they would have been without the Catholic presence, as were other points, including "the concept of the church as communion in a spiritual sense, local and universal."

Held Aug. 4 to 13, 1993, in Santiago de Compostela, Spain, the conference was the first since Catholics joined the Faith and Order Commission of the World Council of Churches in 1968, and the first with official Catholic delegates.

Mr. Gassman said the 26 Catholic delegates made a discernible difference even though they participated as individuals and avoided any appearance of acting as a "pressure group." Conference delegates numbered 205.

Catholics were not alone in the theological emphases they made, Mr. Gassman added, noting that they were joined by Orthodox delegates and many Protestants who felt their own traditions were enriched by the Catholic perspective.

He also said the choice of Santiago de Compostela as the conference site added to the positive atmosphere. "I didn't hear voices who felt oppressed by this very Catholic atmosphere," he said. "That is proof we have come to an appreciation of other traditions."

Among issues at the forefront of the conference's ecumenical agenda, Mr. Gassman said, was that of "primacy" in the church, with reference particularly to the papacy. "Obviously, there is now a moment when many people are thinking we can no longer ignore this difficult issue."

BAPTISM, EUCHARIST, MINISTRY

"Baptism, Eucharist and Ministry," produced under the auspices of the Faith and Order Commission of the World Council of Churches and approved by more than 100 Christian theologians at a meeting held in Lima, Peru, in January, 1982. The Lima Document (also referred to as BEM) is an attempt to state what divided Christians can say in common about baptism, the Eucharist and ministry. It was called a significant development in the ecumenical movement by the Secretariat for Promoting Christian Unity and the Congregation for the Doctrine of the Faith; their response was reported by the NC Documentary Service, Origins, Nov. 19, 1987 (Vol. 17, No. 23).

However, the Vatican agencies declared, it "does not offer a fully systematic treatment of baptism, Eucharist or ministry." Deficiencies have to do with, among other things, the notion of sacrament and the treatment of apostolic tradition and decisive authority in the church. Some passages were judged to be inconsistent with Catholic faith.

THE CHURCH IN COUNTRIES THROUGHOUT THE WORLD __

(Principal sources for statistics: *Statistical Yearbook of the Church, 1991* (the most recent edition); *Annuario Pontificio, 1993*. Figures are as of Dec. 31, 1991, except for cardinals (as of Sept. 10, 1993) and others which are indicated. For 1993 developments, especially in Eastern Europe, see Index entries for individual countries.)

An asterisk indicates that the country has full diplomatic relations with Vatican City (see Index: Diplomats at Vatican).

Abbreviations (in order in which they appear): archd. — archdiocese; dioc. — diocese; ap. ex. — apostolic exarchate; prel. — prelature; abb. — abbacy; v.a. — vicariate apostolic; p.a. — prefecture apostolic; a.a. — apostolic administration; mil. ord. — military ordinariate; card. — cardinal; abp. — archbishops; bp. — bishops (diocesan and titular); priests (dioc. — diocesan or secular priests; rel. — those belonging to religious orders); p.d. — permanent deacons; sem. — major seminarians, diocesan and religious; bros. — brothers; srs. — sisters; bap. — baptisms; Caths. — Catholic population; tot. pop. — total population; (AD), apostolic delegate (see Index: Papal Representatives).

Afghanistan

Republic in south-central Asia (in transition following 15 years of civil war); capital, Kabul. Christianity antedated Muslim conquest in the seventh century but was overcome by it. All inhabitants are subject to the law of Islam. Christian missionaries are prohibited.

Population, 16,430,000.

Albania*

Archd., 2; dioc., 3; abb., 1; a.a. 1; abp. (Dec., 1992) 2; bp. (Dec., 1992), 2. Tot. pop., 3,300,000. (No recent statistics available.)

Emerging democratic republic in the Balkans, bordering the Adriatic Sea; capital, Tirana. Christianity was introduced in apostolic times. The northern part of the country remained faithful to Rome while the south broke from unity following the schism of 1054. A large percentage of the population was forcibly Islamized following the invasion (15th century) and long centuries of occupation by the Ottoman Turks. Many Catholics fled to southern Italy, Sicily and Greece. In 1945, at the time of the communist take-over, an estimated 68 per cent of the population was Muslim; 19 per cent, Orthodox and 13 per cent, Roman Catholic. The Catholic Church prevailed in the north. During 45 years of communist dictatorship, the Church fell victim, as did all religions, to systematic persecution: non-Albanian missionaries were expelled; death, prison sentences and other repressive measures were enacted against church personnel and laity; Catholic schools and churches were closed and used for other purposes, and lines of communication with the Holy See were cut off. In 1967, the government, declaring it had eliminated all religion in the country, proclaimed itself the first atheist state in the world. The right to practice religion was restored in late 1990. In March, 1991, a delegation from the Vatican was allowed to go to Albania; later in the year diplomatic relations were established with the Vatican at the request of the Albanian prime minister. Pope John Paul II made a historic one-day visit to the country April 25, 1993, during which he ordained four bishops appointed by him in December, 1992, to fill long-vacant sees. (See Index for papal visit.)

Algeria*

Archd., 1; dioc., 3; card., 1; abp., 2; bp., 4; parishes, 67; priests, 162 (80 dioc., 82 rel.); p.d., 2; sem., 1; bros., 20; srs., 371; bap., 11; Caths., 27,000 (.11%); tot. pop., 25,660,000.

Republic in northwest Africa: capital, Algiers. Christianity, introduced at an early date, succumbed to Vandal devastation in the fifth century and Muslim conquest in 709, but survived for centuries in small communities into the 12th century. Missionary work was unsuccessful except in service to traders, military personnel and captives along the coast. Church organization was established after the French gained control of the territory in the 1830s. A large number of Catholics were among the estimated million Europeans who left the country after it secured independence from France July 5, 1962. Sunni-Muslim is the state religion.

Andorra

Parishes, 7; priests, 18 (12 dioc., 6 rel.); p.d., 1; srs., 17; bap., 436; Caths., 48,000 (92%); tot. pop., 52,000.

Autonomous principality in the Pyrenees, under the rule of co-princes — the French head of state and the bishop of Urgel, Spain; capital, Andorra la Vella. Christianity was introduced at an early date. Catholicism is the state religion. The principality is under the ecclesiastical jurisdiction of the Spanish diocese of Urgel.

Angola

Archd., 3; dioc., 12; card., 1; abp., 5; bp., 12; parishes, 253; priests, 383 (130 dioc., 253 rel.); p.d., 3; sem., 437; bros., 95; srs., 1,088; catechists, 17,973; bap., 118,904; Caths., 5,728,000 (55.6%); tot. pop., 10,300,000. (AD)

Republic in southwest Africa; capital, Luanda. Evangelization by Catholic missionaries, from Portugal, dating from 1491, reached high points in the 17th and 18th centuries. Independence from Portugal in 1975 and the long civil war which followed (peace accord signed in 1991) left the Church with a heavy loss of personnel through the departure of about half of the foreign missionaries and the persecution and martyrdom experienced by the Church during the war. Renewed fighting following elections in late 1992 brought repeated appeals for peace from the nation's bishops and religious. (See News Events.) The first Angolan cardinal (Alexandre do Nascimento) was named in 1983.

Anguilla

Parish, 1; priests, 2 (1 dioc., 1 rel.); bap., 5; Caths., 100; tot. pop., 7,000. (AD)

Self-governing British island territory in the Caribbean; capital, The Valley. Under ecclesiastical jurisdiction of St. John's-Basseterre diocese, Antigua.

Antigua and Barbuda*

Dioc., 1; bp., 1; parishes, 2; priests, 7 (1 dioc., 6 rel.); bros., 4; srs., 8; catechists, 51; bap., 81; Caths., 7,000 (8.7%); tot. pop., 80,000.

Independent (1981) Caribbean island nation; capital, St. John's, Antigua.

Arabian Peninsula

Christianity, introduced in various parts of the peninsula in early Christian centuries, succumbed to Islam in the seventh century. The native population is entirely Muslim. The only Christians are foreign workers mainly from the Philippines, India and Korea. Most of the peninsula is under the ecclesiastical jurisdiction of the Vicariate Apostolic of Arabia with its seat in Abu Dhabi, United Arab Emirates. See indvidual countries: Bahrain, Oman, Qatar, Saudi Arabia, United Arab Emirates and Yemen.

Argentina*

Archd., 13; dioc. (as of July, 1993), 49; prel., 3; ap. ex., 1 (for Armenians of Latin America); ord., 1; mil. ord.; card., 4; abp., 3; bp., 75; parishes, 2,437; priests, 5,791 (3,189 dioc., 2,602 rel.); p.d., 240; sem., 2,112; bros., 1,083; srs., 11,095; bap., 586,578; Caths., 29,965,000 (91.6%); tot. pop., 32,710,000

Republic in southeast South America, bordering on the Atlantic; capital, Buenos Aires. Priests were with the Magellan exploration party and the first Mass in the country was celebrated Apr. 1, 1519. Missionary work began in the 1530s, diocesan organization in the late 1540s, and effective evangelization about 1570. Independence from Spain was proclaimed in 1816. Since its establishment in the country, the Church has been influenced by Spanish cultural and institutional forces, antagonistic liberalism, government interference and opposition; the latter reached a climax during the last five years of the first presidency of Juan Peron (1946-1955). Widespread human rights violations including the disappearance of thousands of people marked the period of military rule from 1976 to December, 1983, when an elected civilian government took over. The bishops' conference published in book form in September, 1983, communiques they had sent to the military government during those years concerning human right abuses. Catholicism is the state religion.

Armenia*

Ord., 1 (for Armenia and Eastern Europe, with seat in Armenia). Parish, 1; priests, 1 (rel.); srs., 6; Caths., 30,000; tot. Pop., 3,350,000.

Republic in Asia Minor; capital Yerevan. Part of the USSR from 1920, Armenia declared its sovereignty September, 1991. Ancient Armenia, which also included territory annexed by Turkey in 1920, was Christianized in the fourth century. Diplomatic relations were established with the Vatican May 23, 1992.

Australia*

Archd., 7; dioc., 24; mil. ord., 1; card., 2; abp., 13; bp., 41; parishes, 1,434; priests, 3,588 (2,138 dioc., 1,450 rel.); p.d., 31; sem., 312; bros., 1,638; srs., 9,838; bap., 78,914; Caths., 4,762,000 (27.5%); tot. pop. 17,340,000.

Commonwealth; island continent southeast of Asia; capital, Canberra. The first Catholics in the country were Irish under penal sentence, 1795-1804; the first public Mass was celebrated May 15, 1803. Official organization of the Church dates from 1820. The country was officially removed from mission status in March, 1976.

Austria*

Archd., 2; dioc., 7; abb., 1; ord., 1; mil. ord.; card., 3; abp., 3; bp., 17; parishes, 3,088; priests, 5,013 (3,038 dioc., 1,975 rel.); p.d., 266; sem., 536; bros., 554; srs., 8,106; bap., 77,263; Caths., 6,293,000 (80.5%); tot. pop., 7,820,000.

Republic in central Europe; capital, Vienna. Christianity was introduced by the end of the third century, strengthened considerably by conversion of the Bavarians from about 600, and firmly established in the second half of the eighth century. Catholicism survived and grew stronger as the principal religion in the country in the post-Reformation period, but suffered from Josephinism in the 18th century. Although liberated from much government harassment in the aftermath of the Revolution of 1848, it came under pressure again some 20 years later in the Kulturkampf. During this time the Church became involved with a developing social movement. The Church faced strong opposition from Socialists after World War I and suffered persecution from 1938 to 1945 during the Nazi regime. Some Church-state matters are regulated by a concordat originally concluded in 1934.

Azerbaijan*

Independent republic (1991) bordering Iran and Turkey; capital, Baku. Islam is the prevailing religion. There is a small Catholic community of Polish and Armenian origin near the capital. Population, 7,220,000.

Azores

North Atlantic island group 750 miles west of Portugal, of which it is part. Christianity was introduced in the second quarter of the 15th century. The diocese of Angra was established in 1534. Statistics are included in Portugal.

Bahamas*

Dioc., 1; bp., 1; parishes, 29; priests, 33 (13 dioc., 20 rel.); p.d., 4; sem., 3; bros., 4; srs., 42; catechists, 117; bap., 1,021; Caths., 45,000 (17.6%); tot. pop., 255,000.

Independent (July 10, 1973) island group consisting of some 700 (30 inhabited) small islands southeast of Florida and north of Cuba; capital, Nassau. On Oct. 12, 1492, Columbus landed on one of these islands, where the first Mass was celebrated in the New World. Organization of the Catholic Church in the Bahamas dates from about the middle of the 19th century.

Bahrain

Parish, 1; priests, 3 (2 dioc., 1 rel.); srs., 6; bap., 228; Caths., 21,000; tot. pop., 520,000. (AD)

Island state in Persian Gulf; capital, Manama. Population is Muslim; Catholics are foreign workers. Under ecclesiastical jurisdiction of Arabia vicariate apostolic.

Balearic Islands

Spanish province consisting of an island group in the western Mediterranean. Statistics are included in those for Spain.

Bangladesh*

Archd., 1; dioc., 5; abp., 2; bp., 5; parishes, 77; priests, 225 (95 dioc., 130 rel.); sem., 120; bros., 47; srs., 679; catechists, 1,151; bap., 6,454; Caths., 209,000 (.18%); tot. pop. 118,740,000.

Formerly the eastern portion of Pakistan. Officially constituted as a separate nation Dec. 16, 1971; capital, Dhaka. Islam, the principal religion, was declared the state religion in 1988; freedom of religion is granted. There were Jesuit, Dominican and Augustinian missionaries in the area in the 16th century. A vicariate apostolic (of Bengali) was established in 1834; the hierarchy was erected in 1950.

Barbados*

Dioc., 1; bp., 2; parishes, 6; priests, 11 (3 dioc., 8 rel.); p.d., 2; bros., 1; srs., 12; bap., 180; Caths., 11,000 (4%); tot. pop., 275,000.

Parliamentary democracy (independent since 1966), easternmost of the Caribbean islands; capital, Bridgetown. About 70 per cent of the people are Anglicans.

Belarus*

Archd., 1; dioc., 2; abp., 1; bp., 2; parishes, 248; priests 146 (85 dioc., 61 rel.); sem., 73; bros., 2; srs., 82; bap., 10,346; Caths., 1,500,000 (14.3%); tot. pop., 10,478,000.

Independent republic (1991) in eastern Europe; former Soviet republic (Byelorussia); capital, Minsk.

Belgium*

Archd., 1; dioc., 7; mil ord.; card., 3; bp., 25; parishes, 3,955; priests, 10,045 (6,290 dioc., 3,755 rel.); p.d., 425; sem., 350; bros., 1,667; srs., 22,528; bap., 94,216; Caths., 8,498,000 (86.3%); tot. pop., 9,840,000.

Constitutional monarchy in northwestern Europe; captial, Brussels. Christianity was introduced about the first quarter of the fourth century and major evangelization was completed about 730. During the rest of the medieval period the Church had firm diocesan and parochial organization, generally vigorous monastic life, and influential monastic and cathedral schools. Lutherans and Calvinists made some gains during the Reformation period but there was a strong Catholic restoration in the first half of the 17th century, when the country was under Spanish rule. Jansenism disturbed the Church from about 1640 into the 18th century. Josephinism, imposed by an Austrian regime, hampered the Church late in the same century. Repressive and persecutory measures were enforced during the Napoleonic con-

quest. Freedom came with separation of Church and state in the wake of the Revolution of 1830, which ended the reign of William I. Thereafter, the Church encountered serious problems with philosophical liberalism and political socialism. Catholics have long been engaged in strong educational, social and political movements. Except for one five-year period (1880-84), Belgium has had diplomatic relations with Vatican City since 1835.

Belize*

Dioc., 1; bp., 1; parishes, 13; priests, 44 (13 dioc., 31 rel.); p.d., 1; sem., 1; bros., 7; srs., 79; catechists, 359; bap., 3,332; Caths., 122,000 (62.6%); tot. pop., 196,000.

Formerly British Honduras. Independent (Sept. 21, 1981) republic on east coast of Central America; capital, Belmopan. Its history has points in common with Guatemala, where evangelization began in the 16th century.

Benin*

Archd., 1; dioc., 5; card., 1; abp., 2; bp., 5; parishes, 132; priests, 280 (181 dioc., 99 rel.); sem., 168; bros., 36; srs., 476; catechists, 5,701; bap., 34,289; Caths., 1,015,000 (20.7%); tot. pop., 4,890,000.

Formerly Dahomey. Democratic republic in west Africa, bordering on the Atlantic; capital, Porto Novo. Missionary work was very limited from the 16th to the 18th centuries. Effective evangelization dates from 1861. The hierarchy was established in 1955. The majority of Christians are Catholics. (See Index for 1993 papal visit.)

Bermuda

Dioc., 1; bp., 1; parishes, 7; priests, 7 (1 dioc., 6 rel.); srs., 5; catechists, 109; bap., 138; Caths., 9,000 (15%); tot. pop., 60,000. (AD)

British dependency, consisting of 360 islands (20 of them inhabited) nearly 600 miles east of Cape Hatteras; capital, Hamilton. Catholics were not permitted until about 1800. Occasional pastoral care was provided the few Catholics there by visiting priests during the 19th century. Early in the 1900s priests from Halifax began serving the area. A prefecture apostolic was set up in 1953. The first bishop assumed jurisdiction in 1956 when it was made a vicariate apostolic; diocese established, 1967.

Bhutan

Parish, 1; priest, 1 (rel.); bap., 9; Caths., 1,000; tot. pop., 1,480,000.

Kingdom in the Himalayas, northeast of India; capital, Thimphu. Most of the population are Buddhists. Jesuits (1963) and Salesians (1965) were invited to country to direct schools. Salesians were expelled in February, 1982, on disputed charges of proselytism. Ecclesiastical jurisdiction is under the Darjeeling diocese, India.

Bolivia*

Archd., 4; dioc., 4; prel., 2; v.a., 6; mil. ord.; abp., 9; bp., 28; parishes, 501; priests, 924 (271 dioc., 653 rel.); p.d., 46; sem., 386; bros., 184; srs., 1,933;

catechists, 1,627; bap., 224,394; Caths., 7,016,000 (92.1%); tot. pop., 7,610,000.

Republic in central South America; capital, Sucre; seat of government, La Paz. Catholicism, the official religion, was introduced in the 1530s and the first bishopric was established in 1552. Effective evangelization among the Indians, slow to start, reached high points in the middle of the 18th and the beginning of the 19th centuries and was resumed about 1840. Independence from Spain was proclaimed in 1825, at the end of a campaign that started in 1809. Church-state relations are regulated by a 1951 concordat with the Holy See. In recent years, human rights violations in conditions of political, economic and social turmoil have occasioned strong protests by members of the hierarchy and other people of the Church.

Bosnia-Herzegovina*

Archd., 1; dioc., 2; abp., 2; bp., 3; parishes, 268; priests, 528 (229 dioc., 299 rel.); sem., 65; bros., 128; srs., 647; bap., 11,536; Caths., 841,981 (18.9%); tot. pop., 4,446,569. (1993 Annuario Pontificio.)

Independent republic (1992) in southeastern Europe; formerly part of Yugoslavia; capital Saravejo. (See Index for ethnic warfare and related events.)

Botswana

Dioc., 1; bp., 1 (native); parishes, 26; priests, 33 (3 dioc., 30 rel.); p.d., 1; sem., 7; bros., 5; srs., 59; catechists, 112; bap., 1,674; Caths., 49,000 (3.6%); tot. pop., 1,350,000. (AD)

Republic (independent since 1966) in southern Africa; capital, Gaborone. The first Catholic mission was opened in 1928 near Gaborone; earlier attempts at evangelization dating from 1879 were unsuccessful.

Brazil*

Archd., 37; dioc., 199; prel., 13; abb., 2; ord., 1; mil. ord.; card., 7; abp., 47; bp., 320; parishes, 7,760; priests, 14,343 (6,821 dioc., 7,522 rel.); p.d., 577; sem., 5,837; bros., 2,254; srs., 36,595; bap., 2,410,297; Caths., 135,160,000 (88.1%); tot. pop., 153,320,000.

Federal republic in northeast South America; capital, Brasilia. One of several priests with the discovery party celebrated the first Mass in the country Apr. 26, 1500. Evangelization began some years later and the first diocese was erected in 1551. During the colonial period, which lasted until 1822, evangelization made some notable progress — especially in the Amazon region between 1680 and 1750 — but was seriously hindered by government policy and the attitude of colonists regarding Amazon Indians the missionaries tried to protect from exploitation and slavery. The Jesuits were suppressed in 1782 and other missionaries expelled as well. Liberal anti-Church influence grew in strength. The government gave minimal support but exercised maximum control over the Church. After the proclamation of independence from Portugal in 1822 and throughout the regency, government control was tightened and the Church suffered greatly

from dissident actions of ecclesiastical brotherhoods, Masonic anticlericalism and general decline in religious life. Church and state were separated by the constitution of 1891, proclaimed two years after the end of the empire. The Church carried into the 20th century a load of inherited liabilities and problems amid increasingly difficult political, economic and social conditions affecting the majority of the population. A number of bishops, priests, religious and lay persons have been active in movements for social and religious reform.

Brunei Darussalam

Parishes, 5; priests, 3 (dioc.); srs., 4; bap., 137; Caths., 6,000; tot. pop., 270,000.

Independent state (1984) on the northern coast of Borneo; capital, Bandar Seri Begawan. Islam is the official religion; other religions are allowed with some restrictions. Most of the Catholics are technicians and skilled workers from other countries who are not permanent residents; under ecclesiastical jurisdiction of Miri diocese, Malaysia.

Bulgaria*

Dioc., 2; ap. ex., 1; bp., 3; parishes, 55; priests, 63 (41 dioc., 22 rel.); sem., 15; bros., 5; srs., 61; bap., 927; Caths., 80,000 (.89%) tot. pop., 8,980,000.

Republic in southeastern Europe on the eastern part of the Balkan peninsula; capital, Sofia. Christianity was introduced before 343 but disappeared with the migration of Slavs into the territory. The baptism of Boris I about 865 ushered in a new period of Christianity which soon became involved in switches of loyalty between Constantinople and Rome. Through it all the Byzantine, and later Orthodox, element remained stronger and survived under the rule of Ottoman Turks into the 19th century. The few modern Latin Catholics in the country are traceable to 17th century converts from heresy. The Byzantines are products of a reunion movement of the 19th century. In 1947 the constitution of the new republic decreed the separation of Church and state. Catholic schools and institutions were abolished and foreign religious banished in 1948. A year later the apostolic delegate was expelled. Ivan Romanoff, vicar general of Plovdiv, died in prison in 1952. Bishop Eugene Bossilkoff, imprisoned in 1948, was sentenced to death in 1952; his fate remained unknown until 1975 when the Bulgarian government informed the Vatican that he had died in prison shortly after being sentenced. Roman and Bulgarian Rite vicars apostolic were permitted to attend the Second Vatican Council from 1962 to 1965. All church activity was under surveillance and/or control by the government, which professed to be atheistic. Pastoral and related activities were strictly limited. Most of the population is Orthodox. There was some improvement in Bulgarian-Vatican relations in 1975, following a visit of Bulgarian President Todor Zhivkov to Pope Paul VI June 19 and talks between Vatican and Bulgarian representatives at the Helsinki Conference in late July. The needs of the church in Bulgaria were outlined by Pope John Paul II in a private audience with the Bulgarian foreign minister in December, 1978. In

1979, the Sofia-Plovdiv vicariate apostolic was raised to a diocese and a bishop was appointed for the vacant see of Nicopoli. Diplomatic relations with the Vatican were established in 1990.

Burkina Faso*

Archd., 1; dioc., 8; card., 1; bp., 10; parishes, 107; priests, 439 (255 dioc., 184 rel.); sem., 245; bros., 146; srs., 748; catechists, 5,781; bap., 39,893; Caths., 853,000 (9.2%); tot. pop., 9,240,000.

Formerly Upper Volta. Republic inland in western Africa; capital, Ouagadougou. White Fathers (now known as Missionaries of Africa) started the first missions in 1900 and 1901. White Sisters began work in 1911. A minor and a major seminary were established in 1926 and 1942, respectively. The first native bishop in modern times from West Africa was ordained in 1956 and the first cardinal created in 1965. The hierarchy was established in 1955.

Burma
(See Myanmar)

Burundi*

Archd., 1; dioc., 6; abp., 3; bp., 7; parishes, 116; priests, 302 (231 dioc., 71 rel.); sem., 186; bros., 137; srs., 811; catechists, 4,326; bap., 117,354; Caths., 3,366,000 (59.9%); tot. pop., 5,620,000.

Republic since 1966, near the equator in east-central Africa; capital, Bujumbura. The first permanent Catholic mission station was established late in the 19th century. Large numbers of persons were received into the Church following the ordination of the first Burundi priests in 1925. The first native bishop was appointed in 1959. In 1972-73, the country was torn by tribal warfare between the Tutsis, the ruling minority, and the Hutus. Since 1979, approximately 100 Catholic missionaries have been expelled. In 1986, seminaries were nationalized. There has been a gradual resumption of church activity following a change of government in September, 1987.

Cambodia

V.a., 1; p.a., 2. No statistics available. Catholics numbered 13,835 in 1973. International Fides Service (Feb. 6, 1993) reported an approximate estimate of 7,000 Catholics. Tot. pop., 8,440,000.

Republic in southeast Asia, bordering on the Gulf of Siam, Thailand, Laos and Vietnam; capital Phnom Penh. Evangelization dating from the second half of the 16th century had limited results, more among Vietnamese than Khmers. Thousands of Catholics of Vietnamese origin were forced to flee in 1970 because of Khmer hostility. The status of the Church remained uncertain following the Khmer Rouge take-over in April, 1975, the Vietnamese invasion in 1979 and the long civil war which followed. Foreign missionaries were expelled, local clergy and religious were sent to work the land and a general persecution followed. Religious freedom was reestablished in 1990. Buddhism is the state religion.

Cameroon*

Archd., 4; dioc., 17 (1993); card., 1; abp., 3; bp., 17; parishes, 529; priests, 927 (497 dioc., 430 rel.); p.d., 21; sem., 661; bros., 186; srs., 1,386;

catechists, 12,579; bap., 111,964; Caths., 3,446,000 (28.1%); tot. pop., 12,240,000.

Republic in west Africa, bordering on the Gulf of Guinea; capital, Yaounde. Effective evangelization began in 1890, although Catholics had been in the country long before that time. In the 40-year period from 1920 to 1960, the number of Catholics increased from 60,000 to 700,000. The first native priests were ordained in 1935. Twenty years later the first native bishops were ordained and the hierarchy established. The first Cameroonian cardinal (Christian Wiyghan Tumi) was named in 1988.

Canada*

Archd., 19; dioc., 53; abb., 1; ap. ex., 1; mil. ord.; card., 4 (1 is Curia official; 3 are retired); abp., 29 (19 archdiocesan, 1 heads eparchy with personal title of archbishop; 9 retired); bp., 92 (49 diocesan, 17 auxiliary, 1 bishop of Military Ordinariate; 1 bishop for Hungarian Emigrants; 24 retired); abbots, 2 (1 retired); parishes, 5,323; priests, 10,788 (6,502 dioc., 4,286 rel.); p.d., 787; sem., 660; bros., 3,045; srs., 29,821; bap., 177,167; Caths., 11,971,562 (45%); tot. pop., 26,656,320. (Principal sources: 1991-1992 Report of Statistics of the Catholic Church in Canada; Statistical Yearbook of the Church; 1993 Annuario Pontificio.)

Independent federation comprising the northern half of North America; capital, Ottawa. (See Index.)

Canary Islands

Two Spanish provinces, consisting of seven islands, off the northwest coast of Africa. Evangelization began about 1400. Almost all of the one million inhabitants are Catholics. Statistics are included in those for Spain.

Cape Verde*

Dioc., 1; bp., 1; parishes, 30; priests, 49 (15 dioc., 34 rel.); sem., 2; bros., 7; srs., 100; catechists, 2,221; bap., 9,386; Caths., 353,000 (92.9%); tot. pop., 380,000.

Independent (July 5, 1975) island group in the Atlantic 300 miles west of Senegal; formerly a Portuguese overseas province; capital, Praia, San Tiago Island. Evangelization began some years before the establishment of the first diocese in 1532.

Cayman Islands

Parish, 1; priests, 2 (dioc.); srs., 2; catechists, 8; bap., 37; Caths. 200; tot. pop., 9,000. (AD)

British dependency in Caribbean; capital, George Town on Grand Cayman. Under ecclesiastical jurisdiction of Kingston archdiocese, Jamaica.

Central African Republic*

Archd., 1; dioc., 5; abp., 2; bp., 7; parishes, 128; priests, 255 (86 dioc., 169 rel.); p.d., 1; sem., 110; bros., 52; srs., 328; catechists, 3,735; bap., 18,618; Caths., 558,000 (17.8%); tot. pop., 3,130,000.

Former French colony (independent since 1960) in central Africa; capital, Bangui. Effective evangelization dates from 1894. The region was organized as a mission territory in 1909. The first native priest was ordained in 1938. The hierarchy was organized in 1955.

Ceuta

Spanish possession (city) on the northern tip of Africa, south of Gibraltar. Statistics are included in those for Spain.

Chad*

Archd., 1; dioc., 4; abp., 1; bp., 7; parishes, 94; priests, 185 (53 dioc., 132 rel.); sem., 63; bros., 32; srs., 242; catechists, 6,032; bap., 13,281; Caths., 350,000 (6%); tot. pop., 5,820,000.

Republic (independent since 1960) in north-central Africa; former French possession; capital, N'-Djamena. Evangelization began in 1929, leading to firm organization in 1947 and establishment of the hierarchy in 1955.

Chile*

Archd., 5; dioc., 17; prel., 2; v.a., 2; mil. ord.; card., 2; abp., 8; bp., 33; parishes, 866; priests, 2,157 (941 dioc., 1,216 rel.); p.d., 237; sem., 898; bros., 431; srs., 6,949; catechists, 1,315; bap., 189,110; Caths., 10,761,000 (80.3%); tot. pop., 13,390,000.

Republic on the southwestern coast of South America; capital, Santiago. Priests were with the Spanish conquistadores on their entrance into the territory early in the 16th century. The first parish was established in 1547 and the first bishopric in 1561. Overall organization of the Church took place later in the century. By 1650 most of the peaceful Indians in the central and northern areas were evangelized. Missionary work was more difficult in the southern region. Church activity was hampered during the campaign for independence, 1810 to 1818, and through the first years of the new government, to 1830. Later gains were made, into this century, but hindering factors were shortages of native clergy and religious and attempts by the government to control church administration through the patronage system in force while the country was under Spanish control. Separation of Church and state was decreed in the constitution of 1925. Church-state relations were strained during the regime of Marxist president Salvator Allende Gossens (1970-73). He was overthrown in a bloody coup and was reported to have committed suicide Sept. 11, 1973. Conditions remained unsettled under the military government which assumed control after the coup. The Chilean bishops issued numerous statements strongly critical of human rights abuses by the military dictatorship which remained in power until 1990 when an elected president took office.

China

Archd., 20; dioc., 92; p.a., 29. No Catholic statistics are available. In 1949 there were between 3,500,000-4,000,000 Catholics, about .7 per cent of the total population. Tot. pop. 1,118,135,000.

People's republic in eastern part of Asia (mainland China under communist control since 1949); capital, Peking (Beijing). Christianity was introduced by Nestorians who had some influence on part of the area from 635 to 845 and again from the 11th century until 1368. John of Monte Corvino started a Franciscan mission in 1294; he was ordained an archbishop about 1307. Missionary activity involving more priests increased for a while thereafter but the Franciscan mission ended in 1368. The Jesuit Matteo Ricci initiated a remarkable period of activity in the 1580s. By 1700 the number of Catholics was reported to be 300,000. The Chinese Rites controversy, concerning the adaptation of rituals and other matters to Chinese traditions and practices, ran throughout the 17th century, ending in a negative decision by mission authorities in Rome. Bl. Francis de Capillas, the protomartyr of China, was killed in 1648. Persecution, a feature of Chinese history as recurrent as changes in dynasties, occurred several times in the 18th century and resulted in the departure of most missionaries from the country. The Chinese door swung open again in the 1840s and progress in evangelization increased with an extension of legal and social tolerance. At the turn of the 20th century, however, the Boxer Rebellion took one or the other kind of toll among an estimated 30,000 victims. Missionary work in the 1900s reached a new high in every respect before the disaster of persecution initiated by Communists before and especially since they established the republic in 1949. The Reds began a savage persecution as soon as they came into power. Among its results were the expulsion of over 5,000 foreign missionaries, 510 of whom were American priests, brothers and nuns; the arrest, imprisonment and harassment of all members of the native religious, clergy and hierarchy; the forced closing of 3,932 schools, 216 hospitals, 781 dispensaries, 254 orphanages, 29 printing presses and 55 periodicals; denial of the free exercise of religion to all the faithful; the detention of hundreds of priests, religious and lay persons in jail and their employment in slave labor; the proscription of the Legion of Mary and other Catholic Action groups for "counter-revolutionary activities" and "crimes against the new China"; complete outlawing of missionary work and pastoral activity. The government formally established a Patriotic Association of Chinese Catholics in July, 1957. Relatively few priests and lay persons joined the organization, which was condemned by Pius XII in 1958. The government formed the nucleus of what it hoped might become the hierarchy of a schismatic Chinese church in 1958 by "electing" 26 bishops and having them consecrated validly but illicitly between Apr. 13, 1958, and Nov. 15, 1959, without the permission or approval of the Holy See. By 1983, an estimated 60 bishops were consecrated in this manner. In March, 1960, Bishop James E. Walsh, M.M., the last American missionary in China, was sentenced and placed in custody for a period of 20 years. He was released in the summer of 1970. (He died in 1981.) Activity of the Patriotic Association and official policy of the government are in direct opposition to any connection between the Church in China and the Vatican. Bishop Ignatius Gong (Kung) Pin-Mei, imprisoned for 30 years, was paroled in 1985; his 1979 "in pectore" election to the college of cardinals was revealed in 1991. The Vatican confirmed in 1993 that China and the Vatican had indirect contacts aimed at improving relations. (See Index.)

Colombia*

Archd., 12; dioc., 40; prel., 2; v.a., 8; p.a., 5; mil. ord., card., 2; abp., 13; bp., 59; parishes, 2,955;

*priests, 6,280 (4,220 dioc., 2,060 rel.); p.d., 88;
sem., 3,952; bros., 812; srs., 19,007; catechists,
2,965; bap., 794,890; Caths., 31,298,000 (93.1%);
tot. pop.,33,610,000.*

Republic in northwest South America, with Atlantic and Pacific borders; capital, Bogota. Evangelization began in 1508. The first two dioceses were established in 1534. Vigorous development of the Church was reported by the middle of the 17th century despite obstacles posed by the multiplicity of Indian languages, government interference through patronage rights and otherwise, rivalry among religious orders and the small number of native priests among the predominantly Spanish clergy. Some persecution, including the confiscation of property, followed in the wake of the proclamation of independence from Spain in 1819. The Church was affected in many ways by the political and civil unrest of the nation through the 19th century and into the 20th. Various aspects of Church-state relations are regulated by a concordat with the Vatican signed July 12, 1973, and ratified July 2, 1975. The new concordat replaced one which had been in effect with some modifications since 1887. Guerrilla warfare aimed at Marxist-oriented radical social reform and redistribution of land has plagued the country since the 1960s, posing problems for the Church which backed reforms but rejected actions of radical groups.

Comoros

*A.a., 1; parishes, 2; priests, 2 (rel.); srs., 7; bap.,
30; Caths.,3,000 (.5%); tot. pop.,570,000. (AD)*

Consists of main islands of Grande Comore, Anjouan and Moheli in Indian Ocean off southeast coast of Africa; capital, Moroni, Grande Comore Island. Former French territory; independent (July 6, 1975). The majority of the population is Muslim. An apostolic administration was established in 1975.

Congo*

*Archd., 1; dioc., 5; abp., 2; bp., 7; parishes, 99;
priests, 186 (103 dioc., 83 rel.); sem., 183; bros.,
58; srs., 285; catechists, 3,085; bap., 42,033;
Caths.,925,000 (39.3%); tot. pop., 2,350,000.*

Republic (independent since 1960) in west central Africa; former French possession; capital, Brazzaville. Small-scale missionary work with little effect preceded modern evangelization dating from the 1880s. The work of the Church has been affected by political instability, Communist influence, tribalism and hostility to foreigners. The hierarchy was established in 1955.

Cook Islands

*Dioc., 1; bp., 1; parishes, 11; priests, 11 (4 dioc.,
7 rel.); sem., 2; bros., 3; srs., 6; bap., 138; Caths.,
3,000; tot. pop., 19,000.*

Self-governing territory of New Zealand, an archipelago of small islands in Oceania. Evangelization by Protestant missionaries started in 1821, resulting in a predominantly Protestant population. The first Catholic missionary work began in 1894. The hierarchy was established in 1966.

Costa Rica*

*Archd., 1; dioc., 3; v.a., 1; abp., 2; bp., 7;
parishes, 230; priests, 605 (389 dioc., 216 rel.);
sem., 317; bros., 35; srs., 924; catechists, 2,146;
bap., 77,717; Caths., 2,805,000 (91.6%); tot. pop.,
3,060,000.*

Republic in Central America; capital, San Jose. Evangelization began about 1520 and proceeded by degrees to real development and organization of the Church in the 17th and 18th centuries. The republic became independent in 1838. Twelve years later church jurisdiction also became independent with the establishment of a bishopric in the present capital.

Côte d'Ivoire (Ivory Coast)*

*Archd., 1; dioc., 12; card., 1; bp., 12; parishes,
198 priests, 493 (231 dioc., 262 rel.); p.d., 1; sem.,
306; bros., 144; srs., 640; catechists, 7,661; bap.,
37,599; Caths., 1,585,000 (12.7%); tot. pop.,
12,460,000.*

Republic in western Africa; capital, Abidjan. The Holy Ghost Fathers began systematic evangelization in 1895. The first native priests from the area were ordained in 1934. The hierarchy was set up in 1955; the first native cardinal (Bernard Yago) was named in 1983.

Croatia*

*Archd., 4; dioc., 7; card., 1; abp., 6; bp., 17;
parishes, 1,551; priests, 2,218 (1,443 dioc., 775
rel.); p.d., 1; sem., 524; bros., 111; srs., 3,598; bap.,
46,925; Caths., 3,696,000 (67.6%); tot. pop.,
5,467,000.*

Independent (1992) republic in southeastern Europe; capital Zagreb; formerly a constituent republic of Yugoslavia. Christianity was introduced in the seventh century. From the ninth century on the Church in Croatia was allowed to celebrate Mass not only in Latin but in the language of the people. (See Yugoslavia for earlier history and events following communist takeover.) Croatian involvement in the Bosnian-Herzegovina war brought urgent appeals from Cardinal Kuharic and the Croatian Catholic Bishops' Conference condemning crimes on both sides and calling for the establishment of a just peace. (See News Events.)

Cuba*

*Archd., 2; dioc., 5; abp., 2; bp., 10; parishes, 236;
priests, 214 (116 dioc., 98 rel.); p.d., 13; sem., 42;
bros., 27; srs., 353; bap., 68,948; Caths. 4,421,000
(41.2%); tot. pop., 10,730,000.*

Republic under Communist dictatorship, south of Florida; capital, Havana. Effective evangelization began about 1514, leading eventually to the predominance of Catholicism on the island. Native vocations to the priesthood and religious life were unusually numerous in the 18th century but declined in the 19th. The island became independent of Spain in 1902 following the Spanish-American War. Fidel Castro took control of the government Jan. 1, 1959. In 1961, after Cuba was officially declared a socialist state, the University of Villanueva was closed, 350 Catholic schools were nationalized and 136 priests expelled. A greater number of foreign priests and religious had already left the country. Freedom of worship and religious instruction are limited to church premises and no social action is permitted the Church, which survives under surveillance. A new constitution approved in 1976 guaranteed freedom of conscience but restricted its exercise.

Cyprus*

Archd., 1 (Maronite); abp., 1; parishes, 13; priests, 15 (5 dioc., 10 rel.); sem., 1; bros., 6; srs., 53; bap., 109; Caths., 11,000; tot. pop., 710,000.

Republic in the eastern Mediterranean; capital, Nicosia. Christianity was preached on the island in apostolic times and has a continuous history from the fourth century. Latin and Eastern rites were established but the latter prevailed and became Orthodox after the schism of 1054. Roman and Orthodox Christians have suffered under many governments, particularly during the period of Turkish dominion from late in the 16th to late in the 19th centuries, and from differences between the 80 per cent Greek majority and the Turkish minority. About 80 per cent of the population are Orthodox. Catholics are under the jurisdiction of the archdiocese of Cyprus (of the Maronites).

Czech Republic*

Archd., 2; dioc. (1993), 5; abp., 2; bp., 9; parishes, 3,105; priests, 1,846 (1,330 dioc., 516 rel.); p.d., 27; sem., 251; bros., 219; srs., 2,326; bap., 45,381; Caths., 4,681,000 (44.8%); tot. pop., 10,436,800. (1993 Annuario Pontificio.)

Independent state (Jan. 1, 1993); formerly part of Czechoslovakia; capital, Prague. (For background history of the Church and the persecution during the years of communist domination, see Czechoslovakia, below.)

Czechoslovakia

The Czech and Slovak Federal Republic dissolved Jan. 1, 1993, and became two independent states (see Czech Republic and Slovakia entries for statistics). Information below covers the early history of the Church in the Czech and Slovak regions and its situation during the long period of communist domination.

The Czech and Slovak regions of the country have separate religious and cultural backgrounds. Christianity was introduced in Slovakia in the 8th century by Irish and German missionaries and the area was under the jurisdiction of German bishops. In 863, at the invitation of the Slovak ruler Rastislav who wanted to preserve the cultural and liturgical heritage of the people, Sts. Cyril and Methodius began pastoral and missionary work in the region, ministering to the people in their own language. The saints introduced Old Slovak (Old Church Slavonic) into the liturgy and did so much to evangelize the territory that they are venerated as the apostles of Slovakia. A diocese established at Nitra in 880 had a continuous history except for a century ending in 1024. The Church in Slovakia was severely tested by the Reformation and political upheavals. After World War I, when it became part of the Republic of Czechoslovakia, it was 75 per cent Catholic. In the Czech lands, the martyrdom of Prince Wenceslaus in 929 triggered the spread of Christianity.

Prague has had a continuous history as a diocese since 973. A parish system was organized about the 13th century in Bohemia and Moravia, the land of the Czechs. Mendicant orders strengthened relations with the Latin Rite in the 13th century. In the next century the teachings of John Hus in Bohemia brought trouble to the Church in the forms of schism and heresy, and initiated a series of religious wars which continued for decades following his death at the stake in 1415. Church property was confiscated, monastic communities were scattered and even murdered, ecclesiastical organization was shattered, and so many of the faithful joined the Bohemian Brethren that Catholics became a minority. The Reformation, with the way prepared by the Hussites and cleared by other factors, affected the Church seriously. A Counter Reformation got under way in the 1560s and led to a gradual restoration through the thickets of Josephinism, the Enlightenment, liberalism and troubled politics. In 1920, two years after the establishment of the Republic of Czechoslovakia, the schismatic Czechoslovak Church was proclaimed at Prague, resulting in numerous defections from the Catholic Church in the Czech region. In Ruthenia, 112,000 became Russian Orthodox between 1918 and 1930. Vigorous persecution of the church began in Slovakia before the end of World War II when Communists mounted a 1944 offensive against bishops, priests and religious. In 1945, church schools were nationalized, youth organizations were disbanded, the Catholic press was curtailed, the training of students for the priesthood was seriously impeded. Msgr. Josef Tiso, president of the Slovak Republic, was tried for "treason" in December, 1946, and was executed the following April. Between 1945 and 1949 approximately 10 per cent of the Slovak population spent some time in jail or a concentration camp. Persecution began later in the Czech part of the country, following the accession of the Gottwald regime to power early in 1948. Hospitals, schools and property were nationalized and Catholic organizations were liquidated. A puppet organization was formed in 1949 to infiltrate the Church and implement an unsuccessful plan for establishing a schismatic church. In the same year Archbishop Josef Beran of Prague was placed under house arrest. (He left the country in 1965, was made a cardinal, and died in 1969 in Rome.) A number of theatrical trials of bishops and priests were staged in 1950. All houses of religious were taken over between March, 1950, and the end of 1951. Pressure was applied on the clergy and faithful of the Eastern Rite in Slovakia to join the Orthodox Church. Diplomatic relations with Vatican City were terminated in 1950. About 3,000 priests were deprived of liberty in 1951 and attempts were made to force "peace priests" on the people. In 1958 it was reported that 450 to 500 priests were in jail; an undisclosed number of religious and Byzantine-Rite priests had been deported; two bishops released from prison in 1956 were under house arrest; one bishop was imprisoned at Leopoldov and two at the Mirov reformatory. In Bohemia, Moravia and Silesia, five of six dioceses were without ruling bishops; one archbishop and two bishops were active but subject to "supervision"; most of the clergy refused to join the "peace priests." In 1962 only three bishops were permitted to attend the first session of the Second Vatican Council. From January to October, 1968, Church-state relations improved to some extent under the Dubcek regime: a number of bishops were reinstated; some 3,000 priests were engaged in the pastoral ministry, although 1,500 were still barred from priestly work; the "peace priests" organization was disbanded; the Eastern-Rite Church, with 147 parishes, was reestablished. In 1969, an end was ordered to rehabilitation trials for priests and religious, but no wholesale restoration of priests and religious to their proper ways of life and work was in prospect. In 1972, the government ordered the removal of nuns from visible but limited apostolates to farms and mental hospitals where they would be out of sight. In 1973, the government allowed the ordination of four bishops — one in the Czech region and three in the Slovak region. Reports from Slovakia late in the same year stated that authorities there had placed severe restrictions on the education of seminarians and the functioning of priests. Government restrictions continued to hamper the work of priests and nuns. Signatories of the human rights declaration called Charter 77 were particular objects of government repression and retribution. In December, 1983, the Czechoslovakian foreign minister met with the Pope at Vatican City — the first meeting of a high Czech official with a pope since the country came under communist rule. In 1984, two Vatican officials visited Czechoslovakia. Despite the communication breakthrough, there was no indication of any change of policy toward the Church in the country. In 1988, three new bishops were ordained in Czechoslovakia — the first since 1973. Three more episcopal appointments were made in 1989. The communist government fell in late 1989. In 1990: bishops were appointed to fill the remaining vacant sees; announcement was made of the reestablishment of diplomatic relations between the Holy See and Czechoslovakia after 40 years and Pope John Paul II paid a historic visit to the country. (See Czech Republic; Slovakia.)

Denmark*

Dioc., 1; bp., 2; parishes, 50; priests, 94 (35 dioc., 59 rel.); p.d., 1; sem., 7; bros., 5; srs., 318; bap., 531; Caths., 30,000 (.6%); tot. pop., 5,150,000.

Includes the Faroe Islands and Greenland. Constitutional monarchy in northwestern Europe, north of West Germany; capital, Copenhagen. Christianity was introduced in the ninth century and the first diocese for the area was established in 831. Intensive evangelization and full-scale organization of the Church occurred from the second half of the 10th century and ushered in a period of great development and influence in the 12th and 13th centuries. Decline followed, resulting in almost total loss to the Church during the Reformation when Lutheranism became the national religion. Catholics were considered foreigners until religious freedom was legally assured in 1849. Modern development of the Church dates from the second half of the 19th century. About 95 per cent of the population are Evangelical Lutherans.

Djibouti

Dioc., 1; parishes, 6; priests, 5 (rel.); bros., 9; srs., 19; bap., 26; Caths., 8,000; tot. pop., 420,000. (AD)

Formerly French Territory of Afars and Issas. Independent (1977) republic in east Africa, on the Gulf of Aden; capital, Djibouti. Christianity in the area, formerly part of Ethiopia, antedated but was overcome by the Arab invasion of 1200. Modern evangelization, begun in the latter part of the 19th century, had meager results. The hierarchy was established in 1955.

Dominica*

Dioc., 1; bp., 1; parishes, 17; priests, 42 (7 dioc., 35 rel.); sem., 1; bros., 6; srs., 28; 480 catechists; bap., 1,016; Caths., 57,000; tot. pop., 72,000.

Independent (Nov. 3, 1978) state in Caribbean; capital, Roseau. Evangelization began in 1642.

Dominican Republic*

Archd., 1; dioc., 8; mil. ord.; card., 1; abp., 1; bp., 12; parishes, 272; priests, 597 (220 dioc., 377 rel.); p.d., 106; sem., 403; bros., 88; srs., 1,390; bap., 97,199; Caths., 6,699,000 (91.2%); tot. pop., 7,310,000.

Caribbean republic on the eastern two-thirds of the island of Hispaniola, bordering on Haiti; capital, Santo Domingo. Evangelization began shortly after discovery by Columbus in 1492 and church organization, the first in America, was established by 1510. Catholicism is the state religion. (See Index for October, 1992, papal visit.)

Ecuador*

Archd., 4; dioc., 9; prel., 1; v.a., 7; p.a., 1; mil. ord., card., 1; abp., 5; bp., 25; parishes, 991; priests, 1,529 (742 dioc., 787 rel.); p.d., 31; sem., 686; bros., 378; srs., 4,293; catechists, 3,284; bap., 193,322; Caths., 10,081,000 (93%); tot. pop., 10,780,000.

Republic on the west coast of South America, includes Gallapogos Islands; capital, Quito. Evangelization began in the 1530s. The first diocese was established in 1545. A synod, one of the first in the Americas, was held in 1570 or 1594. Multiphased missionary work, spreading from the coastal and mountain regions into the Amazon, made the Church highly influential during the colonial period. The Church was practically enslaved by the constitution enacted in 1824, two years after Ecuador, as part of Colombia, gained independence from Spain. Some change for the better took place later in the century, but from 1891 until the 1930s the Church labored under serious liabilities imposed by liberal governments. The concordat of 1866 was violated; foreign missionaries were barred from the country for some time; the property of religious orders was confiscated; education was taken over by the state; traditional state support was refused; legal standing was denied; attempts to control church offices were made through insistence on rights of patronage. A period of harmony and independence for the Church began after agreement was reached on Church-state relations in 1937.

Egypt*

Patriarchates, 2 (Alexandria for the Copts and for the Melkites); dioc., 9; v.a., 1; patriarch, 1; abp., 2; bp., 14; parishes, 217; priests, 411 (197 dioc., 214 rel.); p.d., 3; sem., 172; bros., 76; srs., 1,423; bap., 3,178; Caths., 206,000 (.37%); tot. pop., 54,690,000.

Arab Republic in northeastern Africa, bordering on the Mediterranean; capital, Cairo. Alexandria was the influential hub of a Christian community established by the end of the second century; it became a patriarchate and the center of the Coptic Church, and had great influence on the spread of Christianity in various parts of Africa. Monasticism developed from desert communities of hermits in the third and fourth centuries. Arianism was first preached in Egypt in the 320s. In the fifth century, the Coptic church went Monophysite through failure to accept doctrine formulated by the Council of Chalcedon in 451 with respect to the two natures of Christ. The country was thoroughly Arabized after 640 and was under the rule of Ottoman Turks from 1517 to 1798. English influence was strong during the 19th century. A monarchy established in 1922 lasted about 30 years, ending with the proclamation of a republic in 1953-54. By that time Egypt had become the leader of pan-Arabism against Israel. It waged two unsuccessful wars against Israel in 1948-49 and 1967. Between 1958 and 1961 it was allied with Syria and Yemen, in the United Arab Republic. In 1979, following negotiations initiated by Pres. Anwar el-Sadat in 1977, Egypt and Israel signed a peace agreement. Islam, the religion of some 90 percent of the population, is the state religion.

El Salvador*

Archd., 1; dioc., 7; mil. ord.; abp., 1; bp., 13; parishes, 266; priests, 485 (282 dioc., 203 rel.); p.d., 1; sem., 249; bros., 119; srs., 1,225; bap., 198,795; Caths., 5,035,000 (93.6%); tot. pop., 5,380,000.

Republic in Central America; capital, San Salvador. Evangelization affecting the whole territory followed Spanish occupation in the 1520s. The country was administered by the captaincy general of Guatemala until 1821 when independence from Spain was declared and it was annexed to Mexico. El Salvador joined the Central American Federation in 1825, decreed its own independence in 1841 and became a republic formally in 1856. Church efforts in recent years to achieve social justice have resulted in persecution of the Church. Archbishop Oscar Romero of San Salvador, peace advocate and outspoken champion of human rights, was murdered Mar. 24, 1980, while celebrating Mass.

England*

Archd., 4; dioc., 15; ap. ex., 1; mil. ord. (Great Britain); card., 1; abp., 3; bp., 35; parishes, 2,540; priests, 5,446 (3,666 dioc., 1,780 rel.); p.d., 257; sem., 365; bros., 728; srs., 9,805; bap., 77,912; Caths., 4,179,177 (9%); tot. pop., 46,472,413. (1993 Annuario Pontificio).

Center of the United Kingdom of Great Britain (England, Scotland, Wales) and Northern Ireland, off the northwestern coast of Europe; capital, London. The arrival of St. Augustine of Canterbury and a band of monks in 597 marked the beginning of evangelization. Real organization of the Church took place some years after the Synod of Whitby, held in 663. Heavy losses were sustained in the wake of the Danish invasion in the 780s, but recovery starting from the time of Alfred the Great and dating especially from the middle of the 10th century led to Christianization of the whole country and close Church-state relations. The Norman Conquest of 1066 opened the Church in England to European influence. The 13th century was climactic, but decline had already set in by 1300 when the country had an all-time high of 17,000 religious. In the 14th century, John Wycliff presaged the Protestant Reformation. Henry VIII, failing in 1529 to gain annulment of his marriage to Catherine of Aragon, refused to acknowledge papal authority over the Church in England, had himself proclaimed its head, suppressed all houses of religious, and persecuted persons — Sts. Thomas More and John Fisher, among others — for not subscribing to the Oath of Supremacy and Act of Succession. He held the line on other-than-papal doctrine, however, until his death in 1547. Doctrinal aberrations were introduced during the reign of Edward VI (1547-53), through the Order of Communion, two books of Common Prayer, and the Articles of the Established Church. Mary Tudor's attempted Catholic restoration (1553-58) was a disaster, resulting in the deaths of more than 300 Protestants. Elizabeth (1558-1603) firmed up the Established Church with formation of a hierarchy, legal enactments and multi-phased persecution. One hundred and 11 priests and 62 lay persons were among the casualties of persecution during the underground Catholic revival which followed the return to England of missionary priests from France and The Lowlands. Several periods of comparative toleration ensued after Elizabeth's death. The first of several apostolic vicariates was established in 1685; this form of church government was maintained until the restoration of the hierarchy and diocesan organization in 1850. The revolution of 1688 and subsequent developments to about 1781 subjected Catholics to a wide variety of penal laws and disabilities in religious, civic and social life. The situation began to improve in 1791, and from 1801 Parliament frequently considered proposals for the repeal of penal laws against Catholics. The Act of Emancipation restored citizenship rights to Catholics in 1829. Restrictions remained in force for some time afterwards, however, on public religious worship and activity. The hierarchy was restored in 1850. Since then the Catholic Church, existing side by side with the Established Churches of England and Scotland, has followed a general pattern of growth and development.

Equatorial Guinea*

Archd., 1; dioc., 2; abp., 1; bp., 2; parishes, 54; priests, 89 (42 dioc., 47 rel.); p.d. 1; sem., 37; bros., 34; srs., 205; catechists, 1,485; bap., 10,584; Caths., 354,000 (98%); tot. pop., 360,000.

Republic on the west coast of Africa, consisting of Rio Muni on the mainland and the islands of Fernando Po and Annobon in the Gulf of Guinea: capital, Malabo (Santa Isabel). Evangelization began in 1841. The country became independent of Spain in 1968. The Church was severely repressed during the 11-year rule of Pres. Macias (Masie) Nguema. Developments since his overthrow (August, 1979) indicated some measure of improvement. An ecclesiastical province was established in October, 1982.

Eritrea

Independent state (May 24, 1993) in northeast Africa; formerly a province of Ethiopia. Christianity was introduced in the fourth century. Population is evenly divided between Christians and Muslims. Catholics form a small minority; most of the population is Orthodox Christian or Muslim. Statistics are included in Ethiopia.

Estonia*

A.a., 1; abp., 1 (apostolic administrator); parishes, 4; priests, 2 (1 dioc., 1 rel); bap., 44; Caths., 3,000; tot. pop., 1,500,000. (1993 Annuario Pontificio.)

Independent (1991) Baltic republic; capital, Tallinn. (Forcibly absorbed by the U.S.S.R. in 1940; it regained independence in 1991.) Catholicism was introduced in the 11th and 12th centuries. Jurisdiction over the area was made directly subject to the Holy See in 1215. Lutheran penetration was general in the Reformation period and Russian Orthodox influence was strong from early in the 18th century until 1917 when independence was attained. The first of several apostolic administrators was appointed in 1924. The small Catholic community was hard hit during the 1940-91 Soviet occupation (not recognized by the Holy See or the United States). (See Index for 1993 papal visit.)

Ethiopia*

Archd., 1; dioc., 2; v.a., 6; card., 1; bp., 7; parishes, 279; priests, 506 (176 dioc., 330 rel.); p.d., 4; sem., 301; bros., 86; srs., 941; bap., 18,340; Caths., 361,000 (.67%); tot. pop., 53,380,000. (Statistics include Eritrea which became an independent state May 24, 1993.)

People's republic in northeast Africa; capital, Addis Ababa. The country was evangelized by missionaries from Egypt in the fourth century and had a bishop by about 340. Following the lead of its parent body, the Egyptian (Coptic) Church, the Church in the area succumbed to the Monophysite heresy in the sixth century. Catholic influence was negligible for centuries. An ordinariate for the Ethiopian Rite was established in Eritrea in 1930. An apostolic delegation was set up in Addis Ababa in 1937 and several jurisdictions were organized, some under the Congregation for the Oriental Churches and others under the Congregation for the Evangelization of Peoples. Most of the Catholics in the country are in the former Italian colony of Eritrea. The first Ethiopian cardinal (Abp. Paulos Tzadua of Addis Ababa) was named in 1985.

Falkland Islands

P.a., 1; parish, 1; priests, 3 (rel.); bap., 2; Caths., 300; tot. pop., 2,000.

British colony off the southern tip of South America; capital, Port Stanley. The islands are called Islas Malvinas by Argentina which also claims sovereignty.

Faroe Islands

Parish, 1; priest, 1 (rel.); p.d., 1; srs., 10; Caths., 100; tot. pop., 47,000.

Self-governing island group in North Atlantic; Danish possession. Under ecclesiastical jurisdiction of Copenhagen diocese.

Fiji*

Archd., 1; abp., 1; parishes, 34; priests, 99 (21 dioc., 78 rel.); sem., 56; bros., 83; srs., 186; bap., 1,100; Caths., 71,000 (9%); tot. pop., 780,000.

Independent island group (100 inhabited) in the southwest Pacific; capital, Suva. Marist missionaries began work in 1844 after Methodism had been firmly established. A prefecture apostolic was organized in 1863. The hierarchy was established in 1966.

Finland*

Dioc., 1; bp., 1; parishes, 7; priests, 22 (5 dioc., 17 rel.); p.d., 2; sem., 1; bros., 1; srs., 41; bap., 120; Caths., 5,000 (.1%); tot. pop., 5,030,000.

Republic in northern Europe; capital, Helsinki. Swedes evangelized the country in the 12th century. The Reformation swept the country, resulting in the prohibition of Catholicism in 1595, general reorganization of ecclesiastical life and affairs, and dominance of the Evangelical Lutheran Church. Catholics were given religious liberty in 1781 but missionaries and conversions were forbidden by law. The first Finnish priest since the Reformation was ordained in 1903 in Paris. A vicariate apostolic for Finland was erected in 1920 (made a diocese in 1955). A law on religious liberty, enacted in 1923, banned the foundation of monasteries.

France*

Archd., 19; dioc., 75; prel., 1; ap. ex., 1; ord., 1; mil. ord.; card., 8; abp., 31; bp., 164; parishes, 34,522; priests, 31,564 (24,624 dioc., 6,940 rel.); p.d., 749; sem., 1,524; bros., 4,572; srs., 63,794; bap., 462,779; Caths., 47,625,000 (83.5%); tot. pop., 57,050,000.

Republic in western Europe; capital, Paris. Christianity was known around Lyons by the middle of the second century. By 250 there were 30 bishoprics. The hierarchy reached a fair degree of organization by the end of the fourth century. Vandals and Franks subsequently invaded the territory and caused barbarian turmoil and doctrinal problems because of their Arianism. The Frankish nation was converted following the baptism of Clovis about 496. Christianization was complete by some time in the seventh century. From then on the Church, its leaders and people, figured in virtually every important development — religious, cultural, political and social — through the periods of the Carolingians, feudalism, the Middle Ages and monarchies to the end of the 18th century. The great University of Paris became one of the intellectual centers of the 13th century. Churchmen and secular rulers were involved with developments surrounding the Avignon residence of the popes and curia from 1309 until near the end of the 14th century and with the disastrous Western Schism that followed. Strong currents of Gallicanism and conciliarism ran through ecclesiastical and secular circles in France; the former was an ideology and movement to restrict papal control of the Church in the country, the latter sought to make the pope subservient to a general council. Calvinism invaded the country about the middle of the 16th century and won a strong body of converts. Jansenism with its rigorous spirit and other aberrations appeared in the next century, to be followed by the highly influential Enlightenment. The Revolution which started in 1789 and was succeeded by the Napoleonic period completely changed the status of the Church, taking a toll of numbers by persecution and defection and disenfranchising the Church in practically every way. Throughout the 19th century the Church was caught up in the whirl of imperial and republican developments and made the victim of official hostility, popular indifference and liberal opposition. In this century, the Church has struggled with problems involving the heritage of the Revolution and its aftermath, the alienation of intellectuals, liberalism, the estrangement of the working classes because of the Church's former identification with the ruling class, and the massive needs of contemporary society.

French Guiana

Dioc., 1; bp., 1; parishes, 24; priests, 30 (8 dioc., 22 rel.); p.d., 1; bros., 4; srs., 103; bap., 1,892; Caths., 95,000; tot. pop., 130,000. (AD)
French overseas department on the northeast coast of South America; capital, Cayenne. Catholicism was introduced in the 17th century. The Cayenne diocese was established in 1956.

French Polynesia

Archd., 1; dioc., 1; abp., 1; bp., 2; parishes, 78; priests, 36 (10 dioc., 26 rel.); p.d., 11; sem., 14; bros., 37; srs., 67; bap., 1,568; Caths., 77,000; tot. pop., 208,000. (AD)
French overseas territory in the southern Pacific, including Tahiti and the Marquesas Islands; capital, Papeete. The first phase of evangelization in the Marquesas Islands, begun in 1838, resulted in 216 baptisms in 10 years. A vicariate was organized in 1848 but real progress was not made until after the baptism of native rulers in 1853. Persecution caused missionaries to leave the islands several times. By the 1960s, more than 95 per cent of the population was Catholic. Isolated attempts to evangelize Tahiti were made in the 17th and 18th centuries. Two Picpus Fathers began missionary work in 1831. A vicariate was organized in 1848. By 1908, despite the hindrances of Protestant opposition, disease and other factors, the Church had firm roots.

Gabon*

Archd., 1; dioc., 3; abp., 1; bp., 3; parishes, 74; priests, 86 (28 dioc., 58 rel.); sem., 49; bros., 29; srs., 154; catechists, 1,238; bap., 8,627; Caths., 638,000 (52.7%); tot. pop., 1,210,000.
Republic on the west coast of central Africa; capital Libreville. Sporadic missionary effort took place

before 1881 when effective evangelization began. The hierarchy was established in 1955.

The Gambia*

Dioc., 1; bp., 1; parishes, 13; priests, 25 (7 dioc., 18 rel.); sem., 11; bros., 10; srs., 47; bap., 1,105; Caths., 19,000 (2%); tot. pop., 880,000.
Republic (1970) on the northwestern coast of Africa, capital, Banjui. Christianity was introduced by Portuguese explorers in the 15th century; effective evangelization began in 1822. The country was under the jurisdiction of a vicariate apostolic until 1931. The hierarchy was established in 1957.

Georgia*

Parish, 1; priests, 4(rel); srs., 10; Caths., 60,000 (1%); tot. pop., 5,470,000
Independent (1991) state in the Caucasus; former Soviet republic; capital, Tbilisi. Christianity came to the area under Roman influence and, according to tradition, was spread through the efforts of St. Nino (or Christiana), a maiden who was brought as a captive to the country and is venerated as its apostle.

Germany*

Archd., 5; dioc., 18; ap. ex., 1; a.a., 4 (includes 3 areas with permanent apostolic administrators); mil. ord.; card., 5 (3 head sees); abp., 4; bp., 94; parishes, 12,945; priests, 22,025 (16,728 dioc., 5,297 rel.); p.d., 1,597; sem., 2,608; bros., 2,257; srs., 50,316; bap., 298,635; Caths., 28,599,000 (35.6%); tot. pop., 80,211,000.
Country in northern Europe; capital, Berlin. From 1949-90 it was partitioned into the Communist German Democratic Republic in the East (capital, East Berlin) and the German Federal Republic in the West (capital, Bonn). Christianity was introduced in the third century, if not earlier. Trier, which became a center for missionary activity, had a bishop by 400. Visigoth invaders introduced Arianism in the fifth century but were converted in the seventh century by the East Franks, Celtic and other missionaries. St. Boniface, the apostle of Germany, established real ecclesiastical organization in the eighth century. The Church had great influence during the Carolingian period. Bishops from that time onward began to act in dual roles as pastors and rulers, a state of affairs which led inevitably to confusion and conflict in Church-state relations and perplexing problems of investiture. The Church developed strength and vitality through the Middle Ages but succumbed to abuses which antedated and prepared the ground for the Reformation. Luther's actions from 1517 made Germany a confessional battleground. Religious strife continued until conclusion of the Peace of Westphalia at the end of the Thirty Years' War in 1648. Nearly a century earlier the Peace of Augsburg (1555) had been designed, without success, to assure a degree of tranquillity by recognizing the legitimacy of different religious confessions in different states, depending on the decisions of princes. The implicit principle that princes should control the churches emerged in practice into the absolutism and Josephinism of subsequent

years. St. Peter Canisius and his fellow Jesuits spearheaded a Counter Reformation in the second half of the 16th century. Before the end of the century, however, 70 per cent of the population of north and central Germany were Lutheran. Calvinism also had established a strong presence. The Church gained internal strength in a defensive position. Through much of the 19th century, however, its influence was eclipsed by Protestant intellectuals and other influences. It suffered some impoverishment also as a result of shifting boundaries and the secularization of property shortly after 1800. It came under direct attack in the Kulturkampf of the 1870s but helped to generate the opposition which resulted in a dampening of the campaign of Bismarck against it. Despite action by Catholics on the social front and other developments, discrimination against the Church spilled over into the 20th century and lasted beyond World War I. Catholics in politics struggled with others to pull the country through numerous postwar crises. The dissolution of the Center Party, agreed to by the bishops in 1933 without awareness of the ultimate consequences, contributed negatively to the rise of Hitler to supreme power. Church officials protested the Nazi anti-Church and anti-Semitic actions, but to no avail. After World War II Christian leadership had much to do with the recovery of Western Germany. East Germany, gone Communist under Russian auspices, initiated a program of control and repression of the Church in 1948 and 1949. With no prospect of success for measures designed to split bishops, priests, religious and lay persons, the regime concentrated most of its attention on mind control, especially of the younger generation, by the elimination of religious schools, curtailment of freedom for religious instruction and formation, severe restriction of the religious press, and the substitution from the mid-50s of youth initiation and Communist ceremonies for the rites of baptism, confirmation, marriage, and funerals. Bishops were generally forbidden to travel outside the Republic. The number of priests decreased, partly because of reduced seminary enrollments ordered by the East German government. In 1973, the Vatican appointed three apostolic administrators and one auxiliary (all titular bishops) for the areas of three West German dioceses located in East Germany. The official reunification of Germany took place Oct. 3, 1990. The separate episcopal conferences for East and West Germany were merged to form one conference in November, 1990.

Ghana*

Archd., 3; dioc., 7; abp., 2; bp., 8; parishes, 213; priests, 703 (506 dioc., 197 rel.); p.d., 2; sem., 341; bros., 181; srs., 727; catechists, 3,782; bap., 46,118; Caths., 1,958,000 (12.6%); tot. pop., 15,510,000.

Republic on the western coast of Africa, bordering on the Gulf of Guinea; capital, Accra. Priests visited the country in 1482, 11 years after discovery by the Portuguese, but missionary effort — hindered by the slave trade and other factors — was slight until 1880 when systematic evangelization began. A prefecture apostolic was set up in 1879. The hierarchy was established in 1950.

Gibraltar

Dioc., 1; bp., 1; parishes, 5; priests, 11 (9 dioc., 2 rel.); sem., 6; srs., 6 ; bap., 284; Caths., 24,000; tot. pop., 34,000.

British dependency on the tip of the Spanish Peninsula on the Mediterranean. Evangelization took place after the Moors were driven out near the end of the 15th century. The Church was hindered by the British who acquired the colony in 1713. Most of the Catholics were, and are, Spanish and Italian immigrants and their descendants. A vicariate apostolic was organized in 1817. The diocese was erected in 1910.

Greece*

Archd., 4; dioc., 4; v.a., 1; ap. ex., 1; ord., 1; abp., 5; bp., 2; parishes, 64; priests, 105 (55 dioc., 50 rel.); sem., 5; bros., 37; srs., 144; bap., 637; Caths., 57,000 (.5%); tot. pop., 10,060,000.

Republic in southeastern Europe on the Balkan Peninsula; capital, Athens. St. Paul preached the Gospel at Athens and Corinth on his second missionary journey and visited the country again on his third tour. Other Apostles may have passed through also. Two bishops from Greece attended the First Council of Nicaea. After the division of the Roman Empire, the Church remained Eastern in rite and later broke ties with Rome as a result of the schism of 1054. A Latin-Rite jurisdiction was set up during the period of the Latin Empire of Constantinople, 1204-1261, but crumbled afterwards. Unity efforts of the Council of Florence had poor results. The country now has Greek Catholic and Latin jurisdictions. The Greek Orthodox Church is predominant.

Greenland (Kalaallit Nunaat)

Parish, 1; priest, 1 (rel.); Caths., 100; tot. pop., 56,000.

Danish island province northeast of North America; granted self rule in 1979; capital, Nuuk (Godthaab). Catholicism was introduced about 1000. The first diocese was established in 1124 and a line of bishops dated from then until 1537. The first known churches in the western hemisphere, dating from about the 11th century, were on Greenland; the remains of 19 have been unearthed. The departure of Scandinavians and spread of the Reformation reduced the Church to nothing. The Moravian Brethren evangelized the Eskimos from the 1720s to 1901. By 1930 the Danish Church — Evangelical Lutheran — was in full possession. Since 1930, priests have been in Greenland, which is part of the Copenhagen diocese.

Grenada*

Dioc., 1; bp., 1; parishes, 20; priests, 24 (6 dioc., 18 rel.); p.d., 4; sem., 2; bros., 4; srs., 36; catechists, 110; bap., 1,065; Caths., 60,000; tot. pop., 91,000.

Independent island state in the West Indies; capital, St. George's.

Guadeloupe

Dioc., 1; bp., 2; parishes, 43; priests, 64 (45 dioc., 19 rel.); p.d., 3; sem., 6; bros., 3; srs., 226; catechists, 2,654; bap., 5,051; Caths., 350,000; tot. pop., 387,000 (AD).

French overseas department in the Leeward Islands of the West Indies; capital, Basse-Terre. Catholicism was introduced in the islands in the 16th century.

Guam

Archd., 1; archbp., 1; parishes, 25; priests, 48 (20 dioc., 28 rel.); p.d., 7; sem., 8; bros., 2; srs., 121; bap., 2,666; Caths., 117,000; tot. pop., 130,000.

Outlying area of U.S. in the southwest Pacific; capital, Agana. The first Mass was offered in the Mariana Islands in 1521. The islands were evangelized by the Jesuits, from 1668, and other missionaries. The first native Micronesian bishop was ordained in 1970. The Agana diocese, which had been a suffragan of San Francisco, was made a metropolitan see in 1984.

Guatemala*

Archd., 1; dioc., 8; prel., 2; v.a., 2; abp., 2; bp., 19; parishes, 383; priests, 766 (254 dioc., 512 rel.); p.d., 5; sem., 672; bros., 418; srs., 1,539; bap., 253,210; Caths. 7,634,000 (80.6%); tot. pop. 9,470,000.

Republic in Central America; capital, Guatemala City. Evangelization dates from the beginning of Spanish occupation in 1524. The first diocese, for all Central American territories administered by the captaincy general of Guatemala, was established in 1534. The country became independent in 1839, following annexation to Mexico in 1821, secession in 1823 and membership in the Central American Federation from 1825. In 1870, a government installed by a liberal revolution repudiated the concordat of 1853 and took active measures against the Church. Separation of Church and state was decreed; religious orders were suppressed and their property seized; priests and religious were exiled; schools were secularized. Full freedom was subsequently granted. In recent years, the bishops have repeatedly condemned political violence and social injustice which have created a crisis in the country.

Guinea*

Archd., 1; dioc., 1; p.a., 1; abp., 1; bp., 1; parishes, 24; priests, 46 (43 dioc., 3 rel.); sem., 36; bros., 3; srs., 45; bap., 1,988; Caths., 127,000 (2%); tot. pop., 5,930,000.

Republic on the west coast of Africa; capital, Conakry. Occasional missionary work followed exploration by the Portuguese about the middle of the 15th century; organized effort dates from 1877. The hierarchy was established in 1955. Following independence from France in 1958, Catholic schools were nationalized, youth organizations banned and missionaries restricted. Foreign missionaries were expelled in 1967. Archbishop Tchidimbo of Conakry, sentenced to life imprisonment in 1971 on a charge of conspiring to overthrow the government, was released in August, 1979; he resigned his see. Private schools, suppressed by the government for more than 20 years, were again authorized in 1984.

Guinea-Bissau*

Dioc., 1; bp., 1; parishes, 25; priests, 67 (4 dioc., 63 rel.); p.d., 1; sem., 19; bros., 9; srs., 94; bap., 1,000; Caths., 70,000 (7.1%); tot. pop., 980,000.

Formerly Portuguese Guinea. Independent state on the west coast of Africa; capital, Bissau. Catholicism was introduced in the second half of the 15th century but limited missionary work, hampered by the slave trade, had meager results. Missionary work in this century dates from 1933. A prefecture apostolic was established in 1955 (made a diocese in 1977).

Guyana

Dioc., 1; bp., 1; parishes, 30; priests, 39 (6 dioc., 33 rel.); sem., 2; bros., 2; srs., 40; catechists, 599; bap., 1,644; Caths., 87,000 (8%); tot. pop., 1,100,000.

Republic on the northern coast of South America; capital, Georgetown. In 1899 the Catholic Church and other churches were given equal status with the Church of England and the Church of Scotland, which had sole rights up to that time. Most of the Catholics are Portuguese. The Georgetown diocese was established in 1956, 10 years before Guyana became independent of England. The first native bishop was appointed in 1971. Schools were nationalized in 1976. Increased government interference was reported in 1980-81.

Haiti*

Archd., 2; dioc., 7; abp., 2; bp., 9; parishes, 223; priests, 491 (285 dioc., 206 rel.); p.d., 3; sem., 226; bros., 255; srs., 1,081; bap., 111,714; Caths., 5,926,000 (89.5%); tot. pop., 6,620,000.

Caribbean republic on the western third of Hispaniola adjacent to the Dominican Republic; captial, Port-au-Prince. Evangelization followed discovery by Columbus in 1492. Capuchins and Jesuits did most of the missionary work in the 18th century. From 1804, when independence was declared, until 1860, the country was in schism. Relations were regularized by a concordat concluded in 1860, when an archdiocese and four dioceses were established. Factors hindering the development of the Church have been a shortage of native clergy, inadequate religious instruction and the prevalence of voodoo. Political upheavals in the 1960s had serious effects on the Church. In 1984, a new concordat was concluded replacing the one in effect since 1860.

Honduras*

Archd., 1; dioc., 6; abp., 1; bp., 8; parishes, 141; priests, 310 (101 dioc., 209 rel.); p.d., 4; sem., 110; bros., 23; srs., 489; bap., 63,985; Caths., 4,920,000 (93.5%); tot. pop., 5,260,000.

Republic in Central America; capital, Tegucigalpa. Evangelization preceded establishment of the first diocese in the 16th century. Under Spanish rule and after independence from 1823, the Church held a favored position until 1880 when equal legal status was given to all religions. Harassment of priests and nuns working among peasants and Salvadoran refugees was reported in recent years.

Hong Kong

Dioc., 1; card., 1; bp., 1; parishes, 62; priests, 356 (78 dioc., 278 rel.); sem., 33; bros., 69; srs., 670; bap., 4,683; Caths., 255,000; tot. pop., 5,835,000.

British crown colony at the mouth of the Canton River, adjacent to the southeast Chinese province of Kwangtung. Most of the territory, leased from China, is scheduled for return in 1997. A prefecture apostolic was established in 1841. Members of the Pontifical Institute for Foreign Missions began work there in 1858. The Hong Kong diocese was erected in 1946.

Hungary*

Archd.(1993), 4; dioc. (1993), 7; abb., 1; ap. ex., 1; card., 1; abp., 3; bp., 18; parishes, 2,264; priests, 3,055 (2,435 dioc., 620 rel.); p.d., 7; sem., 432; bros., 111; srs., 2,109; bap., 82,653; Caths., 6,536,000 (63.2%); tot. pop., 10,340,000.

Republic in east central Europe; capital, Budapest. The early origins of Christianity in the country, whose territory was subject to a great deal of change, is not known. Magyars accepted Christianity about the end of the 10th century. St. Stephen I (d. 1038) promoted its spread and helped to organize some of its historical dioceses. Bishops early became influential in politics as well as in the Church. For centuries the country served as a buffer for the Christian West against barbarians from the East, notably the Mongols in the 13th century. Religious orders, whose foundations started from the 1130s, provided the most effective missionaries, pastors and teachers. Outstanding for years were the Franciscans and Dominicans; the Jesuits were noted for their work in the Counter-Reformation from the second half of the 16th century onwards. Hussites and Waldensians prepared the way for the Reformation which struck at almost the same time as the Turks. The Reformation made considerable progress after 1526, resulting in the conversion of large numbers to Lutheranism and Calvinism by the end of the century. Most of them or their descendants returned to the Church later, but many Magyars remained staunch Calvinists. Turks repressed the churches, Protestant as well as Catholic, during a reign of 150 years but they managed to survive. Domination of the Church was one of the objectives of government policy during the reigns of Maria Theresa and Joseph II in the second half of the 18th century; their Josephinism affected Church-state relations until the first World War. More than 100,000 Eastern-Rite schismatics were reunited with Rome about the turn of the 18th century. Secularization increased in the second half of the 19th century, which also witnessed the birth of many new Catholic organizations and movements to influence life in the nation and the Church. Catholics were involved in the social chaos and anti-religious atmosphere of the years following World War I, struggling with their compatriots for religious as well as political survival. After World War II Communist strength, which had manifested itself with less intensity earlier in the century, was great long before it forced the legally elected president out of office in 1947 and imposed a Soviet type of constitution on the country in 1949. The campaign against the Church started with the disbanding of Catholic organizations in 1946. In 1948, "Caritas," the Catholic charitable organization, was taken over and all Catholic schools, colleges and institutions were sup-

pressed. Interference in church administration and attempts to split the bishops preceded the arrest of Cardinal Mindszenty on Dec. 26, 1948, and his sentence to life imprisonment in 1949. (He was free for a few days during the unsuccessful uprising of 1956. He then took up residence at the U.S. Embassy in Budapest where he remained until September, 1971, when he was permitted to leave the country. He died in 1975 in Vienna.) In 1950, religious orders and congregations were suppressed and 10,000 religious were interned. At least 30 priests and monks were assassinated, jailed or deported. About 4,000 priests and religious were confined in jail or concentration camps. The government sponsored a national "Progressive Catholic" church and captive organizations for priests and "Catholic Action," which attracted only a small minority. Signs were clear in 1965 and 1966 that a 1964 agreement with the Holy See regarding episcopal appointments had settled nothing. Six bishops were appointed by the Holy See and some other posts were filled, but none of the prelates were free from government surveillance and harassment. Four new bishops were appointed by the Holy See in January and ordained in Budapest in February, 1969; three elderly prelates resigned their sees. Shortly thereafter, peace priests complained that the "too Roman" new bishops would not deal with them. Talks between Vatican and Hungarian representatives during the past several years resulted in the appointment of diocesan bishops to fill long-vacant sees. On Feb. 9, 1990, an accord was signed between the Holy See and Hungary reestablishing diplomatic relations. Pope John Paul II reorganized the ecclesiastical structure of Hungary in May, 1993.

Iceland*

Dioc., 1; bp., 1; parishes, 4; priests, 13 (8 dioc., 5 rel.); sem., 2; srs., 47; bap., 42; Caths., 3,000; tot. pop., 260,000.

Island republic between Norway and Greenland; capital, Reykjavik. Irish hermits were there in the eighth century. Missionaries subsequently evangelized the island and Christianity was officially accepted about 1000. The first bishop was ordained in 1056. The Black Death had dire effects and spiritual decline set in during the 15th century. Lutheranism was introduced from Denmark between 1537 and 1552 and made the official religion. Some Catholic missionary work was done in the 19th century. Religious freedom was granted to the few Catholics in 1874. A vicariate was erected in 1929 (made a diocese in 1968).

India*

Patriarchate, 1 (titular of East Indies); major archbishopric (1993; Syro-Malabar), 1; archd., 18; dioc. (1993), 107; card., 3; patr., 1; abp., 22; bp., 122; parishes, 6,847; priests, 15,215 (8,812 dioc., 6,403 rel.); p.d., 26; sem., 9,113; bros., 2,714; srs., 66,465; catechists, 30,719; bap., 310,966; Caths., 14,585,000 (1.7%); tot. pop. 849,640,000.

Republic on the subcontinent of south central Asia; capital, New Delhi. Long-standing tradition credits the Apostle Thomas with the introduction of Christianity in the Kerala area. Evangelization followed the establishment of Portuguese posts and the conquest of Goa in 1510. Jesuits, Franciscans, Dominicans, Augustinians and members of other religious orders figured in the early missionary history. An archdiocese for Goa, with two suffragan sees, was set up in 1558. Five provincial councils were held between 1567 and 1606. The number of Catholics in 1572 was estimated to be 280,000. This figure rose to 800,000 in 1700 and declined to 500,000 in 1800. Missionaries had some difficulties with the British East India Co. which exercised virtual government control from 1757 to 1858. They also had trouble because of a conflict that developed between policies of the Portuguese government, which pressed its rights of patronage in episcopal and clerical appointments, and the Congregation for the Propagation of the Faith, which sought greater freedom of action in the same appointments. This struggle eventuated in the schism of Goa between 1838 and 1857. In 1886, when the number of Catholics was estimated to be one million, the hierarchy for India and Ceylon was restored. Jesuits contributed greatly to the development of Catholic education from the second half of the 19th century. A large percentage of the Catholic population is located around Goa and Kerala and farther south. The country is predominantly Hindu. So-called anti-conversion laws in effect in several states have had a restrictive effect on pastoral ministry and social service.

Indonesia*

Archd., 8; dioc. (1993), 26; mil. ord.; card., 1; abp., 9; bps., 33; parishes, 871; priests, 2,176 (579 dioc., 1,597 rel.); p.d., 16; sem., 2,337; bros., 1,000; srs., 5,702; bap., 163,254; Caths., 4,871,000 (2.6%); tot. pop., 187,760,000.

Eastern Timor (former Portuguese Timor annexed by Indonesia in 1976): Dioc., 1; bp., 1; parishes, 24; priests, 66 (25 dioc., 41 rel.); p.d., 1; sem., 40; bros., 22; srs., 125; bap., 36,660; Caths., 632,000; tot. pop., 744,000.

Republic southeast of Asia, consisting of some 3,000 islands including Kalimantan (most of Borneo), Sulawesi (Celebes), Java, the Lesser Sundas, Moluccas, Sumatra, Timor and West Irian (Irian Jaya, western part of New Guinea); capital, Jakarta. Evangelization by the Portuguese began about 1511. St. Francis Xavier, greatest of the modern missionaries, spent some 14 months in the area. Christianity was strongly rooted in some parts of the islands by 1600. Islam's rise to dominance began at this time. The Dutch East Indies Co., which gained effective control in the 17th century, banned evangelization by Catholic missionaries for some time but Dutch secular and religious priests managed to resume the work. A vicariate of Batavia for all the Dutch East Indies was set up in 1841. About 90 per cent of the population is Muslim. The hierarchy was established in 1961.

Iran*

Archd., 4; dioc., 2; abp., 4; bp., 1; parishes, 24; priests, 21 (10 dioc., 11 rel.); sem., 2; bros., 3; srs., 34; bap., 122; Caths., 13,000 (.02%); tot. pop., 57,730,000.

Islamic republic (Persia until 1935) in southwestern Asia, between the Caspian Sea and the Persian Gulf; capital, Teheran. Some of the earliest Christian communities were established in this area outside the (then) Roman Empire. They suffered persecution in the fourth century and were then cut off from the outside world. Nestorianism was generally professed in the late fifth century. Islam became dominant after 640. Some later missionary work was attempted but without success. Religious liberty was granted in 1834, but Catholics were the victims of a massacre in 1918. Islam is the religion of perhaps 98 per cent of the population. In 1964 the country had approximately 120,000 Orthodox Oriental Christians (not in union with Rome). Catholics belong to the Latin, Armenian and Chaldean rites.

Iraq*

Patriarchate, 1; archd., 9; dioc., 5; patriarch, 1; abp., 11; bp., 3; parishes, 107; priests, 139 (112 dioc., 27 rel.); p.d., 3; sem., 81; bros., 27; srs., 337; bap., 6,497; Caths., 642,000 (3.2%); tot. pop., 19,580,000.

Republic in southwestern Asia, between Iran and Saudi Arabia; capital, Baghdad. Some of the earliest Christian communities were established in the area, whose history resembles that of Iran. Catholics belong to the Armenian, Chaldean, Latin and Syrian rites; Chaldeans are most numerous. Islam is the religion of some 90 per cent of the population.

Ireland*

Archd., 4; dioc., 22; card., 1; abp., 5; bp., 39; parishes, 1,353; priests, 6,410 (3,659 dioc., 2,751 rel.); p.d., 1; sem., 823; bros., 1,237; srs., 10,957; bap., 64,973 (preceding figures include Northern Ireland); Catholics in Ireland were about 95% of the estimated total population of 3,500,000.

Republic in the British Isles; capital, Dublin. St. Patrick, who is venerated as the apostle of Ireland, evangelized parts of the island for some years after the middle of the fifth century. Conversion of the island was not accomplished, however, until the seventh century or later. Celtic monks were the principal missionaries. The Church was organized along monastic lines at first, but a movement developed in the 11th century for the establishment of jurisdiction along episcopal lines. By that time many Roman usages had been adopted. The Church gathered strength during the period from the Norman Conquest of England to the reign of Henry VIII despite a wide variety of rivalries, wars, and other disturbances. Henry introduced an age of repression of the faith which continued for many years under several of his successors. The Irish suffered from proscription of the Catholic faith, economic and social disabilities, subjection to absentee landlords and a plantation system designed to keep them from owning property, and actual persecution which took an uncertain toll of lives up until about 1714. Some penal laws remained in force until emancipation in 1829. Nearly 100 years later Ireland was divided by two enactments which made Northern Ireland, consisting of six counties, part of the United Kindgom (1920) and gave dominion status to the Irish Free

State, made up of the other 26 counties (1922). This state (Eire, in Gaelic) was proclaimed the Republic of Ireland in 1949. The Catholic Church predominates but religious freedom is guaranteed for all.

Northern Ireland

Tot. pop., 1,578,000; Catholics comprise more than one third. (Other statistics are included in Ireland).

Part of the United Kingdom, it consists of six of the nine counties of Ulster in the northeast corner of Ireland; capital, Belfast. History is given under Ireland.

Israel

Patriarchates, 2 (Jerusalem for Latins; patriarchal vicariate for Greek-Melkites); archd., 1; patriarch, 1; abp., 2; bp., 2; parishes, 72; priests, 596 (74 dioc., 522 rel.); p.d., 3; sem., 112; bros., 141; srs., 968; bap., 793; Caths., 83,000; tot. pop., 4,970,000. (AD)

Parliamentary democracy in the Middle East, at the eastern end of the Mediterranean; capitals, Jerusalem and Tel Aviv (diplomatic). Israel was the birthplace of Christianity, the site of the first Christian communities. Some persecution was suffered in the early Christian era and again during the several hundred years of Roman control. Muslims conquered the territory in the seventh century and, except for the period of the Kingdom of Jerusalem established by Crusaders, remained in control most of the time up until World War I. The Church survived in the area, sometimes just barely, but it did not prosper greatly or show any notable increase in numbers. The British took over the protectorate of the area after World War I. Partition into Israel for the Jews and Palestine for the Arabs was approved by the United Nations in 1947. War broke out a year later with the proclamation of the Republic of Israel. The Israelis won the war and 50 percent more territory than they had originally been ceded. War broke out again for six days in June, 1967, and in October, 1973, resulting in a Middle East crisis which persists to the present time. Caught in the middle of the conflict are hundreds of thousands of dispossessed Palestinian refugees. Judaism is the faith professed by about 85 percent of the inhabitants; approximately one-third of them are considered observants. Most of the Arab minority are Muslims.

Italy*

Patriarchate, 1; archd. 58 (37 are metropolitan sees); dioc., 158; prel., 2; abb., 7; mil. ord.; card. (as of Sept. 15, 1993), 34; abp., 150; bps., 276 (hierarchy includes 220 residential, 26 coadjutors or auxiliaries, 84 in Curia offices, remainder in other offices or retired); parishes, 25,860; priests, 57,274 (37,765 dioc., 19,509 rel.); p.d., 1,146; sem., 6,172; bros., 4,947; srs., 125,887; bap., 514,378; Caths., 55,728,000 (97.6%); tot. pop., 57,050,000.

Republic in southern Europe; capital, Rome. A Christian community was formed early at Rome, probably by the middle of the first century. St. Peter established his see there. He and St. Paul suffered death for the faith there in the 60s. The early Christians were persecuted at various times there, as in other parts of the empire, but the Church developed in numbers and influence, gradually spreading out from towns and cities in the center and south to rural areas and the north. Organization, in the process of formation in the second century, developed greatly between the fifth and eighth centuries. By the latter date the Church had already come to grips with serious problems, including doctrinal and disciplinary disputes that threatened the unity of faith, barbarian invasions, and the need for the pope and bishops to take over civil responsibilities because of imperial default. The Church has been at the center of life on the peninsula throughout the centuries. It emerged from underground in 313, with the Edict of Milan, and rose to a position of prestige and lasting influence. It educated and converted the barbarians, preserved culture through the early Middle Ages and passed it on to later times, suffered periods of decline and gained strength through recurring reforms, engaged in military combat for political reasons and intellectual combat for the preservation and development of doctrine, saw and patronized the development of the arts, experienced all human strengths and weaknesses in its members, knew triumph and the humiliation of failure. For long centuries, from the fourth to the 19th, the Church was a temporal as well as spiritual power. This temporal aspect complicated its history in Italy. Since the 1870s, however, when the Papal States were annexed by the Kingdom of Italy, the history became simpler — but remained complicated — as the Church, shorn of temporal power, began to find new freedom for the fulfillment of its spiritual mission. In 1985, a new concordat was ratified between the Vatican and Italy, replacing one in effect since 1929.

Jamaica*

Archd., 1; dioc., 1; v.a., 1; abp., 1; bp., 2; parishes, 72; priests, 90 (33 dioc., 57 rel.); p.d., 14; sem., 5; bros., 8; srs., 214; bap., 1,591; Caths., 105,000; tot. pop., 2,370,000.

Republic in the West Indies; capital, Kingston. Franciscans and Dominicans evangelized the island from about 1512 until 1655. Missionary work was interrupted after the English took possession but was resumed by Jesuits about the turn of the 19th century. A vicariate apostolic was organized in 1837. The hierarchy was established in 1967. (See Index for 1993 papal visit.)

Japan*

Archd., 3; dioc., 13; p.a., 1; card., 1; abp., 4; bp., 20; parishes, 909; priests, 1,907 (535 dioc., 1,372 rel.); p.d., 6; sem., 222; bros., 313; srs., 6,892; bap., 9,758; Caths., 436,000 (.35%); tot. pop., 123,920,000.

Archipelago in the northwest Pacific; capital, Tokyo. Jesuits began evangelization in the middle of the 16th century and about 300,000 converts, most of them in Kyushu, were reported at the end of the century. The Nagasaki Martyrs were victims of persecution in 1597. Another persecution took some 4,000 lives between 1614 and 1651. Missionaries, banned for two centuries, returned about the middle of the 19th century and found Christian communities still surviving in Nagasaki and other places in Kyushu. A vicariate was organized in 1866. Religious freedom was guaranteed in 1889. The hierarchy was established in 1891.

Jerusalem

The entire city, site of the first Christian community has been under Israeli control since the Israeli-Arab war of June, 1967. There are two patriarchates of Jerusalem, Melkite and Latin. (AD)

Jordan

Archd., 1; abp., 1; bp., 1; parishes, 65; priests, 65 (58 dioc., 7 rel.); p.d., 2; sem., 13; bros., 5; srs., 261; bap., 1,217; Caths., 51,000 (1.2%); tot. pop., 4,140,000.

Constitutional monarchy in the Middle East; capital, Amman. Christianity there dates from apostolic times. Survival of the faith was threatened many times under the rule of Muslims from 636 and Ottoman Turks from 1517 to 1918, and in the Islamic Emirate of Trans-Jordan from 1918 to 1949. Since the creation of Israel, some 500,000 Palestinian refugees, some of them Christians, have been in Jordan. Islam is the state religion but religious freedom is guaranteed for all. The Greek Melkite-Rite Archdiocese of Petra and Philadelphia is located in Jordan. Latin (Roman)-Rite Catholics are under the jurisdiction of the Latin Patriarchate of Jerusalem.

Kazakhstan*

A.a., 1; bp., 1; priests, 17 (10 dioc., 7 rel.); srs., 8; Caths., 500,000; tot. pop., 16,871,000.

Independent republic (1991); formerly part of USSR; capital, Alma-Ata. A Latin-rite apostolic administration was established in 1991.

Kenya*

Archd. 4; dioc., 14; mil. ord.; card., 1; abp. 4; bp. 15; parishes, 482; priests, 1,195 (591 dioc., 604 rel.); sem., 1,369; bros., 477; srs., 2,784; catechists, 8,679; bap., 237,280; Caths., 5,621,000 (21.7%); tot. pop., 25,910,000.

Republic in eastern Africa bordering on the Indian Ocean; capital, Nairobi. Systematic evangelization by the Holy Ghost Missionaries began in 1889, nearly 40 years after the start of work by Protestant missionaries. The hierarchy was established in 1953. Three metropolitan sees were established in 1990.

Kiribati

Dioc., 1; bp., 1; parishes, 23; priests, 19 (5 dioc., 14 rel.); sem., 10; bros., 21; srs., 68; bap., 1,715; Caths., 38,000 (52.7%); tot.pop., 72,000.

Former British colony (Gilbert Islands) in Oceania; became independent July 12, 1979; capital, Bairiki on Tarawa. French Missionaries of the Sacred Heart began work in the islands in 1888. A vicariate for the islands was organized in 1897. The hierarchy was established in 1966.

Korea

North Korea: Dioc., 2; abb., 1; bp., 1 (exiled); tot. pop., 22,190,000. No recent Catholic statistics available; there were an estimated 100,000 Catholics reported in 1969.

South Korea: *Archd., 3; dioc., 11; mil. ord.; card., 1; abp., 2; bp., 17; parishes, 820; priests, 1,760 (1,422 dioc., 338 rel.); sem., 1,748; bros., 406; srs., 5,683; bap., 166,096; Caths., 2,886,000 (6.6%); tot. pop., 43,270,000.*

Peninsula in eastern Asia, east of China, divided into the (Communist) Democratic People's Republic in the North, formed May 1, 1948, with Pyongyang as its capital; and the Republic of Korea in the South, with Seoul as the capital. Some Catholics may have been in Korea before it became a "hermit kingdom" toward the end of the 16th century and closed its borders to foreigners. The real introduction to Catholicism came in 1784 through lay converts. A priest arriving in the country in 1794 found 4,000 Catholics there who had never seen a priest. A vicariate was erected in 1831 but was not manned for several years thereafter. There were 15,000 Catholics by 1857. Four persecutions in the 19th century took a terrible toll; several thousands died in the last one, 1866-69. (One hundred and three martyrs of this period were canonized by Pope John Paul II during his 1984 apostolic visit to South Korea.) Freedom of religion was granted in 1883 when Korea opened its borders. Progress was made thereafter. The hierarchy was established in 1962. Since the war of 1950-53, there have been no signs of Catholic life in the North which has been blanketed by a news blackout. In July 1972, both Koreas agreed to seek peaceful means of reunification. Bishop Tji of Won Ju, South Korea, convicted and sentenced to 15 years' imprisonment in 1974 on a charge of inciting to rebellion, was released in February, 1975. The 44th International Eucharistic Congress was held in Seoul, South Korea, Oct. 5-8, 1989.

Kuwait*

V.a., 1; bp., 1; parishes, 5; priests, 6 (2 dioc., 4 rel.); sem., 1; srs., 17; bap., 203; Caths., 15,000; tot. pop., 2,100,000.

Constitutional monarchy (sultanate or sheikdom) in southwest Asia bordering on the Persian Gulf. Remote Christian origins probably date to apostolic times. Islam is the predominant and official religion.

Kyrgyzstan*

Independent republic bordering China; former Soviet republic; capital, Bishkek (former name, Frunze). Established diplomatic relations with the Vatican, August, 1992. No statistics available. Total population, 4,450,000.

Laos

V.a., 4; bp., 3. No statistics available. Catholics numbered 35,000 (1% of the total population) in 1974. Tot. Pop., 4,260,000. (AD)

People's republic in southeast Asia, surrounded by China, Vietnam, Cambodia, Thailand and Myanmar (Burma); capital, Vientiane. Systematic evangelization by French missionaries started about 1881; earlier efforts ended in 1688. The first mission was established in 1885 by Father Xavier Guégo. A vicariate apostolic was organized in 1899 when there were 8,000 Catholics and 2,000 catechumens in the country. Most of the foreign missionaries were expelled following the communist take-over in 1975. Buddhism is the state religion.

Latvia*
Archd., 1; dioc., 1; bp., 3; parishes, 192; priests, 175 (163 dioc., 12 rel.); sem., 34; srs., 30; bap., 10,695; Caths., 506,000 (18.6%); tot. pop., 2,710,000.
Independent (1991) Baltic republic; capital, Riga. (Forcibly absorbed by the U.S.S.R. in 1940; it regained independence in 1991). Catholicism was introduced late in the 12th century. Lutheranism became the dominant religion after 1530. Catholics were free to practice their faith during the long period of Russian control and during independence from 1918 to 1940. The relatively small Catholic community was repressed during the 1940-91 Soviet take-over of Latvia which was not recognized by the Holy See or the United States. (See Index for 1993 papal visit.)

Lebanon*
Archd., 12 (1 Armenian, 4 Maronite, 7 Greek Melkite); dioc., 7 (1 Chaldean, 6 Maronite); v.a., 1 (Latin); card., 1 (Patr. Antoine Khoraiche of Maronites); patriarchs, 3 (patriarchs of Antioch of the Maronites, Antioch of the Syrians and Cilicia of the Armenians who reside in Lebanon); abp. and bp., 35; parishes, 1,029; priests, 1,304 (655 dioc., 649 rel.); p.d., 4; sem., 365; bros., 126; srs., 2,861; bap., 16,249; Caths., 2,233,000; tot. pop., 3,300,000.
Republic in the Middle East, north of Israel; capital, Beirut. Christianity, introduced in apostolic times, was firmly established by the end of the fourth century and has remained so despite heavy Muslim influence since early in the seventh century. The country is the center of the Maronite Rite. In the 1980s, the country was torn by violence and often heavy fighting among rival political-religious factions drawn along Christian-Muslim lines.

Lesotho*
Archd., 1; dioc., 3; abp., 1; bp., 3; parishes, 76; priests, 134 (38 dioc., 96 rel.); sem., 38; bros., 22; srs., 646; bap., 28,679; Caths., 693,000 (37.8%); tot. pop., 1,830,000.
Constitutional monarchy, an enclave in the southeastern part of the Republic of South Africa; capital, Maseru. Oblates of Mary Immaculate, the first Catholic missionaries in the area, started evangelization in 1862. A prefecture apostolic was organized in 1894. The hierarchy was established in 1951.

Liberia*
Archd., 1; dioc., 2; abp., 1; bp., 2; parishes, 58; priests, 42 (18 dioc., 24 rel.); p.d., 4; sem., 21; bros., 19; srs., 61; bap. 3,761; Caths., 79,000 (3%); tot. pop., 2,520,000.
Republic in western Africa, bordering on the Atlantic; capital, Monrovia. Missionary work and influence, dating interruptedly from the 16th century, were slight before the Society of African Missions undertook evangelization in 1906. The hierarchy was established in 1982. In July, 1993, a peace ac-

cord was signed ending the civil war which began in 1989. The war had claimed the lives of 150,000 and made refugees of 100,000. (See Index for deaths of American Missionary Sisters.)

Libya
V.a., 3; p.a., 1; bp., 1; parishes, 2; priests, 11 (1 dioc., 10 rel.); srs., 97; bap., 185; Caths., 40,000 (.84%); tot. pop., 4,710,000. (AD)
Arab state in northern Africa, on the Mediterranean between Egypt and Tunisia; capital, Tripoli. Christianity was probably preached in the area at an early date but was overcome by the spread of Islam from the 630s. Islamization was complete by 1067 and there has been no Christian influence since then. The Catholics in the country belong to the foreign colony. Islam is the state religion.

Liechtenstein*
Parishes, 10; priests, 32 (20 dioc., 12 rel); bros., 4; srs., 86; bap., 300; Caths., 22,000; tot. pop., 29,000.
Constitutional monarchy in central Europe, in the Alps and on the Rhine between Switzerland and Austria; capital, Vaduz. Christianity in the country dates from the fourth century; the area has been under the jurisdiction of Chur, Switzerland, since about that time. The Reformation had hardly any influence in the country. Catholicism is the state religion but religious freedom for all is guaranteed by law.

Lithuania*
Archd., 2; dioc., 4; card., 1; abp., 2; bp., 8; parishes, 662; priests, 724 (640 dioc., 84 rel.); p.d., 3; sem., 242; bros., 20; srs., 770; bap., 24,675; Caths., 2,992,000 (80%); tot. pop., 3,740,000.
Baltic republic forcibly absorbed and under Soviet domination from 1940; regained independence, 1991; captial, Vilna (Vilnius). Catholicism was introduced in 1251 and a short-lived diocese was established by 1260. Effective evangelization took place between 1387 and 1417, when Catholicism became the state religion. Losses to Lutheranism in the 16th century were overcome. Efforts of czars to "russify" the Church between 1795 and 1918 were strongly resisted. Concordat relations with the Vatican were established in 1927, nine years after independence from Russia and 13 years before the start of another kind of Russian control with the following results, among others: all convents closed since 1940; four seminaries shut down; appointment to one seminary (Kaunas) only with government approval; priests restricted in pastoral ministry and subject to appointment by government officials; no religious services outside churches; no religious press; religious instruction banned; parish installations and activities controlled by directives enacted in 1976; two bishops — Vincentas Sladkevicius and Julijonas Steponavicius — forbidden to act as bishops and relegated to remote parishes in 1957 and 1961, respectively; arrest, imprisonment or detention in Siberia for four bishops, 185 priests, 275 lay persons between 1945 and 1955. Despite such developments and conditions, there was a strong and vigorous underground Church in

Lithuania, where the Soviet government found its repressive potential limited by the solidarity of popular resistance. In July, 1982, Rev. Antanas Vaicius was ordained apostolic administrator of the Telsiai diocese and Klaipeda prelature. Auxiliary Bishop Vincentas Sladkevicius, of Kaisiadorys, under severe government restrictions since 1957, was allowed to return to his see in 1982 following his appointment as apostolic administrator. (He was made a cardinal in 1988 and appointed archbishop of Kaunas in March, 1989.) In 1983, four of the five bishops were allowed to go to Rome for their *ad limina* visit. In December, 1988, Bishop Steponavicius was allowed to return to his diocese and was named an archbishop in 1989. (He died in 1991.) The Vatican announcement in March, 1989, of the reorganizaton of the hierarchy indicated some change of attitude on the part of the government. Three former apostolic administrators (titular bishops) were named ordinaries; three apostolic administrators (two of them new) were appointed. The Soviet 1940-91 take-over of Lithuania was not recognized by the Holy See or the United States. (See Index for 1993 papal visit.)

Luxembourg*

Archd., 1; abp., 1; parishes, 274; priests, 344 (260 dioc., 84 rel.); p.d., 2; sem., 7; bros., 26; srs., 899; bap., 3,807; Caths. 356,000 (94.9%); tot. pop., 375,000.

Constitutional monarchy in western Europe, between Belgium, Germany and France; capital, Luxembourg. Christianity, introduced in the fifth and sixth centuries, was firmly established by the end of the eighth century. A full-scale parish system was in existence in the ninth century. Monastic influence was strong until the Reformation, which had minimal influence in the country. The Church experienced some adverse influence from the currents of the French Revolution.

Macau (Macao)

Dioc., 1; bp., 1; parishes, 9; priests, 72 (39 dioc., 33 rel.); sem., 2; bros., 13; srs., 150; bap., 443; Caths., 22,000; tot. pop., 500,000.

Portuguese-administered territory in southeast Asia across the Pearl River estuary from Hong Kong; scheduled to revert to China in 1999. Christianity was introduced by the Jesuits in 1557. Diocese was established in 1576. Macau served as a base for missionary work in Japan and China.

Macedonia

Former Yugoslav republic; declared independence in 1992; capital, Skopje. There is a diocese, Skopje (Macedonia)-Prizren (Serbia); statistics are included in Yugoslavia.

Madagascar*

Archd., 3; dioc., 14; card., 1; abp., 3; bp., 18; parishes, 264; priests, 737 (221 dioc., 516 rel.); p.d., 3; sem., 463; bros., 418; srs., 2,570; bap., 96,314; Caths., 2,618,000 (22.7%); tot. pop. 11,490,000.

Republic (Malagasy Republic) off the eastern coast of Africa; capital, Antananarivo. Missionary

efforts were generally fruitless from early in the 16th century until the Jesuits were permitted to start open evangelization about 1845. A prefecture apostolic was set up in 1850 and a vicariate apostolic in the north was placed in charge of the Holy Ghost Fathers in 1898. There were 100,000 Catholics by 1900. The first native bishop was ordained in 1936. The hierarchy was established in 1955.

Madeira Islands

Portuguese province, an archipelago 340 miles west of the northwestern coast of Africa; capital, Funchal. Catholicism has had a continuous history since the first half of the 15th century. The diocese of Funchal was established in 1514. Statistics are included in Portugal.

Malawi*

Archd., 1; dioc., 6; abp., 1; bp., 5; parishes, 136; priests, 387 (214 dioc., 173 rel.); sem., 221; bros., 63; srs., 686; bap., 137,282; catechists, 7,702; Caths., 1,893,000 (22.1%); tot. pop., 8,560,000.

Republic in the interior of eastern Africa; capital, Lilongwe. Missionary work, begun by Jesuits in the late 16th and early 17th centuries, was generally ineffective until the end of the 19th century. The Missionaries of Africa (White Fathers) arrived in 1889 and later were joined by others. A vicariate was set up in 1897. The hierarchy was established in 1959.

Malaysia

Archd., 2; dioc. (1993), 6; abp., 2; bp., 6; parishes, 137; priests, 219 (157 dioc., 62 rel.); p.d., 2; sem., 63; bros., 77; srs., 587; bap., 20,726; Caths., 558,000 (3%); tot. pop., 18,330,000. (AD)

Parliamentary democracy in southeastern Asia; federation of former states of Malaya, Sabah (former Br. North Borneo), and Sarawak; capital, Kuala Lumpur. Christianity, introduced by Portuguese colonists about 1511, was confined almost exclusively to Malacca until late in the 18th century. The effectiveness of evangelization increased from then on because of the recruitment and training of native clergy. Singapore (see separate entry), founded in 1819, became a center for missionary work. Seventeen thousand Catholics were in the Malacca diocese in 1888. Effective evangelization in Sabah and Sarawak began in the second half of the 19th century. The hierarchy was established in 1973.

Maldives

Republic, an archipelago 400 miles southwest of India and Ceylon; capital, Male. No serious attempt was ever made to evangelize the area, which is completely Muslim. Population, 220,000.

Mali*

Archd., 1; dioc., 5; abp., 1; bp., 5; parishes, 38; priests, 149 (46 dioc., 103 rel.); sem., 58; bros., 21; srs., 171; bap., 3,428; Caths., 96,000 (1%); tot. pop., 9,510,000.

Republic, inland in western Africa; capital, Bamako. Catholicism was introduced late in the second half of the 19th century. Missionary work made little progress in the midst of the predominantly Muslim population. A vicariate was set up in 1921. The hierarchy was established in 1955.

Malta*
Archd., 1; dioc., 1; abp., 2; bp., 1; parishes, 80; priests, 1,016 (522 dioc., 494 rel.); p.d., 1; sem., 85; bros., 110; srs., 1,377; bap., 5,593; Caths., 356,000 (98.6%); tot. pop., 361,000.

Republic 58 miles south of Sicily; capital, Valletta. Early catacombs and inscriptions are evidence of the early introduction of Christianity. St. Paul was shipwrecked on Malta in 60. Saracens controlled the island(s) from 870 to 1090, a period of difficulty for the Church. The line of bishops extends from 1090 to the present. Church-state conflict developed in recent years over passage of government-sponsored legislation affecting Catholic schools and church-owned property. An agreement reached in 1985 ended the dispute and established a joint commission to study other church-state problems.

The Marianas
Dioc., 1; bp., 1; parishes, 22; priests, 13 (10 dioc., 3 rel.); p.d., 3; sem., 2; srs., 25; bap., 1,023; Caths., 56,000; tot. pop., 63,000.

Commonwealth of Northern Mariana Islands, under U.S. sovereignty; formerly part of Trust Territory of Pacific Islands assigned to the U.S. in 1947. Under ecclesiastical jurisdiction of Chalan Kanoa diocese established in 1984.

Marshall Islands
Island republic in central Pacific Ocean; capital, Majura. Formerly administered by U.S. as part of UN Trust Territory of the Pacific; independent nation, 1991. A prefecture apostolic was erected May 25, 1993 (formerly part of Carolines-Marshall diocese), with U.S. Jesuit Rev. James Gould as first prefect apostolic. No separate statistics available. L'-Osservatore Romano (English edition, June 2, 1993) reported about 3,440 Catholics in population of 43,000, under pastoral care of 5 Jesuit priests of New York province and women religious from various congregations.

Martinique
Archd., 1; abp., 1; parishes, 47; priests, 68 (38 dioc., 30 rel.); sem., 6; bros., 10; srs., 214; bap., 5,710; Caths., 318,000; tot. pop., 360,000.

French overseas department in the West Indies, about 130 miles south of Guadeloupe; capital, Fort-de-France. Catholicism was introduced in the 16th century. The hierarchy was established in 1967.

Mauritania
Dioc., 1; bp., 1; parishes, 7; priests, 8 (2 dioc., 6 rel.); bros., 2; srs., 33; bap., 19; Caths., 4,000 (.2%); tot. pop., 2,040,000. (AD)

Islamic republic on the northwest coast of Africa; capital, Nouakchott. With few exceptions, the Catholics in the country are members of the foreign colony.

Mauritius*
Dioc., 1; card., 1; bp., 1; parishes, 44; priests, 87 (53 dioc., 34 rel.); sem., 11; bros., 28; srs., 273;

bap., 6,793; Caths., 288,000 (26.7%); tot. pop., 1,078,000.

Island republic in the Indian Ocean about 500 miles east of Madagascar; capital, Port Louis. Catholicism was introduced by Vincentians in 1722. Port Louis, made a vicariate in 1819 and a diocese in 1847, was a jumping-off point for missionaries to Australia, Madagascar and South Africa.

Mayotte
French overseas island territory, in Indian Ocean off southeast coast of Africa; formerly part of Comoros. Statistics included in Comoros.

Melilla
Spanish possession in northern Africa. Statistics are included in those for Spain.

Mexico*
Archd., 14; dioc., 58; prel., 7; v.a., 1; card., 1; abp., 18; bp., 90; parishes, 4,990; priests, 11,696 (8,404 dioc., 3,292 rel.); p.d., 237; sem., 6,368; bros., 1,355; srs., 25,877; bap., 1,926,719; Caths., 83,815,000 (95.4%); tot. pop., 87,840,000.

Republic in Middle America (United States of Mexico); capital, Mexico City. Christianity was introduced early in the 16th century. Mexico City, made a diocese in 1530, became the missionary and cultural center of the whole country. Missionary work, started in 1524 and forwarded principally by Franciscans, Dominicans, Augustinians and Jesuits, resulted in the baptism of all persons in the central plateau by the end of the century. Progress there and in the rest of the country continued in the following century but tapered off and went into decline in the 18th century, for a variety of reasons ranging from diminishing government support to relaxations of Church discipline. The wars of independence, 1810-21, in which some Catholics participated, created serious problems of adjustment for the Church. Social problems, political unrest and government opposition climaxed in the constitution of 1917 which practically outlawed the Church. Persecution took serious tolls of life and kept the Church underground, under Calles, 1924-1928, again in 1931, and under Cardenas in 1934. President Camacho, 1940-1946, ended persecution and instituted a more lenient policy. The Church, however, still labors under some legal and practical disabilities. In 1990, the Mexican president and the Vatican agreed to exchange permanent personal representatives; full diplomatic relations were established in 1992. Cardinal Juan Jesus Posadas Ocampo, Archbishop of Guadalajara, was shot to death May 24, 1993; see May News Events. (See Index for 1993 papal visit.)

Micronesia
Dioc., 1 (Carolines-Marshalls); bp., 2; parishes, 26; priests, 45 (6 dioc., 39 rel.); p.d., 43; sem., 9; bros., 2; srs., 54; catechists, 456; bap., 2,837; Caths., 70,000 (42.4%); tot. pop., 165,000. (Statistics include Marshall Islands which was established as a separate prefecture apostolic in 1993).

Federated States of Micronesia (Caroline archipelago) in southwest Pacific; former U.S. trust territory; independent nation September 1991. Effective evangelization began in the late 1880s.

Moldava*

Dioc., 1; Caths., 15,000; tot. pop., 4,500,000.

Independent republic bordering Romania; former constituent republic of the USSR; capital, Kishinev. The majority of people belong to the Orthodox Church. Catholics are mostly of Polish or German descent.

Monaco*

Archd., 1; abp., 1, parishes, 6; priests, 24 (12 dioc., 12 rel.); p.d., 1; sem., 5; srs., 27; bap., 272; Caths., 27,000; tot. pop., 30,000.

Constitutional monarchy, an enclave on the Mediterranean coast of France near the Italian border; capital, Monaco-Ville. Christianity was introduced before 1000. Catholicism is the official religion but freedom is guaranteed for all.

Mongolia*

Mission, 1; priests, 3 (rel.); srs., 3; Caths., 200; tot. pop., 2,250,000.

Republic in north central Asia; formerly under communist control; capital Ulaanbaatar. Christianity was introduced by Oriental Orthodox. Some Franciscans were in the country in the 13th and 14th centuries, en route to China. Limited evangelization efforts from the 18th century had little success among the Mongols in Outer Mongolia, where Buddhism has predominated for hundreds of years. There may be a few Catholics in Inner Mongolia. No foreign missionaries have been in the country since 1953. Freedom of worship is guaranteed under the new constitution which went into effect in 1992. The government established relations with the Vatican in 1992 and indicated that missionaries would be welcome to help rebuild the country.

Montserrat

Parish, 1; priests, 2 (rel.); p.d., 1; srs., 4; bap., 22; Caths., 1,000; tot. pop., 12,000.

British island possession in Caribbean; capital, Plymouth. Under ecclesiastical jurisdiction of St. John's-Basseterre diocese, Antigua.

Morocco*

Archd., 2; abp., 2; parishes, 41; priests, 70 (16 dioc., 54 rel.); sem., 1; bros., 17; srs., 293; bap., 90; Caths., 28,000 (.1%); tot. pop., 25,700,000.

Constitutional monarchy in northwest Africa with Atlantic and Mediterranean coastlines; capital, Rabat. Christianity was known in the area by the end of the third century. Bishops from Morocco attended a council at Carthage in 484. Catholic life survived under Visigoth and, from 700, Arab rule; later it became subject to influence from the Spanish, Portuguese and French. Islam is the state religion. The hierarchy was established in 1955.

Mozambique

Archd., 3; dioc., 8; card., 1; abp. 2; bp., 8; parishes, 282; priests, 285 (30 dioc., 255 rel.); sem., 173; bros., 79; srs., 651; bap., 45,816; Caths., 2,011,000 (12.5%); tot. pop., 16,080,000. (AD)

People's republic in southeast Africa, bordering on the Indian Ocean; former Portuguese territory (independent, 1975); capital, Maputo (formerly Lourenco Marques). Christianity was introduced by Portuguese Jesuits about the middle of the 16th century. Evangelization continued from then until the 18th century when it went into decline largely because of the Portuguese government's expulsion of the Jesuits. Conditions worsened in the 1830s, improved after 1881, but deteriorated again during the anticlerical period from 1910 to 1925. Conditions improved in 1940, the year Portugal concluded a new concordat with the Holy See and the hierarchy was established. Outspoken criticism by missionaries of Portuguese policies in Mozambique resulted in Church-state tensions in the years immediately preceding independence. The first two native bishops were ordained March 9, 1975. Two ecclesiastical provinces were established in 1984.

Myanmar

Archd., 2; dioc. (1993), 10; abp., 2; bp., 12; parishes, 205; priests, 314 (290 dioc., 24 rel.); sem., 231; bros., 54; srs., 983; bap., 27,814; Caths., 499,000 (1.1%); tot. pop., 42,560,000. (AD)

A socialist republic in southeast Asia, on the Bay of Bengal, formerly Burma; name changed to Myanmar in 1989; capital, Yangon (Rangoon). Christianity was introduced about 1500. Small-scale evangelization had limited results from the middle of the 16th century until the 1850s when effective organization of the Church began. The hierarchy was established in 1955. Buddhism was declared the state religion in 1961, but the state is now officially secular. In 1965, church schools and hospitals were nationalized. In 1966, all foreign missionaries who had entered the country after 1948 for the first time were forced to leave when the government refused to renew their work permits. Despite these setbacks, the Church has shown some progress in recent years.

Namibia (South West Africa)

V.a., 2; bp., 1 (native); parishes, 71; priests, 65 (3 dioc., 62 rel.); p.d., 1; sem., 12; bros., 32; srs., 267; bap., 8,525; Caths., 244,000 (13.2%); tot. pop., 1,840,000. (AD)

Independent (Mar. 21, 1990) state in southern Africa; capital, Windhoek. The area shares the history of South Africa.

Nauru*

Parishes, 2; priest, 1 (rel.); srs., 5; bap., 113; Caths., 3,000; tot. pop., 8,000.

Independent republic in western Pacific; capital, Yaren. Forms part of the Tarawa and Nauru diocese (Kiribati). Established diplomatic relations with the Vatican in 1992.

Nepal*

Independent mission, 1; parishes, 17; priests, 28 (1 dioc.; 27 rel.); sem., 14; bros., 8; srs., 73; bap., 87; Caths., 4,000; tot. pop., 19,600,000.

Constitutional monarchy, the only Hindu kingdom in the world, in central Asia south of the Himalayas between India and Tibet; capital, Kathmandu. Little is known of the country before the 15th century. Some Jesuits passed through from 1628 and some sections were evangelized in the 18th century, with minimal results, before the country was closed to foreigners. Conversions from Hinduism, the state religion, are not recognized in law and punishable by imprisonment. Christian missionary work is not allowed.

Netherlands*

Archd., 1; dioc., 6; mil ord.; card., 2; bp., 11; parishes, 1,753; priests 5,070 (1,992 dioc., 3,078 rel.); p.d., 162; sem., 176; bros., 2,154; srs., 16,685; bap., 51,633; Caths., 5,537,000 (36.7%); tot. pop., 15,060,000.

Constitutional monarchy in northwestern Europe; capital, Amsterdam (seat of the government, The Hague). Evangelization, begun about the turn of the sixth century by Irish, Anglo-Saxon and Frankish missionaries, resulted in Christianization of the country by 800 and subsequent strong influence on The Lowlands. Invasion by French Calvinists in 1572 brought serious losses to the Catholic Church and made the Reformed Church dominant. Catholics suffered a practical persecution of official repression and social handicap in the 17th century. The schism of Utrecht occurred in 1724. Only one-third of the population was Catholic in 1726. The Church had only a skeleton organization from 1702 to 1853, when the hierarchy was reestablished. Despite this upturn, cultural isolation was the experience of Catholics until about 1914. From then on new vigor came into the life of the Church, and a whole new climate of interfaith relations began to develop. Before and for some years following the Second Vatican Council, the thrust and variety of thought and practice in the Dutch Church moved it to the vanguard position of "progressive" renewal. A particular synod of Dutch bishops held at the Vatican in January, 1980, and aimed at internal improvement of the Church in the Netherlands, had disappointing results, according to reports in 1981.

Netherlands Antilles

Dioc., 1; bp., 1; parishes, 49; priests, 62 (26 dioc., 36 rel.); p.d., 1; sem., 2; bros., 27; srs., 89; bap., 3,225; Caths., 227,000; tot. pop., 270,000. (AD)

Autonomous part of The Netherlands. Consists of two groups of islands in the Caribbean: Curacao, Aruba and Bonaire, off the northern coast of Venezuela; and St. Eustatius, Saba and the southern part of St. Maarten, southeast of Puerto Rico; capital, Willemstad on Curacao. Christianity was introduced in the 16th century.

New Caledonia

Archd., 1; abp., 1; parishes, 37; priests, 52 (10 dioc., 42 rel.); sem., 8; bros., 50; srs., 210; bap., 2,497; Caths., 100,000; tot. pop., 165,000.

French territory consisting of several islands in Oceania east of Queensland, Australia; capital, Noumea. Catholicism was introduced in 1843, nine years after Protestant missionaries began evangelization. A vicariate was organized in 1847. The hierarchy was established in 1966.

New Zealand*

Archd., 1; dioc., 5; mil. ord.; card., 1; bp., 8; parishes, 274; priests, 669 (383 dioc., 286 rel.); p.d., 2; sem., 41; bros., 209; srs., 1,447; bap., 8,883; Caths. 476,000 (14%); tot. pop., 3,380,000.

Independent nation in Commonwealth, a group of islands in Oceania 1,200 miles southeast of Australia: capital, Wellington. Protestant missionaries were the first evangelizers. On North Island, Catholic missionaries started work before the establishment of two dioceses in 1848; their work among the Maoris was not organized until about 1881. On South Island, whose first resident priest arrived in 1840, a diocese was established in 1869. These three jurisdictions were joined in a province in 1896. The Marists were the outstanding Catholic missionaries in the area.

Nicaragua*

Archd., 1; dioc., 6; v.a., 1; card., 1; bp., 10; parishes, 205; priests, 325 (143 dioc., 182 rel.); p.d., 35; sem., 135; bros., 41; srs., 662; bap., 87,042; Caths., 3,575,000 (89.3%); tot. pop., 4,000,000.

Republic in Central America: capital, Managua. Evangelization began shortly after the Spanish conquest about 1524 and eight years later the first bishop took over jurisdiction of the Church in the country. Jesuits were leaders in missionary work during the colonial period, which lasted until the 1820s. Evangelization endeavor increased after establishment of the republic in 1838. In this century it was extended to the Atlantic coastal area where Protestant missionaries had begun work about the middle of the 1900s. Many church leaders, clerical and lay, supported the aims but not necessarily all the methods of the revolution which forced the resignation and flight July 17, 1979, of Anastasio Somoza Debayle, whose family had controlled the government since the early 1930s.

Niger*

Dioc., 1; bp., 2; parishes, 21; priests, 39 (6 dioc., 33 rel.); sem., 3; bros., 7; sem., 2; srs., 78; bap., 428; Caths., 17,000 (.2%); tot. pop., 7,980,000.

Republic in west central Africa; capital, Niamey. The first mission was set up in 1831. A prefecture apostolic was organized in 1942 and the first diocese was established in 1961. The country is predominantly Muslim.

Nigeria*

Archd., 3; dioc., 33; independent missions, 2; card., 2; abp., 3; bp., 36; parishes, 1,023; priests, 2,130 (1,598 dioc., 532 rel.); p.d., 6; sem., 3,146; bros., 400; srs., 2,207; bap., 313,498; Caths., 10,587,000 (9.4%); tot. pop., 112,160,000.

Republic in western Africa; capital, Lagos. The Portuguese introduced Catholicism in the coastal region in the 15th century. Capuchins did some evangelization in the 17th century but systematic missionary work did not get under way along the coast until about 1840. A vicariate for this area was organized in 1870. A prefecture was set up in 1911 for missions in the northern part of the country where Islam was strongly entrenched. From 1967, when Biafra seceded, until early in 1970 the country was torn by civil war. The hierarchy was established in 1950.

Niue

Parish,. 1; priests, 2 (dioc.); srs., 2; bap., 7; Caths., 200; tot. pop., 3,000.

New Zealand self-governing territory in South Pacific. Under ecclesiastical jurisdiction of Rarotonga diocese, Cook Islands.

Norway*

Dioc., 1; prel., 2; bp., 3; parishes, 30; priests, 62 (17 dioc., 45 rel.); p.d., 1; sem., 8; bros., 3; srs., 248; bap., 715; Caths., 36,000 (.8%); tot. pop., 4,260,000.

Constitutional monarchy in northern Europe, the western part of the Scandinavian peninsula; capital, Oslo. Evangelization begun in the ninth century by missionaries from England and Ireland put the Church on a firm footing about the turn of the 11th century. The first diocese was set up in 1153 and development of the Church progressed until the Black Death in 1349 inflicted losses from which it never recovered. Lutheranism, introduced from outside in 1537 and furthered cautiously, gained general acceptance by about 1600 and was made the state religion. Legal and other measures crippled the Church, forcing priests to flee the country and completely disrupting normal activity. Changes for the better came in the 19th century, with the granting of religious liberty in 1845 and the repeal of many legal disabilities in 1897. Norway was administered as a single apostolic vicariate from 1892 to 1932, when it was divided into three jurisdictions under the supervision of the Congregation for the Propagation of the Faith.

Oman

Parishes, 3; priests, 4 (rel.); bap., 159; Caths., 25,000; tot. pop., 1,560,000.

Independent monarchy in eastern corner of Arabian Peninsula; capital, Muscat. Under ecclesiastical jurisdiction of Arabia vicariate apostolic.

Pakistan*

Archd., 1; dioc., 5; card., 1; bp., 8; parishes, 94; priests, 263 (125 dioc., 138 rel.); p.d., 2; sem., 177; bros., 31; srs., 713; bap., 24,344; Caths., 912,000 (.78%); tot. pop., 115,520,000.

Islamic republic in southwestern Asia; capital, Islamabad. (Formerly included East Pakistan which became the independent nation of Bangladesh in 1971.) Islam, firmly established in the eighth century, is the state religion. Christian evangelization of the native population began about the middle of the 19th century, years after earlier scattered attempts. The hierarchy was established in 1950.

Panama*

Archd., 1; dioc., 4; prel., 1; v.a., 1; abp., 1; bp., 8; parishes, 179; priests, 355 (120 dioc., 235 rel.); p.d., 20; sem., 173; bros., 58; srs., 513; bap., 32,890; Caths., 2,172,000 (87.9%); tot. pop., 2,470,000.

Republic in Central America; capital, Panama.

Catholicism was introduced by Franciscan missionaries and evangelization started in 1514. The Panama diocese, oldest in the Americas was set up at the same time. The Catholic Church has favored status and state aid for missions, charities and parochial schools, but religious freedom is guaranteed to all religions.

Papua New Guinea*

Archd., 4; dioc., 14; abp., 5; bp., 17; parishes, 329; priests, 560 (116 dioc., 444 rel.); p.d., 9; sem., 239; bros., 334; srs., 911; bap., 34,669; Caths., 1,226,000 (32.5%); tot. pop., 3,770,000.

Independent (Sept. 16, 1975) republic (formerly under Australian administration) in southwest Pacific. Consists of the eastern half of the southwestern Pacific island of New Guinea and the Northern Solomon Islands; capital, Port Moresby. Marists began evangelization about 1844 but were handicapped by many factors, including "spheres of influence" laid out for Catholic and Protestant missionaries. A prefecture apostolic was set up in 1896 and placed in charge of the Divine Word Missionaries. The territory suffered greatly during World War II. Hierarchy was established for New Guinea and adjacent islands in 1966.

Paraguay*

Archd., 1; dioc. (1993), 10; v.a., 3; mil. ord.; abp., 1; bp., 14; parishes, 339; priests, 571 (203 dioc., 368 rel.); p.d., 33; sem., 357; bros., 116; srs., 1,156; bap., 99,392; Caths., 4,098,000 (93.1%); tot. pop., 4,400,000.

Republic in central South America; capital, Asuncion. Catholicism was introduced in 1542, evangelization began almost immediately. A diocese erected in 1547 was occupied for the first time in 1556. On many occasions thereafter dioceses in the country were left unoccupied because of political and other reasons. Jesuits who came into the country after 1609 devised the reductions system for evangelizing the Indians, teaching them agriculture, husbandry, trades and other useful arts, and giving them experience in property use and community life. The reductions were communes of Indians only, under the direction of the missionaries. About 50 of them were established in southern Brazil, Uruguay and northeastern Argentina as well as in Paraguay. They had an average population of three to four thousand. At their peak, some 30 reductions had a population of 100,000. Political officials regarded the reductions with disfavor because they did not control them and feared that the Indians trained in them might foment revolt and upset the established colonial system under Spanish control. The reductions lasted until about 1768 when their Jesuit founders and directors were expelled from Latin America. Church-state relations following independence from Spain in 1811 were tense as often as not because of government efforts to control the Church through continued exercise of Spanish patronage rights and by other means. The Church as well as the whole country suffered a great deal during the War of the Triple Alliance from 1865-70. After that time, the Church had the same kind of experience in Paraguay as in the rest of Latin America with forces of liberalism, anticlericalism, massive educational needs, poverty, a shortage of priests and other personnel. Most recently church leaders have been challenging the government to initiate long-needed economic and social reforms.

Peru*

Archd., 7; dioc., 15; prel., 11; v.a., 8; mil. ord.; card., 1; abp., 8; bp., 48; parishes, 1,316; priests, 2,419 (1,058 dioc., 1,361 rel.); p.d., 63; sem., 1,169; bros., 494; srs., 5,094; bap., 391,599; Caths., 20,380,000 (92%); tot. pop., 22,000,000.

Republic on the western coast of South America; capital, Lima. An effective diocese became operational in 1537, five years after the Spanish conquest. Evangelization, already under way, developed for some time after 1570 but deteriorated before the end of the colonial period in the 1820s. The first native-born saint of the new world was a Peruvian, Rose of Lima, a Dominican tertiary who died in 1617 and was canonized in 1671. In the new republic founded after the wars of independence the Church experienced problems of adjustment and many of the difficulties that cropped up in other South American countries: government efforts to control it through continuation of the patronage rights of the Spanish crown; suppression of houses of religious and expropriation of church property; religious indifference and outright hostility. The Church was given special status but was not made the established religion. Repressive measures by the government against labor protests have been condemned by Church leaders in the past several years.

Philippines*

Archd., 16; dioc., 50; prel., 6; v.a., 7; mil. ord.; card., 3; abp., 21; bp., 92; parishes, 2,445; priests, 5,805 (3,631 dioc., 2,174 rel.); p.d., 2; sem., 6,530; bros., 552; srs., 8,711; bap., 1,526,735; Caths., 52,325,000 (83%); tot. pop., 62,870,000.

Republic, an archipelago of 7,000 islands off the southeast coast of Asia; capital, Quezon City (de facto, Manila). Systematic evangelization was begun in 1564 and resulted in firm establishment of the Church by the 19th century. During the period of Spanish rule, which lasted from the discovery of the islands by Magellan in 1521 to 1898, the Church experienced difficulties with the patronage system under which the Spanish crown tried to control ecclesiastical affairs through episcopal and other appointments. This system ended in 1898 when the United States gained possession of the islands and instituted a policy of separation of Church and state. Anticlericalism flared late in the 19th century. The Aglipayan schism, an attempt to set up a nationalist church, occurred a few years later, in 1902. The government of Ferdinand Marcos, under attack by people of the church for a number of years for violations of human rights, was replaced in 1986.

Poland*

Archd., 13; dioc., 26; ordinariate, 1; cards., 4 (3 head metropolitan sees); abps., 11; bps., 99; parishes, 9,086; priests, 24,115 (18,763 dioc., 5,352 rel.); p.d., 2; sem., 8,072; bros., 1,452; srs., 27,079;

bap., 565,442; Caths., 36,616,000 (95.7%); tot. pop., 38,240,000.

Republic in eastern Europe; capital, Warsaw. The first traces of Christianity date from the second half of the ninth century. Its spread was accelerated by the union of the Slavs in the 10th century. The first bishopric was set up in 968. The Gniezno archdiocese, with suffragan sees and a mandate to evangelize the borderlands as well as Poland, was established in 1000. Steady growth continued thereafter, with religious orders and their schools playing a major role. Some tensions with the Orthodox were experienced. The Reformation, supported mainly by city dwellers and the upper classes, peaked from about the middle of the 16th century, resulting in numerous conversions to Lutheranism, the Reformed Church and the Bohemian Brethren. A successful Counter-Reformation, with the Jesuits in a position of leadership, was completed by about 1632. The movement served a nationalist as well as religious purpose; in restoring religious unity to a large degree, it united the country against potential invaders, the Swedes, Russians and Turks. The Counter-Reformation had bad side effects, leading to the repression of Protestants long after it was over and to prejudice against Orthodox who returned to allegiance with Rome in 1596 and later. The Church, in the same manner as the entire country, was adversely affected by the partitions of the 18th and 19th centuries. Russification hurt the Orthodox who had reunited with Rome and the Latins who were in the majority. Germans extended their Kulturkampf to the area they controlled. The Austrians exhibited some degree of tolerance. In the republic established after World War I the Church reorganized itself, continued to serve as a vital force in national life, and enjoyed generally harmonious relations with the state. Progressive growth was strong until 1939 when disaster struck in the form of invasion by German and Russian forces and six years of war. In 1945, seven years before the adoption of a Soviet-type of constitution, the Communist-controlled government initiated a policy that included a constant program of atheistic propaganda; a strong campaign against the hierarchy and clergy; the imprisonment in 1948 of 700 priests and even more religious; rigid limitation of the activities of religious; censorship and curtailment of the Catholic press and Catholic Action; interference with church administration and appointments of the clergy; the "deposition" of Cardinal Wyszynski in 1953 and the imprisonment of other members of the hierarchy; the suppression of "Caritas," the Catholic charitable organization; promotion of "Progressive Catholic" activities and a small minority of "patriotic priests." Establishment of the Gomulka regime, the freeing of Cardinal Wyszynski in October, 1956, and the signing of an agreement two months later by bishops and state officials, led to some improvement of conditions. The underlying fact, however, was that the regime conceded to Catholics only so much as was necessary to secure support of the government as a more tolerable evil than the harsh and real threat of a Russian-imposed puppet government like that in Hungary. This has been the controlling principle in Church-state relations. Auxiliary Bishop Ladislaw Rubin of Gniezno sketched the general state of affairs in March, 1968. He said that there was no sign that the government had any intention of releasing its oppressive grip on the Church. As evidence of the "climate of asphyxiation" in the country he cited: persistent questioning of priests by officials concerning their activities; the prohibition against Catholic schools, hospitals and charitable works; the financial burden of a 60 per cent tax on church income. Cardinal Wyszynski denounced "enforced atheism" in a Lenten pastoral in the same year. In May, 1969, the bishops drafted a list of grievances against the government which, they said, were "only some examples of difficulties which demonstrated the situation of the Church in our homeland." The grievances were: refusal of permits to build new churches and establish new parishes; refusal of permission "for the organization of new religion classes"; pressure on Catholics who attend religious ceremonies; censorship and the lack of an independent Catholic daily newspaper; lack of representation in public life; restriction of "freedom to conduct normal pastoral work" in the western portion of the country. There was a move toward improvement in Church-state relations in 1971-72. In 1973, the Polish bishops issued a pastoral letter urging Catholics to resist the official atheism imposed by the government. In 1974 the bishops expressed approval of renewed Vatican efforts at regularizing Church-state relations but insisted that they (the bishops) be consulted on every step of the negotiations. The bishops have continued their sharp criticism of anti-religious policies and human rights violations of the government. Regular contacts on a working level were initiated by the Vatican and Poland in 1974; regular diplomatic relations were established in 1989. Cardinal Karol Wojtyla of Cracow was elected to the papacy in 1978. Church support was strong for the independent labor movement, Solidarity, which was recognized by the government in August, 1980, but outlawed in December, 1981, when martial law was imposed (martial law was suspended in 1982). In May, 1989, following recognition of Solidarity and a series of political changes, the Catholic Church was given legal status for the first time since the communists took control of the government in 1944. In 1990, a new constitution was adopted declaring Poland a democratic state. In 1992, the Pope restructured the Church in Poland, establishing 8 more provinces and 13 new dioceses. A new concordat between the Polish government and the Holy See was signed in 1993.

Portugal*
Patriarchate, 1; archd., 2; dioc., 17; mil. ord.; card., 1; abp., 3; bp., 39; parishes, 4,333; priests, 4,526 (3,453 dioc., 1,073 rel.); p.d., 44; sem., 790; bros., 465; srs., 7,310; bap., 103,296; Caths., 9,869,000 (93.2%); tot. pop., 10,580,000.

Republic in the western part of the Iberian peninsula; capital, Lisbon. Christianity was introduced before the fourth century. From the fifth century to early in the eighth century the Church experienced difficulties from the physical invasion of barbarians

and the intellectual invasion of doctrinal errors in the forms of Arianism, Priscillianism and Pelagianism. The Church survived under the rule of Arabs from about 711 and of the Moors until 1249. Ecclesiastical life was fairly vigorous from 1080 to 1185, and monastic influence became strong. A decline set in about 1450. Several decades later Portugal became the jumping-off place for many missionaries to newly discovered colonies. The Reformation had little effect in the country. Beginning about 1750, Pombal, minister of foreign affairs and prime minister, mounted a frontal attack on the Jesuits whom he succeeded in expelling from Portugal and the colonies. His anti-Jesuit campaign successful Pombal also attempted, and succeeded to some extent, in controlling the Church in Portugal until his fall from power about 1777. Liberal revolutionaries with anti-Church policies made the 19th century a difficult one for the Church. Similar policies prevailed in Church-state relations in this century until the accession of Salazar to power in 1928. In 1940 he concluded a concordat with the Holy See which regularized Church-state relations but still left the Church in a subservient condition. The prevailing spirit of church authorities in Portugal has been conservative. In 1971 several priests were tried for subversion for speaking out against colonialism and for taking part in guerrilla activities in Angola. A military coup of Apr. 25, 1974, triggered a succession of chaotic political developments which led to an attempt by Communists, after receiving only 18 per cent of the votes cast in a national election, to take over the government in the summer of 1975.

Puerto Rico
Archd., 1; dioc., 4; card., 1; bp., 10; parishes, 317; priests, 776 (368 dioc., 408 rel.); p.d., 334; sem., 132; bros., 61; srs., 1,257; bap., 47,663; Caths., 2,859,000 (80%); tot. pop., 3,550,000. (AD)

A U.S. commonwealth, the smallest of the Greater Antilles, 885 miles southeast of the southern coast of Florida; capital, San Juan. Following its discovery by Columbus in 1493, the island was evangelized by Spanish missionaries and remained under Spanish ecclesiastical as well as political control until 1898 when it became a possession of the United States. The original diocese, San Juan, was erected in 1511. The present hierarchy was established in 1960.

Qatar
Parish, 1; priest, 1 (dioc.); bap., 66; Caths., 11,000; tot. pop., 380,000.

Independent state in the Persian Gulf; capital, Doha. Under ecclesiastical jurisdiction of Arabia vicariate apostolic.

Reunion
Dioc., 1; bp., 1; parishes, 75; priests, 103 (56 dioc., 47 rel.); p.d., 4; sem., 10; bros., 42; srs., 423; bap., 12,069; Caths., 539,000 (88.3%); tot. pop., 610,000. (AD)

French overseas department, 450 miles east of Madagascar; capital, Saint-Denis. Catholicism was introduced in 1667 and some intermittent missionary work was done through the rest of the century. A prefecture apostolic was organized in 1712. Vincentians began work there in 1817 and were joined later by Holy Ghost Fathers.

Rhodes

Greek island in the Aegean Sea, 112 miles from the southwestern coast of Asia Minor. A diocese was established about the end of the third century. A bishop from Rhodes attended the Council of Nicaea in 325. Most of the Christians followed the Eastern Churches into schism in the 11th century and became Orthodox. Turks controlled the island from 1522 to 1912. The small Catholic population, for whom a diocese existed from 1328 to 1546, lived in crossfire between Turks and Orthodox. After 1719 Franciscans provided pastoral care for the Catholics, for whom an archdiocese was erected in 1928. Statistics are included in Greece.

Romania*

Archd., 3; dioc., 8; ord., 1; card., 1; abp., 3; bp., 10; parishes, 1,171; priests, 1,297 (1,177 dioc., 120 rel.); p.d., 3; sem., 569; bros., 70; srs., 791; bap., 16,374; Caths., 3,280,000 (14.1%); tot. pop., 23,190,000.

Socialist republic in southeastern Europe; capital, Bucharest. Latin Christianity, introduced in the third century, all but disappeared during the barbarian invasions. The Byzantine Rite was introduced by the Bulgars about the beginning of the eighth century and established firm roots. It eventually became Orthodox, but a large number of its adherents returned later to union with Rome. Attempts to reintroduce the Latin Rite on any large scale have been unsuccessful. Communists took over the government following World War II, forced the abdication of Michael I in 1947, and enacted a Soviet type of constitution in 1952. By that time a campaign against religion was already in progress. In 1948 the government denounced a concordat concluded in 1929, nationalized all schools and passed a law on religions which resulted in the disorganization of Church administration. The 1.5 million-member Romanian Byzantine Rite Church, by government decree, was incorporated into the Romanian Orthodox Church, and the Orthodox bishops then seized the cathedrals of Roman Catholic bishops. Five of the six Latin Rite bishops were immediately disposed of by the government, and the last was sentenced to 18 years' imprisonment in 1951, when a great many arrests of priests and laymen were made. Religious orders were suppressed in 1949. Since 1948 more than 50 priests have been executed and 200 have died in prison. One hundred priests were reported in prison at the end of 1958. Some change for the better in Church-state relations was reported after the middle of the summer of 1964, although restrictions were still in effect. About 1,200 priests were engaged in parish work in August, 1965. Conditions improved in 1990 with the change of government. The hierarchy was restored and diplomatic relations with the Vatican were reestablished.

Russian Federation

Dioc., 1; a.a., 2 (1 for European Russia, 1 for Siberia); ap. ex., 1; abp., 1 (titular); bp., 1;

parishes, 29; priests, 50 (9 dioc., 41 rel.); p.d., 2; sem., 4; bro., 1; srs., 76; bap., 1,000; Caths., 372,000; tot. pop., 165,162,000.

Federation comprising Russia and Siberia in Europe and Asia; capital, Moscow. (See Union of Soviet Socialist Republic.)

Rwanda*

Archd., 1; dioc., 8; abp., 1; bp., 8; parishes, 122; priests, 557 (353 dioc., 204 rel.); sem., 292; bros., 288; srs., 1,161; bap., 136,062; Caths., 3,323,000 (44%); tot. pop., 7,490,000.

Republic in east central Africa; capital, Kigali. Catholicism was introduced about the turn of the 20th century. The hierarchy was established in 1959. Intertribal warfare between the ruling Hutus (90 per cent of the population) and the Tutsis (formerly the ruling aristocracy) plagued the country for a number of years.

Saint Christopher and Nevis

Parishes, 4; priests, 6 (3 dioc., 3 rel.); bro., 1; srs., 4; bap., 44; Caths., 5,000; tot. pop., 46,000. (AD)

Independent (Sept. 19, 1983) island states in West Indies; capital, Basseterre, on St. Christopher; Charlestown, on Nevis. Under ecclesiastical jurisdiction of St. John's-Basseterre diocese, Antigua.

Saint Helena

Independent mission, 1; parish, 1; priest, 1 (religious; head of the mission); bap., 3; Caths., 100; tot. pop., 7,000.

Comprises British Island possessions of St. Helena, Ascension and Tristan da Cunha in the South Atlantic; formerly under ecclesiastical jurisdiction of Cape Town archdiocese (South Africa).

Saint Lucia*

Archd., 1; abp., 1; parishes, 22; priests, 37 (17 dioc., 20 rel.); p.d., 4; sem., 3; bros., 3; srs., 39, bap., 2,858; Caths., 136,000; tot. pop., 151,000.

Independent (Feb. 22, 1979) island state in West Indies; capital, Castries.

Saint Pierre and Miquelon

V.a., 1; bp., 1; parishes, 3; priests, 3 (rel.); srs., 7; bap., 75; Caths., 6,000; tot. pop., 6,000.

French overseas department, two groups of islands near the southwest coast of Newfoundland; capital, St. Pierre. Catholicism was introduced about 1689.

Saint Vincent and the Grenadines*

Dioc., 1; bp., 1; parishes, 6; priests, 8 (5 dioc., 3 rel.); sem., 1; bros., 6; srs., 12; bap., 105; Caths., 12,000; tot. pop., 120,000.

Independent state (1979) in West Indies; capital, Kingstown. The Kingstown diocese (St. Vincent) was established in 1989; it was formerly part of Bridgetown-Kingstown diocese with see in Barbados.

American Samoa

Dioc., 1; bp., 1; parishes 8; priests, 12 (10 dioc., 2 rel.); p.d., 1; sem., 3; bros., 2; srs., 14; bap., 421; Caths., 9,000; tot. pop., 46,000.

Unincorporated U.S. territory in southwestern Pacific, consisting of six small islands; seat of government, Pago Pago on the Island of Tutuila. Samoa-Pago Pago diocese established in 1982.

Western Samoa

Archd., 1; card., 1; bp., 1; parishes, 32; priests, 45 (17 dioc., 28 rel.); p.d., 3; sem., 18; bros., 25; srs., 100; bap., 1,404; Caths., 37,000; tot. pop., 166,000.

Independent state in the southwestern Pacific; capital, Apia. Catholic missionary work began in 1845. Most of the missions now in operation were established by 1870 when the Catholic population numbered about 5,000. Additional progress was made in missionary work from 1896. The first Samoan priest was ordained in 1892. A diocese was established in 1966; elevated to a metropolitan see in 1982.

San Marino*

Parishes, 12; priests, 26 (14 dioc., 12 rel.); bro., 1; srs., 30; bap., 320; Caths., 23,000; tot. pop., 23,000.

Republic, a 24-square-mile enclave in northeastern Italy; capital, San Marino. The date of initial evangelization is not known, but a diocese was established by the end of the third century. Ecclesiastically, it forms part of the diocese of San Marino-Montefeltro in Italy.

Sao Tome and Principe*

Dioc., 1; bp., 1; parishes, 12; priests, 7 (rel.); sem. 18; bros., 4; srs., 26; bap., 2,296; Caths., 99,000 (82.5%); tot. pop., 120,000.

Independent republic (July 12, 1975), consisting of two islands off the western coast of Africa in the Gulf of Guinea; former Portuguese territory; capital, Sao Tome. Evangelization was begun by the Portuguese who discovered the islands in 1471-72. The Sao Tome diocese was established in 1534.

Saudi Arabia

Monarchy occupying four-fifths of Arabian peninsula; capital, Riyadh. Population is Muslim; all other religions are banned. Christians in the area are workers from other countries. Under ecclesiastical jurisdiction of Arabia vicariate apostolic. Population, 14,690,000.

Scotland

Archd., 2; dioc., 6; abp., 2; bp., 7; parishes, 468; priests, 930 (720 dioc., 210 rel.); p.d. 3; sem., 95; bros., 93; srs., 953; bap., 11,999; Caths., 758,003 (14.7%); tot. pop., 5,131,300. (1993 Annuario Pontificio.)

Part of the United Kingdom, in the northern British Isles; capital, Edinburgh. Christianity was introduced by the early years of the fifth century. The arrival of St. Columba and his monks in 563 inaugurated a new era of evangelization which reached into remote areas by the end of the sixth century. He was extremely influential in determining the character of the Celtic Church, which was tribal, monastic, and in union with Rome. Considerable disruption of church activity resulted from Scandinavian invasions in the late eighth and ninth centuries. By 1153 the Scottish Church took a turn away from its insularity and was drawn into closer contact with the European community. Anglo-Saxon religious and political relations, complicated by rivalries between princes and ecclesiastical superiors, were not always the happiest. Religious orders expanded greatly in the 12th century. From shortly after the Norman Conquest of England to 1560 the Church suffered adverse effects from the Hundred Years' War, the Black Death, the Western Schism and other developments. In 1560 parliament abrogated papal supremacy over the Church in Scotland and committed the country to Protestantism in 1567. The Catholic Church was proscribed, to remain that way for more than 200 years, and the hierarchy was disbanded. Defections made the Church a minority religion from that time on. Presbyterian church government was ratified in 1690. Priests launched the Scottish Mission in 1653, incorporating themselves as a mission body under a prefect apostolic and working underground to serve the faithful in much the same way their confreres did in England. About 100 heather priests, trained in clandestine places in the heather country, were ordained by the early 19th century. Catholics got some relief from legal disabilities in 1793 and more later. Many left the country about that time. Some of their numbers were filled subsequently by immigrants from Ireland. The hierarchy was restored in 1878. Scotland, though predominantly Protestant, has a better record for tolerance than Northern Ireland.

Senegal*

Archd., 1; dioc., 5; card., 1; bp., 5; parishes, 100; priests, 286 (151 dioc., 135 rel.); sem., 125; bros., 166; srs., 593; bap., 17,558; Caths., 360,000 (4.6%); tot. pop., 7,530,000.

Republic in western Africa; capital, Dakar. The country had its first contact with Catholicism through the Portuguese some time after 1460. Some incidental missionary work was done by Jesuits and Capuchins in the 16th and 17th centuries. A vicariate for the area was placed in charge of the Holy Ghost Fathers in 1779. More effective evangelization efforts were accomplished after the Senegambia vicariate was erected in 1863; the hierarchy was established in 1955.

Seychelles*

Dioc., 1; bp., 1 (native); parishes, 17; priests, 18 (7 dioc., 11 rel.); sem., 3; bros., 9; srs., 57; bap., 1,512; Caths., 62,000; tot. pop., 68,000.

Independent (1976) group of 92 islands in the Indian Ocean 970 miles east of Kenya; capital, Victoria. Catholicism was introduced in the 18th century. A vicariate apostolic was organized in 1852. All education in the islands was conducted under Catholic auspices until 1954.

Sierra Leone

Archd., 1; dioc., 2; abp., 1; bp., 2; parishes, 39; priests, 121 (36 dioc., 85 rel.); sem., 49; bros., 30; srs., 138; bap., 3,648; Caths., 91,000 (2.1%); tot. pop., 4,260,000. (AD)

Republic on the western coast of Africa; capital, Freetown. Catholicism was introduced in 1858.

Members of the African Missions Society, the first Catholic missionaries in the area, were joined by Holy Ghost Fathers in 1864. Protestant missionaries were active in the area before their Catholic counterparts. Educational work had a major part in Catholic endeavor. The hierarchy was established in 1950.

Singapore*

Archd., 1; abp., 1; parishes, 30; priests, 132 (74 dioc., 58 rel.); sem., 28; bros., 58; srs., 232; bap., 3,718; Caths., 116,000 (4.2%); tot. pop., 2,760,000.
Independent island republic off the southern tip of the Malay Peninsula; capital, Singapore. Christianity was introduced in the area by Portuguese colonists about 1511. Singapore was founded in 1819; the first parish church was built in 1846.

Slovakia*

Archd., 1; dioc., 6; card., 2; abp., 4; bp., 14; parishes, 1,350; priests, 1,743 (1,401 dioc., 342 rel.); p.d., 1; sem., 658; bros., 197; srs., 2,327; bap., 63,645; Caths., 3,859,604 (74%); tot. pop., 5,214,006. (1993 Annuario Pontificio.)
Independent state (Jan. 1, 1993); formerly part of Czechoslovakia; capital, Bratislava. For background history of the Church and its status during communist domination, see Czechoslovakia.

Slovenia*

Archd., 1; dioc., 2; abp., 1; bp., 6; parishes, 792; priests, 1,118 (830 dioc., 288 rel.); p.d., 8; sem., 195; bros., 60; srs., 945; bap., 18,669; Caths., 1,633,000 (83.5%); tot. pop., 1,954,000.
Independent republic (1991) in southeastern Europe; formerly part of Yugoslavia; capital, Ljubljana. Established diplomatic relations with the Vatican in 1992.

Solomon Islands*

Archd., 1; dioc., 2; abp., 1; bp., 2; parishes, 27; priests, 56 (13 dioc., 43 rel.); sem., 29; bros., 25; srs., 125; bap., 2,309; Caths., 63,000 (19%); tot. pop., 330,000.
Independent (July 7, 1978) island group in Oceania; capital, Honiara, on Guadalcanal. Evangelization of the Southern Solomons, begun earlier but interrupted because of violence against them, was resumed by the Marists in 1898. A vicariate apostolic was organized in 1912. A similar jurisdiction was set up for the Western Solomons in 1959. World War II caused a great deal of damage to mission installations.

Somalia

Dioc., 1; parishes, 4; priests, 2 (rel.); sem., 1; srs., 4; bap., 2; Caths., 100; tot. pop., 7,690,000. (AD)
Republic on the eastern coast of Africa; capital, Mogadishu. The country has been Muslim for centuries. Pastoral activity has been confined to immigrants. Schools and hospitals were nationalized in 1972, resulting in the departure of some foreign missionaries.

South Africa

Archd., 4; dioc., 21; v.a., 1; mil. ord.; card., 1; abp., 4; bp., 27; parishes, 721; priests, 1,038 (293
dioc., 745 rel.); p.d., 172; sem., 265; bros., 268; srs., 3,339; bap., 61,397; Caths., 2,851,000 (7.9%); tot. pop., 36,070,000. (AD)
Republic in the southern part of Africa; capitals, Cape Town (legislative), Pretoria (administrative) and Bloemfontein (judicial). Christianity was introduced by the Portuguese who discovered the Cape of Good Hope in 1488. Boers, who founded Cape Town in 1652, expelled Catholics from the region. There was no Catholic missionary activity from that time until the 19th century. After a period of British opposition, a bishop established residence in 1837 and evangelization got under way thereafter among the Bantus and white immigrants. The hierarchy was established in 1951. In recent years church authorities strongly protested the white supremacy policy of apartheid which seriously infringes the human rights of the native blacks and impedes the Church from carrying out its pastoral, educational and social service functions.

Spain*

Archd., 13; dioc., 55; mil. ord.; card., 6; abp., 13; bp., 83; parishes, 21,487; priests, 30,699 (20,231 dioc., 10,468 rel.); p.d., 146; sem., 3,199; bros., 6,566; srs., 71,451; bap., 340,653; Caths., 37,039,000 (94.9%); tot. pop., 39,020,000.
Constitutional monarchy on the Iberian peninsula in southwestern Europe; capital, Madrid. Christians were on the peninsula by 200; some of them suffered martyrdom during persecutions of the third century. A council held in Elvira about 304/6 enacted the first legislation on clerical celibacy in the West. Vandals invaded the peninsula in the fifth century, bringing with them an Arian brand of Christianity which they retained until their conversion following the baptism of their king Reccared, in 589. One of the significant developments of the seventh century was the establishment of Toledo as the primatial see. The Visigoth kingdom lasted to the time of the Arab invasion, 711-14. The Church survived under Muslim rule but experienced some doctrinal and disciplinary irregularities as well as harassment. Reconquest of most of the peninsula was accomplished by 1248; unification was achieved during the reign of Ferdinand and Isabella. The discoveries of Columbus and other explorers ushered in an era of colonial expansion in which Spain became one of the greatest mission-sending countries in history. In 1492, in repetition of anti-Semitic actions of 694, the expulsion of unbaptized Jews was decreed, leading to mass baptisms but a questionable number of real conversions in 1502. (The Jewish minority numbered about 165,000.) Activity by the Inquisition followed. Spain was not seriously affected by the Reformation. Ecclesiastical decline set in about 1650. Anti-Church actions authorized by a constitution enacted in 1812 resulted in the suppression of religious and other encroachments on the leaders, people and goods of the Church. Political, religious and cultural turmoil recurred during the 19th century and into the 20th. A revolutionary republic was proclaimed in 1931, triggering a series of developments which led to civil war from 1936 to 1939. During the conflict, which pitted leftist Loyalists against the forces of

Francisco Franco, 6,632 priests and religious and an unknown number of lay persons perished in addition to thousands of victims of combat. One-man, one-party rule, established after the civil war and with rigid control policies with respect to personal liberties and social and economic issues, continued for more than 35 years before giving way after the death of Franco to democratic reforms. The Catholic Church, long the established religion, was disestablished under a new constitution providing guarantees of freedom for other religions as well. Disestablishment was ratified with modifications of a 1976 revision of the earlier concordat of 1953. (See Index for 1993 papal visit and International Eucharistic Congress.)

Sri Lanka*

Archd., 1; dioc., 9; abp., 1; bp., 12; parishes, 357; priests, 792 (511 dioc., 281 rel.); p.d., 2; sem., 287; bros., 220; srs., 2,379; bap., 29,676; Caths., 1,156,000 (6.7%); tot. pop., 17,240,000.

Independent socialist republic, island southeast of India (formerly Ceylon); capital, Colombo. Effective evangelization began in 1543 and made great progress by the middle of the 17th century. The Church was seriously hampered during the Dutch period from about 1650 to 1795. Anti-Catholic laws were repealed by the British in 1806. The hierarchy was established in 1886. Leftist governments and other factors have worked against the Church since the country became independent in 1948. The high percentage of indigenous clergy and religious has been of great advantage to the Church.

Sudan*

Archd., 2; dioc., 7; abp., 2; bp., 5; parishes, 93; priests, 191 (68 dioc., 123 rel.); p.d., 1; sem., 145; bros., 58; srs., 277; bap., 39,214; Caths., 1,952,000 (7.5%); tot. pop., 25,940,000.

Republic in northeastern Africa, the largest country on the continent; capital, Khartoum. Christianity was introduced from Egypt and gained acceptance in the sixth century. Under Arab rule, it was eliminated in the northern region. No Christians were in the country in 1600. Evangelization attempts begun in the 19th century in the south yielded hard-won results. By 1931 there were nearly 40,000 Catholics there, and considerable progress was made by missionaries after that time. In 1957, a year after the republic was established, Catholic schools were nationalized. An act restrictive of religious freedom went into effect in 1962, resulting in the harassment and expulsion of foreign missionaries. By 1964 all but a few Sudanese missionaries had been forced out of the southern region. The northern area, where Islam predominates, is impervious to Christian influence. Late in 1971 some missionaries were allowed to return to work in the South. Southern Sudan was granted regional autonomy within a unified country in March, 1972, thus ending often bitter fighting between the North and South dating back to 1955. The hierarchy was established in 1974. The imposition of Islamic penal codes in 1984 was a cause of concern to all Christian churches. (See Index for 1993 papal visit.)

Suriname

Dioc., 1; bp., 1; parishes, 20; priests, 26 (6 dioc., 20 rel.); sem., 4; bros., 14; srs., 50; bap., 1,987; Caths., 86,000 (20%); tot. pop., 430,000. (AD)

Independent (Nov. 25, 1975) state in northern South America (formerly Dutch Guiana); capital, Paramaribo, Catholicism was introduced in 1683. Evangelization began in 1817.

Swaziland*

Dioc., 1; bp., 1; parishes, 14; priests, 39 (6 dioc., 33 rel.); sem., 8; bros., 5; srs., 82; bap., 1,106; Caths., 44,000 (5.3%); tot. pop., 820,000.

Monarchy in southern Africa; almost totally surrounded by South Africa; capital, Mbabane. Missionary work was entrusted to the Servites in 1913. A prefecture apostolic was organized in 1923. The hierarchy was established in 1951. Established diplomatic relations with the Vatican in 1992.

Sweden*

Dioc., 1; bp., 2; parishes, 40; priests, 119 (54 dioc., 65 rel.); p.d., 11; sem., 15; bros., 13; srs., 248; bap., 1,347; Caths., 148,000 (1.7%); tot. pop., 8,640,000.

Constitutional monarchy in northwestern Europe; capital, Stockholm. Christianity was introduced by St. Ansgar, a Frankish monk, in 829/30. The Church became well established in the 12th century and was a major influence at the end of the Middle Ages. Political and other factors favored the introduction and spread of the Lutheran Church which became the state religion in 1560. The Augsburg Confession of 1530 was accepted by the government; all relations with Rome were severed; monasteries were suppressed; the very presence of Catholics in the country was forbidden in 1617. A decree of tolerance for foreign Catholics was issued about 1781. Two years later a vicariate apostolic was organized for the country. In 1873 Swedes were given the legal right to leave the Lutheran Church and join another Christian church. (Membership in the Lutheran Church is presumed by law unless notice is given of membership in another church.) In 1923 there were only 11 priests and five churches in the country. Since 1952 Catholics have enjoyed almost complete religious freedom. The hierarchy was reestablished in 1953. Hindrances to growth of the Church are the strongly entrenched established church, limited resources, a clergy shortage and the size of the country.

Switzerland*

Dioc., 6; abb., 2; card., 1; bp. (1993), 17; parishes, 1,706; priests, 3,650 (2,153 dioc., 1,497 rel.); p.d., 54; sem., 209; bros., 389; srs., 7,848; bap., 33,087; Caths., 3,150,000 (46.3%); tot. pop., 6,790,000.

Confederation in central Europe; capital, Bern. Christianity was introduced in the fourth century or earlier and was established on a firm footing before the barbarian invasions of the sixth century. Constance, established as a diocese in the seventh century, was a stronghold of the faith against the pagan Alamanni, in particular, who were not converted until some time in the ninth century. During this period of struggle with the barbarians, a number of monasteries of great influence were established. The Reformation in Switzerland was triggered by Zwingli in 1519 and furthered by him at Zurich until his death in battle against the Catholic cantons in 1531. Calvin set in motion the forces that made Geneva the international capital of the Reformation and transformed it into a theocracy. Catholics mobilized a Counter-Reformation in 1570, six years after Calvin's death. Struggle between Protestant and Catholic cantons was a fact of Swiss life for several hundred years. The Helvetic Constitution enacted at the turn of the 19th century embodied anti-Catholic measures and consequences, among them the dissolution of 130 monasteries. The Church was reorganized later in the century to meet the threats of liberalism, radicalism and the Kulturkampf. In the process, the Church, even though on the defensive, gained the strength and cohesion that characterizes it to the present time. The six dioceses in the country are immediately subject to the Holy See. In 1973, constitutional articles banning Jesuits from the country and prohibiting the establishment of convents and monasteries were repealed.

Syria*

Patriarchates, 3 (Antioch of Maronites, Greek Melkites and Syrians; patriarchs of Maronites and Syrians reside in Lebanon); archd., 12 (1 Armenian, 2 Maronite, 5 Greek Melkite, 4 Syrian); dioc., 3 (Armenian, Chaldean, Maronite); v.a., 1 (Latin); patriarch, 1; abp., 15; bp., 5; parishes, 190; priests, 226 (151 dioc., 75 rel.); p.d., 2; sem., 54; bros., 7; srs., 410; bap., 2,310; Caths., 274,000 (2.1%); tot. pop., 12,990,000.

Arab socialist republic in southwest Asia; capital, Damascus. Christian communities were formed in apostolic times. It is believed that St. Peter established a see at Antioch before going to Rome. Damascus became a center of influence. The area was the place of great men and great events in the early history of the Church. Monasticism developed there in the fourth century. So did the Monophysite and Monothelite heresies to which portion of the Church succumbed. Byzantine Syrians who remained in communion with Rome were given the name Melkites. Christians of various persuasions — Jacobites, Orthodox and Melkites — were subject to various degrees of harassment from the Arabs who took over in 638 and from the Ottoman Turks who isolated the country and remained in control from 1516 to the end of World War II.

Taiwan

Archd., 1; dioc., 6; abp., 1; bp., 7; parishes, 462; priests, 758 (227 dioc., 531 rel.); sem., 105; bros., 113; srs., 1,177; bap., 3,681; Caths., 296,000 (1.4%); tot. pop., 21,405,000.

Location of the Nationalist Government of the Republic of Chinaa, an island 100 miles off the southern coast of mainland China (also known as Formosa); capital, Taipei. Attempts to introduce Christianity in the 17th century were unsuccessful. Evangelization in the 19th century resulted in some 1,300 converts in 1895. Missionary endeavor was hampered by the Japanese who occupied the island following the Sino-Japanese war of 1894-95. Nine thousand Catholics were reported in 1938. Great progress was made in missionary endeavor among the Chinese who emigrated to the island following the Communist take-over of the mainland in 1949. The hierarchy was established in 1952.

Tajikistan

Independent republic bordering China and Afghanistan; formerly part of the USSR; capital, Dushanbc. Total population, 5,420,000.

Tanzania*

Archd., 4; dioc., 25; card., 1; abp., 6; bp., 29; parishes, 767; priests, 1,659 (1,044 dioc., 615 rel.); p.d. 2; sem., 813; bros., 430; srs., 5,930; bap., 212,873; Caths., 5,860,000 (20.6%); tot. pop., 28,360,000.

Republic (consisting of former Tanganyika on the eastern coast of Africa and former Zanzibar, an island group off the eastern coast); capital, Dar es Salaam. The first Catholic mission in the former Tanganyikan portion of the republic was manned by Holy Ghost Fathers in 1868. The hierarchy was established there in 1953. Zanzibar was the landing place of Augustinians with the Portuguese in 1499. Some evangelization was attempted between then and 1698 when the Arabs expelled all priests from the territory. There was no Catholic missionary activity from then until the 1860s. The Holy Ghost Fathers arrived in 1863 and were entrusted with the mission in 1872. Zanzibar was important as a point of departure for missionaries to Tanganyika, Kenya and other places in East Africa. A vicariate for Zanzibar was set up in 1906.

Thailand*

Archd., 2; dioc., 8; card., 1; abp., 3; bp., 14; parishes, 306; priests, 556 (307 dioc., 249 rel.); p.d., 1; sem., 297; bros., 134; srs., 1,313; bap., 7,210; Caths., 240,000 (.4%); tot. pop., 56,920,000.

Constitutional monarchy in southeastern Asia (formerly Siam); capital, Bangkok. The first Christians in the region were Portuguese traders who arrived early in the 16th century. A number of missionaries began arriving in 1554 but pastoral care was confined mostly to the Portuguese until the 1660s. Evangelization of the natives got under way from about that time. A seminary was organized in 1665, a vicariate was set up four years later, and a point of departure was established for missionaries to Tonkin, Cochin China and China. Persecution and death for some of the missionaries ended evangelization efforts in 1688. It was resumed, however, and made progress from 1824 onwards. In 1881 missionaries were sent from Siam to neighboring Laos. The hierarchy was established in 1965. Abp. Michai Kitbunchu was named the first Thai cardinal in 1983.

Togo*

Archd., 1; dioc., 3; abp., 1; bp., 3; parishes, 95; priests, 284 (163 dioc., 121 rel.); sem., 182; bros., 139; srs., 488; bap., 32,446; Caths., 822,000 (22.6%); tot. pop., 3,640,000.

Republic on the western coast of Africa; capital, Lome. The first Catholic missionaries in the area, where slave raiders operated for nearly 200 years, were members of the African Missions Society who arrived in 1563. They were followed by Divine Word Missionaries in 1914, when a prefecture apostolic was organized. At that time the Catholic population numbered about 19,000. The African Missionaries returned after their German predecessors were deported following World War I. The first native priest was ordained in 1922. The hierarchy was established in 1955.

Tokelau
Independent Mission (1992), 1; parish, 1; priest, 1 (dioc.); p.d., 1; srs., 3; bap., 28; Caths., 500; tot. pop., 2,000. (AD)
Pacific islands administered by New Zealand. Established as an independent mission in 1992.

Tonga
Dioc., 1; bp., 1; parishes, 13; priests, 26 (14 dioc., 12 rel.); sem., 14; bros., 11; srs., 63; bap., 527; Caths., 14,000 (14%); tot. pop., 96,000. (AD)
Polynesian monarchy in the southwestern Pacific, consisting of about 150 islands; capital Nuku'alofa. Marists started missionary work in 1842, some years after Protestants had begun evangelization. By 1880 the Catholic population numbered about 1,700. A vicariate was organized in 1937. The hierarchy was established in 1966.

Trinidad and Tobago*
Archd., 1; abp., 1; bp., 1; parishes, 62; priests, 123 (48 dioc., 75 rel.); sem., 22; bros., 17; srs., 170; bap., 6,200; Caths., 395,000 (31.6%); tot. pop., 1,250,000.
Independent nation, consisting of two islands in the Caribbean; capital, Port-of-Spain. The first Catholic church in Trinidad was built in 1591, years after several missionary ventures had been launched and a number of missionaries killed. Capuchins were there from 1618 until about 1802. Missionary work continued after the British gained control early in the 19th century. Cordial relations have existed between the Church and state, both of which have manifested their desire for the development of native clergy.

Tunisia*
Prel., 1; parishes, 15; priests, 43 (19 dioc., 24 rel.); sem., 1; bros., 6; srs., 172; bap., 14; Caths., 12,000 (.14%); tot. pop., 8,360,000.
Republic on the northern coast of Africa; capital, Tunis. There were few Christians in the territory until the 19th century. A prefecture apostolic was organized in 1843 and the Carthage archdiocese was established in 1884. The Catholic population in 1892 consisted of most of the approximately 50,000 Europeans in the country. When Tunis became a republic in 1956, most of the Europeans left the country. The Holy See and the Tunisian government concluded an agreement in 1964 which changed the Carthage archdiocese into a prelacy and handed over some ecclesiastical property to the republic. A considerable number of Muslim students are in Catholic schools, but the number of Muslim converts to the Church has been small.

Turkey*
Patriarchate, 1 (Cilicia for the Armenians; the patriarch resides in Lebanon); archd., 3; v.a., 2; ap. ex., 1; abp., 3; bp., 2; parishes, 54; priests, 68 (15 dioc., 53 rel.); p.d., 15; sem., 5; bros., 16; srs., 118; bap., 88; Caths., 15,000; tot. pop., 67,330,000.
Republic in Asia Minor and southeastern Europe, capital, Ankara. Christian communities were established in apostolic times, as attested in the Acts of the Apostles, some of the Letters of St. Paul, and Revelation. The territory was the scene of heresies and ecumenical councils, the place of residence of Fathers of the Church, the area in which ecclesiastical organization reached the dimensions of more than 450 sees in the middle of the seventh century. The region remained generally Byzantine except for the period of the Latin occupation of Constantinople from 1204 to 1261, but was conquered by the Ottoman Turks in 1453 and remained under their domination until establishment of the republic in 1923. Christians, always a minority, numbered more Orthodox than Latins; they were all under some restrictions during the Ottoman period. They suffered persecution in the 19th and 20th centuries, the Armenians being the most numerous victims. Turkey is overwhelmingly Muslim. Catholics are tolerated to a degree.

Turkmenistan
Former constituent republic of USSR; independent, 1991; capital, Ashkabad. Total population, 3,760,000.

Turks and Caicos Islands
Independent mission, 1; parishes, 2; priests, 2 (1 dioc., 1 rel.); bap., 11; Caths., 2,000; tot. pop., 11,000. (AD, Antilles)
British possession in West Indies; capital, Grand Turk.

Tuvalu
Independent mission, 1; priest, 1 (rel.); bap., 3; Caths., 100; tot. pop., 9,000.
Independent state (1978) in Oceania, consisting of 9 islands (formerly Ellice Islands); capital, Funafuti.

Uganda*
Archd., 1; dioc., 15; mil. ord.; abp., 1; bp., 19; parishes, 358; priests, 1,242 (902 dioc., 340 rel.); p.d., 2; sem., 712; bros., 404; srs., 2,784; bap., 266,408; Caths., 8,013,000 (41%); tot. pop., 19,520,000.
Republic in eastern Africa; capital, Kampala. The Missionaries of Africa (White Fathers) were the first Catholic missionaries, starting in 1879. Persecution broke out from 1885 to 1887, taking a toll of 22 Catholic martyrs, who were canonized in 1964, and a number of Anglican victims. (Pope Paul honored all those who died for the faith during a visit to Kampala in 1969.) By 1888, there were more than 8,000 Catholics. Evangelization was resumed in 1894, after being interrupted by war, and proceeded thereafter. The first native African bishop was ordained in 1939. The hierarchy was established in 1953. The Church was suppressed during the erratic

regime of Pres. Idi-Amin, who was deposed in the spring of 1979. (See Index for 1993 papal visit.)

Ukraine*

Major archbishopric, 1 (Ukrainian); archd., 2 (1 Armenian and 1 Latin rite); dioc. (1993), 9 (6 Byzantine rite, 3 Latin); a.a. (1993), 1; card., 1 (Ukrainian Major Archbishop Lubachivsky); abp., 2; bp., 14; parishes, 3,000; priests, 1,514 (1,245 dioc., 269 rel.); p.d., 1; sem., 1,348; bros., 288; srs., 875; bap., 18,203; Caths., 5,157,000 (14.7%); tot. pop., 35,080,000.

Independent republic bordering on the Black Sea; former USSR republic; capital, Kiev. The baptism of Vladimir and his people in 988 marked the beginning of Christianity in the territory of Kievan Rus which is included in today's Ukraine. The Byzantine-Rite Catholic Church was officially suppressed and underground in the USSR from the late 1940s. (See USSR below for situation during communist control.)

Union of Soviet Socialist Republics

(The Union of Soviet Socialist Republics disbanded Dec. 25, 1991. Background history of the USSR especially during communist domination is given below. See also separate entries: Armenia, Azerbaijan, Belarus, Estonia, Georgia, Kazakhstan, Kyrgyzstan, Latvia, Lithuania, Moldava, Russian Federation, Tajikistan, Turkmenistan, Ukraine, Uzbekistan.) The Orthodox Church has been predominant in Russian history. It developed from the Byzantine Church before 1064. Some of its members subsequently established communion with Rome as the result of reunion movements but most of them remained Orthodox. The government has always retained some kind of general or particular control of this church. Latins, always a minority, had a little more freedom. From the beginning of the Communist government in 1917, all churches of whatever kind — including Jews and Muslims — became the targets of official campaigns designed to negate their influence on society and/or to eliminate them entirely. An accurate assessment of the situation of the Catholic Church in Russia was difficult to make. Its dimensions, however, could be gauged from the findings of a team of research specialists made public by the Judiciary Committee of the U.S. House of Representatives in 1964. It was reported: "The fate of the Catholic Church in the USSR and countries occupied by the Russians from 1917 to 1959 shows the following: (a) the number killed: 55 bishops; 12,800 priests and monks; 2.5 million Catholic believers; (b) imprisoned or deported: 199 bishops; 32,000 priests and 10 million believers; (c) 15,700 priests were forced to abandon their priesthood and accept other jobs; and (d) a large number of seminaries and religious communities were dissolved; 1,600 monasteries were nationalized, 31,779 churches were closed. 400 newspapers were prohibited, and all Catholic organizations were dissolved." Several Latin Rite churches were open; e.g., in Moscow, Leningrad, Odessa and Tiflis. An American chaplain was stationed in Moscow to serve Catholics at the U.S. embassy there. Despite repression and attempts at Sovietization, Lithuania

and the Ukraine remained strongholds of Catholicism. In 1991, the Pope reconstituted the Byzantine hierarchy in the Ukraine. He also established: two Latin rite apostolic administrations in the Russian Republic; one Latin-rite apostolic administration in the Kazakhstan Republic; a metropolitan see and two suffragans in Byelorussia (now Belarus).

United Arab Emirates

V.a, 1; bp., 1; parishes, 4; priests, 13 (2 dioc., 11 rel.); sem., 3; srs., 35; bap., 1,046; Caths., 100,000; tot. pop., 1,630,000.

Independent state along Persian Gulf; capital, Abu Dhabi.

United States*

See Catholic History in the United States, Statistics of the Church in the United States.

Uruguay*

Archd., 1; dioc., 9; abp., 2; bp., 13; parishes, 227; priests, 537 (218 dioc., 319 rel.); p.d., 40; sem., 104; bros., 126; srs., 1,859; bap., 39,506; Caths., 2,434,000 (78.2%); tot. pop., 3,110,000.

Republic (called the Eastern Republic of Uruguay) on the southeast coast of South America; capital, Montevideo. The Spanish established a settlement in 1624 and evangelization followed. Missionaries followed the reduction pattern to reach the Indians, form them in the faith and train them in agriculture, husbandry, other useful arts, and the experience of managing property and living in community. Montevideo was made a diocese in 1878. The constitution of 1830 made Catholicism the religion of the state and subsidized some of its activities, principally the missions to the Indians. Separation of Church and state was provided for in the constitution of 1917.

Uzbekistan*

Former republic of USSR; independent, 1991; capital, Tashkent. Tot. pop., 20,960,000.

Vanuatu

Dioc., 1; bp., 1; parishes, 25; priests, 23 (6 dioc., 17 rel.); p.d., 1; sem., 20; bros., 14; srs., 65; bap., 821; Caths., 21,000 (14.7%); tot. pop., 142,000.

Independent (July 29, 1980) island group in the southwest Pacific, about 500 miles west of Fiji (formerly New Hebrides); capital, Vila. Effective, though slow, evangelization by Catholic missionaries began about 1887. A vicariate apostolic was set up in 1904. The hierarchy was established in 1966.

Vatican City

See separate entry.

Venezuela*

Archd., 7; dioc., 19; v.a., 4; ap. ex., 1; card., 2; abp., 8; bp., 34; parishes, 1,069; priests, 2,049 (954 dioc., 1,095 rel.); p.d., 56, sem., 861; bros., 308; srs., 4,328; bap., 368,493; Caths., 18,638,000 (92.1%); tot. pop., 20,230,000.

Republic in northern South America; capital, Caracas. Evangelization began in 1513-14 and involved members of a number of religious orders who worked in assigned territories, developing missions into pueblos or towns and villages of Indian converts. Nearly 350 towns originated as missions. Fifty-four missionaries met death by violence from the start of missionary work until 1817. Missionary work was seriously hindered during the wars of independence in the second decade of the 19th century and continued in decline through the rest of the century as dictator followed dictator in a period of political turbulence. Restoration of the missions got under way in 1922. The first diocese was established in 1531. Most of the bishops have been native Venezuelans. The first diocesan synod was held in 1574. Church-state relations are regulated by an agreement concluded with the Holy See in 1964.

Vietnam

Archd., 3; dioc., 22; abp., 2; bp., 29; parishes, 1,738; priests, 1,794 (1,493 dioc., 301 rel.); p.d., 2; sem., 880; bros., 541; srs., 6,265; bap., 104,726; Caths., 4,595,000 (6.7%); tot. pop., 68,180,000.

Country in southeastern Asia, reunited officially July 2, 1976, as the Socialist Republic of Vietnam; capital, Hanoi. Previously, from 1954, partitioned into the Democratic Peoples' Republic of Vietnam in the North (capital, Hanoi) and the Republic of Vietnam in the South (capital, Saigon). Catholicism was introduced in 1533 but missionary work was intermittent until 1615 when Jesuits arrived to stay. One hundred thousand Catholics were reported in 1639. Two vicariates were organized in 1659. A seminary was set up in 1666 and two native priests were ordained two years later. A congregation of native women religious formed in 1670 is still active. Severe persecution broke out in 1698, three times in the 18th century, and again in the 19th. Between 100,000 and 300,000 persons suffered in some way from persecution during the 50 years before 1883 when the French moved in to secure religious liberty for the Catholics. Most of the 117 beatified Martyrs of Vietnam were killed during this 50-year period. After the French were forced out of Vietnam in 1954, the country was partitioned at the 17th parallel. The North went Communist and the Viet Cong, joined by North Vietnamese regular army troops in 1964, fought to gain control of the South. In 1954 there were approximately 1,114,000 Catholics in the North and 480,000 in the South. More than 650,000 fled to the South to avoid the government repression that silenced the Church in the North. In South Vietnam, the Church continued to develop during the war years. Fragmentary reports about the status of the Church since the end of the war in 1975 have been ominous. Freedom of religious belief, promised by the Revolutionary Government in May, 1975, shortly after its capture of Saigon (Ho Chi Min City), is denied in practice. Late in 1983, the government initiated support for a "patriotic" Catholic church analogous to the communist-sponsored church in China. The hierarchy was established in 1960. The apostolic delegation, formerly in Saigon, was transferred to Hanoi in 1976; it is presently vacant.

Virgin Islands

Dioc., 1 (St. Thomas, suffragan of Washington, D.C.); parishes, 8; priests, 15 (10 dioc., 5 rel.); p.d.,

22; sem., 8; bros., 1; srs., 23; bap., 593; Caths., 33,000; tot. pop., 102,000.

Organized unincorporated U.S. territory, about 34 miles east of Puerto Rico; capital, Charlotte Amalie on St. Thomas (one of the three principal islands). The islands were discovered by Columbus in 1493 and named for St. Ursula and her virgin companions. Missionaries began evangel- ization in the 16th century. A church on St. Croix dates from about 1660; another, on St. Thomas, from 1774. The Baltimore archdiocese had jurisdiction over the islands from 1804 to 1820 when it was passed on to the first of several places in the Caribbean area. Some trouble arose over a pastoral appointment in the 19th century, resulting in a small schism. The Redemptorists took over pastoral care in 1858; normal conditions have prevailed since.

British Virgin Islands

Parishes, 2; priests, 2 (rel.); bap., 29; Caths., 1,000; tot. pop., 10,000.

British possession in Caribbean; capital, Road Town.

Wales

Archd., 1; dioc., 2; abp., 1; bp., 2; parishes, 186; priests, 294 (170 dioc., 124 rel.); p.d., 8; sem., 21; bros., 20; srs., 575; bap., 2,996; Caths., 153,736 (5%); tot. pop., 3,010,000 (1993 Annuario Pontificio.)

Part of the United Kingdom, on the western part of the island of Great Britain. Celtic missionaries completed evangelization by the end of the sixth century, the climax of what has been called the age of saints. Welsh Christianity received its distinctive Celtic character at this time. Some conflict developed when attempts were made — and proved successful later — to place the Welsh Church under the jurisdiction of Canterbury; the Welsh opted for direct contact with Rome. The Church made progress despite the depredations of Norsemen in the eighth and ninth centuries. Norman infiltration occurred near the middle of the 12th century, resulting in a century-long effort to establish territorial dioceses and parishes to replace the Celtic organizational plan of monastic centers and satellite churches. The Western Schism produced split views and allegiances. Actions of Henry VIII in breaking away from Rome had serious repercussions. Proscription and penal laws crippled the Church, resulted in heavy defections and touched off a 150-year period of repression in which more than 91 persons died for the faith. Methodism prevailed by 1750. Modern Catholicism came to Wales with Irish immigrants in the 19th century, when the number of Welsh Catholics was negligible. Catholic emancipation was granted in 1829. The hierarchy was restored in 1850.

Wallis and Futuna Islands

Dioc., 1; bp., 1; priests, 10 (6 dioc., 4 rel.); bros., 6; srs., 39; bap., 788; Caths., 13,000; tot. pop., 15,000.

French overseas territory in the southwestern Pacific; capital Mata-Utu. Marists, who began evangelizing the islands in 1836-7, were the first

Catholic missionaries. The entire populations of the two islands were baptized by the end of 1842 (Wallis) and 1843 (Futuna). The first missionary to the latter island was killed in 1841. Most of the priests on the islands are native Polynesians. The hierarchy was established in 1966.

Western Sahara

P.a., 1; parishes, 2; priests, 3 (rel.); bros., 3; Caths., 500; tot. pop., 180,000.

Former Spanish overseas province (Spanish Sahara) on the northwestern coast of Africa. Territory is under control of Morocco. Islam is the religion of non-Europeans. A prefecture apostolic was established in 1954 for the European Catholics there.

Yemen

Parishes, 4; priests, 3 (rel.); srs., 24; bap., 9; Caths., 4,000; tot. pop., 11,290,000.

Republic on southern coast of Arabian peninsula; capital, Sanaa. Formerly North Yemen (Arab Republic of Yemen) and South Yemen (People's Republic of Yemen); formally reunited in 1990. Christians perished in the first quarter of the sixth century. Muslims have been in control since the seventh century. The state religion is Islam. Under ecclesiastical jurisdiction of Arabia vicariate apostolic.

Yugoslavia*

Archd., 2; dioc., 4; abp., 3; bp., 5; parishes, 281; priests, 248 (195 dioc., 53 rel.); p.d., 1; sem., 40; bros., 10; srs., 539; bap., 6,370; Caths., 549,954 (4.5%); tot. pop., 12,226,960. (Figures, compiled from diocesan statistics in the 1993 Annuario Pontificio, are approximate; they include the Skopje-Prizren diocese which includes territory in Macedonia.)

Republic in southeastern Europe formed in 1992, consisting of Serbia and Montenegro; captial, Belgrade. The four other republics (Croatia, Slovenia, Bosnia-Herzegovina, and Macedonia) which made up the federation of Yugoslavia created after World War II proclaimed their independence in 1991-1992; see separate entries. Background history of the Church in pre-1991 Yugoslavia, especially during communist domination, is given below. (See Index for war in the area.)

Socialist republic in southeastern Europe; capital, Belgrade. Christianity was introduced from the seventh to ninth centuries in the regions which were combined to form the nation after World War I. Since these regions straddled the original line of demarcation for the Western and Eastern Empires (and churches), and since the Reformation had little lasting effect, the Christians are nearly all either Roman Catholics or Byzantines (some in communion with Rome, the majority Orthodox). Yugoslavia was proclaimed a Socialist republic in 1945, the year in which began years of the harshest kind of total persecution of the Church. Cardinal Stepinac, one of its major victims, died in 1960. In an agreement signed June 25, 1966, the government recognized the Holy See's spiritual jurisdiction over the Church in the country and guaranteed to bishops the possibility of maintaining contact with Rome in ecclesiastical and religious matters. The Holy See confirmed the principle that the activity of ecclesiastics, in the exercise of priestly functions, must take place within the religious and ecclesiastical sphere, and that abuse of these functions for political ends would be illegal.

Zaire*

Archd., 6; dioc., 41; card., 1; abp., 8; bp., 50; parishes, 1,160; priests, 3,303 (1,811 dioc., 1,492 rel.); p.d., 11; sem., 2,764; bros., 1,038; srs., 5,468; bap., 442,589; Caths., 18,583,000 (50.6%); tot. pop., 36,670,000.

Republic in south central Africa; (formerly the Congo); capital, Kinshasa. Christianity was introduced in 1484 and evangelization began about 1490. The first native bishop in black Africa was ordained in 1518. Subsequent missionary work was hindered by factors including 18th and 19th century anticlericalism. Modern evangelization started in the second half of the 19th century. The hierarchy was established in 1959. In the civil disorders which followed independence in 1960, some missions and other church installations were abandoned, thousands of people reverted to tribal religions and many priests and religious were killed. Church-state tensions have developed in recent years because of the Church's criticism of the anti-Christian thrust of Pres. Mobutu's "Africanization" policies.

Zambia*

Archd., 2; dioc., 7; abp., 2; bp., 7; parishes, 233; priests, 560 (193 dioc., 367 rel.); p.d., 2; sem., 267; bros., 146; srs., 902; bap., 78,582; Caths., 2,377,000 (27%); tot. pop., 8,780,000.

Republic in central Africa; capital, Lusaka. Portuguese priests did some evangelizing in the 16th and 17th centuries but no results of their work remained in the 19th century. Jesuits began work in the south in the 1880s and White Fathers in the north and east in 1895. Evangelization of the western region began for the first time in 1931. The number of Catholics doubled in the 20 years following World War II.

Zimbabwe*

Archd., 1; dioc., 6; abp., 1; bp., 8; parishes, 131; priests, 338 (96 dioc., 242 rel.); p.d., 8; sem., 143; bros., 97; srs., 1,119; bap., 36,695; Caths., 872,000 (8.7%); tot. pop., 10,020,000.

Independent republic (Apr. 18, 1980) in south central Africa (formerly Rhodesia); capital, Harare (Salisbury). Earlier unsuccessful missionary ventures preceded the introduction of Catholicism in 1879. Missionaries began to make progress after 1893. The hierarchy was established in 1955; the first black bishop was ordained in 1973. In 1969, four years after the government of Ian Smith made a unilateral declaration of independence from England, a new constitution was enacted for the purpose of assuring continued white supremacy over the black majority. Catholic and Protestant prelates in the country protested vigorously against the constitution and related enactments as opposed to human rights of the blacks and restrictive of the Church's freedom to carry out its pastoral, educational and social service functions. The Smith regime was ousted in 1979 after seven years of civil war in which at least 25,000 people were killed.

CATHOLIC WORLD STATISTICS

(Principal sources: *Statistical Yearbook of the Church, 1991*, the latest edition; *Annuario Pontificio, 1993*. Figures are as of Dec. 31, 1991, unless indicated otherwise.)

	Africa	North America[1]	South America	Asia	Europe	Oceania	WORLD TOTALS
Patriarchates[2]	2	—	—	8	2	—	12
Archdioceses	64	82	88	106	148	18	506
Dioceses	335	332	372	292	483	54	1,868
Prelatures	1	10	36	6	5	—	58
Abbacies	—	1	2	—	11	—	14
Exarchates/Ords.	—	1	4	1	13	—	19
Military Ords.	3	4	8	3	10	2	30
Vicariates Apostolic	12	8	37	11	1	—	69
Prefectures	4	—	7	1	—	—	12
Independent Missions	3	1	—	2	—	1	7
Apostolic Admin.	1	—	—	2	6	—	9
Cardinals[3]	17	19	19	14	75	4	148
Patriarchs[2]	1	—	—	8	1	—	10
Archbishops	87	110	123	147	285	25	777[4]
Bishops	394	658	658	410	1,050	80	3,250[4]
Priests	20,768	82,018	36,698	34,931	224,299	5,317	404,031
Diocesan	10,903	51,086	18,637	19,502	155,670	2,792	258,590
Religious	9,865	30,932	18,061	15,429	68,629	2,525	145,441
Perm. Deacons	290	11,569	1,412	89	4,936	112	18,408
Brothers	6,073	12,649	6,206	6,703	28,091	2,462	62,184
Sisters	43,976	169,413	92,502	113,967	442,125	13,349	875,332
Maj. Seminarians	14,649	15,034	16,368	22,864	29,968	785	99,668
Sec. Inst. Mbrs. (Men)	35	33	16	31	733	2	850
Sec. Inst. Mbrs. (Women)	401	1,462	3,294	877	24,923	51	31,008
Lay Missionaries	1,392	226	478	356	—	187	2,639
Catechists	264,114	12,320	14,596	85,235	338	6,457	383,060
Parishes	9,189	33,322	18,536	16,993	138,783	2,408	219,231[5]
Kindergartens	6,506	7,794	4,998	8,046	23,429	354	51,127
Students	534,273	336,222	601,377	1,080,086	1,863,560	27,449	4,442,967
Elem./Primary Schools	24,193	12,697	8,578	12,692	18,407	2,574	79,141
Students	8,405,084	3,825,819	3,473,230	4,345,391	3,598,622	533,872	24,182,018
Secondary Schools	4,551	3,514	4,974	7,652	10,022	693	31,406
Students	1,325,125	1,412,148	1,996,797	3,906,361	3,340,735	341,565	12,322,731
Students in Higher Insts.[6]	20,501	329,486	121,436	541,880	162,037	3,366	1,178,706
Social Service Facilities	12,999	12,044	22,225	16,921	30,912	1,340	96,441
Hospitals	884	1,122	989	998	1,468	156	5,617
Dispensaries	3,692	1,742	3,241	3,092	2,815	166	14,748
Leprosariums	260	14	44	437	16	3	774
Homes for Aged/Handic.	390	1,383	1,406	882	6,568	231	10,860
Orphanages	583	678	1,040	2,208	1,947	203	6,659
Nurseries	744	980	3,256	1,937	2,100	20	9,037
Matrimonial Advice Ctrs.	896	1,880	1,109	975	2,922	192	7,974
Social Educ. Ctrs.	1,074	1,476	1,996	2,016	2,436	82	9,080
Other Institutions	4,476	2,769	9,144	4,376	10,640	287	31,692
Baptisms	2,862,484	4,284,286	5,303,106	2,476,492	3,071,043	141,981	18,139,392
Under Age 7	1,887,511	4,071,685	4,990,289	2,122,061	3,008,516	125,593	16,205,655
Over Age 7	974,973	212,601	312,817	354,431	62,527	16,388	1,933,737
Marriages	242,864	876,156	961,080	493,134	1,252,781	33,132	3,859,147
Between Catholics	206,640	752,571	943,021	436,465	1,157,207	18,908	3,514,812
Mixed Marriages	36,224	123,585	18,059	56,669	95,574	14,224	344,335
Catholic Pop.[7]	92,078,000	198,621,000	270,099,000	89,164,000	287,460,000	7,156,000	944,578,000
World Population	664,913,000	431,565,000	302,892,000	3,224,912,000	716,240,000	26,909,000	5,367,431,000

[1] Includes Middle America. [2] For listing and description, see Index. [3] As of Sept. 10, 1993. [4] Figures for the hierarchy (cardinals, archbishops and bishops) included 2,456 ordinaries, 615 coadjutors or auxiliaries, 180 with offices in the Roman Curia, 33 in other offices, 912 retired. [5] 161,400 have parish priests; 54,056 are administered by other priests; 313 are entrusted to permanent deacons; 71 to brothers; 1,069 to women Religious; 1,322 to lay people; 1,000 vacant. [6] Thereare also approximately 91,597 in universities for ecclesiastical studies and 1,638,381 other university students. [7] Percentages of Catholics in world population: Africa, 13.8; North America (Catholics 66,903,000; tot. pop., 279,801,000), 23.9; Middle America (131,718,000; tot. pop., 151,764,000) 86.9; South America, 89.1; Asia, 2.8; Europe, 40.1; Oceania, 26.6; World, 17.6. (Catholic totals do not include those in areas that could not be surveyed, estimated to be 5 million.)

EPISCOPAL CONFERENCES

(Principal source: *Annuario Pontificio*.)

Episcopal conferences, organized and operating under general norms and particular statutes approved by the Holy See, are official bodies in and through which the bishops of a given country or territory act together as pastors of the Church.

Listed below according to countries or regions are titles and addresses of conferences and names and sees of presidents (archbishops unless noted otherwise).

Africa, North: Conference Episcopale Regionale du Nord de l'Afrique (CERNA), 13 rue Khelifa-Boukhalfa, Algiers, Algeria. Henri Teissier (Algiers).

Africa, South: Southern African Catholic Bishops' Conference (SACBC), P.O. Box 941, Pretoria 0001, S. Africa. Wilfred Fox Napier, O.F.M. (Durban).

Angola and Sao Tome: Conferencia Episcopal de Angola e Sao Tome (CEAST), C.P. 87 Luanda, Angola. Card. Alexandre do Nascimento (Luanda).

Antilles: Antilles Episcopal Conference (AEC), P.O. Box 3086, St. James (Trinidad and Tobago), W.I. Kelvin Edward Felix (Castries).

Arab Countries: Conference des Eveques Latins dans les Regions Arabes (CELRA), Latin Patriarchate, P.O. Box 14152, Jerusalem (Old City). Patriarch Michel Sabbah (Jerusalem).

Argentina: Conferencia Episcopal Argentina (CEA), Calle Suipacha 1034, 1008 Buenos Aires. Card. Antonio Quarracino (Buenos Aires).

Australia: Australian Catholic Bishops' Conference, 63 Currong St., Braddon, A.C.T. 2601. Card. Edward Bede Clancy (Sydney).

Austria: Osterreichische Bischofkonferenz, Rotenturmstrasse 2, A1010 Vienna. Card. Hans Hermann Groër, O.S.B. (Vienna).

Bangladesh: Catholic Bishops' Conference of Bangladesh (CBCB), P.O. Box 3, Dhaka-2. Michael Rozario (Dhaka).

Belgium: Bisschoppenconferentie van Belgie — Conference Episcopale de Belgique, Rue Guimard 1, B-1040 Brussel. Card. Godfried Danneels (Mechelen-Brussel).

Benin: Conference Episcopale du Benin, B.P. 491, Cotonou. Bp. Lucien Monsi-Agboka (Abomey).

Bolivia: Conferencia Episcopal de Bolivia (CEB), Casilla 2309, Calle Potosi 814, La Paz. Bp. Edmundo Luis Flavio Abastoflor Montero (Potosi).

Bosnia-Herzegovina: Held first meeting Aug. 2, 1993.

Brazil: Conferencia Nacional dos Bispos do Brasil (CNBB), C.P. 02067, SE/Sul Quadra 801, Conjunto "B," 70259-970 Brasilia, D.F. Luciano Pedro Mendes de Almeida, S.J. (Mariana).

Bulgaria: Ulitza Pashovi 10-B, Sofia VI. Bp. Metodio Dimitrow Stratiew, A.A. (Apostolic Exarch, Sofia).

Burkina Faso and Niger: Conference des Eveques de Burkina Faso et du Niger, B.P. 1195, Ouagadougou, Burkina Faso. Bp. Jean-Marie Compaore (Fada N'Gourma).

Burma: See Myanmar.

Burundi: Conference des Eveques Catholiques du Burundi, B. P. 1390, 5 Blvd. de l'Uprona, Bujumbura. Bp. Bernard Bududira (Bururi).

Cameroon: Conference Episcopale Nationale du Cameroun (CENC), BP 807, Yaoundé. Bp. Jean-Baptiste Ama (Ebolowa-Kribi).

Canada: See Canadian Conference of Catholic Bishops.

Central African Republic: Conference Episcopale Centrafricaine (CECA), B.P. 798, Bangui. Joachim N'Dayen (Bangui).

Chad: Conference Episcopale du Tchad, B.P. 456, N'Djamena. Charles Vandame, S.J. (N'Djamena).

Chile: Conferencia Episcopal de Chile (CECH), Casilla 517-V, Correo 21, Cienfuegas 47, Santiago. Bp. Fernando Ariztia Ruiz (Copiapo).

China (Republic of China, Taiwan): Regional Episcopal Conference of China, 34 Lane 32, Kwang Fu South Rd., Taipeh 10552, Taiwan. Bp. Paul Shan Kuo-hsi, S.J. (Kaohsiung). Statutes approved Apr. 16, 1991.

Colombia: Conferencia Episcopal de Colombia, Apartado 7448, Carrera 8, N. 84-87, Santafe de Bogota D.E. Pedro Rubiano Saenz (Cali).

Congo: Conference Episcopale du Congo, B.P. 200, Brazzaville. Barthelemy Batantu (Brazzaville).

Costa Rica: Conferencia Episcopal de Costa Rica (CECOR), Apartado 497, San Jose. Roman Arrieta Villalobos (San Jose de Costa Rica).

Côte d'Ivoire: Conference Episcopale de la Côte d'Ivoire, B.P. 1287, Abidjan 01. Card. Bernard Yago (Abidjan).

Croatia: Hrvatska Biskupska Konferencija, Kaptol 22, 4100 Zagreb. Card. Franjo Kuharic (Zagreb).

Cuba: Conferencia Episcopal de Cuba (CEC), Apartado 594, Calle 26 n. 314 Miramar, Havana 1. Jaime Lucas Ortega y Alamino (Havana).

Czech Republic: Ceska Biskupska Konference, Hradcanske nam. 16, 119 02 Praha (Prague). Miloslav Vlk (Prague).

Dominican Republic: Conferencia del Episcopado Dominicano (CED), Apartado 186, Santo Domingo. Card. Nicolas de Jesus Lopez Rodriguez (Santo Domingo).

Ecuador: Conferencia Episcopal Ecuatoriana, Apartado 1081, Avenida America 1805 y Lagasca, Quito. Antonio Jose Gonzalez Zumarraga (Quito).

El Salvador: Conferencia Episcopal de El Salvador (CEDES). 15 Av. Norte 1420, Col. Layco, Apartado 1310, San Salvador. Arturo Rivera Damas, S.D.B. (San Salvador).

Equatorial Guinea: Conferencia Episcopal de Guinea Ecuatorial. Apartado 106, Malabo. Bp. Anacleto Sima Ngua (Bata).

Ethiopia: Ethiopian Episcopal Conference, P.O. Box 2454, Addis Ababa. Card. Paulos Tzadua (Addis Ababa).

France: Conference des Evêques de France, 106 rue du Bac, 75341 Paris CEDEX 07. Joseph Duval (Rouen).

Gabon: Conference Episcopale du Gabon, B.P. 209, Oyem. Bp. Basile Mvé Engone, S.D.B. (Oyem).

Gambia, Liberia and Sierra Leone: Inter-Territorial Catholic Bishops' Conference of the Gambia, Liberia and Sierra Leone (ITCABIC), Santanno House, P.O. Box 893, Freetown, Sierra Leone. Bp. John C. O'Riordan, C.S.Sp. (Kenema, Sierra Leone).

Germany: Deutsche Bischofskonferenz, Kaiserstrasse 163, D-W-5300 Bonn 1. Bp. Karl Lehmann (Mainz). Statutes approved Nov. 14, 1992.

Ghana: Ghana Bishops' Conference, National Catholic Secretariat, P.O. Box 9712 Airport, Accra. Bp. Francis Anani Kofi Lodonu (Keta-Ho).

Great Britain: Bishops' Conference of England and Wales, General Secretariat, 39 Eccleston Square, London, SWIV IPD. Card. George Basil Hume, O.S.B. (Westminster). Bishops' Conference of Scotland, Archbishop's House, 196 Clyde St., Glasgow GI 4JY. Thomas Winning (Glasgow).

Greece: Conferentia Episcopalis Graeciae, Odos Homirou 9, 106 72 Athens. Nicolaos Foscolos (Athens).

Guatemala: Conferencia Episcopal de Guatemala (CEG), Apartado 1698, 26 Calle 8-90, zona 12, Ciudad de Guatemala. Bp. Gerardo Humberto Flores Reyes (Vera Paz).

Guinea: Conference Episcopale de la Guinee, B.P. 1006 Bis, Conakry. Robert Sarah (Conakry).

Haiti: Conference Episcopale de Haiti (CEH). B.P. 1572, Angle rues Piquant et Lammarre, Port-au-Prince. Francois Gayot, S.M.M. (Cap Haïtien).

Honduras: Conferencia Episcopal de Honduras (CEH), Apartado 847, Tegucigalpa. Hector Enrique Santos Hernandez, S.D.B. (Tegucigalpa).

Hungary: Magyar Püspöki Kar Konferenciája, Széchenyi u. 1, Pf. 80, H-3301 Eger. István Seregély (Eger).

India: Catholic Bishops' Conference of India (CBCI), CBCI Centre, Ashok Place, Goldakkhana, New Delhi-110001. Alphonsus Mathias (Bangalore).

Indian Ocean: Conference Episcopale de l'Ocean Indien (CEDOI) (includes Islands of Mauritus, Seychelles, Comore and La Reunion), B.P. 55, 97462 St. Denis-de-La Reunion (La Reunion). Bp. Gilbert Aubry (St. Denis-de-La Reunion) .

Indonesia: Konperensi Waligereja Indonesia (KWI), Taman Cut Mutiah 10, Tromolpos 3044, Jakarta 10002. Julius Riyadi Darmaatmadja, S.J. (Semerang).

Ireland: Irish Episcopal Conference, "Ara Coeli," Armagh BT61 7QY. Card. Cahal Brendan Daly (Armagh).

Italy: Conferenza Episcopale Italiana (CEI), Circonvallazione Aurelia, 50, 00165 Roma. Card. Camillo Ruini (Vicar General, Rome).

Ivory Coast: See Côte d'Ivoire.

Japan: Catholic Bishops' Conference of Japan, Chiomi 2-10-10, Koto-Ku, Tokyo 135. Francis Xavier Kaname Shimamoto (Nagasaki).

Kenya: Kenya Episcopal Conference (KEC), National Catholic Secretariat, P.O. Box 48062, Nairobi. Zacchaeus Okoth (Kisumu).

Korea: Catholic Bishops' Conference of Korea, Box 16, Seoul. Bp. Angelo Nam Sou Kim (Su Won).

Laos and Cambodia: Conference Episcopale du Laos et du Cambodge, Centre Catholique, Thakhek, Khammouane, Laos. Bp. Jean-Baptiste Outhay Thepmany (vicar apostolic, Savannakhet).

Latvia: Conferentia Episcopalis Lettoniae, Pils Jela, 2, Riga 226050. Vacant.

Lesotho: Lesotho Catholic Bishops' Conference, P.O. Box 200, Maseru 100. Bp. Evaristus Thatho Bitsoane (Qacha's Nek).

Liberia: See Gambia, Liberia and Sierra Leone.

Lithuania: Conferentia Episcopalis Lituaniae, Vilniaus gatve 4, 233000 Kaunas. Card. Vincentas Sladkevicius (Kaunas).

Madagascar: Conference Episcopale de Madagascar, 102 bis Av. Marechal Joffre, Antanimena, B. P 667, Antananarivo. Bp. Jean-Guy Rakotondravahatra, M.S. (Ilhosy).

Malawi: Episcopal Conference of Malawi, Catholic Secretariat of Malawi, P.O. Box 30384, Lilongwe 3. James Chiona (Blantyre).

Malaysia-Singapore-Brunei: Catholic Bishops' Conference of Malaysia, Singapore and Brunei (BCMSB), Archbishop's House, 31 Victoria St., Singapore 0718. Gregory Yong Sooi Ngean (Singapore).

Mali: Conference Episcopale du Mali, B.P. 298, Bamako. Bp. Jean-Marie Cissé (Sikasso).

Malta: Konferenza Episkopali Maltija, Archbishop's Curia, Floriana. Joseph Mercieca (Malta).

Mexico: Conferencia del Episcopado Mexicano (CEM), Prolongacion Rio Acatlan, Lago de Guadalupe, 54760 Cuautitlan Izcalli, Mex. Adolfo Suarez Rivera (Monterrey).

Mozambique: Conferencia Episcopal de Mocambique (CEM), C.P. 286, Maputo. Bp. Paulo Mandlate, S.S.S. (Tete).

Myanmar: Myanmar Catholic Bishops' Conference (MCBC), 292 Pyi Rd., Sanchaung P.O., Yangon. Alphonse U Than Aung (Mandalay).

Netherlands: Nederlandse Bisschoppenconferentie, Postbus 13049, NL-3507 LA, Utrecht. Card. Adrianus J. Simonis (Utrecht).

New Zealand: New Zealand Episcopal Conference, Private Bag 1937, Wellington 1. Bp. Leonard Anthony Boyle (Dunedin).

Nicaragua: Conferencia Episcopal de Nicaragua (CEN), Apartado Postal 2407, Ferreteria Lang, Zona 3, Las Piedrecitas, Managua. Bp. Bosco Vivas Robelo (Leon en Nicaragua).

Niger: See Burkina Faso.

Nigeria: Catholic Bishops Conference of Nigeria, P.O. Box 951, 6 Force Rd., Lagos. Anthony O. Okogie (Lagos).

Pacific: Conferentia Episcopalis Pacifici (CE PAC), P.O. Box 289, Suva (Fiji). Anthony Sablan Apuron, O.F.M. Cap. (Agaña).

Pakistan: Pakistan Episcopal Conference, St. Patrick's Cathedral, Shahrah-Iraq, Karachi 74400. Card. Joseph Cordeiro (Karachi).

Panama: Conferencia Episcopal de Panama (CEP), Apartado 870033, Panama 7. Marcos Mc-Grath, C.S.C. (Panama).

Papua New Guinea and Solomon Islands: Catholic Bishops' Conference of Papua New Guinea and Solomon Islands, Archbishop's Office, P.O. Box 54, Mount Hagen W.H.P. Michael Meier, S.V.D. (Mount Hagen).

Paraguay: Conferencia Episcopal Paraguaya (CEP), Alberdi 782, Casilla Correo 1436, Asuncion. Bp. Jorge Adolfo Livieres Banks (Encarnacion).

Peru: Conferencia Episcopal Peruana, Apartado 310, Rio de Janeiro 488, Lima 100. Vacant.

Philippines: Catholic Bishops' Conference of the Philippines (CBCP), P.O. Box 3601, 470 General Luna St., 1099 Manila. Bp. Carmelo Dominador F. Morelos (Butuan).

Poland: Konferencja Episkopatu Polski, Skwer Kardynala Stefana Wyszynskiego 6, 01-015 Warsaw. Card. Jozef Glemp (Warsaw).

Portugal: Conferencia Episcopal Portuguesa, Campo dos Martires da Patria, 43-1 Esq., 1100 Lisbon. Card. Antonio Ribeiro (Patriarch of Lisbon).

Puerto Rico: Conferencia Episcopal Puertorriqueña (CEP), Apartado 205, Estacion 6, Ponce 00732. Bp. Juan Fremiot Torres Olivier (Ponce).

Romania: Conferinte Episcopala Romania, Palatul Arhiepiscopiei, Str. P.P. Aroni 2, RO-3175 Blaj. Card. Alexandru Todea (Fagaras e Alba Julia).

Rwanda: Conference Episcopale du Rwanda (C.Ep.R.), B.P. 357, Kigali. Bp. Thaddée Nsengiyumva (Kabgayi).

Scandinavia: Conferentia Episcopalis Scandiae, Akersveien 5, P.B. 8270 Hammersborg, N-0129 Oslo 1, Norway. Bp. Paul Verschuren, S.C.I. (Helsinki, Finland).

Senegal, Mauritania, Cape Verde and Guinea Bissau: Conference Episcopale du Senegal, de la Mauritanie, du Cap-Vert et de Guinée-Bissau, B.P. 941, Dakar, Senegal. Bp. Theodore Adrien Sarr (Kaolack, Senegal).

Sierra Leone: See Gambia, Liberia and Sierra Leone.

Slovakia: Biskupská Konferencia Slovenska Kapitulska 11, 81521 Bratislava. Card. Jan Chryzostom Korec, S.J. (bp. Nitra).

Slovenia: Slovenska Skofovska Konferencia, Ciril-Metodov trg 4, 61001 Ljubljana. Alojzij Sustar (Ljubljana).

Spain: Conferencia Episcopal Española, Calle Añastro 1, 28033 Madrid. Card. Angel Suquía Goicoechea (Madrid).

Sri Lanka: Catholic Bishops' Conference of Sri Lanka, 19 Balcombe Place, Cotta Rd., Borella, Colombo 8. Nicholas Marcus Fernando (Colombo).

Sudan: Sudan Catholic Bishops' Conference (SCBC), P.O. Box 6011, Khartoum. Paulino Lukudu, M.C.C.I. (Juba).

Switzerland: Conference des Eveques Suisses, Secretariat, C.P. 22, av. Moleson 21, CH-1700 Fribourg 6. Bp. Pierre Mamie (Lausanne, Geneva and Fribourg).

Tanzania: Tanzania Episcopal Conference (TEC), P.O. Box 2133, Mansfield St., Dar-es-Salaam. Bp. Louis Josaphat Lebulu (Same).

Thailand: Bishops' Conference of Thailand, 57 Oriental Ave., Praetham Bldg., Bangrak, Bangkok 10500. Bp. George Yod Phimphisan, C.SS.R. (Udon Thani).

Togo: Conference Episcopale du Togo, B.P. 348, Lomé. Bp. Philippe Fanoro Kossi Kpodzro (Atakpamé).

Uganda: Uganda Episcopal Conference, P.O. Box 2886, Kampala. Emmanuel Wamala (Kampala).

United States: See National Conference of Catholic Bishops.

Uruguay: Conferencia Episcopal Uruguaya (CEU), Avenida Uruguay 1319, 11100 Montevideo. Bp. Raul Horacio Scarrone Carrero (Florida).

Venezuela: Conferencia Episcopal de Venezuela (CEV), Apartado 4897, Torre a Madrices, Edificio Juan XXIII, Piso 4, Caracas 1010-A. Ramon Ovidio Perez Morales (Maracaibo).

Vietnam: Conference Episcopale du Viêtnam, Toa Giam Muc, B.P. 11, 70 Hung Vuong, Xuân Lôc, Dong Noi. Bp. Paul Marie Nguyên Minh Nhât (Xuân Lôc).

Yugoslavia: . . . . .

Zaire: Conférence Episcopale du Zaïre (CEZ), B.P. 3258, Kinshasa-Gombe. Bp. Faustin Ngabu (Goma).

Zambia: Zambia Episcopal Conference, P.O. Box 31965, Lusaka. Bp. Dennis Harold De Jong (Ndola).

Zimbabwe: Zimbabwe Catholic Bishops' Conference (ZCBC), P.O. Box 8135, Causeway, Harare. Bp. Helmut Reckter, S.J. (Chinhoyi).

Territorial Conferences

(Sources: Almanac survey; *Annuario Pontificio*.)
Territorial as well as national episcopal conferences have been established in some places. Some conferences of this kind are still in the planning stage.

Africa: Symposium of Episcopal Conferences of Africa and Madagascar (SECAM) (Symposium des Conferences Episcopales d'Afrique et de Madagascar, SCEAM): Card. Christian Wiyghan Tumi, archbishop of Douala, Cameroon, president. Address: Secretariat, P.O. Box 9156 Airport, Accra, Ghana.

Association of Episcopal Conferences of Central Africa (Association des Conferences Episcopales de l'Afrique Centrale, ACEAC): Comprises Burundi, Rwanda and Zaire. Bp. Evariste Ngoyagoye, Bubanza, Burundi, president. Address: B.P. 20511, Kinshasa, Zaire.

Association of Episcopal Conferences of the Region of Central Africa (Association des Conferences Episcopales de la Region de l'Afrique Central (ACERAC): Comprises Cameroon, Chad, Congo, Equatorial Guinea, Central African Republic and Gabon. Abp. Joachim N'Dayen, Bangui, Central African Republic, president. Address: Secretariat, B.P. 1518, Bangui, Central African Republic.

Association of Episcopal Conferences of Anglophone West Africa (AECAWA): Comprises Gambia, Ghana, Liberia, Nigeria and Sierra Leone. Abp. Michael Kpakala Francis, Monrovia, Liberia, president. Address: P.O. Box 10-502, Monrovia, Liberia.

Association of Member Episcopal Conferences in Eastern Africa (AMECEA): Represents Ethiopia, Kenya, Malawi, Sudan, Tanzania, Uganda and Zambia. The Seychelles was accepted as an affiliate member in 1979. Abp. Nicodemus Kirima, Nyeri, Kenya, president. Address: P.O. Box 21191, Nairobi, Kenya.

Regional Episcopal Conference of French-Speaking West Africa (Conference Episcopale Regionale de l'Afrique de l'Ouest Francophone, CERAO): Comprises Benin, Burkina Faso, Cape Verde, Côte d'Ivoire, Guinea, Guinea-Bissau, Mali, Mauritania,

Niger, Senegal and Togo. Bp. Anselme Titianma Sanon, Bobo-Dioulasso, Burkina Faso, president. Address: Secretariat General, 06 B.P. 470 Cidex 1, Abidjan 06, Côte d'Ivoire.

Inter-Regional Meeting of Bishops of Southern Africa (IMBISA): Bishops of Angola, Botswana, Lesotho, Mozambique, Namibia, Sao Tome e Principe, South Africa, Swaziland and Zimbabwe. Abp. Patrick Chakaipa (Harare, Zimbabwe), president. Address: P.O. Box BE 230, Belvedere, Harare, Zimbabwe.

Asia: Federation of Asian Bishops' Conferences (FABC): Represents 14 Asian episcopal conferences as regular members (excluding the Middle East). Established in 1970; statutes approved experimentally Dec. 6, 1972. Abp. Oscar Cruz, Lingayen-Dagupan, Philippines (elected 1993), secretary general. Address: 16 Caine Road, Hong Kong.

Oceania: Federation of Catholic Bishops' Conferences of Oceania (FCBCO). Statutes approved experimentally July 28, 1992. Card. Thomas Stafford Williams, archbishop of Wellington, New Zealand, president. Address: P.O. Box 14-044, 112 Queen's Drive, Wellington 3, New Zealand.

Europe: Council of European Bishops' Conferences (Consilium Conferentiarum Episcopalium Europae, CCEE): Abp. Miroslav Vlk, Prague, Czech Republic, president. Address of

secretariat: Klosterhof 6b, CH-9000 Sankt Gallen, Switzerland. Reorganized in 1993 in accordance with suggestions made during the 1991 Synod of Bishops on Europe.

Commission of the Episcopates of the European Community (Commissio Episcopatuum Communitatis Europaeae, COMECE): Established in 1980; represents episcopates of states which belong to European Community. Abp. Charles-Amarin Brand, Strasbourg, France, president. Address of secretariat: 13 Avenue Pere Damien, B-1150 Brussels, Belgium.

Central and South America: Latin American Bishops' Conference (Consejo Episcopal Latino-Americano, CELAM): Established in 1956; statutes approved Nov. 9, 1974. Represents 22 Latin American national bishops' conferences. Card. Nicolas de Jesus Lopez Rodriguez, Santo Domingo, Dominican Republic, president. Address of the secretariat: Carrera 5 No. 118-31, Usaquén, Bogota, Colombia.

Episcopal Secretariat of Central America and Panama (Secretariado Episcopal de America Central y Panama, SEDAC): Statutes approved experimentally Sept. 26, 1970. Bp. Jose Cedeño Delgado, Santiago de Veraguas, Panama, president. Address of secretary general: Calle 20 y Av. Mexico 24-45, Apartado 6386, Panama 5, Panama.

INTERNATIONAL CATHOLIC ORGANIZATIONS

(Principal sources: Conference of International Catholic Organizations; Pontifical Council for the Laity; Almanac survey.)

Guidelines

International organizations wanting to call themselves "Catholic" are required to meet standards set by the Vatican's Council for the Laity and to register with and get the approval of the Papal Secretariat of State, according to guidelines dated Dec. 3 and published in *Acta Apostolicae Sedis* under date of Dec. 23, 1971.

Among conditions for the right of organizations to "bear the name Catholic" are:

● leaders "will always be Catholics," and candidates for office will be approved by the Secretariat of State;

● adherence by the organization to the Catholic Church, its teaching authority and teachings of the Gospel;

● evidence that the organization is really international with a universal outlook and that it fulfills its mission through its own management, meetings and accomplishments.

The guidelines also stated that leaders of the organizations "will take care to maintain necessary reserve as regards taking a stand or engaging in public activity in the field of politics or trade unionism. Abstention in these fields will normally be the best attitude for them to adopt during their term of office."

The guidelines were in line with a provision stated by the Second Vatican Council in the *Decree on the Apostolate of the Laity*: "No project may claim the name 'Catholic' unless it has obtained the consent of the lawful church authority."

They made it clear that all organizations are not obliged to apply for recognition, but that the Church "reserves the right to recognize as linked with her mission and her aims those organizations or movements which see fit to ask for such recognition."

Conference

Conference of International Catholic Organizations: A permanent body for collaboration among various organizations which seek to promote the development of international life along the lines of Christian principles. Eleven international Catholic organizations participated in its foundation and first meeting in 1927 at Fribourg, Switzerland. In 1951, the conference established its general secretariat and adopted governing statutes which were approved by the Vatican Secretariat of State in 1953.

The permanent secretariat is located at 37-39 rue de Vermont, CH-1202 Geneva, Switzerland. Other office addresses are: 1 rue Varembe, CH-1211 Geneva 20, Switzerland (Information Center); 9, rue Cler, F-75007 Paris, France (International Catholic Center for UNESCO); ICO Information Center, 323 East 47th St., New York, N.Y. 10017.

International Organizations

International Catholic organizations are listed below. Information includes name, date and place of establishment (when available), address of general secretariat. An asterisk indicates that the organization is a member of the Conference of International Catholic Organizations. Approximately 30 of the organizations have consultative status with other international or regional non-governmental agencies.

Apostleship of Prayer (1849): Borgo Santo Spirito 5, I-00193 Rome, Italy. National secretariat in most countries. (See Index.)

Apostolatus Maris (Apostleship of the Sea) (1922, Glasgow, Scotland): Pontifical Commission for Migration and Tourism, Piazza San Calisto 16, 00153 Rome, Italy. (See Index.)

L'Arche Communities: B.P. 35, 60350 Cuise Lamotte, France.

Associationes Juventutis Salesianae (Associations of Salesian Youth) (1847): Via della Pisana, 1111, 00163 Rome, Italy.

Blue Army of Our Lady of Fatima: (See Index.)

Caritas Internationalis* (1951, Rome, Italy): Piazza San Calisto 16, I-00153, Rome, Italy. Coordinates and represents its 117 national member organizations (in 113 countries) operating in the fields of development, emergency aid, social action.

Catholic International Education Office* (1952): 60, rue des Eburons, B-1040 Brussels, Belgium.

Catholic International Federation for Physical and Sports Education (1911; present name, 1957): 5, rue Cernuschi, F-75017 Paris, France.

Catholic International Union for Social Service* (1925, Milan, Italy): rue de la Poste 111, B-1030 Brussels, Belgium (general secretariat).

Christian Fraternity of the Sick and Handicapped: 9, Avenue de la Gare, CH-1630, Bulle, Switzerland.

"Communione e Liberazione" Fraternity (1955, Milan, Italy): Via Marcello Malpighi 2, 00161 Rome, Italy. Catholic renewal movement.

European Forum of National Committees of the Laity: 12 Brookwood Lawn Artane, Dublin 5, Ireland.

"Focolare Movement" or "Work of Mary" (1943, Trent, Italy): Via di Frascati, 304, I-00040 Rocca di Papa (Rome), Italy. (See Index: Focolare Movement.)

Foi et Lumiere: 8 rue Serret, 75015 Paris, France.

Inter Cultural Association, formerly International Catholic Auxiliaries (1937, Belgium): 91, rue de la Servette, CH-1202 Geneva, Switzerland.

International Association of Charities of St. Vincent de Paul* (1617, Chatillon les Dombes, France): Rue Brand, 118, B-1050 Brussels, Belgium. (See Index: St. Vincent de Paul Society.)

International Association of Children of Mary (1847): 67 rue de Sèvres, F-75006 Paris, France.

International Catholic Association for Service to Young Women* (1897): 37-39, rue de Vermont, CH-1202 Geneva, Switzerland. Welfare of Catholic girls living away from home.

International Catholic Child Bureau* (1948, in Paris): 65, rue de Lausanne, CH-1202 Geneva, Switzerland.

International Catholic Conference of Guiding* (1965): Rue Paul-Emile Janson, 35, B-1050 Brussels, Belgium. Founded by member bodies of interdenominational World Association of Guides and Girl Scouts.

International Catholic Conference of Scouting* (1948): Piazza Pasquale Paoli, 18, I-00186 Rome, Italy.

International Catholic Migration Commission* (1951): 37-39 rue de Vermont, C.P. 96, CH-1211 Geneva 20, Switzerland. Coordinates activities worldwide on behalf of refugees and migrants, both administering programs directly and supporting the efforts of national affiliated agencies.

International Catholic Organization for Cinema and Audiovisual* (1928, The Hague, The Netherlands): Rue de l'Orme, 8, B-1040 Brussels, Belgium (general secretariat). Federation of national Catholic film offices.

International Catholic Rural Association (1962, Rome): Piazza San Calisto, 00153 Rome, Italy. International body for agricultural and rural organizations.

International Catholic Union of Esperanto: Via Berni 9, 00185 Rome, Italy.

International Catholic Union of the Press*: 37-39 rue de Vermont, Case Postale 197, CH-1211 Geneva 20 CIC, Switzerland. Coordinates and represents at the international level the activities of Catholics and Catholic federations or associations in the field of press and information. Has six specialized branches: International Federation of Catholic Journalists; International Federation of Dailies; International Federation of Periodicals; International Federation of Catholic News Agencies; International Catholic Federation of Teachers and Researchers in the Science and Techniques of Information; International Federation of Church Press Associations.

International Centre for Studies in Religious Education LUMEN VITAE* (1934-35, Louvain, Belgium, under name Catechetical Documentary Centre; present name, 1956): 184, rue Washington, B-1050 Brussels, Belgium. Also referred to as Lumen Vitae Centre; concerned with all aspects of religious formation.

International Committee of Catholic Nurses and Medical Social Workers* (1933): Square Vergote, 43, B-1040 Brussels, Belgium.

International Cooperation for Socio-Economic Development (1965, Rome, Italy): Avenue des ARTS-1, 2, Boite 6, 1040 Brussels, Belgium.

International Federation of Catholic Medical Associations (1954): Palazzo San Calisto, I-00120 Vatican City.

International Federation of Catholic Men* (Unum Omnes) (1948): Piazza San Calisto 16, 00153 Rome, Italy.

International Federation of Catholic Parochial Youth Communities* (1962, Rome, Italy): Kipdorp 30, B-2000 Antwerp, Belgium.

International Federation of Catholic Pharmacists* (1954): 59, Bergstrasse, B-4700 Eupen, Belgium.

International Federation of Catholic Rural Movements* (1964, Lisbon, Portugal): 92, rue Africaine, B-1050 Brussels, Belgium.

International Federation of Catholic Universities* (1949): 51, rue orfila, F-75020 Paris, France.

International Federation of the Catholic Associations of the Blind: c/o Mr. Dooghe, Avenue Dailly, 90, B-1030 Brussels, Belgium. Coordinates actions of Catholic groups and assciations for the blind and develops their apostolate.

International Military Apostolate (1967): Gablenzgasse 62, A-1160 Vienna, Austria. Comprised of organizations of military men.

International Movement of Apostolate of Children* (1929, France): 8, rue Duguay-Trouin, F-75006 Paris, France.

International Movement of Apostolate in Middle and Upper Classes* (1963): Piazza San Calisto 16, 00153 Rome, Italy. Evangelization of adults of the independent milieus (that part of population known as old or recent middle class, aristocracy, bourgeoisie or "white collar").

International Movement of Catholic Agricultural and Rural Youth* (1954, Annevoie, Belgium): Tiensevest 68, B-3000 Leuven, Belgium (permanent secretariat).

International Young Catholic Students* (1946, Fribourg, Switzerland; present name, 1954): 171 rue de Rennes, F-75006 Paris, France.

International Young Christian Workers* (1925, Belgium): 11, rue Plantin, B-1070 Brussels, Belgium.

Legion of Mary (1921, Dublin, Ireland): De Montfort House, North Brunswick St., Dublin, Ireland. (See Index.)

Medicus Mundi Internationalis: (1964. Bensberg. Germany FR): P.O. Box 1547, 6501 BM Nijmegen, Netherlands. Promote health and medicosocial services, particularly in developing countries; recruit essential health and medical personnel for developing countries; contribute to training of medical and auxiliary personnel; undertake research in the field of health.

NOVALIS, Marriage Preparation Center: University of St. Paul, 1 rue Stewart, Ottawa 2, Ont. Canada.

Our Lady's Teams (Equipes Notre-Dame) (1937, France): 49, rue de la Glacière, F-75013 Paris, France. Movement for spiritual formation of couples.

Pax Christi International (1950): Plantin en Moretuslei, 174, B. 2038, Antwerpen, Belgium. International Catholic peace movement. Originated in Lourdes, France in 1948 by French and German Catholics to reconcile enemies from World War II; spread to Italy and Poland and acquired its international title when it merged with the English organization Pax. (See Index: Pax Christi USA.)

Pax Romana* (1921, Fribourg, Switzerland, divided into two branches, 1947):

Pax Romana — IMCS* (International Movement of Catholic Students) (1921): 171, rue de Rennes, F-75006, Paris, France. For undergraduates.

Pax Romana — ICMICA* (International Catholic Movement for Intellectual and Cultural Affairs) (1947): 37-39 rue de Vermont, Case Postale n 85, CH-1211 Geneva 20 CIC, Switzerland. For Catholic intellectuals and professionals.

Pro Sanctity Movement: Piazza S. Andrea della Valle 3, 00166 Rome, Italy.

St. Joan's International Alliance (1911, in England, as Catholic Women's Suffrage Society): 15 London Rd., Canterbury, Kent CT2 8LR, England. Associate member of ICO.

Salesian Cooperators (1876): Don Bosco College, Newton, N.J. 07860. Third Salesian family founded by St. John Bosco. Members commit themselves to an apostolate at the service of the Church, giving particular attention to youth in the Salesian spirit and style.

Secular Franciscan Order (1221, first Rule approved): Via Piemonte, 70, 00187, Rome, Italy. (See Index.)

Secular Fraternity of Charles de Foucauld: Katharinenweg 4, B4700 Eupen, Belgium.

Serra International (1953, in U.S.): (See Index.)

Society of St. Vincent de Paul* (1833, Paris): 5, rue du Pré-aux-Clercs, F-75007 Paris, France.

The Grail (1921, Nijmegen, The Netherlands): Duisburgerstrasse 470, D-4330, Mulheim, West Germany. (See Index.)

Third Order of St. Dominic (1285): Convento Santa Sabina, Piazza Pietro d'Illiria, Aventino, I-00153 Rome, Italy. (See Index.)

Unda: International Catholic Association for Radio and Television* (1928, Cologne, Germany): rue de l'Orme, 12, B-1040 Brussels, Belgium. (See Index.)

Unio Internationalis Laicorum in Servitio Ecclesiae (1965, Aachen, Germany): Postfach 990125, Am Kielshof 2, 5000 Cologne, Germany 91. Consists of national and diocesan associations of persons who give professional services to the Church.

Union of Adorers of the Blessed Sacrament (1937): Largo dei Monti Parioli 3, I-00197, Rome, Italy.

World Catholic Federation for the Biblical Apostolate (1969, Rome): Mittelstrasse, 12, P.O. Box 601, D-7000, Stuttgart 1, Germany.

World Federation of Christian Life Communities* (1953): 8, Borgo Santo Spirito, 00193 Rome, Italy. First Sodality of Our Lady founded in 1563.

World Movement of Christian Workers* (1961): 90, rue des Palais, 1210 Brussels, Belgium.

World Organization of Former Students of Catholic Schools (1967, Rome): Largo Nazareno 25, I-00187 Rome, Italy.

World Union of Catholic Philosophical Societies (1948, Amsterdam, The Netherlands): The Catholic University of America, Washington, D.C. 20064.

World Union of Catholic Teachers* (1951): Piazza San Calisto, 16, 00153 Rome, Italy.

World Union of Catholic Women's Organizations* (1910): 20, rue Notre Dame des Champs, F-75006 Paris, France.

Regional Organizations

European Federation for Catholic Adult Education (1963, Lucerne, Switzerland): Kapuzinestrasse 84, A-4020 Linz, Austria.

European Forum of National Committees of the Laity (1968): 12, Brookwood Lawn Artane, Dublin 5, Ireland.

Movimiento Familiar Cristiano (1949-50, Montevideo and Buenos Aires): Carrera 17 n. 4671, Bogota, D.E., Colombia. Christian Family Movement of Latin America.

THE CATHOLIC CHURCH IN CANADA

The first date in the remote background of the Catholic history of Canada was July 7, 1534, when a priest in the exploration company of Jacques Cartier celebrated Mass on the Gaspe Peninsula.

Successful colonization and the significant beginnings of the Catholic history of the country date from the foundation of Quebec in 1608 by Samuel de Champlain and French settlers. Montreal was established in 1642.

The earliest missionaries were Franciscan Récollets (Recollects) and Jesuits who arrived in 1615 and 1625, respectively. They provided some pastoral care for the settlers but worked mainly among the 100,000 Indians — Algonquins, Hurons and Iroquois — in the interior and in the Lake Ontario region. Eight of the Jesuit missionaries, killed in the 1640s, were canonized in 1930. (See Index: Jesuit North American Martyrs.) Sulpician Fathers, who arrived in Canada late in the 1640s, played a part in the great missionary period which ended about 1700.

Kateri Tekakwitha, "Lily of the Mohawks," who was baptized in 1676 and died in 1680, was declared "Blessed" June 22, 1980.

The communities of women religious with the longest histories in Canada are the Canonesses of St. Augustine and the Ursulines, since 1639; and the Hospitallers of St. Joseph, since 1642. Communities of Canadian origin are the Congregation of Notre Dame, founded by St. Marguerite Bourgeoys in 1658, and the Grey Nuns, formed by St. Marie Marguerite d'Youville in 1737.

Mother Marie (Guyard) of the Incarnation, an Ursuline nun, was one of the first three women missionaries to New France; called "Mother of the Church in Canada," she was declared "Blessed" June 22, 1980.

Start of Church Organization

Ecclesiastical organization began with the appointment in 1658 of Francois De Montmorency-Laval, "Father of the Church in Canada," as vicar apostolic of New France. He was the first bishop of Quebec from 1674 to 1688, with jurisdiction over all French-claimed territory in North America. He was declared "Blessed" June 22, 1980.

In 1713, the French Canadian population numbered 18,000. In the same year, the Treaty of Utrecht ceded Acadia, Newfoundland and the Hudson Bay Territory to England. The Acadians were scattered among the American Colonies in 1755.

The English acquired possession of Canada and its 70,000 French-speaking inhabitants in virtue of the Treaty of Paris in 1763. Anglo-French and Anglican-Catholic differences and tensions developed. The pro-British government at first refused to recognize the titles of church officials, hindered the clergy in their work and tried to install a non-Catholic educational system. Laws were passed which guaranteed religious liberties to Catholics (Quebec Act of 1774, Constitutional Act

of 1791, legislation approved by Queen Victoria in 1851), but it took some time before actual respect for these liberties matched the legal enactments. The initial moderation of government antipathy toward the Church was caused partly by the loyalty of Catholics to the Crown during the American Revolution and the War of 1812.

Growth

The 15 years following the passage in 1840 of the Act of Union, which joined Upper and Lower Canada, were significant. New communities of men and women religious joined those already in the country. The Oblates of Mary Immaculate, missionaries par excellence in Canada, advanced the penetration of the West which had been started in 1818 by Abbe Provencher. New jurisdictions were established, and Quebec became a metropolitan see in 1844. The first Council of Quebec was held in 1851. The established Catholic school system enjoyed a period of growth.

Laval University was inaugurated in 1854 and canonically established in 1876.

Archbishop Elzear-Alexandre Taschereau of Quebec was named Canada's first cardinal in 1886.

The apostolic delegation to Canada was set up in 1899. It became a nunciature October 16, 1969, with the establishment of diplomatic relations with the Vatican.

Early in this century, Canada had eight ecclesiastical provinces, 23 dioceses, three vicariates apostolic, 3,500 priests, 2.4 million Catholics, about 30 communities of men religious, and 70 or more communities of women religious. The Church in Canada was phased out of mission status and removed from the jurisdiction of the Congregation for the Propagation of the Faith in 1908.

Diverse Population

The greatest concentration of Catholics is in the eastern portion of the country. In the northern and western portions, outside metropolitan centers, there are some of the most difficult parish and mission areas in the world. Bilingual (English-French) differences in the general population are reflected in the Church; for example, in the parallel structures of the Canadian Conference of Catholic Bishops, which was established in 1943. Quebec is the center of French cultural influence. Many language groups are represented among Catholics, who include about 211,265 members of Eastern Rites in one metropolitan see, six eparchies and an apostolic exarchate.

Education, a past source of friction between the Church and the government, is administered by the civil provinces in a variety of arrangements authorized by the Canadian Constitution. Denominational schools have tax support in one way in Quebec and Newfoundland, and in another way in Alberta, Ontario and Saskatchewan. Several provinces provide tax support only for public schools, making private financing necessary for separate church-related schools.

ECCLESIASTICAL JURISDICTIONS OF CANADA

Provinces

Names of ecclesiastical provinces and metropolitan sees in bold face: suffragan sees in parentheses.

Edmonton (Calgary, St. Paul).

Gatineau-Hull (Amos, Mont-Laurier, Rouyn Noranda).

Grouard-McLennan (Mackenzie-Ft. Smith, Prince George, Whitehorse).

Halifax (Antigonish, Charlottetown, Yarmouth).

Keewatin-LePas (Churchill-Hudson Bay, Labrador-Schefferville, Moosonee).

Kingston (Alexandria-Cornwall, Peterborough, Sault Ste. Marie).

Moncton (Bathurst, Edmundston, St. John).

Montreal (Joliette, St. Jean-Longueuil, St. Jerome, Valleyfield).

Ottawa (Hearst, Pembroke, Timmins).

Quebec (Chicoutimi, Ste.-Anne-de-la-Pocatiere, Trois Rivieres).

Regina (Gravelbourg, Prince Albert, Saskatoon, Abbey of St. Peter).

Rimouski (Baie-Comeau, Gaspe).

St. Boniface (no suffragans).

St. John's (Grand Falls, St. George).

Sherbrooke (Nicolet, St. Hyacinthe).

Toronto (Hamilton, London, St. Catharines, Thunder Bay).

Vancouver (Kamloops, Nelson, Victoria).

Winnipeg — Ukrainian (Edmonton, New Westminster, Saskatoon, Toronto).

Jurisdictions immediately subject to the Holy See: Roman-Rite Archdiocese of Winnipeg, Byzantine Eparchy of Sts. Cyril and Methodius for Slovaks, Byzantine Eparchy of St. Sauveur de Montreal for Greek Melkites; Antiochene Eparchy of St. Maron of Montreal for Maronites.

Jurisdictions, Hierarchy

(Principal sources: Information office, Canadian Conference of Catholic Bishops; Catholic Almanac survey; *Annuario Pontificio; L'Osservatore Romano; Catholic News Service.* As of July 15, 1993.)

Information includes names of archdioceses (indicated by asterisk) and dioceses, date of foundation, present ordinaries and auxiliaries; addresses of chancery office/bishop's residence; cathedral; former ordinaries. For biographies of current hierarchy, see Index.

Alexandria-Cornwall, Ont. (1890 as Alexandria; name changed to Alexandria-Cornwall, 1976): Eugene Philippe LaRocque, bishop, 1974.

Diocesan Center: 220, chemin Montreal, C.P. 1388, Cornwall, Ont. K6H 5V4. Cathedral: St. Finnans (Alexandria); Nativity Co-Cathedral (Cornwall).

Former bishops: Alexander Macdonell, 1890-1905; William A. Macdonell, 1906-20; Felix Couturier, O.P., 1921-41; Rosario Brodeur, 1941-66; Adolphe E. Proulx, 1967-74.

Amos, Que. (1938): Gerard Drainville, bishop, 1978.

Bishop's Residence: 450, rue Principale Nord, Amos, Que. J9T 2M1. Cathedral: St. Theresa of Avila.

Former bishops: Joseph Aldee Desmarais, 1939-68; Gaston Hains, 1968-78.

Antigonish, N.S. (Arichat, 1844; transferred, 1886): Colin Campbell, bishop, 1987.

Chancery Office: 155 Main St., P.O. Box 1330, Antigonish, N.S., B2G 2L7. Cathedral: St. Ninian.

Former bishops: William Fraser, 1844-51; Colin Francis MacKinnon, 1852-77; John Cameron, 1877-1910; James Morrison, 1912-50; John Roderick MacDonald, 1950-59; William E. Power, 1959-86.

Baie-Comeau, Que. (p.a., 1882; v.a., 1905; diocese Gulf of St. Lawrence, 1945; name changed, to Hauterive, 1960; present title, 1986): Pierre Morissette, bishop, 1990.

Bishop's Residence: 639, rue de Bretagne, Baie-Comeau, Que., G5C 1X2. Cathedral: Paroisse St. Jean-Eudes.

Former bishops: Napoleon-Alexandre Labrie, C.J.M., v.a., 1938-45, first bishop, 1945-56; Gerard Couturier, 1957-74; Jean-Guy Couture, 1975-79; Roger Ebacher, 1979-88; Maurice Couture, R.S.V., 1988-90.

Bathurst, N.B. (Chatham, 1860; transferred, 1938): Andre Richard, C.S.C., bishop, 1989.

Bishop's Residence: 645, avenue Murray, C.P. 460, Bathurst, N.-B., E2A 3Z4. Cathedral: Sacred Heart of Jesus.

Former bishops: James Rogers, 1860-1902; Thomas F. Barry, 1902-20; Patrice-Alexandre Chiasson, C.J.M., 1920-42; Camille-Andre Le Blanc, 1942-69; Edgar Godin, 1969-85; Arsene Richard, 1986-89.

Calgary, Alta. (1912): Paul J. O'Byrne, bishop, 1968.

Former bishops: John Thomas McNally, 1913-24; John T. Kidd, 1925-31; Peter J. Monahan, 1932-35; Francis P. Carroll, 1936-66; Francis J. Klein, 1967-68.

Address: Room 205, Catholic Pastoral Center, 1916 Second St. SW. Calgary, Alta. T2S 1S3. Cathedral: St. Mary.

Charlottetown, P.E.I. (1829): Joseph Vernon Fougère, bishop, 1992.

Bishop's Residence: P.O. Box 907, Charlottetown, P.E.I., C1A 7L9. Cathedral: St. Dunstan's.

Former bishops: Bernard Angus McEachern, 1829-35; Bernard Donald McDonald, 1837-59; Peter McIntyre, 1860-91; James Charles McDonald, 1891-1912; Henry Joseph O'Leary, 1913-20; Louis James O'Leary, 1920-30; J.A. Sullivan, 1931-44; James Boyle, 1944-54; Malcolm A. MacEachern, 1955-70; Francis J. Spence, 1970-82; James H. MacDonald, 1982-91.

Chicoutimi, Que. (1878): Jean-Guy Couture, bishop, 1979. Roch Pedneault, auxiliary.

Bishop's Residence: 602, Racine Est, Chicoutimi, Que. G7H 6J6. Cathedral: St. Francois-Xavier.

Former bishops: Dominique Racine, 1878-88; Louis-Nazaire Begin (later cardinal), 188-92; Michel-Thomas Labrecque, 1892-1927; Charles Lamarche, 1928-40; Georges Melancon, 1940-61; Marius Pare, 1961-79.

Churchill-Hudson Bay, Man. (p.a., 1925; v.a. Hudson Bay, 1931; diocese of Churchill, 1967; present title, 1968): Reynald Rouleau, O.M.I., bishop, 1987.

Diocesan Office: P.O. Box 10, Churchill, Man. ROB OEO. Cathedral: Holy Canadian Martyrs.

Former bishops: Arsene Turquetil, O.M.I., 1931-43; Armand Clabaut, O.M.I., coadjutor, 1937-40; Marc LaCroix, O.M.I., 1943-68; Omer Alfred Robidoux, 1970-86.

Edmonton,* Alta. (St. Albert, 1871; archdiocese, transferred Edmonton, 1912): Joseph N. MacNeil, archbishop, 1973.

Archdiocesan Office: 8421-101 Avenue, Edmonton, Alta. T6A OL1. Cathedral: Basilica of St. Joseph.

Former bishops: Vital-Justin Grandin, O.M.I., 1871-1902; Emile Legal, O.M.I., 1902-20, first archbishop; Henry Joseph O'Leary, 1920-38; John Hugh MacDonald, 1938-64; Anthony Jordan, O.M.I., 1964-73.

Edmonton, Alta. (Ukrainian Byzantine Rite) (ap. ex. of western Canada, 1948; eparchy, 1956): Myron Michael Daciuk, O.S.B.M., eparch, 1991.

Eparch's Residence: 6240 Ada Boulevard, Edmonton, Alta. T5W 4P1. Cathedral: St. Josaphat.

Former bishops: Neil Nicholas Savaryn, O.S.B.M., 1948-86; Demetrius Martin Greschuk, 1986-90.

Edmundston, N.B. (1944): Gérard Dionne, bishop, 1984.

Diocesan Center: 60 rue Bouchard, Edmundston, N.B. E3V 3K1. Cathedral: Immaculate Conception.

Former bishops: Marie-Antoine Roy, O.F.M., 1945-48; Joseph-Roméo Gagnon, 1949-70; Fernand Lacroix, C.J.M., 1970-83.

Gaspe, Que. (1922): Vacant as of July 15, 1993.

Bishop's House: 172, Jacques-Cartier St., C.P. 440, Gaspe, Que. GOC 1RO. Cathedral: Christ the King.

Former bishops: Francois-Xavier Ross, 1922-45; Albini LeBlanc, 1945-57; Paul Bernier (personal title of Archbishop), 1957-64; Jean Marie Fortier, 1965-68; Gilles Ouellet, 1968-73; Bertrand Blanchet, 1973-93.

Gatineau-Hull,* Que. (1963, as Hull; name changed, 1982; archdiocese, 1990): Roger Ebacher, bishop, 1988; first archbishop, Oct.31, 1990.

Former bishops: Emile Charbonneau, 1963-73; Adolph Proulx, 1974-87.

Diocesan Center: 180 Boul. Mont-Bleu, Hull, Que. J8Z 3J5.

Grand Falls, Nfld. (Harbour Grace, 1856; present title, 1964): Joseph Faber MacDonald, bishop, 1980.

Chancery Office: P.O. Box 397, Grand Falls, Nfld. A2A 2M4. Cathedral: Immaculate Conception.

Former bishops: John Dalton, 1856-69; Henry Carfagnini, 1870-80; R. McDonald, 1881-1906; John March, 1906-40; John M. O'Neill, 1940-72; Alphonsus S. Penney, 1973-79.

Gravelbourg, Sask. (1930): Noel Delaquis, bishop, 1974.

Bishop's Residence: C.P. 690, Gravelbourg, Sask. SOH 1XO. Cathedral: Our Lady of the Assumption.

Former bishops: Jean-Marie Villeneuve, O.M.I., 1930-31; Arthur Melanson, 1932-36; Joseph Guy, O.M.I., 1937-42; M.-Joseph Lemieux, 1944-53; Aime Decosse, 1954-73.

Grouard-McLennan,* Alta. (v.a. Athabaska-Mackenzie, 1862; Grouard, 1927; archdiocese Grouard-McLennan, 1967); Henri Legare, O.M.I., archbishop, 1972.

Archbishop's Residence: C.P. 388, McLennan, Alta. TOH 2LO. Cathedral: St. Jean-Baptiste (McLennan).

Former ordinaries: Henri Faraud, O.M.I., 1864-90; Emile Grouard, O.M.I., 1891-1929; Joseph Guy, O.M.I., 1930-38; Ubald Langlois, O.M.I., 1938-53; Henri Routhier, O.M.I., 1953-72, first archbishop.

Halifax,* N.S. (1842; archdiocese, 1852): Austin E. Burke, archbishop, 1991.

Former ordinaries: Edmund Burke, vicar apostolic, 1818-20; William Fraser, 1842-44; William Walsh, 1844-58, first archbishop; Thomas L. Connolly, 1859-76; Michael Hannan, 1877-82; Cornelius O'Brien, 1883-1906; Edward J. McCarthy, 1906-31; Thomas O'Donnell, 1931-36; John T. McNally, 1937-52; Joseph G. Berry, 1953-67; James Martin Hayes, 1967-90.

Chancery Office: P.O. Box 1527, 1531 Grafton St., Halifax, N.S. B3J 2Y3.

Hamilton, Ont. (1856): Anthony Tonnos, bishop, 1984. Matthew Ustrzycki, auxiliary.

Chancery Office: 700 King St. West, Hamilton, Ont. L8P1C7. Cathedral: Christ the King.

Former bishops: John Farrell, 1856-73; Peter F. Crinnon, 1874-82; James Joseph Carbery, 1884-87; Thomas J. Dowling, 1889-1924; J. T. McNally, 1924-37; Joseph F. Ryan, 1937-73; Paul F. Reding, 1973-83.

Hearst, Ont. (p.a., 1918; v.a., 1920; diocese, 1938): Vacant as of July 15, 1993.

Bishop's Residence: C.P. 1330, 68 Neuvieme Rue, Hearst, Ont. POL INO. Cathedral: Notre Dame of the Assumption.

Former bishops: Joseph Halle, 1919-38; Joseph Charbonneau, 1939-40; A. LeBlanc, 1941-45; Georges Landry, 1946-52; Louis Levesque, 1952-64; Jacques Landriault, 1964-71; Roger Despatie, 1973-93.

Joliette, Que. (1904): Gilles Lussier, bishop, 1991.

Bishop's Residence: C.P. 470, 2 rue Saint-Charles-Borromeo Nord, Joliette, Que. J6E 6H6. Cathedral: St. Charles Borromeo.

Former bishops: Joseph Archambault, 1904-13; Guillaume Forbes, 1913-28; Joseph A. Papineau, 1928-68; Rene Audet, 1968-90.

Kamloops, B.C. (1945): Lawrence Sabatini, C.S., bishop, 1982.

Bishop's Residence: 635A Tranquille Rd., Kamloops, B.C. V2B 3H5. Cathedral: Sacred Heart.

Former bishops: Edward Q. Jennings, 1946-52; Michael A. Harrington, 1952-73; Adam Exner, O.M.I., 1974-82.

Keewatin-Le Pas,* Man. (v.a., 1910; archdiocese, 1967): Peter-Alfred Sutton, O.M.I., archbishop, 1986.

Archbishop's Residence: 108, 1st St. West, P.O. Box 270, The Pas, Man. R9A 1K4. Cathedral: Our Lady of the Sacred Heart.

Former bishops: Ovide Charlebois, O.M.I., 1910-33; Martin LaJeunesse, O.M.I., 1933-44; Paul Dumouchel, O.M.I., 1955-86, first archbishop.

Kingston,* Ont. (1826; archdiocese, 1889): Francis J. Spence, archbishop, 1982.

Chancery Office: 390 Palace Rd., Kingston, Ont. K7L 4T3. Cathedral: St. Mary of the Immaculate Conception.

Former bishops: Alexander Macdonell, 1826-40; Remigius Gaulin, 1840-57; Patrick Phelan, 1843-57; Edward J. Horan, 1858-75; John O'Brien, 1875-79;

J. V. Cleary, 1880-98, first archbishop; **C.-H.** Gauthier, 1898-1910; Michael Joseph Spratt, 1911-38; Michael-Joseph O'Brien, 1939-43; Joseph A. O'Sullivan, 1944-66; Joseph L. Wilhelm 1966-82.

Labrador City (Nfld.)-Schefferville, Que. (v.a. Labrador, 1946; diocese, 1967): Henri Goudreault, O.M.I., 1987.
Bishop's Residence: 318 avenue Elizabeth, C.P. 545, Labrador City, Nfld. A2V 2K7. Cathedral: Our Lady of Perpetual Help.
Former bishops: Lionel Scheffer, O.M.I., 1946-66; Henri Legare, O.M.I., 1967-72; Peter A. Sutton, 1974-86.

London, Ont. (1855; transferred Sandwich, 1859; London, 1869): John M. Sherlock, bishop, 1978. Frederick Henry, auxiliary.
Bishop's Residence: 90 Central Avenue, London, Ont. N6A 1M4. Cathedral: St. Peter's Cathedral Basilica.
Former bishops: Pierre Adolphe Pinsoneault, 1856-66; John Walsh, 1867-89; Dennis O'Connor, C.S.B., 1890-99; F.P. McEvay 1899-1908; Michael F. Fallon, 1910-31; J. Thomas Kidd, 1931-50; John C. Cody, 1950-63; Gerald E. Carter, 1964-78.

Mackenzie-Fort Smith, N.W.T. (v.a. Mackenzie, 1902; diocese Mackenzie-Fort Smith, 1967): Denis Croteau, O.M.I., bishop, 1986.
Diocesan Office: 5117-52nd St., Bag 8900, Yellowknife, NWT X1A 2R3. Cathedral: St. Joseph (Ft. Smith).
Former bishops: Gabriel Breynat, O.M.I. (1902-43); Joseph Trocellier, O.M.I., 1943-58); Paul Piche, 1959-86.

Moncton,* N.B. (1936): Donat Chiasson, archbishop, 1972.
Archbishop's Residence: 452, rue Amirault, Dieppe, C.P. 248, Moncton, N.B. E1C 8K9. Cathedral: Our Lady of the Assumption.
Former bishops: L.J.-Arthur Melanson, 1937-41; Norbert Robichaud, 1942-72.

Mont-Laurier, Que. (1913): Jean Gratton, bishop, 1978.
Bishop's Residence: 435, rue de la Madone, Mont-Laurier, Que. J9L 1S1. Cathedral: Notre Dame de Fourvières.
Former bishops: Francois-Xavier Brunet, 1913-22; Joseph-Eugene Limoges, 1922-63; Joseph Louis Andre Ouellette, apostolic administrator sede plena, 1963-65; bishop, 1965-78.

Montreal,* Que. (1836; archdiocese, 1886): Jean-Claude Turcotte, archbishop, 1990. Andre Cimichella, O.S.M., Leonard Crowley, Jude Saint-Antoine, auxiliaries.
Archbishop's Residence: 2000, rue Sherbrooke Ouest, Montreal, Que. H3H 1G4. Cathedral: Basilica of Mary Queen of the World and Saint James.
Former bishops: Jean-Jacques Lartigue, P.S.S., 1836-40; Ignace Bourget, 1840-76; Edouard-Charles Fabre, first archbishop, 1876-96; Paul Bruchési, 1897-1939; Georges Gauthier, administrator 1921-39; archbishop, 1939-40; Joseph Charbonneau, 1940-50; Cardinal Paul-Emile Leger, 1950-67; Cardinal Paul Gregoire, 1968-90.

Moosonee, Ont. (v.a. James Bay, 1938; diocese Moosonee, 1967): Vincent Cadieux, O.M.I, bishop, 1991.

Bishop's Residence: C.P. 40, Moosonee, Ont. POL IYO. Cathedral: Christ the King.
Former bishops: Henri Belleau, O.M.I., 1940-64; Jules LeGuerrier, O.M.I., 1964-67.

Nelson, B.C. (1936): Peter J. Mallon, bishop, 1989.
Bishop's Residence: 813 Ward St., Nelson, B.C. VIL IT4. Cathedral: Mary Immaculate.
Former bishops: Martin M. Johnson, 1936-54; Thomas J. McCarthy, 1955-58; Wilfrid E. Doyle, 1958-89.

New Westminster, B.C. (Ukrainian Byzantine Rite) (1974): Vacant as of April 15, 1993.
Former eparch: Jerome Chimy, O.S.B.M., 1974-92.

Nicolet, Que. (1885): Raymond Saint-Gelais, bishop, 1989.
Bishop's Residence: 49, rue Mgr Brunault, C.P. 820, Nicolet, Que. JOG 1EO. Cathedral: St.-Jean-Baptiste.
Former bishops: Elphege Gravel, 1885-1904; Joseph-Simon-Hermann Brunault, 1904-38; Albini Lafortune, 1938-50; Albert Martin, 1950-89.

Ottawa,* Ont. (Bytown, 1847, name changed, 1854; archdiocese, 1886): Marcel Gervais, archbishop, 1989. Paul Marchand, S.M.M., auxiliary.
Archbishop's Residence: 1247 Place Kilborn, Ottawa, Ont. YIH 6K9. Cathedral: Basilica of Notre Dame-of-Ottawa.
Former bishops: Joseph-Eugene-Bruno Guigues, 1848-74; Joseph Tomas Duhamel, first archbishop, 1874-1909; Charles Hughes Gauthier, 1910-22; Joseph-Medard Emard, 1922-27; Joseph Guillaume Forbes, 1928-40; Alexandre Vachon, 1940-53; Marie-Joseph Lemieux, O.P., 1953-66; Joseph Aurele Plourde, 1967-89.

Pembroke, Ont. (v.a. 1882; diocese, 1898): Brendan M. O'Brien, bishop, 1993.
Chancery Office: 188 Renfrew St., P.O. Box 7, Pembroke, Ont. K8A 6XI. Cathedral: St. Columbkille.
Former bishops: Narcisse-Zephirin Lorrain, 1882-1915; Patrick T. Ryan, 1916-37; Charles-Leo Nelligan, 1937-45; William J. Smith, 1945-71; Joseph R. Windle, 1971-93.

Peterborough, Ont. (1882): James L. Doyle, bishop, 1976.
Bishop's Residence: 350 Hunter St. West, PO Box 175, Peterborough, Ont. K9J 6Y8. Cathedral: St. Peter-in-Chains.
Former bishops: John Francis Jamot, 1882-86; Thomas J. Dowling, 1887-89; Richard A. O'Connor, 1889-1913; Michael J. O'Brien, 1913-29; Denis O'Connor, 1930-42; John R. McDonald, 1943-45; Joseph G. Berry, 1945-53; Benjamin I. Webster, 1954-68; Francis A. Marrocco, 1968-75.

Prince Albert, Sask. (v.a., 1890; diocese, 1907): Blaise Morand, bishop, 1983.
Address: 1415-4th Ave. Ouest, Prince-Albert, Sask S6V 5HI. Cathedral: Sacred Heart.
Former bishops: Albert Pascal, O.M.I., 1907-20; Joseph Henri Prud'homme, 1921-37; R. Duprat, O.P., 1938-52; Leo Blais, 1952-59; Laurent Moran, 1959-83.

Prince George, B.C. (p.a., 1908; v.a. Yukon and

Prince Rupert, 1944; diocese Prince George, 1967): Gerald Wiesner, O.M.I., bishop, 1993.

Chancery Office: P.O. Box 7000, Prince George, B.C. V2N 3Z2. Cathedral: Sacred Heart.

Former bishops: Emile-Marie Bunoz, O.M.I., 1917-45; John-Louie Coudert, O.M.I., coadjutor, 1936-44; Anthony Jordan, O.M.I., 1945-55; John F. O'Grady, O.M.I. 1955-86; Hubert P. O'Connor, 1986-91.

Quebec,* Que. (v.a., 1658; diocese, 1674; archdiocese, 1819; metropolitan, 1844; primatial see, 1956): Maurice Couture, R.S.V., archbishop, 1990. Jean-Paul Labrie, Marc Leclerc, Clement Fecteau, auxiliaries.

Chancery Office: 1073, boul. St-Cyrille Ouest, Quebec, Que. G1S 4R5. Cathedral: Notre-Dame-de-Quebec (Basilica).

Former bishops: Francois de Laval, vicar apostolic, 1658; bishop 1674-88 (beatified 1980); Jean-Baptiste de La Croix de Chevrières de Saint-Vallier, 1688-1727; Louis-Francois Duplessis de Mornay, 1727-33; Pierre-Herman Dosquet, 1733-39; Francois-Louis de Pourroy de Lauberivière, 1739-40; Henri-Marie Dubreil de Pontbriand, 1741-60; Jean-Olivier Briand, 1766-84; Louis-Philippe Mariauchau d'Esgly, 1784-88; Jean-Francois Hubert, 1788-97; Pierre Denaut, 1797-1806; Joseph-Octave Plessis, first archbishop, 1806-25; Bernard-Claude Panet, 1825-33; Joseph Signay, 1833-50; Pierre-Flavien Turgeon, 1850-67; Charles-Francois Baillargeon, 1867-70; Cardinal Elzear-Alexandre Taschereau, 1870-98; Cardinal Louis-Nazaire Begin, 1898-1925; Paul-Eugène Roy, 1925-26; Cardinal Raymond-Marie Rouleau, O.P., 1926-31; Cardinal Jean-Marie-Rodrigue Villeneuve, O.M.I., 1931-47; Cardinal Maurice Roy, 1947-81; Cardinal Louis-Albert Vachon, 1981-90.

Regina,* Sask. (1910; archdiocese, 1915): Charles A. Halpin, archbishop, 1973.

Chancery Office: 445 Broad St. North, Regina, Sask. S4R 2X8. Cathedral: Our Lady of the Most Holy Rosary.

Former bishops: Olivier-Elzear Mathieu, 1911-29; James Charles McGuigan, 1930-34; Peter Joseph Monahan, 1935-47; Michael C.O'Neill, 1948-73.

Rimouski,* Que. (1867; archdiocese, 1946): Bertrand Blanchet, archbishop, 1992.

Archbishop's Residence: 34, rue de l'Évêché Ouest, C.P. 730, Rimouski, Que. G5L 7C7.

Former bishops: Jean Langevin, 1867-91; Andre-Albert Blais, 1891-1919; J.-R. Leonard, 1919-26; Georges Courchesne, 1928-50; Charles-Eugene Parent, 1951-67; Louis Lévesque, 1967-73; Gilles Ouellet, P.M.E., 1973-92.

Rouyn-Noranda, Que. (1973): Jean-Guy Hamelin, bishop, 1974.

Bishop's Residence: 515, avenue Cuddihy, C.P. 1060, Rouyn-Noranda, Que. J9X 5W9. Cathedral: St. Michael the Archangel.

Saint-Boniface,* Man. (1847; archdiocese, 1871): Antoine Hacault, archbishop, 1974.

Archbishop's Residence: 151, avenue de la Cathedrale, Saint-Boniface, Man. R2H OH6. Cathedral: Basilica of St. Boniface.

Former bishops: Joseph-Norbert Provencher, 1847-53; Alexandre-Antonin Tache, O.M.I.,

1853-94, first archbishop; Vital-Justin Grandin, O.M.I., coadjutor, 1857-71; Louis-Philippe-Adelard Langevin, O.M.I., 1895-1915; Arthur Beliveau, 1915-55; Emile Yelle, P.S.S., coadjutor, 1933-41; Georges Cabana, coadjutor, 1941-52; Maurice Baudoux, coadjutor 1952-55, archbishop, 1955-74.

St. Catharines, Ont. (1958): Thomas B. Fulton, bishop, 1978.

Bishop's Residence: 122 Riverdale Ave., St. Catharines, Ont. L2R 4C2. Cathedral: St. Catherine of Alexandria.

Former bishop: Thomas J. McCarthy, 1958-78.

St. George's, Nfld. (p.a., 1870; v.a., 1890; diocese, 1904): Raymond J. Lahey, bishop, 1986.

Bishop's Residence: 16 Hammond Dr., Corner Brook, Nfld. A2H 2W2. Cathedral: Most Holy Redeemer and Immaculate Conception.

Former bishops: Neil McNeil, 1904-10; Michael Power, 1911-20; Henry T. Renouf, 1920-41; Michael O'Reilly, 1941-70; Richard T. McGrath, 1970-85.

Saint-Hyacinthe,   Que.   (1852): Louis-de-Gonzague Langevin, M.Afr., bishop, 1979.

Bishop's Residence: 1900, rue Girouard Ouest, C.P. 190, Saint-Hyacinthe, Que. J2S 7B4. Cathedral. St. Hyacinthe the Confessor.

Former bishops: Jean-Charles Prince, 1852-60; Joseph Larocque, 1860-65; Charles Larocque, 1866-75; Louis-Zéphirin Moreau, 1875-1901 (beatified 1987); Maxime Decelles, 1901-05; Alexis-Xyste Bernard, 1906-23; Fabien-Zoël Decelles, 1924-42; Arthur Doubille, 1942-67; Albert Sanschagrin, O.M.I., 1967-79.

Saint-Jean-Longueuil,   Que.   (1933   as St.-Jean-de-Quebec; named changed, 1982): Bernard Hubert, bishop, 1978. Jacques Berthelet, C.S.V., auxiliary.

Bishop's Residence: 740, boulevard Sainte-Foy, C.P. 40, Longueuil, Que. J4K 4X8. Cathedral: St. John the Evangelist.

Former bishops: Anastase Forget, 1934-55; Gerard-Marie Coderre, 1955-78.

St. Jerome, Que. (1951): Charles Valois, bishop, 1977.

Bishop's Residence: 355, rue Saint-Georges, C.P. 580, Saint-Jerome, Que. J7X 5V3. Cathedral: St. Jerome.

Former bishops: Emilien Frenette, 1951-71; Bernard Hubert, 1971-77.

Saint John, N.B. (1842): J. Edward Troy, bishop, 1986.

Chancery Office: 1 Bayard Dr., Saint John, N.B. E2L 3L5. Cathedral: Immaculate Conception.

Former bishops: William Dollard, 1843-51; Thomas L. Connolly, 1852-59; John Sweeney, 1860-1901; Timothy Casey, 1901-12; Edward A. LeBlanc, 1912-35; Patrick A. Bray, C.J.M., 1936-53; Alfred B. Leverman, 1953-68; Joseph N. MacNeil, 1969-73; Arthur J. Gilbert, 1974-86.

St. John's,* Nfld. (p.a., 1784; v.a., 1796; diocese, 1847; archdiocese, 1904): James H. MacDonald, C.S.C., archbishop, 1991. Chancery Office: P.O. Box 1363, St. John's, Nfld. A1C 5H5. Cathedral: St. john the Baptist.

Former bishops: James O'Donel, O.S.F.,

1784-1807; Patrick Lambert, O.S.F., 1807-17; Patrick Lambert, O.S.F., 1807-17; Thomas Scallan, O.S.F., 1817-30; Michael A. Fleming, O.S.F., 1830-50; John T. Mullock, O.S.F., 1850-69; Thomas J. Power, 1870-93; Michael Howley, first archbishop, 1895-1914; Edward P. Roche, 1915-50; Patrick J. Skinner, C.J.M., 1951-79; Alphonsus L. Penney, 1979-91.

St. Maron of Montreal (Maronites) (1982): Georges Abi-Saber, eparch, 1991.

Chancery Office: 12475 rue Grenet, Montreal, Que. H4J 2K4. Cathedral: St. Maron.

Former bishop: Elias Shaheen, 1982-90.

St. Paul in Alberta (1948): Raymond Roy, bishop, 1972.

Bishop's Residence: 4410, 51e avenue, Saint Paul, Alta. TOA 3A2. Cathedral: St. Paul.

Former bishops: Maurice Baudoux, 1948-52; Philippe Lussier, C.Ss.R., 1952-68; Edouard Gagnon, P.S.S., 1969-72.

St. Sauveur de Montreal (Greek Melkites) (ap. ex. 1980; eparchy, 1984): Archeparch Michel Hakim, 1980.

Address: 34 Maplewood, Outremont, Que. H2V 2MI.

Sts. Cyril and Methodius, Toronto, Ont. (Slovakian Byzantine Rite) (1980): Michael Rusnak, C.Ss.R., eparch, 1981.

Address: P.O. Box 70, 223 Carlton Rd., Unionville, Ont. L3R 2L8.

Sainte-Anne-de-la-Pocatiere, Que. (1951): Andre Gaumond, bishop, 1989.

Bishop's Residence: 1200, 4e avenue, C.P. 430, La Pocatière, Que. GOR 1ZO. Cathedral: St. Anne.

Former bishops: Bruno Desrochers, 1951-68; Charles Henri Levesque, 1968-84.

Saskatoon, Sask. (1933): James P. Mahoney, bishop, 1967.

Chancery Office: 106-5th Avenue North, Saskatoon, Sask. S7K 2N7. Cathedral: St. Paul.

Former bishops: Gerald C. Murray, C.SS.R., 1934-44; Philip F. Pocock, 1944-51; F. Klein, 1951-67.

Saskatoon, Sask. (Ukrainian Byzantine Rite) (ap. ex., 1951; diocese, 1956): Basil (Wasyl) Filevich, eparch, 1984.

Address: 866 Saskatchewan Crescent East, Saskatoon, Sask. S7N OL4.

Former bishop: Andrew J. Roborecki, 1951-82.

Sault Ste. Marie, Ont. (1904): Jean-Louis Plouffe, bishop, 1990. Bernard F. Pappin, auxiliary.

Chancery Office: 480 McIntyre St. West, P.O. Box 510, North Bay, Ont. P1B 8J1. Cathedral: Pro-Cathedral of the Assumption, North Bay.

Former bishops: David Joseph Scollard, 1905-34; Ralphael Hubert Dignan, 1934-58; Alexander Carter, 1958-85; Marcel Gervais, 1985-89.

Sherbrooke,* Que. (1874; archdiocese, 1951): J.-M. Fortier, archbishop, 1968.

Archbishop's Residence: 130, rue de la Cathedrale, C.P. 430, Sherbrooke, Que. J1H 5K1. Cathedral: St. Michel.

Former ordinaries: Antoine Racine, 1874-93; Paul Larocque, 1893-1926; Alphonse-Osias Gagnon, 1927-41; Philippe Desranleau, first archbishop, 1941-52; Georges Cabana, 1952-68.

Thunder Bay, Ont. (Ft. William, 1952;

transferred, 1970): John A. O'Mara, bishop, 1976.

Bishop's Residence: P.O. Box 756, Thunder Bay, Ont. P7C 4W6. Cathedral: St. Patrick.

Former bishops: Edward Q. Jennings, 1952-69; Norman J. Gallagher, 1970-75.

. Timmins, Ont. (v.a. Temiskaming, 1908; diocese Haileybury, 1915; present title, 1938): Gilles Cazabon, O.M.I., bishop, 1992.

Address: 65, Ave. Jubilee Est, Timmins, Ont. P4N 5W4. Cathedral: St. Anthony of Padua.

Former bishops: Elie-Anicet Latulippe, 1908-22; Louis Rheaume, O.M.I., 1922-55; Maxime Tessier, 1955-71; Jacques Landriault, 1971-90.

Toronto,* Ont. (1841; archdiocese, 1870): Aloysius M. Ambrozic, archbishop, 1990. Robert B. Clune, John Stephen Knight, C.H., Nicola De Angelis, C.F.I.C., auxiliaries.

Chancery Office: 335 Church St., Toronto, Ont. M5B 1Z8. Cathedral: St. Michael.

Former ordinaries: Michael Power, 1842-47; Armand-Francois-Marie de Charbonnel, 1850-60; John Joseph Lynch, first archbishop, 1860-88; John Walsh, 1889-98; Denis O'Connor, 1899-1908; Fergus P. McEvay, 1908-11; Neil McNeil, 1912-34; Cardinal James Charles McGuigan, 1934-71; Philip F. Pocock, 1971-78; Cardinal G. Emmett Carter, 1978-90.

Toronto, Ont. (Ukrainian Byzantine Rite) (ap. ex., 1948; eparchy, 1956): Isidore Borecky (exarch 1948-56), first eparch, 1956. Roman Danylak, apostolic administrator, 1993.

Chancery Office: 61 Glen Edyth Dr., Toronto, Ont. M4V 2V8. Cathedral: St. Josaphat.

Trois-Rivieres, Que. (1852): Laurent Noel, bishop, 1975. Martin Veillette, auxiliary.

Bishop's Residence: 362, rue Bonaventure, C.P. 879, Trois-Rivieres, Que. G9A 5J9. Cathedral: The Assumption.

Former bishops: Thomas Cooke, 1852-70; L.-F. Lafleche, 1870-98; F.-X. Cloutier, 1899-1934; A.-O. Comtois, 1935-45; Maurice Roy, 1946-47; Georges-Leon Pelletier, 1947-75.

Valleyfield, Que. (1892): Robert Lebel, bishop, 1976.

Bishop's Residence: 11, rue de l'Eglise, Valleyfield, Que. J6T 1J5. Cathedral: St. Cecilia.

Former bishops: Joseph Médard Emard, 1892-1922; Raymond-M. Rouleau, O.P., 1922-26; Joseph Alfred Langlois, 1926-66; Percival Caza, 1966-69; Guy Belanger, 1969-75.

Vancouver,* B. C. (v.a. British Columbia, 1863; diocese New Westminster, 1890; archdiocese Vancouver, 1908): Adam Exner, O.M.I., archbishop, 1991.

Chancery Office: 150 Robson St., Vancouver, B.C. V6B 2A7. Cathedral: Holy Rosary.

Former ordinaries: Louis-Joseph d'Herbomez, O.M.I., 1864-90; Paul Durieu, O.M.I., 1890-99; Augustin Dontenwill, O.M.I., 1899-1908; Neil McNeil, first archbishop, 1910-12; Timothy Casey, 1912-31; William M. Duke, 1931-64; Martin Michael Johnson, 1964-69; James F. Carney, 1969-90.

Victoria, B.C. (diocese Vancouver Is., 1846; archdiocese, 1903; diocese Victoria, 1908): Remi J. De Roo, bishop, 1962.

Chancery Office: Diocesan Pastoral Centre, #1-4044 Nelthorpe St., Victoria, B.C. V8X 2A1. Cathedral: St. Andrew.

Former bishops: Modeste Demers, 1847-71; Charles J. Seghers, 1873-78; Jean Baptiste Brondel, 1879-84; Charles J. Seghers (2nd time), 1885-86; J. N. Lemmens, 1888-97; Alexander Christie, 1898-99; Bertram Orth, 1900-08; Alexander Macdonald, 1909-23; Thomas O'Donnell, 1924-29; Gerald Murray, C.SS.R., 1930-33; John H. MacDonald, 1933-37; John C. Cody, 1937-46; James M. Hill, 1946-62.

Whitehorse, Y.T. (v.a., 1944; diocese 1967): Thomas Lobsinger, O.M.I., bishop, 1987.

Bishop's Residence: 5119-5th Avenue, Whitehorse, Yukon Y1A 2C8. Cathedral: Sacred Heart.

Former bishops: Jean-Louis Coudert, O.M.I., 1944-65(?); James Mulvihill, O.M.I., 1966-71; Hubert P. O'Connor, O.M.I., 1971-86.

Winnipeg,* Man. (1915): Leonard J. Wall, archbishop, 1992.

Chancery Office: 1495 Pembina Highway, Winnipeg, Man., R3T 2C6. Cathedral: St. Mary.

Former bishops: Alfred Sinnott, 1915-52; Gerald Murray, coadjutor, 1944-51; Philip F. Pocock, 1952-61; Cardinal George B. Iahiff, 1961-82; Adam Exner, O.M.I., 1982-91.

Winnipeg,* Man. (Ukrainian Byzantine Rite) (Ordinariate of Canada, 1912; ap. ex. Central Canada, 1948; ap. ex. Manitoba, 1951; archeparchy Winnipeg, 1956): Michael Bzdel, C.Ss.R., archeparch, 1993.

Archeparchy Office: 235 Scotia St., Winnipeg,

Man., R2V 1V7. Cathedral: Sts. Vladimir and Olga.

Former ordinaries: Niceta Budka, 1912-28; Basile-Vladimir Ladyka, O.S.B.M., 1929-56; Maxim Hermaniuk, C.Ss.R., first archbishop, 1956-92.

Yarmouth, N.S. (1953): James M. Wingle, bishop, 1993.

Address: C.P. 278, 53 rue Park, Yarmouth, N.S. B5a 4B2. Cathedral: St. Ambrose.

Former bishops: Albert Lemenager, 1953-67; Austin E. Burke, 1968-91.

Military Ordinariate of Canada (1951): André Vallée, P.M.E., military ordinary, 1988.

Address: Catholic Chaplain General, National Defense Headquarters, Ottawa, Ont. K1A OK2.

Former military ordinaries: Cardinal Maurice Roy, archbishop of Quebec, 1946-82; John S. Spence, Archbishop of Kingston, 1982-87.

Abbacy of St. Peter, Muenster, Sask. (1921): Peter Novecosky, O.S.B., abbatial blessing, 1990.

Abbot's Residence: St. Peter's Abbey, Muenster, Sask. SOK 2YO.

Former abbots: Bruno Doerfler, 1911-19; Michael Ott, 1921-26; Severinus Gertken, 1927-60; Jerome Weber, 1960-90.

An **Apostolic Exarchate for Armenian-Rite Catholics in Canada and the United States** was established in July, 1981, with headquarters in New York City. Nerses Mikaël Setian, exarch.

Most Rev. Attila Mikloshazy, S.J., titular bishop of Castel Minore and bishop for **Hungarian Emigrants throughout the world**, resides in Canada. Address: 2661 Kingston Rd., Scarborough, Ont. M1M 1M3.

Dioceses with Interprovincial Lines

The following dioceses, indicated by + in the table, have interprovincial lines.

Churchill-Hudson Bay includes part of Northwest Territories.

Keewatin-LePas includes part of Manitoba and Saskatchewan provinces.

Labrador City-Schefferville includes the Labrador region of Newfoundland and the northern part of Quebec province.

Mackenzie-Fort Smith, Northwest Territories, includes part of Alberta and Saskatchewan provinces.

Moosonee, Ont., includes part of Quebec province.

Pembroke, Ont., includes one county of Quebec province.

Whitehorse, Y.T., includes part of British Columbia.

SUNDAY CELEBRATIONS IN THE ABSENCE OF A PRIEST

(Source: Newsletter of the U.S. Bishops' Committee on the Liturgy, July/August, 1988.)

A "Directory for Sunday Celebrations in the Absence of a Priest" was approved by Pope John Paul May 21, 1988.

The first chapter states the meaning of Sunday as "a synthesis of the Church's understanding of the nature and purpose of Sunday and the divine command to worship on the Day of the Lord."

The Directory "indicates the conditions upon which a decision can be made to have Sunday celebrations in the absence of a priest." Specifically:

• "There should be no confusion in the mind of the faithful about the difference between these

celebrations and the celebration of the Eucharist."

• "The diocesan bishop ... is to establish regulations for Sunday celebrations in the absence of a priest. All such celebrations must be approved by the bishop and be under the supervision of a pastor."

• "Sunday celebrations may be led by deacons or by suitably prepared lay people."

• "In no case should there be a presentation (and preparation) of the gifts or the proclamation of the Eucharistic Prayer."

• "The Opening Prayer and Prayer after Communion are taken from the Sacramentary, and the readings are taken from the Lectionary for Mass."

STATISTICS OF THE CATHOLIC CHURCH IN CANADA

(Principal source: *Canadian Conference of Catholic Bishops, Statistics of the Catholic Church in Canada, 1991-1992 Report, published January, 1993* (figures as of Dec. 31, 1991). Statistics for Brothers are from the *1993 Annuario Pontificio*. Archdioceses are indicated by an asterisk. For dioceses marked +, see Canadian Dioceses with Interprovincial Lines.)

Canada's 10 civil provinces and two territories are divided into 18 ecclesiastical provinces consisting of 18 metropolitan sees (archdioceses) and 51 suffragan sees (50 dioceses and one territorial abbacy); there are also one archdiocese, and three eparchies immediately subject to the Holy See. (See listing of Ecclesiastical Provinces elsewhere in this section.)

This table presents a regional breakdown of Catholic statistics. In some cases, the totals are approximate because diocesan boundaries fall within several civil provinces.

Civil Province Diocese	Cath. Pop.	Dioc. Priests	Rel. Priests	Total Priests	Perm. Deacs.	Bro-thers	Sis-ters	Par-ishes
Newfoundland	**211,896**	**107**	**28**	**135**	**—**	**37**	**421**	**120**
*St. John's	127,466	49	18	67	—	22	301	44
Grand Falls	30,470	29	—	29	—	3	40	28
Labrador City-Schefferville+	14,215	—	9	9	—	7	32	25
St. George's	39,745	29	1	30	—	5	48	23
Prince Edward Island								
Charlottetown	**58,668**	**66**	**3**	**69**	**1**	**—**	**197**	**59**
Nova Scotia	**304,310**	**264**	**50**	**314**	**24**	**14**	**877**	**220**
*Halifax	141,500	66	23	89	23	2	370	53
Antigonish	127,810	173	11	184	—	9	465	128
Yarmouth	35,000	25	16	41	1	3	42	39
New Brunswick	**354,234**	**265**	**71**	**336**	**2**	**35**	**979**	**206**
*Moncton	86,917	67	28	95	1	25	356	52
Bathurst	116,470	71	17	88	—	7	272	62
Edmundston	52,847	45	13	58	—	2	162	34
St. John	98,000	82	13	95	1	1	189	58
Quebec	**5,910,300**	**3,572**	**2,284**	**5,856**	**281**	**2,457**	**20,258**	**1,852**
*Gatineau-Hull	195,000	70	49	119	2	13	267	60
*Montreal	1,375,000	700	916	1,616	81	745	6,738	254
*Quebec	1,066,352	670	390	1,060	70	504	4,553	273
*Rimouski	155,341	169	59	228	—	41	873	117
*Sherbrooke	282,344	260	124	384	20	113	1,325	130
Amos	107,488	74	25	99	—	13	197	69
Baie-Comeau	93,844	53	22	75	6	23	142	49
Chicoutimi	269,065	232	68	300	28	73	814	97
Gaspe	90,816	78	21	99	2	7	205	63
Joliette	185,857	113	60	173	2	59	420	57
Mont Laurier	74,125	56	33	89	—	36	155	59
Nicolet	177,220	196	41	237	16	115	863	85
Rouyn-Noranda	57,043	31	19	50	—	6	129	37
Ste.-Anne-de-la-Pocatiere	89,388	160	4	164	4	9	303	54
St. Hyacinthe	335,225	207	96	303	26	228	1,252	113
St. Jean-Longueuil	487,114	140	83	223	1	87	506	90
St. Jerome	316,009	103	121	224	—	144	286	68
St. Maron, Mtrl (Maronites)	80,000	6	12	18	—	—	10	9
St. Sauveur-Montreal (Greek Melkites)	38,000	2	7	9	—	—	—	9
Trois Rivieres	254,969	159	98	257	16	173	910	94
Valleyfield	180,100	93	36	129	7	68	310	65
Ontario	**3,240,197**	**1,452**	**1,137**	**2,589**	**413**	**301**	**4,242**	**1,174**
*Kingston	79,511	73	9	82	4	—	221	52
*Ottawa	347,628	149	218	367	25	69	1,017	112
*Toronto	1,233,785	262	548	810	208	132	1,016	212
Alexandria-Cornwall	55,890	42	6	48	14	4	89	34

Civil Province Diocese	Cath. Pop.	Dioc. Priests	Rel. Priests	Total Priests	Perm. Deacs.	Bro- thers	Sis- ters	Par- ishes
Ontario								
Hamilton	374,585	139	124	263	1	36	381	122
Hearst	30,859	39	—	39	2	—	31	30
London	387,135	234	90	324	—	17	531	147
Moosonee+	4,000	—	8	8	1	4	12	16
Pembroke+	65,164	81	6	87	6	10	250	72
Peterborough	76,016	101	3	104	6	—	144	40
St. Catharines	129,075	61	32	93	—	3	80	47
Sts. Cyril and Methodius- Toronto (Slovaks)	30,000	16	—	16	—	—	—	17
Sault Ste. Marie	224,469	112	40	152	109	11	310	125
Thunder Bay	71,700	27	30	57	15	3	67	41
Timmins	50,380	30	7	37	7	8	55	34
Toronto (Ukrainians)	80,000	86	16	102	15	4	38	73
Manitoba	**319,384**	**175**	**186**	**361**	**47**	**63**	**836**	**359**
*Keewatin-LePas+	38,289	1	26	27	1	3	38	53
*St. Boniface	82,000	92	66	158	9	53	509	70
*Winnipeg	148,215	51	64	115	17	3	240	149
*Winnipeg (Ukrainians)	46,000	31	14	45	20	1	38	69
Churchill-Hudson Bay+	4,880	—	16	16	—	3	11	18
Saskatchewan	**240,906**	**191**	**103**	**294**	**7**	**30**	**682**	**508**
*Regina	80,000	78	—	78	—	5	171	168
Gravelbourg	12,121	17	3	20	—	—	67	39
Prince Albert	49,035	33	15	48	1	3	126	89
Saskatoon	64,250	40	47	87	—	3	176	61
Saskatoon (Ukrainians)	23,500	23	14	37	6	2	32	130
St. Peter-Muenster (Abb.)	12,000	—	24	24	—	17	110	21
Alberta	**632,057**	**230**	**227**	**457**	**6**	**51**	**825**	**481**
*Edmonton	252,484	83	121	204	—	33	541	176
*Grouard-McLennan	40,000	7	28	35	—	2	42	65
Calgary	261,448	82	61	143	2	12	158	78
Edmonton (Ukrainians)	35,000	31	17	48	3	4	32	93
St. Paul	43,125	27	—	27	1	—	52	69
British Columbia	**557,930**	**175**	**151**	**326**	**6**	**58**	**468**	**227**
*Vancouver	325,822	84	82	166	—	41	232	74
Kamloops	26,250	13	12	25	1	5	30	25
Nelson	62,475	31	20	51	—	—	50	31
New Westminster (Ukrainians)	7,700	14	3	17	3	—	5	22
Prince George	56,977	4	16	20	1	8	36	19
Victoria	78,706	29	18	47	1	4	115	56
Yukon Territory								
Whitehorse+	**7,284**	**3**	**13**	**16**	**—**	**4**	**6**	**24**
Northwest Territories								
MacKenzie-Ft. Smith+	**20,477**	**2**	**21**	**23**	**—**	**4**	**30**	**40**
Military Ordinariate	**113,919**	**—**	**19**	**19**	**—**	**—**	**—**	**53**
TOTALS	**11,971,562**	**6,502**	**4,286**	**10,788**	**787**	**3,045+**	**29,821**	**5,323**

+Diocesan and total figures for brothers are from *1993 Annuario Pontificio*. The 1991-1992 Report of Statistics of the Catholic Church in Canada, reported a total of 2,921 brothers; no diocesan breakdown was available.

CANADIAN CONFERENCE OF CATHOLIC BISHOPS

The Canadian Conference of Catholic Bishops was established Oct. 12, 1943, as a permanent voluntary association of the bishops of Canada, was given official approval by the Holy See in 1948, and acquired the status of an episcopal conference after the Second Vatican Council.

The CCCB acts in two ways: (1) as a strictly ecclesiastical body through which the bishops act together with pastoral authority and responsibility for the Church throughout the country; (2) as an operational secretariat through which the bishops act on a wider scale for the good of the Church and society.

At the top of the CCCB organizational table are the president, an executive committee, a permanent council and a plenary assembly. The membership consists of all the bishops of Canada.

Departments and Offices

The CCCB's work is planned and co-ordinated by the Programmes and Priorities Committee composed of the six chairmen of the national episcopal commissions and the two general secretaries. It is chaired by the vice-president of the CCCB.

The CCCB's nine episcopal commissions undertake study and projects in special areas of pastoral work. Six serve nationally (social affairs, canon law/inter-rite, ministries, missions, ecumenism, theology); three relate to French and English sectors (social communications, Christian education, liturgy).

The general secretariat consists of a French and an English general secretary and their assistants and directors of public relations.

Administrative services for purchasing, archives and library, accounting, personnel, publications, printing and distribution are supervised by directors who relate to the general secretaries.

Various advisory councils and committees with mixed memberships of lay persons, religious, priests and bishops also serve the CCCB on a variety of topics.

Operations

Meetings for the transaction of business are held at least once a year by the plenary assembly, six times a year by the executive committee, and four times a year by the permanent council.

Bishop Jean-Guy Hamelin of Rouyn-Noranda, Que., is president of the CCCB and Archbishop Francis J. Spence of Kingston, Ont., is vice president for the 1993-95 term.

Secretariat is located at 90 Parent Ave., Ottawa, K1N 7B1, Canada.

PERCENTAGE OF CATHOLICS

Sources: *Statistics of the Church in Canada, 1991-1992 Report,* Canadian Conference of Catholic Bishops; the *1993 Annuario Pontificio.*

The table presents a regional breakdown of Catholic percentage in total population. In some cases, the Catholic totals are approximate because diocesan boundaries fall within several civil provinces. See Index: Canadian Dioceses with Interprovincial Lines.

Civil Province Territory	Cath. Pop.	Total Pop.	Cath. Pct.	Civil Province Territory	Cath. Pop.	Total Pop.	Cath. Pct.
Alberta	632,057	2,397,700	26.3	Prince Edward Is.	58,668	130,100	45.1
British Columbia	557,930	3,014,530	18.5	Quebec	5,910,300	6,870,814	86.0
Manitoba	319,384	1,148,061	27.8	Saskatchewan	240,906	984,500	24.4
New Brunswick	354,234	668,503	53.0	Yukon	7,284	36,413	20.0
Newfoundland	211,896	617,645	34.3	Northwest Territories	20,477	38,347	53.3
Nova Scotia	304,310	932,200	32.6	Military Ordinariate	113,919	—	—
Ontario	3,240,197	9,817,507	33.0	**TOTALS**	**11,971,562**	**26,656,320**	**45.0**

BIOGRAPHIES OF CANADIAN BISHOPS

(Sources: *Information office of Canadian Conference of Catholic Bishops; Annuario Pontificio; L'Osservatore Romano.* Data as of Aug. 20, 1993.)

Abi-Saber, Georges, O.L.M.: b May 12, 1923, Lebanon; ord. priest July 16, 1952; ord. bishop of Lattaquie of the Maronites, Nov. 12, 1977; titular bishop of Arado and auxiliary of patriarchate of Antioch of the Maronites, May 2, 1986; eparch of St. Maron of Montreal, Nov. 23, 1990.

Ambrozic, Aloysius M.: b. Jan. 27, 1930; ord. priest June 4, 1955; ord. titular bishop of Valabria and auxiliary bishop of Toronto, May 27, 1976; coadjutor archbishop of Toronto, May 28, 1986; archbishop of Toronto, Mar. 17, 1990.

Audet, Rene: b. Jan. 18, 1920, Montreal, Que.; ord. priest May 30, 1948; ord. titular bishop of Chonochora and auxiliary bishop of Ottawa, July 31, 1963; bishop of Joliette, Jan. 3, 1968; retired Oct. 31, 1990.

Belisle, Gilles: b. Oct. 7, 1923, Clarence Creek, Ont.; ord. priest Feb. 2, 1950; ord. titular bishop of Uccula and auxiliary bishop of Ottawa, June 21, 1977; resigned Aug. 19, 1993.

Berthelet, Jacques, C.S.V.: b. Oct. 24, 1934, Montreal, Que.; ord. priest June 16, 1962; ord. titular bishop of Lamsorti and auxiliary of Saint-Jean-Longueuil, Mar. 21, 1987.

Blanchet, Bertrand: b. Sept. 19, 1932, Saint

Thomas de Montmagny, Que.; ord. priest May 20, 1956; ord. bishop of Gaspe, Dec. 8, 1973; archbishop of Rimouski, Oct. 16, 1992.

Borecky, Isidore: b. Oct. 1, 1911, Ostrovec, Ukraine; ord. priest July 17, 1938; ord. titular bishop of Amathus in Cypro and exarch of Toronto, May 27, 1948; eparch of Toronto (Ukrainians), Nov. 3, 1956.

Burke, Austin-Emile: b. Jan. 11, 1922, Sluice Point, N.S.; ord. priest Mar. 25, 1950; ord. bishop of Yarmouth, May 14, 1968; archbishop of Halifax, July 8, 1991.

Bzdel, Michael, C.Ss.R.: b. July 7, 1930, Wishart, Sask.; ord. priest July 7, 1954; ord. archeparch of Winnipeg of the Ukrainians, Mar. 9, 1993.

Cadieux, Vincent, O.M.I.: b. Feb. 16, 1940, Alfred, Ont.; ord. priest Dec. 17, 1966; ord. bishop of Moosonee, Mar. 29, 1992.

Campbell, Colin: b. June 12, 1931, Antigonish, N.S.; ord. priest May 26, 1956; ord. bishop of Antigonish, Mar. 19, 1987.

Carew, William A.: b. Oct. 23, 1922, St. John's, Nfld., ord. priest June 15, 1947; ord. titular archbishop of Telde, Jan. 4, 1970; nuncio to Rwanda and Burundi, 1970-74; apostolic delegate to Jerusalem and Palestine and pro-nuncio to Cyprus, 1974-83; pro-nuncio to Japan, Aug. 30, 1983.

Carter, Alexander: b. Apr. 16, 1909, Montreal, Que.; ord. priest June 6, 1936; ord. titular bishop of Sita and coadjutor bishop of Sault Ste. Marie, Feb. 2, 1957; bishop of Sault Ste. Marie, Nov. 22, 1958; retired May 8, 1985.

Carter, G. Emmett: (See Cardinals, Biographies.)

Cazabon, Gilles, O.M.I.: b. Apr. 5, 1933, Verner, Ont.; ord. priest June 11, 1960; ord. bishop of Timmins, June 29, 1992.

Charbonneau, Paul E.: b. May 4, 1922, Ste. Therese de Blainville, Que.; ord. priest May 31, 1947; ord. titular bishop of Thapsus and auxiliary bishop of Ottawa, Jan. 18, 1961; first bishop of Hull (now Gatineau-Hull), May 21, 1963; retired Apr. 12, 1973, because of ill health.

Chiasson, Donat: b. Jan. 2, 1930, Paquetville, N.B.; ord. priest May 6, 1956; ord. archbishop of Moncton, June 1, 1972.

Cimichella, Andre, O.S.M.: b. Feb. 21, 1921, Grotte Santo Stefano, Italy; ord. priest May 26, 1945; ord. titular bishop of Quiza and auxiliary of Montreal, July 16, 1964.

Clune, Robert B.: b. Sept. 18, 1920, Toronto, Ont.; ord. priest May 26, 1945; ord. titular bishop of Lacubaza and auxiliary bishop of Toronto, June 21, 1979.

Coderre, Gerard-Marie: b. Dec. 19, 1904, St. Jacques de Montcalm, Que.; ord. priest May 30, 1931; ord. titular bishop of Aegae and coadjutor bishop of St.-Jean-de-Quebec, Sept. 12, 1951; bishop of St.-Jean-de-Quebec (now Saint-Jean-Longueuil), Feb. 3, 1955; retired May 3, 1978.

Couture, Jean-Guy: b. May 6, 1929, St.-Jean-Baptiste de Quebec, Que.; ord. priest May 30, 1953; ord. bishop of Hauterive (now Baie-Comeau), Que., Aug. 15, 1975; bishop of Chicoutimi, Apr. 5, 1979.

Couture, Maurice, R.S.V.: b. Nov. 3, 1926, Saint-Pierre-de-Broughton, Que.; ord. priest June

17, 1951; ord. titular bishop of Talaptula and auxiliary bishop of Quebec, Oct. 22, 1982; bishop of Baie Comeau, Dec. 1, 1988; archbishop of Quebec and primate of Canada, Mar. 17, 1990.

Couturier, Gerard: b. Jan. 12, 1913, St. Louis du Ha Ha, Que; ord. priest Mar. 25, 1938; ord. bishop of Hauterive (now Baie-Comeau), Feb. 28, 1957; resigned Sept. 7, 1974.

Croteau, Denis, O.M.I: b. Oct. 23, 1932, Thetford Mines, Que., ord. priest Aug. 31, 1958; ord. bishop of MacKenzie-Fort Smith, June 8, 1986.

Crowley, Leonard: b. Dec. 28, 1921, Montreal, Que.; ord. priest May 31, 1947; ord. titular bishop of Mons and auxiliary bishop of Montreal, Mar. 24, 1971.

Daciuk, Myron, O.S.B.M.: b. Nov. 16, 1919, Mundare, Alta; ord. priest June 10, 1945; ord. titular bishop of Thyatira and auxiliary eparch of Winnipeg (Ukrainians), Oct. 14, 1982; eparch of Edmonton (Ukrainians), Oct. 28, 1991.

Danylak, Roman: b. Dec. 29, 1930, Toronto, Ont.; ord. priest Oct. 3, 1957; ord. titular bishop of Nissa and apostolic administrator of Toronto Eparchy (Ukrainians), Mar. 25, 1993.

De Angelis, Nicola, C.F.I.C.: b. Jan. 23, 1939, in Pozzaglia Sabino, Italy; ord. priest for the Conceptionists, Dec. 6, 1970; became Canadian citizen, 1975; ord. titular bishop of Remesiana and auxiliary bishop of Toronto, June 24, 1992.

Delaquis, Noel: b. Dec. 25, 1934, Notre-Dame-de-Lourdes, Man.; ord. priest June 5, 1958; ord. bishop of Gravelbourg, Feb. 19, 1974.

De Roo, Remi J.: b. Feb. 24, 1924, Swan Lake, Man.; ord. priest June 8, 1950; ord. bishop of Victoria, Dec. 14, 1962.

Despatie, Roger: b. Apr. 12, 1927, Sudbury, Ont.; ord. priest Apr. 12, 1952; ord. titular bishop of Usinaza and auxiliary bishop of Sault Ste. Marie, June 28, 1968; bishop of Hearst, Feb. 8, 1973; retired Apr. 13, 1993.

Dionne, Gerard: b. June 19, 1919, Saint-Basile, N.B.; ord. priest May 1, 1948; ord. titular bishop of Garba and auxiliary bishop of Sault Ste. Marie, Apr. 8, 1975; bishop of Edmundston, Nov. 17, 1983.

Doyle, James L.: b. June 20, 1929, Chatham, Ont.; ord. priest June 12, 1954; ord. bishop of Peterborough June 28, 1976.

Doyle, W. Emmett: b. Feb. 18, 1913, Calgary, Alta.: ord. priest June 5, 1938; ord. bishop of Nelson, Dec. 3, 1958; retired Nov. 16, 1989.

Drainville, Gerard: b. May 20, 1930, L'Isle-du-Pas, Que.; ord. priest May 30, 1953; ord. bishop of Amos, June 12, 1978.

Dumouchel, Paul, O.M.I.: b. Sept. 19, 1911, St. Boniface, Man.; ord. priest June 24, 1936; ord. titular bishop of Sufes and vicar apostolic of Keewatin, May 24, 1955; archbishop of Keewatin-Le Pas, July 13, 1967; retired 1986.

Ebacher, Roger: b. Oct. 6, 1936, Amos, Que.; ord. priest May 27, 1961; ord. bishop of Hauterive, July 31, 1979; title of see changed to Baie-Comeau, 1986; bishop of Gatineau-Hull, May 6, 1988; first archbishop, Oct 31, 1990, when Gatineau-Hull was made a metropolitan see.

Exner, Adam, O.M.I.: b. Dec. 24, 1928, Killaly, Sask.; ord. priest July 7, 1957; ord. bishop of Kamloops,

B.C., Mar. 12, 1974; archbishop of Winnipeg, Mar. 31, 1982; archbishop of Vancouver, 1991.

Fecteau, Clement: b. Apr. 20, 1933, Sainte-Marie-de-Beauce, Que.; ord. priest June 16, 1957; ord. titular bishop of Talattula and auxiliary bishop of Quebec, Oct. 20, 1989.

Filevich, Basil (Wasyl): b. Jan. 13, 1918; ord. priest Apr. 12, 1942; ord. eparch of Ukrainian eparchy of Saskatoon Feb. 27, 1984.

Fortier, Jean-Marie: b. July 1, 1920, Quebec, Que.; ord. priest June 16, 1944; ord. titular bishop of Pomaria and auxiliary bishop of Ste. Anne-de-la-Pocatiere, Jan. 23, 1961; bishop of Gaspe, Jan. 19, 1965; archbishop of Sherbrooke, Apr. 20, 1968.

Fougère, Joseph Vernon: b. May 20, 1943, Petit Grat, N.S.; ord. priest May 31, 1969; ord. bishop of Charlottetown, Mar. 19, 1992.

Fulton, Thomas B.: b. Jan. 13, 1918, St. Catharines, Ont.; ord. priest June 7, 1941; ord. titular bishop of Cursola and auxiliary bishop of Toronto, Jan. 6, 1969; bishop of St. Catharines, July 7, 1978.

Gagnon, Edouard, P.S.S.: (See Cardinals, Biographies.)

Gaumond, Andre: b. June 3, 1936, St. Thomas de Montmagny, Que.; ord. priest May 27, 1961; ord. bishop of Ste.Anne-de-la-Pocatiere, Aug. 15, 1985.

Gervais, Marcel A.: b. Sept. 21, 1931, Elie, Man.; ord. priest May 31, 1958; ord. titular bishop of Rosmarkaeum and auxiliary bishop of London, Ont., June 11, 1980; bishop of Sault Ste. Marie, May 8, 1985; coadjutor archbishop of Ottawa, June 21, 1989; archbishop of Ottawa, Sept. 27, 1989.

Gilbert, Arthur J.: b. Oct. 26, 1915, Oromocto, N.B.; ord. priest June 3, 1943; ord. bishop of St. John, N.B., June 19, 1974; retired Apr. 2, 1986.

Goudreault, Henri, O.M.I.: b. Apr. 30, 1928, Belle-Vallee, Ont.; ord. priest June 17, 1956; ord. bishop of Labrador City-Schefferville, June 17, 1987.

Gratton, Jean: b. Dec. 4, 1924, Wendover, Ont.; ord. priest Apr. 27, 1952; ord. bishop of Mont Laurier, June 29, 1978.

Gregoire, Paul: (See Cardinals, Biographies.)

Hacault, Antoine: b. Jan. 17, 1926, Bruxelles, Man.; ord. priest May 20, 1951; ord. titular bishop of Media and coadjutor of St. Boniface, Sept. 8, 1964; archbishop of St. Boniface, Sept. 7, 1974.

Hakim, Michel: b. Apr. 21, 1921, Magdouche, South Lebanon; ord. priest Nov. 10, 1947; ord. archbishop of Saida of Greek Melkites, Sept. 10, 1977; app. titular archbishop of Caesarea in Cappadocia and apostolic exarch of Greek Melkite Catholics in Canada, Oct. 13, 1980; first eparch (with personal title of archbishop), Sept. 1, 1984, when exarchate was raised to eparchy with title St. Sauveur de Montreal.

Halpin, Charles A.: b. Aug. 30, 1930, St. Eustache, Man.; ord. priest May 27, 1956; ord. archbishop of Regina, Nov. 26, 1973.

Hamelin, Jean-Guy: b. Oct. 8, 1925, St. Severin-de-Proulxville, Que.; ord. priest June 11, 1949; ord. first bishop of Rouyn-Noranda, Que., Feb. 9, 1974.

Hayes, James M.: b. May 27, 1924, Halifax, N.S.; ord. priest June 15, 1947; ord. titular bishop of Reperi and apostolic administrator of Halifax, Apr.

20, 1965; archbishop of Halifax, June 22, 1967; retired Nov. 6, 1990. President of Canadian Conference of Catholic Bishops, 1987-89.

Henry, Frederick: b. Apr. 11, 1943, London, Ont.; ord. priest May 25, 1968; ord. titular bishop of Carinola and auxiliary bishop of London, Ont., June 24, 1986.

Hermaniuk, Maxim, C.Ss.R.: b. Oct. 30, 1911, Nove Selo, Ukraine; ord. priest Sept. 4, 1938; ord. titular bishop of Sinna and exarch of Manitoba (Ukrainians), June 29, 1951; archeparch of Winnipeg (Ukrainians), Nov. 3, 1956; retired Dec. 17, 1992.

Hubert, Bernard: b. June 1, 1929, Beloeil, Que.; ord. priest May 30, 1953; ord. bishop of St. Jerome, Sept. 12, 1971; coadjutor bishop of Saint-Jean-de-Quebec, 1977; succeeded as bishop of Saint-Jean-de-Quebec, May 3, 1978; title of see changed to Saint-Jean-Longueuil, 1982. President of Canadian Conference of Catholic Bishops, 1985-87.

Knight, John Stephen: b. Apr. 10, 1942, Binghamton, N. Y.; moved to Ontario as a child; ord. priest June 2, 1967; ord. titular bishop of Taraqua and auxiliary bishop of Toronto, June 24, 1992.

Labrie, Jean-Paul: b. Nov. 4, 1922, Laurieville, Que.; ord. priest May 20, 1951; ord. titular bishop of Urci and auxiliary bishop of Quebec, May 14, 1977.

Lacey, Michael Pearse: b. Nov. 27, 1916, Toronto, Ont.; ord. priest May 23, 1943; ord. titular bishop of Diana and auxiliary bishop of Toronto, June 21, 1979; retired May 31, 1993.

Lacroix, Fernand, C.J.M.: b. Oct. 16, 1919, Quebec; ord. priest Feb. 10, 1946; ord. bishop of Edmundston, Oct. 20, 1970; retired May 31, 1983.

Lahey, Raymond: b. May 29, 1940, St. John's Nfld.; ord. priest June 13, 1963; ord. bishop of St. George's, Nfld., Aug. 3, 1986.

Landriault, Jacques: b. Sept. 23, 1921, Alfred, Ont.; ord. priest Feb. 9, 1947; ord. titular bishop of Cadi and auxiliary bishop of Alexandria, July 25, 1962; bishop of Hearst, May 27, 1964; app. bishop of Timmins, Mar. 24, 1971; retired Dec. 13, 1990.

Langevin, Louis-de-Gonzague, M. Afr.: b. Oct. 31, 1921, Oka, Que.; ord. priest Feb. 2, 1950; ord. titular bishop of Rosemarkie and auxiliary of St. Hyacinthe Sept. 23, 1974; bishop of St. Hyacinthe, July 18, 1979.

LaRocque, Eugene-Philippe: b. Mar. 27, 1927, Windsor, Ont.; ord. priest June 7, 1952; ord. bishop of Alexandria, Ont., Sept. 3, 1974; title of see changed to Alexandria-Cornwall, 1976.

Lebel, Robert: b. Nov. 8, 1924, Trois-Pistoles, Que.; ord. priest June 18, 1950; ord. titular bishop of Alinda and auxiliary of St. Jean de Quebec, May 12, 1974; bishop of Valleyfield, Mar. 26, 1976. President of Canadian Conference of Catholic Bishops, 1989-91.

LeBlanc, Camille-Andre: b. Aug. 25, 1898, Barachois, N.B.; ord. priest Apr. 5, 1924; ord. bishop of Bathurst, Sept. 8, 1942; retired Jan. 8, 1969.

Leclerc, Marc: b. Jan. 9, 1933, Saint-Gregoire de Montmorency, Que.; ord. priest May 31, 1958; ord. titular bishop of Eguga and auxiliary bishop of Quebec, Oct. 22, 1982.

Legare, Henri, O.M.I.: b. Feb. 20, 1918, Willow

Bunch, Sask.; ord. priest June 29, 1943; ord. first bishop of Labrador-Schefferville, Sept. 9, 1967; archbishop of Grouard-McLennan, Nov. 21, 1972. President of Canadian Conference of Catholic Bishops, 1981-83.

Leguerrier, Jules, O.M.I.: b. Feb. 18, 1915, Clarence Creek, Ont.; ord. priest June 19, 1943; ord. titular bishop of Bavagaliana and vicar apostolic of James Bay, June 29, 1964; first bishop of Moosonee, July 13, 1967; retired Dec. 5, 1991.

Lemieux, Marie Joseph, O.P.: b. May 10, 1902, Quebec, Que.; ord. priest Apr. 15, 1928; ord. bishop of Sendai, Japan, June 29, 1936; titular bishop of Calydon, 1941; apostolic administrator of Gravelbourg, 1942; bishop of Gravelbourg, Apr. 15, 1944; archbishop of Ottawa, 1953-66; titular archbishop of Salde, Nov. 16, 1966, apostolic nuncio. Retired. Archbishop emeritus of Ottawa.

Levesque, Louis: b. May 27, 1908, Amqui, Que.; ord. priest June 26, 1932; ord. bishop of Hearst, Aug. 15, 1952; titular archbishop of Egnatia and coadjutor of Rimouski, Apr. 13, 1964; archbishop of Rimouski, Feb. 25, 1967; retired May 14, 1973.

Lobsinger, Thomas J., O.M.I.: b. Nov. 17, 1927, Ayton, Ont.; ord. priest May 29, 1954; ord. bishop of Whitehorse, Y.T., Oct. 1, 1987.

Lussier, Gilles: b. June 5, 1940, Montreal, Que.; ord. priest Dec. 19, 1964; ord. titular bishop of Augurus and auxiliary bishop of Saint Jerome, Feb. 28, 1989; bishop of Joliette, Sept. 7, 1991.

MacDonald, James H., C.S.C.: b. Apr. 28, 1925, Wycogama, N.S.; ord. priest June 29, 1953; ord. titular bishop of Gibba and auxiliary bishop of Hamilton April 17, 1978; app. bishop of Charlottetown, Aug. 12, 1982; archbishop of St. John's, Nfld., 1991.

MacDonald, Joseph Faber: b. Jan. 20, 1932, Little Pond, P.E.I.; ord. priest Mar. 9, 1963; ord. bishop of Grand Falls, Mar. 19, 1980.

MacNeil, Joseph N.: b. Apr. 15, 1924, Sydney, N.S.; ord. priest May 23, 1948; ord. bishop of St. John, N.B., June 24, 1969; archbishop of Edmonton, July 6, 1973. President Canadian Conference of Catholic Bishops, 1979-81.

Mahoney, James P.: b. Dec. 7, 1927, Saskatoon, Sask.; ord. priest June 7, 1952; ord. bishop of Saskatoon, Dec. 13, 1967.

Mallon, Peter J.: b. Dec. 5, 1929, Prince Rupert, B.C.; ord. priest May 27, 1956; ord. bishop of Nelson, Feb. 2, 1990.

Marchand, Paul, S.M.M.: b. 1937; solemnly professed, Montfort Missionaries, 1961; ord. priest 1962; app. titular bishop of Tamata and auxiliary of Ottawa, May 31, 1993.

Mikloshazy, Attila, S.J.: b. Apr. 5, 1931, Diósgyör, Hungary; ord. priest, June 18, 1961; ord. titular bishop of Castel Minore, Nov. 4, 1989. Bishop for Hungarian emigrants (resides in Canada).

Morand, Blaise E.: b. Sept. 12, 1932, Tecumseh, Ont.; ord. priest Mar. 22, 1958; ord. coadjutor bishop of Prince Albert, June 29, 1981; bishop of Prince Albert, Apr. 9, 1983.

Morin, Laurent: b. Feb. 14, 1908, Montreal,

Que.; ord. priest May 27, 1934; ord. titular bishop of Arsamosata and auxiliary bishop of Montreal, Oct. 30, 1955; bishop of Prince Albert, Feb. 28, 1959; retired Apr. 9, 1983.

Morissette, Pierre: b. Nov. 22, 1944, Thetford-Mines, Que.; ord. priest June 8, 1968; ord. titular bishop of Mesarfelta and auxiliary of Quebec, June 12, 1987; app. bishop of Baie Comeau, Mar. 17, 1990.

Noel, Laurent: b. Mar. 19, 1920, Saint-Just-de-Bretenieres, Que.; ord. priest June 16, 1944; ord. titular bishop of Agathopolis and auxiliary bishop of Quebec, Aug. 29, 1963; bishop of Trois Rivieres, Nov. 5, 1975.

Novecosky, Peter, O.S.B.: b. Apr. 27, 1945, Humboldt, Saskatchewan; ord. priest July 11, 1970; app. abbot-ordinary of St. Peter Muenster, July 23, 1990; abbatial blessing Nov. 26, 1990.

O'Brien, Brendan M.: b. Sept. 28, 1943, Ottawa, Ont.; ord. priest June 1, 1968; ord. titular bishop of Numana and auxiliary of Ottawa, June 29, 1987; app. bishop of Pembroke, Apr. 5, 1993.

O'Byrne, Paul J.: b. Dec. 12, 1922, Calgary, Alta.; ord. priest Feb. 21, 1948; ord. bishop of Calgary, Aug. 22, 1968.

O'Connor, Hubert P., O.M.I.: b. Feb. 17, 1928, Huntingdon, Que.; ord. priest June 5, 1955; ord. bishop of Whitehorse, Dec. 8, 1971; bishop of Prince George, June 9, 1986; retired 1991.

O'Grady, John Fergus, O.M.I.: b. July 27, 1908, Macton, Ont.; ord. priest June 29, 1934; ord. titular bishop of Aspendus and vicar apostolic of Prince Rupert, Mar. 7, 1956; first bishop of Prince George, July 13, 1967; retired June 9, 1986.

O'Mara, John A.: b. Nov. 17, 1924, Buffalo, N.Y.; ord. priest June 1, 1951; ord. bishop of Thunder Bay, June 29, 1976.

Ouellet, Gilles, P.M.E.: b. Aug. 14, 1922, Bromptonville, Que.; ord. priest June 30, 1946; ord. bishop of Gaspe, Nov. 23, 1968; app. archbishop of Rimouski, Apr. 27, 1973; retired Oct. 16, 1992. President Canadian Conference of Catholic Bishops, 1977-79.

Ouellette, Andre: b. Feb. 4, 1913, Salem, Mass.; ord. priest June 11, 1938; ord. titular bishop of Carre and auxiliary bishop of Mont-Laurier, Feb. 25, 1957; bishop of Mont-Laurier, Mar. 27, 1965; retired Feb. 15. 1978.

Pappin, Bernard F.: b. July 10, 1928, Westmeath, Ont.; ord. priest May 27, 1954; ord. titular bishop of Aradi and auxiliary bishop of Sault Ste. Marie, Apr. 11, 1975.

Pare, Marius: b. May 22, 1903, Montmagny, Que.; ord. priest July 3, 1927; ord. titular bishop of Aegae and auxiliary bishop of Chicoutimi, May 1, 1956; bishop of Chicoutimi, Feb. 18, 1961; retired Apr. 5, 1979.

Pedneault, Roch: b. Apr. 10, 1927, Saint Joseph d'Alma, Que.; ord. priest Feb. 8, 1953; ord. titular bishop of Aggersel and auxiliary of Chicoutimi, Que., June 29, 1974.

Penney, Alphonsus L.: b. Sept. 17, 1924, St. John's, Nfld.; ord. priest June 29, 1949; ord. bishop of Grand Falls, Jan. 18, 1973; archbishop of St. John's, Nfld., Apr. 5, 1979; retired 1991.

Piche, Paul, O.M.I.: b. Sept. 14, 1909, Gravelbourg, Sask.; ord. priest Dec. 23, 1934; ord. titular bishop of

Orcistus and vicar apostolic of Mackenzie, June 11, 1959; first bishop of Mackenzie-Fort Smith, July 13, 1967; retired Feb. 6, 1986.

Plouffe, Jean-Louis: b. Oct. 29, 1940, Ottawa, Ont.; ord. priest June 12, 1965; ord. titular bishop of Lamzella and auxiliary of Sault Ste. Marie, Feb. 24, 1987; bishop of Sault Ste. Marie, Dec. 9, 1989.

Plourde, Joseph-Aurele: b. Jan. 12, 1915, St. Francois de Madawaska, N.B.; ord. priest May 7, 1944; ord. titular bishop of Lapda and auxiliary bishop of Alexandria, Aug. 26, 1964; archbishop of Ottawa, Jan. 2, 1967; retired Sept. 27, 1989.

Power, William E.: b. Sept. 27, 1915; Montreal, Que.; ord. priest June 7, 1941; ord. bishop of Antigonish, July 20, 1960 (retired Dec. 12, 1986); president Canadian Conference of Catholic Bishops, 1971-73.

Richard, Andre, C.S.C.: b. June 30, 1937, St. Ignace, N.B.; ord. priest Feb. 17, 1963; ord. bishop of Bathurst, Aug. 9, 1989.

Rouleau, Reynald, O.M.I.: b. Nov. 30, 1935, Saint-Jean-de-Dieu, Que.; ord. priest Feb. 2, 1963; ord. bishop of Churchill-Hudson Bay, July 29, 1987.

Roy, Raymond: b. May 3, 1919, St. Boniface, Man.; ord. priest May 31, 1947; ord. bishop of St. Paul in Alberta, July 18, 1972.

Rusnak, Michael, C.Ss.R.: b. Aug. 21, 1921, Beaverdale, Pa.; ord. priest July 4, 1949; ord. titular bishop of Tzernicus and auxiliary eparch of Toronto of the Ukrainians and apostolic visitator to Slovak Catholics of Byzantine rite in Canada, Jan. 2, 1965; first eparch of Sts Cyril and Methodius Eparchy for Slovaks of Byzantine Rite, Feb. 28, 1981.

Sabatini, Lawrence, C.S.: b. May 15, 1930, Chicago, Ill.; ord. priest Mar. 19, 1957; ord. titular bishop of Nasai and auxiliary bishop of Vancouver, Sept. 21, 1978; bishop of Kamloops, Sept. 30, 1982.

Saint-Antoine, Jude: b. Oct. 29, 1930, Montreal, Que.; ord. priest May 31, 1956; ord. titular bishop of Scardona and auxiliary bishop of Montreal, May 22, 1981. Episcopal vicar of west central region.

Saint-Gelais, Raymond: b. Mar. 23, 1936, Baie St. Paul, Que.; ord. priest June 12, 1960; ord. titular bishop of Diana and auxiliary bishop of St. Jerome, July 31, 1980; coadjutor bishop of Nicolet, Feb. 19, 1988; bishop of Nicolet, Mar. 14, 1989.

Sanschagrin, Albert, O.M.I.: b. Aug. 5, 1911, Saint-Tite, Que.; ord. priest May 24, 1936; ord. titular bishop of Bagi and coadjutor bishop of Amos Sept. 14, 1957; bishop of Saint-Hyacinthe, June 13, 1967; retired July 18, 1979.

Setian, Nerses Mikaäl: Apostolic Exarch of Armenian Catholics in Canada and the U.S. (see Index).

Sherlock, John M.: b. Jan. 20, 1926, Regina, Sask.; ord. priest June 3, 1950; ord. titular bishop of Macriana and auxiliary of London, Ont., Aug. 28, 1974; bishop of London, July 7, 1978. President of the Canadian Conference of Catholic Bishops, 1983-85.

Spence, Francis J.: b. June 3, 1926, Perth, Ont.; ord. priest Apr. 16, 1950; ord. titular bishop of Nova and auxiliary bishop of the military vicariate, June 15, 1967; bishop of Charlottetown, Aug. 15, 1970; military vicar of Canada, 1982-87; archbishop of Kingston, Apr. 24, 1982.

Sutton, Peter Alfred, O.M.I.: b. Oct. 18, 1934, Chandler, Que.; ord. priest Oct. 22, 1960; ord. bishop of Labrador-Schefferville, July 18, 1974; coadjutor archbishop of Keewatin-Le Pas, Jan. 24, 1986; archbishop of Keewatin-LePas, Nov. 7, 1986.

Tonnos, Anthony: b. Aug. 1, 1935, Port Colborne, Ont.; ord. priest May 27, 1961; ord. titular bishop of Naziona and auxiliary bishop of Hamilton, July 12, 1983; bishop of Hamilton, May 2, 1984.

Tremblay, Gerard, P.S.S.: b. Oct. 27, 1918, Montreal, Que.; ord. priest June 16, 1946; ord. titular bishop of Trisipa and auxiliary bishop of Montreal, May 22, 1981; retired 1991.

Troy, J. Edward: b. Sept. 3, 1931, Chatham, N.B.; ord. priest May 28, 1959; ord. coadjutor bishop of St. John, N.B., May 22, 1984; bishop of St. John, N.B., Apr. 2, 1986.

Turcotte, Jean-Claude: b. June 26, 1936, Montreal, Que.; ord. priest May 24, 1959; ord. titular bishop of Suas and auxiliary bishop of Montreal, June 29, 1982; archbishop of Montreal, Mar. 17, 1990.

Ustrzycki, Matthew: b. Mar. 25, 1932, Saint Catharines, Ont.; ord. priest May 30, 1959; ord. titular bishop of Nationa and auxiliary of Hamilton, July 3, 1985.

Vachon, Louis-Albert: (See Cardinals, Biographies.)

Vallée, Andre, P.M.E.: b. July 31, 1930, Sainte-Anne-de-Perade, Que.; ord. priest June 24, 1956; ord. titular bishop of Sufasar and bishop of the Military Ordinariate of Canada, Jan. 28, 1988.

Valois, Charles: b. Apr. 24, 1924, Montreal, Que.; ord. priest June 3, 1950; ord. bishop of St. Jerome, June 29, 1977.

Veillette, Martin: b. Nov. 16, 1936, Saint-Zephirin de Courval, Que., ord. priest June 12, 1960; ord. titular bishop of Valabria and auxiliary of Trois-Rivieres, Dec. 13, 1986.

Wall, Leonard J.: b. Sept. 27, 1924, Windsor, Ont.; ord. priest June 11, 1949; ord. titular bishop of Leptiminus and auxiliary bishop of Toronto, June 21, 1979; archbishop of Winnipeg, Feb. 25, 1992.

Weber, Jerome, O.S.B.: b. Sept. 14, 1915, Muenster, Sask., Canada; ord. priest June 8, 1941; app. abbot-ordinary of St. Peter Muenster, Apr. 6, 1960; abbatial blessing, Aug. 24, 1960; retired June, 1990.

Wiesner, Gerald, O.M.I.: b. June 25, 1937, Danzil, Sask.; ord. priest Feb. 23, 1963; ord. bishop of Prince George, B.C., Feb. 22, 1993.

Wilhelm, Joseph L.: b. Nov. 16, 1909, Walkerton, Ont.; ord. priest June 9, 1934; ord. titular bishop of Saccaea and auxiliary bishop of Calgary, Aug. 22, 1963; archbishop of Kingston, Dec. 14, 1966; retired Mar. 12, 1982.

Windle, Joseph R.: b. Aug. 28, 1917, Ashdad, Ont.; ord. priest May 16, 1943; ord. titular bishop of Uzita and auxiliary bishop of Ottawa, Jan. 18, 1961; coadjutor bishop of Pembroke, 1969; bishop of Pembroke, Feb. 15, 1971; retired Apr. 5, 1993.

Wingle, James Matthew: b. 1947; ord. priest 1977 (Pembroke diocese); app. bishop of Yarmouth, May 31, 1993.

CANADIAN SHRINES

Our Lady of the Cape (Cap de la Madeleine), Queen of the Most Holy Rosary: The Three Rivers, Quebec, parish church, built of fieldstone in 1714 and considered the oldest stone church on the North American continent preserved in its original state, was rededicated June 22, 1888, as a shrine of the Queen of the Most Holy Rosary. Thereafter, the site increased in importance as a pilgrimage and devotional center, and in 1904 St. Pius X decreed the crowning of a statue of the Blessed Virgin which had been donated 50 years earlier to commemorate the dogma of the Immaculate Conception. In 1909, the First Plenary Council of Quebec declared the church a shrine of national pilgrimage. In 1964, the church at the shrine was given the status and title of minor basilica.

St. Anne de Beaupre: The devotional history of this shrine in Quebec, began with the reported cure of a cripple, Louis Guimont, on Mar. 16, 1658, the starting date of construction work on a small chapel of St. Anne. The original building was successively enlarged and replaced by a stone church which was given the rank of minor basilica in 1888. The present structure, a Romanesque-Gothic basilica, houses the shrine proper in its north transept. The centers of attraction are an eight-foot-high oaken statue and the great relic of St. Anne, a portion of her forearm.

St. Joseph's Oratory: The massive oratory basilica standing on the western side of Mount Royal and overlooking the city of Montreal had its origin in a primitive chapel erected there by Blessed Andre Bessette, C.S.C., in 1904. Eleven years later, a large crypt was built to accommodate an increasing number of pilgrims, and in 1924 construction work was begun on the large church. A belfry, housing a 60-bell carillon and standing on the site of the original chapel, was dedicated May 15, 1955, as the first major event of the jubilee year observed after the oratory was given the rank of minor basilica.

Martyrs' Shrine: A shrine commemorating several of the Jesuit Martyrs of North America who were killed between 1642 and 1649 in the Ontario and northern New York area is located on the former site of old Fort Sainte Marie. Before its location was fixed near Midland, Ont., in 1925, a small chapel had been erected in 1907 at old Mission St. Ignace to mark the martyrdom of Fathers Jean de Brebeuf and Gabriel Lalemant. This sanctuary has a U.S. counterpart in the Shrine of the North American Martyrs near Auriesville, N.Y., under the care of the Jesuits.

Others

Other shrines and historic churches in Canada include the following.

In Quebec City: the Basilica of Notre Dame, dating from 1650, once the cathedral of a diocese stretching from Canada to Mexico; Notre Dame des Victoires, on the waterfront, dedicated in 1690; the Ursuline Convent, built in 1720, on du Parloir St.

In Montreal: Notre Dame Basilica, patterned after the famous basilica of the same name in Paris, constructed in 1829; the Shrine of Mary, Queen of All Hearts.

Near Montreal: the Chapel of St. Marie Marguerite d'Youville, foundress of the Grey Nuns; Notre Dame de Lourdes, at Rigaud.

CANADIAN CATHOLIC PUBLICATIONS

(Principal source: 1993 *Catholic Press Directory.*)

Newspapers

B. C. Catholic, The, w; 150 Robson St., Vancouver, B.C. V6B 2A7.

Catholic New Times (national), biweekly; 80 Sackville St., Toronto, Ont. M5A 3E5.

Catholic Register, The (national), w; 67 Bond St., Toronto, Ont. M5B 1X6. Lay edited.

Catholic Times, The, 10 times a year; 2005 St. Marc St., Montreal, Que. H3H 2G8.

Diocesan Review, The, m; 16 Hammond Dr., Corner Brook, Nfld. A2H 2W2.

L'Informateur Catholique, semimonthly; C.P. 330, Chertsey, Que. J0K 3K0.

Monitor, The, m; P.O. Box 986, St. John's, Nfld. A1C 5M3.

New Freeman, The, w; 1 Bayard Dr., St. John, N.B. E2L 3L5.

Our Diocese, bm; 8A Church Rd., Grand Falls-Windsor, Nfld. A2A 2J8.

Pastoral Reporter, The, 4 times a year; 1916 Second St. S.W., Calgary. Alta. T2S 1S3.

Prairie Messenger, w; Box 190, Muenster, Sask. S0K 2Y0.

Teviskes, Ziburiai (The Lights of the Homeland) (Lithuanian), w; 2185 Stavebank Rd., Mississauga, Ont. L5C 1T3.

Magazines, Other Periodicals

Annals of St. Anne de Beaupre, m; Box 1000, Ste. Anne de Beaupre, Que. G0A 3C0; Basilica of St. Anne.

Apostolat, bm; 460 Primiere Rue, Richelieu, Que. J3L 4B5. Oblates of Mary Immaculate.

Bread of Life, The, 6 times a year; 370 Main St., Suite B1, Hamilton, Ont. L8N 1J6.

Bulletin (French-English), q; 324 E. Laurier St., Ottawa, Ont. K1N 6P6 Canadian Religious Conference.

Canadian Catholic Review, 11 times a year; 1437 College Dr., Saskatoon, Saskatchewan S7N 0W6.

Canadian League, The, 4 times a year; 1-660 Murray Park Rd., Winnipeg, Man. R3J 3X5. Catholic Women's League of Canada.

Caravan, 4 times a year; 90 Parent Ave., Ottawa, Ont. K1N 7B1. Canadian Conference of Catholic Bishops.

Casket, The, w; 88 College St., Antigonish, N.S. B2G 2L7.

Catholic Communicator, m; 222 Albert St. East, Sault Ste. Marie, Ont. P6A 2J4

Catholic International, 22 times a year; 6255 Hutchinson St., Suite 103, Montreal, Que. H2V 4C7.

Chesterton Review, q; 1437 College Dr., Saskatoon, Sask. S7N 0W6.

Companion of St. Francis and St. Anthony, m; P. O. Box 535, Sta. F., Toronto, Ont. M4Y 2L8; Conventual Franciscan Fathers.

Compass — A Jesuit Journal, bm (Jan.-Nov.); 10 St. Mary St., Toronto, Ont. M4Y 1P9.

Fatima Crusader, 4 times a year; P.O. Box 602, Fort Erie, Ont. L2A 5X3.

Global Village Voice, 4 times a year; 3028 Danforth Ave., Toronto, Ont. M4C 1N2. Canadian Organization for Development and Peace.

Grail: An Ecumenical Journal, q; Univ. of St. Jerome's College, Waterloo, Ont. N2L 3G3.

Home Missions, q; 67 Bond St., Suite 101, Toronto, Ont. M5B 1X5.

Insight, a; 90 Parent Ave., Ottawa, Ont. K1N 7B1.

Kateri (English-French), q; P.O. Box 70, Kahnawake, Que. JOL 1BO.

L'Almanach Populaire Catholique (French), a; P.O. Box 1000, St. Anne de Beaupre, Que. GOA 3CO.

La Revue d'Sainte Anne de Beaupre (French), m; P.O. Box 1000, Ste. Anne de Beaupre, Quebec GOA 3CO.

La Voix de l'Archdiocese de Grouard-McLennan (French-English), m; 210 First St. W., Box 388, McLennan, Alberta T0H 2L0.

L'Eglise Canadienne (French), 15 times a year; 1073 Boulevard Saint Cyrille Ouest, 1073 Que. G1S 4R5.

Martyrs' Shrine Message, 2 times a year; Midland, Ont. L4R 4K5. Newsletter.

Messager de Saint Antoine, Le, 10 times a year; Lac-Bouchette, Que. GOW 1VO.

Messenger of the Sacred Heart, m; 661 Greenwood Ave., Toronto, Ont. M4J 4B3. Apostleship of Prayer.

Missions Etrangeres, 6 times a year; 180 Place Juge-Desnoyers, Laval, Que. H7G 1A4.

Oratory, 6 times a year; 3800 Ch. Reine-Marie, Montreal, Que. H3V 1H6.

Our Family, m; P.O. Box 249, Battleford, Sask.; S0M 0E0; Oblates of Mary Immaculate.

Prete et Pasteur, m; 4450 St. Hubert St., Montreal, Que. H2J 2W9.

Relations (French), 10 times a year; 25 Rue Jarry Ouest, Montreal, Que. H2P 1S6.

Restoration, 10 times a year; Madonna House, Combemere, Ont. KOJ 1LO.

Scarboro Missions, m; 2685 Kingston Rd., Scarboro, Ont. M1M 1M4.

Spiritan Missionary News, 4 times a year; 14420 McQueen Rd., Edmonton, Alta. T5N 3L2.

Unity, bm; 308 Young St., Montreal, Que. H3C 2G2.

Vox Benedictina, 4 times a year; 180 Sherwood Ave., Toronto, Ont. M4P 2A8.

MISSIONARIES TO THE AMERICAS

An asterisk with a feast date indicates that the saint or blessed is listed in the General Roman Calendar or the proper calendar for U.S. dioceses.

Allouez, Claude Jean (1622-1689): French Jesuit; missionary in Canada and midwestern U.S.; preached to 20 different tribes of Indians and baptized over 10,000; vicar general of Northwest.

Altham, John (1589-1640): English Jesuit; missionary among Indians in Maryland.

Anchieta, Jose de, Bl. (1534-1597): Portuguese Jesuit, b. Canary Islands; missionary in Brazil; writer; beatified 1980; feast, June 9.

Andreis, Felix de (1778-1820): Italian Vincentian; missionary and educator in western U.S.

Aparicio, Sebastian, Bl. (1502-1600): Franciscan brother, born Spain; settled in Mexico, c. 1533; worked as road builder and farmer before becoming Franciscan at about the age of 70; beatified, 1787; feast, Feb. 25.

Badin, Stephen T. (1768-1853): French missioner; came to U.S., 1792, when Sulpician seminary in Paris was closed; ordained, 1793, Baltimore, the first priest ordained in U.S.; missionary in Kentucky, Ohio and Michigan; bought land on which Notre Dame University now stands; buried on its campus.

Baraga, Frederic (1797-1868): Slovenian missionary bishop in U.S.; studied at Ljubljana and Vienna, ordained, 1823; came to U.S., 1830; missionary to Indians of Upper Michigan; first bishop of Marquette, 1857-1868; wrote Chippewa grammar, dictionary, prayer book and other works.

Bertran, Louis, St. (1526-1581): Spanish Dominican; missionary in Colombia and Caribbean, 1562-69; canonized, 1671; feast, Oct. 9.

Betancur, Pedro de San Jose, Bl. (1626-1667): Secular Franciscan, b. Canary Islands; arrived in Guatemala, 1651; established hospital, school and homes for poor; beatified 1980; feast, Apr. 25.

Bourgeoys, Marguerite, St. (1620-1700): French foundress, missionary; settled in Canada, 1653; founded Congregation of Notre Dame, 1658; beatified, 1950; canonized 1982; feast, Jan. 12.

Brebeuf, John de, St. (1593-1649): French Jesuit; missionary among Huron Indians in Canada; martyred by Iroquois, Mar. 16, 1649; canonized, 1930; one of Jesuit North American martyrs; feast, Oct. 19* (U.S.).

Cancer de Barbastro, Louis (1500-1549): Spanish Dominican; began missionary work in Middle America, 1533; killed at Tampa Bay, Fla.

Castillo, John de, St. (1596-1628): Spanish Jesuit; worked in Paraguay Indian mission settlements (reductions); martyred; beatified, 1934; canonized, 1988; feast, Nov. 16.

Catala, Magin (1761-1830): Spanish Franciscan; worked in California mission of Santa Clara for 36 years.

Chabanel, Noel, St. (1613-1649): French Jesuit; missionary among Huron Indians in Canada; murdered by renegade Huron, Dec. 8, 1649; canonized, 1930; one of Jesuit North American martyrs; feast, Oct. 19* (U.S.).

Chaumonot, Pierre Joseph (1611-1693): French Jesuit; missionary among Indians in Canada.

Claver, Peter, St. (1581-1654): Spanish Jesuit; missionary among Negroes of South America and West Indies; canonized, 1888; patron of Catholic missions among black people; feast, Sept. 9* (U.S.).

Daniel, Anthony, St. (1601-1648): French Jesuit; missionary among Huron Indians in Canada; martyred by Iroquois, July 4, 1648; canonized, 1930; one of Jesuit North American martyrs; feast, Oct. 19* (U.S.).

De Smet, Pierre Jean (1801-1873): Belgian-born Jesuit; missionary among Indians of northwestern U.S.; served as intermediary between Indians and U.S. government; wrote on Indian culture.

Duchesne, Rose Philippine, St. (1769-1852): French nun; educator and missionary in the U.S.; established first convent of the Society of the Sacred Heart in the U.S., at St. Charles, Mo.; founded schools for girls; did missionary work among Indians; beatified, 1940; canonized, 1988; feast, Nov. 18* (U.S.).

Farmer, Ferdinand (family name, Steinmeyer) (1720-1786): German Jesuit; missionary in Philadelphia, where he died; one of the first missionaries in New Jersey.

Flaget, Benedict J. (1763-1850): French Sulpician bishop; came to U.S., 1792; missionary and educator in U.S.; first bishop of Bardstown, Ky. (now Louisville), 1810-32; 1833-50.

Gallitzin, Demetrius (1770-1840): Russian prince, born The Hague; convert, 1787; ordained priest at Baltimore, 1795; frontier missionary, known as Father Smith; Gallitzin, Pa., named for him.

Garnier, Charles, St. (c. 1606-1649): French Jesuit; missionary among Hurons in Canada; martyred by Iroquois, Dec. 7, 1649; canonized, 1930; one of Jesuit North American martyrs; feast, Oct. 19* (U.S.).

Gibault, Pierre (1737-1804): Canadian missionary in Illinois and Indiana; aided in securing states of Ohio, Indiana, Illinois, Michigan and Wisconsin for the Americans during Revolution.

Gonzalez, Roch, St. (1576-1628): Paraguayan Jesuit; worked in Paraguay Indian mission settlements (reductions); martyred; beatified, 1934; canonized, 1988; feast, Nov. 16.

Goupil, Rene, St. (1607-1642): French lay missionary; had studied surgery at Orleans, France; missionary companion of St. Isaac Jogues among the Hurons; martyred, Sept. 29, 1642; canonized, 1930; one of Jesuit North American martyrs; feast, Oct. 19* (U.S.).

Gravier, Jacques (1651-1708): French Jesuit; missionary among Indians of Canada and midwestern U.S.

Hennepin, Louis (d. c. 1701): Belgian-born Franciscan missionary and explorer of Great Lakes region and Upper Mississippi, 1675-81, when he returned to Europe; first European to see and describe Niagara Falls.

Jesuit North American Martyrs: Isaac Jogues, Anthony Daniel, John de Brebeuf, Gabriel Lalemant, Charles Garnier, Noel Chabanel (Jesuit priests), and Rene Goupil and John Lalande (lay missionaries) who were martyred between Sept. 29, 1642, and Dec. 9, 1649, in the missions of New France; canonized June 29, 1930; feast, Oct. 19* (U.S.). See separate entries.

Jogues, Isaac, St. (1607-1646): French Jesuit; missionary among Indians in Canada; martyred near present site of Auriesville, N.Y., by Mohawks, Oct. 18, 1646; canonized, 1930; one of Jesuit North American martyrs; feast, Oct. 19* (U.S.).

Kino, Eusebio (1645-1711): Italian Jesuit; missionary and explorer in U.S.; arrived Southwest, 1681; established 25 Indian missions, took part in 14 exploring expeditions in northern Mexico, Arizona and southern California; helped develop livestock raising and farming in the area. He was selected in 1965 to represent Arizona in Statuary Hall.

Lalande, John, St. (d. 1646): French lay missionary, companion of Isaac Jogues; martyred by Mohawks at Auriesville, N.Y., Oct. 19, 1646; canonized, 1930; one of Jesuit North American martyrs; feast, Oct. 19* (U.S.).

Lalemant, Gabriel, St. (1610-1649): French Jesuit; missionary among the Hurons in Canada; martyred by the Iroquois, Mar. 17, 1649; canonized, 1930; one of Jesuit North American martyrs; feast, Oct. 19* (U.S.).

Lamy, Jean Baptiste (1814-1888): French prelate; came to U.S., 1839; missionary in Ohio and Kentucky; bishop in Southwest from 1850; first bishop (later archbishop) of Santa Fe, 1850-1885. He was nominated in 1951 to represent New Mexico in Statuary Hall.

Las Casas, Bartolome (1474-1566): Spanish Dominican; missionary in Haiti, Jamaica and Venezuela; reformer of abuses against Indians and black people; bishop of Chalapas, Mexico, 1544-47; historian.

Laval, Francoise de Montmorency, Bl. (1623-1708): French-born missionary bishop in Canada; named vicar apostolic of Canada, 1658; first bishop of Quebec, 1674; jurisdiction extended over all French-claimed territory in New World; beatified 1980; feast, May 6.

Manogue, Patrick (1831-1895): Missionary bishop in U.S., b. Ireland; migrated to U.S.; miner in California; studied for priesthood at St. Mary's of the Lake, Chicago, and St. Sulpice, Paris; ordained, 1861; missionary among Indians of California and Nevada; coadjutor bishop, 1881-84, and bishop, 1884-86, of Grass Valley; first bishop of Sacramento, 1886-1895, when see was transferred there.

Margil, Antonio (1657-1726): Spanish Franciscan; missionary in Middle America; apostle of Guatemala; established missions in Texas.

Marie of the Incarnation, Bl. (Marie Guyard Martin) (1599-1672): French widow; joined Ursuline Nuns; arrived in Canada, 1639; first superior of Ursulines in Quebec; missionary to Indians; writer; beatified 1980; feast, Apr. 30.

Marquette, Jacques (1637-1675): French Jesuit; missionary and explorer in America; sent to New France, 1666; began missionary work among Ottawa Indians on Lake Superior, 1668; accompanied Joliet down the Mississippi to mouth of the Arkansas, 1673, and returned to Lake Michigan by way of Illinois River; made a second trip over the same route; his diary and map are of historical significance. He was selected in 1895 to represent Wisconsin in Statuary Hall.

Massias (Macias), John de, St. (1585-1645); Dominican brother, a native of Spain; entered Dominican Friary at Lima, Peru, 1622; served as doorkeeper until his death; beatified, 1837; canonized 1975; feast, Sept. 16.

Mazzuchelli, Samuel C. (1806-1864): Italian Dominican; missionary in midwestern U.S.; called builder of the West; writer. A decree advancing his beatification cause was promulgated July 6, 1993.

Membre, Zenobius (1645-1687): French Franciscan; missionary among Indians of Illinois; accompanied LaSalle expedition down the Mississippi (1681-1682) and Louisiana colonizing expedition (1684) which landed in Texas; murdered by Indians.

Nerinckx, Charles (1761-1824): Belgian priest; missionary in Kentucky; founded Sisters of Loretto at the Foot of the Cross.

Nobrega, Manoel (1517-1570): Portuguese Jesuit; leader of first Jesuit missionaries to Brazil, 1549.

Padilla, Juan de (d. 1542): Spanish Franciscan; missionary among Indians of Mexico and southwestern U.S.; killed by Indians in Kansas; protomartyr of the U.S.

Palou, Francisco (c. 1722-1789): Spanish Franciscan; accompanied Junipero Serra to Mexico, 1749; founded Mission Dolores in San Francisco; wrote history of the Franciscans in California.

Pariseau, Mother Mary Joseph (1833-1902): Canadian Sister of Charity of Providence; missionary in state of Washington from 1856; founded first hospitals in northwest territory; artisan and architect. Represents Washington in National Statuary Hall.

Peter of Ghent (d. 1572): Belgian Franciscan brother; missionary in Mexico for 49 years.

Porres, Martin de, St. (1579-1639): Peruvian Dominican oblate; his father was a Spanish soldier and his mother a black freedwoman from Panama; called wonder worker of Peru; beatified, 1837; canonized, 1962; feast, Nov. 3*.

Quiroga, Vasco de (1470-1565): Spanish missionary in Mexico; founded hospitals; bishop of Michoacan, 1537.

Ravalli, Antonio (1811-1884): Italian Jesuit; missionary in far-western United States, mostly Montana, for 40 years.

Raymbaut, Charles (1602-1643): French Jesuit; missionary among Indians of Canada and northern U.S.

Richard, Gabriel (1767-1832): French Sulpician; missionary in Illinois and Michigan; a founder of University of Michigan; elected delegate to Congress from Michigan, 1823; first priest to hold seat in the House of Representatives.

Rodriguez, Alfonso, St. (1598-1628): Spanish Jesuit; missionary in Paraguay; martyred; beatified, 1934; canonized, 1988; feast, Nov. 16.

Rosati, Joseph (1789-1843): Italian Vincentian; missionary bishop in U.S. (vicar apostolic of Mississippi and Alabama, 1822; coadjutor of

Louisiana and the Two Floridas, 1823-26; administrator of New Orleans, 1826-29; first bishop of St. Louis, 1826-1843).

Sahagun, Bernardino de (c. 1500-1590): Spanish Franciscan; missionary in Mexico for over 60 years; expert on Aztec archaeology.

Seelos, Francis X. (1819-1867): Redemptorist missionary, born Bavaria; ordained, 1844, at Baltimore; missionary in Pittsburgh and New Orleans.

Serra, Junipero, Bl. (1713-1784): Spanish Franciscan, b. Majorca; missionary in America; arrived Mexico, 1749, where he did missionary work for 20 years; began work in Upper California in 1769 and established nine of the 21 Franciscan missions along the Pacific coast; baptized some 6,000 Indians and confirmed almost 5,000; a cultural pioneer of California. Represents California in Statuary Hall. He was declared venerable May 9, 1985, and was beatified Sept. 25, 1988; feast, July 1* (U.S.).

Seghers, Charles J. (1839-1886): Belgian missionary bishop in North America; Apostle of Alaska; archbishop of Oregon City (now Portland), 1880-1884; murdered by berserk companion while on missionary journey.

Solanus, Francis, St. (1549-1610): Spanish Franciscan; missionary in Paraguay, Argentina and Peru; wonder worker of the New World; canonized, 1726; feast, July 14.

Sorin, Edward F. (1814-1893): French priest; member of Congregation of Holy Cross; sent to U.S. in 1841; founder and first president of the University of Notre Dame; missionary in Indiana and Michigan.

Todadilla, Anthony de (1704-1746): Spanish Capuchin; missionary to Indians of Venezuela; killed by Motilones.

Turibius de Mogrovejo, St. (1538-1606): Spanish archbishop of Lima, Peru, c. 1580-1606; canonized 1726; feast, Mar. 23*.

Twelve Apostles of Mexico (early 16th century): Franciscan priests; arrived in Mexico, 1524: Fathers Martin de Valencia (leader), Francisco de Soto, Martin de la Coruna, Juan Suares, Antonio de Ciudad Rodrigo, Toribio de Benevente, Garcia de Cisneros, Luis de Fuensalida, Juan de Ribas, Francisco Ximenes; Brothers Andres de Coroboda, Juan de Palos.

Valdivia, Luis de (1561-1641): Spanish Jesuit; defender of Indians in Peru and Chile.

Vasques de Espinosa, Antonio (early 17th century): Spanish Carmelite; missionary and explorer in Mexico, Panama and western coast of South America.

Vieira, Antonio (1608-1687): Portuguese Jesuit; preacher; missionary in Peru and Chile; protector of Indians against exploitation by slave owners and traders; considered foremost prose writer of 17th-century Portugal.

White, Andrew (1579-1656): English Jesuit; missionary among Indians in Maryland.

Wimmer, Boniface (1809-1887): German Benedictine; missionary among German immigrants in the U.S..

Youville, Marie Marguerite d', St. (1701-1771):

Canadian widow; foundress of Sisters of Charity (Grey Nuns), 1737, at Montreal: beatified, 1959; canonized 1990, first native Canadian saint; feast, Dec. 23.

Zumarraga, Juan de (1468-1548): Spanish Franciscan; missionary; first bishop of Mexico; introduced first printing press in New World, published first book in America, a catechism for Aztec Indians; extended missions in Mexico and Central America; vigorous opponent of exploitation of Indians; approved of devotions at Guadalupe; leading figure in early church history in Mexico.

FRANCISCAN MISSIONS

The 21 Franciscan missions of Upper California were established during the 54-year period from 1769 to 1822. Located along the old El Camino Real, or King's Highway, they extended from San Diego to San Francisco and were the centers of Indian civilization, Christianity and industry in the early history of the state.

Junipero Serra (beatified 1988) was the great pioneer of the missions of Upper California. He and his successor as superior of the work, Fermin Lasuen, each directed the establishment of nine missions. One hundred and 46 priests of the Order of Friars Minor, most of them Spaniards, labored in the region from 1769 to 1845; 67 of them died at their posts, two as martyrs. The regular time of mission service was 10 years.

The missions were secularized by the Mexican government in the 1830s but were subsequently restored to the Church by the U.S. government. They are now variously used as the sites of parish churches, a university, houses of study and museums.

The names of the missions and the order of their establishment were as follows:

San Diego de Alcala, San Carlos Borromeo (El Carmelo), San Antonio de Padua, San Gabriel Arcangel, San Luis Obispo de Tolosa, San Francisco de Asis (Dolores), San Juan Capistrano;

Santa Clara de Asis, San Buenaventura, Santa Barbara, La Purisima Concepcion de Maria Santisima, Santa Cruz, Nuestra Senora de la Soledad, San Jose de Guadalupe;

San Juan Bautista, San Miguel Arcangel, San Fernando Rey de Espana, San Luis Rey de Francia, Santa Ines, San Rafael Arcangel, San Francisco Solano de Sonoma (Sonoma).

SHRINES AND PLACES OF HISTORIC INTEREST IN THE UNITED STATES

(Principal source: *Catholic Almanac* survey.)

Listed below, according to state, are shrines, other centers of devotion and some places of historic interest with special significance for Catholics. The list is necessarily incomplete because of space limitations.

Information includes: name and location of shrine or place of interest, date of foundation, sponsoring agency or group, and address for more informa- tion.

Alabama: St. Jude Church of the City of St. Jude, Montgomery (1934; dedicated, 1938); Mobile Archdiocese. Address: 2048 W. Fairview Ave., Montgomery 36108.

• Shrine of the Most Blessed Trinity, Holy Trinity (1924); Missionary Servants of the Most Blessed Trinity. Address: Holy Trinity 36875.

Arizona: Chapel of the Holy Cross, Hwy 179 and Chapel Rd., Sedona (1956); Phoenix Diocese: P.O. Box 1043, Sedona 86339.

• Mission San Francis Xavier del Bac, near Tucson (1700); National Historic Landmark; Franciscan Friars and Tucson Diocese; Address: 1950 W. San Xavier Rd., Tucson 85746.

• Shrine of St. Joseph of the Mountains, Yarnell (1939); erected by Catholic Action League; currently maintained by Board of Directors. Address: P.O. Box 267, Yarnell 85362.

California: Mission San Diego de Alcala (July 16, 1769); first of the 21 Franciscan missions of Upper California; Minor Basilica; National Historic Landmark; San Diego Diocese. Address: 10818 San Diego Mission Rd., San Diego 92108.

• Carmel Mission (Mission San Carlos Borromeo del Rio Carmelo), Carmel by the Sea (June 3, 1770); Monterey Diocese. Address: 3080 Rio Rd., Carmel 93923.

• Old Mission San Luis Obispo de Tolosa, San Luis Obispo (Sept. 1, 1772); Monterey Diocese (Parish Church). Address: P.O. Box 1483, San Luis Obispo 93406.

• San Gabriel Mission, San Gabriel (Sept. 8, 1771); Los Angeles Archdiocese (Parish Church, staffed by Claretians). Address: 537 W. Mission, San Gabriel 91776.

• Mission San Francisco de Asis (Oct. 9, 1776) and Mission Dolores Basilica (1860s); San Francisco Archdiocese. Address: 3321 Sixteenth St., San Francisco 94114.

• Mission San Juan Capistrano, San Juan Capistrano (Nov. 1, 1776); Orange Diocese. Address: 31882 Camino Capistrano, No. 107, San Juan Capistrano 92675.

• Old Mission Santa Barbara, Santa Barbara (Dec. 4, 1786); National Historic Landmark; Parish Church, staffed by Franciscan Friars. Address: 2201 Laguna St., Santa Barbara 93105.

• Old Mission San Juan Bautista, San Juan Bautista (June 24, 1797); Monterey Diocese (Parish Church). Address: P.O. Box 410, San Juan Bautista 95045.

• Mission San Miguel, San Miguel (July 25, 1797); Franciscan Friars. Address: P.O. Box 69, San Miguel 93451.

• Old Mission Santa Ines, Solvang (1804); Los Angeles Archdiocese (Parish Church, staffed by Capuchin Franciscan Friars). Address: P.O. Box 408, Solvang 93463.

Franciscan Friars founded 21 missions in California. (See Index: Franciscan Missions.)

• Shrine of Our Lady of Sorrows, Colusa (1883): Sacramento Diocese. Address: c/o Our Lady of Lourdes Church, 745 Ware Ave., Colusa 95932.

Connecticut: Lourdes in Litchfield (Shrine of Our Lady of Lourdes), Litchfield (1958); Montfort Missionaries. Address: P.O. Box 667, Litchfield 06759.

• Shrine of the Infant of Prague, New Haven (1945); Dominican Friars. Address: P.O. Box 1202, 5 Hillhouse Ave., New Haven 06505.

District of Columbia: Mount St. Sepulchre, Franciscan Monastery of the Holy Land (1897; church dedicated, 1899); Order of Friars Minor. Address: 1400 Quincy St. N.E., Washington, D.C. 20017.

• Basilica of the National Shrine of the Immaculate Conception. See Index for separate entry.

Florida: Our Lady of La Leche Shrine (Patroness of Mothers and Mothers-to-be) and Mission of Nombre de Dios, Saint Augustine (1565); Angelus Crusade Headquarters. St. Augustine Diocese. Address: 30 Ocean Ave., St. Augustine 32084.

• Our Lady of Guadalupe, Patroness of Unborn, Miami (1981; dedicated, 1984); Respect Life Apostolate, Miami Archdiocese. Address: 18340 N. W. 12th Ave., Miami 33169.

Illinois: Holy Family Log Church, Cahokia (1799; original log church erected 1699); Belleville Diocese (Parish Church). Address: 116 Church St., Cahokia 62206.

• National Shrine of Our Lady of the Snows, Belleville (1958); Missionary Oblates of Mary Immaculate. Address: 9500 W. Illinois, Hwy. 15, Belleville 62223.

• National Shrine of St. Jude, Chicago (1929); located in Our Lady of Guadalupe Church, founded and staffed by Claretians. Address: 3200 E. 91st St., Chicago 60617.

• National Shrine of St. Therese, Darien (1930, at St. Clara's Church, Chicago; new shrine, 1987, after original destroyed by fire); Carmelites of Most Pure Heart of Mary Province. Address: 8501 Bailey Rd., Darien 60561.

• Shrine of St. Jude Thaddeus, Chicago (1929) located in St. Pius V Church, staffed by Dominicans, Central Province. Address: 1909 S. Ashland Ave., Chicago 60608.

Indiana: Our Lady of Monte Cassino Shrine, St. Meinrad (1870); Benedictines. Address: St. Meinrad Archabbey, 401 Hill Dr., St. Meinrad 47577.

• Old Cathedral (Basilica of St. Francis Xavier), Vincennes (1826, parish records go back to 1749); Evansville Diocese. Minor Basilica, 1970. Address: 205 Church St., Vincennes 47591.

Iowa: Grotto of the Redemption, West Bend (1912); Sioux City Diocese. Life of Christ in stone. Mailing address: P.O. Box 376, West Bend 50597.

Louisiana: National Votive Shrine of Our Lady of Prompt Succor, New Orleans (1810); located in the Chapel of the Ursuline Convent (a National Historic Landmark). Address: 2635 State St., New Orleans 70118.

• Shrine of St. Roch, New Orleans (1876); located in St. Roch's *Campo Santo* (Cemetery); New Orleans Archdiocese. Address: 1725 St. Roch Ave., New Orleans 70117.

Maryland: National Shrine Grotto of Our Lady of Lourdes, Emmitsburg (1809, Grotto of Our Lady; 1875, National Shrine Grotto of Lourdes); Public oratory, Archdiocese of Baltimore. Address: Mount St. Mary's College and Seminary, Emmitsburg 21727.

• National Shrine of St. Elizabeth Ann Seton, Emmitsburg (1975); Minor Basilica; Daughters of Charity of St. Vincent de Paul. Address: 333 South Seton Ave., Emmitsburg 21727.

• St. Francis Xavier Shrine, "Old Bohemia", near Warwick (1704), located in Wilmington, Del.,

Diocese; restoration under aupices of Old Bohemia Historical Society, Inc. Address: P.O. Box 61, Warwick 21912.

• St. Anthony Shrine, Emmitsburg (1893); attached to St. Anthony Parish, Baltimore Archdiocese. Address: 16150 St. Anthony Rd., Emmitsburg 21727.

Massachusetts: National Shrine of Our Lady of La Salette, Ipswich (1945); Missionaries of Our Lady of La Salette. Address: 315 Topsfield Rd., Ipswich 01938.

• Our Lady of Fatima Shrine, Holliston (1950); Xaverian Missionaries. Address: 101 Summer St., Holliston 01746.

• St. Anthony Shrine, Boston (1947); downtown Service Church with shrine; Boston Archdiocese and Franciscans of Holy Name Province. Address: 100 Arch St., Boston 02107.

• Saint Clement's Eucharistic Shrine, Boston (1945); Boston Archdiocese, staffed by Oblates of the Virgin Mary. Address: 1105 Boylston St., Boston 02215.

• National Shrine of The Divine Mercy, Stockbridge (1960); Congregaton of Marians. Address: Eden Hill, Stockbridge 01262.

Michigan: Cross in the Woods, Indian River (1947); Gaylord diocese; staffed by Franciscan Friars of Sacred Heart Province, St. Louis. Address: 7078 M-68, Indian River 49749.

• Shrine of the Little Flower, Royal Oak (c. 1929, by Father Coughlin); Detroit archdiocese. Address: 2123 Roseland, Royal Oak 48073.

Missouri: Memorial Shrine of St. Rose Philippine Duchesne, St. Charles (1940); Religious of the Sacred Heart of Jesus. Address: 619 N. Second St., St. Charles 63301.

• National Shrine of Our Lady of the Miraculous Medal, Perryville; located in St. Mary of the Barrens Church (1837); Vincentians. Address: 1811 W. St. Joseph St., Perryville 63775.

• Old St. Ferdinand's Shrine, Florissant (1819, Sacred Heart Convent; 1821, St. Ferdinand's Church); Friends of Old St. Ferdinand's, Inc. Address: No. 1 Rue St. Francois, Florissant 63031.

• Shrine of Our Lady of Sorrows, Starkenburg (1888; shrine building, 1910); Jefferson City Diocese. Address: c/o Risen Savior Parish, Rt. 1, Box 17, Rhineland 65069.

Nebraska: The Eucharistic Shrine of Christ the King (1973); Lincoln diocese and Holy Spirit Adoration Sisters. Address: 1040 South Cotner Blvd., Lincoln 68510.

New Hampshire: Our Lady of Grace, Colebrook (1948); Oblates of Mary Immaculate. Address: R.R. 1, Box 521, Colebrook 03576.

• Shrine of Our Lady of La Salette, Enfield (1951); Missionaries of Our Lady of La Salette. Address: Rt. 4A, P.O. Box 420, Enfield 03748.

New Jersey: Shrine of the Immaculate Heart of Mary (National Blue Army Shrine) (1978); World Apostolate of Fatima. Address: Mountain View Rd., P.O. Box 976, Washington 07882.

• Shrine of St. Joseph, Stirling (1924); Missionary Servants of the Most Holy Trinity. Address: 1050 Long Hill Rd., Stirling 07980.

New Mexico: St. Augustine Mission, Isleta

(1613); Santa Fe Archdiocese. Address: P.O. Box 463, Isleta, Pueblo 87022.

• San Miguel Chapel, Santa Fe (1610); Private Chapel; Brothers of the Christian Schools. Address: 410 Old Santa Fe Trail, Santa Fe 87501.

• Santuario de Nuestro Senor de Esquipulas, Chimayo (1816); Santa Fe archdiocese, Sons of the Holy Family; national historic landmark, 1970. Address: Santuario de Chimayo, P.O. Box 235; Chimayo 87522.

New York: National Shrine of Bl. Kateri Tekakwitha, Fonda (1938); Order of Friars Minor Conventual. Address: P.O. Box 627, Fonda 12068.

• Infant Jesus Shrine, North Tonawanda (1958); Society of the Catholic Apostolate. Address: 3452 Niagara Falls Blvd., N. Tonawanda 14120.

• Marian Shrine (National Shrine of Mary Help of Christians), West Haverstraw (1953); Salesians of St. John Bosco. Address: Filors Lane, W. Haverstraw 10993.

• National Shrine of St. Frances Xavier Cabrini, New York (1938; new shrine dedicated 1960); Missionary Sisters of the Sacred Heart. Address: St. Frances Cabrini Chapel, 701 Fort Washington Ave., New York 10040.

• Original Shrine of St. Ann in New York City (1892); located in St. Jean Baptiste Church; Blessed Sacrament Fathers. Address: 184 E. 76th St., New York 10021.

• Our Lady of Fatima Shrine, Youngstown (1954); Barnabite Fathers. Address: 1023 Swan Rd., Youngstown 14174.

• Our Lady of Victory National Shrine, Lackawanna (1926); Minor Basilica. Address: 767 Ridge Rd., Lackawanna 14218.

• Shrine Church of Our Lady of Mt. Carmel, Brooklyn (1888); Brooklyn Diocese (Parish Church). Address: 275 N. 8th St., Brooklyn 11218.

• Shrine of Our Lady of Martyrs, Auriesville (1885); Society of Jesus. Address: Auriesville 12016.

• Shrine of Our Lady of the Island, Eastport (1975); Montfort Missionaries. Address: Box 26, Eastport, L.I., 11941.

• Shrine of St. Elizabeth Ann Seton, New York City (1975); located in Our Lady of the Rosary Church. Address: 7 State St., New York 10004.

Ohio: Basilica and National Shrine of Our Lady of Consolation, Carey (1867); Minor Basilica; Toledo Diocese; staffed by Conventual Franciscan Friars. Address: 315 Clay St., Carey 43316.

• National Shrine of Our Lady of Lebanon, North Jackson (1965); St. Maron diocese (Brooklyn). Address: 2759 N. Lipkey Rd., N. Jackson 44451.

• Our Lady of Czestochowa, Garfield Heights (1939); Sisters of St. Joseph, Third Order of St. Francis. Address: 12215 Granger Rd., Garfield Hts. 44125.

• Our Lady of Fatima, Ironton (1954); Watterson Council of Knights of Columbus. Address: P.O. Box, 112, Ironton 45638.

• Our Lady Queen of the Most Holy Rosary, Parma Heights (1936); Sisters of the Incarnate Word. Address: 6618 Pearl Rd., Parma Hts. 44130.

• St. Anthony Shrine, Cincinnati (1888); Franciscan Friars, St. John Baptist Province. Address: 5000 Colerain Ave., Cincinnati 45223.

• Shrine and Oratory of the Weeping Madonna of Mariapoch, Burton (1956); Social Mission Sisters. Parma Diocese. Address: 17486 Mumford Rd., Burton 44021.

• Shrine of the Holy Relics (1892); Sisters of the Precious Blood. Address: 2291 St. John's Rd., Maria Stein 45860.

• Sorrowful Mother Shrine, Bellevue (1850); Society of the Precious Blood. Address: 4106 State Rt. 269, Bellevue 44811.

Oklahoma: National Shrine of the Infant Jesus of Prague, Prague (1949); Oklahoma City Archdiocese. Address: P.O. Box 488, Prague 74864.

Oregon: The Grotto (National Sanctuary of Our Sorrowful Mother), Portland (1924); Servite Friars. Address: P.O. Box 20008, Portland 97220.

Pennsylvania: Basilica of the Sacred Heart of Jesus (1741; present church, 1787); Minor Basilica; Harrisburg Diocese. Address: 30 Basilica Dr., Hanover 17331.

• National Shrine Center of Our Lady of Guadalupe, Mother of the Americas, Allentown (1974); located in Immaculate Conception Church; Allentown Diocese. Address: 501 Ridge Ave., Allentown 18102.

• National Shrine of Our Lady of Czestochowa (1955); Order of St. Paul the Hermit (Pauline Fathers). Address: P.O. Box 2049, Doylestown 18901.

• National Shrine of St. John Neumann, Philadelphia (1860); Redemptorist Fathers, St. Peter's Church. Address: 1019 N. 5th St., Philadelphia 19123.

• National Shrine of the Sacred Heart, Harleigh (1975); Scranton Diocese. Address: P.O. Box 500, Harleigh 18225.

• Old St. Joseph's National Shrine, a unit of the Independence National Historical Park, Philadelphia (1733); Philadelphia Archdiocese (Parish Church). Address: 321 Willings Alley, Philadelphia 19106.

• St. Ann's Monastery Shrine, Scranton (1902); Passionist Community. Address: 1230 St. Ann's St., Scranton 18504.

• St. Anthony's Chapel, Pittsburgh (1883); Pittsburgh Diocese. Address: 1700 Harpster St., Pittsburgh 15212.

• Shrine of St. Walburga, Greensburg (1974); Sisters of St. Benedict. Address: 1001 Harvey Ave., Greensburg 15601.

Texas: Virgen de San Juan del Valle Shrine, San Juan (1949); Brownsville Diocese; staffed by Oblates of Mary Immaculate. Address: 400 N. Nebraska, P.O. Box 747, San Juan 78589.

Vermont: St. Anne's Shrine, Isle La Motte (1666); Burlington Diocese, conducted by Edmundites. Address: West Shore Rd., Isle La Motte 05463.

Wisconsin: Holy Hill — National Shrine of Mary, Help of Christians (1857); Discalced Carmelite Friars. Address: 1525 Carmel Rd., Hubertus 53033.

• National Shrine of St. Joseph, De Pere (1889); Norbertine Fathers. Address: 1016 N. Broadway, De Pere 54115.

• Shrine of Mary, Mother Thrice Admirable, Queen and Victress of Schoenstatt (1914, original shrine in Germany), Waukesha; International Schoenstatt Center. Address: W284 N698 Cherry Lane, Waukesha 53188.

THE CATHOLIC CHURCH IN THE UNITED STATES

The starting point of the mainstream of Catholic history in the United States was Baltimore at the end of the Revolutionary War, although before that time Catholic explorers had traversed much of the country and missionaries had done considerable work among the Indians in the Southeast, Northeast and Southwest. (See Index: Chronology of Church in U.S.)

Beginning of Organization

Father John Carroll's appointment as superior of the American missions on June 9, 1784, was the first step toward organization of the Church in this country.

At that time, according to a report he made to Rome in 1785, there were approximately 25,000 Catholics in the general population of four million. Many of them had been in the Colonies for several generations. Among them were such outstanding figures as Charles Carroll, a member of the Continental Congress and signer of the Declaration of Independence; Thomas FitzSimons of Philadelphia and Oliver Pollock, the Virginia agent, who raised funds for the militia; Commander John Barry, father of the American Navy, and numerous high-ranking army officers. For the most part, however, Catholics were an unknown minority laboring under legal and social handicaps.

Father Carroll, the cousin of Charles Carroll, was named the first American bishop in 1789 and placed in charge of the Diocese of Baltimore, whose boundaries were coextensive with those of the United States. He was ordained in England Aug. 15, 1790, and installed in his see the following Dec. 12.

Ten years later, Father Leonard Neale became his coadjutor and the first bishop ordained in the United States. Bishop Carroll became an archbishop in 1808 when Baltimore was designated a metropolitan see and the new dioceses of Boston, New York, Philadelphia and Bardstown were established. These jurisdictions were later subdivided, and by 1840 there were, in addition to Baltimore, 15 dioceses, 500 priests and 663,000 Catholics in the general population of 17 million.

Priests and First Seminaries

The original number of 24 priests noted in Bishop Carroll's 1785 report was gradually augmented with the arrival of others from France, after the Civil Constitution on the Clergy went into effect there, and other countries. Among the earliest arrivals were several Sulpicians who established the first seminary in the U.S., St. Mary's, Baltimore, in 1791. By 1815, 30 alumni of the school had been ordained to the priesthood. By that time, two additional seminaries were in operation: Mt. St. Mary's, established in 1809 at Emmitsburg, Md., and St. Thomas, founded two years later, at Bardstown, Ky. These and similar institutions founded later played key roles in the development and growth of the American clergy.

Early Schools

Early educational enterprises included the establishment in 1791 of a school at Georgetown which later became the first Catholic university in the U.S.; the opening of a secondary school for girls, conducted by Visitation Nuns, in 1799 at Georgetown; and the start of a similar school in the first decade of the 19th century at Emmitsburg, Md., by Saint Elizabeth Ann Seton and the Sisters of Charity of St. Joseph, the first religious community of American foundation.

By the 1840s, which saw the beginnings of the present public school system, more than 200 Catholic elementary schools, half of them west of the Alleghenies, were in operation. From this start, the Church subsequently built the greatest private system of education in the world.

Trusteeism

The initial lack of organization in ecclesiastical affairs, nationalistic feeling among Catholics and the independent action of some priests were factors involved in several early crises.

In Philadelphia, some German Catholics, with the reluctant consent of Bishop Carroll, founded Holy Trinity, the first national parish in the U.S. They refused to accept the pastor appointed by the bishop and elected their own. This and other abuses led to formal schism in 1796, a condition which existed until 1802 when they returned to canonical jurisdiction. Philadelphia was also the scene of the Hogan Schism, which developed in the 1820s when Father William Hogan, with the aid of lay trustees, seized control of St. Mary's Cathedral. His movement, for churches and parishes controlled by other than canonical procedures and run in extralegal ways, was nullified by a decision of the Pennsylvania Supreme Court in 1822.

Similar troubles seriously disturbed the peace of the Church in other places, principally New York, Baltimore, Buffalo, Charleston and New Orleans.

Dangers arising from the exploitation of lay control were gradually diminished with the extension and enforcement of canonical procedures and with changes in civil law about the middle of the century.

Bigotry

Bigotry against Catholics waxed and waned during the 19th century and into the 20th. The first major campaign of this kind, which developed in the wake of the panic of 1819 and lasted for about 25 years, was mounted in 1830 when the number of Catholic immigrants began to increase to a noticeable degree. Nativist anti-Catholicism generated a great deal of violence, represented by climaxes in loss of life and property in Charlestown, Mass., in 1834, and in Philadelphia 10 years later. Later bigotry was fomented by the Know-Nothings, in the 1850s; the Ku Klux Klan, from 1866; the American Protective Association, from 1887, and the Guardians of Liberty. Perhaps the last eruption of virulently overt anti-Catholicism occurred during the campaign of Alfred E. Smith for the presidency in 1928. Observers feel the issue was muted to a considerable extent in the political area with the election of John F. Kennedy to the presidency in 1960.

Growth and Immigration

Between 1830 and 1900, the combined factors of natural increase, immigration and conversion raised the Catholic population to 12 million. A large percentage of the growth figure represented immigrants: some 2.7 million, largely from Ireland, Germany and France, between 1830 and 1880; and another 1.25 million during the 1880s when Eastern and Southern Europeans came in increasing numbers. By the 1860s the Catholic Church, with most of its members concentrated in urban areas, was one of the largest religious bodies in the country.

The efforts of progressive bishops to hasten the acculturation of Catholic immigrants occasioned a number of controversies, which generally centered around questions concerning national or foreign-language parishes. One of them, called Cahenslyism, arose from complaints that German Catholic immigrants were not being given adequate pastoral care.

Immigration continued after the turn of the century, but its impact was more easily cushioned through the application of lessons learned earlier in dealing with problems of nationality and language.

Councils of Baltimore

The bishops of the growing U.S. dioceses met at Baltimore for seven provincial councils between 1829 and 1849.

In 1846, they proclaimed the Blessed Virgin Mary patroness of the United States under the title of the Immaculate Conception, eight years before the dogma was proclaimed.

After the establishment of the Archdiocese of Oregon City in 1846 and the elevation to metropolitan status of St. Louis, New Orleans, Cincinnati and New York, the first of the three plenary councils of Baltimore was held.

The first plenary assembly was convoked on May 9, 1852, with Archbishop Francis P. Kenrick of Baltimore as papal legate. The bishops drew up regulations concerning parochial life, matters of church ritual and ceremonies, the administration of church funds and the teaching of Christian doctrine.

The second plenary council, meeting from Oct. 7 to 21, 1866, under the presidency of Archbishop Martin J. Spalding, formulated a condemnation of several current doctrinal errors and established norms affecting the organization of dioceses, the education and conduct of the clergy, the management of ecclesiastical property, parochial duties and general education.

Archbishop (later Cardinal) James Gibbons called into session the third plenary council which lasted from Nov. 9 to Dec. 7, 1884. Among highly significant results of actions taken by this assembly were the preparation of the line of Baltimore catechisms which became a basic means of religious instruction in this country; legislation which fixed the pattern of Catholic education by requiring the building of elementary schools in all parishes; the establishment of the Catholic University of America in Washington, D.C., in 1889; and the determination of six holy days of obligation for observance in this country.

The enactments of the three plenary councils have had the force of particular law for the Church in the United States.

The Holy See established the Apostolic Delegation in Washington, D.C., on Jan. 24, 1893.

Slavery

In the Civil War period, as before, Catholics reflected attitudes of the general population with respect to the issue of slavery. Some supported it, some opposed it, but none were prominent in the Abolition Movement. Gregory XVI had condemned the slave trade in 1839, but no contemporary pope or American bishop published an official document on slavery itself. The issue did not split Catholics in schism as it did Baptists, Methodists and Presbyterians.

Catholics fought on both sides in the Civil War. Five hundred members of 20 or more sisterhoods served the wounded of both sides.

One hundred thousand of the four million slaves emancipated in 1863 were Catholics; the highest concentrations were in Louisiana, about 60,000, and Maryland, 16,000. Three years later, their pastoral care was one of the subjects covered in nine decrees issued by the Second Plenary Council of Baltimore. The measures had little practical effect with respect to integration of the total Catholic community, predicated as they were on the proposition that individual bishops should handle questions regarding segregation in churches and related matters as best they could in the pattern of local customs.

Long entrenched segregation practices continued in force through the rest of the 19th century and well into the 20th. The first effective efforts to alter them were initiated by Cardinal Joseph Ritter of St. Louis in 1947, Cardinal (then Archbishop) Patrick O'Boyle of Washington in 1948, and Bishop Vincent Waters of Raleigh in 1953.

Friend of Labor

The Church became known during the 19th century as a friend and ally of labor in seeking justice for the working man. Cardinal Gibbons journeyed to Rome in 1887, for example, to defend and prevent a condemnation of the Knights of Labor by Leo XIII. The encyclical *Rerum Novarum* was hailed by many American bishops as a confirmation, if not vindication, of their own theories. Catholics have always formed a large percentage of union membership, and some have served unions in positions of leadership.

The American Heresy

Near the end of the century some controversy developed over what was characterized as Americanism or the phantom heresy. It was alleged that Americans were discounting the importance of contemplative virtues, exalting the practical virtues, and watering down the purity of Catholic doctrine for the sake of facilitating convert work.

The French translation of Father Walter Elliott's *Life of Isaac Hecker*, which fired the controversy, was one of many factors that led to the issuance of Leo XIII's *Testem Benevolentiae* in January, 1899, in an attempt to end the matter. It was the first time the orthodoxy of the Church in the U.S. was called into question.

Schism

In the 1890s, serious friction developed between Poles and Irish in Scranton, Buffalo and Chicago, resulting in schism and the establishment of the Polish National Church. A central figure in the affair was Father Francis Hodor, who was excommunicated by Bishop William O'Hara of Scranton in 1898. Nine Years Later, his ordination by an Old Catholic Archbishop of Utrecht gave the new church its first bishop.

Another schism of the period led to formation of the American Carpatho-Russian Orthodox Greek Catholic Church.

Coming of Age

In 1900, there were 12 million Catholics in the total U.S. population of 76 million, 82 dioceses in 14 provinces, and 12,000 priests and members of about 40 communities of men Religious. Many sisterhoods, most of them of European origin and some of American foundation, were engaged in Catholic educational and hospital work, two of their traditional apostolates.

The Church in the United States was removed from mission status with promulgation of the apostolic constitution *Sapienti Consilio* by Pope St. Pius X on June 29, 1908.

Before that time, and even into the early 1920s, the Church in this country received financial assistance from mission-aid societies in France, Bavaria and Austria. Already, however, it was making increasing contributions of its own. At the present time, it is one of the major national contributors to the worldwide Society for the Propagation of the Faith.

American foreign missionary personnel increased from 14 or less in 1906 to an all-time high in 1968 of 9,655 priests, brothers, sisters, seminarians, and lay persons. The first missionary seminary in the U.S. was in operation at Techny, Ill., in 1909, under the auspices of the Society of the Divine Word. Maryknoll, the first American missionary society, was established in 1911 and sent its first priests to China in 1918. Despite these contributions, the Church in the U.S. has not matched the missionary commitment of some other nations.

Bishops' Conference

A highly important apparatus for mobilizing the Church's resources was established in 1917 under the title of the National Catholic War Council. Its name was changed to National Catholic Welfare Conference several years later, but its objectives remained the same: to serve as an advisory and coordinating agency of the American bishops for advancing works of the Church in fields of social significance and impact — education, communications, immigration, social action, legislation, youth and lay organizations.

The forward thrust of the bishops' social thinking was evidenced in a program of social reconstruction they recommended in 1919. By 1945, all but one of their twelve points had been enacted into legislation. The NCWC was renamed the United States Catholic Conference (USCC) in November, 1966, when the hierarchy also organized itself as a territorial conference with pastoral-juridical authority under the title, National Conference of Catholic Bishops. The USCC is carrying on the functions of the former NCWC.

Pastoral Concerns

The potential for growth of the Church in this country by immigration was sharply reduced but not entirely curtailed after 1921 with the passage of restrictive federal legislation. As a result, the Catholic population became more stabilized and, to a certain extent and for many reasons, began to acquire an identity of its own.

Some increase from outside has taken place in the past 50 years, however; from Canada, from Central and Eastern European countries, and from Puerto Rico and Latin American countries since World War II. This influx, while not as great as that of the 19th century and early 20th, has enriched the Church here with a sizable body of Eastern- Rite Catholics for whom twelve ecclesiastical jurisdictions have been established. It has also created a challenge for pastoral care of millions of Hispanics in urban centers and in agricultural areas where migrant workers are employed.

The Church continues to grapple with serious pastoral problems in rural areas, where about 600 counties are no-priest land. The National Catholic Rural Life Conference was established in 1922 in an attempt to make the Catholic presence felt on the land, and the Glenmary Society since its foundation in 1939 has devoted itself to this single apostolate. Religious communities and diocesan priests are similarly engaged.

Other challenges lie in the cities and suburbs where 75 percent of the Catholic population lives. Conditions peculiar to each segment of the metropolitan area have developed in recent years as the flight to the suburbs has not only altered some traditional aspects of parish life but has also, in combination with many other factors, left behind a complex of special problems in inner city areas.

Contemporary Factors

The Church in the U.S. is in a stage of transition from a relatively stable and long established order of life and action to a new order of things. Some of the phenomena of this period are:

- differences in trends and emphasis in theology, and in interpretation and implementation of directives of the Second Vatican Council, resulting in situations of conflict;

- the changing spiritual formation, professional education, style of life and ministry of priests and Religious (men and women), which are altering influential patterns of pastoral and specialized service;

- vocations to the priesthood and religious life, which are generally in decline;

- departures from the priesthood and religious life which, while small percentage-wise, are numerous enough to be a matter of serious concern;

- decline of traditional devotional practices, along with the emergence of new ones.

● exercise of authority along the lines of collegiality and subsidiarity;

● structure and administration, marked by a trend toward greater participation in the life and work of the Church by its members on all levels, from the parish on up;

● alienation from the Church, leading some persons into the catacombs of an underground church, "anonymous Christianity" and religious indifferentism;

● education, undergoing crisis and change in Catholic schools and seeking new ways of reaching out to the young not in Catholic schools and to adults;

● social witness in ministry to the world, which is being shaped by the form of contemporary needs — e.g., race relations, poverty, the peace movement, the Third World;

● ecumenism, involving the Church in interfaith relations on a wider scale than before.

BACKGROUND DATES IN U.S. CATHOLIC CHRONOLOGY

Dates in this section refer mostly to earlier "firsts" and developments in the background of Catholic history in the United States. For other dates, see various sections of the Almanac.

Alabama

1540: Priests crossed the territory with De Soto's expedition.

1560: Five Dominicans in charge of mission at Santa Cruz des Nanipacna.

1682: La Salle claimed territory for France.

1704: First parish church established at Fort Louis de la Mobile under the care of diocesan priests.

1829: Mobile diocese established (redesignated Mobile-Birmingham, 1954-69).

1830: Spring Hill College, Mobile, established.

1834: Visitation Nuns established an academy at Summerville.

1969: Birmingham diocese established.

1980: Mobile made metropolitan see.

Alaska

1779: Mass celebrated for first time on shore of Port Santa Cruz on lower Bucareli Bay on May 13 by Franciscan Juan Riobo.

1868: Alaska placed under jurisdiction of Vancouver Island.

1879: Father John Althoff became first resident missionary.

1886: Archbishop Charles J. Seghers, "Apostle of Alaska," murdered by a guide; had surveyed southern and northwest Alaska in 1873 and 1877, respectively.

Sisters of St. Ann first nuns in Alaska.

1887: Jesuits enter Alaska territory.

1894: Alaska made prefecture apostolic.

1902: Sisters of Providence opened hospital at Nome.

1916: Alaska made vicariate apostolic.

1917: In first ordination in territory, Rev. G. Edgar Gallant raised to priesthood.

1951: Juneau diocese established.

1962: Fairbanks diocese established.

1966: Anchorage archdiocese established.

Arizona

1539: Franciscan Marcos de Niza explored the state.

1540: Franciscans Juan de Padilla and Marcos de Niza accompanied Coronado expedition through the territory.

1629: Spanish Franciscans began work among Moqui Indians.

1632: Franciscan Martin de Arvide killed by Indians.

1680: Franciscans Jose de Espeleta, Augustin de Santa Maria, Jose de Figueroa and Jose de Trujillo killed in Pueblo Revolt.

1700: Jesuit Eusebio Kino, who first visited the area in 1692, established mission at San Xavier del Bac, near Tucson. In 1783, under Franciscan administration, construction was begun of the Mission Church of San Xavier del Bac near the site of the original mission; it is still in use as a parish church.

1767: Jesuits expelled; Franciscans took over 10 missions.

1828: Spanish missionaries expelled by Mexican government.

1863: Jesuits returned to San Xavier del Bac briefly.

1869: Sisters of Loretto arrived to conduct schools at Bisbee and Douglas.

1897: Tucson diocese established.

1969: Phoenix diocese established.

Arkansas

1541: Priests accompanied De Soto expedition through the territory.

1673: Marquette visited Indians in east.

1686: Henri de Tonti established trading post, first white settlement in territory.

1700-1702: Fr. Nicholas Foucault working among Indians.

1805: Bishop Carroll of Baltimore appointed Administrator Apostolic of Arkansas.

1838: Sisters of Loretto opened first Catholic school.

1843: Little Rock diocese established. There were about 700 Catholics in state, two churches, one priest.

1851: Sisters of Mercy founded St. Mary's Convent in Little Rock.

California

1542: Cabrillo discovered Upper (Alta) California; name of priest accompanying expedition unknown.

1602: On Nov. 12 Carmelite Anthony of the Ascension offered first recorded Mass in California on shore of San Diego Bay.

1697: Missionary work in Lower and Upper Californias entrusted to Jesuits.

1767: Jesuits expelled from territory. Spanish Crown confiscated their property, including the

Pious Fund for Missions. Upper California missions entrusted to Franciscans.

1769: Franciscan Junipero Serra, missionary in Mexico for 20 years, began establishment of Franciscan missions in California, in present San Diego. He was beatified in 1988.

1775: Franciscan Luis Jayme killed by Indians at San Diego Mission.

1779: Diocese of Sonora, Mexico, which included Upper California, established.

1781: On Sept. 4 an expedition from San Gabriel Mission founded present city of Los Angeles — Pueblo "de Nuestra Senora de los Angeles."

Franciscans Francisco Hermenegildo Garces, Juan Antonio Barreneche, Juan Marcello Diaz and Jose Matias Moreno killed by Indians.

1812: Franciscan Andres Quintana killed at Santa Cruz Mission.

1822: Dedication on Dec. 8 of Old Plaza Church, "Assistant Mission of Our Lady of the Angels."

1833: Missions secularized, finally confiscated.

1840: Pope Gregory XVI established Diocese of Both Californias.

1846: Peter H. Burnett, who became first governor of California in 1849, received into Catholic Church.

1848: Mexico ceded California to the United States.

1850: Monterey diocese erected; title changed to Monterey-Los Angeles, 1859; and to Los Angeles-San Diego, 1922.

1851: University of Santa Clara chartered.

Sisters of Notre Dame de Namur opened women's College of Notre Dame at San Jose; chartered in 1868; moved to Belmont, 1923.

1852: Baja California detached from Monterey diocese.

1853: San Francisco archdiocese established.

1855: Negotiations inaugurated to restore confiscated California missions to Church.

1868: Grass Valley diocese established; transferred to Sacramento in 1886.

1922: Monterey-Fresno diocese established; became separate dioceses, 1967.

1934: Sesquicentennial of Serra's death observed; Serra Year officially declared by Legislature and Aug. 24 observed as Serra Day.

1936: Los Angeles made archdiocese. San Diego diocese established.

1952: Law exempting non-profit, religious-sponsored elementary and secondary schools from taxation upheld in referendum, Nov. 4.

1953: Archbishop James Francis McIntyre of Los Angeles made cardinal by Pius XII.

1962: Oakland, Santa Rosa and Stockton dioceses established.

1973: Archbishop Timothy Manning of Los Angeles made cardinal by Pope Paul VI.

1976: Orange diocese established.

1981: San Jose diocese established.

Byzantine-Rite eparchy of Van Nuys established.

1991: Archbishop Roger Mahony of Los Angeles made cardinal by Pope John Paul II.

Colorado

1858: First parish in Colorado established.

1864: Sisters of Loretto at the Foot of the Cross,

first nuns in the state, established academy at Denver.

1868: Vicariate Apostolic of Colorado and Utah established.

1887: Denver diocese established.

1888: Regis College founded.

1941: Denver made archdiocese.

Pueblo diocese established.

1983: Colorado Springs diocese established.

Connecticut

1651: Probably first priest to enter state was Jesuit Gabriel Druillettes; ambassador of Governor of Canada, he participated in a New England Colonial Council at New Haven.

1756: Catholic Acadians, expelled from Nova Scotia, settled in the state.

1791: Rev. John Thayer, first native New England priest, offered Mass at the Hartford home of Noah Webster, his Yale classmate.

1808: Connecticut became part of Boston diocese.

1818: Religious freedom established by new constitution, although the Congregational Church remained, in practice, the state church.

1829: Father Bernard O'Cavanaugh became first resident priest in state.

Catholic Press of Hartford established.

1830: First Catholic church in state dedicated at Hartford.

Father James Fitton (1805-81), New England missionary, was assigned to Hartford for six years. He ministered to Catholics throughout the state.

1843: Hartford diocese established.

1882: Knights of Columbus founded by Father Michael J. McGivney.

1942: Fairfield University founded.

1953: Norwich and Bridgeport dioceses established. Hartford made archdiocese.

1956: Byzantine Rite Exarchate of Stamford established; made eparchy, 1958.

Delaware

1730: Mount Cuba, New Castle County, the scene of Catholic services.

1750: Jesuit mission at Apoquiniminck administered from Maryland.

1772: First permanent parish established at Coffee Run.

1792: French Catholics from Santo Domingo settled near Wilmington.

1816: St. Peter's Church, later the cathedral of the diocese, erected at Wilmington.

1830: Daughters of Charity opened school and orphanage at Wilmington.

1868: Wilmington diocese established.

1869: Visitation Nuns established residence in Wilmington.

District of Columbia

1641: Jesuit Andrew White evangelized Anacosta Indians.

1774: Father John Carroll ministered to Catholics.

1789: Georgetown, first Catholic college in U.S., established.

1791: Pierre Charles L'Enfant designed the Federal City of Washington. His plans were not fully implemented until the early 1900s.

1792: James Hoban designed the White House.
1794: Father Anthony Caffrey began St. Patrick's Church, first parish church in the new Federal City.
1801: Poor Clares opened school for girls in Georgetown.
1802: First mayor of Washington, appointed by President Jefferson, was Judge Robert Brent.
1889: Catholic University of America founded.
1893: Apostolic Delegation established; became an Apostolic Nunciature in 1984 with the establishment of full diplomatic relations between the U.S. and the Vatican.
1919: National Catholic Welfare Conference (now the United States Catholic Conference) organized by American hierarchy to succeed National Catholic War Council.
1920: Cornerstone of National Shrine of Immaculate Conception laid. The crypt church was completed in 1926. The entire structure was completed in 1959 and dedicated Nov. 20, 1959. In 1990 it was designated a minor basilica.
1939: Washington made archdiocese of equal rank with Baltimore, under direction of same archbishop.
1947: Washington archdiocese received its own archbishop, was separated from Baltimore; became a metropolitan see in 1965.
1967: Archbishop Patrick A. O'Boyle of Washington made cardinal by Pope Paul VI.
1976: Archbishop William Baum of Washington made a cardinal by Pope Paul VI; transferred to Roman Curia in 1980. (See Index.)
1988: Archbishop James A. Hickey of Washington made a cardinal by Pope John Paul II.

Florida

1513: Ponce de Leon discovered Florida.
1521: Missionaries accompanying Ponce de Leon and other explorers probably said first Masses within present limits of U.S.
1528: Franciscans landed on western shore.
1539: Twelve missionaries landed with De Soto at Tampa Bay.
1549: Dominican Luis Cancer de Barbastro and two companions slain by Indians near Tampa Bay.
1565: City of St. Augustine, oldest in U.S., founded by Pedro Menendez de Aviles, who was accompanied by four secular priests.
America's oldest mission, Nombre de Dios, was established.
Father Martin Francisco Lopez de Mendoza Grajales became the first parish priest of St. Augustine, where the first parish in the U.S. was established.
1572: St. Francis Borgia, general of the Society, withdrew Jesuits from Florida.
1606: Bishop Juan de las Cabeyas de Altamirano, O.P., conducted the first episcopal visitation in the U.S.
1620: The chapel of Nombre de Dios was dedicated to Nuestra Senora de la Leche y Buen Parto (Our Nursing Mother of the Happy Delivery); oldest shrine to the Blessed Mother in the U.S.
1704: Destruction of Florida's northern missions by English and Indian troops led by Governor James Moore of South Carolina. Franciscans Juan de

Parga, Dominic Criodo, Tiburcio de Osorio, Augustine Ponze de Leon, Marcos Delgado and two Indians, Anthony Enixa and Amador Cuipa Feliciano, were slain by the invaders.
1735: Bishop Francis Martinez de Tejadu Diaz de Velasco, auxiliary of Santiago, was the first bishop to take up residence in U.S., at St. Augustine.
1793: Florida and Louisiana were included in Diocese of New Orleans.
1857: Eastern Florida made a vicariate apostolic.
1870: St. Augustine diocese established.
1917: Convent Inspection Bill passed; repealed 1935.
1958: Miami diocese established.
1968: Miami made metropolitan see; Orlando and St. Petersburg dioceses established.
1976: Pensacola-Tallahassee diocese established.
1984: Palm Beach and Venice dioceses established.

Georgia

1540: First priests to enter were chaplains with De Soto. They celebrated first Mass within territory of 13 original colonies.
1566: Pedro Martinez, first Jesuit martyr of the New World, was slain by Indians on Cumberland Island.
1569: Jesuit mission was opened at Guale Island by Father Antonio Sedeno.
1572: Jesuits withdrawn from area.
1595: Five Franciscans assigned to Province of Guale.
1597: Five Franciscan missionaries (Fathers Pedro de Corpa, Blas de Rodriguez, Miguel de Anon, Francisco de Berascolo and Brother Antonio de Badajoz) killed in coastal missions. Their cause for beatification was formally opened in 1984.
1606: Bishop Altamirano, O.P., conducted visitation of the Georgia area.
1612: First Franciscan province in U.S. erected under title of Santa Elena; it included Georgia, South Carolina and Florida.
1655: Franciscans had nine flourishing missions among Indians.
1742: Spanish missions ended as result of English conquest at Battle of Bloody Marsh.
1796: Augustinian Father Le Mercier was first post-colonial missionary to Georgia.
1798: Catholics granted right of refuge.
1800: First church erected in Savannah on lot given by city council.
1810: First church erected in Augusta on lot given by State Legislature.
1850: Savannah diocese established; became Savannah-Atlanta, 1937; divided into two separate sees, 1956.
1864: Father Emmeran Bliemel, of the Benedictine community of Latrobe, Pa., was killed at the battle of Jonesboro while serving as chaplain of the Confederate 10th Tennessee Artillery.
1962: Atlanta made metropolitan see.

Hawaii

1825: Pope Leo XII entrusted missionary efforts in Islands to Sacred Hearts Fathers.
1827: The first Catholic missionaries arrived — Fathers Alexis Bachelot, Abraham Armand and

Patrick Short, along with three lay brothers. After three years of persecution, the priests were forcibly exiled.

1836: Father Arsenius Walsh, SS. CC., a British subject, was allowed to remain in Islands but was not permitted to proselytize or conduct missions.

1839: Hawaiian government signed treaty with France granting Catholics freedom of worship and same privileges as Protestants.

1844: Vicariate Apostolic of Sandwich Islands (Hawaii) erected.

1873: Father Damien de Veuster of the Sacred Hearts Fathers arrived in Molokai and spent the remainder of his life working among lepers.

1941: Honolulu diocese established, made a suffragan of San Francisco.

Idaho

1840: Jesuit Pierre de Smet preached to the Flathead and Pend d'Oreille Indians; probably offered first Mass in state.

1842: Jesuit Nicholas Point opened a mission among Coeur d'Alene Indians near St. Maries.

1863: Secular priests sent from Oregon City to administer to incoming miners.

1867: Sisters of Holy Names of Jesus and Mary opened first Catholic school at Idaho City.

1868: Idaho made a vicariate apostolic.

1870: First church in Boise established.
Church lost most of missions among Indians of Northwest Territory when Commission on Indian Affairs appointed Protestant missionaries to take over.

1893: Boise diocese established.

Illinois

1673: Jesuit Jacques Marquette, accompanying Joliet, preached to Indians.

1674: Father Marquette set up a cabin for saying Mass in what later became City of Chicago.

1675: Father Marquette established Mission of the Immaculate Conception among Kaskaskia Indians, near present site of Utica; transferred to Kaskaskia, 1703.

1679: La Salle brought with him Franciscans Louis Hennepin, Gabriel de la Ribourde, and Zenobius Membre.

1680: Father Ribourde was killed by Kickapoo Indians.

1689: Jesuit Claude Allouez died after 32 years of missionary activity among Indians of Midwest; he had evangelized Indians of 20 different tribes. Jesuit Jacques Gravier succeeded Allouez as vicar general of Illinois.

1699: Mission established at Cahokia, first permanent settlement in state.

1730: Father Gaston, a diocesan priest, was killed at the Cahokia Mission.

1763: Jesuits were banished from the territory.

1778: Father Pierre Gibault championed Colonial cause in the Revolution and aided greatly in securing states of Ohio, Indiana, Illinois, Michigan and Wisconsin for Americans.

1827: The present St. Patrick's Parish at Ruma,

oldest English-speaking Catholic congregation in state, was founded.

1833: Visitation Nuns established residence in Kaskaskia.

1843: Chicago diocese established.

1853: Quincy diocese established; transferred to Alton, 1857; Springfield, 1923.

1860: Quincy College founded.

1877: Peoria diocese established.

1880: Chicago made archdiocese.

1887: Belleville diocese established.

1894: Franciscan Sisters of Bl. Kunegunda (now the Franciscan Sisters of Chicago) founded by Mother Marie Therese (Josephine Dudzik).

1908: Rockford diocese established.
First American Missionary Congress held in Chicago.

1924: Archbishop Mundelein of Chicago made cardinal by Pope Pius XI.

1926: The 28th International Eucharistic Congress, first held in U.S., convened in Chicago.

1946: Blessed Frances Xavier Cabrini, former resident of Chicago, was canonized; first U.S. citizen raised to dignity of altar.
Archbishop Samuel A. Stritch of Chicago made cardinal by Pope Pius XII.

1948: Joliet diocese established.

1958: Cardinal Stritch appointed Pro-Prefect of the Sacred Congregation for the Propagation of the Faith — the first U.S.-born prelate to be named to the Roman Curia.

1959: Archbishop Albert G. Meyer of Chicago made cardinal by Pope John XXIII.

1961: Eparchy of St. Nicholas of the Ukrainians established at Chicago.

1967: Archbishop John P. Cody of Chicago made cardinal by Pope Paul VI.

1983: Archbishop Joseph L. Bernardin of Chicago made cardinal by Pope John Paul II.

Indiana

1679: Recollects Louis Hennepin and Gabriel de la Ribourde passed through state.

1686: Land near present Notre Dame University at South Bend given by French government to Jesuits for mission.

1749: Beginning of the records of St. Francis Xavier Church, Vincennes. These records continue with minor interruptions to the present.

1778: Father Gibault aided George Rogers Clark in campaign against British in conquest of Northwest Territory.

1824: Sisters of Charity of Nazareth, Ky., opened St. Clare's Academy in Vincennes.

1825: Laying of cornerstone of third church of St. Francis Xavier, which later (from 1834-98) was the cathedral of the Vincennes diocese. The church was designated a minor basilica in 1970 and is still in use as a parish church.

1834: Vincennes diocese established with Simon Gabriel Brute as bishop; title changed to Indianapolis, 1898.

1840: Sisters of Providence founded St. Mary-of-the-Woods College for women.

1842: University of Notre Dame founded by Holy Cross Father Edward Sorin and Brothers of St.

Joseph on land given the diocese of Vincennes by Father Stephen Badin.

1853: First Benedictine community established in state at St. Meinrad. It became an abbey in 1870 and an archabbey in 1954.

1857: Fort Wayne diocese established; changed to Fort Wayne-South Bend, 1960.

1944: Indianapolis made archdiocese. Lafayette and Evansville dioceses established.

1957: Gary diocese established.

Iowa

1673: A Peoria village on Mississippi was visited by Father Marquette.

1679: Fathers Louis Hennepin and Gabriel de la Ribourde visited Indian villages.

1836: First permanent church, St. Raphael's, founded at Dubuque by Dominican Samuel Mazzuchelli.

1837: Dubuque diocese established.

1838: St. Joseph's Mission founded at Council Bluffs by Jesuit Father De Smet.

1843: Sisters of Charity of the Blessed Virgin Mary was first sisterhood in state.

Sisters of Charity opened Clarke College, Dubuque.

1850: First Trappist Monastery in state, Our Lady of New Melleray, was begun.

1881: Davenport diocese established.

1882: St. Ambrose College, Davenport, established.

1893: Dubuque made archdiocese.

1902: Sioux City diocese established.

1911: Des Moines diocese established.

Kansas

1542: Franciscan Juan de Padilla, first martyr of the United States, was killed in central Kansas.

1858: St. Benedict's College founded.

1863: Sisters of Charity opened orphanage at Leavenworth, and St. John's Hospital in following year.

1877: Leavenworth diocese established; transferred to Kansas City in 1947.

1887: Dioceses of Concordia (transferred to Salina in 1944) and Wichita established.

1888: Oblate Sisters of Providence opened an orphanage for African-American boys at Leavenworth, first west of Mississippi.

1951: Dodge City diocese established.

1952: Kansas City made archdiocese.

Kentucky

1775: First Catholic settlers came to Kentucky.

1787: Father Charles Maurice Whelan, first resident priest, ministered to settlers in the Bardstown district.

1793: Father Stephen T. Badin began missionary work in Kentucky.

1806: Dominican Fathers built Priory at St. Rose of Lima.

1808: Bardstown diocese established with Benedict Flaget as its first bishop; transferred to Louisville, 1841.

1811: Rev. Guy I. Chabrat first priest ordained west of the Allegheny Mountains.

St. Thomas Seminary founded.

1812: Sisters of Loretto founded by Rev. Charles Nerinckx; first religious community in the United States without foreign affiliation.

Sisters of Charity of Nazareth founded, the second native community of women founded in the West.

1814: Nazareth College for women established.

1816: Cornerstone of St. Joseph's Cathedral, Bardstown, laid.

1836: Hon. Benedict J. Webb founded *Catholic Advocate* first Catholic weekly newspaper in Kentucky.

1848: Trappist monks took up residence in Gethsemani.

1849: Cornerstone of Cathedral of the Assumption laid at Louisville.

1852: Know-Nothing troubles in state.

1853: Covington diocese established.

1937: Louisville made archdiocese. Owensboro diocese established.

1988: Lexington diocese established.

Louisiana

1682: La Salle's expedition, accompanied by two priests, completed discoveries of De Soto at mouth of Mississippi. LaSalle named territory Louisiana.

1699: French Catholics founded colony of Louisiana.

First recorded Mass offered Mar. 3, by Franciscan Father Anastase Douay.

1706: Father John Francis Buisson de St. Cosme was killed near Donaldsonville.

1717: Franciscan Anthony Margil established first Spanish mission in north central Louisiana.

1718: City of New Orleans founded by Jean Baptiste Le Moyne de Bienville.

1720: First resident priest in New Orleans was the French Recollect Prothais Boyer.

1725: Capuchin Fathers opened school for boys.

1727: Ursuline Nuns founded convent in New Orleans, oldest convent in what is now U.S.; they conducted a school, hospital and orphan asylum.

1793: New Orleans diocese established.

1842: Sisters of Holy Family, a black congregation, founded at New Orleans by Henriette Delille and Juliette Gaudin.

1850: New Orleans made archdiocese.

1853: Natchitoches diocese established; transferred to Alexandria in 1910; became Alexandria-Shreveport in 1977; redesignated Alexandria, 1986.

1912: Loyola University of South established.

1918: Lafayette diocese established.

1925: Xavier University established in New Orleans.

1961: Baton Rouge diocese established.

1962: Catholic schools on all levels desegregated in New Orleans archdiocese.

1977: Houma-Thibodaux diocese established.

1980: Lake Charles diocese established.

1986: Shreveport diocese established.

Maine

1604: First Mass in territory celebrated by Father Nicholas Aubry, accompanying De Monts' expedition which was authorized by King of France to begin colonizing region.

1605: Colony founded on St. Croix Island; two secular priests served as chaplains.

1613: Four Jesuits attempted to establish permanent French settlement near mouth of Kennebec River.

1619: French Franciscans began work among settlers and Indians; driven out by English in 1628.

1630: New England made a prefecture apostolic in charge of French Capuchins.

1633: Capuchin Fathers founded missions on Penobscot River.

1646: Jesuits established Assumption Mission on Kennebec River.

1688: Church of St. Anne, oldest in New England, built at Oldtown.

1704: English soldiers destroyed French missions.

1724: English forces again attacked French settlements, killed Jesuit Sebastian Rale.

1853: Portland diocese established.

1854: Know-Nothing uprising resulted in burning of church in Bath.

1856: Anti-Catholic feeling continued; church at Ellsworth burned.

1864: Sisters of Congregation of Notre Dame from Montreal opened academy at Portland.

1875: James A. Healy, first bishop of Negro blood consecrated in U.S., became second Bishop of Portland.

Maryland

1634: Maryland established by Lord Calvert. Two Jesuits among first colonists.

First Mass offered on Island of St. Clement in Lower Potomac by Jesuit Father Andrew White.

St. Mary's founded by English and Irish Catholics.

1641: St. Ignatius Parish founded by English Jesuits at Chapel Point, near Port Tobacco.

1649: Religious Toleration Act passed by Maryland Assembly. It was repealed in 1654 by Puritan-controlled government.

1651: Cecil Calvert, second Lord Baltimore, gave Jesuits 10,000 acres for use as Indian mission.

1658: Lord Baltimore restored Toleration Act.

1672: Franciscans came to Maryland under leadership of Father Massius Massey.

1688: Maryland became royal colony as a result of the Revolution in England; Anglican Church became the official religion (1692); Toleration Act repealed; Catholics disenfranchised and persecuted until 1776.

1704: Jesuits founded St. Francis Xavier Mission, Old Bohemia, to serve Catholics of Delaware, Maryland and southeastern Pennsylvania; its Bohemia Academy established in the 1740s and attended by sons of prominent Catholics in the area.

1784: Father John Carroll appointed prefect apostolic for the territory embraced by new Republic.

1789: Baltimore became first diocese established in U.S., with John Carroll as first bishop.

1790: Carmelite Nuns founded convent at Port Tobacco, the first in the English-speaking Colonies.

1791: First Synod of Baltimore held.

St. Mary's Seminary, first seminary in U.S., established.

1793: Rev. Stephen T. Badin first priest ordained by Bishop Carroll.

1800: Jesuit Leonard Neale became first bishop consecrated in present limits of U.S.

1806: Cornerstone of Assumption Cathedral, Baltimore, was laid.

1808: Baltimore made archdiocese.

1809: St. Joseph's College, first women's college in U.S., founded.

Sisters of Charity of St. Joseph founded by St. Elizabeth Ann Seton; first native American sisterhood.

1821: Assumption Cathedral, Baltimore, formally opened.

1829: Oblate Sisters of Providence, first congregation of black sisters, established at Baltimore by Mother Mary Elizabeth Lange.

First Provincial Council of Baltimore held; six others followed, in 1833, 1837, 1840, 1843, 1846 and 1849.

1836: Roger B. Taney appointed Chief Justice of Supreme Court by President Jackson.

1852: First of the three Plenary Councils of Baltimore convened. Subsequent councils were held in 1866 and 1884.

1855: German Catholic Central Verein founded.

1886: Archbishop James Gibbons of Baltimore made cardinal by Pope Leo XIII.

1965: Archbishop Lawrence Shehan of Baltimore made cardinal by Pope Paul VI.

Massachusetts

1630: New England made a prefecture apostolic in charge of French Capuchins.

1647: Massachusetts Bay Company enacted an anti-priest law.

1688: Hanging of Ann Glover, an elderly Irish Catholic widow, who refused to renounce her Catholic religion.

1732: Although Catholics were not legally admitted to colony, a few Irish families were in Boston; a priest was reported working among them.

1755-56: Acadians landing in Boston were denied services of a Catholic priest.

1775: General Washington discouraged Guy Fawkes Day procession in which pope was carried in effigy, and expressed surprise that there were men in his army "so void of common sense as to insult the religious feelings of the Canadians with whom friendship and an alliance are being sought."

1780: The Massachusetts State Constitution granted religious liberty, but required a religious test to hold public office and provided for tax to support Protestant teachers of piety, religion and morality.

1788: First public Mass said in Boston on Nov. 2 by Abbe de la Poterie, first resident priest.

1803: Church of Holy Cross erected in Boston with financial aid given by Protestants headed by John Adams.

1808: Boston diocese established.

1831: Irish Catholic immigration increased.

1832: St. Vincent's Orphan Asylum, oldest charitable institution in Boston, opened by Sisters of Mercy.

1834: Ursuline Convent in Charlestown burned by a Nativist mob.

1843: Holy Cross College founded.

1855: Catholic militia companies disbanded; nunneries' inspection bill passed.

1859: St. Mary's, first parochial school in Boston, opened.

1860: Portuguese Catholics from Azores settled in New Bedford.

1870: Springfield diocese established.

1875: Boston made archdiocese.

1904: Fall River diocese established.

1911: Archbishop O'Connell of Boston made cardinal by Pope Pius X.

1950: Worcester diocese established.

1958: Archbishop Richard J. Cushing of Boston made cardinal by Pope John XXIII.

1966: Apostolic Exarchate for Melkites in the U.S. established, with headquarters in Boston; made an eparchy (Newton) in 1976.

1973: Archbishop Humberto S. Medeiros of Boston made cardinal by Pope Paul VI.

1985: Archbishop Bernard F. Law of Boston made a cardinal by Pope John Paul II.

Michigan

1641: Jesuits Isaac Jogues and Charles Raymbaut preached to Chippewas; named the rapids Sault Sainte Marie.

1660: Jesuit Rene Menard opened first regular mission in Lake Superior region.

1668: Father Marquette founded Sainte Marie Mission at Sault Sainte Marie.

1671: Father Marquette founded St. Ignace Mission on north shore of Straits of Mackinac.

1701: Fort Pontchartrain founded on present site of Detroit and placed in command of Antoine de la Mothe Cadillac. The Chapel of Sainte-Anne-de-Detroit founded.

1706: Franciscan Father Delhalle killed by Indians at Detroit.

1823: Father Gabriel Richard elected delegate to Congress from Michigan territory; he was the first priest chosen for the House of Representatives.

1833: Father Frederic Baraga celebrated first Mass in present Grand Rapids.

Detroit diocese established, embracing whole Northwest Territory.

1843: *Western Catholic Register* founded at Detroit.

1845: St. Vincent's Hospital, Detroit, opened by Sisters of Charity.

1848: Cathedral of Sts. Peter and Paul, Detroit, consecrated.

1853: Vicariate Apostolic of Upper Michigan established.

1857: Sault Ste. Marie diocese established; later transferred to Marquette.

1877: University of Detroit founded.

1882: Grand Rapids diocese established.

1897: Nazareth College for women founded.

1937: Detroit made archdiocese. Lansing diocese established.

1938: Saginaw diocese established.

1946: Archbishop Edward Mooney of Detroit created cardinal by Pope Pius XII.

1949: Opening of St. John's Theological (major) Seminary at Plymouth; this was first seminary in U.S. serving an entire ecclesiastical province (Detroit).

1966: Apostolic Exarchate for Maronites in the United States established, with headquarters in Detroit; made an eparchy in 1972; transferred to Brooklyn, 1977.

1969: Archbishop John Dearden of Detroit made cardinal by Pope Paul VI.

1971: Gaylord and Kalamazoo dioceses established.

1982: Apostolic Exarchate for Chaldean-Rite Catholics in United States established. Detroit designated see city; made an eparchy, 1985, under title St. Thomas Apostle of Detroit.

1988: Archbishop Edmund C. Szoka of Detroit made a cardinal by Pope John Paul II; transferred to Roman Curia in 1990. (See Index.)

Minnesota

1680: Falls of St. Anthony discovered by Franciscan Louis Hennepin.

1727: First chapel, St. Michael the Archangel, erected near town of Frontenac and placed in charge of French Jesuits.

1732: Fort St. Charles built; Jesuits ministered to settlers.

1736: Jesuit Jean Pierre Aulneau killed by Indians.

1839: Swiss Catholics from Canada settled near Fort Snelling; Bishop Loras of Dubuque, accompanied by Father Pellamourgues, visited the Fort and administered sacraments.

1841: Father Lucian Galtier built Church of St. Paul, thus forming nucleus of modern city of same name.

1850: St. Paul diocese established.

1851: Sisters of St. Joseph arrived in state.

1857: St. John's University founded.

1888: St. Paul made archdiocese; name changed to St. Paul and Minneapolis in 1966.

1889: Duluth, St. Cloud and Winona dioceses established.

1909: Crookston diocese established.

1957: New Ulm diocese established.

Mississippi

1540: Chaplains with De Soto expedition entered territory.

1682: Franciscans Zenobius Membre and Anastase Douay preached to Taensa and Natchez Indians. Father Membre offered first recorded Mass in the state on Mar. 29, Easter Sunday.

1698: Priests of Quebec Seminary founded missions near Natchez and Fort Adams.

1702: Father Nicholas Foucault murdered by Indians near Fort Adams.

1721: Missions practically abandoned, with only Father Juif working among Yazoos.

1725: Jesuit Mathurin de Petit carried on mission work in northern Mississippi.

1729: Indians tomahawked Jesuit Paul du Poisson near Fort Rosalie; Father Jean Souel shot by Yazoos.

1736: Jesuit Antoine Senat and seven French officers burned at stake by Chickasaws.

1822: Vicariate Apostolic of Mississippi and Alabama established.

1825: Mississippi made a separate vicariate apostolic.

1837: Natchez diocese established; became Natchez-Jackson in 1956; transferred to Jackson in 1977.

1848: Sisters of Charity opened orphan asylum and school in Natchez.

1977: Biloxi diocese established.

Missouri

1700: Jesuit Gabriel Marest established a mission among Kaskaskia Indians near St. Louis.

1734: French Catholic miners and traders settled Old Mines and Sainte Genevieve.

1750: Jesuits visited French settlers.

1762: Mission established at St. Charles.

1767: Carondelet mission established.

1770: First church founded at St. Louis.

1811: Jesuits established Indian mission school at Florissant.

1818: Bishop Dubourg arrived at St. Louis, with Vincentians Joseph Rosati and Felix de Andreis. St. Louis University, the diocesan (Kenrick) seminary and the Vincentian Seminary in Perryville trace their origins to them.
Rose Philippine Duchesne arrived at St. Charles; founded first American convent of the Society of the Sacred Heart; missionary; beatified 1940; canonized 1988.

1826: St. Louis diocese established.

1828: Sisters of Charity opened first hospital west of the Mississippi, at St. Louis.

1832: *The Shepherd of the Valley,* first Catholic paper west of the Mississippi.

1845: First conference of Society of St. Vincent de Paul in U.S. founded at St. Louis.

1847: St. Louis made archdiocese.

1865: A Test Oath Law passed by State Legislature (called Drake Convention) to crush Catholicism in Missouri. Law declared unconstitutional by Supreme Court in 1866.

1867: College of St. Teresa for women founded at Kansas City.

1868: St. Joseph diocese established.

1880: Kansas City diocese established.

1946: Archbishop John J. Glennon of St. Louis made cardinal by Pope Pius XII.

1956: Kansas City and St. Joseph dioceses combined into one see. Jefferson City and Springfield-Cape Girardeau dioceses established.

1961: Archbishop Joseph E. Ritter of St. Louis made cardinal by Pope John XXIII.

1969: Archbishop John J. Carberry of St. Louis made cardinal by Pope Paul VI.

Montana

1743: Pierre and Francois Verendrye, accompanied by Jesuit Father Coquart, may have explored territory.

1833: Indian missions handed over to care of Jesuits by Second Provincial Council of Baltimore.

1840: Jesuit Pierre De Smet began missionary work among Flathead and Pend d'Oreille Indians.

1841: St. Mary's Mission established by Father De Smet and two companions on the Bitter Root River in present Stevensville.

1845: Jesuit Antonio Ravalli arrived at St. Mary's Mission; Ravalli County named in his honor.

1859: Fathers Point and Hoecken established St. Peter's Mission near the Great Falls.

1869: Sisters of Charity founded a hospital and school in Helena.

1884: Helena diocese established.

1904: Great Falls diocese established; redesignated Great Falls-Billings in 1980.

1910: Carroll College founded.

1935: Rev. Joseph M. Gilmore became first Montana priest elevated to hierarchy.

Nebraska

1541: Coronado expedition, accompanied by Franciscan Juan de Padilla, reached the Platte River.

1673: Father Marquette visited Nebraska Indians.

1720: Franciscan Juan Miguel killed by Indians near Columbus.

1855: Father J. F. Tracy administered to Catholic settlement of St. Patrick and to Catholics in Omaha.

1856: Land was donated by Governor Alfred Cumming for a church in Omaha.

1857: Nebraska vicariate apostolic established.

1878: Creighton University established.

1881: Poor Clares, first contemplative group in state, arrived in Omaha.
Duchesne College established.

1885: Omaha diocese established.

1887: Lincoln diocese established.

1912: Kearney diocese established; name changed to Grand Island, 1917.

1917: Father Edward Flanagan founded Boy's Town for homeless boys, an institution which gained national and international recognition in subsequent years.

1945: Omaha made archdiocese.

Nevada

1774: Franciscan missionaries passed through Nevada on way to California missions.

1860: First parish, serving Genoa, Carson City and Virginia City, established.

1862: Rev. Patrick Manogue appointed pastor of Virginia City. He established a school for boys and girls, an orphanage and hospital.

1871: Church erected at Reno.

1931: Reno diocese established; name changed to Reno-Las Vegas, 1977.

New Hampshire

1630: Territory made part of a prefecture apostolic embracing all of New England.

1784: State Constitution included a religious test which barred Catholics from public office; local support was provided for public Protestant teachers of religion.

1818: The Barber family of Claremont was visited by their son Virgil (converted to Catholicism in 1816) accompanied by Father Charles Ffrench, O.P. The visit led to the conversion of the entire Barber family.

1823: Father Virgil Barber, minister who became a Jesuit priest, built first Catholic church and school at Claremont.

1830: Church of St. Aloysius dedicated at Dover.
1853: New Hampshire made part of the Portland diocese.
1858: Sisters of Mercy began to teach school at St. Anne's, Manchester.
1877: Catholics obtained full civil liberty and rights.
1884: Manchester diocese established.
1893: St. Anselm's College opened; St. Anselm's Abbey canonically erected.
1937: Francis P. Murphy became first Catholic governor of New Hampshire.

New Jersey

1668: William Douglass of Bergen was refused a seat in General Assembly because he was a Catholic.
1672: Fathers Harvey and Gage visited Catholics in Woodbridge and Elizabethtown.
1701: Tolerance granted to all but "papists." 1744: Jesuit Theodore Schneider of Pennsylvania visited German Catholics of New Jersey.
1762: Fathers Ferdinand Farmer and Robert Harding working among Catholics in state.
1765: First Catholic community organized in New Jersey at Macopin in Passaic County.
1776: State Constitution tacitly excluded Catholics from office.
1799: Foundation of first Catholic school in state, St. John's at Trenton.
1814: First church in Trenton erected.
1820: Father Richard Bulger, of St. John's, Paterson, first resident pastor in state.
1844: Catholics obtained full civil liberty and rights.
1853: Newark diocese established.
1856: Seton Hall University established.
1878: John P. Holland, teacher at St. John's School, Paterson, invented first workable submarine.
1881: Trenton diocese established.
1937: Newark made archdiocese. Paterson and Camden dioceses established.
1947: U.S. Supreme Court ruled on N.J. bus case, permitting children attending non-public schools to ride on buses and be given other health services provided for those in public schools.
1957: Seton Hall College of Medicine and Dentistry established: the first medical school in state; it was run by Seton Hall until 1965.
1963: Byzantine Eparchy of Passaic established.
1981: Metuchen diocese established.

New Mexico

1539: Territory explored by Franciscan Marcos de Niza.
1581: Franciscans Agustin Rodriguez, Juan de Santa Maria and Francisco Lopez named the region "New Mexico"; they later died at hands of Indians.
1598: Juan de Onate founded a colony at Chamita, where first chapel in state was built.
1609-10: Santa Fe founded.
1631: Franciscan Pedro de Miranda was killed by Indians.
1632: Franciscan Francisco Letrado was killed by Indians.
1672: Franciscan Pedro de Avila y Ayala was killed by Indians.

1675: Franciscan Alonso Gil de Avila was killed by Indians.
1680: Pueblo Indian revolt; 21 Franciscan missionaries massacred; missions destroyed.
1692: Franciscan missions refounded and expanded.
1696: Indians rebelled, five more Franciscan missionaries killed.
1850: Jean Baptiste Lamy appointed head of newly established Vicariate Apostolic of New Mexico.
1852: Sisters of Loretto arrived in Santa Fe.
1853: Santa Fe diocese established.
1859: Christian Brothers arrived, established first school for boys in New Mexico (later St. Michael's College).
1865: Sisters of Charity started first orphanage and hospital in Santa Fe. It was closed in 1966.
1875: Santa Fe made archdiocese.
1939: Gallup diocese established.
1982: Las Cruces diocese established.

New York

1524: Giovanni da Verrazano was first white man to enter New York Bay.
1642: Jesuits Isaac Jogues and Rene Goupil were mutilated by Mohawks; Rene Goupil was killed by them shortly afterwards. Dutch Calvinists rescued Father Jogues.
1646: Jesuit Isaac Jogues and John Lalande were martyred by Iroquois at Ossernenon, now Auriesville.
1654: The Onondagas were visited by Jesuits from Canada.
1655: First permanent mission established near Syracuse.
1656: Church of St. Mary erected on Onondaga Lake, in first French settlement within state. Kateri Tekakwitha, "Lily of the Mohawks," was born at Ossernenon, now Auriesville (d. in Canada, 1680). She was beatified in 1980.
1658: Indian uprisings destroyed missions among Cayugas, Senecas and Oneidas.
1664: English took New Amsterdam. Freedom of conscience allowed by the Duke of York, the new Lord Proprietor.
1667: Missions were restored under protection of Garaconthie, Onondaga chief.
1678: Franciscan Louis Hennepin, first white man to describe Niagara Falls, celebrated Mass there.
1682: Thomas Dongan appointed governor by Duke of York.
1683: English Jesuits came to New York, later opened a school.
1700: Although Assembly enacted a bill calling for religious toleration of all Christians in 1683, other penal laws were now enforced against Catholics; all priests were ordered out of the province.
1709: French Jesuit missionaries obliged to give up their central New York missions.
1741: Because of an alleged popish plot to burn city of New York, four whites were hanged and 11 blacks burned at stake.
1774: Elizabeth Bayley Seton, foundress of the American Sisters of Charity, was born in New York City on Aug. 28. She was canonized in 1975.
1777: State Constitution gave religious liberty, but

the naturalization law required an oath to renounce allegiance to any foreign ruler, ecclesiastical as well as civil.

1785: Cornerstone was laid for St. Peter's Church, New York City, first permanent structure of Catholic worship in state.
Trusteeism began to cause trouble at New York.

1806: Anti-Catholic 1777 Test Oath for naturalization repealed.

1808: New York diocese established.

1823: Father Felix Varela of Cuba, educator, theologian and social reformer, arrived in New York; established churches and charitable organizations; published journals and philosophical works.

1828: New York State Legislature enacted a law upholding sanctity of seal of confession.

1834: First native New Yorker to become a secular priest, Rev. John McCloskey, was ordained.

1836: John Nepomucene Neumann arrived from Bohemia and was ordained a priest in Old St. Patrick's Cathedral, New York City. He was canonized in 1977.

1841: Fordham University and Manhattanville College established.

1847: Albany and Buffalo dioceses established.

1850: New York made archdiocese.

1853: Brooklyn diocese established.

1856: Present St. Bonaventure University and Christ the King Seminary founded at Allegany.

1858: Cornerstone was laid of second (present) St. Patrick's Cathedral, New York City. The cathedral was completed in 1879.

1868: Rochester diocese established.

1872: Ogdensburg diocese established.

1875: Archbishop John McCloskey of New York made first American cardinal by Pope Pius IX.

1878: Franciscan Sisters of Allegany were first native American community to send members to foreign missions.

1880: William R. Grace was first Catholic mayor of New York City.

1886: Syracuse diocese established.

1889: Mother Frances Xavier Cabrini arrived in New York City to begin work among Italian immigrants. She was canonized in 1946.

1911: Archbishop John M. Farley of New York made cardinal by Pope Pius X.
Catholic Foreign Mission Society of America (Maryknoll) opened a seminary for foreign missions, the first of its kind in U.S. The Maryknollers were also unique as the first U.S.-established foreign mission society.

1917: Military Ordinariate established with headquarters at New York; renamed Military Archdiocese and transferred to Washington, D.C., in 1985.

1919: Alfred E. Smith became first elected Catholic governor.

1924: Archbishop Patrick Hayes of New York made cardinal by Pope Pius XI.

1930: Jesuit Martyrs of New York and Canada were canonized on June 29.

1946: Archbishop Francis J. Spellman of New York made cardinal by Pope Pius XII.

1957: Rockville Centre diocese established.

1969: Archbishop Terence Cooke of New York made cardinal by Pope Paul VI.

1981: Apostolic Exarchate for Armenian-Rite Catholics in the United States and Canada established. New York designated see city.

1985: Archbishop John J. O'Connor of New York made cardinal by Pope John Paul II.

North Carolina

1526: The Ayllon expedition attempted to establish a settlement on Carolina coast.

1540: De Soto expedition, accompanied by chaplains, entered state.

1776: State Constitution denied office to "those who denied the truths of the Protestant religion."

1805: The few Catholics in state were served by visiting missionaries.

1821: Bishop John England of Charleston celebrated Mass in the ballroom of the home of William Gaston at New Bern, marking the start of organization of the first parish, St. Paul's, in the state.

1835: William Gaston, State Supreme Court Justice, succeeded in having the article denying religious freedom repealed.

1852: First Catholic church erected in Charlotte.

1868: North Carolina vicariate apostolic established. Catholics obtained full civil liberty and rights.

1874: Sisters of Mercy arrived, opened an academy, several schools, hospitals and an orphanage.

1876: Benedictine priory and school (later Belmont Abbey College) founded at Belmont; priory designated an abbey in 1884.

1910: Belmont Abbey established as an abbacy nullius; abbacy nullius status suppressed in 1977.

1924: Raleigh diocese established.

1971: Charlotte diocese established.

North Dakota

1742: Pierre and Francois Verendrye, accompanied by Jesuit Father Coquart, explored territory.

1818: Canadian priests ministered to Catholics in area.

1840: Jesuit Father De Smet made first of several trips among Mandan and Gros Ventre Indians.

1848: Father George Belcourt, first American resident priest in territory, reestablished Pembina Mission.

1874: Grey Nuns arrived at Fort Totten to conduct a school.

1889: Jamestown diocese established; transferred to Fargo in 1897.

1893: Benedictines founded St. Gall Monastery at Devil's Lake. (It was moved to Richardton in 1899 and became an abbey in 1903.)

1909: Bismarck diocese established.

1959: Archbishop Aloysius J. Muench, bishop of Fargo, made cardinal by Pope John XXIII.

Ohio

1749: Jesuits in expedition of Céleron de Blainville preached to Indians.
First religious services were held within present limits of Ohio. Jesuit Joseph de Bonnecamps celebrated Mass at mouth of Little Miami River and in other places.

1751: First Catholic settlement founded among Huron Indians near Sandusky by Jesuit Father de la Richardie.

1790: Benedictine Pierre Didier ministered to French immigrants.

1812: Bishop Flaget of Bardstown visited and baptized Catholics of Lancaster and Somerset Counties.

1818: Dominican Father Edward Fenwick (later first bishop of Cincinnati) built St. Joseph's Church and established first Dominican convent in Ohio.

1821: Cincinnati diocese established.

1831: Xavier University founded.

1843: Members of Congregation of Most Precious Blood arrived in Cincinnati from Switzerland.

1845: Cornerstone laid for St. Peter's Cathedral, Cincinnati.

1847: Cleveland diocese established.

1850: Cincinnati made archdiocese.
Marianists opened St. Mary's Institute, now University of Dayton.

1865: Sisters of Charity opened hospital in Cleveland, first institution of its kind in city.

1868: Columbus diocese established.

1871: Ursuline College for women opened at Cleveland.

1910: Toledo diocese established.

1935: Archbishop John T. McNicholas, O.P., founded the Institutum Divi Thomae in Cincinnati for fundamental research in natural sciences.

1943: Youngstown diocese established.

1944: Steubenville diocese established.

1969: Byzantine Rite Eparchy of Parma (for Ruthenians) established.

1982: Apostolic Exarchate for Romanian Byzantine-Rite Catholics in the United States established. Canton designated see city. Raised to an eparchy (St. George Martyr) 1987.

1983: Byzantine Rite Eparchy of Saint Josaphat in Parma (for Ukraianians) established.

Oklahoma

1540: De Soto expedition, accompanied by chaplains, explored territory.

1541: Coronado expedition, accompanied by Franciscan Juan de Padilla, explored state.

1630: Spanish Franciscan Juan de Salas labored among Indians.

1700: Scattered Catholic families were visited by priests from Kansas and Arkansas.

1874: First Catholic church built by Father Smyth at Atoka.

1876: Prefecture Apostolic of Indian Territory established with Benedictine Isidore Robot as its head.

1886: First Catholic day school for Choctaw and white children opened by Sisters of Mercy at Krebs.

1891: Vicariate Apostolic of Oklahoma and Indian Territory established.

1905: Oklahoma diocese established; title changed to Oklahoma City and Tulsa, 1930.

1917: Benedictine Heights College for women founded.
Carmelite Sisters of St. Theresa of the Infant Jesus founded at Oklahoma City.

1972: Oklahoma City made archdiocese. Tulsa diocese established.

Oregon

1603: Vizcaino explored northern Oregon coast.

1774: Franciscan missionaries accompanied Juan Perez on his expedition to coast, and Heceta a year later.

1811: Catholic Canadian trappers and traders with John J. Astor expedition founded first American settlement — Astoria.

1834: Indian missions in Northwest entrusted to Jesuits by Holy See.

1838: Abbe Blanchet appointed vicar general to Bishop of Quebec with jurisdiction over area which included Oregon Territory.

1839: First Mass celebrated at present site of St. Paul.

1843: Oregon vicariate apostolic established.
St. Joseph's College for boys opened.

1844: Jesuit Pierre de Smet established Mission of St. Francis Xavier near St. Paul.
Sisters of Notre Dame de Namur, first to enter Oregon, opened an academy for girls.

1846: Vicariate made an ecclesiastical province with Bishop Blanchet as first Archbishop of Oregon City (now Portland).
Walla Walla diocese established; suppressed in 1853.

1847: First priest was ordained in Oregon.

1848: First Provincial Council of Oregon.

1857: Death of Dr. John McLoughlin, "Father of Oregon."

1865: Rev. H. H. Spalding, a Protestant missionary, published the Whitman Myth to hinder work of Catholic missionaries.

1874: Catholic Indian Mission Bureau established.

1875: St. Vincent's Hospital, first in state, opened at Portland.

1903: Baker diocese established.

1922: Anti-private school bill sponsored by Scottish Rite Masons was passed by popular vote, 115,506 to 103,685.

1925: U.S. Supreme Court declared Oregon anti-private school bill unconstitutional.

1953: First Trappist monastery on West Coast established in Willamette Valley north of Lafayette.

Pennsylvania

1673: Priests from Maryland ministered to Catholics in the Colony.

1682: Religious toleration was extended to members of all faiths.

1729: Jesuit Joseph Greaton became first resident missionary of Philadelphia.

1734: St. Joseph's Church, first Catholic church in Philadelphia, was opened by Father Greaton.

1741: Jesuit Fathers Schneider and Wappeler ministered to German immigrants.
Conewego Chapel, a combination chapel and dwelling, was built by Father William Wappeler, S.J., a priest sent to minister to the German Catholic immigrants who settled in the area in the 1730s.

1782: St. Mary's Parochial School opened at Philadelphia.

1788: Holy Trinity Church, Philadelphia, was incorporated; first exclusively national church organized in U.S.

1797: Augustinian Matthew Carr founded St. Augustine parish, Philadelphia.

1799: Prince Demetrius Gallitzin (Father Augustine Smith) built church in western Pennsylvania, at Loretto.

1808: Philadelphia diocese established.

1814: St. Joseph's Orphanage was opened at Philadelphia; first Catholic institution for children in U.S.

1842: University of Villanova founded by Augustinians.

1843: Pittsburgh diocese established.

1844: Thirteen persons killed, two churches and a school burned in Know-Nothing riots at Philadelphia.

1846: First Benedictine Abbey in New World founded near Latrobe by Father Boniface Wimmer.

1852: Redemptorist John Nepomucene Neumann became fourth bishop of Philadelphia. He was beatified in 1963 and canonized in 1977.

1853: Erie diocese established.

1868: Scranton and Harrisburg dioceses established.

1871: Chestnut Hill College, first for women in state, founded.

1875: Philadelphia made archdiocese.

1891: Katharine Drexel founded Sisters of Blessed Sacrament for Indians and Colored Peoples. She was beatified in 1988. (See Index.)

1901: Altoona-Johnstown diocese established.

1913: Byzantine Rite Apostolic Exarchate of Philadelphia established; became metropolitan see, 1958.

1921: Archbishop Dennis Dougherty made cardinal by Pope Benedict XV.

1924: Byzantine Rite Apostolic Exarchate of Pittsburgh established; made an eparchy in 1963; raised to metropolitan status and transferred to Munhall, 1969; transferred back to Pittsburgh in 1977.

1951: Greensburg diocese established.

1958: Archbishop John O'Hara, C.S.C., of Philadelphia made cardinal by Pope John.

1961: Allentown diocese established.

1967: Archbishop John J. Krol of Philadelphia made cardinal by Pope Paul VI.

1969: Bishop John J. Wright of Pittsburgh made cardinal by Pope Paul VI and transferred to Curia post.

1976: The 41st International Eucharistic Congress, the second held in the U.S., convened in Philadelphia, August 1-8.

1985: Major Archbishop Myroslav Lubachivsky of the Major Archbishopric of Lviv of the Ukrainians, former metropolitan of Byzan- tine-rite Philadelphia archeparchy (1979-80), made cardinal by Pope John Paul II.

1991: Archbishop Anthony J. Bevilacqua of Phildelphia made cardinal by Pope John Paul II.

Rhode Island

1663: Colonial Charter granted freedom of conscience.

1719: Laws denied Catholics the right to hold public office.

1829: St. Mary's Church, Pawtucket, was first Catholic church in state.

1837: Parochial schools inaugurated in state.

First Catholic church in Providence was built.

1851: Sisters of Mercy began work in Rhode Island.

1872: Providence diocese established.

1900: Trappists took up residence in state.

1917: Providence College founded.

South Carolina

1569: Jesuit Juan Rogel was the first resident priest in the territory.

1573: First Franciscans arrived in southeastern section.

1606: Bishop Altamirano conducted visitation of area.

1655: Franciscans had two missions among Indians; later destroyed by English.

1697: Religious liberty granted to all except "papists."

1790: Catholics given right to vote.

1820: Charleston diocese established.

1822: Bishop England founded *U.S. Catholic Miscellany*, first Catholic paper of a strictly religious nature in U.S.

1830: Sisters of Our Lady of Mercy, first in state, took up residence at Charleston.

1847: Cornerstone of Cathedral of St. John the Baptist, Charleston, was laid.

1861: Cathedral and many institutions destroyed in Charleston fire.

South Dakota

1842: Father Augustine Ravoux began ministrations to French and Indians at Fort Pierre, Vermilion and Prairie du Chien; printed devotional book in Sioux language the following year.

1867: Parish organized among the French at Jefferson.

1878: Benedictines opened school for Sioux children at Fort Yates.

1889: Sioux Falls diocese established.

1902: Lead diocese established; transferred to Rapid City, 1930.

1950: Mount Marty College for women established.

1952: Blue Cloud Abbey, first Benedictine foundation in state, was dedicated.

Tennessee

1541: Cross planted on shore of Mississippi by De Soto; accompanying the expedition were Fathers John de Gallegos and Louis De Soto.

1682: Franciscan Fathers Membre and Douay accompanied La Salle to present site of Memphis; may have offered the first Masses in the territory.

1800: Catholics were served by priests from Bardstown, Ky.

1822: Non-Catholics assisted in building church in Nashville.

1837: Nashville diocese established.

1843: Sisters of Charity opened a school for girls in Nashville.

1871: Christian Brothers opened a school for boys in Memphis; it later became Christian Brothers College (now University).

1921: Sisters of St. Dominic opened Siena College for women at Memphis; closed in 1971.

1970: Memphis diocese established.

1988: Knoxville diocese established.

Texas

1541: Missionaries with Coronado expedition probably entered territory.

1553: Dominicans Diego de la Cruz, Hernando Mendez, Juan Ferrer, Brother Juan de Mina killed by Indians.

1675: Bosque-Larios missionary expedition entered region; Father Juan Larios offered first recorded high Mass.

1682: Mission Corpus Christi de Isleta (Ysleta) founded by Franciscans near El Paso, first mission in present-day Texas.

1690: Mission San Francisco de los Tejas founded in east Texas.

1703: Mission San Francisco de Solano founded on Rio Grande; rebuilt in 1718 as San Antonio de Valero or the Alamo.

1717: Franciscan Antonio Margil founded six missions in northeast.

1720: San Jose y San Miguel de Aguayo Mission founded by Fray Antonio Margil de Jesus.

1721: Franciscan Brother Jose Pita killed by Indians at Carnezeria.

1728: Site of San Antonio settled.

1738: Construction of San Fernando Cathedral at San Antonio.

1744: Mission church of the Alamo built.

1750: Franciscan Francisco Xavier was killed by Indians; so were Jose Ganzabal in 1752, and Alonzo Ferrares and Jose San Esteban in 1758.

1793: Mexico secularized missions.

1825: Governments of Cohuila and Texas secularized all Indian missions.

1838-39: Irish priests ministered to settlements of Refugio and San Patricio.

1841: Vicariate of Texas established.

1847: Ursuline Sisters established their first academy in territory at Galveston.
Galveston diocese established.

1852: Oblate Fathers and Franciscans arrived in Galveston to care for new influx of German Catholics.
St. Mary's College founded at San Antonio.

1854: Know-Nothing Party began to stir up hatred against Catholics.

1858: Texas Legislature passed law entitling all schools granting free scholarships and meeting state requirements to share in school fund.

1874: San Antonio diocese established.
Vicariate of Brownsville established.

1881: St. Edward's College founded: became first chartered college in state in 1889.
Sisters of Charity founded Incarnate Word College at San Antonio.

1890: Dallas diocese established; changed to Dallas-Ft. Worth, 1953; made two separate dioceses, 1969.

1912: Corpus Christi diocese established.

1914: El Paso diocese established.

1926: San Antonio made archdiocese. Amarillo diocese established.

1947: Austin diocese established.

1959: Galveston diocese redesignated Galveston-Houston.

1961: San Angelo diocese established.

1965: Brownsville diocese established.

1966: Beaumont diocese established.

1982: Victoria diocese established.

1983: Lubbock diocese established.

1986: Tyler diocese established.

Utah

1776: Franciscans Silvestre de Escalante and Atanasio Dominguez reached Utah (Salt) Lake; first white men known to enter the territory.

1858: Jesuit Father De Smet accompanied General Harney as chaplain on expedition sent to settle troubles between Mormons and U.S. Government.

1866: On June 29 Father Edward Kelly offered first Mass in Salt Lake City in Mormon Assembly Hall.

1886: Utah vicariate apostolic established.

1891: Salt Lake City diocese established.

1926: College of St. Mary-of-the-Wasatch for women was founded.

Vermont

1609: Champlain expedition passed through territory.

1666: Captain La Motte built fort and shrine of St. Anne on Isle La Motte; Sulpician Father Dollier de Casson celebrated first Mass.

1668: Bishop Laval of Quebec (beatified in 1980), administered confirmation in region; this was the first area in northeastern U.S. to receive an episcopal visit.

1710: Jesuits ministered to Indians near Lake Champlain.

1793: Discriminatory measures against Catholics were repealed.

1830: Father Jeremiah O'Callaghan became first resident priest in state.

1853: Burlington diocese established.

1854: Sisters of Charity of Providence arrived to conduct St. Joseph's Orphanage at Burlington.

1904: St. Michael's College founded.

1951: First Carthusian foundation in America established at Whitingham.

Virginia

1526: Dominican Antonio de Montesinos offered first Mass on Virginia soil.

1561: Dominicans visited the coast.

1571: Father John Baptist de Segura and seven Jesuit companions killed by Indians.

1642: Priests outlawed and Catholics denied right to vote.

1689: Capuchin Christopher Plunket was captured and exiled to a coastal island where he died in 1697.

1776: Religious freedom granted.

1791: Father Jean Dubois arrived at Richmond with letters from Lafayette. The House of Dele- gates was placed at his disposal for celebration of Mass.
A church was built in Norfolk (St. Mary of the Immaculate Conception). It was designated a minor basilica in 1991.

1796: A church was built at Alexandria.

1820: Richmond diocese established.

1822: Trusteeism created serious problems in diocese; Bishop Kelly resigned the see.

1848: Sisters of Charity opened an orphan asylum at Norfolk.
1866: School Sisters of Notre Dame and Sisters of Charity opened academies for girls at Richmond.
1974: Arlington diocese established.

Washington

1774: Spaniards explored the region.
1838: Fathers Blanchet and Demers, "Apostles of the Northwest," were sent to territory by archbishop of Quebec.
1840: Cross erected on Whidby Island, Puget Sound.
1843: Vicariate Apostolic of Oregon, including Washington, was established.
1844: Mission of St. Paul founded at Colville. Six Sisters of Notre Dame de Namur began work in area.
1850: Nesqually diocese established; transferred to Seattle, 1907.
1856: Providence Academy, the first permanent Catholic school in the Northwest, was built at Fort Vancouver by Mother Joseph Pariseau of the Sisters of Charity of Providence.
1887: Gonzaga University founded.
1913: Spokane diocese established.
1951: Seattle made archdiocese. Yakima diocese established.

West Virginia

1749: Father Joseph de Bonnecamps, accompanying the Bienville expedition, may have offered first Mass in the territory.
1821: First Catholic church in Wheeling.
1838: Sisters of Charity founded school at Martinsburg.
1848: Visitation Nuns established academy for girls in Wheeling.
1850: Wheeling diocese established; name changed to Wheeling-Charleston, 1974. Wheeling Hospital incorporated, the oldest Catholic charitable institution in territory.
1955: Wheeling College established.

Wisconsin

1661: Jesuit Rene Menard, first known missionary in the territory, was killed or lost in the Black River district.
1665: Jesuit Claude Allouez founded Mission of the Holy Ghost at La Pointe Chegoimegon, now Bayfield; was the first permanent mission in region.
1673: Father Marquette and Louis Joliet traveled from Green Bay down the Wisconsin and Mississippi rivers.
1762: Suppression of Jesuits in French Colonies closed many missions for 30 years.
1843: Milwaukee diocese established.
1853: St. John's Cathedral, Milwaukee, was built.
1864: State charter granted for establishment of Marquette University. First students admitted, 1881.
1868: Green Bay and La Crosse dioceses established.
1875: Milwaukee made archdiocese.
1905: Superior diocese established.
1946: Madison diocese established.

Wyoming

1840: Jesuit Pierre de Smet offered first Mass near Green River.
1851: Father De Smet held peace conference with Indians near Fort Laramie.
1867: Father William Kelly, first resident priest, arrived in Cheyenne and built first church a year later.
1873: Father Eugene Cusson became first resident pastor in Laramie.
1875: Sisters of Charity of Leavenworth opened school and orphanage at Laramie.
1884: Jesuits took over pastoral care of Shoshone and Arapaho Indians.
1887: Cheyenne diocese established.
1949: Weston Memorial Hospital opened near Newcastle.

Puerto Rico

1493: Island discovered by Columbus on his second voyage; he named it San Juan de Borinquen (the Indian name for Puerto Rico).
1509: Juan Ponce de Leon, searching for gold, colonized the island and became its first governor; present population descended mainly from early Spanish settlers.
1511: Diocese of Puerto Rico established as suffragan of Seville, Spain; Bishop Alonso Manso, sailing from Spain in 1512, became first bishop to take up residence in New World.
1645: Synod held in Puerto Rico to regulate frequency of Masses according to distances people had to walk.
1898: Puerto Rico ceded to U.S. (became self-governing Commonwealth in 1952); inhabitants granted U.S. citizenship in 1917.
1924: Diocese of Puerto Rico renamed San Juan de Puerto Rico and made immediately subject to the Holy See; Ponce diocese established.
1948: Catholic University of Puerto Rico founded at Ponce through efforts of Most Rev. James E. McManus, C.SS.R., bishop of Ponce, 1947-63.
1960: San Juan made metropolitan see. Arecibo diocese established.
1964: Caguas diocese established.
1973: Archbishop Luis Aponte Martinez of San Juan made first native Puerto Rican cardinal by Pope Paul VI.
1976: Mayaguez diocese established. Virgin of Providence officially approved as Patroness of Puerto Rico by Pope Paul VI.

CATHOLICS IN PRESIDENTS' CABINETS

From 1789 to 1940, nine Catholics were appointed to cabinet posts by six of 32 presidents. The first was Roger Brooke Taney (later named first Catholic Supreme Court Justice) who was appointed in 1831 by Pres. Andrew Jackson. Catholics have been appointed to cabinet posts from the time of Pres. Franklin D. Roosevelt to the present.

Listed below in chronological order are presidents, Catholic cabinet officials, posts held, dates.

Andrew Jackson — Roger B. **Taney,** Attorney General, 1831-33, Secretary of Treasury, 1833-34.

Franklin Pierce — James **Campbell,** Postmaster General, 1853-57.

James Buchanan — John B. **Floyd,** Secretary of War, 1857-61.

William McKinley — Joseph **McKenna,** Attorney General, 1897-98.

Theodore Roosevelt — Robert J. **Wynne,** Postmaster General, 1904-05; Charles **Bonaparte,** Secretary of Navy, 1905-06, Attorney General, 1906-09.

Franklin D. Roosevelt — James A. **Farley,** Postmaster General, 1933-40; Frank **Murphy,** Attorney General, 1939-40; Frank C. **Walker,** Postmaster General, 1940-45.

Harry S. Truman — Robert E. **Hannegan,** Postmaster General, 1945-47; J. Howard **McGrath,** Attorney General, 1949-52; Maurice J. **Tobin,** Secretary of Labor, 1948-53; James P. **McGranery,** Attorney General, 1952-53.

Dwight D. Eisenhower — Martin P. **Durkin,** Secretary of Labor, 1953; James P. **Mitchell,** Secretary of Labor, 1953-61.

John F. Kennedy — Robert F. **Kennedy,** Attorney General, 1961-63; Anthony **Celebrezze,** Secretary of Health, Education and Welfare, 1962-63; John S. **Gronouski,** Postmaster General, 1963.

Lyndon B. Johnson — (Robert F. **Kennedy,** 1963-65, Anthony **Celebrezze,** 1963-65, and John S. **Gronouski,** 1963-65, reappointed to posts held in Kennedy Cabinet — see above.) John T. **Connor,** Secretary of Commerce, 1965-67; Lawrence **O'Brien,** Postmaster General, 1965-68.

Richard M. Nixon — Walter J. **Hickel,** Secretary of Interior, 1969-71; John A. **Volpe,** Secretary of Transportation, 1969-72; Maurice H. **Stans,** Secretary of Commerce, 1969-72; Peter J. **Brennan,** Secretary of Labor, 1973-74; William E. **Simon,** Secretary of Treasury, 1974.

Gerald R. Ford — (Peter J. **Brennan,** 1974-75, and William E. **Simon,** 1974-76, reappointed to posts held above.)

Jimmy Carter — Joseph **Califano, Jr.,** Secretary of Health, Education and Welfare, 1977-79; Benjamin **Civiletti,** Attorney General, 1979-81; Moon **Landrieu,** Secretary of Housing and Urban Development, 1979-81; Edmund S. **Muskie,** Secretary of State, 1980-81.

Ronald Reagan — Alexander M. **Haig,** Secretary of State, 1981-82; Raymond J. **Donovan,** Secretary of Labor, 1981-84; Margaret M. **Heckler,** Secretary of Health and Human Services, 1983-85; William J. **Bennett,** Secretary of Education, 1985-88; Ann Dore **McLaughlin,** Secretary of Labor, 1988-89; Lauro F. **Cavazos,** Secretary of Education, 1988-89; Nicholas F. **Brady,** Secretary of Treasury, 1988-89.

George Bush — Lauro F. **Cavazos** (reappointed), Secretary of Education, 1989-90; Nicholas F. **Brady** (reappointed), Secretary of Treasury, 1989-93 ; James D. **Watkins,** Secretary of Energy, 1989-93; Manuel **Lujan, Jr.,** Secretary of Interior, 1989-93 ; Edward J. **Derwinski,** Secretary of Veteran Affairs, 1989-93; Lynn **Martin,** Secretary of Labor, 1990-93; Edward **Madigan,** Secretary of Agriculture, 1991-93; William P. **Barr,** Attorney General, 1991-93.

Cabinet members who became Catholics after leaving their posts were: Thomas Ewing, Secretary of Treasury under William A. Harrison, and Secretary of Interior under Zachary Taylor; Luke E. Wright, Secretary of War under Theodore Roosevelt; Albert B. Fall, Secretary of Interior under Warren G. Harding.

CATHOLIC SUPREME COURT JUSTICES

Roger B. Taney, Chief Justice 1836-64; app. by Andrew Jackson.

Edward D. White, Associate Justice 1894-1910, app. by Grover Cleveland; Chief Justice 1910-21, app. by William H. Taft.

Joseph McKenna, Associate Justice 1898-1925; app. by William McKinley.

Pierce Butler, Associate Justice 1923-39; app. by Warren G. Harding.

Frank Murphy, Associate Justice 1940-49; app. by Franklin D. Roosevelt.

William Brennan, Associate Justice 1956-90; app. by Dwight D. Eisenhower.

Antonin Scalia, Associate Justice 1986-; app. by Ronald Reagan.

Anthony M. Kennedy, Associate Justice 1988-; app. by Ronald Reagan.

Sherman Minton, Associate Justice from 1949 to 1956, became a Catholic several years before his death in 1965.

CATHOLICS IN STATUARY HALL

Statues of 13 Catholics deemed worthy of national commemoration by the donating states are among those enshrined in National Statuary Hall and other places in the U.S. Capitol. The Hall, formerly the chamber of the House of Representatives, was erected by Act of Congress July 2, 1864.

Donating states, names and years of placement are listed.

Arizona: Rev. Eusebio Kino, S. J., missionary, 1965.

California: Rev. Junipero Serra, O. F. M. missionary, 1931. (Beatified 1988.)

Hawaii: Father Damien, missionary, 1969.

Illinois: Gen. James Shields, statesman, 1893.

Louisiana: Edward D. White, Justice of the U.S. Supreme Court (1894-1921), 1955.

Maryland: Charles Carroll, statesman, 1901.

Nevada: Patrick A. McCarran, statesman, 1960.

New Mexico: Dennis Chavez, statesman, 1966. (Archbishop Jean B. Lamy, pioneer prelate of Santa Fe, was nominated for Hall honor in 1951.)

North Dakota: John Burke, U.S. treasurer, 1963.

Oregon: Dr. John McLoughlin, pioneer, 1953.

Washington: Mother Mary Joseph Pariseau, pioneer missionary and humanitarian.

West Virginia: John E. Kenna, statesman, 1901.

Wisconsin: Rev. Jacques Marquette, S.J., missionary, explorer, 1895.

CHURCH-STATE DECISIONS OF THE SUPREME COURT

(Among sources of this selected listing of U.S. Supreme Court decisions was *The Supreme Court on Church and State,* Joseph Tussman, editor; Oxford University Press, New York, 1962.)

Watson v. Jones, 13 Wallace 679 (1872): The Court declared that a member of a religious organization may not appeal to secular courts against a decision made by a church tribunal within the area of its competence.

Polygamy: The Mormon practice of polygamy was at

issue in three decisions and was declared unconstitutional: Reynolds v. United States, 98 US 145 (1879); Davis v. Beason, 133 US 333 (1890); Church of Latter-Day Saints v. United States, 136 US 1 (1890).

Bradfield v. Roberts, 175 US 291 (1899): The Court denied that an appropriation of government funds for an institution (Providence Hospital, Washington, D.C.) run by Roman Catholic sisters violated the No Establishment Clause of the First Amendment.

Pierce v. Society of Sisters, 268 US 510 (1925): The Court denied that a state can require children to attend public schools only. The Court held that the liberty of the Constitution forbids standardization by such compulsion, and that the parochial schools involved had claims to protection under the Fourteenth Amendment.

Cochran v. Board of Education, 281 US 370 (1930): The Court upheld a Louisiana statute providing textbooks at public expense for children attending public or parochial schools. The Court held that the children and state were beneficiaries of the appropriations, with incidental secondary benefit going to the schools.

United States v. MacIntosh, 283 US 605 (1931): The Court denied that anyone can place allegiance to the will of God above his allegiance to the government since such a person could make his own interpretation of God's will the decisive test as to whether he would or would not obey the nation's law. The Court stated that the nation, which has a duty to survive, can require citizens to bear arms in its defense.

Everson v. Board of Education, 330 US 1 (1947): The Court upheld the constitutionality of a New Jersey statute authorizing free school bus transportation for parochial as well as public school students. The Court expressed the opinion that the benefits of public welfare legislation, included under such bus transportation, do not run contrary to the concept of separation of Church and State.

McCollum v. Board of Education, 333 US 203 (1948): The Court declared unconstitutional a program for releasing children, with parental consent, from public school classes so they could receive religious instruction on public school premises from representatives of their own faiths.

Zorach v. Clauson, 343 US 306 (1952): The Court upheld the constitutionality of a New York statute permitting, on a voluntary basis, the release during school time of students from public school classes for religious instruction given off public school premises.

Torcaso v. Watkins, 367 US 488 (1961): THe Court declared unconstitutional a Maryland requirement that one must make a declaration of belief in the existence of God as part of the oath of office for notaries public.

McGowan v. Maryland, 81 Sp Ct 1101; **Two Guys from Harrison v. McGinley,** 81 Sp Ct 1135; **Gallagher v. Crown Kosher Super Market,** 81 Sp Ct 1128; **Braunfield v. Brown,** 81 Sp Ct 1144 (1961): The Court ruled that Sunday closing laws do not violate the No Establishment of Religion Clause of the First Amendment, even though the laws were religious in their inception and still have some religious overtones. The Court held that, "as presently written and administered, most of them, at least, are of a secular rather than of a religious character, and that presently they bear no relationship to establishment of religion as those words are used in the Constitution of the United States."

Engel v. Vitale, 370 US 42 (1962): The Court declared that the voluntary recitation in public schools of a prayer composed by the New York State Board of Regents is unconstitutional on the ground that it violates the No Establishment of Religion Clause of the First Amendment.

Abington Township School District v. Schempp and Murray v. Curlett, 83 Sp Ct 1560 (1963): The Court ruled that Bible reading and recitation of the Lord's Prayer in public schools, with voluntary participation by students, are unconstitutional on the ground that they violate the No Establishment of Religion Clause of the First Amendment.

Chamberlin v. Dade County, 83 Sp Ct 1864 (1964): The Court reversed a decision of the Florida Supreme Court concerning the constitutionality of prayer and devotional Bible reading in public schools during the school day, as sanctioned by a state statute which specifically related the practices to a sound public purpose.

Board of Education v. Allen, No. 660 (1968): The Court declared constitutional the New York school book loan law which requires local school boards to purchase books with state funds and lend them to parochial and private school students.

Walz v. Tax Commission of New York (1970): The Court upheld the constitutionality of a New York statute exempting church-owned property from taxation.

Earle v. DiCenso, Robinson v. DiCenso, Lemon v. Kurtzman, Tilton v. Richardson (1971): In Earle v. DiCenso and Robinson v. DiCenso, the Court ruled unconstitutional a 1969 Rhode Island statute which provided salary supplements to teachers of secular subjects in parochial schools; in Lemon v. Kurtzman, the Court ruled unconstitutional a 1968 Pennsylvania statute which authorized the state to purchase services for the teaching of secular subjects in nonpublic schools. The principal argument against constitutionality in these cases was that the statutes and programs at issue entailed excessive entanglement of government with religion. In Tilton v. Richardson, the Court held that this argument did not apply to a prohibitive degree with respect to federal grants, under the Higher Education Facilities Act of 1963, for the construction of facilities for nonreligious purposes by four church-related institutions of higher learning, three of which were Catholic, in Connecticut.

Amish Decision (1972): In a case appealed on behalf of Yoder, Miller and Yutzy, the Court ruled that Amish parents were exempt from a Wisconsin statute requiring them to send their children to school until the age of 16. The Court said in its decision that secondary schooling exposed Amish children to attitudes, goals and values contrary to their beliefs, and substantially hindered "the religious development of the Amish child and his integration into the way of life of the Amish faith-community at the crucial adolescent state of development."

Committee for Public Education and Religious Liberty, et al., v. Nyquist, et al., No. 72-694 (1973): The Court ruled that provisions of a 1972 New York statute were unconstitutional on the grounds that they were violative of the No Establishment Clause of the First Amendment and had the "impermissible effect" of advancing the sectarian activities of church-affiliated schools. The programs ruled unconstitutional concerned: (1) maintenance and repair grants, for facilities and equipment, to ensure the health, welfare and safety of students in nonpublic, non-profit elementary and secondary schools serving a high concentration of students from low income families; (2) tuition reimbursement ($50 per grade school child, $100 per high school student) for parents (with income less than $5,000) of children attending nonpublic elementary or secondary schools; tax deduction from adjusted gross income for parents failing to qualify under the above reimbursement plan, for each child attending a nonpublic school.

Sloan, Treasurer of Pennsylvania, et al., v. Lemon, et al., No. 72-459 (1973): The Court ruled unconstitutional a Pennsylvania Parent Reimbursement Act for Nonpublic Education which provided funds to reimburse parents (to a maximum of $150) for a portion of tuition expenses incurred in sending their children to nonpublic schools. The Court held that there was no significant difference between this and the New York tuition reimbursement program (above), and declared that the Equal Protection Clause of the Fourteenth Amendment cannot be relied upon to sustain a program held to be violative of the No Establishment Clause.

Levitt, et al., v. Committee for Public Education and Religious Liberty, et al., No. 72-269 (1973): The Court ruled unconstitutional the Mandated Services Act of 1970 under which New York provided $28 million ($27 per pupil from first to seventh grade, $45 per pupil from seventh to 12th grade) to reimburse nonpublic schools for testing, recording and reporting services required by the state. The Court declared that the act provided "impermissible aid" to religion in contravention of the No Establishment Clause.

In related decisions handed down June 25, 1973, the Court: (1) affirmed a lower court decision against the constitutionality of an Ohio tax credit law benefiting parents with children in nonpublic schools; (2) reinstated an injunction against a parent reimbursement program in New Jersey; (3) affirmed South Carolina's right to grant construction loans to church-affiliated colleges, and dismissed an appeal contesting its right to provide loans to students attending church-affiliated colleges (**Hunt v. McNair, Durham v. McLeod).**

Wheeler v. Barrera (1974): The Court ruled that nonpublic school students in Missouri must share in federal funds for educationally deprived students on a comparable basis with public school students under Title I of the Elementary and Secondary Education Act of 1965.

Norwood v. Harrison (93 S. Ct. 2804): The Court ruled that public assistance which avoids the prohibitions of the "effect" and "entanglement" tests (and which therefore does not substantially promote the religious mission of sectarian schools) may be confined to the secular functions of such schools.

Wiest v. Mt. Lebanon School District (1974): The Court upheld a lower court ruling that invocation and benediction prayers at public high school commencement ceremonies do not violate the principle of separation of Church and state.

Meek v. Pittenger (1975): The Court ruled unconstitutional portions of a Pennsylvania law providing auxiliary services for students of nonpublic schools; at the same time, it ruled in favor of provisions of the law permitting textbook loans to students of such schools. In denying the constitutionality of auxiliary services, the Court held that they had the "primary effect of establishing religion" and involved "excessive entanglement" of Church and state officials with respect to supervision; objection was also made against providing such services only on the premises of non-public schools and only at the request of such schools.

TWA, Inc., v. Hardison, 75-1126; **International Association of Machinists and Aero Space Workers v. Hardison,** 75-1385 (1977): The Court ruled that federal civil rights legislation does not require employers to make more than minimal efforts to accommodate employees who want a particular working day off as their religion's Sabbath Day, and that an employer cannot accommodate such an employee by violating seniority systems determined by a union collective bargaining agreement. The Court noted that its ruling was not a constitutional judgment but an interpretation of existing law.

Wolman v. Walter (1977): The Court ruled constitutional portions of an Ohio statute providing tax-paid textbook loans and some auxiliary services (standardized and diagnostic testing, therapeutic and remedial services, off school premises) for nonpublic school students. It decided that other portions of the law, providing state funds for nonpublic school field trips and instructional materials (audio-visual equipment, maps, tape recorders), were unconstitutional.

Parochiaid (1979): The Court decided, in Byrne v. Public Funds for Public Schools, against the constitutionality of a 1976 New Jersey law providing state income tax deductions for tuition paid by parents of students attending parochial and other private schools.

Student Bus Transportation (1979): The Court upheld a Pennsylvania law providing bus transportation at public expense for students to non-public schools up to 10 miles away from the boundaries of the public school districts in which they lived.

Reimbursement (1980): The Court upheld the constitutionality of a 1974 New York law providing direct cash payment to non-public schools for the costs of state-mandated testing and record-keeping.

Ten Commandments (1980): The Court struck down a 1978 Kentucky law requiring the posting of the Ten Commandments in public school classrooms in the state.

Campus Worship (1981): The Court ruled, in Widmar v. Vincent, that the University of Missouri at Kansas City could not deny student religious groups the use of campus facilities for worship services. The Court also, in Brandon v. Board of Education of Guilderland Schools, declined without comment to hear an appeal for reversal of lower court decisions denying a group of New York high school students the right to meet for prayer on public school property before the beginning of the school day.

No Meeting on Public School Property (1983): By refusing to hear an appeal in Lubbock v. Lubbock Civil Liberties Union, the Court upheld a lower court ruling against a public policy of permitting student religious groups to meet on public school property before and after school hours.

Tuition Tax Deduction (1983): In Mueller v. Allen, the Court upheld a Minnesota law allowing parents of students in public and non-public (including parochial) schools to take a tax deduction for the expenses of tuition, textbooks and transportation. Maximum allowable deductions were $500 per child in elementary school and $700 per child in grades seven through 12.

Christmas Nativity Scene (1984): The Court ruled 5-to-4 in Lynch v. Donnelly that the First Amendment does not mandate "complete separation of church and state," and that, therefore, the sponsorship of a Christmas nativity scene by the City of Pawtucket, R.I., was not unconstitutional. The case involved a scene included in a display of Christmas symbols sponsored by the city in a park owned by a non-profit group. The majority opinion said "the Constitution (does not) require complete separation of church and state; it affirmatively mandates accommodation, not merely tolerance, of all religions and forbids hostility toward any. Anything less" would entail callous indifference not intended by the Constitution. Moreover, "such hostility would bring us into 'war with our national tradition as embodied in the First Amendment's guaranty of the free exercise of religion.' " (The additional quotation was from the 1948 decision in McCollum v. Board of Education.)

Christmas Nativity Scene (1985): The Court upheld a lower court ruling that the Village of Scarsdale, N.Y., must make public space available for the display of privately sponsored nativity scenes.

Wallace v. Jaffree, No. 83-812 (1985): The Court ruled against the constitutionality of a 1981 Alabama law calling for a public-school moment of silence that specifically included optional prayer.

Grand Rapids v. Ball, No. 83-990, and **Aguilar v. Felton**, No. 84-237 (1985): The Court ruled against the constitutionality of programs in Grand Rapids and New York City allowing public school teachers to teach remedial entitlement subjects (under the Elementary and Secondary Education Act of 1965) in private schools, many of which were Catholic.

Creche and Menorah: In County of Allegheny v.

American Civil Liberties Union, the Court ruled in 1989 (1) The display of a Christmas nativity scene in the Allegheny County Courthouse in Pittsburgh, Pa., violated the principle of separation of church and state because it appeared to be a government-sponsored endorsement of Christian belief. (2) The display of a Hanukkah menorah outside the Pittsburgh-Allegheny city-county building was constitutional because of its "particular physical setting" with secular symbols.

CHURCH TAX EXEMPTION

The exemption of church-owned property was ruled constitutional by the U.S. Supreme Court May 4, 1970, in the case of Walz v. The Tax Commission of New York.

Suit in the case was brought by Frederick Walz, who purchased in June, 1967, a 22-by-29-foot plot of ground in Staten Island valued at $100 and taxable at $5.24 a year. Shortly after making the purchase, Walz instituted a suit in New York State, contending that the exemption of church property from taxation authorized by state law increased his own tax rate and forced him indirectly to support churches in violation of his constitutional right to freedom of religion under the First Amendment. Three New York courts dismissed the suit, which had been instituted by mail. The Supreme Court, judging that it had probable jurisdiction, then took the case.

In a 7-1 decision affecting Church-state relations in every state in the nation, the Court upheld the New York law under challenge.

For and Against

Chief Justice Warren E. Burger, who wrote the majority opinion, said that Congress from its earliest days had viewed the religion clauses of the Constitution as authorizing statutory real estate tax exemption to religious bodies. He declared: "Nothing in this national attitude toward religious tolerance and two centuries of uninterrupted freedom from taxation has given the remotest sign of leading to an established church or religion, and on the contrary it has operated affirmatively to help guarantee the free exercise of all forms of religious beliefs."

Justice William O. Douglas wrote in dissent that the involvement of government in religion as typified in tax exemption may seem inconsequential but: "It is, I fear, a long step down the establishment path. . . . Perhaps I have been misinformed. But, as I read the Constitution and the philosophy, I gathered that independence was the price of liberty."

Burger rejected Douglas' "establishment" fears. If tax exemption is the first step toward establishment, he said, "the second step has been long in coming."

The basic issue centered on the following question: Is there a contradiction between federal constitutional provisions against the establishment of religion, or the use of public funds for religious purposes, and state statutes exempting church property from taxation?

In the Walz decision, the Supreme Court ruled that there is no contradiction.

Legal Background

The U.S. Constitution makes no reference to tax exemption.

There was no discussion of the issue in the Constitutional Convention nor in debates on the Bill of Rights.

In the Colonial and post-Revolutionary years, some churches had established status and were state-supported. This state of affairs changed with enactment of the First Amendment, which laid down no-establishment as the federal norm. This norm was adopted by the states which, however, exempted churches from tax liabilities.

No establishment, no hindrance, was the early American view of Church-state relationships.

This view, reflected in custom law, was not generally formulated in statute law until the second half of the 19th century, although specific tax exemption was provided for churches in Maryland in 1798, in Virginia in 1800, and in North Carolina in 1806.

The first major challenge to church property exemption was initiated by the Liberal League in the 1870s. It reached the point that President Grant included the recommendation in a State of the Union address in 1875, stating that church property should bear its own proportion of taxes. The plea fell on deaf ears in Congress, but there was some support for the idea at state levels. The exemption, however, continued to survive various challenges.

About 36 state constitutions contain either mandatory or permissive provisions for exemption. Statutes provide for exemption in all other states.

There has been considerable litigation challenging this special exemption, but most of it focused on whether a particular property satisfied statutory requirements. Few cases before Walz focused on the strictly constitutional question, whether directly under the First Amendment or indirectly under the Fourteenth Amendment.

Objections

Objectors to the tax exempt status of churches feel that churches should share, through taxation, in the cost of the ordinary benefits of public services they enjoy, and/or that the amount of "aid" enjoyed through exemption should be proportionate to the amount of social good they do.

According to one opinion, exemption is said to weaken the independence of churches from the political system which benefits them by exemption.

In another view, exemption is said to involve the government in decisions regarding what is and what is not religion.

THE WALL OF SEPARATION

Thomas Jefferson, in a letter written to the Danbury (Conn.) Baptist Association Jan. 1, 1802, coined the metaphor, "a wall of separation between Church and State," to express a theory concerning interpretation of the religion clauses of the First Amendment: "Congress shall make no law respecting an establishment of religion or prohibiting the free exercise thereof."

The metaphor was cited for the first time in

judicial proceedings in 1879, in the opinion by Chief Justice Waite in Reynolds v. United States. It did not, however, figure substantially in the decision.

Accepted as Rule

In 1947 the wall of separation gained acceptance as a constitutional rule, in the decision handed down in Everson v. Board of Education. Associate Justice Black, in describing the principles involved in the No Establishment Clause, wrote:

"Neither a state nor the Federal Government can set up a church. Neither can pass laws which aid one religion, aid all religions, or prefer one religion over another. Neither can force nor influence a person to go to or to remain away from church against his will or force him to profess a belief or disbelief in any religion. No person can be punished for entertaining or professing religious beliefs or disbeliefs, for church attendance or non-attendance. No tax in any amount, large or small, can be levied to support any religious activities or institutions, whatever they may be called, or whatever form they may adopt to teach or practice religion. Neither a state nor the Federal Government can, openly or secretly, participate in the affairs of any religious organizations or groups and vice versa. In the words of Jefferson, the clause against establishment of religion by law was intended to erect 'a wall of separation between Church and State.'"

Mr. Black's associates agreed with his statement of principles, which were framed without reference to the Freedom of Exercise Clause. They disagreed, however, with respect to application of the principles, as the split decision in the case indicated. Five members of the Court held that the benefits of public welfare legislation — in this case, free bus transportation to school for parochial as well as public school students — did not run contrary to the concept of separation of Church and State embodied in the First Amendment.

Different Opinions

Inside and outside the legal profession, opinion is divided concerning the wall of separation and the balance of the religion clauses of the First Amendment.

The view of absolute separationists, carried to the extreme, would make government the adversary of religion. The bishops of the United States, following the McCollum decision in 1948, said that the wall metaphor had become for some persons the "shibboleth of doctrinaire secularism."

Proponents of governmental neutrality toward religion are of the opinion that such neutrality should not be so interpreted as to prohibit incidental aid to religious institutions providing secular services.

In the realm of practice, federal and state legislatures have enacted measures involving incidental benefits to religious bodies. Examples of such measures are the tax exemption of church property; provision of bus rides, book loans and lunch programs to students in church-related as well as public schools; military chaplaincies; loans to church-related hospitals; the financing of studies by military veterans at church-related colleges under GI bills of rights.

U.S. CATHOLIC JURISDICTIONS, HIERARCHY, STATISTICS

The organizational structure of the Catholic Church in the United States consists of 33 provinces with as many archdioceses (metropolitan sees); 150 suffragan sees (dioceses); four Eastern-Rite jurisdictions immediately subject to the Holy See —the eparchies of St. Maron (Maronites), Newton (Melkites), St. Thomas Apostle of Detroit (Chaldeans) and St. George Martyr of Canton, Ohio (Romanians); and the Military Services Archdiocese. An Armenian-Rite apostolic exarchate for the United States and Canada has its seat in New York. Each of these jurisdictions is under the direction of an archbishop or bishop, called an ordinary, who has apostolic responsibility and authority for the pastoral service of the people in his care.

The structure includes the territorial episcopal conference known as the National Conference of Catholic Bishops. In and through this body, which is strictly ecclesiastical and has defined juridical authority, the bishops exercise their collegiate pastorate over the Church in the entire country (see Index).

Related to the NCCB is the United States Catholic Conference, a civil corporation and operational secretariat through which the bishops, in cooperation with other members of the Church, act on a wider-than-ecclesiastical scale for the good of the Church and society in the United States (see Index).

The representative of the Holy See to the Church in this country is an Apostolic Pro-Nuncio.

ECCLESIASTICAL PROVINCES

(Sources: *The Official Catholic Directory*, Catholic News Service.)

The 33 ecclesiastical provinces bear the names of archdioceses, i.e., of metropolitan sees.

Anchorage: Archdiocese of Anchorage and suffragan sees of Fairbanks, Juneau. Geographical area: Alaska.

Atlanta: Archdiocese of Atlanta (Ga.) and suffragan sees of Savannah (Ga.); Charlotte and Raleigh (N.C.), Charleston (S.C.). Geographical area: Georgia, North Carolina, South Carolina.

Baltimore: Archdiocese of Baltimore (Md.) and suffragan sees of Wilmington (Del.); Arlington and Richmond (Va.); Wheeling-Charleston (W. Va.). Geographical area: Maryland (except five counties), Delaware, Virginia, West Virginia.

Boston: Archdiocese of Boston (Mass.) and suffragan sees of Fall River, Springfield and Worcester (Mass.); Portland (Me.); Manchester (N.H.); Burlington (Vt.). Geographical area: Massachusetts, Maine, New Hampshire, Vermont.

Chicago: Archdiocese of Chicago and suffragan sees of Belleville, Joliet, Peoria, Rockford, Springfield. Geographical area: Illinois.

Cincinnati: Archdiocese of Cincinnati and suffragan sees of Cleveland, Columbus, Steubenville, Toledo, Youngstown. Geographical area: Ohio.

Denver: Archdiocese of Denver (Colo.) and suffragan sees of Colorado Springs and Pueblo (Colo.); Cheyenne (Wyo.). Geographical area: Colorado, Wyoming.

Detroit: Archdiocese of Detroit and suffragan sees of Gaylord, Grand Rapids, Kalamazoo, Lan-sing, Marquette, Saginaw. Geographical area: Michigan.

Dubuque: Archdiocese of Dubuque and suffragan sees of Davenport, Des Moines, Sioux City. Geographical area: Iowa.

Hartford: Archdiocese of Hartford (Conn.) and suffragan sees of Bridgeport and Norwich (Conn.); Providence (R.I.). Geographical area: Connecticut, Rhode Island.

Indianapolis: Archdiocese of Indianapolis and suffragan sees of Evansville, Fort Wayne-South Bend, Gary, Lafayette. Geographical area: Indiana.

Kansas City (Kans.): Archdiocese of Kansas City and suffragan sees of Dodge City, Salina, Wichita. Geographical area: Kansas.

Los Angeles: Archdiocese of Los Angeles and suffragan sees of Fresno, Monterey, Orange, San Bernardino, San Diego. Geographical area: Southern and Central California.

Louisville: Archdiocese of Louisville (Ky.) and suffragan sees of Covington, Lexington and Owensboro (Ky.); Knoxville, Memphis and Nashville (Tenn.). Geographical area: Kentucky, Tennessee.

Miami: Archdiocese of Miami and suffragan sees of Orlando, Palm Beach, Pensacola-Tallahassee, St. Augustine, St. Petersburg, Venice. Geographical area: Florida.

Milwaukee: Archdiocese of Milwaukee and suffragan sees of Green Bay, La Crosse, Madison, Superior. Geographical area: Wisconsin.

Mobile: Archdiocese of Mobile, Ala., and suffragan sees of Birmingham (Ala.); Biloxi and Jackson (Miss.). Geographical area: Alabama, Mississippi.

Newark: Archdiocese of Newark and suffragan sees of Camden, Metuchen, Paterson, Trenton. Geographical area: New Jersey.

New Orleans: Archdiocese of New Orleans and suffragan sees of Alexandria, Baton Rouge, Houma-Thibodaux, Lafayette, Lake Charles and Shreveport. Geographical area: Louisiana.

New York: Archdiocese of New York and suffragan sees of Albany, Brooklyn, Buffalo, Ogdensburg, Rochester, Rockville Centre, Syracuse. Geographical area: New York.

Oklahoma City: Archdiocese of Oklahoma City (Okla.) and suffragan sees of Tulsa (Okla.) and Little Rock (Ark.). Geographical area: Oklahoma, Arkansas.

Omaha: Archdiocese of Omaha and suffragan sees of Grand Island, Lincoln. Geographical area: Nebraska.

Philadelphia: Archdiocese of Philadelphia and suffragan sees of Allentown, Altoona-Johnstown, Erie, Greensburg, Harrisburg, Pittsburgh, Scranton. Geographical area: Pennsylvania.

Philadelphia (Byzantine Rite, Ukrainians): Metropolitan See of Philadelphia (Byzantine Rite) and Eparchies of St. Josaphat in Parma (Ohio), St. Nicholas of the Ukrainians in Chicago and Stamford, Conn. The jurisdiction extends to all Ukrainian Catholics in the U.S. from the ecclesiastical province of Galicia in the Ukraine.

Pittsburgh (Byzantine Rite, Ruthenians): Metropolitan See of Pittsburgh, Pa. and Eparchies of Passaic (N.J.), Parma (Ohio), Van Nuys (Calif.).

Portland: Archdiocese of Portland (Ore.) and suffragan sees of Baker (Ore.); Boise (Ida.); Great Falls-Billings and Helena (Mont.). Geographical area: Oregon, Idaho, Montana.

St. Louis: Archdiocese of St. Louis and suffragan sees of Jefferson City, Kansas City-St. Joseph, Springfield-Cape Girardeau. Geographical area: Missouri.

St. Paul and Minneapolis: Archdiocese of St. Paul and Minneapolis (Minn.) and suffragan sees of Crookston, Duluth, New Ulm, St. Cloud and Winona (Minn.); Bismarck and Fargo (N.D.); Rapid City and Sioux Falls (S.D.). Geographical area: Minnesota, North Dakota, South Dakota.

San Antonio: Archdiocese of San Antonio (Tex.) and suffragan sees of Amarillo, Austin, Beaumont, Brownsville, Corpus Christi, Dallas, El Paso, Fort Worth, Galveston-Houston, Lubbock, San Angelo, Tyler and Victoria (Tex.). Geographical area: Texas.

San Francisco: Archdiocese of San Francisco (Calif.) and suffragan sees of Oakland, Sacramento, San Jose, Santa Rosa and Stockton (Calif.); Honolulu (Hawaii); Reno-Las Vegas (Nev.); Salt Lake City (Utah). Geographical area: Northern California, Nevada, Utah, Hawaii.

Santa Fe: Archdiocese of Santa Fe (N.M.) and suffragan sees of Gallup and Las Cruces (N.M.); Phoenix and Tucson (Ariz.). Geographical area: New Mexico, Arizona.

Seattle: Archdiocese of Seattle and suffragan sees of Spokane, Yakima. Geographical area: Washington.

Washington: Archdiocese of Washington, D.C., and suffragan see of St. Thomas (Virgin Islands). Geographical area: District of Columbia, five counties of Maryland, Virgin Islands.

ARCHDIOCESES, DIOCESES, ARCHBISHOPS, BISHOPS

(Sources: *The Official Catholic Directory;* Catholic News Service; *L'Osservatore Romano.* As of Sept. 2, 1993.)

Information includes name of diocese, year of foundation (as it appears on the official document erecting the see), present ordinaries (year of installation), auxiliaries and former ordinaries (for biographies, see Index).

Archdioceses are indicated by an asterisk.

Albany, N.Y. (1847): Howard J. Hubbard, bishop, 1977.

Former bishops: John McCloskey, 1847-64; John J. Conroy, 1865-77; Francis McNeirny, 1877-94; Thomas M. Burke, 1894-1915; Thomas F. Cusack, 1915-18; Edmund F. Gibbons, 1919-54; William A. Scully, 1954-69; Edwin B. Broderick, 1969-76.

Alexandria, La. (1853): Sam G. Jacobs, bishop, 1989.

Established at Natchitoches, transferred to Alexandria 1910; title changed to Alexandria-Shreveport, 1977; redesignated Alexandria, 1986, when Shreveport was made a diocese.

Former bishops: Augustus M. Martin, 1853-75; Francis X. Leray, 1877-79, administrator, 1879-83; Anthony Durier, 1885-1904; Cornelius Van de Ven, 1904-32; Daniel F. Desmond, 1933-45; Charles P. Greco, 1946-73; Lawrence P. Graves, 1973-82; William B. Friend, 1983-86; John C. Favalora, 1986-89.

Allentown, Pa. (1961): Thomas J. Welsh, bishop, 1983.

Former bishop: Joseph McShea, 1961-83.

Altoona-Johnstown, Pa. (1901): Joseph V. Adamec, bishop, 1987.

Established as Altoona, name changed, 1957.

Former bishops: Eugene A. Garvey, 1901-20; John J. McCort, 1920-36; Richard T. Guilfoyle, 1936-57; Howard J. Carroll, 1958-60; J. Carroll McCormick, 1960-66; James J. Hogan, 1966-86.

Amarillo, Tex. (1926): Leroy T. Matthiesen, bishop, 1980.

Former bishops; Rudolph A. Gerken, 1927-33; Robert E. Lucey, 1934-41; Laurence J. Fitzsimon, 1941-58; John L. Morkovsky, 1958-63; Lawrence M. De Falco, 1963-79.

Anchorage,* Alaska (1966): Francis T. Hurley, archbishop, 1976.

Former archbishop: Joseph T. Ryan, 1966-75.

Arlington, Va. (1974): John R. Keating, bishop, 1983.

Former bishop: Thomas J. Welsh, 1974-83.

Atlanta,* Ga. (1956; archdiocese, 1962): John F. Donoghue, archbishop, 1993.

Former ordinaries: Francis E. Hyland, 1956-61; Paul J. Hallinan, first archbishop, 1962-68; Thomas A. Donnellan, 1968-87; Eugene A. Marino, S.S.J., 1988-90; James P. Lyke, 1991-92.

Austin, Tex. (1947): John E. McCarthy, bishop, 1986.

Former bishops: Louis J. Reicher, 1947-71; Vincent M. Harris, 1971-86.

Baker, Ore. (1903): Thomas J. Connolly, bishop, 1971.

Established as Baker City, name changed, 1952.

Former bishops: Charles J. O'Reilly, 1903-18; Joseph F. McGrath, 1919-50; Francis P. Leipzig, 1950-71.

Baltimore,* Md. (1789; archdiocese, 1808): William H. Keeler, archbishop, 1989. P. Francis Murphy, William C. Newman, John H. Ricard, S.S.J., auxiliaries.

Former ordinaries: John Carroll, 1789-1815, first archbishop; Leonard Neale, 1815-17; Ambrose Marechal, S.S., 1817-28; James Whitfield, 1828-34; Samuel Eccleston, S.S., 1834-51; Francis P. Kenrick, 1851-63; Martin J. Spalding, 1864-72; James R. Bayley, 1872-77; Cardinal James Gibbons, 1877-1921; Michael J. Curley, 1921-47; Francis P.

Keough, 1947-61; Cardinal Lawrence J. Shehan, 1961-74; William D. Borders, 1974-89.
Baton Rouge, La. (1961): Vacant as of Aug. 15, 1993.
Former bishops: Robert E. Tracy, 1961-74; Joseph V. Sullivan, 1974-82; Stanley J. Ott (1983-93).
Beaumont, Tex. (1966): Bernard J. Ganter, bishop, 1977.
Former bishops: Vincent M. Harris, 1966-71; Warren L. Boudreaux, 1971-77.
Belleville, Ill. (1887): Vacant as of Aug. 15, 1993.
Former bishops: John Janssen, 1888-1913; Henry Althoff, 1914-47; Albert R. Zuroweste, 1948-76; William M. Cosgrove, 1976-81; John N. Wurm, 1981-84; James P. Keleher, 1984-93.
Biloxi, Miss. (1977): Joseph Lawson Howze, bishop, 1977.
Birmingham, Ala. (1969): Vacant as of Aug. 15, 1993.
Former bishops: Joseph G. Vath, 1969-87; Raymond J. Boland, 1988-93.
Bismarck, N. Dak. (1909): John F. Kinney, bishop, 1982.
Former bishops: Vincent Wehrle, O.S.B., 1910-39; Vincent J. Ryan, 1940-51; Lambert A. Hoch, 1952-56; Hilary B. Hacker, 1957-82.
Boise, Ida. (1893): Tod David Brown, bishop, 1989.
Former bishops: Alphonse J. Glorieux, 1893-1917; Daniel M. Gorman, 1918-27; Edward J. Kelly, 1928-56; James J. Byrne, 1956-62; Sylvester Treinen, 1962-88.
Boston,* Mass. (1808; archdiocese, 1875): Cardinal Bernard F. Law, archbishop, 1984. Daniel A. Hart, Alfred C. Hughes, Roberto O. Gonzalez, O.F.M., John R. McNamara, John P. Boles, auxiliaries.
Former ordinaries: John L. de Cheverus, 1810-23; Benedict J. Fenwick, S.J., 1825-46; John B. Fitzpatrick, 1846-66; John J. Williams, 1866-1907, first archbishop; Cardinal William O'Connell, 1907-44; Cardinal Richard Cushing, 1944-70; Cardinal Humberto Medeiros, 1970-83.
Bridgeport, Conn. (1953): Edward M. Egan, bishop, 1988.
Former bishops: Lawrence J. Shehan, 1953-61; Walter W. Curtis, 1961-88.
Brooklyn, N.Y. (1853): Thomas V. Daily, bishop, 1990. Joseph M. Sullivan, Rene A. Valero, auxiliaries.
Former bishops: John Loughlin, 1853-91; Charles E. McDonnell, 1892-1921; Thomas E. Molloy, 1921-56; Bryan J. McEntegart, 1957-68; Francis J. Mugavero, 1968-90.
Brownsville, Tex. (1965): Enrique San Pedro, S.J., bishop, 1991.
Former bishops: Adolph Marx, 1965; Humberto S. Medeiros, 1966-70; John J. Fitzpatrick, 1971-91.
Buffalo, N.Y. (1847): Edward D. Head, bishop, 1973. Edward M. Grosz, auxiliary.
Former bishops: John Timon, C.M., 1847-67; Stephen V. Ryan, C.M., 1868-96; James E. Quigley, 1897-1903; Charles H. Colton, 1903-15; Dennis J. Dougherty, 1915-18; William Turner, 1919-36; John A. Duffy, 1937-44; John F. O'Hara, C.S.C., 1945-51; Joseph A. Burke, 1952-62; James McNulty, 1963-72.

Burlington, Vt. (1853): Kenneth A. Angell, bishop, 1992.
Former bishops: Louis De Goesbriand, 1853-99; John S. Michaud, 1899-1908; Joseph J. Rice, 1910-38; Matthew F. Brady, 1938-44; Edward F. Ryan, 1945-56; Robert F. Joyce, 1957-71; John A. Marshall, 1972-91.
Camden, N.J. (1937): James T. McHugh, bishop, 1989.
Former bishops: Bartholomew J. Eustace, 1938-56; Justin J. McCarthy, 1957-59; Celestine J. Damiano, 1960-67; George H. Guilfoyle, 1968-89.
Charleston, S.C. (1820): David B. Thompson, bishop, 1990.
Former bishops: John England, 1820-42; Ignatius W. Reynolds, 1844-55; Patrick N. Lynch, 1858-82; Henry P. Northrop, 1883-1916; William T. Russell, 1917-27; Emmet M. Walsh, 1927-49; John J. Russell, 1950-58; Paul J. Hallinan, 1958-62; Francis F. Reh, 1962-64; Ernest L. Unterkoefler, 1964-90.
Charlotte, N.C. (1971): Vacant as of Aug. 15, 1993.
Former bishops: Michael J. Begley, 1972-84; John F. Donoghue, 1984-93.
Cheyenne, Wyo. (1887): Joseph Hart, bishop, 1978.
Former bishops: Maurice F. Burke, 1887-93; Thomas M. Lenihan, 1897-1901; James J. Keane, 1902-11; Patrick A. McGovern, 1912-51; Hubert M. Newell, 1951-78.
Chicago,* Ill. (1843; archdiocese, 1880): Cardinal Joseph L. Bernardin, archbishop, 1982. Alfred L. Abramowicz, Placido Rodriguez, C.M.F., Timothy J. Lyne, Wilton D. Gregory, Thad J. Jakubowski, John R. Gorman, Raymond E. Goedert, auxiliaries.
Former ordinaries: William Quarter, 1844-48; James O. Van de Velde, S.J., 1849-53; Anthony O'Regan, 1854-58; James Duggan, 1859-70; Thomas P. Foley, administrator, 1870-79; Patrick A. Feehan, 1880-1902, first archbishop; James E. Quigley, 1903-15; Cardinal George Mundelein, 1915-39; Cardinal Samuel Stritch, 1939-58; Cardinal Albert Meyer, 1958-65; Cardinal John Cody, 1965-82.
Cincinnati,* Ohio (1821; archdiocese, 1850): Daniel E. Pilarczyk, archbishop, 1982. Carl K. Moeddel, auxiliary.
Former ordinaries: Edward D. Fenwick, O.P., 1822-32; John B. Purcell, 1833-83, first archbishop; William H. Elder, 1883-1904; Henry Moeller, 1904-1925; John T. McNicholas, O.P., 1925-50; Karl J. Alter, 1950-69; Paul F. Leibold, 1969-72; Joseph L. Bernardin, 1972-82.
Cleveland, Ohio (1847): Anthony M. Pilla, bishop, 1980. A. Edward Pevec, A. James Quinn, auxiliaries.
Former bishops: L. Amadeus Rappe, 1847-70; Richard Gilmour, 1872-91; Ignatius F. Horstmann, 1892-1908; John P. Farrelly, 1909-21; Joseph Schrembs, 1921-45; Edward F. Hoban, 1945-66; Clarence G. Issenmann, 1966-74; James A. Hickey, 1974-80.
Colorado Springs, Colo. (1983): Richard C. Hanifen, bishop, 1984.
Columbus, Ohio (1868): James A. Griffin, bishop, 1983.
Former bishops: Sylvester H. Rosecrans, 1868-78;

John A. Watterson, 1880-99; Henry Moeller, 1900-03; James J. Hartley, 1904-44; Michael J. Ready, 1944-57; Clarence Issenmann, 1957-64; John J. Carberry, 1965-68; Clarence E. Elwell, 1968-73; Edward J. Herrmann, 1973-82.

Corpus Christi, Tex. (1912): Rene H. Gracida, bishop, 1983.
Former bishops: Paul J. Nussbaum, C.P., 1913-20; Emmanuel B. Ledvina, 1921-49; Mariano S. Garriga, 1949-65; Thomas J. Drury, 1965-83.

Covington, Ky. (1853): William A. Hughes, bishop, 1979.
Former bishops: George A. Carrell, S.J., 1853-68; Augustus M. Toebbe, 1870-84; Camillus P. Maes, 1885-1914; Ferdinand Brossart, 1916-23; Francis W. Howard, 1923-44; William T. Mulloy, 1945-59; Richard Ackerman, C.S.Sp., 1960-78.

Crookston, Minn. (1909): Victor H. Balke, bishop, 1976.
Former bishops: Timothy Corbett, 1910-38; John H. Peschges, 1938-44; Francis J. Schenk, 1945-60; Laurence A. Glenn, 1960-70; Kenneth J. Povish, 1970-75.

Dallas, Tex. (1890): Charles V. Grahmann, bishop, 1990.
Established 1890, as Dallas, title changed to Dallas-Ft. Worth 1953; redesignated Dallas, 1969, when Ft. Worth was made diocese.
Former bishops: Thomas F. Brennan, 1891-92; Edward J. Dunne, 1893-1910; Joseph P. Lynch, 1911-54; Thomas K. Gorman, 1954-69; Thomas Tschoepe, 1969-90.

Davenport, Ia. (1881): Gerald F. O'Keefe, bishop, 1966.
Former bishops: John McMullen, 1881-83; Henry Cosgrove, 1884-1906; James Davis, 1906-26; Henry P. Rohlman, 1927-44; Ralph L. Hayes, 1944-66.

Denver,* Colo. (1887; archdiocese, 1941): J. Francis Stafford, archbishop, 1986.
Former ordinaries: Joseph P. Machebeuf, 1887-89; Nicholas C. Matz, 1889-1917; J. Henry Tihen, 1917-31; Urban J. Vehr, 1931-67, first archbishop; James V. Casey, 1967-86.

Des Moines, Ia. (1911): Vacant as of Aug. 15, 1993.
Former bishops: Austin Dowling, 1912-19; Thomas W. Drumm, 1919-33; Gerald T. Bergan, 1934-48; Edward C. Daly, O.P., 1948-64; George J. Biskup, 1965-67; Maurice J. Dingman, 1968-86; William H. Bullock, 1987-93.

Detroit,* Mich. (1833; archdiocese, 1937): Adam J. Maida, archbishop, 1990. Thomas J. Gumbleton, Walter J. Schoenherr, Moses B. Anderson, S.S.E., Dale J. Melczek, auxiliaries.
Former ordinaries: Frederic Rese, 1833-71; Peter P. Lefevere, administrator, 1841-69; Caspar H. Borgess, 1871-88; John S. Foley, 1888-1918; Michael J. Gallagher, 1918-37; Cardinal Edward Mooney, 1937-58, first archbishop; Cardinal John F. Dearden, 1958-80; Cardinal Edmund C. Szoka, 1981-90.

Dodge City, Kans. (1951): Stanley G. Schlarman, bishop, 1983.
Former bishops: John B. Franz, 1951-59; Marion F. Forst, 1960-76; Eugene J. Gerber, 1976-82.

Dubuque,* Iowa (1837; archdiocese, 1893):

Daniel W. Kucera, O.S.B., archbishop, 1984. William E. Franklin, auxiliary.
Former ordinaries: Mathias Loras, 1837-58; Clement Smyth, O.C.S.O., 1858-65; John Hennessy, 1866-1900, first archbishop; John J. Keane, 1900-11; James J. Keane, 1911-29; Francis J. Beckman, 1930-46; Henry P. Rohlman, 1946-54; Leo Binz, 1954-61; James J. Byrne, 1962-83.

Duluth, Minn. (1889): Roger L. Schwietz, O.M.I., bishop, 1990.
Former bishops: James McGolrick, 1889-1918; John T. McNicholas, O.P., 1918-25; Thomas A. Welch, 1926-59; Francis J. Schenk, 1960-69; Paul F. Anderson, 1969-82; Robert H. Brom, 1983-89.

El Paso, Tex. (1914): Raymundo J. Pena, bishop, 1980.
Former bishops: Anthony J. Schuler, S.J., 1915-42; Sidney M. Metzger, 1942-78. Patrick F. Flores, 1978-79.

Erie, Pa. (1853): Donald W. Trautman, bishop, 1990.
Former bishops: Michael O'Connor, 1853-54; Josue M. Young, 1854-66; Tobias Mullen, 1868-99; John E. Fitzmaurice, 1899-1920; John M. Gannon, 1920-66; John F. Whealon, 1966-69; Alfred M. Watson, 1969-82; Michael J. Murphy, 1982-90.

Evansville, Ind. (1944): Gerald A. Gettelfinger, bishop, 1989.
Former bishops: Henry J. Grimmelsman, 1944-65; Paul F. Leibold, 1966-69; Francis R. Shea, 1970-89.

Fairbanks, Alaska (1962): Michael J. Kaniecki, S.J., bishop, 1985.
Former bishops: Francis D. Gleeson, S.J., 1962-68; Robert L. Whelan, S.J., 1968-85.

Fall River, Mass. (1904): Sean O'Malley, O.F.M. Cap., bishop, 1992.
Former bishops: William Stang, 1904-07; Daniel F. Feehan, 1907-34; James E. Cassidy, 1934-51; James L. Connolly, 1951-70; Daniel A. Cronin, 1970-91.

Fargo, N. Dak. (1889): James S. Sullivan, bishop, 1985.
Established at Jamestown, transferred, 1897.
Former bishops: John Shanley, 1889-1909; James O'Reilly, 1910-34; Aloysius J. Muench, 1935-59; Leo F. Dworschak, 1960-70; Justin A. Driscoll, 1970-84.

Fort Wayne-South Bend, Ind. (1857): John M. D'Arcy, bishop, 1985. John R. Sheets, S.J., auxiliary.
Established as Fort Wayne, name changed, 1960.
Former bishops: John H. Luers, 1858-71; Joseph Dwenger, C.Pp. S., 1872-93; Joseph Rademacher, 1893-1900; Herman J. Alerding, 1900-24; John F. Noll, 1925-56; Leo A. Pursley, 1957-76; William E. McManus, 1976-85.

Fort Worth, Tex. (1969): Joseph P. Delaney, bishop, 1981.
Former bishop: John J. Cassata, 1969-80.

Fresno, Calif. (1967): John T. Steinbock, bishop, 1991.
Formerly Monterey-Fresno, 1922.
Former bishops (Monterey-Fresno): John J. Cantwell, administrator, 1922-24; John B. MacGinley, first bishop, 1924-32; Philip G. Sher, 1933-53; Aloysius J. Willinger, 1953-67.

Former bishops (Fresno): Timothy Manning, 1967-69; Hugh A. Donohoe, 1969-80; Joseph J. Madera, M.Pp.S., 1980-91.

Gallup, N. Mex. (1939): Donald Pelotte, S.S.S., bishop, 1990.

Former bishops: Bernard T. Espelage, O.F.M., 1940-69; Jerome J. Hastrich, 1969-90.

Galveston-Houston, Tex. (1847): Joseph A. Fiorenza, bishop, 1985. Curtis J. Guillory, S.V.D.; James A. Tamayo, auxiliaries.

Established as Galveston, name changed, 1959.

Former bishops: John M. Odin, C.M., 1847-61; Claude M. Dubuis, 1862-92; Nicholas A. Gallagher, 1892-1918; Christopher E. Byrne, 1918-50; Wendelin J. Nold, 1950-75; John L. Morkovsky, 1975-84.

Gary, Ind. (1956): Norbert F. Gaughan, bishop, 1984. Dale J. Melczek, auxiliary of Detroit, apostolic administrator, Aug. 1992.

Former bishop: Andrew G. Grutka, 1957-84.

Gaylord, Mich. (1971): Patrick R. Cooney, bishop, 1989, installed 1990.

Former bishops: Edmund C. Szoka, 1971-81; Robert J. Rose, 1981-89.

Grand Island, Neb. (1912): Lawrence McNamara, bishop, 1978.

Established at Kearney, transferred, 1917.

Former bishops: James A. Duffy, 1913-31; Stanislaus V. Bona, 1932-44; Edward J. Hunkeler, 1945-51; John L. Paschang, 1951-72; John J. Sullivan, 1972-77.

Grand Rapids, Mich. (1882): Robert J. Rose, bishop, 1989. Joseph C. McKinney, auxiliary.

Former bishops: Henry J. Richter, 1883-1916; Michael J. Gallagher, 1916-18; Edward D. Kelly, 1919-26; Joseph G. Pinten, 1926-40; Joseph C. Plagens, 1941-43; Francis J. Haas, 1943-53; Allen J. Babcock, 1954-69; Joseph M. Breitenbeck, 1969-89.

Great Falls-Billings, Mont. (1904): Anthony M. Milone, bishop, 1988.

Established as Great Falls; name changed, 1980.

Former bishops: Mathias C. Lenihan, 1904-30; Edwin V. O'Hara, 1930-39; William J. Condon, 1939-67; Eldon B. Schuster, 1968-77; Thomas J. Murphy, 1978-87.

Green Bay, Wis. (1868): Robert J. Banks, bishop, 1990. Robert F. Morneau, auxiliary.

Former bishops: Joseph Melcher, 1868-73; Francis X. Krautbauer, 1875-85; Frederick X. Katzer, 1886-91; Sebastian G. Messmer, 1892-1903; Joseph J. Fox, 1904-14; Paul P. Rhode, 1915-45; Stanislaus V. Bona, 1945-67; Aloysius J. Wycislo, 1968-83; Adam J. Maida, 1984-90.

Greensburg, Pa. (1951): Anthony G. Bosco, bishop, 1987.

Former bishops: Hugh L. Lamb, 1951-59; William G. Connare, 1960-87.

Harrisburg, Pa. (1868): Nicholas C. Dattilo, bishop, 1990.

Former bishops: Jeremiah F. Shanahan, 1868-86; Thomas McGovern, 1888-98; John W. Shanahan,1899-1916; Philip R. McDevitt, 1916-35; George L. Leech, 1935-71; Joseph T. Daley, 1971-83; William H. Keeler, 1984-89.

Hartford,* Conn. (1843; archdiocese, 1953): Daniel A. Cronin, archbishop, 1991, installed, 1992. Peter A. Rosazza, Paul S. Loverde, auxiliaries.

Former ordinaries: William Tyler, 1844-49; Bernard O'Reilly, 1850-56; F. P. MacFarland, 1858-74; Thomas Galberry, O.S.A., 1876-78; Lawrence S. McMahon, 1879-93; Michael Tierney, 1894-1908; John J. Nilan, 1910-34; Maurice F. McAuliffe, 1934-44; Henry J. O'Brien, 1945-68, first archbishop; John F. Whealon, 1969-91.

Helena, Mont. (1884): Vacant as of Aug. 15, 1993.

Former bishops: John B. Brondel, 1884-1903; John P. Carroll, 1904-25; George J. Finnigan, C.S.C., 1927-32; Ralph L. Hayes, 1933-35; Joseph M. Gilmore, 1936-62; Raymond Hunthausen, 1962-75; Elden F. Curtiss, 1976-93.

Honolulu, Hawaii (1941): Joseph A. Ferrario, bishop, 1982.

Former bishops: James J. Sweeney, 1941-68; John J. Scanlan, 1968-81.

Houma-Thibodaux, La. (1977): Charles Michael Jarrell, bishop, 1993.

Former bishop: Warren L. Boudreaux, 1977-92.

Indianapolis,* Ind. (1834; archdiocese, 1944): Daniel M. Buechlein, O.S.B., archbishop, 1992.

Established at Vincennes, transferred, 1898.

Former ordinaries: Simon G. Bruté, 1834-39; Celestine de la Hailandière, 1839-47; John S. Bazin, 1847-48; Maurice de St. Palais, 1849-77; Francis S. Chatard, 1878-1918; Joseph Chartrand, 1918-33; Joseph E. Ritter, 1934-46, first archbishop; Paul C. Schulte, 1946-70; George J. Biskup, 1970-79; Edward T. O'Meara, 1980-92.

Jackson, Miss. (1837): William R. Houck, bishop, 1984.

Established at Natchez; title changed to Natchez-Jackson, 1956; transferred to Jackson, 1977 (Natchez made titular see).

Former bishops: John J. Chanche, S.S., 1841-52; James Van de Velde, S.J., 1853-55; William H. Elder, 1857-80; Francis A. Janssens, 1881-88; Thomas Heslin, 1889-1911; John E. Gunn, S.M., 1911-24; Richard O. Gerow, 1924-67; Joseph B. Brunini, 1968-84.

Jefferson City, Mo. (1956): Michael F. McAuliffe, bishop, 1969.

Former bishop: Joseph Marling, C.Pp.S., 1956-69.

Joliet, Ill. (1948): Joseph L. Imesch, bishop, 1979. Roger L. Kaffer, auxiliary.

Former bishops: Martin D. McNamara, 1949-66; Romeo Blanchette, 1966-79.

Juneau, Alaska (1951): Michael H. Kenny, bishop, 1979.

Former bishops: Dermot O'Flanagan, 1951-68; Joseph T. Ryan, administrator, 1968-71; Francis T. Hurley, 1971-76, administrator, 1976-79.

Kalamazoo, Mich. (1971): Paul V. Donovan, bishop, 1971.

Kansas City,* Kans. (1877; archdiocese, 1952): James P. Keleher, archbishop, 1993.

Established as vicariate apostolic, 1850, became Diocese of Leavenworth, 1877, transferred to Kansas City 1947.

Former ordinaries: J. B. Miege, vicar apostolic, 1851-74; Louis M. Fink, O.S.B., vicar apostolic,

1874-77, first bishop, 1877-1904; Thomas F. Lillis, 1904-10; John Ward, 1910-29; Francis Johannes, 1929-37; Paul C. Schulte, 1937-46; George J. Donnelly, 1946-50; Edward Hunkeler, 1951-69, first archbishop; Ignatius J. Strecker, 1969-93.

Kansas City-St. Joseph, Mo. (Kansas City, 1880; St. Joseph, 1868; united 1956): Raymond J. Boland, bishop, 1993.

Former bishops: John J. Hogan, 1880-1913; Thomas F. Lillis, 1913-38; Edwin V. O'Hara, 1939-56; John P. Cody, 1956-61; Charles H. Helmsing, 1962-77; John J. Sullivan, 1977-93.

Former bishops (St. Joseph): John J. Hogan, 1868-80, administrator, 1880-93; Maurice F. Burke, 1893-1923; Francis Gilfillan, 1923-33; Charles H. Le Blond, 1933-56.

Knoxville, Tenn. (1988): Anthony J. O'Connell, bishop, 1988.

La Crosse, Wis. (1868): John J. Paul, bishop, 1983.

Former bishops: Michael Heiss, 1868-80; Kilian C. Flasch, 1881-91; James Schwebach, 1892-1921; Alexander J. McGavick, 1921-48; John P. Treacy, 1948-64; Frederick W. Freking, 1965-83.

Lafayette, Ind. (1944): William L. Higi, bishop, 1984.

Former bishops: John G. Bennett, 1944-57; John J. Carberry, 1957-65; Raymond J. Gallagher, 1965-82; George A. Fulcher, 1983-84.

Lafayette, La. (1918): Harry J. Flynn, bishop, 1989.

Former bishops: Jules B. Jeanmard, 1918-56; Maurice Schexnayder, 1956-72; Gerard L. Frey, 1973-89.

Lake Charles, La. (1980): Jude Speyrer, bishop, 1980.

Lansing, Mich. (1937): Kenneth J. Povish, bishop, 1975.

Former bishops: Joseph H. Albers, 1937-65; Alexander Zaleski, 1965-75.

Las Cruces, N. Mex. (1982): Ricardo Ramirez, C.S.B., bishop, 1982.

Lexington, Ky. (1988): James Kendrick Williams, bishop, 1988.

Lincoln, Neb. (1887): Fabian W. Bruskewitz, bishop, 1992.

Former bishops: Thomas Bonacum, 1887-1911; J. Henry Tihen, 1911-17; Charles J. O'Reilly, 1918-23; Francis J. Beckman, 1924-30; Louis B. Kucera, 1930-57; James V. Casey, 1957-67; Glennon P. Flavin, 1967-72.

Little Rock, Ark. (1843): Andrew J. McDonald, bishop, 1972.

Former bishops: Andrew Byrne, 1844-62; Edward Fitzgerald, 1867-1907; John Morris, 1907-46; Albert L. Fletcher, 1946-72.

Los Angeles,* Calif. (1840; archdiocese, 1936): Cardinal Roger M. Mahony, archbishop, 1985. John J. Ward, Juan A. Arzube, Armando Ochoa, Stephen E. Blaire, auxiliaries.

Founded as diocese of Two Californias, 1840; became Monterey diocese, 1850; Baja California detached from Monterey diocese, 1852; title changed to Monterey-Los Angeles, 1859; Los Angeles-San Diego, 1922; became archdiocese under present title, 1936 (San Diego became separate see).

Former ordinaries: Francisco Garcia Diego y Moreno, O.F.M., 1840-46; Joseph S. Alemany, O.P., 1850-53; Thaddeus Amat, C.M., 1854-78; Francis Mora, 1878-96; George T. Montgomery, 1896-1903; Thomas J. Conaty, 1903-15; John J. Cantwell, 1917-47, first archbishop; Cardinal James McIntyre, 1948-70; Cardinal Timothy Manning, 1970-85.

Louisville,* Ky. (1808; archdiocese, 1937): Thomas C. Kelly, O.P., archbishop, 1982.

Established at Bardstown, transferred, 1841.

Former ordinaries: Benedict J. Flaget, S.S., 1810-32; John B. David, S.S., 1832-33; Benedict J. Flaget, S.S., 1833-50; Martin J. Spalding, 1850-64; Peter J. Lavialle, 1865-67; William G. McCloskey, 1868-1909; Denis O'Donaghue, 1910-24; John A. Floersh, 1924-67, first archbishop; Thomas J. McDonough, 1967-81.

Lubbock, Tex. (1983): Vacant as of Aug. 20, 1993.

Fromer bishop: Michael J. Sheehan, 1983-93.

Madison, Wis. (1946): William H. Bullock, bishop, 1993. George O. Wirz, auxiliary.

Former bishops: William P. O'Connor, 1946-67; Cletus F. O'Donnell, 1967-92.

Manchester, N.H. (1884): Leo E. O'Neil, bishop, 1990.

Former bishops: Denis M. Bradley, 1884-1903; John B. Delany, 1904-06; George A. Guertin, 1907-32; John B. Peterson, 1932-44; Matthew F. Brady, 1944-59; Ernest J. Primeau, 1960-74; Odore J. Gendron, 1975-90.

Marquette, Mich. (1857): James H. Garland, bishop, 1992.

Former bishops: Frederic Baraga, 1857-68; Ignatius Mrak, 1869-78; John Vertin, 1879-99; Frederick Eis, 1899-1922; Paul J. Nussbaum, C.P., 1922-35; Joseph C. Plagens, 1935-40; Francis Magner, 1941-47; Thomas L. Noa, 1947-68; Charles A. Salatka, 1968-77; Mark F. Schmitt, 1978-92.

Memphis, Tenn. (1970): J. Terry Steib, S.V.D., bishop, 1993.

Former bishops: Carroll T. Dozier, 1971-82; J. Francis Stafford, 1982-86; Daniel M. Buechlein, O.S.B.,1987-92.

Metuchen, N.J. (1981): Edward T. Hughes, bishop, 1987.

Former bishop: Theodore E. McCarrick, 1981-86.

Miami,* Fla. (1958; archdiocese, 1968): Edward A. McCarthy, archbishop, 1977. Agustin A. Roman, auxiliary.

Former ordinary: Coleman F. Carroll, 1958-77, first archbishop.

Milwaukee,* Wis. (1843; archdiocese, 1875): Rembert G. Weakland, O.S.B., archbishop, 1977. Richard J. Sklba, auxiliary.

Former ordinaries: John M. Henni, 1844-81, first archbishop; Michael Heiss, 1881-90; Frederick X. Katzer, 1891-1903; Sebastian G. Messmer, 1903-30; Samuel A. Stritch, 1930-39; Moses E. Kiley, 1940-53; Albert G. Meyer, 1953-58; William E. Cousins, 1959-77.

Mobile,* Ala. (1829; archdiocese, 1980): Oscar H. Lipscomb, first archbishop, 1980.

Founded as Mobile, 1829; title changed to Mobile-Birmingham, 1954; redesignated Mobile, 1969.

Former bishops: Michael Portier, 1829-59; John Quinlan, 1859-83; Dominic Manucy, 1884; Jeremiah O'Sullivan, 1885-96; Edward P. Allen, 1897-1926; Thomas J. Toolen, 1927-69; John L. May, 1969-80.

Monterey in California (1967): Sylvester D. Ryan, bishop, 1992.

Formerly Monterey-Fresno, 1922. (Originally established in 1850, see Los Angeles listing.)

Former bishops (Monterey-Fresno): John J. Cantwell, administrator, 1922-24; John B. MacGinley, first bishop, 1924-32; Philip G. Sher, 1933-53; Aloysius J. Willinger, 1953-67.

Former bishops (Monterey): Harry A. Clinch, 1967-82; Thaddeus A. Shubsda, 1982-91.

Nashville, Tenn. (1837): Edward U. Kmiec, bishop, 1992.

Former bishops: Richard P. Miles, O.P., 1838-60; James Whelan, O.P., 1860-64; Patrick A. Feehan, 1865-80; Joseph Rademacher, 1883-93; Thomas S. Byrne, 1894-1923; Alphonse J. Smith, 1924-35; William L. Adrian, 1936-69; Joseph A. Durick, 1969-75; James D. Niedergeses, 1975-92.

Newark,* N.J. (1853; archdiocese, 1937): Theodore E. McCarrick, archbishop, 1986. Robert F. Garner, Joseph A. Francis, S.V.D., Dominic A. Marconi, David Arias, O.A.R., Michael A. Saltarelli, auxiliaries.

Former ordinaries: James R. Bayley, 1853-72; Michael A. Corrigan, 1873-80; Winand M. Wigger, 1881-1901; John J. O'Connor, 1901-27; Thomas J. Walsh, 1928-52, first archbishop; Thomas A. Boland, 1953-74; Peter L. Gerety, 1974-86.

New Orleans,* La. (1793; archdiocese, 1850): Francis B. Schulte, archbishop, 1988. Robert W. Muench, Dominic Carmon, S.V.D. auxiliaries.

Former ordinaries: Luis Penalver y Cardenas, 1793-1801; John Carroll, administrator, 1805-15; W. Louis Dubourg, S.S., 1815-25; Joseph Rosati, C.M., administrator, 1826-29; Leo De Neckere, C.M., 1829-33; Anthony Blanc, 1835-60, first archbishop; Jean Marie Odin, C.M., 1861-70; Napoleon J. Perche, 1870-83; Francis X. Leray, 1883-87; Francis A. Janssens, 1888-97; Placide L. Chapelle, 1897-1905; James H. Blenk, S.M., 1906-17; John W. Shaw, 1918-34; Joseph F. Rummel, 1935-64; John P. Cody, 1964-65; Philip M. Hannan, 1965-88.

Newton, Mass. (Melkite Rite) (1966; eparchy, 1976): Vacant as of Aug. 15, 1993. John A. Elya, B.S.O., Nicholas Samra, auxiliaries.

Former ordinaries: Justin Najmy, exarch, 1966-68; Joseph Tawil, exarch, 1969-76, first eparch, 1976-89; Ignatius Ghattas, B.S.O., 1990-92.

New Ulm, Minn. (1957): Raymond A. Lucker, bishop, 1975.

Former bishop: Alphonse J. Schladweiler, 1958-75.

New York,* N.Y. (1808; archdiocese, 1850): Cardinal John J. O'Connor, archbishop, 1984. Patrick V. Ahern, James P. Mahoney, Anthony F. Mestice, Austin B. Vaughan, Francisco Garmendia, Emerson J. Moore, William J. McCormack, Patrick J. Sheridan, Henry J. Mansell, auxiliaries.

Former ordinaries: Richard L. Concanen, O.P., 1808-10; John Connolly, O.P., 1814-25; John

Dubois, S.S., 1826-42; John J. Hughes, 1842-64, first archbishop; Cardinal John McCloskey, 1864-85; Michael A. Corrigan, 1885-1902; Cardinal John Farley, 1902-18; Cardinal Patrick Hayes, 1919-38; Cardinal Francis Spellman, 1939-67; Cardinal Terence J. Cooke, 1968-83.

Norwich, Conn. (1953): Daniel P. Reilly, bishop, 1975.

Former bishops: Bernard J. Flanagan, 1953-59; Vincent J. Hines, 1960-75.

Oakland, Calif. (1962): John S. Cummins, bishop, 1977.

Former bishop: Floyd L. Begin, 1962-77.

Ogdensburg, N.Y. (1872): Stanislaus J. Brzana, bishop, 1968.

Former bishops: Edgar P. Wadhams, 1872-91; Henry Gabriels, 1892-1921; Joseph H. Conroy, 1921-39; Francis J. Monaghan, 1939-42; Bryan J. McEntegart, 1943-53; Walter P. Kellenberg, 1954-57; James J. Navagh, 1957-63; Leo R. Smith, 1963; Thomas A. Donnellan, 1964-68.

Oklahoma City,* Okla. (1905; archdiocese, 1972): Eusebius J. Beltran, archbishop, 1993.

Former ordinaries: Theophile Meerschaert, 1905-24; Francis C. Kelley, 1924-48; Eugene J. McGuinness, 1948-57; Victor J. Reed, 1958-71; John R. Quinn, 1971-77, first archbishop; Charles A. Salatka, 1977-92.

Omaha,* Nebr. (1885; archdiocese, 1945): Elden F. Curtiss, archbishop, 1993.

Former ordinaries: James O'Gorman, O.C.S.O., 1859-74, vicar apostolic; James O'Connor, vicar apostolic, 1876-85, first bishop, 1885-90; Richard Scannell, 1891-1916; Jeremiah J. Harty, 1916-27; Francis Beckman, administrator, 1926-28; Joseph F. Rummel, 1928-35; James H. Ryan, 1935-47, first archbishop; Gerald T. Bergan, 1948-69; Daniel E. Sheehan, 1969-93.

Orange, Calif. (1976): Norman F. McFarland, bishop, 1986, installed, 1987. Michael P. Driscoll, auxiliary.

Former bishop: William R. Johnson, 1976-86.

Orlando, Fla. (1968): Norbert M. Dorsey, C.P., bishop, 1990.

Former bishops: William Borders, 1968-74; Thomas J. Grady, 1974-89.

Owensboro, Ky. (1937): John J. McRaith, bishop, 1982.

Former bishops: Francis R. Cotton, 1938-60; Henry J. Soenneker, 1961-82.

Palm Beach, Fla. (1984): J. Keith Symons, bishop, 1990.

Former bishop: Thomas V. Daily, 1984-90.

Parma, Ohio (Byzantine Rite) (1969): Andrew Pataki, eparch, 1984.

Former bishop: Emil Mihalik, 1969-84.

Passaic, N.J. (Byzantine Rite) (1963): Michael J. Dudick, eparch, 1968.

Former bishop: Stephen Kocisko, 1963-68.

Paterson, N.J. (1937): Frank J. Rodimer, bishop, 1978.

Former bishops: Thomas H. McLaughlin, 1937-47; Thomas A. Boland, 1947-52; James A. McNulty, 1953-63; James J. Navagh, 1963-65; Lawrence B. Casey, 1966-77.

Pensacola-Tallahassee, Fla. (1975): John M. Smith, bishop, 1991.

Former bishops: Rene H. Gracida, 1975-83; J. Keith Symons, 1983-90.

Peoria, Ill. (1877): John J. Myers, bishop, 1990. Former bishops: John L. Spalding, 1877-1908; Edmund M. Dunne, 1909-29; Joseph H. Schlarman, 1930-51; William E. Cousins, 1952-58; John B. Franz, 1959-71; Edward W. O'Rourke, 1971-90.

Philadelphia,* Pa. (1808; archdiocese, 1875): Cardinal Anthony J. Bevilacqua, archbishop, 1988. Martin J. Lohmuller, Louis A. DeSimone, auxiliaries.

Former ordinaries: Michael Egan, O.F.M., 1810-14; Henry Conwell, 1820-42; Francis P. Kenrick, 1842-51; John N. Neumann, C.SS.R., 1852-60; James F. Wood, 1860-83, first archbishop; Patrick J. Ryan, 1884-1911; Edmond F. Prendergast, 1911-18; Cardinal Dennis Dougherty, 1918-51; Cardinal John O'Hara, C.S.C., 1951-60; Cardinal John Krol, 1961-88.

Philadelphia,* Pa. (Byzantine Rite, Ukrainians) (1924; metropolitan, 1958): Stephen Sulyk, archbishop, 1981. Walter Paska, auxiliary.

Former ordinaries: Stephen Ortynsky, O.S.B.M., 1907-16; Constantine Bohachevsky, 1924-61; Ambrose Senyshyn, O.S.B.M., 1961-76; Joseph Schmondiuk, 1977-78; Myroslav J. Lubachivsky, 1979-80, apostolic administrator, 1980-81.

Phoenix, Ariz. (1969): Thomas J. O'Brien, bishop, 1982.

Former bishops: Edward A. McCarthy, 1969-76; James S. Rausch, 1977-81.

Pittsburgh,* Pa. (Byzantine Rite, Ruthenians) (1924; metropolitan, 1969): Vacant as of Aug. 15, 1993. John M. Bilock, auxiliary.

Former ordinaries: Basil Takach 1924-48; Daniel Ivancho, 1948-54; Nicholas T. Elko, 1955-67; Stephen J. Kocisko, 1968-91, first metropolitan; Thomas V. Dolinay, 1991-93.

Pittsburgh, Pa. (1843): Donald W. Wuerl, bishop, 1988. John B. McDowell, William J. Winter, Thomas J. Tobin, auxiliaries.

Former bishops: Michael O'Connor, 1843-53, 1854-60; Michael Domenec, C.M., 1860-76; J. Tuigg, 1876-89; Richard Phelan, 1889-1904; J.F. Regis Canevin, 1904-20; Hugh C. Boyle, 1921-55; John F. Dearden, 1950-58; John J. Wright, 1959-69; Vincent M. Leonard, 1969-83; Anthony J. Bevilacqua, 1983-88.

Portland, Me. (1853): Joseph J. Gerry, O.S.B., bishop, 1989. Amedee W. Proulx, auxiliary.

Former bishops: David W. Bacon, 1855-74; James A. Healy, 1875-1900; William H. O'Connell, 1901-06; Louis S. Walsh, 1906-24; John G. Murray, 1925-31; Joseph E. McCarthy, 1932-55; Daniel J. Feeney, 1955-69; Peter L. Gerety, 1969-74; Edward C. O'Leary, 1974-88.

Portland,* Ore. (1846): William J. Levada, archbishop, 1986. Kenneth D. Steiner, auxiliary.

Established as Oregon City, name changed, 1928. Former ordinaries: Francis N. Blanchet, 1846-80 vicar apostolic, first archbishop; Charles J. Seghers, 1880-84; William H. Gross, C.SS.R., 1885-98; Alexander Christie, 1899-1925; Edward D. Howard, 1926-66; Robert J. Dwyer, 1966-74; Cornelius M. Power, 1974-86.

Providence, R.I. (1872): Louis E. Gelineau, bishop, 1972.

Former bishops: Thomas F. Hendricken, 1872-86; Matthew Harkins, 1887-1921; William A. Hickey, 1921-33; Francis P. Keough, 1934-47; Russell J. McVinney, 1948-71.

Pueblo, Colo. (1941): Arthur N. Tafoya, bishop, 1980.

Former bishops: Joseph C. Willging, 1942-59; Charles A. Buswell, 1959-79.

Raleigh, N.C. (1924): F. Joseph Gossman, bishop, 1975.

Former bishops: William J. Hafey, 1925-37; Eugene J. McGuinness, 1937-44; Vincent S. Waters, 1945-75.

Rapid City, S. Dak. (1902): Charles J. Chaput, O.F.M. Cap., bishop, 1988.

Established at Lead, transferred, 1930.

Former bishops: John Stariha, 1902-09; Joseph F. Busch, 1910-15; John J. Lawler, 1916-48; William T. McCarty, C.SS.R., 1948-69; Harold J. Dimmerling, 1969-87.

Reno-Las Vegas, Nev. (1931): Daniel F. Walsh, bishop, 1987.

Established at Reno; title changed to Reno-Las Vegas, 1976.

Former bishops: Thomas K. Gorman, 1931-52; Robert J. Dwyer, 1952-66; Joseph Green, 1967-74; Norman F. McFarland, 1976-86.

Richmond, Va. (1820): Walter F. Sullivan, bishop, 1974. David E. Foley, auxiliary.

Former bishops: Patrick Kelly, 1820-22; Ambrose Marechal, S.S., administrator, 1822-28; James Whitfield, administrator, 1828-34; Samuel Eccleston, S.S., administrator, 1834-40; Richard V. Whelan, 1841-50; John McGill, 1850-72; James Gibbons, 1872-77; John J. Keane, 1878-88; Augustine Van de Vyver, 1889-1911; Denis J. O'Connell, 1912-26; Andrew J. Brennan, 1926-45; Peter L. Ireton, 1945-58; John J. Russell, 1958-73.

Rochester, N.Y. (1868): Matthew H. Clark, bishop, 1979.

Former bishops: Bernard J. McQuaid, 1868-1909; Thomas F. Hickey, 1909-28; John F. O'Hern, 1929-33; Edward F. Mooney, 1933-37; James E. Kearney, 1937-66; Fulton J. Sheen, 1966-69; Joseph L. Hogan, 1969-78.

Rockford, Ill. (1908): Arthur J. O'Neill, bishop, 1968.

Former bishops: Peter J. Muldoon, 1908-27; Edward F. Hoban, 1928-42; John J. Boylan, 1943-53; Raymond P. Hillinger, 1953-56; Loras T. Lane, 1956-68.

Rockville Centre, N.Y. (1957): John R. McGann, bishop, 1976. James Daly, Alfred J. Markiewicz, John C. Dunne, Emil A. Wcela, auxiliaries.

Former bishop: Walter P. Kellenberg, 1957-76.

Sacramento, Calif. (1886): Francis A. Quinn, bishop, 1979.

Former bishops: Patrick Manogue, 1886-95; Thomas Grace, 1896-1921; Patrick J. Keane, 1922-28; Robert J. Armstrong, 1929-57; Joseph T. McGucken, 1957-62; Alden J. Bell, 1962-79.

Saginaw, Mich. (1938): Kenneth E. Untener, bishop, 1980.

Former bishops: William F. Murphy, 1938-50;

Stephen S. Woznicki, 1950-68; Francis F. Reh, 1969-80.

St. Augustine, Fla. (1870): John J. Snyder, bishop, 1979.

Former bishops: Augustin Verot, S.S., 1870-76; John Moore, 1877-1901; William J. Kenny, 1902-13; Michael J. Curley, 1914-21; Patrick J. Barry, 1922-40; Joseph P. Hurley, 1940-67; Paul F. Tanner, 1968-79.

St. Cloud, Minn. (1889): Jerome Hanus, O.S.B., bishop, 1987.

Former bishops: Otto Zardetti, 1889-94; Martin Marty, O.S.B., 1895-96; James Trobec, 1897-1914; Joseph F. Busch, 1915-53; Peter Bartholome, 1953-68; George H. Speltz, 1968-87.

St. George's in Canton, Ohio (Byzantine Rite, Romanians) (1982; eparchy, 1987): Vacant as of Aug. 15, 1993. Rev. John Michael Botean, apostolic administrator, 1993.

Former bishop: Vasile Louis Puscas, 1983-93.

St. Josaphat in Parma, Ohio (Byzantine Rite, Ukrainians) (1983): Robert M. Moskal, bishop, 1984.

St. Louis,* Mo. (1826; archdiocese, 1847): Vacant as of Aug. 15, 1993. Edward J. O'Donnell, Paul A. Zipfel, auxiliaries.

Former ordinaries: Joseph Rosati, C.M., 1827-43; Peter R. Kenrick, 1843-95, first archbishop; John J. Kain, 1895-1903; Cardinal John Glennon, 1903-46; Cardinal Joseph Ritter, 1946-67; Cardinal John J. Carberry, 1968-79; John L. May, 1980-92.

St. Maron, Brooklyn, N.Y. (Maronite Rite) (1966; diocese, 1971): Francis Zayek (titular archbishop), exarch, 1966, first eparch, 1972. John Chedid, auxiliary.

Established at Detroit; transferred to Brooklyn, 1977.

St. Nicholas in Chicago (Byzantine Rite Eparchy of St. Nicholas of the Ukrainians) (1961): Michael Wiwchar, C.SS.R., bishop, 1993.

Former bishops: Jaroslav Gabro, 1961-80; Innocent H. Lotocky, O.S.B.M., 1981-93.

St. Paul and Minneapolis,* Minn. (1850; archdiocese, 1888): John R. Roach, archbishop, 1975. Robert J. Carlson, Joseph L. Charron, C.PP.S., Lawrence H. Welsh, auxiliaries.

Former ordinaries: Joseph Cretin, 1851-57; Thomas L. Grace, O.P., 1859-84; John Ireland, 1884-1918, first archbishop; Austin Dowling, 1919-30; John G. Murray, 1931-56; William O. Brady, 1956-61; Leo Binz, 1962-75.

St. Petersburg, Fla. (1968): John C. Favalora, bishop, 1989.

Former bishops: Charles McLaughlin, 1968-78; W. Thomas Larkin, 1979-88.

St. Thomas the Apostle of Detroit (Chaldean Rite) (1982; eparchy, 1985): Ibrahim N. Ibrahim, exarch, 1982; first eparch, 1985.

Salina, Kans. (1887): George K. Fitzsimons, bishop, 1984.

Established at Concordia, transferred, 1944.

Former bishops: Richard Scannell, 1887-91; John J. Hennessy, administrator, 1891-98; John F. Cunningham, 1898-1919; Francis J. Tief, 1921-38; Frank A. Thill, 1938-57; Frederick W. Freking, 1957-64; Cyril J. Vogel, 1965-79; Daniel W. Kucera, O.S.B., 1980-84.

Salt Lake City, Utah (1891): William K. Weigand, bishop, 1980.

Former bishops: Lawrence Scanlan, 1891-1915; Joseph S. Glass, C.M., 1915-26; John J. Mitty, 1926-32; James E. Kearney, 1932-37; Duane G. Hunt, 1937-60; J. Lennox Federal, 1960-80.

San Angelo, Tex. (1961): Michael D. Pfeifer, O.M.I., bishop, 1985.

Former bishops: Thomas J. Drury, 1962-65; Thomas Tschoepe, 1966-69; Stephen A. Leven, 1969-79; Joseph A. Fiorenza, 1979-84.

San Antonio,* Tex. (1874; archdiocese, 1926): Patrick F. Flores, archbishop, 1979. Joseph A. Galante, auxiliary.

Former ordinaries: Anthony D. Pellicer, 1874-80; John C. Neraz, 1881-94; John A. Forest, 1895-1911; John W. Shaw, 1911-18; Arthur Jerome Drossaerts, 1918-40, first archbishop; Robert E. Lucey, 1941-69; Francis Furey, 1969-79.

San Bernardino, Calif. (1978): Phillip F. Straling, bishop, 1978. Gerald R. Barnes, auxiliary.

San Diego, Calif. (1936): Robert H. Brom, bishop, 1990. Gilbert Espinoza Chavez, auxiliary.

Former bishops: Charles F. Buddy, 1936-66; Francis J. Furey, 1966-69; Leo T. Maher, 1969-90.

San Francisco,* Calif. (1853): John R. Quinn, archbishop, 1977. Patrick J. McGrath, Carlos A. Sevilla, S.J., auxiliaries.

Former ordinaries: Joseph S. Alemany, O.P., 1853-84; Patrick W. Riordan, 1884-1914; Edward J. Hanna, 1915-35; John Mitty, 1935-61; Joseph T. McGucken, 1962-77.

San Jose, Calif. (1981): R. Pierre DuMaine, first bishop, 1981.

Santa Fe*, N. Mex. (1850; archdiocese, 1875): Michael J. Sheehan, archbishop, 1993.

Former ordinaries: John B. Lamy, 1850-85; first archbishop; John B. Salpointe, 1885-94; Placide L. Chapelle, 1894-97; Peter Bourgade, 1899-1908; John B. Pitaval, 1909-18; Albert T. Daeger, O.F.M., 1919-32; Rudolph A. Gerken, 1933-43; Edwin V. Byrne, 1943-63; James P. Davis, 1964-74; Robert Sanchez, 1974-93.

Santa Rosa, Calif. (1962): G. Patrick Ziemann, bishop, 1992.

Former bishops: Leo T. Maher, 1962-69; Mark J. Hurley, 1969-86; John T. Steinbock, 1987-91.

Savannah, Ga. (1850): Raymond W. Lessard, bishop, 1973.

Former bishops: Francis X. Gartland, 1850-54; John Barry, 1857-59; Augustin Verot, S.S., 1861-70; Ignatius Persico, O.F.M. Cap., 1870-72; William H. Gross, C.SS.R., 1873-85; Thomas A. Becker, 1886-99; Benjamin J. Keiley, 1900-22; Michael Keyes, S.M., 1922-35; Gerald P. O'Hara, 1935-59; Thomas J. McDonough, 1960-67; Gerard L. Frey, 1967-72.

Scranton, Pa. (1868): James C. Timlin, bishop, 1984. Francis X. Di Lorenzo, auxiliary.

Former bishops: William O'Hara, 1868-99; Michael J. Hoban, 1899-1926; Thomas C. O'Reilly, 1928-38; William J. Hafey, 1938-54; Jerome D. Hannan, 1954-65; J. Carroll McCormick, 1966-83; John J. O'Connor, 1983-84.

Seattle,* Wash. (1850; archdiocese, 1951): Thomas J. Murphy, archbishop, 1991.

Established as Nesqually, name changed, 1907.
Former ordinaries; Augustin M. Blanchet, 1850-79; Aegidius Junger, 1879-95; Edward J. O'Dea, 1896-1932; Gerald Shaughnessy, S.M., 1933-50; Thomas A. Connolly, first archbishop, 1950-75; Raymond G. Hunthausen, 1975-91.

Shreveport, La. (1986): William B. Friend, bishop, 1986.

Sioux City, Ia. (1902): Lawrence D. Soens, bishop, 1983.
Former bishops: Philip J. Garrigan, 1902-19; Edmond Heelan, 1919-48; Joseph M. Mueller, 1948-70; Frank H. Greteman, 1970-83.

Sioux Falls, S. Dak. (1889): Paul V. Dudley, bishop, 1978.
Former bishops: Martin Marty, O.S.B., 1889-94; Thomas O'Gorman, 1896-1921; Bernard J. Mahoney, 1922-39; William O. Brady, 1939-56; Lambert A. Hoch, 1956-78.

Spokane, Wash. (1913): William S. Skylstad, bishop, 1990.
Former bishops: Augustine F. Schinner, 1914-25; Charles D. White, 1927-55; Bernard J. Topel, 1955-78; Lawrence H. Welsh, 1978-90.

Springfield, Ill. (1853): Daniel L. Ryan, bishop, 1984. Established at Quincy, transferred to Alton 1857; transferred to Springfield 1923.
Former bishops: Henry D. Juncker, 1857-68; Peter J. Baltes, 1870-86; James Ryan, 1888-1923; James A. Griffin, 1924-48; William A. O'Connor, 1949-75; Joseph A. McNicholas, 1975-83.

Springfield, Mass. (1870): John A. Marshall, bishop, 1991, installed, 1992. Thomas L. Dupre, auxiliary.
Former bishops: Patrick T. O'Reilly, 1870-92; Thomas D. Beaven, 1892-1920; Thomas M. O'Leary, 1921-49; Christopher J. Weldon, 1950-77; Joseph F. Maguire, 1977-91.

Springfield-Cape Girardeau, Mo. (1956): John J. Leibrecht, bishop, 1984.
Former bishops: Charles Helmsing, 1956-62; Ignatius J. Strecker, 1962-69; William Baum, 1970-73; Bernard F. Law, 1973-84.

Stamford, Conn. (Byzantine Rite, Ukrainians) (1956): Basil Losten, eparch, 1977.
Former eparchs: Ambrose Senyshyn, O.S.B.M., 1956-61; Joseph Schmondiuk, 1961-77.

Steubenville, Ohio (1944): Gilbert I. Sheldon, bishop, 1992.
Former bishops: John K. Mussio, 1945-77; Albert H. Ottenweller, 1977-92.

Stockton, Calif. (1962): Donald W. Montrose, bishop, 1986.
Former bishops: Hugh A. Donohoe, 1962-69; Merlin J. Guilfoyle, 1969-79; Roger M. Mahony, 1980-85.

Superior, Wis. (1905): Raphael M. Fliss, bishop, 1985.
Former bishops: Augustine F. Schinner, 1905-13; Joseph M. Koudelka, 1913-21; Joseph G. Pinten, 1922-26; Theodore M. Reverman, 1926-41; William P. O'Connor, 1942-46; Albert G. Meyer, 1946-53; Joseph Annabring, 1954-59; George A. Hammes, 1960-85.

Syracuse, N.Y. (1886): Joseph T. O'Keefe, bishop, 1987. Thomas J. Costello, auxiliary.

Former bishops: Patrick A. Ludden, 1887-1912; John Grimes, 1912-22; Daniel J. Curley, 1923-32; John A. Duffy, 1933-37; Walter A. Foery, 1937-70; David F. Cunningham, 1970-76; Frank J. Harrison, 1976-87.

Toledo, Ohio (1910): James R. Hoffman, bishop, 1980. Robert Donnelly, auxiliary.
Former bishops: Joseph Schrembs, 1911-21; Samuel A. Stritch, 1921-30; Karl J. Alter, 1931-50; George J. Rehring, 1950-67; John A. Donovan, 1967-80.

Trenton, N.J. (1881): John C. Reiss, bishop, 1980.
Former bishops: Michael J. O'Farrell, 1881-94; James A. McFaul, 1894-1917; Thomas J. Walsh, 1918-28; John J. McMahon, 1928-32; Moses E. Kiley, 1934-40; William A. Griffin, 1940-50; George W. Ahr, 1950-79.

Tucson, Ariz. (1897): Manuel D. Moreno, bishop, 1982.
Former bishops: Peter Bourgade, 1897-99; Henry Granjon, 1900-22; Daniel J. Gercke, 1923-60; Francis J. Green, 1960-81.

Tulsa, Okla. (1972): Vacant as of Aug. 15, 1993.
Former bishop: Bernard J. Ganter, 1973-77; Eusebius J. Beltran, 1978-92.

Tyler, Tex. (1986): Edmond Carmody, bishop, 1992.
Former bishop: Charles E. Herzig, 1987-91.

Van Nuys, Calif. (Byzantine Rite, Ruthenians) (1981): George M. Kuzma, eparch, 1991.
Former bishop: Thomas V. Dolinay, 1982-90.

Venice, Fla. (1984): John J. Nevins, bishop, 1984.
Victoria, Tex. (1982): David E. Fellhauer, bishop, 1990.
Former bishop: Charles V. Grahmann, 1982-89.

Washington,* D.C. (1939): Cardinal James A. Hickey, archbishop, 1980. Alvaro Corrada del Rio, S.J., William G. Curlin, Leonard Olivier, S.V.D., auxiliaries.
Former ordinaries: Michael J. Curley, 1939-47; Cardinal Patrick O'Boyle, 1948-73; Cardinal William Baum, 1973-80.

Wheeling-Charleston, W. Va. (1850): Bernard W. Schmitt, bishop, 1989.
Established as Wheeling; name changed, 1974.
Former bishops: Richard V. Whelan, 1850-74; John J. Kain, 1875-93; Patrick J. Donahue, 1894-1922; John J. Swint, 1922-62; Joseph H. Hodges, 1962-85; Francis B. Schulte, 1985-88.

Wichita, Kans. (1887): Eugene J. Gerber, bishop, 1982, installed, 1983.
Former bishops: John J. Hennessy, 1888-1920; Augustus J. Schwertner, 1921-39; Christian H. Winkelmann, 1940-46; Mark K. Carroll, 1947-67; David M. Maloney, 1967-82.

Wilmington, Del. (1868): Robert E. Mulvee, bishop, 1985.
Former bishops: Thomas A. Becker, 1868-86; Alfred A. Curtis, 1886-96; John J. Monaghan, 1897-1925; Edmond Fitzmaurice, 1925-60; Michael Hyle, 1960-67; Thomas J. Mardaga, 1968-84.

Winona, Minn. (1889): John G. Vlazny, bishop, 1987.
Former bishops: Joseph B. Cotter, 1889-1909; Patrick R. Heffron, 1910-27; Francis M. Kelly, 1928-49; Edward A. Fitzgerald, 1949-69; Loras J. Watters, 1969-86.

Worcester, Mass. (1950): Timothy J. Harrington, bishop, 1983. George E. Rueger, auxiliary.
Former bishops: John J. Wright, 1950-59; Bernard J. Flanagan, 1959-83.
Yakima, Wash. (1951): Francis E. George, O.M.I., bishop, 1990.
Former bishops: Joseph P. Dougherty, 1951-69; Cornelius M. Power, 1969-74; Nicholas E. Walsh, 1974-76; William Skylstad, 1977-90.
Youngstown, Ohio (1943): James W. Malone, bishop, 1968. Benedict C. Franzetta, auxiliary.
Former bishops: James A. McFadden, 1943-52; Emmet M. Walsh, 1952-68.
Apostolic Exarchate for Armenian-Rite Catholics in the United States and Canada, New York, N.Y. (1981); Nerses Mikael Setian, exarch, 1981.

Archdiocese for the Military Services, U.S.A., Washington, D.C. (1957; restructured, 1985): Archbishop Joseph T. Dimino, military ordinary, 1991. Francis X. Roque, John G. Nolan, Joseph J. Madera, M.Pp.S., John J. Glynn, auxiliaries.
Military vicar appointed, 1917; canonically established, 1957, as U.S. Military Vicariate under jurisdiction of New York archbishop; name changed, restructured as independent jurisdiction, 1985.
Former military vicars: Cardinal Patrick Hayes, 1917-38; Cardinal Francis Spellman, 1939-67; Cardinal Terence J. Cooke, 1968-83; Cardinal John J. O'Connor, apostolic administrator, 1984-85.
Former military ordinary: Archbishop Joseph T. Ryan, 1985-91.

MISSIONARY BISHOPS

Africa
South Africa: Keimoes-Upington (diocese), John B. Minder, O.S.F.S.
De Aar (diocese), Joseph J. Potocnak, S.C.J.

Asia
Indonesia: Agats (diocese), Alphonse A. Sowada, O.S.C.
Iraq: Mossul (Chaldean-rite archdiocese), George Garmo.
Korea: Inchon (diocese), William J. McNaughton, M.M.
Philippines: Cotabato (archdiocese), Philip F. Smith, O.M.I.

Central America, West Indies
Honduras: Comayagua (diocese), Gerald Scarpone Caporale, O.F.M.
Jamaica: Mandeville (vicariate apostolic), Paul M. Boyle, C.P.
Nicaragua: Bluefields (vicariate apostolic), Salvator Schlaefer Berg, O.F.M. Cap., vicar apostolic; Paul Schmitz Simon, O.F.M. Cap., auxiliary.
Virgin Islands: St. Thomas (diocese), Vacant as of Aug. 15, 1993.

North America
Mexico: Nuevo Laredo (diocese), Ricardo Watty Urquidi, M.Sp.S., first bishop.

Europe
Iceland: Reykjavik (diocese), Alfred Jolson, S.J.

Oceania
American Samoa: Samoa-Pago Pago (diocese), John Quinn Weitzel, M.M.
Caroline and Marshall Islands: Carolines-Marshalls (diocese), Martin J. Neylon, S.J.
Papua New Guinea: Mendi (diocese), Firmin Schmidt, O.F.M.Cap.
Wewak (diocese), Raymond P. Kalisz, S.V.D.
Vanuatu (New Hebrides): Port Vila (diocese), Francis Lambert, S.M.

South America
Bolivia: Coroico (diocese), Thomas R. Manning, O.F.M.
Pando (vicariate apostolic), Luis Morgan Casey.
Santa Cruz (archdiocese), Charles A. Brown, M.M., auxiliary.
Brazil: Abaetetuba (diocese), Angelo Frosi, S.X.
Cristalandia (prelacy), Herbert Hermes, O.S.B.
Itaituba (prelacy), Capistran Heim, O.F.M.
Jatai (diocese), Benedict D. Coscia, O.F.M., bishop; Michael P. Mundo, auxiliary.
Paranagua (diocese), Alfred Novak, C.Ss.R.
Sao Salvador da Bahia (archdiocese), Thomas W. Murphy, C.SS.R., auxiliary.
Valenca (diocese), Elias James Manning, O.F.M. Conv., bishop.
Peru: Chulucanas (diocese), John C. McNabb, O.S.A.

MARIAN SHRINES

Renewed prayer and outreach at Marian shrines can help the Church prepare to celebrate the 2,000th anniversary of the birth of Christ. So stated the Holy Father in a letter released Sept. 7, 1993, marking the 700th anniversary of the Holy House of the Blessed Virgin in Loreto, Italy.

Meditating on Mary as a model of grace and faith open to doing God's will can help people rediscover "the awe, the adoration, the necessary silence" preceding the great mystery of God becoming human and dwelling on earth, the Pope said. "Historically, Mary was the dawn which preceded the rising of the Son of Justice, Christ our God."

The world's newest Marian shrine, dedicated Aug. 20, 1993, near the Disney theme parks in Florida, marks a new beginning of ministry to travelers and vacationers, providing them with the opportunity to be pilgrims, not just tourists. The shrine includes an evangelization center, a Mother and Child Chapel, and a Rosary Walk and Garden. It has a seating capacity of 2,000.

CATHOLIC POPULATION OF THE UNITED STATES

(Source: *The Official Catholic Directory, 1993;* figures as of Jan. 1, 1993. Archdioceses are indicated by an asterisk; for dioceses marked+, see Dioceses with Interstate Lines.)

State Diocese	Catholics	Dioc. Priests	Rel. Priests	Total Priests	Perm. Deacons	Bros.	Sisters	Par- ishes
Alabama	**131,323**	**166**	**91**	**257**	**43**	**30**	**386**	**151**
*Mobile	67,595	100	66	166	22	12	237	75
Birmingham	63,728	66	25	91	21	18	149	76
Alaska	**48,663**	**43**	**41**	**84**	**66**	**7**	**86**	**69**
*Anchorage	25,408	22	12	34	14	3	54	20
Fairbanks	17,704	6	25	31	43	4	23	41
Juneau	5,551	15	4	19	9	—	9	8
Arizona	**698,888**	**257**	**192**	**449**	**204**	**33**	**562**	**149**
Phoenix	345,079	146	123	269	134	18	247	85
Tucson	353,809	111	69	180	70	15	315	64
Arkansas, Little Rock	**76,070**	**100**	**68**	**168**	**47**	**47**	**364**	**87**
California	**7,696,890**	**2,256**	**1,733**	**3,989**	**576**	**543**	**5,768**	**1,070**
*Los Angeles	3,527,481	639	659	1,298	131	214	2,158	284
*San Francisco	410,943	256	240	496	34	50	1,028	102
Fresno	351,660	114	44	158	3	6	137	85
Monterey	167,850	77	35	112	3	29	130	45
Oakland	472,821	168	208	376	54	44	442	87
Orange	588,105	176	71	247	44	9	391	53
Sacramento	337,176	166	79	245	96	34	250	98
San Bernardino	561,188	175	59	234	74	18	202	99
San Diego	618,408	223	86	309	80	16	390	99
San Jose	374,412	119	213	332	20	86	449	45
Santa Rosa	112,212	81	15	96	10	34	115	41
Stockton	174,634	62	24	86	27	3	76	32
Colorado	**497,555**	**287**	**206**	**493**	**140**	**45**	**867**	**195**
*Denver	332,000	172	146	318	119	32	573	112
Colorado Springs	75,163	36	20	56	15	4	175	29
Pueblo	90,392	79	40	119	6	9	119	54
Connecticut	**1,350,377**	**868**	**305**	**1,173**	**396**	**154**	**1,987**	**389**
*Hartford	793,007	475	144	619	286	122	1,114	223
Bridgeport	342,893	255	93	348	64	6	568	88
Norwich+	214,477	138	68	206	46	26	305	78
Delaware, Wilmington+	**152,452**	**131**	**86**	**217**	**41**	**35**	**348**	**56**
District of Columbia								
*Washington+	**440,000**	**335**	**675**	**1,010**	**205**	**178**	**1,010**	**138**
Florida	**1,768,707**	**811**	**462**	**1,273**	**378**	**134**	**1,408**	**439**
*Miami	681,228	238	127	365	103	56	406	107
Orlando	254,125	123	52	175	86	1	126	69
Palm Beach	174,686	80	44	124	32	2	180	45
Pensacola-Tallahassee	58,225	79	12	91	45	—	62	49
St. Augustine	105,910	87	23	110	15	1	130	50
St. Petersburg	324,221	125	147	272	62	52	360	71
Venice	170,312	79	57	136	35	22	144	48
Georgia	**244,517**	**165**	**120**	**285**	**155**	**25**	**317**	**117**
*Atlanta	187,000	100	86	186	121	7	152	67
Savannah	57,517	65	34	99	34	18	165	50
Hawaii, Honolulu	**248,136**	**83**	**94**	**177**	**28**	**47**	**277**	**66**
Idaho, Boise	**106,640**	**103**	**17**	**120**	**31**	**8**	**116**	**73**
Illinois	**3,527,051**	**1,972**	**1,300**	**3,272**	**934**	**569**	**6,776**	**1,068**
*Chicago	2,306,000	1,048	912	1,960	602	413	3,971	382
Belleville	119,540	150	40	190	26	14	320	129
Joliet	466,500	214	122	336	136	92	868	117
Peoria	230,700	244	71	315	88	15	414	168
Rockford	235,729	152	68	220	82	17	444	101
Springfield	168,582	164	87	251	—	18	759	171
Indiana	**703,659**	**672**	**431**	**1,103**	**97**	**125**	**2,257**	**448**
*Indianapolis	196,848	188	122	310	—	66	880	142

State Diocese	Catholics	Dioc. Priests	Rel. Priests	Total Priests	Perm. Deacons	Bros.	Sisters	Par- ishes
Indiana								
Evansville	84,975	112	10	122	24	2	318	73
Ft. Wayne-South Bend	152,561	119	211	330	37	30	800	90
Gary	185,129	138	60	198	32	22	167	80
Lafayette	84,146	115	28	143	4	5	92	63
Iowa	**517,339**	**779**	**49**	**828**	**190**	**32**	**1,745**	**530**
*Dubuque	222,184	307	32	339	57	31	1,145	217
Davenport	105,866	167	12	179	53	1	316	109
Des Moines	92,115	117	3	120	42	—	143	87
Sioux City	97,174	188	2	190	38	—	141	117
Kansas	**371,091**	**375**	**110**	**485**	**9**	**29**	**1,725**	**385**
*Kansas City	176,520	105	67	172	—	22	872	122
Dodge City	39,363	63	5	68	7	—	106	59
Salina	53,588	67	26	93	—	7	288	95
Wichita	101,620	140	12	152	2	—	459	109
Kentucky	**357,684**	**464**	**110**	**574**	**113**	**108**	**2,151**	**297**
*Louisville	190,180	208	73	281	80	91	1,182	121
Covington	77,104	121	2	123	9	10	505	49
Lexington	40,266	52	22	74	24	6	200	49
Owensboro	50,134	83	13	96	—	1	264	78
Louisiana	**1,361,103**	**713**	**434**	**1,147**	**286**	**197**	**1,367**	**495**
*New Orleans	516,592	240	268	508	150	132	857	145
Alexandria	48,050	62	15	77	8	5	62	48
Baton Rouge	227,355	94	49	143	27	12	121	70
Houma-Thibodaux	112,634	68	8	76	22	13	37	40
Lafayette	338,153	155	59	214	53	29	188	121
Lake Charles	82,079	50	25	75	19	5	25	36
Shreveport	36,240	44	10	54	7	1	77	35
Maine, Portland	**253,861**	**201**	**65**	**266**	**11**	**34**	**595**	**144**
Maryland, *Baltimore	**464,008**	**305**	**273**	**578**	**176**	**94**	**1,388**	**152**
Massachusetts	**2,966,024**	**1,741**	**1,155**	**2,896**	**319**	**357**	**5,213**	**771**
*Boston	1,979,534	1,013	768	1,781	180	215	3,522	398
Fall River	350,450	192	117	309	33	30	416	111
Springfield	321,961	244	85	329	38	20	689	135
Worcester	314,079	292	185	477	68	92	586	127
Michigan	**2,264,449**	**1,194**	**384**	**1,578**	**302**	**122**	**3,454**	**801**
*Detroit	1,477,567	537	257	794	163	96	1,957	304
Gaylord	84,628	71	17	88	9	4	99	81
Grand Rapids	148,579	133	28	161	19	3	350	90
Kalamazoo	101,953	61	17	78	20	7	281	47
Lansing	226,431	148	40	188	64	9	524	85
Marquette	76,282	118	10	128	8	1	85	84
Saginaw	149,000	126	15	141	19	2	158	110
Minnesota	**1,153,736**	**897**	**331**	**1,228**	**191**	**160**	**3,007**	**747**
*St. Paul and Minneapolis	681,755	360	146	506	142	71	1,268	218
Crookston	41,645	49	10	59	3	1	221	77
Duluth	85,500	87	20	107	18	1	210	99
New Ulm	70,310	103	2	105	3	—	99	85
St. Cloud	149,094	157	138	295	25	66	648	144
Winona	125,432	141	15	156	—	21	561	124
Mississippi	**107,237**	**131**	**54**	**185**	**18**	**50**	**356**	**119**
Biloxi	62,897	57	26	83	7	38	71	44
Jackson	44,340	74	28	102	11	12	285	75
Missouri	**834,362**	**881**	**590**	**1,471**	**307**	**284**	**3,313**	**479**
*St. Louis	558,692	545	413	958	183	183	2,668	235
Jefferson City	78,005	117	13	130	52	3	111	96
Kansas City-St. Joseph	147,354	138	100	238	64	44	372	84
Springfield-Cape Girardeau	50,311	81	64	145	8	54	162	64
Montana	**128,483**	**180**	**29**	**209**	**27**	**4**	**177**	**115**
Great Falls-Billings	62,170	82	22	104	3	4	108	57
Helena	66,313	98	7	105	24	—	69	58
Nebraska	**337,226**	**464**	**114**	**578**	**124**	**24**	**725**	**323**
*Omaha	205,280	240	103	343	124	13	473	140
Grand Island	49,967	88	—	88	—	—	106	50

State Diocese	Catholics	Dioc. Priests	Rel. Priests	Total Priests	Perm. Deacons	Bros.	Sisters	Parishes
Nebraska								
Lincoln	81,979	136	11	147	—	11	146	133
Nevada, Reno-Las Vegas	**185,000**	**52**	**34**	**86**	**9**	**9**	**102**	**50**
New Hampshire, Manchester	309,848	258	107	365	18	56	927	131
New Jersey	**3,201,479**	**1,858**	**644**	**2,502**	**689**	**241**	**4,189**	**712**
*Newark	1,305,297	770	311	1,081	225	98	1,634	241
Camden	402,216	349	52	401	103	17	429	126
Metuchen	477,900	206	48	254	81	30	500	110
Paterson	364,185	277	172	449	98	39	1,009	111
Trenton	651,881	256	61	317	182	57	617	124
New Mexico	**466,068**	**243**	**173**	**416**	**144**	**106**	**625**	**194**
*Santa Fe	288,710	152	97	252	98	91	322	91
Gallup	39,744	63	30	93	21	11	217	59
Las Cruces	137,614	25	46	71	25	4	86	44
New York	**7,275,348**	**3,863**	**1,884**	**5,747**	**958**	**682**	**9,332**	**1,691**
*New York	2,263,960	959	1,058	2,017	289	199	1,415	412
Albany	390,000	340	137	477	84	64	1,132	193
Brooklyn	1,602,763	763	179	942	140	164	1,811	217
Buffalo	753,095	496	227	723	86	59	1,622	280
Ogdensburg	161,722	183	22	205	53	17	241	122
Rochester	389,523	304	86	390	84	51	837	162
Rockville Centre	1,352,994	471	100	571	172	108	1,694	133
Syracuse	361,291	347	75	422	50	20	580	172
North Carolina	**181,393**	**146**	**126**	**272**	**51**	**16**	**249**	**139**
Charlotte	94,169	79	78	157	42	6	157	66
Raleigh	87,224	67	48	115	9	10	92	73
North Dakota	**167,462**	**203**	**49**	**252**	**78**	**26**	**450**	**182**
Bismarck	68,559	71	35	106	47	25	194	67
Fargo	98,903	132	14	146	31	1	256	115
Ohio	**2,212,148**	**1,743**	**635**	**2,378**	**554**	**343**	**5,241**	**943**
*Cincinnati	537,400	400	284	684	130	195	1,557	242
Cleveland	812,483	557	172	729	127	91	1,852	240
Columbus	215,924	210	64	274	55	12	461	110
Steubenville	44,729	132	20	152	2	7	94	73
Toledo	325,217	227	61	288	193	10	954	163
Youngstown	276,395	217	34	251	47	28	323	115
Oklahoma	**132,568**	**187**	**63**	**250**	**90**	**20**	**324**	**154**
*Oklahoma City	84,761	113	37	150	52	14	171	72
Tulsa	47,807	74	26	100	38	6	153	82
Oregon	**293,961**	**196**	**229**	**425**	**12**	**77**	**692**	**161**
*Portland	265,636	156	221	377	10	77	656	125
Baker	28,325	40	8	48	2	—	36	36
Pennsylvania	**3,659,657**	**2,868**	**1,053**	**3,921**	**270**	**317**	**10,201**	**1,417**
*Philadelphia	1,456,208	880	461	1,341	105	189	4,535	302
Allentown	258,655	279	75	354	62	15	735	153
Altoona-Johnstown	128,164	167	75	242	11	14	200	125
Erie	210,431	274	21	295	1	—	634	127
Greensburg	204,436	170	102	272	—	32	362	111
Harrisburg	226,325	169	51	220	59	3	611	116
Pittsburgh	810,826	556	171	727	24	56	2,149	274
Scranton	364,612	373	97	470	8	8	975	209
Rhode Island, Providence	**645,608**	**336**	**133**	**469**	**65**	**132**	**922**	**159**
South Carolina, Charleston	**94,036**	**79**	**53**	**132**	**53**	**25**	**167**	**85**
South Dakota	**149,642**	**171**	**83**	**254**	**44**	**29**	**579**	**264**
Rapid City	34,418	41	39	80	22	16	85	109
Sioux Falls	115,224	130	44	174	22	13	494	155
Tennessee	**147,002**	**173**	**49**	**222**	**81**	**56**	**318**	**130**
Knoxville	34,468	35	17	52	22	14	49	38
Memphis	61,073	81	12	93	29	40	108	42
Nashville	51,461	57	20	77	30	2	161	50
Texas	**3,745,960**	**1,141**	**918**	**2,059**	**1,002**	**252**	**3,310**	**948**
*San Antonio	619,367	157	225	382	214	111	1,079	138
Amarillo	39,038	57	6	63	30	1	140	33
Austin	210,000	121	60	181	77	46	113	87

State Diocese	Catholics	Dioc. Priests	Rel. Priests	Total Priests	Perm. Deacons	Bros.	Sisters	Parishes
Texas								
Beaumont	89,124	63	17	80	31	4	60	43
Brownsville	573,165	58	56	114	82	13	146	61
Corpus Christi	348,500	101	63	164	62	28	356	84
Dallas	262,605	100	92	192	121	5	202	56
El Paso	459,479	79	48	127	23	17	199	55
Fort Worth	158,586	59	56	115	48	7	118	84
Galveston-Houston	714,898	186	214	400	210	18	599	146
Lubbock	48,194	31	14	45	25	—	41	36
San Angelo	78,850	53	26	79	41	—	35	49
Tyler	35,581	24	23	47	28	1	76	27
Victoria	108,573	52	18	70	10	1	146	49
Utah, Salt Lake City	**72,335**	**56**	**38**	**94**	**26**	**6**	**99**	**43**
Vermont, Burlington	**145,543**	**149**	**56**	**205**	**32**	**25**	**292**	**97**
Virginia	**442,961**	**348**	**114**	**462**	**75**	**35**	**566**	**191**
Arlington	270,650	121	84	205	69	25	241	60
Richmond	172,311	227	30	257	6	10	325	131
Washington	**480,453**	**342**	**247**	**589**	**154**	**48**	**1,102**	**258**
*Seattle	343,062	200	143	343	100	33	658	137
Spokane	78,491	89	93	182	37	14	398	81
Yakima	58,900	53	11	64	17	1	46	40
West Virginia								
Wheeling-Charleston	**105,724**	**128**	**65**	**193**	**32**	**7**	**326**	**126**
Wisconsin	**1,549,854**	**1,283**	**582**	**1,865**	**266**	**172**	**4,479**	**921**
*Milwaukee	620,409	545	374	919	144	102	2,519	269
Green Bay	373,601	262	140	402	71	51	789	210
La Crosse	223,256	212	24	236	19	11	612	190
Madison	247,991	180	25	205	—	7	429	137
Superior	84,597	84	19	103	32	1	130	115
Wyoming, Cheyenne+	**47,154**	**52**	**8**	**60**	**1**	**4**	**47**	**37**
EASTERN RITES	**518,061**	**568**	**111**	**679**	**131**	**46**	**322**	**563**
*Philadelphia	74,421	60	10	70	5	3	79	79
St. Nicholas	17,981	36	13	49	14	4	9	31
Stamford	36,089	41	16	57	5	2	35	51
St. Josaphat (Parma)	11,823	39	1	40	5	—	11	35
*Pittsburgh	103,651	67	6	73	—	11	115	86
Parma	16,650	46	2	48	—	—	15	42
Passaic	74,500	94	22	116	18	7	24	99
Van Nuys	3,170	16	2	18	4	2	2	16
St. Maron (Maronites)	54,076	86	8	94	12	10	5	51
Newton (Melkites)	27,000	44	25	69	25	7	5	40
St. Thomas Apostle of Detroit (Chaldean)	55,000	17	—	17	43	—	10	12
St. George Martyr (Romanian)	5,200	20	2	22	—	—	—	15
Armenian Ex. (U.S.-Canada)	38,500	2	4	6	—	—	12	6
MILITARY ARCHDIOCESE	**1,361,900**	**424**	**162**	**586**	**79**	**—**	**15**	**—**
U.S. TOTALS 1993	**56,398,696**	**32,872**	**17,135**	**50,007**	**10,328**	**6,205**	**92,621**	**19,469**
U.S. Totals 1992	**55,337,316**	**33,835**	**17,523**	**51,358**	**9,987**	**6,550**	**97,751**	**19,581**
U.S. Totals 1983	**52,088,744**	**35,356**	**22,514**	**57,870**	**6,066**	**7,658**	**120,699**	**18,939**

CATHOLIC POPULATION OF OUTLYING U.S. AREAS

	Catholics	Dioc. Priests	Rel. Priests	Total Priests	Perm. Deacons	Bros.	Sisters	Parishes
Puerto Rico	**2,563,915**	**407**	**388**	**795**	**437**	**52**	**1,202**	**318**
Am.Samoa, Samoa-Pago Pago	9,248	9	2	11	2	—	14	8
Carolines-Marshalls	**70,542**	**8**	**22**	**30**	**42**	**1**	**39**	**27**
Guam, *Agana	**101,000**	**25**	**21**	**46**	**6**	**1**	**104**	**24**
Northern Mariana Islands								
Chalan Kanoa	**47,322**	**2**	**3**	**5**	**3**	**—**	**22**	**9**
Virgin Islands								
St. Thomas	**30,000**	**8**	**5**	**13**	**22**	**1**	**20**	**8**
TOTALS	**2,822,027**	**459**	**441**	**900**	**512**	**55**	**1,401**	**394**
GRAND TOTALS 1993	**59,220,723**	**33,331**	**17,576**	**50,907**	**10,840**	**6,260**	**94,022**	**19,863**

PERCENTAGE OF CATHOLICS IN TOTAL POPULATION IN U.S.

(Source: *The Official Catholic Directory, 1993;* figures are as of Jan. 1, 1993. Total general population figures at the end of the table are U.S. Census Bureau estimates for Jan. 1 of the respective years. Archdioceses are indicated by an asterisk; for dioceses marked +, see Dioceses with Interstate Lines.)

State Diocese	Catholic Pop.	Total Pop.	Cath. Pct.	State Diocese	Catholic Pop.	Total Pop.	Cath. Pct.
Alabama	131,323	4,010,579	3.3	Ft. Wayne-S. Bend	152,561	1,096,876	13.9
*Mobile	67,595	1,452,506	4.7	Gary	185,129	734,339	25.2
Birmingham	63,728	2,558,073	2.5	Lafayette	84,146	1,022,916	8.2
Alaska	48,663	505,888	9.6	Iowa	517,339	2,771,857	18.7
*Anchorage	25,408	300,000	8.5	*Dubuque	222,184	923,454	24.1
Fairbanks	17,704	133,467	13.3	Davenport	105,866	707,123	15.0
Juneau	5,551	72,421	7.6	Des Moines	92,115	671,381	13.7
Arizona	698,888	3,608,676	19.4	Sioux City	97,174	469,899	20.7
Phoenix	345,079	2,502,600	13.8	Kansas	371,091	2,380,675	15.6
Tucson	353,809	1,106,076	32.0	*Kansas City	176,520	952,000	18.5
Arkansas, Little Rock	76,070	2,372,000	3.2	Dodge City	39,363	209,536	18.8
California	7,696,890	30,502,653	25.2	Salina	53,588	333,539	16.1
*Los Angeles	3,527,481	10,105,825	34.9	Wichita	101,620	885,600	11.5
*San Francisco	410,943	1,700,000	24.2	Kentucky	357,684	3,694,474	9.7
Fresno	351,660	1,923,433	18.2	*Louisville	190,180	1,139,022	16.7
Monterey	167,850	839,253	20.0	Covington	77,104	403,024	19.1
Oakland	472,821	2,082,914	22.7	Lexington	40,266	1,376,114	2.9
Orange	588,105	2,512,198	23.4	Owensboro	50,134	776,314	6.5
Sacramento	337,176	2,699,140	12.5	Louisiana	1,361,103	4,232,137	32.2
San Bernardino	561,188	2,820,300	19.9	*New Orleans	516,592	1,307,576	39.5
San Diego	618,408	2,607,319	23.7	Alexandria	48,050	400,478	12.0
San Jose	374,412	1,497,648	25.0	Baton Rouge	227,355	754,933	30.0
Santa Rosa	112,212	771,950	14.5	Houma-Thibodaux	112,634	202,000	55.8
Stockton	174,634	942,673	18.5	Lafayette	338,153	540,143	62.6
Colorado	497,555	3,363,204	14.8	Lake Charles	82,079	259,425	31.6
*Denver	332,000	2,358,754	14.1	Shreveport	36,240	767,582	4.7
Colorado Springs	75,163	519,450	14.5	Maine, Portland	253,861	1,227,927	20.7
Pueblo	90,392	485,000	18.6	Maryland, *Baltimore	464,008	2,722,904	17.0
Connecticut	1,350,377	3,248,714	41.6	Massachusetts	2,966,024	6,006,284	49.4
*Hartford	793,007	1,830,094	43.3	*Boston	1,979,534	3,783,817	52.3
Bridgeport	342,893	817,900	41.9	Fall River	350,450	700,440	50.0
Norwich+	214,477	600,720	35.7	Springfield	321,961	812,322	39.6
Delaware, Wilmington+	152,452	1,009,937	15.1	Worcester	314,079	709,705	44.3
District of Columbia				Michigan	2,264,449	9,382,028	24.1
*Washington+	440,000	2,312,795	19.0	*Detroit	1,477,567	4,266,654	34.6
Florida	1,768,707	13,589,620	13.0	Gaylord	84,628	421,449	20.1
*Miami	681,228	3,270,606	20.8	Grand Rapids	148,579	1,109,795	13.4
Orlando	245,125	2,800,000	9.1	Kalamazoo	101,953	968,535	10.5
Palm Beach	174,686	1,337,610	13.0	Lansing	226,431	1,616,148	14.0
Pensacola-Tallahassee	58,225	1,168,012	5.0	Marquette	76,282	313,915	24.3
St. Augustine	105,910	1,404,260	7.5	Saginaw	149,009	685,532	21.7
St. Petersburg	324,221	2,189,864	14.8	Minnesota	1,153,736	4,414,545	26.1
Venice	170,312	1,419,268	12.0	*St. Paul and			
Georgia	244,517	6,578,292	3.7	Minneapolis	681,755	2,533,701	26.9
*Atlanta	187,000	3,810,625	4.9	Crookston	41,645	236,100	17.6
Savannah	57,517	2,768,292	2.1	Duluth	85,500	404,500	21.1
Hawaii, Honolulu	248,136	1,134,800	21.8	New Ulm	70,310	278,514	25.2
Idaho, Boise	106,640	1,039,000	10.2	St. Cloud	149,094	433,427	34.4
Illinois	3,527,051	11,434,102	30.8	Winona	125,432	528,303	23.7
*Chicago	2,306,000	5,621,485	41.0	Mississippi	107,237	2,643,827	4.1
Belleville	119,540	861,193	13.9	Biloxi	62,897	663,802	9.5
Joliet	466,500	1,352,000	34.5	Jackson	44,340	1,980,025	2.2
Peoria	230,700	1,413,800	16.3	Missouri	834,362	5,114,960	16.3
Rockford	235,729	1,079,500	21.8	*St. Louis	558,692	2,005,499	27.9
Springfield	168,582	1,106,124	15.2	Jefferson City	78,005	750,700	10.4
Indiana	703,659	5,519,297	12.7	Kansas City-St. Joseph	147,354	1,299,555	11.3
*Indianapolis	196,848	2,201,503	8.9	Springfield-			
Evansville	84,975	463,663	18.3	Cape Girardeau	50,311	1,059,206	4.7

State Diocese	Catholic Pop.	Total Pop.	Cath. Pct.	State Diocese	Catholic Pop.	Total Pop.	Cath. Pct.
Montana	128,483	776,230	16.5	Greensburg	204,436	679,144	30.1
Great Falls-Billings	62,170	351,858	17.7	Harrisburg	226,325	1,867,124	12.1
Helena	66,313	424,372	15.6	Pittsburgh	810,826	2,069,118	39.2
Nebraska	337,226	1,582,128	21.3	Scranton	364,612	1,006,170	36.2
*Omaha	205,280	775,037	26.5	Rhode Island, Providence	645,608	1,004,000	64.3
Grand Island	49,967	290,429	17.2	South Carolina			
Lincoln	81,979	516,662	15.8	Charleston	94,036	3,486,703	2.7
Nevada, Reno-Las Vegas	185,000	1,296,340	14.3	South Dakota	149,642	711,591	21.0
New Hampshire				Rapid City	34,418	211,591	16.3
Manchester	309,848	1,105,000	28.0	Sioux Falls	115,224	500,000	23.0
New Jersey	3,201,479	7,730,188	41.4	Tennessee	147,002	4,920,157	3.0
*Newark	1,305,297	2,650,504	49.2	Knoxville	34,468	1,860,218	1.9
Camden	402,216	1,255,669	32.0	Memphis	61,073	1,359,225	4.5
Metuchen	477,900	1,111,442	43.0	Nashville	51,461	1,700,714	3.0
Paterson	364,185	1,005,356	36.2	Texas	3,745,960	17,302,893	21.6
Trenton	651,881	1,707,217	38.2	*San Antonio	619,367	1,639,283	37.8
New Mexico	466,068	1,705,640	27.3	Amarillo	39,038	371,403	10.5
*Santa Fe	288,710	900,000	32.1	Austin	210,000	1,638,245	12.8
Gallup	39,744	355,640	11.2	Beaumont	89,124	528,500	16.9
Las Cruces	137,614	450,000	30.6	Brownsville	573,165	701,888	88.7
New York	7,275,348	18,209,391	40.0	Corpus Christi	348,500	720,700	48.3
*New York	2,263,960	5,096,270	44.4	Dallas	262,605	2,546,402	10.3
Albany	390,000	1,312,411	29.7	El Paso+	459,479	706,891	65.0
Brooklyn	1,602,763	4,252,262	37.7	Fort Worth	158,586	2,061,632	7.7
Buffalo	753,095	1,600,000	47.1	Galveston-Houston	714,898	3,883,265	18.4
Ogdensburg	161,722	430,000	37.6	Lubbock	48,194	448,312	10.7
Rochester	389,523	1,458,749	26.7	San Angelo	78,850	674,500	11.7
Rockville Centre	1,352,994	2,836,108	47.7	Tyler	35,581	1,126,596	3.2
Syracuse	361,291	1,223,591	29.5	Victoria	108,573	255,276	42.5
North Carolina	181,393	6,744,304	2.7	Utah, Salt Lake City	72,335	1,722,850	4.2
Charlotte	94,169	3,443,145	2.7	Vermont, Burlington	145,543	562,758	25.9
Raleigh	87,224	3,301,159	2.6	Virginia	442,961	6,337,597	7.0
North Dakota	167,462	651,707	25.7	Arlington	270,650	1,937,597	14.0
Bismarck	68,559	261,307	26.2	Richmond	172,311	4,400,000	3.9
Fargo	98,903	390,400	25.3	Washington	480,453	5,053,991	9.5
Ohio	2,212,148	10,943,329	20.2	*Seattle	343,062	3,985,500	8.6
*Cincinnati	537,400	2,840,500	18.9	Spokane	78,491	606,891	12.9
Cleveland	812,483	2,766,206	29.4	Yakima	58,900	461,600	12.8
Columbus	215,924	2,127,520	10.1	West Virginia			
Steubenville	44,729	511,607	8.7	Wheeling-Charleston	105,724	1,793,477	5.9
Toledo	325,217	1,486,610	21.9	Wisconsin	1,549,854	5,062,146	30.6
Youngstown	276,395	1,210,886	22.8	*Milwaukee	620,409	2,080,883	29.8
Oklahoma	132,568	3,100,003	4.3	Green Bay	373,601	836,600	44.7
*Oklahoma City	84,761	1,843,503	4.6	La Crosse	223,256	781,763	28.5
Tulsa	47,807	1,256,500	3.8	Madison	247,991	991,964	25.0
Oregon	293,961	2,930,000	10.0	Superior	84,597	370,936	22.8
*Portland	265,636	2,555,100	10.4	Wyoming, Cheyenne	47,154	467,000	10.1
Baker	28,325	374,918	7.6	EASTERN RITES	518,061	—	—
Pennsylvania	3,659,657	11,934,548	30.7	MILITARY			
*Philadelphia	1,456,208	3,729,737	39.0	ARCHDIOCESE	1,361,900	—	—
Allentown	258,655	1,084,189	23.9	U.S. TOTALS 1993	56,398,696	256,561,239	22.0
Altoona-Johnstown	128,164	636,571	20.1	U.S. Totals 1992	55,337,316	253,572,640	21.8
Erie	210,431	862,495	24.4	U.S. Totals 1983	52,088,744	233,267,000	22.3

NATIONAL SHRINE OF THE IMMACULATE CONCEPTION

The National Shrine of the Immaculate Conception is dedicated to the honor of the Blessed Virgin Mary who, by decision of the nation's bishops, was declared patroness of the United States under this title in 1846, eight years before the proclamation of the dogma of the Immaculate Conception. The church was designated a minor basilica by Pope John Paul II Oct. 12, 1990. The church is the seventh largest religious building in the world and the largest Catholic church in the Western Hemisphere, with numerous special chapels and with normal seating and standing accommodations for 6,000 people. Open daily, it is adjacent to The Catholic University of America, at Michigan Ave. and Fourth St. N.E., Washington, D.C. 20017. Msgr. Michael Bramsfield is the rector.

RECEPTIONS INTO THE CHURCH
AND MARRIAGES IN THE UNITED STATES

(Source: *The Official Catholic Directory, 1993;* figures as of Jan. 1, 1993. Archdioceses are indicated by an asterisk; for dioceses marked +, see Dioceses with Interstate Lines.)

State Diocese	Rec'd into Church	Mar- riages	State Diocese	Rec'd into Church	Mar- riages
Alabama	3,397	861	Gary	2,980	988
*Mobile	1,696	419	Lafayette	2,261	639
Birmingham	1,701	442	Iowa	11,253	4,401
Alaska	1,595	273	*Dubuque	4,530	1,947
*Anchorage	936	169	Davenport	2,364	859
Fairbanks	479	74	Des Moines	2,188	776
Juneau	180	30	Sioux City	2,171	819
Arizona	16,788	2,954	Kansas	9,546	2,737
Phoenix	9,553	1,860	*Kansas City	4,351	1,285
Tucson	7,235	1,094	Dodge City	1,020	264
Arkansas, Little Rock	2,110	649	Salina	1,260	412
California	209,093	33,121	Wichita	2,915	776
*Los Angeles	98,783	12,688	Kentucky	8,181	2,707
*San Francisco	8,735	2,095	*Louisville	3,878	1,193
Fresno	17,433	2,153	Covington	1,843	691
Monterey	5,183	1,038	Lexington	1,055	341
Oakland	9,996	1,964	Owensboro	1,405	482
Orange	18,622	3,501	Louisiana	25,461	7,614
Sacramento	10,042	1,971	*New Orleans	8,932	2,589
San Bernardino	10,162	2,249	Alexandria	1,108	305
San Diego	11,815	2,598	Baton Rouge	3,504	1,360
San Jose	9,868	1,325	Houma-Thibodaux	2,147	617
Santa Rosa	3,314	752	Lafayette	6,980	1,914
Stockton	5,140	787	Lake Charles	1,930	598
Colorado	14,693	2,913	Shreveport	860	231
*Denver	10,563	2,118	Maine, Portland	4,632	1,857
Colorado Springs	1,624	347	Maryland, *Baltimore	11,317	5,186
Pueblo	2,506	448	Massachusetts	50,401	16,957
Connecticut	24,499	7,488	*Boston	32,549	10,899
*Hartford	14,031	4,443	Fall River	6,362	2,299
Bridgeport	6,428	2,124	Springfield	5,511	1,986
Norwich+	4,040	921	Worcester	5,979	1,773
Delaware, Wilmington+	3,681	1,203	Michigan	39,303	13,470
District of Columbia, *Washington+	9,471	2,666	*Detroit	20,928	7,137
Florida	42,553	10,153	Gaylord	1,606	610
*Miami	17,948	3,362	Grand Rapids	4,199	1,312
Orlando	6,682	1,844	Kalamazoo	2,182	632
Palm Beach	4,678	1,128	Lansing	5,669	1,951
Pensacola-Tallahassee	1,474	382	Marquette	1,448	636
St. Augustine	2,540	750	Saginaw	3,271	1,192
St. Petersburg	5,943	1,880	Minnesota	23,357	8,027
Venice	3,288	807	*St. Paul and Minneapolis	13,836	4,293
Georgia	5,550	1,334	Crookston	978	320
*Atlanta	3,884	911	Duluth	1,782	724
Savannah	1,666	423	New Ulm	1,445	534
Hawaii, Honolulu	5,171	1,124	St. Cloud	2,957	1,202
Idaho, Boise	2,671	580	Winona	2,359	954
Illinois	69,915	20,995	Mississippi	2,607	797
*Chicago	42,667	12,775	Biloxi	1,469	464
Belleville	2,318	897	Jackson	1,138	333
Joliet	10,336	2,864	Missouri	16,924	5,841
Peoria	4,807	1,550	*St. Louis	10,379	3,520
Rockford	6,026	1,514	Jefferson City	1,934	736
Springfield	3,761	1,395	Kansas City-St. Joseph	3,270	1,112
Indiana	15,866	5,283	Springfield-Cape Girardeau	1,341	473
*Indianapolis	5,343	1,726	Montana	2,629	844
Evansville	1,950	680	Great Falls-Billings	1,350	380
Ft. Wayne-South Bend	3,332	1,250	Helena	1,279	464

State Diocese	Rec'd into Church	Mar- riages	State Diocese	Rec'd into Church	Mar- riages
Nebraska	8,296	2,434	Tennessee	4,119	1,192
*Omaha	5,159	1,582	Knoxville	946	322
Grand Island	1,280	373	Memphis	1,467	424
Lincoln	1,857	479	Nashville	1,706	446
Nevada, Reno-Las Vegas	4,091	814	Texas	83,692	16,564
New Hampshire, Manchester	6,561	1,743	*San Antonio	14,223	2,838
New Jersey	58,861	17,868	Amarillo	1,224	272
*Newark	20,772	6,905	Austin	6,119	1,418
Camden	9,530	2,432	Beaumont	1,775	457
Metuchen	8,169	2,584	Brownsville	8,152	1,365
Paterson	8,836	2,701	Corpus Christi	6,883	1,316
Trenton	11,554	3,246	Dallas	8,784	1,937
New Mexico	12,254	2,225	El Paso	6,588	988
*Santa Fe	7,957	1,587	Fort Worth	5,314	1,022
Gallup	1,124	163	Galveston-Houston	16,734	3,410
Las Cruces	3,173	475	Lubbock	2,342	331
New York	122,591	38,555	San Angelo	2,688	522
*New York	37,863	9,958	Tyler	1,093	244
Albany	7,227	2,878	Victoria	1,773	444
Brooklyn	27,096	6,463	Utah, Salt Lake City	2,274	419
Buffalo	9,160	3,772	Vermont, Burlington	2,599	903
Ogdensburg	2,905	1,057	Virginia	11,551	2,881
Rochester	6,762	2,241	Arlington	7,054	1,772
Rockville Centre	23,536	9,279	Richmond	4,497	1,109
Syracuse	8,042	2,907	Washington	12,141	3,150
North Carolina	5,322	1,499	*Seattle	7,948	2,226
Charlotte	2,793	773	Spokane	1,734	460
Raleigh	2,529	726	Yakima	2,459	464
North Dakota	3,508	1,246	West Virginia, Wheeling-Charleston	1,992	753
Bismarck	1,614	574	Wisconsin	27,284	13,215
Fargo	1,894	672	*Milwaukee	11,605	4,230
Ohio	40,924	14,735	Green Bay	6,126	2,353
*Cincinnati	10,876	3,437	La Crosse	4,048	4,505
Cleveland	13,740	5,392	Madison	3,823	1,465
Columbus	5,043	1,487	Superior	1,682	662
Steubenville	1,304	433	Wyoming, Cheyenne+	1,454	372
Toledo	5,277	2,247	**EASTERN CHURCHES**	**5,504**	**2,303**
Youngstown	4,684	1,739	*Philadelphia	761	320
Oklahoma	3,861	1,110	St. Nicholas	351	191
*Oklahoma City	2,540	672	Stamford	252	117
Tulsa	1,321	438	St. Josaphat (Parma)	162	61
Oregon	6,074	1,565	*Pittsburgh	798	579
*Portland	5,046	1,432	Parma	219	84
Baker	1,028	224	Passaic	534	195
Pennsylvania	59,048	22,269	Van Nuys	102	30
*Philadelphia	23,470	8,424	St. Maron (Maronites)	854	283
Allentown	4,688	1,729	Newton (Melkites)	453	194
Altoona-Johnstown	2,202	966	St. Thomas Apostle of		
Erie	3,926	1,519	Detroit (Chaldeans)	864	186
Greensburg	3,164	1,322	St. George Martyr (Romanian)	77	26
Harrisburg	4,679	1,398	Armenian Ex. (U.S.-Can.)	77	37
Pittsburgh	10,825	4,554	**MILITARY ARCHDIOCESE**	**11,871**	**2,240**
Scranton	6,094	2,357	**U.S. TOTALS 1993**	**1,142,270***	**316,675**
Rhode Island, Providence	7,829	2,741	**U.S. Totals 1992**	**1,128,376***	**322,550**
South Carolina, Charleston	2,560	719	**U.S. Totals 1983**	**1,059,300****	**347,445**
South Dakota	3,345	1,034			
Rapid City	1,037	229			
Sioux Falls	2,308	805			

* Includes infant and adult baptisms, and already baptized persons received into full communion with the Church.

** Includes infant baptisms and converts.

North American College

The North American College, founded by the U.S. bishops in 1859, is a residence and house of formation for U.S. seminarians and graduate students in Rome. The first ordination of an alumnus took place June 14, 1862. Pontifical status was granted the college by Pope Leo XIII Oct. 25, 1884. Students pursue theological and related studies principally at the Pontifical Gregorian University.

STATISTICAL SUMMARY OF THE CHURCH IN THE U.S.

(Principal source: *The Official Catholic Directory, 1993. Comparisons, where given, are with figures reported in the previous edition of the Directory.*)

Catholic Population: 56,398,696; increase, 1,061,380. Percent of total population, 22.

Jurisdictions: 34 archdioceses (includes Military Archdiocese), 154 dioceses (includes St. Thomas, Virgin Islands), 1 apostolic exarchate (New York-based Armenian exarchate for U.S. and Canada).

Vacant jurisdictions (as of Sept 1, 1993), 13: Baton Rouge, Belleville, Birmingham, Charlotte, Des Moines, Helena, Lubbock, Newton (Melkites), Pittsburgh archdiocese (Ukrainians), St. George's in Canton (Romanian), St. Louis archdiocese, Tulsa and St. Thomas (Virgin Islands).

Cardinals: 11 (6 head archiepiscopal sees in U.S., 1, in Europe; 2 are Roman Curia officials; 2 are retired). As of Sept. 1, 1993.

Archbishops: 60. Diocesan, in U.S., 32 (includes 6 cardinals and the Military Archbishop); retired, 20 (includes 2 cardinals); outside U.S., 8 (includes 3 cardinals). As of Sept. 1, 1993.

Bishops: 382. Diocesan, in U.S., 144 (1 is titular archbishop); exarch, 1; auxiliaries, 105; retired, 103; serving outside U.S., 29. As of Sept. 1, 1993.

Priests: 50,007; decrease, 1,351. Diocesan, 32,872 (decrease, 963); religious order priests (does not include those assigned overseas), 17,135 (decrease, 388).

Permanent Deacons: 10,328; increase, 341.

Brothers: 6,205; decrease, 345.

Sisters: 92,621; decrease, 5,130.

Seminarians: 5,715. Diocesan seminarians, 4,219; religious order seminarians, 1,496.

Receptions into Church: 1,142,270. Includes infant and adult baptisms and already baptized persons received into full communion with the Church.

First Communions: 765,208.

Confirmations: 533,852.

Marriages: 316,675.

Deaths: 449,043.

Parishes: 19,469.

Seminaries, Diocesan: 70.

Religious Seminaries: 128.

Colleges and Universities: 226. Students, 638,728.

High Schools: 1,271. Students, 604,545.

Elementary Schools: 7,187. Students 1,951,595.

Non-Residential Schools for Handicapped: 94. Students, 8,765.

Teachers: 164,661 (priests, 2,738; brothers, 1,756; scholastics, 78; sisters, 15,735; laity, 144,354).

Public School students in Religious Instruction Programs: 4,041,285. High school students 759,656; elementary school students, 3,281,629.

Hospitals: 621; patients treated, 50,216,423.

Health Care Centers: 245; patients treated, 2,249,694.

Specialized Homes: 1,531; patients assisted, 671,525.

Residential Care of Children (Orphanages): 240; total assisted, 212,042.

Day Care and Extended Day Care Centers: 950; total assisted, 102,957.

Special Centers for Social Services: 1,926; assisted annually, 16,751,938.

CATHEDRALS IN THE UNITED STATES

A cathedral is the principal church in a diocese, the one in which the bishop has his seat (cathedra). He is the actual pastor, although many functions of the church, which usually serves a parish, are the responsibility of a priest serving as the rector. Because of the dignity of a cathedral, the dates of its dedication and its patronal feast are observed throughout a diocese.

The pope's cathedral, the Basilica of St. John Lateran, is the highest-ranking church in the world.

(Archdioceses are indicated by asterisk.)

Albany, N.Y.: Immaculate Conception.
Alexandria, La.: St. Francis Xavier.
Allentown, Pa.: St. Catharine of Siena.
Altoona-Johnstown, Pa.: Blessed Sacrament (Altoona); St. John Gualbert (Johnstown).
Amarillo, Tex.: St. Laurence.
Anchorage,* Alaska: Holy Family.
Arlington, Va: St. Thomas More.
Atlanta,* Ga.: Christ the King.
Austin, Tex.: St. Mary (Immaculate Conception).
Baker, Ore.: St. Francis de Sales.
Baltimore,* Md.: Mary Our Queen; Basilica of the Assumption of the Blessed Virgin Mary (Co-Cathedral).
Baton Rouge, La.: St. Joseph.
Beaumont, Tex.: St. Anthony (of Padua).

Belleville, Ill.: St. Peter.
Biloxi, Miss.: Nativity of the Blessed Virgin Mary.
Birmingham, Ala.: St. Paul.
Bismarck, N.D.: Holy Spirit.
Boise, Ida.: St. John the Evangelist.
Boston,* Mass.: Holy Cross.
Bridgeport, Conn.: St. Augustine.
Brooklyn, N.Y.: St. James (Minor Basilica).
Brownsville, Tex.: Immaculate Conception.
Buffalo, N.Y.: St. Joseph.
Burlington, Vt.: Immaculate Conception.
Camden, N.J.: Immaculate Conception.
Charleston, S.C.: St. John the Baptist.
Charlotte, N.C.: St. Patrick.
Cheyenne, Wyo.: St. Mary.
Chicago,* Ill.: Holy Name (of Jesus).
Cincinnati,* Ohio: St. Peter in Chains.
Cleveland, Ohio: St. John the Evangelist.
Colorado Springs, Colo: St. Mary.
Columbus, Ohio: St. Joseph.
Corpus Christi, Tex.: Corpus Christi.
Covington, Ky.: Basilica of the Assumption.
Crookston, Minn.: Immaculate Conception.
Dallas, Tex.: Cathedral-Santuario de Guadalupe.
Davenport, Ia.: Sacred Heart.
Denver,* Colo.: Immaculate Conception (Minor Basilica).

Des Moines, Ia.: St. Ambrose.
Detroit,* Mich.: Most Blessed Sacrament.
Dodge City, Kans.: Sacred Heart.
Dubuque,* Ia.: St. Raphael.
Duluth, Minn.: Our Lady of the Rosary.
El Paso, Tex.: St. Patrick.
Erie, Pa.: St. Peter.
Evansville, Ind.: Most Holy Trinity (Pro-Cathedral).
Fairbanks, Alaska: Sacred Heart.
Fall River, Mass.: St. Mary of the Assumption.
Fargo, N.D.: St. Mary.
Fort Wayne-S. Bend, Ind.: Immaculate Conception (Fort Wayne); St. Matthew (South Bend).
Fort Worth, Tex.: St. Patrick.
Fresno, Calif.: St. John (the Baptist).
Gallup, N.M.: Sacred Heart.
Galveston-Houston, Tex.: St. Mary (Minor Basilica, Galveston); Sacred Heart Co-Cathedral (Houston).
Gary, Ind.: Holy Angels.
Gaylord, Mich.: St. Mary, Our Lady of Mt. Carmel.
Grand Island, Nebr.: Nativity of Blessed Virgin Mary.
Grand Rapids, Mich.: St. Andrew.
Great Falls-Billings, Mont.: St. Ann (Great Falls); St. Patrick Co-Cathedral (Billings).
Green Bay, Wis.: St. Francis Xavier.
Greensburg, Pa.: Blessed Sacrament.
Harrisburg, Pa.: St. Patrick.
Hartford,* Conn.: St. Joseph.
Helena, Mont.: St. Helena.
Honolulu, Hawaii: Our Lady of Peace; St. Theresa of the Child Jesus (Co-Cathedral).
Houma-Thibodaux, La.: St. Francis de Sales (Houma); St. Joseph Co-Cathedral (Thibodaux).
Indianapolis,* Ind.: Sts. Peter and Paul.
Jackson, Miss.: St. Peter.
Jefferson City, Mo.: St. Joseph.
Joliet, Ill.: St. Raymond Nonnatus.
Juneau, Alaska: Nativity of the Blessed Virgin Mary.
Kalamazoo, Mich.: St. Augustine.
Kansas City,* Kans.: St. Peter the Apostle.
Kansas City-St. Joseph, Mo.: Immaculate Conception (Kansas City); St. Joseph Co-Cathedral (St. Joseph).
Knoxville, Tenn.: Sacred Heart of Jesus.
La Crosse, Wis.: St. Joseph the Workman.
Lafayette, Ind.: St. Mary.
Lafayette, La.: St. John the Evangelist.
Lake Charles, La.: Immaculate Conception.
Lansing, Mich.: St. Mary.
Las Cruces, N. Mex.: Immaculate Heart of Mary.
Lexington, Ky.: Christ the King.
Lincoln, Nebr.: Cathedral of the Risen Christ.
Little Rock, Ark.: St. Andrew.
Los Angeles,* Calif.: St. Vibiana.
Louisville,* Ky.: Assumption.
Lubbock, Tex.: Christ the King.
Madison, Wis.: St. Raphael.
Manchester, N.H.: St. Joseph.
Marquette, Mich.: St. Peter.
Memphis, Tenn.: Immaculate Conception.
Metuchen, N.J.: St. Francis (of Assisi).
Miami,* Fla.: St. Mary (Immaculate Conception).

Milwaukee,* Wis.: St. John.
Mobile,* Ala.: Immaculate Conception (Minor Basilica).
Monterey, Calif.: San Carlos Borromeo.
Nashville, Tenn.: Incarnation.
Newark,* N.J.: Sacred Heart.
New Orleans,* La.: Cathedral (Basilica) of St. Louis.
Newton, Mass. (Melkite Rite): Our Lady of the Annunciation (Boston).
New Ulm, Minn.: Holy Trinity.
New York,* N.Y.: St. Patrick.
Norwich, Conn.: St. Patrick.
Oakland, Calif.: St. Francis de Sales.
Ogdensburg, N.Y.: St. Mary (Immaculate Conception).
Oklahoma City,* Okla.: Our Lady of Perpetual Help.
Omaha,* Nebr.: St. Cecilia.
Orange, Calif.: Holy Family.
Orlando, Fla.: St. James.
Owensboro, Ky.: St. Stephen.
Palm Beach, Fla.: St. Ignatius Loyola, Palm Beach Gardens.
Parma, Ohio (Byzantine Rite): St. John the Baptist.
Passaic, N.J. (Byzantine Rite): St. Michael.
Paterson, N.J.: St. John the Baptist.
Pensacola-Tallahassee, Fla.: Sacred Heart (Pensacola); Co-Cathedral of St. Thomas More (Tallahassee).
Peoria, Ill.: St. Mary.
Philadelphia,* Pa.: Sts. Peter and Paul (Minor Basilica).
Philadelphia,* Pa. (Byzantine Rite): Immaculate Conception of Blessed Virgin Mary.
Phoenix, Ariz.: Sts. Simon and Jude.
Pittsburgh,* Pa. (Byzantine Rite): St. John the Baptist, Munhall.
Pittsburgh, Pa.: St. Paul.
Portland, Me.: Immaculate Conception.
Portland,* Ore.: Immaculate Conception.
Providence, R.I.: Sts. Peter and Paul.
Pueblo, Colo.: Sacred Heart.
Raleigh, N.C.: Sacred Heart.
Rapid City, S.D.: Our Lady of Perpetual Help.
Reno-Las Vegas, Nev.: St. Thomas Aquinas (Reno), Guardian Angel (Las Vegas).
Richmond, Va.: Sacred Heart.
Rochester, N.Y.: Sacred Heart.
Rockford, Ill.: St. Peter.
Rockville Centre, N.Y.: St. Agnes.
Sacramento, Calif.: Blessed Sacrament.
Saginaw, Mich.: St. Mary.
St. Augustine, Fla.: St. Augustine (Minor Basilica).
St. Cloud, Minn.: St. Mary.
St. George's in Canton, Ohio (Byzantine Rite, Romanians): St. George (Pro-Cathedral).
St. Josaphat in Parma, Ohio (Byzantine Rite): St. Josaphat.
St. Louis,* Mo.: St. Louis.
St. Maron, Brooklyn, N.Y. (Maronite Rite): Our Lady of Lebanon.
St. Nicholas in Chicago (Byzantine Rite): St. Nicholas.
St. Paul and Minneapolis,* Minn.: St. Paul (St.

Paul); Basilica of St. Mary Co-Cathedral (Minneapolis).

St. Petersburg, Fla.: St. Jude the Apostle.

St. Thomas the Apostle of Detroit (Chaldean Rite): Our Lady of Chaldeans Cathedral (Mother of God Church), Southfield, Mich.

Salina, Kans.: Sacred Heart.

Salt Lake City, Utah: The Madeleine.

San Angelo, Tex.: Sacred Heart.

San Antonio,* Tex.: San Fernando.

San Bernardino, Calif: Our Lady of the Rosary.

San Diego, Calif.: St. Joseph.

San Francisco,* Calif.: St. Mary (Assumption).

San Jose, Calif.: St. Joseph; St. Patrick, Proto-Cathedral.

Santa Fe,* N.M.: San Francisco de Asis.

Santa Rosa, Calif.: St. Eugene.

Savannah, Ga.: St. John the Baptist.

Scranton, Pa.: St. Peter.

Seattle,* Wash.: St. James.

Shreveport, La.: St. John Berchmans.

Sioux City, Ia.: Epiphany.

Sioux Falls, S.D.: St. Joseph.

Spokane, Wash.: Our Lady of Lourdes.

Springfield, Ill.: Immaculate Conception.

Springfield, Mass.: St. Michael.

Springfield-Cape Girardeau, Mo.: St. Agnes (Springfield): St. Mary (Cape Girardeau).

Stamford, Conn. (Byzantine Rite): St. Vladimir.

Steubenville, Ohio: Holy Name.

Stockton, Calif: Annunciation.

Superior, Wis.: Christ the King.

Syracuse, N.Y.: Immaculate Conception.

Toledo, Ohio: Queen of the Most Holy Rosary.

Trenton, N.J.: St. Mary (Assumption).

Tucson, Ariz.: St. Augustine.

Tulsa, Okla.: Holy Family.

Tyler, Tex.: Immaculate Conception.

Van Nuys, Calif. (Byzantine Rite): St. Mary (Patronage of the Mother of God).

Venice, Fla: Epiphany.

Victoria, Tex.: Our Lady of Victory.

Washington,* D.C.: St. Matthew.

Wheeling-Charleston, W. Va.: St. Joseph (Wheeling); Sacred Heart (Charleston).

Wichita, Kans.: Immaculate Conception.

Wilmington, Del.: St. Peter.

Winona, Minn.: Sacred Heart.

Worcester, Mass.: St. Paul.

Yakima, Wash.: St. Paul.

Youngstown, Ohio: St. Columba.

Apostolic Exarchate for Armenian-Rite Catholics in the U.S. and Canada: St. Ann (110 E. 12th St., New York, N.Y. 10003).

BASILICAS IN U.S. AND CANADA

Basilica is a title assigned to certain churches because of their antiquity, dignity, historical importance or significance as centers of worship. Major basilicas have the papal altar and holy door, which is opened at the beginning of a Jubilee Year; minor basilicas enjoy certain ceremonial privileges.

Among the major basilicas are the patriarchal basilicas of St. John Lateran, St. Peter, St. Paul Outside the Walls and St. Mary Major in Rome; St. Francis and St. Mary of the Angels in Assisi, Italy.

The patriarchal basilica of St. Lawrence, Rome, is a minor basilica.

The dates in the listings below indicate when the churches were designated as basilicas.

Minor Basilicas in U.S., Puerto Rico, Guam

Alabama: Mobile, Cathedral of the Immaculate Conception (Mar. 10, 1962).

Arizona: Phoenix, St. Mary's (Immaculate Conception) (Sept. 11, 1985).

California: San Francisco, Mission Dolores (Feb. 8, 1952); Carmel, Old Mission of San Carlos (Feb. 5, 1960); Alameda, St. Joseph (Jan. 21, 1972); San Diego, Mission San Diego de Alcala (Nov. 17, 1975).

Colorado: Denver, Cathedral of the Immaculate Conception (Nov. 3, 1979).

District of Columbia: National Shrine of the Immaculate Conception (Oct. 12, 1990).

Florida: St. Augustine, Cathedral of St. Augustine (Dec. 4, 1976).

Illinois: Chicago, Our Lady of Sorrows (May 4, 1956), Queen of All Saints (Mar. 26, 1962).

Indiana: Vincennes, Old Cathedral (Mar. 14, 1970). Notre Dame, Parish Church of Most Sacred Heart Church, Univ. of Notre Dame (Nov. 23, 1991).

Iowa: Dyersville, St. Francis Xavier (May 11, 1956); Des Moines, St. John the Apostle (Oct. 4, 1989).

Kentucky: Trappist, Our Lady of Gethsemani (May 3, 1949); Covington, Cathedral of Assumption (Dec. 8, 1953).

Louisiana: New Orleans, St. Louis King of France (Dec. 9, 1964).

Maryland: Baltimore, Assumption of the Blessed Virgin Mary (Sept. 1, 1937); Emmitsburg, Shrine of St. Elizabeth Ann Seton (Feb. 13, 1991).

Massachusetts: Roxbury, Perpetual Help ("Mission Church") (Sept. 8, 1954); Chicopee, St. Stanislaus (June 25, 1991).

Michigan: Grand Rapids, St. Adalbert (Aug. 22, 1979).

Minnesota: Minneapolis. St. Mary (Feb. 1, 1926).

Missouri: Conception, Basilica of Immaculate Conception (Sept. 14, 1940); St. Louis, St. Louis King of France (Jan. 27, 1961).

New York: Brooklyn, Our Lady of Perpetual Help (Sept. 5, 1969), Cathedral-Basilica of St. James (June 22, 1982); Lackawanna, Our Lady of Victory (1926); Youngstown, Blessed Virgin Mary of the Rosary of Fatima (Oct. 7, 1975).

North Carolina: Asheville, St. Lawrence (1993)

North Dakota: Jamestown, St. James (Oct. 26, 1988).

Ohio: Carey, Shrine of Our Lady of Consolation (Oct. 21, 1971).

Pennsylvania: Latrobe, St. Vincent Basilica, Benedictine Archabbey (Aug. 22, 1955); Conewago, Basilica of the Sacred Heart (June 30, 1962); Philadelphia, Sts. Peter and Paul (Sept. 27, 1976); Danville, Sts. Cyril and Methodius (chapel at the motherhouse of the Sisters of Sts. Cyril and Methodius) (June 30, 1989).

Texas: Galveston, St. Mary Cathedral (Aug. 11, 1979).

Virginia: Norfolk, St. Mary of the Immaculate Conception (July 9, 1991).

Wisconsin: Milwaukee, St. Josaphat (Mar. 10, 1929).

Puerto Rico: San Juan, Cathedral of San Juan (Jan. 25, 1978).

Guam: Agana, Cathedral of Dulce Nombre de Maria (Sweet Name of Mary) (1985).

Minor Basilicas in Canada

Alberta: Edmonton, Cathedral Basilica of St. Joseph (Mar. 15, 1984).

Manitoba: St. Boniface, Cathedral Basilica of St. Boniface (June 10, 1949).

New Brunswick: Chatham, St. Michael the Archangel (Dec. 9, 1988).

Newfoundland: St. John's, Cathedral Basilica of St. John the Baptist.

Nova Scotia: Halifax, St. Mary's Basilica (June 14, 1950).

Ontario: Ottawa, Basilica of Notre Dame; London, St. Peter's Cathedral (Dec. 13, 1961).

Prince Edward Island: Charlottetown, Basilica of St. Dunstan.

Quebec: Sherbrooke, Cathedral Basilica of St. Michael (July 31, 1959). Montreal, Cathedral Basilica of Our Lady Queen of the World; St. Joseph of Mount Royal; Basilica of Notre Dame (Feb. 15, 1982); St. Patrick (Dec. 9, 1988). Cap-de-la-Madeleine, Basilica of Our Lady of the Cape (Aug. 15, 1964). Quebec, Basilica of Notre Dame; St. Anne de Beaupre, Basilica of St. Anne. Valleyfield, Cathedral Basilica of St. Cecilia (Feb. 9, 1991).

CHANCERY OFFICES OF U.S. ARCHDIOCESES AND DIOCESES

A chancery office, under this or another title, is the central administrative office of an archdiocese or diocese.

(Archdioceses are indicated by asterisk.)

Albany, N.Y.: 40 N. Main Ave. 12203.

Alexandria, La.: P.O. Box 7417. 71306.

Allentown, Pa.: 202 N. 17th St., P.O. Box F. 18105.

Altoona-Johnstown, Pa.: 126 Logan Blvd., Hollidaysburg. 16648.

Amarillo, Tex.: 1800 N. Spring St., P.O. Box 5644. 79117.

Anchorage,* Alaska: P.O. Box 102239. 99510.

Arlington, Va.: Suite 704, 200 N. Glebe Rd. 22203.

Atlanta,* Ga.: Catholic Center, 680 W. Peachtree St. N.W. 30308.

Austin, Tex.: N. Congress and 16th, P.O. Box 13327, Capitol Sta. 78711.

Baker, Ore.: P.O. Box 5999, Bend 97708.

Baltimore,* Md.: 320 Cathedral St. 21201.

Baton Rouge, La.: P.O. Box 2028. 70821.

Beaumont, Tex.: 703 Archie St., P.O. Box 3948. 77704.

Belleville, Ill.: 222 S. Third St., 62220.

Biloxi, Miss.: P.O. Box 1189. 39533.

Birmingham, Ala.: P.O. Box 12047. 35202.

Bismarck, N.D.: 420 Raymond St., Box 1575. 58502.

Boise, Ida.: Box 769. 83701.

Boston,* Mass.: 2121 Commonwealth Ave., Brighton. 02135.

Bridgeport, Conn.: The Catholic Center, 238 Jewett Ave. 06606.

Brooklyn, N.Y.: 75 Greene Ave., P.O. Box C. 11202.

Brownsville, Tex.: P.O. Box 2279. 78522.

Buffalo, N.Y.: 795 Main St. 14203.

Burlington, Vt.: 351 North Ave. 05401.

Camden, N.J.: 1845 Haddon Ave., P.O. Box 709, 08101.

Charleston, S.C.: 119 Broad St., P.O. Box 818. 29402.

Charlotte, N.C.: P.O. Box 36776. 28236.

Cheyenne, Wyo.: Box 426. 82003.

Chicago,* Ill.: P.O. Box 1979. 60690.

Cincinnati,* O.: 100 E. 8th St. 45202.

Cleveland, O.: Chancery Bldg., 1027 Superior Ave. 44114.

Colorado Springs, Colo.: 29 W. Kiowa. 80903.

Columbus, O.: 198 E. Broad St. 43215.

Corpus Christi, Tex.: 620 Lipan St. P.O. Box 2620. 78403.

Covington, Ky.: P.O. Box 18548, Erlanger 41018.

Crookston, Minn.: 1200 Memorial Dr., P.O. Box 610. 56716.

Dallas, Tex.: 3725 Blackburn, P.O. Box 190507. 75219.

Davenport, Ia.: St. Vincent Center, 2706 N. Gaines St. 52804.

Denver,* Colo.: 200 Josephine St. 80206.

Des Moines, Ia.: P.O. Box 1816. 50306.

Detroit,* Mich.: 1234 Washington Blvd. 48226.

Dodge City, Kans.: 910 Central Ave., P.O. Box 137. 67801.

Dubuque,* Ia.: P.O. Box 479. 52004.

Duluth, Minn.: 2830 E. 4th St. 55812.

El Paso, Tex.: 499 St. Matthews St. 79907.

Erie, Pa.: P.O. Box 10397. 16514.

Evansville, Ind.: P.O. Box 4169. 47724.

Fairbanks, Alaska: 1316 Peger Rd. 99709.

Fall River, Mass.: 47 Underwood St., Box 2577. 02722.

Fargo, N.D.: 1310 Broadway, Box 1750. 58107.

Fort Wayne-South Bend, Ind.: P.O. Box 390, Fort Wayne. 46801.

Fort Worth, Tex.: 800 W. Loop 820 South. 76108.

Fresno, Calif.: P.O. Box 1668, 1550 N. Fresno St. 93717.

Gallup, N. Mex.: 711 S. Puerco Dr., P.O. Box 1338. 87305.

Galveston-Houston, Tex.: 1700 San Jacinto St., Houston. 77002.

Gary, Ind.: 9292 Broadway, Merrillville. 46410.

Gaylord, Mich.: 1665 W. M-32 West, Seton Bldg. 49735.

Grand Island, Nebr.: 311 W. 17th St., P.O. Box 996. 68802.

Grand Rapids, Mich.: 660 Burton St., S.E. 49507.

Great Falls-Billings, Mont.: P.O. Box 1399, Great Falls. 59403.

Green Bay, Wis.: P.O. Box 23066. 54305.

Greensburg, Pa.: 723 E. Pittsburgh St. 15601.
Harrisburg, Pa.: P.O. Box 2153. 17105.
Hartford,* Conn.: 134 Farmington Ave. 06105.
Helena, Mont.: 515 North Ewing, P.O. Box 1729. 59624.
Honolulu, Hawaii: 1184 Bishop St. 96813.
Houma-Thibodaux, La.: P.O. Box 9077, Houma, La. 70361.
Indianapolis,* Ind.: 1400 N. Meridian St., P.O. Box 1410. 46206.
Jackson, Miss.: 237 E. Amite St., P.O. Box 2248. 39225.
Jefferson City, Mo.: 605 Clark Ave., P.O. Box 417. 65101.
Joliet, Ill.: 425 Summit St. 60435.
Juneau, Alaska: 419 6th St., No. 200. 99801.
Kalamazoo, Mich.: 215 N. Westnedge Ave., P.O. Box 949. 49005.
Kansas City,* Kans.: 12615 Parallel. 66109.
Kansas City-St. Joseph, Mo.: P.O. Box 419037, Kansas City. 64141.
Knoxville, Tenn.: 417 Erin Dr., P.O. Box 11127. 37939.
La Crosse, Wis.: 3710 East Ave. S., Box 4004. 54602.
Lafayette in Indiana: P.O. Box 260. 47902.
Lafayette, La.: 1408 Carmel Ave. 70501.
Lake Charles, La.: P.O. Box 3223. 70602.
Lansing, Mich.: 300 W. Ottawa. 48933.
Las Cruces, N. Mex.: 1280 Med Park Dr., 88005.
Lexington, Ky.: P.O. Box 12350. 40582.
Lincoln, Nebr.: P.O. Box 80328. 68501.
Little Rock, Ark.: 2415 N. Tyler St. P.O. Box 7239. 72217.
Los Angeles,* Calif.: 1531 W. 9th St. 90015.
Louisville,* Ky.: 212 E. College St., P.O. Box 1073. 40201.
Lubbock, Tex.: P.O. Box 98700. 79499.
Madison, Wis.: 15 E. Wilson St., P.O. Box 111. 53701.
Manchester, N. H.: 153 Ash St., P.O. Box 310. 03105.
Marquette, Mich.: 444 S. Fourth St., P.O. Box 550. 49855.
Memphis, Tenn.: 1325 Jefferson St., P.O. Box 41679. 38174.
Metuchen, N.J.: P.O. Box 191. 08840.
Miami,* Fla.: 9401 Biscayne Blvd., Miami Shores. 33138.
Milwaukee,* Wis.: P.O. Box 07912. 53207.
Mobile,* Ala.: 400 Government St., P.O. Box 1966. 36633.
Monterey, Calif.: P.O. Box 2048. 93942.
Nashville, Tenn.: 2400 21st Ave. S. 37212.
Newark,* N.J.: 31 Mulberry St. 07102.
New Orleans,* La.: 7887 Walmsley Ave. 70125.
Newton, Mass. (Melkite Rite): 19 Dartmouth St., W. Newton, Mass. 02165.
New Ulm, Minn.: 1400 Sixth North St. 56073.
New York,* N.Y.: 1011 First Ave. 10022.
Norwich, Conn.: 201 Broadway, P.O. Box 587. 06360.
Oakland, Calif.: 2900 Lakeshore Ave. 94610.
Ogdensburg, N.Y.: 622 Washington St., P.O. Box 369. 13669.
Oklahoma City,* Okla.: P.O. Box 32180. 73123.

Omaha,* Nebr.: 100 N. 62nd St. 68132.
Orange, Calif.: 2811 E. Villa Real Dr. 92667.
Orlando, Fla.: P.O. Box 1800. 32802.
Owensboro, Ky.: 600 Locust St. 42301.
Palm Beach, Fla.: 9995 N. Military Trail, Palm Beach Gardens 33410.
Parma, Ohio (Byzantine Rite): 1900 Carlton Rd. 44134.
Passaic, N.J. (Byzantine Rite): 445 Lackawanna Ave., W. Paterson. 07424.
Paterson, N.J.: 777 Valley Rd., Clifton. 07013.
Pensacola-Tallahassee, Fla.: P.O. Drawer 17329, Pensacola. 32522.
Peoria, Ill.: 607 N.E. Madison Ave., P.O. Box 1406. 61655.
Philadelphia,* Pa.: 222 N. 17th St. 19103.
Philadelphia,* Pa. (Byzantine Rite): 827 N. Franklin St. 19123.
Phoenix, Ariz.: 400 E. Monroe St. 85004.
Pittsburgh,* Pa. (Byzantine Rite): 925 Liberty Ave. 15222.
Pittsburgh, Pa.: 111 Blvd. of the Allies. 15222.
Portland, Me.: 510 Ocean Ave., P.O. Box 11559. 04101.
Portland in Oregon*: 2838 E. Burnside St. 97214.
Providence, R.I.: One Cathedral Sq. 02903.
Pueblo, Colo.: 1001 N. Grand Ave. 81003.
Raleigh, N.C.: 300 Cardinal Gibbons Dr. 27606.
Rapid City, S.D.: 606 Cathedral Dr., P.O. Box 678. 57709.
Reno-Las Vegas, Nev.: P.O. Box 1211, Reno. 89504; P.O. Box 18316, Las Vegas. 89114..
Richmond, Va.: 811 Cathedral Pl., 23220.
Rochester, N.Y.: 1150 Buffalo Rd. 14624.
Rockford, Ill.: 1245 N. Court St. 61103.
Rockville Centre, N.Y.: 50 N. Park Ave. 11570.
Sacramento, Calif.: 1119 K St., P.O. Box 1706. 95812.
Saginaw, Mich.: 5800 Weiss St. 48603.
St. Augustine, Fla.: P.O. Box 24000, Jacksonville, Fla. 32241.
St. Cloud, Minn.: P.O. Box 1248. 56302.
St. George's in Canton, Ohio (Byzantine Rite, Romanian): 1121 44th St. N.E., Canton, O. 44714.
St. Josaphat in Parma, Ohio (Byzantine Rite): P.O. Box 347180, Parma. 44134.
St. Louis,* Mo.: 4445 Lindell Blvd. 63108.
St. Maron (Maronite Rite), Brooklyn, N.Y.: 8120 15th Ave., Brooklyn. 11228.
St. Nicholas in Chicago (Byzantine Rite): 2245 W. Rice St. 60622.
St. Paul and Minneapolis,* Minn.: 226 Summit Ave., St. Paul. 55102.
St. Petersburg, Fla.: P.O. Box 40200. 33743.
St. Thomas the Apostle of Detroit (Chaldean Rite): 25585 Berg Rd., Southfield, Mich. 48034.
Salina, Kans.: P.O. Box 980. 67402.
Salt Lake City, Utah: 27 C St. 84103.
San Angelo, Tex.: 804 Ford, P.O. Box 1829. 76902.
San Antonio,* Tex.: P.O. Box 28410. 78228.
San Bernardino, Calif.: 1450 North D St. 92405.
San Diego, Calif.: P.O. Box 85728. 92186.
San Francisco,* Calif.: 445 Church St. 94114.
San Jose, Calif.: 900 Lafayette St., Suite 301, Santa Clara 95050.
Santa Fe,* N. Mex.: 4000 St. Joseph's Pl. N.W., Albuquerque. 87120.

Santa Rosa, Calif.: P.O. Box 1297. 95402.
Savannah, Ga.: 601 E. Liberty St. 31401.
Scranton, Pa.: 300 Wyoming Ave. 18503.
Seattle,* Wash.: 910 Marion St. 98104.
Shreveport, La.: 2500 Line Ave. 71104.
Sioux City, Ia.: P.O. Box 3379. 51102.
Sioux Falls, S.D.: 609 W. 5th St., Box 5033. 57117.
Spokane, Wash.: 1023 W. Riverside Ave., P.O. Box 1453. 99210.
Springfield, Ill.: P.O. Box 3187. 62708.
Springfield, Mass.: P.O. Box 1730. 01101.
Springfield-Cape Girardeau, Mo.: 601 S. Jefferson, Springfield. 65806.
Stamford, Conn. (Byzantine Rite): 161 Glenbrook Rd. 06902.
Steubenville, Ohio: P.O. Box 969. 43952.
Stockton, Calif.: P.O. Box 4237. 95204.
Superior, Wis.: 1201 Hughitt Ave., Box 969. 54880.
Syracuse, N.Y.: P.O. Box 511. 13201.
Toledo, Ohio: P.O. Box 985. 43696.
Trenton, N.J.: P.O. Box 5309. 08638.

Tucson, Ariz.: 192 S. Stone Ave., Box 31. 85702.
Tulsa, Okla.: P.O. Box 2009. 74101.
Tyler, Tex.: 1920 Sybil Lane. 75703.
Van Nuys, Calif. (Byzantine Rite): 18024 Parthenia St., Northridge, Calif. 91325.
Venice, Fla.: P.O. Box 2006. 34284.
Victoria, Tex.: P.O. Box 4070. 77903.
Washington,* D.C.: P.O. Box 29260. 20017.
Wheeling-Charleston, W. Va.: 1300 Byron St., P.O. Box 230, Wheeling. 26003.
Wichita, Kans.: 424 N. Broadway. 67202.
Wilmington, Del.: P.O. Box 2030. 19899.
Winona, Minn.: P.O. Box 588. 55987.
Worcester, Mass.: 49 Elm St. 01609.
Yakima, Wash.: 5301-A Tieton Dr. 98908.
Youngstown, Ohio: 144 W. Wood St. 44503.
Military Archdiocese: 962 Wayne Ave., Silver Spring, MD 20910.
Armenian-Rite Apostolic Exarchate for the United States and Canada: 110 E. 12th St., New York, NY 10003.

NATIONAL CATHOLIC CONFERENCES

The two conferences described below are related in membership and directive control but distinct in nature, purpose and function.

The National Conference of Catholic Bishops (NCCB) is a strictly ecclesiastical body in and through which the bishops of the United States act together, officially and with authority as pastors of the Church. It is the sponsoring organization of the United States Catholic Conference.

The United States Catholic Conference (USCC) is a civil corporation and operational secretariat in and through which the bishops, together with other members of the Church, act on a wider scale for the good of the Church and society. It is sponsored by the National Conference of Catholic Bishops.

The principal officers of both conferences are: Archbishop William H. Keeler, president; Bishop Anthony M. Pilla, vice president; Archbishop Daniel W. Kucera, O.S.B., treasurer; Bishop Joseph A. Fiorenza, secretary.

The membership of the Administrative Committee of the NCCB and the Administrative Board of the USCC is identical.

Headquarters of both conferences are located at 3211 Fourth St. N.E., Washington, D.C. 20017.

CONFERENCE OF CATHOLIC BISHOPS

The National Conference of Catholic Bishops (NCCB), established by action of the U.S. hierarchy Nov. 14, 1966, is a strictly ecclesiastical body with defined juridical authority over the Church in this country. It was set up with the approval of the Holy See and in line with directives from the Second Vatican Council. Its constitution was formally ratified during the November, 1967, meeting of the U.S. hierarchy.

The NCCB is a development from the Annual Meeting of the Bishops of the United States, whose pastoral character was originally approved by Pope Benedict XV Apr. 10, 1919.

The address of the Conference is 3211 Fourth St. N.E., Washington, D.C. 20017. Rev. Msgr. Robert N. Lynch is general secretary.

Pastoral Council

The conference, one of many similar territorial conferences envisioned in the conciliar Decree on the Pastoral Office of Bishops in the Church (No. 38), is "a council in which the bishops of a given nation or territory (in this case, the United States) jointly exercise their pastoral office to promote the greater good which the Church offers mankind, especially through the forms and methods of the apostolate fittingly adapted to the circumstances of the age."

Its decisions, "provided they have been approved legitimately and by the votes of at least two-thirds of the prelates who have a deliberative vote in the conference, and have been recognized by the Apostolic See, are to have juridically binding force only in those cases prescribed by the common law or determined by a special mandate of the Apostolic See, given either spontaneously or in response to a petition of the conference itself."

All bishops who serve the Church in the U.S., its territories and possessions, have membership and voting rights in the NCCB. Retired bishops cannot be elected to conference offices nor can they vote on matters which by law are binding by two-thirds of the membership. Only diocesan bishops can vote on diocesan quotas, assessments or special collections.

Officers, Committees

The conference operates through a number of bishops' committees with functions in specific areas of work and concern. Their basic assignments are to prepare materials on the basis of which the bishops, assembled as a conference, make decisions, and to put suitable action plans into effect.

The principal officers are: Archbishop William H. Keeler, president; Bishop Anthony M. Pilla, vice president; Archbishop Daniel W. Kucera, O.S.B., treasurer; Bishop Joseph A. Fiorenza, secretary.

These officers, with several other bishops, hold positions on executive-level committees — Executive Committee, the Committee on Budget and Finance, the Committee on Personnel, and the Committee on Priorities and Plans. They also, with other bishops, serve on the NCCB Administrative Committee.

The standing committees and their chairmen (Archbishops and Bishops) are as follows.

African American Catholics, J. Terry Steib, S.V.D.

American Board of Catholic Missions, J. Keith Symons.

American College, Louvain, Daniel P. Reilly.

Bishops' Welfare Emergency Relief, William H. Keeler.

Boundaries of Dioceses and Provinces, William H. Keeler.

Canonical Affairs, Cardinal Anthony Bevilacqua.

Church in Latin America, Arthur N. Tafoya.

Doctrine, Alfred C. Hughes.

Ecumenical and Interreligious Affairs, Rembert G. Weakland, O.S.B.

Evangelization, William R. Houck.

Hispanic Affairs, Enrique San Pedro, S.J.

Laity, Robert F. Morneau.

Liturgy, Wilton D. Gregory.

Marriage and Family Life, Cardinal Joseph Bernardin.

Migration, Theodore E. McCarrick.

Missions, Edmond Carmody.

North American College, Rome, Edward M. Egan.

Pastoral Research and Practices, Emil A. Wcela.

Permanent Diaconate, Dale J. Melczek.

Priestly Formation, Daniel Buechlein, O.S.B.

Priestly Life and Ministry, Robert H. Brom.

Pro-Life Activities, Cardinal Roger M. Mahony.

Religious Life and Ministry, Carlos A. Sevilla, S.J.

Science and Human Values, William B. Friend.

Selection of Bishops, William H. Keeler.

Vocations, Robert J. Carlson.

Women in Society and in the Church, John J. Snyder.

Ad hoc committees and their chairmen are as follows.

Aid to the Church in Central and Eastern Europe and the USSR, Theodore E. McCarrick.

Bishops Life and Ministry, Robert H. Brom.

Canonical Determination of Age of Confirmation, Emil A. Wcela.

Catholic Charismatic Renewal, Joseph McKinney.

Economic Concerns of the Holy See, James P. Keleher.

Liaison Committee for Eastern and Latin Church, Stephen Sulyk.

Liaison Committee with CNS (Catholic News Service), Edward J. O'Donnell.

Mission and Structure of the NCCB, Cardinal Joseph Bernardin.

Native American Catholics, Donald E. Pelotte, S.S.S.

1994 Special Assembly, Harry J. Flynn.

Nomination of Conference Offices, Michael Sheehan.

Review of Scripture Translations, Richard J. Sklba.

Sexual Abuse, John F. Kinney.

Shrines, James P. Keleher.

Stewardship, Thomas J. Murphy.

UNITED STATES CATHOLIC CONFERENCE

The United States Catholic Conference, Inc. (USCC), is the operational secretariat and service agency of the National Conference of Catholic Bishops for carrying out the civic-religious work of the Church in this country. It is a civil corporation related to the NCCB in membership and directive control but distinct from it in purpose and function.

The address of the Conference is 3211 Fourth St. N.E., Washington, D.C. 20017. Rev. Msgr. Robert N. Lynch is general secretary.

Service Secretariat

The USCC, as of Jan. 1, 1967, took over the general organization and operations of the former National Catholic Welfare Conference, Inc., whose origins dated back to the National Catholic War Council of 1917. The council underwent some change after World War I and was established on a permanent basis Sept. 24, 1919, as the National Catholic Welfare Council to serve as a central agency for organizing and coordinating the efforts of U.S. Catholics in carrying out the social mission of the Church in this country. In 1923, its name was changed to National Catholic Welfare Conference, Inc., and clarification was made of its nature as a service agency of the bishops and the Church rather than as a conference of bishops with real juridical authority in ecclesiastical affairs.

The Official Catholic Directory states that the USCC assists "the bishops in their service to the Church in this country by uniting the people of God where voluntary collective action on a broad interdiocesan level is needed. The USCC provides an organizational structure and the resources needed to insure coordination, cooperation, and assistance in the public, educational and social concerns of the Church at the national, regional, state and, as appropriate, diocesan levels."

Officers, Departments

The principal officers of the USCC are Archbishop William H. Keeler, president; Bishop Anthony M. Pilla, vice president; Archbishop Daniel W. Kucera, O.S.B., treasurer; Bishop Joseph A. Fiorenza, secretary. These officers, with several other bishops, hold positions on executive-level committees — the Executive Committee; the Committee on Priorities and Plans; the Committee on Budget and Finance; the Committee on Personnel. They also serve on the Administrative Board.

The Executive Committee, organized in 1969, is authorized to handle matters of urgency between meetings of the Administrative Board and the general conference, to coordinate items for the agenda of general meetings, and to speak in the name of the USCC.

The major departments are: Campaign for Human Development; Communications; Education; Social Development and World Peace. A National Advisory Council of bishops, priests, men and women religious, lay men and women advises the Administrative Board on overall plans and operations of the USCC.

The administrative general secretariat, in addition to other duties, supervises staff-service offices of Finance, General Counsel, Government Liaison,

Priorities and Plans, Management Information Services, Human Resources, General Services, Research.

Most of the organizations and associations affiliated with the USCC are covered in separate Almanac entries.

MEETINGS OF THE U.S. BISHOPS

NOVEMBER 16 TO 19, 1992

About 250 bishops attended the annual meeting of the National Conference of Catholic Bishops and the U.S. Catholic Conference Nov. 16 to 19, 1992, in Washington.

Presidential Address: Archbishop Daniel E. Pilarczyk, retiring president, recounted impressions gained on travels abroad with respect to conditions facing the Church in other countries, especially in Poland, Ireland and Latin America. His purpose was to remind his fellow bishops "that the Church in other parts of the world has challenges and problems, even as we do, although the challenges and problems may be different, and that the Church in other parts of the world strives to come to grips with those challenges and problems in the context of the same gifts of faith, hope and love that we rely on in our work as bishops of the United States." He said he had "come to a deepened awareness of the great constant in the life of the Church ... the Lord's promise of hope: 'See, I am coming soon.'"

Business Items

The bishops acted on the following subjects.

Budget: Approved a 1993 budget of nearly $41.4 million for the two conferences, along with a set of future priorities and plans.

Eastern European Collection: Extended for one year a special national collection to help churches in Eastern Europe.

Elections: Elected Archbishop William H. Keeler of Baltimore and Bishop Anthony M. Pilla of Cleveland to three-year terms as president and vice president, respectively, of the two conferences. Archbishop Daniel W. Kucera of Dubuque was elected to serve as treasurer for the remainder of the term of Bishop Pilla, former treasurer.

Evangelization: "Go and Make Disciples: A National Plan and Strategy for Catholic Evangelization in the United States," was approved by a vote of 229 to 2. Turned down was a move to fund a conference staff position to promote evangelization.

Liturgy: (1) Accepted by a vote of 190 to 29 a new edition of Volume 2 of the Lectionary for Mass, providing readings for weekdays, feasts of saints, common and ritual Masses; (2) adopted by a vote of 210 to 3 the text of a Mass of Thanksgiving for the Gift of Human Life: both actions require ratification by the Vatican. (3) Set policy for adding saints' observances to the calendar of celebrations.

Reports: Reports were submitted on a variety of subjects, including plans for the World Youth Day celebration in August, 1993, in Denver, the new Universal Catechism, the worldwide activities of Catholic Relief Services, and the Catholic Telecommunications Network of America.

Seminary Training: Approved by a vote of 230 to 3 a revised national plan for the formation of students for the priesthood, with emphasis on tighter requirements for philosophical and pre-theological studies along with formation for celibate life in the priesthood.

Sexual Abuse by Clergy: Passed a resolution reiterating the need to take quick action on accusations of abuse and to be a "healing" presence in the wake of such allegations.

Stewardship: Endorsed by a vote of 208 to 12 a pastoral letter on the responsibilities of Christian stewardship, stating: "While many Catholics are generous in giving of themselves and their resources (time, talent, treasure) to the Church, others do not respond to the need in proportion to what they possess. The result now is a lack of resources which seriously hampers the Church's ability to carry out its mission and obstructs peoples' growth as disciples."

Women: Failed to approve publication of a controversial pastoral letter on the concerns of women, entitled "One in Christ Jesus," remanding it instead as a report to the executive committee for appropriate action on its recommendations. The vote for publication was 137 with 110 opposed; 190 favorable votes were required for approval. The letter, in its fourth draft after more than nine years of work by a special committee, was sharply criticized on various counts.

JUNE 17 TO 19, 1993

More than 200 bishops attended the semi-annual meeting of their conferences June 17 to 19 in New Orleans. They acted on the following subjects.

Catechism: Passed a resolution urging the Vatican to end delays in approving the English translation (from the original French) of the *Catechism of the Catholic Church*.

Communications: Endorsed a plan to revamp the Catholic Telecommunications Network of America, making it directly accessible by parishes for the first time in its 12-year history.

Confirmation: Voted to have the sacrament of confirmation administered in the United States between the ages of 7 and 18.

Discussions: Discussed: (1) religious life in the United States, in preparation for the 1994 assembly of the Synod of Bishops; (2) the translation of Latin liturgical texts into English, current translation projects and related matters.

Eucharistic Prayers: Initiated voting on a request for permission from the Vatican to write two new Eucharistic Prayers for use in the United States.

Health Care: Issued a resolution endorsing comprehensive health care reform in the United States and spelling out Catholic principles for reform, among them insistence on universal access to health care and rejection of abortion coverage.

Meeting Theme: Adopted "Shepherding a Future of Hope" as the theme of their June, 1994, retreat-style assembly in San Diego.

Sexual Abuse: Took a new offensive against

sexual abuse of minors by priests, forming a committee headed by Bishop John F. Kinney of Bismarck to recommend responses to the problem.

Youth Celebration: Extended an additional $2 million line of credit to World Youth Day, to be held in August in Denver, increasing the budget to accommodate much larger crowds than originally expected.

STATE CATHOLIC CONFERENCES

These conferences are agencies of bishops and dioceses in the various states. Their general purposes are to develop and sponsor cooperative programs designed to cope with pastoral and common-welfare needs, and to represent the dioceses before governmental bodies, the public, and in private sectors. Their membership consists of representatives from the dioceses in the states — bishops, clergy and lay persons in various capacities.

The **National Association of State Catholic Conference Directors** maintains liaison with the general secretariat of the United States Catholic Conference. Pres., Dr. M. Desmond Ryan, executive director of Indiana Catholic Conference.

Arizona Catholic Conference, 400 E. Monroe St., Phoenix, AZ 85004; exec. dir., Rev. Msgr. Edward J. Ryle.

California Catholic Conference, Cathedral Square, 1010 11th St., Suite 200, Sacramento, CA 95814; exec. dir., Rev. Msgr. E. James Petersen.

Colorado Catholic Conference, 200 Josephine St., Denver, CO 80206; exec. dir., Doug Delaney.

Connecticut Catholic Conference, 134 Farmington Ave., Hartford, CT 06105; exec. dir., Rev. Thomas J. Barry.

Florida Catholic Conference, P.O. Box 1638, Tallahassee, FL 32302; exec. dir., Thomas A. Horkan, Jr.

Georgia Catholic Conference, Office Bldg., 3200 Deans Bridge Rd., Augusta, GA 30906; exec. dir., Cheatham E. Hodges, Jr.

Illinois, Catholic Conference of, 500 North Clark St., Chicago, IL 60610; 200 Broadway, Springfield, Ill. 62701; exec. dir., Jimmy M. Lago.

Indiana Catholic Conference, 1400 N. Meridian St., P.O. Box 1410, Indianapolis, IN 46206; exec. dir., M. Desmond Ryan.

Iowa Catholic Conference, 818 Insurance Exchange Building, Des Moines, IA 50309; exec. dir., Timothy McCarthy.

Kansas Catholic Conference, 6301 Antioch, Merriam, KS 66202; exec. dir., Robert Runnels, Jr.

Kentucky, Catholic Conference of, 1042 Burlington Lane, Frankfort, KY 40601; exec. dir., Kenneth J. Dupre.

Louisiana Catholic Conference, P.O. Box 52948, New Orleans, LA 70152; exec. dir., Emile Comar.

Maryland Catholic Conference, 188 Duke of Gloucester St., Annapolis, MD 21401; exec. dir., Richard J. Dowling.

Massachusetts Catholic Conference, 60 School St., Boston, MA 02108; exec. dir., Gerald D. D'-Avolio, Esq.

Michigan Catholic Conference, 505 N. Capitol Ave., Lansing, MI 48933; exec. dir., Sr. Monica Kostielney, R.S.M.

Minnesota Catholic Conference, 475 University Ave. W., St. Paul, MN 55103; exec. dir., Rev. Msgr. James D. Habiger.

Missouri Catholic Conference, P.O. Box 1022, 600 Clark Ave., Jefferson City, MO 65102; exec. dir., Louis C. DeFeo, Jr.

Montana Catholic Conference, P.O. Box 1708, Helena, MT 59624; exec. dir., Sharon Hoff.

Nebraska Catholic Conference, 521 S. 14th St., Lincoln, NE 68508; exec. dir., James R. Cunningham.

New Jersey Catholic Conference, 211 N. Warren St., Trenton, NJ 08618; exec. dir., William F. Bolan, Jr.

New York State Catholic Conference, 119 Washington Ave., Albany, NY 12210; exec. dir., John M. Kerry.

North Dakota Catholic Conference, 227 West Broadway Suite No. 2, Bismarck, ND 58501; exec. dir., Sr. Paula Ringuette, P.B.V.M.

Ohio, Catholic Conference of, 35 E. Gay St., Suite 502, Columbus, OH 43215; exec. dir., Timothy V. Luckhaupt.

Oregon Catholic Conference, 2838 E. Burnside, Portland, OR 97214; exec. dir., Robert J. Castagna.

Pennsylvania Catholic Conference, 223 North St., Box 2835, Harrisburg, PA 17105; exec. dir., Howard J. Fetterhoff.

Texas Catholic Conference, 3001 S. Congress Ave., Austin, TX 78704; exec. dir., Bro. Richard Daly, C.S.C.

Washington State Catholic Conference, 419 Occidental Ave. S, Suite 608, Seattle, WA 98104; exec. dir., Edward J. Dolejsi.

Wisconsin Catholic Conference, 30 W. Mifflin St., Suite 302, Madison, WI 53703; exec. dir., John A. Huebscher.

Dioceses with Interstate Lines

Diocesan lines usually fall within a single state and in some cases include a whole state.

The following dioceses, with their statistics as reported in tables throughout the Almanac, are exceptions.

Norwich, Conn., includes Fisher's Island, N.Y.

Wilmington, Del., includes all of Delaware and nine counties of Maryland.

Washington, D.C., includes five counties of Maryland.

Gallup, N.M., has jurisdiction over several counties of Arizona.

Cheyenne, Wyo., includes all of Yellowstone National Park.

NCCB-USCC REGIONS

I. Maine, Vermont, New Hampshire, Massachusetts, Rhode Island, Connecticut. **II.** New York. **III.** New Jersey, Pennsylvania. **IV.** Delaware, District of Columbia, Florida, Georgia, Maryland,

North Carolina, South Carolina, Virgin Islands, Virginia, West Virginia. **V.** Alabama, Kentucky, Louisiana, Mississippi, Tennessee. **VI.** Michigan, Ohio. **VII.** Illinois, Indiana, Wisconsin. **VIII.** Minnesota, North Dakota, South Dakota. **IX.** Iowa, Kansas, Missouri, Nebraska. **X.** Arkansas, Oklahoma, Texas. **XI.** California, Hawaii, Nevada. **XII.** Idaho, Montana, Alaska, Washington, Oregon. **XIII.** Utah, Arizona, New Mexico, Colorado, Wyoming.

OUR LADY OF CZESTOCHOWA

The Black Madonna, the icon of Our Lady of Czestochowa, is enshrined on the "Hill of Light," Jasna Gora, above the city of Czestochowa in south central Poland. Long the center and focus of Marian devotion since it was brought there in 1382, it is the primary symbol of Polish religious faith and freedom.

The icon is a portrayal of Mary holding the Child Jesus. Their faces and hands are dark, as though they had been burned or stained by smoke. Three cuts are on one of Mary's cheeks, put there by robbers who desecrated the icon in 1430.

The origin of the icon is not clear. Elements of the legend say it was painted by St. Luke on a panel made by St. Joseph for the home of the Holy Family in Nazareth; that it was transported from the Holy Land to Constantinople; that it was given in 988 to a Ukrainian princess, Anna, the wife of Vladimir of Kiev; and that it eventually was brought to Czestochowa in 1382. The *Catholic Encyclopedia* notes another possibility, that the icon was of Greek-Italian origin in the ninth century.

The location of the icon on the hill above Czestochowa was related to the establishment of a priory of Pauline monks there, also in 1382. A shrine was built some time after 1386. A church was erected in 1644, and a 344-foot tower was raised in 1702.

Our Lady of Czestochowa was declared the Queen of Poland in 1656, and the icon was solemnly crowned in 1717 during the pontificate of Pope Clement XI.

The shrine has a long history as the greatest pilgrimage and religious center in Central Europe. Hundreds of thousands of young people from many countries gathered at the shrine Aug. 14 and 15, 1991, to celebrate World Youth Day with Pope John Paul II.

The shrine has undergone changes, some of them violent, in the years since 1382. Even in this century it has been a target of search and harassment by officials of the communist government of Poland in the years following World War II.

GALILEO REVISITED

Early in the 17th century Italian astronomer and physicist Galilei Galileo proposed an unproven hypothesis (advanced earlier by Copernicus) in opposition to the general view that the earth was the center of the universe and that the sun revolved around the earth rather than the other way around. The geocentric theory was supported by the contemporary literal interpretation of the Genesis account of creation. Galileo's view, therefore, was regarded as a threat to belief in the doctrine of creation and for that reason was denounced by church authorities in 1616. Galileo was tried by a church court in 1633 and was prevailed upon to abjure his view.

An imprimatur granted for publication of his writings in 1741 was equivalent to an implicit withdrawal or non-recognition of the sentence of 1663. Galileo was further vindicated in 1758 with the disappearance of his writings from the revised Index of Forbidden Books. The infallible teaching authority of the Church was not involved in handling the Galileo case.

Really, the whole affair was a product of inadequate understanding of the nature of religious truth and scientific truth or theory, and of the relationship between them. This, basically, was the substance of an address by Pope John Paul to the Pontifical Academy of Sciences Oct. 31, 1992, and of an ancillary report by a special commission charged with re-examining and clarifying the Galileo case. Both documents were circulated by the CNS Documentary Service, Origins, Nov. 12, 1992 (Vol. 22, No. 22).

The commission's report said in part: "The philosophical and theological qualifications wrongly granted to the then new theories about the centrality of the sun and the movement of the earth were the result of a transitional situation in the field of astronomical knowledge and of an exegetical confusion regarding cosmology. Certain theologians, Galileo's contemporaries, being heirs of a unitarian concept of the world universally accepted until the dawn of the 17th century, failed to grasp the profound, non-literal meaning of the Scriptures when they describe the physical structure of the created universe. This led them unduly to transpose a question of factual observation into the realm of faith."

"It is in that historical and cultural framework that Galileo's judges, incapable of dissociating faith from an age-old cosmology, believed quite wrongly that the adoption of the Copernican revolution ... was such as to undermine Catholic tradition, and that it was their duty to forbid its' being taught." The commission quoted comment by Cardinal (St.) Robert Bellarmine: "I say that, if it were really demonstrated that the sun is at the center of the world and the earth is in the third heaven, and that it is not the sun which revolves around the earth but the earth around the sun, then it would be necessary, ... in the explanation of scriptural texts which seem contrary to this assertion, to say that we do not understand them, rather than to say that what is demonstrated is false."

BIOGRAPHIES OF AMERICAN BISHOPS

(Sources: Almanac survey, *The Official Catholic Directory, Annuario Pontificio,* Catholic News Service. As of Sept. 2, 1993. For former bishops of the U.S., see "American Bishops of the Past," elsewhere in this section.)

Information includes: date and place of birth; educational institutions attended; date of ordination to the priesthood with, where applicable, name of archdiocese (*) or diocese in parentheses; date of episcopal ordination; episcopal appointments; date of resignation/retirement.

A

Abramowicz, Alfred L.: b. Jan. 27, 1919, Chicago, Ill.; educ. St. Mary of the Lake Seminary (Mundelein, Ill.), Gregorian Univ. (Rome); ord. priest (Chicago*) May 1, 1943; ord. titular bishop of Paestum and auxiliary bishop of Chicago, June 13, 1968.

Adamec, Joseph V.: b. Aug. 13, 1935, Bannister, Mich.; educ. Michigan State Univ. (East Lansing), Nepomucene College and Lateran Univ. (Rome); ord. priest (for Nitra diocese, Czechoslovakia), July 3, 1960; ord. bishop of Altoona-Johnstown, May 20, 1987.

Ahern, Patrick V.: b. Mar. 8, 1919, New York, N.Y.; educ. Manhattan College and Cathedral College (New York City), St. Joseph's Seminary (Yonkers, N.Y.), St. Louis Univ. (St. Louis, Mo.), Notre Dame Univ. (Notre Dame, Ind.); ord. priest (New York*) Jan. 27, 1945; ord. titular bishop of Naiera and auxiliary bishop of New York, Mar. 19, 1970.

Anderson, Moses B., S.S.E.: b. Sept. 9, 1928, Selma, Ala.; educ. St. Michael's College (Winooski, Vt.), St. Edmund Seminary (Burlington, Vt.), Univ. of Legon (Ghana); ord. priest May 30, 1958; ord. titular bishop of Vatarba and auxiliary bishop of Detroit, Jan. 27, 1983.

Angell, Kenneth A.: b. Aug. 3, 1930, Providence, R.I.; educ. St. Mary's Seminary (Baltimore, Md.); ord. priest (Providence) May 26, 1956; ord. titular bishop of Septimunicia and auxiliary bishop of Providence, R.I., Oct. 7, 1974; bishop of Burlington, Vt. Oct. 6, 1992; installed Nov. 9, 1992.

Apuron, Anthony Sablan, O.F.M. Cap.: b. Nov. 1, 1945, Agana, Guam; educ. St. Anthony College and Capuchin Seminary (Hudson, N.H.), Capuchin Seminary (Garrison, N.Y.), Maryknoll Seminary (New York), Notre Dame Univ. (Notre Dame, Ind.); ord. priest Aug. 26, 1972, in Guam; ord. titular bishop of Muzuca in Proconsulari and auxiliary bishop of Agana, Guam (U.S. Trust Territory), Feb. 19, 1984; archbishop of Agana, Mar. 10, 1986.

Arias, David, O.A.R.: b. July 22, 1929, Leon, Spain; educ. St. Rita's College (San Sebastian, Spain), Our Lady of Good Counsel Theologate (Granada, Spain), Teresianum Institute (Rome, Italy); ord. priest May 31, 1952; ord. titular bishop of Badie and auxiliary bishop of Newark, Apr. 7, 1983; episcopal vicar for Hispanic affairs.

Arkfeld, Leo, S.V.D.: b. Feb. 4, 1912, Butte, Nebr.; educ. Divine Word Seminary (Techny, Ill.), Sacred Heart College (Girard, Pa.); ord. priest Aug.

15, 1943; ord. titular bishop of Bucellus and vicar apostolic of Central New Guinea, Nov. 30, 1948; name of vicariate changed to Wewak, May 15, 1952; first bishop of Wewak, Nov. 15, 1966; app. archbishop of Madang, Papua New Guinea, Dec. 19, 1975; resigned Dec. 31, 1987.

Arliss, Reginald, C.P.: b. Sept. 8, 1906, East Orange, N.J.; educ. Immaculate Conception Seminary (Jamaica, N.Y.) and other Passionist houses of study; ord. priest Apr. 28, 1934; missionary in China for 16 years, expelled 1951; missionary in Philippines; rector of the Pontifical Philippine College Seminary in Rome, 1961-69; ord. titular bishop of Cerbali and prelate of Marbel, Philippines (now a diocese), Jan. 30, 1970; resigned from titular see and prelature, Oct. 1, 1981.

Arzube, Juan A.: b. June 1, 1918, Guayaquil, Ecuador; educ. Rensselaer Polytechnic Institute (Troy, N.Y.), St. John's Seminary (Camarillo, Calif.); ord. priest (Los Angeles*) May 5, 1954; ord. titular bishop of Civitate and auxiliary bishop of Los Angeles, Mar. 25, 1971.

B

Balke, Victor: b. Sept. 29, 1931, Meppen, Ill.; educ. St. Mary of the Lake Seminary (Mundelein, Ill.), St. Louis Univ. (St. Louis, Mo.); ord. priest (Springfield, Ill.) May 24, 1958; ord. bishop of Crookston, Sept. 2, 1976.

Baltakis, Paul Antanas, O.F.M.: b. Jan. 1, 1925, Troskunai, Lithuania; educ. seminaries of the Franciscan Province of St. Joseph (Belgium); ord. priest Aug. 24, 1952, in Belgium; served in U.S. as director of Lithuanian Cultural Center, New York, and among Lithuanian youth; head of U.S. Lithuanian Franciscan Vicariate, Kennebunkport, Maine, from 1979; ord. titular bishop of Egara, Sept. 24, 1984; assigned to pastoral assistance to Lithuanian Catholics living outside Lithuania.

Banks, Robert J.: b. Feb. 26, 1928, Winthrop, Mass.; educ. St. John's Seminary (Brighton, Mass.), Gregorian Univ., Lateran Univ. (Rome); ord. priest (Boston*) Dec. 20, 1952, in Rome; rector of St. John's Seminary, Brighton, Mass., 1971-81; vicar general of Boston archdiocese, 1984; ord. titular bishop of Taraqua and auxiliary bishop of Boston, Sept. 19, 1985; bishop of Green Bay, Oct. 16, 1990, installed Dec. 5, 1990.

Barnes, Gerald R.: b. June 22, 1945, Phoenix, Ariz., of Mexican descent; educ. St. Leonard Seminary (Dayton, O.), Assumption-St. John's Seminary (San Antonio, Tex.); ord. priest (San Antonio*) Dec. 20, 1975; ord. titular bishop of Montefiascone and auxiliary bishop of San Bernardino, Mar. 18, 1992.

Baum, William W.: (See Cardinals, Biographies.)

Begley, Michael J.: b. Mar. 12, 1909, Mattineague, Mass.; educ. Mt. St. Mary Seminary (Emmitsburg, Md.); ord. priest (Raleigh) May 26, 1934; ord. first bishop of Charlotte, N.C., Jan. 12, 1972; retired May 29, 1984.

Beltran, Eusebius J.: b. Aug. 31, 1934, Ashley, Pa.; educ. St. Charles Seminary (Philadelphia, Pa.); ord. priest (Atlanta*) May 14, 1960; ord. bishop of

Tulsa, Apr. 20, 1978; app. archbishop of Oklahoma City, Nov. 24, 1992; installed Jan 22, 1993.

Bernardin, Joseph L.: (See Cardinals, Biographies.)

Bevilacqua, Anthony J.: (See Cardinals, Biographies.)

Bilock, John M.: b. June 20, 1916, McAdoo, Pa.; educ. St. Procopius College and Seminary (Lisle, Ill.); ord. priest (Pittsburgh,* Byzantine Rite) Feb. 3, 1946; vicar general of Byzantine archdiocese of Munhall, 1969; ord. titular bishop of Pergamum and auxiliary bishop of Munhall, May 15, 1973; title of see changed to Pittsburgh, 1977.

Blaire, Stephen E.: b. Dec. 22, 1942, Los Angeles, Calif; educ. St. John's Seminary (Camarillo, Calif.); ord. priest (Los Angeles*) Apr. 29, 1967; ord. titular bishop of Lamzella and auxiliary of Los Angeles, May 31, 1990.

Boland, Ernest B., O.P.: b. July 10, 1925, Providence, R.I.; educ. Providence College (Rhode Island), Dominican Houses of Study (Somerset, Ohio; Washington, D.C.); ord. priest June 9, 1955; ord. bishop of Multan, Pakistan, July 25, 1966; resigned Oct. 20, 1984.

Boland, Raymond J.: b. Feb. 8, 1932, Tipperary, Ireland; educ. National Univ. of Ireland and All Hallows Seminary (Dublin); ord. priest (Washington*) June 16, 1957, in Dublin; vicar general and chancellor of Washington archdiocese; ord. bishop of Birmingham, Ala., Mar. 25, 1988; app. bishop of Kansas City-St. Joseph, Mo., June 22, 1993.

Boles, John P.: b. 1930, Boston, Mass.; educ. St. John Seminary, Boston College (Boston, Mass.); ord. priest (Boston*) 1955; ord. titular bishop of Nova Sparsa and auxiliary bishop of Boston, May 21, 1992.

Borders, William D.: b. Oct. 9, 1913, Washington, Ind.; educ. St. Meinrad Seminary (St. Meinrad, Ind.), Notre Dame Seminary (New Orleans, La.), Notre Dame Univ. (Notre Dame, Ind.); ord. priest (New Orleans*) May 18, 1940; ord. first bishop of Orlando, June 14, 1968; app. archbishop of Baltimore, Apr. 2, 1974, installed June 26, 1974; retired Apr. 11, 1989.

Bosco, Anthony G.: b. Aug. 1, 1927, New Castle, Pa.; educ. St. Vincent Seminary (Latrobe, Pa.), Lateran Univ. (Rome); ord. priest (Pittsburgh) June 7, 1952; ord. titular bishop of Labicum and auxiliary of Pittsburgh, June 30, 1970; app. bishop of Greensburg, Apr. 14, 1987, installed June 30, 1987.

Boudreaux, Warren L.: b. Jan. 25, 1918, Berwick, La.; educ. St. Joseph's Seminary (St. Benedict, La.), St. Sulpice Seminary (Paris, France), Notre Dame Seminary (New Orleans, La.), Catholic Univ. (Washington, D.C.); ord. priest (Lafayette, La.) May 30, 1942; ord. titular bishop of Calynda and auxiliary bishop of Lafayette, La., July 25, 1962; app. bishop of Beaumont, June 5, 1971; app. first bishop of Houma-Thibodaux, installed June 5, 1977; retired Dec. 29, 1992.

Boyle, Paul M., C.P.: b. May 28, 1926, Detroit, Mich.; educ. Passionist houses of study, Lateran Univ. (Rome); professed in Congregation of the Passion July 9, 1946; ord. priest May 30, 1953; professor of canon law and homiletics at Sacred

Heart Seminary, Louisville, Ky.; professor of canon law at St. Meinrad Seminary, St. Meinrad, Ind.,1965-68; pres. of Conference of Major Superiors of Men, 1969-74; superior general of Passionists, 1976-88; ord. titular bishop of Canapium and first vicar apostolic of newly established vicariate apostolic of Mandeville, Jamaica, July 9, 1991.

Breitenbeck, Joseph M.: b. Aug. 3, 1914, Detroit, Mich.; educ. University of Detroit, Sacred Heart Seminary (Detroit, Mich.), North American College and Lateran Univ. (Rome), Catholic Univ. (Washington, D.C.); ord. priest (Detroit*) May 30, 1942; ord. titular bishop of Tepelta and auxiliary bishop of Detroit, Dec. 20, 1965; app. bishop of Grand Rapids, Oct. 15, 1969, installed Dec. 2, 1969; retired July 11, 1989.

Broderick, Edwin B.: b. Jan. 16, 1917, New York, N.Y.; educ. Cathedral College (New York City), St. Joseph's Seminary (Yonkers, N.Y.), Fordham Univ. (New York City); ord. priest (New York*) May 30, 1942; ord. titular bishop of Tizica and auxiliary of New York, Apr. 21, 1967; bishop of Albany, 1969-76; executive director of Catholic Relief Services, 1976-82. Bishop emeritus of Albany.

Brom, Robert H.: b. Sept. 18, 1938, Arcadia, Wis.; educ. St. Mary's College (Winona, Minn.), Gregorian Univ. (Rome); ord. priest (Winona) Dec. 18, 1963, in Rome; ord. bishop of Duluth, May 23, 1983; coadjutor bishop of San Diego, May, 1989; bishop of San Diego, July 10, 1990.

Brown, Charles A., M.M.: b. Aug. 20, 1919, New York, N.Y.; educ. Cathedral College (New York City), Maryknoll Seminary (Maryknoll, N.Y.); ord. priest June 9, 1946; ord. titular bishop of Vallis and auxiliary bishop of Santa Cruz, Bolivia, Mar. 27, 1957.

Brown, Tod D.: b. Nov. 15, 1936, San Francisco, Calif.; educ. St. John's Seminary (Camarillo, Calif.), North American College (Rome); ord. priest (Monterey-Fresno) May 1, 1963; ord. bishop of Boise, Apr. 3, 1989.

Brunini, Joseph B.: b. July 24, 1909, Vicksburg, Miss.; educ. Georgetown Univ. (Washington, D.C.), North American College (Rome), Catholic Univ. (Washington, D.C.); ord. priest (Jackson) Dec. 5, 1933; ord. titular bishop of Axomis and auxiliary bishop of Natchez-Jackson, Jan. 29, 1957; apostolic administrator of Natchez-Jackson, 1966; app. bishop of Natchez-Jackson, Dec. 2, 1967; installed Jan. 29, 1968; title of see changed to Jackson, 1977; retired Jan. 24, 1984.

Bruskewitz, Fabian W.: b. Sept. 6, 1935, Milwaukee, Wis.; educ. North American College, Gregorian Univ. (Rome); ord. priest (Milwaukee*) July 17, 1960; ord. bishop of Lincoln, May, 1992.

Brust, Leo J.: b. Jan. 7, 1916, St. Francis, Wis.; educ. St. Francis Seminary (Milwaukee, Wis.), Canisianum (Innsbruck, Austria), Catholic Univ. (Washington, D.C.); ord. priest (Mlwaukee*) May 30, 1942; ord. titular bishop of Suelli and auxiliary bishop of Milwaukee, Oct. 16, 1969; retired Jan. 7, 1991.

Brzana, Stanislaus J.: b. July 1, 1917, Buffalo, N.Y.; educ. Christ the King Seminary (St. Bonaventure, N.Y.), Gregorian Univ. (Rome); ord. priest (Buffalo) June 7, 1941; ord. titular bishop of Cufruta and auxiliary bishop of Buffalo, June 29, 1964; bishop of Ogdensburg, Oct. 22, 1968.

Buechlein, Daniel M., O.S.B.: b. Apr. 20, 1938; educ. St. Meinrad College and Seminary (St. Meinrad, Ind.), St. Anselm Univ. (Rome); solemn profession as Benedictine monk, Aug. 15, 1963; ord. priest (St. Meinrad Archabbey) May 3, 1964; ord. bishop of Memphis, Mar. 2, 1987; app. archbishop of Indianapolis, July 14, 1992.

Bullock, William H.: b. Apr. 13, 1927, Maple Lake, Minn.; educ. St. Thomas College and St. Paul Seminary (St. Paul, Minn.), Notre Dame Univ. (Notre Dame, Ind.); ord. priest (St. Paul-Minneapolis*) June 7, 1952; ord. titular bishop of Natchez and auxiliary bishop of St. Paul and Minneapolis, Aug. 12, 1980; app. bishop of Des Moines, Feb. 10, 1987, installed Apr. 2, 1987; app. bishop of Madison, Wis., Apr. 13, 1993.

Burke, James C., O.P.: b. Nov. 30, 1926, Philadelphia, Pa.; educ. King's College (Wilkes-Barre, Pa.), Providence College (R.I.); ord. priest June 8, 1956; ord. titular bishop of Lamiggiga and prelate of Chimbote, Peru, May 25, 1967, resigned from prelature (now a diocese), June 8, 1978. Titular bishop of Lamiggiga.

Buswell, Charles A.: b. Oct. 15, 1913, Homestead, Okla.; educ. St. Louis Preparatory Seminary (St. Louis, Mo.), Kenrick Seminary (Webster Groves, Mo.), American College, Univ. of Louvain (Belgium); ord. priest (Oklahoma City*) July 9, 1939; ord. bishop of Pueblo, Sept. 30, 1959; resigned Sept. 18, 1979.

Byrne, James J.: b. July 28, 1908, St. Paul, Minn.; educ. Nazareth Hall Preparatory Seminary and St. Paul Seminary (St. Paul, Minn.), Univ. of Minnesota (Minneapolis, Minn.); Louvain Univ. (Belgium); ord. priest (St. Paul-Minneapolis*) June 3, 1933; ord. titular bishop of Etenna and auxiliary bishop of St. Paul, July 2, 1947; app. bishop of Boise, June 16, 1956; app. archbishop of Dubuque, Mar. 19, 1962, installed May 8, 1962; retired Aug. 23, 1983.

C

Camacho, Tomas Aguon: b. Sept. 18, 1933, Chalon Kanoa, Saipan; educ. St. Patrick's Seminary (Menlo Park, Calif.); ord. priest June 14, 1961; ord. first bishop of Chalan Kanoa, Northern Marianas (U.S. Commonwealth), Jan. 13, 1985.

Carberry, John J.: (See Cardinals, Biographies.)

Carlson, Robert J.: b. June 30, 1944, Minneapolis, Minn.; educ. Nazareth Hall and St. Paul Seminary (St. Paul, Minn.), Catholic Univ. (Washington, D.C.): ord. priest (St. Paul-Minneapolis*) May 23, 1970; ord. titular bishop of Avioccala and auxiliary bishop of St. Paul and Minneapolis, Jan. 11, 1984; vicar of eastern vicariate.

Carmody, Edmond: b. Jan. 12, 1934, Ahalena, Kerry, Ireland; educ. St. Brendan's College (Killarney), St. Patrick Seminary (Carlow, Ire.); ord. priest (San Antonio*) June 8, 1957; missionary in Peru 1984-89; ord. titular bishop of Mortlach and auxiliary bishop of San Antonio, Dec. 15, 1988; app. bishop of Tyler, Mar. 24, 1992.

Carmon, Dominic, S.V.D.: b. Dec. 13, 1930, Opelousas, La.; entered Society of Divine Word, 1946; ord. priest Feb. 2, 1960; missionary in Papua-New Guinea, 1961-68; ord. titular bishop of Rusicade and auxiliary bishop of New Orleans, Feb. 11, 1993.

Casey, Luis Morgan: b. June 23, 1935, Portageville, Mo.; ord. priest (St. Louis*) Apr. 7, 1962; missionary in Bolivia from 1965; ord. titular bishop of Mibiarca and auxiliary of La Paz, Jan. 28, 1984; vicar apostolic of Pando, Bolivia, Jan. 18, 1988.

Chaput, Charles J., O.F.M. Cap.: b. Sept. 26, 1944, Concordia, Kans.; educ. St. Fidelis College (Herman, Pa.), Capuchin College and Catholic Univ. (Washington, D.C.), Univ. of San Francisco; solemn vows as Capuchin, July 14, 1968; ord. priest Aug. 29, 1970; ord. bishop of Rapid City, S.D., July 26, 1988, the second priest of Native American ancestry (member of Prairie Band Potawatomi Tribe) ordained a bishop in the U.S.

Charron, Joseph L., C.PP.S.: b. Dec. 30, 1939, Redfield, S.D.; educ. St. John's Seminary (Collegeville, Minn.); ord. priest June 3, 1967; ord. titular bishop of Bencenna and auxiliary bishop of St. Paul and Minneapolis, Jan. 25, 1990.

Chavez, Gilbert Espinoza: b. May 9, 1932, Ontario, Calif.; educ. St. Francis Seminary (El Cajon, Calif.), Immaculate Heart Seminary (San Diego), Univ. of California; ord. priest (San Diego) Mar. 19, 1960; ord. titular bishop of Magarmel and auxiliary of San Diego, June 21, 1974.

Chedid, John: b. July 4, 1923, Eddid, Lebanon; educ. seminaries in Lebanon and Pontifical Urban College (Rome); ord. priest Dec. 21, 1951, in Rome; ord. titular bishop of Callinico and auxiliary bishop of St. Maron of Brooklyn for the Maronites, Jan. 25, 1981.

Clark, Matthew H.: b. July 15, 1937, Troy, N.Y.; educ. St. Bernard's Seminary (Rochester, N.Y.), Gregorian Univ. (Rome); ord. priest (Albany) Dec. 19, 1962; ord. bishop of Rochester, May 27, 1979; installed June 26, 1979.

Clinch, Harry A.: b. Oct. 27, 1908, San Anselmo, Calif.; educ. St. Joseph's College (Mountain View, Calif.), St. Patrick's Seminary (Menlo Park, Calif.); ord. priest (Monterey-Fresno) June 6, 1936; ord. titular bishop of Badiae and auxiliary bishop of Monterey-Fresno, Feb. 27, 1957; app. first bishop of Monterey in California, installed Dec. 14, 1967; resigned Jan. 19, 1982.

Coggin, Walter A., O.S.B.: b. Feb. 10, 1916, Richmond, Va.; ord. priest June 19, 1943; app. abbot ordinary of abbacy nullius of Mary Help of Christians, Belmont N.C., 1959; blessed Mar. 28, 1960; resigned 1970.

Cohill, John Edward, S.V.D.: b. Dec. 13, 1907, Elizabeth, N.J.; educ. Divine Word Seminary (Techny, Ill.); ord. priest Mar. 20, 1936; ord. first bishop of Goroko, Papua New Guinea, Mar. 11, 1967; resigned Aug. 30, 1980.

Comber, John W., M.M.: b. Mar. 12, 1906, Lawrence, Mass.; educ. St. John's Preparatory College (Danvers, Mass.), Boston College (Boston, Mass.), Maryknoll Seminary (Maryknoll, N.Y.); ord. priest Feb. 1, 1931; superior general of

Maryknoll, 1956-66; ord. titular bishop of Foratiana, Apr. 9, 1959.

Connare, William G.: b. Dec. 11, 1911, Pittsburgh, Pa.; educ. Duquesne Univ. (Pittsburgh, Pa.), St. Vincent Seminary (Latrobe, Pa.); ord. priest (Pittsburgh) June 14, 1936; ord. bishop of Greensburg, May 4, 1960; retired Jan. 20, 1987.

Connolly, Thomas J.: b. July 18, 1922, Tonopah, Nev.; educ. St. Patrick's Seminary (Menlo Park, Calif.), Catholic Univ. (Washington, D.C.), Lateran Univ. (Rome); ord. priest (Reno-Las Vegas) Apr. 8, 1947; ord. bishop of Baker, June 30, 1971.

Connors, Ronald G., C.SS.R.: b. Nov. 1, 1915, Brooklyn, N.Y.; ord. priest June 22, 1941; ord. titular bishop of Equizetum and coadjutor bishop of San Juan de la Maguana, Dominican Republic, July 20, 1976; succeeded as bishop of San Juan de la Maguana, July 20, 1977; retired Feb. 20, 1991.

Cooney, Patrick R.: b. Mar. 10, 1934, Detroit, Mich.; educ. Sacred Heart Seminary (Detroit), Gregorian Univ. (Rome), Notre Dame Univ. (Notre Dame, Ind.); ord. priest (Detroit*) Dec. 20, 1959; ord. titular bishop of Hodelm and auxiliary bishop of Detroit, Jan. 27, 1983; app. bishop of Gaylord, November, 1989; installed Jan. 28, 1990.

Corrada del Rio, Alvaro, S.J.: b. May 13, 1942, Santurce, Puerto Rico; entered Society of Jesus, 1960, at novitiate of St. Andrew-on-Hudson (Poughkeepsie, N.Y.); educ. Jesuit seminaries, Fordham Univ. (New York), Institut Catholique (Paris); ord. priest July 6, 1974, in Puerto Rico; pastoral coordinator of Northeast Catholic Hispanic Center, New York, 1982-85; ord. titular bishop of Rusticiana and auxiliary bishop of Washington, D.C., Aug. 4, 1985.

Coscia, Benedict Dominic, O.F.M.: b. Aug. 10, 1922, Brooklyn, N.Y.; educ. St. Francis College (Brooklyn, N.Y.), Holy Name College (Washington, D.C.); ord. priest June 11, 1949; ord. bishop of Jatai, Brazil, Sept. 21, 1961.

Costello, Thomas J.: b. Feb. 23, 1929, Camden, N.Y.; educ. Niagara Univ. (Niagara Falls, N.Y.), St. Bernard's Seminary (Rochester, N.Y.), Catholic Univ. (Washington, D.C.); ord. priest (Syracuse) June 5, 1954; ord. titular bishop of Perdices and auxiliary bishop of Syracuse Mar. 13, 1978.

Cotey, Arnold R., S.D.S.: b. June 15, 1921, Milwaukee, Wis.; educ. Divine Savior Seminary (Lanham, Md.), Marquette Univ. (Milwaukee, Wis.); ord. priest June 7, 1949; ord. first bishop of Nachingwea (now Lindi), Tanzania, Oct. 20, 1963; retired Nov. 11, 1983.

Cronin, Daniel A.: b. Nov. 14, 1927, Newton, Mass.; educ. St. John's Seminary (Boston, Mass.), North American College and Gregorian Univ. (Rome); ord. priest (Boston*) Dec. 20, 1952; attaché apostolic nunciature (Addis Ababa), 1957-61; served in papal Secretariat of State, 1961-68; ord. titular bishop of Egnatia and auxiliary bishop of Boston, Sept. 12, 1968; bishop of Fall River, Dec. 16, 1970; archbishop of Hartford, Dec. 10, 1991.

Crowley, Joseph R.: b. Jan. 12, 1915, Fort Wayne, Ind.; educ. St. Mary's College (St. Mary, Ky.), St. Meinrad Seminary (St. Meinrad, Ind.); served in US Air Force, 1942-46; ord. priest (Ft. Wayne-S. Bend) May 1, 1953; editor of *Our Sunday Visitor* 1958-67; ord. titular bishop of Maraguis and

auxiliary bishop of Fort Wayne-South Bend, Aug. 24, 1971; retired May 8, 1990.

Cummins, John S.: b. Mar. 3, 1928, Oakland, Calif.; educ. St. Patrick's Seminary (Menlo Park, Calif.), Catholic Univ. (Washington, D.C.), Univ. of California; ord. priest (San Francisco*) Jan. 24, 1953; executive director of the California Catholic Conference 1971-76; ord. titular bishop of Lambaesis and auxiliary bishop of Sacramento, May 16, 1974; app. bishop of Oakland, installed June 30, 1977.

Curlin, William G.: b. Aug. 30, 1927, Portsmouth, Va.; educ. Georgetown Univ. (Washington, D.C.), St. Mary's Seminary (Baltimore, Md.); ord. priest (Washington*), May 25, 1957; ord. titular bishop of Rosemarkie and auxiliary bishop of Washington, Dec. 20, 1988.

Curtis, Walter W.: b. May 3, 1913, Jersey City, N.J.; educ. Fordham Univ. (New York City), Seton Hall Univ. (South Orange, N.J.), Immaculate Conception Seminary (Darlington, N.J.), North American College and Gregorian Univ. (Rome), Catholic Univ. (Washington, D.C.); ord. priest (Newark*) Dec. 8, 1937; ord. titular bishop of Bisica and auxiliary bishop of Newark, Sept. 24, 1957; app. bishop of Bridgeport, 1961, installed Nov. 21, 1961; retired June 28, 1988.

Curtiss, Elden F.: b. June 16, 1932, Baker, Ore.; educ. St. Edward Seminary College and St. Thomas Seminary (Kenmore, Wash.); ord. priest (Baker) May 24, 1958; ord. bishop of Helena, Mont., Apr. 28, 1976; app. archbishop of Omaha, Nebr., May 4, 1993.

D

Daily, Thomas V.: b. Sept. 23, 1927, Belmont, Mass.; educ. Boston College, St. John's Seminary (Brighton, Mass.); ord. priest (Boston*) Jan. 10, 1952; missionary in Peru for five years as a member of the Society of St. James the Apostle; ord. titular bishop of Bladia and auxiliary bishop of Boston, Feb. 11, 1975; app. first bishop of Palm Beach, Fla., July 17, 1984, installed Oct. 24, 1984; app. bishop of Brooklyn, Feb. 20, 1990; installed Apr. 18, 1990.

Daly, James: b. Aug. 14, 1921, New York, N.Y.; educ. Cathedral College (Brooklyn, N.Y.), Immaculate Conception Seminary (Huntington, L.I.); ord. priest (Buffalo) May 22, 1948; ord. titular bishop of Castra Nova and auxiliary bishop of Rockville Centre, May 9, 1977.

D'Antonio, Nicholas, O.F.M.: b. July 10, 1916, Rochester, N.Y.; educ. St. Anthony's Friary (Catskill, N.Y.); ord. priest June 7, 1942; ord. titular bishop of Giufi Salaria and prelate of Olancho, Honduras, July 25, 1966; resigned 1977; vicar general of New Orleans archdiocese and episcopal vicar for Spanish Speaking, 1977-92.

D'Arcy, John M.: b. Aug. 18, 1932, Brighton, Mass.; educ. St. John's Seminary (Brighton, Mass.), Angelicum Univ. (Rome); ord. priest (Boston*) Feb. 2, 1957; spiritual director of St. John's Seminary; ord. titular bishop of Mediana and auxiliary bishop of Boston, Feb. 11, 1975; app. bishop of Fort Wayne-South Bend, Feb. 26, 1985, installed May 1, 1985.

Dattilo, Nicholas C.: b. Mar. 8, 1932, Mahoningtown, Pa.; educ. St. Vincent Seminary

(Latrobe, Pa.), St. Charles Borromeo Seminary (Philadelphia, Pa.); ord. priest (Pitsburgh) May 31, 1958; ord. bishop of Harrisburg, Jan. 26, 1990.

Deksnys, Antanas L.: b. May 9, 1906, Buteniskiai, Lithuania; educ. Metropolitan Seminary and Theological and Philosophical Faculty at Vytautas the Great Univ. (all at Kaunas, Lithuania), Univ. of Fribourg (Switzerland); ord. priest May 30, 1931; served in U.S. parishes at Mt. Carmel, Pa., and East St. Louis, Ill.; ord. titular bishop of Lavellum, June 15, 1969; assigned to pastoral work among Lithuanians in Western Europe; retired June 5, 1984.

Delaney, Joseph P.: b. Aug. 29, 1934, Fall River, Mass.; educ. Cardinal O'Connell Seminary (Boston, Mass.), Theological College (Washington, D.C.), North American College (Rome), Rhode Island College (Providence, R.I.); ord. priest (Fall River) Dec. 18, 1960; ord. bishop of Fort Worth, Tex., Sept. 13, 1981.

Dempsey, Michael J., O.P.: b. Feb. 22, 1912, Providence,R.I.; entered Order of Preachers (Dominicans), Chicago, province, 1935; ord. priest June 11, 1942; ord. bishop of Sokoto, Nigeria, Aug. 15, 1967; resigned Dec. 31, 1984.

De Palma, Joseph A., S.C.J.: b. Sept. 4, 1913, Walton, N.Y.; ord. priest May 20, 1944; superior general of Congregation of Priests of the Sacred Heart, 1959-67; ord. first bishop of De Aar, South Africa, July 19, 1967; retired Nov. 18, 1987.

De Paoli, Ambrose: b. Aug. 19, 1934, Jeannette, Pa., moved to Miami at age of nine; educ. St. Joseph Seminary (Bloomfield, Conn.), St. Mary of the West Seminary (Cincinnati, O.), North American College and Lateran Univ. (Rome); ord. priest (Miami*) Dec. 18, 1960, in Rome; served in diplomatic posts in Canada, Turkey, Africa and Venezuela; ord. titular archbishop of Lares, Nov. 20, 1983, in Miami; apostolic pro-nuncio to Sri Lanka, 1983-88; apostolic delegate in southern Africa and pro-nuncio to Lesotho, 1988.

De Simone, Louis A.: b. Feb. 21, 1922, Philadelphia, Pa.; educ. Villanova Univ. (Villanova, Pa.), St. Charles Borromeo Seminary (Overbrook, Pa.); ord. priest (Philadelphia*) May 10, 1952; ord. titular bishop of Cillium and auxiliary bishop of Philadelphia, Aug. 12, 1981.

Di Lorenzo, Francis X.: b. Apr. 15, 1942, Philadelphia, Pa.; educ. St. Charles Borromeo Seminary (Philadelphia), Univ. of St. Thomas (Rome); ord. priest (Philadelphia*) May 18, 1968; ord. titular bishop of Tigia and auxiliary bishop of Scranton, Mar. 8, 1988.

Dimino, Joseph T.: b. Jan. 7, 1923, New York, N.Y.; educ. Cathedral College (New York, N.Y.), St. Joseph's Seminary (Yonkers, N.Y.), Catholic Univ. (Washington, D.C.); ord. priest (New York*) June 4, 1949; ord. titular bishop of Carini and auxiliary bishop of the Military Services archdiocese, May 10, 1983; app. ordinary of Military Services archdiocese, May 14, 1991.

Dion, Georges E., O.M.I.: b. Sept. 25, 1911, Central Falls, R.I.; educ. Holy Cross College (Worcester, Mass.), Oblate Juniorate (Colebrook, N.H.), Oblate Scholasticates (Natick, Mass., and Ottawa, Ont.); ord. priest June 24, 1936; ord. titular bishop

of Arpaia and vicar apostolic of Jolo, Philippines Apr. 23, 1980; retired 1992.

Donnelly, Robert William: b. Mar. 22, 1931, Toledo, O.; educ. St. Meinrad Seminary College (St. Meinrad, Ind.), Mount St. Mary's in the West Seminary (Norwood, O.); ord. priest (Toledo) May 25, 1957; ord. titular bishop of Garba and auxiliary bishop of Toledo, May 3, 1984.

Donoghue, John F.: b. Aug. 9, 1928, Washington, D.C.; educ. St. Mary's Seminary (Baltimore, Md.); Catholic Univ. (Washington, D.C.); ord. priest (Washington*) June 4, 1955; chancellor and vicar general of Washington archdiocese, 1973-84; ord. bishop of Charlotte, N.C., Dec. 18, 1984; app. archbishop of Atlanta, June 22, 1993; installed Aug. 19, 1993.

Donovan, Paul V.: b. Sept. 1, 1924, Bernard, Iowa; educ. St. Gregory's Seminary (Cincinnati, Ohio), Mt. St. Mary's Seminary (Norwood, Ohio), Lateran Univ. (Rome); ord. priest (Lansing) May 20, 1950; ord. first bishop of Kalamazoo, Mich., July 21, 1971.

Dorsey, Norbert M., C.P.: b. Dec. 14, 1929, Springfield, Mass.; educ. Passionist seminaries, (eastern U.S. province), Pontifical Institute of Sacred Music and Gregorian Univ. (Rome, Italy); professed in Passionists, Aug. 15, 1949; ord priest Apr. 28, 1956; assistant general of Passionists, 1976-86; ord. titular bishop of Mactaris and auxiliary bishop of Miami, Mar. 19, 1986; app. bishop of Orlando, Mar. 20, 1990, installed May 25, 1990.

Driscoll, Michael P.: b. Aug. 8, 1939, Long Beach, Calif.; educ. St. John Seminary (Camarillo, Calif), Univ. of Southern Calif.; ord. priest (Los Angeles*) May 1, 1965; ord. titular bishop of Massita and auxiliary bishop of Orange, Mar. 6, 1990.

Dudick, Michael J.: b. Feb. 24, 1916, St. Clair, Pa.; educ. St. Procopius College and Seminary (Lisle, Ill.); ord. priest (Passaic, Byzantine Rite) Nov. 13, 1945; ord. bishop of Byzantine Rite Eparchy of Passaic, Oct. 24, 1968.

Dudley, Paul: b. Nov. 27, 1926, Northfield, Minn.; educ. Nazareth College and St. Paul Seminary (St. Paul, Minn.); ord. priest (St. Paul-Minneapolis*) June 2, 1951; ord. titular bishop of Ursona and auxiliary bishop of St. Paul and Minneapolis, Jan. 25, 1977; app. bishop of Sioux Falls, installed Dec. 13, 1978.

Duhart, Clarence James, C.SS.R.: b. Mar. 23, 1912, New Orleans, La.; ord, priest June 29, 1937; ord. bishop of Udon Thani, Thailand, Apr. 21, 1966; resigned Oct. 2, 1975.

DuMaine, (Roland) Pierre: b. Aug. 2, 1931, Paducah, Ky.; educ. St. Joseph's College (Mountain View, Calif.), St. Patrick's College and Seminary (Menlo Park, Calif.), Univ. of California (Berkeley), Catholic Univ. (Washington, D.C.); ord. priest (San Francisco) June 15, 1957; ord. titular bishop of Sarda and auxiliary bishop of San Francisco, June 29, 1978; app. first bishop of San Jose, Jan. 27, 1981; installed Mar. 18, 1981.

Dunne, John C.: b. Oct. 30, 1937, Brooklyn, N.Y.; educ. Cathedral College (Brooklyn, N.Y.). Immaculate Conception Seminary (Huntington, N.Y.), Manhattan College (New York); ord. priest

(Rockville Centre) June 1, 1963; ord. titular bishop of Abercorn and auxiliary bishop of Rockville Centre, Dec. 13, 1988. Vicar for Central Vicariate.

Dupre, Thomas L.: b. Nov. 10, 1933, South Hadley Falls, Mass.; educ. College de Montreal, Assumption College (Worcester, Mass.), Catholic Univ. (Washington, D.C.), ord. priest (Springfield, Mass.) 1959; ord. titular bishop of Hodelm and auxiliary bishop of Springfield, Mass. May 31, 1990.

Durick, Joseph Aloysius: b. Oct. 13, 1914, Dayton, Tenn.; educ. St. Bernard Minor Seminary (St. Bernard, Ala.), St. Mary's Seminary (Baltimore, Md.), Urban Univ. (Rome); ord. priest (Mobile*) May 23, 1940; ord. titular bishop of Cerbal and auxiliary bishop of Mobile-Birmingham, Mar. 24, 1955; app. coadjutor bishop of Nashville, Tenn., installed Mar. 3, 1964; apostolic administrator, 1966; bishop of Nashville, Sept. 10, 1969; resigned Apr. 4, 1975, to work with inmates of Federal correctional institutions and their families.

Durning, Dennis V., C.S.Sp.: b. May 18, 1923, Germantown, Pa.; educ. St. Mary's Seminary (Ferndale, Conn.); ord. priest June 3, 1949; ord. first bishop of Arusha, Tanzania, May 28, 1963; resigned Mar. 6, 1989.

E

Egan, Edward M.: b. Apr. 2, 1932, Oak Park, Ill.; educ. Quigley Preparatory Seminary (Chicago, Ill.), St. Mary of the Lake Seminary (Mundelein, Ill.), Gregorian Univ. (Rome); ord. priest (Chicago*) Dec. 15, 1957, in Rome; judge of Roman Rota, 1972-85; ord. titular bishop of Allegheny and auxiliary bishop of New York, May 22, 1985; bishop of Bridgeport, Nov. 5, 1988.

Elya, John A., B.S.O.: b. Sept. 16, 1928, Maghdouche, Lebanon; educ. diocesan monastery (Sidon, Lebanon), Gregorian Univ. (Rome, Italy); professed as member of Basilian Salvatorian Order, 1949; ord. priest Feb. 17, 1952, in Rome; came to U.S., 1958; ord. titular bishop of Abilene of Syria and auxiliary bishop of Melkite-Rite diocese of Newton, Mass., June 29, 1986.

F

Favalora, John C.: b. Dec. 5, 1935, New Orleans, La.; educ. St. Joseph Seminary (St. Benedict, La.), Notre Dame Seminary (New Orleans, La.), Gregorian Univ. (Rome), Catholic Univ. of America (Washington, D.C.), Xavier Univ. and Tulane Univ. (New Orleans); ord. priest (New Orleans*) Dec. 20, 1961; ord. bishop of Alexandria, La., July 29, 1986; bishop of St. Petersburg, March 14, 1989.

Federal, Joseph Lennox: b. Jan. 13, 1910, Greensboro, N.C.; educ. Belmont Abbey College (Belmont Abbey, N.C.), Niagara Univ. (Niagara Falls, N.Y.), Univ. of Fribourg (Switzerland), North American College and Gregorian Univ. (Rome); ord. priest (Raleigh) Dec. 8, 1934; ord. titular bishop of Appiaria and auxiliary bishop of Salt Lake City, Apr. 11, 1951; app. coadjutor with right of succession, May, 1958; bishop of Salt Lake City, Mar. 31, 1960; retired Apr. 22, 1980.

Fellhauer, David E.: b. Aug. 19, 1939, Kansas City, Mo.; educ. Pontifical College Josephinum

(Worthington, O.), St. Paul Univ. (Ottawa, Ont.); ord. priest (Dallas), 1965; ord. bishop of Victoria, May 28, 1990.

Ferrario, Joseph A.: b. Mar. 3, 1926, Scranton, Pa.; educ. St. Charles College (Catonsville, Md.), St. Mary's Seminary (Baltimore, Md.), Catholic Univ. (Washington, D.C.); Univ. of Scranton; ord. priest (Honolulu) May 19, 1951; ord. titular bishop of Cuse and auxiliary bishop of Honolulu, Jan. 13, 1978; bishop of Honolulu, May 13, 1982.

Fiorenza, Joseph A.: b. Jan. 25, 1931, Beaumont, Tex.; educ. St. Mary's Seminary (LaPorte, Tex.); ord. priest (Galveston-Houston) May 29, 1954; ord. bishop of San Angelo, Oct. 25, 1979; app. bishop of Galveston-Houston, Dec. 18, 1984, installed Feb. 18, 1985.

Fitzpatrick, John J.: b. Oct. 12, 1918, Trenton, Ont., Canada; educ. Urban Univ. (Rome), Our Lady of the Angels Seminary (Niagara Falls, N.Y.); ord. priest (Buffalo) Dec. 13, 1942; ord. titular bishop of Cenae and auxiliary bishop of Miami, Aug. 28, 1968; bishop of Brownsville, Tex., May 28, 1971; retired Nov. 30, 1991.

Fitzsimons, George K.: b. Sept. 4, 1928, Kansas City, Mo.; educ. Rockhurst College (Kansas City, Mo.), Immaculate Conception Seminary (Conception, Mo.); ord. priest (Kansas City-St. Joseph) Mar. 18, 1961; ord. titular bishop of Pertusa and auxiliary bishop of Kansas City-St. Joseph, July 3, 1975; app. bishop of Salina, Mar. 28, 1984, installed May 29, 1984.

Flanagan, Bernard Joseph: b. Mar. 31, 1908, Proctor, Vt.; educ. Holy Cross College (Worcester, Mass.), North American College (Rome), Catholic Univ. (Washington, D.C.); ord. priest (Burlington) Dec. 8, 1931; ord. first bishop of Norwich, Nov. 30, 1953; app. bishop of Worcester, installed, Sept. 24, 1959; resigned Mar. 31, 1983.

Flavin, Glennon P.: b. Mar. 2, 1916, St. Louis, Mo.; educ. Kenrick Seminary (St. Louis, Mo.); ord. priest (St. Louis*) Dec. 20, 1941; ord. titular bishop of Joannina and auxiliary bishop of St. Louis, May 30, 1957; app. bishop of Lincoln, installed Aug. 17, 1967; retired Mar. 24, 1992.

Fliss, Raphael M.: b. Oct. 25, 1930, Milwaukee, Wis.; educ. St. Francis Seminary (Milwaukee, Wis.), Catholic University (Washington, D.C.), Pontifical Lateran Univ. (Rome); ord. priest (Milwaukee*) May 26, 1956; ord. coadjutor bishop of Superior with right of succession, Dec. 20, 1979; bishop of Superior, June 27, 1985.

Flores, Patrick F.: b. July 26, 1929, Ganado, Tex.; educ. St. Mary's Seminary (Houston, Tex.); ord. priest (Galveston-Houston) May 26, 1956; ord. titular bishop of Itolica and auxiliary bishop of San Antonio, May 5, 1970 (first Mexican-American bishop); app. bishop of El Paso, Apr. 4, 1978, installed May 29, 1978; app. archbishop of San Antonio 1979; installed Oct. 13, 1979.

Flynn, Harry J.: b. May 2, 1933, Schenectady, N.Y.; educ. Siena College (Loudonville, N.Y.), Mt. St. Mary's College (Emmitsburg, Md.); ord. priest (Albany) May 28, 1960; ord. coadjutor bishop of Lafayette, La., June 24, 1986; bishop of Lafayette, La., May 15, 1989.

Foley, David E.: b. Feb. 3, 1930, Worcester,

Mass.; educ. St. Charles College (Catonsville, Md.), St. Mary's Seminary (Baltimore, Md.); ord. priest (Washington*) May 26, 1952; ord. titular bishop of Octaba and auxiliary bishop of Richmond, June 27, 1986.

Foley, John Patrick: b. Nov. 11, 1935, Sharon Hill, Pa.; educ. St. Joseph's Preparatory School (Philadelphia, Pa.), St. Joseph's College (now University) (Philadelphia, Pa.), St. Charles Borromeo Seminary (Overbrook, Pa.), St. Thomas Univ. (Rome), Columbia School of Journalism (New York); ord. priest (Philadelphia*) May 19, 1962; assistant editor (1967-70) and editor (1970-84) of *The Catholic Standard and Times,* Philadelphia archdiocesan paper; ord. titular archbishop of Neapolis in Proconsulari, May 8, 1984, in Philadelphia; app. president of the Pontifical Council for Social Communications, Apr. 5, 1984.

Forst, Marion F.: b. Sept. 3, 1910, St. Louis, Mo.; educ. St. Louis Preparatory Seminary (St. Louis, Mo.), Kenrick Seminary (Webster Groves, Mo.); ord. priest (St. Louis*) June 10, 1934; ord. bishop of Dodge City, Mar. 24, 1960; app. titular bishop of Scala and auxiliary bishop of Kansas City, Kans. Oct. 16, 1976; retired Dec. 23, 1986. Bishop emeritus of Dodge City.

Francis, Joseph A., S.V.D.: b. Sept. 30, 1923, Lafayette, La.; educ. St. Augustine Seminary (Bay St. Louis, Miss.), St. Mary Seminary (Techny, Ill.), Catholic Univ. (Washington, D.C.); ord. priest Oct. 7, 1950; president Conference of Major Superiors of Men, 1974-76, and the National Black Catholic Clergy Caucus; ord. titular bishop of Valliposita and auxiliary bishop of Newark, June 25, 1976.

Franklin, William Edwin: b. May 3, 1930, Parnell, Iowa; educ. Loras College and Mt. St. Bernard Seminry (Dubuque, Iowa); ord. priest (Dubuque*) Feb. 4, 1956; ord. titular bishop of Surista and auxiliary bishop of Dubuque, Apr. 1, 1987.

Franzetta, Benedict C.: b. Aug. 1, 1921, East Liverpool, O.; educ. St. Charles College (Catonsville, Md.), St. Mary Seminary (Cleveland, O.); ord. priest (Youngstown) Apr. 29, 1950; ord. titular bishop of Oderzo and auxiliary bishop of Youngstown, Sept. 4, 1980.

Freking, Frederick W.: b. Aug. 11, 1913, Heron Lake, Minn.; educ. St. Mary's College (Winona, Minn.), North American College and Gregorian Univ. (Rome), Catholic Univ. (Washington, D.C.); ord. priest (Winona) July 31, 1938; ord. bishop of Salina, Nov. 30, 1957; app. bishop of La Crosse, Dec. 30, 1964, installed Feb. 24, 1965; resigned May 10, 1983.

Frey, Gerard L.: b. May 10, 1914, New Orleans, La.; educ. Notre Dame Seminary (New Orleans, La.); ord. priest (New Orleans*) Apr. 2, 1938; ord. bishop of Savannah, Aug. 8, 1967; app. bishop of Lafayette, La., Nov. 7, 1972, installed Jan, 7, 1973; retired May 15, 1989.

Friend, William B.: b. Oct. 22, 1931, Miami, Fla.; educ. St. Mary's College (St. Mary, Ky.), Mt. St. Mary Seminary (Emmitsburg, Md.), Catholic Univ. (Washington, D.C.), Notre Dame Univ. (Notre Dame, Ind.); ord. priest (Mobile*) May 7, 1959; ord. titular bishop of Pomaria and auxiliary bishop of Alexandria-Shreveport, La., Oct. 30, 1979; app. bishop of Alexandria-Shreveport, Nov.

17, 1982, installed Jan 11, 1983; app. first bishop of Shreveport, June, 1986; installed July 30, 1986.

Frosi, Angelo, S.X.: b. Jan. 31, 1924, Baffano Cremona, Italy; ord. priest May 6, 1948; U.S. citizen; ord. titular bishop of Magneto, May 1, 1970, and prelate of Abaete do Tocantins, Brazil; app. first bishop of Abaetetuba, Brazil, Sept. 17, 1981.

G

Galante, Joseph A.: b. July 2, 1938, Philadelphia, Pa.; educ. St. Joseph Preparatory School, St. Charles Seminary (Philadelphia, Pa.); Lateran Univ., Angelicum, North American College (Rome); ord. priest (Philadelphia*) May 16, 1964; on loan to diocese of Brownsville, Tex., 1968-72, where he served in various diocesan posts; returned to Philadelphia, 1972; assistant vicar (1972-79) and vicar (1979-87) for religious; undersecretary of Congregation for Institutes of Consecrated Life and Societies of Apostolic Life (Rome), 1987-92; ord. titular bishop of Equilium and auxiliary bishop of San Antonio, Dec. 11, 1992.

Ganter, Bernard J.: b. July 17, 1928, Galveston, Tex.; educ. Texas A & M Univ. (College Sta., Tex.), St. Mary's Seminary (La Porte, Tex.), Catholic Univ. (Washington, D.C.); ord. priest (Galveston-Houston) May 22, 1952; chancellor of Galveston-Houston diocese, 1966-73; ord. first bishop of Tulsa, Feb. 7, 1973; app. bishop of Beaumont, Tex., Oct. 18, 1977, installed Dec. 13, 1977.

Garland, James H.: b. Dec. 13, 1931, Wilmington, Ohio; educ. Wilmington College (Ohio), Ohio State Univ. (Columbus, O.); Mt. St. Mary's Seminary (Cincinnati, O.), Catholic Univ. (Washington,D.C.); ord. priest (Cincinnati*) Aug. 15, 1959; ord. titular bishop of Garriana and auxiliary bishop of Cincinnati, July 25, 1984; director of department of social services; app. bishop of Marquette, Oct. 6, 1992; installed Nov. 11, 1992.

Garmendia, Francisco: b. Nov. 6, 1924, Lozcano, Spain; ord. priest June 29, 1947, in Spain; came to New York in 1964; became naturalized citizen; ord. titular bishop of Limisa and auxiliary bishop of New York, June 29, 1977. Vicar for Spanish pastoral development in New York archdiocese.

Garmo, George: b. Dec. 8, 1921, Telkaif, Iraq; educ. St. Peter Chaldean Patriarchal Seminary (Mossul, Iraq), Pontifical Urban Univ. (Rome); ord. priest Dec. 8, 1945; pastor of Chaldean parish in Detroit archdiocese, 1960-64, 1966-80; ord. archbishop of Chaldean-Rite archdiocese of Mossul, Iraq, Sept. 14, 1980.

Garner, Robert F.: b. Apr. 27, 1920, Jersey City, N.J.; educ. Seton Hall Univ. (S. Orange, N.J.), Immaculate Conception Seminary (Darlington, N.J.); ord. priest (Newark*) June 15, 1946; ord. titular bishop of Blera and auxiliary bishop of Newark, June 25, 1976.

Gaughan, Norbert F.: b. May 30, 1921, Pittsburgh, Pa.; educ. St. Vincent College (Latrobe, Pa.), Univ. of Pittsburgh; ord. priest (Pittsburgh) Nov. 4, 1945; ord. titular bishop of Taraqua and auxiliary bishop of Greensburg, June 26, 1975; app. bishop of Gary, July 24, 1984, installed Oct. 1, 1984.

Gelineau, Louis E.: b. May 3, 1928, Burlington, Vt.; educ. St. Michael's College (Winooski, Vt.), St. Paul's Univ. Seminary (Ottawa, Ont.), Catholic Univ. (Washington, D.C.); ord. priest (Burlington) June 5, 1954; ord. bishop of Providence, R.I., Jan. 26, 1972.

Gendron, Odore: b. Sept. 13, 1921, Manchester, N.H.; educ. St. Charles Borromeo Seminary (Sherbrooke, Que., Canada), Univ. of Ottawa, St. Paul Univ. Seminary (Ottawa, Ont., Canada); ord. priest (Manchester) May 31, 1947; ord. bishop of Manchester, Feb. 3, 1975; resigned June 12, 1990.

George, Francis E., O.M.I.: b. Jan. 16, 1937, Chicago, Ill.; educ. Univ. of Ottawa (Canada); Catholic Univ. (Washington, D.C.), Tulane Univ. (New Orleans), Urban Univ. (Rome); ord. priest Dec. 21, 1963; provincial of central region of Oblates of Mary Immaculate, 1973-74, vicar general, 1974-86; ord. bishop of Yakima, Sept. 21, 1990.

Gerber, Eugene J.: b. Apr. 30, 1931, Kingman, Kans.; educ. St. Thomas Seminary (Denver, Colo.), Wichita State Univ.; Catholic Univ. (Washington, D.C.), Angelicum (Rome); ord. priest (Wichita) May 19, 1959; ord. bishop of Dodge City, Dec. 14, 1976; app. bishop of Wichita, Nov. 17, 1982.

Gerbermann, Hugo, M.M.: b. Sept. 11, 1913, Nada, Tex.; educ. St. John's Minor and Major Seminary (San Antonio, Tex.), Maryknoll Seminary (Maryknoll, N.Y.); ord. priest Feb. 7, 1943; missionary work in Ecuador and Guatemala; ord. titular bishop of Amathus and prelate of Huehuetenango, Guatemala, July 22, 1962; first bishop of Huehuetenango, Dec. 23, 1967; app. titular bishop of Pinkel and auxiliary bishop of San Antonio, July 24, 1975; resigned June 30, 1982.

Gerety, Peter L.: b. July 19, 1912, Shelton, Conn.; educ. Sulpician Seminary (Paris, France); ord. priest (Hartford*) June 29, 1939; ord. titular bishop of Crepedula and coadjutor bishop of Portland, Me., with right of succession, June 1, 1966; app. apostolic administrator of Portland, 1967; bishop of Portland, Me., Sept. 15, 1969; app. archbishop of Newark, Apr. 2, 1974; installed June 28, 1974; retired June 3, 1986.

Gerry, Joseph, O.S.B.: b. Sept. 12, 1928, Millinocket, Me.; educ. St. Anselm Abbey Seminary (Manchester, N.H.), Univ. of Toronto (Canada), Fordham Univ. (New York); ord. priest June 12, 1954; abbot of St. Anselm Abbey, Manchester, N.H., 1972; ord. titular bishop of Praecausa and auxiliary of Manchester, Apr. 21, 1986; bishop of Portland, Me., Dec. 27, 1988, installed Feb. 21, 1989.

Gettelfinger, Gerald A.: b. Oct. 20, 1935, Ramsey, Ind.; educ. St. Meinrad Seminary (St. Meinrad, Ind.), Butler Univ. (Indianapolis, Ind.); ord. priest (Indianapolis*) May 7, 1961; ord. bishop of Evansville, Apr. 11, 1989.

Glennie, Ignatius T., S.J.: b. Feb. 5, 1907, Mexico City; educ. Mt. St. Michael's Scholasticate (Spokane, Wash.), Pontifical Seminary (Kandy, Ceylon), St. Mary's College (Kurdeong, India); entered Society of Jesus, 1924; ord. priest Nov. 21, 1938; ord. bishop of Trincomalee, Ceylon, Sept. 21,

1947; title of see changed to Trincomalee-Batticaloa (Sri Lanka), 1967; resigned Feb. 15, 1974.

Glynn, John J.: b. Aug. 6, 1926, Boston, Mass.; educ. St. John's Seminary (Brighton, Mass.); ord. priest (Boston*), Apr. 11, 1951; Navy chaplain, 1960-85; ord. titular bishop of Monteverde and auxiliary bishop of Military Services archdiocese, Jan. 6, 1992.

Goedert, Raymond E.: b. Oct. 15, 1927, Oak Park, Ill.; educ. Quigley Preparatory Seminary (Chicago, Ill.), St. Mary of the Lake Seminary and Loyola Univ. (Chicago, Ill.), Gregorian Univ. (Rome); ord. priest (Chicago*), 1952; ord. titular bishop of Tamazeni and auxiliary bishop of Chicago, Aug. 29, 1991.

Gonzalez, Roberto O., O.F.M.: b. June 2, 1950, Elizabeth, N.J.; educ. St. Joseph Seraphic Seminary (Callicoon, N.Y.), Siena College (Loudonville, N.Y.), Washington Theological Union (Silver-Spring, Md.), Fordham Univ. (New York, N.Y.); solemnly professed in Franciscan Order, 1976; ord. priest May 8, 1977; ord. titular bishop of Ursona and auxiliary bishop of Boston, Oct. 3, 1988.

Gorman, John R.: b. Dec. 11, 1925, Chicago, Ill.; educ. St. Mary of the Lake Seminary (Mundelein, Ill.), Loyola Univ. (Chicago, Ill.); ord. priest (Chicago*) May 1, 1956; ord. titular bishop of Catula and auxiliary bishop of Chicago, Apr. 11, 1988.

Gossman, F. Joseph: b. Apr. 1, 1930, Baltimore, Md.; educ. St. Charles College (Catonsville, Md.), St. Mary's Seminary (Baltimore, Md.), North American College (Rome), Catholic Univ. (Washington, D.C.); ord. priest (Baltimore*) Dec. 17, 1955; ord. titular bishop of Agunto and auxiliary bishop of Baltimore, Sept. 11, 1968; named urban vicar, June 13, 1970; app. bishop of Raleigh April 8, 1975.

Gottwald, George J.: b. May 12, 1914, St. Louis, Mo.; educ. Kenrick Seminary (Webster Groves, Mo.); ord. priest (St. Louis*) June 9, 1940; ord. titular bishop of Cedamusa and auxiliary bishop of St. Louis, Aug. 8, 1961; resigned Aug. 2, 1988.

Gracida, Rene H.: b. June 9, 1923, New Orleans, La.; educ. Rice Univ. and Univ. of Houston (Houston, Tex.), Univ. of Fribourg (Switzerland); ord. priest (Miami*) May 23, 1959; ord. titular bishop of Masuccaba and auxiliary bishop of Miami, Jan. 25, 1972; app. first bishop of Pensacola-Tallahassee, Oct. 1, 1975, installed Nov. 6, 1975; app. bishop of Corpus Christi, May 24, 1983, installed July 11, 1983.

Grady, Thomas J.: b. Oct. 9, 1914, Chicago, Ill.; educ. St. Mary of the Lake Seminary (Mundelein, Ill.), Gregorian Univ. (Rome), Loyola Univ. (Chicago, Ill.); ord. priest (Chicago*) Apr. 23, 1938; ord. titular bishop of Vamalla and auxiliary bishop of Chicago, Aug. 24, 1967; app. bishop of Orlando, Fla., Nov. 11, 1974, installed Dec. 16, 1974; resigned Dec. 12, 1989.

Graham, John J.: b. Sept. 11, 1913, Philadelphia, Pa.; educ. St. Charles Borromeo Seminary (Philadelphia, Pa.), Pontifical Roman Seminary (Rome, Italy); ord. priest (Philadelphia*) Feb. 26, 1938; ord. titular bishop of Sabrata and auxiliary bishop of Philadelphia, Jan. 7, 1964; retired Nov. 8, 1988.

Grahmann, Charles V.: b. July 15, 1931, Halletsville, Tex.; educ. The Assumption-St. John's Seminary (San Antonio, Tex.); ord. priest (San Antonio*) Mar. 17, 1956; ord. titular bishop of Equilium and auxiliary bishop of San Antonio, Aug. 20, 1981; app. first bishop of Victoria, Tex., Apr. 13, 1982; app. coadjutor bishop of Dallas, Dec. 9, 1989; bishop of Dallas, July, 1990.

Graves, Lawrence P.: b. May 4, 1916, Texarkana, Ark.; educ. St. John's Seminary (Little Rock, Ark.), North American College (Rome), Catholic Univ. (Washington, D.C.); ord. priest (Little Rock) June 11, 1942; ord. titular bishop of Vina and auxiliary bishop of Little Rock, Apr. 25, 1969; app. bishop of Alexandria, May 22, 1973, installed Sept. 18, 1973; title of see changed to Alexandria-Shreveport, Jan. 12, 1977; resigned July 20, 1982.

Green, Francis J.: b. July 7, 1906, Corning, N.Y.; educ. St. Patrick's Seminary (Menlo Park, Calif.); ord. priest (Tucson) May 15, 1932; ord. titular bishop of Serra and auxiliary bishop of Tucson, Sept. 17, 1953; named coadjutor of Tucson with right of succession, May 11, 1960; bishop of Tucson, Oct. 26, 1960; retired July 27, 1981.

Gregory, Wilton D.: b. Dec. 7, 1947, Chicago, Ill.; educ. Quigley Preparatory Seminary South, Niles College of Loyola Univ. (Chicago, Ill.), St. Mary of the Lake Seminary (Mundelein, Ill.), Pontifical Liturgical Institute, Sant'Anselmo (Rome); ord. priest (Chicago*) May 9, 1973; ord. titular bishop of Oliva and auxiliary bishop of Chicago, Dec. 13, 1983.

Griffin, James A.: b. June 13, 1934, Fairview Park, O.; educ. St. Charles College (Baltimore, Md.), Borromeo College (Wicklife, O.); St. Mary Seminary (Cleveland, O.); Lateran Univ. (Rome); Cleveland State Univ.; ord. priest (Cleveland) May 28, 1960; ord. titular bishop of Holar and auxiliary bishop of Cleveland, Aug. 1, 1979; app. bishop of Columbus, Feb. 8, 1983.

Grosz, Edward M.: b. Feb. 16, 1945, Buffalo, N.Y.; educ. St. John Vianney Seminary (East Aurora, N.Y.), Notre Dame Univ. (Notre Dame, Ind.); ord. priest (Buffalo) May 29, 1971; ord. titular bishop of Morosbisdus and auxiliary bishop of Buffalo, Feb. 2, 1990.

Grutka, Andrew G.: b. Nov. 17, 1908, Joliet, Ill.; educ. St. Procopius College and Seminary (Lisle, Ill.), Urban Univ. and Gregorian Univ. (Rome); ord. priest (Ft. Wayne-S. Bend) Dec. 5, 1933; app. moderator of lay activities in Gary diocese, 1955; ord. first bishop of Gary, Feb. 25, 1957; app. member of Pontifical Marian Academy, Jan. 5, 1970; retired July 24, 1984.

Guillory, Curtis J., S.V.D.: b. Sept. 1, 1943, Mallet, La.; educ. Divine Word College (Epworth, Iowa), Chicago Theological Union (Chicago), Creighton Univ. (Omaha, Neb.); ord. priest Dec. 16, 1972; ord. titular bishop of Stagno and auxiliary bishop of Galveston-Houston, Feb 19, 1988.

Gumbleton, Thomas J.: b. Jan. 26, 1930, Detroit, Mich.; educ. St. John Provincial Seminary (Detroit, Mich.), Pontifical Lateran Univ. (Rome); ord. priest

(Detroit*) June 2, 1956; ord. titular bishop of Ululi and auxiliary bishop of Detroit, May 1, 1968.

H

Ham, J. Richard, M.M.: b. July 11, 1921, Chicago, Ill.; educ. Maryknoll Seminary (New York); ord. priest June 12, 1948; missionary to Guatemala, 1958; ord. titular bishop of Puzia di Numidia and auxiliary bishop of Guatemala, Jan. 6, 1968; resigned see 1979; app. vicar for Hispanic ministry in St. Paul and Minneapolis archdiocese, January, 1980; auxiliary bishop of St. Paul and Minneapolis, October, 1980; retired Oct. 29, 1990.

Hanifen, Richard C.: b. June 15, 1931, Denver, Colo,; educ. Regis College and St. Thomas Seminary (Denver, Colo.), Catholic Univ. (Washington, D.C.), Lateran Univ. (Rome); ord. priest (Denver*) June 6, 1959; ord. titular bishop of Abercorn and auxiliary bishop of Denver, Sept. 20, 1974; app. first bishop of Colorado Springs, 1983; installed Jan. 30, 1984.

Hannan, Philip M.: b. May 20, 1913, Washington, D.C.; educ. St. Charles College (Catonsville, Md.), Catholic Univ. (Washington, D.C.), North American College (Rome); ord. priest (Washington*) Dec. 8, 1939; ord. titular bishop of Hieropolis and auxiliary bishop of Washington, D.C., Aug. 28, 1956; app. archbishop of New Orleans, installed Oct. 13, 1965; retired Dec. 6, 1988.

Hanus, Jerome George, O.S.B.: b. May 25, 1940, Brainard, Nebr.; educ. Conception Seminary (Conception, Mo.), St. Anselm Univ. (Rome), Princeton Theological Seminary (Princeton, N.J.); ord. priest (Conception Abbey, Mo.) July 30, 1966; abbot of Conception Abbey, 1977-87; president of Swiss American Benedictine Congregation, 1984-87; ord. bishop of St. Cloud, Aug. 24, 1987.

Harrington, Timothy J.: b. Dec. 19, 1918, Holyoke, Mass.; educ. Holy Cross College (Worcester, Mass.), Grand Seminary (Montreal, Que.), Boston College School of Social Work; ord. priest (Springfield, Mass.) Jan. 19, 1946; ord. titular bishop of Rusuca and auxiliary bishop of Worcester, Mass., July 2, 1968; app. bishop of Worcester, Sept. 1, 1983, installed Oct. 13, 1983.

Harrison, Frank J.: b. Aug. 12, 1912; Syracuse, N.Y.; educ. Notre Dame Univ. (Notre Dame, Ind.), St. Bernard's Seminary (Rochester, N.Y.), ord. priest (Syracuse) June 4, 1937; ord. titular bishop of Aquae in Numidia and auxiliary bishop of Syracuse, Apr. 22, 1971; app. bishop of Syracuse, Nov. 9, 1976, installed Feb. 6, 1977; retired June 16, 1987.

Hart, Daniel A.: b. Aug. 24, 1927, Lawrence, Mass.; educ. St. John's Seminary (Brighton, Mass.); ord. priest (Boston*) Feb. 2, 1953; ord. titular bishop of Tepelta and auxiliary bishop of Boston, Oct. 18, 1976.

Hart, Joseph: b. Sept. 26, 1931, Kansas City, Missouri; educ. St. John Seminary (Kansas City, Mo.), St. Meinrad Seminary (Indianapolis, Ind.); ord. priest (Kansas City-St. Joseph) May 1, 1956; ord. titular bishop of Thimida Regia and auxiliary bishop of Cheyenne, Wyo., Aug. 31, 1976; app. bishop of Cheyenne, installed June 12, 1978.

Hastrich, Jerome J.: b. Nov. 13, 1914, Milwaukee, Wis.; educ. Marquette Univ., St. Francis

Seminary (Milwaukee, Wis.); ord. priest (Milwaukee*) Feb. 9, 1941; ord. titular bishop of Gurza and auxiliary bishop of Madison, Sept. 3, 1963; app. bishop of Gallup, N. Mex., Sept. 3, 1969; retired Mar. 20, 1990.

Head, Edward D.: b. Aug. 5, 1919, White Plains, N.Y.; educ. Cathedral College, St. Joseph's Seminary, Columbia Univ. (New York City); ord. priest (New York*) Jan. 27, 1945; director of New York Catholic Charities; ord. titular bishop of Ardsratha and auxiliary bishop of New York, Mar. 19, 1970; app. bishop of Buffalo, Jan. 23, 1973, installed Mar. 19, 1973.

Heim, Capistran F., O.F.M.: b. Jan. 21, 1934, Catskill, N.Y.; educ. Franciscan Houses of Study; ord. priest Dec. 18, 1965; missionary in Brazil; ord. first bishop of prelature of Itaituba, Brazil, Sept. 17, 1988; installed Oct. 2, 1988.

Helmsing, Charles H.: b. Mar. 23, 1908, Shrewsbury, Mo.; educ. St. Louis Preparatory Seminary (St. Louis, Mo.), Kenrick Seminary (Webster Groves, Mo.); ord. priest (St. Louis*) June 10, 1933; ord. titular bishop of Axomis and auxiliary bishop of St. Louis, Apr. 19, 1949; first bishop of Springfield-Cape Girardeau, Aug. 24, 1956; bishop of Kansas City-St. Joseph, 1962, installed Apr. 3, 1962; resigned June 25, 1977.

Hermes, Herbert, O.S.B.: b. May 25, 1933, Scott City, Kans.; ord. priest (St. Benedict Abbey, Atchison, Kans.), May 26, 1960; missionary in Brazil; ord. bishop of territorial prelature of Cristalandia, Brazil, Sept. 2, 1990.

Herrmann, Edward J.: b. Nov. 6, 1913, Baltimore, Md.; educ. Mt. St. Mary's Seminary (Emmitsburg, Md.), Catholic Univ. (Washington, D.C.); ord. priest (Washington*) June 12, 1947; ord. titular bishop of Lamzella and auxiliary bishop of Washington, D.C., Apr. 26, 1966; app. bishop of Columbus, June 26, 1973; resigned Sept. 18, 1982.

Hettinger, Edward Gerhard: b. Oct. 14, 1902, Lancaster, O.; educ. St. Vincent's College (Beatty, Pa.); ord. priest (Columbus) June 2, 1928; ord. titular bishop of Teos and auxiliary bishop of Columbus, Feb. 24, 1942; retired Oct. 18, 1977.

Hickey, Dennis W.: b. Oct. 28, 1914, Dansville, N.Y.; educ. Colgate Univ. and St. Bernard's Seminary (Rochester, N.Y.); ord. priest (Rochester) June 7, 1941; ord. titular bishop of Rusuccuru and auxiliary bishop of Rochester, N.Y., Mar. 14, 1968; retired Jan. 16, 1990.

Hickey, James A.: (See Cardinals, Biographies.)

Higi, William L.: b. Aug. 29, 1933, Anderson, Ind.; educ. Our Lady of the Lakes Preparatory Seminary (Wawasee, Ind.), Mt. St. Mary of the West Seminary and Xavier Univ. (Cincinnati, O.); ord. priest (Lafayette, Ind.) May 30, 1959; ord. bishop of Lafayette, Ind., June 6, 1984.

Hoffman, James R.: b. June 12, 1932, Fremont, O.; educ. Our Lady of the Lake Minor Seminary (Wawasee, Ind.), St. Meinrad College (St. Meinrad, Ind.); Mt. St. Mary Seminary (Norwood, O.); Catholic Univ. (Washington, D.C.); ord. priest (Toledo) July 28, 1957; ord. titular bishop of Italica and auxiliary bishop of Toledo, June 23, 1978; bishop of Toledo, Dec. 16, 1980.

Hogan, James J.: b. Oct. 17, 1911, Philadelphia, Pa.; educ. St. Charles College (Catonsville, Md.), St.

Mary's Seminary (Baltimore), Gregorian Univ. (Rome), Catholic Univ. (Washington, D.C.); ord. priest (Trenton) Dec. 8, 1937; ord. titular bishop of Philomelium and auxiliary bishop of Trenton, Feb. 25, 1960; app. bishop of Altoona-Johnstown, installed July 6, 1966; retired Nov. 4, 1986.

Hogan, Joseph L.: b. Mar. 11, 1916, Lima, N.Y.; educ. St. Bernard's Seminary (Rochester, N.Y.), Canisius College (Buffalo, N.Y.), Angelicum (Rome); ord. priest (Rochester) June 6, 1942; ord. bishop of Rochester, Nov. 28, 1969; resigned Nov. 28, 1978.

Houck, William Russell: b. June 26, 1926, Mobile Ala.; educ. St. Bernard Junior College (Cullman, Ala.), St. Mary's Seminary College and St. Mary's Seminary (Baltimore, Md.), Catholic Univ. (Washington, D.C.); ord. priest (Mobile*) May 19, 1951; ord. titular bishop of Alessano and auxiliary bishop of Jackson, Miss., May 27, 1979, by Pope John Paul II; app. bishop of Jackson, Apr. 11, 1984, installed June 5, 1984.

Howze, Joseph Lawson E.: b. Aug. 30, 1923, Daphne, Ala.; convert to Catholicism, 1948; educ. St. Bonaventure Univ. (St. Bonaventure, N.Y.); priest (Raleigh) May 7, 1959; ord. titular bishop of Massita and auxiliary bishop of Natchez-Jackson, Jan. 28, 1973; app. first bishop of Biloxi, Miss., Mar. 8, 1977; installed June 6, 1977.

Hubbard, Howard J.: b. Oct. 31, 1938, Troy, N.Y.; educ. St. Joseph's Seminary (Dunwoodie, N.Y.); North American College and Gregorian Univ. (Rome), Catholic Univ. (Washington, D.C.); ord. priest (Albany) Dec. 18, 1963; ord. bishop of Albany, Mar. 27, 1977.

Hughes, Alfred C.: b. Dec. 2, 1932, Boston, Mass.; educ. St. John Seminary (Brighton, Mass.), Gregorian Univ. (Rome); ord. priest (Boston*) Dec. 15, 1957, in Rome; ord. titular bishop of Maximiana in Byzacena and auxiliary bishop of Boston, Sept. 14, 1981.

Hughes, Edward T.: b. Nov. 13, 1920, Lansdowne, Pa.; educ. St. Charles Seminary, Univ. of Pennsylvania (Philadelphia); ord. priest (Philadelphia*) May 31, 1947; ord. titular bishop of Segia and auxiliary bishop of Philadelphia, July 21, 1976; app. bishop of Metuchen, Dec. 11, 1986, installed Feb. 5, 1987.

Hughes, William A.: b. Sept. 23, 1921, Youngstown, O.; educ. St. Charles College (Catonsville, Md.), St. Mary's Seminary (Cleveland, O.), Notre Dame Univ. (Notre Dame, Ind.); ord. priest (Youngstown) Apr. 6, 1946; ord. titular bishop of Inis Cathaig and auxiliary bishop of Youngstown, Sept. 12, 1974; app. bishop of Covington, installed May 8, 1979.

Hunthausen, Raymond G.: b. Aug. 21, 1921, Anaconda, Mont.; educ. Carroll College (Helena, Mont.), St. Edward's Seminary (Kenmore, Wash.), St. Louis Univ. (St. Louis, Mo.), Catholic Univ. (Washington, D.C.), Fordham Univ. (New York City), Notre Dame Univ. (Notre Dame, Ind.); ord. priest (Helena) June 1, 1946; ord. bishop of Helena, Aug. 30, 1962; app. archbishop of Seattle, Feb. 25, 1975; retired 1991.

Hurley, Francis T.: b. Jan. 12, 1927, San Francisco, Calif.; educ. St. Patrick's Seminary (Menlo Park,

Calif.), Catholic Univ. (Washington, D.C.); ord. priest (San Francisco*) June 16, 1951; assigned to NCWC in Washington, D.C., 1957; assistant (1958) and later (1968) associate secretary of NCCB and USCC; ord. titular bishop of Daimlaig and auxiliary bishop of Juneau, Alaska, Mar. 19, 1970; app. bishop of Juneau, July 20, 1971, installed Sept. 8, 1971; app. archbishop of Anchorage, May 4, 1976, installed July 8, 1976.

Hurley, Mark J.: b. Dec. 13, 1919, San Francisco, Calif.; educ. St. Patrick's Seminary (Menlo Park, Calif.), Univ. of California (Berkeley), Catholic Univ. (Washington, D.C.), Lateran Univ. (Rome), Univ. of Portland (Portland, Ore.); ord. priest (San Francisco*) Sept. 23, 1944; ord. titular bishop of Thunusuda and auxiliary bishop of San Francisco, Jan. 4, 1968; app. bishop of Santa Rosa, Nov. 19, 1969; resigned Apr. 15, 1986.

I-J

Ibrahim, Ibrahim N.: b. Oct. 1, 1937, Telkaif, Mosul, Iraq.; educ. Patriarchal Seminary (Mosul, Iraq), St. Sulpice Seminary (Paris, France); ord. priest Dec. 30, 1962, in Baghdad, Iraq; ord. titular bishop of Anbar and apostolic exarch for Chaldean-Rite Catholics in the United States, Mar. 8, 1982, in Baghdad; installed in Detroit, Apr. 18, 1982; app. first eparch, Aug. 3, 1985, when exarchate was raised to eparchy of St. Thomas Apostle of Detroit.

Imesch, Joseph L.: b. June 21, 1931, Detroit, Mich.; educ. Sacred Heart Seminary (Detroit, Mich.), North American College, Gregorian Univ. (Rome); ord. priest (Detroit*) Dec. 16, 1956; ord. titular bishop of Pomaria and auxiliary bishop of Detroit, Apr. 3, 1973; app. bishop of Joliet, June 30, 1979.

Jacobs, Sam Galip: b. Mar. 4, 1938, Greenwood, Miss.; educ. Immaculata Seminary (Lafayette, La.), Catholic Univ. (Washington, D.C.); ord. priest (Lafayette) June 6, 1964; became priest of Lake Charles diocese, 1980, when that see was established; ord. bishop of Alexandria, La., Aug. 24, 1989.

Jakubowski, Thad J.: b. Apr. 5, 1924, Chicago, Ill.; educ. Mundelein Seminary, St. Mary of the Lake Univ., Loyola Univ. (Chicago); ord priest (Chicago*) May 3, 1950; ord. titular bishop of Plestia and auxiliary bishop of Chicago, Apr. 11, 1988.

Jarrell, C. Michael: b. May 15, 1940, Opelousas, La.; educ. Immaculata Minor Seminary (Lafayette, La.); Catholic Univ. (Washington, D.C.); ord. priest (Lafayette, La.) June 3, 1967; ord. bishop of Houma-Thibodaux, Mar. 4, 1993.

Jolson, Alfred, S.J.: b. June 18, 1928, Bridgeport, Conn.; educ. Weston College (Weston, Mass.), Gregorian Univ. (Rome); ord. priest June 14, 1958; ord. bishop of Reykjavik, Iceland, Feb. 6, 1988.

K

Kaffer, Roger L.: b. Aug. 14, 1927, Joliet, Ill.; educ. Quigley Preparatory Seminary (Chicago, Ill.), St. Mary of the Lake Seminary (Mundelein, Ill.), Gregorian Univ. (Rome); ord. priest (Joliet) May 1, 1954; ord. titular bishop of Dusa and auxiliary bishop of Joliet, June 26, 1985.

Kalisz, Raymond P., S.V.D.: b. Sept. 25, 1927, Melvindale, Mich.; educ. St. Mary's Seminary (Techny, Ill.); ord. priest Aug. 15, 1954; ord. bishop of Wewak, Papua New Guinea, August 15, 1980.

Kaniecki, Michael Joseph, S.J.: b. Apr. 13, 1935, Detroit Mich.; joined Jesuits 1953; educ. Xavier Univ. (Milford, O.), Mt. St. Michael's Seminary (Spokane, Wash.), Regis College (Willowdale, Ont.); ord. priest June 5, 1965; ord. coadjutor bishop of Fairbanks, May 1, 1984; bishop of Fairbanks, June 1, 1985.

Keating, John Richard: b. July 20, 1934, Chicago, Ill.; educ. Quigley Preparatory Seminary (Chicago, Ill.), St. Mary of the Lake Seminary (Mundelein, Ill.), Gregorian Univ. (Rome); ord. priest (Chicago*) Dec. 20, 1958; ord. bishop of Arlington, Aug. 4, 1983.

Keeler, William Henry: b. Mar. 4, 1931, San Antonio, Tex.; educ. St. Charles Seminary (Overbrook, Pa.), North American College, Pontifical Gregorian Univ. (Rome); ord. priest (Harrisburg) July 17, 1955; ord. titular bishop of Ulcinium and auxiliary bishop of Harrisburg, Sept. 21, 1979; app. bishop of Harrisburg, Nov. 15, 1983; installed Jan. 4, 1984; archbishop of Baltimore, Apr. 11, 1989.

Keleher, James P.: b. July 31, 1931, Chicago, Ill.; educ. Quigley Preparatory Seminary (Chicago, Ill.), St. Mary of the Lake Seminary (Mundelein, Ill.); ord. priest (Chicago*) Apr. 12, 1958; ord. bishop of Belleville, Dec. 11, 1984; app. archbishop of Kansas City, Kans., June 28, 1993.

Kelly, Thomas C., O.P.: b. July 14, 1931, Rochester, N.Y.; educ. Providence College (Providence, R.I.), Immaculate Conception College (Washington, D.C.), Angelicum (Rome); professed in Dominicans, Aug. 26, 1952; secretary, apostolic delegation, Washington, D.C., 1965-71; associate general secretary, 1971-77, and general secretary, 1977-81, NCCB/USCC; ord. titular bishop of Tusurus and auxiliary bishop of Washington, D.C., Aug. 15, 1977; app. archbishop of Louisville, Dec. 28, 1981, installed Feb. 18, 1982.

Kenny, Michael H.: b. June 26, 1937, Hollywood, Calif.; educ. St. Joseph College (Mountain View, Calif.), St. Patrick's Seminary (Menlo Park, Calif.), Catholic Univ. (Washington, D.C.); ord. priest (Santa Rosa) Mar. 30, 1963; ord. bishop of Juneau, May 27, 1979.

Kinney, John F.: b. June 11, 1937, Oelwein, Iowa; educ. Nazareth Hall and St. Paul Seminaries (St. Paul, Minn.); Pontifical Lateran University (Rome); ord. priest (St. Paul-Minneapolis*) Feb. 2, 1963; ord. titular bishop of Caorle and auxiliary bishop of St. Paul and Minneapolis, Jan. 25, 1977; app. bishop of Bismarck June 30, 1982.

Kmiec, Edward U.: b. June 4, 1936, Trenton, N.J.; educ. St. Charles College (Catonsville, Md.), St. Mary's Seminary (Baltimore, Md.), Gregorian Univ. (Rome); ord. priest (Trenton) Dec. 20, 1961; ord. titular bishop of Simidicca and auxiliary bishop of Trenton, Nov. 3, 1982; app. bishop of Nashville, Oct. 13, 1992; installed Dec. 3, 1992.

Kocisko, Stephen: b. June 11, 1915, Minneapolis, Minn.; educ. Nazareth Hall Minor Seminary (St. Paul, Minn.), Pontifical Ruthenian College, Urban Univ. (Rome); ord. priest (Pittsburgh*, Byzantine Rite) Mar. 30, 1941; ord. titular bishop of Teveste and auxiliary bishop of apostolic exarchate of Pittsburgh, Oct. 23, 1956; installed as first eparch of the eparchy of Passaic, Sept. 10, 1963; app. eparch of Byzantine-Rite diocese of Pittsburgh, installed Mar. 5, 1968; app. first metropolitan of Munhall, installed June 11, 1969; title of see changed to Pittsburgh, 1977; retired June 12, 1991.

Koester, Charles R.: b. Sept. 16, 1915, Jefferson City, Mo.; educ. Conception Academy (Conception, Mo.), St. Louis Preparatory Seminary and Kenrick Seminary (St. Louis, Mo.), North American College (Rome); ord. priest (St. Louis*) Dec. 20, 1941; ord. titular bishop of Suacia and auxiliary bishop of St. Louis, Feb. 11, 1971; retired.

Krawczak, Arthur H.: b. Feb. 2, 1913, Detroit, Mich.; educ. Sacred Heart Seminary, Sts. Cyril and Methodius Seminary (Orchard Lake, Mich.), Catholic Univ. (Washington, D.C.); ord. priest (Detroit*) May 18, 1940; ord. titular bishop of Subbar and auxiliary bishop of Detroit, Apr. 3, 1973; retired Aug. 17, 1982.

Krol, John J.: (See Cardinals, Biographies.)

Kucera, Daniel, O.S.B.: b. May 7, 1923, Chicago, Ill.; educ. St. Procopius College (Lisle, Ill.), Catholic Univ. (Washington, D.C.); professed in Order of St. Benedict, June 16, 1944; ord. priest May 26, 1949; abbot, St. Procopius Abbey, 1964-71; pres. Illinois Benedictine College, 1959-65 and 1971-76; ord. titular bishop of Natchez and auxiliary bishop of Joliet, July 21, 1977; app. bishop of Salina, Mar. 5, 1980, installed May 7, 1980; app. archbishop of Dubuque, installed Feb. 23, 1984.

Kuchmiak, Michael, C.SsR.: b. Feb. 5, 1923, Obertyn, Horodenka, Western Ukraine; left during World War II; educ. St. Josaphat Ukrainian Seminary (Rome, Italy), St. Mary's Seminary (Meadowvale, Ont., Canada); ord. priest May 13, 1956; in the U.S. from 1967; ord. titular bishop of Agathopolis and auxiliary bishop of Ukrainian metropolitan of Philadelphia, Apr. 27, 1988; exarch of apostolic exarchate for Ukrainian Catholics in Great Britain, July, 1989.

Kupfer, William F., M.M.: b. Jan. 28, 1909, Brooklyn, N.Y.; educ. Cathedral College (Brooklyn, N.Y.), Maryknoll Seminary (Maryknoll, N.Y.); ord. priest June 11, 1933; missionary in China; app. prefect apostolic of Taichung, Taiwan, 1951; ord. first bishop of Taichung, July 25, 1962; retired Sept. 3, 1986.

Kuzma, George M.: b. July 24, 1925, Widber, Pa.; educ. St. Francis Seminary (Loretto, Pa.), St. Procopius College (Lisle, Ill.), Sts. Cyril and Methodius Byzantine Catholic Seminary, Duquesne Univ. (Pittsburgh, Pa.); ord. priest (Pittsburgh*, Byzantine Rite), May 5, 1955; ord. titular bishop of Telmisso and auxiliary bishop of Byzantine Rite eparchy of Passaic, 1987; app. bishop of Byzantine-Rite diocese of Van Nuys, Calif., Oct. 23, 1990, installed Jan. 15, 1991.

L

Lambert, Francis, S.M.: b. Feb. 7, 1921, Lawrence, Mass.; educ. Marist Seminary (Framingham, Mass.); ord. priest, June 29, 1946; served in Marist missions in Oceania; provincial of Marist Oceania province, 1971; ord. bishop of Port Vila, Vanuatu (New Hebrides), Mar. 20, 1977.

Larkin, W. Thomas: b. Mar. 31, 1923, Mt. Morris, N.Y.; educ. St. Andrew Seminary and St. Bernard Seminary (Rochester, N.Y.); Angelicum Univ. (Rome); ord. priest (St. Augustine) May 15, 1947; ord. bishop of St. Petersburg, May 27, 1979; retired Nov. 29, 1988.

Law, Bernard F.: (See Cardinals, Biographies.)

Leibrecht, John J.: b. Aug. 30, 1930, Overland, Mo.; educ. Catholic Univ. (Washington, D.C.); ord. priest (St. Louis*) Mar. 17, 1956; superintendent of schools of St. Louis archdiocese, 1962-1981; ord. bishop of Springfield-Cape Girardeau, Mo., Dec. 12, 1984.

Leonard, Vincent M.: b. Dec. 11, 1908, Pittsburgh, Pa.; educ. Duquesne Univ. (Pittsburgh, Pa.), St. Vincent Seminary (Latrobe, Pa.); ord. priest (Pittsburgh) June 16, 1935; ord. titular bishop of Arsacal and auxiliary bishop of Pittsburgh, Apr. 21, 1964; app. bishop of Pittsburgh, installed July 2, 1969; resigned June 30, 1983.

Lessard, Raymond W.: b. Dec. 21, 1930, Grafton, N.D.; educ. St. Paul Seminary (St. Paul, Minn.), North American College (Rome); ord. priest (Fargo) Dec. 16, 1956; served on staff of the Congregation for Bishops in the Roman Curia, 1964-73; ord. bishop of Savannah, Apr. 27, 1973.

Levada, William J.: b. June 15, 1936, Long Beach, Calif.; educ. St. John's College (Camarillo, Calif.), Gregorian Univ. (Rome); ord. priest (Los Angeles*) Dec. 20, 1961; ord. titular bishop of Capri and auxiliary bishop of Los Angeles, May 12, 1983; app. archbishop of Portland, Ore., July 3, 1986.

Lipscomb, Oscar H.: b. Sept. 21, 1931, Mobile, Ala.; educ. McGill Institute, St. Bernard College (Cullman, Ala.), North American College and Gregorian Univ. (Rome), Catholic Univ. (Washington, D.C.); ord. priest (Mobile*) July 15, 1956; ord. first archbishop of Mobile, Nov. 16, 1980.

Lohmuller, Martin N.: b. Aug. 21, 1919, Philadelphia, Pa.; educ. St. Charles Borromeo Seminary (Philadelphia, Pa.), Catholic Univ. (Washington, D.C.); ord. priest (Philadelphia*) June 3, 1944; ord. titular bishop of Ramsbury and auxiliary bishop of Philadelphia, Apr. 2, 1970.

Losten, Basil: b. May 11, 1930, Chesapeake City, Md.; educ. St. Basil's College (Stamford, Conn.), Catholic University (Washington, D.C.); ord. priest (Philadelphia*, Byzantine Rite) June 10, 1957; ord. titular bishop of Arcadiopolis in Asia and auxiliary bishop of Ukrainian archeparchy of Philadelphia, May 25, 1971; app. apostolic administrator of archeparchy, 1976; app. bishop of Ukrainian eparchy of Stamford, Sept. 20, 1977.

Lotocky, Innocent Hilarius, O.S.B.M.: b. Nov. 3, 1915, Petlykiwci, Ukraine; educ. seminaries in Ukraine, Czechoslovakia and Austria; ord. priest Nov. 24, 1940; ord. bishop of St. Nicholas of Chicago for the Ukrainians, Mar. 1, 1981; retired July 15, 1993.

Loverde, Paul S.: b. Sept. 3, 1940, Framingham, Mass.; educ. St. Thomas Seminary (Bloomfield, Conn.), St. Bernard Seminary (Rochester, N.Y.), Gregorian Univ. (Rome), Catholic Univ. (Washington, D.C.); ord. priest (Norwich), Dec. 18,

1965; ord. titular bishop of Ottabia and auxiliary bishop of Hartford, Apr. 12, 1988.

Lubachivsky, Myroslav I.: (See Cardinals, Biographies.)

Lucker, Raymond A.: b. Feb. 24, 1927, St. Paul, Minn.; educ. St. Paul Seminary (St. Paul, Minn.); University of Minnesota (Minneapolis), Angelicum (Rome); ord. priest (St. Paul-Minneapolis*) June 7, 1952; director of USCC department of education, 1968-71; ord. titular bishop of Meta and auxiliary bishop of St. Paul and Minneapolis, Sept. 8, 1971; app. bishop of New Ulm, Dec. 23, 1975, installed Feb. 19, 1976.

Lynch, George E.: b. Mar. 4, 1917, New York, N.Y.; educ. Fordham Univ. (New York), Mt. St. Mary's Seminary (Emmitsburg, Md.), Catholic Univ. (Washington, D.C.); ord. priest (Raleigh) May 29, 1943; ord. titular bishop of Satafi and auxiliary of Raleigh Jan. 6, 1970; retired Apr. 16, 1985.

Lyne, Timothy J.: b. Mar. 21, 1919, Chicago, Ill.; educ. Quigley Preparatory Seminary, St. Mary of the Lake Seminary (Mundelein, Ill.); ord. priest (Chicago*) May 1, 1943; ord. titular bishop of Vamalla and auxiliary bishop of Chicago, Dec. 13, 1983.

M

McAuliffe, Michael F.: b. Nov. 22, 1920, Kansas City, Mo.; educ. St. Louis Preparatory Seminary (St. Louis, Mo.), Catholic Univ. (Washington, D.C.): ord. priest (Kansas City-St. Joseph) May 31, 1945; ord. bishop of Jefferson City, Aug. 18, 1969.

McCarrick, Theodore E.: b. July 7, 1930, New York, N.Y.; educ. Fordham Univ. (Bronx, N.Y.), St. Joseph's Seminary (Dunwoodie, N.Y.), Catholic Univ. (Washington, D.C.); ord. priest (New York*) May 31, 1958; dean of students Catholic Univ. of America, 1961-63; pres., Catholic Univ. of Puerto Rico, 1965-69; secretary to Cardinal Cooke, 1970; ord. titular bishop of Rusubisir and auxiliary bishop of New York, June 29, 1977; app. first bishop of Metuchen, N.J., Nov. 19, 1981, installed Jan. 31, 1982; app. archbishop of Newark, June 3, 1986, installed July 25, 1986.

McCarthy, Edward A.: b. Apr. 10, 1918, Cincinnati, O.; educ. Mt. St. Mary Seminary (Norwood, O.), Catholic Univ. (Washington, D.C.), Lateran and Angelicum (Rome); ord. priest (Cincinnati*) May 29, 1943; ord. titular bishop of Tamascani and auxiliary bishop of Cincinnati, June 15, 1965; first bishop of Phoenix, Ariz., Dec. 2, 1969; app. coadjutor archbishop of Miami, Fla., July 7, 1976; succeeded as archbishop of Miami, July 26, 1977.

McCarthy, John E.: b. June 21, 1930, Houston, Tex.; educ. Univ. of St. Thomas (Houston, Tex.); ord. priest (Galveston-Houston) May 26, 1956; assistant director Social Action Dept. USCC, 1967-69; executive director Texas Catholic Conference; ord. titular bishop of Pedena and auxiliary bishop of Galveston-Houston, Mar. 14, 1979; app. bishop of Austin, Dec. 19, 1985, installed Feb. 25, 1986.

McCormack, William J.: b. Jan. 24, 1924, New York, N.Y.; educ. Christ the King Seminary, St. Bonaventure Univ. (St. Bonaventure, N.Y.); ord. priest (New York*) Feb. 21, 1959; national director of the Society for the Propagation of the Faith,

1980- ; ord. titular bishop of Nicives and auxiliary bishop of New York, June 6, 1987.

McCormick, J. Carroll: b. Dec. 15, 1907, Philadelphia, Pa.; educ. College Ste. Marie (Montreal), St. Charles Seminary (Overbrook, Pa.), Minor and Major Roman Seminary (Rome); ord. priest (Philadelphia*) July 10, 1932; ord. titular bishop of Ruspae and auxiliary bishop of Philadelphia, Apr. 23, 1947; app. bishop of Altoona-Johnstown, installed Sept. 21, 1960; app. bishop of Scranton, installed May 25, 1966; resigned Feb. 15, 1983.

McDonald, Andrew J.: b. Oct. 24, 1923, Savannah, Ga.; educ. St. Mary's Seminary (Baltimore, Md.), Catholic Univ. (Washington, D.C.), Lateran Univ. (Rome); ord. priest (Savannah) May 8, 1948; ord. bishop of Little Rock, Sept. 5, 1972.

McDonough, Thomas J.: b. Dec. 5, 1911, Philadelphia, Pa.; educ. St. Charles Seminary (Overbrook, Pa.), Catholic Univ. (Washington, D.C.); ord. priest (Philadelphia*) May 26, 1938; ord. titular bishop of Thenae and auxiliary bishop of St. Augustine, Apr. 30, 1947; app. auxiliary bishop of Savannah, Jan. 2, 1957; named bishop of Savannah, installed Apr. 27, 1960; app. archbishop of Louisville, installed May 2, 1967; resigned Sept. 29, 1981.

McDowell, John B.: b. July 17, 1921, New Castle, Pa.; educ. St. Vincent College, St. Vincent Theological Seminary (Latrobe, Pa.), Catholic Univ. (Washington, D.C.); ord. priest (Pittsburgh) Nov. 4, 1945; superintendent of schools, Pittsburgh diocese, 1955-70; ord. titular bishop of Tamazuca, and auxiliary bishop of Pittsburgh, Sept. 8, 1966.

McFarland, Norman F.: b. Feb. 21, 1922, Martinez, Calif.; educ. St. Patrick's Seminary (Menlo Park, Calif.), Catholic Univ. (Washington, D.C.); ord. priest (San Francisco*) June 15, 1946; ord. titular bishop of Bida and auxiliary bishop of San Francisco, Sept. 8, 1970; apostolic adminstrator of Reno, 1974; app. bishop of Reno, Feb. 10, 1976, installed Mar. 31, 1976; title of see changed to Reno-Las Vegas; app. bishop of Orange, Calif., Dec. 29, 1986; installed Feb. 24, 1987.

McGann, John R.: b. Dec. 2, 1924, Brooklyn, N.Y.; educ. Cathedral College (Brooklyn, N.Y.), Immaculate Conception Seminary (Huntington, L.I.); ord. priest (Rockville Centre) June 3, 1950; ord. titular bishop of Morosbisdus and auxiliary bishop of Rockville Centre, Jan. 7, 1971; vicar general and episcopal vicar; app. bishop of Rockville Centre May 3, 1976, installed June 24, 1976.

McGarry, Urban, T.O.R.: b. Nov. 11, 1911, Warren, Pa.; ord. priest Oct. 3, 1942, in India; prefect apostolic of Bhagalpur, Aug. 7, 1956; ord. first bishop of Bhagalpur, India, May 10, 1965; resigned Nov. 30, 1987.

McGrath, Joseph P.: b. July 11, 1945, Dublin, Ire.; educ. St. John's College Seminary (Waterford, Ire.), Lateran Univ. (Rome, Italy); ord. priest in Ireland June 7, 1970; came to U.S. same year and became San Francisco archdiocesan priest; ord. titular bishop of Allegheny and auxiliary bishop of San Francisco, Jan. 25, 1989.

McHugh, James T.: b. Jan. 3, 1932, Orange, N.J. educ. Seton Hall Univ. (S. Orange, N.J.), Immaculate Conception Seminary (Darlington, N.J.), Fordham Univ. (New York, N.Y.), Catholic Univ. (Washington, D.C.), Angelicum (Rome, Italy); ord. priest (Newark*) May 25, 1957; assistant director. 1965-67, and director, 1967-75, of Family Life Division, USCC; director, 1972-78, of NCCB Office for Pro-Life Activities; special advisor to Mission of Permanent Observer of Holy See to UN; ord. titular bishop of Morosbisdo and auxiliary of Newark, Jan. 25, 1988; bishop of Camden, May 22, 1989.

McKinney, Joseph C.: b. Sept. 10, 1928, Grand Rapids, Mich.: educ. St. Joseph's Seminary (Grand Rapids, Mich.), Seminaire de Philosophie (Montreal, Canada), Urban Univ. (Rome, Italy); ord. priest (Grand Rapids) Dec. 20, 1953; ord. titular bishop of Lentini and auxiliary bishop of Grand Rapids, Sept. 26, 1968.

McLaughlin, Bernard J.: b. Nov. 19, 1912, Buffalo, N.Y.; educ. Urban Univ. (Rome, Italy); ord. priest (Buffalo) Dec. 21, 1935, at Rome; ord. titular bishop of Mottola and auxiliary bishop of Buffalo, Jan. 6, 1969; resigned Jan. 5, 1988.

McManus, William E.: b. Jan. 27, 1914, Chicago, Ill.; educ. St. Mary of the Lake Seminary (Mundelein, Ill.), Catholic Univ. (Washington, D.C.); ord. priest (Chicago*) Apr. 15, 1939; ord. titular bishop of Mesarfelta and auxiliary bishop of Chicago, Aug. 24, 1967; app. bishop of Fort Wayne-South Bend, Aug. 31, 1976, installed Oct. 19, 1976; retired Feb. 26, 1985.

McNabb, John C., O.S.A.: b. Dec. 11, 1925, Beloit, Wis.; educ. Villanova Univ. (Villanova, Pa.), Augustinian College and Catholic Univ. (Washington, D.C.), De Paul Univ. (Chicago, Ill.); ord. priest May 24, 1952; ord. titular bishop of Saia Maggiore, June 17, 1967 (resigned titular see, Dec. 27, 1977); prelate of Chulucanas, Peru, 1967; first bishop of Chulucanas, Dec. 12, 1988.

McNamara, John R.: b. 1928, Worcester, Mass.; educ. Holy Cross College (Worcester, Mass.), St. John's Seminary (Boston, Mass.); ord. priest (Boston*) 1952; served as chaplain in the U.S. Navy 1962-88; attained the rank of Rear Admiral and was Chief of Naval Chaplains; ord. titular bishop of Risinium and auxiliary bishop of Boston, May 21, 1992.

McNamara, Lawrence J.: b. Aug. 5, 1928, Chiccago, Ill.; educ. St. Paul Seminary (St. Paul, Minn.), Catholic Univ. (Washington, D.C.); ord. priest (Kansas City-St. Joseph) May 30, 1953; executive director of Campaign for Human Development 1973-77; ord. bishop of Grand Island, Nebr., Mar. 28, 1978.

McNaughton, William J., M.M.: b. Dec. 7, 1926, Lawrence, Mass.; educ. Maryknoll Seminary (Maryknoll, N.Y.); ord. priest June 13, 1953; ord. titular bishop of Thuburbo Minus and vicar apostolic of Inchon, Korea, Aug. 24, 1961; first bishop of Inchon, Mar. 10, 1962, when vicariate was raised to diocese.

McRaith, John Jeremiah: b. Dec. 6, 1934, Hutchinson, Minn.; educ. St. John Preparatory School (Collegeville, Minn.), Loras College, St. Bernard Seminary (Dubuque, Ia); ord. priest (New Ulm) Feb. 21, 1960; exec. dir. of Catholic Rural Life Conference, 1971-78; ord. bishop of Owensboro, Ky., Dec. 15, 1982.

Madera, Joseph J., M.Sp.S.: b. Nov. 27, 1927, San Francisco, Calif.; educ. Domus Studiorum of the Missionaries of the Holy Spirit (Coyoacan, D.F. Mexico); ord. priest June 15, 1957; ord. coadjutor bishop of Fresno, Mar. 4, 1980; bishop of Fresno, July 1, 1980; app. titular bishop of Orte and auxiliary of Military Services archdiocese, June 30, 1991.

Maguire, Joseph F.: b. Sept. 4, 1919, Boston, Mass.; educ. Boston College, St. John's Seminary (Boston, Mass.); ord. priest (Boston*) June 29, 1945; ord. titular bishop of Macteris and auxiliary bishop of Boston, Feb. 2, 1972; app. coadjutor bishop of Springfield, Mass., Apr. 13, 1976; succeeded as bishop of Springfield, Mass., Oct. 15, 1977; retired Dec. 27, 1991.

Mahoney, James P.: b. Aug. 16, 1925, Kingston, N.Y.; educ. St. Joseph's Seminary (Dunwoodie, N.Y.); ord. priest (New York*) May 19, 1951; ord. titular bishop of Ipagro and auxiliary bishop of New York, Sept. 15, 1972.

Mahony, Roger M.: (See Cardinals, Biographies.)

Maida, Adam J.: b. Mar. 18, 1930, East Vandergrift, Pa.; educ. St. Vincent College (Latrobe, Pa.). St. Mary Univ. (Baltimore, Md.), Lateran Univ. (Rome), Duquesne Univ. (Pittsburgh, Pa.); ord. priest (Pittsburgh) May 26, 1956; ord. bishop of Green Bay, Jan. 25, 1984; app. archbishop of Detroit, May 8, 1990, installed June 11, 1990.

Malone, James W.: b. Mar. 8, 1920, Youngstown, O.; educ. St. Charles Preparatory Seminary (Catonsville, Md.), St. Mary's Seminary (Cleveland, O.), Catholic Univ. (Washington, D.C.); ord. priest (Youngstown) May 26, 1945; ord. titular bishop of Alabanda and auxiliary bishop of Youngstown, Mar. 24, 1960; apostolic administrator, 1966; bishop of Youngstown, installed June 20, 1968; president of NCCB/USCC, 1983-86.

Maloney, Charles G.: b. Sept. 9, 1912, Louisville, Ky.; educ. St. Joseph's College (Rensselaer, Ind.), North American College (Rome); ord. priest (Louisville*) Dec. 8, 1937; ord. titular bishop of Capsa and auxiliary bishop of Louisville, Feb. 2, 1955; resigned Jan. 8, 1988.

Maloney, David M.: b. Mar. 15, 1912, Littleton, Colo.; educ. St. Thomas Seminary (Denver, Colo.), Gregorian Univ. and Apollinare Univ. (Rome); ord. priest (Denver*) Dec. 8, 1936; ord. titular bishop of Ruspe and auxiliary bishop of Denver, Jan. 4, 1961; app. bishop of Wichita, Kans., Dec. 6, 1967; resigned July 16, 1982.

Manning, Elias (James), O.F.M. Conv.: b. Apr. 14, 1938, Troy, N.Y.; educ. Sao José Seminary (Rio de Janeiro, Brazil); ord. priest Oct. 30, 1965, in New York; ord. bishop of Valenca, Brazil, May 13, 1990.

Manning, Thomas R., O.F.M.: b. Aug. 29, 1922, Baltimore, Md.; educ. Duns Scotus College (Southfield, Mich.), Holy Name College (Washington, D.C.); ord. priest June 5, 1948; ord. titular bishop of Arsamosata, July 14, 1959 (resigned titular see Dec. 30, 1977); prelate of Coroico, Bolivia, July 14, 1959; became first bishop, 1983, when prelature was raised to diocese.

Mansell, Henry J.: b. Oct. 10, 1937, New York, N.Y.; educ. Cathedral College, St. Joseph's Seminary and College (New York); North American College, Gregorian Univ. (Rome); ord. priest (New York*) Dec. 19, 1962; ord. titular bishop of Marazane and auxiliary bishop of New York, Jan. 6, 1993.

Marcinkus, Paul C.: b. Jan. 15, 1922, Cicero, Ill.; ord. priest (Chicago*) May 3, 1947; served in Vatican secretariat from 1952; ord. titular bishop of Orta, Jan. 6, 1969; secretary (1968-71) and president (1971-89) of Institute for Works of Religion (Vatican Bank); titular archbishop, Sept. 26, 1981; former pro-president of Pontifical Commission for the State of Vatican City (resigned in 1990).

Marconi, Dominic A.: b. Mar. 13, 1927, Newark, N.J.; educ. Seton Hall Univ. (S. Orange, N.J.), Immaculate Conception Seminary (Darlington, N.J.), Catholic Univ. (Washington, D.C.); ord. priest (Newark*) May 30, 1953; ord. titular bishop of Bure and auxiliary bishop of Newark, June 25, 1976.

Marino, Eugene A., S.S.J.: b. May 29, 1934, Biloxi, Miss.; educ. Epiphany Apostolic College and Mary Immaculate Novitiate (Newburgh, N.Y.), St. Joseph's Seminary (Washington, D.C.), Catholic Univ. (Washington, D.C.), Loyola Univ. (New Orleans, La.), Fordham Univ. (New York City); ord. priest June 9, 1962; ord. titular bishop of Walla Walla and auxiliary bishop of Washington, D.C., Sept. 12, 1974; archbishop of Atlanta, installed May 5, 1988; resigned July 10, 1990.

Markiewicz, Alfred J.: b. May 17, 1928, Brooklyn, N.Y.; educ. St. Francis College (Brooklyn, N.Y.), Immaculate Conception Seminary (Huntington, N.Y.); ord. priest (Brooklyn) June 6, 1953; ord. titular bishop of Afufenia and auxiliary bishop of Rockville Centre, Sept. 17, 1986. Vicar for Nassau.

Marshall, John A.: b. Apr. 26, 1928, Worcester, Mass.; educ. Holy Cross College (Worcester, Mass.), Sulpician Seminary (Montreal), North American College and Gregorian Univ. (Rome), ssumption College (Worcester); ord. priest (Worcester) Dec. 19, 1953; ord. bishop of Burlington, Jan. 25, 1972; app. bishop of Springfield, Mass., Dec. 27, 1991.

Matthiesen, Leroy Theodore: b. June 11, 1921, Olfen, Tex.; educ. Josephinum College (Columbus, O.), Catholic Univ. (Washington, D.C.), Register School of Journalism; ord. priest (Amarillo) Mar. 10, 1946; ord. bishop of Amarillo, May 30, 1980.

May, John L.: b. Mar. 31, Evanston, Ill.; educ. St. Mary of the Lake Seminary (Mundelein, Ill.); ord. priest (Chicago*) May 3, 1947; general secretary and vice-president of the Catholic Church Extension Society, 1959; ord. titular bishop of Tagarbala and auxiliary bishop of Chicago, Aug. 24, 1967; bishop of Mobile, Ala., Sept. 29, 1969; app. archbishop of St. Louis, installed Mar. 25, 1980; president of NCCB/USCC, 1986-89; retired Dec. 9, 1992.

Melczek, Dale J.: b. Nov. 9, 1938, Detroit, Mich.; educ. St. Mary's College (Orchard Lake, Mich.), St. John's Provincial Seminary (Plymouth, Mich.), Univ. of Detroit; ord. priest (Detroit*) June 6, 1964; ord. titular bishop of Trau and auxiliary bishop of Detroit, Jan. 27, 1983; vicar general; regional bishop of northwest region of Detroit archdiocese; apostolic administrator of Gary.

Mendez, Alfred, C.S.C.: b. June 3, 1907, Chicago,

Ill.; educ. Notre Dame Univ. (Notre Dame, Ind.), Institute of Holy Cross (Washington, D.C.); ord. priest June 24, 1935; ord. first bishop of Arecibo, Puerto Rico, Oct. 28, 1960; resigned Jan. 24, 1974.

Mestice, Anthony F.: b. Dec. 6, 1923, New York, N.Y.; educ. St. Joseph Seminary (Yonkers, N.Y.); ord. priest (New York*) June 4, 1949; ord. titular bishop of Villa Nova and auxiliary bishop of New York, Apr. 27, 1973.

Michaels, James E., S.S.C.: b. May 30, 1926, Chicago, Ill.; educ. Columban Seminary (St. Columban, Neb.), Gregorian Univ. (Rome); ord. priest Dec. 21, 1951; ord. titular bishop of Verbe and auxiliary bishop of Kwang Ju, Korea, Apr. 14, 1966; app. auxiliary bishop of Wheeling, Apr. 3, 1973; title of see changed to Wheeling-Charleston, 1974; resigned Sept. 22, 1987.

Milone, Anthony: b. Sept. 24, 1932, Omaha, Nebr.; educ. North American College (Rome); ord. priest (Omaha*) Dec. 15, 1957, in Rome; ord. titular bishop of Plestia and auxiliary bishop of Omaha, Jan. 6, 1982; app. bishop of Great Falls-Billings, Dec. 14, 1987, installed Feb. 23, 1988.

Minder, John, O.S.F.S.: b. Nov. 1, 1923, Philadelphia, Pa.; educ. Catholic Univ. (Washington, D.C.); ord. priest June 3, 1950; ord. bishop of Keimos (renamed Keimos-Upington, 1985), South Africa, Jan. 10, 1968.

Moeddel, Carl K.: b. Dec. 28, 1937, Cincinnati, Ohio; educ. Athenaeum of Ohio, Mt. St. Mary's Seminary (Cincinnati); ord. priest (Cincinnati*) Aug. 15, 1962; ord. titular bishop of Bistue and auxiliary bishop of Cincinnati, Aug. 24, 1993. Vicar general.

Montrose, Donald: b. May 13, 1923, Denver, Colo.; educ. St. John's Seminary (Camarillo, Calif.); ord. priest (Los Angeles*) May 7, 1949; ord. titular bishop of Forum Novum and auxiliary bishop of Los Angeles, May 12, 1983; app. bishop of Stockton, Dec. 17, 1985.

Moore, Emerson John: b. May 16, 1938, New York, N.Y.; educ. Cathedral College (New York City), St. Joseph's Seminary (Yonkers, N.Y.); New York University, Columbia Univ. School of Social Work (New York City); ord. priest (New York*) May 30, 1964; ord. auxiliary bishop of Curubi and auxiliary bishop of New York, Sept. 8, 1982.

Moran, William J.: b. Jan. 15, 1906, San Francisco, Calif.; educ. St. Patrick's Seminary (Menlo Park, Calif.); ord. priest (San Francisco*) June 20, 1931; Army chaplain, 1933; ord. titular bishop of Centuria and auxiliary to the military vicar, Dec. 13, 1965; retired Jan. 15, 1981.

Moreno, Manuel D.: b. Nov. 27, 1930, Placentia, Calif.; educ. Univ. of California (Los Angeles), Our Lady Queen of Angels (San Fernando, Calif.), St. John's Seminary (Camarillo, Calif.); ord. priest (Los Angeles*) Apr. 25, 1961; ord. titular bishop of Tanagra and auxiliary bishop of Los Angeles, Feb. 19, 1977; bishop of Tucson, Jan. 12, 1982, installed Mar. 11, 1982.

Morneau, Robert F.: b. Sept. 10, 1938, New London, Wis.; educ. St. Norbert's College (De Pere, Wis.), Sacred Heart Seminary (Oneida, Wis.), Catholic Univ. (Washington, D.C.); ord. priest (Green Bay) May 28, 1966; ord. titular bishop of

Massa Lubrense and auxiliary bishop of Green Bay, Feb. 22, 1979.

Moskal, Robert M.: b. Oct. 24, 1937, Carnegie, Pa.; educ. St. Basil Minor Seminary (Stamford, Conn.), St. Josaphat Seminary and Catholic Univ. (Washington, D.C.); ord. priest (Philadelphia*, Byzantine Rite) Mar. 25, 1963; ord. titular bishop of Agatopoli and auxiliary bishop of the Ukrainian-Rite archeparchy of Philadelphia, Oct. 13, 1981; app. first bishop of St. Josaphat in Parma, Dec. 5, 1983.

Muench Robert W.: b. Dec. 28, 1942, Louisville, Ky.; educ. St. Joseph Seminary and Notre Dame Seminary (New Orleans, La.), Catholic Univ. (Washington, D.C.); ord. priest (New Orleans*) June 18, 1968; ord. titular bishop of Mactaris and auxiliary bishop of New Orleans, June 29, 1990.

Mulcahy, John J.: b. June 26, 1922, Dorchester, Mass.; educ. St. John's Seminary (Brighton, Mass.); ord. priest (Boston*) May 1, 1947; rector Pope John XXIII Seminary for Delayed Vocations, 1969-73; ord. titular bishop of Penafiel and auxiliary bishop of Boston, Feb. 11, 1975; retired July, 1992.

Mulvee, Robert E.: b. Feb. 15, 1930, Boston, Mass.; educ. St. Thomas Seminary (Bloomfield, Conn.), University Seminary (Ottawa, Ont., Canada), American College (Louvain, Belgium), Lateran Univ. (Rome); ord. priest (Manchester) June 30, 1957; ord. titular bishop of Summa and auxiliary bishop of Manchester, N.H., Apr. 14, 1977; app. bishop of Wilmington, Del., Feb. 19, 1985.

Mundo, Michael P.: b. July 25, 1937, New York, N.Y.; educ. Fordham Univ. (Bronx, N.Y.), St. Jerome's College (Kitchener, Ont., Canada), St. Francis Seminary (Loretto, Pa.); ord. priest (Camden) May 19, 1962; missionary in Brazil from 1963; ord. titular bishop of Blanda Julia and auxiliary bishop of Jatai, Brazil, June 2, 1978.

Murphy, Michael J.: b. July 1, 1915, Cleveland, O.; educ. Niagara Univ. (Niagara Falls, N.Y.); North American College (Rome), Catholic Univ. (Washington, D.C.); ord. priest (Cleveland) Feb. 28, 1942; ord. titular bishop of Ariendela and auxiliary bishop of Cleveland, June 11, 1976; app. coadjutor bishop of Erie, Nov. 20, 1978; bishop of Erie, July 16, 1982; retired June 12, 1990.

Murphy, Philip Francis: b. Mar. 25, 1933, Cumberland, Md.; educ. St. Mary Seminary (Baltimore, Md.), North American College (Rome); ord. priest (Baltimore*) Dec. 20, 1958; ord. titular bishop of Tacarata and auxiliary bishop of Baltimore, Feb. 29, 1976.

Murphy, Thomas J.: b. Oct. 3, 1932, Chicago, Ill.; educ. Quigley Preparatory Seminary (Chicago, Ill.), St. Mary of the Lake Seminary (Mundelein, Ill.); ord. priest (Chicago*) Apr. 12, 1958; ord. bishop of Great Falls, Mont. Aug. 21, 1978; title of see changed to Great Falls-Billings, 1980; app. coadjutor archbishop of Seattle, May 27, 1987; archbishop of Seattle, 1991.

Murphy, Thomas W., C.SS.R.: b. Dec. 17, 1917, Omaha, Nebr.; educ. St. Joseph's College (Kirkwood, Mo.); ord. priest June 29, 1943; ord. first bishop of Juazeiro, Brazil, Jan. 2, 1963; resigned Dec. 29, 1973; app. titular bishop of Sululos and auxiliary bishop of Sao Salvador da Bahia, Brazil, Jan. 31, 1974.

Myers, John Joseph: b. July 26, 1941, Ottawa, Ill.; educ. Loras College (Dubuque, Ia.), North American College and Gregorian Univ. (Rome), Catholic Univ. of America (Washington, D.C.); ord. priest (Peoria) Dec. 17, 1966, in Rome; ord. coadjutor bishop of Peoria, Sept. 3, 1987; bishop of Peoria, Jan. 23, 1990.

N

Nevins, John J.: b. Jan. 19, 1932, New Rochelle, N.Y.; educ. Iona College (New Rochelle, N.Y.), Catholic Univ. (Washington, D.C.); ord. priest (Miami*) June 6, 1959; ord. titular bishop of Rusticana and auxiliary bishop of Miami, Mar. 24, 1979; app. first bishop of Venice, Fla., July 17, 1984; installed Oct. 25, 1984.

Newman, William C.: b. Aug. 16, 1928, Baltimore, Md.; educ. St. Mary Seminary (Baltimore, Md.), Catholic Univ. (Washington, D.C.), Loyola College (Baltimore, Md.); ord. priest (Baltimore*) May 29, 1954; ord. titular bishop of Numluli and auxiliary bishop of Baltimore, July 2, 1984.

Neylon, Martin J., S.J.: b. Feb. 13, 1920, Buffalo, N.Y.; ord. priest June 18, 1950; ord. titular bishop of Libertina and coadjutor vicar apostolic of the Caroline and Marshall Islands, Feb. 2, 1970; vicar apostolic of Caroline and Marshall Is., Sept. 20, 1971; first bishop of Carolines-Marshalls when vicariate apostolic was raised to diocese, 1979.

Niedergeses, James D.: b. Feb. 2, 1917, Lawrenceburg, Tenn.; educ. St. Bernard College (St. Bernard, Ala.), St. Ambrose College (Davenport, Ia.), Mt. St. Mary Seminary of the West and Athenaeum (Cincinnati, Ohio); ord. priest (Nashville) May 20, 1944; ord. bishop of Nashville, May 20, 1975; retired Oct. 13, 1992..

Nolan, John G.: b. Mar. 15, 1924, Mechanicville, N.Y.; educ. Siena College (Loudonville, N.Y.), St. Charles College (Catonsville, Md.), St. Mary's Seminary (Baltimore, Md.); Catholic Univ. (Washington, D.C.), Fordham Univ. (New York, N.Y.); ord. priest (Albany) June 11, 1949; ord. titular bishop of Natchez and auxiliary bishop of Military Services archdiocese Jan. 6, 1988; vicar general for Europe.

Nolker, Bernard, C.SS.R.: b. Sept. 25, 1912, Baltimore, Md.; educ. St. Mary's College (North East, Pa.), St. Mary's College (Ilchester, Md.), Mt. St. Alphonsus Seminary (Esopus, N.Y.); ord. priest June 18, 1939; ord. first bishop of Paranagua, Brazil, Apr. 25, 1963; retired Mar. 14, 1989.

Novak, Alfred, C.SS.R.: b. June 2, 1930, Dwight, Nebr.; educ. Immaculate Conception Seminary (Oconomowoc, Wis.); ord. priest July 2, 1956; ord. titular bishop of Vardimissa and auxiliary bishop of Sao Paulo, Brazil, May 25, 1979; bishop of Paranagua, Brazil, Mar. 14, 1989.

O

O'Brien, Thomas Joseph: b. Nov. 29, 1935, Indianapolis, Ind.; educ. St. Meinrad High School Seminary, St. Meinrad College Seminary (St. Meinrad, Ind.); ord. priest (Tucson) May 7, 1961; ord. bishop of Phoenix, Jan. 6, 1982.

Ochoa, Armando: b. Apr. 3, 1943, Oxnard, Calif.; educ. Ventura College (Ventura, Calif.), St.

John's College and St. John's Seminary (Camarillo, Calif.); ord. priest (Los Angeles*) May 23, 1970; ord. titular bishop of Sitifi and auxiliary bishop of Los Angeles, Feb. 23, 1987.

O'Connell, Anthony J.: b. May 10, 1938, Lisheen, Co. Clare, Ireland; came to U.S. at the age of 20; educ. Mt. St. Joseph College (Cork, Ire.), Mungret College (Limerick, Ire.), Kenrick Seminary (St. Louis, Mo.); ord. priest (Jefferson City) Mar. 30, 1963; ord. first bishop of Knoxville, Tenn., Sept. 8, 1988.

O'Connor, John J.: (See Cardinals, Biographies.)

O'Donnell, Edward J.: b. July 4, 1931, St. Louis, Mo.; educ. St. Louis Preparatory Seminary and Kenrick Seminary (St. Louis, Mo.); ord. priest (St. Louis*) Apr. 6, 1957; ord. titular bishop of Britania and auxiliary bishop of St. Louis Feb. 10, 1984.

O'Keefe, Gerald F.: b. Mar. 30, 1918, St. Paul, Minn.; educ. College of St. Thomas, St. Paul Seminary (St. Paul, Minn.); ord. priest (St. Paul-Minneapolis*) Jan. 29, 1944; ord. titular bishop of Candyba and auxiliary bishop of St. Paul, July 2, 1961; bishop of Davenport, Oct. 20, 1966, installed Jan. 4, 1967.

O'Keefe, Joseph Thomas: b. Mar. 12, 1919, New York, N.Y.; educ. Cathedral College (New York City), St. Joseph's Seminary (Yonkers, N.Y.), Catholic Univ. (Washington, D.C.); ord. priest (New York*) Apr. 17, 1948; ord. titular bishop of Tre Taverne and auxiliary bishop of New York, Sept. 8, 1982; app. bishop of Syracuse, June 16, 1987, installed Aug. 3, 1987.

O'Leary, Edward C.: b. Aug. 21, 1920, Bangor, Me.; educ. Holy Cross College (Worcester, Mass.), St. Paul's Seminary (Ottawa, Canada); ord. priest (Portland, Me.) June 15, 1946; ord. titular bishop of Moglena and auxilary b ishop of Portland, Me., Jan. 25, 1971; app. bishop of Portland, installed Dec. 18, 1974; retired Sept. 27, 1988.

Olivier, Leonard J., S.V.D.: b. Oct. 12, 1923, Lake Charles, La.; educ. St. Augustine Major Seminary (Bay St. Louis, Miss.), Catholic Univ. (Washington, D.C.), Loyola Univ. (New Orleans, La.); ord. priest June 29, 1951; ord. titular bishop of Leges in Numidia and auxiliary bishop of Washington, Dec. 20, 1988.

O'Malley, Sean, O.F.M.Cap.: b. June 29, 1944, Lakewood, O.; educ. St. Fidelis Seminary (Herman, Pa.), Capuchin College and Catholic Univ. (Washington, D.C.); ord. priest Aug. 29, 1970; episcopal vicar of priests serving Spanish speaking in Washington archdiocese, 1974-84; executive director of Spanish Catholic Center, Washington, from 1973; ord. coadjutor bishop of St. Thomas, Virgin Islands, Aug. 2, 1984; bishop of St. Thomas, Oct. 16, 1985; app. bishop of Fall River, June 16, 1992.

O'Neil, Leo E.: b. Jan. 31, 1928, Holyoke, Mass.; educ. Maryknoll Seminary (Maryknoll, N.Y.), St. Anselm's College (Manchester, N.H.), Grand Seminary (Montreal, Canada); ord. priest (Springfield, Mass.) June 4, 1955; ord. titular bishop of Bencenna and auxiliary bishop of Springfield, Mass., Aug. 22, 1980; app. coadjutor bishop of Manchester, Oct. 17, 1989; bishop of Manchester, June 12, 1990.

O'Neill, Arthur J.: b. Dec. 14, 1917, East Dubuque, Ill.; educ. Loras Collge (Dubuque, Ia.), St. Mary's Seminary (Baltimore, Md.); ord. priest (Rockford) Mar. 27, 1943; ord. bishop of Rockford, Oct. 11, 1968.

O'Rourke, Edward W.: b. Oct. 31, 1917, Downs, Ill.; educ. St. Mary's Seminary (Mundelein, Ill.), Aquinas Institute of Philosophy and Theology (River Forest, Ill.); ord. priest (Peoria) May 28, 1944; executive director of National Catholic Rural Life Conference, 1960-71; ord. bishop of Peoria, July 15, 1971; retired Jan. 22, 1990.

Ottenweller, Albert H.: b. Apr. 5, 1916, Stanford, Mont.; educ. St. Joseph's Seminary (Rensselaer, Ind.), Catholic Univ. (Washington, D.C.); ord. priest (Toledo) June 19, 1943; ord. titular bishop of Perdices and auxiliary bishop of Toledo, May 29, 1974; app. bishop of Steubenville, Oct. 11, 1977, installed Nov. 22, 1977; retired 1992.

P

Paschang, John L.: b. Oct. 5, 1895, Hemingford, Nebr.; educ. Conception College (Conception, Mo.), St. John Seminary (Collegeville, Minn.), Catholic Univ. (Washington, D.C.); ord. priest (Omaha*) June 12, 1921; ord. bishop of Grand Island, Oct. 9, 1951; resigned July 25, 1972.

Paska, Walter: b. Nov. 29, 1923, Elizabeth, N.J.; educ. St. Charles Seminary (Catonsville, Md.), Catholic Univ. (Washington, D.C.); Fordham Univ. (New York); ord. priest (Philadelphia of Ukrainians*) 1947; ord. titular bishop of Tigilava and auxiliary of Ukrainian archdiocese of Philadelphia, Mar. 19, 1992.

Pataki, Andrew: b. Aug. 30, 1927, Palmerton, Pa.; educ. St. Vincent College (Latrobe, Pa.), St. Procopius College, St. Procopius Seminary (Lisle, Ill.), Sts. Cyril and Methodius Byzantine Catholic Seminary (Pittsburgh, Pa.), Gregorian Univ. and Oriental Pontifical Institute (Rome, Italy); ord. priest (Pittsburgh,a Byzantine Rite) Feb. 24, 1952; ord. titular bishop of Telmisso and auxiliary bishop of Byzantine diocese of Passaic, Aug. 23, 1983; vicar general; episcopal vicar of Pennsylvania; app. bishop of Ruthenian Byzantine diocese of Parma, July 3, 1984.

Paul, John J.: b. Aug. 17, 1918, La Crosse, Wis.; educ. Loras College (Dubuque, Iowa), St. Mary's Seminary (Baltimore, Md.), Marquette Univ. (Milwaukee, Wis.), ord. priest (Lincoln) Jan. 24, 1943; ord. titular bishop of Lambaesis and auxiliary bishop of La Crosse, Aug. 4, 1977; app. bishop of La Crosse, Oct. 18, 1983, installed Dec. 5, 1983.

Pearce, George H., S.M.: b. Jan. 9, 1921, Brighton, Mass.; educ. Marist College and Seminary (Framington, Mass.); ord. priest Feb. 2, 1947; ord. titular bishop of Attalea in Pamphylia and vicar apostolic of the Samoa and Tokelau Islands, June 29, 1956; title changed to bishop of Apia, June 21, 1966; app. archbishop of Suva, Fiji Islands, June 22, 1967; resigned Apr. 10, 1976.

Pelotte, Donald E., S.S.S.: b. Apr. 13, 1945, Waterville, Me.; educ. Eymard Seminary and Junior College (Hyde Park, N.Y.), John Carroll Univ. (Cleveland, O.), Fordham Univ. (Bronx, N.Y.); ord. priest Sept. 2, 1972; ord. coadjutor bishop of Gallup, May 6, 1986 (first priest of Native American ancestry to be named U.S. bishop); bishop of Gallup, Mar. 20, 1990.

Pena, Raymundo J.: b. Feb. 19, 1934, Robstown, Tex.; educ. Assumption Seminary (San Antonio, Tex.); ord. priest (Corpus Christi) May 25, 1957; ord. titular bishop of Trisipa and auxiliary bishop of San Antonio, Dec. 13, 1976; app. bishop of El Paso, Apr. 29, 1980.

Pevec, A. Edward: b. Apr. 16, 1925, Cleveland, O.; educ. St. Mary's Seminary, John Carroll Univ. (Cleveland, O.); ord. priest (Cleveland) Apr. 29, 1950; ord. titular bishop of Mercia and auxiliary bishop of Cleveland, July 2, 1982.

Pfeifer, Michael, O.M.I.: b. May 18, 1937, Alamo, Tex.; educ. Oblate school of theology (San Antonio, Tex.); ord. priest Dec. 21, 1964; provincial of southern province of Oblates of Mary Immaculate, 1981; ord. bishop of San Angelo, July 26, 1985.

Pilarczyk, Daniel E.: b. Aug. 12, 1934, Dayton, Ohio; educ. St. Gregory's Seminary (Cincinnati, O.), Urban Univ. (Rome), Xavier Univ. and Univ. of Cincinnati (Cincinnati, O.); ord. priest (Cincinnati*) Dec. 20, 1959; ord. titular bishop of Hodelm and auxiliary bishop of Cincinnati, Dec. 20, 1974; app. archbishop of Cincinnati, Oct. 30, 1982; installed Dec. 20, 1982. President of NCCB/USCC, 1989- .

Pilla, Anthony M.: b. Nov. 12, 1932, Cleveland, O.; educ. St. Gregory College Seminary (Cincinnati, O.), Borromeo College Seminary (Wickliffe, O.), St. Mary Seminary and John Carroll Univ. (Cleveland, O.); ord. priest (Cleveland) May 23, 1959; ord. titular bishop of Scardona and auxiliary bishop of Cleveland, Aug. 1, 1979; app. apostolic administrator of Cleveland, 1980; bishop of Cleveland, Nov. 13, 1980.

Popp, Bernard F.: b. Dec. 6, 1917, Nada, Tex.; educ. St. John's Seminary and St. Mary's Univ. (San Antonio, Tex.); ord. priest (San Antonio*) Feb. 24, 1943; ord. titular bishop of Capsus and auxiliary bishop of San Antonio, July 25, 1983; retired Mar. 23, 1993.

Potacnak, Joseph, J. S.C.J.: b. May 13, 1933, Berwick, Pa.; educ. Dehon Seminary (Great Barrington, Mass.); Kilroe Seminary (Honesdale, Pa.), Sacred Heart (Hales Corners, Wis.); ord. priest 1966; missionary in South Africa from 1973; ord. bishop of De Aar, South Africa, May 1, 1992.

Povish, Kenneth J.: b. Apr. 19, 1924, Alpena, Mich.; educ. St. Joseph's Seminary (Grand Rapids, Mich.), Sacred Heart Seminary (Detroit, Mich.), Catholic Univ. (Washington, D.C.); ord. priest (Saginaw) June 3, 1950; ord. bishop of Crookston, Sept. 29, 1970; app. bishop of Lansing, Oct. 8, 1975, installed Dec. 11, 1975.

Power, Cornelius M.: b. Dec. 18, 1913, Seattle, Wash.; educ. St. Patrick's College (Menlo Park, Calif.), St. Edward's Seminary (Kenmore, Wash.), Catholic Univ. (Washington, D.C.); ord. priest (Seattle*) June 3, 1939; ord. bishop of Yakima, May 1, 1969, installed May 20, 1969; app. archbishop of Portland, Ore., Jan. 22, 1974, installed Apr. 17, 1974; retired 1986.

Prost, Jude, O.F.M.: b. Dec. 6, 1915, Chicago, Ill.; educ. Our Lady of the Angels Seminary (Cleveland, O.), St. Joseph's Seminary (Teutopolis, Ill.); ord. priest June 24, 1942; ord. titular bishop of Fronta and auxiliary bishop of Belem do Para, Brazil, Nov. 1, 1962; retired March, 1992.

Proulx, Amedee W.: b. Aug. 31, 1932, Sanford, Me.; educ. St. Hyacinthe Seminary (Quebec), St. Paul Univ. Seminary (Ottawa), Catholic Univ. (Washington, D.C.); ord. priest (Portland, Me.) May 31, 1958; ord. titular bishop of Clipia and auxiliary bishop of Portland, Me., Nov. 12, 1975.

Pursley, Leo A.: b. Mar. 12, 1902, Hartford City, Ind.; educ. Mt. St. Mary's Seminary (Cincinnati, O.); ord. priest (Ft. Wayne-S. Bend) June 11, 1927; ord. titular bishop of Hadrianapolis in Pisidia and auxiliary bishop of Fort Wayne, Sept. 19, 1950; app. apostolic administrator of Fort Wayne, Mar. 9, 1955; installed as bishop of Fort Wayne, Feb. 26, 1957; title of see changed to Fort Wayne-South Bend, 1960; resigned Aug. 31, 1976.

Puscas, Vasile Louis: b. Sept. 13, 1915, Aurora, Ill.; educ. Quigley Preparatory Seminary (Chicago, Ill.), seminary in Oradea-Mare (Romania), Propaganda Fide Seminary (Rome), Illinois Benedictine College (Lisle, Ill.); ord. priest (Erie) May 14, 1942; ord. titular bishop of Leuce and first exarch of apostolic exarchate for Romanians of the Byzantine Rite in the U.S., June 26, 1983 (seat of the exarchate is Canton, Ohio); app. first eparch, Apr. 11, 1987, when exarchate was raised to eparchy of St. George Martyr; retired July 15, 1993.

Q

Quinn, Alexander James: b. Apr. 8, 1932, Cleveland, O.; educ. St. Charles College (Catonsville, Md.), St. Mary Seminary (Cleveland, O.), Lateran Univ. (Rome), Cleveland State Univ.; ord. priest (Cleveland) May 24, 1958; ord. titular bishop of Socia and auxiliary bishop of Cleveland, Dec. 5, 1983; vicar of western region of Cleveland diocese.

Quinn, Francis A.: b. Sept. 11, 1921, Los Angeles, Calif.; educ. St. Joseph's College (Mountain View, Calif.), St. Patrick's Seminary (Menlo Park, Calif.), Catholic Univ. (Washington, D.C.);Univ. of California (Berkley); ord. priest (San Francisco*) June 15, 1946; ord. titular bishop of Numana and auxiliary bishop of San Francisco, June 29, 1978; app. bishop of Sacramento Dec. 18, 1979.

Quinn, John R.: b. Mar. 28, 1929, Riverside, Calif.; educ. St. Francis Seminary (El Cajon, Calif.), North American College (Rome); ord. priest (San Diego) July 19, 1953; ord. titular bishop of Thisiduo and auxiliary bishop of San Diego, Dec. 12, 1967; bishop of Oklahoma City and Tulsa, Nov. 30, 1971; first archbishop of Oklahoma City, Dec. 19, 1972; app. archbishop of San Francisco Feb. 22, 1977, installed Apr. 26, 1977; president NCCB/USCC, 1977-80.

R

Ramirez, Ricardo, C.S.B.: b. Sept. 12, 1936, Bay City, Tex.; educ. Univ. of St. Thomas (Houston, Tex.), Univ. of Detroit (Detroit, Mich.), St. Basil's Seminary (Toronto, Ont.); Seminario Concilium (Mexico City, Mexico), East Asian Pastoral Institute (Manila, Philippines); ord. priest Dec. 10, 1966; ord titular bishop of Vatarba and auxiliary of San Antonio, Dec. 6, 1981; app. first bishop of Las Cruces, N. Mex., Aug. 17, 1982; installed Oct. 18, 1982.

Raya, Joseph M.: b. July 20, 1917, Zahle,

Lebanon; educ. St. Louis College (Paris, France), St. Anne's Seminary (Jerusalem); ord. priest July 20, 1941; came to U.S., 1949, became U.S. citizen; ord. archbishop of Acre, Israel, of the Melkites, Oct. 20, 1968; resigned Aug. 20, 1974; assigned titular metropolitan see of Scytopolis.

Regan, Joseph W., M.M.: b. Apr. 5, 1905, Boston, Mass.; educ. Boston College (Boston, Mass.), St. Bernard's Seminary (Rochester, N.Y.), Maryknoll Seminary (Maryknoll, N.Y.); ord. priest Jan. 27, 1929; missionary in China 15 years; in Philippines since 1952; ord. titular bishop of Isinda and prelate of Tagum, Philippines, Apr. 25, 1962; resigned May 16, 1980.

Reh, Francis F.: b. Jan. 9, 1911, New York, N.Y.; educ. St. Joseph's Seminary (Dunwoodie, N.Y.), North American College and Gregorian Univ. (Rome); ord. priest (New York*) Dec. 8, 1935; ord. bishop of Charleston, S.C., June 29, 1962; named titular bishop of Macriana in Mauretania, 1964; rector of North American College, 1964-68; bishop of Saginaw, installed Feb. 26, 1969; resigned Apr. 28, 1980.

Reilly, Daniel P.: b. May 12, 1928, Providence, R.I.; educ. Our Lady of Providence Seminary (Warwick, R.I.), St. Brieuc Major Seminary (Cotes du Nord, France); ord. priest (Providence) May 30, 1953; ord. bishop of Norwich, Aug. 6, 1975.

Reiss, John C.: b. May 13, 1922, Red Bank, N.J.; educ. Catholic Univ. (Washington, D.C.), Immaculate Conception Seminary (Darlington, N.J.); ord. priest (Trenton) May 31, 1947; ord. titular bishop of Simidicca and auxiliary bishop of Trenton, Dec. 12, 1967; app. bishop of Trenton, Mar. 11, 1980.

Riashi, Georges, B.C.O.: b. Nov. 25, 1933, Kaael-Rim, Lebanon; ord. priest Apr. 4, 1965; parish priest of Our Lady of Redemption Parish, Warren, Mich. (Newton Greek-Catholic Melkite eparchy); U.S. citizen; ord. first bishop of eparchy of St. Michael's of Sydney (Australia) for Greek-Catholic Melkites, July 19, 1987.

Ricard, John H., S.S.J.: b. Feb. 29, 1940, Baton Rouge, La.; educ. St. Joseph's Seminary (Washington, D.C.), Tulane Univ. (New Orleans, La.); ord. priest May 25, 1968; ord. titular bishop of Rucuma and auxiliary of Baltimore, July 2, 1984; urban vicar, Baltimore.

Rigali, Justin: b. Apr. 19, 1935, Los Angeles, Calif.; educ. St. John's Seminary (Camarillo, Calif.); ord. priest (Los Angeles*) Apr. 25, 1961; in Vatican diplomatic service from 1964; ord. titular archbishop of Bolsena, Sept. 14, 1985, by Pope John Paul II; president of the Pontifical Ecclesiastical Academy, 1985-89; app. secretary of Congregation for Bishops (1989) and College of Cardinals (1990).

Riley, Lawrence J.: b. Sept. 6, 1914; Boston, Mass.; educ. Boston College and St. John's Seminary (Boston, Mass.), North American College and Gregorian Univ. (Rome), Catholic Univ. (Washington, D.C.); ord. priest (Boston*) Sept. 21, 1940; ord. titular bishop of Daimlaig and auxiliary bishop of Boston, Feb. 2, 1972; retired Jan. 22, 1990.

Roach, John R.: b. July 31, 1921, Prior Lake, Minn.; educ. St. Paul Seminary (St. Paul, Minn.), Univ. of Minnesota (Minneapolis); ord. priest (St.

Paul and Minneapolis*) June 18, 1946; ord. titular bishop of Cenae and auxiliary bishop of St. Paul and Minneapolis, Sept. 8, 1971; app. archbishop of St. Paul and Minneapolis, May 28, 1975; vice-president NCCB/USCC, 1977-80; president, 1980-83.

Rodimer, Frank J.: b. Oct. 25, 1927, Rockaway, N.J.; educ. Seton Hall Prep (South Orange, N.J.), St. Charles College (Catonsville, Md.), St. Mary's Seminary (Baltimore, Md.), Immaculate Conception Seminary (Darlington, N.J.), Catholic Univ. (Washington, D.C.); ord. priest (Paterson) May 19, 1951; ord. bishop of Paterson, Feb. 28, 1978.

Rodriguez, Migúel, C.SS.R.: b. Apr. 18, 1931, Mayaguez, P.R.; educ. St. Mary's Minor Seminary (North East, Pa.), Mt. St. Alphonsus Major Seminary (Esopus, N.Y.); ord. priest June 22, 1958; ord. bishop of Arecibo, P.R., Mar. 23, 1974; resigned Mar. 20, 1990.

Rodriguez, Placido, C.M.F.: b. Oct. 11, 1940, Celaya, Guanajuato, Mexico; educ. Claretian Novitate (Los Angeles, Calif.), Claretville Seminary College (Calabasas, Calif.), Catholic Univ. (Washington, D.C.), Loyola Univ. (Chicago, Ill.); ord. priest May 23, 1968; ord. titular bishop of Fuerteventura and auxiliary bishop of Chicago, Dec. 13, 1983.

Roman, Agustin A.: b. May 5, 1928, San Antonio de los Banos, Havana, Cuba; educ. San Alberto Magno Seminary (Matanzas, Cuba), Missions Etrangeres (Montreal, Canada), Barry College (Miami, Fla.); ord. priest July 5, 1959, Cuba; vicar for Spanish speaking in Miami archdiocese, 1976; ord. titular bishop of Sertei and auxiliary bishop of Miami, Mar. 24, 1979.

Roque, Francis: b. Oct. 9, 1928, Providence R.I.; educ. St. John's Seminary (Brighton, Mass.); ord. priest (Providence) Sept. 19, 1953; became chaplain in U.S. Army 1961; ord. titular bishop of Bagai and auxiliary bishop of Military Services archdiocese, May 10, 1983.

Rosazza, Peter Anthony: b. Feb. 13, 1935, New Haven, Conn.; educ. St. Thomas Seminary (Bloomfield, Conn.), Dartmouth College (Hanover, N.H.), St. Bernard's Seminary (Rochester, N.Y.), St. Sulpice (Issy, France); ord. priest (Hartford*) June 29, 1961; ord. titular bishop of Oppido Nuovo and auxiliary bishop of Hartford, June 24, 1978.

Rose, Robert John: b. Feb. 28, 1930, Grand Rapids, Mich.; educ. St. Joseph's Seminary (Grand Rapids, Mich.), Seminaire de Philosophie (Montreal, Canada), Pontifical Urban University (Rome), Univ. of Michigan (Ann Arbor, Mich.); ord. priest (Grand Rapids) Dec. 21, 1955; ord. bishop of Gaylord, Dec. 6, 1981; bishop of Grand Rapids, July, 1989.

Rudin, John J., M.M.: b. Nov. 27, 1916, Pittsfield, Mass.; educ. Maryknoll Seminary (Maryknoll, N.Y.), Gregorian Univ. (Rome); ord. priest June 11, 1944; ord. first bishop of Musoma, Tanzania, Oct. 3, 1957; retired Jan. 12, 1979.

Rueger, George E.: b. Sept. 3, 1933, Framingham, Mass; educ. Holy Cross College (Worcester, Mass.), St. John's Seminary (Brighton), Harvard University (Cambridge, Mass.); ord. priest (Worcester), Jan. 6, 1958; ord. titular bishop of Maronana and auxiliary bishop of Worcester Feb. 25, 1987.

Ryan, Daniel L.: b. Sept. 28, 1930, Mankato, Minn.; educ. St. Procopius Seminary (Lisle, Ill.), Lateran Univ. (Rome); ord. priest (Joliet) May 3, 1956; ord. titular bishop of Surista and auxiliary bishop of Joliet, Sept. 30, 1981; app. bishop of Springfield, Ill., Nov. 22, 1983, installed Jan. 18, 1984.

Ryan, James C., O.F.M.: b. Nov. 17, 1912, Chicago, Ill.; educ. St. Joseph's Seraphic Seminary (Westmont, Ill.), Our Lady of the Angels Seminary (Cleveland, O.); ord. priest June 24, 1938; ord. titular bishop of Margo and prelate of Santarem, Brazil, April 9, 1958; first bishop of Santarem, Dec. 4, 1979; retired Nov. 27, 1985.

Ryan, Joseph T.: b. Nov. 1, 1913, Albany, N.Y.; educ. Manhattan College (New York City); ord. priest (Albany) June 3, 1939; national secretary of Catholic Near East Welfare Assn. 1960-65; ord. first archbishop of Anchorage, Alaska, Mar. 25, 1966; app. titular archbishop of Gabi and coadjutor archbishop of the military ordinariate, Oct. 24, 1975, installed Dec. 13, 1975; app. military vicar of U.S. military archdiocese, Mar. 16, 1985, installed Apr. 30, 1985, at National Shrine of the Immaculate Conception, Washington, D.C.; resigned May 14, 1991.

Ryan, Sylvester D.: b. Mar. 3, 1930, Catalina Is. Calif.; educ. St. John's Seminary (Camarillo, Calif.); ord. priest (Los Angeles*) May 3, 1957; ord. titular bishop of Remesiana and auxiliary bishop of Los Angeles, May 31, 1990; app. bishop of Monterey Jan. 28, 1992.

S

Salatka, Charles A.: b. Feb. 26, 1918, Grand Rapids, Mich.; educ. St. Joseph's Seminary (Grand Rapids, Mich.), Catholic Univ. (Washington, D.C.), Lateran Univ. (Rome); ord. priest (Grand Rapids) Feb. 24, 1945; ord. titular bishop of Cariana and auxiliary bishop of Grand Rapids, Mich., Mar. 6, 1962; app. bishop of Marquette, installed Mar. 25, 1968; app. archbishop of Oklahoma City, Sept. 27, 1977; installed Dec. 15, 1977; retired Nov. 24, 1992.

Saltarelli, Michael A.: b. Jan. 17, 1932, Jersey City, N.J.; educ. Seton Hall College and Immaculate Conception Seminary (S. Orange, N.J.); ord. priest (Newark*), 1960; ord. titular bishop of Mesarfelta and auxiliary bishop of Newark, July 30, 1990.

Samra, Nicholas J.: b. Aug. 15, 1944, Paterson, N.J.; educ. St. Anselm College (Manchester, N.H.), St. Basil Seminary (Methuen, Mass.), St. John Seminary (Brighton, Mass.); ord. priest (Newton) May 10, 1970; ord. titular bishop of Gerasa and auxiliary bishop of Melkite-rite diocese of Newton, July 6, 1989. Regional bishop for Midwest/West.

Sanchez, Robert: b. Mar. 20, 1934, Socorro, N.M.; educ. Immaculate Heart Seminary (Santa Fe, N.M.), Gregorian Univ. (Rome), Catholic Univ. (Washington, D.C.); ord. priest (Santa Fe*) Dec. 20, 1959; ord. archbishop of Santa Fe, N.M., July 25, 1974; resigned Apr. 6, 1993.

San Pedro, Enrique, S.J.: b. Mar. 9, 1926, Havana, Cuba; educ. Cuba, Spain, Philippines, Leopold-Franzens Univ. (Innsbruck, Austria); Pontifical Biblical Institute (Rome), ord. priest Mar. 18, 1957; taught Scripture and did missionary work in Vietnam, 1965-75, when he was expelled; visiting Scripture professor at St. Vincent de Paul Regional Seminary, Florida, from 1981; ord. titular bishop of Siccesi and auxiliary bishop of Galveston-Houston, June 29, 1986; app. coadjutor of Brownsville, August, 1991; bishop of Brownsville Nov. 30, 1991.

Scanlan, John J.: b. May 24, 1906, County Cork, Ireland; educ. National Univ. of Ireland (Dublin), All Hallows College (Dublin); ord. priest (San Francisco*) June 22, 1930; U.S. citizen 1938; ord. titular bishop of Cenae and auxiliary bishop of Honolulu, Sept. 21, 1954; bishop of Honolulu, installed May 1, 1968; retired June 30, 1981.

Scarpone Caporale, Gerald, O.F.M.: b. Oct. 1, 1928, Watertown, Mass.; ord. priest June 24, 1956; ord. coadjutor bishop of Comayagua, Honduras, Feb. 21, 1979; succeeded as bishop of Comayagua, May 30, 1979.

Schad, James L.: b. July 20, 1917, Philadelphia, Pa.; educ. St. Mary's Seminary (Baltimore, Md.); ord. priest (Camden) Apr. 10, 1943; ord. titular bishop of Panatoria and auxiliary bishop of Camden, Dec. 8, 1966; retired Jan 26, 1993.

Schladweiler, Alphonse: b. July 18, 1902, Milwaukee, Wis.; educ. St. Joseph College (Teutopolis, Ill.), St. Paul's Seminary (St. Paul, Minn.), Univ. of Minnesota (Minneapolis, Minn.); ord. priest (St. Paul and Minneapolis*) June 9, 1929; ord. first bishop of New Ulm, Jan. 29, 1958; retired Dec. 23, 1975.

Schlaefer Berg, Salvator, O.F.M. Cap.: b. June 27, 1920, Campbellsport, Wis.; ord. priest June 5, 1946; missionary in Bluefields, Nicaragua from 1947; ord. titular bishop of Fiumepiscense and vicar apostolic of Bluefields, Nicaragua, Aug. 12, 1970.

Schlarman, Stanley Gerard: b. July 27, 1933, Belleville, Ill.; educ. St. Henry Prep Seminary (Belleville, Ill.), Gregorian Univ. (Rome), St. Louis Univ. (St. Louis, Mo.); ord. priest (Belleville) July 13, 1958, Rome; ord. titular bishop of Capri and auxiliary bishop of Belleville, May 14, 1979; app. bishop of Dodge City, Mar. 1, 1983.

Schlotterback, Edward F., O.S.F.S.: b. Mar. 2, 1912, Philadelphia, Pa.; educ. Catholic Univ. (Washington, D.C.); ord. priest Dec. 17, 1938; ord. titular bishop of Balanea and vicar apostolic of Keetmanshoop, Namibia, June 11, 1956; retired Oct. 2, 1989.

Schmidt, Firmin M., O.F.M.Cap.: b. Oct. 12, 1918, Catherine, Kans.; educ. Catholic Univ. (Washington, D.C.); ord. priest June 2, 1946; app. prefect apostolic of Mendi, Papua New Guinea, Apr. 3, 1959; ord. titular bishop of Conana and first vicar apostolic of Mendi, Dec.15, 1965; became first bishop of Mendi when vicariate apostolic was raised to a diocese, Nov. 15, 1966.

Schmitt, Bernard W.: b. Aug. 17, 1928, Wheeling, W. Va.; educ. St. Joseph College (Catonsville, Md.), St. Mary's Seminary (Baltimore, Ohio Univ. (Athens, O.). ord. priest (Wheeling-Charleston) May 28, 1955; ord. titular bishop of Walla Walla and auxiliary bishop of Wheeling-Charleston, Aug. 1, 1988; bishop of Wheeling-Charleston, March, 1989.

Schmitt, Mark: b. Feb. 14, 1923, Algoma, Wis., educ. Salvatorian Seminary (St. Nazianz, Wis.), St. John's Seminary (Collegeville, Minn.); ord. priest (Green Bay) May 22, 1948; ord. titular bishop of

Ceanannus Mor and auxiliary bishop of Green Bay, June 24, 1970; app. bishop of Marquette, Mar. 21, 1978, installed May 8, 1978; retired Oct. 6, 1992.

Schmitz Simon, Paul, O.F.M. Cap.: b. Dec. 4, 1943, Fond du Lac, Wis.; ord. priest Sept. 3, 1970; missionary in Nicaragua from 1970; superior of vice province of Capuchins in Central America (headquartered in Managua), 1982-84; ord. titular bishop of Elepla and auxiliary bishop of the vicariate apostolic of Bluefields, Nicaragua, Sept. 17, 1984.

Schoenherr, Walter J.: b. Feb. 28, 1920, Detroit, Mich.; educ. Sacred Heart Seminary (Detroit, Mich.), Mt. St. Mary Seminary (Norwood, O.); ord. priest (Detroit*) Oct. 27, 1945; ord. titular bishop of Timidana and auxiliary bishop of Detroit, May 1, 1968.

Schulte, Francis B.: b. Dec. 23, 1926, Philadelphia, Pa.; educ. St. Charles Borromeo Seminary (Overbrook, Pa.): ord. priest (Philadelphia*) May 10, 1952; ord. titular bishop of Afufenia and auxiliary bishop of Philadelphia, Aug. 12, 1981; app. bishop of Wheeling-Charleston, June 4, 1985; archbishop of New Orleans, Dec. 6, 1988.

Schuster, Eldon B.: b. Mar. 10, 1911, Calio, N. Dak.; educ. Loras College (Dubuque, Ia.), Catholic Univ. (Washington, D.C.), Oxford Univ. (England), St. Louis Univ. (St. Louis, Mo.); ord. priest (Great Falls) May 27, 1937; ord. titular bishop of Amblada and auxiliary bishop of Great Falls, Mont., Dec. 21, 1961; app. bishop of Great Falls, Dec. 2, 1967, installed Jan. 23, 1968; resigned Dec. 28, 1977.

Schweitz, Roger L., O.M.I.: b. July 3, 1940, St. Paul, Minn.; educ. Univ. of Ottawa (Canada), Gregorian Univ. (Rome); ord. priest Dec. 20, 1967; ord. bishop of Duluth Feb. 2, 1990.

Setian, Nerses Mikail: b. Oct. 18,1918, Sebaste, Turkey; educ. Armenian Pontifical College and Gregorian Univ. (Rome); ord. priest Apr. 13, 1941, in Rome; ord. titular bishop of Ancira of the Armenians and first exarch of the apostolic exarchate for Armenian-Rite Catholics in Canada and the United States (see city New York), Dec. 5, 1981.

Sevilla, Carlos A., S.J.: b. Aug. 9, 1935, San Francisco, Calif.; entered Jesuits Aug. 14, 1953; educ. Gonzaga Univ. (Spokane, Wash.), Santa Clara Univ. (Santa Clara, Calif.), Jesuitenkolleg (Innsbruck, Austria), Catholic Institute of Paris (France); ord. priest June 3, 1966; ord. titular bishop of Mina and auxiliary bishop of San Francisco, Jan. 25, 1989.

Shea, Francis R.: b. Dec. 4, 1913, Knoxville, Tenn.; educ. St. Mary's Seminary (Baltimore, Md.), North American College (Rome), Peabody College (Nashville, Tenn.); ord. priest (Nashville) Mar. 19, 1939; ord. bishop of Evansville, Ind., Feb. 3, 1970; retired Mar. 27, 1989.

Sheehan, Daniel E.: b. May 14, 1917, Emerson, Nebr.; educ. Creighton Univ. (Omaha, Nebr.), Kenrick Seminary (Webster Groves, Mo.), Catholic Univ. (Washington, D.C.): ord. priest (Omaha*) May 23, 1942; ord. titular bishop of Capsus and auxiliary bishop of Omaha, Mar. 19, 1964; app. archbishop of Omaha, installed Aug. 11, 1969; retired May 4, 1993.

Sheehan, Michael J.: b. July 9, 1939, Wichita, Kans.; educ. Assumption Seminary (San Antonio,

Tex.), Gregorian Univ. and Lateran Univ. (Rome); ord. priest (Dallas) July 12, 1964; ord. first bishop of Lubbock, Tex., June 17, 1983; apostolic administrator of Santa Fe, Apr. 6, 1993; app. archbishop of Santa Fe, Aug. 17, 1993.

Sheets, John R., S.J.: b. Sept. 21, 1922, Omaha, Neb.; joined Jesuits, 1940; educ. St. Louis Univ. (St. Louis, Mo.), St. Mary's College (St. Mary's, Kans.), Univ. of Innsbruck (Austria); ord. priest June 17, 1953; final profession of vows as Jesuit, Aug. 15, 1957; ord. titular bishop of Murcona and auxiliary bishop of Fort Wayne-South Bend, Ind., June 25, 1991.

Sheldon, Gilbert I.: b. Sept. 20, 1926, Cleveland, O.; educ. John Carroll Univ. and St. Mary Seminary (Cleveland, O.); ord. priest (Cleveland) Feb. 28, 1953; ord. titular bishop of Taparura and auxiliary bishop of Cleveland, June 11, 1976; app. bishop of Steubenville, Jan. 28, 1992.

Sheridan, Patrick J.: b. Mar. 10, 1922, New York, N.Y.; educ St. Joseph's Seminary (Yonkers, N.Y.), University of Chicago; ord. priest (New York*), Mar. 1, 1947; ord. titular bishop of Curzola and auxiliary bishop of New York, Dec. 12, 1990.

Sklba, Richard J.: b. Sept. 11, 1935, Racine, Wis.; educ. Old St. Francis Minor Seminary (Milwaukee, Wis.), North American College, Gregorian Univ., Pontifical Biblical Institute, Angelicum (Rome); ord. priest (Milwaukee*) Dec. 20, 1959; ord. titular bishop of Castra and auxiliary bishop of Milwaukee, Dec. 19, 1979.

Skylstad, William: b. Mar. 2, 1934, Omak, Wash.; educ. Pontifical College Josephinum (Worthington, Ohio), Washington State Univ. (Pullman, Wash.), Gonzaga Univ. (Spokane, Wash.); ord. priest (Spokane) May 21, 1960; ord. bishop of Yakima, May 12, 1977; app. bishop of Spokane, Apr. 17, 1990.

Smith, John M.: b. June 23, 1935, Orange, N.J.; educ. Immaculate Conception Seminary (Darlington, N.J.), Seton Hall Univ. (South Orange, N.J.), Catholic Univ. (Washington, D.C.); ord. priest (Newark*) May 27, 1961; ord. titular bishop of Tre Taverne and auxiliary bishop of Newark, Jan. 25, 1988; app. bishop of Pensacola-Tallahassee, Fla., June 25, 1991.

Smith, Philip F., O.M.I.: b. Oct. 16, 1924, Lowell, Mass.; ord. priest Oct. 29, 1950; ord. titular bishop of Lamfua and vicar apostolic of Jolo, Philippine Islands, Sept. 8, 1972; app. coadjutor archbishop of Cotabato, Philippines, April 11, 1979; archbishop of Cotabato, Mar. 14, 1980.

Snyder, John J.: b. Oct. 25, 1925, New York, N.Y.; educ. Cathedral College (Brooklyn, N.Y.), Immaculate Conception Seminary (Huntington, N.Y.); ord. priest (Brooklyn) June 9, 1951; ord. titular bishop of Forlimpopli and auxiliary bishop of Brooklyn, Feb. 2, 1973; app. bishop of St. Augustine, installed Dec. 5, 1979.

Soens, Lawrence D.: b. Aug. 26, 1926, Iowa City, Ia.; educ. Loras College (Dubuque, Ia.), St. Ambrose College (Davenport, Ia.), Kenrick Seminary (St. Louis, Mo.), Univ. of Iowa; ord. priest (Davenport) May 6, 1950; ord. bishop of Sioux City, Aug. 17, 1983.

Sowada, Alphonse A., O.S.C.: b. June 23, 1933,

Avon, Minn.; educ. Holy Cross Scholasticate (Fort Wayne, Ind.), Catholic Univ. (Washington, D.C.), ord. priest May 31, 1958; missionary in Indonesia from 1958; ord. bishop of Agats, Indonesia, Nov. 23, 1969.

Speltz, George H.: b. May 29, 1912, Altura, Minn.; educ. St. Mary's College, St. Paul's Seminary (St. Paul, Minn.), Catholic Univ. (Washington, D.C.); ord. priest (St. Cloud) June 2, 1940; ord. titular bishop of Claneus and auxiliary bishop of Winona, Mar. 25, 1963; app. coadjutor bishop of St. Cloud, Apr. 4, 1966; bishop of St. Cloud, Jan. 31, 1968; retired Jan. 13, 1987.

Speyrer, Jude: b. Apr. 14, 1929, Leonville, La.; educ. St. Joseph Seminary (Covington, La.), Notre Dame Seminary (New Orleans, La.), Gregorian Univ. (Rome), Univ. of Fribourg (Switzerland); ord. priest (Lafayette, La.) July 25, 1953; ord. first bishop of Lake Charles, La., Apr. 25, 1980.

Stafford, James Francis: b. July 26, 1932, Baltimore, Md.; educ. St. Mary's Seminary (Baltimore, Md.), North American College and Gregorian Univ. (Rome); ord. priest (Baltimore*) Dec. 15, 1957; ord. titular bishop of Respecta and auxiliary bishop of Baltimore, Feb. 29, 1976; app. bishop of Memphis, Nov. 17, 1982; app. archbishop of Denver, June 3, 1986, installed July 30, 1986.

Steib, J. (James) Terry, S.V.D.: b. May 17, 1940, Vacherie, La.; educ. Divine Word seminaries (Bay St. Louis, Miss., Conesus, N.Y., Techny, Ill.), Xavier Univ. (New Orleans, La.); ord. priest Jan. 6, 1967; ord. titular bishop of Fallaba and auxiliary bishop of St. Louis, Feb. 10, 1984; app. bishop of Memphis, Mar. 24, 1993.

Steinbock, John T.: b. July 16, 1937, Los Angeles, Calif.; educ. Los Angeles archdiocesan seminaries; ord. priest (Los Angeles*) May 1, 1963; ord. titular bishop of Midila and auxiliary bishop of Orange, Calif., July 14, 1984; app. bishop of Santa Rosa, Jan. 27, 1987; app. bishop of Fresno, Oct. 15, 1991.

Steiner, Kenneth Donald: b. Nov. 25, 1936, David City, Nebr.; educ. Mt. Angel Seminary (St. Benedict, Ore), St. Thomas Seminary (Seattle, Wash); ord. priest (Portland,* Ore.) May 19, 1962; ord. titular bishop of Avensa and auxiliary bishop of Portland, Ore., Mar. 2, 1978.

Straling, Phillip F.: b. Apr. 25, 1933, San Bernardino, Calif.; educ. Immaculate Heart Seminary, St. Francis Seminary, Univ. of San Diego and San Diego State University (San Diego, Calif.), North American College (Rome); ord. priest (San Diego) Mar. 19, 1959; ord. first bishop of San Bernardino, Nov. 6, 1978.

Strecker, Ignatius J.: b. Nov. 23, 1917, Spearville, Kans.; educ. St. Benedict's College (Atchison, Kans.), Kenrick Seminary (Webster Groves, Mo.), Catholic Univ. (Washington, D.C.); ord. priest (Wichita) Dec. 19, 1942; ord. bishop of Springfield-Cape Girardeau, Mo., June 20, 1962; archbishop of Kansas City, Kans., Oct. 28, 1969; retired June 28, 1993.

Sullivan, James S.: b. July 23, 1929, Kalamazoo, Mich.; educ. Sacred Heart Seminary (Detroit, Mich.), St. John Provincial Seminary (Plymouth, Mich.); ord. priest (Lansing) June 4, 1955; ord.

titular bishop of Siccessi and auxiliary bishop of Lansing, Sept. 21, 1972; app. bishop of Fargo, Apr. 2, 1985; installed May 30, 1985.

Sullivan, John J.: b. July 5, 1920, Horton, Kans.; educ. Kenrick Seminary (St. Louis, Mo.); ord. priest (Oklahoma City*) Sept. 23, 1944; vice-president of Catholic Church Extension Society and national director of Extension Lay Volunteers, 1961-68; ord. bishop of Grand Island, Sept. 19, 1972; app. bishop of Kansas City-St. Joseph, June 27, 1977, installed Aug. 17, 1977; retired June 22, 1993.

Sullivan, Joseph M.: b. Mar. 23, 1930, Brooklyn, N.Y.; educ. Immaculate Conception Seminary (Huntington, N.Y.), Fordham Univ. (New York); ord. priest (Brooklyn) June 2, 1956; ord. titular bishop of Suliana and auxiliary bishop of Brooklyn, Nov. 24, 1980.

Sullivan, Walter F.: b. June 10, 1928, Washington, D.C.; educ. St. Mary's Seminary (Baltimore, Md.), Catholic Univ. (Washington, D.C.); ord. priest (Richmond) May 9, 1953; ord. titular bishop of Selsea and auxiliary bishop of Richmond, Va., Dec. 1, 1970; app. bishop of Richmond, June 4, 1974.

Sulyk, Stephen: b. Oct. 2, 1924, Balnycia, Western Ukraine; migrated to U.S. 1948; educ. Ukrainian Catholic Seminary of the Holy Spirit (Hirschberg, Germany), St. Josaphat's Seminary and Catholic Univ. (Washington, D.C.); ord. priest (Philadelphia,* Byzantine Rite) June 14, 1952; ord. archbishop of the Ukrainian-Rite archeparcy of Philadelphia, Mar. 1, 1981.

Symons, J. Keith: b. Oct. 14, 1932, Champion, Mich.; educ. St. Thomas Seminary (Bloomfield, Conn.), St. Mary Seminary (Baltimore, Md.); ord. priest (St. Augustine) May 18, 1958; ord. titular bishop of Siguitanus and auxiliary bishop of St. Petersburg, Mar. 19, 1981; app. bishop of Pensacola-Tallahassee, Oct. 4, 1983, installed Nov. 8, 1983; app. bishop of Palm Beach, June 12, 1990.

Szoka, Edmund C.: (See Cardinals, Biographies.)

T

Tafoya, Arthur N.: b. Mar. 2, 1933, Alameda, N.M.; educ. St. Thomas Seminary (Denver, Colo.), Conception Seminary (Conception, Mo.); ord. priest (Santa Fe*) May 12, 1962; ord. bishop of Pueblo, Sept. 10, 1980.

Tamayo, James A.: b. Oct. 23, 1949, Brownsville, Tex.; educ. Del Mar College (Corpus Christi, Tex.); Univ. of St. Thomas and Univ. of St. Thomas School of Theology (Houston); ord. priest (Corpus Christi) June 11, 1976; ord. titular bishop of Ita and auxiliary bishop of Galveston-Houston, Mar. 10, 1993. Episcopal vicar for Hispanics.

Tanner, Paul F.: b. Jan. 15, 1905, Peoria, Ill.; educ. Marquette Univ. (Milwaukee, Wis.), Kenrick Seminary (Webster Groves, Mo.), St. Francis Seminary (Milwaukee, Wis.), Catholic Univ. (Washington, D.C.): ord. priest (Milwaukee*) May 30, 1931; assistant director NCWC Youth Department 1940-45; assistant general secretary of NCWC 1945-58; general secretary of NCWC (now USCC) 1958-68; ord. titular bishop of Lamasba, Dec. 21, 1965; bishop of St. Augustine, Mar. 27, 1968; resigned Apr. 21, 1979.

Tawil, Joseph: b. Dec. 25, 1913, Damascus, Syria; ord. priest July 20, 1936; ord. titular archbishop of Mira and patriarchal vicar for eparchy of Damascus of the Patriarchate of Antioch for the Melkites, Jan. 1, 1960; apostolic exarch for faithful of the Melkite rite in the U.S., Oct. 31, 1969; app. first eparch with personal title of archbishop when exarchate was raised to eparchy, July 15, 1976; title of see changed to Newton, 1977; retired Dec. 2, 1989.

Thompson, David B.: b. May 29, 1923, Philadelphia, Pa.; educ. St. Charles Seminary (Overbrook, Pa.), Catholic Univ. (Washington, D.C.); ord. priest (Philadelphia*) May 27, 1950; ord. coadjutor bishop of Charleston, May 24, 1989; bishop of Charleston, Feb. 22, 1990.

Timlin, James C.: b. Aug. 5, 1927, Scranton, Pa.; educ. St. Charles College (Catonsville, Md.), St. Mary's Seminary (Baltimore, Md.), North American College (Rome); ord. priest (Scranton) July 16, 1951; ord. titular bishop of Gunugo and auxiliary bishop of Scranton, Sept. 21, 1976; app. bishop of Scranton, Apr. 24, 1984.

Tobin, Thomas J.: b. Apr. 1, 1948, Pittsburgh, Pa.; educ. St. Mark Seminary High School, Gannon College (Erie, Pa.), St. Francis College (Loretto, Pa.), North American College (Rome); ord. priest (Pittsburgh) July 21, 1973; ord. titular bishop of Novica and auxiliary bishop of Pittsburgh, Dec. 27, 1992.

Trautman, Donald W.: b. June 24, 1936, Buffalo, N.Y.; educ. Our Lady of Angels Seminary (Niagara Falls, N.Y.), Theology Faculty (Innsbruck, Austria), Pontifical Biblical Institute (Rome), Catholic Univ. (Washington, D.C.); ord. priest (Buffalo) Apr. 7, 1962, in Innsbruck; ord. titular bishop of Sassura and auxiliary of Buffalo, Apr. 16, 1985; app. bishop of Erie, June 12, 1990.

Treinen, Sylvester: b. Nov. 19, 1917, Donnelly, Minn.; educ. Crosier Seminary (Onamia, Minn.), St. Paul Seminary (St. Paul, Minn.); ord. priest (Bismarck) June 11, 1946; ord. bishop of Boise, July 25, 1962; resigned Aug. 17, 1988.

Tschoepe, Thomas: b. Dec. 17, 1915, Pilot Point, Tex.; educ. Pontifical College Josephinum (Worthington, O.); ord. priest (Dallas) May 30, 1943; ord. bishop of San Angelo, Tex., Mar. 9, 1966; app. bishop of Dallas, Tex., Aug. 27, 1969; retired July 14, 1990.

U-V

Untener, Kenneth E.: b. Aug. 3, 1937, Detroit, Mich.; educ. Sacred Heart Seminary (Detroit, Mich.), St. John's Provincial Seminary (Plymouth, Mich.), Gregorian Univ. (Rome); ord. priest (Detroit*) June 1, 1963; ord. bishop of Saginaw, Nov. 24, 1980.

Valero, René A.: b. Aug. 15, 1930, New York, N.Y.; educ. Cathedral College, Immaculate Conception Seminary (Huntington, N.Y.), Fordham Univ. (New York); ord. priest (Brooklyn) June 2, 1956; ord. titular bishop of Turris Vicus and auxiliary bishop of Brooklyn, Nov. 24, 1980.

Vaughan, Austin B.: b. Sept. 27, 1927, New York, N.Y.; educ. North American College and Gregorian Univ. (Rome), ord. priest (New York*) Dec. 8, 1951; pres. Catholic Theological Society of America, 1967; rector of St. Joseph's Seminary (Dunwoodie, N.Y.), 1973; ord. titular bishop of Cluain Iraird and auxiliary bishop of New York, June 29, 1977.

Veigle, Adrian J.M., T.O.R.: b. Sept. 15, 1912, Lilly, Pa.; educ. St. Francis College (Loretto, Pa.), Pennsylvania State College; ord. priest May 22, 1937; ord. titular bishop of Gigthi June 9, 1966 (resigned titular see May 26, 1978); prelate of Borba, Brazil, 1966; retired July 6, 1988.

Vlazny, John G.: b. Feb. 22, 1937, Chicago, Ill.; educ. Quigley Preparatory Seminary (Chicago, Ill.), St. Mary of the Lake Seminary (Mundelein, Ill.), Gregorian Univ. (Rome), Univ. of Michigan, Loyola Univ. (Chicago, Ill.); ord. priest (Chicago*) Dec. 20, 1961; ord. titular bishop of Stagno and auxiliary bishop of Chicago, Dec. 13, 1983; episcopal vicar; app. bishop of Winona, Minn., May 19, 1987.

W

Waldschmidt, Paul E., C.S.C.: b. Jan. 7, 1920, Evansville, Ind.; educ. Notre Dame Univ. (Notre Dame, Ind.), Holy Cross College (Washington, D.C.), Laval Univ. (Quebec), Angelicum (Rome), Louvain (Belgium), Sorbonne (Paris), ord. priest June 24, 1946; president University of Portland, 1962-77; ord. titular bishop of Citium and auxiliary bishop of Portland, Ore., Mar. 2, 1978; resigned Jan. 8, 1990.

Walsh, Daniel Francis: b. Oct. 2, 1937, San Francisco, Calif.; educ. St. Joseph Seminary (Mountain View, Calif.), St. Patrick Seminary (Menlo Park, Calif.) Catholic Univ. (Washington, D.C.); ord. priest (San Francisco*) Mar. 30, 1963; ord. titular bishop of Tigia and auxiliary bishop of San Francisco, Sept. 24, 1981; app. bishop of Reno-Las Vegas, June 9, 1987.

Walsh, Nicolas E.: b. Oct. 20, 1916, Burnsville, Minn.; educ. St. Paul Seminary (St. Paul, Minn.), Catholic Univ. (Washington, D.C.), Pontifical Palafoxianum Seminary (Puebla, Mexico), Register College of Journalism (Denver, Colo.); ord. priest (Boise) June 6, 1942; first editor of *Idaho Register;* diocesan vicar for Mexican Americans; ord. bishop of Yakima, Oct. 28, 1974; app. titular bishop of Bolsena and auxiliary bishop of Seattle, Aug. 10, 1976; retired Sept. 6, 1983. Bishop emeritus of Yakima.

Ward, John J.: b. Sept. 28, 1920, Los Angeles, Calif.; educ. St. John's Seminary (Camarillo, Calif.), Catholic Univ. (Washington, D.C.); ord. priest (Los Angeles*) May 4, 1946; ord. titular bishop of Bria and auxiliary of Los Angeles, Dec. 12, 1963.

Watters, Loras J.: b. Oct. 14, 1915, Dubuque, Ia.; educ. Loras College (Dubuque, Ia.), Gregorian Univ. (Rome), Catholic Univ. (Washington, D.C.); ord. priest (Dubuque*) June 7, 1941; ord. titular bishop of Fidoloma and auxiliary bishop of Dubuque, Aug. 26, 1965; bishop of Winona, installed Mar. 13, 1969; retired Oct. 14, 1986.

Watty Urquidi, Ricardo, M.Sp.S.: b. July 16, 1938, San Diego, Calif.; ord. priest June 8, 1968; ord. titular bishop of Macomedes and auxiliary bishop of Mexico City, July 19, 1980; app. first bishop of Nuevo Laredo, Mexico, Nov. 6, 1989.

Wcela, Emil A.: b. May 1, 1931, Bohemia, N.Y.; educ. St. Francis College (Brooklyn, N.Y.), Immaculate Conception Seminary (Huntington, N.Y.), Catholic Univ. (Washington, D.C.), Pontifical Biblical Institute (Rome, Italy); ord. priest (Brooklyn) June 2, 1956; ord. titular bishop of Filaca and auxiliary bishop of Rockville Centre, Dec. 13, 1988. Vicar, Eastern Vicariate.

Weakland, Rembert G., O.S.B.: b. Apr. 2, 1927, Patton, Pa.; joined Benedictines, 1945; ord. priest June 24, 1951; abbot-primate of Benedictine Confederation, 1967-77; ord. archbishop of Milwaukee, Nov. 8, 1977.

Weigand, William K.: b. May 23, 1937, Bend, Ore.; educ. Mt. Angel Seminary (St. Benedict, Ore.), St. Edward's Seminary and St. Thomas Seminary (Kenmore, Wash.); ord. priest (Boise) May 25, 1963; ord. bishop of Salt Lake City, Nov. 17, 1980.

Weitzel, John Quinn, M.M.: b. May 10, 1928, Chicago, Ill.; educ. Maryknoll Seminary (Maryknoll, N.Y.); ord. priest Nov. 5, 1955, missionary to Samoa, 1979; ord. bishop of Samoa-Pago Pago, American Samoa, Oct. 29, 1986.

Welsh, Lawrence H.: b. Feb. 1, 1935, Winton, Wyo.; educ. Univ. of Wyoming (Laramie, Wyo.), St. John's Seminary (Collegeville, Minn.), Catholic Univ. (Washington, D.C.); ord. priest (Rapid City) May 26, 1962; ord. bishop of Spokane, Dec. 14, 1978; resigned Apr. 17, 1990; app. titular bishop of Aulon and auxiliary bishop of St. Paul and Minneapolis, Nov. 5, 1991.

Welsh, Thomas J.: b. Dec. 20, 1921, Weatherly, Pa.; educ. St. Charles Borromeo Seminary (Philadelphia, Pa.), Catholic Univ. (Washington, D.C.); ord. priest (Philadelphia*) May 30, 1946; ord. titular bishop of Scattery Island and auxiliary bishop of Philadelphia, Apr. 2, 1970; app. first bishop of Arlington, Va., June 4, 1974, installed Aug. 13, 1974; app. bishop of Allentown, Feb. 8, 1983, installed Mar. 21, 1983.

Whelan, Robert L., S.J.: b. Apr. 16, 1912, Wallace, Ida.; educ. St. Michael's College (Spokane, Wash.), Alma College (Alma, Calif.); ord. priest June 17, 1944; ord. titular bishop of Sicilibba and coadjutor bishop of Fairbanks, Alaska, with right of succession, Feb. 22, 1968; bishop of Fairbanks, Nov. 30, 1968; retired June 1, 1985.

Wildermuth, Augustine F., S.J.: b. Feb. 20, 1904, St. Louis, Mo.; educ. St. Stanislaus Seminary (Florissant, Mo.), St. Michael's Scholasticate (Spokane, Wash.), Sacred Heart College (Shembaganur, S. India), St. Mary's College (Kurseong, India), Gregorian Univ. (Rome); entered Society of Jesus, 1922; ord. priest July 25, 1935; ord. bishop of Patna, India, Oct. 28, 1947; retired Mar. 6, 1980.

Williams, James Kendrick: b. Sept. 5, 1936, Athertonville, Ky.; educ. St. Mary's College (St. Mary's, Ky.), St. Maur's School of Theology (South Union, Ky.); ord. priest (Louisville*) May 25, 1963; ord. titular bishop of Catula and auxiliary bishop of Covington, June 19, 1984; first bishop of Lexington, Ky., installed Mar. 2, 1988.

Winter, William J.: b. May 20, 1930, Pittsburgh, Pa.; educ. St. Vincent College and Seminary (Latrobe, Pa.), Gregorian Univ. (Rome, Italy); ord. priest (Pittsburgh), Dec. 17, 1955; ord. titular bishop of Uthina and auxiliary bishop of Pittsburgh, Feb. 13, 1989.

Wirz, George O.: b. Jan. 17, 1929, Monroe, Wis.; educ. St. Francis Seminary and Marquette Univ. (Milwaukee, Wis.); Cath. Univ. (Washington, D.C.); ord. priest (Madison) May 31, 1952; ord. titular bishop of Municipa and auxiliary bishop of Madison, Mar. 9, 1978.

Wiwchar, Michael, C.SS.R.: b. May 9, 1932, Komarno, Manitoba, Canada; educ. Redemptorist Seminary (Windsor, Ontario); made solemn vows as Redemptorist, 1956; ord. priest, June 28, 1959; pastor St. John the Baptist Parish, Newark, N.J., 1990-93; app. bishop of St. Nicholas of Chicago for the Ukrainians, July 15, 1993.

Wuerl, Donald: b. Nov. 12, 1940, Pittsburgh, Pa.; educ. Catholic Univ. of America (Washington, D.C.), North American College, Angelicum (Rome); ord. priest (Pittsburgh) Dec. 17, 1966, in Rome; ord. titular bishop of Rosemarkie Jan. 6, 1986, in Rome; auxiliary bishop of Seattle, 1986-87; app. bishop of Pittsburgh Feb. 11, 1988, installed Mar. 25, 1988.

Wycislo, Aloysius John: b. June 17, 1908, Chicago, Ill.; educ. St. Mary's Seminary (Mundelein, Ill.), Catholic Univ. (Washington, D.C.); ord. priest (Chicago*) Apr. 4, 1934; ord. titular bishop of Stadia and auxiliary bishop of Chicago, Dec. 21, 1960; app. bishop of Green Bay, installed Apr. 16, 1968; resigned May 10, 1983.

Z

Zayek, Francis: b. Oct. 18, 1920, Manzanillo, Cuba; ord. priest Mar. 17, 1946; ord. titular bishop of Callinicum and auxiliary bishop for Maronites in Brazil, Aug. 5, 1962; named apostolic exarch for Maronites in U.S., with headquarters in Detroit; installed June 11, 1966; first eparch of St. Maron of Detroit, Mar. 25, 1972; see transferred to Brooklyn, June 27, 1977; given personal title of archbishop, Dec. 22, 1982.

Ziemann, G. Patrick: b. Sept. 13, 1941, Pasadena, Calif.; educ. St. John's College Seminary and St. John's Seminary (Camarillo, Calif.), Mt. St. Mary's College (Los Angeles, Calif.); ord. priest (Los Angeles*) Apr. 29, 1967; ord. titular bishop of Obba and auxiliary bishop of Los Angeles, Feb. 23, 1987; app. bishop of Santa Rosa, July 14, 1992.

Zipfel, Paul A.: b. Sept. 22, 1935, St. Louis, Mo.; educ. Cardinal Glennon College, Kenrick Seminary (St. Louis, Mo.), Catholic Univ. (Washington, D.C.), St. Louis Univ. (St. Louis, Mo.); ord. priest (St. Louis*) Mar. 18, 1961; ord. titular bishop of Walla Walla and auxiliary bishop of St. Louis, June 29, 1989.

BISHOP-BROTHERS

(The asterisk indicates brothers who were bishops at the same time.)

There have been nine pairs of brother-bishops in the history of the U.S. hierarchy.

Living: Francis T. Hurley,* archbishop of Anchorage and Mark J. Hurley,* bishop emeritus of Santa Rosa.

Deceased: Francis Blanchet* of Oregon City (Portland) and Augustin Blanchet* of Walla Walla; John S. Foley of Detroit and Thomas P. Foley of Chicago; Francis P. Kenrick,* apostolic administrator of Philadelphia, bishop of Philadelphia and Baltimore, and Peter R. Kenrick* of St. Louis; Matthias C. Lenihan of Great Falls and Thomas M. Lenihan of Cheyenne; James O'Connor, vicar apostolic of Nebraska and bishop of Omaha, and Michael O'Connor of Pittsburgh and Erie; Jeremiah F. and John W. Shanahan, both of Harrisburg; Sylvester J. Espelage, O.F.M.* of Wuchang, China, who died 10 days after the ordination of his brother, Bernard T. Espelage, O.F.M.* of Gallup; Coleman F. Carroll* of Miami and Howard Carroll* of Altoona-Johnstown.

U.S. BISHOPS OVERSEAS

Cardinal William W. Baum, major penitentiary; Cardinal Myroslav Ivan Lubachivsky, major archbishop of Lviv of the Ukrainians; Cardinal Edmund C. Szoka, president of Prefecture for Economic Affairs of the Holy See; Archbishop Ambrose de Paoli, apostolic delegate to southern Africa and pro-nuncio to Lesotho; Archbishop John P. Foley, president of Pontifical Commission for Social Communications; Archbishop Justin Rigali, secretary of the Congregation for Bishops and the College of Cardinals; Most Rev. George Riashi, B.C.O., bishop of eparchy of St. Michael of Sydney, (Australia) for Greek-Catholic Melkites; Most Rev. Michael R. Kuchmiak, exarch of apostolic exarchate of Great Britain for Ukrainian Catholics.

(See also Missionary Bishops.)

RETIRED/RESIGNED U.S. PRELATES

Information, as of Aug. 1, 1993, includes name of the prelate and see held at the time of retirement or resignation; archbishops are indicated by an asterisk. Most of the prelates listed below resigned their sees because of age in accordance with church law. See Index: Biographies, U.S. Bishops.

Forms of address of retired residential prelates (unless they have a titular see): *Archbishop or Bishop Emeritus of* (last see held); *Former Archbishop or Bishop of* (last see held).

Leo Arkfeld, S.V.D.* (Madang, Papua New Guinea), Reginald Arliss, C.P. (Marbel, Philippines, prelate), Michael J. Begley (Charlotte), Ernest B. Boland, O.P. (Multan, Pakistan), William D. Borders* (Baltimore), Warren L. Boudreaux (Houma-Thibodaux), Joseph M. Breitenbeck (Grand Rapids), Edwin B. Broderick (Albany), Joseph Brunini (Jackson), Leo J. Brust (Milwaukee, auxiliary), James C. Burke, O.P. (Chimbote, Peru, prelate), Charles A. Buswell (Pueblo), James J. Byrne* (Dubuque).

Cardinal John Carberry* (St. Louis), Harry A. Clinch (Monterey), John E. Cohill, S.V.D. (Goroka, Papua New Guinea), John W. Comber, M.M. (Foratiano, titular see), William G. Connare (Greensburg), Ronald G. Connors, C.SS.R. (San Juan de la Maguana, Dominican Republic), Arnold R. Cotey, S.D.S. (Nachingwea, now Lindi, Tanzania), Joseph R. Crowley (Ft. Wayne-S. Bend, auxiliary), Walter W. Curtis (Bridgeport), Nicholas D'Antonio, O.F.M. (Olancho, Honduras).

Antanas L. Deksnys (Lavellum, titular see), Michael J. Dempsey, O.P. (Sokoto, Nigeria), Joseph A. DePalma, S.C.J. (DeAar, South Africa), Georges Dion, O.M.I. (Jolo, Philippines, vicar apostolic),

Clarence J. Duhart, C.SS.R. (Udon Thani, Thailand), Joseph A. Durick (Nashville), Dennis V. Durning, C.S.Sp. (Arusha, Tanzania), J. Lennox Federal (Salt Lake City), John J. Fitzpatrick (Brownsville), Bernard J. Flanagan (Worcester), Glennon Flavin (Lincoln), Marion F. Forst (Dodge City), Frederick W. Freking (La Crosse), Gerard L. Frey (Lafayette, La.).

Odore Gendron (Manchester), Hugo Gerbermann, M.M. (San Antonio, auxiliary), Peter L. Gerety* (Newark), Ignatius T. Glennie, S.J. (Trincomalee-Batticaloa, Sri Lanka), George J. Gottwald (St. Louis, auxiliary), Thomas J. Grady (Orlando), John J. Graham (Philadelphia, auxiliary), Lawrence P. Graves (Alexandria-Shreveport), Francis J. Green (Tucson), Andrew G. Grutka (Gary). J. Richard Ham, M.M. (St. Paul and Minneapolis, auxiliary), Philip M. Hannan* (New Orleans), Frank J. Harrison (Syracuse).

Jerome J. Hastrich (Gallup), Charles H. Helmsing (Kansas City-St. Joseph), Edward J. Herrmann (Columbus), Edward G. Hettinger (Columbus, auxiliary), Dennis W. Hickey (Rochester, auxiliary), James J. Hogan (Altoona-Johnstown), Joseph L. Hogan (Rochester), Raymond G. Hunthausen* (Seattle), Mark J. Hurley (Santa Rosa), Stephen Kocisko* (Pittsburgh, Byzantine-Rite), Charles B. Koester (St. Louis, auxiliary), Arthur H. Krawczak (Detroit, auxiliary), Cardinal John Krol* (Philadelphia), William F. Kupfer, M.M. (Taichung, Taiwan), W. Thomas Larkin (St. Petersburg), Vincent M. Leonard (Pittsburgh), Innocent Hilarius Lotocky, O.S.B.M. (St. Nicholas of Chicago for Ukrainians), George E. Lynch (Raleigh, auxiliary).

J. Carroll McCormick (Scranton), Thomas J. McDonough* (Louisville), Bernard J. McLaughlin (Buffalo, auxiliary), William E. McManus (Fort Wayne-South Bend), Joseph F. Maguire (Springfield, Mass.), Charles G. Maloney (Louisville, auxiliary), David M. Maloney (Wichita), Paul C. Marcinkus* (titular see of Orta), Eugene A. Marino, S.S.J.* (Atlanta), John L. May* (St. Louis), Alfred Mendez, C.S.C. (Arecibo, P.R.), James E. Michaels (Wheeling-Charleston, auxiliary), William J. Moran (Military Vicariate, delegate), John J. Mulcahy (Boston, auxiliary), Michael J. Murphy (Erie), James D. Niedergeses (Nashville), Bernard Nolker, C.Ss. R. (Parangua, Brazil), Edward C. O'Leary (Portland, Me.).

Edward W. O'Rourke (Peoria), Albert H. Ottenweller (Steubenville), John L. Paschang (Grand Island), George H. Pearce, S.M.* (Suva, Fiji Islands), Bernard F. Popp (San Antonio, auxiliary), Cornelius M. Power* (Portland, Ore.), Leo A. Pursley (Fort Wayne-South Bend), Vasile Louis Puscas (St.George's in Canton of the Romanians), Joseph M. Raya* (Acre), Joseph W. Regan, M.M. (Tagum, P.I., Prelate), Francis F. Reh (Saginaw), Lawrence J. Riley (Boston, auxiliary), Miguel Rodriguez, C.SS.R. (Areciba, P.R.), John J. Rudin, M.M. (Musoma, Tanzania), James C. Ryan, O.F.M. (Santarem, Brazil), Joseph T. Ryan* (Military Services archdiocese).

Charles A. Salatka* (Oklahoma City), Robert Sanchez* (Santa Fe), John J. Scanlan (Honolulu), James L. Schad (Camden, auxiliary), Alphonse

Schladweiler (New Ulm), Edward F. Schlotterback, O.S.F.S. (Keetmanshoop, Namibia, vicar apostolic), Mark Schmitt (Marquette), Eldon B. Schuster (Great Falls), Francis R. Shea (Evansville), Daniel E. Sheehan* (Omaha), George H. Speltz (St. Cloud), Ignatius J. Strecker* (Kansas City, Kans.), John J. Sullivan (Kansas City-St. Joseph, Mo.).

Paul F. Tanner (St. Augustine), Joseph Tawil* (titular) (Newton, Greek Melkites), Sylvester Treinen (Boise), Thomas Tschoepe (Dallas), Adrian Veigle, T.O.R. (Borba, Brazil, Prelate), Paul E. Waldschmidt, C.S.C. (Portland, Ore., auxiliary), Nicolas Walsh (Yakima), Loras J. Watters (Winona), Robert L. Whelan (Fairbanks), Augustine Wildermuth, S.J. (Patna, India), Aloysius J. Wycislo (Green Bay).

AMERICAN BISHOPS OF THE PAST

Information includes: dates; place of birth if outside the U.S.; date of ordination to the priesthood; titular see in parentheses of bishops who were not ordinaries; indication, where applicable, of date of resignation.

Abbreviation code: abp., archbishop; bp., bishop; v.a., vicar apostolic; aux., auxiliary bishop; coad., coadjutor; ord., ordained priest; res., resigned.

A

Acerra, Angelo Thomas, O.S.B. (1925-90): ord. May 20, 1950; aux. Military Services archdiocese (Lete), 1983-90.

Ackerman, Richard H., C.S.Sp. (1903-92): ord. Aug. 28, 1926; aux. San Diego (Lares), 1956-60; bp. Covington 1960-78 (res.).

Adrian, William L. (1883-1972): ord. Apr. 15, 1911; bp. Nashville, 1936-69 (res.).

Ahr, George W. (1904-93): ord. July 29, 1928; bp. Trenton, 1950-79 (res.).

Albers, Joseph (1891-1965): ord. June 17, 1916; aux. Cincinnati (Lunda), 1929-37; first bp. Lansing, 1937-65.

Alemany, Joseph Sadoc, O.P. (1814-88): b. Spain; ord. Mar. 11, 1837; bp. Monterey, 1850-53; first abp. San Francisco, 1853-84 (res.).

Alencastre, Stephen P., SS.CC. (1876-1940): b. Madeira; ord. Apr. 5, 1902; coad. v.a. Sandwich Is. (Arabissus), 1924-36; v.a. Sandwich (Hawaiian) Is., 1936-40.

Alerding, Herman J. (1845-1924): b. Germany; ord. Sept. 22, 1869; bp. Fort Wayne, 1900-24.

Allen, Edward P. (1853-1926): ord. Dec. 17, 1881; bp. Mobile, 1897-1926.

Alter, Karl J. (1885-1977): ord. June 4, 1910; bp. Toledo, 1931-50; abp. Cincinnati, 1950-69 (res.).

Althoff, Henry (1873-1947): ord. July 26, 1902; bp. Belleville, 1914-47.

Amat, Thaddeus, C.M. (1811-78): b. Spain; ord. Dec. 23, 1837; bp. Monterey (title changed to Monterey-Los Angeles, 1859), 1854-78.

Anderson, Joseph (1865-1927): ord. May 20, 1892; aux. Boston (Myrina), 1909-27.

Anderson, Paul F. (1917-87): ord. Jan. 6, 1943; coad. bp. Duluth (Polignana), 1968-69; bp. Duluth, 1969-82 (res.); aux. Sioux Falls, 1983-87.

Anglim, Robert, C.SS.R. (1922-73): ord. Jan. 6, 1948; prelate Coari, Brazil (Gaguari), 1966-73.

Annabring, Joseph (1900-59): b. Hungary; ord. May 3, 1927; bp. Superior, 1954-59.

Appelhans, Stephen A., S.V.D. (1905-51): ord. May 5, 1932; v.a. East New Guinea (Catula), 1948-51.

Armstrong, Robert J. (1884-1957): ord. Dec. 10, 1910; bp. Sacramento, 1929-57.

Arnold, William R. (1881-1965): ord. June 13, 1908; delegate of U.S. military vicar (Phocaea), 1945-65.

Atkielski, Roman R. (1898-1969): ord. May 30, 1931; aux. Milwaukee (Stobi), 1947-69.

B

Babcock, Allen J. (1898-1969): ord. Mar. 7, 1925; aux. Detroit (Irenopolis), 1947-54; bp. Grand Rapids, 1954-69.

Bacon, David W. (1815-74): ord. Dec. 13, 1838; first bp. Portland, Me., 1855-74.

Baldwin, Vincent J. (1907-79): ord. July 26, 1931; aux. Rockville Centre (Bencenna), 1962-79.

Baltes, Peter J. (1827-86): b. Germany; ord. May 31, 1852; bp. Alton (now Springfield), Ill., 1870-86.

Baraga, Frederic: See Index.

Barron, Edward (1801-54): b. Ireland; ord. 1829; v.a. The Two Guineas (Constantina), 1842-44 (res.) missionary in U.S.

Barry, John (1799-1859): b. Ireland; ord. Sept. 24, 1825; bp. Savannah, 1857-59.

Barry, Patrick J. (1868-1940): b. Ireland; ord. June 9, 1895; bp. St. Augustine, 1922-40.

Bartholome, Peter W. (1893-1982): ord. June 12, 1917; coad. St. Cloud (Lete), 1942-53; bp. St. Cloud, 1953-68 (res.).

Baumgartner, Apollinarls, O.F.M. Cap. (1899-1970): ord. May 30, 1926; v.a. Guam (Joppa), 1945-65; first bp. Agana, Guam, 1965-70.

Bayley, James Roosevelt (1814-77): convert, 1842; ord. Mar. 2, 1843; first bp. Newark, 1853-72; abp. Baltimore, 1872-77.

Bazin, John S. (1796-1848): b. France; ord. July 22, 1822; bp. Vincennes (now Indianapolis), 1847-48.

Beaven, Thomas D. (1851-1920): ord. Dec. 18, 1875; bp. Springfield, Mass., 1892-1920.

Becker Thomas A. (1832-99): ord. June 18, 1859; first bp. Wilmington, 1868-86; bp. Savannah, 1886-99.

Beckman, Francis J. (1875-1948): ord. June 20, 1902; bp. Lincoln, 1924-30; abp. Dubuque, 1930-46 (res.).

Begin, Floyd L. (1902-77): ord. July 31, 1927; aux. Cleveland (Sala), 1947-62; first bp. Oakland, 1962-77.

Bell, Alden J. (1904-82): b. Canada; ord. May 14, 1932; aux. Los Angeles (Rhodopolis), 1956-62; bp. Sacramento, 1962-79 (res.).

Benincasa, Pius A. (1913-86): ord. Mar. 27, 1937; aux. Buffalo (Buruni), 1964-86.

Benjamin, Cletus J. (1909-61): ord. Dec. 8, 1935; aux. Philadelphia (Binda), 1960-61.

Bennett, John G. (1891-1957): ord. June 27, 1914; first bp. Lafayette, Ind. 1944-57.

Bergan, Gerald T. (1892-1972): ord. Oct. 28, 1915; bp. Des Moines, 1934-48; abp. Omaha, 1948-69 (res.).

Bernarding, George, S.V.D. (1912-87): ord. Aug. 13, 1939; first v.a. Mount Hagen, Papua New Guinea (Belabitene), 1960-66; first bp., 1966-82, and first abp., 1982-87 (res.), Mount Hagen.

Bidawid, Thomas M. (1910-71): b. Iraq; ord. May 15, 1935; U.S. citizen; first abp. Ahwaz, Iran (Chaldean Rite), 1968-70; Chaldean patriarchal vicar for United Arab Republic, 1970-71.

Binz, Leo (1900-79): ord. Mar. 15, 1924; coad. bp. Winona (Pinara) 1942-49; coad. abp. Dubuque (Silyum), 1949-54; abp. Dubuque, 1954-61; abp. St. Paul and Minneapolis, 1962-75 (res.).

Biskup, George J. (1911-79): ord. Mar. 19, 1937; aux. Dubuque (Hemeria), 1957-65; bp. Des Moines, 1965-67; coad. abp. Indianapolis (Tamalluma), 1969-70; abp. Indianapolis, 1970-79 (res.).

Blanc, Anthony (1792-1860): b. France; ord. July 22, 1916; bp. New Orleans, 1835-50; first abp. New Orleans, 1850-60.

Blanchet (brothers): **Augustin M.** (1797-1887): b. Canada; ord. June 3, 1821; bp. Walla Walla, 1846-50; first bp. Nesqually (now Seattle), 1850-79 (res.). **Francis N.** (1795-1883): b. Canada; ord. July 19, 1819; v.a. Oregon Territory (Philadelphia, Adrasus), 1843-46; first abp. Oregon City (now Portland), 1846-80 (res.).

Blanchette, Romeo R. (1913-82): ord. Apr. 3, 1937; aux. Joliet (Maxita), 1965-66; bp. Joliet, 1966-79 (res.).

Blenk, James H., S.M. (1856-1917): b. Germany; ord. Aug. 16, 1885; bp. San Juan, 1899-1906; abp. New Orleans, 1906-17.

Boardman, John J. (1894-1978): ord. May 21, 1921; aux. Brooklyn (Gunela), 1952-77 (res.).

Boccella, John H., T.O.R. (1912-92): b. Italy, came to U.S. at age of two; ord. Mar. 29, 1941; abp. Izmir, Turkey, 1968-78 (res.); tit. abp. Ephesus.

Boeynaems, Libert H., SS.CC. (1857-1926): b. Belgium; ord. Sept. 11, 1881; v.a. Sandwich (Hawaiian) Is. (Zeugma), 1903-26.

Bohachevsky, Constantine (1884-1961): b. Austrian Galicia; ord. Jan. 31, 1909; ap. ex. Ukrainian Byzantine Catholics in U.S. (Amisus), 1924-58; first metropolitan of Byzantine Rite archeparchy of Philadelphia, 1958-61.

Boileau, George, S.J. (1912-65): ord. June 13, 1948; coad. bp. Fairbanks (Ausuccura), 1964-65.

Bokenfohr, John, O.M.I. (1903-82): ord. July 11, 1927; bp. Kimberley, S. Africa, 1953-74 (res,).

Boland, Thomas A. (1896-1979): ord. Dec. 23, 1922; aux. Newark (Irina), 1940-47; bp. Paterson, 1947-52; abp. Newark, 1953-74 (res.).

Bona, Stanislaus (1888-1967): ord. Nov. 1, 1912; bp. Grand Island, 1932-44; coad. bp. Green Bay (Mela), 1944-45; bp. Green Bay, 1945-67.

Bonacum, Thomas (1847-1911): b. Ireland; ord. June 18, 1870; bp. Lincoln, 1887-1911.

Borgess, Caspar H. (1826-90): b. Germany; ord. Dec. 8, 1848; coad. bp. and ap. admin. Detroit (Calydon), 1870-71; bp. Detroit, 1871-87 (res.).

Bourgade, Peter (1845-1908): b. France; ord. Nov. 30, 1869; v.a. Arizona (Thaumacus), 1885-97; first bp. Tucson, 1897-99; abp. Santa Fe, 1899-1908.

Boylan, John J. (1889-1953): ord. July 28, 1915; bp. Rockford, 1943-53.

Boyle, Hugh C. (1873-1950): ord. July 2, 1898; bp. Pittsburgh, 1921-50.

Bradley, Denis (1846-1903):b. Ireland; ord. June 3, 1871; first bp. Manchester, 1884-1903.

Brady, John (1842-1910): b. Ireland; ord. Dec. 4, 1864; aux. Boston (Alabanda), 1891-1910.

Brady, Matthew F. (1893-1959): ord. June 10, 1916; bp. Burlington, 1938-44 bp. Manchester, 1944-59.

Brady, William O. (1899-1961): ord. Dec. 21, 1923; bp. Sioux Falls, 1939-56; coad. abp. St. Paul (Selymbria), June-Oct, 1956; abp. St. Paul, 1956-61.

Brennan, Andrew J. (1877-1956): ord. Dec. 17, 1904; aux. Scranton (Thapsus), 1923-26; bp. Richmond, 1926-45 (res.).

Brennan, Francis J. (1894-1968): ord. Apr. 3, 1920; judge (1940-59) and dean (1959-67) of Roman Rota; ord. bp. 1967; cardinal 1967.

Brennan, Thomas F. (1853-1916): b. Ireland; ord. July 14, 1880; first bp. Dallas, 1881-93; aux. St. John's, Newfoundland (Usula), 1893-1905 (res.).

Brizgys, Vincas (1903-92): b. Lithuania; U.S. citizen, 1958; ord. June 5, 1927; aux. Kaunas, Lithuania (Bosano), 1940; exiled 1944; resided in U.S. (Chicago archdiocese) from 1951.

Broderick, Bonaventure (1868-1943): ord. July 26, 1896; aux. Havana, Cuba (Juliopolis), 1903-05 (res.).

Brondel, John B. (1842-1903): b. Belgium; ord. Dec. 17, 1864; bp. Vancouver Is., 1879-84; first bp. Helena, 1884-1903.

Brossart, Ferdinand (1849-1930): b. Germany; ord. Sept. 1, 1892; bp. Covington, 1916-23 (res.).

Brute, Simon G. (1779-1839): b. France; ord. June 11, 1808; first bp. Vincennes (now Indianapolis), 1834-39.

Buddy, Charles F. (1887-1966): ord. Sept. 19, 1914; first bp. San Diego, 1936-66.

Burke, Joseph A. (1886-1962): ord. Aug. 3, 1912; aux. Buffalo (Vita), 1943-52; bp. Buffalo, 1952-62.

Burke, Maurice F. (1845-1923): b. Ireland; ord. May 22, 1875; first bp. Cheyenne, 1887-93; bp. St. Joseph, 1893-1923.

Burke, Thomas M. (1840-1915): b. Ireland; ord. June 30, 1864; bp. Albany, 1894-1915.

Busch, Joseph F. (1866-1953): ord. July 28, 1889; bp. Lead (now Rapid City), 1910-15; bp. St. Cloud, 1915-53.

Byrne, Andrew (1802-62): b. Ireland; ord. Nov. 11, 1827; first bp. Little Rock, 1844-62.

Byrne, Christopher E. (1867-1950): ord. Sept. 23, 1891; bp. Galveston, 1918-50.

Byrne, Edwin V. (1891-1963): ord. May 22, 1915; first bp. Ponce, 1925-29; bp. San Juan, 1929-43; abp. Santa Fe, 1943-63.

Byrne, Leo C. (1908-74): ord. June 10, 1933; aux. St. Louis (Sabadia), 1954-61; coad. bp. Wichita, 1961-67; coad. abp. (Plestra) St. Paul and Minneapolis, 1967-74.

Byrne, Patrick J., M.M. (1888-1950): ord. June 23, 1915; apostolic delegate to Korea (Gazera), 1949-50).

Byrne, Thomas S. (1841-1923): ord. May 22, 1869; bp. Nashville, 1894-1923.

C

Caesar, Raymond R., S.V.D. (1932-87): ord. June 4, 1961; coad. bp. Goroka, Papua New Guinea, 1978-80; bp. Goroka, 1980-87.

Caillouet, L. Abel (1900-84): ord. May 7, 1925; aux. New Orleans (Setea), 1947-76 (res.).

Canevin, J. F. Regis (1853-1927): ord. June 4, 1879; coad. bp. Pittsburgh (Sabrata), 1903-04; bp. Pittsburgh, 1904-21 (res.).

Cantwell, John J. (1874-1947): b. Ireland; ord. June 18, 1899; bp. Monterey-Los Angeles, 1917-22; bp. Los Angeles-San Diego, 1922-36; first abp. Los Angeles, 1936-47.

Carrell, George A., S.J. (1803-68): ord. Dec. 20, 1827; first bp. Covington, 1853-68.

Carroll (brothers) **Coleman F.** (1905-77): ord. June 15, 1930; aux. Pittsburgh (Pitanae), 1953-58; first bp. Miami, 1958-68 and first abp., 1968-77. **Howard J.** (1902-60): ord. Apr. 2, 1927; bp. Altoona-Johnstown, 1958-60.

Carroll, James J. (1862-1913): ord. June 15, 1889; bp. Nueva Segovia, P.I., 1908-12 (res.).

Carroll, John (1735-1815): ord. Feb. 14, 1761; first bishop of the American hierarchy; first bp., 1789-1808, and first abp., 1808-15, of Baltimore.

Carroll, John P. (1864-1925): ord. July 7, 1886; bp. Helena, 1904-25.

Carroll, Mark K. (1896-1985): ord. June 10, 1922; bp. Wichita, 1947-67 (res.).

Cartwright, Hubert J. (1900-58): ord. June 11, 1927; coad. bp. Wilmington (Neve), 1956-58.

Caruana, George (1882-1951): b. Malta; ord. Oct. 28, 1905; bp. Puerto Rico (name changed to San Juan, 1924), 1921-25; ap. del. Mexico (Sebastea in Armenia), 1925-27; internuncio to Haiti, 1927-35; nuncio to Cuba, 1935-47 (res.).

Casey, James V. (1914-86): ord. Dec. 8, 1939; aux. Lincoln (Citium), Apr.-June, 1957; bp. Lincoln, 1957-67; abp. Denver 1967-86.

Casey, Lawrence B. (1905-77): ord. June 7, 1930; aux. Rochester (Cea), 1953-66; bp. Paterson, 1966-77.

Cassata, John J. (1908-89): ord. Dec. 8, 1932; aux. Dallas-Ft. Worth (Bida), 1968-69; bp. Ft. Worth 1969-80 (res.).

Cassidy, James E. (1869-1951): ord. Sept. 8, 1898; aux. Fall River (Ibora), 1930-34; bp. Fall River, 1934-51.

Chabrat, Guy Ignatius, S.S. (1787-1868): b. France; ord. Dec. 21, 1811; coad. bp. Bardstown (Bolina), 1834-47 (res.).

Chanche, John J., S.S. (1795-1852): ord. June 5, 1819; bp. Natchez (now Jackson), 1841-52.

Chapelle, Placide L. (1842-1905): b. France; ord. June 28, 1865; coad. abp. Santa Fe (Arabissus), 1891-94; abp. Santa Fe, 1894-97; abp. New Orleans 1897-1905.

Chartrand, Joseph (1870-1933): ord. Sept. 24, 1892; coad. bp. Indianapolis (Flavias), 1910-18; bp. Indianapolis, 1918-33.

Chatard, Francis S. (1834-1918): ord. June 14, 1862; bp. Vincennes (now Indianapolis — title changed in 1898), 1878-1918.

Cheverus, John Lefebvre de (1768-1836): b. France; ord. Dec. 18, 1790; bp. Boston, 1810-23 (returned to France, made cardinal 1836).

Christie, Alexander (1848-1925): ord. Dec. 22,

1877; bp. Vancouver Is., 1898-99; abp. Oregon City (now Portland), 1899-1925.

Clancy, William (1802-47): b. Ireland; ord. May 24, 1823; coad. bp. Charleston (Oreus), 1834-37; v.a. British Guiana, 1837-43.

Clavel Mendez, Tomas Alberto (1921-88): b. Panama; ord. Dec. 7, 1947; bp. David, Panama, 1955-64; abp. Panama, 1964-68 (res.); vicar for Hispanics, Orange, Calif., diocese.

Cody, John P. (1907-82): ord. Dec. 8, 1931; aux. St. Louis (Apollonia), 1947-54; coad. bp. St. Joseph, Mo., 1954-55; bp. Kansas City-St. Joseph, 1956-61; coad. abp. 1961-62; ap. admin., 1962-64, and abp., 1964-65, New Orleans; abp. Chicago, 1965-82; cardinal, 1967.

Collins, John J., S.J. (1856-1934): ord. Aug. 29, 1891; v.a. Jamaica (Antiphellus), 1907-18 (res.).

Collins, Thomas P., M.M. (1915-73): ord. June 21, 1942; v.a. Pando, Bolivia (Sufetula), 1961-68 (res.).

Colton, Charles H. (1848-1915): ord. June 10, 1876; bp. Buffalo, 1903-15.

Conaty, Thomas J. (1847-1915): b. Ireland; ord. Dec. 21, 1872; rector of Catholic University, 1896-1903; tit. bp. Samos, 1901-03; bp. Monterey- Los Angeles (now Los Angeles), 1903-15.

Concanen, Richard L., O.P. (1747-1810): b. Ireland; ord. Dec. 22, 1770; first bp. New York, 1808-10 (detained in Italy, never reached his see).

Condon, William J. (1895-1967): ord. Oct. 14, 1917; bp. Great Falls, 1939-67.

Connolly, James L. (1894-1986): ord. Dec. 21, 1923; coad bp. Fall River (Mylasa), 1945-51; bp. Fall River, 1951-70 (res.).

Connolly, John, O.P. (1750-1825): b. Ireland; ord. Sept. 24, 1774; bp. New York, 1814-25.

Connolly, Thomas A. (1899-1991): ord. June 11, 1926; aux. San Francisco (Sila), 1939-48; coad. bp. Seattle, 1948-50; bp, 1950-51, and first abp. Seattle, 1951-75 (res.).

Conroy, John J. (1819-95): b. Ireland; ord. May 21, 1842; bp. Albany, 1865-77 (res.).

Conroy, Joseph H. (1858-1939): ord. June 11, 1881; aux. Ogdensburg (Arindela), 1912-21; bp. Ogdensburg, 1921-39.

Conwell, Henry (1748-1842): b. Ireland; ord. 1776; bp. Philadelphia, 1820-42.

Cooke, Terence J. (1921-83): ord. Dec. 1, 1945; aux. New York (Summa), 1965-68; abp. New York, 1965-83; cardinal 1969.

Corbett, Timothy (1858-1939): ord. June 12, 1886; first bp. Crookston, 1910-38 (res.).

Corrigan, Joseph M. (1879-1942): ord. June 6, 1903; rector of Catholic University, 1936-42; tit. bp. Bilta, 1940-42.

Corrigan, Michael A. (1839-1902): ord. Sept. 19, 1863; bp. Newark, 1873-80; coad. abp. New York (Petra), 1880-85; abp. New York, 1885-1902.

Corrigan, Owen (1849-1929): ord. June 7, 1873; aux. Baltimore (Macri), 1908-29.

Cosgrove, Henry (1834-1906): ord. Aug. 27, 1857; bp. Davenport, 1884-1906.

Cosgrove, William M. (1916-92): ord. Dec. 18, 1943; aux. Cleveland (Trisipa), 1968-76; bp. Belleville, 1976-81 (res.).

Costello, Joseph A. (1915-78): ord. June 7, 1941; aux. Newark (Choma), 1963-78.

Cote, Philip, S.J. (1896-1970): ord. Aug. 14, 1927; v.a. Suchow, China (Polystylus), 1935-46; first bp. Suchow, 1946-70 (imprisoned by Chinese Communists, 1951; expelled from China, 1953; ap. admin. Islands of Quemoy and Matsu, 1969-70.

Cotter, Joseph B. (1844-1909): b. England; ord. May 3, 1871; first bp. Winona, 1889-1909.

Cotton, Francis R. (1895-1960): ord. June 17, 1920; first bp. Owensboro, 1938-60.

Cousins, William E. (1902-88): ord. Apr. 23, 1927, aux. Chicago (Forma), 1949-52; bp. Peoria, 1952-59; abp. Milwaukee 1959-77 (res.).

Cowley, Leonard P. (1913-73): ord. June 4, 1938; aux. St. Paul and Minneapolis (Pertusa), 1958-73.

Crane, Michael J. (1863-1928): ord. June 15, 1889; aux. Philadelphia (Curium), 1921-28.

Cretin, Joseph (1799-1857): b. France; ord. Dec. 20, 1823; bp. St. Paul, 1851-57.

Crimont, Joseph R., S.J. (1858-1945): b. France; ord. Aug. 26, 1888; v.a. Alaska (Ammaedara), 1917-45.

Crowley, Timothy J., C.S.C. (1880-1945): b. Ireland; ord. Aug. 2, 1906; coad. bp. Dacca (Epiphania), 1927-29; bp. Dacca, 1929-45.

Cunningham, David F. (1900-79): ord. June 12, 1926; aux., 1950-67, and coad. bp., 1967-79, Syracuse (Lampsacus); bp. Syracuse, 1970-76 (res.).

Cunningham, John F. (1842-1919): b. Ireland; ord. Aug. 8, 1865; bp. Concordia, 1898-1919.

Curley, Daniel J. (1869-1932): ord. May 19, 1894; bp. Syracuse, 1923-32.

Curley, Michael J. (1879-1947): b. Ireland; ord. Mar. 19, 1904; bp. St. Augustine, 1914-21; abp. Baltimore, 1921-39; title changed to abp. Baltimore and Washington, 1939-47.

Curtis, Alfred A. (1831-1908): convert, 1872; ord. Dec. 19, 1874; bp. Wilmington, 1886-96 (res.).

Cusack, Thomas F. (1862-1918): ord. May 30, 1885; aux. New York (Temiscyra), 1904-15; bp. Albany, 1915-18.

Cushing, Richard J. (1895-1970): ord. May 26, 1921; aux. Boston (Mela), 1939-44; abp. Boston, 1944-70; cardinal 1958.

D

Daeger, Albert T., O.F.M. (1872-1932): ord. July 25, 1896; abp. Santa Fe, 1919-32.

Daley, Joseph T. (1915-83): ord. June 7, 1941; aux. Harrisburg (Barca), 1964-67; coad., 1967-71, and bp., 1971-83, Harrisburg.

Daly, Edward C., O.P. (1894-1964): ord. June 12, 1921; bp. Des Moines, 1948-64.

Damiano, Celestine (1911-67): ord. Dec. 21, 1935; apostolic delegate to South Africa (Nicopolis in Epiro), 1952-60; bp. Camden, 1960-67.

Danehy, Thomas J., M.M. (1914-59): ord. Sept. 17, 1939; ap. admin. v.a. Pando, Bolivia (Bita), 1953-59.

Danglmayr, Augustine (1898-1992): ord. June 10, 1922; aux. Dallas-Ft. Worth (Olba), 1942-69 (res.).

Dargin, Edward V. (1898-1981): ord. Sept. 23, 1922; aux. New York (Amphipolis), 1953-73 (res.).

David, John B., S.S. (1761-1841): b. France; ord. Sept. 24, 1785; coad. bp. Bardstown (Mauri-castrum), 1819-32; bp. Bardstown (now Louisville), 1832-33 (res.).

Davis, James (1852-1926): b. Ireland; ord. June 21, 1878; coad. bp. Davenport (Milopotamus), 1904-06; bp. Davenport, 1906-26.

Davis, James P. (1904-88): ord. May 19, 1929; bp. 1943-60, and first abp., 1960-64, San Juan, P.R.; abp. Santa Fe, 1964-74 (res.).

Dearden, John F. (1907-88): ord. Dec. 8, 1932; coad. bp. Pittsburgh (Sarepta), 1948-50; bp. Pittsburgh, 1950-58; abp. Detroit, 1958-80 (res.); cardinal 1969.

De Cheverus, John L.: See Cheverus, John

De Falco, Lawrence M. (1915-79): ord. June 11, 1942; bp. Amarillo, 1963-79 (res.).

De Goesbriand, Louis (1816-99): b. France; ord. July 13, 1840; first bp. Burlington, 1853-99.

De la Hailandiere, Celestine (1798-1882): b. France; ord. May 28, 1825; bp. Vincennes (now Indianapolis), 1839-47 (res.).

Delany, John B. (1864-1906): ord. May 23, 1891; bp. Manchester, 1904-06.

Demers, Modeste (1809-71): b. Canada; ord. Feb. 7, 1836; bp. Vancouver Is., 1846-71.

Dempsey, Michael R. (1918-74): ord. May 1, 1943; aux. Chicago (Truentum), 1968-74.

De Neckere, Leo, C.M. (1799-1833): b. Belgium; ord. Oct. 13, 1822; bp. New Orleans, 1829-33.

Denning, Joseph P. (1907-90): ord. May 21, 1932; aux. Brooklyn (Mallus), 1959-82 (res.).

De Saint Palais, Maurice (1811-77): b. France; ord. May 28, 1836; bp. Vincennes (now Indianapolis), 1849-77.

Desmond, Daniel F. (1884-1945): ord. June 9, 1911; bp. Alexandria, 1933-45.

Dimmerling, Harold J. (1914-87): ord. May 2, 1940; bp. Rapid City, 1969-87.

Dinand, Joseph N., S.J. (1869-1943): ord. June 25, 1903; v.a. Jamaica (Selinus), 1927-29 (res.).

Dingman, Maurice J. (1914-92): ord. Dec. 8, 1939; bp. Des Moines, 1968-86 (res.).

Dobson, Robert (1867-1942): ord. May 23, 1891; aux. Liverpool, Eng. (Cynopolis), 1922-42.

Dolinay, Thomas V. (1923-93): ord. May 16, 1948; aux. Passaic Byzantine Rite (Tiatira); 1976-81; first bp. Van Nuys Byzantine Rite, 1981-90; coad. abp., 1990-91, and abp., 1991-93, Pittsburgh Byzantine Rite.

Domenec, Michael, C.M. (1816-78): b. Spain; ord. June 30, 1839; bp. Pittsburgh, 1860-76; bp. Allegheny, 1876-77 (res.).

Donaghy, Frederick A., M.M. (1903-88): ord. Jan. 29, 1929; v.a. Wuchow, China (Setea), 1939; first bp. Wuchow, 1946, expelled from China, 1955.

Donahue, Joseph P. (1870-1959): ord. June 8, 1895; aux. New York (Emmaus), 1945-59.

Donahue, Patrick J. (1849-1922): b. England; ord. Dec. 19, 1885; bp. Wheeling, 1894-1922.

Donahue, Stephen J. (1893-1982): ord. May 22, 1918; aux. New York (Medea), 1934-69 (res.).

Donnellan, Thomas A. (1914-87): ord. June 3, 1939; bp. Ogdensburg, 1964-68; abp. Atlanta, 1968-87.

Donnelly, George J. (1889-1950): ord. June 12, 1921; aux. St. Louis (Coela), 1940-46; bp. Leavenworth (now Kansas City — title changed in 1947), 1946-50.

Donnelly, Henry E. (1904-67): ord. Aug. 17, 1930; aux. Detroit (Tymbrias), 1954-67.

Donnelly, Joseph F. (1909-77): ord. June 29, 1934; aux. Hartford (Nabala), 1965-77.

Donohoe, Hugh A. (1905-87): ord. June 14, 1930; aux. bp. San Francisco (Taium), 1947-62; first bp. Stockton, 1962-69; bp. Fresno, 1969-80 (res.).

Donovan, John A. (1911-91): b. Canada; ord. Dec. 8, 1935; aux. Detroit (Rhasus), 1954-67; bp. Toledo, 1967-80 (res.).

Doran, Thomas F. (1856-1916): ord. July 4, 1880; aux. Providence (Halicarnassus), 1915-16.

Dougherty, Dennis (1865-1951): ord. May 31, 1890; bp. Nueva Segovia, P.I., 1903-08; bp. Jaro, P.I., 1980-15; bp. Buffalo, 1915-18; abp. Philadelphia, 1918-51; cardinal, 1921.

Dougherty, John J. (1907-86): ord. July 23, 1933; aux. Newark (Cotena), 1963-82 (res.).

Dougherty, Joseph P. (1905-70): ord. June 14, 1930; first bp. Yakima, 1951-69; aux. Los Angeles (Altino), 1969-70.

Dowling, Austin (1868-1930): ord. June 24, 1891; first bp. Des Moines, 1912-19; abp. St. Paul, 1919-30.

Dozier, Carroll T. (1911-85): ord. Mar. 19, 1937; first bp. Memphis, 1971-82 (res.).

Driscoll, Justin A. (1920-84): ord. July 28, 1945; bp. Fargo, 1970-84.

Drossaerts, Arthur J. (1862-1940): b. Holland; ord. June 15, 1889; bp. San Antonio 1918-26; first abp. San Antonio, 1926-40.

Drumm, Thomas W. (1871-1933): b. Ireland; ord. Dec. 21, 1901; bp. Des Moines, 1919-33.

Drury, Thomas J. (1908-92): ord. June 2, 1935; first bp. San Angelo, 1962-65; bp. Corpus Christi, 1965-83 (res.).

Dubois, John, S.S. (1764-1842): b. France; ord. Sept. 28, 1787; bp. New York, 1826-42.

Dubourg, Louis William, S.S. (1766-1833): b. Santo Domingo; ord. 1788; bp. Louisiana and the Two Floridas (now New Orleans), 1815-25; returned to France; bp. Montauban, 1826-33; abp. Besancon 1833.

Dubuis, Claude M. (1817-95): b. France; ord. June 1, 1844; bp. Galveston, 1862-92 (res.).

Dufal, Peter, C.S.C. (1822-98): b. France; ord. Sept. 29, 1852; v.a. Eastern Bengal (Delcon), 1860-78; coad. bp. Galveston, 1878-80 (res.).

Duffy, James A. (1873-1968): ord. May 27, 1899; bp. Kearney (see transferred to Grand Island, 1917), 1913-31 (res.).

Duffy, John A. (1884-1944): ord. June 13, 1908; bp. Syracuse, 1933-37; bp. Buffalo, 1937-44.

Duggan, James (1825-99): b. Ireland; ord. May 29, 1847; coad. bp. St. Louis (Gabala), 1857-59; bp. Chicago, 1859-80 (res.). Inactive from 1869 because of illness.

Dunn, Francis J. (1922-89): ord. Jan. 11, 1948; aux. Dubuque (Turris Tamallani), 1969-89.

Dunn, John J. (1869-1933): ord. May 30, 1896; aux. New York (Camuliana), 1921-33.

Dunne, Edmund M. (1864-1929): ord. June 24, 1887; bp. Peoria, 1909-29.

Dunne, Edward (1848-1910): b. Ireland; ord. June 29, 1871; bp. Dallas, 1893-1910.

Durier, Anthony (1832-1904): b. France; ord.

Oct. 28, 1856; bp. Natchitoches (now Alexandria), La., 1885-1904.

Dwenger, Joseph, C.Pp.S. (1837-93): ord. Sept. 4, 1859; bp. Fort Wayne, 1872-93.

Dworschak, Leo F. (1900-76): ord. May 29, 1926; coad. bp. Rapid City (Tium), 1946-47; aux. Fargo, 1947-60; bp. Fargo, 1960-70 (res.).

Dwyer, Robert J. (1908-76): ord. June 11, 1932; bp. Reno, 1952-66; abp. Portland, Ore., 1966-74 (res.).

E

Eccleston, Samuel, S.S. (1801-51): ord. Apr. 24, 1825; coad. bp. Baltimore (Thermae), Sept.-Oct., 1834; abp. Baltimore, 1834-51.

Egan, Michael, O.F.M. (1761-1814): b. Ireland; first bp. Philadelphia, 1810-14.

Eis, Frederick (1843-1926): b. Germany; ord. Oct. 30, 1870; bp. Sault Ste. Marie and Marquette (now Marquette), 1899-1922 (res.).

Elder, William (1819-1904): ord. Mar. 29, 1846; bp. Natchez (now Jackson), 1857-80; coad. bp. Cincinnati (Avara), 1880-83; abp. Cincinnati, 1883-1904.

Elko, Nicholas T. (1909-91): ord. Sept. 30, 1934; ap. admin. Byzantine exarchy of Pittsburgh (Apollonias), Mar.-Sept. 1955; exarch, Sept., 1955-63, and first eparch, 1963-67, of Pittsburgh; tit. abp. Dara, 1967, with assignment in Rome; aux. bp. Cincinnati, 1971-85 (res.).

Elwell, Clarence E. (1904-73): ord. Mar. 17, 1929; aux. Cleveland (Cone) 1962-68; bp. Columbus, 1968-73.

Emmet, Thomas A., S.J. (1873-1950): ord. July 30, 1909; v.a. Jamaica (Tuscamia), 1930-49 (res.).

England, John (1786-1842): b. Ireland; ord. Oct. 11, 1808; first bp. Charleston, 1820-42.

Escalante, Alonso Manuel, M.M. (1906-67): b. Mexico; ord. Feb. 1, 1931; v.a. Pando, Bolivia (Sora), 1943-60 (res.).

Espelage (brothers): Bernard T., O.F.M. (1892-1971): ord. May 16, 1918; bp. Gallup, 1940-69 (res.).
Sylvester J., O.F.M. (1877-1940): ord. Jan. 18, 1900; v.a. Wuchang, China (Oreus), 1930-40.

Etteldorf, Raymond P. (1911-86): ord. Dec. 8, 1937; apostolic delegate, 1969-73, and nuncio, 1973-74, to New Zealand (Tindari); pro-nuncio to Ethiopia, 1947-82.

Eustace, Bartholomew J. (1887-1956): ord. Nov. 1, 1914; bp. Camden, 1938-56.

Evans, George R. (1922-85): ord. May 31, 1947; aux. Denver (Tubyza), 1969-85.

F

Fahey, Leo F. (1898-1950): ord. May 29, 1926; coad. bp. Baker City (Ipsus), 1948-50.

Falconio, Diomede, O.F.M. (1842-1917): b. Italy; ord. Jan. 3, 1866, Buffalo, N.Y.; missionary in U.S. and Canada; returned to Italy; bp. Lacedonia, 1892-95; abp. Acerenza e Matera, 1895-99; ap. del. Canada (Larissa), 1899-1902, U.S., 1902-11; cardinal 1911.

Farley, John (1842-1918): b. Ireland; ord. June 11, 1870; aux. New York (Zeugma), 1895-1902; abp. New York, 1902-18; cardinal 1911.

Farrelly, John P. (1856-1921): ord. Mar. 22, 1880; bp. Cleveland, 1909-21.

Fearns, John M. (1897-1977): ord. Feb. 19, 1922; aux. New York (Geras), 1957-72 (res.).

Fedders, Edward L., M.M. (1913-73): ord. June 11, 1944; prelate Juli, Peru (Antiochia ad Meadrum), 1963-73.

Feehan, Daniel F. (1855-1934): ord. Dec. 29, 1879; bp. Fall River, 1907-34.

Feehan, Patrick A. (1829-1902): b. Ireland; ord. Nov. 1, 1852; bp. Nashville, 1865-80; first abp. Chicago, 1880-1902.

Feeney, Daniel J. (1894-1969): ord. May 21, 1921; aux. Portland, Me. (Sita), 1946-52; coad. bp. Portland, 1952-55; bp. Portland, 1955-69.

Feeney, Thomas J., S.J. (1894-1955): ord. June 23, 1927; v.a. Caroline and Marshall Is. (Agnus), 1951-55.

Fenwick, Benedict J., S.J. (1782-1846): ord. June 11, 1808; bp. Boston, 1825-46.

Fenwick, Edward D., O.P. (1768-1832): ord. Feb. 23, 1793; first bp. Cincinnati, 1822-32.

Fink, Michael, O.S.B. (1834-1904): b. Germany; ord. May 28, 1857; coad. v.a., 1871-74, and v.a., 1874-77, Kansas and Indian Territory (Eucarpia); first bp. Leavenworth (now Kansas City), 1877-1904.

Finnigan, George, C.S.C. (1885-1932): ord. June 13, 1915; bp. Helena, 1927-32.

Fisher, Carl, S.S.J. (1945-93): ord. June 2, 1973; aux. Los Angeles (Tlos), 1987-93.

Fitzgerald, Edward (1833-1907): b. Ireland; ord. Aug. 22, 1857; bp. Little Rock, 1867-1907.

Fitzgerald, Edward A. (1893-1972): ord. July 25, 1916; aux. Dubuque (Cantanus), 1946-49; bp. Winona, 1949-69 (res.).

Fitzgerald, Walter J., S.J. (1883-1947): ord. May 16, 1918; coad. v.a. Alaska (Tymbrias), 1939-45; v.a. Alaska, 1945-47.

Fitzmaurice, Edmond (1881-1962): b. Ireland; ord. May 28, 1904; bp. Wilmington, 1925-60 (res.).

Fitzmaurice, John E. (1837-1920): b. Ireland; ord. Dec. 21, 1862; coad. bp. Erie (Amisus), 1898-99; bp. Erie, 1899-1920.

Fitzpatrick, John B. (1812-66): ord. June 13, 1840; aux. Boston (Callipolis), 1843-46; bp. Boston, 1846-66.

Fitzsimon, Laurence J. (1895-1958): ord. May 17, 1921; bp. Amarillo, 1941-58.

Flaget, Benedict, S.S.: See Index.

Flaherty, J. Louis (1910-75): ord. Dec. 8, 1936; aux. Richmond (Tabudo), 1966-75.

Flannelly, Joseph F. (1894-1973): ord. Sept. 1, 1918; aux. New York (Metelis), 1948-70 (res.).

Flasch, Kilian C. (1831-91): b. Germany; ord. Dec. 16, 1859; bp. La Crosse, 1881-91.

Fletcher, Albert L. (1896-1979): ord. June 4, 1920; aux. Little Rock (Samos), 1940-46; bp. Little Rock, 1946-72 (res.).

Floersh, John (1886-1968): ord. June 10, 1911; coad. bp. Louisville (Lycopolis), 1923-24; bp. Louisville, 1924-37; first abp. Louisville, 1937-67 (res.).

Flores, Felixberto C. (1921-85): b. Gaum; ord. Apr. 30, 1949; ap. admin. Agana, Guam (Stonj), 1970-72; bp., 1977-84, and first abp. Agana, 1984-85.

Foery, Walter A. (1890-1978): ord. June 10, 1916; bp. Syracuse, 1937-70 (res.).

Foley (brothers): **John S.** (1833-1918): ord. Dec. 20, 1856; bp. Detroit, 1888-1918. **Thomas** (1822-79): ord. Aug. 16, 1846; coad. bp. and ap. admin. Chicago (Pergamum), 1870-79.

Foley, Maurice P. (1867-1919): ord. July 25, 1891; bp. Tuguegarao, P.I., 1910-16; bp. Jaro, P.I., 1916-19.

Ford, Francis X., M.M. (1892-1952): ord. Dec. 5, 1917; v.a. Kaying, China (Etenna), 1935-46; first bp. Kaying, 1946-52.

Forest, John A. (1838-1911): b. France; ord. Apr. 12, 1863; bp. San Antonio, 1895-1911.

Fox, Joseph J. (1855-1915): ord. June 7, 1879; bp. Green Bay, 1904-14 (res.).

Franz, John B. (1896-1992): ord. June 13, 1920; first bp. Dodge City, 1951-59; bp. Peoria, 1959-71 (res.).

Fulcher, George A. (1922-84): ord. Feb. 28, 1948; aux. Columbus (Morosbisdus), 1976-83; bp. Lafayette, 1983-84.

Furey, Francis J. (1905-79): ord. Mar. 15, 1930; aux. Philadelphia (Temnus), 1960-63; coad bp. San Diego, 1963-66; bp. San Diego, 1966-69; abp. San Antonio, 1969-79.

Furlong, Philip J. (1892-1989): ord. May 18, 1918; aux. Military Vicar (Araxa), 1956-71 (res.).

G

Gabriels, Henry (1838-1921): b. Belgium; ord. Sept. 21, 1861; bp. Ogdensburg, 1892-1921.

Gabro, Jaroslav (1919-80): ord. Sept. 27, 1945; bp. St. Nicholas of Chicago (Byzantine Rite, Ukrainians), 1961-80.

Galberry, Thomas, O.S.A. (1833-78): b. Ireland; ord. Dec. 20, 1856; bp. Hartford, 1876-78.

Gallagher, Michael J. (1866-1937): ord. Mar. 19, 1893; coad. bp. Grand Rapids (Tiposa in Mauretania), 1915-16; bp. Grand Rapids, 1916-18; bp. Detroit, 1918-37.

Gallagher, Nicholas (1846-1918): ord. Dec. 25, 1868; coad. bp. Galveston (Canopus), 1882-92; bp. Galveston, 1892-1918.

Gallagher, Raymond J. (1912-91): ord. Mar. 25, 1939; bp. Lafayette, Ind., 1965-82 (res.).

Gallegos, Alphonse, O.A.R. (1931-91): ord. May 24, 1958; aux. Sacramento (Sassabe), 1981-91.

Gannon, John M. (1877-1968): ord. Dec. 21, 1901; aux. Erie (Nilopolis), 1918-20; bp. Erie, 1920-66 (res.).

Garcia Diego y Moreno, Francisco, O.F.M. (1785-1846): b. Mexico; ord. Nov. 14, 1808; bp. Two Californias (now Los Angeles), 1840-46.

Garriga, Mariano S. (1886-1965): ord. July 2, 1911; coad. bp. Corpus Christi (Syene), 1936-49; bp. Corpus Christi, 1949-65.

Garrigan, Philip (1840-1919): b. Ireland; ord. June 11, 1870; first bp. Sioux City, 1902-19.

Gartland, Francis X. (1808-54): b. Ireland; ord. Aug. 5, 1832; first bp. Savannah, 1850-54.

Garvey, Eugene A. (1845-1920): ord. Sept. 22, 1869; first bp. Altoona (now Altoona-Johnstown), 1901-20.

Gercke, Daniel J. (1874-1964): ord. June 1, 1901; bp. Tucson, 1923-60 (res.).

Gerken, Rudolph A. (1887-1943): ord. June 10, 1917; first bp. Amarillo, 1927-33; abp. Santa Fe, 1933-43.

Gerow, Richard O. (1885-1976): ord. June 5, 1909; bp. Natchez-Jackson (now Jackson), 1924-67 (res.).

Gerrard, James J. (1897-1991): ord. May 26, 1923; aux. Fall River (Forma), 1959-76 (res.).

Ghattas, Ignatius, B.S.O. (1920-92): b. Nazareth, Israel; ord. July 7, 1946; bp. Newton for Greek Melkites, 1990-92.

Gibbons, Edmund F. (1868-1964): ord. May 27, 1893; bp. Albany, 1919-54 (res.).

Gibbons, James (1834-1921): ord. June 30, 1861; v.a. North Carolina (Adramyttium), 1868-72; bp. Richmond, 1872-77; coad. Baltimore (Jonopolis), May-Oct., 1877; abp. Baltimore, 1877-1921; cardinal 1886.

Gilfillan, Francis (1872-1933): b. Ireland; ord. June 24, 1895; coad. bp. St. Joseph (Spiga), 1922-23; bp. St. Joseph, 1923-33.

Gill, Thomas E. (1908-73): ord. June 10, 1933; aux. Seattle (Lambesis) 1956-73.

Gilmore, Joseph M. (1893-1962): ord. July 25, 1915; bp. Helena, 1936-62.

Gilmour, Richard (1824-91): b. Scotland; ord. Aug. 30, 1852; bp. Cleveland, 1872-91.

Girouard, Paul J., M.S. (1898-1964): ord. July 26, 1927; first bp. Morondava, Madagascar, 1956-64.

Glass, Joseph S., C.M. (1874-1926): ord. Aug. 15, 1897; bp. Salt Lake City, 1915-26.

Gleeson, Francis D., S.J. (1895-1983): ord. July 29, 1926; v.a. Alaska (Cotenna), 1948-62; first bp. Fairbanks, 1962-68 (res.).

Glenn, Lawrence A. (1900-85): ord. June 11, 1927; aux. Duluth (Tuscamia), 1956-60; bp. Crookston, 1960-70 (res.).

Glennon, John J. (1862-1946): b. Ireland; ord. Dec. 20, 1884; coad. bp. Kansas City, Mo. (Pinara), 1896-1903; coad. St. Louis, April-Oct., 1903; abp. St. Louis, 1903-46; cardinal 1946.

Glorieux, Alphonse J. (1844-1917): b. Belgium; ord. Aug. 17, 1867; v.a. Idaho (Apollonia), 1885-93; bp. Boise, 1893-1917.

Gorman, Daniel (1861-1927): ord. June 24, 1893; bp. Boise, 1918-27.

Gorman, Thomas K. (1892-1980): ord. June 23, 1917; first bp. Reno 1931-52; coad. bp. Dallas-Ft. Worth (Rhasus), 1952-54; bp. Dallas-Fort Worth (now Dallas), 1954-69 (res.).

Grace, Thomas (1841-1921): b. Ireland; ord. June 24, 1876; bp. Sacramento, 1896-1921.

Grace, Thomas L., O.P. (1814-97): ord. Dec. 21, 1839; bp. St. Paul, 1859-84 (res.).

Graner, Lawrence L., C.S.C. (1901-82): ord. June 24, 1928; bp. Dacca, 1947-50, and first abp., 1950-67 (res.).

Granjon, Henry (1863-1922): b. France; ord. Dec. 17, 1887; bp. Tucson, 1900-22.

Graziano, Lawrence, O.F.M. (1921-90): ord. Jan. 26, 1947; aux. Santa Ana, El Salvador (Limata), 1961-65; coad. San Miguel, El Salvador, 1965-68; bp. San Miguel, 1968-69 (res.).

Greco, Charles P. (1894-1987): ord. July 25, 1918; bp. Alexandria, La., 1946-73 (res.).

Green, Joseph J. (1917-82): ord. July 14, 1946;

aux. Lansing (Trisipa), 1962-67; bp. Reno 1967-74 (res.).

Grellinger, John B. (1899-1984): ord. priest July 14, 1929; aux. Green Bay (Syene), 1949-74 (res.).

Greteman, Frank H. (1907-87): ord. Dec. 8, 1932; aux. Sioux City (Vissala), 1965-70; bp. Sioux City, 1970-83 (res.).

Griffin, James A. (1883-1948): ord. July 4, 1909; bp. Springfield, Ill., 1924-48.

Griffin, William A. (1885-1950): ord. Aug. 15, 1910; aux. Newark (Sanavus), 1938-40; bp. Trenton, 1940-50.

Griffin, William R. (1883-1944): ord. May 25, 1907; aux. La Crosse (Lydda), 1935-44.

Griffiths, James H. (1903-64): ord. Mar. 12, 1927; aux. New York and delegate of U.S. military vicar (Gaza), 1950-64.

Grimes, John (1852-1922): b. Ireland; ord. Feb. 19, 1882; coad. bp. Syracuse (Hemeria), 1909-12; bp. Syracuse, 1912-22.

Grimmelsman, Henry J. (1890-1972); ord. Aug. 15, 1915; first bp. Evansville, 1945-65 (res.).

Gross, William H., C.SS.R. (1837-98): ord. Mar. 21, 1863; bp. Savannah, 1873-85; abp. Oregon City (now Portland), 1885-98.

Grovas Felix, Rafael (1905-91): b. San Juan, Puerto Rico; ord. Apr. 7, 1928; bp. Caguas, P.R., 1965-81 (res.).

Guertin, George A. (1869-1932): ord. Dec. 17, 1892; bp. Manchester, 1907-32.

Guilfoyle, George H. (1913-91): ord. Mar. 25, 1944; aux. New York (Marazane), 1964-68; bp. Camden 1968-89 (res.).

Guilfoyle, Richard T. (1892-1957): ord. June 2, 1917; bp. Altoona (now Altoona-Johnstown), 1936-57.

Guilfoyle, Merlin J. (1908-81): ord. June 10, 1933; aux. San Francisco (Bulla), 1950-69; bp. Stockton, 1969-79 (res.).

Gunn, John E., S.M. (1863-1924): b. Ireland; ord. Feb. 2, 1890; bp. Natchez (now Jackson), 1911-24.

H

Haas, Francis J. (1889-1953): ord. June 11, 1913; bp. Grand Rapids, 1943-53.

Hacker, Hilary B. (1913-90): ord. June 4, 1938; bp. Bismarck, 1957-82 (res.).

Hackett, John F. (1911-90): ord. June 29, 1936; aux. Hartford (Helenopolis in Palaestina),1953-86 (res.).

Hafey, William (1888-1954): ord. June 16, 1914; first bp. Raleigh, 1925-37; coad. bp. Scranton (Appia), 1937-38; bp. Scranton, 1938-54.

Hagan, John R. (1890-1946): ord. Mar. 7, 1914; aux. Cleveland (Limata), 1946.

Hagarty, Paul L., O.S.B. (1909-84): ord. June 6, 1936; v.a. Bahamas (Arba), 1950-60; first bp. Nassau, Bahamas, 1960-81 (res.).

Haid, Leo M., O.S.B. (1849-1924): ord. Dec. 21, 1872; v.a. N. Carolina (Messene), 1888-1910; abbot Mary Help of Christians abbacy, 1910-24.

Hallinan, Paul J. (1911-68): ord. Feb. 20, 1937; bp. Charleston, 1958-62; first abp. Atlanta, 1962-68.

Hammes, George A. (1911-93): ord. May 22, 1937; bp. Superior 1960-85 (res.).

Hanna, Edward J. (1860-1944): ord. May 30,

1885; aux. San Francisco (Titiopolis). 1912-15; abp. San Francisco, 1915-35 (res.).

Hannan, Jerome D. (1896-1965): ord. May 22, 1921; bp. Scranton, 1954-65.

Harkins, Matthew (1845-1921): ord. May 22, 1869; bp. Providence, 1887-1921.

Harper, Edward, C.SS.R. (1910-90): ord. June 18, 1939; first prelate Virgin Islands (Heraclea Pontica), 1960-77, and first bishop (prelacy made diocese of St. Thomas), 1977-85 (res.).

Harris, Vincent M. (1913-88): ord. Mar. 19, 1938; first bp. Beaumont, 1966-71; coad. bp. Austin (Rotaria), Apr. 27-Nov. 16, 1971; bp. Austin, 1971-85 (res.).

Hartley, James J. (1858-1944): ord. July 10, 1882; bp. Columbus, 1904-44.

Harty, Jeremiah J. (1853-1927): ord. Apr. 28, 1878; abp. Manila, 1903-16; abp. Omaha, 1916-27.

Hayes, James T., S.J. (1889-1980): ord. June 29, 1921; bp. of Cagayan, Philippines, 1933-51; first abp. Cagayan, 1951-70 (res.).

Hayes, Nevin W., O. Carm. (1922-88): ord. June 8, 1946; prelate Sicuani, Peru (Nova Sinna), 1965-70; aux. bp. Chicago, 1971-88.

Hayes, Patrick J. (1867-1938): ord. Sept. 8, 1892; aux. New York (Thagaste), 1914-19; abp. New York, 1919-38; cardinal 1924.

Hayes, Ralph L. (1884-1970): ord. Sept. 19, 1909; bp. Helena 1933-35; rector North American College (Hieropolis) 1935-44; bp. Davenport, 1944-66 (res.).

Healy, James A. (1830-1900): ord. June 10, 1854; bp. Portland 1875-1900.

Heelan, Edmond (1868-1948): b. Ireland; ord. June 24, 1890; aux. Sioux City (Gerasa), 1919-20; bp. Sioux City, 1920-48.

Heffron, Patrick (1860-1927): ord. Dec. 22, 1884; bp. Winona, 1910-27.

Heiss, Michael (1818-90): b. Germany; ord. Oct. 18, 1840; bp. La Crosse, 1868-80; coad. abp. Milwaukee (Hadrianopolis), 1880-81; abp. Milwaukee, 1881-90.

Hendrick, Thomas A. (1849-1909): ord. June 7, 1873; bp. Cebu, P.I., 1904-09.

Hendricken, Thomas F. (1827-86): b. Ireland; ord. Apr. 25, 1853; bp. Providence, 1872-86.

Hennessy, John (1825-1900): b. Ireland; ord. Nov. 1, 1850; bp. Dubuque, 1866-93; first abp. Dubuque, 1893-1900.

Hennessy, John J. (1847-1920): b. Ireland; ord. Nov. 28, 1869; first bp. Wichita, 1888-1920; ap. admin. Concordia (now Salina), 1891-98.

Henni, John M. (1805-81): b. Switzerland; ord. Feb. 2, 1829; first bp. Milwaukee, 1844-75; first abp. Milwaukee, 1875-81.

Henry, Harold W., S.S.C. (1909-76): ord. Dec. 21, 1932; v.a. Kwang Ju, Korea (Coridala), 1957-62; first abp. Kwang Ju, 1962-71; ap. admin. p.a. Cheju-Do, Korea (Thubunae), 1971-76.

Herzig, Charles E. (1929-91): ord. May 31, 1955; first bp. Tyler, 1987-91.

Heslin, Thomas (1845-1911): b. Ireland; ord. Sept. 8, 1869; bp. Natchez (now Jackson), 1889-1911.

Heston, Edward L. (1907-73): ord. Dec. 22, 1934; sec. Sacred Congregation for Religious and Secular Institutes, 1969-71; pres. Pontifical Commission for Social Communications, 1971-73; tit. abp. Numidea, 1972.

Hickey, David F., S.J. (1882-1973): ord. June 27, 1917; v.a. Belize, Br. Honduras (Bonitza), 1948-56; first bp. Belize, 1956-57 (res.); tit. abp. Cabasa, 1957-73.

Hickey, Thomas F. (1861-1940): ord. Mar. 25, 1884; coad. bp. Rochester (Berenice), 1905-09; bp. Rochester, 1909-28 (res.).

Hickey, William A. (1869-1933): ord. Dec. 22, 1893; coad. bp. Providence (Claudiopolis), 1919-21; bp. Providence, 1921-33.

Hillinger, Raymond P. (1904-71): ord. Apr. 2, 1932; bp. Rockford, 1953-56; aux. Chicago (Derbe), 1956-71.

Hines, Vincent J. (1912-90): ord. May 2, 1937; bp. Norwich, 1960-75 (res.).

Hoban, Edward F. (1878-1966): ord. July 11, 1903; aux. Chicago (Colonia), 1921-28; bp. Rockford, 1928-42; coad. bp. Cleveland (Lystra), 1942-45; bp. Cleveland, 1945-66.

Hoban, Michael J. (1853-1926): ord. May 22, 1880; coad. bp. Scranton (Halius), 1896-99; bp. Scranton, 1899-1926.

Hoch, Lambert A. (1903-90): ord. May 30, 1928; bp. Bismarck, 1952-56; bp. Sioux Falls, 1956-78 (res.).

Hodapp, Robert L., S.J. (1910-89): ord. June 18, 1941; bp. Belize (now Belize-Belmopan), 1958-83 (res.).

Hodges, Joseph H. (1911-85): ord. Dec. 8, 1935; aux. Richmond (Rusadus), 1952-61; coad. Wheeling, 1961-62; bp. Wheeling (now Wheeling- Charleston), 1962-85.

Hogan, John J. (1829-1913): b. Ireland; ord. Apr. 10, 1852; first bp. St. Joseph, 1868-80; first bp. Kansas City, 1880-1913.

Horstmann, Ignatius (1840-1908): ord. June 10, 1865; bp. Cleveland, 1892-1908.

Howard, Edward D. (1877-1983): ord. June 12, 1906; aux. Davenport (Isauropolis), 1924-26; abp. Oregon City (title changed to Portland, 1928), 1926-66 (res.).

Howard, Francis W. (1867-1944): ord. June 16, 1891; bp. Covington, 1923-44.

Hughes, John J. (1797-1864): b. Ireland; ord. Oct. 15, 1826; coad. bp. New York (Basilinopolis), 1837-42; bp. New York, 1842-50, and first abp., 1850-64.

Hunkeler, Edward J. (1894-1970): ord. June 14, 1919; bp. Grand Island, 1945-51; bp. Kansas City, Kans. 1951-52; first abp. Kansas City, 1952-69 (res.).

Hunt, Duane G. (1884-1960): ord. June 27, 1920; bp. Salt Lake City, 1937-60.

Hurley, Joseph P. (1894-1967): ord. May 29, 1919; bp. St. Augustine, 1940-67.

Hyland, Francis E. (1901-68): ord. June 11, 1927; aux. Savannah-Atlanta (Gomphi), 1949-56; bp. Atlanta, 1956-61 (res.).

Hyle, Michael W. (1901-67): ord. Mar. 12, 1927; coad. bp. Wilmington, 1958-60; bp. Wilmington, 1960-67.

I

Iranyi, Ladislaus A., Sch. P. (1923-87): ord. Mar. 13, 1948; U.S. citizen, 1958; ord. bp. (Castel

Mediano), July 27, 1983, for spiritual care of Hungarian Catholics living outside Hungary.

Ireland, John (1838-1918): b. Ireland; ord. Dec. 21, 1861; coad. bp. St. Paul (Marobea), 1875-84; bp. St. Paul, 1884-88, and first abp. St. Paul, 1888-1918.

Ireton, Peter L. (1882-1958): ord. June 20, 1906; coad. bp. Richmond (Cyme), 1935-45; bp. Richmond, 1945-58.

Issenmann, Clarence G. (1907-82): ord. June 29, 1932; aux. Cincinnati (Phytea), 1954-57; bp. Columbus, 1957-64; coad. bp. Cleveland (Filaca), 1964-66; bp. Cleveland, 1966-74 (res.).

Ivancho, Daniel (1908-72): b. Austria-Hungary; ord. Sept. 30, 1934; coad. bp. Pittsburgh Ruthenian Rite (Europus), 1946-48; bp. Pittsburgh Ruthenian Rite, 1948-54 (res.).

J

Janssen, John (1835-1913): b. Germany; ord. Nov. 19, 1858; first bp. Belleville, 1888-1913.

Janssens, Francis A. (1843-97): b. Holland; ord. Dec. 21, 1867; bp. Natchez (now Jackson) 1881-88; abp. New Orleans, 1888-97.

Jeanmard, Jules B. (1879-1957): ord. June 10, 1903; first bp. Lafayette, La., 1918-56 (res.).

Johannes, Francis (1874-1937): b. Germany; ord. Jan. 3, 1897; coad. bp. Leavenworth (Thasus), 1928-29; bp. Leavenworth (now Kansas City), 1929-37.

Johnson, William R. (1918-86): ord. May 28, 1944; aux. Los Angeles (Blera), 1971-76; first bp. Orange, 1976-86.

Jones, William A., O.S.A. (1865-1921): ord. Mar. 15, 1890; bp. San Juan, 1907-21.

Joyce, Robert F. (1896-1990): ord. May 26, 1923; aux. Burlington (Citium), 1954-57; bp. Burlington 1957-71 (res.).

Juncker, Henry D. (1809-68): b. Lorraine (France); ord. Mar. 16, 1834; first bp. Alton (now Springfield), Ill., 1857-68.

Junger, Aegidius (1833-95): b. Germany; ord. June 27, 1862; bp. Nesqually (now Seattle), 1879-95.

K

Kain, John J. (1841-1903): ord. July 2, 1866; bp. Wheeling, 1875-93; coad. abp. St. Louis (Oxyrynchus), 1893-95; abp. St. Louis, 1895-1903.

Katzer, Frederick X. (1844-1903): b. Austria; ord. Dec. 21, 1866; bp. Green Bay, 1886-91; abp. Milwaukee, 1891-1903.

Keane, James J. (1856-1929): ord. Dec. 23, 1882; bp. Cheyenne, 1902-11; abp. Dubuque, 1911-29.

Keane, John J. (1839-1918): b. Ireland; ord. July 2, 1866; bp. Richmond, 1878-88; rector of Catholic University, 1888-97; consultor of Congregation for Propagation of the Faith, 1897-1900; abp. Dubuque, 1900-11 (res.).

Keane, Patrick J. (1872-1928): b. Ireland; ord. June 20, 1895; aux. Sacramento (Samaria), 1920-22; bp. Sacramento, 1922-28.

Kearney, James E. (1884-1977): ord. Sept. 19, 1908; bp. Salt Lake City, 1932-37; bp. Rochester, 1937-66 (res.).

Kearney, Raymond A. (1902-56): ord. Mar. 12, 1927; aux. Brooklyn (Lysinia), 1935-56.

Keiley, Benjamin J. (1847-1925): ord. Dec. 31, 1873; bp. Savannah, 1900-22 (res.).

Kelleher, Louis F. (1889-1946): ord. Apr. 3, 1915; aux. Boston (Thenae), 1945-46.

Kellenberg, Walter P. (1901-86): ord. June 2, 1928; aux. New York (Joannina), 1953-54; bp. Ogdensburg, 1954-57; first bp. Rockville Centre, 1957-76 (res.).

Kelley, Francis C. (1870-1948): b. Canada; ord. Aug. 23, 1893; bp. Oklahoma, 1924-48.

Kelly, Edward D. (1860-1926): ord. June 16, 1886; aux. Detroit (Cestrus), 1911-19; bp. Grand Rapids, 1919-26.

Kelly, Edward J. (1890-1956): ord. June 2, 1917; bp. Boise, 1928-56.

Kelly, Francis M. (1886-1950): ord. Nov. 1, 1912; aux. Winona (Mylasa), 1926-28; bp. Winona, 1928-49 (res.).

Kelly, Patrick (1779-1829): b. Ireland; ord. July 18, 1802; first bp. Richmond, 1820-22 (returned to Ireland; bp. Waterford and Lismore, 1822-29).

Kennally, Vincent, S.J. (1895-1977): ord. June 20, 1928; v.a. Caroline and Marshall Islands (Sassura), 1957-71 (res.).

Kennedy, Thomas F. (1858-1917): ord. July 24, 1887; rector North American College, 1901-17; tit. bp. Hadrianapolis, 1907-15; tit. abp. Seleucia, 1915-17.

Kenney, Lawrence J. (1930-90): ord. June 2, 1956; aux. Military Services archdiocese (Holar),1983-90.

Kenny, William J. (1853-1913): ord. Jan. 15, 1879; bp. St. Augustine, 1902-13.

Kenrick (brothers): Francis P. (1796-1863): b. Ireland; ord. Apr. 7, 1821; coad. bp. Philadelphia (Aratha), 1830-42; bp. Philadelphia, 1842-51; abp. Baltimore, 1851-63. **Peter** (1806-96): b. Ireland; ord. Mar. 6, 1832; coad. bp. St. Louis (Adrasus), 1841-43; bp. 1843-47, and first abp. 1847-95, St. Louis (res.).

Keough, Francis P. (1890-1961): ord. June 10, 1916; bp. Providence, 1943-47; abp. Baltimore, 1947-61.

Kevenhoerster, John B., O.S.B. (1869-1949): b. Germany; ord. June 24, 1896, Collegeville, Minn.; ord. tit. bp. Camuliana, 1933; p.a., 1933-41, and v.a., 1941-49, of Bahamas.

Keyes, Michael, S.M. (1876-1959): b. Ireland; ord. June 21, 1907; bp. Savannah, 1922-35 (res.).

Kiley, Moses E. (1876-1953): b. Nova Scotia; ord. June 10, 1911; bp. Trenton, 1934-40; abp. Milwaukee, 1940-53.

Killeen, James (1917-78): ord. May 30, 1942; aux. Military Vicariate (Valmalla), 1975-78.

Klonowski, Henry T. (1898-1977): ord. Aug. 8, 1920; aux. Scranton (Daldis), 1947-73 (res.).

Kogy, Lorenz S., O.M. (1895-1963): b. Georgia, Russia; ord. Nov. 15, 1917; U.S. citizen, 1944; patriarchal vicar for Armenian diocese of Beirut (Comana), 1951-63.

Koudelka, Joseph (1852-1921): b. Austria; ord. Oct. 8, 1875; aux. Cleveland (Germanicopolis), 1908-11; aux. Milwaukee, 1911-13; bp. Superior, 1913-21.

Kowalski, Rembert, O.F.M. (1884-1970): ord. June 22, 1911; v.a. Wuchang, China (Ipsus), 1942-46; first bp. Wuchang, 1946-70 (in exile from 1953).

Kozlowski, Edward (1860-1915): b. Poland; ord. June 29, 1887; aux. Milwaukee (Germia), 1914-15.

Krautbauer, Francix X. (1824-85): b. Germany; ord. July 16, 1850; bp. Green Bay, 1875-85.

Kucera, Louis B. (1888-1957): ord. June 8, 1915; bp. Lincoln, 1930-57.

L

Lamb, Hugh (1890-1959): ord. May 29, 1915; aux. Philadelphia (Helos), 1936-51; first bp. Greensburg, 1951-59.

Lamy, Jean B.: See Index.

Lane, Loras (1910-68): ord. Mar. 19, 1937; aux. Dubuque (Bencenna), 1951-56; bp. Rockford, 1956-68.

Lane, Raymond A., M.M. (1894-1974): ord. Feb. 8, 1920; v.a. Fushun, Manchukuo (Hypaepa), 1940-46; sup. gen. Maryknoll, 1946-56.

Lardone, Francesco (1887-1980): b. Italy; ord. June 29, 1910; U.S. citizen 1937; nuncio to various countries (tit. abp. Rhizaeum), 1949-66 (res.).

Laval, John M. (1854-1937): b. France; ord. Nov. 10, 1877; aux. New Orleans (Hierocaesarea), 1911-37.

Lavialle, Peter J. (1819-67): b. France; ord. Feb. 12, 1844; bp. Louisville, 1865-67.

Lawler, John J. (1862-1948): ord. Dec. 19, 1885; aux. St. Paul (Hermopolis), 1910-16; bp. Lead (now Rapid City), 1916-48.

Le Blond, Charles H. (1883-1958): ord. June 29, 1909; bp. St. Joseph, 1933-56 (res.).

Ledvina, Emmanuel (1868-1952): ord. Mar. 18, 1893; bp. Corpus Christi, 1921-49 (res.).

Leech, George L. (1890-1985): ord. May 29, 1920; aux. Harrisburg (Mela), Oct.-Dec., 1935; bp. Harrisburg, 1935-71 (res.).

Lefevere, Peter P. (1804-69): b. Belgium; ord. Nov. 30, 1831; coad. bp. and admin. Detroit (Zela), 1841-69.

Leibold, Paul F. (1914-72): ord. May 18, 1940; aux. Cincinnati (Trebenna), 1958-66; bp. Evansville, 1966-69; abp. Cincinnati, 1969-72.

Leipzig, Francis P. (1895-1981): ord. Apr. 17, 1920; bp. Baker, 1950-71 (res.).

Lemay, Leo, S.M. (1909-83): ord. Apr. 15, 1933; v.a. North Solomon Is. (Agbia), 1961-66; first bp. Bougainville, 1966-74 (res.).

Lenihan (brothers): **Mathias C.** (1854-1943): ord. Dec. 20, 1879; first bp. Great Falls, 1904-30 (res.). **Thomas M.** (1844-1901): b. Ireland; ord. Nov. 19, 1868; bp. Cheyenne, 1897-1901.

Leray, Francis X. (1825-87): b. France; ord. Mar. 19, 1852; bp. Natchitoches (now Alexandria, La.), 1877-79; coad. bp. New Orleans and admin. of Natchitoches (Jonopolis), 1879-83; abp. New Orleans, 1883-87.

Leven, Stephen A. (1905-83): ord. June 10, 1928; aux. San Antonio (Bure), 1956-69; bp. San Angelo, 1969-79 (res.).

Ley, Felix, O.F.M. Cap. (1909-72): ord. June 14, 1936; ap. admin. Ryukyu Is. (Caporilla), 1968-72.

Lillis, Thomas F. (1861-1938): ord. Aug. 15, 1885; bp. Leavenworth (now Kansas City, Kans.), 1904-10; coad. bp. Kansas City, Mo. (Cibyra), 1910-13; bp. Kansas City, Mo., 1913-38.

Lootens, Louis (1827-98): b. Belgium; ord. June 14, 1851; v.a. Idaho and Montana (Castabala), 1868-75 (res.).

Loras, Mathias (1792-1858): b. France; ord. Nov. 12, 1815; first bp. Dubuque, 1837-58.

Loughlin, John (1817-91): b. Ireland; ord. Oct. 18, 1840; first bp. Brooklyn, 1853-91.

Lowney, Denis M. (1863-1918): b. Ireland; ord. Dec. 17, 1887; aux. Providence (Hadrianopolis), 1917-18.

Lucey, Robert E. (1891-1977): ord. May 14, 1916; bp. Amarillo, 1934-41; abp. San Antonio, 1941-69 (res.).

Ludden, Patrick A. (1838-1912): b. Ireland; ord. May 21, 1865; first bp. Syracuse, 1887-1912.

Luers, John (1819-71): b. Germany; ord. Nov. 11, 1846; first bp. Fort Wayne, 1858-71.

Lyke, James P., O.F.M. (1939-92): ord. June 24, 1966; aux. Cleveland (Furnes Maior) 1979-90; ap. admin. Atlanta, 1990-91; abp. Atlanta, 1991-92.

Lynch, Joseph P. (1872-1954): ord. June 9, 1900; bp. Dallas, 1911-54.

Lynch, Patrick N. (1817-82): b. Ireland; ord. Apr. 5, 1840; bp. Charleston, 1858-82.

Lyons, Thomas W. (1923-88): ord. May 22, 1948; aux. bp. Washington, D.C. (Mortlach), 1974-88.

M

McAuliffe, Maurice F. (1875-1944): ord. July 29, 1900; aux. Hartford (Dercos), 1923-34; bp. Hartford, 1934-44.

McCafferty, John E. (1920-80): ord. Mar. 17, 1945; aux. Rochester (Tanudaia), 1968-80.

McCarthy, Joseph E. (1876-1955): ord. July 4, 1903; bp. Portland, Me., 1932-55.

McCarthy, Justin J. (1900-59): ord. Apr. 16, 1927; aux. Newark (Doberus), 1954-57; bp. Camden, 1957-59.

McCarty, William T., C.SS.R. (1889-1972): ord. June 10, 1915; military delegate (Anea), 1943-47; coad. bp. Rapid City, 1947-48; bp. Rapid City, 1948-69 (res.).

McCauley, Vincent J., C.S.C. (1906-82): ord. June 24, 1943; first bp. Fort Portal, Uganda, 1961-72 (res.).

McCloskey, James P. (1870-1945): ord. Dec. 17, 1898; bp. Zamboanga, P.I., 1917-20; bp. Jaro, P.I., 1920-45.

McCloskey, John (1810-85): ord. Jan. 12, 1834; coad. bp. New York (Axiere), 1843-47; first bp. Albany, 1847-64; abp. New York, 1864-85; first U.S. cardinal 1875.

McCloskey, William G. (1823-1909): ord. Oct. 6, 1852; bp. Louisville, 1868-1909.

McCormick, Patrick J. (1880-1953): ord. July 6, 1904; aux. Washington (Atenia), 1950-53.

McCort, John J. (1860-1936): ord. Oct. 14, 1883; aux. Philadelphia (Azotus), 1912-20; bp. Altoona, 1920-36.

McDevitt, Gerald V. (1917-80): ord. May 30, 1942; aux. Philadelphia (Tigias), 1962-80.

McDevitt, Philip R. (1858-1935): ord. July 14, 1885; bp. Harrisburg, 1916-35.

McDonald, William J. (1904-89): b. Ireland; ord. June 10, 1928; aux. Washington (Aquae Regiae), 1964-67; aux. San Francisco, 1967-79 (res.).

McDonnell, Charles E. (1854-1921): ord. May 19, 1878; bp. Brooklyn, 1892-1921.

McDonnell, Thomas J. (1894-1961): ord. Sept. 20, 1919; aux. New York (Sela), 1947-51; coad. bp. Wheeling, 1951-61.

McEleney, John J., S.J. (1895-1986): ord. June 18, 1930; v.a. Jamaica (Zeugma), 1950-56; bp. Kingston, 1956-67; abp. Kingston 1967-70 (res.)

McEntegart, Bryan (1893-1968): ord. Sept. 8, 1917; bp. Ogdensburg, 1943-53; rector Catholic University (Aradi), 1953-57; bp. Brooklyn, 1957-68.

McFadden, James A. (1880-1952): ord. June 17, 1905; aux. Cleveland (Bida), 1932-43; first bp. Youngstown, 1943-52.

MacFarland, Francis P. (1819-74): ord. May 1, 1845; bp. Hartford, 1858-74.

McFaul, James A. (1850-1917): b. Ireland; ord. May 26, 1877; bp. Trenton, 1894-1917.

McGavick, Alexander J. (1863-1948): ord. June 11, 1887; aux. Chicago (Marcopolis), 1899-1921; bp. La Crosse, 1921-48.

McGeough, Joseph F. (1903-70): ord. Dec. 20, 1930; internuncio Ethiopia, 1957-60; apostolic delegate (Hemesa) S. Africa, 1960-67; nuncio Ireland, 1967-69.

McGill, John (1809-72): ord. June 13, 1835; bp. Richmond, 1850-72.

MacGinley, John B. (1871-1969): b. Ireland; ord. June 8, 1895; bp. Nueva Caceres, 1910-24; first bp. Monterey-Fresno, 1924-32 (res.).

McGolrick, James (1841-1918): b. Ireland; ord. June 11, 1867; first bp. Duluth, 1889-1918.

McGovern, Patrick A. (1872-1951): ord. Aug. 18, 1895; bp. Cheyenne, 1912-51.

McGovern, Thomas (1832-98): b. Ireland; ord. Dec. 27, 1861; bp. Harrisburg, 1888-98.

McGrath, Joseph F. (1871-1950): b. Ireland; ord. Dec. 21, 1895; bp. Baker City (now Baker), 1919-50.

McGucken, Joseph T. (1902-84): ord. Jan. 15, 1928; aux. Los Angeles (Sanavus), 1940-55; coad. bp. Sacramento, 1957-62; abp. San Francisco, 1962-77 (res.).

McGuinness, Eugene (1889-1957): ord. May 22, 1915; bp. Raleigh, 1937-44; coad. bp. Oklahoma City and Tulsa (Ilium), 1944-48; bp. Oklahoma City and Tulsa, 1948-57.

McGurkin, Edward A., M.M. (1905-83): ord. Sept. 14, 1930; bp. Shinyanga, Tanzania, 1956-75 (res.).

McIntyre, James F. (1886-1979): ord. May 21, 1921; aux. New York (Cirene), 1941-46; coad. abp. New York (Palto), 1946-48; abp. Los Angeles, 1948-70 (res.); cardinal, 1953.

MacKenzie, Eric F. (1893-1969): ord. Oct. 20, 1918; aux. Boston (Alba), 1950-69.

McLaughlin, Charles B. (1913-78): ord. June 6, 1941; aux. Raleigh (Risinium), 1964-68; first bp. St. Petersburg, 1968-78.

McLaughlin, Thomas H. (1881-1947): ord. July 26, 1904; aux. Newark (Nisa), 1935-37; first bp. Paterson, 1937-47.

McMahon, John J. (1875-1932): ord. May 20, 1900; bp. Trenton, 1928-32.

McMahon, Lawrence S. (1835-93): ord. Mar. 24, 1860; bp. Hartford, 1879-93.

McManaman, Edward P. (1900-64): ord. Mar. 12, 1927; aux. Erie (Floriana), 1948-64.

McManus, James E., C.SS.R. (1900-76): ord. June 19, 1927; bp. Ponce, P.R., 1947-63; aux. New York (Banda), 1963-70 (res.).

McMullen, John (1832-83): b. Ireland; ord. June 20, 1858; first bp. Davenport, 1881-83.

McNamara, John M. (1878-1960): ord. June 21, 1902; aux. Baltimore (Eumenia), 1928-47; aux. Washington, 1947-60.

McNamara, Martin D. (1898-1966): ord. Dec. 23, 1922; first bp. Joliet, 1949-66.

McNeirny, Francis (1828-94): ord. Aug. 17, 18554; coad. bp. Albany (Rhesaina), 1872-77; bp. Albany, 1877-94.

McNicholas, John T., O.P. (1877-1950): b. Ireland; ord. Oct. 10, 1901; bp. Duluth, 1918-25; abp. Cincinnati, 1925-50.

McNicholas, Joseph A. (1923-83): ord. June 7, 1949; aux. St. Louis (Scala), 1969-75; bp. Springfield, Ill., 1975-83.

McNulty, James A. (1900-72): ord. July 12, 1925; aux. Newark (Methone), 1947-53; bp. Paterson, 1953-63; bp. Buffalo, 1963-72.

McQuaid, Bernard J. (1823-1909): ord. Jan. 16, 1848; first bp. Rochester, 1868-1909.

McShea, Joseph M. (1907-91): ord. Dec. 6, 1931; aux. Philadelphia (Mina), 1952-61; first bp. Allentown, 1961-83 (res.).

McSorley, Francis J., O.M.I. (1913-71): ord. May 30, 1939; v.a. Jolo, P.I. (Sozusa), 1958-71.

McVinney, Russell J. (1898-1971): ord. July 13, 1924; bp. Providence, 1948-71.

Macheboeuf, Joseph P. (1812-89): b. France; ord. Dec. 17, 1836; v.a. Colorado and Utah (Epiphania), 1868-87; first bp. Denver, 1887-89.

Maes, Camillus P. (1846-1915): b. Belgium; ord. Dec. 19, 1868; bp. Covington, 1885-1915.

Maginn, Edward J. (1897-1984): b. Scotland; ord. June 10, 1922; aux. Albany (Curium), 1957-72 (res.).

Magner, Francis (1887-1947): ord. May 17, 1913; bp. Marquette, 1941-47.

Maguire, John J. (1904-89): ord. Dec. 22, 1928; aux. New York (Antiphrae), 1959-65; coad. abp. New York (Tabalta), 1965-80 (res.).

Maher, Leo H. (1915-91): ord. Dec. 18, 1943; first bp. Santa Rosa, 1962-69; bp. San Diego, 1969-90 (res.).

Mahoney, Bernard (1875-1939): ord. Feb. 27, 1904; bp. Sioux Falls, 1922-39.

Maloney, Thomas F. (1903-62): ord. July 13, 1930; aux. Providence (Andropolis), 1960-62.

Manning, Timothy (1909-89): b. Ireland; ord. June 16, 1934 (Los Angeles archd.); American citizen, 1944; aux. Los Angeles (Lesvi), 1946-67; first bp. Fresno, 1967-69; coad. abp. Los Angeles (Capri), 1969-70; abp. Los Angeles, 1970-85 (res.); cardinal 1973.

Manogue, Patrick: See Index.

Manucy, Dominic (1823-85): ord. Aug. 15, 1850; v.a. Brownsville (Dulma), 1874-84; bp. Mobile, Mar.-Sept., 1884 (res.); reappointed v.a. Brownsville (Maronea) (now diocese of Corpus Christi), 1884-85.

Mardaga, Thomas J. (1913-84): ord. May 14, 1940; aux. Baltimore (Mutugenna), 1967-68; bp. Wilmington, 1968-84.

Marechal, Ambrose, S.S. (1766-1828): b. France; ord. June 2, 1792; abp. Baltimore, 1817-28.

Markham, Thomas F. (1891-1952): ord. June 2, 1917; aux. Boston (Acalissus), 1950-52.

Marling, Joseph M., C.Pp.S. (1904-79): ord. Feb. 21, 1929; aux. Kansas City, Mo. (Thasus), 1947-56; first bp. Jefferson City, 1956-69 (res.).

Martin, Augustus M. (1803-75): b. France; ord. May 31, 1828; first bp. Natchitoches (now Alexandria), 1853-75.

Marty, Martin, O.S.B. (1834-96): b. Switzerland; ord. Sept. 14, 1856; v.a. Dakota (Tiberias), 1880-89; first bp. Sioux Falls, 1889-95; bp. St. Cloud, 1895-96.

Marx, Adolph (1915-65): b. Germany; ord. May 2, 1940; aux. Corpus Christi (Citrus), 1956-65; first bp. Brownsville, 1965.

Matz, Nicholas C. (1850-1917): b. France; ord. May 31, 1874; coad. bp. Denver (Telmissus), 1887-89; bp. Denver, 1889-1917.

Mazzarella, Bernardino N., O.F.M. (1904-79): ord. June 5, 1931; prelate Olancho, Honduras (Hadrianopolis in Pisidia), 1957-63; first bp. Comayagua, Honduras, 1963-79.

Medeiros, Humberto S. (1915-83): b. Azores; U.S. citizen, 1940; ord. June 15, 1946; bp. Brownsville, 1966-70; abp. Boston, 1970-83; cardinal 1973.

Meerschaert, Theophile (1847-1924): b. Belgium; ord. Dec. 23, 1871; v.a. Oklahoma and Indian Territory (Sidyma), 1891-1905; first bp. Oklahoma, 1905-24.

Melcher, Joseph (1806-73): b. Austria; ord. Mar. 27, 1830; first bp. Green Bay, 1868-73.

Messmer, Sebastian (1847-1930): b. Switzerland; ord. July 23, 1871; bp. Green Bay, 1892-1903; abp. Milwaukee, 1903-30.

Metzger, Sidney M. (1902-86): ord. Apr. 3, 1926; aux. Santa Fe (Birtha), 1940-41; coad. bp. El Paso, 1941-42; bp. El Paso, 1942-78 (res.).

Meyer, Albert (1903-65): ord. July 11, 1926; bp. Superior, 1946-53; abp. Milwaukee, 1953-58; abp. Chicago, 1958-65; cardinal, 1959.

Michaud, John S. (1843-1908): ord. June 7, 1873; coad. bp. Burlington (Modra), 1892-99; bp. Burlington, 1899-1908.

Miege, John B., S.J. (1815-84): b. France; ord. Sept. 12, 1844; v.a. Kansas and Indian Territory (now Kansas City) (Messene), 1851-74 (res.).

Mihalik, Emil J. (1920-84): ord. Sept. 21, 1945; first bp. Parma (Byzantine Rite, Ruthenians), 1969-84.

Miles, Richard P., O.P. (1791-1860): ord. Sept. 21, 1816; first bp. Nashville, 1838-60.

Minihan, Jeremiah F. (1903-73): ord. Dec. 21, 1929; aux. Boston (Paphus), 1954-73.

Misner, Paul B., C.M. (1891-1938): ord. Feb. 23, 1919; v.a. Yukiang, China (Myrica), 1935-38.

Mitty, John J. (1884-1961): ord. Dec. 22, 1906; bp. Salt Lake, 1926-32; coad. abp. San Francisco (Aegina), 1932-35; abp. San Francisco, 1935-61.

Moeller, Henry (1849-1925): ord. June 10, 1876; bp. Columbus, 1900-03; coad. abp. Cincinnati (Areopolis), 1903-04; abp. Cincinnati, 1904-25.

Molloy, Thomas E. (1884-1956): ord. Sept. 19, 1908; aux. Brooklyn (Lorea), 1920-21; bp. Brooklyn, 1921-56.

Monaghan, Francis J. (1890-1942): ord. May 29, 1915; coad. bp. Ogdensburg (Mela), 1936-39; bp. Ogdensburg, 1939-42.

Monaghan, John J. (1856-1935): ord. Dec. 18, 1880; bp. Wilmington, 1897-1925 (res.).

Montgomery, George T. (1847-1907): ord. Dec. 20, 1879; coad. bp. Monterey-Los Angeles (Thmuis), 1894-96; bp. Monterey-Los Angeles (now Los Angeles), 1896-1903; coad. abp. San Francisco (Auxum), 1903-07.

Mooney, Edward (1882-1958): ord. Apr. 10, 1909; ap. del. India (Irenopolis), 1926-31; ap. del. Japan, 1931-33; bp. Rochester, 1933-37; first abp. Detroit, 1937-58; cardinal, 1946.

Moore, John (1835-1901): b. Ireland; ord. Apr. 9, 1860; bp. St. Augustine, 1877-1901.

Mora, Francis (1827-1905); b. Spain; ord. Mar. 19, 1856; coad. bp. Monterey-Los Angeles (Mosynopolis), 1873-78; bp. Monterey-Los Angeles (now Los Angeles), 1878-96 (res.).

Morkovsky, John L. (1909-90): ord. Dec. 5, 1933; aux. Amarillo (Hieron), 1956-58; bp. Amarillo, 1958-63; coad. bp. Galveston-Houston (Tigava), 1963-75; bp. Galveston, 1975-84 (res.).

Morris, John (1866-1946): ord. June 11, 1892; coad. bp. Little Rock (Acmonia), 1906-07; bp. Little Rock, 1907-46.

Morrow, Louis La Ravoire, S.D.B. (1892-1987): ord. May 21, 1921; bp. Krishnagar, India, 1939-69 (res.).

Mrak, Ignatius (1810-1901): b. Austria; ord. July 31, 1837; bp. Sault Ste. Marie and Marquette (now Marquette), 1869-78 (res.).

Mueller, Joseph M. (1894-1981): ord. June 14, 1919; coad. bp. Sioux City (Sinda), 1947-48; bp. Sioux City, 1948-70 (res.).

Muench, Aloysius (1889-1962): ord. June 8, 1913; bp. Fargo, 1935-59 (res.); apostolic visitator to Germany, 1946; nuncio to Germany 1951-59; cardinal 1959.

Mugavero, Francis J. (1914-91): ord. May 18, 1940; bp. Brooklyn, 1968-90 (res.).

Muldoon, Peter J. (1862-1927): ord. Dec. 18, 1886; aux. Chicago (Tamasus), 1901-08; first bp. Rockford, 1908-27.

Mullen, Tobias (1818-1900): b. Ireland; ord. Sept. 1, 1844; bp. Erie, 1868-99 (res.).

Mulloy, William T. (1892-1959): ord. June 7, 1916; bp. Covington, 1945-59.

Mulrooney, Charles R. (1906-89): ord. June 10, 1930; aux. Brooklyn (Valentiniana), 1959-81 (res.).

Mundelein, George (1872-1939): ord. June 8, 1895; aux. Brooklyn (Loryma), 1909-15; abp. Chicago, 1915-39; cardinal, 1924.

Murphy, Joseph A., S.J. (1857-1939): b. Ireland; ord. Aug. 26, 1888; v.a. Belize, Br. Honduras (Birtha), 1923-39.

Murphy, T.(Thomas) Austin (1911-91): ord. June 10, 1937; aux. Baltimore (Appiaria), 1962-84 (res.).

Murphy, William F. (1885-1950): ord. June 13, 1908; first bp. Saginaw, 1938-50.

Murray, John G. (1877-1956): ord. Apr. 14, 1900; aux. Hartford (Flavias), 1920-25; bp. Portland, 1925-31; abp. St. Paul, 1931-56.

Mussio, John K. (1902-78): ord. Aug. 15, 1935; bp. Steubenville, 1945-77 (res.).

N

Najmy, Justin, O.S.B.M. (1898-1968): b. Syria; ord. Dec. 25, 1926; ap. ex. Melkites (Augustopolis in Phrygia), 1966-68.

Navagh, James J. (1901-65): ord. Dec. 21, 1929; aux. Raleigh (Ombi), 1952-57; bp. Ogdensburg, 1957-63; bp. Paterson, 1963-65.

Neale, Leonard (1746-1817): ord. June 5, 1773; coad. bp. Baltimore (Gortyna), 1800-15; abp. Baltimore, 1815-17.

Nelson, Knute Ansgar, O.S.B. (1906-90): b. Denmark; ord. May 22, 1937; U.S. citizen, 1941; coad. bp. Stockholm, Sweden (Bilta), 1947-57; bp. Stockholm, 1957-62 (res.)

Neraz, John C. (1828-94): b. France; ord. Mar. 19, 1853; bp. San Antonio, 1881-1894.

Neumann, John, St.: See Index.

Newell, Hubert M. (1904-87): ord. June 15, 1930; coad. bp. Cheyenne (Zapara), 1947-51; bp. Cheyenne, 1951-78 (res.).

Newman, Thomas A., M.S. (1903-78): ord. June 29, 1929; first bp. Prome, Burma, 1961-75 (res.).

Niedhammer, Matthew A., O.F.M. Cap. (1901-70): ord. June 8, 1927; v.a. Bluefields, Nicaragua (Caloe), 1943-70.

Nilan, John J. (1855-1934): ord. Dec. 2, 1878; bp. Hartford, 1910-34.

Noa, Thomas L. (1892-1977): ord. Dec. 23, 1916; coad. bp. Sioux City (Salona), 1946-47; bp. Marquette, 1947-68 (res.).

Nold, Wendelin J. (1900-81): ord. Apr. 11, 1925; coad. bp. Galveston (Sasima), 1948-50; bp. Galveston-Houston, 1950-75 (res.).

Noll, John F. (1875-1956): ord. June 4, 1898; bp. Fort Wayne, 1925-56 (pers. tit. abp., 1953).

Northrop, Henry P. (1842-1916): ord. June 25, 1865; v.a. North Carolina (Rosalia), 1881-83; bp. Charleston, 1883-1916.

Noser, Adolph, S.V.D. (1900-81): ord. Sept. 27, 1925; v.a. Accra, British W. Africa (now Ghana) (Capitolias), 1947-50; bp. Accra, 1950-53; v.a. Alexishafen, New Guinea (Hierpiniana), 1953-66; abp. Madang, Papua New Guinea, 1966-75 (res.).

Nussbaum, Paul J., C.P. (1870-1935): ord. May 20, 1894; first bp. Corpus Christi, 1913-20 (res.); bp. Sault Ste. Marie and Marquette (now Marquette), 1922-35.

O

O'Boyle, Patrick A. (1896-1987): ord. May 21, 1921; abp. Washington, D.C., 1948-73 (res.); cardinal 1967.

O'Brien, Henry J. (1896-1976): ord. July 8, 1923; aux. Hartford (Sita), 1940-45; bp. Hartford, 1945-53, and first abp. Hartford, 1953-68 (res.).

O'Brien, William D. (1878-1962): ord. July 11, 1903; aux. Chicago (Calynda), 1934-62.

O'Connell, Denis J. (1849-1927): b. Ireland; ord. May 26, 1877; aux. San Francisco (Sebaste), 1908-12; bp. Richmond, 1912-26 (res.).

O'Connell, Eugene (1815-91): b. Ireland; ord. May 21, 1842; v.a. Marysville (Flaviopolis), 1861-68; first bp. Grass Valley, 1868-84 (res.).

O'Connell, William H. (1859-1944): ord. June 7, 1884; bp. Portland, 1901-06; coad. bp. Boston (Con-

stantia), 1906-07; abp. Boston, 1907-44; cardinal, 1911.

O'Connor (brothers), James (1823-90): b. Ireland; ord. Mar. 25, 1848; v.a. Nebraska (Dibon), 1876-85; first bp. Omaha, 1885-90. **Michael, S.J.** (1810-72): b. Ireland; ord. June 1, 1833; first bp. Pittsburgh, 1843-53; first bp. Erie, 1853-54; bp. Pittsburgh, 1854-60 (resigned, joined Jesuits).

O'Connor, John J. (1855-1927): ord. Dec. 22, 1877; bp. Newark, 1901-27.

O'Connor, Martin J. (1900-86): ord. Mar. 15, 1924; aux. Scranton (Thespia), 1943-46; rector North American College, Rome, 1946-64; abp., 1959 (Laodicea); nuncio to Malta, 1965-69; pres. Pontifical Commission for Social Communications, 1964-71.

O'Connor, William A. (1903-83): ord. Sept. 24, 1927; bp. Springfield, Ill., 1949-75 (res.).

O'Connor, William P. (1886-1973): ord. Mar. 10, 1912; bp. Superior, 1942-46; first bp. Madison, 1946-67 (res.).

O'Dea, Edward J. (1856-1932): ord. Dec. 23, 1882; bp. Nesqually (now Seattle — title changed in 1907), 1896-1932.

Odin, John M., C.M. (1800-70): b. France; ord. May 4, 1823; v.a. Texas (Claudiopolis), 1842-47; first bp. Galveston, 1847-61; abp. New Orleans, 1861-70.

O'Donaghue, Denis (1848-1925): ord. Sept. 6, 1874; aux. Indianapolis (Pomaria), 1900-10; bp. Louisville, 1910-24 (res.).

O'Donnell, Cletus F. (1917-92): ord. May 3, 1941; aux. Chicago (Abritto), 1960-67; bp. Madison, 1967-92 (res.).

O'Dowd, James T. (1907-50): ord. June 4, 1932; aux. San Francisco (Cea), 1948-50.

O'Farrell, Michael J. (1832-94): b. Ireland; ord. Aug. 18, 1855; first bp. Trenton, 1881-94.

O'Flanagan, Dermot (1901-73): b. Ireland; ord. Aug. 27, 1929; first bp. Juneau, 1951-68 (res.).

O'Gara, Cuthbert, C.P. (1886-1968): b. Canada; ord. May 26, 1915; v.a. Yuanling, China (Elis), 1934-46; first bp. Yuanling, 1946-68 (imprisoned, 1951, and then expelled, 1953, by Chinese Communists).

O'Gorman, James, O.C.S.O. (1804-74): b. Ireland; ord. Dec. 23, 1843; v.a. Nebraska (now Omaha) (Raphanea), 1859-74.

O'Gorman, Thomas (1843-1921): ord. Nov. 5, 1865; bp. Sioux Falls, 1896-1921.

O'Hara, Edwin V. (1881-1956): ord. June 9, 1905; bp. Great Falls, 1930-39; bp. Kansas City, Mo., 1939-56 (title changed to Kansas City-St. Joseph, 1956).

O'Hara, Gerald P. (1895-1963): ord. Apr. 3, 1920; aux. Philadelphia (Heliopolis), 1929-35; bp. Savannah (title changed to Savannah-Atlanta in 1937), 1935-59 (res.); regent of Romania nunciature, 1946-50 (expelled); nuncio to Ireland, 1951-54; ap. del. to Great Britain, 1954-63; tit. abp. Pessinus, 1959-63.

O'Hara, John F., C.S.C. (1888-1960): ord. Sept. 9, 1916; delegate of U.S. military vicar (Mylasa), 1940-45; bp. Buffalo, 1945-51; abp. Philadelphia, 1951-60; cardinal, 1958.

O'Hara, William (1816-99): b. Ireland; ord. Dec. 21, 1842; first bp. Scranton, 1868-99.

O'Hare, William F., S.J. (1870-1926): ord. June 25, 1903; v.a. Jamaica (Maximianopolis), 1920-26.

O'Hern, John F. (1874-1933): ord. Feb. 17, 1901; bp. Rochester, 1929-33.

O'Leary, Thomas (1875-1949): ord. Dec. 18, 1897; bp. Springfield, Mass., 1921-49.

Olwell, Quentin, C.P. (1898-1972): ord. Feb. 4, 1923; prelate Marbel, P.I. (Thabraca), 1961-69 (res.).

O'Meara, Edward T. (1921-92): ord. Dec. 21, 1946; aux. St. Louis (Thisiduo), 1972-80; abp. Indianapolis, 1980-92.

O'Regan, Anthony (1809-66): b. Ireland; ord. Nov. 29, 1834; bp. Chicago, 1854-58 (res.).

O'Reilly, Bernard (1803-56): b. Ireland; ord. Oct. 16, 1831; bp. Hartford, 1850-56.

O'Reilly, Charles J. (1860-1923): b. Canada; ord. June 29, 1890; first bp. Baker City (now Baker), 1903-18; bp. Lincoln, 1918-23.

O'Reilly, James (1855-1934): b. Ireland; ord. June 24, 1880; bp. Fargo, 1910-34.

O'Reilly, Patrick T. (1833-92): b. Ireland; ord. Aug. 15, 1857; first bp. Springfield, Mass., 1870-92.

O'Reilly, Peter J. (1850-1924): b. Ireland; ord. June 24, 1877; aux. Peoria (Lebedus), 1900-24.

O'Reilly, Thomas C. (1873-1938): ord. June 4, 1898; bp. Scranton, 1928-38.

Ortynsky, Stephen, O.S.B.M. (1866-1916): b. Poland; ord. July 18, 1891; first Ukrainian Byzantine Rite bishop in U.S. (Daulia), 1907-16.

O'Shea, John A., C.M. (1887-1969): ord. May 30, 1914; v.a. Kanchow, China (Midila), 1928-46; first bp. Kanchow, 1949-69 (expelled by Chinese Communists, 1953).

O'Shea, William F., M.M. (1884-1945): ord. Dec. 5, 1917; v.a. Heijon, Japan (Naissusz), 1939-45; prisoner of Japanese 1941-42.

O'Sullivan, Jeremiah (1842-96): b. Ireland; ord. June 30, 1868; bp. Mobile, 1885-96.

Ott, Stanley J. (1927-92) ord. Dec. 8, 1951; aux. New Orleans (Nicives), 1976-83; bp. Baton Rouge, 1983-92.

Oves Fernandez, Ricardo (1928-90) b. Cuba; ord. Apr. 13, 1952; aux. Cienfuegas, Cuba (Montecorvino), 1969-70; abp. Havana, 1970-81 (res.); resided in El Paso, Tex., diocese from 1982.

P

Pardy, James V., M.M. (1898-1983): ord. Jan. 26, 1930; v.a. Cheong-Ju, Korea (Irenopolis), 1958-62; first bp. Cheong-Ju, 1962-69 (res.).

Paschang, Adolph J., M.M. (1895-1968): ord. May 21, 1921; v.a. Kong Moon, China (Sasima), 1937-46; first bp. Kong Moon, 1946-68 (expelled by Communists, 1951).

Pechillo, Jerome, T.O.R. (1919-91): ord. June 10, 1947; prelate Coronel Oviedo, Paraguay (Novasparsa), 1966-76; aux. Newark, 1976-91.

Pellicer, Anthony (1824-80): ord. Aug. 15, 1850; first bp. San Antonio, 1874-80.

Penalver y Cardenas, Luis (1749-1810): b. Cuba; ord. Apr. 4, 1772; first bp. Louisiana and the Two Floridas (now New Orleans), 1793-1801; abp. Guatemala, 1801-06 (res.).

Perche, Napoleon J. (1805-83): b. France; ord. Sept. 19, 1829; abp. New Orleans, 1870-83.

Pernicone, Joseph M. (1903-85): b. Sicily; ord.

Dec. 18, 1926; aux. New York (Hadrianapolis) 1954-78 (res.).

Perry, Harold R., S.V.D. (1916-91), ord. Jan. 6, 1944; aux. New Orleans (Mons in Mauretania), 1966-91.

Persico, Ignatius, O.F.M. Cap. (1823-95): b. Italy; ord. Jan. 24, 1846; bishop from 1854; bp. Savannah, 1870-72; cardinal, 1893.

Peschges, John H. (1881-1944): ord. Apr. 15, 1905; bp. Crookston, 1938-44.

Peterson, John B. (1871-1944): ord. Sept. 15, 1899; aux. Boston (Hippos), 1972-32: bp. Manchester, 1932-44.

Phelan, Richard (1828-1904): b. Ireland; ord. May 4, 1854; coad. bp. Pittsburgh (Cibyra), 1885-89; bp. Pittsburgh, 1889-1904.

Pinger, Henry A., O.F.M. (1897-1988): ord. June 27, 1927; v.a. Chowtsun, China (Capitolias), 1937-46; first bp. Chowtsun, 1946 (imprisoned, 1951 then released, 1956 and expelled by Chinese Communists).

Pinten, Joseph G. (1867-1945): ord. Nov. 1, 1890; bp. Superior, 1922-26; bp. Grand Rapids, 1926-40 (res.).

Pitaval, John B. (1858-1928): b. France; ord. Dec. 24, 1881; aux. Santa Fe (Sora), 1902-09; abp. Santa Fe, 1909-18 (res.).

Plagens, Joseph C. (1880-1943): b. Poland; ord. July 5, 1903; aux. Detroit (Rhodiapolis), 1924-35; bp. Sault Ste. Marie and Marquette (title changed to Marquette, 1937), 1935-40; bp. Grand Rapids, 1941-43.

Portier, Michael (1795-1859): b. France; ord. May 16, 1818; v.a. Two Floridas and Alabama (Olena), 1826-29; first bp. Mobile, 1829-59.

Prendergast, Edmond (1843-1918): b. Ireland; ord. Nov. 17, 1865; aux. Philadelphia (Scilium), 1897-1911; abp. Philadelphia, 1911-18.

Primeau, Ernest J. (1909-89): ord. Apr. 7, 1934; bp. Manchester, 1960-74 (res.); director Villa Stritch, Rome, 1974-79 (ret.).

Purcell, John B. (1800-83): b. Ireland; ord. May 20, 1826; bp., 1833-50, and first abp., 1850-83, Cincinnati.

Q

Quarter, William (1806-48): b. Ireland; ord. Sept. 19, 1829; first bp. Chicago, 1844-48.

Quigley, James E. (1855-1915): b. Canada; ord. Apr. 13, 1879; bp. Buffalo, 1897-1903; abp. Chicago, 1903-15.

Quinlan, John (1826-83): b. Ireland; ord. Aug. 30, 1852; bp. Mobile, 1859-83.

Quinn, William Charles, C.M. (1905-60): ord. Oct. 11, 1931; v.a. Yukiang, China (Halicarnassus), 1940-46; first bp. Yukiang, 1946-60 (expelled by Chinese Communists, 1951).

R

Rademacher, Joseph (1840-1900): ord. Aug. 2, 1863; bp. Nashville, 1883-93; bp. Fort Wayne, 1893-1900.

Rappe, Louis Amadeus (1801-77): b. France; ord. Mar. 14, 1829; first bp. Cleveland, 1847-70 (res.).

Rausch, James S. (1928-81): ord. June 2, 1956; aux. St. Cloud (Summa), 1973-77; bp. Phoenix, 1977-81.

Ready, Michael J. (1893-1957): ord. Sept. 14, 1918; bp. Columbus, 1944-57.

Reed, Victor J. (1905-71): ord. Dec. 21, 1929; aux. Oklahoma City and Tulsa (Limasa), 1957-58; bp. Oklahoma City and Tulsa, 1958-71.

Rehring, George J. (1890-1976): ord. Mar. 28, 1914; aux. Cincinnati (Lunda), 1937-50; bp. Toledo, 1950-67 (res.).

Reicher, Louis J. (1890-1984): ord. Dec. 6, 1918; first bp. Austin, 1948-71 (res.).

Reilly, Edmond J. (1897-1958): ord. Apr. 1, 1922; aux. Brooklyn (Nepte), 1955-58.

Reilly, Thomas F., C.SS.R. (1908-92): ord. June 10, 1933; prelate San Juan de la Maguana, Dominican Republic (Themisonium), 1956-69; first bp. San Juan de la Maguana, 1969-77 (res.).

Rese, Frederic (1791-1871): b. Germany; ord. Mar. 15, 1823; first bp. Detroit, 1833-71. Inactive from 1841 because of ill health.

Reverman, Theodore (1877-1941): ord. July 26, 1901; bp. Superior, 1926-41.

Reynolds, Ignatius A. (1798-1855): ord. Oct. 24, 1823; bp. Charleston, 1844-55.

Rhode, Paul P. (1871-1945): b. Poland; ord. June 17, 1894; aux. Chicago (Barca), 1908-15; bp. Green Bay, 1915-45.

Rice, Joseph J. (1871-1938): ord. Sept. 29, 1894; bp. Burlington, 1910-38.

Rice, William A., S.J. (1891-1946): ord. Aug. 27, 1925; v.a. Belize, Br. Honduras (Rusicade), 1939-46.

Richter, Henry J. (1838-1916): b. Germany; ord. June 10, 1865; first bp. Grand Rapids, 1883-1916.

Riley, Thomas J. (1900-1977): ord. May 20, 1927; aux. Boston (Regiae), 1956-76 (res.).

Riordan, Patrick W. (1841-1914): b. Canada; ord. June 10, 1865; coad. abp. San Francisco (Cabasa), 1883-84; abp. San Francisco, 1884-1914.

Ritter, Joseph E. (1892-1967): ord. May 30, 1917; aux. Indianapolis (Hippos), 1933-34; bp., 1934-44, and first abp. Indianapolis, 1944-46; abp. St. Louis, 1946-67; cardinal 1961.

Robinson, Pascal C., O.F.M. (1870-1948): b. Ireland; ord. Dec. 21, 1901; ap. visitor to Palestine, Egypt, Syria and Cyprus (Tyana), 1927-29; ap. nuncio to Ireland, 1929-48.

Rohlman, Henry P. (1876-1957): b. Germany; ord. Dec. 21, 1901; bp. Davenport, 1927-44; coad. abp. Dubuque (Macra), 1944-46; abp. Dubuque, 1946-54 (res.).

Rooker, Fraderick Z. (1861-1907): ord. July 25, 1888; bp. Jaro, P.I., 1903-07.

Ropert, Gulstan F., SS.CC. (1839-1903): b. France; ord. May 26, 1866; v.a. Sandwich (now Hawaiian) Is. (Panopolis), 1892-1903.

Rosati, Joseph, C.M.: See Index.

Rosecrans, Sylvester (1827-78): ord. June 5, 1853; aux. Cincinnati (Pompeiopolis), 1862-68; first bp. Columbus, 1868-78.

Rouxel, Gustave A. (1840-1908): b. France, ord. Nov. 4, 1863; aux. New Orleans (Curium), 1899-1908.

Rummel, Joseph (1876-1964): b. Germany; ord. May 24, 1902; bp. Omaha, 1928-35; abp. New Orleans, 1935-64.

Ruocco, Joseph J. (1922-80): ord. May 6, 1948; aux. Boston (Polignano), 1975-80.

Russell, John J. (1897-1993): ord. July 8, 1923;

bp. Charleston, 1950-58; bp. Richmond, 1958-73 (res.).

Russell, William T. (1863-1927): ord. June 21, 1889; bp. Charleston, 1917-27.

Ryan, Edward F. (1879-1956): ord. Aug. 10, 1905; bp. Burlington, 1945-56.

Ryan, Gerald J. (1923-85): ord. June 3, 1950; aux. Rockville Centre (Munatiana), 1977-85.

Ryan, James (1848-1923): b. Ireland; ord. Dec. 24, 1871; bp. Alton (now Springfield), Ill., 1888-1923.

Ryan, James H. (1886-1947): ord. June 5, 1909; rector Catholic University, 1928-35; tit. bp. Modra, 1933-35; bp., 1935-45, and first abp. Omaha, 1945-47.

Ryan, Patrick J. (1831-1911): b. Ireland; ord. Sept. 8, 1853; coad. bp. St. Louis (Tricomia), 1872-84; abp. Philadelphia, 1884-1911.

Ryan, Stephen, C.M. (1826-96): b. Canada; ord. June 24, 1849; bp. Buffalo, 1868-96.

Ryan, Vincent J. (1884-1951): ord. June 7, 1912; bp. Bismarck, 1940-41.

S

Salpointe, John B. (1825-98): b. France; ord. Dec. 20, 1851; v.a. Arizona (Dorylaeum), 1869-84; coad. abp. Santa Fe (Anazarbus), 1884-85; abp. Santa Fe, 1885-94 (res.).

Scanlan, Lawrence (1843-1915): b. Ireland; ord. June 28, 1868; v.a. Utah (Laranda), 1887-91; bp. Salt Lake (now Salt Lake City), 1891-1915.

Scannell, Richard (1845-1916): b. Ireland; ord. Feb. 26, 1871; first bp. Concordia (now Salina), 1887-91; bp. Omaha, 1891-1916.

Scheerer, Louis A., O.P. (1909-66): ord. June 13, 1935; bp. Multan, Pakistan, 1960-66.

Schenk, Francis J. (1901-69): ord. June 13, 1926; bp. Crookston, 1945-60; bp. Duluth, 1960-69.

Scher, Philip G. (1880-1953): ord. June 6, 1904; bp. Monterey-Fresno, 1933-53.

Schexnayder, Maurice (1895-1981): ord. Apr. 11, 1925; aux. Lafayette (Tuscamia), 1951-56; bp. Lafayette, La., 1956-72 (res.).

Schierhoff, Andrew B. (1922-87): ord. Apr. 14, 1948; aux. La Paz, Bolivia (Gerenza), 1969-82; v.a. Pando, Bolivia, 1982-87.

Schinner, Augustine (1863-1937): ord. Mar. 7, 1886; first bp. Superior, 1905-13; first bp. Spokane, 1914-25 (res.).

Schlarman, Joseph H. (1879-1951): ord. June 29, 1904; bp. Peoria, 1930-51.

Schmidt, Matthias W., O.S.B. (1931-92): ord. May 30, 1957; aux. Jatai, Brazil (Mutugenna), 1972-76; bp. Ruy Barbosa, Brazil, 1976-92.

Schmitt, Adolph G., C.M.M. (1905-76): b. Bavaria; U.S. citizen 1945; v.a. Bulawayo (Nasai), Rhodesia (now Zimbabwe), 1951-55; first bp. Bulawayo, 1955-74 (res.). Murdered by terrorists.

Schmondiuk, Joseph (1912-1978): ord. Mar. 29, 1936; aux. Philadelphia exarchate (Zeugma in Syria), 1956-61; eparch Stamford, 1961-77; abp. Philadelphia, 1977-78.

Schott, Lawrence F. (1907-63): ord. July 15, 1935; aux. Harrisburg (Eluza), 1956-63.

Schrembs, Joseph (1866-1945): b. Germany; ord. June 29, 1889; aux. Grand Rapids (Sophene), 1911; first bp. Toledo, 1911-21; bp. Cleveland, 1921-45.

Schuck, James A., O.F.M. (1913-93): ord. June 11, 1940; prelate Cristalandia, Brazil (Avissa, 1959-78), 1959-88 (res.).

Schuler, Anthony J., S.J. (1869-1944): ord. June 27, 1901; first bp. El Paso, 1915-42 (res.).

Schulte, Paul (1890-1984): ord. June 11, 1915; bp. Leavenworth, 1937-46; abp. Indianapolis, 1946-70 (res.).

Schwebach, James (1847-1921): b. Luxembourg; ord. June 16, 1870; bp. La Crosse, 1892-1921.

Schwertner, August J. (1870-1939): ord. June 12, 1897; bp. Wichita, 1921-39.

Scully, William (1894-1969): ord. Sept. 20, 1919; coad. bp. Albany (Pharsalus), 1945-54; bp. Albany, 1954-69.

Sebastian, Jerome D. (1895-1960): ord. May 25, 1922; aux. Baltimore (Baris in Hellesponto), 1954-60.

Seghers, Charles J.: See Index.

Seidenbusch, Rupert, O.S.B. (1830-95): b. Germany; ord. June 22, 1853; v.a. Northern Minnesota (Halia), 1875-88 (res.).

Senyshyn, Ambrose, O.S.B.M. (1903-76): b. Galicia; ord. Aug. 23, 1931; aux. Ukrainian Catholic Diocese of U.S. (Maina), 1942-56; first bp. Stamford (Byzantine Rite), 1958-61; abp. Philadelphia (Byzantine Rite), 1961-76.

Seton, Robert J. (1839-1927): b. Italy, ord. Apr. 15, 1865; tit. abp. Heliopolis, 1903-27. Grandson of St. Elizabeth Seton.

Shahan, Thomas J. (1857-1932): ord. June 3, 1882; rector, Catholic University of America, 1909-27; tit. bp. Germanicopolis, 1914-32.

Shanahan (brothers): Jeremiah F. (1834-86): ord. July 3, 1859; first bp. Harrisburg, 1868-86. **John W.** (1846-1916): ord. Jan. 2, 1869; bp. Harrisburg, 1899-1916.

Shanley, John (1852-1909): ord. May 30, 1874; first bp. Jamestown (see transferred to Fargo in 1897), 1889-1909.

Shanley, Patrick H., O.C.D. (1896-1970): b. Ireland; ord. Dec. 21, 1930; U.S. citizen; prelate Infanta, P.I. (Sophene), 1953-60 (res.).

Shaughnessy, Gerald, S.M. (1887-1950): ord. June 20, 1920; bp. Seattle, 1933-50.

Shaw, John W. (1861-1934): ord. May 26, 1888; coad. bp. San Antonio (Castabala), 1910-11; bp. San Antonio, 1911-18; abp. New Orleans, 1918-34.

Sheehan, Edward T., C.M. (1888-1933): ord. June 7, 1916, v.a. Yukiang, China (Calydon), 1929-33.

Sheen, Fulton J. (1895-1979): ord. Sept. 20, 1919; aux. New York (Caesarina), 1951-66; bp. Rochester, 1966-69 (res.); tit. abp. Newport.

Shehan, Lawrence J. (1898-1984): ord. Dec. 23, 1922; aux. Baltimore and Washington (Lidda), 1945-53; bp. Bridgeport, 1953-61; coad. abp. Baltimore (Nicopolis ad Nestum), Sept.-Dec., 1961; abp. Baltimore, 1961-74 (res.); cardinal 1965.

Sheil, Bernard J. (1886-1969); ord. May 21, 1910; aux. bp. Chicago (Pegae), 1928-69; tit. abp. Selge, 1959-69.

Shubsda, Thaddeus A. (1925-91): ord. Apr. 26, 1950; aux. Los Angeles (Trau), 1977-82; bp. Monterey, 1982-91.

Smith, Alphonse (1883-1935): ord. Apr. 18, 1908; bp. Nashville, 1924-35.

Smith, Eustace, O.F.M. (1908-75): ord. June 12, 1934; v.a. Beirut, Lebanon (Apamea Cibotus), 1958-73 (res.).

Smith, Leo R. (1905-63): ord. Dec. 21, 1929; aux. Buffalo (Marida), 1952-63; bp. Ogdensburg, 1963.

Smyth, Clement, O.C.S.O. (1810-65): b. Ireland; ord. May 29, 1841; coad. bp. Dubuque (Thennesus), 1857-58; bp. Dubuque, 1858-65.

Soenneker, Henry J. (1907-87): Ord. May 26, 1934; bp. Owensboro, 1961-82 (res.).

Spalding, John L. (1840-1916): ord. Dec. 19, 1863, first bp. Peoria, 1876-1908 (res.).

Spalding, Martin J. (1810-72): ord. Aug. 13, 1834; aux. Louisville (Lengone), 1848-50; bp. Louisville, 1850-64; abp. Baltimore, 1864-72.

Spellman, Francis J. (1889-1967): ord. May 14, 1916; aux. Boston (Sila), 1932-39; abp. New York, 1939-67; cardinal 1946.

Spence, John S. (1909-73): ord. Dec. 5, 1933; aux. Washington (Aggersel), 1964-73.

Stang, William (1854-1907): b. Germany; ord. June 15, 1878; first bp. Fall River, 1904-07.

Stanton, Martin W. (1897-1977): ord. June 14, 1924; aux. Newark (Citium) 1957-72 (res.).

Stariha, John (1845-1915): b. Austria; ord. Sept. 19, 1869; first bp. Lead (now Rapid City), 1902-09 (res.).

Steck, Leo J. (1898-1950): ord. June 8, 1924; aux. Salt Lake City (Ilium), 1948-50.

Stemper, Alfred M., M.S.C. (1913-84): ord. June 26, 1940; v.a. Kavieng (Eleutheropolis), 1957-66; first bp. Kavieng, 1966-80 (res.).

Stock, John (1918-72): ord. Dec. 4, 1943; aux. Philadelphia (Ukrainian Rite) (Pergamum), 1971-72.

Stritch, Samuel (1887-1958): ord. May 21, 1909; bp. Toledo, 1921-30; abp. Milwaukee, 1930-39; abp. Chicago, 1939-58; cardinal 1946.

Sullivan, Bernard, S.J. (1889-1970): ord, June 26, 1921; bp. Patna, India, 1929-46 (res.).

Sullivan, Joseph V. (1919-82): ord. June 1, 1946; aux. Kansas City-St. Joseph (Tagamuta), 1964-74; bp. Baton Rouge, 1974-82.

Swanstrom, Edward E. (1903-85): ord. June 2, 1928; aux. New York (Arba), 1960-78 (res.).

Sweeney, James J. (1898-1968): ord. June 20, 1925; first bp. Honolulu, 1941-68.

Swint, John J. (1879-1962): ord. June 23, 1904; aux. Wheeling (Sura), 1922; bp. Wheeling, 1922-62.

T

Takach, Basil (1879-1948): b. Austria-Hungary; ord. Dec. 12, 1902; first ap. ex. Pittsburgh Byzantine Rite (Zela), 1924-48.

Tarasevitch, Vladimir L., O.S.B. (1921-86): b. Byelorussia (White Russia); ord. May 26, 1949; ap. visitator (with residence in Chicago) for Byelorussians outside Soviet Union (Mariamme), 1983-86.

Taylor, John E., O.M.I. (1914-76): ord. May 25, 1940; bp. Stockholm, Sweden, 1962-76.

Thill, Francis A. (1893-1957): ord. Feb. 28, 1920; bp. Concordia (title changed to Salina in 1944), 1938-57.

Tief, Francis J. (1881-1965): ord. June 11, 1908; bp. Concordia (now Salina), 1921-38 (res.).

Tierney, Michael (1839-1908): b. Ireland; ord. May 26, 1866; bp. Hartford, 1894-1908.

Tihen, J. Henry (1861-1940): ord. Apr. 26, 1886; bp. Lincoln, 1911-17; bp. Denver, 1917-31 (res.).

Timon, John, C.M. (1797-1867): ord. Sept. 23, 1826; first bp. Buffalo, 1847-67.

Toebbe, Augustus M. (1829-84): b. Germany; ord. Sept. 14, 1854; bp. Covington, 1870-84.

Toolen, Thomas J. (1886-1976): ord. Sept. 27, 1910; bp. (pers. tit. abp., 1954), Mobile, 1927-69 (res.).

Topel, Bernard J. (1903-86): ord. June 7, 1927; coad. bp. Spokane (Binda), Sept. 21-25, 1955; bp. Spokane, 1955-78 (res.).

Tracy, Robert E. (1909-80): ord. June 12, 1932; aux. Lafayette, La. (Sergentiza), 1959-61; first bp. Baton Rouge, 1961-74 (res.).

Treacy, John P. (1890-1964): ord. Dec. 8, 1918; coad. bp. La Crosse (Metelis), 1945-48; bp. La Crosse, 1948-64.

Trobec, James (1838-1921): b. Austria; ord. Sept. 8, 1865; bp. St. Cloud, 1897-1914 (res.).

Tuigg, John (1820-89): b. Ireland; ord. May 14, 1850; bp. Pittsburgh, 1876-89.

Turner, William (1871-1936): b. Ireland; ord. Aug. 13, 1893; bp. Buffalo, 1919-36.

Tyler, William (1806-49): ord. June 3, 1829; first bp. Hartford, 1844-49.

U-V

Unterkoefler, Ernest L. 1917-93): ord. May 18, 1944; aux. Richmond (Latopolis) 1962-64; bp. Charleston, 1964-90 (res.).

Van de Velde, James O., S.J. (1795-1855): b. Belgium; ord. Sept. 16, 1827; bp. Chicago, 1849-53; bp. Natchez (now Jackson), 1953-55.

Van de Ven, Cornelius (1865-1932): b. Holland; ord. May 31, 1890; bp. Natchitoches (title changed to Alexandria, 1910), 1904-32.

Van de Vyver, Augustine (1844-1911): b. Belgium; ord. July 24, 1870; bp. Richmond, 1889-1911.

Vath, Joseph G. (1918-87): ord. June 7, 1941; aux. Mobile-Birmingham (Novaliciana), 1966-69; first bp. Birmingham, 1969-87.

Vehr, Urban J. (1891-1973): ord. May 29, 1915; bp. 1931-41, and first abp. Denver, 1941-67 (res.).

Verdaguer, Peter (1835-1911): b. Spain; ord. Dec. 12, 1862; v.a. Brownsville (Aulon), 1890-1911.

Verot, Augustin, S.S. (1805-76): b. France; ord. Sept. 20, 1828; v.a. Florida (Danaba), 1856-61; bp. Savannah, 1861-70; bp. St. Augustine, 1870-76.

Vertin, John (1844-99): b. Austria; ord. Aug. 31, 1866; bp. Sault Ste. Marie and Marquette (now Marquette), 1879-99.

Vogel, Cyril J. (1905-79): ord. June 7, 1931; bp. Salina, 1965-79.

Vonesh, Raymond J. (1916-91): ord. May 3, 1941; aux. Joliet (Vanariona), 1968-1991 (res. May; d. Aug.).

W

Wade, Thomas, S.M. (1893-1969): ord. June 15, 1922; v.a. Northern Solomons (Barbalissus), 1930-69.

Wadhams, Edgar (1817-91): convert, 1846; ord. Jan. 15, 1850; first bp. Ogdensburg, 1872-91.

Walsh, Emmet (1892-1968): ord. Jan. 15, 1916;

bp. Charleston, 1927-49; coad. bp. Youngstown (Rhaedestus), 1949-52; bp. Youngstown, 1952-68.

Walsh, James A., M.M. (1867-1936): ord. May 20, 1892; co-founder (with Thomas F. Price) of Maryknoll, first U.S. established foreign mission society and first sponsor of a U.S. foreign mission seminary; superior of Maryknoll, 1911-36; tit. bp. Syene, 1933-36.

Walsh, James E., M.M. (1891-1981): ord. Dec. 7, 1915; v.a. Kongmon, China (Sata), 1927-36; superior of Maryknoll, 1936-46; general secretary, Catholic Central Bureau, Shanghai, China, 1948; imprisoned by Chinese communists, 1958-70.

Walsh, Louis S. (1858-1924): ord. Dec. 23, 1882; bp. Portland, Me., 1906-24.

Walsh, Thomas J. (1873-1952): ord. Jan. 27, 1900; bp. Trenton, 1918-28; bp., 1928-37, and first abp. 1937-52, Newark.

Ward, John (1857-1929): ord. July 17, 1884; bp. Leavenworth (now Kansas City), 1910-29.

Waters, Vincent S. (1904-74): ord. Dec. 8, 1931; bp. Raleigh, 1945-74.

Watson, Alfred M. (1907-90): ord. May 10, 1934; aux. Erie (Nationa), 1965-69; bp. Erie 1969-82 (res.).

Watterson, John A. (1844-99): ord. Aug. 9, 1868; bp. Columbus, 1880-99.

Wehrle, Vincent, O.S.B. (1855-1941): b. Switzerland; ord. Apr. 23, 1882; first bp. Bismarck, 1910-39 (res.).

Welch, Thomas A. (1884-1959): ord. June 11, 1909; bp. Duluth, 1926-59.

Weldon, Christopher J. (1905-82): ord. Sept. 21, 1939; bp. Springfield, Mass., 1950-77 (res.).

Whealon, John F. (1921-91): ord. May 26, 1945; aux. Cleveland (Andrapa), 1961-66; bp. Erie, 1966-69; abp. Hartford, 1969-91.

Whelan, James O.P. (1822-78): b. Ireland; ord. Aug. 2, 1846; coad. bp. Nashville (Marcopolis), 1859-60; bp. Nashville, 1860-64 (res.).

Whelan, Richard V. (1809-74): ord. May 1, 1831; bp. Richmond, 1841-50; bp. Wheeling, 1850-74.

White, Charles (1879-1955): ord. Sept. 24, 1910; bp. Spokane, 1927-55.

Whitfield, James (1770-1834): b. England; ord. July 24, 1809; coad. bp. Baltimore (Apollonia), 1828; abp. Baltimore, 1828-34.

Wigger, Winand (1841-1901): ord. June 10, 1865; bp. Newark, 1881-1901.

Willging, Joseph C. (1884-1959): ord. June 20, 1908; first bp. Pueblo, 1942-59.

Williams, John J. (1822-1907): ord. May 17, 1845; bp., 1866-75, and first abp., 1875-1907, Boston.

Willinger, Aloysius J., C.SS.R. (1886-1973): ord. July 2, 1911; bp. Ponce, P.R., 1929-46; coad. bp. Monterey-Fresno, 1946-53; bp. Monterey-Fresno, 1953-67 (res.).

Winkelmann, Christian H. (1883-1946): ord. June 11, 1907; aux. St. Louis (Sita), 1933-39; bp. Wichita, 1939-46.

Wood, James F. (1813-83): convert, 1836; ord. Mar. 25, 1844; coad. bp. Philadelphia (Antigonea), 1857-60;

bp., 1860-75, and first abp., 1875-83, Philadelphia.
Woznicki, Stephen (1894-1968): ord. Dec. 22, 1917; aux. Detroit (Peltae), 1938-50; bp. Saginaw, 1950-68.
Wright, John J. (1909-79): ord. Dec. 8, 1935; aux. Boston (Egee), 1947-50; bp. Worcester, 1950-59; bp. Pittsburgh, 1959-69; cardinal, 1969; prefect Congregation of the Clergy, 1969-79.
Wurm, John N. (1927-84): ord. Apr. 3, 1954; aux. St. Louis (Plestia), 1976-81; bp. Belleville, 1981-84.

Y-Z
Young, Josue (1808-66): ord. Apr. 1, 1838; bp. Erie, 1854-66.
Zaleski, Alexander, M. (1906-75): ord. July 12, 1931; aux. Detroit (Lybe), 1950-64; coad. bp. Lansing, 1964-65; bp. Lansing 1966-75.
Zardetti, Otto (1847-1902): b. Switzerland; ord. Aug. 21, 1870; first bp. St. Cloud, 1889-94; abp. Bucharest, Rumania, 1894-95 (res.).
Zuroweste, Albert R. (1901-87): ord. June 8, 1924; bp. Belleville, 1948-76 (res.).

HISPANICS

The nation's Hispanic population totaled 22.4 million, according to figures reported by the U.S. Census Bureau in 1990. It was estimated that 80 percent of the Hispanics were baptized Catholics.

Pastoral Patterns

Pastoral ministry to Hispanics varies, depending on differences among the people and the availability of personnel to carry it out.

The pattern in cities with large numbers of Spanish-speaking is built around special and bilingual churches, centers or other agencies where pastoral and additional forms of service are provided in a manner suited to the needs, language and culture of the people. Services in some places are extensive and include legal advice, job placement, language instruction, recreational and social assistance, specialized counseling, replacement services. In many places, however, even where there are special ministries, the needs are generally greater than the means required to meet them.

Some urban dwellers have been absorbed into established parishes and routines of church life and activity. Many Spanish-speaking communities remain in need of special ministries. An itinerant form of ministry best meets the needs of the thousands of migrant workers who follow the crops.

Demographic and ministerial data were the subjects of a national survey commissioned by the Bishops' Commission for Hispanic Affairs and carried out by its secretariat. It was reported in November, 1990, that responses were received from 152 archdioceses and dioceses. Twelve or more dioceses and archdioceses had Hispanic populations of more than 50 percent; 27 others were a quarter or more Hispanic. Fifty-five percent of the reporting jurisdictions had Hispanic apostolates. Overall, ministerial emphasis was reported in six areas: youth, small Christian communities, the Cursillo movement, Catholic Charities and social ministry, lay leadership formation, and charismatic renewal. Other sources reported that well over 80 percent of Hispanics were located in urban areas, and that 54 percent were 25 years of age or younger. It was estimated that perhaps 100,000 Catholic Hispanics a year were being lost, principally to fundamentalist and pentecostal sects. (See related entries in News Events.)

Pastoral ministry to Hispanics was the central concern of three national meetings, *Encuentros,* held in 1972, 1977 and 1985.

The third National *Encuentro* in 1985 produced a master pastoral plan for ministry which the National Conference of Catholic Bishops approved in 1987. Its four keys are collaborative ministry; evangelization; a missionary option regarding the poor, the maginalized, the family, women and youth; the formation of lay leadership.

The U.S. bishops, at their annual meeting in November, 1983, approved and subsequently published a pastoral letter on Hispanic Ministry under the title, "The Hispanic Presence: Challenge and Commitment." (For text, see pp. 46-49 of the 1985 *Catholic Almanac*.)

Bishops

As of Aug 20, 1993, there were 22 (21 active) bishops of Hispanic origin in the United States; all were named since 1970 (for biographies, see Index). Seven were heads of archdioceses or dioceses: Archbishop Patrick F. Flores (San Antonio); Bishops Raymundo J. Pena (El Paso), Ricardo Ramirez, C.S.B. (Las Cruces), Rene H. Gracida (Corpus Christi), Arthur N. Tafoya (Pueblo), Manuel D. Moreno (Tucson) and Enrique San Pedro S.J. (Brownsville). Fourteen were auxiliary bishops: Juan Arzube and Armando Ochoa (Los Angeles), Gilbert Espinoza Chavez (San Diego), Joseph J. Madera (Military Services), Francisco Garmendia (New York), Agustin Roman (Miami), Rene Valero (Brooklyn), David Arias, O.A.R. (Newark), Placido Rodriguez, C.M.F. (Chicago), Alvaro Corrada del Rio, S.J. (Washington, D.C.), Roberto O. Gonzalez, O.F.M. (Boston), Carlos A. Sevilla, S.J. (San Francisco), Gerald R. Barnes (San Bernardino) and James A. Tamayo (Galveston-Houston). Archbishop Robert F. Sanchez of Santa Fe resigned in April, 1993.

Hispanic priests and nuns in the U.S. number about 1,600 and 2,000, respectively, according to an estimate made in June, 1988, by Father Gary Riebe Estrella, S.V.D., director of a Hispanic vocational recruitment program.

Secretariat for Hispanic Affairs

The national secretariat was established by the U.S. Catholic Conference for service in promoting and coordinating pastoral ministry to the Spanish-speaking. Its basic orientation is toward integral evangelization, combining religious ministry with development efforts in programs geared to the culture and needs of Hispanics. Its concerns are urban and migrant Spanish-speaking people; communications and publications in line with secretariat purposes and the service of people; bilingual and bicultural religious and general education; liaison for and representation of Hispanics with church, civic and governmental agencies.

The secretariat publishes a newsletter, *En Marcha,* available to interested parties for a subscription fee.

Ronaldo M. Cruz is executive director of the national office at 3211 Fourth St. N.E., Washington, D.C. 20017.

The secretariat works in collaboration with regional offices and pastoral institutes throughout the country.

The Northeast Regional Office, officially the Northeast Hispanic Catholic Center, was established in 1976 under the auspices of the bishops in 14 states from Maine to Virginia. It has established the Conference of Diocesan Directors of the Hispanic Apostolate, the Association of Hispanic Deacons, a Regional Youth Task Force and a Regional Committee of Diocesan Coordinators of Religious Educators for the Hispanics. The office is the official publishing house for the Hispanic Lectionary approved by the National Conference of Catholic Bishops for the United States. The center has liturgical, evangelization and youth ministry departments and an office of cultural affairs. Mario J. Paredes is executive director. The center is located at 1011 First Ave., New York, NY 10022.

The Southeast Regional Office serves 26 dioceses in Tennessee, North and South Carolina, Florida, Georgia, Mississippi, Alabama and Louisiana. Father Mario Vizcaino, Sch. P., is director of the region and institute. The office is located at 2900 S.W. 87th Ave., Miami, Fla. 33165. The Southeast Pastoral Institute serves as the educational arm of the regional office by providing formation programs for the development of leadership skills focused on ministry among Hispanics, at the Miami site and in the various dioceses of the region.

The Midwest Hispanic Catholic Commission serves 29 archdioceses/dioceses in the five states of the Midwest's Episcopal Regions VI and VII (Ohio, Indiana, Illinois, Michigan, Wisconsin). The executive director is Maria Teresa Garza. The mailing address is 18965 Douglas Rd., P.O. Box 703, Notre Dame, IN 46556.

In the Southwest, the Mexican American Cultural Center serves as convener of diocesan directors and representatives of Hispanic ministry in Arkansas, Oklahoma and Texas.

A regional office serving the **Mountain States** (Arizona, New Mexico, Utah, Colorado and Wyoming) is under the direction of Rev. Lorenzo Ruiz, O.F.M., Hispanic Ministry Office, P.O. Box 11295, Denver, CO 80211.

National Hispanic Priests Association

The National Association of Hispanic Priests of the USA (ANSH — *La Asociación Nacional de Sacerdotes Hispanos,* EE. UU.) was established in September, 1989, with a representation of about 3,000 Hispanic clergy residing and ministering in the United States. The association is a product of a long process. In 1970, a group of priests formally organized under the name of PADRES, an acronym for the Spanish title, "Padres Asociados para Derechos Religiosos, Educativos y Sociales." They advocated for and organized the first National Hispanic Encounters with important support and leadership of Las Hermanas. Among the early issues was the naming of the first Hispanic bishops. After annual conventions held from 1985 to 1988, they organized as a national association in Miami in 1989 with Rev. Eduardo Salazar, S.J., as first president. The association collaborates with the laity and bishops in implementing the National Plan for Hispanic Ministry and in developing approaches for a more meaningful ministry. The president is Rev. Juan Castro, O.M.I., 555 West St. Francis St., Brownsville, TX 78520.

National Catholic Council for Hispanic Ministry (NCCHM)

The council is a volunteer umbrella association of Roman Catholic organizations, agencies and movements committed to the development of Hispanics/Latinos in Church and society. It was established June 17, 1990, at a gathering at Mundelein College, Chicago; its by-laws were adopted in January, 1991, at Mercy Center, Burlingame, Calif. The council convokes a national gathering every three years called the Hispanic Congress. NCCHM has 44 member organizations. It publishes *Puentes,* a newsletter. The president is Rev. Allan Figueroa Deck, S.J., 8601 Lincoln Blvd., Suite 320A, Los Angeles, CA 90045.

Mexican American Cultural Center

This national center, specializing in pastoral studies and language education, was founded in 1972 to provide programs focused on ministry among Hispanics and personnel working with Hispanics in the U.S. and Latin America. Courses — developed according to the see-judge-act methodology — include culture, faith development, Scripture, theology, and praxis; some are offered in Spanish, others in English. Intensive language classes are offered in Spanish and English as second languages, with emphasis on pastoral usage.

The center also conducts workshops for the development of leadership skills and for a better understanding of Hispanic communities. Faculty members serve as resource personnel for pastoral centers, dioceses and parishes throughout the U.S. The center offers master-degree programs in pastoral ministry in cooperation with Incarnate Word College, Boston College, the Oblate School of Theology, St. Mary's University and Loyola University, New Orleans. Participants attending summer study weeks can obtain a Certificado de Pastoralista.

The center is a distribution agency for the circulation of pastoral materials in the U.S. and Latin America.

Father Rosendo Urrabazo, C.M.F., is president of the center which is located at 3019 W. French Place, San Antonio, TX 78228.

Hispanic Liturgy

Spanish-speaking communities in the U.S. are served by the Institute of Hispanic Liturgy, a national organization of liturgists, musicians, artists and pastoral agents, funded in part by the U.S. Bishops. The institute promotes the study of liturgical texts, art, music and popular religiosity in an effort to develop liturgical spirituality among

Hispanics. It works closely with the U.S. Bishops' Committee on the Liturgy, and has published liturgical materials. Sister Rosa Maria Icaza is the president. Address: P.O. Box 28229, San Antonio, Tex. 78228.

BLACK CATHOLICS IN THE UNITED STATES

National Office

The National Office for Black Catholics, organized in July, 1970, is a central agency with the general purposes of promoting active and full participation by black Catholics in the Church and of making more effective the presence and ministry of the Church in the black community.

Its operations are in support of the aspirations and calls of black Catholics for a number of objectives, including the following:

● representation and voice for blacks among bishops and others with leadership and decision-making positions in the Church;

● promoting vocations to the priesthood and religious life;

● sponsoring programs of evangelization, pastoral ministry, education and liturgy on a national level;

● recognition of the black heritage in liturgy, community life, theology and education.

Walter T. Hubbard is executive director of the NOBC.

The NOBC office is located at 3025 Fourth St. N.E., Washington, D.C. 20017.

Clergy Caucus

The National Black Catholic Clergy Caucus, founded in 1968 in Detroit, is a fraternity of several hundred back priests, permanent deacons and brothers pledged to mutual support in their vocations and ministries.

The Caucus develops programs of spiritual, theological, educational and ministerial growth for its members, to counteract the effects of institutionalized racism within the Church and American society. A bimonthly newsletter is published.

Rev. Donald Sterlings is president of the Caucus.

The NBCCC office is located at 343 N. Walnut St., P.O. Box 1088, Opelousas, La. 70571.

Other peer and support groups were the National Black Sisters' Conference and the National Black Catholic Seminarians Association.

National Black Catholic Congress

The National Black Catholic Congress, Inc., was formed in 1985 exclusively to assist in the development of the Roman Catholic Church in the African American community and to devise effective means of evangelization of African American peoples in the United States. Its fundamental purpose is the formation and development of concrete approaches toward the evangelization of African Americans through revitalization of African American Catholic life.

The Congress is under the sponsorship of the African American Roman Catholic bishops of the United States, the National Black Catholic Clergy Caucus, the National Black Sisters' Conference, the National Association of Black Catholic Administrators and the Knights of Peter Claver and the Ladies Auxiliary Knights of Peter Claver. The Con-

gress is also in consultation with African American clergy and vowed religious women communities. The Congress sponsors *Pastoring in Black Parishes*, an annual workshop first held in 1988 and *An African American Catholic Ministries Program*, a week-long curriculum presented twice a year, usually in January and June.

The National Black Catholic Congress sponsored the seventh general assembly of African-American Catholics and those serving in African American communities, July 9 to 12, 1992, in New Orleans. (See separate article.)

The office of the Congress is located at The Catholic Center, 320 Cathedral St., Room 712, Baltimore, MD 21201. The executive director is Dr. Hilbert D. Stanley.

Committee and Secretariat

The **Committee on African American Catholics,** established by the National Conference of Catholic Bishops in 1987, is chaired by Bishop J. Terry Steib of Memphis. The purpose of the committee is to assist the bishops in their evangelization efforts to the African American community by initiating, encouraging and supporting programs which recognize and respect African American genius and values. Priorities of the Committee include implementation of the National Black Catholic Pastoral Plan of 1987, inculturation of liturgy and ministry, and increasing lay leadership and vocations.

Also established as a service agency to the committee was a **Secretariat for African American Catholics** under the executive direction of Beverly Carroll. The secretariat is the officially recognized voice of the African American community as it articulates its gifts and aspirations regarding ministry, evangelization and worship. It also serves as a liaison to the National Black Catholic Clergy Caucus, the National Black Catholic Seminarians Association, the National Black Sisters' Conference, National Black Catholic Administrators, Knights of St. Peter Claver and Ladies Auxiliary, and the National Black Catholic Congress.

The committee and secretariat have offices at 3211 Fourth St. N.E., Washington, D.C. 20017.

Bishops

There were 11 (10 active) black bishops, as of Sept. 3, 1993: Bishops Joseph L. Howze of Biloxi, and J. Terry Steib, S.V.D., of Memphis; and Auxiliary Bishops Joseph A. Francis, S.V.D., of Newark, Emerson Moore of New York, Moses Anderson, S.S.E., of Detroit, Wilton D. Gregory of Chicago, John H. Ricard, S.S.J., of Baltimore, Curtis J. Guillory, S.V.D., of Galveston-Houston, Leonard J. Olivier, S.V.D., of Washington, and Dominic Carmon, S.V.D., of New Orleans. Archbishop Eugene A. Marino, S.S.J., of Atlanta, resigned in July, 1990.

Josephite Pastoral Center

The Josephite Pastoral Center was established in September, 1968, as an educational and pastoral service agency for the Josephites in their mission work, specifically in the black community, subsequently to all those who minister in the African American community. St. Joseph's Society of the Sacred Heart, the sponsoring body has about 156 priests and 12 brothers in 75 mostly southern parishes in 18 dioceses. The staff of the center includes Father John G. Harfmann, S.S.J., director, and Maria M. Lannon, associate director. The center is located at St. Joseph Seminary 1200 Varnum St. N.E., Washington, D.C. 20017.

AFRICAN-AMERICAN EVANGELIZATION

The National Black Catholic Pastoral Plan adopted by the National Black Catholic Congress in May, 1987, was approved and recommended for implementation by the National Conference of Catholic Bishops in November, 1989. The conference statement bears the title, "Here I Am, Send Me: A Conference Response to the Evangelization of African-Americans and the National Black Catholic Pastoral Plan."

Following is an account of several points in the bishops' statement, based on coverage by the CNS Documentary Service, Origins, Dec. 28, 1989 (Vol. 19, No. 30).

Evangelization

"Evangelization," wrote the bishops, "would not be complete if it did not take account of the unceasing interplay of the Gospel and of man's concrete life, both personal and social. . . . Evangelization involves an explicit message, adapted to the different situations constantly being realized, about the rights and duties of every human being, about family life, without which personal growth and development are hardly possible, about life in society, about international life, peace, justice and development — a message especially energetic today about liberation."

The Plan

The pastoral plan "embraces three broad areas: 1) the Catholic identity of African-American Catholics; 2) ministry and leadership within the African-American community; and 3) the responsibility of this community to reach out to the broader society.

Within these areas are such issues as culture, family, youth, spirituality, liturgy, ministry, lay leadership, parishes, education, social action and community development."

Recommendation

Reflecting a recommendation of the pastoral plan, the bishops encourage African-American Catholics to "discover their past" since "the possession of one's history is the first step in an appreciation of one's culture."

On the parish level, it is suggested that African-American Catholics "take a leadership role in the formation of neighborhood outreach programs within the African-American community."

The bishops urge parishes to institute "courses in Scripture, catechetics and lay-minister formation within the African-American community," and suggest that dioceses establish offices of black Catholic ministries.

Among other points of concern, the bishops encourage the work of inner-city Catholic schools and stress the need for the local church to tailor activities "to the cultural dimensions of African-American youth."

Liturgy

"It is essential that pastors and parish associates working within the African-American community become familiar with the richness of African-American art and music . . . so that they may cooperate with their parishioners in making the liturgical celebration an authentic and true representation of the African-American Catholic cultural experience."

NATIVE AMERICAN TEKAKWITHA CONFERENCE

The Kateri Tekakwitha Conference is so named in honor of Blessed Kateri Tekakwitha, "Lily of the Mohawks," who was born in 1656 at Ossernenon (Auriesville), N.Y. in 1656, was baptized in 1676, lived near Montreal, died in 1680 and was beatified in 1980 by Pope John Paul.

The conference was established in 1939 as a missionary-priest advisory group in the Diocese of Fargo. It was a missionary-priest support group from 1946 to 1977. Since 1977 it has been a gathering of Catholic Native peoples together with men and women — clerical, religious and lay persons — who minister with Native Catholic communities.

The primary focus of conference concern and activity is evangelization, with specific emphasis on development of Native ministry and leadership.

Other priorities include catechesis, liturgy, family life, social justice ministry, chemical dependency, youth ministry, spirituality and native Catholic dialogue. Annual conferences, regional conferences and local Kateri Circles serve as occasions for the exchange of ideas, approaches, prayer and mutual support. Since 1980, the national center has promoted and registered 81 Kateri Circles in the U.S. and Canada. Publications include a quarterly newsletter.

The conference has a board of 12 directors, the majority of whom are Native people. Bishop Donald Pelotte, S.S.S., is the episcopal moderator. Address: Tekakwitha Conference National Center, P.O. Box 6768, Great Falls, Mont. 59406.

The 54th annual Tekakwitha Conference, was held Aug. 4 to 8, 1993, in Seattle, Wash.

RELIGIOUS

Institutes of Consecrated Life

Religious institutes and congregations are special societies in the Church — institutes of consecrated life — whose members, called Religious, commit themselves, by public vows to observance of the evangelical counsels of poverty, chastity and obedience in a community kind of life in accordance with rules and constitutions approved by church authority.

Secular institutes (covered in its own Almanac entry) are also institutes of consecrated life.

The particular goal of each institute and the means of realizing it in practice are stated in the rule and constitutions proper to the institute. Local bishops can give approval for rules and constitutions of institutes of diocesan rank. Pontifical rank belongs to institutes approved by the Holy See. General jurisdiction over all Religious is exercised by the Congregation for Institutes of Consecrated Life and Societies of Apostolic Life. General legislation concerning Religious is contained in Canons 573 to 709 in Book II, Part III, of the Code of Canon Law.

All institutes of consecrated life are commonly called religious orders, despite the fact that there are differences between orders and congregations. The best known orders include the Benedictines, Trappists, Franciscans, Dominicans, Carmelites and Augustinians, for men; and the Carmelites, Benedictines, Poor Clares, Dominicans of the Second Order and Visitation Nuns, for women. The orders are older than the congregations, which did not appear until the 16th century.

Contemplative institutes are oriented to divine worship and service within the confines of their communities, by prayer, penitential practices, other spiritual activities and self-supporting work. Examples are the Trappists and Carthusians, the Carmelite and Poor Clare nuns. Active institutes are geared for pastoral ministry and various kinds of apostolic work. Mixed institutes combine elements of the contemplative and active ways of life. While most institutes of men and women can be classified as active, all of them have contemplative aspects.

Clerical communities of men are those whose membership is predominantly composed of priests.

Non-clerical or lay institutes of men are the various brotherhoods.

Societies of Apostolic Life

Some of the institutes listed below have a special kind of status because their members, while living a common life like that which is characteristic of Religious, do not profess the vows of Religious. Examples are the Maryknoll Fathers, the Oratorians of St. Philip Neri, the Paulists and Sulpicians. They are called societies of apostolic life and are the subject of Canons 731 to 746 in the Code of Canon Law.

RELIGIOUS INSTITUTES OF MEN IN THE UNITED STATES

(Sources: *Official Catholic Directory;* Catholic Almanac survey.)

Africa, Missionaries of (M. Afr.): Founded 1868 at Algiers by Cardinal Charles M. Lavigerie; known as White Fathers until 1984. Generalate, Rome Italy; U.S. headquarters, 1624 21st St. N.W., Washington, DC 20009. Missionary work in Africa.

African Missions, Society of, S.M.A.: Founded 1856, at Lyons, France, by Bishop Melchior de Marion Brésillac. Generalate, Rome, Italy; American province (1941), 23 Bliss Ave., Tenafly, NJ 07670. Missionary work.

Alexian Brothers, C.F.A.: Founded 14th century in western Germany and Belgium during the Black Plague. Motherhouse, Aachen, Germany; generalate, Signal Mountain, TN 37377. Hospital and general health work.

Assumptionists (Augustinians of the Assumption), A.A.: Founded 1845, at Nimes, France, by Rev. Emmanuel d'Alzon; in U.S., 1946. General house, Rome, Italy; U.S. province, 330 Market St., Brighton, MA 02135. Educational, parochial, ecumenical, retreat, foreign mission work.

Atonement, Franciscan Friars of the, S.A.: Founded as an Anglican Franciscan community in 1898 at Garrison, N.Y., by Rev. Paul Wattson. Community corporately received into the Catholic Church in 1909. Generalate, St. James Friary, P.O. Box 5, Graymoor, Garrison NY 10524. Ecumenical, mission, retreat and charitable works.

Augustinian Recollects, O.A.R.: Founded 1588: in U.S., 1944. General motherhouse, Rome, Italy. Missionary, parochial, education work.

St. Augustine Province (1944), 29 Ridgeway Ave., W. Orange, NJ 07052.

St. Nicholas Province: U.S. Delegates, 2800 Schurz Ave., Bronx, NY 10465 (New York); P.O. Box 310, Mesilla, NM 88044 (South).

Augustinians (Order of St. Augustine), O.S.A.: Established canonically in 1256 by Pope Alexander IV; in U.S., 1796. General motherhouse, Rome, Italy.

St. Thomas of Villanova Province (1796), P.O. Box 338, Villanova, PA 19085.

Our Mother of Good Counsel Province (1941), Tolentine Center, 20300 Governors Hwy., Olympia Fields, IL 60461.

St. Augustine Province (1969), 1605 28th St., San Diego, CA 92102.

Good Counsel Vice-Province, St. Augustine Preparatory School, Richland, NJ 08350.

U.S. Address of King City, Ont., Canada, Province: 3103 Arlington Ave., Bronx, NY 10463.

U.S. Vicariate of Castile, Spain, Province (1963), Vicar, 3648 61st St., Port Arthur, TX 77642.

Barnabites (Clerics Regular of St. Paul), C.R.S.P.: Founded 1530, in Milan, Italy, by St. Anthony M. Zaccaria; approved 1533; in U.S., 1952. Historical motherhouse, Church of St. Barnabas (Milan). Generalate, Rome, Italy; North American province, 1023 Swann Rd., Youngstown, NY 14174. Parochial, educational, mission work.

Basil the Great, Order of St. (Basilian Order of

St. Josaphat), O.S.B.M.: General motherhouse, Rome, Italy; U.S. province, 31-12 30th St., Long Island City, NY 11106. Parochial work among Byzantine Ukrainian Rite Catholics.

Basilian Fathers (Congregation of the Priests of St. Basil), C.S.B.: Founded 1822, at Annonay, France. General motherhouse, Milton, Ont., Canada. U.S. addresses: 445 King's Hwy., Rochester, NY 14617 (East); 106 Fifth St., Sugar Land, TX 77478 (West). Educational, parochial work.

Basilian Salvatorian Fathers: Founded 1684, at Saida, Lebanon, by Eftimios Saifi; in U.S., 1953. General motherhouse, Saida, Lebanon; American headquarters, 30 East St., Methuen, MA 01844. Educational, parochial work among Eastern Rite peoples.

Benedictine Monks (Order of St. Benedict), O.S.B.: Founded 529, in Italy, by St. Benedict of Nursia; in U.S., 1846.

● American Cassinese Congregation (1855). Pres., Rt. Rev. Melvin J. Valvano, O.S.B., Newark Abbey, 528 Dr. Martin Luther King Blvd., Newark, NJ 07102. Abbeys and Priories belonging to the congregation:

St. Vincent Archabbey, Fraser Purchase Rd., Latrobe, PA 15650; St. John's Abbey, Collegeville, MN 56321; St. Benedict's Abbey, Atchison, KS 66002; St. Mary's Abbey, Delbarton, Morristown, NJ 07960; Newark Abbey, 528 Dr. Martin Luther King, Jr., Blvd., Newark, NJ 07102; Belmont Abbey, Belmont, NC 28012; St. Bernard Abbey, Cullman, AL 35055; St. Procopius Abbey, 5601 College Rd., Lisle, IL 60532; St. Gregory's Abbey, Shawnee, OK 74801; St. Leo Abbey, St. Leo, FL 33574; Assumption Abbey, P.O. Box A, Richardton, ND 58652;

St. Bede Abbey, Peru, IL 61354; St. Martin's Abbey, Lacey, WA 98503; Holy Cross Abbey, P.O. Box 1510, Canon City, CO 81215; St. Anselm's Abbey, 87 St. Anselm, Manchester, NH 03102; St. Andrew's Abbey, 10510 Buckeye Rd., Cleveland, OH 44104; Holy Trinity Priory, P.O. Box 990, Butler, PA 16003; St. Maur Priory, 4615 N. Michigan Rd., Indianapolis, IN 46208; Benedictine Priory, 6502 Seawright Dr., Savannah, GA 31406; Woodside Priory, 302 Portola Rd., Portola Valley, CA 94025; Mary Mother of the Church Abbey, 304 N. Sheppard St., Richmond, VA 23221 ; Abadia de San Antonio Abad, P.O. Box 729, Humacao, PR 00661.

● Swiss-American Congregation (1870). Abbeys and priory belonging to the congregation:

St. Meinrad Archabbey, St. Meinrad, IN 47577; Conception Abbey, Conception, MO 64433; Mt. Michael Abbey, Elkhorn, NE 68022; New Subiaco Abbey, Subiaco, AR 72865; St. Joseph's Abbey, St. Benedict, LA 70457; Mt. Angel Abbey, St. Benedict, OR 97373; Marmion Abbey, Butterfield Rd., Aurora, IL 60504;

St. Benedict's Abbey, Benet Lake, WI 53102; Glastonbury Abbey, 16 Hull St., Hingham, MA 02043; Blue Cloud Abbey, Marvin, SD 57251; Corpus Christi Abbey, HCR2, Box 6300, Sandia, TX 78383; Prince of Peace Abbey, 650 Benet Hill Rd., Oceanside, CA 92054; St. Benedict Priory, 252 Still River Rd., Still River-Harvard, MA 01467.

● Congregation of St. Ottilien for Foreign Missions: St. Paul's Abbey, Newton, NJ 07860; Christ the King Priory, Schuyler, NE 68661.

● Congregation of the Annunciation, St. Andrew Abbey, Valyermo, CA 93563.

● English Benedictine Congregation: St. Anselm's Abbey, 4501 S. Dakota Ave. N.E., Washington, DC 20017; Abbey of St. Gregory, Cory's Lane, Portsmouth, RI 02871; Abbey of St. Mary and St. Louis, 500 S. Mason Rd., St. Louis, MO 63141.

● Houses not in Congregations: Mount Saviour Monastery, Pine City, NY 14871; Conventual Priory of St. Gabriel the Archangel, Weston, VT 05161.

Benedictines, Camaldolese Congregation, Cam. O.S.B.: Founded 1012, at Camaldoli, near Arezzo, Italy, by St. Romuald; in U.S. 1958. General motherhouse, Arezzo, Italy; U.S. foundation, Immaculate Heart Hermitage, Big Sur, CA 93920.

Benedictines,   Olivetan,   O.S.B.: General motherhouse, Siena, Italy. U.S. monasteries, Our Lady of Guadalupe Abbey, Pecos, NM 87552; Holy Trinity Monastery, P.O. Box 298, St. David, AZ 85630; Benedictine Monastery of Hawaii, P.O. Box 490, Waialua, Hawaii 96791; Monastery of the Risen Christ, P.O. Box 3931, San Luis Obispo, CA 93403.

Benedictines, Subiaco Congregation, O.S.B.: Independent priory, 1983. Monastery of Christ in the Desert, Abiquiu, NM 87510; St, Mary's Monastery, P.O. Box 345, Petersham, MA 01366.

Benedictines, Sylvestrine, O.S.B.: Founded 1231, in Italy by Sylvester Gozzolini. General motherhouse, Rome, Italy; U.S. foundations; 17320 Rosemont Rd., Detroit, MI 48219; 2711 E. Drahner Rd., Oxford, MI 48051; 1697 State Highway 3, Clifton, NJ 07012.

Bethany, Brothers of: Founded in 1984. Holy Trinity Monastery, Dunhamtown Rd., Palmer, MA 01069.

Bethlehem Missionaries, Society of, S.M.B.: Founded 1921, at Immensee, Switzerland, by Rt. Rev. Canon Peter Bondolfi. General motherhouse, Immensee, Switzerland. Foreign mission work.

Blessed Sacrament, Congregation of the, S.S.S.: Founded 1856, at Paris, France, by St. Pierre Julien Eymard; in U.S., 1900. General motherhouse, Rome, Italy; U.S. province, 5384 Wilson Mills Rd., Cleveland, OH 44143. Eucharistic apostolate.

Brigittine Monks (Order of the Most Holy Savior), O.Ss.S.: Monastery of Our Lady of Consolation, 23300 Walker Lane, Amity, OR 97101.

Camaldolese Hermits of the Congregation of Monte Corona, Er. Cam.: Founded 1520, from Camaldoli, Italy, by Bl. Paul Giustiniani. General motherhouse, Frascati (Rome), Italy; U.S. foundation, Holy Family Hermitage, Rt. 2, Box 36, Bloomingdale, OH 43910.

Camillian Fathers and Brothers (Order of St. Camillus; Order of Servants of the Sick), O.S.Cam.: Founded 1582, at Rome, by St. Camillus de Lellis; in U.S., 1923. General motherhouse, Rome, Italy; North American province, 10213 W. Wisconsin Ave., Wauwatosa, WI 53226.

Carmelites (Order of Our Lady of Mt. Carmel), O. Carm.: General motherhouse, Rome, Italy. Educational, charitable work.

Most Pure Heart of Mary Province (1864), 1317 Frontage Rd., Darien, IL 60559.

St. Elias Province (1931), P.O. Box 868, Middletown, NY 10940.

Mt. Carmel Hermitage, Pineland, R.D. 3, Box 36, New Florence, PA 15944 (immediately subject to Prior General.)

Carmelites, Order of Discalced, O.C.D.: Established 1562, a Reform Order of Our Lady of Mt. Carmel; in U.S., 1924. Generalate, Rome, Italy. Spiritual direction, retreat, parochial work.

California-Arizona Province, Central Office, (1924), 926 E. Highland Ave., P.O. Box 2178, Redlands, CA 92373.

St. Therese of Oklahoma Province (1935), P.O. Box 26127, Oklahoma City, OK 73126.

Immaculate Heart of Mary Province (1947), 1233 S. 45th St., Milwaukee, WI 53214.

Polish Province of the Holy Spirit (1949), 1628 Ridge Rd., Munster, IN 46321.

Carmelites of Mary Immaculate, C.M.I.: Founded 1855, in India, by Bl. Kuriakose Elias Chavara. Generalate, Kerala, India; North American headquarters, Holy Family Church, 21 Nassau Ave., Brooklyn, NY 11222.

Carthusians, Order of, O. Cart.: Founded 1084, in France, by St. Bruno; in U.S., 1951. General motherhouse, St. Pierre de Chartreuse, France; U.S. charterhouse, R.R. 2, Box 2411, Arlington, VT 05250. Cloistered contemplatives; semi-eremitic.

Charity, Brothers of, F.C.: Founded 1807, in Belgium, by Canon Peter J. Triest. General motherhouse, Rome, Italy: American District (1963), Emeric House, 13 Wren Ct., Edison, NJ 08820. Charitable, educational work.

Charity, Servants of (Guanellians), S.C.: Founded 1908, in Italy, by Bl. Luigi Guanella. General motherhouse, Rome, Italy; U.S. headquarters, St. Louis School, 16195 Old U.S. 12, Chelsea, MI 48118.

Christ, Society of, S.Ch.: Founded 1932, General Motherhouse, Poznan, Poland; U.S.-Canadian Province, 3000 Eighteen Mile Rd., Sterling Heights, MI 48311.

Christian Brothers, Congregation of, C.F.C. (formerly Christian Brothers of Ireland): Founded 1802 at Waterford, Ireland, by Edmund Ignatius Rice; in U.S., 1906. General motherhouse, Rome, Italy. Educational work.

American Province, Eastern U.S. (1916), 21 Pryer Terr., New Rochelle, NY 10804.

Brother Rice Province, Western U.S. (1966), 9237 S. Avalon Ave., Chicago, IL 60619.

Christian Instruction, Brothers of (La Mennais Brothers), F.I.C.: Founded 1817, at Ploermel, France, by Abbe Jean Marie de la Mennais and Abbe Gabriel Deshayes. General motherhouse, Rome, Italy; American province, Notre Dame Institute, P.O. Box 159, Alfred, ME 04002.

Christian Schools, Brothers of the (Christian Brothers), F.S.C.: Founded 1680, at Reims, France, by St. Jean Baptiste de la Salle. General motherhouse, Rome, Italy; U.S. Conference, 100 De La Salle Dr., Romeoville, IL 60441. Educational, charitable work.

Baltimore Province (1845), Box 29, Adamstown, MD 21710.

Chicago Province (1966), 200 De La Salle Dr., Romeoville, IL 60441.

New York Province (1848), 800 Newman Springs Rd., Lincroft, NJ 07738.

Long Island-New England Province (1957), Christian Brothers Center, 635 Ocean Ave., Narragansett, RI 02882.

St. Louis Province (1886), 2101 Rue de la Salle, Glencoe, MO 63038.

San Francisco Province (1868), P.O. Box 3720, Napa, CA 94558.

New Orleans-Santa Fe Province (1921), De La Salle Christian Brothers, 1522 Breaux Bridge Rd., Lafayette, LA 70501.

St. Paul-Minneapolis Province (1963), 807 Summit Ave., St. Paul, MN 55105.

Cistercians, Order of, O.Cist.: Founded 1098, by St. Robert. Headquarters, Rome, Italy.

Our Lady of Spring Bank Abbey, Rt. 3, Box 211, Sparta, WI 54656.

Our Lady of Dallas Monastery, 1 Cistercian Rd., Irving, TX 75039.

Cistercian Monastery of Our Lady of Fatima, Hainesport-Mt. Laurel Rd., Mt. Laurel, NJ 08054.

Cistercian Conventual Priory, St. Mary's Priory, R.D. 1, Box 206, New Ringgold, PA 17960.

Cistercians of the Strict Observance, Order of (Trappists), O.C.S.O.: Founded 1098, in France, by St. Robert; in U.S., 1848. Generalate, Rome, Italy.

Our Lady of Gethsemani Abbey (1848), Trappist, KY 40051.

Our Lady of New Melleray Abbey (1849), 6500 Melleray Circle, Peosta, IA 52068.

St. Joseph's Abbey (1825), Spencer, MA 01562.

Holy Spirit Monastery (1944), 2625 Hwy. 212 S.W., Conyers, GA 30208.

Our Lady of Guadalupe Abbey (1947), Lafayette, OR 97127.

Our Lady of the Holy Trinity Abbey (1947), Huntsville, Utah 84317.

Abbey of the Genesee (1951), Piffard, NY 14533.

Mepkin Abbey (1949), HC 69, Box 800, Moncks Corner, SC 29461.

Our Lady of the Holy Cross Abbey (1950), Rt. 2, Box 3870, Berryville, VA 22611.

Assumption Abbey (1950), Rt. 5, Box 1056, Ava, MO 65608.

Abbey of New Clairvaux (1955), Vina, CA 96092.

St. Benedict's Monastery (1956), 1012 Monastery Rd., Snowmass, CO 81654.

Claretians (Missionary Sons of the Immaculate Heart of Mary), C.M.F.: Founded 1849, at Vich, Spain, by St. Anthony Mary Claret. General headquarters, Rome, Italy. Missionary, parochial, educational, retreat work.

Western Province, 1119 Westchester Pl., Los Angeles, CA 90019.

Eastern Province, 400 N. Euclid Ave. Oak Park, IL 60302.

Clerics Regular Minor (Adorno Fathers) C.R.M.: Founded 1588, at Naples, Italy, by Ven. Augustine Adorno and St. Francis Caracciolo. General motherhouse, Rome, Italy; U.S. address, 575 Darlington Ave., Ramsey, NJ 07446.

Columban, Society of St. (St. Columban

Foreign Mission Society, S.S.C.): Founded 1918. General headquarters, Dublin, Ireland. U.S. headquarters, P.O. Box 10, St. Columbans, NE 68056. Foreign mission work.

Comboni Missionaries of the Heart of Jesus (Verona Fathers), M.C.C.J.: Founded 1867, in Italy by Bp. Daniele Comboni; in U.S., 1939. General motherhouse, Rome, Italy; North American headquarters, Comboni Mission Center, 8108 Beechmont Ave., Cincinnati, OH 45230. Mission work in Africa and the Americas.

Consolata Missionaries, I.M.C.: Founded 1901, at Turin, Italy, by Bl. Joseph Allamano. General motherhouse, Rome, Italy; U.S. headquarters, P.O. Box 5550, Rt. 27, Somerset, NJ 08873.

Crosier Fathers (Canons Regular of the Order of the Holy Cross), O.S.C.: Founded 1210, in Belgium by Bl. Theodore De Celles. Generalate, Rome, Italy; U.S. Province of St. Odilia, 3204 E. 43rd St., Minneapolis, MN 55406. Mission, retreat, educational work.

Cross, Brothers of the Congregation of Holy, C.S.C.: Founded 1837, in France, by Rev. Basil Moreau; U.S. province, 1841. Generalate, Rome, Italy. Educational, social work; missions.

Midwest Province (1841), Box 460, Notre Dame, IN 46556.

Southwest Province (1956), St. Edward's University, Austin, TX 78704.

Eastern Province (1956), 85 Overlook Circle, New Rochelle, NY 10804.

Cross, Priests of the Congregation of Holy, C.S.C.: Founded 1837, in France; in U.S., 1841. Generalate, Rome, Italy. Educational and pastoral work; home missions and retreats; foreign missions; social services and apostolate of the press.

Indiana Province (1841), 1304 E. Jefferson Blvd., South Bend, IN 46617.

Eastern Province (1952), 835 Clinton Ave., Bridgeport, CT 06604.

Southern Province (1968), 2111 Brackenridge St., Austin, TX 78704.

Divine Word, Society of the, S.V.D.: Founded 1875, in Holland, by Bl. Arnold Janssen. North American Province founded 1897 with headquarters in Techny, IL General motherhouse, Rome, Italy.

Province of Bl. Joseph Freinademetz (Chicago Province) (1985, from merger of Eastern and Northern provinces), 1985 Waukegan Rd., Techny, IL 60082.

St. Augustine's Province (Southern Province) (1940), 201 Ruella Ave., Bay St. Louis, MS 39520.

St. Therese Province (Western Province) (1964), 2737 Pleasant Ave., Riverside, CA 92507.

Dominicans (Order of Friars Preachers), O.P.: Founded early 13th century by St. Dominic de Guzman. General headquarters, Santa Sabina, Rome, Italy. Preaching, teaching, missions, research, parishes.

St. Joseph Eastern Province (1805), 869 Lexington Ave., New York, NY 10021.

Most Holy Name of Jesus (Western) Province (1912), 5877 Birch Ct., Oakland, CA 94618.

St. Albert the Great (Central) Province (1939), 1909 S. Ashland Ave., Chicago, IL 60608.

Southern Dominican Province (1979), 3407 Napoleon Ave., New Orleans, LA 70125.

Spanish Province, U.S. foundation (1926), P.O. Box 279, San Diego, TX 78384.

Edmund, Society of St., S.S.E.: Founded 1843, in France, by Fr. Jean Baptiste Muard. General motherhouse, Edmundite Generalate, Fairholt, S. Prospect St., Burlington, VT 05401. Educational, missionary work.

Eudists (Congregation of Jesus and Mary), C.J.M.: Founded 1643, in France, by St. John Eudes. General motherhouse, Rome, Italy; North American province, 6125 Premiere Ave., Charlesbourg, Quebec G1H 2V9, Canada; U.S. community, 71 Burke Dr., Buffalo, NY 14215. Parochial, educational, pastoral, missionary work.

Francis, Brothers of Poor of St., C.F.P.: Founded 1857. Motherhouse, Aachen, Germany; U.S. province, P.O. Box 187, Burlington, IA 52601. Educational work, especially with poor and emotionally disturbed youth.

Francis, Third Order Regular of St., T.O.R.: Founded 1221, in Italy; in U.S., 1910. General motherhouse, Rome, Italy. Educational, parochial, missionary work.

Most Sacred Heart of Jesus Province (1910), 393 Valley Rd., Etters, PA 17319.

Immaculate Conception Province (1925), P.O. Box 29655, Brookland Sta., Washington, DC 20017.

Commissariat of the Spanish Province (1924), 301 Jefferson Ave., Waco, TX 76702.

Francis de Sales, Oblates of St., O.S.F.S.: Founded 1871, by Fr. Louis Brisson. General motherhouse, Rome, Italy. Educational, missionary, parochial work.

Wilmington-Philadelphia Province (1906), 2200 Kentmere Parkway, Box 1452, Wilmington, DE 19899.

Toledo-Detroit Province (1966), Box 4683, Toledo, Ohio 43610.

Francis Xavier, Brothers of St. (Xaverian Brothers), C.F.X.: Founded 1839, in Belgium, by Theodore J. Ryken. Generalate, Twickenham, Middlesex, England. Educational work.

Sacred Heart Province, 10318B Baltimore National Pike, Ellicott City, MD 21043.

St. Joseph Province, 704 Brush Hill Rd., Milton, MA 02186.

Franciscan Brothers of Brooklyn, O.S.F.: Founded in Ireland; established at Brooklyn, 1858. Generalate, 135 Remsen St., Brooklyn, NY 11201. Educational work.

Franciscan Brothers of Christ the King, O.S.F.: Founded 1961. General motherhouse, 3737 N. Marybelle Ave., Peoria, IL 61615.

Franciscan Brothers of the Holy Cross, F.F.S.C.: Founded 1862, in Germany. Generalate, Hausen, Linz Rhein, West Germany; U.S. region, 2500 St. James Rd., Springfield, IL 62707. Educational work.

Franciscan Brothers of the Third Order Regular, O.S.F.: Generalate, Mountbellew, Ireland; U.S. region, 5430 Torrance Blvd., Torrance, CA 90503.

Franciscan Friars of the Immaculate: Founded

1990, Italy. U.S. address, Our Lady's Chapel, 600 Pleasant St., New Bedford, MA. 02740.

Franciscan Friars of the Renewal, C.F.R.: Community established under jurisdiction of the archbishop of New York. Central House, St. Crispin Friary, 420 E. 156th St., Bronx, NY 10455.

Franciscan Missionary Brothers of the Sacred Heart of Jesus, O.S.F.: Founded 1927, in the St. Louis, MO, archdiocese. Motherhouse, St. Joseph Rd., Box 39, Eureka, MO 63025. Care of aged, infirm, homeless men and boys.

Franciscans (Order of Friars Minor), O.F.M.: A family of the First Order of St. Francis (of Assisi) founded in 1209 and established as a separate jurisdiction in 1517; in U.S., 1844. General headquarters, Rome, Italy. English-speaking conference: 3140 Meramec St., St. Louis, MO 63118. Preaching, missionary, educational, parochial, charitable work.

St. John the Baptist Province (1844), 1615 Vine St., Cincinnati, Ohio 45210.

Immaculate Conception Province (1855), 147 Thompson St., New York, NY 10012.

Sacred Heart Province (1858), 3140 Meramec St., St. Louis, MO 63118.

Assumption of the Blessed Virgin Mary Province (1887), Pulaski, WI 54162.

Most Holy Name of Jesus Province (1901), 58 W. 88th St., New York, NY 10024.

St. Barbara Province (1915), 1500 34th Ave., Oakland, CA 94601.

Our Lady of Guadalupe Province (1985), 1350 Lakeview Rd. S.W., Albuquerque, NM 87105.

Holy Cross Custody (1912), 1400 Main St., P.O. Box 608, Lemont, IL 60439.

Most Holy Savior Vice-Province, 232 S. Home Ave., Pittsburgh, PA 15202.

St. John Capistran Custody (1928), 209 E. 83rd St., New York, NY 10028.

St. Stephen King Custody (1948), 517 S. Belle Vista Ave., Youngstown, Ohio 44509.

Holy Family Croatian Custody (1927), 4848 S. Ellis Ave., Chicago, IL 60615.

St. Casimir Lithuanian Vice-Province, P.O. Box 980, Kennebunkport, ME 04046.

Holy Gospel Province (Mexico), U.S. foundation, 2400 Marr St., El Paso, TX 79903.

Saints Francis and James Province (Jalisco, Mexico), U.S. foundation, 504 E. Santa Clara St., Hebbronville, TX 78361.

Commissariat of the Holy Land, Mt. St. Sepulchre, 1400 Quincy St. N.E., Washington, DC 20017.

St. Mary of the Angels Custody, Byzantine Slavonic Rite, P.O. Box 270, Sybertsville, PA 18251.

Academy of American Franciscan History, 1712 Euclid Ave., Berkeley, CA 94709.

Franciscans (Order of Friars Minor Capuchin), O.F.M. Cap.: A family of the First Order of St. Francis (of Assisi) founded in 1209 and established as a separate jurisdiction in 1528. General motherhouse, Rome, Italy. Missionary, parochial work, chaplaincies.

St. Joseph Province (1857), 1740 Mt. Elliott Ave., Detroit, MI 48207.

St. Augustine Province (1873), 220 37th St., Pittsburgh, PA 15201.

St. Mary Province (1952), 30 Gedney Park Dr., White Plains, NY 10605.

Province of the Stigmata (1918), P.O. Box 809, Union City, NJ 07087.

Western American Capuchin Province, Our Lady of the Angels, 1345 Cortez Ave., Burlingame, CA 94010.

Sts. Adalbert and Stanislaus Province (1948), Manor Dr., Oak Ridge, NJ 07438.

Province of Mid-America (1977), St. Elizabeth Friary, 1060 St. Francis Way, Denver, CO 80204.

Vice-Province of Texas, 5707 Bernal Dr., Dallas, TX 75212.

St. John the Baptist Vice-Province, 216 Arzuaga St., P.O. Box 21350, Rio Piedras, Puerto Rico 00928.

Franciscans (Order of Friars Minor Conventual), O.F.M. Conv.: A family of the First Order of St. Francis (of Assisi) founded in 1209 and established as a separate jurisdiction in 1517; first U.S. foundation, 1852. General curia, Rome, Italy. Missionary, educational, parochial work.

Immaculate Conception Province (1852), Immaculate Conception Friary, Rensselaer, NY 12144.

St. Anthony of Padua Province (1906), 12300 Folly Quarter Rd., Ellicott City, MD 21043.

St. Bonaventure Province (1939), 6107 Kenmore Ave., Chicago, IL 60660.

Our Lady of Consolation Province (1926), 101 Anthony Dr., Mt. St. Francis, IN 47146.

Our Lady of Guadalupe Custody (vice-province), Holy Cross Friary, P.O. Box 158, Mesilla Park, NM 88047.

St. Joseph of Cupertino Province (1981), P.O. Box 820, Arroyo Grande, CA 93420.

Glenmary Missioners (The Home Missioners of America): Founded 1939, in U.S. General headquarters, P.O. Box 465618, Cincinnati, Ohio 45246. Home mission work.

Good Shepherd, Little Brothers of the, B.G.S.: Founded 1951, by Bro. Mathias Barrett. Motherhouse, P.O. Box 389, Albuquerque, NM 87102. Operate shelters and refuges for aged and homeless; homes for handicapped men and boys, alcoholic rehabilitation center.

Holy Eucharist, Brothers of the, F.S.E.: Founded in U.S., 1957. Generalate, P.O. Box 25, Plaucheville, LA 71362. Teaching, social, clerical, nursing work.

Holy Family, Congregation of the Missionaries of the, M.S.F.: Founded 1895, in Holland, by Rev. John P. Berthier. General motherhouse, Rome, Italy; U.S. provincial house, 10415 Midland Blvd., St. Louis, MO 63114. Belated vocations for the missions.

Holy Family, Sons of the, S.F.: Founded 1864, at Barcelona, Spain, by Bl. Jose Mañanet y Vives; in U.S., 1920. General motherhouse, Barcelona, Spain; U.S. address, 401 Randolph Rd., P.O. Box 4138, Silver Spring, MD 20904.

Holy Ghost Fathers, C.S.Sp.: Founded 1703, in Paris, by Claude Francois Poullart des Places; in U.S., 1872. Generalate, Rome, Italy. Missions, education.

Eastern Province (1872), 6230 Brush Run Rd.,

Bethel Park, PA 15102. Western Province (1964), 919 Briarcliff, San Antonio, TX 78213.

Holy Ghost Fathers of Ireland (1971), U.S. delegates: 4849 37th St., Long Island City, NY 11101 (East); Laguna Honda Hospital, 375 Laguna Honda Blvd., San Francisco, CA 94116 (West); St. John Baptist Church, 1139 Dryades St., New Orleans, LA 70113.

Holy Spirit, Missionaries of the, M.Sp.S.: Founded 1914, at Mexico City, Mexico, by Felix Rougier. General motherhouse, Mexico City; U.S. headquarters, Our Lady of Guadalupe, 500 N. Juanita Ave., P.O. Box 1091, Oxnard, CA 93030. Missionary work.

Immaculate Heart of Mary, Brothers of the, F.I.C.M.: Founded 1948, at Steubenville, Ohio, by Bishop John K. Mussio. Motherhouse, 609 N. 7th St., Steubenville, Ohio 43952. Educational, charitable work.

Jesuits (Society of Jesus), S.J.: Founded 1534, in France, by St. Ignatius of Loyola; received papal approval, 1540; first U.S. province, 1833. Generalate, Rome, Italy; U.S. national office, Jesuit Conference, 1424 16th St. N.W., Suite 300, Washington, DC 20036. Missionary, educational, literary work.

Maryland Province (1833), 5704 Roland Ave., Baltimore, MD 21210.

New York Province (1943), 501 E. Fordham Rd., Bronx, NY 10458.

Missouri Province (1863), 4511 W. Pine Blvd., St. Louis, MO 63108.

New Orleans Province (1907), 500 S. Jefferson Davis Pkwy., New Orleans, LA 70119.

California Province (1909), 300 College Ave., P.O. Box 519, Los Gatos, CA 95031.

New England Province (1926), 775 Harrison Ave., Boston, MA 02118.

Chicago Province (1928), 2050 N. Clark St., Chicago, IL 60614.

Oregon Province (1932), 2222 N.W. Hoyt, Portland, OR 97210.

Detroit Province (1955), 7303 W. Seven Mile Rd., Detroit, MI 48221.

Wisconsin Province (1955), 1434 W. State St., Milwaukee, WI 53233.

Province of the Antilles (1947), U.S. address, 1339 S.W. 9 Terrace, Miami, FL 33184.

John of God, Brothers of the Hospitaller Order of St., O.H.: Founded 1537, in Spain. General motherhouse, Rome, Italy; American province, 2425 S. Western Ave., P.O. Box 77627, Los Angeles, CA 90018; Irish Province of Immaculate Conception, 532 Delsea Dr., Westville Grove, NJ 08093. Nursing work and related fields.

Joseph, Congregation of St., C.S.J.: General motherhouse, Rome, Italy; U.S. vice province, 4076 Case Rd., Avon, Ohio 44011. Parochial, missionary, educational work.

Joseph, Oblates of St., O.S.J.: Founded 1878, in Italy, by Bishop Joseph Marello; in U.S., 1929. General motherhouse, Rome, Italy. Parochial, educational work.

Eastern Province, Route 315, Pittston, PA 18640.

California Province, 544 W. Cliff Dr., Santa Cruz, CA 95060.

Josephite Fathers, C.J.: General motherhouse, Ghent, Belgium; U.S. foundation, 989 Brookside Ave., Santa Maria, CA 93455.

Josephites (St. Joseph's Society of the Sacred Heart), S.S.J.: Established 1893, in U.S. as American congregation (originally established in U.S. in 1871 by Mill Hill Josephites from England). General motherhouse, 1130 N. Calvert St., Baltimore, MD 21202. Evangelization in African American community.

LaSalette, Missionaries of Our Lady of, M.S.: Founded 1852, by Msgr. de Bruillard; in U.S., 1892. Motherhouse, Rome, Italy.

Our Lady of Seven Dolors Province (1934), P.O. Box 260127, Hartford, CT 06126.

Immaculate Heart of Mary Province (1945), 947 Park St., Attleboro, MA 02703.

Mary Queen Province (1958), 4650 S. Broadway, St. Louis, MO 63111.

Mary Queen of Peace Province (1967), 1607 E. Howard Ave., Milwaukee, WI 53207.

Lateran, Canons Regular of the, C.R.L.: General house, Rome, Italy; U.S. address: 2317 Washington Ave., Bronx, NY 10458.

Legionaries of Christ, L.C.: Founded 1941, in Mexico, by Rev. Marcial Maciel; in U.S., 1965. General headquarters, Rome, Italy; U.S. novitiate, 475 Oak Ave., Cheshire, CT 06410.

Little Brothers of St. Francis, L.B.S.F.: Founded 1970 in Archdiocese of Boston by Bro. James Curran. General fraternity, 785-789 Parker St., Roxbury (Boston), MA 02120. Combine contemplative life with evangelical street ministry.

Marianist Fathers and Brothers (Society of Mary; Brothers of Mary), S.M.: Founded 1817, at Bordeaux, France, by Rev. William-Joseph Chaminade; in U.S., 1849. General motherhouse, Rome, Italy. Educational work.

Cincinnati Province (1849), 4435 E. Patterson Rd., Dayton, Ohio 45430.

St. Louis Province (1908), 4538 Maryland Ave., St. Louis, MO 63156.

Pacific Province (1948), 22825 San Juan Rd., Cupertino, CA 95015.

New York Province (1961), 4301 Roland Ave., Baltimore, MD 21210.

Province of Meribah (1976), 240 Emory Rd., Mineola, NY 11501.

Mariannhill, Congregation of the Missionaries of, C.M.M.: Trappist monastery, begun in 1882 by Abbot Francis Pfanner in Natal, South Africa, became an independent modern congregation in 1909; in U.S., 1920. Generalate, Rome, Italy; U.S.-Canadian province (1938), Our Lady of Grace Monastery, 23715 Ann Arbor Trail, Dearborn Hts., MI 48127. Foreign mission work.

Marians of the Immaculate Conception, Congregation of, M.I.C.: Founded 1673; U.S. foundation, 1913. General motherhouse, Rome, Italy. Educational, parochial, mission, publication work.

St. Casimir Province (1913), 6336 S. Kilbourn Ave., Chicago, IL 60629.

St. Stanislaus Kostka Province (1948), Eden Hill, Stockbridge, MA 01262.

Marist Brothers, F.M.S.: Founded 1817, in France, by Bl. Marcellin Champagnat. General motherhouse, Rome, Italy. Educational, social, catechetical work.

Esopus Province, 1241 Kennedy Blvd., Bayonne, NJ 07002 (office).

Poughkeepsie Province, 252 School St., Watertown, MA 02172.

Marist Fathers (Society of Mary), S.M.: Founded 1816, at Lyons, France, by Jean Claude Colin; in U.S., 1863. General motherhouse, Rome, Italy. Educational, foreign mission, pastoral work.

Washington Province (1924), 815 Varnum St., N.E., Washington, DC 20017.

Boston Province (1924), 27 Isabella St., Boston, MA 02116.

San Francisco Western Province (1962), 625 Pine St., San Francisco, CA 94108.

Maronite Monks (Cloistered Penitents of St. Francis), O. Mar.: Most Holy Trinity Monastery, Dugway Rd., Petersham, MA 01366.

Mary Immaculate, Oblates of, O.M.I.: Founded 1816, in France, by Bl. Charles Joseph Eugene de Mazenod; in U.S., 1849. General house, Rome, Italy. U.S. consulate, 707 Jefferson St., Oakland, CA 94607. Parochial, foreign mission, educational work; ministry to marginal. Southern U.S. Province (1904), 7711 Madonna Dr., San Antonio, TX 78216.

Our Lady of Hope, Eastern Province (1883), 391 Michigan Ave. N.E., Washington, DC 20017.

St. John the Baptist, Northern Province (1921), 61 Burns Hill Rd., Hudson, NH 03051.

Central Province (1924), 267 E. 8th St., St. Paul, MN 55101.

Western Province (1953), 290 Lenox Ave., Oakland, CA 94610.

Maryknoll (Catholic Foreign Mission Society of America), M.M.: Founded 1911, in U.S., by Frs. Thomas F. Price and James A. Walsh. General Center, Maryknoll, NY 10545.

Mekhitarist Order of Vienna, C.M.Vd.: Established 1773. General headquarters, Vienna, Austria. U.S. address, 4900 Maryland Ave., La Crescenta, CA 91214. Work among Armenians in U.S.

Mercedarians (Order of Our Lady of Mercy), O. de M.: Founded 1218, in Spain, by St. Peter Nolasco. General motherhouse, Rome, Italy; U.S. headquarters, 3205 Fulton Rd., Cleveland, OH 44109.

Mercy, Brothers of, F.M.M.: Founded 1856, in Germany. General motherhouse, Montabaur, Germany. American headquarters, 4520 Ransom Rd., Clarence, NY 14031. Hospital work.

Mercy, Brothers of Our Lady, Mother of, C.F.M.M.: Founded 1844, in The Netherlands by Abp. J. Zwijsen. Generalate, Tilburg, The Netherlands; U.S. region, 2336 S. C St., Oxnard, CA 93033.

Mercy, Congregation of Priests of (Fathers of Mercy), C.P.M.: Founded 1808, in France, by Rev. Jean Baptiste Rauzan; in U.S., 1839. General mission house, South Union, KY 42283. Mission work.

Mill Hill Missionaries (St. Joseph's Society for Foreign Missions), M.H.M.: Founded 1866, in England, by Cardinal Vaughan; in U.S., 1951. International headquarters, London, England;

American headquarters, 12101 Gravois Rd., St. Louis, MO 63127.

Minim Fathers, O.M.: General motherhouse, Rome, Italy. North American delegation (1970), 3431 Portola Ave., Los Angeles, CA 90032.

Missionaries of St. Charles, Congregation of the (Scabrinians), C.S.: Founded 1887, at Piacenza, Italy, by Bishop John Baptist Scalabrini. General motherhouse, Rome, Italy.

St. Charles Borromeo Province (1888), 27 Carmine St., New York, NY 10014.

St. John Baptist Province (1903), 546 N. East Ave., Oak Park, IL 60302.

Missionaries of the Holy Apostles, M.Ss.A.: Founded 1962, Washington, DC, by Very Rev. Eusebe M. Menard. North American headquarters, P.O. Box 7188, New Haven, CT 06519.

Missionhurst — CICM (Congregation of the Immaculate Heart of Mary): Founded 1862, at Scheut, Brussels, Belgium, by Very Rev. Theophile Verbist. General motherhouse, Rome, Italy; U.S. province, 4651 N. 25th St., Arlington, VA 22207. Home and foreign mission work.

Montfort Missionaries (Missionaries of the Company of Mary), S.M.M.: Founded 1715, by St. Louis Marie Grignon de Montfort; in U.S., 1948. General motherhouse, Rome, Italy; U.S. province, 101-18 104th St., Ozone Park, NY 11416. Mission work.

Mother Co-Redemptrix, Congregation of, C.M.C.: Founded 1953 at Lein-Thuy, Vietnam (North), by Fr. Dominic Mary Tran Dinh Thu; in U.S., 1975. General house, Hochiminhville, Vietnam; U.S. provincial house, 1900 Grand Ave., Carthage, MO 64836. Work among Vietnamese Catholics in U.S.

Oblates of the Virgin Mary, O.M.V.: Founded 1815, in Italy; in U.S., 1976; Generalate, Rome, Italy; U.S. provincialate: 65 Father Carney Dr., Milton, MA 02186. Clement's Shrine, 1105 Boylston St., Boston, MA 02215.

Oratorians (Congregation of the Oratory of St. Philip Neri), C.O.: Founded 1575, at Rome, by St. Philip Neri. A confederation of autonomous houses. U.S. addresses: P.O. Box 11586, Rock Hill, SC 29731; P.O. Box 1688, Monterey, CA 93940; 4040 Bigelow Blvd., Pittsburgh, PA 15213; P.O. Drawer ii, Pharr, TX 78577; 109 Willoughby St., Brooklyn, NY 11201.

Pallottines (Society of the Catholic Apostolate), S.A.C.: Founded 1835, at Rome, by St. Vincent Pallotti. Generalate, Rome, Italy. Charitable, educational, parochial, mission work.

Immaculate Conception Province (1953), P.O. Box 573, Pennsauken, NJ 08110.

Mother of God Province (1946), 5424 W. Blue Mound Rd., Milwaukee, WI 53208.

Irish Province (1909), U.S. address: 3352 4th St., P.O. Box 249, Wyandotte, MI 48192.

Queen of Apostles Province (1909), 448 E. 116th St., New York, NY 10029.

Christ the King Province, 3452 Niagara Falls, Blvd., N. Tonawanda, NY 14120.

Paraclete, Servants of the, s.P.: Founded 1947, Santa Fe, NM, archdiocese. Generalate and U.S. motherhouse, Via Coeli, Jemez Springs, N.M. 87025. Devoted to care of priests.

Paris Foreign Missions Society, M.E.P.: Founded 1662, at Paris, France. Headquarters, Paris, France; U.S. establishment, 930 Ashbury St., San Francisco, CA 94117. Mission work and training of native clergy.

Passionists (Congregation of the Passion), C.P.: Founded 1720, in Italy, by St. Paul of the Cross. General motherhouse, Rome, Italy.

St. Paul of the Cross Province (Eastern Province) (1852), 80 David St., South River, NJ 08882.

Holy Cross Province (Western Province), 5700 N. Harlem Ave., Chicago, IL 60631.

Patrician Brothers (Brothers of St. Patrick), F.S.P.: Founded 1808, in Ireland, by Bishop Daniel Delaney; U.S. novitiate, 7820 Bolsa Ave., Midway City, CA 92655. Educational work.

Patrick's Missionary Society, St., S.P.S.: Founded 1932, at Wicklow, Ireland, by Msgr. Patrick Whitney; in U.S., 1953. International headquarters, Kiltegan Co., Wicklow, Ireland. U.S. foundations: 70 Edgewater Rd., Cliffside Park, NJ 07010; 19536 Eric Dr., Saratoga, CA 95070; 1347 W. Granville Ave., Chicago, IL 60660.

Pauline Fathers (Order of St. Paul the First Hermit), O.S.P.P.E.: Founded 1215; established in U.S., 1955. General motherhouse, Czestochowa, Jasna Gora, Poland; U.S. province, P.O. Box 2049, Doylestown, PA 18901.

Pauline Fathers and Brothers (Society of St. Paul for the Apostolate of Communications), S.S.P.: Founded 1914, by Very Rev. James Alberione; in U.S., 1932. Motherhouse, Rome, Italy; New York province (1932), 6746 Lake Shore Rd., Derby, NY 14047; Los Angeles province, 112 S. Herbert Ave., Los Angeles, CA 90063. Social communications work.

Paulists (Missionary Society of St. Paul the Apostle), C.S.P.: Founded 1858, in New York, by Fr. Isaac Thomas Hecker. General offices, 86 Dromore Rd., Scarsdale, NY 10583. Missionary, ecumenical, pastoral work.

Piarists (Order of the Pious Schools), Sch.P.: Founded 1617, at Rome, Italy, by St. Joseph Calasanctius. General motherhouse, Rome, Italy. U.S. province, 363 Valley Forge Rd., Devon, PA 19333. New York-Puerto Rico vice-province (Calasanzian Fathers), P.O. Box 118, Playa Sta., Ponce, PR 00734. California vicariate, 3951 Rogers St., Los Angeles, CA 90063. Educational work.

Pius X, Brothers of St.: Founded 1952, at La Crosse, WI, by Bishop John P. Treacy. Motherhouse, 3710 East Ave. S., La Crosse, WI 54601. Education.

Pontifical Institute for Foreign Missions, P.I.M.E.: Founded 1850, in Italy, at request of Pope Pius IX. General motherhouse, Rome, Italy; U.S. province, 17330 Quincy Ave., Detroit, MI 48221. Foreign mission work.

Precious Blood, Society of, C.Pp.S.: Founded 1815, in Italy, by St. Gaspar del Bufalo. General motherhouse, Rome, Italy.

Cincinnati Province, 431 E. Second St., Dayton, OH 45402.

Kansas City Province, P.O. Box 339, Liberty, MO 64068.

Pacific Province, 2337 134th Ave. W., San Leandro, CA 94577.

Atlantic Province, 540 St. Clair Ave. West, Toronto M6C 14A, Canada.

Premonstratensians (Order of the Canons Regular of Premontre; Norbertines), O. Praem.: Founded 1120, at Premontre, France, by St. Norbert; in U.S., 1893. Generalate, Rome, Italy. Educational, parish work.

St. Norbert Abbey, 1016 N. Broadway, DePere, WI 54115.

Daylesford Abbey, 220 S. Valley Rd., Paoli, PA 19301.

St. Michael's Abbey, 1042 Star Route, Orange, CA 92667.

Providence, Sons of Divine, F.D.P.: Founded 1893, at Tortona, Italy, by Bl. Luigi Orione; in U.S., 1933. General motherhouse, Rome, Italy; U.S. address, 111 Orient Ave., E. Boston, MA 02128.

Redemptorists (Congregation of the Most Holy Redeemer), C.SS.R.: Founded 1732, in Italy, by St. Alphonsus Mary Liguori. Generalate, Rome, Italy. Mission work.

Baltimore Province (1850), 7509 Shore Rd., Brooklyn, NY 11209.

St. Louis Province (1875), Box 6, Glenview, IL 60025.

Oakland Province (1952), 3696 Clay St., San Francisco, CA 94118.

New Orleans Vice-Province, 1527 3rd St., New Orleans, LA 70130.

Richmond Vice-Province (1942), 313 Hillman St., P.O. Box 1529, New Smyrna Beach, FL 32170.

Resurrectionists (Congregation of the Resurrection), C.R.: Founded 1836, in France, under direction of Bogdan Janski. Motherhouse, Rome, Italy.

U.S. Province, 2250 N. Latrobe Ave., Chicago, IL 60639.

Ontario Kentucky Province, U.S. address, 338 N. 25th St., Louisville, KY 40212.

Rogationist Fathers, R.C.J.: Founded by Bl. Annibale (Hannibal) di Francia, 1887. General motherhouse, Rome, Italy. U.S. addresses: 9815 Columbus Ave., North Hills, CA 91343; P.O. Box 37, Sanger, CA 93657. Charitable work.

Rosary, Brothers of Our Lady of the Holy, F.S.R.: Founded 1956, in U.S., Motherhouse and novitiate, 1725 S. McCarran Blvd., Reno, NV 89502.

Rosminians (Institute of Charity), I.C.: Founded 1828, in Italy, by Antonio Rosmini-Serbati. General motherhouse, Rome, Italy; U.S. address, 2327 W. Heading Ave., Peoria, IL 61604. Charitable work.

Sacred Heart, Brothers of the, S.C.: Founded 1821, in France, by Rev. Andre Coindre. General motherhouse, Rome, Italy. Educational work.

New Orleans Province (1847), 4540 Elysian Fields Ave., New Orleans, LA 70122.

New England Province (1945), 685 Steere Farm Rd., Pascoag, RI 02859.

New York Province (1960), P.O. Box 68, Belvidere, NJ 07823.

Sacred Heart, Missionaries of the, M.S.C.: Founded 1854, by Rev. Jules Chevelier. General motherhouse, Rome, Italy; U.S. province, 305 S. Lake St., Aurora, IL 60507.

Sacred Heart of Jesus, Congregation of the

(Sacred Heart Fathers and Brothers), S.C.J.: Founded 1877, in France. General motherhouse, Rome, Italy; U.S. provincial office: P.O. Box 289, Hales Corners, WI 53130. Educational, preaching, mission work.

Sacred Hearts of Jesus and Mary, Congregation of (Picpus Fathers), SS.CC.: Founded 1805, in France, by Fr. Coudrin. General motherhouse, Rome, Italy. Mission, educational work.

Eastern Province (1946), 3 Adams St. (Box 111), Fairhaven, MA 02719.

Western Province (1970), 15201 Rinaldi St., Mission Hills, CA 91345.

Hawaii Province, Box 797, Kaneohe, Oahu, Hawaii 96744.

Sacred Hearts of Jesus and Mary, Missionaries of the, M.SS.CC.: Founded 1833, in Naples, Italy, by Ven. Cajetan Errico. General motherhouse, Rome, Italy; U.S. headquarters, 2249 Shore Rd., Linwood, NJ 08221.

Salesians of St. John Bosco (Society of St. Francis de Sales), S.D.B.: Founded 1859, by St. John (Don) Bosco. Generalate, Rome, Italy.

St. Philip the Apostle Province (1902), 148 Main St., New Rochelle, NY 10802.

San Francisco Province (1926), 1100 Franklin St., San Francisco, CA 94109.

Salvatorians (Society of the Divine Savior), S.D.S.: Founded 1881, in Rome, by Fr. Francis Jordan; in U.S., 1896. General headquarters, Rome, Italy; U.S. province, 1735 Hi-Mount Blvd., Milwaukee, WI 53208. Educational, parochial, mission work; campus ministries, chaplaincies.

Scalabrinians: See Missionaries of St. Charles, Congregation of the.

Servites (Order of Friar Servants of Mary), O.S.M.: Founded 1233, at Florence, Italy, by Seven Holy Founders. Generalate, Rome, Italy. General apostolic ministry.

Eastern Province (1967), 3121 W. Jackson Blvd., Chicago, IL 60612.

Western Province (1967), 5210 Somerset St., Buena Park, CA 90621.

Somascan Fathers, C.R.S.: Founded 1534, at Somasca, Italy, by St. Jerome Emiliani. General motherhouse, Rome, Italy; U.S. address, Pine Haven Boys Center, River Rd., P.O. 162, Suncook, NH 03275.

Sons of Mary Missionary Society (Sons of Mary, Health of the Sick), F.M.S.I.: Founded 1952, in the Boston archdiocese, by Rev. Edward F. Garesche, S.J. Headquarters, 567 Salem End Rd., Framingham, MA 01701. Dedicated to health of the sick; medical, catechetical and social work in home and foreign missions.

Stigmatine Fathers and Brothers (Congregation of the Sacred Stigmata), C.S.S.: Founded 1816, by St. Gaspare Bertoni. General motherhouse, Rome, Italy; North American Province, 554 Lexington St., Waltham, MA 02154. Parish work.

Sulpicians (Society of Priests of St. Sulpice), S.S.: Founded 1641, at Paris, by Rev. Jean Jacques Olier. General motherhouse, Paris, France; U.S. province, 5408 Roland Ave., Baltimore, MD 21210. Education of seminarians and priests.

Theatines (Congregation of Clerics Regular): C.R.: Founded 1524, at Rome, by St. Cajetan. General

motherhouse, Rome, Italy; U.S. headquarters, 1050 S. Birch St., Denver, CO 80222.

Trappists: See Cistercians of the Strict Observance.

Trinitarians (Order of the Most Holy Trinity), O.SS.T.: Founded 1198, by St. John of Matha; in U.S., 1911. General motherhouse, Rome, Italy; U.S. headquarters, P.O. Box 5719, Baltimore, MD 21208.

Trinity Missions (Missionary Servants of the Most Holy Trinity), S.T.: Founded 1929, by Fr. Thomas Augustine Judge. Generalate, 1215 N. Scott St., Arlington, VA 22209. Home mission work.

Viatorian Fathers (Clerics of St. Viator), C.S.V.: Founded 1831, in France, by Fr. Louis Joseph Querbes. General motherhouse, Rome, Italy. Province of Chicago (1882), 1212 E. Euclid St., Arlington Hts., IL 60004. Educational work.

Vincentians (Congregation of the Mission; Lazarists), C.M.: Founded 1625, in Paris, by St. Vincent de Paul; in U.S., 1818. General motherhouse, Rome, Italy. Educational work.

Eastern Province (1867), 500 E. Chelten Ave., Philadelphia, PA 19144.

Midwest Province (1888), 1723 Pennsylvania Ave., St. Louis, MO 63104.

New England Province (1975), 1109 Prospect Ave., W. Hartford, CT 06105.

American Italian Branch, Our Lady of Pompei Church, 3600 Claremont St., Baltimore, MD 21224.

American Spanish Branch (Barcelona, Spain), 234 Congress St., Brooklyn, NY 11201.

American Spanish Branch (Zaragoza, Spain), Holy Agony Church, 1834 3rd Ave., New York, NY 10029.

Western Province (1975), 650 W. 23rd St., Los Angeles, CA 90007.

Southern Province (1975), 3826 Gilbert Ave., Dallas, TX 75219.

Vocationist Fathers (Society of Divine Vocations), S.D.V.: Founded 1920, in Italy; in U.S., 1962. General motherhouse, Naples, Italy; U.S. headquarters, 90 Brooklake Rd., Florham Park, NJ 07932.

Xaverian Missionary Fathers, S.X.: Founded 1895, by Archbishop Conforti, at Parma, Italy. General motherhouse, Rome, Italy; U.S. province, 12 Helene Ct., Wayne, NJ 07470. Foreign mission work.

Other Communications Offices

International Mission Radio Association: Sister Noreen Perelli, P.B.V.M., treasurer-administrator, Presentation Convent, 2755 Woodhull Ave., Bronx, NY 10469.

Jesuits in Communication (JESCOM): Rev. Thomas M. Lucas, S.J., secretary for communications, Jesuit Conference, Suite 300, 1424 16th St. N.W., Washington, DC 20036.

Maryknoll Media Relations: Rev. William J. Grimm, M.M., director, Maryknoll Fathers and Brothers, Maryknoll, NY 10545.

National Franciscan Communications Conference: Rev. James J. Gardiner, S.A., president, Atonement Friars, 138 Waverly Pl., New York, NY 10014.

MEMBERSHIP OF RELIGIOUS INSTITUTES OF MEN

(Principal source: *1993 Annuario Pontificio.* Statistics as of Jan. 1, 1992, unless indicated otherwise.)

Listed below are world membership statistics of institutes of men of pontifical right with 500 or more members; the number of priests is in parentheses. Also listed are institutes with less than 500 members with houses in the United States.

Jesuits (16,699) 23,778
Franciscans (Friars Minor) (12,599) 18,738
Salesians (11,208) 17,555
Franciscans (Capuchins) (7,802) 11,699
Benedictines (5,377) 9,039
Brothers of Christian Schools 8,149
Dominicans (5,053) 6,715
Redemptorists (4,516) 6,135
Marist Brothers 5,791
Society of the Divine Word (3,494) 5,729
Oblates of Mary Immaculate (3,970) 5,331
Franciscans (Conventuals) (2,630) 4,295
Discalced Carmelites (O.C.D.) (2,340) 3,709
Vincentians (3,297) 3,681
Holy Spirit (Holy Ghost),
  Congregation (2,623) 3,323
Augustinians (2,394) 3,105
Claretians (2,036) 2,980
Trappists (1,245) 2,673
Passionists (1,974) 2,663
Missionaries of Africa (2,135) 2,516
Priests of the Sacred Heart (1,776) 2,470
Missionaries of the Sacred Heart
  of Jesus (1,698) 2,402
Pallottines (1,531) 2,217
Christian Brothers 2,124
Carmelites (O.Carm.) (1,486) 2,085
Combonian Missionaries of the Heart of
  Jesus(1,303) 1,960
Holy Cross, Congregation (841) 1,861
Marianists (554) 1,807
Carmelites of BVM (994) 1,702
Marists (1,347) 1,624
Brothers of the Sacred Heart (56) 1,618
Hospitallers of St. John of God (137) 1,533
Piarists (1,196) 1,514
Congregation of the Immaculate Heart
  of Mary (Missionhurst; Scheut Missionaries)
  (1,085) 1,446
Brothers of Christian Instruction
  of Ploermel (6) 1,393
Premonstratensians (974) 1,343
Cistercians (Common Observance) (817) 1,325
Sacred Hearts, Congregation (Picpus)
  (996) 1,296
Brothers of Christian Instruction
  of St. Gabriel (35) 1,285
Augustinians (Recollects) (960) 1,278
Salvatorians (818) 1,264
Legionaries of Christ (282) 1,262
Society of African Missions (1,027) 1,246
Montfort Missionaries (896) 1,218
Society of St. Paul (561) 1,203
Servants of Mary (800) 1,114
Little Workers of Divine Providence (739) 1,100
Blessed Sacrament, Congregation of (725) 1,062

Assumptionists (769) 1,058
Ministers of Sick (Camillians) (636) 1,052
Consolata Missionaries (769) 1,001
Missionaries of Holy Family (713) 968
Viatorians (383) 940
LaSalette Missionaries (646) 933
Xaverian Missionaries (694) 930
Franciscans (Third Order Regular) (584) 875
Canons Regular of St. Augustine (669) 833
Columbans (709) 770
Mercedarians (509) 765
Oblates of St. Francis de Sales (604) 763
Scalabrinians (623) 760
Mill Hill Missionaries (657) 757
Maryknollers (630) 728
Congregation of St. Joseph (526) 707
Brothers of Charity (Ghent) 704
Missionaries of the Most Precious
  Blood (521) 694
Trinitarians (407) 676
Missionaries of St. Francis de Sales
  of Annecy (362) 675
Pontifical Institute for Foreign Missions (542) ... 628
Eudists (407) 572
Brothers of the Immaculate Conception (5) 554
Somascans (329) 536
Order of St. Basil the Great
  (Basilians of St. Josaphat) (286) 525
Society of Christ (350) 511
Brothers of Our Lady Mother of Mercy 505
Crosier Fathers and Brothers (346) 498
Oratorians (355) 489
Servants of Charity (361) 477
Marian Fathers and Brothers (272) 455
Paris Foreign Mission Society (448) 448
Resurrection, Congregation of (336) 443
Oblates of St. Joseph (286) 438
Sulpicians (431) 431
Barnabites (330) 425
Stigmatine Fathers and Brothers (318) 415
Congr. of St. Basil (Canada) *(1990)* (385) 402
Missionaries of the Holy Spirit (248) 400
St. Patrick's Mission Society (371) 399
Order of St. Paul the First Hermit (207) 397
Mariannhill Missionaries (228) 367
Rosminians (270) 366
Carthusians (172) 358
Rogationists (184) 341
Xaverian Brothers 331
Little Brothers of Jesus (74) 261
Bethlehem Missionaries (200) 259
Paulists (222) 242
Oblates of the Virgin Mary (170) 213
Vocationist Fathers (156) 207
Brothers of St. Patrick 203
Sons of the Holy Family (123) 180
Franciscan Friars of the Atonement (115) 172
Josephites (St. Joseph's Society
  of the Sacred Heart — S.S.J.) (149) 163
Missionary Servants
  of the Most Holy Trinity (107) 159
Presentation Brothers 156
Theatines (107) 156
Josephites (C.J.) (93) 129

Alexian Brothers (2) 127	Society of St. Edmund (66) 75
Franciscan Brothers of Brooklyn 120	Brothers of the Good Shepherd 66
Basilian Salvatorian Fathers (84) 114	Congr. of Sacerdotal Fraternity (34) 65
Camaldolese (36) 93	Franciscan Bros. of Holy Cross (2) 62
Brothers of Mercy 80	Servants of Holy Paraclete (28) 34
Glenmary Missioners (67) 77	Mekhitarist Order of Vienna (17) 21
Clerics Regular Minor (Adorno Fathers) (32) 76	Fathers of Mercy (9) 21

RELIGIOUS INSTITUTES OF WOMEN IN THE UNITED STATES

(Sources: *Official Catholic Directory;* Catholic Almanac survey.)

Adorers of the Blood of Christ, A.S.C.: Founded 1834, in Italy; in U.S., 1870. General motherhouse, Rome, Italy. U.S. provinces: Rt. 1, Box 115, Red Bud, Ill. 62278; 1400 South Sheridan, Wichita, Kans. 67213; St. Joseph Convent, Columbia, Pa. 17512. Education, retreats, social services, pastoral ministry.

Africa, Missionary Sisters of Our Lady of (Sisters of Africa), M.S.O.L.A.: Founded 1869, at Algiers, Algeria, by Cardinal Lavigerie; in U.S., 1929. General motherhouse, Frascati, Italy; U.S. headquarters, 5335 16th St., N.W., Washington, DC 20011. Medical, educational, catechetical and social work in Africa.

Agnes, Sisters of St., C.S.A.: Founded 1858, in U.S., by Rev. Caspar Rehrl. General motherhouse, 475 Gillett St., Fond du Lac, WI 54935. Education, health care, social services.

Ann, Sisters of St., S.S.A.: Founded 1834, in Italy; in U.S., 1952. General motherhouse, Rome, Italy; U.S. headquarters, Mount St. Ann, Ebensburg, PA 15931.

Anne, Sisters of St., S.S.A.: Founded 1850, at Vaudreuil, Que., Canada; in U.S., 1866. General motherhouse, Lachine, Que., Canada; U.S. address, 720 Boston Post Rd., Marlboro, MA 01752. Retreat work, pastoral ministry, religious education.

Anthony, Missionary Servants of St., M.S.S.A.: Founded 1929, in U.S., by Rev. Peter Baque. General motherhouse, 100 Peter Baque Rd., San Antonio, TX 78209. Social work.

Antoine Maronite Sisters: Established in U.S., 1966. U.S. address, 2691 N. Lipkey Rd., North Jackson, Ohio 44451.

Apostolate, Sisters Auxiliaries of the, S.A.A.: Founded 1903, in Canada; in U.S., 1911. General motherhouse, 689 Maple Terr., Monongah, WV 26555. Education, nursing.

Assumption, Little Sisters of the, L.S.A.: Founded 1865, in France; in U.S., 1891. General motherhouse, Paris, France; U.S. provincialate, 214 E. 30th St., New York, NY 10016. Social work, nursing, family life education.

Assumption, Religious of the, R.A.: Founded 1839, in France; in U.S., 1919. Generalate, Paris, France; North American province, 11 Old English Rd., Worcester, MA 01609. Educational work.

Assumption of the Blessed Virgin, Sisters of the, S.A.S.V.: Founded 1853, in Canada; in U.S., 1891. General motherhouse, Nicolet, Que., Canada; U.S. province, 316 Lincoln St., Worcester, MA 01605. Education, mission, pastoral ministry.

Augustinian Nuns of Contemplative Life, O.S.A.: Established in Spain in 13th century; U.S. foundation, Convent of Our Mother of Good Counsel, 4328 W. Westminster Pl., St. Louis, MO 63108.

Augustinian Sisters, Servants of Jesus and Mary, Congregation of, O.S.A.: Generalate, Rome, Italy; U.S. foundation, St. John School, Brandenburg, KY 40108.

Basil the Great, Sisters of the Order of St. (Byzantine Rite), O.S.B.M.: Founded fourth century, in Cappadocia, by St. Basil the Great and his sister St. Macrina; in U.S., 1911. Generalate, Rome, Italy; U.S. motherhouses: Philadelphia Ukrainian Byzantine Rite, 710 Fox Chase Rd., Philadelphia, PA 19111; Pittsburgh Ruthenian Byzantine Rite, Mount St. Macrina P.O. Box 878, Uniontown, PA 15401. Education, health care.

Benedict, Sisters of the Order of St., O.S.B.: Our Lady of Mount Caritas Monastery (founded 1979, Ashford, Conn.), Seckar Rd., Ashford, CT 06278. Contemplative.

Benedictine Nuns, O.S.B.: St. Scholastica Priory, Box 606, Petersham, MA 01366. Cloistered.

Benedictine Nuns of the Congregation of Solesmes, O.S.B.: U.S. establishment, 1981, in Burlington diocese. Monastery of the Immaculate Heart of Mary, H.C.R. Box 11, Westfield, VT 05874. Cloistered, papal enclosure.

Benedictine Nuns of the Primitive Observance, O.S.B.; Founded c. 529, in Italy; in U.S., 1948. Abbey of Regina Laudis, Flanders Rd., Bethlehem, CT 06751. Cloistered.

Benedictine Sisters, O.S.B.: Founded c. 529, in Italy; in U.S., 1852. General motherhouse, Eichstatt, Bavaria, Germany. U.S. addresses: St. Emma's Monastery, Motherhouse and Novitiate, 1001 Harvey Ave., Greensburg, PA 15601; Convent of St. Walburga, 6717 S. Boulder Rd., Boulder, CO 80303.

Benedictine Sisters (Regina Pacis), O.S.B.: Founded 1627, in Lithuania as cloistered community; reformed 1918 as active community; established in U.S. 1957, by Mother M. Raphaela Simonis. Regina Pacis, 333 Wallace Rd., Bedford, NH 03102.

Benedictine Sisters, Missionary, O.S.B.: Founded 1885. Generalate, Rome, Italy; U.S. motherhouse, 300 N. 18th St., Norfolk, NE 68701.

Benedictine Sisters, Olivetan, O.S.B.: Founded 1887, in U.S.. General motherhouse, Holy Angels Convent, P.O. Drawer 130, Jonesboro, AK 72403. Educational, hospital work.

Benedictine Sisters of Perpetual Adoration of Pontifical Jurisdiction, Congregation of the, O.S.B.: Founded in U.S., 1874, from Maria Rickenbach, Switzerland. General motherhouse, 8300 Morganford Rd., St. Louis, MO 63123.

Benedictine Sisters of Pontifical Jurisdiction,

O.S.B.: Founded c. 529, in Italy. No general motherhouse in U.S. Three federations.

• Federation of St. Scholastica (1922). Pres., Sister Regina Crowley, O.S.B., 7430 Ridge Blvd. Chicago, IL 60646. Motherhouses belonging to the federation:

Mt. St. Scholastica, 801 S. 8th St., Atchison, Kans. 66002; Benedictine Sisters of Elk Co., St. Joseph's Monastery, St. Mary's, PA 15857; Benedictine Sisters of Erie, 6101 E. Lake Rd., Erie, PA 16511; Benedictine Sisters of Chicago, St. Scholastica Priory, 7430 Ridge Blvd., Chicago, IL 60645; Sacred Heart Monastery, 1910 Maple Ave., Lisle, IL 60532; Benedictine Sisters of Newark, St. Walburga Monastery, 851 N. Broad St., Elizabeth, NJ 07208; Benedictine Sisters of Pittsburgh, 4530 Perrysville Ave., Pittsburgh, PA 15229; Red Plains Priory, 1132 N.W. 32nd, Oklahoma City, OK 73118; St. Joseph's Convent, 2200 S. Lewis, Tulsa, OK 74114; St. Gertrude's Monastery, Ridgely, MD 21660; St. Walburga Monastery, 2500 Amsterdam Rd., Covington, KY 41016; Sacred Heart Monastery, Cullman, AL 35056; St. Scholastica Priory, 75512 LA Hwy 1081,, Covington, LA 70434; St. Benedict's Monastery, Bristow, VA 22013; St. Scholastica Convent, 416 W. Highland Dr., Boerne, TX 78006; St. Lucy's Priory, Glendora, CA 91740; Holy Name Priory, St. Leo, FL 33574; Benet Hill Priory, 2555 N. Chelton Rd., Colorado Springs, CO 80909; Queen of Heaven Convent (Byzantine Rite), 8640 Squires Lane N.E., Warren, OH 44484; Benedictine Sisters of Baltimore, Emmanuel Monastery, 2229 W. Joppa Rd., Lutherville, MD 21093.

• Federation of St. Gertrude the Great (1937). Office: Sacred Heart Monastery, P.O. Box 364, Richardton, ND 58652. Pres., Sister Ruth Fox, O.S.B. Motherhouses belonging to the federation: Mother of God Monastery, R.R. 3, Box 254, Watertown, SD 57201; Sacred Heart Monastery, 1005 W. 8th St., Yankton, SD 57078; Mt. St. Benedict Monastery, 620 E. Summit Ave., Crookston, MN 56716; Sacred Heart Monastery, P.O. Box 364, Richardton, ND 58652; Convent of St. Martin, 2110-C St. Martin's Dr., Rapid City, SD 57702; Monastery of Immaculate Conception, 802 E. 10th St., Ferdinand, IN 47532; Monastery of St. Gertrude, P.O. Box 107, Cottonwood, ID 83522; Monastery of St. Benedict Center, Box 5070, Madison, WI 53705; Queen of Angels Monastery, 840 S. Main St., Mt. Angel, OR 97362; St. Scholastica Monastery, P.O. Box 3489, Fort Smith, AR 72913; Our Lady of Peace Monastery, 1511 Wilson Ave., Columbia, MO 65201; Queen of Peace Monastery, Box 370, Belcourt, ND 58316; Our Lady of Grace Monastery, 1402 Southern Ave., Beech Grove, IN 46107; Holy Spirit Monastery, 22791 Pico St., Grand Terrace, CA 92324; Spirit of Life Monastery, 10760 Glenwood Dr. West, Lakewood, CO 80226. St. Benedict's Monastery 225 Masters Ave., RR #1b, Winnipeg, Man. R3C 4A3, Canada.

• Federation of St. Benedict (1947). Pres., Sister Colleen Haggerty, O.S.B., St. Benedict Convent, St. Joseph, MN 56374. Motherhouses in U.S. belonging to the federation:

St. Benedict's Convent, St. Joseph, MN 56374; St. Scholastica Priory, 1200 Kenwood Ave., Duluth, MN 55811; St. Bede Priory, 1190 Priory Rd., Eau Claire, WI 54702; St. Mary Priory, Nauvoo, IL 62354; Annunciation Priory, 7520 University Dr., Bismarck, ND 58504; St. Paul's Priory, 2675 Larpenteur Ave., E., St. Paul, MN 55109; St. Placid Priory, 500 College St. N.E., Lacey, WA 98516.

Bethany, Sisters of, C.V.D.: Founded 1928, in El Salvador; in U.S. 1949. General motherhouse, Santa Tecla, El Salvador. U.S. address: 850 N. Hobart Blvd., Los Angeles, CA 90029.

Bethlemita Sisters, Daughters of the Sacred Heart of Jesus, S.C.I.F.: Founded 1861, in Guatemala. Motherhouse, Bogota, Colombia; U.S. address, St. Joseph Residence, 330 W. Pembroke St., Dallas, TX 75208.

Blessed Virgin Mary, Institute of the (Loreto Sisters), I.B.V.M.: Founded 17th century in Belgium; in U.S., 1954. Motherhouse, Rathfarnham, Dublin, Ireland; U.S. address: 2520 W. Maryland Ave., Phoenix, AZ 85017.

Blessed Virgin Mary, Institute of the (Loretto Sisters), I.B.V.M.: Founded 1609, in Belgium; in U.S., 1880. U.S. address, Loretto Convent, Box 508, Wheaton, IL 60189. Educational work.

Bon Secours, Sisters of, C.B.S.: Founded 1824, in France; in U.S., 1881. Generalate, Rome, Italy; U.S. provincial house, 1525 Marriottsville Rd., Marriottsville, MD 21104. Hospital work.

Brigid, Congregation of St., C.S.B.: Founded 1807, in Ireland; in U.S., 1953. U.S. regional house, 5118 Loma Linda Dr., San Antonio, TX 78201.

Brigittine Sisters (Order of the Most Holy Savior), O.SS.S.: Founded 1344, at Vadstena, Sweden, by St. Bridget; in U.S., 1957. General motherhouse, Rome, Italy; U.S. address, Vikingsborg, Runkenhage Rd., Darien, CT 06820.

Carmel, Congregation of Our Lady of Mount, O. Carm.: Founded 1825, in France; in U.S., 1833. Generalate, P.O. Box 476, Lacombe, LA 70445. Education, social services, pastoral ministry, retreat work.

Carmel, Institute of Our Lady of Mount, O. Carm.: Founded 1854, in Italy; in U.S., 1947. General motherhouse, Rome, Italy; U.S. novitiate, 5 Wheatland St., Peabody, MA 01960. Apostolic work.

Carmelite Community of the Word, C.C.W.: Motherhouse and Novitiate, Aquinas Hall, Ebensburg, PA 15931.

Carmelite Missionaries of St. Theresa, C.M.S.T.: Founded 1903, in Mexico. General motherhouse, Mexico City, Mexico; U.S. foundation, 9548 Deer Trail Dr., Houston, TX 70038.

Carmelite Nuns, Discalced, O.C.D.: Founded 1562, Spain. First foundation in U.S. in 1790, at Charles County, MD; this monastery was moved to Baltimore. Monasteries in U.S. are listed below, according to states.

Alabama: 716 Dauphin Island Pkwy., Mobile 36606. Arkansas: 7201 W. 32nd St., Little Rock 72204. California: 215 E. Alhambra Rd., Alhambra 91801; 27601 Highway 1, Carmel 93923; 68 Rincon Rd., Kensington 94707; 1883 Ringsted Dr., P.O.

Box 379, Solvang, CA 93463; 6981 Teresian Way, Georgetown 95634; 5158 Hawley Blvd., San Diego 92116; 721 Parker Ave., San Francisco 94118; 530 Blackstone Dr., San Rafael 94903; 1000 Lincoln St., Santa Clara 95050.

Colorado: 6138 S. Gallup St., Littleton 80120. Georgia: Coffee Bluff, 11 W. Back St., Savannah 31419; Illinois: River Rd. and Central, Des Plaines 60016. Indiana: 2500 Cold Springs Rd., Indianapolis 46222; 63 Allendale Pl., Terre Haute 47802. Iowa: 17937 250th St., Eldridge 52748; 2901 S. Cecilia St., Sioux City 51106. Kentucky: 1740 Newburg Rd., Louisville 40205. Louisiana: 1250 Carmel Ave., Lafayette 70507; 1611 Mirabeau Ave., New Orleans 70122.

Maryland: 1318 Dulaney Valley Rd., Towson, Baltimore 21204; R.R. 4, Box 4035A, LaPlata, MD 20646. Massachusetts: 61 Mt. Pleasant Ave., Roxbury, Boston 02119; 15 Mt. Carmel Rd., Danvers 01923. Michigan: 3800 Mt. Carmel Dr. NE, Ada 49301; 16630 Wyoming Ave., Detroit 48221; U.S. 2 Highway, P.O. Box 397, Iron Mountain 49801; 3501 Silver Lake Rd., Traverse City 49684. Minnesota: 8251 De Montreville Trail N., Lake Elmo 55042. Mississippi: 2155 Terry Rd., Jackson 39204.

Missouri: 2201 W. Main St., Jefferson City 65101; 9150 Clayton Rd., Ladue, St. Louis Co. 63124; 424 E. Republic Rd., Springfield 65807. Nevada: 1950 La Fond Dr., Reno 89509. New Hampshire: 275 Pleasant St., Concord, 03301. New Jersey: P.O. Box 785, Flemington 08822; 189 Madison Ave., Morristown 07960. New Mexico: Mt. Carmel Rd., Santa Fe 87501. New York: 745 St. John's Pl., Brooklyn 11216; 139 De Puyster Ave., Beacon 12508; 75 Carmel Rd., Buffalo 14214; 1931 W. Jefferson Rd., Pittsford 14534; 68 Franklin Ave., Saranac Lake 12983; 428 Duane Ave., Schenectady 12304.

Ohio: 3176 Fairmount Blvd., Cleveland Heights 44118. Oklahoma: 20,000 N. County Line Rd., Piedmont 73078. Oregon: 87609 Green Hill Rd., Eugene 97402. Pennsylvania: Elysburg 17824; 510 E. Gore Rd., Erie 16509; R.D. 6, Box 28, Center Dr., Latrobe 15650; P.O. Box 57, Loretto 15940; 66th Ave. and Old York Rd. (Oak Lane), Philadelphia 19126; Byzantine Rite, R.D. No. 1, Box 245, Sugarloaf 18249. Rhode Island: Watson Ave. at Nayatt Rd., Barrington 02806.

Texas: 600 Flowers Ave., Dallas 75211; 5801 Mt. Carmel Dr., Arlington 76017; 1100 Parthenon Pl., Roman Forest, New Caney 77357. 6301 Culebra and St. Joseph Way, San Antonio 78238. Utah: 5714 Holladay Blvd., Salt Lake City 84121. Vermont: Beckley Hill, Barre, 05641. Washington: 2215 N.E. 147th St., Seattle 98155. Wisconsin: W267 N2517 Meadowbrook Rd., Pewaukee 53072.

Carmelite Nuns of the Ancient Observance (Calced Carmelites), O. Carm.: Founded 1452, in The Netherlands; in U.S., 1930, from Naples, Italy, convent (founded 1856). U.S. monasteries: Carmelite Monastery of St. Therese, 3551 Lanark Rd., Coopersburg, PA 18036; Carmel of Mary, Wahpeton, ND 58075; Our Lady of Grace Monastery, 1 St. Joseph Pl., San Angelo, TX 76905; Carmel of the Sacred Heart, 430 Laurel Ave., Hudson, WI 54016. Papal enclosure.

Carmelite Sisters (Corpus Christi), O. Carm.: Founded 1908, in England; in U.S., 1920. General motherhouse, Tunapuna, Trinidad, W.I. U.S. address: Mt. Carmel Home, 412 W. 18th St., Kearney, NE 68847. Home and foreign mission work.

Carmelite Sisters for the Aged and Infirm, O. Carm.: Founded 1929, at New York, by Mother M. Angeline Teresa, O. Carm. Motherhouse, Avila-on-Hudson, Germantown, NY 12526. Social work, nursing and educating in the field of gerontology.

Carmelite Sisters of Charity, C.a.Ch.: Founded 1826 at Vich, Spain, by St. Joaquina de Vedruna. General motherhouse, Rome, Italy; U.S. address, 701 Beacon Rd., Silver Spring, MD 20903.

Carmelite Sisters of St. Therese of the Infant Jesus, C.S.T.: Founded 1917, in U.S.. General motherhouse, 1300 Classen Dr., Oklahoma City, OK 73103. Educational work.

Carmelite Sisters of the Divine Heart of Jesus, Carmel DCJ.: Founded 1891, in Germany; in U.S., 1912. General motherhouse, Sittard, Netherlands. U.S. provincial houses: 1230 Kavanaugh Pl., Milwaukee, WI 52313 (Northern Province); 10341 Manchester Rd., St. Louis, MO 63122 (Central Province); 8585 La Mesa Blvd., La Mesa, CA 92041 (South Western Province). Social services, mission work.

Carmelite Sisters of the Most Sacred Heart of Los Angeles, O.C.D.: Founded 1904, in Mexico. General motherhouse, Guadalajara, Mexico; U.S. provincialate and novitiate, 920 E. Alhambra Rd., Alhambra, CA 91801. Social services, retreat and educational work.

Casimir, Sisters of St., S.S.C.: Founded 1907, in U.S. by Mother Maria Kaupas. General motherhouse, 2601 W. Marquette Rd., Chicago, IL 60629. Education, missions, social services.

Cenacle, Congregation of Our Lady of the Retreat in the, R.C.: Founded 1826, in France; in U.S., 1892. Generalate, Rome, Italy. Eastern Province: Cenacle Rd., Lake Ronkonkoma, L.I., NY 11779; Midwestern Province, 513 Fullerton Pkwy., Chicago, IL 60614.

Charity, Daughters of Divine, F.DC: Founded 1868, at Vienna, Austria; in U.S., 1913. General motherhouse, Rome, Italy. U.S. provinces: 205 Major Ave., Staten Island, NY 10305; 39 N. Portage Path, Akron, OH 44303; 1315 N. Woodward Ave., Bloomfield Hills, MI 48013. Education, social services.

Charity, Little Missionary Sisters of, P.M.C.: Founded 1915, in Italy by Bl. Luigi Orione; in U.S., 1949. General motherhouse, Rome, Italy; U.S. address, 120 Orient Ave., East Boston, MA 02128.

Charity, Missionaries of, M.C.: Founded 1950, in Calcutta, India, by Mother Teresa; first U.S. foundation 1971. General motherhouse, 54A Lower Circular Road, Calcutta 700016, India. U.S. address, 335 E. 145th St., Bronx, NY 10451. Service of the poor.

Charity, Religious Sisters of, R.S.C.: Founded 1815, in Ireland; in U.S., 1953. Motherhouse, Dublin, Ireland; U.S. headquarters, Marycrest Manor, 10664 St. James Dr., Culver City, CA 90230.

Charity, Sisters of (of Seton Hill), S.C.: Founded 1870, at Altoona, PA, from Cincinnati foundation. Generalate, Mt. Thor Rd., Greensburg, PA 15601. Educational, hospital, social, foreign mission work.

Charity, Sisters of (Grey Nuns of Montreal), S.G.M.: Founded 1737, in Canada by St. Marie Marguerite d'Youville; in U.S., 1855. General administration, Montreal, Que. H2Y 2L7, Canada; U.S. provincial house, 10 Pelham Rd., Lexington, MA 02173.

Charity, Sisters of (of Leavenworth), S.C.L.: Founded 1858, in U.S. Motherhouse, 4200 S. 4th St., Leavenworth, KS 66048.

Charity, Sisters of (of Nazareth), S.C.N.: Founded 1812, in U.S. General motherhouse, SCN Center, P.O. Box 172, Nazareth, KY 40048. Education, health services.

Charity, Sisters of (of St. Augustine), C.S.A.: Founded 1851, at Cleveland, Ohio. Motherhouse, 5232 Broadview Rd., Richfield, OH 44286.

Charity, Sisters of Christian, S.C.C.: Founded 1849, in Paderborn, Germany, by Bl. Pauline von Mallinckrodt; in U.S., 1873. General motherhouse, Rome, Italy. U.S. provinces: Mallinckrodt Convent, Mendham, NJ 07945; 1041 Ridge Rd., Wilmette, IL 60091, Education, health services, other apostolic work.

Charity, Vincentian Sisters of, V.S.C.: Founded 1835, in Austria; in U.S., 1902. General motherhouse, 8200 McKnight Rd., Pittsburgh, PA 15237.

Charity, Vincentian Sisters of, V.S.C.: Founded 1928, at Bedford, Ohio. General motherhouse, 1160 Broadway, Bedford, OH 44146.

Charity at Ottawa, Sisters of (Grey Nuns of the Cross), S.C.O.: Founded 1845, at Ottawa, Canada; in U.S., 1857. General motherhouse, Ottawa, Canada; U.S. provincial house, 975 Varnum Ave., Lowell, MA 01854. Educational, hospital work, extended health care.

Charity of Canossa, Daughters of (Canossian Sisters): Founded 1808 in Verona, Italy. General motherhouse, Rome, Italy; U.S. provincial house, 5625 Isleta Blvd. S.W., Albuquerque, NM 87105.

Charity of Cincinnati, Ohio, Sisters of, S.C.: Founded 1809; became independent community, 1852. General motherhouse, Mt. St. Joseph, Ohio 45051. Educational, hospital, social work.

Charity of Our Lady, Mother of Mercy, Sisters of, S.C.M.M.: Founded 1832, in Holland; in U.S., 1874. General motherhouse, Den Bosch, Netherlands; U.S. provincialate, 520 Thompson Ave., East Haven, CT 06512.

Charity of Our Lady of Mercy, Sisters of, O.L.M.: Founded 1829, in Charleston, S.C. Generalate and motherhouse, 424 Fort Johnson Rd., James Island, Charleston, SC 29412. Education, campus ministry, social services.

Charity of Quebec, Sisters of (Grey Nuns), S.C.Q.: Founded 1849, at Quebec; in U.S., 1890. General motherhouse, 2655 Le Pelletier St., Beauport, Quebec GIC 3X7, Canada; U.S. address, 359 Summer St., New Bedford, MA 02740. Social work.

Charity of St. Elizabeth, Sisters of (Convent, NJ), S.C.: Founded 1859, at Newark, N. J. General motherhouse, P.O. Box 476, Convent Station, NJ 07961. Education, pastoral ministry, social services.

Charity of St. Hyacinthe, Sisters of (Grey Nuns), S.C.S.H.: Founded 1840, at St. Hyacinthe, Canada; in U.S., 1878. General motherhouse, 16470 Avenue Bourdages, SUD, St. Hyacinthe, Quebec J2T 4J8, Canada; U.S. regional house, 98 Campus Ave., Lewiston, ME 04240.

Charity of St. Joan Antida, Sisters of, S.C.S.J.A.: Founded 1799, in France; in U.S., 1932. General motherhouse, Rome, Italy; U.S. provincial house, 8560 N. 76th Pl., Milwaukee, WI 53223.

Charity of St. Louis, Sisters of, S.C.S.L.: Founded 1803, in France; in U.S., 1910. Generalate, Rome, Italy; U.S. provincialate, 146 S. Catherine St., Plattsburgh, NY 12901.

Charity of St. Vincent de Paul, Daughters of, DC: Founded 1633, in France; in U.S. 1809, at Emmitsburg, MD, by St. Elizabeth Ann Seton. General motherhouse, Paris, France. U.S. provinces: Emmitsburg, MD 21727; 7800 Natural Bridge Rd., St. Louis, MO 63121; 9400 New Harmony Rd., Evansville, IN 47712; 96 Menands Rd., Albany, NY 12204; 26000 Altamont Rd., Los Altos Hills, CA 94022.

Charity of St. Vincent de Paul, Sisters of, S.V.Z.: Founded 1845, in Croatia; in U.S., 1955. General motherhouse, Zagreb, Croatia; U.S. foundation, 171 Knox Ave., West Seneca, NY 14224.

Charity of St. Vincent de Paul, Sisters of, Halifax, S.C.H.: Founded 1856, at Halifax, N. S., from Emmitsburg, MD, foundation. Generalate, Mt. St. Vincent, Halifax, N. S., Canada. U.S. addresses: Commonwealth of Massachusetts, 125 Oakland St., Wellesley Hills, MA 02181; Boston Province, 26 Phipps St., Quincy, MA 02169; New York Province, 84-32 63rd Ave., Middle Village, NY 11379. Educational, hospital, social work.

Charity of St. Vincent de Paul, Sisters of, New York, S.C.: Founded 1817, from Emmitsburg, MD General motherhouse, Mt. St. Vincent on Hudson, 6301 Riverdale Ave., Bronx, NY 10471. Educational, hospital work.

Charity of the Blessed Virgin Mary, Sisters of, B.V.M.: Founded 1833, in U.S. by Mary Frances Clarke. General motherhouse, Mt. Carmel, 1100 Carmel Dr., Dubuque, IA 52001. Education, pastoral ministry, social services.

Charity of the Immaculate Conception of Ivrea, Sisters of, S.C.I.C.: Founded 18th century, in Italy; in U.S., 1961. General motherhouse, Rome, Italy; U.S. address, Immaculate Virgin of Miracles Convent, R.D. 2, Box 348, Mt. Pleasant, PA 15666.

Charity of the Incarnate Word, Congregation of the Sisters of, C.C.V.I.: Founded 1869, at San Antonio, TX, by Bishop C. M. Dubuis. Provincialate, 2128 Stone Moss Lane, Grapevine, TX 76051.

Charity of the Incarnate Word, Congregation of the Sisters of (Houston, Tex.), C.C.V.I.: Founded 1866, in U.S., by Bishop C. M. Dubuis. General motherhouse, P.O. Box 230969, Houston, TX 77223. Educational, hospital, social work.

Charity of the Sacred Heart, Daughters of, F.C.S.C.J.: Founded 1823, at La Salle de Vihiers,

France; in U.S., 1905. General motherhouse, La Salle de Vihiers, France; U.S. address, Sacred Heart Province, Littleton, NH 03561.

Charles Borromeo, Missionary Sisters of St. (Scalabrini Srs.): Founded 1895, in Italy; in U.S., 1941. American novitiate, 1414 N. 37th Ave., Melrose Park, IL 60601.

Child Jesus, Sisters of the Poor, P.C.J.: Founded 1844, at Aix-la-Chapelle, Germany; in U.S., 1924. General motherhouse, Simpelveld, Netherlands, American provincialate, 4567 Olentangy River Rd., Columbus, OH 43214.

Chretienne, Sisters of Ste., S.S.CH.: Founded 1807, in France; in U.S., 1903. General motherhouse, Metz, France; U.S. provincial house, 297 Arnold St., Wrentham, MA 02093. Educational, hospital, mission work.

Christ the King, Missionary Sisters of, M.S.C.K.: Founded 1959 in Poland; in U.S., 1978. General motherhouse, Poznan, Poland; U.S. regional superior, 3424 W. Adams Blvd., Los Angeles, CA 90018.

Christ the King, Sister Servants of, S.S.C.K.: Founded 1936, in U.S. General motherhouse, Loretto Convent, Mt. Calvary, WI 53057. Social services.

Christ the King, Sisters of, S.C.K.: Hermitage of Christ the King, 6501 Orchard Station Rd., Sebastopol, CA 95472.

Christian Doctrine, Sisters of Our Lady of, R.C.D.: Founded 1910, in New York. Central office, 23 Haskell Ave., Suffern, NY 10901.

Christian Education, Religious of, R.C.E.: Founded 1817, in France; in U.S., 1905. General motherhouse, Farnborough, England; U.S. provincial residence, 36 Hillcrest Rd., Belmont, MA 02178.

Cistercian Nuns, O. Cist.: Headquarters, Rome, Italy; U.S. address, Valley of Our Lady Monastery, E. 11096 Yanke Dr., Prairie du Sac, WI 53578.

Cistercian Nuns of the Strict Observance, Order of, O.C.S.O.: Founded 1125, in France, by St. Stephen Harding; in U.S., 1949. U.S. addresses: Mt. St. Mary's Abbey, 300 Arnold St., Wrentham, MA 02093; Santa Rita Abbey, HCR Box 929, Sonoita, AZ 85637; Our Lady of the Redwoods Abbey, Whitethorn, CA 95489. Our Lady of the Mississippi Abbey, 8400 Abbey Hill Rd., Dubuque, IA 52001; Our Lady of the Angels Monastery, Rt. 2, Box 288-A, Crozet, VA 22932.

Clare, Sisters of St., O.S.C.: General motherhouse, Dublin, Ireland; U.S. foundation, St. Angela Merici Convent, 575 S. Walnut Ave., Brea, CA 92621.

Clergy, Congregation of Our Lady, Help of the, C.L.H.C.: Founded 1961, in U.S. Motherhouse, Maryvale Convent, Rt. 1, Box 164, Vale, NC 28168.

Clergy, Servants of Our Lady Queen of the, S.R.C.: Founded 1929, in Canada; in U.S., 1934. General motherhouse, 57 Jules A. Brillant, Rimouski, Que. G5L 1X1 Canada. Domestic work.

Colettines: See Franciscan Poor Clare Nuns.

Columban, Missionary Sisters of St., S.S.C.: Founded 1922, in Ireland; in U.S., 1930. General motherhouse, Wicklow, Ireland; U.S. region, 73 Mapleton St., Brighton, MA 02135.

Comboni Missionary Sisters (Missionary Sisters of Verona), C.M.S.: Founded 1872, in Italy; in U.S., 1950. U.S. address, 1307 Lakeside Ave., Richmond, VA 23228.

Consolata Missionary Sisters, M.C.: Founded 1910, in Italy; in U.S., 1954. General motherhouse, Turin, Italy; U.S. headquarters, 6801 Belmont Rd., Belmont, MI 49306.

Cross, Daughters of the, DC: Founded 1640, in France; in U.S., 1855. General motherhouse, 1000 Fairview St., Shreveport, LA 71104. Educational work.

Cross, Daughters of, of Liege, F.C.: Founded 1833, in Liege, Belgium; in U.S., 1958. U.S. address, 165 W. Eaton Ave., Tracy, CA 95376.

Cross, Sisters, Lovers of the Holy (Phat Diem): Founded 1670, in Vietnam; in U.S. 1976. U.S. address, Our Lady of Peace Convent, 9028 Langdon Ave., Sepulveda, CA 91343.

Cross, Sisters of the Holy, C.S.C.: Founded 1841, at Le Mans, France, established 1847, in Canada; in U.S., 1881. General motherhouse, St. Laurent, Montreal, Que., Canada; U.S. regional office, 377 Island Pond Rd., Manchester, NH 03109. Educational work.

Cross, Sisters of the Holy, Congregation of, C.S.C.: Founded 1841, at Le Mans, France; in U.S., 1843. General motherhouse, Saint Mary's, Notre Dame, IN 46556. Education, health care, social services, pastoral ministry.

Cross and Passion, Sisters of the (Passionist Sisters), C.P.: Founded 1852; in U.S., 1924. General motherhouse, Northampton, England; U.S. address: Holy Family Convent, One Wright Lane, N. Kingstown, RI 02852.

Cyril and Methodius, Sisters of Sts., SS.C.M.: Founded 1909, in U.S., by Rev. Matthew Jankola. General motherhouse, Villa Sacred Heart, Danville, PA 17821. Education, care of aged.

Divine Compassion, Sisters of, R.DC: Founded 1886, in U.S. General motherhouse, 52 N. Broadway, White Plains, NY 10603. Education, other ministries.

Divine Spirit, Congregation of the, C.D.S.: Founded 1956, in U.S., by Archbishop John M. Gannon. Motherhouse, 409 W. 6th St., Erie, PA 16507. Education, social services.

Dominicans

Nuns of the Order of Preachers (Dominican Nuns), O.P.: Founded 1206 by St. Dominic at Prouille, France. Cloistered, contemplative. Two branches in the United States:

● Dominican Nuns having perpetual adoration. First monastery established 1880, in Newark, NJ, from Oullins, France, foundation (1868). Autonomous monasteries:

St. Dominic, 375 13th Ave., Newark, NJ 07103; Corpus Christi, 1230 Lafayette Ave., Bronx, NY 10474; Blessed Sacrament, 29575 Middlebelt Rd., Farmington Hills, MI 48334; Monastery of the Angels, 1977 Carmen Ave., Los Angeles, CA 90068; Corpus Christi, 215 Oak Grove Ave., Menlo Park, CA 94025; Infant Jesus, 1501 Lotus Lane, Lufkin, TX 75901.

● Dominican Nuns devoted to the perpetual Rosary. First monastery established 1891, in Union City, NJ, from Calais, France, foundation (1880). Twelve autonomous monasteries (some also observe perpetual adoration).

Dominican Nuns of Perpetual Rosary, 14th and West Sts., Union City, NJ 07087; 217 N. 68th St., Milwaukee, WI 53213; Perpetual Rosary, 1500 Haddon Ave., Camden, NJ 08103; Our Lady of the Rosary, 335 Doat St., Buffalo, NY 14211; Our Lady of the Rosary, 543 Springfield Ave., Summit, NJ 07901; Mother of God, 1430 Riverdale St., W. Springfield, MA 01089; Perpetual Rosary, 802 Court St., Syracuse, NY 13208; Immaculate Heart of Mary, 1834 Lititz Pike, Lancaster, PA 17601; Mary the Queen, 1310 W. Church St., Elmira, NY 14905; St. Jude, Marbury, AL 36051; Our Lady of Grace, North Guilford, CT 06437; St. Dominic, 4901 16th St. N.W., Washington, DC 20011.

Dominican Rural Missionaries, O.P.: Founded 1932, in France; in U.S., 1951, at Abbeville, LA General motherhouse, Luzarches, France; U.S. address, 1318 S. Henry St., Abbeville, LA 70510.

Dominican Sisters of Charity of the Presentation, O.P.: Founded 1696, in France; in U.S., 1906. General motherhouse, Tours, France; U.S. headquarters, 3012 Elm St., Dighton, MA 02715. Hospital work.

Dominican Sisters of Our Lady of the Rosary and of St. Catherine of Siena (Cabra): Founded 1644 in Ireland. General motherhouse, Cabra, Dublin, Ireland. U.S. regional house, 1930 Robert E. Lee Rd., New Orleans, LA 70122.

Dominican Sisters of the Roman Congregation of St. Dominic, O.P.: Founded 1621, in France; in U.S., 1904. General motherhouse, Paris, France; U.S. province, Box 570, Riverside, IA 52327. Educational work.

Eucharistic Missionaries of St. Dominic, O.P.: Founded 1927, in Louisiana. General motherhouse, 1101 Aline St., New Orleans, LA 70115. Parish work, social services.

Maryknoll Sisters of St. Dominic, M.M.: Founded 1912, in New York. Center, Maryknoll, NY 10545.

Religious Missionaries of St. Dominic, O.P.: General motherhouse, Rome, Italy. U.S. address (Spanish province), 502 Purdue St., Corpus Christi, TX 74818.

Sisters of St. Dominic, O.P.: Thirty congregations in the U.S. Educational, hospital work. Names of congregations are given below, followed by the date of foundation, and location of motherhouse.

St. Catharine of Siena, 1822. 2645 Bardstown Rd., St. Catharine, KY 40061.

St. Mary of the Springs, 1830. 2320 Airport Dr., Columbus Ohio 43219.

Most Holy Rosary, 1847. Sinsinawa, WI 53824.

Most Holy Name of Jesus, 1850. 1520 Grand Ave., San Rafael, CA 94901.

Holy Cross, 1853. Albany Ave., Amityville, NY 11701.

Most Holy Rosary, 1859. 320 Powell Ave., Newburgh, NY 12550.

St. Cecilia, 1860. 801 Dominican Dr., Nashville, TN 37228.

St. Mary, 1860. 580 Broadway, New Orleans, LA 70118.

St. Catherine of Siena, 1862. 5635 Erie St., Racine, WI 53402.

Our Lady of the Sacred Heart, 1873. 1237 W. Monroe St., Springfield, IL 62704.

Our Lady of the Rosary, 1876. Sparkill, NY 10976.

Queen of the Holy Rosary, 1876. P.O. Box 3908, Mission San Jose, CA 94539.

Most Holy Rosary, 1892. 1257 Siena Heights Dr., Adrian, MI 49221.

Our Lady of the Sacred Heart, 1877. 2025 E. Fulton St., Grand Rapids, MI 49503.

St. Dominic, 1878. Blauvelt, NY 10913.

Immaculate Conception (Dominican Sisters of the Sick Poor), 1879. 299 N. Highland Ave., Ossining, NY 10562. Social work.

St. Catherine de Ricci, 1880. 750 Ashbourne Rd., Elkins Park, PA 19117.

Sacred Heart of Jesus, 1881. 1 Ryerson Ave., Caldwell, NJ 07006.

Sacred Heart, 1882. 6501 Almeda Rd., Houston, TX 77021.

St. Thomas Aquinas, 1888. 935 Fawcett Ave., Tacoma, WA 98402.

Holy Cross, 1890. P.O. Box 280, Edmonds, WA 98020.

St. Catherine of Siena, 1891. 37 Park St., Fall River, MA 02721.

St. Rose of Lima (Servants of Relief for Incurable Cancer), 1896. Hawthorne, NY 10532.

Dominican Sisters of Great Bend, 1902. 3600 Broadway, Great Bend, KS 67530.

St. Catherine of Siena, 1911. 4600 93rd St., Kenosha, WI 53142.

St. Rose of Lima, 1923. 775 Drahner Rd., Oxford, MI 48051.

Immaculate Conception, 1929. 9000 W. 81st St., Justice, IL 60458.

Immaculate Heart of Mary, 1929. 1230 W. Market St., Akron, Ohio 44313.

Dominican Sisters of Spokane. West 3100 Fort George Wright Dr., Spokane, WA 99204.

Dominican Sisters of Oakford (St. Catherine of Siena), 1889. Motherhouse, Oakford, Natal, South Africa. U.S. regional house, 1965. 1855 Miramonte Ave., Mountain View, CA 94040.

(End, Listing of Dominicans)

Dorothy, Institute of the Sisters of St., S.S.D.: Founded 1834, in Italy; by St. Paola Frassinetti; in U.S., 1911. General motherhouse, Rome, Italy; U.S. provincialate, Mt. St. Joseph, 13 Monkeywrench Lane, Bristol, RI 02809.

Eucharist, Religious of the, R.E.: Founded 1857, in Belgium; in U.S., 1900. General motherhouse, Belgium; U.S. foundation, 2907 Ellicott Terr., N.W., Washington, DC 20008.

Family, Congregation of the Sisters of the Holy, S.S.F.: Founded 1842, in Louisiana, by Henriette Delille and Juliette Gaudin. General motherhouse, 6901 Chef Menteur Hwy., New Orleans, LA 70126. Educational, hospital work.

Family, Little Sisters of the Holy, P.S.S.F.: Founded 1880, in Canada; in U.S., 1900. General motherhouse, Sherbrooke, Que., Canada. U.S. novitiate, 285 Andover St., Lowell, MA 01852.

Family, Sisters of the Holy, S.H.F.: Founded 1872, in U.S. General motherhouse, P.O. Box 3248, Mission San Jose, CA 94539. Educational, social work.

Family of Nazareth, Sisters of the Holy, C.S.F.N.: Founded 1875, in Italy; in U.S., 1885. General motherhouse, Rome, Italy. U.S. provinces: Sacred Heart, 353 N. River Rd., Des Plaines, IL 60016; Immaculate Conception BVM, 4001 Grant Ave., Torresdale, Philadelphia, PA 19114; St. Joseph, 285 Bellevue Rd., Pittsburgh, PA 15229; Immaculate Heart of Mary, Marian Heights, 1428 Monroe Turnpike, Monroe, CT 06468; Sacred Heart Vice-Province, 1814 Egyptian Way, Box 530959, Grand Prairie, TX 75053.

Filippini, Religious Teachers, M.P.F.: Founded 1692, in Italy; in U.S., 1910. General motherhouse, Rome, Italy; U.S. provinces: St. Lucy Filippini Province, Villa Walsh, Morristown, NJ 07960; Queen of Apostles Province, 474 East Rd., Bristol, CT 06010. Educational work.

Francis de Sales, Oblate Sisters of St., O.S.F.S.: Founded 1866, in France; in U.S., 1951. General motherhouse, Troyes, France; U.S. headquarters, Villa Aviat Convent, Childs, MD 21916. Educational, social work.

Franciscans

Bernardine Sisters of the Third Order of St. Francis, O.S.F.: Founded 1457, at Cracow, Poland; in U.S., 1894. Generalate, 647 Spring Mill Rd., Villanova, PA 19085. Educational, hospital, social work.

Capuchin Nuns of St. Clare (Madres Clarisas Capuchinas): U.S. establishment, 1981, Amarillo diocese. Convent of the Blessed Sacrament and Our Lady of Guadalupe, 4201 N.E. 18th St., Amarillo, TX 79107. Cloistered.

Congregation of the Servants of the Holy Infancy of Jesus, O.S.F.: Founded 1855, in Germany; in U.S., 1929. General motherhouse, Wuerzburg, Germany; American motherhouse, Villa Maria, P.O. Box 708, North Plainfield, NJ 07061.

Congregation of the Third Order of St. Francis of Mary Immaculate, O.S.F.: Founded 1865, in U.S., by Fr. Pamphilus da Magliano, O.F.M. General motherhouse, 520 Plainfield Ave., Joliet, IL 60435. Educational and pastoral work.

Daughters of St. Francis of Assisi, D.S.F.: Founded 1894, in Hungary; in U.S., 1946. Provincial motherhouse, 507 N. Prairie St., Lacon, IL 61540. Nursing, CCD work.

Eucharistic Franciscan Missionary Sisters, E.F.M.S.: Founded 1943, in Mexico. Motherhouse, 943 S. Soto St., Los Angeles, CA 90023.

Felician Sisters (Congregation of the Sisters of St. Felix), C.S.S.F.: Founded 1855, in Poland by Bl. Mary Angela Truszkowska; in U.S., 1874. General motherhouse, Rome, Italy. U.S. provinces: 36800 Schoolcraft Rd., Livonia, MI 48150; 600 Doat St., Buffalo, NY 14211; 3800 Peterson Ave., Chicago, IL 60659; 260 South Main St., Lodi, NJ 07644; 1500 Woodcrest Ave., Coraopolis, PA 15108; 1315

Enfield St., Enfield, CT 06082; 4210 Meadowlark Lane, S.E., Rio Rancho, NM 87124.

Franciscan Handmaids of the Most Pure Heart of Mary, F.H.M.: Founded 1916, in U.S.. General motherhouse, 15 W. 124th St., New York, NY 10027. Educational, social work.

Franciscan Hospitaller Sisters of the Immaculate Conception, F.H.I.C.: Founded 1876, in Portugal; in U.S., 1960. General motherhouse, Lisbon, Portugal; U.S. novitiate, 300 S. 17th St., San Jose, CA 95112.

Franciscan Missionaries of Mary, F.M.M.: Founded 1877, in India; in U.S., 1904. General motherhouse, Rome, Italy; U.S. provincialate, 3305 Wallace Ave., Bronx, NY 10467. Mission work.

Franciscan Missionaries of Our Lady, O.S.F.: Founded 1854, at Calais, France; in U.S., 1913. General motherhouse, Desvres, France; U.S. provincial house, 4200 Essen Lane, Baton Rouge, LA 70809. Hospital work.

Franciscan Missionaries of St. Joseph (Mill Hill Sisters), F.M.S.J.: Founded 1883, at Rochdale, Lancashire, England; in U.S., 1952. Generalate, Manchester, England; U.S. headquarters, Franciscan House, 1006 Madison Ave., Albany, NY 12208.

Franciscan Missionaries of the Immaculate Heart of Mary, F.M.I.H.M.: Founded at Cairo, Egypt by Bl. Catarino di S. Rosa (Costanzo Troiano). Generalate, Rome, Italy; U.S. address, 400 S. Black Horse Pike, Blackwood, NJ 08302.

Franciscan Missionary Sisters for Africa, O.S.F.: American foundation, 1953. Generalate, Ireland; U.S. headquarters, 172 Foster St., Brighton, MA 02135.

Franciscan Missionary Sisters of Assisi, F.M.S.A.: First foundation in U.S., 1961. General motherhouse, Assisi, Italy; U.S. address, St. Francis Convent, 1039 Northampton St., Holyoke, MA 01040.

Franciscan Missionary Sisters of Our Lady of Sorrows, O.S.F.: Founded 1939, in China, by Bishop Rafael Palazzi, O.F.M.; in U.S., 1949. U.S. address, 3600 S.W. 170th Ave., Beaverton, OR 97006. Educational, social, domestic, retreat and foreign mission work.

Franciscan Missionary Sisters of the Divine Child, F.M.DC: Founded 1927, at Buffalo, NY, by Bishop William Turner. General motherhouse, 6380 Main St., Williamsville, NY 14221. Educational, social work.

Franciscan Missionary Sisters of the Immaculate Conception, O.S.F.: Founded 1874, in Mexico; in U.S., 1926. U.S. provincial house, 11306 Laurel Canyon Blvd., San Fernando, CA 91340.

Franciscan Missionary Sisters of the Infant Jesus, F.M.I.J.: Founded 1879, in Italy; in U.S., 1961. Generalate, Rome, Italy. U.S. provincialate, 1215 Kresson Rd., Cherry Hill, NJ 08003.

Franciscan Missionary Sisters of the Sacred Heart, F.M.S.C.: Founded 1860, in Italy; in U.S., 1865. Generalate, Rome, Italy; U.S. provincialate, 250 South St., Peekskill, NY 10566. Educational and social welfare apostolates and specialized services.

Franciscan Poor Clare Nuns (Poor Clares, Order of St. Clare, Poor Clares of St. Colette),

P.C., O.S.C., P.C.C.: Founded 1212, at Assisi, Italy, by St. Francis of Assisi; in U.S., 1875. Proto-monastery, Assisi, Italy. Addresses of autonomous motherhouses in U.S. are listed below.

3626 N. 65th Ave., Omaha, NE 68104; 720 Henry Clay Ave., New Orleans, LA 70118; 6825 Nurrenbern Rd., Evansville, IN 47712; 1310 Dellwood Ave., Memphis, TN 38127; 920 Centre St., Jamaica Plain, MA 02130; 201 Crosswicks St., Bordentown, NJ 08505; 1271 Langhorne-Newtown Rd., Langhorne, PA 19047; 4419 N. Hawthorne St., Spokane, WA 99205; 142 Hollywood Ave., Bronx, NY 10465; 421 S. 4th St., Sauk Rapids, MN 56379; 8650 Russell Ave. S., Minneapolis, MN 55431; 3501 Rocky River Dr., Cleveland, OH 44111; 1671 Pleasant Valley Rd., Aptos, CA 95001; 2111 S. Main St., Rockford, IL 61102; 215 E. Los Olivos St., Santa Barbara, CA 93105; 460 River Rd., W. Andover, MA 01810; 809 E. 19th St., Roswell, NM 88201; 28210 Natoma Rd., Los Altos Hills, CA 94022; 1916 N. Pleasantburg Dr., Greenville, SC 29609; 28 Harpersville Rd., Newport News, VA 23601; 1175 N. County Rd. 300 W., Kokomo, IN 46901; 3900 Sherwood Blvd., Delray Beach, FL 33445; 200 Marycrest Dr., St. Louis, MO 63129.

Franciscan Sisters, Daughters of the Sacred Hearts of Jesus and Mary, O.S.F.: Founded 1860, in Germany; in U.S., 1872. Generalate, Rome, Italy; U.S. motherhouse, P.O. Box 667, Wheaton, IL 60189. Educational, hospital, foreign mission, social work.

Franciscan Sisters of Allegany, N.Y., O.S.F.: Founded 1859, at Allegany, NY, by Fr. Pamphilus da Magliano, O.F.M. General motherhouse Allegany, NY 14706. Educational, hospital, foreign mission work.

Franciscan Sisters Daughters of Mercy, F.H.M.: Founded 1856, in Spain; in U.S., 1962. General motherhouse, Palma de Mallorca, Spain; U.S. address, 612 N. 3rd St., Waco, TX 76701.

Franciscan Sisters of Baltimore, O.S.F.: Founded 1868, in England; in U.S., 1881. General motherhouse, 3725 Ellerslie Ave., Baltimore, MD 21218. Educational work; social services.

Franciscan Sisters of Chicago, O.S.F.: Founded 1894, in U.S., by Mother Mary Therese (Josephine Dudzik). General motherhouse, 1220 Main St., Lemont, IL 60439. Educational work, social services.

Franciscan Sisters of Christian Charity, O.S.F.: Founded 1869, in U.S. Motherhouse, Holy Family Convent, 2409 S. Alverno Rd., Manitowoc, WI 54220. Educational, hospital work.

Franciscan Sisters of Little Falls, MN, O.S.F.: Founded 1891, in U.S. General motherhouse, Little Falls, MN 56345. Health, education, social services, pastoral ministry, mission work.

Franciscan Sisters of Mary, F.S.M.: Established, 1987, through unification of the Sisters of St. Mary of the Third Order of St. Francis (founded 1872, St. Louis) and the Sisters of St. Francis of Maryville, MO (founded 1894). Address of general superior: 1100 Bellevue Ave., St. Louis, MO 63117. Health care, social services.

Franciscan Sisters of Mary Immaculate of the Third Order of St. Francis of Assisi, F.M.I.: Founded 16th century, in Switzerland; in U.S., 1932. General motherhouse, Bogota, Colombia; U.S. provincial house, 4301 N.E. 18th Ave., Amarillo, TX 79107. Education.

Franciscan Sisters of Our Lady of Perpetual Help, O.S.F.: Founded 1901, in U.S., from Joliet, IL, foundation. General motherhouse, 201 Brotherton Lane, St. Louis, MO 63135. Educational, hospital work.

Franciscan Sisters of Peace, F.S.P.: Established 1986, in U.S., as archdiocesan community, from Franciscan Missionary Sisters of the Sacred Heart. Congregation center, 20 Ridge St., Haverstraw, NY 10927.

Franciscan Sisters of Ringwood, F.S.R.: Founded 1927, at Passaic, New Jersey. General motherhouse, Mt. St. Francis, Ringwood, NJ 07456. Educational work.

Franciscan Sisters of St. Elizabeth, F.S.S.E.: Founded 1866, at Naples, Italy; in U.S., 1919. General motherhouse, Rome; U.S. novitiate, 499 Park Rd., Parsippany, NJ 07054. Educational work, social services.

Franciscan Sisters of St. Joseph, F.S.S.J.: Founded 1897, in U.S. General motherhouse, 5286 S. Park Ave., Hamburg, NY 14075. Educational, hospital work.

Franciscan Sisters of St. Joseph (of Mexico): U.S. foundation, St. Paul College, 3015 4th St. N.E., Washington, DC 20017.

Franciscan Sisters of the Atonement, Third Order Regular of St. Francis (Graymoor Sisters), S.A.: Founded 1898, in U.S., as Anglican community; entered Church, 1909. General motherhouse, Graymoor, Garrison P.O., NY 10524. Mission work.

Franciscan Sisters of St. Paul, Minn., O.S.F.: Founded 1863, at Neuwied, Germany (Franciscan Sisters of the Blessed Virgin Mary of the Holy Angels); in U.S., 1923. General motherhouse, Rhine, Germany; U.S. motherhouse, 1388 Prior Ave. S., St. Paul, MN 55116. Educational, hospital, social work.

Franciscan Sisters of the Immaculate Conception, O.S.F.: Founded in Germany; in U.S., 1928. General motherhouse, Kloster, Bonlanden, Germany; U.S. province, 291 W. North St., Buffalo, NY 14201.

Franciscan Sisters of the Immaculate Conception, Missionary, O.S.F.: Founded 1873, in U.S. General motherhouse, Rome, Italy; U.S. address, 790 Centre St., Newton, MA 02158. Educational work.

Franciscan Sisters of the Immaculate Conception and St. Joseph for the Dying, O.S.F.: Founded 1919, in U.S. General motherhouse, 485 Church St., Monterey, CA 93940.

Franciscan Sisters of the Poor, S.F.P.: Founded 1845, at Aachen, Germany, by Bl. Frances Schervier; in U.S., 1858. Community service center, 133 Remsen St., Brooklyn, NY 11201. Hospital, social work and foreign missions.

Franciscan Sisters of the Sacred Heart, O.S.F.: Founded 1866, in Germany; in U.S., 1876. General motherhouse, St. Francis Woods, R.R. 4, Mokena, IL 60448. Education, health care, other service ministries.

Hospital Sisters of the Third Order of St. Francis, O.S.F.: Founded 1844, in Germany; in U.S., 1875. General motherhouse, Muenster, Germany; U.S. motherhouse, Box 19431, Springfield, IL 62794. Hospital work.

Institute of the Franciscan Sisters of the Eucharist, F.S.E.: Founded 1973. Motherhouse, 405 Allen Ave., Meriden, CT 06450.

Little Franciscans of Mary, P.F.M.: Founded 1889, in U.S. General motherhouse, Baie St. Paul, Que., Canada. U.S. region, 55 Moore Ave., Worcester, MA 01602. Educational, hospital, social work.

Missionary Sisters of the Immaculate Conception of the Mother of God, S.M.I.C.: Founded 1910, in Brazil; in U.S., 1922, U.S. provincialate, P.O. Box 3026, Paterson, NJ 07509. Mission, educational, health work, social services.

Mothers of the Helpless, M.D.: Founded 1873, in Spain; in U.S., 1916. General motherhouse, Valencia, Spain; U.S. address, Sacred Heart Residence, 432 W. 20th St., New York, NY 10011.

Poor Clares of Perpetual Adoration, P.C.P.A.: Founded 1854, at Paris, France; in U.S., 1921, at Cleveland, Ohio. U.S. monasteries: 4200 N. Market Ave., Canton, OH 44714; 2311 Stockham Lane, Portsmouth, OH 45662; 4108 Euclid Ave., Cleveland, OH 44103; 3900 13th St. N.E., Washington, DC 20017; 5817 Old Leeds Rd., Birmingham, AL 35210. Contemplative, cloistered, perpetual adoration.

School Sisters of St. Francis, O.S.F.: Founded 1874, in U.S. General motherhouse, 1501 S. Layton Blvd., Milwaukee, WI 53215.

School Sisters of St. Francis (Bethlehem, Pa.), O.S.F.: Founded in Austria, 1843; in U.S., 1913. General motherhouse, Rome, Italy; U.S. province, 395 Bridle Path Rd., Bethlehem, PA 18017. Educational, mission work.

School Sisters of St. Francis, (Pittsburgh, Pa.), O.S.F.: Established 1913, in U.S. Motherhouse, Mt. Assisi Convent, 934 Forest Ave., Pittsburgh, PA 15202. Education, health care services and related ministries.

School Sisters of the Third Order of St. Francis (Panhandle, Tex.), O.S.F.: Established 1931, in U.S., from Vienna, Austria, foundation (1845). General motherhouse, Vienna, Austria; U.S. center and novitiate, P.O. Box 906, Panhandle, TX 79068. Educational, social work.

Sisters of Charity of Our Lady, Mother of the Church, S.C.M.C.: Established 1970, in U.S. Motherhouse, Baltic, CT 06330. Teaching, nursing, care of aged, and dependent children.

Sisters of Mercy of the Holy Cross, S.C.S.C.: Founded 1856, in Switzerland; in U.S. 1912. General motherhouse, Ingenbohl, Switzerland; U.S. provincial residence, 700 Riverside Ave., Merrill, WI 54452.

Sisters of Our Lady of Mercy (Mercedarians), S.O.L.M.: General motherhouse, Rome, Italy; U.S. addresses: Most Precious Blood, 133 27th Ave., Brooklyn, NY 11214; St. Edward School, Pine Hill, NJ 08021.

Sisters of St. Elizabeth, S.S.E.: Founded 1931, at Milwaukee, WI General motherhouse, 745 N. Brookfield Rd., Brookfield, WI 53005.

Sisters of St. Francis (Clinton, Iowa), O.S.F.: Founded 1868, in U.S. General motherhouse, Bluff Blvd. and Springdale Dr., Clinton, IA 57232. Educational, hospital, social work.

Sisters of St. Francis (Millvale, Pa.), O.S.F.: Founded 1865, Pittsburgh, PA General motherhouse, 146 Hawthorne Rd., Millvale P.O., Pittsburgh, PA 15209. Educational, hospital work.

Sisters of St. Francis (Hastings-on-Hudson), O.S.F.: Founded 1893, in New York. General motherhouse, Hastings-on-Hudson, NY 10706. Education, parish ministry, social services.

Sisters of St. Francis of Christ the King, O.S.F.: Founded 1864, in Austria. General motherhouse, Rome, Italy; U.S. provincial house, 1600 Main St., Lemont, IL 60439. Educational work, home for aged.

Sisters of St. Francis of Penance and Christian Charity, O.S.F.: Founded 1835, in Holland; in U.S., 1874. General motherhouse, Rome, Italy. U.S. provinces: 4421 Lower River Rd., Stella Niagara, NY 14144; 2851 W. 52nd Ave., Denver, CO 80221; 3910 Bret Harte Dr., P.O. Box 1028, Redwood City, CA 94064.

Sisters of St. Francis of Philadelphia, O.S.F.: Founded 1855, at Philadelphia, by Mother Mary Francis Bachmann and St. John N. Neumann. General motherhouse, Convent of Our Lady of the Angels, Glen Riddle-Aston, PA 19014. Education, health care, social services.

Sisters of St. Francis of Savannah, Mo., O.S.F.: Founded 1850, in Austria; in U.S., 1922. Provincial house, La Verna Heights, Box 488, 104 E. Park, Savannah, MO 64485. Educational, hospital work.

Sisters of St. Francis of the Congregation of Our Lady of Lourdes, O.S.F.: Founded 1916, in U.S. General motherhouse, 6832 Convent Blvd., Sylvania, OH 43560. Education, health care, social services, pastoral ministry.

Sisters of St. Francis of the Holy Cross, O.S.F.: Founded 1881, in U.S., by Rev. Edward Daems, O.S.C. General motherhouse, 3025 Bay Settlement Rd., Green Bay, WI 54301. Educational, nursing work, pastoral ministry, foreign missions.

Sisters of St. Francis of the Holy Eucharist, O.S.F.: Founded 1378, in Switzerland; in U.S., 1893. General motherhouse, 2100 N. Noland Rd., Independence, MO 64050. Education, health care, social services, foreign missions.

Sisters of St. Francis of the Holy Family, O.S.F.: U.S. foundation, 1875. Motherhouse, Mt. St. Francis, 3390 Windsor Ave., Dubuque, IA 52001. Varied apostolates.

Sisters of St. Francis of the Immaculate Conception, O.S.F.: Founded 1890, in U.S. General motherhouse, 2408 W. Heading Ave., Peoria, IL 61604. Education, care of aging, pastoral ministry.

Sisters of St. Francis of the Immaculate Heart of Mary, O.S.F.: Founded 1241, in Bavaria; in U.S., 1913. General motherhouse, Rome, Italy; U.S. motherhouse, Hankinson, ND 58041. Education, social services.

Sisters of St. Francis of the Martyr St. George, O.S.F.: Founded 1859, in Germany; in U.S., 1923. General motherhouse, Thuine, Germany; U.S. provincial house, St. Francis Convent, 2120 Central

Ave., Alton, IL 62002. Education, social services, foreign mission work.

Sisters of St. Francis of the Perpetual Adoration, O.S.F.: Founded 1863, in Germany; in U.S., 1875. General motherhouse, Olpe, Germany. U.S. provinces: Box 766, Mishawaka, IN 46544; 7665 Assisi Heights, Colorado Springs, CO 80919. Educational, hospital work.

Sisters of St. Francis of the Providence of God, O.S.F.: Founded 1922, in U.S., by Msgr. M. L. Krusas. General motherhouse, Grove and McRoberts Rds., Pittsburgh, PA 15234. Education, varied apostolates.

Sisters of St. Francis of the Third Order Regular, O.S.F.: Founded 1861, at Buffalo, NY, from Philadelphia foundation. General motherhouse, 400 Mill St., Williamsville, NY 14221. Educational, hospital work.

Sisters of St. Joseph of the Third Order of St. Francis, S.S.J.: Founded 1901, in U.S. Administrative office, P.O. Box 688, South Bend, IN 46624. Education, health care, social services.

Sisters of the Infant Jesus, I.J.: Founded 1662, at Rouen, France; in U.S., 1950. Motherhouse, Paris, France. Generalate, Rome, Italy. U.S. address: 20 Reiner St., Colma, CA 94014.

Sisters of the Sorrowful Mother (Third Order of St. Francis), S.S.M.: Founded 1883, in Italy; in U.S., 1889. General motherhouse, Rome, Italy. U.S. address: 17600 E. 51st St. S., Broken Arrow, OK 74012. Educational, hospital work.

Sisters of the Third Franciscan Order, O.S.F.: Founded 1860, at Syracuse, N.Y. Generalate offices, 2500 Grant Blvd., Syracuse, NY 13208. Educational, hospital work.

Sisters of the Third Order of St. Francis, O.S.F.: Founded 1877, in U.S., by Bishop John L. Spalding. Motherhouse, St. Francis Lane, E. Peoria, IL 61611. Hospital work.

Sisters of the Third Order of St. Francis (Oldenburg, Ind.), O.S.F.: Founded 1851, in U.S. General motherhouse, Convent of the Immaculate Conception, Oldenburg, IN 47036. Education, social services, pastoral ministry, foreign missions.

Sisters of the Third Order of St. Francis of Assisi, O.S.F.: Founded 1849, in U.S. General motherhouse, 3221 S. Lake Dr., Milwaukee, WI 53207. Education, other ministries.

Sisters of the Third Order of St. Francis of Penance and Charity, O.S.F.: Founded 1869, in U.S., by Rev. Joseph Bihn. Motherhouse, St. Francis Ave., Tiffin, OH 44883. Education, social services.

Sisters of the Third Order of St. Francis of the Perpetual Adoration, F.S.P.A.: Founded 1849, in U.S. Generalate, 912 Market St., La Crosse, WI 54601. Education, health care.

Sisters of the Third Order Regular of St. Francis of the Congregation of Our Lady of Lourdes, O.S.F.: Founded 1877, in U.S. General motherhouse, Assisi Heights, Rochester, MN 55901. Education, health care, social services.

(End, Listing of Franciscans)

Good Shepherd Sisters (Servants of the Immaculate Heart of Mary), S.C.I.M.: Founded 1850, in Canada; in U.S., 1882. General motherhouse, Quebec, Canada; Provincial House, Bay View, 313 Seaside Ave., Saco, Maine 04072. Educational, social work.

Good Shepherd, Sisters of Our Lady of Charity of the, R.G.S.: Founded 1835, in France by Mary Euphrasia Pelletier; in U.S., 1843. Generalate, Rome, Italy. U.S. provinces: 2849 Fischer Pl., Cincinnati, OH 45211; 82-31 Doncaster Pl., Jamaica, NY 11432; 504 Hexton Hill Rd., Silver Spring, MD 20904; 7654 Natural Bridge Rd., St. Louis, MO 63121; 5100 Hodgson Rd., St. Paul, MN 55112.

Graymoor Sisters: See Franciscan Sisters of the Atonement.

Grey Nuns of the Sacred Heart, G.N.S.H.: Founded 1921, in U.S. General motherhouse, 1750 Quarry Rd., Yardley, PA 19067.

Guadalupan Missionaries of the Holy Spirit, M.G.Sp.S.: Founded 1930 in Mexico by Rev. Felix de Jesus Rougier, M.Sp.S. General motherhouse, Mexico; U.S. delegation: 2483 S.W. 4th St. Miami, FL 33135.

Guardian Angel, Sisters of the Holy, S.A.C.: Founded 1839, in France. General motherhouse, Madrid, Spain; U.S. foundation, 1245 S. Van Ness, Los Angeles, CA 90019.

Handmaids of Mary Immaculate, A.M.I.: Founded 1952 in Helena, Mont. Address: Mountain View Rd., Washington, NJ 07882.

Handmaids of the Precious Blood, Congregation of, H.P.B.: Founded 1947, at Jemez Springs, N. Mex. Motherhouse and novitiate, Cor Jesu Monastery, Jemez Springs, NM 87025.

Helpers, Society of, H.H.S.: Founded 1856, in France; in U.S., 1892. General motherhouse, Paris, France; American province, 303 W. Barry Ave., Chicago, IL 60657.

Hermanas Catequistas Guadalupanas, H.C.G.: Founded 1923, in Mexico; in U.S., 1950. General motherhouse, Mexico; U.S. foundation, 4110 S. Flores, San Antonio, TX 78214.

Hermanas Josefinas, H.J.: General motherhouse, Mexico; U.S. foundation, Assumption Seminary, 2600 W. Woodlawn Ave., P.O. Box 28240, San Antonio, TX 78284. Domestic work.

Holy Child Jesus, Society of the, S.H.C.J.: Founded 1846, in England; in U.S., 1862. General motherhouse, Rome, Italy. U.S. province: 460 Shadeland Ave., Drexel Hill, PA 19026.

Holy Faith, Congregation of the Sisters of the, C.H.F.: Founded 1856, in Ireland; in U.S., 1953. General motherhouse, Dublin, Ireland; U.S. province, 12322 S. Paramount Blvd., P.O. Box 2085, Downey, CA 90242.

Holy Heart of Mary, Servants of the, S.S.C.M.: Founded 1860, in France; in U.S., 1889. General motherhouse, Montreal, Que., Canada; U.S. province, 145 S. 4th Ave., Kankakee, IL 60901. Educational, hospital, social work.

Holy Names of Jesus and Mary, Sisters of the, S.NJM.: Founded 1843, in Canada by Bl. Marie Rose Durocher; in U.S., 1859. Generalate, Longueuil Que., Canada. U.S. addresses: Oregon Province, Box 25, Marylhurst, OR 97036; California Province, P.O. Box 907, Los Gatos, CA 95031; New York Province, 1061 New Scotland

Rd., Albany, NY 12208; Washington Province, 2911 W. Ft. Wright Dr., Spokane, WA 99204.

Holy Spirit, Community of the: Founded 1970 in San Diego, CA Address: 1275 Nagle Ave., San Jose, CA 95126.

Holy Spirit, Daughters of the, D.H.S.: Founded 1706, in France; in U.S., 1902. Generalate, Bretagne, France; U.S. motherhouse, 72 Church St., Putnam, CT 06260. Educational work, district nursing; pastoral ministry.

Holy Spirit, Mission Sisters of the, M.S.Sp.: Founded 1932, at Cleveland, O. Motherhouse, 1030 N. River Rd., Saginaw, MI 48603.

Holy Spirit, Missionary Sisters, Servants of the: Founded 1889, in Holland; in U.S., 1901. Generalate, Rome, Italy; U.S. motherhouse, Convent of the Holy Spirit, Techny, IL 60082.

Holy Spirit, Sisters of the, C.S.Sp.: Founded 1890, in Rome, Italy; in U.S. as independent diocesan community, 1929. General motherhouse, 10102 Granger Rd., Garfield Hts., Ohio 44125. Educational, social, nursing work.

Holy Spirit, Sisters of the, S.H.S.: Founded 1913, in U.S., by Most Rev. J. F. Regis Canevin. General motherhouse, 5246 Clarwin Ave., Ross Township, Pittsburgh, PA 15229. Educational, nursing work; care of aged.

Holy Spirit and Mary Immaculate, Sisters of, S.H.Sp.: Founded 1893, in U.S. Motherhouse, 301 Yucca St., San Antonio, TX 78203. Education, hospital work.

Holy Spirit of Perpetual Adoration, Sister Servants of the: Founded 1896, in Holland; in U.S., 1915. Generalate, West Germany; U.S. Province, 2212 Green St., Philadelphia, PA 19130.

Home Mission Sisters of America (Glenmary Sisters): Founded 1952, in U.S. Glenmary Center, P.O. Box 2264, Owensboro, KY 42302.

Home Visitors of Mary, Sisters, H.V.M.: Founded 1949, in Detroit, Mich. Motherhouse, 356 Arden Park, Detroit, MI 48202.

Humility of Mary, Congregation of, C.H.M.: Founded 1854, in France; in U.S., 1864. U.S. address, Humility of Mary Center, Davenport, IA 52804.

Humility of Mary, Sisters of the, H.M.: Founded 1854, in France; in U.S., 1864. U.S. address, Villa Maria Community Center, Villa Maria, PA 16155.

Immaculate Conception, Little Servant Sisters of the: Founded 1850, in Poland; in U.S., 1926. General motherhouse, Poland; U.S. provincial house, 1000 Cropwell Rd., Cherry Hill, NJ 08003. Education, social services, African missions.

Immaculate Conception, Sisters of the, R.C.M.: Founded 1892, in Spain; in U.S., 1962. General motherhouse, Madrid, Spain; U.S. address, 2250 Franklin, San Francisco, CA 94109.

Immaculate Conception, Sisters of the, C.I.C.: Founded 1874, in U.S. General motherhouse, 4920 Kent Ave., Metairie, LA 70006.

Immaculate Conception of the Blessed Virgin Mary, Sisters of the (Lithuanian): Founded 1918, at Mariampole, Lithuania; in U.S., 1936. U.S. headquarters, Immaculate Conception Convent, 600 Liberty Hwy., Putnam, CT 06260.

Immaculate Heart of Mary, Missionary Sisters, I.C.M.: Founded 1897, in India; in U.S., 1919.

Generalate, Rome, Italy; U.S. province, 283 E. 15th St., New York, NY 10003. Educational social, foreign mission work.

Immaculate Heart of Mary, Sisters of the: Founded 1848, in Spain; in U.S., 1878. General motherhouse, Rome, Italy. U.S. province, 4100 Sabino Canyon Rd., Tucson, AZ 85715. Educational work.

Immaculate Heart of Mary, Sisters of the (California Institute of the Most Holy and Immaculate Heart of the B.V.M.), I.H.M.: Founded 1848, in Spain; in U.S., 1871. Generalate, 3431 Waverly Dr., Los Angeles, CA 90027.

Immaculate Heart of Mary, Sisters, Servants of the, I.H.M.: Founded 1845, at Monroe, Mich., by Rev. Louis Florent Gillet. Generalate, 610 W. Elm St., Monroe, MI 48161.

Immaculate Heart of Mary, Sisters, Servants of the, I.H.M.: Founded 1845; established in Scranton, Penn., 1871. General motherhouse, Immaculate Heart of Mary Marywood, Scranton, PA 18509.

Immaculate Heart of Mary, Sisters Servants of the, I.H.M.: Founded 1845; established in West Chester, Penn., 1872. General motherhouse, Villa Maria, Immaculata, PA 19345.

Incarnate Word, Religious of, C.V.I.: General motherhouse, Mexico City, Mexico. U.S. address, 153 Rainier Ct., Chula Vista, CA 92011.

Incarnate Word and Blessed Sacrament, Congregation of, C.V.I.: Founded 1625, in France; in U.S., 1853. Incarnate Word Convent, 3400 Bradford Pl., Houston, TX 77028.

Incarnate Word and Blessed Sacrament, Congregation of the, I.W.B.S.: Motherhouse, 1101 Northeast Water St., Victoria, TX 77901.

Incarnate Word and Blessed Sacrament, Congregation of the, I.W.B.S.: Motherhouse, 2930 S. Alameda, Corpus Christi, TX 78404.

Incarnate Word and Blessed Sacrament, Sisters of the, S.I.W.: Founded 1625, in France; in U.S. 1853. Motherhouse, 6618 Pearl Rd., Parma Heights, Cleveland, OH 44130.

Infant Jesus, Congregation of the (Nursing Sisters of the Sick Poor), C.I.J.: Founded 1835, in France; in U.S., 1905. General motherhouse, 310 Prospect Park W., Brooklyn, NY 11215.

Jesus, Daughters of, F.I.: Founded 1871, in Spain; in U.S., 1950. General motherhouse, Rome, Italy; U.S. address, 2021 Stuart Ave., Baton Rouge, LA 70808.

Jesus, Daughters of (Filles de Jesus), F.J.: Founded 1834, in France; in U.S., 1904. General motherhouse, Kermaria, Locmine, France; U.S. address, 4209 3rd Ave. S., Great Falls, Mont. 59405. Educational, hospital, parish and social work.

Jesus, Little Sisters of: Founded 1939, in Sahara; in U.S., 1952. General motherhouse, Rome, Italy; U.S. headquarters, 400 N. Streeper St., Baltimore, MD 21224.

Jesus, Servants of, S.J.: Founded 1974, in U.S. Central Office, 9075 Big Lake Rd., P.O. Box 128, Clarkston, MI 48016.

Jesus, Society of the Sisters, Faithful Companions of, F.C.J.: Founded 1820, in France; in U.S., 1896. General motherhouse, Kent, England.

U.S. province: St. Philomena Convent, Cory's Lane, Portsmouth, RI 02871.

Jesus and Mary, Little Sisters of, L.S.J.M.: Founded 1974 in U.S. Address: Joseph House, P.O. Box 1755, Salisbury, MD 21801.

Jesus and Mary, Religious of, R.J.M.: Founded 1818, at Lyons, France; in U.S., 1877. General motherhouse, Rome, Italy; U.S. province, 3706 Rhode Island Ave., Mt. Ranier, MD 20712. Educational work.

Jesus Crucified, Congregation of: Founded 1930, in France; in U.S., 1955. General motherhouse, Brou, France; U.S. foundations: Regina Mundi Priory, Devon, PA 19333; St. Paul's Priory, 61 Narragansett, Newport, RI 02840.

Jesus Crucified and the Sorrowful Mother, Poor Sisters of, C.J.C.: Founded 1924, in U.S., by Rev. Alphonsus Maria, C.P. Motherhouse, 261 Thatcher St., Brockton, MA 02402. Education, nursing homes, catechetical centers.

Jesus, Mary and Joseph, Missionaries of, M.J.M.J.: Founded 1942, in Spain; in U.S., 1956. General motherhouse, Madrid, Spain; U.S. regional house, 12940 Up River Rd., Corpus Christi, TX 78410.

Joan of Arc, Sisters of St., S.J.A.: Founded 1914, in U.S., by Rev. Marie Clement Staub, A.A. General motherhouse, 1505, rue de l'Assomption Sillery, Que. G1S 4T3, Canada. U.S. novitiate, 529 Eastern Ave., Fall River, MA 02723. Spiritual and temporal service of priests.

John the Baptist, Sisters of St., C.S.J.B.: Founded 1878, in Italy; in U.S., 1906. General motherhouse, Rome, Italy; U.S. provincialate, Anderson Hill Rd., Purchase, NY 10577. Education, parish and retreat work; social services.

Joseph, Poor Sisters of St.: Founded 1880, in Argentina. General motherhouse, Muniz, Buenos Aires, Argentina; U.S. addresses, Casa Belen, 305 E. 4th St., Bethlehem, PA 78015; Casa Nazareth, 532 Spruce St., Reading, PA 19602; St. Gabriel Convent, 4319 Sano St., Alexandria, VA 22312.

Joseph, Religious Daughters of St., F.S.J.: Founded 1875, in Spain. General motherhouse, Spain; U.S. foundation, 319 N. Humphreys Ave., Los Angeles, CA 90022.

Joseph, Religious Hospitallers of St., R.H.S.J.: Founded 1636, in France; in U.S., 1894. Generalate, Montreal, Que., Canada; U.S. address, Holy Family Convent, 438 College St., Burlington, VT 05401. Hospital work.

Joseph, Servants of St., S.S.J.: Founded 1874, in Spain; in U.S., 1957. General motherhouse, Salamanca, Spain; U.S. address, 203 N. Spring St., Falls Church, VA 22046.

Joseph, Sisters of St., C.S.J. or S.S.J.: Founded 1650, in France; in U.S., 1836, at St. Louis. Independent motherhouses in U.S.:

637 Cambridge St., Brighton, MA 02135; 1515 W. Ogden Ave., La Grange Park, IL, 60525; 480 S. Batavia St., Orange, CA 92668.

St. Joseph Convent, Brentwood, NY 11717; 23 Agassiz Circle, Buffalo, NY 14214; Avila Hall, Clement Rd., Rutland, VT 05701; 3430 Rocky River Dr., Cleveland, OH 44111; R.R. No. 3, Box

291A, Tipton, IN 46072; Motherhouse and Novitiate, Nazareth, MI 49074; 1425 Washington St., Watertown, NY 13601; Mt. Gallitzin Academy and Motherhouse, Baden, PA 15005; 819 W. 8th St., Erie, PA 16502.

4095 East Ave., Rochester, NY 14610; 215 Court St., Concordia, KS 66901; Mont Marie, Holyoke, MA 01040; 1412 E. 2nd St., Superior, WI 54880; Pogue Run Rd., Wheeling, WV 26003; 3700 E. Lincoln St., Wichita, KS 67218.

Joseph, Sisters of St. (Lyons, France), C.S.J.: Founded 1650, in France; in U.S., 1906. General motherhouse, Lyons, France; U.S. provincialate, 93 Halifax St., Winslow, ME 04901. Educational, hospital work.

Joseph, Sisters of St., of Peace, C.S.J.P.: Founded 1884, in England; in U.S. 1885. Generalate, 1225 Newton St. N.E., Washington, DC 20017. Educational, hospital, social service work.

Joseph of Carondelet, Sisters of St., C.S.J.: Founded 1650, in France; in U.S., 1836, at St. Louis, MO U.S. headquarters, 2307 S. Lindbergh Blvd., St. Louis, MO 63131.

Joseph of Chambery, Sisters of St.: Founded 1650, in France; in U.S., 1885. Generalate, Rome, Italy; U.S. provincial house, 27 Park Rd., West Hartford, CT 06119. Educational, hospital, social work.

Joseph of Chestnut Hill, Sisters of St., S.S.J.: Founded 1650; Philadelphia foundation, 1847. Motherhouse, Mt. St. Joseph Convent, Chestnut Hill, PA 19118.

Joseph of Cluny, Sisters of St., S.J.C.: Founded 1807, in France. Generalate, Paris, France; U.S. provincial house, Brenton Rd., Newport, RI 02840.

Joseph of Medaille, Sisters of, C.S.J.: Founded 1650, in France; in U.S., 1855. Became an American congregation Nov. 30, 1977. Central office, 1821 Summit Rd., Cincinnati, Ohio 45237.

Joseph of St. Augustine, Florida, Sisters of St., S.S.J.: General motherhouse, 241 St. George St., P.O. Box 3506, St. Augustine, FL 32085. Educational, hospital, pastoral, social work.

Joseph of St. Mark, Sisters of St., S.S.J.S.M.: Founded 1845, in France; in U.S., 1937. General motherhouse, 21800 Chardon Rd., Euclid, Cleveland, OH 44117. Nursing homes.

Joseph the Worker, Sisters of St., S.J.W.: General motherhouse, St. Joseph Convent, 1 St. Joseph Lane, Walton, KY 41094.

Lamb of God, Sisters of the, A.D.: Founded 1945, in France; in U.S., 1958. General motherhouse, France; U.S. address, 2068 Wyandotte Ave., Owensboro, KY 42301.

Little Workers of the Sacred Hearts, P.O.S.C.: Founded 1892, in Italy; in U.S. 1948. General house, Rome, Italy; U.S. address, Our Lady of Grace Convent, 635 Glenbrook Rd., Stamford, CT 06906.

Living Word, Sisters of the, S.L.W.: Founded 1975, in U.S. Motherhouse, The Center, 800 N. Fernandez Ave., Arlington Heights, IL 60004. Education, hospital, parish ministry work.

Loretto at the Foot of the Cross, Sisters of, S.L.: Founded 1812 in U.S., by Rev. Charles Nerinckx.

General motherhouse, Nerinx, KY 40049. Educational work.

Louis, Congregation of Sisters of St., S.S.L.: Founded 1842, in France; in U.S., 1949. General motherhouse, Monaghan, Ireland; U.S. regional house, 22300 Mulholland Dr., Woodland Hills, CA 91364. Educational, medical, parish, foreign mission work.

Marian Sisters of the Diocese of Lincoln: Founded 1954. Motherhouse, Marian Center, R.R. 1, Box 108, Waverly, NE 68462.

Marian Society of Dominican Catechists, O.P.: Founded 1954 in Louisiana. General motherhouse, P.O. Box 176, Boyce, LA 71409. Community of Alexandria, LA, diocese.

Marianites of Holy Cross, Congregation of the Sisters, M.S.C.: Founded 1841, in France; in U.S., 1843. Motherhouse, Le Mans, Sarthe, France. North American headquarters, 4123 Woodland Dr., New Orleans, LA 70131.

Marist Sisters, Congregation of Mary, S.M.: Founded 1824, in France. General motherhouse, Rome, Italy; U.S. convents: St. Albert the Great, 4855 Parker, Dearborn Hts., MI 48125; St. Barnabas, 24262 Johnston, E. Detroit, MI 48021; Our Lady of the Snows, 4810 S. Leamington, Chicago, IL 60638; Marie, Madre de la Iglesia, 4419 St. James, Detroit, MI 48210.

Martha, Sisters of St. (of Antigonish, N.S.), C.S.M.: Founded 1900 in Canada. Motherhouse, Antigonish. U.S. address, Box 30, Lowell, MA 01853.

Marthe, Sisters of Sainte (of St. Hyacinthe), S.M.S.H.: Founded 1883, in Canada; in U.S., 1929. General motherhouse 675 ouest, rue St.-Pierre, Hyacinthe, Que., J2T IN7 Canada; U.S. address, 383 Beech St., Manchester, NH 03103.

Mary, Company of, O.D.N.: Founded 1607, in France; in U.S., 1926. General motherhouse, Rome, Italy; U.S. motherhouse, 16791 E. Main St., Tustin, CA 92680.

Mary, Daughters of the Heart of, D.H.M.: Founded 1790, in France; in U.S., 1851. Generalate, Paris, France; U.S. provincialate, 1339 Northampton St., Holyoke, MA 01040. Education retreat work.

Mary, Missionary Sisters of the Society of (Marist Sisters), S.M.S.M.: Founded 1845, at St. Brieuc, France; in U.S., 1922. General motherhouse, Rome, Italy; U.S. provincial house, 357 Grove St., Waltham, MA 02154. Foreign missions.

Mary, Servants of, O.S.M.: Founded 13th century, in Italy; in U.S., 1893. Generalate, Rome, Italy; U.S. provincial motherhouse, 7400 Military Ave., Omaha, NE 68134.

Mary, Servants of (Servite Sisters), O.S.M.: Founded 13th century, in Italy; in U.S., 1912. General motherhouse, Our Lady of Sorrows Convent, 1000 College Ave., Ladysmith, WI 54848.

Mary, Servants of, of Blue Island (Mantellate Sisters), O.S.M.: Founded 1861, in Italy; in U.S., 1916. Generalate, Rome, Italy; U.S. motherhouse, 13811 S. Western Ave., Blue Island, IL 60406. Educational work.

Mary, Sisters of St., of Oregon, S.S.M.O.: Founded 1886, in Oregon, by Bishop William H. Gross, C.Ss.R. General motherhouse, 4440 S.W. 148th Ave., Beaverton, OR 97007. Educational, nursing work.

Mary, Sisters of the Little Company of, L.C.M.: Founded 1877, in England; in U.S., 1893. Generalate, London, England; U.S. provincial house, 9350 S. California Ave., Evergreen Park, IL 60642.

Mary, Sisters Servants of (Trained Nurses), S.M.: Founded 1851, at Madrid, Spain; in U.S., 1914. General motherhouse, Rome, Italy; U.S. motherhouse, 800 N. 18th St., Kansas City, KS 66102. Home nursing.

Mary and Joseph, Daughters of, D.M.J.: Founded 1817, in Belgium; in U.S., 1926. Generalate, Rome, Italy; American provincialate, 5300 Crest Rd., Rancho Palos Verdes, CA 90274.

Mary Help of Christians, Daughters of (Salesian Sisters of St. John Bosco), F.M.A.: Founded 1872, in Italy, by St. John Bosco and St. Mary Dominic Mazzarello; in U.S., 1908. General motherhouse, Rome, Italy; U.S. provinces, 655 Belmont Ave., Haledon, NJ 07508; 6019 Buena Vista St., San Antonio, TX 78237. Education, youth work.

Mary Immaculate, Daughters of (Marianist Sisters), F.M.I.: Founded 1816, in France, by Very Rev. William-Joseph Chaminade. General motherhouse, Rome, Italy; U.S. foundation, 251 W. Ligustrum Dr., San Antonio, TX 78228. Educational work.

Mary Immaculate, Religious of, R.M.I.: Founded 1876, in Spain; in U.S., 1954. Generalate, Rome, Italy: U.S. foundation, 719 Augusta St., San Antonio, TX 78215.

Mary Immaculate, Religious of (Claretian Missionary Sisters), R.M.I.: Founded 1855, in Cuba; in U.S., 1956. Generalate, Rome, Italy; U.S. address, 9600 W. Atlantic Ave., Delray Beach, FL 33446.

Mary Immaculate, Sister Servants of, S.S.M.I.: Founded 1878 in Poland. General motherhouse, Mariowka-Opoczynska, Poland; American provincialate, 1220 Tugwell Dr., Catonsville, MD 21228.

Mary Immaculate, Sisters of, S.M.I.: Founded 1948, in India, by Bishop Louis LaRavoire Morrow; in U.S., 1981. General motherhouse, Bengal, India; U.S. address, R.D. 5, Box 1231, Leechburg, PA 15656.

Mary Immaculate, Sisters Servants of, S.S.M.I: Founded 1892, in Ukraine; in U.S., 1935. General motherhouse, Rome, Italy; U.S. address, Immaculate Conception Province, Table Rock, Sloatsburg, NY 10974. Educational, hospital work.

Mary of Namur, Sisters of St., S.S.M.N.: Founded 1819, at Namur, Belgium; in U.S., 1863. General motherhouse, Namur, Belgium. U.S. provinces: 3756 Delaware Ave., Kenmore, NY 14217; 909 West Shaw St., Ft. Worth, TX 76110.

Mary of Providence, Daughters of St., D.S.M.P.: Founded 1872, at Como, Italy; in U.S., 1913. General motherhouse, Rome, Italy; U.S. provincial house, 4200 N. Austin Ave., Chicago, IL 60634. Special education for mentally handicapped.

Mary of the Immaculate Conception, Daughters of, D.M.: Founded 1904, in U.S., by

Msgr. Lucian Bojnowski. General motherhouse, 314 Osgood Ave., New Britain, CT 06053. Educational, hospital work.

Mary Queen, Congregation of, C.M.R.: Founded in Vietnam; established in U.S., 1979. U.S. region, 535 S. Jefferson, Springfield, MO 65806.

Mary Reparatrix, Society of, S.M.R.: Founded 1857, in France; in U.S., 1908. Generalate, Rome, Italy. U.S. province, 225 E. 234th St., Bronx, NY 10470.

Medical Mission Sisters (Society of Catholic Medical Missionaries, Inc.), M.M.S.: Founded 1925, in U.S., by Mother Anna Dengel. Generalate, London, Eng.; U.S. headquarters, 8400 Pine Rd., Philadelphia, PA 19111. Medical work, health education, especially in mission areas.

Medical Missionaries of Mary, M.M.M.: Founded 1937, in Ireland, by Mother Mary Martin; in U.S., 1950. General motherhouse, Dublin, Ireland; U.S. headquarters, 563 Minneford Ave., City Island, Bronx, NY 10464. Medical aid in missions.

Medical Sisters of St. Joseph, M.S.J.: Founded 1946, in India; first U.S. foundation, 1985. General motherhouse, Kerala, S. India; U.S. address, 3435 E. Funston, Wichita, KS 67218. Health care apostolate.

Mercedarian Missionaries of Berriz, M.M.B.: Founded 1930, in Spain; in U.S., 1946. General motherhouse, Rome, Italy. U.S. headquarters, 1400 N.E. 42nd Terr., Kansas City, MO 64106.

Mercy, Daughters of Our Lady of, D.M.: Founded 1837, in Italy, by St. Mary Joseph Rossello; in U.S., 1919. General motherhouse, Savona, Italy; U.S. motherhouse, Villa Rossello, Catawba Ave., Newfield, NJ 08344. Educational, hospital work.

Mercy, Missionary Sisters of Our Lady of, M.O.M.: Founded 1938, in Brazil; in U.S., 1955. General motherhouse, Brazil; U.S. address, 388 Franklin St., Buffalo, NY 14202.

Mercy, Religious Sisters of, R.S.M.: Founded 1973 in U.S. Motherhouse, 1417 Michigan Ave., Alma, MI 48801.

Mercy, Sisters of, Daughters of Christian Charity of St. Vincent de Paul, S.M.DC: Founded 1842, in Hungary; U.S. foundation, Rt. 1, Box 353A, 240 Longhouse Dr., Hewitt, NJ 07421.

Mercy, Sisters of, of the Americas: Formed in July, 1991, through union of 25 regional communities of Sisters of Mercy which previously were independent motherhouses or houses which formed the Sisters of Mercy of the Union. Mother Mary Catherine McAuley founded the Sisters of Mercy in Dublin, Ireland, in 1831; the first establishment in the U.S., 1843, in Pittsburgh. Address of administrative office: 8300 Colesville Rd., No. 300, Silver Spring, MD 20910. Pres., Sr. Doris Gottemoeller.

Mercy of the Blessed Sacrament, Sisters of: Founded 1910 in Mexico. U.S. foundation, 555 E. Mountain View, Barstow, CA 92311.

Mill Hill Sisters; See Franciscan Missionaries of St. Joseph.

Minim Daughters of Mary Immaculate, C.F.M.M.: Founded 1886, in Mexico; in U.S. 1926. General motherhouse, Leon, Guanajuato, Mexico;

U.S. address, Our Lady of Lourdes High School, Box 1865, Nogales, AZ 85621.

Misericordia Sisters, S.M.: Founded 1848, in Canada; in U.S., 1887. General motherhouse. 12435 Ave. Misericorde, Montreal H4J 2J3, Canada; U.S. address, 820 Jungles Ave., Aurora, IL 60505. Social work with unwed mothers and their children; hospital work.

Mission Helpers of the Sacred Heart, M.H.S.H.: Founded 1890, in U.S. General motherhouse, 1001 W. Joppa Rd., Baltimore, MD 21204. Religious education, evangelization.

Missionary Catechists of the Sacred Hearts of Jesus and Mary (Violetas), M.C.: Founded 1918, in Mexico; in U.S., 1943. Motherhouse, Tlalpan, Mexico; U.S. address, 209 W. Murray St., Victoria, TX 77901.

Missionary Sisters of the Catholic Apostolate (Pallottine Missionary Sisters), S.A.C.: Founded in Rome, 1838; in U.S., 1912. Generalate, Rome, Italy; U.S. provincialate, 15270 Old Halls Ferry Rd., Florissant, MO 63034.

Mother of God, Missionary Sisters of the, M.S.M.G.: Byzantine, Ukrainian Rite, Stamford. Motherhouse, 711-719 N. Franklin St., Philadelphia, PA 19123.

Mother of God, Sisters Poor Servants of the, S.M.G.: Founded 1869, in London, England; in U.S., 1947. General motherhouse, Maryfield, Roehampton, London. U.S. addresses: Maryfield Nursing Home, Greensboro Rd., High Point, NC 27260; St. Mary's Hospital, 916 Virginia Ave., Norton, VA 24273; Holy Spirit Convent, 1800 Geary St., Philadelphia, PA 19145; 101 Center St., Perth Amboy, NJ 08861. Hospital, educational work.

Nazareth, Poor Sisters of: Founded in England; U.S. foundation, 1924. General motherhouse, Hammersmith, London, England; U.S. novitiate, 3333 Manning Ave., Los Angeles, CA 90064. Social services, education.

Notre Dame, School Sisters of, S.S.N.D.: Founded 1833, in Germany; in U.S., 1847. General motherhouse, Rome, Italy. U.S. motherhouse, 1233 N. Marshall St., Milwaukee, WI 53202. Provinces: 6401 N. Charles St., Baltimore, MD 21212; 320 E. Ripa Ave., St. Louis, MO 63125; Good Counsel Hill, Mankato, MN 56001; 345 Belden Hill Rd., Wilton, CT 06897; P.O. Box 227275. Dallas, TX 75222; 1431 Euclid Ave., Berwyn, IL 60402.

Notre Dame, Sisters of, S.N.D.: Founded 1850, at Coesfeld, Germany; in U.S., 1874. General motherhouse, Rome, Italy. U.S. provinces: 13000 Auburn Rd., Chardon, O. 44024; 1601 Dixie Highway, Covington, KY 41011; 3837 Secor Rd., Toledo, OH 43623; 1776 Hendrix Ave., Thousand Oaks, CA 91360.

Notre Dame, Sisters of the Congregation of, C.N.D.: Founded 1653, in Canada; in U.S., 1860. General motherhouse, Montreal, Que., Canada; U.S. province, 223 West Mountain Rd., Ridgefield, CT 06877. Education.

Notre Dame de Namur, Sisters of, S.N.D.: Founded 1803, in France; in U.S., 1840. General motherhouse, Rome, Italy. U.S. provinces: 400 The Fenway, Boston, MA 02115; 54 Jeffrey's Neck Rd., Ipswich, MA 01938; 468 Poquonock Ave.,

Windsor, CT 06095; P.O. Box 298, 5025 Ilchester Rd., Ellicott City, MD 21041; 701 E. Columbia Ave., Cincinnati, OH 45215; 14800 Bohlman Rd., Saratoga, CA 95070; Base Communities Province, 3037 Fourth St. N.E., Washington, DC Educational work.

Notre Dame de Sion, Congregation of, N.D.S.: Founded 1843, in France; in U.S., 1892. Generalate, Rome, Italy; U.S. province, 349 Westminster Rd., Brooklyn, NY 11218. Creation of better understanding and relations between Christians and Jews.

Notre Dame Sisters: Founded 1853, in Czechoslovakia; in U.S., 1910. General motherhouse, Javornik, Czech Republic; U.S. motherhouse, 3501 State St., Omaha, NE 68112. Educational work.

Oblates of the Mother of Orphans, O.M.O: Founded 1945, in Italy. General motherhouse, Milan, Italy. U.S. address, 20 E. 72nd St., New York, NY 10021.

Our Lady of Charity, North American Union of Sisters of, Eudist Sisters (Sisters of Our Lady of Charity of the Refuge), N.A.U.-O.L.C.: Founded 1641, in Caen, France, by St. John Eudes; in U.S., 1855. Autonomous houses were federated in 1944 and in May, 1978, the North American Union of the Sisters of Our Lady of Charity was established. General motherhouse and administrative center, Box 327, Wisconsin Dells, WI 53965. Primarily devoted to re-education and rehabilitation of women and girls in residential and non-residential settings.

Independent monasteries: 1125 Malvern Ave., Hot Springs, AR 71901; 620 Roswell Rd. N.W., Carrollton, OH 44615; 4500 W. Davis St., Dallas, TX 75211.

Our Lady of Sorrows, Sisters of, O.L.S.: Founded 1839, in Italy; in U.S., 1947. General motherhouse, Rome, Italy; U.S. headquarters, 9894 Norris Ferry Rd., Shreveport, LA 71106.

Our Lady of the Garden, Sisters of, O.L.G.: Founded 1829, in Italy, by St. Anthony Mary Gianelli. Motherhouse, Rome, Italy; U.S. address, 67 Round Hill Rd., Middletown, CT 06457.

Our Lady of Victory Missionary Sisters, O.L.V.M.: Founded 1922, in U.S. Motherhouse, Victory Noll, Box 109, Huntington, IN 46750. Educational, social work.

Pallottine Sisters of the Catholic Apostolate, C.S.A.C.: Founded 1843, at Rome, Italy; in U.S., 1889. General motherhouse, Rome; U.S. motherhouse, St. Patrick's Villa, Harriman Heights, Harriman, NY 10926. Educational work.

Parish Visitors of Mary Immaculate, P.V.M.I.: Founded 1920, in New York. General motherhouse, Box 658, Monroe, NY 10950. Mission work.

Passion of Jesus Christ, Religious of (Passionist Nuns), C.P.: Founded 1771, in Italy, by St. Paul of the Cross; in U.S., 1910. U.S. convents: 2715 Churchview Ave., Pittsburgh, PA 15227; 631 Griffin Pond Rd., Clarks Summit, PA 18411; 1420 Benita Ave., Owensboro, KY 42301; 1151 Donaldson Hwy., Erlanger, KY 41018; 15700 Clayton Rd., Ellisville, MO 63011. Contemplatives.

Passionist Sisters: See Cross and Passion, Sisters of the.

Paul, Daughters of St. (Missionary Sisters of the Media of Communication), D.S.P.: Founded 1915, at Alba, Piedmont, Italy; in U.S., 1932. General motherhouse, Rome, Italy; U.S. provincial house, 50 St. Paul's Ave., Boston, MA 02130. Apostolate of the communications arts.

Paul of Chartres, Sisters of St., S.P.C.: Founded 1696, in France. General house, Rome, Italy; U.S. address, 1300 County Rd. 492, Marquette, MI 49855.

Peter Claver, Missionary Sisters of St., S.S.P.C.: Founded 1894; in U.S., 1914. General motherhouse, Rome, Italy; U.S. address, 667 Woods Mill Rd. S., Chesterfield, MO 63017.

Pious Disciples of the Divine Master, P.D.D.M.: Founded 1924; in U.S., 1948. General motherhouse, Rome, Italy; U.S. headquarters, 60 Sunset Ave., Staten Island, NY 10314.

Pious Schools, Sisters of, Sch. P.: Founded 1829 in Spain; in U.S., 1954. General motherhouse, Rome, Italy; U.S. headquarters, 9925 Mason Ave., Chatsworth, CA 91311.

Poor, Little Sisters of the, L.S.P.: Founded 1839, in France by Bl. Jeanne Jugan; in U.S., 1868. General motherhouse, St. Pern, France. U.S. provinces: 110-30 221st St., Queens Village, NY 11429; 601 Maiden Choice Lane, Baltimore, MD 21228; 80 W. Northwest Hwy., Palatine, IL 60067. Care of aged.

Poor Clare Missionary Sisters (Misioneras Clarisas), M.C.: Founded Mexico. General motherhouse, Rome, Italy; U.S. novitiate, 1019 N. Newhope, Santa Ana, CA 92703.

Poor Clare Nuns: See Franciscan Poor Clare Nuns.

Poor Handmaids of Jesus Christ (Ancilla Domini Sisters), P.H.J.C.: Founded 1851, in Germany by Bl. Mary Kasper; in U.S., 1868. General motherhouse, Dernbach, Westerwald, Germany; U.S. motherhouse, Ancilla Domini Convent, Donaldson, IN 46513. Educational, hospital work, social services.

Precious Blood, Daughters of Charity of the Most: Founded 1872, at Pagani, Italy; in U.S., 1908. General motherhouse, Rome, Italy; U.S. convent, 1482 North Ave., Bridgeport, CT 06604.

Precious Blood, Missionary Sisters of the, C.P.S.: Founded 1885, at Mariannhill, South Africa; in U.S., 1925. Generalate, Rome, Italy: U.S. novitiate, New Holland Ave., P.O. Box 97, Shillington, PA 19607. Home and foreign mission work.

Precious Blood, Sisters Adorers of the, A.P.B.: Founded 1861, in Canada; in U.S., 1890. General motherhouse, Canada. U.S. autonomous monasteries: 54th St. and Fort Hamilton Pkwy., Brooklyn, NY 11219; 700 Bridge St., Manchester, NH 03104; 7408 S.E. Alder St., Portland, OR 97215; 166 State St., Portland, ME 04101; 1106 State St., Lafayette, IN 47905; 400 Pratt St., Watertown, NY 13601. Cloistered, contemplative.

Precious Blood, Sisters of the, C.Pp.S.: Founded 1834, in Switzerland; in U.S., 1844. Generalate, 4000 Denlinger Rd., Dayton, Ohio 45426. Education, health care, other ministries.

Precious Blood, Sisters of the Most, C.Pp.S.:

Founded 1845, in Steinerberg, Switzerland; in U.S., 1870. General motherhouse, 204 N. Main St., O'Fallon, MO 63366. Education, other ministries.

Presentation, Sisters of Mary of the, S.M.P.: Founded 1829, in France; in U.S., 1903. General motherhouse, Broons, Cotes-du-Nord, France. U.S. address, Maryvale Novitiate, 11550 River Rd., Valley City, ND 58072. Educational, hospital work.

Presentation of Mary, Sisters of the, P.M.: Founded 1796, in France by Bl Marie Rivier; in U.S., 1873. General motherhouse, Castel Gandolfo, Italy. U.S. provincial houses: 495 Mammoth Rd., Manchester, NH 03104; 209 Lawrence St., Methuen, MA 01844.

Presentation of the B.V.M., Sisters of the, P.B.V.M.: Founded 1775, in Ireland; in U.S., 1854, in San Francisco. U.S. motherhouses: 2360 Carter Rd., Dubuque, Ia. 52001; R.D. 2, Box 33, Newburgh, NY 12550; 2340 Turk Blvd., San Francisco, CA 94118; ·St. Colman's Convent, Watervliet, NY 12189;
1101 32nd Ave., S. Fargo, ND 58103; 250 S. Davis Dr., P.O. Box 1113, Warner Robbins, GA 31093; 1500 N. Main, Aberdeen, SD 57401; 99 Church St., Leominster, MA 01453; 419 Woodrow Rd., Staten Island, NY 10312.

Presentation of the Blessed Virgin Mary, Sisters of, of Union: Founded in Ireland, 1775; union established in Ireland, 1976; first U.S. vice province, 1979. Generalate, Kildare, Ireland. U.S. provincialate, 729 W. Wilshire Dr., Phoenix, AZ 85007.

Providence, Daughters of Divine, F.D.P.: Founded 1832, Italy; in U.S., 1964. General motherhouse, Rome, Italy; U.S. address, 1625 Missouri St., Chalmette, LA 70043.

Providence, Missionary Catechists of Divine, M.C.D.P.: Administrative house, 2318 Castroville Rd., San Antonio, TX 78237.

Providence, Oblate Sisters of, O.S.P.: Founded 1829, in U.S., by Mother Mary Elizabeth Lange and Father James Joubert, S.S. First order of black nuns in U.S. General motherhouse, 701 Gun Rd., Baltimore, MD 21227. Educational work.

Providence, Sisters of, S.P.: Founded 1861, in Canada; in U.S., 1873. General motherhouse, Our Lady of Victory Convent, Gamelin St., Holyoke, MA 01040.

Providence, Sisters of, S.P.: Founded 1843, in Canada; in U.S., 1854. General motherhouse, Montreal, Canada. U.S. provinces: P.O. Box 11038, Seattle, WA 98111; 9 E. 9th Ave., Spokane, WA 99202; 353 N. River Rd., Des Plaines, IL 60616.

Providence, Sisters of (of St. Mary-of-the-Woods), S.P.: Founded 1806, in France; in U.S., 1840. Generalate, St. Mary-of-the-Woods, IN 47876.

Providence, Sisters of Divine, C.D.P.: Founded 1762, in France; in U.S., 1866. Generalate, Box 197, Helotes, TX 78023. Educational, hospital work.

Providence, Sisters of Divine, C.D.P.: Founded 1851, in Germany; in U.S., 1876. Generalate, Rome, Italy. U.S. provinces: 9000 Babcock Blvd., Allison Park, PA 15101; 8351 Florissant Rd., St. Louis, MO 63121; 363 Bishops Hwy., Kingston, MA 02364. Educational, hospital work.

Providence, Sisters of Divine (of Kentucky),

C.D.P.: Founded 1762, in France; in U.S., 1889. General motherhouse, Fenetrange, France; U.S. province, St. Anne Convent, Melbourne, KY 41059. Education, social services, other ministries.

Redeemer, Oblates of the Most Holy, O.SS.R.: Founded 1864, in Spain. General motherhouse, Spain; U.S. foundation, 60-80 Pond St., Jamaica Plain, MA 02130.

Redeemer, Order of the Most Holy, O.SS.R.: Founded 1731, by St. Alphonsus Liguori; in U.S., 1957. U.S. addresses: Mother of Perpetual Help Monastery, Esopus, NY 12429; St. Alphonsus Monastery, Liguori, MO 63057.

Redeemer, Sisters of the Divine, S.D.R.: Founded 1849, in Niederbronn, France; in U.S., 1912. General motherhouse, Rome, Italy; U.S. province, 999 Rock Run Road, Elizabeth, PA 15037. Educational, hospital work; care of the aged.

Redeemer, Sisters of the Holy, C.S.R.: Founded 1849, in Alsace; in U.S., 1924. General motherhouse, Wuerzburg, Germany; U.S. provincial house, 521 Moredon Rd., Huntingdon Valley, PA 19006. Personalized medical care in hospitals, homes for aged, private homes; retreat work.

Reparation of the Congregation of Mary, Sisters of, S.R.C.M.: Founded 1903, in U.S. Motherhouse, St. Zita's Villa, Monsey, NY 10952.

Resurrection, Sisters of the, C.R.: Founded 1891, in Italy; in U.S., 1900. General motherhouse, Rome, Italy. U.S. provinces: 7432 Talcott Ave., Chicago, IL 60631; Mt. St. Joseph, Castleton-on-Hudson, NY 12033. Education, nursing.

Rita, Sisters of St., O.S.A.: General motherhouse, Wurzburg, Germany. U.S. foundation, St. Monica's Convent, 3920 Green Bay Rd., Racine, WI 53404.

Rosary, Congregation of Our Lady of the Holy, R.S.R.: Founded 1874, in Canada; in U.S., 1899. General motherhouse, Rimouski, Que., Canada. U.S. regional house, 20 Thomas St., Portland, ME 04102. Educational work.

Rosary, Missionary Sisters of the Holy, M.S.H.R.: Founded 1924, in Ireland; in U.S., 1954. Motherhouse, Dublin, Ireland. U.S. regional mailing address, 5334 Vine St., Philadelphia, PA 19139. African missions.

Sacrament, Missionary Sisters of the Most Blessed, M.SS.S.: General motherhouse, Madrid, Spain; U.S. foundation: 1111 Wordin Ave., Bridgeport, CT 06605.

Sacrament, Nuns of the Perpetual Adoration of the Blessed, A.P.: Founded 1807 in Rome, Italy; in U.S., 1925. U.S. monasteries: 145 N. Cotton Ave., El Paso, TX 79901; 771 Ashbury St., San Francisco, CA 94117.

Sacrament, Oblate Sisters of the Blessed, O.S.B.S.: Founded 1935, in U.S.; motherhouse, St. Sylvester Convent, Marty, SD 57361. Care of American Indians.

Sacrament, Religious Sisters of Mercy of the Blessed, H.M.SS.S.: Founded 1910, in Mexico; in U.S. convent, 222 W. Cevallos St., San Antonio, TX 78204.

Sacrament, Servants of the Blessed, S.S.S.: Founded 1858, in France, by St. Pierre Julien Eymard; in U.S., 1947. General motherhouse, Rome, Italy; American provincial house, 1818 Coal Pl. SE, Albuquerque, NM 87106. Contemplative.

Sacrament, Servants of the Blessed, S.J.S.: Founded 1904, in Mexico; in U.S., 1926. General motherhouse, Mexico; U.S. address, 215 Lomita St., El Segundo, CA 90245.

Sacrament, Sisters of the Blessed, for Indians and Colored People, S.B.S.: Founded 1891, in U.S., by Bl. Katharine Drexel. General motherhouse, St. Elizabeth's Convent, Bensalem, PA 19020.

Sacrament, Sisters of the Most Holy, M.H.S.: Founded 1851, in France; in U.S., 1872. Generalate, 313 Corona Dr. (P.O. Box 30727), Lafayette, LA 70593.

Sacrament, Sisters Servants of the Blessed, S.S.B.S.: Founded 1904, in Mexico. General motherhouse, Guadalajara, Mexico. U.S. address, 536 Rockwood Ave., Calexico, CA 92231.

Sacramentine Nuns (Religious of the Order of the Blessed Sacrament and Our Lady), O.S.S.: Founded 1639, in France; in U.S., 1912. U.S. monasteries: 23 Park Ave., Yonkers, NY 10703; US 31, Conway, MI 49722. Perpetual adoration of the Holy Eucharist.

Sacred Heart, Daughters of Our Lady of the: Founded 1882, in France; in U.S., 1955. General motherhouse, Rome, Italy; U.S. address, 424 E. Browning Rd., Bellmawr, NJ 08031. Educational work.

Sacred Heart, Missionary Sisters of the (Cabrini Sisters), M.S.C.: Founded 1880, in Italy, by St. Frances Xavier Cabrini; in U.S., 1889. General motherhouse, Rome, Italy; U.S. provinces: 229 E. 19th St., New York, NY 10003 (Eastern); 434 W. Deming Pl., Chicago, IL 60614 (Western). Educational, health, social and catechetical work.

Sacred Heart, Religious of the Apostolate of the, R.A.: General motherhouse, Madrid, Spain; U.S. address, 1310 W. 42nd Pl., Hialiah, FL 33012.

Sacred Heart, Society Devoted to the, S.D.S.H.: Founded 1940, in Hungary; in U.S., 1956. U.S. motherhouse, 9814 Sylvia Ave., Northridge, CA 91324. Educational work.

Sacred Heart, Society of the, R.S.C.J.: Founded 1800, in France; in U.S., 1818. Generalate, Rome, Italy. U.S. provincial house, 4389 W. Pine Blvd., St. Louis, MO 63108. Educational work.

Sacred Heart of Jesus, Apostles of, A.S.C.J.: Founded 1894, in Italy; in U.S., 1902. General motherhouse, Rome, Italy; U.S. motherhouse, 265 Benham St., Hamden, CT 06514. Educational, social work.

Sacred Heart of Jesus, Handmaids of the, A.C.J.: Founded 1877, in Spain. General motherhouse, Rome, Italy; U.S. province, 616 Coopertown Rd., Haverford, PA 19041. Educational, retreat work.

Sacred Heart of Jesus, Missionary Sisters of the Most (Hiltrup), M.S.C.: Founded 1899, in Germany; in U.S., 1908. General motherhouse, Rome, Italy; U.S. province, 51 Seminary Rd., Reading, PA 19605. Education, health care, pastoral ministry.

Sacred Heart of Jesus, Oblate Sisters of the, O.S.H.J.: Founded 1894; in U.S., 1949. General motherhouse, Rome, Italy; U.S. headquarters, 50 Warner Rd., Hubbard, Ohio 44425. Educational, social work.

Sacred Heart of Jesus, Servants of the Most,

S.S.C.J.: Founded 1894, in Poland; in U.S., 1959. General motherhouse, Cracow, Poland; U.S. address, 231 Arch St., Cresson, PA 16630. Education, health care, social services.

Sacred Heart of Jesus, Sisters of the, S.S.C.J.: Founded 1816, in France; in U.S., 1903. General motherhouse, St. Jacut, Brittany, France; U.S. provincial house, 5922 Blanco Rd., San Antonio, TX 78216. Educational, hospital, domestic work.

Sacred Heart of Jesus and of the Poor, Servants of the (Mexican), S.S.H.J.P.: Founded 1885, in Mexico; in U.S., 1907. General motherhouse, Apartado 92, Puebla, Pue., Mexico; U.S. address, 3317 Sacred heart Dr., Laredo, TX 78040.

Sacred Heart of Jesus for Reparation, Congregation of the Handmaids of the, A.R.: Founded 1918, in Italy; in U.S., 1958. U.S. address, Sunshine Park, R.D. 3, Steubenville, Ohio 43952.

Sacred Heart of Mary, Religious of the, R.S.H.M.: Founded 1848, in France; in U.S., 1877. Generalate, Rome, Italy. U.S. provinces; 50 Wilson Park Dr., Tarrytown, NY 10591; 441 N. Garfield Ave., Montebellow, CA 90640.

Sacred Hearts, Religious of the Holy Union of the, S.U.S.C.: Founded 1826, in France; in U.S., 1886. Generalate, Rome, Italy. U.S. provinces: 550 Rock St., Fall River, MA 02720; Box 993, Main St., Groton, MA 01450. Varied ministries.

Sacred Hearts and of Perpetual Adoration, Sisters of the, SS.CC.: Founded 1797, in France; in U.S., 1908. General motherhouse, Rome, Italy; U.S. provinces: 3253 Waialae Rd., Honolulu, Hawaii 96816 (Pacific); 216 Lawrence St., Lawrence, MA 02720 (East Coast). Varied ministries.

Sacred Hearts of Jesus and Mary, Sisters of the, S.H.J.M.: Established 1953, in U.S. General motherhouse, Essex, England; U.S. address, 844 Don Carlo Dr., El Cerrito, CA 94530.

Savior, Company of the, C.S.: Founded 1952, in Spain; in U.S., 1962. General motherhouse, Madrid, Spain; U.S. foundation, 820 Clinton Ave., Bridgeport, CT 06604.

Savior, Sisters of the Divine, S.D.S.: Founded 1888, in Italy; in U.S., 1895. General motherhouse, Rome, Italy; U.S. province, 4311 N. 100th St., Milwaukee, WI 53222. Educational, hospital work.

Social Service, Sisters of, S.S.S.: Founded in Hungary, 1923, by Sr. Margaret Slachta. U.S. generalate, 296 Summit Ave., Buffalo, NY 14214. Social work.

Social Service, Sisters of, of Los Angeles, S.S.S.: Founded 1908, in Hungary; in U.S., 1926. General motherhouse, 1120 Westchester Pl., Los Angeles, CA 90019.

Teresa of Jesus, Society of St., S.T.J.: Founded 1876, in Spain; in U.S., 1910. General motherhouse, Rome, Italy; U.S. provincial house, 18080 St. Joseph's Way, Covington, LA 70433.

Thomas of Villanova, Congregation of Sisters of St., S.S.T.V.: Founded 1661, in France; in U.S., 1948. General motherhouse, Neuilly-sur-Seine, France; U.S. foundation W. Rocks Rd., Norwalk, CT 06851.

Trinity, Missionary Servants of the Most Blessed, M.S.B.T.: Founded 1912, in U.S., by Very Rev. Thomas A. Judge. General motherhouse, 3501

Solly Ave., Philadelphia, PA 19136. Educational, social work; health services.

Trinity, Sisters Oblates to the Blessed, O.B.T.: Founded 1923, in Italy. U.S. novitiate, Beekman Rd., Hopewell Junction, NY 12533.

Trinity, Sisters of the Most Holy, O.Ss.T.: Founded 1198, in Rome; in U.S., 1920. General motherhouse, Rome, Italy; U.S. address, Immaculate Conception Province, 21281 Chardon Rd., Euclid, Ohio 44117. Educational work.

Ursula of the Blessed Virgin, Society of the Sisters of St., S.U.: Founded 1606, in France; in U.S., 1902. General motherhouse, France; U.S. novitiate, 139 S. Mill Rd., Rhinebeck, NY 12572. Educational work.

Ursuline Nuns (Roman Union), O.S.U.: Founded 1535, in Italy; in U.S., 1727. Generalate, Rome, Italy. U.S. provinces: 323 E. 198th St., Bronx, NY 10458; 210 Glennon Heights Rd., Crystal City, MO 63019; 639 Angela Dr., Santa Rosa, CA 95401; 71 Lowder St., Dedham, MA 02026.

Ursuline Nuns of the Congregation of Paris, O.S.U.: Founded 1535, in Italy; in U.S., 1727, in New Orleans. U.S. motherhouses: St. Martin, OH 45118; 901 E. Miami St., Paola, KS 66071; 3115 Lexington Rd., Louisville, KY 40206; 2600 Lander Rd., Cleveland, O. 44124; Maple Mount, KY 42356; 436 W. Delaware, Toledo, OH 43610; 4250 Shields Rd., Canfield, OH 44406; 1339 E. McMillan St., Cincinnati, OH 45206.

Ursuline Nuns of the Congregation of Tildonk, Belgium, O.S.U.: Founded 1535, in Italy; Tildonk congregation, 1832; in U.S., 1924. Generalate, Tildonk, Belgium; U.S. address, 81-15 Utopia Parkway, Jamaica, NY 11432. Educational, foreign mission work.

Ursuline Sisters of Belleville, O.S.U.: Founded 1535, in Italy; in U.S., 1910; established as diocesan community, 1983. Central house, 1026 N. Douglas Ave., Belleville, IL 62221. Educational work.

Ursuline Sisters (Irish Ursuline Union), O.S.U.: Generalate, Dublin, Ireland; U.S. address, 1973 Torch Hill Rd., Columbus, GA 31903.

Venerini Sisters, Religious, M.P.V.: Founded 1685, in Italy; in U.S., 1909. General motherhouse, Rome, Italy; U.S. provincialate; 23 Edward St., Worcester, MA 01605.

Vincent de Paul, Sisters: See Charity of St. Vincent de Paul, Sisters of.

Visitation Nuns, V.H.M.: Founded 1610, in France; in U.S. (Georgetown, DC), 1799. Contemplative, educational work. Two federations in U.S.

First Federation of North America. Major pontifical enclosure. Pres., Mother Mary Jozefa Kowalewski, Monastery of the Visitation, Snellville, GA 30278. Addresses of monasteries belonging to the federation: 2300 Springhill Ave., Mobile, AL 36607; 2002 Bancroft Pkwy., Wilmington, DE 19806; Rt. 1, Box 2055, Rockville, VA 23146; 5820 City Ave., Philadelphia, PA 19131; 1745 Parkside Blvd., Toledo, OH 43607; 2055 Ridgedale Dr., Snellville, GA 30278.

Second Federation of North America. Constitutional enclosure. Pres., Rev. Mother Mary Philomena Tisinger, Visitation Monastery of Georgetown, Washington, DC 20007. Addresses of monasteries belonging to the federation: 1500 35th St., Washington, DC 20007; 3020 N. Ballas Rd., St. Louis, MO 63131; 200 E. Second St., Frederick, MD 21701; Mt. St. Chantal Monastery of the Visitation, Wheeling, WV 26003; Ridge Blvd. and 89th St., Brooklyn, NY 11209; 1600 Murdoch Ave., Parkersburg, WV 26101; 2000 Sixteenth Ave., Rock Island, IL 61201; 2455 Visitation Dr., Mendota Heights, St. Paul, MN 55120; 3200 S.W. Dash Point Rd., Federal Way, WA 98003.

Visitation of the Congregation of the Immaculate Heart of Mary, Sisters of the, S.V.M.: Founded 1952, in U.S. Motherhouse, 900 Alta Vista St., Dubuque, IA 52001. Educational work, parish ministry.

Vocationist Sisters (Sisters of the Divine Vocations): Founded 1921, in Italy; in U.S., 1967 General motherhouse, Naples, Italy; U.S. foundation, Perpetual Help Nursery, 172 Broad St., Newark, NJ 07104.

Wisdom, Daughters of, D.W.: Founded 1703, in France, by St. Louis Marie Grignion de Montfort; in U.S., 1904. General motherhouse, Vendee, France; U.S. province, 385 S. Ocean Ave., Islip, NY 11751. Education, health care, parish ministry, social services.

Xaverian Missionary Society of Mary, Inc., X.M.M.: Founded 1945, in Italy; in U.S., 1954. General motherhouse, Parma, Italy; U.S. address, 242 Salisbury St., Worcester, MA 01609.

ORGANIZATIONS OF RELIGIOUS

Conferences

Conferences of major superiors of religious institutes, dating from the 1950s and encouraged by the Code of Canon Law (canons 708, 709), have been established in 21 countries of Europe, 14 in North and Central America, 10 in South America, 34 in Africa and 19 in Asia and Oceania.

Listed below are U.S. and international conferences.

Conference of Major Superiors of Men: Founded in 1956; canonically established Sept. 12, 1957. Its purposes are to promote the spiritual and apostolic welfare of men Religious, provide liaison opportunities among Religious and with church officials, and serve as a national voice for the corporate views of superiors. Membership, 269 major superiors representing institutes with a combined membership of approximately 30,000. President Rev. Gerald Brown, S.S.; executive director, Rev. Gregory Reisert, O.F.M. Cap. National office: 8808 Cameron St., Silver Spring, MD 20910.

Leadership Conference of Women Religious: Founded in 1956; canonically established Dec. 12, 1959. Its purposes are to promote the understanding and living of religious life; to promote collaboration among religious institutes and between religious and the Church; and to serve as a voice for the leadership of U.S. women's congregations. Membership, approximately 800. President, Sister

Doris Gottemoeller, R.S.M.; executive director, Sister Margaret Cafferty, P.B.V.M. National office: 8808 Cameron St., Silver Spring, MD 20910.

Council of Major Superiors of Women Religious: Established officially June 13, 1992. Membership, superiors of approximately 84 religious congregations. Head of steering committee, Mother Vincent Marie Finnegan, O.C.D., 920 E. Alhambra Rd., Alhambra, CA 91801.

International Union of Superiors General (Women): Established Dec. 8, 1965; approved, 1967. General secretary, Sister Pamela Dowdell, F.M.M. Address: Piazza di Ponte S. Angelo, 28, 00186, Rome, Italy.

Union of Superiors General (Men): Established in 1957. President, Father Flavio Carraro, O.F.M. Cap. Address: Via dei Penitenzieri 19, 00193 Rome, Italy.

Latin American Confederation of Religious: Established in 1959, approved by the Congregation for Religious and Secular Institutes, 1967. President, Father Benito Blanco Martinez, S.J. Address: Calle 64, No 10-45 Piso 50, Apartado Aereo 90710, Bogota, Colombia.

Union of European Conferences of Major Superiors: Established Dec. 25, 1983. President, Sister Frances Delcourt, S.A.; secretary, Father Joseph Dargan, S.J. Address: Milltown Park, Dublin 6, Ireland.

Other Organizations

Association of Contemplative Sisters (1969): Its principal purpose is development of the contemplative life-style for effective service to the Church. Membership, approximately 525. President, Sr. Ginny Manss, 370 Neeb Rd., Cincinnati, OH 45233.

Institute on Religious Life (1974). To foster more effective understanding and implementation of teachings of the Church on religious life, promote vocations to religious life and the priesthood, and promote growth in sanctity of all the faithful according to their state in life. Executive director, Rev. James Downey. National office, P.O. Box 41007, Chicago, IL 60641.

National Assembly of Religious Brothers (1972): To publicize the unique vocations of brothers, to further communication among brothers and provide liaison with various organizations of the Church. Executive secretary, Bro. Willie Morin, S.C., National office, 1337 West Ohio, Chicago, IL 60622.

National Black Sisters' Conference (1968): To determine priorities in service to Black people, promote Black vocations and the development of religious life in the unique Black life-style. Executive director, Sister Gwynette Proctor, S.N.D.

National Conference of Vicars for Religious (1967): National organization of diocesan officials concerned with relations between their respective dioceses and religious communities engaged therein. President, Sr. Nola Brunner, C.S.J., 40 N. Main Ave., Albany, NY 12203; secretary, Sr. Doris Rauenhorst, O.P., 2220 Summit Ave., St. Paul, MN 55105.

National Religious Vocation Conference (NRVC) (1988, with merger of National Sisters Vocation Conference and National Conference of Religious Vocation Directors): Service organization of men and women committed to the fostering and discernment of vocations, Executive director, Sr. Catherine Bertrand, S.S.N.D. Address: 1603 S. Michigan Ave., No. 400, Chicago, IL 60616.

Religious Formation Conference (1953): Originally the Sister Formation Conference; membership includes women and men Religious and non-canonical groups. Facilitates the ministry of formation, both initial and ongoing, in religious communities. Executive director, Sister Margaret Fitzer, S.S.L. National office: 8820 Cameron St., Silver Spring, MD 20910.

SECULAR INSTITUTES

(Sources: Almanac survey; United States Conference of Secular Institutes; *Annuario Pontificio*.)

Secular institutes are societies of men and women living in the world who dedicate themselves to observe the evangelical counsels and to carry on apostolic works suitable to their talents and opportunities in the areas of their everyday life.

"Secular institutes are not religious communities but they carry with them in the world a profession of evangelical counsels which is genuine and complete, and recognized as such by the Church. This profession confers a consecration on men and women, laity and clergy, who reside in the world. For this reason they should chiefly strive for total self-dedication to God, one inspired by perfect charity. These institutes should preserve their proper and particular character, a secular one, so that they may everywhere measure up successfully to that apostolate which they were designed to exercise, and which is both in the world and, in a sense, of the world" (*Decree on the Appropriate Renewal of Religious Life*, No. 11; Second Vatican Council).

Secular institutes are under the jurisdiction of the Congregation for Institutes of Consecrated Life and Societies of Apostolic Life. General legislation concerning them is contained in Canons 710 to 730 of the Code of Canon Law.

A secular institute reaches maturity in several stages. It begins as an association of the faithful, technically called a pious union, with the approval of a local bishop. Once it has proved its viability, he can give it the status of an institute of diocesan right, in accordance with norms and permission emanating from the Congregation for Institutes of Consecrated Life and Societies of Apostolic Life. On issuance of a separate decree from this congregation, an institute of diocesan right becomes an institute of pontifical right.

Secular institutes, which originated in the latter part of the 18th century, were given full recognition and approval by Pius XII Feb. 2, 1947, in the apostolic constitution *Provida Mater Ecclesia*. On Mar. 25 of the same year a special commission for secular institutes was set up within the Congregation for Religious. Institutes were commended and confirmed by Pius XII in a motu proprio of Mar. 12, 1948, and were the subject of a special instruction issued a week later, Mar. 19, 1948.

The **World Conference of Secular Institutes (CMIS)** was approved by the Vatican May 23, 1974. Address: Via Tullio Levi-Civita 5, 00146 Rome, Italy.

The **United States Conference of Secular Institutes (USCSI)** was established following the organization of the World Conference of Secular Institutes in Rome. Its membership is open to all canonically erected secular institutes with members living in the United States. The conference was organized to offer secular institutes an opportunity to exchange experiences, to do research in order to help the Church carry out its mission, and to search for ways and means to make known the existence of secular institutes in the U.S. Address: P.O. Box 4556, 12th St. NE, Washington, DC 20017.

Institutes in the U.S.

Caritas Christi: Originated in Marseilles, 1937; for women. Established as a secular institute of pontifical right Mar. 19, 1955. Address: P.O. Box 5162, River Forest, IL 60305.

Company of St. Paul: Originated in Milan, Italy, 1920; for lay people and priests. Approved as a secular institute of pontifical right June 30, 1950. Address: 52 Davis Ave., White Plains, NY 10605.

Company of St. Ursula, Secular Institute of St. Angela Merici: Founded in Brescia, Italy, 1535; for women. Approved as a secular institute of pontifical right 1958. Address: 3229 McCort Ave., Fort Worth, TX 76110.

DeSales Secular Institute: Founded in Vienna, Austria, 1940; for women. Pontifical right, 1964. Addresses: Rev. John J. Conmy, 1120 Blue Bell Rd., Childs, MD 21916; Mary Robinson, 420 Biddle St., Chesapeake City, MD 21915.

Diocesan Laborer Priests: Founded in Spain 1885; approved as a secular institute of pontifical right, 1952. The specific aim of the institute is the promotion, sustenance and cultivation of apostolic, religious and priestly vocations. Address: Rev. James Alonso, 3706 15th St. N.E., Washington, DC 20017.

Don Bosco Volunteers: Founded 1917 by Bl. Philip Rinaldi; for women. Approved as a secular institute of pontifical right Aug. 5, 1978. Follow spirituality and charism of St. John Bosco. Address: Rev. Paul P. Avallone, S.D.B., Don Bosco Volunteers, 202 Union Ave., Paterson, NJ 07502. International membership of 1,000 in 30 countries.

Fr. Kolbe Missionaries of the Immaculata: Founded in Bologna, Italy, in 1954, by Fr. Luigi Faccenda, O.F.M. Conv.; for women. Approved as a secular institute of diocesan right Aug. 15, 1985. Live the fullness of baptismal consecration, strive for perfect charity and promote the knowledge and veneration of Mary. Address: 531 E. Merced Ave., West Covina, CA 91790.

Handmaids of Divine Mercy: Founded in Bari, Italy, 1951; for women. Approved as an institute of pontifical right 1972. Address: Mary I. DiFonzo, 2410 Hughes Ave., Bronx, NY 10458. International membership of 980.

Institute of Apostolic Oblates: A secular institute of diocesan right founded in Rome, Italy, 1947; established in the U.S., 1962; for women, as internal or external (vowed) and cooperatives (married). Addresses: 2125 W. Walnut Ave., Fullerton, CA 92633; 6762 Western Ave., Omaha, NE 68132; 730 E. 87th St., Brooklyn, NY 11236.

Institute of Secular Missionaries: Founded in Vitoria, Spain, 1939; for women. Approved as a secular institute, 1955. Address: 2710 Ruberg Ave., Cincinnati, OH 45211, Att. E. Dilger.

Institute of the Heart of Jesus: Originated in France Feb. 2, 1791; restored Oct. 29, 1918; for diocesan priests. Received final approval from the Holy See as a secular institute of pontifical right Feb. 2, 1952. Rev. Yves Gerard, superior general. Addresses: Central House, 202 Avenue du Maine, Pavillion 4, 75014 Paris, France; U.S. address, Rev. Dennis Brennan, 10321 Tujunga Canyon Blvd., Tujunga, CA 91042.

Lay Missionaries of the Passion: Founded in Catania, Sicily; approved as a secular institute of diocesan right July 1, 1980.

To be fully responsible to shape the world, perfect it, sanctify it from within, transform it and to live the spirit of the Passion. Address: 633 Main St., Dicksen City, PA 18519.

Little Franciscan Family: Founded in Italy, 1929, by Father Ireneo Mazotti, O.F.M.; for women. Approved as a secular institute of pontifical right, 1983. Address: Ms. J. Curley, 319 Main St., Cromwell, CT 06416.

Mission of Our Lady of Bethany: Founded in France, 1948; for women. Approved as a secular institute of diocesan right, 1965. Address: P.O. Box 807, Boston, MA 02130.

Missionaries of the Kingship of Christ the King: Under this title are included three distinct and juridically separate institutes founded by Agostino Gemelli, O.F.M. (1878-1959) and Armida Barelli (1882-1952). Two are active in the U.S.

(1) Women Missionaries of the Kingship of Christ — Founded in 1919, in Italy; definitively approved as an institute of pontifical rite 1953. Established in 30 countries. U.S. branch established 1950. Age at time of entrance, 21 to 40.

(2) Men Missionaries of the Kingship of Christ — Founded 1928, in Italy, as an institute of diocesan right. U.S. branch established 1962.

Addresses: Rev. Dominic Monti, O.F.M., 10400 Lorain Ave., Silver Spring, MD 20901 (for Men Missionaries); Rev. Geoffrey Bridges, O.F.M., 3215 Army St., San Francisco, CA 94110 (for Women Missionaries).

Nuestra Senora de Altagracia: Focus on Our Lady to integrate contemplative prayer life with active life in the apostolate. Address: Ms. Christiana Perez, 129 Van Sislen Ave., Brooklyn, NY 11207.

Oblate Missionaries of Mary Immaculate: Founded, 1952; approved as a secular institute of diocesan right Feb. 2, 1962, and of pontifical right Mar. 25, 1984; for women. Addresses: Oblate Missionaries of Mary Immaculate, P.O. Box 10094, San Antonio, TX 78201; P.O. Box 303, Manville, RI 02838. International membership.

Opus Spiritus Sancti: Originated in West

Germany, 1952; for diocesan priests and unmarried permanent deacons. Formally acknowledged by Rome as a secular institute of diocesan right, 1977. Address: Rev. Ronald J. Reicks, P.O. Box 181, Alton, IA 51003.

Schoenstatt Sisters of Mary: Originated in Schoenstatt, Germany, 1926; for women. Established as a secular institute of diocesan right May 20, 1948; of pontifical right Oct. 18, 1948. Addresses: W. 284 N. 404 Cherry Lane, Waukesha, WI 53188; House Schoenstatt, HCO 1, Box 100, Rockport, TX 78382.

Secular Institute of Schoenstatt Fathers: Founded in Germany by Fr. Joseph Kentenich in 1965; for priests serving the International Schoenstatt Movement in over 20 countries. Approved as a secular institute of pontifical right, June 24, 1988. Address: W. 284 N. 746 Cherry Lane, Waukesha, WI 53188.

Secular Institute of Pius X: Originated in Manchester, N.H., 1940; for priests and laymen. Approved as a secular institute, 1959 (first secular institute of diocesan right founded in the U.S. to be approved by the Holy See). Also admits married and unmarried men as associate members. Address: C.P. 1815, Quebec City, P.Q. G1K 7K7, Canada.

Servitium Christi Secular Institute of the Blessed Sacrament: Founded in Holland, 1952; for women. Approved as a secular institute of diocesan right May 8, 1963. Address: Miss Olympia Panagatos, 184 E. 76th St., New York, NY 10021.

Society of Our Lady of the Way: Originated, 1936; for women. Approved as a secular institute of pontifical right Jan. 3, 1953. Addresses: 147 Dorado Terr., San Francisco, CA 94112; P.O. Box 412, Stamford, Conn. 06904; 1116 Cook Ave., Apt. 27, Lakewood, OH 44107; 2339 N. Catalina, Los Angeles, CA 90027.

Voluntas Dei Institute: Originated in Canada, 1958 by Father L. M. Parent; for secular priests and laymen (with married couples as associates). Approved as a secular institute of pontifical right, July 12, 1987. Established in 21 countries. Address: Rev. Michael Craig, 4257 Tazewell Terr., Burtonsville, MD 20866.

The *Annuario Pontificio* lists the following secular institutes of pontifical right which are not established in the U.S.:

For men: Christ the King; Institute of Our Lady of Life; Institute of Prado; Priests of the Sacred Heart of Jesus.

For women: Alliance in Jesus through Mary; Apostles of the Sacred Heart; Catechists of Mary, Virgin and Mother; Catechists of the Sacred Heart of Jesus (Ukrainian); Cordimarian Filiation; Daughters of the Nativity of Mary; Daughters of the Queen of the Apostles; Daughters of the Sacred Heart; Evangelical Crusade; Faithful Servants of Jesus; Handmaids of Our Mother of Mercy; Institute of the Blessed Virgin Mary (della Strada); Institute of Notre Dame du Travail; Institute of Our Lady of Life; Institute of St. Boniface; Little Apostles of Charity;

Life and Peace in Christ Jesus; Missionaries of Royal Priesthood; Missionaries of the Sick; Oblates of Christ the King; Oblates of the Sacred Heart of Jesus; Servants of Jesus the Priest; Servite Secular Institute; Union of the Daughters of God; Workers of Divine Love; Workers of the Cross; Handmaids of Holy Church; Augustinian Auxiliary Missionaries; Heart of Jesus; Apostolic Missionaries of Charity; Combonian Secular Missionaries; Missionaries of the Gospel; Secular Servants of Jesus Christ Priest; Women of Schoenstatt.

Associations

Caritas: Originated in New Orleans, 1950; for women. Follow guidelines of secular institutes. Small self-supporting groups who live and work among the poor and oppressed; work in Louisiana and Guatemala. Address: Box 308, Abita Springs, LA 70420.

Daughters of Our Lady of Fatima: Originated in Lansdowne, Pa., 1949; for women. Received diocesan approval, Jan., 1952. Address: Fatima House, Rolling Hills Rd., Ottsville, PA 18942.

Focolare Movement: Founded in Trent, Italy, in 1943, by Chiara Lubich; for men and women. Approved as an association of the faithful, 1962. It is not a secular institute by statute; however, vows are observed by its totally dedicated core membership of 4,000 who live in small communities called Focolare (Italian word for "hearth") centers. There are 17 resident centers in the U.S. and four in Canada. GEN (New Generation) is the youth organization of the movement. An estimated 70,000 are affiliated with the movement in the U.S. and Canada; 1,200,000, worldwide. Publications include *Living City*, monthly; *GEN II* and *GEN III* for young people and children. Five week-long summer conventions, called "Mariapolis" ("City of Mary"), are held annually. Address for information: P.O. Box 496, New York, NY 10021 (indicate men's or women's branch).

Jesus-Caritas Fraternity of Priests: An international association of diocesan priests who strive to combine an active life with a contemplative calling by their membership in small fraternities. U.S. address for information: Rev. Donald F. Dunn, USA National Responsible, c/o Diocese of Colorado Springs, 29 W. Kiowa, Colorado Springs, CO 80903.

Franciscan Missionaries of Jesus Crucified: Founded in New York in 1987; separate communities for women and men. Approved as an association of the faithful Jan. 7, 1992. To provide an opportunity for persons with disabilities to live a life of total consecration in the pursuit of holiness in the apostolate of service to the Church and to those who suffer in any way. Address: Louise D. Principe, F.M.J.C., 400 Central Ave., Apt. 3D, Albany, NY 12206.

Madonna House Apostolate: Originated in Toronto, Canada, 1930; for priests and lay persons. Public association of the Christian faithful. Address: Madonna House, Combermere, Ontario, Canada KOJ ILO — Jean Fox (women), Albert Osterberger (men), Rev. Robert Pelton (priests). International membership and missions.

Opus Spiritus Sancti: Originated in Germany; for women. An association of the faithful. Address: Bernadette Reilly, 115 W. Nebraska St. Algona, IA 50511.

Pax Christi: Lay institute of men and women dedicated to witnessing to Christ, with special emphasis on service to the poor in Mississippi. Addresses: St. Francis Center, 708 Ave. I, Greenwood, MI 38930; LaVerna House, 2108 Altawoods Blvd., Jackson, Miss. 39204.

Rural Parish Workers of Christ the King: Founded in 1942; for women. An approved lay institute of apostolic action of the Archdiocese of St. Louis. Dedicated to the glory of God in service of neighbor, especially in rural areas. Address: Box 552, Rt. 1, Cadet, MO 63630.

Teresian Institute: Founded in Spain 1911 by Pedro Poveda. Approved as an association of the faithful of pontifical right Jan. 11, 1924. Mailing Address: 3400 S. W. 99th Ave., Miami, FL 33165.

SECULAR ORDERS

Secular orders (commonly called third orders) are societies of the faithful living in the world who seek to deepen their Christian life and apostolic commitment in association with and according to the spirit of various religious institutes. The orders are called "third" because their foundation usually followed the establishment of the first and second religious orders with which they are associated.

Augustine, Third Order Secular of St.: Founded, 13th century; approved Nov. 7, 1400.

Carmelites, Lay (Third Order of Our Lady of Mt. Carmel): Rule for laity approved by Pope Nicholas V, Oct. 7, 1452; new statutes, January, 1991. Addresses: Aylesford, 8501 Bailey Rd., Darien, IL 60561; P.O. Box 613, Williamston, MA 01267. Approximately 235 communities and 8,000 members in the U.S. and Canada.

Carmelites, The Secular Order of Discalced (formerly the Third Order Secular of the Blessed Virgin Mary of Mt Carmel and of St. Teresa of Jesus): Rule based on the Carmelite reform established by St. Teresa and St. John of the Cross, 16th century; approved Mar. 23, 1594. Revised rule approved May 10, 1979. Office of National Secretariat, U.S.A.; P.O. Box 3420, San Jose, CA 95156. Approximately 24,445 members throughout the world; 130 groups/communities and 5,200 members in the U.S. and Canada.

Dominican Laity: Founded in the 13th century. Addresses of provincial coordinators: 487 Michigan Ave. N.E., Washington, DC 20017; 1909 S. Ashland Ave., Chicago, IL 60608; 5890 Birch Ct., Oakland, CA 94618; 3600 Travis, Houston, TX 77002.

Franciscan Order, Secular (SFO): Founded, 1209 by St. Francis of Assisi; approved Aug. 30, 1221. National minister, Richard Morton, SFO, 3191 71st St. E., Inver Grove Heights, MN 55076. Approximately 780,000 throughout the world; 23,000 in U.S.

Mary, Third Order of: Founded, Dec. 8, 1850; rule approved by the Holy See, 1857. Addresses of provincial directors: Marist School, 3790 Ashford-Dunwoody Rd. N.E., Atlanta, GA 30319; Marist House, 518 Pleasant St., Framingham, MA 01701; Notre Dame des Victoires, 566 Bush St., San Francisco, CA 94108. Approximately 14,000 in the world, 5,600 in U.S.

Mary, Secular Order of Servants of (Servite): Founded, 1233; approved, 1304. Revised rule approved 1986. Address: Assistant for Secular Order, 3121 W. Jackson Blvd., Chicago, IL 60612.

Mercy, Secular Third Order of Our Lady of (Mercedarian): Founded, 1219 by St. Peter Nolasco; approved the same year.

Norbert, Associates of St.: Founded, 1122 by St. Norbert; approved by Pope Honorius II, 1126. Address: St. Norbert Abbey, 1016 N. Broadway, De Pere, WI 54115.

Trinity, Third Order Secular of the Most: Founded 1198; approved, 1219.

Oblates of St. Benedict are lay persons affiliated with a Benedictine abbey or monastery who strive to direct their lives, as circumstances permit, according to the spirit and Rule of St. Benedict.

In addition to the recognized secular orders, there are other groups of lay persons with strong ties to religious orders. Relationships of this kind serve the spiritual good of the faithful and also enrich the religious orders in a complementary fashion, with the mutual vitality of prayer in the cloister or convent and action in the marketplace.

CATHOLIC RELIEF SERVICES

Catholic Relief Services is the official overseas aid and development agency of American Catholics; it is a separately incorporated organization of the U.S. Catholic Conference.

Long-term Development Projects

CRS was founded in 1943 by the bishops of the United States to help civilians in Europe and North Africa caught in the disruption and devastation of World War II. As conditions in Europe improved in the late 1940s and early 1950s, the works conducted by CRS spread to other continents and areas — Asia, Africa and Latin America. Although best known for its record of disaster response, compassionate aid to refugees and commitment to reconstruction and rehabilitation, CRS places primary focus on long-term development projects designed to help people to help themselves and to determine their own future. Administrative funding for CRS comes largely from the Catholic Relief Services Annual Appeal. Major support is derived from private, individual donors and through a program of sacrificial giving called Operation Rice Bowl.

Kenneth F. Hackett is executive director. CRS headquarters are located at 209 W. Fayette St., Baltimore, Md. 21201.

MISSIONARY ACTIVITY OF THE CHURCH _____

UNITED STATES OVERSEAS MISSIONARIES

From the 1992-1993 Report on U.S. Catholic Overseas Mission, reproduced with permission of the United States Catholic Mission Association, 3029 Fourth St. N.E., Washington, D.C. 20017.
For additional information about the Church in mission areas, see News Events and other Almanac entries.

Field Distribution, 1992

Under this and following headings, Alaska, Hawaii, etc., are considered abroad because they are outside the 48 contiguous states.

Africa: 949 (483 men; 466 women). Largest numbers in Kenya, 233; Tanzania, 124; Ghana, 86; Zambia, 77; Nigeria, 63; Uganda, 54; South Africa, 54.

Near East: 59 (43 men; 16 women). Largest numbers in Israel, 32; Egypt, 12; Lebanon, 5; Jordan, 4; Cyprus, 3.

Far East: 1,163 (767 men; 396 women). Largest numbers in Philippines, 276; Japan, 247; Taiwan, 142; Korea, 101; Hong Kong, 88; India, 85.

Oceania: 512 (255 men; 257 women). Largest groups in Hawaii, 188; Papua New Guinea, 135; Australia, 48; Micronesia, 40; Guam, 27; Marshall Islands, 21.

North America: 257 (105 men; 152 women). Largest groups in Alaska, 132; Canada, 117.

Caribbean Islands: 431 (238 men; 193 women). Largest groups in Puerto Rico, 139; Jamaica, 95; Haiti, 58; Dominican Republic, 52; Bahamas, 29.

Central America: 810 (439 men; 371 women). Largest groups in Mexico, 296; Guatemala, 179; Nicaragua, 81; Honduras, 78.

South America: 1,286 (655 men; 631 women). Largest groups in Peru, 387; Brazil, 369; Bolivia, 177; Chile, 173.

TOTAL: 5,467 (2,985 men; 2,482 women).

Men Religious, 1992

Eighty-eight mission-sending groups had 2,658 priests and brothers in overseas assignments. Listed below are those with 17 or more members serving abroad.

Jesuits: 477 in 49 countries; largest group, 65 in the Philippines.

Maryknoll Missionaries: 412 in 29 countries; largest groups, 38 in Tanzania.

Franciscans (O.F.M.): 167 in 28 countries; largest group, 43 in Brazil.

Divine Word Missionaries: 135 in 18 countries; largest group, 34 in Papua New Guinea.

Redemptorists: 118 in 11 countries; largest group, 40 in Brazil.

Oblates of Mary Immaculate: 115 in 17 countries; largest group, 27 in Brazil.

Capuchins (O.F.M. Cap): 114 in 13 countries; largest group, 25 in Papua New Guinea.

Congregation of Holy Cross: 97 in 10 countries; largest group, 24 in Bangladesh.

Marianists: 91 in 14 countries; largest group, 25 in Hawaii.

Benedictines: 67 in 13 countries; largest group, 17 in Guatemala.

Brothers of the Christian Schools: 58 in 14 countries; largest group, 16 in Kenya.

Dominicans: 54 in 10 countries; largest group, 10 in Nigeria.

Columbans: 53 in 11 countries; largest group, 19 in the Philippines.

Conventual Franciscans (O.F.M. Conv): 44 in 9 countries; largest group, 12 in Zambia.

Vincentians: 37 in 8 countries; largest group, 18 in Panama.

Passionists: 36 in 12 countries; largest group, 10 in the Philippines.

Holy Ghost Fathers: 35 in 8 countries; largest group, 15 in Tanzania.

Congregation of Christian Brothers: 29 in 5 countries; largest group, 13 in Peru.

Augustinians: 26 in 4 countries; largest group, 15 in Peru.

La Salette Missionaries: 25 in 7 countries; largest group, 12 in Argentina.

Missionaries of the Sacred Heart: 24 in 3 countries; largest group, 19 in Papua New Guinea.

Salesians: 24 in 8 countries; largest group, 12 in Canada.

Marist Brothers: 20 in 5 countries; largest group, 7 each in Japan and the Philippines.

Xaverian Missionary Fathers: 19 in 9 countries; largest group, 6 in Brazil.

Marist Fathers: 18 in 6 countries; largest group, 8 in Hawaii.

Franciscan Friars of the Atonement: 17 in 4 countries; largest group, 10 in Canada.

Missionhurst-CICM: 17 in 8 countries; largest group, 5 in Dominican Republic.

Comboni Missionaries: 17 in 11 countries; largest groups, 3 each in Kenya and Uganda.

Society of the Precious Blood: 17 in 3 countries; largest group, 8 in Peru.

Diocesan Priests, 1992

One hundred and 81 diocesan priests from 90 dioceses were in overseas assignments in 1992.

The largest groups were from: Boston, 19 (Bolivia, 6; Ecuador, 3; Peru, 10); St. Louis, 7 (Bolivia); Cleveland, 6 (El Salvador); Jefferson City, 6 (Peru).

Forty-eight of the U.S. diocesan priests in overseas assignments were members of the Missionary Society of St. James the Apostle, founded by Cardinal Richard J. Cushing of Boston in 1958. Its director is Rev. William T. Pearsall, 24 Clark St., Boston, Massachusetts 02109.

Twenty-nine other U.S. diocesan priests in overseas assignments were working as Priest Associates with the Maryknoll Missionaries, whose headquarters are in Maryknoll, New York 10545.

Sisters, 1992

Two hundred and 61 mission-sending groups had 2,222 sisters in overseas assignments.

Maryknoll Sisters: 331 in 31 countries; largest group, 38 in Hawaii.

School Sisters of Notre Dame: 94 in 17 countries; largest group, 11 in Kenya.

Sisters of Mercy of the Americas: 68 in 20 countries; largest group, 19 in Bolivia.

Sisters of St. Joseph of Carondelet: 60 in 8 countries; largest group, 25 in Hawaii.

Daughters of Charity: 56 in 11 countries; largest group, 19 in Bolivia.

Sisters of the Holy Cross: 47 in 7 countries; largest group, 16 in Brazil.

Sisters of Notre Dame de Namur: 45 in 11 countries; largest group, 10 in Kenya.

Marist Missionary Sisters: 41 in 15 countries; largest group, 8 in Peru.

Medical Mission Sisters: 36 in 11 countries; largest group, 11 in Ghana.

Benedictine Sisters: 31 in 9 countries: largest group, 8 in Brazil.

Sisters, Servants of the Immaculate Heart of Mary (Philadelphia): 29 in 2 countries; larger group, 20 in Peru.

Ursulines of the Roman Union: 27 in 12 countries; largest group, 8 in Thailand.

Franciscan Missionaries of Mary: 26 in 15 countries; largest groups, 4 each in Ghana and Australia.

Sisters, Servants of the Immaculate Heart of Mary (Monroe): 24 in 8 countries; largest group, 6 in South Africa.

Franciscan Sisters of Allegany: 23 in 3 countries; largest group, 14 in Jamaica.

Sisters of Our Lady of the Good Shepherd: 23 in 7 countries; largest group, 7 in Hong Kong.

Little Sisters of the Poor: 22 in 10 countries; largest group, 5 in Canada.

Sisters of the Holy Family of Nazareth: 22 in 3 countries; largest group, 16 in Australia.

Sisters of Notre Dame: 20 in 3 countries; largest group, 11 in Papua New Guinea.

Daughters of St. Paul: 19 in 7 countries; largest groups, 5 each in Hawaii and Canada.

Sisters of St. Francis (Oldenburg): 18 in 3 countries; largest group, 15 in Papua New Guinea.

Sisters of the Third Franciscan Order (Syracuse): 18 in 2 countries; larger group, 15 in Hawaii.

Sisters of the Presentation B.V.M.: 18 in 6 countries; largest group, 6 in Mexico.

Dominican Sisters (Sinsinawa): 18 in 5 countries; largest groups, 8 in Alaska.

Missionary Sisters of the Immaculate Conception: 18 in 2 countries; larger group, 17 in Canada.

Sisters of St. Francis of Philadelphia: 18 in 6 countries; largest group, 5 in Liberia.

The other mission-sending institutes of women had 17 or less members in overseas assignments.

Lay Volunteers, 1992

Four hundred and six lay volunteers of 47 sponsoring organizations were in overseas assignments in 1992.

Maryknoll Lay Missioners: 122 in 16 countries; largest group, 15 each in Venezuela and Peru.

Jesuit International Volunteers: 42 in 6 countries; largest group, 19 in Belize.

Jesuit Volunteer Corps: 32 in Alaska.

Lay Mission Helpers/Mission Doctors: 27 in 8 countries; largest group, 20 in Papua New Guinea.

Volunteer Missionary Movement: 17 in 7 countries; largest group, 6 in Uganda.

Diocese of Davenport: 16 in 8 countries; largest group, 4 each in Brazil and Mexico.

Christian Foundation for Children and Aging: 11 in 7 countries; largest group, 3 in Guatemala.

Salesian Lay Mission Volunteers: 11 in 3 countries; largest group, 4 in Bolivia.

Holy Cross Associates: 10 in Chile.

Catholic Medical Mission Board: 10 in 6 countries; largest groups, 2 each in Ghana and Guatemala. (This figure represents those whose term of service was for at least one year. In addition, 109 short-term volunteers served in 15 countries during the year.)

Society of Our Lady of the Most Holy Trinity: 9 in 3 countries; largest group, 4 in Belize.

Franciscan Mission Service: 8 in 3 countries; largest group, 3 in Guatemala.

Annunciation House: 8 in Mexico.

The other thirty-four sponsoring organizations had seven members or less in overseas assignments.

U.S. MISSION ASSOCIATION

The United States Catholic Mission Association was juridically established Sept. 1, 1981. Its members include U.S. missioners, mission organizations, diocesan mission offices and others concerned about the mission of the Church and global justice. The Association seeks to help missioners stay up to date on mission and world trends, to promote greater global awareness, sensibility, and solidarity in the U.S., and, periodically, to be a voice for U.S. missioners speaking out in defense of the poor and oppressed throughout the world.

The activities of the association include a national conference and regional seminars which highlight specific mission themes and issues; liaison and cooperation with missionary bodies of other Christian churches; training programs and refresher courses for departing and returning missionaries. The USCMA is responsible for gathering statistical data on U.S. missionary personnel overseas, which it publishes in the biannual *Report on U.S. Catholic Overseas Mission*, formerly the *Mission Handbook*. The association also publishes *Mission Update*, a bimonthly newsletter.

The president of the association is Mr. Donald Mueller and the executive director is Sr. Margaret F. Loftus, S.N.D. The office is located at 3029 Fourth St. N.E., Washington, DC 20017.

U.S. OVERSEAS MISSIONARIES, 1960-1992

Year	Diocesan Priests	Religious Priests	Religious Brothers	Religious Sisters	Seminarians	Lay Persons	Total
1960	14	3018	575	2827	170	178	6782
1962	31	3172	720	2764	152	307	7146
1964	80	3438	782	3137	157	532	8126
1966	215	3731	901	3706	201	549	9303
1968	282	3727	869	4150	208	419	9655
1970	373	3117	666	3824	90	303	8373
1972+	246	3182	634	3121	97	376	7656
1973	237	3913*	—	3012	—	529	7691
1974	220	3084	639	2916	101	458	7418
1975	197	3023	669	2850	65	344	7148
1976	193	2961	691	2840	68	257	7010
1977	182	2882	630	2781	42	243	6760
1978	166	2830	610	2673	43	279	6601
1979	187	2800	592	2568	50	258	6455
1980	188	2750	592	2592	50	221	6393
1981	187	2702	584	2574	43	234	6324
1982	178	2668	578	2560	44	217	6245
1983	174	2668	569	2540	48	247	6246
1984	187	2603	549	2492	40	263	6134
1985	171	2500	558	2505	30	292	6056
1986	204	2473	532	2481	30	317	6037
1987	200	2394	570	2505	53	351	6073
1988	200	2420	504	2495	50	394	6063
1989	209	2364	494	2473	51	410	6001
1990	200	2257	477	2347	51	421	5744
1991	187	2200	468	2264	30	446	5595
1992	181	2183	449	2222	26	406	5467

+A corrected total for 1972 should read 7937, indicating losses of 436 from 1970 to 1972 and 246 from 1972 to 1973.

*Includes religious brothers and seminarians.

FIELD DISTRIBUTION BY AREAS, 1960-1992

Year	Africa	Far East	Near East	Oceania	Europe	N. Amer.	Carib. Is.	Cent. Amer.	S. Amer.	Total
1960	781	1959	111	986	203	337	991	433	981	6782
1962	901	2110	75	992	93	224	967	537	1247	7146
1964	1025	2332	122	846	69	220	1056	660	1796	8126
1966	1184	2453	142	953	38	211	1079	857	2386	9303
1968	1157	2470	128	1027	33	251	1198	936	2455	9655
1970	1141	2137	39	900	38	233	1067	738	2080	8373
1972	1107	1955	59	826	39	234	819	728	1889	7656
1973	1229	1962	54	811	40	253	796	763	1783	7691
1974	1121	1845	60	883	43	241	757	752	1716	7418
1975	1065	1814	71	808	37	252	698	734	1669	7148
1976	1042	1757	68	795	34	313	671	712	1618	7010
1977	1003	1659	62	784	34	296	629	702	1591	6760
1978	966	1601	57	769	34	339	593	705	1537	6601
1979	923	1562	65	743	37	332	562	686	1545	6455
1980	909	1576	65	711	35	294	548	699	1556	6393
1981	946	1529	70	696	36	315	511	693	1528	6324
1982	956	1501	62	673	32	319	522	669	1511	6245
1983	990	1468	68	640	34	346	517	650	1533	6246
1984	967	1420	84	644	29	329	513	650	1498	6134
1985	986	1366	78	650	31	312	500	692	1441	6056
1986	944	1356	73	631	28	306	495	743	1461	6037
1987	971	1335	76	635	27	283	499	762	1485	6073
1988	984	1332	72	584	27	289	466	818	1491	6063
1989	968	1299	65	595	28	267	472	832	1475	6001
1990	945	1253	64	560	**	264	449	796	1413	5744
1991	933	1198	65	546	**	265	453	785	1350	5595
1992	949	1163	59	512	**	257	431	810	1286	5467

** Eastern and western Europe not considered to be "mission" areas by the Congregation for the Evangelization of Peoples.

HOME MISSIONS

The expression "home missions" is applied to places in the U.S. where the local church does not have its own resources, human and otherwise, which are needed to begin or, if begun, to survive and grow. These areas share the name "missions" with their counterparts in foreign lands because they too need outside help to provide the personnel and means for making the Church present and active there in carrying out its mission for the salvation of people.

Dioceses in the Southeast, the Southwest, and the Far West are most urgently in need of outside help to carry on the work of the Church. Millions of persons live in counties in which there are no resident priests. Many others live in rural areas beyond the reach and influence of a Catholic center. According to recent statistics compiled by the Glenmary Research Center, there are more than 500 priestless counties in the United States.

Mission Workers

A number of forces are at work to meet the pastoral needs of these missionary areas and to establish permanent churches and operating institutions where they are required. In many dioceses, one or more missions and stations are attended from established parishes and are gradually growing to independent status. Priests, brothers and sisters belonging to scores of religious institutes are engaged full-time in the home missions. Lay persons, some of them in affiliation with special groups and movements, are also involved.

The Society for the Propagation of the Faith, which conducts an annual collection for mission support in all parishes of the U.S., allocates 40 per cent of this sum for disbursement to home missions through the American Board of Catholic Missions.

Various mission-aid societies frequently undertake projects in behalf of the home missions.

The **Glenmary Home Missioners,** founded by Father W. Howard Bishop in 1939, is the only home mission society established for the sole purpose of carrying out the pastoral ministry in small towns and rural districts of the United States. Glenmary serves in many areas where at least 20 per cent of the people live in poverty and less than one per cent are Catholic. With 64 priests and 20 professed brothers as of May, 1993, the Glenmary Missioners had 80 missions in the archdioceses of Atlanta, Cincinnati and Washington, and in the dioceses of Birmingham, Charlotte, Covington, Dallas, Jackson, Knoxville, Lexington, Little Rock, Nashville, Owensboro, Richmond, Savannah, Tulsa, Tyler and Wheeling-Charleston. National headquarters are located at 4119 Glenmary Trace, Fairfield, Ohio. The mailing address is P.O. Box 465618, Cincinnati, Ohio 45246.

Organizations

The Commission for Catholic Missions among the Colored People and the Indians (Black and Indian Mission Office): Organized officially in 1885 by decree of the Third Plenary Council of Baltimore. Provides financial support for religious works among Blacks and Native Americans in 133 archdioceses and dioceses through funds raised by an annual collection in all parishes of the U.S. on the first Sunday of Lent, the designated Sunday. In 1992, more than $6.9 million was raised; disbursements amounted to $4,446,000 for Black missions and $2,454,000 for Native American missions. Cardinal John J. O'Connor is president of the board; Msgr. Paul A. Lenz is secretary. Headquarters: 2021 H St. N.W., Washington, DC 20006.

Bureau of Catholic Indian Missions: Established in 1874 as the representative of Catholic Indian missions before the federal government and the public; made permanent organization in 1884 by Third Plenary Council of Baltimore. After a remarkable history of rendering important services to the Indian people, the bureau continues to represent the Catholic Church in the U.S. in her apostolate to the American Indian. Concerns are evangelization, catechesis, liturgy, family life, education, advocacy. Cardinal John J. O'Connor is president of the board; Msgr. Paul A. Lenz is secretary. Address: 2021 H St., Washington, DC 20006.

Statistics (1991) reported a total Native American population of 2,000,000; an estimated 350,000 are Catholics.

Catholic Negro-American Mission Board (1907): Support priests and sisters in southern states and provide monthly support to sisters and lay teachers in the poorest Black schools. Cardinal John J. O'Connor is president of the board; Msgr. Paul A. Lenz is executive director; Patricia L. O'Rourke, assistant director. Address: 2021 H St. N.W., Washington, DC 20005.

The Catholic Church Extension Society (1905): Established with papal approval for the purpose of preserving and extending the Church in rural and isolated parts of the U.S. and its dependencies through the collection and disbursement of funds for home mission work. Since the time of its founding, more than $200 million have been received and expended for this purpose. Disbursements, made at the requests of bishops in 76 designated mission dioceses, exceeded $12 million for fiscal year 1991-92. The 10,000th church project built with the help of the society was dedicated in 1992. The society also distributes parish calendars and evangelization materials. Works of the society are supervised by a 14-member board of governors: Cardinal Joseph Bernardin, archbishop of Chicago, chancellor; Very Rev. Edward J. Slattery, president; five bishops, one sister and six lay people. Headquarters: 35 E. Wacker Drive, Chicago, IL 60601.

National Catholic Rural Life Conference: Founded in 1923, through the efforts of Bishop Edwin V. O'Hara, is a membership organization that works from a faith perspective to promote a family farm system of agriculture, a healthy environment and strong rural communities. Rev. William Wood, S.J., is president. National headquarters: 4625 Beaver Ave., Des Moines, IA 50310.

LEGAL STATUS OF CATHOLIC EDUCATION

The right of private schools to exist and operate in the United States is recognized in law. It was confirmed by the U.S. Supreme Court in 1925 when the tribunal ruled (Pierce v. Society of Sisters, see Church-State Decisions of the Supreme Court) that an Oregon state law requiring all children to attend public schools was unconstitutional.

Private schools are obliged to comply with the education laws in force in the various states regarding such matters as required basic curricula, periods of attendance, and standards for proper accreditation.

The special curricula and standards of private schools are determined by the schools themselves. Thus, in Catholic schools, the curricula include not only the subject matter required by state educational laws but also other fields of study, principally, education in the Catholic faith.

The Supreme Court has ruled that the First Amendment to the U.S. Constitution, in accordance with the No Establishment of Religion Clause of the First Amendment, prohibits direct federal and state aid from public funds to church-affiliated schools. (See several cases in Church-State Decisions of the Supreme Court.)

Public Aid

This prohibition does not extend to all child-benefit and public-purpose programs of aid to students of non-public elementary and secondary schools.

Statutes authorizing such programs have been ruled constitutional on the grounds that they:
- have a "secular legislative purpose";
- neither inhibit nor advance religion as a "principal or primary effect";
- do not foster "excessive government entanglement with religion."

Aid programs considered constitutional have provided bus transportation, textbook loans, school lunches and health services, and "secular, neutral or non-ideological services, facilities and materials provided in common to all school children," public and non-public.

The first major aid to education program in U.S. history containing provisions benefiting non-public school students was enacted by the 89th Congress and signed into law by President Lyndon B. Johnson Apr. 11, 1965. The Elementary and Secondary Education Act was designed to avoid the separation of Church and state impasse which had blocked all earlier aid proposals pertaining to nonpublic, and especially church-affiliated, schools. The objective of the program, under public control, is to serve the public purpose by aiding disadvantaged pupils in nonpublic as well as public schools.

With respect to college and university education in church-affiliated institutions, the Supreme Court has upheld the constitutionality of statutes providing student loans and, under the Federal Higher Education Facilities Act of 1963, construction loans and grants for secular-purpose facilities.

Catholic schools are exempt from real estate taxation in all of the states. Since Jan. 1, 1959, nonprofit parochial and private schools have also been exempt from several federal excise taxes.

Shared and Released Time

In a shared time program of education, students enrolled in Catholic or other church-related schools take some courses (e.g., religion, social studies, fine arts) in their own schools and others (e.g., science, mathematics, industrial arts) in public schools. Such a program has been given serious consideration in recent years by Catholic and other educators. Its constitutionality has not been seriously challenged, but practical problems — relating to teacher and student schedules, transportation, adjustment to new programs, and other factors — are knotty.

Several million children of elementary and high school age of all denominations have the opportunity of receiving religious instruction on released time. Under released time programs they are permitted to leave their public schools during school hours to attend religious instruction classes held off the public school premises. They are released at the request of their parents. Public school authorities merely provide for their dismissal, and take no part in the program.

NCEA

The National Catholic Educational Association, founded in 1904, is a voluntary organization of educational institutions and individuals concerned with Catholic education in the U.S. Its objectives are to promote and encourage the principles and ideals of Christian education and formation by suitable service and other activities.

The NCEA has 21,000 institutional and individual members. Its official publication is *Momentum*. Numerous service publications are issued to members.

Archbishop Thomas C. Kelly of Louisville is chairman of the association. Sister Catherine T. McNamee, C.S.J., is president.

Headquarters are located at 1077 30th St. N.W., Washington, D.C. 20007.

The American College, Louvain

The American College was founded by the U.S. bishops in 1857 as a house of formation for U.S. seminarians and as a residence of on-going formation for graduate priests pursuing courses in theology and related subjects at The Catholic Universities of Leuven and Louvain-la-Neuve (dating from 1425) in Belgium. The college is administered by an American rector and staff, and operates under the auspices of a special committee of the National Conference of Catholic Bishops. Rev. David Windsor, C.M., is rector. Address: The American College, University of Louvain, Naamsestraat 100, 3000 Leuven, Belgium.

CATHOLIC SCHOOLS AND STUDENTS IN THE UNITED STATES

(Source: The Official Catholic Directory, 1993; figures as of Jan. 1, 1993. Archdioceses are indicated by an asterisk.)

State Diocese	Univs. Colleges	Students	High Schools	Students	Elem. Schools	Students
Alabama	**1**	**1,350**	**6**	**2,583**	**44**	**10,482**
*Mobile	1	1,350	3	1,527	22	5,978
Birmingham	—	—	3	1,056	22	4,504
Alaska	**—**	**—**	**1**	**256**	**4**	**737**
*Anchorage	—	—	—	—	2	321
Fairbanks	—	—	1	256	1	319
Juneau	—	—	—	—	1	97
Arizona	**—**	**—**	**9**	**5,181**	**44**	**11,969**
Phoenix	—	—	5	3,233	24	7,155
Tucson	—	—	4	1,948	20	4,814
Arkansas, Little Rock	**—**	**—**	**5**	**1,675**	**32**	**6,323**
California	**15**	**36,991**	**117**	**66,828**	**601**	**178,919**
*Los Angeles	6	8,994	53	31,175	232	70,436
*San Francisco	3	8,791	14	6,832	66	20,943
Fresno	—	—	2	1,285	23	6,010
Monterey	—	—	4	1,210	15	3,856
Oakland	3	5,116	9	5,612	55	14,923
Orange	1	100	6	5,133	36	12,920
Sacramento	—	—	7	3,753	44	12,732
San Bernardino	—	—	2	923	30	8,493
San Diego	1	6,083	5	3,094	45	12,803
San Jose	1	7,907	6	4,879	29	9,455
Santa Rosa	—	—	7	1,824	14	3,164
Stockton	—	—	2	1,108	12	3,184
Colorado	**1**	**9,249**	**7**	**2,203**	**46**	**12,512**
*Denver	1	9,249	5	2,060	37	10,416
Colorado Springs	—	—	—	—	4	969
Pueblo	—	—	2	143	5	1,127
Connecticut	**6**	**11,397**	**25**	**10,450**	**133**	**31,372**
*Hartford	3	2,586	11	4,803	76	18,472
Bridgeport	2	8,579	9	3,566	36	8,888
Norwich	1	232	5	2,081	21	4,012
Delaware, Wilmington	**—**	**—**	**7**	**4,386**	**29**	**11,234**
District of Columbia, *Washington	**3**	**19,667**	**17**	**7,501**	**85**	**21,720**
Florida	**3**	**9,677**	**35**	**20,711**	**173**	**57,576**
*Miami	2	8,660	17	11,710	55	21,597
Orlando	—	—	4	1,975	27	9,429
Palm Beach	—	—	3	1,605	16	4,759
Pensacola-Tallahassee	—	—	1	437	9	2,485
St. Augustine	—	—	2	1,258	15	5,554
St. Petersburg	1	1,017	5	2,517	42	10,672
Venice	—	—	3	1,209	9	3,080
Georgia	**—**	**—**	**7**	**3,903**	**28**	**9,192**
*Atlanta	—	—	2	1,993	13	4,771
Savannah	—	—	5	1,910	15	4,421
Hawaii, Honolulu	**1**	**2,281**	**7**	**3,395**	**27**	**7,956**
Idaho, Boise	**—**	**—**	**1**	**526**	**12**	**2,142**
Illinois	**15**	**48,937**	**83**	**50,676**	**563**	**170,487**
*Chicago	7	38,216	50	35,466	315	108,865
Belleville	1	951	3	1,410	41	7,749
Joliet	4	7,797	8	5,339	62	17,632
Peoria	1	189	7	2,471	49	12,519
Rockford	—	—	8	3,483	42	11,435
Springfield	2	1,784	7	2,507	54	12,287
Indiana	**10**	**18,087**	**24**	**11,067**	**184**	**43,647**
*Indianapolis	3	2,370	9	4,478	62	16,326
Evansville	—	—	5	1,752	27	5,170
Ft. Wayne-South Bend	5	13,517	4	2,371	42	10,246
Gary	1	1,200	4	2,092	33	8,424

State Diocese	Univs. Colleges	Students	High Schools	Students	Elem. Schools	Students
Indiana						
Lafayette	1	1,000	2	374	20	3,481
Iowa	**6**	**7,658**	**25**	**7,871**	**144**	**32,172**
*Dubuque	3	4,119	8	3,059	56	15,640
Davenport	2	2,792	7	1,120	39	5,355
Des Moines	—	—	2	1,314	19	4,202
Sioux City	1	747	8	2,378	30	6,975
Kansas	**4**	**4,145**	**17**	**5,363**	**95**	**20,630**
*Kansas City	3	2,830	7	2,962	39	10,152
Dodge City	—	—	—	—	11	1,442
Salina	—	—	6	712	12	1,870
Wichita	1	1,315	4	1,689	33	7,166
Kentucky	**5**	**5,912**	**25**	**9,758**	**131**	**31,683**
*Louisville	3	3,813	10	5,602	65	16,597
Covington	1	1,299	9	2,678	32	8,045
Lexington	—	—	3	564	15	2,816
Owensboro	1	800	3	914	19	4,225
Louisiana	**3**	**9,300**	**52**	**25,718**	**179**	**72,158**
*New Orleans	3	9,300	24	15,458	84	37,457
Alexandria	—	—	3	490	9	2,442
Baton Rouge	—	—	8	4,348	25	12,771
Houma-Thibodaux	—	—	3	1,631	12	4,161
Lafayette	—	—	11	2,735	30	10,625
Lake Charles	—	—	1	383	8	2,230
Shreveport	—	—	2	673	11	2,472
Maine, Portland	**1**	**6,650**	**3**	**713**	**19**	**3,928**
Maryland, *Baltimore	**3**	**10,071**	**22**	**8,708**	**76**	**23,231**
Massachusetts	**9**	**31,263**	**52**	**22,968**	**206**	**59,659**
*Boston	4	20,074	37	15,028	131	38,541
Fall River	1	3,025	4	2,330	22	5,705
Springfield	1	1,070	4	2,401	31	9,497
Worcester	3	7,094	7	3,209	22	5,916
Michigan	**6**	**18,150**	**54**	**19,759**	**304**	**74,443**
*Detroit	4	13,863	35	13,307	143	39,671
Gaylord	—	—	4	484	18	3,010
Grand Rapids	1	2,539	4	1,747	42	8,926
Kalamazoo	—	—	3	860	21	4,390
Lansing	1	1,748	5	2,423	39	9,781
Marquette	—	—	—	—	9	1,872
Saginaw	—	—	3	938	32	6,793
Minnesota	**7**	**21,056**	**21**	**8,296**	**204**	**44,126**
*St. Paul and Minneapolis	3	14,037	11	6,186	100	26,078
Crookston	—	—	1	68	9	1,243
Duluth	1	1,985	—	—	13	2,071
New Ulm	—	—	3	446	22	3,466
St. Cloud	2	3,736	2	591	35	5,977
Winona	1	1,298	4	1,005	25	5,291
Mississippi	**1**	**22**	**9**	**3,646**	**26**	**5,843**
Biloxi	—	—	5	1,719	12	2,994
Jackson	1	22	4	1,927	14	2,849
Missouri	**4**	**16,790**	**42**	**18,478**	**263**	**62,909**
*St. Louis	2	12,680	29	14,301	168	44,069
Jefferson City	—	—	2	804	37	5,993
Kansas City-St. Joseph	2	4,110	8	2,792	35	9,403
Springfield-Cape Girardeau	—	—	3	581	23	3,444
Montana	**2**	**2,642**	**4**	**923**	**16**	**2,735**
Great Falls-Billings	1	1,260	2	524	12	1,955
Helena	1	1,382	2	399	4	780
Nebraska	**2**	**7,530**	**27**	**6,833**	**91**	**21,521**
*Omaha	2	7,530	17	4,753	60	14,973
Grand Island	—	—	4	728	7	965
Lincoln	—	—	6	1,352	24	5,583
Nevada, Reno-Las Vegas	—	—	2	1,152	11	3,402
New Hampshire, Manchester	**5**	**6,455**	**4**	**1,800**	**35**	**5,909**

State Diocese	Univs. Colleges	Students	High Schools	Students	Elem. Schools	Students
New Jersey	**7**	**19,424**	**79**	**38,071**	**383**	**108,278**
*Newark	4	15,735	39	16,563	157	44,516
Camden	—	—	11	5,998	63	15,392
Metuchen	—	—	8	3,609	41	11,473
Paterson	2	1,186	10	4,085	61	15,668
Trenton	1	2,503	11	7,816	61	21,229
New Mexico	**1**	**1,411**	**6**	**1,882**	**33**	**6,760**
*Santa Fe	1	1,411	3	1,616	18	4,606
Gallup	—	—	3	266	10	1,472
Las Cruces	—	—	—	—	5	682
New York	**29**	**106,640**	**138**	**75,064**	**757**	**220,297**
*New York	12	59,409	55	28,704	243	77,715
Albany	4	8,417	7	2,990	40	9,080
Brooklyn	2	19,397	22	19,858	162	54,790
Buffalo	6	13,079	17	5,520	94	24,413
Ogdensburg	2	635	2	621	24	4,754
Rochester	—	—	7	3,289	56	12,203
Rockville Centre	2	3,251	22	11,394	82	27,647
Syracuse	1	2,452	6	2,688	56	9,695
North Carolina	**2**	**1,000**	**3**	**1,180**	**30**	**8,192**
Charlotte	2	1,000	2	832	14	4,327
Raleigh	—	—	1	348	16	3,865
North Dakota	**2**	**2,036**	**4**	**1,254**	**28**	**5,454**
Bismarck	1	1,900	3	977	16	3,416
Fargo	1	136	1	277	12	2,038
Ohio	**11**	**32,908**	**80**	**42,659**	**464**	**141,682**
*Cincinnati	4	19,991	22	13,587	116	39,267
Cleveland	3	6,874	24	14,565	145	50,233
Columbus	1	1,220	11	4,654	49	13,264
Steubenville	1	1,790	3	643	16	2,816
Toledo	1	1,483	14	6,397	87	23,438
Youngstown	1	1,550	6	2,813	51	12,664
Oklahoma	**1**	**328**	**4**	**2,124**	**31**	**7,050**
*Oklahoma City	1	328	2	996	18	3,487
Tulsa	—	—	2	1,128	13	3,563
Oregon	**2**	**4,623**	**8**	**3,192**	**46**	**9,093**
*Portland	2	4,623	8	3,192	42	8,549
Baker	—	—	—	—	4	544
Pennsylvania	**26**	**83,073**	**95**	**51,685**	**649**	**188,535**
*Philadelphia	11	36,257	44	30,615	258	96,449
Allentown	2	2,956	9	3,826	56	13,566
Altoona-Johnstown	2	3,943	3	1,183	33	5,704
Erie	2	6,848	8	2,993	45	11,289
Greensburg	2	2,189	2	943	39	7,265
Harrisburg	—	—	8	3,553	44	10,379
Pittsburgh	3	18,869	11	4,917	117	29,721
Scranton	4	12,011	10	3,655	57	14,162
Rhode Island, Providence	**2**	**8,325**	**10**	**4,350**	**55**	**12,079**
South Carolina, Charleston	**—**	**—**	**3**	**1,290**	**26**	**5,505**
South Dakota	**2**	**1,520**	**5**	**1,316**	**26**	**4,804**
Rapid City	—	—	2	347	3	795
Sioux Falls	2	1,520	3	969	23	4,009
Tennessee	**2**	**2,153**	**11**	**4,289**	**37**	**10,517**
Knoxville	—	—	2	655	7	2,170
Memphis	1	1,609	7	2,554	13	4,199
Nashville	1	544	2	1,080	17	4,148
Texas	**7**	**17,646**	**45**	**15,685**	**226**	**60,860**
*San Antonio	4	9,653	9	2,963	42	11,827
Amarillo	—	—	1	155	8	1,398
Austin	1	3,047	2	402	17	3,596
Beaumont	—	—	1	560	7	2,124
Brownsville	—	—	1	726	7	2,495
Corpus Christi	—	—	6	1,650	23	4,696
Dallas	1	2,867	6	2,777	29	9,038

State Diocese	Univs. Colleges	Students	High Schools	Students	Elem. Schools	Students
Texas						
El Paso	—	—	3	1,290	12	3,568
Fort Worth	—	—	4	1,172	13	3,588
Galveston-Houston	1	2,079	8	3,203	47	13,203
Lubbock	—	—	—	—	2	377
San Angelo	—	—	—	—	3	1,053
Tyler	—	—	1	134	4	805
Victoria	—	—	3	653	12	3,092
Utah, Salt Lake City	—	—	2	1,121	9	2,561
Vermont, Burlington	3	4,221	2	599	11	2,244
Virginia	2	3,228	14	4,793	49	16,688
Arlington	2	3,228	4	3,092	28	9,684
Richmond	—	—	10	1,701	21	7,004
Washington	3	15,291	11	6,286	78	20,925
*Seattle	2	5,230	9	4,668	54	15,018
Spokane	1	10,061	2	1,618	17	4,295
Yakima	—	—	—	—	7	1,612
West Virginia, Wheeling-Charleston	1	1,438	8	1,657	30	5,624
Wisconsin	9	27,613	28	11,925	373	66,636
*Milwaukee	5	21,504	13	7,386	150	29,321
Green Bay	2	3,219	6	2,153	82	15,308
La Crosse	1	1,279	7	1,694	77	11,133
Madison	1	1,611	2	692	46	7,813
Superior	—	—	—	—	18	3,061
Wyoming, Cheyenne	—	—	—	—	6	1,127
EASTERN RITES	1	570	5	796	35	5,968
*Philadelphia	1	570	1	321	9	1,312
St. Nicholas (Chicago)	—	—	1	65	2	487
Stamford	—	—	2	150	4	540
St. Josaphat (Parma)	—	—	—	—	2	340
*Pittsburgh	—	—	—	—	6	1,043
Parma	—	—	—	—	3	424
Passaic	—	—	1	260	5	935
Van Nuys	—	—	—	—	—	—
St. Maron (Maronites)	—	—	—	—	—	—
Newton (Melkites)	—	—	—	—	—	—
St. Thomas Apostle of Detroit (Chaldeans)	—	—	—	—	—	—
St. George Martyr (Romanians)	—	—	—	—	—	—
Armenians (Ap. Ex.)	—	—	—	—	4	887
U.S. TOTALS 1993	**226**	**638,728**	**1,271**	**604,545**	**7,187**	**1,951,595**
U.S. Totals 1992	**230**	**633,480**	**1,278**	**602,856**	**7,288**	**1,948,457**
U.S. Totals 1983	**238**	**544,136**	**1,470**	**814,068**	**7,969**	**2,268,453**

SCHOOLS AND STUDENTS IN OUTLYING AREAS

	Univs. Colleges	Students	High Schools	Students	Elem. Schools	Students
American Samoa	—	—	2	346	2	448
Carolines and Marshalls	—	—	7	879	11	3,270
Guam	—	—	3	1,138	7	3,247
Marianas	—	—	1	220	2	349
Puerto Rico	5	22,059	91	28,096	134	47,435
Virgin Islands	—	—	2	516	3	955
TOTALS (Outlying Areas)	**5**	**22,059**	**106**	**31,195**	**159**	**55,704**
GRAND TOTALS, 1993						
U.S. AND OUTLYING AREAS	**231**	**660,787**	**1,377**	**635,740**	**7,346**	**2,007,299**

MOZARABIC RITE

The Mozarabic or Hispano-Mozarabic rite is the Latin liturgy which developed in Spain during the first Christian centuries and was preserved by Hispano-Romans even during the periods of Visigothic and Moorish domination. General use of the rite died out after the reconquest but limited use continued in several parishes in Toledo. The rite may now be used in any part of Spain.

SUMMARY OF SCHOOL STATISTICS

The status of Catholic educational institutions and programs in the United States at the beginning of 1993 was reflected in figures (as of Jan. 1) reported by *The Official Catholic Directory, 1993*.

Colleges and Universities: 226.

College and University Students: 638,728.

High Schools: 1,271 (759 diocesan and parochial; 512 private).

High School Students: 604,545 (345,586 diocesan and parochial; 258,959 private).

Public High School Students Receiving Religious Instruction: 759,656.

Elementary Schools: 7,187 (6,927 diocesan and parochial; 260 private).

Elementary School Students: 1,951,595 (1,891,217 diocesan and parochial; 60,378 private).

Public Elementary School Students Receiving Religious Instruction: 3,281,629.

Non-Residential Schools for Handicapped: 94. **Students:** 8,765.

Teachers — 164,661: Lay Persons, 144,354; Sisters, 15,735; Priests, 2,738; Brothers, 1,756; Scholastics, 78.

Seminaries: 198. Diocesan, 70; religious institutes: 128.

Seminarians: 5,715. Diocesan, 4,219; religious institutes: 1,496.

RELIGIOUS EDUCATION

Religious Education/Catechesis/CCD (Confraternity of Christian Doctrine): Its objective is the catechesis of persons from early childhood through adult life.

The modern expansion of catechesis dates from publication of the encyclical letter *Acerbo Nimis* by Pope St. Pius X in 1905. His directive, that CCD programs be established in every parish, was incorporated in the 1917 Code of Canon Law, reaffirmed by the Second Vatican Council in the *Decree on the Bishops' Pastoral Office in the Church*, and given direction by the publication of the *National Catechetical Directory* in 1978.

Programs for catechesis are parish-based. Policies are developed by parish boards or commissions, and responsibility for administering programs rests

ideally with a coordinator or director who is a trained professional. On the diocesan level, religious education is coordinated by a director with a staff operating under the title of an office of religious education or a similar title.

On the national level, Religious Education/Catechetical Ministry/CCD (formerly called the National Center for the Confraternity of Christian Doctrine is situated in the Division of Catechesis/Religious Education within the Department of Education of the United States Catholic Conference. On the international level, it participates in programs of appropriate Vatican congregations.

Offices are located at 3211 4th St. N.E., Washington, D.C. 20017.

UNIVERSITIES AND COLLEGES IN THE UNITED STATES

(Sources: Almanac survey; *The Official Catholic Directory*.)

Listed below are institutions of higher learning established under Catholic auspices. Some of them are now independent.

Information includes: name of each institution; indication of male (m), female (w), coeducational (c) student body; name of founding group or group with which the institution is affiliated; year of foundation; total number of students, in parentheses.

Albertus Magnus College (c): 700 Prospect St., New Haven, CT 06511. Dominican Sisters; 1925; independent (655).

Allentown College of St. Francis de Sales (c): 2755 Station Ave., Center Valley, PA 18034. Oblates of St. Francis de Sales; 1965 (1,640).

Alvernia College (c): Reading, PA 19607. Bernardine Sisters; 1958 (1,332).

Alverno College (w): 3401 S. 39th St. Milwaukee, WI 53215. School Sisters of St. Francis; 1887; independent (2,414).

Anna Maria College (c): Sunset Lane, Paxton, MA 01612. Sisters of St. Anne; 1946; independent (1,486).

Aquinas College (c): 1607 Robinson Rd. S.E., Grand Rapids, MI 49506. Sisters of St. Dominic; 1922; independent (2,539).

Assumption College (c): 500 Salisbury St., Wor-

cester, MA 01615. Assumptionist Fathers; 1904 (2,792).

Avila College (c): 11901 Wornall Rd., Kansas City, MO 64145. Sisters of St. Joseph of Carondelet; 1916 (1,409).

Barat College (c): 700 Westleigh Rd., Lake Forest, IL 60045. Society of the Sacred Heart; 1919; independent (770).

Barry University (c): 11300 N.E. 2nd Ave., Miami Shores, FL 33161. Dominican Sisters (Adrian, Mich.); 1940 (6,436).

Bellarmine College (c): 2001 Newburg Rd., Louisville, KY 40205; Louisville archdiocese; independent (2,326).

Belmont Abbey College (c): Belmont, NC 28012. Benedictine Fathers; 1876 (1,029).

Benedictine College (c): 1020 N. Second St., Atchison, KS 66002. Benedictines; 1859; independent (953).

Boston College (University Status) (c): Chestnut Hill, MA 02167. Jesuit Fathers; 1863 (14,455).

Brescia College (c): 717 Frederica St., Owensboro, KY 42301. Ursuline Sisters; 1950 (800).

Briar Cliff College (c): 3303 Rebecca St., P.O. Box 2100, Sioux City, IA 51104. Sisters of St. Francis of the Holy Family; 1930 (1,144).

Cabrini College (c): 610 King of Prussia Rd.,

Radnor, PA 19087. Missionary Srs. of Sacred Heart; 1957; private (1,760).

Caldwell College (c): 9 Ryerson Ave., Caldwell, NJ 07006. Dominican Sisters; 1939 (1,306).

Calumet College of St. Joseph (c): 2400 New York Ave., Whiting, IN 46394. Society of the Precious Blood, 1951 (1,000).

Canisius College (c): 2001 Main St., Buffalo, NY 14208. Jesuit Fathers; 1870; independent (4,829).

Cardinal Stritch College (c): 6801 N. Yates Rd., Milwaukee, WI 53217. Sisters of St. Francis of Assisi; 1937 (4,200).

Carlow College (w): 3333 5th Ave., Pittsburgh, PA 15213. Sisters of Mercy; 1929 (1,731).

Carroll College (c): Helena, MT 59625. Diocesan; 1909 (1,382).

Catholic University of America, The (c): 620 Michigan Ave. N.E., Washington, DC 20064. Hierarchy of the United States; 1887. Pontifical University (6,749).

Catholic University of Puerto Rico (c): Ponce, PR 00731. Hierarchy of Puerto Rico; 1948; Pontifical University (12,100).

Chaminade University of Honolulu (c): 3140 Waialae Ave., Honolulu, Hawaii 96816. Marianists; 1955 (2,400).

Chestnut Hill College (w): Philadelphia, PA 19118. Sisters of St. Joseph; 1924 (1,346).

Christendom College (c): 2101 Shenandoah Shores Rd., Front Royal, VA 22630. Founded 1977 (145).

Christian Brothers University (c): 650 E. Parkway S., Memphis, TN 38104. Brothers of the Christian Schools; 1871 (1,725).

Clarke College (c): 1550 Clarke Dr., Dubuque, Iowa 52001. Sisters of Charity, BVM; 1843 (927).

Creighton University (c): California St. at 24th, Omaha, NE 68178. Jesuit Fathers; 1878; independent (6,160).

Dallas, University of (c): 1845 E. Northgate, Irving, TX 75062. Dallas diocese; 1956; independent (2,995).

Dayton, University of (c): 300 College Park Ave., Dayton, Ohio 45469. Marianists; 1850 (10,658).

DePaul University (c): 25 E. Jackson Blvd., Chicago, IL 60604. Vincentians; 1898 (16,414).

Detroit Mercy, University of (c): 4001 W. McNichols Rd., Detroit, MI, P.O. Box 19900, 48219; 8200 W. Outer Dr., Detroit MI 48219. Society of Jesus and Sisters of Mercy; 1877 (7,774).

Dominican College of Blauvelt (c): Orangeburg, NY 10962. Dominican Sisters; 1952; independent (1,500).

Dominican College (c): 1520 Grand Ave.; San Rafael, CA 94901. Dominican Sisters; 1890; independent (953).

Duquesne University (c): 600 Forbes Ave., Pittsburgh, PA 15282. Congregation of the Holy Ghost; 1878 (more than 8,000).

D'Youville College (c): 320 Porter Ave., Buffalo, NY 14201. Grey Nuns of the Sacred Heart; 1908; independent. (1,700).

Edgewood College (c): 855 Woodrow St., Madison, WI 53711. Dominican Sisters; 1927 (1,700).

Emmanuel College (w): 400 The Fenway, Boston, MA 02115. Sisters of Notre Dame de Namur; independent (1,170).

Fairfield University (c): North Benson Rd., Fairfield, CT 06430. Jesuits; 1942 (4,873).

Felician College (c): 260 S. Main St., Lodi, NJ 07644. Felician Sisters; 1942; independent (1,010).

Fontbonne College (c): 6800 Wydown Blvd., St. Louis, MO 63105. Sisters of St. Joseph of Carondelet; 1917; independent (1,245).

Fordham University (c): Fordham Rd. and Third Ave., New York, NY 10458. Society of Jesus (Jesuits); 1841; independent (14,500).

Franciscan University of Steubenville (c): Steubenville, Ohio 43952. Franciscan Fathers; 1946 (1,800).

Gannon University (c): 109 University Square, Erie, PA 16541 (main campus); 2551 W. 8th St., Erie, PA 16505 (Villa Maria branch campus). Diocese of Erie; 1933 (3,715).

Georgetown University (c): 37th and O Sts. N.W., Washington, DC 20057. Jesuit Fathers; 1789 (11,985).

Georgian Court College (w/c): 900 Lakewood Ave., Lakewood, NJ 08701. Sisters of Mercy; 1908 (2,503).

Gonzaga University (c): Spokane, WA 99258. Jesuit Fathers; 1887 (4,200).

Great Falls, College of (c): 1301 20th St. S., Great Falls, MT 59405. Sisters of Providence; 1932; independent (1,400).

Gwynedd-Mercy College (c): Gwynedd Valley, PA 19437. Sisters of Mercy; 1948; independent (2,019).

Holy Cross, College of the (c): Worcester, MA 01610. Jesuit Fathers; 1843 (2,712).

Holy Family College (c): Grant and Frankford Aves., Philadelphia, PA 19114. Sisters of Holy Family of Nazareth; 1954; independent (2,429).

Holy Names College (c): 3500 Mountain Blvd., Oakland, CA 94619. Sisters of the Holy Names of Jesus and Mary; 1868 (891).

Illinois Benedictine College (c): 5700 College Rd., Lisle, IL 60532. Benedictine Monks of St. Procopius Abbey; 1887 (2,675).

Immaculata College (w): Immaculata, PA 19345. Sisters, Servants of the Immaculate Heart of Mary; 1920 (2,522).

Incarnate Word College (c): 4301 Broadway, San Antonio, TX 78209. Sisters of Charity of the Incarnate Word; 1881 (2,861).

Iona College (c): 715 North Ave., New Rochelle, NY 10801. Congregation of Christian Brothers; 1940; independent (7,397).

John Carroll University (c): 20700 North Park Blvd., Cleveland, OH 44118. Jesuits; 1886 (4,500).

Kansas Newman College (formerly Sacred Heart College) (c): 3100 McCormick Ave., Wichita, KS 67213. Sisters Adorers of the Blood of Christ; 1933 (1,610).

King's College (c): Wilkes-Barre, PA 18711. Holy Cross Fathers; 1946 (2,280).

La Roche College (c): 9000 Babcock Blvd., Pittsburgh, PA 15237. Sisters of Divine Providence; 1963 (1,763).

La Salle University (c): 1900 W. Olney Ave., Philadelphia, PA 19141. Christian Brothers; 1863 (6,000).

Le Moyne College (c): Syracuse, NY 13214. Jesuit Fathers; 1946; independent (1,835).

Lewis University (c): Romeoville, IL 60441. Christian Brothers; 1932 (4,102).

Loras College (c): 1450 Alta Vista St., Dubuque, IA 52004. Archdiocese of Dubuque; 1839 (1,776).

Lourdes College (c): 6832 Convent Blvd., Sylvania, OH 43560. Sisters of St. Francis; 1958 (1,628).

Loyola College (c): 4501 N. Charles St., Baltimore, MD 21210. Jesuits; 1852; combined with Mt. St. Agnes College, 1971 (6,249).

Loyola Marymount University (c): 7101 W. 80th St., Los Angeles, CA 90045; Orange campus, St. Joseph College, 480 S. Batavia, Orange, CA 92668. Society of Jesus; Religious of Sacred Heart of Mary, Sisters of St. Joseph of Orange; 1914 (6,429).

Loyola University (c): 6363 St. Charles Ave., New Orleans, LA 70118. Jesuit Fathers; 1912 (4,911).

Loyola University Chicago (c): 820 N. Michigan Ave., Chicago, IL 60611. Jesuit Fathers; 1870 (14,798). Mallinckrodt College (Wilmette) and Mundelein College (Chicago) became part of Loyola University Chicago,in January and June, 1991, respectively.

Madonna University (c): 36600 Schoolcraft Rd., Livonia, MI 48150. Felician Sisters; 1947 (4,400).

Magdalen College (c): RFD #2, Box 375, Warner, NH 03278; Magdalen College Corporation; 1973 (60).

Manhattan College (c): 4513 Manhattan College Pkwy., Riverdale, NY 10471. Brothers of the Christian Schools; 1835; independent (4,000). Cooperative program with College of Mt. St. Vincent.

Marian College (c): 45 S. National Ave., Fond du Lac, WI 54935. Sisters of St. Agnes; 1936 (2,020).

Marian College (c): 3200 Cold Spring Rd., Indianapolis, IN 46222. Sisters of St. Francis (Oldenburg, Ind.); 1851; independent (1,288).

Marist College (c): Poughkeepsie, NY 12601. Marist Brothers of the Schools; 1946; independent (4,100).

Marquette University (c): 615 N. 11th St., Milwaukee, WI 53233. Jesuit Fathers; 1881; independent (11,775).

Mary, University of (c): 7500 University Dr., Bismarck, ND 58504. Benedictine Sisters; 1959 (1,855).

Marygrove College (c): 8425 W. McNichols Rd., Detroit, MI 48221. Sisters, Servants of the Immaculate Heart of Mary; 1910 (1,238).

Marylhurst College (c): Marylhurst, OR 97036. Srs. of Holy Names of Jesus and Mary; 1893; independent (1,240).

Marymount College (w): Tarrytown, NY 10591. Religious of the Sacred Heart of Mary; 1907; independent (1,138). Coed in weekend degree programs.

Marymount Manhattan College (w): 221 E. 71st St., New York, NY 10021. Religious of the Sacred Heart of Mary; 1936; independent (1,332).

Marymount University (c): 2807 N. Glebe Rd., Arlington, VA 22007. Religious of the Sacred Heart of Mary; 1950; independent (3,810).

Marywood College (c): Scranton, PA 18509. Sisters, Servants of the Immaculate Heart of Mary; 1915; independent (2,927).

Mater Dei College (c): R.R. #2, Box 45, Ogdensburg, NY 13669. Sisters of St. Joseph; 1960; independent (506).

Mercyhurst College (c): Glenwood Hills, Erie, PA 16546. Sisters of Mercy; 1926 (2,403).

Merrimack College (c): North Andover, MA 01845. Augustinians; 1947 (2,165).

Misericordia (College Misericordia) (c): Dallas, PA 18612. Religious Sisters of Mercy of the Union; 1924 (1,689).

Molloy College (c): 1000 Hempstead Ave., Rockville Centre, NY 11570. Dominican Sisters; 1955; independent (3,619).

Mount Marty College (c): Yankton, SD 57078. Benedictine Sisters; 1936 (791).

Mount Mary College (w): 2900 N. Menomonee River Pkwy., Milwaukee, WI 53222. School Sisters of Notre Dame; 1913 (1,450).

Mount Mercy College (c): 1330 Elmhurst Dr. N.E., Cedar Rapids, IA 52402. Sisters of Mercy; 1928 (1,529).

Mount St. Clare College (c): 400 N. Bluff Blvd., Clinton, IA 52732. Sisters of St. Francis of Clinton, Iowa; 1918 (396).

Mt. St. Joseph, College of (c): 5900 Delhi Rd., Cincinnati, OH 45233. Sisters of Charity; 1920 (2,648).

Mt. St. Mary College (c): Newburgh, NY 12550. Dominican Sisters; 1959; independent (1,400).

Mount St. Mary's College (c): Emmitsburg, MD 21727. Founded by Fr. John DuBois, S.S., 1808; independent (1,800).

Mount St. Mary's College (w/c): 12001 Chalon Rd., Los Angeles, CA 90049 and 10 Chester Pl., Los Angeles, CA 90007 (Doheny Campus). Sisters of St. Joseph of Carondelet; 1925 (1,179). Coed in music, nursing and graduate programs.

Mt. St. Vincent, College of (c): 6301 Riverdale Ave., Bronx, NY 10471. Sisters of Charity; 1847; independent (1,06080). Cooperative program with Manhattan College.

Neumann College (c): Concord Rd., Aston, PA 19014. Sisters of St. Francis; 1965; independent (1,268).

New Rochelle, College of (w/c): 29 Castle Pl., New Rochelle, NY 10805 (main campus). Ursuline Order; 1904; independent (5,200). Coed in nursing, graduate, new resources divisions.

Niagara University (c): Niagara Univ., NY 14109. Vincentian Fathers and Brothers; 1856 (3,002).

Notre Dame, College of (c): 1500 Ralston Ave., Belmont, CA 94002. Sisters of Notre Dame de Namur; 1868; independent (1,519).

Notre Dame, University of (c): Notre Dame, IN 46556. Congregation of Holy Cross; 1842 (10,000).

Notre Dame College (w): 4545 College Rd., Cleveland, OH 44121. Sisters of Notre Dame; 1922 (849).

Notre Dame College (c): 2321 Elm St., Manchester, NH 03104. Sisters of Holy Cross; 1950; independent (1,100).

Notre Dame of Maryland, College of (w): 4701 N. Charles St., Baltimore, MD 21210. School Sisters of Notre Dame; 1873 (2,679).

Ohio Dominican College (c): Columbus, OH 43219. Dominican Sisters of St. Mary of the Springs; 1911 (1,510).

Our Lady of Holy Cross College (c): 4123 Woodland Dr., New Orleans, LA 70131. Congregation of Sisters Marianites of Holy Cross; 1916 (1,195).

Our Lady of the Elms, College of (w): Chicopee, MA 01013. Sisters of St. Joseph; 1928 (1,073).

Our Lady of the Lake University of San Antonio (c): 411 S.W. 24th St., San Antonio, TX 78207. Sisters of Divine Providence; 1895 (2,947).

Parks College of Saint Louis University (c): Cahokia, IL 62206. Jesuits; 1927; independent (1,047).

Portland, University of (c): 5000 N. Willamette Blvd., Portland, OR 97203. Holy Cross Fathers; 1901; independent (2,800).

Providence College (c): River Ave. and Eaton St., Providence, RI 02918. Dominican Friars; 1917 (6,387).

Quincy University (c): 1800 College Ave., Quincy, IL 62301. Franciscan Friars; 1860 (1,250).

Regis College (w): Weston, MA 02193. Sisters of St. Joseph; 1927; independent (1,145).

Regis University (c): 3333 Regis Blvd. Denver, CO 80221. Jesuits; 1887 (9,249).

Rivier College (c): Nashua, NH 03060. Sisters of the Presentation of Mary; 1933; independent (2,775).

Rockhurst College (c): 1100 Rockhurst Rd., Kansas City, MO 64110. Jesuit Fathers; 1910 (2,806).

Rosary College (c): 7900 Division St., River Forest, IL 60305. Dominican Sisters; 1901 (1,855).

Rosemont College (w): Rosemont, PA 19010. Society of the Holy Child Jesus; 1921 (650).

Sacred Heart University (c): 5151 Park Ave., Fairfield, CT 06432. Diocese of Bridgeport; 1963; independent (5,000).

St. Ambrose University (c): Davenport, IA 52803. Diocese of Davenport; 1882 (2,416).

Saint Anselm College (c): Manchester NH 03102. Benedictine Monks; 1889 (1,900).

Saint Benedict, College of (w): 37 S. College Ave., St. Joseph, MN 56374. Benedictine Sisters; 1913 (1,742). Sister college of St. John's University, Collegeville (see below).

St. Bonaventure University (c): St. Bonaventure, NY 14778. Franciscan Friars; 1856; independent (2,578).

St. Catherine, College of (w): 2004 Randolph Ave., St. Paul, MN 55105. Sisters of St. Joseph of Carondelet; 1905 (3,200).

St. Edward's University (c): 3001 S. Congress Ave., Austin, TX 78704. Holy Cross Brothers; 1885; independent (3,050).

St. Elizabeth, College of (w): 2 Convent Rd., Morristown, NJ 07960. Sisters of Charity; 1899; independent (1,315). Coed in continuing education and weekend college programs.

St. Francis, College of (c): 500 N. Wilcox St., Joliet, IL 60435. Sisters of St. Francis of Mary Immaculate; 1920; independent (1,100).

St. Francis College (c): 180 Remsen St., Brooklyn Heights, NY 11201. Franciscan Brothers; 1884; private, independent in the Franciscan tradition (1,800).

St. Francis College (c): 2701 Spring St., Fort Wayne, IN 46808. Sisters of St. Francis; 1890 (1,042).

St. Francis College (c): Loretto, PA 15940. Franciscan Friars; 1847; independent (1,765).

St. John's University (c): Grand Central and Utopia Pkwys., Jamaica, NY 11439 (Queens Campus); 300 Howard Ave., Grymes Hill, Staten Island, NY 10301 (Staten Island Campus). Vincentians; 1870 (19,105).

St. John's University (m): Collegeville, MN 56321. Benedictines; 1857 (1,812). All classes and programs are coeducational with College of St. Benedict (see above).

St. Joseph, College of (c): Clement Rd., Rutland, VT 05701. Sisters of St. Joseph; 1954; independent (510).

Saint Joseph College (w/c): 1678 Asylum Ave., West Hartford, CT 06117. Sisters of Mercy; 1932 (1,919). Coed in graduate school and in McAuley Program Weekend College.

Saint Joseph's College (c): Windham, ME 04062. Sisters of Mercy; 1912 (650, campus; also has external degree program).

Saint Joseph's College (c): Rensselaer, IN 47978. Society of the Precious Blood; 1891 (1,001).

St. Joseph's College (c): 245 Clinton Ave., Brooklyn, NY 11205 (572) and 155 Roe Blvd., Patchogue, N.Y. 11772 (1,931). Sisters of St. Joseph; 1916; independent.

St. Joseph's University (c): 5600 City Ave., Philadelphia, PA 19131. Jesuit Fathers; 1851 (6,000).

Saint Leo College (c): Saint Leo, FL 33574. Order of St. Benedict; 1889; independent (7,148).

St. Louis University (c): 221 N. Grant Blvd., St. Louis, MO 63103. Society of Jesus; 1818; independent (11,747).

Saint Martin's College (c): Lacey, WA 98503. Benedictine Monks; 1895 (886 main campus; 374 extension campuses).

Saint Mary, College of (w): 1901 S. 72nd St., Omaha, NE 68124. Sisters of Mercy; 1923; independent (1,280).

Saint Mary College (c): Leavenworth, KS 66048. Sisters of Charity of Leavenworth; 1923 (1,000).

St. Mary-of-the-Woods College (w): St. Mary-of-the-Woods, IN 47876. Sisters of Providence; 1840 (1,047).

Saint Mary's College (w): Notre Dame, IN 46556. Sisters of the Holy Cross; 1844 (1,576).

St. Mary's College (c): Orchard Lake, MI 48324. Secular Clergy; 1885 (375).

St. Mary's College (c): Moraga, CA 94575. Brothers of the Christian Schools; 1863 (4,000).

Saint Mary's College of Minnesota (c): Winona, MN 55987. Brothers of the Christian Schools; 1912 (1,260 undergraduate, 5,115 graduate).

St. Mary's University (c): One Camino Santa Maria, San Antonio, TX 78228. Society of Mary (Marianists); 1852 (4,007).

St. Michael's College (c): Colchester, VT 05439. Society of St. Edmund; 1904 (1,723).

St. Norbert College (c): De Pere, WI 54115. Norbertine Fathers; 1898; independent (1,804).

Saint Peter's College (c): 2641 Kennedy Blvd., Jersey City, NJ 07306. Jesuit Fathers; independent; 1872 (3,463).

Saint Rose, College of (c): 432 Western Ave., Albany, NY 12203. Sisters of St. Joseph of Carondelet; 1920; independent (3,800).

St. Scholastica, College of (c): 1200 Kenwood Ave., Duluth, MN 55811. Benedictine Sisters; 1912; independent (1,970).

St. Thomas, University of (c): 2115 Summit Ave., St. Paul, MN 55105. Archdiocese of St. Paul and Minneapolis; 1885 (10,072).

St. Thomas, University of (c): 3812 Montrose Blvd., Houston, TX 77006. Basilian Fathers; 1947 (1,964).

St. Thomas Aquinas College (c): Sparkill, NY 10976. Dominican Sisters of Sparkill; 1952; independent, corporate board of trustees (2,100).

St. Thomas University (c): 16400 N.W. 32nd Ave., Miami, FL 33054. Archdiocese of Miami; 1962 (2,587).

Saint Vincent College (c): Fraser Purchase Rd., Latrobe, PA 15650. Benedictine Fathers; 1846 (1,248).

St. Xavier University (c): 3700 W. 103rd St., Chicago, IL 60655. Sisters of Mercy; chartered 1847 (3,600).

Salve Regina University (c): Ochre Point Ave., Newport, RI 02840. Sisters of Mercy; 1934 (2,314).

San Diego, University of (c): Alcala Park, San Diego, CA 92110. San Diego diocese and Religious of the Sacred Heart; 1949; independent (6,027).

San Francisco, University of (c): Ignatian Heights, San Francisco, CA 94117. Jesuit Fathers; 1855 (7,122).

Santa Clara University (c): Santa Clara, CA 95053. Jesuit Fathers; 1851; independent (7,750).

Santa Fe, College of (c): Santa Fe, NM 87501. Brothers of the Christian Schools; 1947 (1,400).

Scranton, University of (c): Scranton, PA 18510. Society of Jesus; 1888 (5,100).

Seattle University (c): Broadway and East Madison, Seattle, WA 98122. Jesuit Fathers; 1891 (4,769).

Seton Hall University (c): South Orange Ave., South Orange, NJ 07079. Diocesan Clergy; 1856 (9,700).

Seton Hill College (w): Greensburg, PA 15601. Sisters of Charity of Seton Hill; 1883 (1,100).

Siena College (c): Loudonville, NY 12211. Franciscan Friars; 1937 (3,596).

Siena Heights College (c): 1247 E. Siena Heights Dr., Adrian, MI 49221. Dominican Sisters; 1919 (1,850).

Silver Lake College of Holy Family (c): 2406 S. Alverno Rd., Manitowoc, WI 54220. Franciscan Sisters of Christian Charity; 1935 (800).

Spalding University (c): 851 S. 4th Ave., Louisville, KY 40203. Sisters of Charity of Nazareth; 1814; independent (1,141: 949 women; 192 men).

Spring Hill College (c): 400 Dauphin St., Mobile, AL 36608. Jesuit Fathers; 1830 (998).

Stonehill College (c): 320 Washington St., North Easton, MA 02357. Holy Cross Fathers; 1948; independent (3,039).

Thomas Aquinas College (c): 10000 N. Ojai Rd., Santa Paula, CA 93060. Founded 1971 (205).

Thomas More College (c): Crestview Hills, Covington, KY 41017. Diocese of Covington; 1921 (1,297).

Trinity College (w/c): Colchester Ave., Burlington, VT 05401. Sisters of Mercy; 1925 (1,081).

Trinity College (w): 125 Michigan Ave. N.E., Washington, DC 20017. Sisters of Notre Dame de Namur; 1897 (1,100). Coed in graduate school.

Ursuline College (w): 2550 Lander Rd., Cleveland, OH 44124. Ursuline Nuns; 1871 (1,588).

Villanova University (c): Villanova, PA 19085. Order of St. Augustine; 1842 (11,100).

Viterbo College (c): 815 S. 9th, La Crosse, WI 54601. Franciscan Sisters of Perpetual Adoration; 1890 (1,163).

Walsh University (c): 2020 Easton St. N.W., North Canton, Ohio 44720. Brothers of Christian Instruction; 1958 (1,550).

Wheeling Jesuit College (c): 316 Washington Ave., Wheeling, WV 26003. Jesuit Fathers; 1954 (1,400).

Xavier University (c): 3800 Victory Pkwy., Cincinnati, OH 45207. Jesuit Fathers; 1831 (6,680).

Xavier University of Louisiana (c): 7325 Palmetto St., New Orleans, LA 70125. Sisters of Blessed Sacrament; 1925; lay-Religious administrative board (3,330).

Catholic Junior Colleges

Ancilla College (c): Donaldson, IN 46513. Ancilla Domini Sisters; 1937 (682).

Aquinas Junior College (c): 4210 Harding Rd., Nashville, TN 37205. Dominican Sisters; 1961 (380).

Assumption College for Sisters: 350 Bernardsville Rd.,, Mendham, NJ 07945. Sisters of Christian Charity; 1953 (44).

Castle College: Searles Rd., Windham, NH 03087. Sisters of Mercy; 1963; independent (393).

Chatfield College (c): St. Martin, OH 45118. Ursulines; 1971 (300).

Donnelly College (c): 608 N. 18th St., Kansas City, KS 66102. Archdiocesan College; 1949 (882).

Don Bosco Technical Institute (m): 1151 San Gabriel Blvd., Rosemead, CA 91770. Salesians; 1969 (281).

Hilbert College (c): 5200 S. Park Ave., Hamburg, NY 14075. Franciscan Sisters of St. Joseph; 1957; independent (796).

Holy Cross College (c): Notre Dame, IN 46556. Brothers of Holy Cross; 1966 (427).

Manor Junior College (c): Fox Chase Road, Jenkintown, PA 19046. Sisters of St. Basil the Great; 1947 (640).

Maria College (c): 700 New Scotland Ave., Albany, NY 12208. Sisters of Mercy; 1963 (983).

Marymount Palos Verdes College (c): Rancho Palos Verdes, CA 90274. Religious of the Sacred Heart of Mary; independent (1,076).

Mt. Aloysius Junior College (c): Cresson, PA 16630. Sisters of Mercy; 1939 (824).

Presentation College (c): Aberdeen, SD 57401. Sisters of the Presentation; 1951 (500).

St. Catharine College (c); St. Catharine, KY 40061. Dominican Sisters; 1931 (280).

St. Gregory's College (c): Shawnee, OK 74801. Benedictine Monks; 1876 (348).

St. Mary's Campus of the College of St. Catherine (c): 2500 S. 6th St., Minneapolis, MN 55454. Sisters of St. Joseph of Carondelet (1,079).

Springfield College in Illinois (c): 1500 N. Fifth St., Springfield, IL 62702. Ursuline Sisters; 1929 (400).

Trocaire College (c): 110 Red Jacket Pkwy., Buffalo, NY 14220. Sisters of Mercy; 1958; independent (985).

Villa Maria College of Buffalo (c): 240 Pine Ridge Rd., Buffalo, NY 14225. Felician Sisters 1960; independent (400).

CAMPUS MINISTRY

Campus ministry is an expression of the Church's special desire to be present to all who are involved in higher education and to further dialogue between the Church and the academic community. In the words of the U.S. bishops' 1985 pastoral letter entitled "Empowered by the Spirit," this ministry is "the public presence and service through which properly prepared baptized persons are empowered by the Spirit to use their talents and gifts on behalf of the Church in order to be sign and instrument of the Kingdom in the academic world."

Campus ministry, carried on by lay, Religious and ordained ministers, gathers members of the Church on campus to form the faith community, appropriate the faith, form Christian consciences, educate for justice and facilitate religious development.

The dimensions and challenge of this ministry are evident from, among other things, the numbers involved: approximately 550,000 Catholics on more than 230 Catholic college and university campuses; about four million on several thousand non-Catholic private and public institutions; 1,200 or more campus ministers. In many dioceses, the activities of ministers are coordinated by a local diocesan director. Two professional organizations serve the ministry on the national level:

The National Association of Diocesan Directors of Campus Ministry; Rev. Frederick J. Pennett, president, 153 Ash St., P.O. Box 310, Manchester, NH 03105.

The Catholic Campus Ministry Association, with a membership of 1,200, is headquartered at 300 College Park Ave., Dayton, OH 45469. The executive director is Donald R. McCrabb.

DIOCESAN AND INTERDIOCESAN SEMINARIES

(Sources: Almanac survey; *Official Catholic Directory;* Catholic News Service.)

Information, according to states, includes names of archdioceses and dioceses, and names and addresses of seminaries. Types of seminaries, when not clear from titles, are indicated in most cases. Interdiocesan seminaries are generally conducted by religious orders for candidates for the priesthood from several dioceses. The list does not include houses of study reserved for members of religious communities. Archdioceses are indicated by an asterisk.

California: Los Angeles* — St. John's Seminary (major), 5012 Seminary Rd., Camarillo 93012; St. John's Seminary College, 5118 Seminary Rd., Camarillo 93012; Our Lady Queen of the Angels High School Seminary, 15101 San Fernando Mission Blvd., Mission Hills 91345.

San Diego — St. Francis Seminary (college and pre-theology formation program), 1667 Santa Paula Dr., San Diego 92111.

San Francisco* — St. Patrick's Seminary (major), 320 Middlefield Rd., Menlo Park 94025.

Colorado: Denver* — St. Thomas Theological Seminary (interdiocesan, major), 1300 S. Steele St., Denver 80210.

Connecticut: Hartford* — St. Thomas Seminary (college formation program), 467 Bloomfield Ave., Bloomfield 06002.

Norwich — Holy Apostles College and Seminary (adult vocations; minor and major), 33 Prospect Hill Rd., Cromwell 06416.

Stamford Byzantine Rite — Ukrainian Catholic Seminary: St. Basil House of Formation (minor), 195 Glenbrook Rd., Stamford 06902.

District of Columbia: Washington* — Theological College (national, major), The Catholic University of America, 401 Michigan Ave., N.E. 20017.

St. Josaphat's Seminary, 201 Taylor St. N.E., Washington 20017. (Major house of formation serving the four Ukrainian Byzantine-rite dioceses in the U.S.)

Florida: Miami* — St. John Vianney College Seminary, 2900 S.W. 87th Ave., Miami 33165.

Palm Beach — St. Vincent de Paul Regional Seminary (major), 10701 S. Military Trail, Boynton Beach 33436.

Illinois: Chicago* — Archbishop Quigley Preparatory Seminary, 103 East Chestnut St., Chicago 60611; Niles College Seminary of Loyola University, 7135 N. Harlem Ave., Chicago 60631; Mundelein Seminary, University of St. Mary of the Lake, Mundelein 60060.

Indiana: Indianapolis* — St. Meinrad Seminary, College and School of Theology (interdiocesan), St. Meinrad 47577.

Iowa: Davenport — St. Ambrose University Seminary, 518 W. Locust St., Davenport 52803.

Dubuque* — Seminary of St. Pius X (interdiocesan), Loras College, Dubuque 52001.

Louisiana: New Orleans* — Notre Dame Seminary Graduate School of Theology, 2901 S. Carrollton Ave., New Orleans 70118; St. Joseph Seminary College (interdiocesan), St. Benedict 70457.

Maryland: Baltimore* — St. Mary's Seminary and University, 5400 Roland Ave., Baltimore 21210; Mt. St. Mary's Seminary, Emmitsburg 21727.

Massachusetts: Boston* — St. John's Seminary

School of Theology, 127 Lake St., Brighton 02135; St. John's Seminary, College of Liberal Arts, 197 Foster St., Brighton 02135; Pope John XXIII National Seminary (for ages 30-60), 558 South Ave., Weston 02193.

Newton — Melkite Greek Catholic — St. Gregory the Theologian Seminary, 233 Grant Ave., Newton 02159.

Michigan: Detroit* — Sacred Heart Major Seminary (college and theologate), 2701 Chicago Blvd., Detroit 48206; The Orchard Lake Schools (Sts. Cyril and Methodius Seminary, St. Mary's College, St. Mary's Preparatory — graduate, undergraduate, secondary; independent, primarily serving Polish-American community), Orchard Lake 48324.

Grand Rapids — Christopher House Seminary, 723 Rosewood Ave., S.E., East Grand Rapids 49506.

Minnesota: St. John's Seminary/School of Theology, St. John's University, P.O. Box 7288, Collegeville 56321.

St. Paul and Minneapolis* — St. Paul Seminary School of Divinity of the University of St. Thomas, 2260 Summit Ave., St. Paul 55105; St. John Vianney College Seminary, 2115 Summit Ave., St. Paul 55105.

Winona — Immaculate Heart of Mary Seminary, St. Mary's College, No. 43, 700 Terrace Heights, Winona 55987.

Missouri: Jefferson City — St. Thomas Aquinas Preparatory Seminary (High School Seminary), 245 N. Levering Ave., P.O. Box 858, Hannibal 63401.

St. Louis* — St. Louis Roman Catholic Theological Seminary, Kenrick School of Theology, 5200 Glennon Dr., St. Louis 63119; Cardinal Glennon College (major seminary), 5200 Glennon Dr., St. Louis 63119.

Montana: Helena — Pre-Seminary Program, Carroll College, Helena 59625.

New Jersey: Newark* — Immaculate Conception Seminary — college seminary; major seminary; graduate school — Seton Hall University, South Orange Ave., South Orange 07079.

New Mexico: Santa Fe* — Immaculate Heart of Mary Seminary (college level), Mt. Carmel Rd., Santa Fe 87501.

New York: Brooklyn — Cathedral Seminary Residence of the Immaculate Conception (college and pre-theology), 7200 Douglaston Parkway, Douglaston 11362; Cathedral Preparatory Seminary of the Immaculate Conception, 56-25 92nd St., Elmhurst 11373.

Buffalo — Christ the King Seminary (interdiocesan theologate), 711 Knox Rd., East Aurora 14052.

New York* — St. Joseph's Seminary (major), 201 Seminary Ave., Dunwoodie, Yonkers 10704; St. John Neumann Residence (college and pre-theology), 5655 Arlington Ave., Riverdale 10471. Cathedral Preparatory Seminary, 946 Boston Post Rd., Rye 10580.

Ogdensburg — Wadhams Hall Seminary College (interdiocesan), R.R. 4, Box 80, Ogdensburg 13669.

Rockville Centre — Seminary of the Immaculate Conception (major), Lloyd Harbor, Huntington, L.I. 11743.

St. Maron Diocese, Brooklyn — Our Lady of Lebanon Maronite Seminary, 7164 Alaska Ave. N.W., Washington, DC 20012.

North Dakota: Fargo — Cardinal Muench Seminary (interdiocesan high school, college and pretheology), 100 35th Ave. N.E., Fargo 58102.

Ohio: Cincinnati* — Mt. St. Mary's Seminary of the West, 6616 Beechmont Ave., Cincinnati 45230 (division of the Athenaeum of Ohio).

Cleveland — St. Mary Seminary Center for Pastoral Leadership, 28700 Euclid Ave. Wickliffe 44092.

Columbus — Pontifical College Josephinum (national), theologate and college, Columbus 43235.

Oregon: Portland* — Mt. Angel Seminary (interdiocesan, college, pre-theology program, graduate school of theology), St. Benedict 97373.

Pennsylvania: Erie — St. Mark Seminary, P.O. Box 10397, Erie 16514. (College formation and pretheology — interdiocesan). Affiliated with Gannon University.

Greensburg — St. Vincent Seminary (interdiocesan; pre-theology program; graduate program in theology; religious education), Latrobe 15650.

Philadelphia* — Theological Seminary of St. Charles Borromeo, One Thousand East Wynnewood Rd., Overbrook 19096. (College, pre-theology program, theologate.)

Pittsburgh* (Byzantine-Ruthenian Rite) — Byzantine Catholic Seminary of Sts. Cyril and Methodius (college, pre-theology program, theologate), 3605 Perrysville Ave., Pittsburgh 15214.

Pittsburgh — St. Paul Seminary (interdiocesan, college and pre-theology), 2900 Noblestown Rd., Pittsburgh 15205.

Scranton — St. Pius X Seminary (college and pretheology formation; interdiocesan), Dalton 18414. Affiliated with the University of Scranton.

Rhode Island: Providence — Seminary of Our Lady of Providence (House of Formation; college students), 485 Mount Pleasant Ave., Providence 02908.

Texas: Dallas — Holy Trinity Seminary (college and pre-theology; English proficiency and academic foundation programs), P.O. Box 140309, Irving 75014.

El Paso — St. Charles Seminary College, P.O. Box 17548, El Paso 79917.

Galveston-Houston — St. Mary's Seminary (theologate), 9845 Memorial Dr., Houston 77024.

San Antonio* — Assumption Seminary (theologate and pre-theology, Hispanic ministry emphasis), 2600 W. Woodlawn Ave., San Antonio 78228.

Washington: Spokane — Bishop White Seminary, College Formation Program, E. 429 Sharp Ave., Spokane 99202.

Wisconsin: Madison — Holy Name Seminary (High School), 3577 High Point Rd., Madison 53719.

Milwaukee* — St. Francis Seminary, 3257 S. Lake Dr., St. Francis.. 53235; College Program, 2301 W. Wisconsin Ave., Milwaukee 53233. Sacred Heart School of Theology (interdiocesan seminary for second career vocations), P.O. Box 429, Hales Corner, Wis. 53130.

PONTIFICAL UNIVERSITIES

(Principal source: *Annuario Pontificio*.)

These universities, listed according to country of location, have been canonically erected and authorized by the Congregation for Catholic Education to award degrees in stated fields of study.

New laws and norms governing ecclesiastical universities and faculties were promulgated in the apostolic constitution *Sapientia Christiana,* issued Apr. 15, 1979.

Argentina: Pontifical Catholic University of S. Maria of Buenos Aires (June 16, 1960): Juncal 1912, 1116 Buenos Aires.

Belgium: Catholic University of Louvain (Dec. 9, 1425; 1834), with autonomous institutions for French- (Louvain) and Flemish- (Leuven) speaking: Place de l'Universite I, B-1348 Louvain-La-Neuve (French); Naamsestraat 22/b, B-3000 Leuven (Flemish).

Brazil: Pontifical Catholic University of Rio de Janeiro (Jan. 20, 1947): Rua Marques de Sao Vicente 225, 22451. Rio de Janeiro, RJ.

Pontifical Catholic University of Minas Gerais (June 5, 1983): Av. Dom Jose Gaspar 500, C.P. 2686, 30161 Belo Horizonte MG.

Pontifical Catholic University of Parana (Aug. 6, 1985): Rua Imaculada Conceicao, 1155, Prado Velho, C.P. 670, 80001 Curitiba, PR.

Pontifical Catholic University of Rio Grande do Sul (Nov. 1, 1950): Av. Ipiranga 6681, C.P. 1429, 90001 Porto Alegre, RS.

Pontifical Catholic University of Sao Paulo (Jan. 25, 1947): Rua Monte Alegre 984, 05014 Sao Paulo.

Pontifical University of Campinas (Sept. 8, 1956): Rua Marechal Deodoro 1099, 13020 Campinas, Sao Paulo.

Canada: Laval University (Mar. 15, 1876): Case Postale 460, Quebec G1K 7P4.

St. Paul University (formerly University of Ottawa) (Feb. 5, 1889): 223, Rue Main, Ottawa, Ont. K1S 1C4.

University of Sherbrooke (Nov. 21, 1957): Chemin Ste.-Catherine, Cite Universitaire, Sherbrooke, Que. J1K 2R1.

Chile: Pontifical Catholic University of Chile (June 21, 1888): Avenida Bernardo O'Higgins, 340, Casilla 114D. Santiago.

Catholic University of Valparaiso (Nov. 1, 1961): Avenida Brasil 2950, Casilla 4059, Valparaiso.

Colombia: Bolivarian Pontifical Catholic University (Aug. 16, 1945): Calle 52, N. 40-88, Apartado 1178, Medellin.

Pontifical Xaverian University (July 31, 1937): Carrera 7, N. 40-76, Apartado 56710, Bogota D.E. Apartado 26239, Calle 18n. 118.250, Cali (Cali campus).

Cuba: Catholic University of St. Thomas of Villanueva (May 4, 1957): Avenida Quenta 16,660, Marianao, Havana.

Dominican Republic: Pontifical Catholic University "Mother and Teacher" (Sept. 9, 1987): Apartado 822, Santiago de Los Caballeros.

Ecuador: Pontifical Catholic University of Ecuador (July 16, 1954): Doce de Octubre, N. 1076, Apartado 2184, Quito.

Ethiopia: University of Asmara (Sept. 8, 1960): Via Menelik II, 45, Post Office Box 1220, Asmara.

France: Catholic University of Lille (Nov. 18, 1875): Boulevard Vauban 60, 59046 Lille.

Catholic Faculties of Lyon (Nov. 22, 1875): 25, Rue du Plat, 69288 Lyon.

Catholic Institute of Paris (Aug. 11, 1875): 21, Rue d'Assas, 75270 Paris.

Catholic Institute of Toulouse (Nov. 15, 1877): Rue de la Fonderie 31, 31068 Toulouse.

Catholic University of the West (Sept. 16, 1875): 3, Place Andre Leroy, B.P. 808, 49005 Angers.

Germany: Eichstatt Catholic University (Apr. 1, 1980): Ostenstrasse 26, D-8078, Eichstatt, Federal Republic of Germany.

Guatemala: Rafael Landivar University (Oct. 18, 1961): 17 Calle 8-64, zone 10 Guatemala.

Ireland: St. Patrick's College (Mar. 29, 1896): Maynooth, Co. Kildare.

Italy: Catholic University of the Sacred Heart (Dec. 25, 1920): Largo Gemelli 1, 20123 Milan.

Libera University Mary of the Assumption (Oct. 26, 1939): Via della Traspontina 21, 00193 Rome, Italy.

Japan: *Jochi Daigaku* (Sophia University) (Mar. 29, 1913): Chiyoda-Ku, Kioi-cho 7, Tokyo 102.

Lebanon: St. Joseph University of Beirut (Mar. 25, 1881): Rue de l'Universite St.-Joseph, Boite Postale 293, Beyrouth (Beirut).

Netherlands: Nijmegen Roman Catholic University (June 29, 1923): P.B. 9102, 6500 HC, Nijmegen.

Panama: University of S. Maria La Antigua (May 27, 1965): Apartado 2143, Panama 1.

Paraguay: Catholic University of Our Lady of the Assumption (Feb. 2, 1965): Independencia Nacional y Comuneros, Casilla 1718, Asuncion.

Peru: Pontifical Catholic University of Peru (Sept. 30, 1942): Av. Universitaria, Pueblo Libre, Apartado 1761, Lima 100.

Philippines: Pontifical University of Santo Tomas (Nov. 20, 1645): Espana Street, 1008 Manila.

Poland: Catholic University of Lublin (July 25, 1920): Aleje Raclawickie 14, Skr. Poczt. 279, 20-950, Lublin.

Catholic Theological Academy (June 29, 1989): Ul. Dewajtis 5, 01-653, Warsaw.

Pontifical Academy of Theology of Krakow (Dec. 8, 1981): Ul. Kanonicza, 31-002 Krakow.

Portugal: Portuguese Catholic University (Nov. 1, 1967): Palma de Cima, 1600 Lisbon.

Puerto Rico: Catholic University of Puerto Rico (Aug. 15, 1972): Ponce, Puerto Rico 00731.

Spain: Catholic University of Navarra (Aug. 6, 1960): Ciudad Universitaria, 31009 Pamplona.

Pontifical University "Comillas" (Mar. 29, 1904): 28049 Madrid.

Pontifical University of Salamanca (Sept. 25, 1940): Apartado 541, 37080 Salamanca.

University of Deusto (Aug. 10, 1963): Avenida de las Universidades, 28, 48007 Bilbao.

Taiwan (China): Fu Jen Catholic University (Nov. 15, 1923, at Peking; reconstituted at

Taipeh, Sept. 8, 1961): Hsinchuang, Taipeh Hsien 24205.

United States: Catholic University of America (Mar. 7, 1889): 620 Michigan Ave. N.E., Washington, D.C. 20064.

Georgetown University (Mar. 30, 1833): 37th and O Sts. N.W., Washington, D.C. 20057.

Niagara University (June 21, 1956): Niagara University P.O., N.Y. 14109.

Uruguay: Catholic University of Uruguay "Damaso Antonio Larranaga" (Jan. 25, 1985): Avda. 8 de Octubre 2738, Montevideo.

Venezuela: Catholic University "Andres Bello" (Sept. 29, 1963): Esquina Jesuitas, Apartado 29068, Caracas.

ECCLESIASTICAL FACULTIES

(Principal source: *Annuario Pontificio*)

These faculties in Catholic seminaries and universities, listed according to country of location, have been canonically erected and authorized by the Sacred Congregation for Catholic Education to award degrees in stated fields of study. In addition to those listed here, there are other faculties of theology or philosophy in state universities and for members of certain religious orders only.

Argentina: Faculties of Philosophy and Theology, San Miguel (Sept. 8, 1932).

Australia: Institute of Theology, Sydney (Feb. 2, 1954).

Austria: Theological Faculty, Linz (Dec. 25, 1978).

Brazil: Ecclesiastical Faculty of Philosophy "John Paul II," Rio de Janeiro Aug. 6, 1981.

Philosophical and Theological Faculties of the Company of Jesus, Belo Horizonte (July 15, 1941 and Mar. 12, 1949).

Cameroon: Catholic Institute of Yaoundé (Nov. 15, 1991).

Canada: Pontifical Institute of Medieval Studies, Toronto (Oct. 18, 1939).

Dominican Faculty of Theology of Canada, Ottawa (1965; Nov. 15, 1975).

Regis College — Toronto Section of the Jesuit Faculty of Theology in Canada, Toronto (Feb. 17, 1956; Dec. 25, 1977).

College of Immaculate Conception — Montreal Section of Jesuit Faculties in Canada (Sept. 8, 1932).

Cote d'Ivoire (Ivory Coast): Catholic Institute of West Africa, Abidjan (Aug. 12, 1975).

Croatia: Philosophical Faculty, Zagreb (July 31, 1989).

France: Centre Sevres — Faculties of Theology and Philosophy of the Jesuits, Paris (Sept. 8, 1932).

Germany: Theological Faculty, Paderborn (June 11, 1966).

Theological Faculty of the Major Episcopal Seminary, Trier (Sept. 8, 1955).

Philosophical Faculty, Munich (1932; Oct. 25, 1971).

Theological-Philosophical Faculty, Frankfurt (1932; June 7, 1971).

Theological Faculty, Fulda (Dec. 22, 1978).

Philosophical-Theological School of Salesians, Benediktbeuren (May 24, 1992).

Great Britain: Heythrop College, University of London, London (Nov. 1, 1964). Theology, philosophy.

Hungary: Roman Catholic Academy, Budapest (1635).

India: "Jnana Deepa Vidyapeeth" (Pontifical Athenaeum), Institute of Philosophy and Religion, Poona (July 27, 1926).

Pontifical Institute of Theology and Philosophy at the Pontifical Interritual Seminary of St. Joseph, Alwaye, Kerala (Feb. 24, 1972).

"Vidyajyoti," Institute of Religious Studies, Faculty of Theology, Delhi (1932; Dec. 9, 1974).

Dharmaram Pontifical Institute of Theology and Philosophy, Bangalore (theology, Jan. 6, 1976; philosophy, Dec. 8, 1983).

Faculty of Theology, Ranchi (Aug. 15, 1982).

Pontifical Oriental Institute of Religious Studies, Kottayam (July 3, 1982).

St. Peter's Pontifical Institute of Theology, Bangalore (Jan. 6, 1976).

"Satya Nilayam," Institute of Philosophy and Culture. Faculty of Philosophy, Madras (Sept. 8, 1932; Dec. 15, 1976).

Indonesia: Wedabhakti Pontifical Faculty of Theology, Yogyakarta (Nov. 1, 1984).

Ireland: Institute of Theology and Philosophy, Dublin (1932).

Israel: French Biblical and Archeological School, Jerusalem (founded 1890; approved Sept. 17, 1892; canonically approved to confer Doctorate in Biblical Science, June 29, 1983).

Italy: Interregional Theological Faculty, Milan (Aug. 8, 1935; restructured 1969).

Pontifical Theological Faculty of Sardinia, Cagliari, (Aug. 5, 1927).

Pontifical Ambrosian Institute of Sacred Music, Milan (Mar. 12, 1940).

Theological Faculty of Sicily, Palermo (Dec. 8, 1980).

Theological Faculty of Southern Italy, Naples. Two sections: St. Thomas Aquinas Capodimonte (Oct. 31, 1941) and St. Louis Posillipo (Mar. 16, 1918). Theological Institute Pugliese, Molfetta (Jan. 24, 1992).

Faculty of Philosophy "Aloisianum," Gallarate (1937; Mar. 20, 1974).

Japan: Faculty of Theology, Nagoya (May 25, 1984).

Kenya: Catholic Higher Institute of Eastern Africa, Nairobi (May 2, 1984).

Lebanon: Faculty of Theology, University of the Holy Spirit, Kaslik (May 30, 1982).

Madagascar: Superior Institute of Theology, at the Regional Seminary of Antananarivo, Ambatoroka-Antananarivo (Apr. 21, 1960).

Malta: Faculty of Theology, Tal-Virtu (Nov. 22, 1769), with Institute of Philosophy and Human Studies (Sept. 8, 1984).

Mexico: Theological Faculty of Mexico (June 29, 1982) and Philosophy (Jan. 6, 1986), Mexico City.

Netherlands: International Academic Institute, Kerkrade (Apr. 4, 1990)

Nigeria: Catholic Institute of West Africa, Port Harcourt (Nov. 30, 1981).

Peru: Pontifical and Civil Faculty of Theology, Lima (July 25, 1571).

Poland: Theological Faculty, Poznan (1969; pontifical designation, June 2, 1974).

Philosophical Faculty, Krakow (1932; Sept. 20, 1984).

Pontifical Theological Faculty, Warsaw (May 3, 1988) with St. John Baptist section (1837, 1920, Nov. 8, 1962) at the "Metropolitan Seminary Duchowne" and "St. Andrew Bobola"-"Bobolanum" section (Sept. 8, 1932).

Spain: Theological Faculty of Catalunya, (Mar. 7, 1968), with the Institutes of Fundamental Theology (Dec. 28, 1984), Liturgy (Aug. 15, 1986) and Philosophy (July 26, 1988), Barcelona.

Theological Faculty, Granada (1940; July 31, 1973).

Theological Faculty of the North, of the Metropolitan Seminary of Burgos and the Diocesan Seminary of Vitoria (Feb. 6, 1967).

Theological Faculty "San Vicente Ferrer" (two sections), Valencia (Jan. 23, 1974).

Switzerland: Theological Faculty, Chur (Jan. 1, 1974).

Theological Faculty, Luzerne (Dec. 25, 1973).

United States: St. Mary's Seminary and University. School of Theology, Baltimore (May 1, 1822).

St. Mary of the Lake Faculty of Theology, Mundelein, Ill. (Sept. 30, 1929).

Weston School of Theology, Cambridge, Mass. (Oct. 18, 1932).

The Jesuit School of Theology, Berkeley, Calif. (Feb. 2, 1934, as "Alma College," Los Gatos, Calif.).

Faculty of Philosophy and Letters, St. Louis, Mo. (Feb. 2, 1934).

St. Michael's Institute, Jesuit School of Philosophy and Letters, Spokane, Wash. (Feb. 2, 1934).

Pontifical Faculty of Theology of the Immaculate Conception, Washington, D.C. (Nov. 15, 1941).

International Marian Research Institute (IMRI), U.S. branch of Pontifical Theological Faculty "Marianum," University of Dayton, Dayton, O. 45459 (affil. 1976, inc. 1983).

John Paul II Institute for Studies on Marriage and the Family, U.S. section of Pontifical Institute of Studies of Marriage and the Family at the Pontifical Lateran University, Dominican House of Studies, 487 Michigan Ave. NE, Washington, DC 20017 (Aug. 22, 1988).

Vietnam: Theological Faculty of the Pontifical National Seminary of St. Pius X, Dalat (July 31, 1965). Activities suppressed.

Zaire: Catholic Faculties of Kinshasa, Kinshasa (theology, Apr. 25, 1957; philosophy, Nov. 25, 1987).

Pontifical College Josephinum (Theologate and College) at Columbus, Ohio, is a national pontifical seminary. Established Sept. 1, 1888, it is immediately subject to the Holy See.

PONTIFICAL UNIVERSITIES AND INSTITUTES IN ROME

(Source: *Annuario Pontificio.*)

Pontifical Gregorian University (1552): Piazza della Pilotta, 4, 00187 Rome. Associated with the university are:

The **Pontifical Biblical Institute** (May 7, 1909): Via della Pilotta, 25, 00187 Rome.

The **Pontifical Institute of Oriental Studies** (Oct. 15, 1917): Piazza S. Maria Maggiore, 7, 00185 Rome.

Pontifical Lateran University (1773). Piazza S. Giovanni in Laterano, 4, 00184 Rome. Annexed to the university is the Pontifical Institute of Studies of Marriage and the Family, erected by Pope John Paul II, Oct 7, 1982; a section of the Institute was established at the Dominican House of Studies, Washington, D.C., by a decree dated Aug. 22, 1988.

Pontifical Urban University (1627): Via Urbano VIII, 16, 00165 Rome.

Pontifical University of St. Thomas Aquinas (Angelicum) (1580), of the Order of Preachers: Largo Angelicum, 1, 00184 Rome.

Pontifical University Salesianum (May 3, 1940; university designation May 24, 1973), of the Salesians of Don Bosco: Piazza dell' Ateneo Salesiano, 1, 00139 Rome. Associated with the university is the **Pontifical Institute of Higher Latin Studies**, known as the **Faculty of Christian and Classical Letters** (June 4, 1971).

Pontifical Athenaeum of St. Anselm (1687), of the Benedictines: Piazza dei Cavalieri di Malta, 5, 00153 Rome.

Pontifical Athenaeum "Antonianum" (of St. Anthony) (May 17, 1933), of the Order of Friars Minor: Via Merulana, 124, 00185 Rome.

Pontifical Institute of Sacred Music (1911; May 24, 1931): Via di Torre Rossa, 21, 00165 Rome.

Pontifical Institute of Christian Archeology (Dec. 11, 1925): Via Napoleone III, 1, 00185 Rome.

Pontifical Theological Faculty "St. Bonaventure" (Dec. 18, 1587), of the Order of Friars Minor Conventual: Via del Serafico, 1, 00142 Rome.

Pontifical Theological Faculty, Pontifical Institute of Spirituality "Teresianum" (1935), of the Discalced Carmelites: Piazza San Pancrazio, 5-A, 00152 Rome.

Pontifical Theological Faculty "Marianum" (1398), of the Servants of Mary: Viale Trente Aprile, 6, 00153 Rome.

Pontifical Institute of Arabic and Islamic Studies (1926), of the Missionaries of Africa: Viale di Trastevere, 89, 00153 Rome.

Pontifical Faculty of Educational Science "Auxilium" (June 27, 1970), of the Daughters of Mary, Help of Christians: Via Cremolino, 141, 00166 Rome.

Roman Athenaeum of the Holy Cross (Jan. 9, 1985), of Personal Prelature of Opus Dei: Piazza S. Apollinare, 49, 00186 Rome.

Pontifical Institute "Regina Mundi" (1970): Lungotevere Tor di Nona, 7, 00186 Rome.

PONTIFICAL ACADEMY OF SCIENCES

(Sources: *Annuario Pontificio*, Catholic News Service.)

The Pontifical Academy of Sciences was constituted in its present form by Pius XI Oct. 28, 1936, in virtue of *In Multis Solaciis*, a document issued on his own initiative.

The academy is the only supranational body of its kind in the world with a pope-selected, life-long membership of outstanding mathematicians and experimental scientists regardless of creed from many countries. The normal complement of 70 members was increased to 80 in 1985-86 by John Paul II. There are additional honorary and supernumerary members.

Purposes of the academy are to honor pure science and its practitioners, to promote the freedom of pure science and to foster research.

The academy traces its origin to the *Linceorum Academia* (Academy of the Lynxes — its symbol) founded in Rome Aug. 17, 1603. Pius IX reorganized this body and gave it a new name — *Pontificia Accademia dei Nuovi Lincei* — in 1847. It was taken over by the Italian state in 1870 and called the *Accademia Nazionale dei Lincei*. Leo XIII reconstituted it with a new charter in 1887. Pius XI designated the Vatican Gardens as the site of academy headquarters in 1922 and gave it its present title and status in 1936. In 1940, Pius XII gave the title of Excellency to its members; John XXIII extended the privilege to honorary members in 1961.

Members in U.S.

Scientists in the U.S. who presently hold membership in the Academy are listed below according to year of appointment.

1936 (Oct. 28): Franco Rasetti, professor emeritus of physics at Johns Hopkins University, Baltimore, Md.

1964 (Sept. 24): William Wilson Morgan, professor emeritus of astronomy at the University of Chicago.

1970 (Apr. 10): Christian de Duve (Nobel Prize, 1974), professor of biochemistry at the International Institute of Cellular and Molecular Pathology at Brussels, Belgium, and Rockefeller Institute (University), New York.

1974 (June 24): Marshall Warren Nirenberg (Nobel Prize, 1968), director of Laboratory on genetics and biochemistry at the National Institutes of Health, Bethesda, Md.

1975 (Dec. 2): George Palade (Nobel Prize, 1974), professor of cellular biology at University of California, San Diego; Victor Weisskopf, professor of physics at the Massachusetts Institute of Technology, Cambridge, Mass.

1978 (Apr. 17): David Baltimore (Nobel Prize, 1975), professor of biology and president of Rockefeller Institute (University), New York; Har Gobind Khorana (Nobel Prize, 1968), professor of biochemistry, and Alexander Rich, professor of molecular biology — both at the Massachusetts Institute of Technology, Cambridge, Mass.; Roger Walcott Sperry (Nobel Prize, 1981), professor of psychobiology, California Institute of Technology, Pasadena, Calif.

1981 (May 12): Christian Anfinsen (Nobel Prize, 1972), professor of biology at Johns Hopkins University, Baltimore, Md.

1983 (Jan. 26): Charles Townes (Nobel Prize, 1964), professor emeritus of physics at the University of California at Berkeley.

1986 (June 9): Beatrice Mintz, chief researcher, Cancer Research Institute of Philadelphia; Maxine Singer, biochemist, president of Carnegie Institution, Washington, D.C.

1990 (Oct. 4): Roald Z. Sagdeev, professor of physics at University of Maryland, College Park; Peter Hamilton Raven, professor of biology at the Boston Botanical Garden of St. Louis, Mo.

Members in Other Countries

Other members of the Academy are listed below according to country of location; dates of their selection are given in parentheses.

Austria: Hans Tuppy (Apr. 10, 1970); Walter Thirring (June 9, 1986).

Belgium: Paul Adriaan Jan Janssen (June 25, 1990).

Brazil: Carlos Chagas, former president of the academy (Aug. 18, 1961); Johanna Dobereiner (Apr. 17, 1978); Crodowaldo Pavan (Apr. 17, 1978).

Canada: Gerhard Herzberg (Sept. 24, 1964), Nobel Prize,1971; John Charles Polanyi (June 9, 1986), Nobel Prize, 1986.

Chile: Hector Croxatto Rezzio (Dec. 2, 1975).

Denmark: Aage Bohr (Apr. 17, 1978), Nobel Prize, 1975.

France: Louis Leprince-Ringuet (Aug. 18, 1961); Jerome Lejeune (June 24, 1974); Andre Blanc-La-Pierre (Apr. 17, 1978), Andre Lichnerowicz (May 12, 1981), Bernard Pullman (May 12, 1981); Paul Germain (June 9, 1986); Jacques Louis Lions (Oct. 4, 1990).

Germany: Rudolf L. Mossbauer (Apr. 10, 1970), Nobel Prize, 1961; Manfred Eigen (May 12, 1981), Nobel Prize, 1967; Wolf Joachim Singer (Sept. 18, 1992).

Ghana: Daniel Adzei Bekoe (Sept. 26, 1983).

Great Britain: Hermann Alexander Bruck (Apr. 5, 1955); Percy C.C. Garnham (Apr. 10, 1970); George Porter (June 24, 1974), Nobel Prize, 1967; Max Ferdinand Perutz (May 12, 1981), Nobel Prize, 1962; Stanley Keith Runcorn (Sept. 12, 1981); Stephen William Hawking (Jan. 9, 1986); Martin John Rees (June 25, 1990); Sir Richard Southwood (Sept. 18, 1992).

Hungary: Janos Szentagothai (May 12, 1981).

India: Mambillikalathil Govind Kumar Menon (May 12, 1981); Chintamani N.R. Rao (June 25, 1990).

Ireland: James Robert McConnell (June 25, 1990).

Israel: Michael Sela (Dec. 2, 1975).

Italy: Giovanni Battista Marini-Bettolo Marconi (Apr. 22, 1968); Rita Levi-Montalcino (June 24, 1974), Nobel Prize, 1986; Giampietro Puppi (Apr. 17, 1978), Ennio De Giorgi (May 12, 1981), Abdus Salam (May 12, 1981), Nobel Prize, 1979; Nicola Cabibbo (June 9, 1986); Bernardo Maria Colombo (Sept. 18, 1992).

Japan: Kenichi Fukui (Dec. 14, 1985) Nobel Prize, 1981; Minoru Oda (Sept. 18, 1992).

Kenya: Thomas R. Odhiambo (May 12, 1981).

Mexico: Marcos Moshinsky (June 9, 1986).

Nigeria: Thomas Adeoye Lambo (June 24, 1974).

Pakistan: Salimuzzaman Siddiqui (Sept. 24, 1964).

Poland: Stanislaw Lojasiewicz (Jan. 28, 1983); Czeslaw Olech (June 9, 1986); Michal Heller (Oct. 4, 1990).

Spain: Manuel Lora-Tamayo (Sept. 24, 1964); Severo Ochoa (June 24, 1974), Nobel Prize, 1959.

Sweden: Sven Horstadius (Aug. 18, 1961); Sune Bergstrom (Dec. 14, 1985), Nobel Prize, 1982; Kai Siegbahn (Dec. 14, 1985), Nobel Prize, 1981.

Switzerland: John Carew Eccles (Apr. 8, 1961), Nobel Prize, 1963; Werner Arber (May 12, 1981), Nobel Prize, 1978; Vladimir Prelog (Dec. 14, 1985), Nobel Prize, 1975; Carlo Rubbia (Dec. 14, 1985), Nobel Prize, 1984; Albert Eschenmoser (June 9, 1986).

Venezuela: Marcel Roche (Apr. 10, 1970).

Zaire: Wa Kalengo Malu (Sept. 26, 1983).

Ex officio members: Rev. George V. Coyne, S.J., director of Vatican Observatory (Sept. 2, 1978);

Very Rev. Leonard E. Boyle, O.P., prefect of the Vatican Library (May 24, 1984); Very Rev. Joseph Metzler, O.M.I., prefect of the Secret Vatican Archives (May 24, 1984).

Honorary members: Silvio Ranzi, professor emeritus of zoology and embryology of the University of Milan (May 12, 1981); Enrico di Rovasenda, O.P., civil engineer and doctor of theology; former chancellor of the Pontifical Academy of Sciences (Nov. 13, 1986); Nicola Dallaporta, professor of theoretic astrophysics at the University of Padua (Oct. 5, 1989); Carlo Pietrangeli, director general of pontifical monuments, museums and galleries (Oct. 5, 1989); Stanley L. Jaki, O.S.B., professor of physics and philosophy of science at Seton Hall University, South Orange, N.J. (Sept. 5, 1990); Georges Marie Martin Cottier, O.P., theologian of Pontifical Household and secretary general of the International Theological Commission (Oct. 28, 1992).

President: Nicola Cabibbo, professor of theoretical physics at Univ. of Rome (app. Apr. 6, 1993, for next four years).

1993 CHRISTOPHER AWARDS

Christopher Awards are given each year to recognize the creative writers, producers and directors who have achieved artistic excellence in films, books and television specials affirming the highest values of the human spirit.

The 1993 awards were presented as follows:

Books: *The Book of the Just: The Unsung Heroes who Rescued Jews from Hitler,* by Eric Silver (Grove Press); *Choteau Creek: A Sioux Reminiscence,* by Joseph Iron Eye Dudley (Univ. of Nebraska Press); *Fritz Eichenberg: Works of Mercy,* edited by Robert Ellsberg (Orbis Books); *The Measure of Our Success: A Letter to My Children and Yours,* by Marian Wright Edelman (Beacon Press); *There's a Boy in Here,* by Judy Barron and Sean Barron (Simon & Schuster); *A Year in Saigon,* by Katie Kelly (Simon & Schuster).

Books for Young People: *The Rainbow Fish,* by Marcus Pfister, translated by J. Alison James (Ages 5-8, North-South Books); *Rosie and the Yellow Ribbon,* by Paula De Paolo, pictures by Janet Wolf (Ages 6-8, Little, Brown); *Letters from Rifka,* by Karen Hesse (Ages 8-12, Henry Holt); *Mississippi Challenge,* by Mildred Pitts Walter (Ages 12 and up, Bradbury Press).

Motion Pictures: Producers, directors and writers of: "Enchanted April" (Miramax Films); "Howard's End" (Sony Pictures Classics); "Lorenzo's Oil" (Universal); "Serafina!" (Hollywood Pictures and Miramax Films).

Television Specials: Producers, directors and writers of: "Against Her Will: An Incident in Baltimore" (CBS); "The Broken Cord" (ABC); "Father/Son" (Independent Network); "Jonathan: The Boy Nobody Wanted" (NBC); "Miles from Nowhere" (CBS); "Sr. Thea: Her Own Story" (NBC); "A Town Torn Apart" (NBC).

James Keller Youth Award: Vincent J. Fontana, M.D., New York Foundling Hospital's medical director, for his commitment to children and pioneering efforts and advocacy in child abuse prevention.

Life Achievement Award: Robert G. Schwartz, for outstanding corporate leadership and community service.

Order of St. George

The Sacred Military Constantinian Order of St. George was established by Pope Clement XI in 1718. The purposes of the order are to work for the preaching and defense of the Catholic faith and to promote the spiritual and physical welfare of sick, disabled, homeless and other unfortunate persons. The principal officer is Prince Carlo of Bourbon-Two Sicilies, Duke of Calabria. Addresses: Via Duomo 149, 80138 Nanples, Italy; Via Sistina 23, 00187, Rome, Italy.

Beatifications

(Continued from page 142.)

1991 (contd): Edoardo Giuseppe Rosaz (July 14, Susa, Italy); Pauline of the Heart of Jesus in Agony Visintainer (Oct. 18, during papal visit to Florianapols, Brazil); Adolph Kolping (Oct. 27).

1992: Josephine Bakhita, Josemaria Escriva de Balaguer (May 17); Francesco Spinelli (June 21, Caravaggio, Italy); 17 Irish Martyrs, Rafael Arnáiz Barón, Nazaria Ignacia March Mesa, Léonie Françoise de Sales Aviat, and Maria Josefa Sancho de Guerra (Sept. 27); 121 Martyrs of Spanish Civil War, Narcisa Martillo Morán (Oct. 25); Cristóbal Magellanes and 24 companions, Mexican martyrs, and Maria de Jesús Sacramentado Venegas (Nov. 22).

1993 (as of Aug. 25): Dina Belanger (Mar. 20); John Duns Scotus (Mar. 20, cult solemnly recognized); Mary Angela Truszkowska, Ludovico of Casoria, Faustina Kowalska, Stanislaus Kazimierczyk and Paula Montal Fornés (Apr. 18); Maurice Tornay, Marie-Louise Trichet, Columba Gabriel and Florida Cevoli (May 16).

SOCIAL SERVICES

Catholic Charities USA (formerly National Conference of Catholic Charities): Founded in 1910 by Most Rev. Thomas J. Shahan and Rt. Rev. Msgr. William J. Kerby in cooperation with lay leaders of the Society of St. Vincent de Paul to help advance and promote the charitable programs and activities of Catholic community and social service agencies in the United States. As the central and national organization for this purpose, it services a network of more than 1,200 agencies and institutions by consultation, information and assistance in planning and evaluating social service programs under Catholic auspices.

Diocesan member agencies provide shelter, food, counseling, services to children, teen parents and the elderly, and a variety of other services to people in need — without regard to religion, gender, age or national origin. Each year millions of people receive help from Catholic Charities; in 1991, more than 12 million turned to Catholic Charities agencies for help. In addition, Catholic Charities is an advocate for persons and families in need.

Catholic Charities USA serves members through national and regional meetings, training programs, literature and social policy advocacy on the national level. It is charged by the U.S. bishops with responding to disasters in this country. Catholic Charities USA's president represents North America before Caritas Internationalis, the international conference of Catholic Charities, and thus maintains contact with the Catholic Charities movement throughout the world. Publications include *Charities USA*, a quarterly membership magazine, and a biannual directory of U.S. Catholic Charities agencies and institutions.

Rev. Fred Kammer, S.J., is president of Catholic Charities USA. Address: 1731 King St., Suite 200, Alexandria, VA 22314.

The Society of St. Vincent de Paul, originally called the Conference of Charity: An association of Catholic lay men and women devoted to personal service of the poor through the spiritual and corporal works of mercy. The first conference was formed at Paris in 1833 by Frederic Ozanam and his associates.

The first conference in the U.S. was organized in 1845 at St. Louis. There are now approximately 4,700 units of the society in this country, with a membership of about 59,000.

In the fiscal year 1990-91, members of the society in this country distributed among poor persons financial and other forms of assistance valued at approximately $160,000,000.

Besides person-to-person assistance, increasing emphasis is being given to stores and rehabilitation workshops of the society through which persons with marginal income can purchase refurbished goods at minimal cost. Handicapped persons are employed in renovating goods and store operations. The society also operates food centers, shelters, criminal justice and other programs.

Address of the National Council: 58 Progress Parkway, St. Louis, MO 63043. John F. Coppinger, president; Rita W. Porter, executive director.

Catholic Health Association of the United States is the national leadership organization of Catholic health-care sponsors, systems, facilities and related organizations and services. CHA enables its members to accomplish collective goals. It asserts leadership in society and the Church by advancing the health-care ministry through programs of advocacy, facilitation and education.

Composed of more than 1,200 organizational and personal members, CHA maintains its national headquarters office at 4455 Woodson Road, St. Louis, MO 63134, and its government services office at 1776 K Street N.W., Suite 204, Washington, DC 20006.

National Association of Catholic Chaplains: Founded in 1965. membership is over 3,700. Address: P.O. Box 07473, Milwaukee, WI 53207.

FACILITIES FOR RETIRED AND AGED PERSONS

(Sources: Almanac survey, *The Official Catholic Directory*.)

This list covers residence, health care and other facilities for the retired and aged under Catholic auspices. Information includes name, type of facility if not evident from the title, address, and total capacity (in parentheses); unless noted otherwise, facilities are for both men and women. Many facilities for the aged offer intermediate nursing care.

Alabama: Allen Memorial Home (Skilled Nursing), 735 S. Washington Ave., Mobile 36603 (94).

Cathedral Place Apartments (Retirement Complex), 351 Conti St., Mobile 36602 (192).

Mercy Medical (Specialized Hospital, Skilled Nursing Facility, Hospice, Home Health and Domiciliary), P.O. Box 1090, Daphne 36526 (137). Not restricted to elderly.

Sacred Heart Residence Little Sisters of the Poor, 1655 McGill Ave., Mobile 36604 (100).

Seton Haven, 3721 Wares Ferry Rd., Montgomery 36193 (104).

Arizona: Desert Crest Campus (Retirement Complex), 2101 E. Maryland Ave., Phoenix 85016 (114 apartments and cottages) and Crestview Lodge (Skilled, Intermediate and Personal Nursing Services), 2151 E. Maryland Ave., Phoenix 85016 (66).

Villa Maria (Skilled Nursing Facility; Assisted and Independent Living Apartments), 4310 E. Grant Rd., Tucson 85712 (93 beds, 50 apartments).

Arkansas: Benedictine Manor (Retirement Home), 100 2nd St., Hot Springs 71913 (59).

California: Alexis Apartments of St. Patrick's Parish, 756 Mission St. 94103; 390 Clementina St., San Francisco 94103 (240).

Casa Manana Inn, 3700 N. Sutter St., Stockton

95204 (162). Non-profit housing for low-income elderly over 62.

Cathedral Plaza, 1551 Third Ave., San Diego 92101 (222 apartments).

Guadalupe Plaza, 4142 42nd St., San Diego 92105 (127 apartments).

Jeanne d'Arc Manor, 85 S. Fifth St., San Jose 95112 (121). For elderly and handicapped.

La Paz Villas, 43-555 Deep Canyon Dr., Palm Desert 92260 (30 units).

Little Flower Haven (Residential Care Facility for Retired), 8585 La Mesa Blvd., La Mesa 91941 (90).

Little Sisters of the Poor, St. Anne's Home, 300 Lake St., San Francisco 94118 (103).

Little Sisters of the Poor, Jeanne Jugan Residence, 2100 South Western Ave., San Pedro, Calif. 90732 (104).

Madonna Residence (Housing for low-income women over 60), 1055 Pine St., San Francisco 94109 (57).

Marian Residence (Retirement Home), 124 S. College Dr., Santa Maria 93454 (58).

Mercy McMahon Terrace, 3865 J St., Sacramento 96816 (118 units).

Mercy Retirement and Care, 3431 Foothill Blvd., Oakland 94601 (135).

Mother Gertrude Balcazar Home for Senior Citizens, 11320 Laurel Canyon Blvd., San Fernando 91340 (114).

Nazareth House (Residential and Skilled Care), 2121 N. 1st St., Fresno 93703 (91).

Nazareth House (Residential and Skilled Nursing), 3333 Manning Ave., Los Angeles 90064 (118 residential; 20 skilled nursing).

Nazareth House (Retirement Home), 245 Nova Albion Way, Terra Linda, San Rafael 94903 (139).

Nazareth House Retirement Home, 6333 Rancho Mission Rd., San Diego 92108 (122).

O'Connor Woods (Residential), 3400 Wagner Heights, Stockton 95209.

Our Lady of Fatima Villa (Skilled Nursing Facility), 20400 Saratoga/Los Gatos Rd., Saratoga 95070 (85).

St. Bernardine Plaza (Retirement Home), 550 W. 5th St., San Bernardino 92401 (150 units).

St. Francis Home (Elderly Retired Women), 1718 W. 6th St., Santa Ana 92703 (80).

St. John of God (Retirement and Care Center), 2035 W. Adams Blvd., Los Angeles 90018.

St. John's Plaza, 8080 La Mesa Blvd., La Mesa 91941..

Vigil Light Apartments, 1945 Long Dr., Santa Rosa 95405 (48).

Villa Scalabrini (Retirement and Skilled Nursing Care Center), 10631 Vinedale St., Sun Valley 91352 (130 residence; 58 skilled nursing).

Villa Siena (Residence and Skilled Nursing Care), 1855 Miramonte Ave., Mountain View 94040 (50, residence; 20, skilled nursing care).

Colorado: Francis Heights, Inc., 2626 Osceola St., Denver 80212 (400 units; 431 residents).

Gardens at St. Elizabeth (Congregate Housing and Assisted Living), 2835 W. 32nd Ave., Denver 80211 (209 congregate; 81 assisted living).

Little Sisters of the Poor, 3629 W. 29th Ave., Denver 80211 (85).

Connecticut: Augustana Homes (Residence), Simeon Rd., Bethel 06801.

Carmel Ridge Estates, Gramco Management Co., 6454 Main St., Trumbull 06611.

Holy Family Home and Shelter, Inc., 88 Jackson St., P.O. Box 884, Willimantic 06226.

Matulaitis Nursing Home, 10 Thurber Rd., Putnam 06260 (119).

Monsignor Bojnowski Manor, Inc. (Skilled Nursing Facility), 50 Pulaski St., New Britain 06053 (48; also 6 residential rooms).

Notre Dame Convalescent Home, 76 West Rocks Rd., Norwalk 06851 (60).

St. Joseph Living Center, 14 Club Rd., Windham 06280 (120).

St. Joseph's Manor (Health Care Facility; Home for Aged), Carmelite Srs. for Aged and Infirm, 6448 Main St., Trumbull 06611 (297).

St. Joseph's Residence, Little Sisters of the Poor, 1365 Enfield St., Enfield, Conn. 06082 (94)

St. Lucian's Home for the Aged, 532 Burritt St., New Britain 06053 (55).

St. Mary's Home (Residence and Health Care Facility) 291 Steele Rd., W. Hartford 06117 (113).

Teresian Towers, Gramco Management Co., 6448 Main St., Trumbull 06611.

Delaware: The Antonian, 1701 W. 10th St., Wilmington 19805 (136 apartments).

Jeanne Jugan Residence, Little Sisters of the Poor, 185 Salem Church Rd., Newark 19713 (107).

Marydale Retirement Village, 135 Jeandell Dr., Newark 19713 (108 apartments).

St. Patrick's House, Inc., 14th and French Sts., Wilmington 19801 (16).

District of Columbia: Jeanne Jugan Residence — St. Joseph Villa, Little Sisters of the Poor, 4200 Harewood Rd., N.E. Washington 20017 (117).

Florida: All Saints Home for the Aged, 2040 Riverside Ave., Jacksonville 32204 (60).

Bon Secour-Maria Manor Nursing Care Center, 10300 4th St. N., St. Petersburg 33702 (274).

Carroll Manor (Retirement Apartments), 3667 S. Miami Ave., Miami 33133 (236 apartments).

Casa Calderon, Inc. (Retirement Apartments), 800 W. Virginia St., Tallahassee 32304 (111).

Haven of Our Lady of Peace (Residence and Health Care Facility), 5203 N. 9th Ave., Pensacola 32504 (89).

Marian Towers, Inc. (Retirement Apartments), 17505 North Bay Rd., Miami Beach 33160.

Noreen McKeen Residence for Geriatric Care, 315 Flagler Dr. S., W. Palm Beach 33401.

Opa Locka Village, Inc., 13201 N.W. 28 Avenue, Opa Locka 33054 (113 apartments).

Palmer House, Inc., 1225 S.W. 107th Ave., Miami 33174 (120 apartments).

Pennsylvania Retirement Residence, 208 Evernia St., W. Palm Beach 33401 (190).

St. Andrew Towers (Retirement Apartments), 2700 N.W. 99th Ave., Coral Springs 33065.

St. Catherine Laboure (Skilled and Intermediate Care), 1717 Barrs St., Jacksonville 33204 (232).

St. Dominic Gardens (Retirement Apartments), 5849 N.W. 7th St., Miami 33126 (149 apartments).

St. Elizabeth Gardens, Inc. (Retirement Apartments), 801 N.E. 33rd St., Pompano Beach 33064 (150).

St. John's Rehabilitation Hospital/St. John Health Care Center, 3075 N.W. 35th Ave., Lauderdale Lakes 33311.

Stella Maris House, Inc., 8636 Harding Ave., Miami Beach 33141 (136 apartments).

Illinois: Addolorata Villa (Sheltered, Intermediate, Skilled Care Facility; Apartments), 555 McHenry Rd., Wheeling 60090 (135 health care; 100 apartments).

Alvernia Manor (Sheltered Care), 1598 Main St., Lemont 60439 (50).

Carlyle Healthcare Center, 501 Clinton St., Carlyle 62231 (131).

Carmelite Carefree Village, 8419 Bailey Rd., Darien 60561 (96 units, 115 residents).

Cortland Manor Retirement Home, 1900 N. Karlov, Chicago 60639. (56).

Holy Family Health Center, 2380 Dempster, Des Plaines 60016 (362).

Holy Family Villa (Intermediate Care Facility), 123rd St. and Father Linkus Dr., Lemont 60439 (99).

Jugan Terrace, Little Sisters of the Poor, 2300 N. Racine, Chicago 60614 (50 apartments).

Little Sisters of the Poor Center for the Aging, 2325 N. Lakewood Ave., Chicago, Ill. 60614 (102).

Maria Care Center (Nursing Facility), 350 W. S. First St., Red Bud 62278 (115).

Marian Heights Apartments (Elderly, Handicapped), 20 Marian Heights Dr., Alton 62002 (127).

Marian Park, Inc., 2126 W. Roosevelt Rd., Wheaton 60187 (117 apartments).

Maryhaven, Inc. (Skilled and Intermediate Care Facility), 1700 E. Lake Ave., Glenview 60025 (147).

Mayslake Village (Retirement Apartments), 1801 35th St., Oak Brook 60521 (630 apartments).

Mercy Residence at Tolentine Center, 20300 Governors Hwy., Olympia Fields 60461 (52).

Meredith Memorial Home, 16 S. Illinois St., Belleville 62220 (90).

Merkle-Knipprath (Apartments and Nursing Facility), Rt. 1, Franciscan Brothers. Clifton 60927 (130).

Mother Theresa Home (Skilled, Intermediate and Sheltered Care), 1270 Franciscan Dr., Lemont 60439 (150).

Nazarethville (Intermediate and Sheltered Care), 300 N. River Rd., Des Plaines 60016 (83).

Our Lady of Angels Retirement Home, 1201 Wyoming, Joliet 60435 (100).

Our Lady of the Snows, Apartment Community, 9500 West Illinois Highway 15, Belleville 62223. Retirement community (166 apartments); adjoining skilled-care facility (57 beds).

Our Lady of Victory Nursing Home (Intermediate and Skilled Care), 20 Briarcliff Lane, Bourbonnais 60914 (97).

Pope John Paul I Apartments (Elderly and Handicapped), 1 Pope John Paul Plaza, Springfield 62703 (150).

Resurrection Nursing Pavilion (Skilled Care), 1001 N. Greenwood, Park Ridge 60068 (295).

Resurrection Retirement Community, 7262 W. Peterson Ave., Chicago, 60631 (473 apartments).

Rosary Hill Home (Women), 9000 W. 81st St., Justice 60458 (50).

St. Andrew Home (Retirement Residence), 7000 N. Newark Ave., Niles 60648 (198).

St. Ann's Healthcare Center, 770 State St., Chester 62233 (157).

St. Anne Center, 4405 Highcrest Rd., Rockford 61107 (120).

St. Benedict Home, 6930 W. Touhy Ave., Niles 60648 (52).

St. Elizabeth Home, 704 W. Marion St., Joliet 60436.

St. James Manor, 1251 East Richton Rd., Crete 60417 (110).

St. Joseph's Home (Sheltered and Intermediate Care), 3306 S. 6th St. Rd., Springfield 62703 (133).

St. Joseph's Home (Sheltered and Intermediate Care), 2223 W. Heading Ave., Peoria 61604 (187).

St. Joseph's Home for the Aged, 659 E. Jefferson St., Freeport 61032 (108).

St. Joseph's Home for the Elderly, 80 W. Northwest Hwy., Palatine 60067 (132).

St. Joseph Home of Chicago, Inc. (Skilled Care), 2650 N. Ridgeway Ave., Chicago 60647 (173).

St. Patrick's Residence (Sheltered and Intermediate Care), 22 E. Clinton St., Joliet 60431 (197).

Villa Franciscan, Franciscan Sisters Health Care Corporation, 210 N. Springfield, Joliet 60435 (129).

Villa Saint Cyril (Intermediate Care), 1111 St. John's Ave., Highland Park 60035 (80).

Villa Scalabrini (Sheltered, Intermediate and Skilled), 480 N. Wolf Rd., Northlake 60164 (265).

Indiana: Albertine Home, 1501 Hoffman St., Hammond 46327 (33).

Little Company of Mary Health Facility (Comprehensive Nursing), 7520 S. 421, San Pierre 46374 (200).

Providence Retirement Home, 703 E. Spring St., New Albany 47150 (95).

Regina Continuing Care Center (Skilled Nursing and Intermediate Care Facility), 3900 Washington Ave., Evansville 47715 (154).

Sacred Heart Home (Comprehensive Nursing), R.R. 2, Box 2A, Avilla 46710 (133). LaVerna Terrace, same address; independent living for senior citizens, handicapped and disabled (51 units).

St. Anne Home (Residential and Comprehensive Nursing), 1900 Randallia Dr., Ft. Wayne 46805 (205).

St. Anthony Medical Center and St. Anthony Home, Inc., 201 Franciscan Rd., Crown Point 46307 (219).

St. Augustine Home for the Aged, Little Sisters of the Poor, 2345 W. 86th St., Indianapolis 46260 (101).

St. John's Home for the Aged, Little Sisters of the Poor, 1236 Lincoln Ave., Evansville 47714 (71).

St. Paul Hermitage (Residential and Intermediate Care Nursing), 501 N. 17th St., Beech Grove 46107 (95).

Iowa: The Alverno Health Care Facility (Nursing Care), 849 13th Ave. N., Clinton 52732 (138).

Bishop Drumm Retirement Center, 5837 Winwood Dr., Johnston 50131 (120). McAuley Apartments (87 units).

Hallmar-Mercy Hospital, 701 Tenth St. S.E., Cedar Rapids 52403 (62).

Holy Spirit Retirement Home (Intermediate Care), 1701 W. 25th St., Sioux City 51103 (94).

Kahl Home for the Aged and Infirm (Skilled and Intermediate Care Facility), 1101 W. 9th St., Davenport 52804 (135).

The Marian Home, 2400 6th Ave. North, Fort Dodge 50501 (Intermediate Care, 97) and Marian Village (Apartments), 2320 6th Ave. North, Fort Dodge 50501.

Padre Pio Health Care Center, Stonehill Care Center (Residence, Nursing Home), 3485 Windsor, Dubuque 52001 (250). Stonehill Adult Center (Day Care), same address.

St. Anthony Nursing Home (Intermediate Care), 406 E. Anthony St., Carroll 51401 (80). Orchard View, same address (50 apartments).

St. Francis Continuation Care and Nursing Home Center, Burlington 52601 (29 skilled nursing; 59 intermediate care). Orchard City of St. Francis, same address (16 independent living apartment units).

Kansas: Catholic Care Center (Skilled and Intermediate Care Facility), 6700 E. 45th St, Wichita 67226 (180 beds — includes 15 Alzheimer and 6 AIDS).

Mt. Joseph Senior Community (Intermediate Care Facility), 1110 W. 11, Concordia 66901 (125 nursing; 12 apartments).

St. Elizabeth Home Health Agency, 2225 Canterbury Rd., Hays 67601.

St. John Rest Home (Intermediate Care Facility), 701 Seventh St., Victoria 67671 (90 nursing).

St. John's of Hays (Nursing Facility), 2010 E. 25th, Hays 67601 (60).

St. Joseph Care Center (Intermediate and Skilled Care Facility), 759 Vermont Ave., Kansas City 66101 (201 nursing; 36 apartments).

Villa Maria, Inc. (Intermediate Care Facility), 116 S. Central, Mulvane 67110 (66).

Kentucky: Bishop Soenneker Personal Care Home, 9545 Ky. 144, Philpot 42366 (60).

Carmel Home (Residence, Adult Day Care, Respite Care and Nursing Care), 2501 Old Hartford Rd., Owensboro 42303 (115).

Carmel Manor (Skilled, Intermediate and Personal Care Home), Carmel Manor Rd., Ft. Thomas, 41075 (132).

Madonna Manor Nursing Home, 2344 Amsterdam Rd., Villa Hills 41016 (60). Also has 49 senior citizen apartments.

Marian Home, 3105 Lexington Rd., Louisville 40206 (70).

Nazareth Home, 2000 Newburg Rd., Louisville 40205 (168).

St. Charles Care Center and Village, 500 Farrell Dr., Covington 41011 (147). Nursing home; adult day health program. Independent living cottages (35). Assisted living (60). Independent living apartments (18).

Louisiana: Annunciation Inn, 1220 Spain St., New Orleans 70117 (106 residential units).

Bethany M.H.S. Health Care Center (Women), P.O. Box 2308, Lafayette 70502 (42).

Chateau de Notre Dame (Residence and Nursing Home), 2832 Burdette St., New Orleans 70125 (110 residential units, 180 nursing beds).

Christopher Inn Apartments, 2110 Royal St., New Orleans 70116 (144 residential units).

Consolata Home (Nursing Home), 2319 E. Main St., New Iberia 70560 (114).

Haydel Heights (Apartments), 6655 Ransom St., New Orleans 70126.

Lafon Nursing Home of the Holy Family, 6900 Chef Menteur Hwy., New Orleans 70126 (171).

Mary-Joseph Residence for the Elderly, 4201 Woodland Dr., New Orleans 70131 (122).

Metairie Manor, 4929 York St., Metairie 70001 (287 residential units).

Nazareth Inn, 9630 Haynes Blvd., New Orleans 70127 (270 apartments).

Ollie Steele Burden Manor (Nursing Home), 4200 Essen Lane, Baton Rouge 70809 (184).

Our Lady of Prompt Succor Home, 751 E. Prudhomme Lane, Opelousas 70570 (80).

Our Lady's Manor, Inc., 402 Monroe St., Alexandria 71301 (104 apartments).

Place Dubourg, 201 Rue Dubourg, LaPlace 70068 (115 residential units).

Rouquette Lodge, 4300 Hwy 22, Mandeville 70448 (119 residential units).

St. John Berchmans Manor, 3400 St. Anthony Ave., New Orleans 70122 (150 residential units).

St. Joseph's Home (Nursing Home), 2301 Sterlington Rd., Monroe 71201 (132).

St. Margaret's Daughters Home (Nursing Home, Women), 6220 Chartres St., New Orleans 70117 (112).

St. Martin Manor, 1501 N. Johnson St., New Orleans 70116 (140 residential units).

Villa St. Maurice, 500 St. Maurice Ave., New Orleans 70117. (110 residential units).

Villa St. Maurice II, 6101 Douglas St., New Orleans 70117 (75 residential units).

Village du Lac, Inc., 1404 Carmel Ave., Lafayette 70501 (200). For handicapped and elderly.

Wynhoven Apartments (Residence for Senior Citizens), 4600-10th St., Marrero 70072 (200).

Wynhoven II, 4606-10th St., Marrero 70072 (150).

Maine: Deering Pavilion (Apartments for Senior Citizens), 880 Forest Ave., Portland 04103 (200 units).

Marcotte Nursing Home-D'Youville Pavilion, 102 Campus Ave., Lewiston 04240 (280). Marcotte Congregate Housing, 100 Campus Ave., Lewiston 04240 (128 apartments).

Mt. St. Joseph (Nursing Home), Highwood St., Waterville 04901 (78). St. Andre Health Care

Facility, Inc. (Nursing Home), 407 Pool St., Biddeford 04005 (96).
St. Joseph's Manor (Nursing Care Facility), 1133 Washington Ave., Portland 04103 (200). Adult day care center, same address.
St. Xavier's Home, 199 Somerset St., Bangor 04401 (19 units).
Seton Village, Inc., 1 Carver St., Waterville 04901 (140 housing units).

Maryland: Cardinal Shehan Center, Inc., 2300 Dulaney Valley Rd., Towson 21204 (438).
Carroll Manor (Residence and Nursing Home), 4922 La Salle Rd., Hyattsville 20782 (242).
Little Sisters of the Poor, St. Martin's Home (for the Aged), 601 Maiden Choice Lane, Baltimore 21228 (120).
Sacred Heart Home (Women), 5805 Queens Chapel Rd., Hyattsville 20782 (102).
St. Joseph Nursing Home, 1222 Tugwell Dr., Baltimore 21228 (40).
Villa Rosa (Nursing Home), 3800 Lottsford Vista Rd., Mitchellville 20721 (101).

Massachusetts: Beaven-Kelly Home for Elderly (Rest Home), 1245 Main St., Holyoke 01040 (55).
Catholic Memorial Home (Nursing Home), 2446 Highland Ave., Fall River 02720 (288).
Don Orione Nursing Home, 111 Orient Ave., East Boston 02128 (194). Adult day care center (30).
D'Youville Manor (Nursing Home), 981 Varnum Ave., Lowell 01854 (196). Day care program (20).
Jeanne Jugan Residence, Little Sisters of the Poor (Nursing Home), 186 Highland Ave., Somerville 02143 (95). Jeanne Jugan Pavilion, 190 Highland Ave., Somerville 02143 (apartments, 27; residents, 28).
Madonna Manor (Nursing Home), 85 N. Washington St., N. Attleboro 02760 (121).
Marian Manor, for the Aged and Infirm (Nursing Home), 130 Dorchester St., S. Boston, 02127 (376).
Marian Manor of Taunton (Nursing Home), 33 Summer St., Taunton 02780 (83).
Maristhill Nursing Home, 66 Newton St., Waltham 02154 (120).
MI Nursing/Restorative Center, Zero Bennington St., Lawrence 01841 (250). Alzheimer beds (42).
MI Residential Community, 189 Maple St., Lawrence 01841 (304 apartments). Adult Day Health Care Center (42), Social Day Care (30).
Mt. St. Vincent Nursing Home, 35 Holy Family Rd., Holyoke 01040 (125).
Our Lady's Haven (Nursing Home), 71 Center St., Fairhaven 02719 (110).
Sacred Heart Home (Nursing Home), 359 Summer St., New Bedford 02740 (217).
St. John's Nursing Home of Lowell, 500 Wentworth Ave., Lowell 01852 (103)
St. Joseph Manor Nursing Home, 215 Thatcher St., Brockton 02402 (120).
St. Joseph's Home (Nursing Home), 321 Centre St., Dorchester, Boston 02122 (118).

St. Luke's Home (Rest Home), 85 Spring St., Springfield 01105 (89).
St. Patrick's Manor (Nursing Home), 863 Central St., Framingham 01701 (332).

Michigan: Bishop Noa Home for Senior Citizens, Escanaba 49829 (109).
Casa Maria (Residence), 600 Maple Vista, Imlay City 48444 (96).
Kundig Center (Residence), 3300 Jefferies Freeway, Detroit 48208 (168). Rooms and apartments.
Lourdes Nursing Home (Skilled Facility), 2300 Watkins Lake Rd., Waterford 48328 (108).
Madonna Villa Senior Residence, 17825 Fifteen Mile Rd., Fraser, 48026 (90).
Marian Hall (Residence), 529 M.L. King Ave., Flint 48502 (124).
Marian-Oakland West, 29250 W. Ten Mile Rd., Farmington Hills 48336 (100). Rooms and apartments.
Marian Place (Residence), 408 W. Front St., Monroe 48161 (52).
Marycrest Manor (Skilled Nursing Facility), 15475 Middlebelt Rd., Livonia 48154 (55).
Marydale Center for Senior Citizens (Board and Apartments), 3147 Tenth Ave., Port Huron 48060 (71).
Maryhaven (Residence), 11350 Reeck Rd., Southgate 48195 (93).
St. Ann's Home, (Residence and Nursing Home), 2161 Leonard St. N.W., Grand Rapids 49504 (120).
St. Catherine Cooperative House, 1641 Webb Ave., Detroit 48206 (12).
St. Elizabeth Briarbank (Women, Residence), 1315 N. Woodward Ave., Bloomfield Hills 48013 (54).
St. Francis Home (Nursing Home), 915 N. River Rd., Saginaw 48609 (100).
St. Joseph's Home for the Aged, 4800 Cadieux Rd., Detroit 48224 (104).
St. Jude Home, Inc., (Residence), 2270 Marwood, Waterford 48328.
Stapleton Center (Residence), 9341 Agnes St., Detroit 48214 (65).
Villa Elizabeth (Nursing Home), 2100 Leonard St. N.E., Grand Rapids 49505 (136). Country Villa (Assisted Living Apartments), 2110 Leonard N.E., Grand Rapids 49505 (48 units).
Villa Francesca (Residence, Women), 565 W. Long Lake Rd., Bloomfield Hills 48302 (18).
Villa Marie (Board and Apartments), 15131 Newburgh Rd., Livonia 48154 (100).

Minnesota: Alverna Apartments, 300 8th Ave. S.E., Little Falls 56345 (60). Retirement community.
Assumption Home, 715 North First St., Cold Spring 56320 (Skilled nursing beds, 95). Respite care.
Benedictine Health Center, 935 Kenwood Ave., Duluth 55811 (Nursing home, 120; day care, 25). Respite care.
Divine Providence Community Home (Intermediate Care), 700 Third Ave. N.W., Sleepy Eye 56085 (58).

Divine Providence Home (Skilled Nursing Home), Ivanhoe 56142 (51).

Health One St. Mary's (Nursing Home), P.O. Box 357, Winsted 55395 (95).

John Paul Apartments, 200 8th Ave. N., Cold Spring 56320 (61).

Little Sisters of the Poor, Holy Family Residence (Skilled Nursing and Intermediate Care), 330 S. Exchange St., St. Paul 55102 (111).

Madonna Towers (Retirement Apartments and Nursing Home), 4001 19th Ave. N.W., Rochester 55901 (200).

Mary Rondorf Retirement Home, 222 N. 5th St., Staples 56479 (50).

Mille Lacs Nursing Home, 200 N. Elm, Onamia 56359 (80).

Mother of Mercy Nursing Home and Retirement Center, Albany 56307 (Skilled nursing home, 84; retirement housing, 33).

Regina Nursing Home and Retirement Residence, Hastings 55033. Nursing home (61); retirement home (56); boarding care (32).

Sacred Heart Hospice (Skilled Nursing Home, Adult Day Care, Home Health Care) 1200 Twelfth St. S.W., Austin 55912 (59).

St. Ann's Residence, 330 E. 3rd St., Duluth 55805 (200).

St. Anne Hospice, Inc. (Nursing Home), 1347 W. Broadway, Winona 55987 (134).

St. Benedict's Center (Nursing Home), 1810 Minnesota Blvd. S.E., St. Cloud 56304 (222). Skilled and intermediate nursing, adult day care, respite care. Benedict Village (Retirement Apartments), 2000 15th Ave. S.E., St. Cloud 56304. Benedict Homes (Alzheimer Residential Care) and Benedict Court (Assisted Living).

St. Elizabeth's Hospital, Nursing Home and Health Care Center, 1200-5th Grant Blvd., Wabasha 55981 (157). Assisted living apartments (23).

St. Francis Home, 501 Oak St., Breckenridge 56520 (124).

St. Mary's Home (Nursing Home), 1925 Norfolk Ave., St. Paul 55116 (140).

St. Mary's Regional Health Center (Hospital and Nursing Center), 1027 Washington Ave., Detroit Lakes 56501 (100).

St. Mary's Villa (Nursing Home), Box 397, Pierz 56364 (101).

St. Otto's Care Center (Nursing Home), 920 S.E. 4th St., Little Falls 56345 (150).

St. William's Nursing Home, Parkers Prairie 56361.

Villa of St. Francis Nursing Home, Morris 56267 (140).

Villa St. Vincent (Skilled Nursing Home and Residence), 516 Walsh St., Crookston 56716. Nursing home (80); residence (95).

Mississippi: Santa Maria Retirement Apartments, 674 Beach Blvd., Biloxi, 39530.

Villa Maria Retirement Apartments, 921 Porter Ave., Ocean Springs 39564.

Missouri: Cathedral Square Towers, 444 W. 12th St., Kansas City 64105. Apartments for elderly and handicapped.

Chariton Apartments (Retirement Apartments), 4249 Michigan Ave., St. Louis 63111 (122 units; 143 residents).

DePaul Health Center — St. Anne's Division (Skilled Nursing), 12303 DePaul Dr., Bridgeton 63044 (96).

LaVerna Heights Retirement Home (Women), 104 E. Park Ave., Savannah 64485 (40). Nursing facility.

LaVerna Village Nursing Home, 904 Hall Ave., Savannah 64485 (120).

Little Sisters of the Poor (Home for Aged), 3225 N. Florissant Ave., St. Louis 63107 (135).

Mary, Queen and Mother Center (Nursing Care), 7601 Watson Rd., St. Louis 63119 (220).

Mother of Good Counsel Home (Skilled Nursing, Women), 6825 Natural Bridge Rd., Northwoods, 63121 (114).

Our Lady of Mercy Country Home, 2205 Hughes Rd., Liberty 64068 (115).

Price Memorial Skilled Nursing Facility Forby Rd., P.O. Box 476, Eureka 63025 (120).

St. Agnes Home for the Elderly, 10341 Manchester Rd., Kirkwood 63122 (122).

St. Joseph Hill Infirmary, Inc., (Nursing Care Facility, Men), St. Joseph Road, Eureka 63025 (127).

St. Joseph's Home, 723 First Capitol Dr., St. Charles 63301 (100).

St. Joseph's Home for the Aged (Residential and Intermediate Care Facility), 1306 W. Main St., Jefferson City 65109 (89).

Nebraska: Bergan Mercy Medical Center, Mercy Care Center (Skilled Nursing Facility), 1870 S. 75th St., Omaha 68124 (250).

Madonna Centers, 5401 South St., Lincoln 68506 (252).

Mercy Villa, 1845 S. 72nd St., Omaha 68124 (36).

Mt. Carmel Home, Keens' Memorial (Nursing Home), 412 W. 18th St., Kearney 68847 (76).

New Cassel Retirement Center, 900 N. 90th St., Omaha 68114 (156).

St. Joseph's Retirement Community, 320 E. Decatur St., West Point 68788 (70). Assisted living.

St. Joseph's Nursing Home, 401 N. 18th St., Norfolk 68701 (75).

St. Joseph's Villa (Nursing Home), David City 68632. (65).

New Hampshire: Mount Carmel Nursing Home, 235 Myrtle St., Manchester 03104 (120).

St. Ann Home (Nursing Home), 195 Dover Point Rd., Dover 03820 (53).

St. Francis Home (Nursing Home), Court St., Laconia 03246 (51). Apartments (24).

St. Teresa Manor (Nursing Home), 519 Bridge St., Manchester 03104 (51). Bishop Primeau Apartments, same address (25).

St. Vincent de Paul Nursing Home, 29 Providence Ave., Berlin 03570 (80).

New Jersey: Holy Family Residence (Women), 44 Rifle Camp Rd., P.O. Box 536, W. Paterson 07424 (64).

Little Sisters of the Poor, St. Joseph Home, 140

Shepherd Lane, Totowa 07512 (130; also, 18 independent living units).

McCarrick Care Center, 15 Dellwood Lane, Somerset 08873 (120).

Mater Dei Nursing Home, RD 3, Box 164, Rt. 40, P.O. Newfield 08344 (64).

Morris Hall, Home for the Aged (Residence and Skilled Nursing Home), 2361 Lawrenceville Rd., Lawrenceville 08648 (115).

Mount St. Andrew Villa (Residence), 55 W. Midland Ave., Paramus 07652 (56).

Our Lady's Residence (Nursing Home), Glendale and Clematis Aves., Pleasantville 08232 (104).

St. Ann's Home for the Aged (Skilled and Intermediate Nursing Care Home, Women), 198 Old Bergen Rd., Jersey City 07305 (106). Adult Medical Day Care.

St. Francis Health Resort (Residence), Denville 07834 (100), Apartments, 56.

St. Joseph's Home (Women), 240 Longhouse Dr., Hewitt 07421.

St. Joseph's Rest Home for Aged Women, 46 Preakness Ave., Paterson 07522 (35).

St. Joseph's Senior Residence (Sheltered Care), 1 St. Joseph Terr., Woodbridge 07095 (60).

St. Joseph's Catholic Nursing Home, 1B St. Joseph Terr., Woodbridge 07095 (40).

St. Mary's Catholic Home (Skilled Nursing Home), 1730 Kresson Rd., Cherry Hill 08003 (215).

St. Vincent's Nursing Home, 45 Elm St., Montclair 07042 (135).

Villa Maria (Residence and Infirmary, Women), 641 Somerset St., N. Plainfield 07061 (70).

New Mexico: Good Shepherd Manor (Residential Care for Aged Persons), Little Brothers of the Good Shepherd, P.O. Box 10248, Albuquerque 87184 (40).

New York: Bernardine Apartments, 417 Churchill Ave., Syracuse 13205.

Brothers of Mercy Sacred Heart Home (Residence) 4520 Ransom Rd., Clarence 14031 (82). Brothers of Mercy Nursing Home, 10570 Bergtold Rd., Clarence 14031 (240). Brothers of Mercy Housing Co., Inc. (Apartments), 10500 Bergtold Rd., Clarence 14031 (100 units).

Carmel Richmond Nursing Home, 88 Old Town Rd., Staten Island 10304 (300).

Consolation Residence (Skilled Nursing and Health Related), 111 Beach Dr., West Islip 11795 (250).

Ferncliff Nursing Home, 52 River Rd., Rhinebeck 12572 (328).

Frances Schervier Home and Hospital, 2975 Independence Ave., Bronx 10463 (364). Frances Schervier Long Term Health Care Program, same address (150 slots). Frances Schervier Housing Development Fund Corporation, 2995 Independence Ave., Bronx 10463 (154 units).

Good Samaritan Nursing Home (Skilled Nursing), 101 Elm St., Sayville, N.Y. 11782 (100).

Holy Family Home, 1740-84th St., Brooklyn 11214 (105).

Holy Family Home (Adult Home), 410 Mill St., Williamsville 14221 (85).

Kateri Residence (Skilled Nursing), 150 Riverside Dr., New York 10024 (520).

Little Sisters of the Poor, Jeanne Jugan Residence (Skilled Nursing and Health Related; Adult Care), 3200 Baychester Ave., Bronx 10475 (120).

Little Sisters of the Poor, Queen of Peace Residence, 110-30 221st St., Queens Village 11429 (130).

Mercy Center for Health Services (Residential Health Care Facility), 218 Stone St., Watertown 13601 (300).

Madonna Residence, Inc. (Nursing Home), 1 Prospect Park W., Brooklyn, 11215 (290).

Mary Manning Walsh Home (Nursing Home), 1339 York Ave., New York 10021 (362).

Mercy Healthcare Center (Skilled Nursing Facility), Tupper Lake 12986 (54).

Mt. Loretto Nursing Home, (Skilled Nursing Facility), Sisters of the Resurrection, R.D., 3, Amsterdam 12010 (82).

Nazareth Nursing Home (Women), 291 W. North St., Buffalo 14201 (125).

Our Lady of Hope Residence (Home for the Aged), Little Sisters of the Poor, 1 Jeanne Jugan Lane, Latham 12210 (110; also 16 apartments).

Ozanam Hall of Queens Nursing Home, Inc., 42-41 201st St., Bayside 11361 (432).

Providence Rest, 3304 Waterbury Ave., Bronx 10465 (200).

Resurrection Rest Home (Skilled Nursing Facility, Women), Castleton 12033 (48).

Sacred Heart Home (Skilled Nursing Facility), 8 Mickle St., Plattsburgh 12901 (89).

St. Ann's Home / The Heritage (Nursing Facility), 1500 Portland Ave., Rochester 14621 (591). Home Connection (Adult Day Care), same address (55).

St. Cabrini Nursing Home, 115 Broadway, Dobbs Ferrry 10522 (200).

St. Clare Manor, 543 Locust St., Lockport 14094 (28).

St. Columban's on the Lake (Retirement Home), 2546 Lake Rd., Silver Creek 14136 (50).

St. Elizabeth Home (Adult Home), 5539 Broadway, Lancaster 14086 (102).

St. Francis Home (Skilled Nursing Facility), 147 Reist St., Williamsville 14221 (142).

St. Joseph Manor (Nursing Home), W. State St., Olean 14760 (22).

St. Joseph Nursing Home, 2535 Genesee St., Utica 13501 (120).

St. Joseph's Guest Home, Missionary Sisters of St. Benedict,, 350 Cuba Hill Rd., Huntington 11743 (48).

St. Joseph's Home (Nursing Home), 420 Lafayette St., Ogdensburg 13669 (82).

St. Joseph's Villa (Residence), 38 Prospect Ave., Catskill 12414 (60).

St. Luke Manor, 17 Wiard St., Batavia 14020 (20).

St. Mary's Manor, 515 Sixth St., Niagara Falls 14301 (119).

St. Patrick's Home for the Aged and Infirm, 66 Van Cortland Park S., Bronx 10463 (264).

St. Teresa Nursing Home, 120 Highland Ave., Middletown 10940 (92).

St. Vincent's Home for the Aged, 319 Washington Ave., Dunkirk 14048 (34).

Terence Cardinal Cooke Health Care Center

(Skilled Nursing), 1249 Fifth Ave., New York 10029 (237).

Teresian House, Washington Ave. Extension, Albany 12203 (300).

Uihlein Mercy Center (Nursing Home), Lake Placid 12946 (156).

North Carolina: Maryfield Nursing Home (115 beds) and Maryfield Acres (26 retirement homes), Greensboro Rd., High Point 27260.

North Dakota: Carrington Health Center (Nursing Home), Carrington 58421 (40).

Manor St. Joseph Home for Aged and Infirm, Edgeley 58433 (40).

Marillac Manor (Retirement Apartments), 1016 N. 28th St., Bismarck 58501 (78 apartments).

St. Anne's Guest Home, 524 N. 17th St., Grand Forks 58203 (56) Apartments (30). Adult basic care facility.

St. Vincent's Nursing Home, 1021 N. 26th St., Bismarck 58501 (101).

Ohio: Archbishop Leibold Home for the Aged, Little Sisters of the Poor, 476 Riddle Rd., Cincinnati 45220 (118).

Assumption Nursing Home, 550 W. Chalmers Ave., Youngstown 44511 (126).

Francesca Residence (Retirement), 39 N. Portage Path, Akron 44303 (41).

House of Loreto (Nursing Home), 2812 Harvard Ave. N.W., Canton 44709 (100).

Jennings Hall, Inc. (Nursing Care), 10204 Granger Rd., Garfield Heights 44125 (100).

Little Sisters of the Poor, Sacred Heart Home, 4900 Navarre Ave., Oregon 43616 (126).

Little Sisters of the Poor, Sts. Mary and Joseph Home for Aged, 4291 Richmond Rd., Cleveland 44122 (133).

The Maria-Joseph Living Care Center, 4830 Salem Ave., Dayton 45416 (440).

Mercy St. Theresa Center (Rest Home and Nursing Facility), 6760 Belkenton Ave., Cincinnati 45236 (100).

Mercy Siena Woods (Nursing Home, Skilled and Intermediate Care), 235 W. Orchard Spring Dr., Dayton 45415 (99).

Mount Alverna (Residence for Aged), 6765 State Rd., Cleveland 44134 (203).

Mt. St. Joseph (Skilled Nursing Facility, Dual Certified), 21800 Chardon Rd., Cleveland 44117 (100).

Nazareth Towers, 300 E. Rich St., Columbus 43215. Hi-rise apartments for independent living for senior citizens (208).

St. Augustine Manor (Skilled Nursing Facility), 7800 Detroit Ave., Cleveland 44102 (194).

St. Clare Retirement Community (Nursing Home, Rest Home, Apartments), Franciscan Sisters of the Poor, 100 Compton Rd., Cincinnati 45215 (171).

St. Francis Home, Inc. (Residence and Nursing Care), 182 St. Francis Ave., Tiffin 44883 (116).

St. Francis Rehabilitation Hospital and Nursing Home, 401 N. Broadway St., Green Springs 44836 (186).

St. Joseph's Hospice (Nursing Home), 2308 Reno Dr., Louisville 44641 (100).

St. Margaret Hall (Rest Home and Nursing Facility), 1960 Madison Rd., Cincinnati 45206 (135).

St. Raphael Home (Nursing Home), 1550 Roxbury Rd., Columbus 43212 (78).

St. Rita's Home (Skilled Nursing Home), 880 Greenlawn Ave., Columbus 43223 (100).

Schroder Manor (Residence, Skilled Nursing Care and Independent Living Units), Franciscan Sisters of the Poor, 1302 Millville Ave., Hamilton 45013 (173).

The Villa Sancta Anna Home for the Aged, Inc., 25000 Chagrin Blvd., Beachwood 44122 (68).

The Village at St. Edward (Apartments, Nursing Care and Assisted Living), 3131 Smith Rd., Fairlawn 44333 (276).

Oklahoma: Franciscan Villa, 17110 E. 51st St. S., Broken Arrow 74012. Intermediate nursing care (60); apartments (40 independent; 22 assisted living).

St. Ann's Home, 9400 St. Ann's Dr., Oklahoma City 73162 (82).

Westminster Village, Inc. (Residence), 1601 Academy, Ponca City 74604. Apartments, 50 units; residential care, 20; nursing care, 38.

Oregon: Benedictine Nursing Center and Home Health Agency, S. Main St., Mt. Angel 97362 (130).

Evergreen Court Retirement Apartments, 451 O'-Connell St., North Bend 97459 (77).

Maryville Nursing Home, 14645 S.W. Farmington, Beaverton 97007 (137).

Mt. St. Joseph Residence and Extended Care Center, 3060 S.E. Stark St., Portland 97214 (280).

St. Catherine's Residence and Nursing Center, 3959 Sheridan Ave., North Bend 97459 (166).

St. Elizabeth Health Care Center, 3985 Midway, Baker City 97814 (120).

Pennsylvania: Ascension Manor I (Senior Citizen Housing), 911 N. Franklin St., Philadelphia 19123 (140 units).

Ascension Manor II (Senior Citizen Housing), 970 N. 7th St., Philadelphia 19123 (140 units).

Benetwood Apartments for Elderly and Handicapped (Low Income), 641 Troupe Rd., Harborcreek 16421 (75).

Bethlehem Retirement Village, 100 W. Wissahickon Ave., Flourtown 19031. Apartments for well elderly (100).

Christ the King Manor, 1100 W. Long Ave., Du Bois 15801 (160).

D'Youville Manor (Personal Care Residence), 1750 Quarry Rd., Yardley 19067.

Garvey Manor (Nursing Home), Logan Blvd., Hollidaysburg 16648 (150).

Holy Family Apartments (Low Income), Clay and Valley Sts., New Philadelphia 17959 (11).

Holy Family Home, Little Sisters of the Poor, 5300 Chester Ave., Philadelphia 19143 (111).

Holy Family Manor (Skilled and Intermediate Nursing Facility), 1200 Spring St., Bethlehem 18018 (210).

Holy Family Residence (Residential Care Facility), 417 Hayes St., Bethlehem 18015 (15).

Holy Family Residence (Residential Care Facility), 217 Spring Garden St., Easton 18042 (14).

Holy Family Residence (Personal Care Facility), 570 Wood St., Emmaus 18049 (14).

Holy Family Residence (Personal Care Facility), 900 W. Market St., Orwigsburg 17961 (50).

Holy Redeemer Health System, Inc. (Sisters of the Holy Redeemer), sponsor: Redeemer Village I & II (Senior Citizen Housing), 1551 Huntingdon Pike, Huntingdon Valley 19006 (199 apartments); St. Joseph's Manor (Long-Term Care for Elderly), 1616 Huntingdon Pike, Meadowbrook 19046 (200 skilled nursing and 65 personal care beds). Also sponsor home-care and hospice programs at two other locations.

Immaculate Mary Home (Nursing Care Facility), 2990 Holme Ave., Philadelphia 19136 (296).

John XXIII Home (Silled, Inermediate and Personal Care), 2250 Shenango Freeway, Hermitage 16148 (142).

Little Flower Manor Nursing Home (Skilled Nursing), 1201 Springfield Rd., Darby 19023 (125).

Little Flower Manor of Diocese of Scranton, (Long-Term Skilled Nursing Care Facility), 200 S. Meade St., Wilkes-Barre 18702 (133).

Little Sisters of the Poor, 1028 Benton Ave. N.S., Pittsburgh 15212 (127).

Little Sisters of the Poor, Holy Family Residence, 2500 Adams Ave., Scranton 18509 (59).

Maria Joseph Manor (Skilled, Intermediate and Personal Care Facility), 875 Montour Blvd., Danville 17821 (96).

Marian Hall Home for the Aged (Women), 934 Forest Ave., Pittsburgh 15202 (25).

Marian Manor (Intermediate Care), 2695 Winchester Dr., Pittsburgh 15220 (170).

Mount Macrina Manor (Skilled Nursing Facility), P.O. Box 548, Uniontown 15401 (160).

Neumann Apartments (Low Income), 25 N. Nichols St., St. Clair 17970 (25).

Queen of Angels Apartments (Elderly and Handicapped), 22 Rothermel St., Hyde Park, Reading 19605 (45 units).

Queen of Peace Apartments (Low Income), 777 Water St., Pottsville 17901 (65).

Sacred Heart Manor (Nursing Home and Independent Living), 6445 Germantown Ave., Philadelphia 19119 (267).

St. Anne's Home and Village, 3952 Columbia Ave., Columbia 17512 (Nursing home, 121; personal care, 16; independent living, 36 cottages).

St. Anne Home for the Elderly (Nursing Facility), 685 Angela Dr., Greensburg 15601 (125).

St. Basil's Home for Aged Women (Residential), 530 W. Main St., Box 878, Uniontown 15401 (11).

St. Ignatius Nursing Home, 4401 Haverford Ave., Philadelphia 19104 (176).

St. John Neumann Nursing Home, 10400 Roosevelt Blvd., Philadelphia 19116 (224).

St. Joseph Home for the Aged (Residential and Skilled Nursing Facility), 1182 Holland Rd., Holland 18966 (96).

St. Joseph Nursing and Health Care Center (Skilled Nursing Facility), 5324 Penn Ave., Pittsburgh 15224 (158).

St. Joseph's House of Hospitality (Low Income

Senior Citizen Residence for Men and Women), 1635 Bedford Ave., Pittsburgh 15219 (65).

St. Joseph's Residence, 1111 1/2 S. Cascade St., New Castle 16101.

St. Leonard's Home Inc. (Personal Care Facility), 601 N. Montgomery St., Hollidaysburg 16648 (21).

St. Mary of Providence Center, R.D. 2, Box 145, Elverson 19520 (Senior Citizen Housing, 39 units). Center is also a House of Spirituality.

St. Mary's Home of Erie, 607 E. 26th St., Erie 16504. Residential and personal care (131); skilled and intermediate nursing care (227, includes Alzheimer Center, 35); adult day care (22).

Saint Mary's Manor (Residential, Personal Care, Short-Term Rehabilitation and Nursing Care), 701 Lansdale Ave., Lansdale 19446 (160).

St. Mary's Villa Nursing Home, Elmhurst 18416 (112).

Villa de Marillac Nursing Home, 5300 Stanton Ave., Pittsburgh 15206 (52).

Villa St. Teresa (Residence, Women), 1215 Springfield Rd., Darby 19023 (53).

Villa Teresa (Nursing Home), 1051 Avila Rd., Harrisburg 17109 (184).

Vincentian Home for the Chronically Ill., Perrymont Rd., Pittsburgh 15237 (221).

Rhode Island: Jeanne Jugan Residence of the Little Sisters of the Poor, 964 Main St., Pawtucket 02860 (99).

Saint Antoine Residence (Nursing Facility), 400 Mendon Rd., North Smithfield 02895 (243).

St. Clare Home (Nursing Facility), 309 Spring St., Newport 02840 (46).

St. Francis House, 167 Blackstone St., Woonsocket 02895 (50).

Scalabrini Villa (Convalescent, Rest — Nursing Home). 860 N. Quidnessett Rd., North Kingstown 02852 (70).

South Carolina: Carter-May Home, 1660 Ingram Rd., Charleston 29407 (12). Personal care home for elderly ladies.

South Dakota: Brady Memorial Home (Skilled Nursing Facility), 500 S. Ohlman St., Mitchell 57301 (83). Independent living units (3); congregate apartments (6); adult day care.

Maryhouse, Inc. (Skilled Nursing Facility), 717 E. Dakota, Pierre 57501 (105).

Mother Joseph Manor (Skilled Nursing Facility), 1002 North Jay St., Aberdeen 57401. Apartment units (7). Adult day care program. Respite nursing care.

Prince of Peace Retirement Community, 4500 Prince of Peace Pl., Sioux Falls 57103. Skilled nursing home (90 beds); independent living apartments (51).

St. William's Home for the Aged (Intermediate Care, 60), and Angela Hall (Supervised Living, 20), 901 E. Virgil, Box 432, Milbank 57252. Adult day care program (10).

Sister James Nursing Home, Yankton, SD 57078.

Tekakwitha Nursing Home (Skilled and Intermediate Care), Sisseton 57262 (101). Tekakwitha

Housing Corp. (Independent Living), P.O. Box 208, Sisseton 57262 (24 units).

Tennessee: Alexian Village of Tennessee (Retired Men and Women), 100 James Blvd., Signal Mountain 37377 (235 retirement apartments) and Health Care Center (124).

St. Mary Manor, 1771 Highway 45 Bypass, Jackson 38305 (149 retirement apartments).

St. Peter Manor, 108 N. Auburndale, Memphis 38104.

St. Peter Villa (Intermediate and Skilled Care), 141 N. McLean, Memphis 38104 (180).

Villa Maria Manor, 2400 21st Ave., Nashville 37212 (238).

Texas: Casa Housing for Elderly and Handicapped, 3201 Sondra Dr., Fort Worth 76107 (200).

Casa Brendan and Casa II Housing for the Elderly and Handicapped, 1300 Hyman St., Stephenville 76401 (86).

Home for Aged Women-Men, 920 S. Oregon St., El Paso 79901 (24).

John Paul II Nursing Home (Intermediate Care and Personal Care), 215 Tilden St., Kenedy 78219.

Mother of Perpetual Help Home (Intermediate Care Facility), 519 E. Madison Ave., Brownsville 78520 (38).

Mt. Carmel Home (Personal Care Home), 4130 S. Alameda St., Corpus Christi 78411 (92).

Nuestro Hogar Housing for Elderly and Handicapped, 709 Magnolia St., Arlington 76012 (65).

The Regis Retirement Home and St. Elizabeth Nursing Home, 400 Austin Ave., Waco 76701 (291).

St. Ann's Nursing Home, P.O. Box 1179, Panhandle 79068 (52).

St. Dominic Nursing Home, 6502 Grand Ave., Houston 77021 (120).

St. Dominic Residence Hall, 2401 E. Holcombe Blvd., Houston 77021 (80).

St. Francis Nursing Home (Home for Aged and Convalescents), 2717 N. Flores St., San Antonio 78212 (143).

St. Francis Village, Inc. (Retired and Elderly), 1 Chapel Plaza, Crowley 76036 (450).

St. Joseph Residence (Custodial Care Home), 330 W. Pembroke St., Dallas 75208 (49).

San Juan Nursing Home, Inc. (Skilled and Intermediate Care Facility), P.O. Box 1238, San Juan 78589 (127).

Villa Maria, Inc. (Apartment Complex), 3146 Saratoga Blvd., Corpus Christi 78415 (48 units). Corpus Christi diocese.

Utah: St. Joseph Villa (Nursing Care Facility), 475 Ramona Ave., Salt Lake City 84115 (175).

Vermont: Loretto Home for Aged, 59 Meadow St., Rutland 05701 (57).

Michaud Memorial Manor (Home for Aged), Derby Line 05830 (24).

St. Joseph's Home for Aged, 243 N. Prospect St., Burlington 05401 (52).

Virginia: Madonna Home, 814 W. 37th St., Norfolk 23508 (15).

Marian Manor (Assisted Living, Nursing Care), 5345 Marian Lane, Virginia Beach 23462 (100 units; 30 beds nursing care).

Marywood Apartments, 1261 Marywood Lane, Marywood 23229 (112 units).

McGurk House Apartments, 2425 Tate Springs Rd., Lynchburg 24501 (88 units).

Our Lady of the Valley Retirement Community, 650 N. Jefferson St., Roanoke 24016. Assisted living units (85); nursing centr (30 beds).

Russell House Apartments, 900 First Colonial Rd., Virginia Beach 23454 (127).

St. Francis Home, 2511 Wise St., Richmond 23225 (31).

St. Joseph's Home for the Aged, Little Sisters of the Poor, 1503 Michael Rd., Richmond 23229 (91).

St. Mary's Woods (Apartments, Assisted Living), 1257 Marywood Lane, Richmond 23229 (112 units).

Seton Manor (Apartments), 215 Marcella Rd., Hampton 23666 (112).

Washington: Cathedral Plaza Apartments (Retirement Apartments), W. 1120 Sprague Ave., Spokane 99204 (150).

Chancery Place (Retirement Apartments), 910 Marion, Seattle 98104.

The Delaney, W. 242 Riverside Ave., Spokane 99201 (84).

Elbert House, 16000 N.E. 8th St., Bellevue 98008.

Emma McRedmond Manor, 7960-169th N.E., Redmond 98052.

Fahy Garden Apartments, W. 1411 Dean Ave., Spokane 99201 (31).

Fahy West Apartments, W. 1523 Dean Ave., Spokane 99201 (55).

The Franciscan (Apartments), 15237-21st Ave. S.W., Seattle 98166 (38).

The Josephinum (Apartments), 1902 2nd Ave., Seattle 98101 (221).

Mt. St. Vincent Nursing Center and Retirement Apartments, 4831 35th Ave. S.W., Seattle 98126.

The O'Malley, E. 707 Mission, Spokane 99202 (100).

St. Brendan Nursing Home, E. 17 8th Ave., Spokane 99202.

St. Joseph Care Center (Skilled Long-Term Care), West 20-9th Ave., Spokane 99204 (103).

Tumwater Apartments, 5701-6th Ave. S.W.,Tumwater 98501 (50).

West Virginia: Welty Home for the Aged (Women), 21 Washington Ave., Wheeling 26003 (44).

Wisconsin: Alexian Village of Milwaukee (Retirement Community/Skilled Nursing Home), 7979 W. Glenbrook Rd., Milwaukee 53223 (324 apartments; 87 skilled nursing; 30 assisted living; adult day care).

Bethany-St. Joseph Health Care Center, 2501 Shelby Rd., La Crosse 54601 (226).

Clement Manor (Retirement Community and Skilled Nursing), 3939 S. 92nd St., Greenfield 53228 (164 skilled nursing; 99 apartments). Senior day care.

Divine Savior Nursing Home, 715 W. Pleasant St., Portage 53901 (111 skilled nursing; 14 self care).

Felician Village (Independent Living), 1700 S. 18th St., Manitowoc 54020 (119 apartments).

Franciscan Care Center, 2915 North Meade St., Appleton 54911 (235).

Franciscan Villa (Skilled Nursing Home), 3601 S. Chicago Ave., S. Milwaukee 53172 (150).

Hope Nursing Home, 438 Ashford Ave., Lomira 53048 (42).

McCormick Memorial Home, 212 Iroquois St., Green Bay 54301 (74).

Marian Catholic Home (Skilled Care Nursing Home), 3333 W. Highland Blvd., Milwaukee 53208 (360).

Marian Franciscan Home, 9632 W. Appleton Ave., Milwaukee 53225.

Marian Housing Center (Independent Living), 4105 Spring St., Racine 53405 (40).

Maryhill Manor Nursing Home, 501 Madison Ave., Niagara 54151 (49 skilled nursing; 6 assisted living units).

Milwaukee Catholic Home, Inc., 2462 N. Prospect Ave., Milwaukee 53211 (44 skilled nursing; 168 apartments).

Nazareth House (Skilled Nursing Facility), 814 Jackson St., Stoughton 53589 (99).

St. Ann Rest Home (Intermediate Care Facility, Women), 2020 S. Muskego Ave., Milwaukee 53204 (54).

St. Anne's Home for the Elderly (Aged Poor), 3800 N. 92nd St., Milwaukee 53222 (116 skilled nursing; 16 independent living units).

St. Camillus Campus (Skilled Care Nursing Home, Retirement Community, Community Based Residential Facility, Home Health), 10100 West Bluemound Road, Wauwatosa 53226 (188 skilled nursing, 297 apartments).

St. Catherine Infirmary (Nursing Home), 5635 Erie St., Racine 53402 (41).

St. Elizabeth Nursing Home, 502 St. Lawrence Ave., Janesville 53545 (43).

St. Francis Home, 620 S. 11th St., La Crosse 54601 (95).

St. Francis Home (Skilled Nursing Facility), 1800 New York Ave., Superior 54880 (192).

St. Francis Home (Skilled Nursing), 365 Gillett St., Fond du Lac 54935 (70).

St. Joan Antida Home, 6700 W. Beloit Rd., W. Allis 53219 (73).

St. Joseph's Home, 705 Clyman St., Watertown 53094 (28).

St. Joseph's Home, 9244 29th Ave., Kenosha 53140 (93). Independent living apartments; skilled nursing home; adult day care.

St. Joseph's Home, 5301 W. Lincoln Ave., W. Allis 53219 (136).

St. Joseph's Nursing Home, 464 S. St. Joseph Ave., Arcadia 54612 (75).

St. Joseph's Nursing Home, 2902 East Ave. S., La Crosse 54601 (80).

St. Joseph's Nursing Home, 400 Water Ave., Hillsboro 54634 (65).

St. Joseph Residence, Inc. (Nursing Home), 107 E. Beckert Rd., New London 54961 (107 skilled nursing; 10 apartments).

St. Mary's Home for the Aged (Residence and Skilled Nursing), 2005 Division St., Manitowoc 54220 (297).

St. Mary's Nursing Home (Skilled Nursing and Respite Care), 3516 W. Center St., Milwaukee 53210 (130).

St. Monica's Senior Citizens Home, 3920 N. Green Bay Rd., Racine 53404 (125).

St. Paul Home, Inc. (Intermediate and Skilled Nursing Home), 1211 Oakridge Ave., Kaukauna 54130 (129).

Villa Clement (Nursing Home), 9047 W. Greenfield Ave., W. Allis 53214 (190).

Villa Loretto Nursing Home, Mount Calvary 53057 (52).

Villa St. Anna (Residential Facility), 5737 Erie St., Racine, 53402.

Villa St. Francis, Inc., 1910 W. Ohio Ave., Milwaukee 53215.

FACILITIES FOR CHILDREN AND ADULTS WITH DISABILITIES

Sources: Almanac survey; *Directory of Catholic Special Educational Programs and Facilities, 1989,* published by the National Catholic Educational Association, Washington, D.C.; *Official Catholic Directory.*

This listing covers facilities and programs with educational and training orientation. Information about other services for the handicapped can generally be obtained from the Catholic Charities Office or its equivalent (c/o Chancery Office) in any diocese. (See Index for listing of addresses of chancery offices in the U.S.)

Abbreviation code: b, boys; c, coeducational; d, day; g, girls; r, residential. Other information includes chronological age for admission. The number in parentheses at the end of an entry indicates total capacity or enrollment.

Deaf and Hearing Impaired

California: St. Joseph's Center for Deaf and Hard of Hearing, 3880 Smith St., Union City 94587.

Colorado: Excelsior Youth Centers (r,g; 12-18 yrs.), 15001 E. Oxford, Aurora 80014 (147).

Iowa: Happy World Pre-School (d,c; 3-5 yrs.), 509 Ave. F., Ft. Madison 52627.

Louisiana: Chinchuba Institute (d,c; birth through 16 yrs.), 1131 Barataria Blvd., Marrero 70072.

Massachusetts: Boston School for the Deaf (d,c; 3-21 yrs.), 800 N. Main St., Randolph 02368 (85).

Missouri: St. Joseph Institute for the Deaf (r,d,c; birth to 14 years), 1483 82nd Blvd., St. Louis 63132 (120).

New Jersey: Mt. Carmel Guild Communication Disorders Program (c), 17 Mulberry St., Newark 07102.

New York: Cleary School for the Deaf (d,c; infancy through high school), 301 Smithtown Blvd., Nesconset, NY 11767 (105).

St. Francis de Sales School for the Deaf (d,c; infant through elementary grades), 260 Eastern Parkway, Brooklyn 11225 (220).

St. Joseph's School for the Deaf (d,c; parent-infant through 14 yrs.), 1000 Hutchinson River Pkwy, Bronx 10465 (160).

St. Mary's School for the Deaf (r,d,c; birth to 21 yrs.), 2253 Main St., Buffalo 14214 (165).

Ohio: St. Rita School for the Deaf (r,d,c; birth to 21 yrs.), 1720 Glendale-Milford Rd., Cincinnati 45215 (140).

Pennsylvania: Archbishop Ryan School for Hearing Impaired Children (d,c; parent-infant programs through 8th grade), 3509 Spring Garden St., Philadelphia 19104 (62).

De Paul Institute (d,c; birth through 15 yrs.), Castlegate Ave., Pittsburgh 15226 (115).

Emotionally and/or Socially Maladjusted

This listing includes facilities for abused, abandoned and neglected as well as emotionally disturbed children and youth.

Alabama: St. Mary's Home for Children (r,c; referred from agencies), 4350 Moffat Rd., Mobile 36618 (44).

California: Hanna Boys Center (r; 10-15 yrs. at intake; school goes to 10th grade), Box 100, Sonoma 95476 (95).

Rancho San Antonio (r,b; 13-17 yrs.), 21000 Plummer St., Chatsworth 91311 (102).

Colorado: Excelsior Youth Centers (r,g; 12-18 yrs.), 15001 E. Oxford, Aurora 80014 (141).

Mt. St. Vincent Home (r,c; 5-13 yrs.), 4159 Lowell Blvd., Denver 80211 (45).

Connecticut: St. Francis Home for Children (r,d,c; 4-17 yrs.), 651 Prospect St., New Haven 06511 (70).

Mt. St. John (r,b; 11-16 yrs.), 135 Kirtland St., Deep River 06417 (75). Home and school for boys.

Delaware: Our Lady of Grace Home for Children (r,d,c; 6-12 yrs.), 487 E. Chestnut Hill Rd., Newark 19713 (16).

Seton Villa and Siena Hall (c; group home; 5-18 yrs,), c/o 2307 Kentmere Pkwy, Wilmington 19806.

Florida: Boystown of Florida (r,b; 12-16 yrs.; group home), 11400 S.W. 137th Ave., Miami 33186 (43).

Georgia: Village of St. Joseph (r,c; 6-16 yrs.), 2969 Butner Rd. S.W., Atlanta 30331 (39). Residential treatment center and therapeutic special school for children with emotional problems, behavior disorders, learning disabilities.

Illinois: Guardian Angel (d,c), 1550 Plainfield Rd., Joliet 60435 (50).

Loyola Day School (d,c; 3-12 yrs.), 1043 W. Loyola Ave., Chicago 60626 (22).

Maryville Academy (r,c; 6-18 yrs.), 1150 North River Rd., Des Plaines 60016.

Mission of Our Lady of Mercy, Mercy Home for Boys and Girls (r,d,c; 15-18 yrs.), 1140 W. Jackson Blvd., Chicago 60607 (150).

St. Joseph Carondelet Child Center (r,b; d,c); 739 E. 35th St., Chicago 60616 (44 r, boys 5-18 yrs.; 76 d, coed 4-15 yrs.)

Indiana: Gibault School for Boys (r; 10-18 yrs.), 6301 South U.S. Highway 41, P.P. Box 2316, Terre Haute 47802 (135).

Hoosier Boys Town (r; 10-18 yrs.), 7403 Cline Ave., Schererville 46375 (60).

Kentucky: Boys' Haven (r; 12-18 yrs.), 2301 Goldsmith Lane, Louisville 40218 (32).

Maryhurst School (r,g; 13-17 yrs.), 1015 Dorsey Lane, Louisville 40223 (42).

Louisiana: Hope Haven Center (r,c; 5-18 yrs.), 1101 Barataria Blvd., Marrero 70072 (150). Residential treatment center and school.

Maison Marie Group Home (r,g; 14-18 yrs.), 3020 Independence St., Metairie 70006.

Maryland: Good Shepherd Center (r,g; 13-17 yrs.), 4100 Maple Ave., Baltimore. 21227 (105).

Massachusetts: McAuley Nazareth Home for Boys (r; 6-13 yrs.), 77 Mulberry St., Leicester 01524 (16). Residential treatment center.

Our Lady of Providence Children's Center/The Brightside for Families and Children (r,d,c; 6-16 yrs.), 2112 Riverdale St., W. Springfield 01089 (66). Diagnostic treatment program also.

St. Vincent Home (r,c 6-18 yrs.), 2425 Highland Ave., Fall River 02720 (62). Residential treatment center.

Michigan: Barat House, Barat Human Services, League of Catholic Women (r,g; 13-17 yrs.), 5250 John R., Detroit 48202 (24).

Boysville of Michigan, Inc. (r; 13-17 yrs.), 8744 Clinton-Macon Rd., Clinton 49236. Facilities located throughout the state.

Don Bosco Hall (r,b; 13-17 years.), 10001 Petoskey Ave., Detroit 48204 (35).

St. Vincent Home for Children (r,c; 10-16 yrs.), 2800 W. Willow St., Lansing 48917 (30).

Vista Maria (r,g; 11-18 yrs.), 20651 W. Warren Ave., Dearborn Heights 48127 (150).

Minnesota: St. Cloud Children's Home (r,c; 8-18 yrs.), 1726 7th Ave. S., St. Cloud 56301 (83). Day Treatment Program (d,c; 7-14 yrs.), same address (12). Intensive Care Unit (r,c; 13-17 yrs.), Box 1006, Fergus Falls 56538 (12).

St. Elizabeth Home (r,c; 18 yrs. and older), 306 15th Ave. N., St. Cloud 56301 (14). Primarily for mentally ill.

Missouri: Child Center of Our Lady (r,d,c; 5-14 yrs. — d,c; 4-14 yrs.), 7900 Natural Bridge Rd., St. Louis. 63121 (40).

Marygrove (r,d,c; 6-21 yrs.), 2705 Mullanphy Lane, Florissant. 63031 (97).

St. Joseph's Home for Boys (r,d,b), 4753 S. Grand Blvd., St. Louis 63111.

Nebraska: Father Flanagan's Boys' Home (r,c; 10-16 yrs.), Boys Town 68010 (556). Boys Town National Research Hospital (r,d,c; 1-18 yrs.), 555 N. 30th St., Omaha 68131. Center for Abused Handicapped Children; diagnosis of speech, language and hearing problems in children. Boys Town also has various facilities or programs in Brooklyn, N.Y.; Portsmouth, R.I.; Philadelphia, Pa.; Washington, D.C.; Tallahassee, Orlando and Delray Beach, Fla.; New Orleans, La.; San Antonio, Tex., Las Vegas, Nev., and southern California.

New Jersey: Catholic Community Service/Mt. Carmel Guild (d,c; 3-20 yrs.), 17 Mulberry St., Newark 07102. Day school, four locations.

Christopher House (c; 18 and over), 55 N. Clinton Ave., Trenton 08607 (90). Psychiatric day treatment.

Collier Group Home (r,g; 13-18 yrs.), 180 Spring St., Red Bank 07701 (12).

Collier High School (d,c; 13-18 yrs.), Conover Rd., Wickatunk 07765 (140).

Guidance Clinic of Catholic Charities (c), 39 N.

Clinton Ave., Trenton 08607. Psychiatric counseling for children and adults.

Mt. St. Joseph Children's Center (r,d,b; 6-12 yrs.), Shepherd Lane, Totowa 07512 (32).

New York: The Astor Home for Children (r,d,c; 5-12 yrs.), 36 Mill St., P.O. Box 5000, Rhinebeck 12572 (75). Group Home (7-12 yrs.), same address (10). Child Guidance Clinics/Day Treatment (Rhinebeck, Poughkeepsie, Beacon, Bronx). Head Start — Day Care (Poughkeepsie, Beacon, Red Hook, Dover, Millerton).

Baker Hall (r,d,c; 10-17 yrs.), 150 Martin Rd., Lackawanna 14218. Special services (18), institution (24), residential treatment facility (45), group homes (27), foster homes (10), preventive services (250), special education school (100), day treatment (52), out-patient clinic (75).

Good Shepherd Services, 337 W. 17th St., New York 10003. Residential programs for adolescents; community-based neighborhood family services in Park Slope and Red Hook, Brooklyn.

LaSalle School (r,d,b; 12-18 yrs.), 391 Western Ave., Albany. 12203 (145). Also conducts independent living apartments and prevention programs.

Madonna Heights Services (r,d,g; 12-18 yrs.), 151 Burrs Lane, Dix Hills 11746 (110). Also conducts group homes on Long Island and outpatient programs.

Saint Anne Institute (r,d,g; 12-18 yrs.), 160 N. Main Ave., Albany 12206 (140). Critical level, preventive services. Sex abuse prevention and juvenile sex offender programs, substance abuse program. Regents accredited school. Non-residential pre-school for 3-4 year olds.

St. Catherine's Center for Children (r,d,c; birth through 12 yrs.), 40 N. Main Ave., Albany 12203 (150). Group homes, day treatment, prevention and specialized foster care programs.

St. John's of Rockaway Beach (r,b; 9-21 yrs.), 144 Beach 111th St., Rockaway Park 11694 (100). Also conducts a non secured detention facility with the Dept. of Juvenile Justice in Richmond Hill, N.Y. Rockaway Beach programs include Diagnostic centers and independent living programs.

North Dakota: Home on the Range (r,c; 11-18 yrs.), HC1, Box 41, Sentinel Butte. 58654 (79). Residential and emergency shelter therapeutic programs.

Ohio: Diocesan Child Guidance Center, Inc. (d,c; preschool) Outpatient counseling program (c; 2-18 yrs.), 840 W. State St., Columbus 43222.

Marycrest (r,g; 13-18 yrs.), 7800 Brookside Rd., Independence 44131 (70). Residential treatment and transitional living for adolescent girls and adolescent mothers.

Parmadale Family Services Village (r,c; 12 -18 yrs.), 6753 State Rd., Parma 44134.

Rosemont (r,g;d,c; 11-18 yrs.), 2440 Dawnlight Ave., Columbus 43211 (150). Baby day care (birth-3 yrs.); outreach to single parents; home-based services (2-19 yrs.).

Oregon: St. Mary's Home for Boys (r; 9-18 yrs.), 16535 S.W. Tualatin Valley Highway, Beaverton 97006 (56).

Pennsylvania: De LaSalle in Towne (d,b; 14-17 yrs.), 25 S. Van Pelt St., Philadelphia 19103 (80).

De LaSalle Vocational Day Treatment (b; 15-17 yrs.), P.O. Box 344 — Street Rd. and Bristol Pike, Bensalem 19020 (120).

Gannondale (r; 12-17 yrs.), 4635 E. Lake Rd., Erie 16511 (57).

Harborcreek Youth Services (r,d,c; 10-17 yrs.), 5712 Iroquois Ave., Harborcreek 16421 (150). Also conducts group homes.

Holy Family Institute (r,d,c; 7-17 yrs.), 8235 Ohio River Blvd., Pittsburgh 15202 (75). Also conducts in-home services.

Lourdesmont Good Shepherd Youth and Family Services (r,g;d,c; 13-17 yrs.), 537 Venard Rd., Clarks Summit 18411 (100).

Pauline Auberle Foundation (r,c; 7-18 yrs.), 1101 Hartman St., McKeesport 15132 (57). Residential treatment for boys; emergency shelter care, foster care, group home for girls and family preservation program.

St. Gabriel's Hall (r,b; 10-18 yrs.), P.O. Box 7280, Audubon 19407 (220). Also conducts group homes.

St. Michael's School (r,b; d,c; 12-17 yrs.), Box 370, Tunkhannock 18657 (150). Also conducts group homes, day treatment program and foster care.

Tennessee: DeNeuville Heights School for Girls (r; 12-17 yrs.), 3060 Baskin St., Memphis 38127 (52).

St. Peter Home (r,g), 1805 Poplar, Memphis 38104.

Texas: St. Joseph Youth Center (r,c; 13-17 yrs.), 901 S. Madison St., Dallas 75208 (52).

Washington: Morning Star Boys Ranch (Spokane Boys' Ranch, Inc.), (r,b; 10-18 yrs.), Box 8087 Manito Station, Spokane 99203 (30).

Wisconsin: Our Lady of Charity Family Program (r,c; 10-17 yrs.), 2640 West Point Rd., P.O. Box 11737, Green Bay 54304 (27).

St. Charles Youth and Family Services (r,d,b; 12-18 yrs.), 151 S. 84th St., Milwaukee 53214 (63).

Wyoming: St. Joseph's Children's Home (r,c; 6-18 yrs.), P.O. Box 1117, Torrington 82240 (50). Also conducts group home. Newell Children's Center (r,c; 6-18 years), same address (12).

Developmentally Disabled

This listing includes facilities for children, youth and adults with learning disabilities.

Alabama: Father Purcell Memorial Exceptional Children's Center (r, c; birth to 10 yrs.), 2048 W. Fairview Ave., Montgomery 36108 (58). Skilled nursing facility.

Father Walter Memorial Child Care Center (r,c; birth-12 yrs.), 2815 Forbes Dr., Montgomery 36110 (44). Skilled nursing facility.

California: Child Study Center of St. John's Hospital (d,c; birth-18 yrs.), 1339 - 20th St., Santa Monica. 90404 (80).

Helpers of the Mentally Retarded, Inc., 2626 Fulton St., San Francisco 94118. Conducts three homes: Helpers Home for Girls (18 years and older), 2608 Fulton St. and 2626 Fulton St., San Francisco 94118; Helpers Home for Men (18 years and older), 2750 Fulton St., San Francisco 94118.

St. Madeleine Sophie's Center (d,c; 18 yrs. and older), 2111 E. Madison Ave., El Cajon 92019 (142).

St. Vincent's (r,d,c; 7-21 yrs.), 4200 Calle Real, P.O. Box 669, Santa Barbara 93102 (90).

Tierra del Sol Foundation (d,c; 18 yrs. and older), 9919 Sunland Blvd., Sunland 91040 (200); 7033 Hayvenhurst Ave., Van Nuys 91406 (38); Claremont (25).

Connecticut: Gengras Center (d,c; 3-21 yrs.), St. Joseph College, 1678 Asylum Ave., W. Hartford 06117 (112).

Special Education Office, Diocese of Bridgeport, 238 Jewett Ave., Bridgeport 06606.

Villa Maria Education Center (d,c), 159 Sky Meadow Dr., Stamford 06903 (55). For children with learning disabilities.

District of Columbia: Lt. Joseph P. Kennedy, Jr., Institute (d,c; 6 weeks to 5 yrs. for preschool program; 5-21 yrs. for school program; 18 yrs. and older for other programs which include continuing education, training and employment, therapeutic and residential services. Headquarters: 801 Buchanan St. N.E. Washington 20017. Other locations in District of Columbia and Maryland (Prince George and Montgomery counties). No enrollment limit.

St. Gertrude's School and Development Program (d,c;r,g; 6-19 yrs.), 4801 Sargent Rd. N.E., Washington 20017.

Florida: Harbor House, (c; 18 yrs. and older; group home), 700-2 Arlington Rd., Jacksonville 32211.

Marian Center Services for Developmentally Handicapped and Mentally Retarded (r,d,c; 2-21 yrs.), 15701 Northwest 37th Ave., Opa Locka 33054. Offers variety of services.

Morning Star School (d,c; 4-14 yrs.), 725 Mickler Rd., Jacksonville 32211 (100). For children with learning disabilities.

Morning Star School (d,c; school age), 954 Leigh Ave., Orlando 32804 (55).

Morning Star School (d,c; 6-10 yrs.), 4661-80th Ave. N., Pinellas Park 34665 (60). For children with learning disabilities and other learning handicaps.

Morning Star School (d,c; 6-16 yrs.), 210 E. Linebaugh Ave., Tampa 33612. (95). For children with learning disabilities.

Georgia: St. Mary's Home (r,c), 2170 E. Victory Dr., Savannah 31404.

Illinois: Bartlett Learning Center (r,d,c; 3-21 yrs.), 801 W. Bartlett Rd., Bartlett 60103 (121).

Brother James Court (r, men over 18 yrs.), 2500 St. James Rd., Springfield 62707 (96).

Good Shepherd Manor (r,b; 18 yrs. and older), Little Brothers of the Good Shepherd, P.O. Box 260, Momence. 60954 (120). Resident care for adult males.

Misericordia Home South (r,c), 2916 W. 47th St., Chicago 60632 (110).

Misericordia Home - Heart of Mercy Village (r,c; 6-35 yrs.), 6300 North Ridge, Chicago 60660 (232).

Mt. St. Joseph (developmentally disabled women; over age 25), 24955 N. Highway 12, Lake Zurich 60047 (160).

St. Coletta's of Illinois (r,d,c; 6 to adult), 123rd and Wolf Rd., Palos Park 60464: St. Coletta's Residential Program (111 in 19 group homes and apartments); Lt. Joseph P. Kennedy, Jr., School (50d, 80r); Kennedy Job Training Center (100d, 40r).

St. Francis School for Exceptional Children (r,c; 2-12 yrs.), 1209 S. Walnut Ave., Freeport 61032 (40).

St. Jude Special Education Center (d,c), 2nd and Spring Ave., Aviston 62216.

St. Mary of Providence (r,g; 6 to adult), 4200 N. Austin Ave., Chicago 60634 (110). Day program (c; 6-21 yrs.).

St. Rose Center (d,c; 3-21 yrs.), 4911 S. Hoyne Ave., Chicago 60609 (60). For mentally handicapped children.

St. Vincent Community Living Facility (adults, over 18 yrs.) (20), and St. Vincent Supported Living Arrangement (adults, over 18 yrs.) (20), 659 E. Jefferson St., Freeport 61032.

Springfield Developmental Center (m; 21 yrs. and over), 2500 St. James Rd., Springfield 62707. Vocational training.

Indiana: Marian Day Program (d,c; 6-16 yrs.), 700 Herndon Dr., Evansville 47711 (35). For learning disabled.

Providence House (nursing facility, men; 18 yrs. and up), 520 W. 9th St., Jasper 47546 (58).

Kansas: Lakemary Center, Inc. (r,c), 100 Lakemary Dr., P.O. Box 449, Paola 66071. Children education and training (3-16 yrs.); adult residence and training (16 yrs. and up).

Kentucky: Ursuline-Pitt School (d,c), 2117 Payne St., Louisville 40206 (75).

Ursuline Speech Clinic (d,c; 3 yrs.-adult), 3105 Lexington Rd., Louisville 40206 (65).

Louisiana: Department of Special Education, Archdiocese of New Orleans, St. Michael Special School (d,c; 6-16 yrs.), 1522 Chippewa St., New Orleans 70130.

Holy Angels Residential Facility (r,c; teen-age, 14 yrs. and older), 10450 Ellerbe Rd., Shreveport 71106 (180).

Ocean Avenue Community House, 361 Ocean Ave., Gretna 70053. Group home (6).

Padua Community Services (r,c; birth-21 yrs.), 200 Beta St., Belle Chase 70037 (32).

St. Jude the Apostle, 1430 Claire Ave., Gretna 70053. Group home (6).

St. Mary's Residential Training School (r,c: 3-22 yrs.), P.O. Drawer 7768, Alexandria 71306 (152).

Sts. Mary and Elizabeth, 720 N. Elm St., Metairie 70003. Group home (6).

St. Peter the Fisherman, 235 Airport Dr., Slidell 70458. Group home (6).

St. Rosalie (r; men 18 and up), 119 Kass St., Gretna 70056. Group home (6).

Maryland: The Benedictine School for Exceptional Children (r,c; 6-21 yrs.), Ridgely 21660 (145). Also conducts Habilitation Center (r,c; 17 yrs. and older) (50) and 17 community-based homes (21 yrs. and older).

Francis X. Gallagher Services (r), 2520 Pot Spring Rd., Timonium 21093 (186). Adult day activity (180).

St. Elizabeth School and Habilitation Center (d,c; 12-21 yrs.), 801 Argonne Dr., Baltimore 21218 (99).

Massachusetts: Cardinal Cushing School and Training Center (r,d,c; 10-22 yrs.), Hanover 02339 (130 r; 40 d).

Mercy Centre for Developmental Disabilities (d,c; 3-22 yrs. and over), 25 West Chester St., Worcester 01605 (176).

St. Coletta Day School (d,c; 5-22 yrs.), 85 Washington St., Braintree 02184 (132).

Michigan: Our Lady of Providence Center, 16115 Beck Rd., Northville. 48167.

St. Louis Center and School (r,d,b; 6-18 yrs. child care; 18-26 yrs. adult foster care), 16195 Old U.S. 12, Chelsea 48118 (68).

Minnesota: Mother Teresa Home (r,c; 18 yrs. and older), 101-10th Ave. N., Cold Spring 56320 (14).

St. Francis Home (r,c; 9-12 yrs.), 25-2nd St. N., Waite Park 56387.

Missouri: Department of Special Education, Archdiocese of St. Louis, 4472 Lindell Blvd., St. Louis. 63108. Conducts St. Mary's Special School and St. Joseph's Vocational Center (see separate entries) and special ungraded day classes in 15 parish schools (c; 5-16 yrs.). Total number of children served, 700.

Good Shepherd Homes (residential for developmentally disabled men; 18 yrs. and up), The Community of the Good Shepherd, 10101 James A. Reed Rd., Kansas City 64134 (30).

St. Casimir Group Home (r; young women, 16-21 yrs.), 10735 Vorhof Dr., St. Louis 63136.

St. Joseph's Vocational Center (d,c; 15-21 yrs.), 5341 Emerson Ave., St. Louis 63120 (150).

St. Mary's Special School (r,d,c; 5-16 yrs.), 5341 Emerson Ave., St. Louis 63120 (123).

Vogelweid Learning Center (d,c; 5-14 yrs.), 314 W. High St., Jefferson City 65101 (25).

Nebraska: Madonna School for Exceptional Children (d,c; 5-21 yrs.), 2537 N. 62nd St., Omaha 68104 (65). Children with learning problems.

Villa Marie School and Home for Exceptional Children (r,d,c; 6-18 yrs.), P.O. Box 80328, Lincoln 68501 (18).

New Jersey: Alhambra Child Study Center (d,c; 5-12 yrs.), 31 Centre St., Newark 07102 (35).

Archbishop Boland Rehabilitation Center (d,c; 16-60 yrs.), 450 Market St. Newark 07105 (350).

Archbishop Damiano School (d,c; 5-21 yrs.), 532 Delsea Dr., Westville Grove 08093.

Catholic Communities Services, Archdiocese of Newark, 17 Mulberry St., Newark 07102. Services include: Alhambra Child Study Center, Archbishop Boland Rehabilitation Center, Mt. Carmel Guild, St. Anthony's and St. Patrick's Special Education Schools (see separate entries).

Department of Special Education, Diocese of Camden, 1845 Haddon Ave., Camden 08101. Services include: Archbishop Damiano School (above), and full time programs at 6 Catholic Schools; religious education programs.

Department for Persons with Disabilities, Diocese of Paterson, 1049 Weldon Rd., Oak Ridge, N.J. 07438. Services include 8 residential programs for adults, one adult training center, family support services.

Felician School for Exceptional Children (d,c; 5-21 yrs.), 260 S. Main St., Lodi 07644 (145).

McAuley School for Exceptional Children (d,c; 5-21 yrs.), 1633 Rt. 22 at Terrill Rd., Watchung 07060 (48).

St. Anthony's Special Education School (d,c; 10-20 yrs.), 25 N. 7th St., Belleville 07109 (40).

Sr. Georgine Learning Center (d,c; 6-17 yrs.), 544 Chestnut Ave., Trenton 08611 (30).

St. Patrick's Special Education School (d,c; 6-16 yrs.), 72 Central Ave., Newark 07102 (64).

New York: Cantalician Center for Learning (d,c; birth-21 yrs.), 3233 Main St., Buffalo 14214. Infant and pre-school; elementary and secondary; workshop (600). Two group homes.

Catholic Charities Residential Services (21 years and up), 155 Indian Head Rd., Commack 11725. Conducts eight residences for developmentally disabled adults; Regina Residence for unwed mothers; Siena Residence for mental health.

Cobb Memorial School (r,d,c; 5-21 yrs.), Altamont 12009 (32).

L'Arche (r, adults), 1701 James St., Syracuse 13206 (12). Homes where assistants and persons with developmental disabilities share life, following the philosophy of Jean Vanier. Member of International L'Arche Federation.

Maryhaven Center of Hope (r,d,c; school age to adult), Myrtle Ave., Port Jefferson 11777. Offers variety of services.

Mercy Home for Children (r,c), 310 Prospect Park West, Brooklyn 11215. Conducts six residences for adolescents and young adults who are developmentally disabled. (72)

Office for Disabled Persons, Catholic Charities, Diocese of Brooklyn, 191 Joralemon St., Brooklyn 11201. Services include: adult day treatment center; 17 community residences for mentally retarded adults; special events for disabled children (from age 3) and adults.

Office for Disabled Persons, Archdiocese of New York, 1011 First Ave., New York 10022. Services include consultation and referral, variety of services for deaf, blind, mentally retarded, mentally ill.

Our Lady of Victory Infant Home (r), 790 Ridge Rd., Lackawanna, N.Y. 14218. Residential care for handicapped and retarded children; nursery school program for emotionally disturbed pre-school children.

School of the Holy Childhood (d,c; 5-21 yrs.), 100 Groton Parkway, Rochester 14623 (94). Adult program, 18-50 yrs.

Seton Foundation for Learning (d,c; 5-15 yrs.), 30 Manor Rd., Staten Is. 10310.

North Carolina: Holy Angels (r,c; birth to adult), 427 E. Wilkinson Blvd., Belmont 28012 (65).

North Dakota: Friendship (r,c; 5 and older), 3004 11th St. South, Fargo 58103.

Ohio: Good Shepherd Manor (residential care and programming for developmentally disabled men 22 years and older), Little Brothers of the Good Shepherd, P.O. Box 387, Wakefield 45687 (110).

Julie Billiart School (d,c; 6-12 yrs.), 4982 Clubside Rd., Cleveland 44124 (125). Non-graded school for children with learning problems.

Mary Immaculate School (d,c; 6-14 yrs.), 3837 Secor Rd., Toledo 43623 (80). For children with learning disabilities.

Mount Aloysius, Inc. (r, adult men), Little Brothers of the Good Shepherd, 5375 Tile Plant Rd., New Lexington 43764 (80).

OLA/St. Joseph Center (d,c; 6-16 yrs.), 2346 W. 14th St., Cleveland 44113 (80).

Our Lady of the Elms Special School (d,c; 4-14

yrs.), Dominican Sisters, 1230 W. Market St., Akron 44313 (59). For learning disabled.

Rose Mary, The Johanna Graselli Rehabilitation and Education Center (r,c; 3-12 yrs.), 19350 Euclid Ave., Cleveland 44117 (40).

St. John's Villa (r,c; continued care and training, 15 yrs. and over), 620 Roswell Rd. N.W., Carrollton 44615 (143).

Oregon: Emily School Early Intervention Program (d,c; 3-5 yrs.), 830 N.E. 47th Ave., Portland 97213 (12).

Pennsylvania: Clelian Heights School for Exceptional Children (r,d,c; 5-21 yrs.), R.D. 9, Box 607, Greensburg 15601 (140). Also conducts resocialization program (r,d,c; young adults).

Divine Providence Village (children/young adults), 686 Old Marple Rd., Springfield 19064 (96).

Don Guanella School (r,d,b; 6-21 yrs.) and C.K. Center (r,; adults, post-school age), 1797-1799 S. Sproul Rd., Springfield 19064. Don Guanella Village (residential for children/adult male) with mental retardation), same address.

John Paul II, Center for Special Learning (d,c; 5-21 yrs.), 450 S. 6th St., Reading 19602 (40).

McGuire Memorial (r,d,c; infancy to 7 yrs.), 2119 Mercer Rd., New Brighton 15066 (99).

Mercy Special Learning Center (d,c; 3-21 yrs. and early intervention), 830 S. Woodward St., Allentown 18103 (100).

Our Lady of Confidence Day School (d,c; 4½-21 yrs.), 10th and Lycoming Sts., Philadelphia 19140 (140).

Queen of the Universe Day Center (d,c; 4½-16 yrs.), Trenton Rd., Levittown 19056 (48).

St. Anthony School Programs (d,c; 5-21 yrs.), 2718 Custer Ave., Pittsburgh 15227 (75).

St. Joseph Center for Special Learning (d,c), 2075 W. Norwegian St., Pottsville 17901 (50).

St. Joseph's Center (r,d,c; birth-10 yrs.), 2010 Adams Ave., Scranton 18509 (93).

St. Katherine Day School (d,c; 4½-21 yrs.), 930 Bowman Ave., Wynnewood 19096.

Tennessee: Madonna Day School for Retarded Children (d,c; 5-16 yrs.), 4189 Leroy Ave., Memphis 38108 (52).

St. Bernard School for Exceptional Children, (c,d; 4-8 yrs.), 2021 21st Ave. S., Nashville 37212 (25).

Texas: Notre Dame of Dallas Special School and Vocational Center (d,c; 3-21 yrs.), 2018 Allen St., Dallas, Tex. 75204. Academic and vocational training for developmentally handicapped.

Virginia: St. Coletta School (d,c; 5-25 yrs.), 1305 N. Jackson St., Arlington 22201 (25). For developmentally disabled. Services include: occupational, physical and language therapy; vocational program with job search, placement, training and follow-up services.

St. Mary's Infant Home (r,c; 3 days-9 yrs.), 317 Chapel St., Norfolk 23504 (88). For multiple handicapped.

Washington: St. Anne's Children's Home (r,c), North 707 Cedar St., Spokane 99201.

St. Margaret's Hall (r,g; 18 yrs. and up), S. 707 McClellan, Spokane 99204.

Wisconsin: St. Coletta School, W4955, Jefferson. Academic or school program (r,c; 6-21 yrs.); Habilitation Program to prepare adolescents and young adults for gainful employment in community; employment for limited number of post adolescents; Alverno Personal Care Program; Coletta-James Transitional Group Home. (580)

St. Coletta Day School (c; 8-17 yrs.), 1740 N. 55th St., Milwaukee. 53208 (12).

Orthopedically/Physically Handicapped

Pennsylvania: St. Edmond's Home for Crippled Children (r,c; 6-21 yrs.)., 320 S. Roberts Rd., Rosemont 19010 (40).

Virginia: St. Joseph Villa Housing Corp. (adults), 8000 Washington Brook Rd., Richmond 23227 (30 apartments).

Visually Handicapped

Maine: Visually Handicapped Services (Diocesan Human Relations Services), 87 High St., Portland 04101; 15 Vaughn St., Caribou 04736; 382 Sabattus St., Lewiston 04240; 35 Elm St., Waterville 04901; 1066 Kenduskeag Ave., Bangor 04401. Itinerant teacher and other services.

New Jersey: St. Joseph's School for the Blind (r,d,c; 3-21 yrs.), 253 Baldwin Ave., Jersey City 07306 (40). For visually impaired, multiple handicapped.

New York: Lavelle School for the Blind, East 221st St. and Paulding Ave., Bronx 10469. Day program for pre-school, elementary and high school with support services. Additional unity for multi-handicapped visually impaired children ages 3-7. (120).

Pennsylvania: St. Lucy Day School (d,c; pre-K to 8th grade), 929 S. Farragut St., Philadelphia 19143. Also has part-time program for infants and toddlers (birth to 3 yrs.).

OTHER SOCIAL SERVICES

Cancer Hospitals or Homes: The following homes or hospitals specialize in the care of cancer patients. They are listed according to state.

Our Lady of Perpetual Help Home, Servants of Relief for Incurable Cancer, 760 Washington St., S.W., Atlanta, GA 30315 (48).

Rose Hawthorne Lathrop Home, Servants of Relief for Incurable Cancer, 1600 Bay St., Fall River, MA 02724 (35).

Our Lady of Good Counsel Home, Servants of

Relief for Incurable Cancer, 2076 St. Anthony Ave., St. Paul, MN 55104 (40).

Calvary Hospital, Inc., 1740 Eastchester Rd., Bronx, NY 10461 (200). Operated in connection with Catholic Charities, Department of Health and Hospitals, Archdiocese of New York.

St. Rose's Home, Servants of Relief for Incurable Cancer), 71 Jackson St., New York, NY 10002 (60).

Rosary Hill Home, Servants of Relief for Incurable Cancer, 600 Linda Ave., Hawthorne, NY 10532 (72).

Holy Family Home, Servants of Relief for Incurable Cancer, 6707 State Rd., Parma, OH 44134 (50).

Sacred Heart Free Home for Incurable Cancer, Servants of Relief for Incurable Cancer, 1315 W. Hunting Park Ave., Philadelphia, PA 19140 (45).

Substance Abuse: Facilities for substance abuse (alcohol and other drugs) include:

Daytop Village, Inc., 54 W. 40th St., New York, NY 10018. Msgr. William B. O'Brien, president. Fifteen residential facilities and nine day care centers in New York, New Jersey, Texas and California.

Good Shepherd Gracenter, Convent of the Good Shepherd, 1310 Beacon St., San Francisco, CA 94134. Residential program for chemically dependent women.

New Hope Manor, 35 Hillside Rd., Barryville, NY 12719. Residential substance abuse treatment center for teen-age girls and women ages 13-30. Residential; half-way house and aftercare program totaling 6 months or more.

St. Joseph's Hospital, L.E. Phillips Libertas Center for the Chemically Dependent, 2661 County Road I, Chippewa Falls, WI 54729 (46). Residential and outpatient. Adult and adolescent programs. Hospital Sisters of the Third Order of St. Francis.

St. Luke's Addiction Recovery Services, 7707 NW 2nd Ave., Miami, FL 33150. A program of Catholic Community Services, Miami. Adult residential and family outpatient recovery services for drug, alcohol addiction and DUI. New EXODUS 12-step Christian recovery component for impaired clergy and lay employees.

Miami DARE, 9401 Biscayne Blvd., Miami Shores, FL 33138. Trains parents, youth, priests and teachers as prevention volunteers in the area of substance abuse.

Transitus House for Chemically Dependent Women. 1835 Wheaton St., Chippewa Falls, WI 54729 (20). Six-month residential transitional living after primary treatment. Hospital Sisters of the Third Order of St. Francis.

Matt Talbot Inn, 2270 Professor St., Cleveland, OH 44113 (capacity 25 men; Halfway House; residential treatment for alcoholics and other drug-addicted males).

Sacred Heart Rehabilitation Center, Inc., 569 E. Elizabeth St., Detroit, MI 48201 (10 beds, detoxification; 70 beds, early treatment); 400 Stoddard Rd., Memphis, MI 48041 (120 beds, advance treatment). Both facilities serve male and female live-in clients. Outpatient services available for male and female clients.

Straight and Narrow, Inc., 396 Straight St., Paterson, NJ 07501. Facilities and services include (at various locations): Straight and Narrow Hospital (Mount Carmel Guild), substance abuse, detoxification (20 beds); Alpha House for Drug and Alcohol Rehabilitation (women; 30 beds — 25 adults, 5 children), Dismas House for Drug and Alcohol Rehabilitation (men; 78 beds); The Guild for Drug and Alcohol Rehabilitation (men, 56 beds); juvenile residential units; outpatient services and facility; three halfway houses; counseling services; employment assistance; intoxicated driver's resource cen-

ter; medical day care center (available to HIV infected persons and persons diagnosed with AIDS).

The National Catholic Conference on Alcoholism and Related Drug Problems, 1200 Varnum St., N.E., Washington, DC 20017, offers educational material to those involved in pastoral ministry on ways of dealing with problems related to alcoholism and medication dependency.

Convicts: Priests serve as full- or part-time chaplains in penal and correctional institutions throughout the country. Limited efforts have been made to assist in the rehabilitation of released prisoners in Halfway House establishments.

Dining Rooms; Facilities for Homeless: Representative of places where meals are provided, and in some cases lodging and other services as well, are:

St. Anthony Foundation, 121 Golden Gate Ave., San Francisco, CA 94102. Founded in 1950 by the Franciscan Friars. Dining room serves 2,100 meals daily; more than 23 million since its founding. Other services include free clothing and furniture, free medical care, drug and alcohol rehabilitation and employment programs, emergency shelter and daytime facility for homeless women, residence for low-income senior women, free hygiene services, case management for seniors, social services.

St. Vincent de Paul Free Dining Room, 675 23rd St., Oakland, CA 94612. Administered by Daughters of Charity of St. Vincent de Paul, under sponsorship of St. Vincent de Paul Society. Hot meals served at lunch time 7 days a week; clothing, lodging provided those in need.

St. Vincent's Dining Room, 505 W. 3rd St., Reno, NV 89503. Hot meals at lunch time, Monday through Saturdays; continental breakfast on Sunday.

St. Vincent Dining Room, 1501 Las Vegas Blvd., Las Vegas, NV 89101. Hot meal every day at noon. At same address: St. Vincent Shelter (overnight facilities for 138 men) and St. Vincent Job Development Office (finds jobs for homeless).

Good Shepherd Center, Little Brothers of the Good Shepherd, 218 Iron St. S.W., P.O. Box 749, Albuquerque, NM 87103.

Holy Name Centre for Homeless Men, Inc., 18 Bleeker St., New York, NY 10012. A shelter for alcoholic, homeless men. Provides social services and aid to transients and those in need. Affiliated with New York Catholic Charities.

St. Francis Inn, 2441 Kensington Ave., Philadelphia, PA 19125. Serves hot meals. Temporary shelter for men. Day center for women. Thrift shop.

St. John's Hospice for Men, staffed by Little Brothers of the Good Shepherd, 1221 Race St., Philadelphia, PA 19107. Founded in 1963. Hot meals Monday through Friday; accommodations for 35 men for night shelter; clothing distributed daily to needy.

Camillus House, Little Brothers of the Good Shepherd, 726 N.E. First Ave., Miami, FL 33132. Free comprehensive services for the poor and homeless including daily dinner; night lodging for 70; clothing distribution; showers; mail distribution; drug/alcohol rehabilitation program.

Camillus Health Concern, Little Brothers of the Good Shepherd, 708 N.E. First Ave., Miami, FL

33132. Free comprehensive medical and social services for the homeless.

Shelters: Facilities for runaways, the abused, exploited and homeless include:

Anthony House, supported by St. Anthony's Guild (see Index). Four locations: 246 2nd St., Jersey City, NJ 07302 (for homeless women and children); 38 E. Roosevelt Ave., Roosevelt, NY 11575 (with St. Vincent de Paul Society — for homeless men); 128 W. 112th St., New York, NY 10026 (emergency food and clothing); 6215 Holly St., P.O. Box 880, Zellwood, FL 32798 (for migrant workers and their families).

Covenant House, 346 W. 17th St., New York, NY 10011. Non-sectarian. President, Sister Mary Rose McGeady, D.C. Provides shelter and services for homeless, runaway and exploited youth under the age of 21, in New York, New Jersey (Newark, Atlantic City), Houston, Ft. Lauderdale, New Orleans, Anchorage, Los Angeles; Toronto (Canada), Tegucigalpa (Honduras), Guatemala City (Guatemala), Mexico City (Mexico).

Crescent House, 1000 Howard Ave., Suite 1200, New Orleans, LA 70113. Provides temporary shelter, counseling and advocacy for battered women and their children.

The Dwelling Place, 409 W. 40th St., New York, NY 10018. For homeless women 30 years of age and over.

Good Shepherd Shelter, 2561 Venice Blvd., Los Angeles, CA 90019. For battered women with children.

House of the Good Shepherd, 1114 W. Grace St., Chicago, IL 60613. For abused women with children.

Mercy Hospice, Sisters of Mercy, 334 S. 13th St., Philadelphia, PA 19107. Temporary shelter and relocation assistance for homeless women and children.

Mt. Carmel House, Carmelite Sisters, 471 G Pl., N.W., Washington, DC 20001. For homeless women.

Ozanam Inn, 843 Camp St., New Orleans, LA 70130. Under sponsorship of the St. Vincent de Paul Society. Hospice for homeless men.

St. Christopher Inn, Graymoor, Garrison, NY 10524. Temporary shelter (21 days) for alcohol- and drug-free homeless and needy men.

Siena-Francis House, Inc., P.O. Box 217 D.T.S., Omaha, NE 68102. Two facilities: Siena House, 804 N. 19th St., Omaha, NE 68102 (for homeless and abused women or women with children; provides 24-hour assistance and advocacy services); Francis House, 1902 Cuming St., Omaha, NE 68102 (temporary shelter for homeless men).

Unwed Mothers: Residential and care services for unwed mothers are available in many dioceses.

ORGANIZATIONS

(See separate article for a listing of facilities for the handicapped.)

The Carroll Center for the Blind (formerly the Catholic Guild for All the Blind): Located at 770 Centre St., Newton, MA 02158, the center conducts diagnostic evaluation and rehabilitation programs for blind people over 16 years of age, and maintains programs in community services for all ages, volunteer and special services, computer access training, low-vision training and professional training. It offers a large range of services for blind people who are not in residence, and maintains an office of public education and information. The president is Rachel Rosenbaum.

Xavier Society for the Blind: The Society is located at 154 E. 23rd St., New York, NY 10010. Founded in 1900 by Rev. Joseph Stadelman, S.J., it is a center for publications for the blind and partially sighted and for the deaf blind and maintains a circulating library of approximately 8,000 volumes in Braille, large type and on tape. Its many publications include *The Catholic Review*, a monthly selection of articles of current interest from the Catholic press. The director is Rev. Thomas R. Fitzpatrick, S.J.

International Catholic Deaf Association: Established by deaf adults in Toronto, Canada, in 1949, the association has more than 8,000 members in 128 chapters, mostly in the U.S. It is the only international lay association founded and controlled by deaf Catholic adults. The ICDA publishes *The Deaf Catholic* bimonthly, sponsors regional conferences, workshops and an annual convention. The ICDA-US secretary is Kathleen Kush, 8002 S. Sawyer Rd., Darien, IL 60559.

National Catholic Office for the Deaf: Formally established in 1976, at Washington, D.C., to provide pastoral service to those who teach deaf children and adults, to the parents of deaf children, to pastors of deaf persons, and to organizations of the deaf. The office develops liturgical and religious education materials; organizes workshops, pastoral weeks, leadership programs, cursillos; and serves as a clearinghouse for information concerning ministry with Catholic deaf communities. It publishes *Vision*, four times a year, and a newsletter, three times a year. The executive director is Nora Letourneau, Ph.D. Address: 814 Thayer Ave., Silver Spring, MD 20910.

According to the National Catholic Office for the Deaf, percentages of the general population who are deaf are: deaf from birth (.5%); later deafened (1.5%); hard of hearing (8%). These percentages should be of assistance to dioceses in determining the number of Catholics in each group in need of specialized services to meet their pastoral needs.

National Apostolate with People with Mental Retardation: Established in 1968 to promote the full participation in the Church by persons who are mentally retarded. It publishes the *NAMRP Quarterly* and a newsletter six times a year, and provides information and referral services on Church-related questions. The executive director is Charles M. Luce. Address: P.O. Box 4711, Columbia, SC 29240.

National Catholic Office for Persons with Disabilities: Established in 1982 to assist dioceses in developing pastoral services with people with disabilities. The executive director is Ms. Mary Jane Owen. Address: P.O. Box 29113, Washington, DC 20017.

RETREATS, SPIRITUAL RENEWAL PROGRAMS

There is great variety in retreat and renewal programs, with orientations ranging from the traditional to teen encounters. Central to all of them are celebration of the liturgy and deepening of a person's commitment to faith and witness in life. Features of many of the forms are as follows.

Traditional Retreats: Centered around conferences and the direction of a retreat master; oriented to the personal needs of the retreatants; including such standard practices as participation in Mass, reception of the sacraments, private and group prayer, silence and meditation, discussions.

Team Retreat: Conducted by a team of several leaders or directors (priests, religious, lay persons) with division of subject matter and activities according to their special skills and the nature and needs of the group.

Closed Retreat: Involving withdrawal for a period of time — overnight, several days, a weekend — from everyday occupations and activities.

Open Retreat: Made without total disengagement from everyday involvements, on a part-time basis.

Private Retreat: By one person, on a kind of do-it-yourself basis with the one-to-one assistance of a director.

Special Groups: With formats and activities geared to particular groups; e.g., members of Alcoholics Anonymous, vocational groups and apostolic groups.

Marriage Encounters: Usually weekend periods of husband-wife reflection and dialogue; introduced into the U.S. from Spain in 1967.

Charismatic Renewal: Featuring elements of the movement of the same name; "Spirit-oriented," communitarian and flexible, with spontaneous and shared prayer, personal testimonies of faith and witness.

Christian Community: Characterized by strong community thrust.

Teens Encounter Christ (TEC), SEARCH: Formats adapted to the mentality and needs of youth, involving experience of Christian faith and commitment in a community setting.

Christian Maturity Seminars: Similar to teen encounters in basic concept but different to suit persons of greater maturity.

Cursillo: see separate entry.

Conference

Retreats International Inc.: The first organization for promoting retreats in the U.S. was started in 1904 in New York. Its initial efforts and the gradual growth of the movement led to the formation in 1927 of the National Catholic Laymen's Retreat Conference, the forerunner of the men's division of Retreats International. The women's division developed from the National Laywomen's Retreat Movement which was founded in Chicago in 1936. The men's and women's divisions merged July 9, 1977. The services of the organization include an annual summer institute for retreat and pastoral ministry, regional conferences for retreat center leadership and area meetings of directors and key leadership in the retreat movement. The officers are: Auxiliary Bishop Robert Morneau of Green Bay, episcopal advisor; Sr. Barbara Hagedorn, S.C., president; Rev. Thomas W. Gedeon, S.J., executive director. National office: Box 1067, Notre Dame, IN 46556.

HOUSES OF RETREAT AND RENEWAL

(Principal sources: Almanac survey; *The Official Catholic Directory*.)

Abbreviation code: m, men; w, women; mc, married couples; y, youth. Houses and centers without code generally offer facilities to most groups. An asterisk after an abbreviation indicates that the facility is primarily for the group designated but that special groups are also accommodated. Houses furnish information concerning the types of programs they offer.

Alabama: Blessed Trinity Shrine Retreat, 107 Holy Trinity Rd., Holy Trinity 36859.

Visitation Sacred Heart Retreat House, 2300 Spring Hill Ave., Mobile 36607.

Alaska: Holy Spirit Retreat House, 10980 Hillside Dr., Anchorage 99516.

Arizona: Franciscan Renewal Center, 5802 E. Lincoln Dr., Box 220, Scottsdale 85252.

Mount Claret Retreat Center, 4633 N. 54th St., Phoenix 85018.

Our Lady of Solitude House of Prayer, P.O. Box 1140, Black Canyon City 85324.

Redemptorist Picture Rocks Retreat House, 7101 W. Picture Rocks Rd., Tucson 85743.

Arkansas: Brothers and Sisters of Charity, Little Portion Hermitage, Rt. 3, Box 608, Eureka Springs 72632.

Little Portion Retreat and Training Center, Rt. 4, Box 430, Eureka Springs 72632.

St. Scholastica Retreat Center, P.O. Box 3489, Ft. Smith 72913.

California: Angela Center, 535 Angela Dr., Santa Rosa 95401.

Christ the King Retreat Center, 6520 Van Maren Lane, Citrus Heights 95621.

Claretian Retreat Center, 1119 Westchester Pl., Los Angeles 90019.

De Paul Center, 1105 Bluff Rd., Montebello 90640.

El Carmelo Retreat House, P.O. Box 446, Redlands 92373.

Heart of Jesus Retreat Center, 2927 S. Greenville St., Santa Ana 92704.

Holy Spirit Retreat Center, 4316 Lanai Rd., Encino 91436.

Holy Transfiguration Monastery, Monks of Mt. Tabor (Byzantine Ukrainian), 17001 Tomki Rd., P.O. Box 217, Redwood Valley, Calif. 95470.

Immaculate Heart Hermitage, New Camaldoli, Big Sur 93920.

Jesuit Retreat House, 330 Manresa Way, Los Altos 94022.

Madonna of Peace Renewal Center (y), P.O. Box 71, Copperopolis 95228.

Manresa Retreat House, 801 E. Foothill Blvd., P.O. Box 1330, Azusa 91702.

Mary and Joseph Retreat Center, 5300 Crest Rd., Rancho Palos Verdes 90274.

Marywood Retreat Center, 2811 E. Villa Real Dr., Orange 92667.

Mater Dolorosa Retreat Center, 700 N. Sunnyside Ave., Sierra Madre 91024.

Mercy Center, 2300 Adeline Dr., Burlingame 94010.

Mission San Luis Rey Retreat, P.O. Box 409, San Luis Rey 92068.

Mother of Mercy Convent, 20301 Elkwood St., Canoga Park 91306.

Mount Alverno Retreat and Conference Center, 3910 Bret Harte Dr., Redwood City 94061.

Mount Mary Immaculate Center for Spiritual Growth, 3254 Gloria Terr., Lafayette 94549.

Poverello of Assisi Retreat House, 1519 Woodworth St., San Fernando 91340.

Presentation Education and Retreat Center, 19480 Bear Creek Rd., Los Gatos 95030.

Prince of Peace Abbey, 650 Benet Hill Rd., Oceanside 92054.

Pro Sanctity Spirituality Center, 205 S. Pine St., Fullerton 92633. For day use.

Sacred Heart Retreat House (w), 920 E. Alhambra Rd., Alhambra 91801.

St. Andrew's Abbet Retreat House, Valyermo 93563.

St. Anthony's Retreat House, P.O. Box 249, Three Rivers 93271.

St. Clare's Retreat, 2381 Laurel Glen Rd., Soquel 95073.

St. Francis Retreat, P.O. Box 1070, San Juan Bautista 95045.

St. Francis Salesian Retreat (Camp St. Francis) (y), 75 Dalton Lane, Watsonville 95076.

St. Joseph's Salesian Youth Center (y), P.O. Box 1639, 8301 Arroyo Dr., Rosemead 91770.

St. Mary's Seminary and Retreat House, 1964 Las Conoas Rd., Santa Barbara 93105.

San Damiano Retreat, P.O. Box 767, Danville 94526.

San Miguel Retreat House, P.O. Box 69, San Miguel 93451.

Santa Sabina Center, 1520 Grand Ave., San Rafael 94901.

Serra Retreat, 3401 S. Serra Rd., Box 127, Malibu 90265.

Starcross Community, P.O. Box 14279, Santa Rosa, CA 95402.

Villa Maria del Mar, Santa Cruz. Mailing address, 2-1918 E. Cliff Dr., Santa Cruz 95062.

Villa Maria — House of Prayer (w), 1252 N. Citrus Dr., La Habra 90631.

Colorado: Benet Hill Monastery, 2555 N. Chelton Rd., Colorado Springs 80909.

Benet Pines Retreat Center, 15780 Highway 83, Colorado Springs 80921.

Sacred Heart Retreat House, Box 185, Sedalia 80135.

Spiritual Life Institute (individuals only), Nada Hermitage, P.O. Box 219, Crestone 81131. Private desert retreats with minimal direction.

Connecticut: Archdiocesan Spiritual Life Center, 467 Bloomfield Ave., Bloomfield 06002.

Edmundite Apostolate and Conference Center, Enders Island, Mystic 06355.

Emmaus Spiritual Life Center, 24 Maple Ave., Uncasville 06382.

Holy Family Retreat, 303 Tunxis Rd., West Hartford 06107.

Immaculata Retreat House, P.O. Box 55, Willimantic 06226.

Mercy Center, P.O. Box 191, 167 Neck Rd., Madison 06443.

Montfort Missionaries Retreat Center, P.O. Box 667, Litchfield 06759.

My Father's House, Box 22, North Moodus Rd., Moodus 06469.

Our Lady of Calvary Retreat (w*), 31 Colton St., Farmington 06032.

Trinita Retreat Center, 595 Town Hill Rd., Rt. 219, New Hartford 06057.

Villa Maria Retreat House, 159 Sky Meadow Dr., Stamford 06903.

Delaware: St. Francis Renewal Center, 1901 Prior Rd., Wilmington 19809.

District of Columbia: Washington Retreat House, 4000 Harewood Rd. N.E., Washington 20017.

Florida: Cenacle Retreat House, 1400 S. Dixie Highway, Lantana 33462.

Dominican Retreat House, Inc., 7275 S.W. 124th St., Miami 33156.

Franciscan Center, 3010 Perry Ave., Tampa 33603.

John Paul II Retreat House, 720 N.E. 27th St., Miami 33137.

Saint John Neumann Renewal Center, 685 Miccosukee Rd., Tallahassee 32308.

St. Leo Abbey Retreat Center, P.O. Box 2157, St. Leo 33574.

Georgia: Ignatius House, 6700 Riverside Dr. N.W., Atlanta 30328.

Idaho: Nazareth Retreat Center, 4450 N. Five Mile Rd., Boise 83704.

Illinois: Aylesford Carmelite Spiritual Center, 8433 Bailey Rd., Darien 60559.

Bellarmine Hall (ma), Box 268, Barrington 60010.

Bishop Lane Retreat House, 7708 E. McGregor Rd., Rockford 61102.

Cabrini Retreat Center (m, w, y), 9430 Golf Rd., Des Plaines 60016.

Cenacle Retreat House, 513 Fullerton Parkway, Chicago 60614.

Cenacle Retreat House, P.O. Box 797, Warrenville 60555.

Divine Word International, 2001 Waukegan Rd., Techny 60082.

King's House, 700 N. 66th St., Belleville 62223.

King's House of Retreats, Henry 61537.

La Salle Manor, Christian Brothers Retreat House, 12480 Galena Rd., Plano 60545.

La Sallette Retreat Center, R.R. 1, Box 403, Georgetown 61846.

Sacred Heart Center, 3000 Central Rd., Rolling Meadows 60008.

St. Joseph Retreat Center, 353 N. River Rd., Des Plaines 60016.

St. Mary's Retreat House, P.O. Box 608, 1400 Main St., Lemont 60439.

Tolentine Center, 20300 Governors Highway, Olympia Fields 60461.

Villa Desiderata Retreat House, 3015 N. Bayview Lane, McHenry 60050.

Villa Redeemer Retreat Center, P.O. Box 6, Glenview 60025.

Indiana: Beech Grove Benedictine Center, 1402 Southern Ave., Beech Grove 46107.

Fatima Retreat House, 5353 E. 56th St., Indianapolis 46226.

John XXIII Center, 407 W. McDonald St., Hartford City 47348.

Kordes Enrichment Center, 841 E. 14th St., Ferdinand 47532.

Lindenwood, PHJC Ministry Center, P.O. Box 1, Donaldson 46513.

Mount Saint Francis Retreat Center, Mount Saint Francis 47146.

Our Lady of Fatima Retreat Center, Notre Dame 46556.

St. Jude Guest House, St. Meinrad Archabbey, St. Meinrad 47577.

Sarto Retreat House, 4200 N. Kentucky Ave., Evansville 47711.

Solitude of St. Joseph, Box 983, Notre Dame, Ind. 46556.

Iowa: American Martyrs Retreat House, 2209 N. Union Rd., P.O. Box 605, Cedar Falls 50613.

Emmanuel House of Prayer and Retreat Center, R.R. 2, Box 83, Iowa City 52240.

New Melleray Guest House, 6500 Melleray Circle, Peosta 52068.

Shalom Renewal Center, 1001 Davis Ave., Dubuque 52001.

Kansas: Manna House of Prayer, 323 East 5th St., Box 675, Concordia 66901.

Spiritual Life Center, 7100 E. 45th St., N. Wichita 67226.

Kentucky: Catherine Spalding Center, P.O. Box 24, Nazareth 40048.

Flaget Center, 1935 Lewiston Pl., Louisville 40216.

Marydale Retreat Center, 945 Donaldson Hwy., Erlanger 41018.

Mt. St. Joseph Retreat Center, 8001 Cummings Rd., Maple Mount 42356.

Our Lady of Gethsemani (m, w, private), The Guestmaster, Abbey of Gethsemani, Trappist 40051.

Louisiana: Abbey Christian Life Center, St. Joseph's Abbey, St. Benedict 70457.

Ave Maria Retreat House, Route 1, Box 0368 AB, Marrero 70072.

Cenacle Retreat House, 5500 St. Mary St., P.O. Box 8115, Metairie 70011.

Jesuit Spirituality Center, P.O. Box C, Grand Coteau 70541.

Lumen Christi Retreat Center, 100 Lumen Christi Lane, Hwy. 311, Schriever 70395.

Manresa House of Retreats (m), P.O. Box 89, Convent 70723.

Maryhill Renewal Center, 600 Maryhill Rd., Pineville 71360.

Our Lady of the Oaks Retreat House, P.O. Box D, Grand Coteau 70541.

Regina Coeli Retreat Center, 1725 Regina Coeli Rd., Covington 70433.

Maine: Marie Joseph Spiritual Center, RFD 2, Biddeford 04005.

St. Paul Retreat and Cursillo Center, 136 State St., Augusta 04330.

Maryland: Bon Secours Spiritual Center, Marriottsville 21104.

Christian Brothers Spiritual Center (m,w,y), P.O. Box 29, 2535 Buckeyestown Pike, Adamstown 21710.

Loyola Retreat House-on-Potomac, Faulkner 20632.

Msgr. Clare J. O'Dwyer Retreat House (y), 15523 York Rd., P.O. Box 310, Sparks 21152.

Our Lady of Mattaponi Youth Retreat and Conference Center, 11000 Mattaponi Rd., Upper Marlboro 20772.

Villa Cortona, 7007 Bradley Blvd., Bethesda 20817.

Massachusetts: Calvary Retreat Center, 59 South St., P.O. Box 219, Shrewsbury 01545.

Campion Renewal Center, 319 Concord Rd., Weston 02193.

Cenacle Retreat House, 200 Lake St., Brighton, Boston 02135.

Eastern Point Retreat House, Gonzaga Hall, Gloucester 01930.

Espousal Center, 554 Lexington St., Waltham 02154.

Esther House of Spiritual Renewal, Sisters of St. Anne, 1015 Pleasant St., Worcester 01602.

Genesis Spiritual Life Center, 53 Mill St., Westfield 01085.

Glastonbury Abbey (Benedictine Monks), 16 Hull St., Hingham 02043.

Holy Cross Fathers Retreat House, 490 Washington St., N. Easton 02356.

Jesuit Center, Sullivan Square, Charlestown, Boston 02129.

La Salette Center for Christian Living, 947 Park St., Attleboro 02703.

LaSalette Retreat House, 315 Topsfield Rd., Ipswich 01938.

Marian Center, 1365 Northampton St., Holyoke 01040. Day and evening programs.

Mater Dei Retreat House (boys), Old Groveland Rd., Bradford 01830.

Miramar Retreat Center, P.O. Box M, Duxbury, 02331.

Mother of Sorrows Retreat House, 110 Monastery Ave., W. Springfield 01089.

Mt. Carmel Retreat Center, Oblong Rd., Box 613, Williamstown 01267.

Retreat Center, Sisters of St. Joseph, 339 Jerusalem Rd., Cohasset 02025.

Sacred Heart Retreat House, Salesians of St. John Bosco, P.O. Box 567, Ipswich 01938.

St. Benedict Abbey, 252 Still River Rd., P.O. Box 67, Still River 01467.

St. Joseph's Abbey Retreat House (m) (Trappist Monks), North Spencer Rd., Spencer 01562.

St. Stephen Priory Spiritual Life Center (Dominican), 20 Glen St., Box 370, Dover 02030.

Michigan: Augustine Center, Box 84, Conway 49722.

Capuchin Retreat, 62460 Mt. Vernon, Box 188, Washington 48094.

Colombiere Conference Center, Box 139, 9075 Big Lake Rd., Clarkston 48347.

Manresa Jesuit Retreat House, 1390 Quarton Rd., Bloomfield Hills 48304.

Marygrove Retreat Center, Garden 49835.

Queen of Angels Retreat, 3400 S. Washington Rd., Box 2026, Saginaw 48605.

St. Clare Capuchin Retreat (y*), 1975 N. River Rd., St. Clair 48079.

St. Francis Retreat Center, Diocese of Lansing, 703 E. Main St., De Witt 48820.

St. Lazare Retreat House, 18600 W. Spring Lake Rd., Spring Lake 49456.

St. Mary's Retreat House (w*), 775 W. Drahner Rd., Oxford 48371.

St. Paul of the Cross Retreat Center (m*), 23333 Schoolcraft, Detroit 48223.

Minnesota: Benedictine Center, St. Paul's Priory, 2675 E. Larpenteur Ave., St. Paul 55109.

Catholic Youth Ministry Services (y*), 2120 Park Ave. S., Minneapolis 55404.

The Cenacle, 1221 Wayzata Blvd., Wayzata 55391.

Center for Spiritual Development, 211 Tenth St. S., P.O. Box 538, Bird Island 55310.

Christ the King Retreat House, 621 First Ave. S., Buffalo 55313.

Christian Brothers Retreat Center, 15525 St. Croix Trail North, Marine-on-St. Croix 55047.

Franciscan Retreats, Conventual Franciscan Friars, 16385 St. Francis Lane, Prior Lake 55372.

Jesuit Retreat House (m), 8243 DeMontreville Trail North, Lake Elmo 55042.

Maryhill Retreat Center, Society of Daughters of the Heart of Mary, 260 Summit Ave., St. Paul 55102.

Retreat House, 116 S.E. Eighth Ave., Little Falls 56345. St. Francis Center, same address.

Villa Maria Center, Ursuline Sisters, Frontenac 55026.

Missouri: The Cenacle, 7654 Natural Bridge Rd., St. Louis 63121.

Christina House Hermitages, Abbey Lane, P.O. Box 69, Pevely 63070.

Il Ritiro - The Little Retreat, P.O. Box 38, Eime Rd., Dittmer 63023.

Maria Fonte Solitude (private; individual hermitages), P.O. Box 322, High Ridge 63049.

Marianist Retreat and Conference Center, P.O. Box 718, Eureka 63025.

Mercy Center, 2039 N. Geyer Rd., St. Louis 63131.

Nazareth House, 716 Geyer Ave., St. Louis 63104.

Our Lady of Assumption Abbey (m,w), Trappists, Rt. 5, Box 1056, Ava 65608.

Our Lady's Retreat House, Passionist Community, 3036 Bellerive Dr., St. Louis 63121.

Pallottine Renewal Center, 15270 Old Halls Ferry Rd., Florissant 63034.

Queen of Heaven Solitude (private, individual hermitages), Rt. 1, Box 107A, Marionville 65705.

White House Retreat, 7400 Christopher Dr., St. Louis 63129.

Montana: Christhaven - Diocesan Retreat Center, P.O. Box 948, Anaconda 59711.

Emmaus Retreat House, Box 407, Havre 59501.

Ursuline Retreat Centre, 2300 Central Ave., Great Falls 59401.

Nebraska: Crosier Renewal Center, 223 E. 14th St., P.O. Box 789, Hastings 68902.

Good Counsel, R.R. 1, Box 110, Waverly 68462.

New Hampshire: The Common - St. Joseph Monastery, Discalced Carmelite Friars, 174 Old Street Rd., Peterborough 03458.

La Salette Conference and Retreat Center, Enfield 03748.

New Hampshire Monastery, Hundred Acres, New Boston 03070.

Oblates of Mary Immaculate Retreat House, 200 Lowell Rd., Hudson 03051.

St. Francis Retreat Center, 860 Central Rd., Rye Beach 03871.

New Jersey: Bethlehem Hermitage, Pleasant Hill Rd., Box 315, Chester 07930.

Carmel Retreat House, 1071 Ramapo Valley Rd., Mahwah 07430.

Cenacle Retreat House, 411 River Rd., Highland Park 08904.

Felician Retreat House, 35 Windemere Ave., Mt. Arlington 07856.

Good Shepherd Center, 74 Kahdena Rd., Morristown 07960.

Loyola House of Retreats, 161 James St., Morristown 07960.

Marianist Retreat House (families*, mc), 415 Yale Ave., Box D-2, Cape May Point 08212.

Maris Stella (Vacation Home for Sisters*), 7201 Long Beach Blvd., Harvey Cedars 08008.

Mission and Ministry Center, 44 Rifle Camp Rd., W. Paterson 07424. Mailing address: P.O. Box 3026, Paterson 07509.

Mt. St. Francis Retreat House, 474 Sloatsburg Rd., Ringwood 07456.

Queen of Peace Retreat House, St. Paul's Abbey, P.O. Box 7, Newton 07860.

St. Joseph by the Sea Retreat House, 400 Rte. 35 N., South Mantoloking 08738.

St. Joseph's Villa (w, guest and retreat house), Srs. of St. John the Baptist, Peapack 07977.

St. Pius X Retreat House, P.O. Box 216, Blackwood 08012.

San Alfonso Retreat House, P.O. Box 3098, 755 Ocean Ave., Long Branch 07740.

Sanctuary of Mary, R.R. 1, Box 106, Branchville 07826. Days of Recollection.

Stella Maris Retreat House, 981 Ocean Ave., Elberon 07740.

Trinity Ministries Center, 1292 Long Hill Rd., Stirling 07980.

Villa Pauline Retreat House (w*), Hilltop Rd., Mendham 07945.

Xavier Retreat and Conference Center, P.O. Box 211, Convent Station 07961.

New Mexico: Dominican Retreat House, 5825 Coors Rd. S.W., Albuquerque 87121.

Holy Cross Retreat, Conventual Franciscan Friars, P.O. Box 158, Mesilla Park 88047.

Pecos Benedictine Abbey, Pecos 87552.

Sacred Heart Retreat, P.O. Box 1989, Gallup 87301.

New York: Bethany Retreat House, County Road 105, Box 1003, Highland Mills 10930.

Bethlehem Retreat House, Abbey of the Genesee, Piffard 14533.

Bishop Molloy Retreat House, 86-45 Edgerton Blvd., Jamaica, L.I. 11432.

Blessed Kateri Retreat House, National Kateri Shrine, P.O. Box 627, Fonda, N.Y. 12068.

Cardinal Spellman Retreat House, Passionist Community, 5801 Palisade Ave., Bronx (Riverdale) 10471.

Cenacle Center for Spiritual Renewal, 310 Cenacle Rd., Lake Ronkonkoma 11779.

Cenacle Retreat House, State Rd., P.O. Box 467, Bedford Village 10506.

Christ the King Retreat House, 500 Brookford Rd., Syracuse 13224.

Cormaria Retreat House, Sag Harbor, L.I. 11963.

Diocesan Cursillo Center (Spanish), 118 Congress St., Brooklyn 11201.

Dominican Retreat House, 1945 Union St., Schenectady 12309.

Don Bosco Retreat Center, Box 9000, Filor's Lane, West Haverstraw 10993.

Graymoor Christian Unity Center, Graymoor, Garrison 10524.

Jesuit Retreat House, North American Martyrs Shrine, Auriesville 12016.

Monastery of the Precious Blood (w), Ft. Hamilton Parkway and 54th St., Brooklyn 11219. Single day retreats.

Mount Alvernia Retreat House, Box 858, Wappingers Falls 12590.

Mount Irenaeus Franciscan Mountain Retreat, Holy Peace Friary, P.O. Box 100, West Clarksville, NY 14786.

Mount Manresa Retreat House, 239 Fingerboard Rd., Staten Island 10305.

Notre Dame Retreat House, Box 342, 5151 Foster Rd., Canandaigua 14424.

Our Lady of Hope Center, 434 River Rd., Newburgh 12550.

Regina Maria Retreat House, 77 Brinkerhoff St., Plattsburgh 12901.

St. Andrew's House, 257 St. Andrew's Rd., Walden 12586.

St. Columban Center, Diocese of Buffalo, 6892 Lake Shore Rd., P.O. Box 816, Derby 14047.

St. Gabriel Retreat House (y, mc), 64 Burns Rd., P.O. Box P, Shelter Island 11965.

St. Ignatius Center for Spirituality, P.O. Box 723, 711 Knox Rd., E. Aurora 14050.

St. Ignatius Retreat House, Searingtown Rd., Manhasset, L.I. 11030.

St. Josaphat's Retreat House, Basilian Monastery, East Beach Rd., Glen Cove 11542.

St. Joseph Center (Spanish Center), 523 W. 142nd St., New York 10031.

St. Mary's Villa, 50 Table Rock Rd., Sloatsburg 10974.

St. Paul Center, 21-35 Crescent St., Astoria 11105.

St. Ursula Center, P.O. Box 86, Middle Rd., Blue Point 11715.

Stella Maris Retreat Center, 130 E. Genesee St., Skaneateles 13152.

Stella Niagara Center of Renewal, 4421 Lower River Rd., Stella Niagara 14144.

Tagaste Monastery Retreat House (m, y), Suffern 10901.

Trinity Retreat, 1 Pryer Manor Rd., Larchmont 10538.

North Carolina: Avila Retreat Center, 711 Mason Rd., Durham 27712.

Living Waters Catholic Reflection Center, 1420 Soco Rd., Maggie Valley 28751.

North Dakota: Presentation Prayer Center, 1101 32nd Ave. S., Fargo 58103.

Queen of Peace Retreat, Dominican Fathers and Sisters, 1310 Broadway, Fargo 58102.

Ohio: Bergamo, 4400 Shakertown Rd., Dayton 45430.

Franciscan Renewal Center (Retreat Center and Pilgrim House), 320 West St., Carey 43316.

Friarhurst Retreat House, 8136 Wooster Pike, Cincinnati 45227.

Jesuit Renewal Center, 5361 S. Milford Rd., Milford 45150.

Jesuit Retreat House, 5629 State Rd., Cleveland 44134.

Loyola of the Lakes, 700 Killinger Rd., Clinton 44216.

Maria Stein Center, 2365 St. Johns Rd., Maria Stein 45860.

Milford Retreat House, Box 348, Milford 45150.

Our Lady of the Pines, 1250 Tiffin St., Fremont 43420.

Sacred Heart Retreat and Renewal Center, 3128 Logan Ave., P.O. Box 6074, Youngstown 44501.

St. Joseph Christian Life Center, 18485 Lake Shore Blvd., Cleveland 44119.

St. Joseph Renewal Center, 200 St. Francis Ave., Tiffin 44883.

Shrine Center for Renewal, Diocese of Columbus, 5277 E. Broad St., Columbus 43213.

Oklahoma: St. Gregory's Abbey, Shawnee 74801.

Oregon: Franciscan Renewal Center, 0858 S.W. Palatine Hill Rd., Portland 97219.

Loyola Retreat House (Jesuit Center for Spiritual Renewal), 3220 S.E. 43rd St., Portland 97206.

Mount Angel Abbey Retreat House, St. Benedict 97373.

Our Lady of Peace Retreat, 3600 S. W. 170th Ave., Beaverton 97006.

St. Rita Retreat Center, P.O. Box 310, Gold Hill 97525.

Shalom Prayer Center, Benedictine Sisters, Mt. Angel 97362.

Trappist Abbey Retreat (m,w), P.O. Box 97, Lafayette 97127.

Pennsylvania: Byzantine Catholic Seminary (m), 3605 Perrysville Ave., Pittsburgh 15214.

Cenacle Retreat House, 4723 Fifth Ave., Pittsburgh 15213.

Dominican Retreat House, 750 Ashbourne Rd., Elkins Park 19117.

Doran Hall Retreat and Renewal Center, 443 Mt. Thor Rd., Greensburg 15601.

Fatima House, Rolling Hills Rd., Ottsville 18942.

Fatima Renewal Center, 1000 Seminary Rd., Dalton 18414.

Gilmary Diocesan Center, Flaugherty Run Rd., Coraopolis 15108.

Jesuit Center for Spiritual Growth, Box 223, Church Rd., Wernersville 19565.

Maria Wald Retreat House, Convent of the Precious Blood, Box 97, New Holland Ave., Shillington 19607.

Mount St. Macrina Retreat Center, 510 W. Main St., Box 878, Uniontown 15401.

St. Emma Retreat House, 1001 Harvey St., Greensburg 15601.

St. Francis Center (y*), 900 W. Market St., Orwigsburg 17961.

St. Francis Center for Renewal, Monocacy Manor, 395 Bridle Path Rd., Bethlehem 18017.

St. Francis Retreat House, 3918 Chipman Rd., Easton 18042.

St. Gabriel's Retreat House, 631 Griffin Pond Rd., Clarks Summit 18411.

St. Joseph's in the Hills (m), Men of Malvern, 313 Warren Ave., Malvern 19355.

St. Paul of the Cross Retreat Center, 148 Monastery Ave., Pittsburgh 15203.

Saint Raphaela Mary Retreat House, 616 Coopertown Rd., Haverford 19041.

St. Vincent Retreat Program, Latrobe 15650.

Villa of Our Lady Retreat Center (w, mc, y), HCR No. 1, Box 41, Mt. Pocono 18344.

Rhode Island: Bethany House, 397 Fruit Hill Ave., N. Providence 02911.

Ephpheta House — A Center for Renewal, 10 Manville Hill Rd; mailing address, P.O. Box 1, Manville 02838.

Father Marot CYO Center (y), 53 Federal St., Woonsocket 02895.

Our Lady of Peace Spiritual Life Center, 333 Ocean Rd., Box 507, Narragansett 02882.

St. Dominic Savio Youth Center (y*), Broad Rock Rd., Box 67, Peace Dale 02883.

South Carolina: Springbank Retreat Center, Rt. 2, Box 180, Kingstree 29556.

South Dakota: St. Martin's Community Center, 2110C St. Martin's Dr., Rapid City 57702.

Sioux Spiritual Center (for Native Americans), Diocese of Rapid City, HC 77, Box 271, Howes 57748.

Tennessee: House of the Lord, 1306 Dellwood Ave., Memphis 38127.

Texas: Bishop DeFalco Retreat Center, 2100 N. Spring, Amarillo 79107.

Bishop Thomas J. Drury Retreat Center, 1200 Lantana St., Corpus Christi 78407.

Catholic Renewal Center of North Texas, 4503 Bridge St., Ft. Worth 76103.

Cenacle Retreat House, 420 N. Kirkwood, Houston 77079.

Christian Renewal Center (Centro de Renovacion Cristiana), Oblates of Mary Immaculate, P.O. Box 635, Dickinson 77539.

Holy Family Retreat Center, 9920 N. Major Dr., Beaumont 77713.

Holy Name Retreat Center, 430 Bunker Hill Rd., Houston 77024.

Montserrat Jesuit Retreat House, P.O. Box 398, Lake Dallas 75065.

Moye Center, 600 London, Castroville 78009.

Oblate Renewal Center (Casa San Jose), 127 Oblate Dr., San Antonio 78216.

Our Lady of the Pillar Marianist Retreat Center, 2507 N.W. 36th St., San Antonio 78228.

San Juan Retreat House, Diocese of Brownsville, P.O. Box 998, San Juan 78589.

Utah: Our Lady of the Holy Trinity Retreat House (m), Huntsville 84317.

Our Lady of the Mountains, 1794 Lake St., Ogden 84401.

Virginia: Dominican Retreat, 7103 Old Dominion Dr., McLean 22101.

Holy Family Retreat House, The Redemptorists, P.O. 3151, 1414 N. Mallory St., Hampton 23663.

Missionhurst Mission Center, 4651 N. 25th St., Arlington 22207.

Retreat House, Holy Cross Abbey, Rt. 2, Box 3870, Berryville 22611.

Washington: Camp Field Retreat Center, P.O. Box 128, Leavenworth 98826.

Immaculate Heart Retreat Center, 6910 S. Ben Burr Rd., Spokane 99223.

Palisades Retreat House, P.O. Box 3739, Federal Way 98063.

Visitation Retreat Center (w), 3200 S.W. Dash Point Rd., Federal Way 98023.

West Virginia: Bishop Hodges Pastoral Center, P.O. Box 60, Huttonsville, 26273.

Cenacle Retreat House, 1114 Virginia St. E., Charleston 25301.

Good Counsel Friary, Rt. 7, Box 183, Morgantown 26505.

John XXIII Pastoral Center, 100 Hodges Rd., Charleston, W. Va. 25314.

Paul VI Pastoral Center, 667 Stone and Shannon Rd., Wheeling 26003.

Priest Field Pastoral Center, Rt. 51, Box 133, Kearneysville 25430.

Wisconsin: Archdiocesan Retreat Center, 3501 S. Lake Dr., P.O. Box 07912, Milwaukee 53207.

Cardoner Jesuit Retreat Center, 1501 S. Layton Blvd., Milwaukee 53215.

Holy Name Retreat House, Chambers Island; mailing address, 1825 Riverside Drive, P.O. Box 23825, Green Bay 54305.

Jesuit Retreat House, 4800 Fahrnwald Rd., Oshkosh 54901.

Marynook Retreat and Conference Center (ecumenically owned), Box 9, Galesville 54630.

Monte Alverno Retreat Center, 1000 N. Ballard Rd., Appleton 54911.

Perpetual Help Retreat Center, 1800 N. Timber Trail Lane, Oconomowoc 53066.

St. Anthony Retreat Center, 300 E. 4th St., Marathon 54448.

St. Benedict Center (ecumenical retreat and conference center), P.O. Box 5070, Madison 53705.

St. Francis Friary and Retreat Center, 503 S. Browns Lake Dr., Burlington 53105.

St. Joseph's Retreat Center, 3035 O'Brien Rd., Bailey's Harbor 54202.

St. Vincent Pallotti Center, N6409 Bowers Rd., Elkhorn 53121.

Schoenstatt Center, W. 284 N. 698 Cherry Lane, Waukesha 53188.

1993 CPA AWARDS

Catholic Press Association Awards for material published in 1992 were presented during the annual CPA convention held May 26 to 28, 1993, in Cincinnati, Ohio. Some of the awards are listed below.

Newspapers — General Excellence
National Newspapers: *National Catholic Reporter* (first place); *National Catholic Register* (second place); *Our Sunday Visitor* (third place).

Diocesan Newspapers, to 17,000 circulation: *The Valley Catholic,* Santa Clara, Calif. (first place); *The Observer,* Monterey, Calif. (second); *Hawaii Catholic Herald,* Honolulu, Hawaii. (third).

Diocesan Newspapers, 17,001 to 40,000 circulation: *The Florida Catholic,* Combined Staff: Miami, Palm Beach, St. Petersburg, Orlando, Pensacola-Tallahassee, Venice (first place); *The Providence Visitor,* Providence, R.I. (second); *The Catholic Herald,* Milwaukee, Wis. (third).

Diocesan Newspapers, 40,001 and over circulation: *Catholic New York,* New York, N.Y. (first place); *Catholic Courier,* Rochester, N.Y. (second); *Catholic Times,* Springfield, Ill. (third).

Magazines — General Excellence
General Interest: *Notre Dame Magazine* (first place); *Liguorian* (second place).

Mission: *Comboni Missions* (first place); *Extension Magazine* (second).

Religious Order: *Salt* (first place); *National Jesuit News* (second).

Professional and Special Interest: *My Friend* (first place); *Health Progress* (second).

Magazines for Clergy and Religious: *The Priest* (first place); *Chicago Studies* (second).

Scholarly: *Communio* and *Horizons* (first place, tie); *Catholic Update* (second).

Prayer and Spirituality: *Spiritual Life* (first place); *Queen of All Hearts* (second).

Newsletters, General Interest: *Context* (first place); *Youth Update* (second).

Newsletters, Special Interest: *Chariscenter USA* (first place); *Missionaries of Africa Report* (second).

Spanish-Language Awards
General Excellence: *Nuevo Amanecer,* Brooklyn, N.Y. (first place); *La Voz Catolica,* Miami, Fla. (second place).

Books — First Place Awards
Popular Presentation of Catholic Faith: Harper San Francisco, *The Year That Shook Catholic America,* by Kenneth Briggs.

Spirituality: Orbis Books, *Works of Mercy,* by Fritz Eichenberg.

Theology: Crossroad, *The Craft of Theology: From Symbol to System,* by Avery Dulles.

Scripture: Doubleday, *The Pentateuch,* by Joseph Blenkinsopp.

Liturgy: Crossroad, *WomanWitness: A Feminist Lectionary and Psalter,* by Miriam Therese Winter.

Pastoral Ministry: Doubleday, *Lead Us Not into Temptation: Catholic Priests and the Sexual Abuse of Children,* by Jason Berry.

Professional Books: *Sexuality, Celibacy, and Relationships among Catholic Clergy and Religious,* by Sheila Murphy.

Educational Books: The Liturgical Press,*The New Jerome Bible Handbook,* by Ronald E. Murphy, O.Carm., Joseph A. Fitzmyer, S.J., Raymond E. Brown, S.S.

Design and Production: ACTA Publications, *Playing with God,* by Jean Morman Unsworth.

Children's Books: Winston Press, *Me at Four,* Mary Irene Flanagan.

LAY PERSONS AND THEIR APOSTOLATE _____

RIGHTS AND OBLIGATIONS OF ALL THE FAITHFUL

The following rights are listed in Canons 208-223 of the revised Code of Canon Law; additional rights are specified in other canons.

They are all equal in dignity because of their baptism and regeneration in Christ.

They are bound always to preserve communion with the Church.

According to their condition and circumstances, they should strive to lead a holy life and promote the growth and holiness of the Church.

They have the right and duty to work for the spread of the divine message of salvation to all peoples of all times and places.

They are bound to obey declarations and orders given by their pastors in their capacity as representatives of Christ, teachers of the faith and rectors of the Church.

They have the right to make known their needs, especially their spiritual needs, to pastors of the Church.

They have the right, and sometimes the duty, of making known to pastors and others of the faithful their opinions about things pertaining to the good of the Church.

They have the right to receive help from their pastors, from the spiritual goods of the Church and especially from the word of God and the sacraments.

They have the right to divine worship performed according to prescribed rules of their rite, and to follow their own form of spiritual life in line with the doctrine of the Church.

They have the right to freely establish and control associations for good and charitable purposes, to foster the Christian vocation in the world, and to hold meetings related to the accomplishment of these purposes.

They have the right to promote and support apostolic action but may not call it "Catholic" unless they have the consent of competent authority.

They have a right to a Christian education.

They have a right to freedom of inquiry in sacred studies, in accordance with the teaching authority of the Church.

They have a right to freedom in the choice of their state of life.

No one has the right to harm the good name of another person or to violate his or her right to maintain personal privacy.

They have the right to vindicate the rights they enjoy in the Church, and to defend themselves in a competent ecclesiastical forum.

They have the obligation to provide for the needs of the Church, with respect to things pertaining to divine worship, apostolic and charitable works, and the reasonable support of ministers of the Church.

They have the obligation to promote social justice and to help the poor from their own resources.

In exercising their rights, the faithful should have regard for the common good of the Church and for the rights and duties of others.

Church authority has the right to monitor the exercise of rights proper to the faithful, with the common good in view.

RIGHTS AND OBLIGATIONS OF LAY PERSONS

In addition to rights and obligations common to all the faithful and those stated in other canons, lay persons are bound by the obligations and enjoy the rights specified in these canons (224-231).

Lay persons, like all the faithful, are called by God to the apostolate in virtue of their baptism and confirmation. They have the obligation and right, individually or together in associations, to work for the spread and acceptance of the divine message of salvation among people everywhere; this obligation is more urgent in those circumstances in which people can hear the Gospel and get to know Christ only through them (lay persons).

They are bound to bring an evangelical spirit to bear on the order of temporal things and to give Christian witness in carrying out their secular pursuits.

Married couples are obliged to work for the building up of the people of God through their marital and family life.

Parents have the most serious obligation to provide for the Christian education of their children according to the doctrine handed down by the Church.

Lay persons have the same civil liberty as other citizens. In the use of this liberty, they should take care that their actions be imbued with an evangelical spirit. They should attend to the doctrine proposed by the magisterium of the Church but should take care that, in questions of opinion, they do not propose their own opinion as the doctrine of the Church.

Qualified lay persons are eligible to hold and perform the duties of ecclesiastical offices open to them in accord with the provisions of law.

Properly qualified lay persons can assist pastors of the Church as experts and counselors.

Lay persons have the obligation and enjoy the right to acquire knowledge of doctrine commensurate with their capacity and condition.

They have the right to pursue studies in the sacred sciences in pontifical universities or facilities and in institutes of religious sciences, and to obtain academic degrees.

If qualified, they are eligible to receive from ecclesiastical authority a mandate to teach sacred sciences.

Lay men can be invested by liturgical rite and in a stable manner in the ministries of lector and acolyte.

Lay persons, by temporary assignment, can fulfill the office of lector in liturgical actions; likewise, all lay persons can perform the duties of commentator or cantor.

In cases of necessity and in the absence of the usual ministers, lay persons — even if not lectors or acolytes — can exercise the ministry of the word, lead liturgical prayers, confer baptism and distribute Communion, according to the prescripts of law.

Lay persons who devote themselves permanently or temporarily to the service of the Church are obliged to acquire the formation necessary for carrying out their duties in a proper manner. They have a right to remuneration for their service which is just and adequate to provide for their own needs and those of their families; they also have a right to insurance, social security and health insurance.

SPECIAL APOSTOLATES AND GROUPS

Apostleship of the Sea (1920, Glasgow, Scotland; 1947 in U.S.): 3211 Fourth St. NE, Washington, DC 20017 (national office). An international Catholic organization for the moral, social and spiritual welfare of seafarers and those involved in the maritime industry. Formally instituted by the Holy See in 1952 (apostolic constitution Exul Familia), it is a sector of the Pontifical Council for Migrants and Itinerant Peoples. The U.S. unit, an affiliate of the NCCB-USCC, serves port chaplains in 63 U.S. ports. Nat. Dir., Robert Mario Balderas, a permanent deacon.

Auxiliaries of Our Lady of the Cenacle (1878, France): An association of Catholic laywomen, under the direction of the Congregation of Our Lady of the Cenacle, who serve God through their own professions and life styles by means of vows. Members live a fully secular life consecrated according to the spirituality of the Cenacle and pursue individual apostolates. They number approximately 150 throughout the world. U.S. address: 7654 Natural Bridge Rd., St. Louis, MO 63121.

Catholic Central Union of America (1855): 3835 Westminster Pl., St. Louis, MO 63108; membership, 8,100; *Social Justice Review*, bimonthly. One of the oldest Catholic lay organizations in the U.S.and the first given an official mandate for Catholic Action by a committee of the American bishops (1936). Devoted to the development and vigor of Christian principles in personal, social, cultural, economic and civic life.

Catholic Medical Mission Board (1928): 10 W. 17th Street, New York, NY 10011. A charitable, non-profit organization dedicated to providing health care supplies and support for the medically disadvantaged in developing and transitional countries. CMMB depends upon the financial generosity of over 25,000 individual donors and through product contributions by major pharmaceutical corporations. In 1992, over $19 million worth of medical assistance was provided to medical facilities in Latin America, the Caribbean, Africa, Asia, Oceania, and Central and Eastern Europe. CMMB's medical program includes a placement service for health care specialists who volunteer at Catholic medical facilities in developing countries. In 1992, over 65 medical specialists served worldwide for diverse tours of service. Director, Rev. James J. Yannarell, S.J.

Catholic Movement for Intellectual and Cultural Affairs of Pax Romana: The U.S. affiliate of Pax Romana — ICMICA (see International Catholic Organizations); *The Notebook*, quarterly. President, Dr. Anthony Cernera, Sacred Heart University, Park Ave., Fairfield, CT 06430.

Catholic Volunteers in Florida (1983, formerly Augustinian Volunteers): P.O. Box 702, Goldenrod, FL 32733. Co-sponsored by the bishops of Florida to promote values of social justice by direct service to farm workers, homeless, hungry, low-income people, unwed mothers and others in need. Volunteers, 20 years of age and older, serve for a one-year period in urban and rural settings.

Center for Applied Research in the Apostolate (CARA): Georgetown University, P.O. Box 1601, Washington, DC 20057. A non-profit research center serving the planning needs of the Catholic Church. CARA gathers empirical data (from attitudinal surveys, demographic projections, etc.) for use by bishops, diocesan agencies, parishes and congregations of men and women religious. Executive director, Gerald H. Early.

Christian Family Movement (CFM) (1947): Originated in Chicago to Christianize family life and create communities conducive to Christian family life. Since 1968, CFM in the U.S. has included couples from all Christian churches. National office, Box 272, Ames, IA 50010.

Christian Life Communities (1971, promulgation of revised norms by Pope Paul VI; originated, 1563, as Sodalities of Our Lady, at the Jesuit College in Rome): Director, Tage Howes, 3601 Lindell Blvd., St. Louis, MO 63108 (national office); the world CLC office is in Rome. Small communities of primarily lay persons who come together to form committed individuals for service to the world and the Church. The Spiritual Exercises of St. Ignatius are the specific source of the spiritual life of the movement.

Cursillo Movement (1949, in Spain; in U.S., 1957): National Cursillo Center, P.O. Box 210226, Dallas, TX 75211. An instrument of Christian renewal designed to form and stimulate persons to engage in apostolic action individually and in the organized apostolate, in accordance with the mission which individuals have to transform the environments in which they live into Christian environments. The method of the movement involves a three-day weekend called a cursillo and a follow-up program known as the post-cursillo. Episcopal moderator, Bishop James S. Sullivan of Fargo, N. Dak.; executive director, Thomas E. Sarg.

Franciscan World Care, an Overseas Lay Ministry Program directed by Franciscan Mission Service (1990): P.O. Box 29034, Washington, DC 20017. Laypeople serve overseas, in any part of the world, for a period of three years, in collaboration with other Franciscans overseas.

Grail, The (1921, in The Netherlands, by Rev. Jacques van Ginneken, S.J.; 1940, in U.S.): Grailville, 932 O'Bannonville Rd., Loveland, Ohio 45140 (U. S. headquarters); Duisburger Strasse 470, 4330 Mulheim, Germany (international secretariat). An international movement of women concerned about the full development of all peoples, working in education, religious, social and cultural areas.

Catholic Network of Volunteer Service (formerly, International Liaison of Lay Volunteers in Mission, ILLVIM - 1963): 4121 Harewood Rd. N.E., Washington, DC 20017. Network for lay mission programs, coordinating and facilitating efforts of volunteer mission organizations. Communicates to the laity the urgency of their role in the mission of the Church. Maintains contact with U.S. dioceses, religious communities and the private sector to connect the laity with the immediate and projected needs in mission areas worldwide. Publishes annual directory, *The Response.* Executive director, Sister Ellen Cavanaugh, R.S.M.

Jesuit Volunteer Corps (1956): 18th and Thompson Sts., Philadelphia, PA 19121 (address for information). Sponsored by the Society of Jesus in the U.S. Men and women volunteers work throughout the U.S. serving the poor directly and working for structural change. They live a simple life-style in community and seek to develop spiritually.

LAMP Ministries (Lay Apostolic Ministries with the Poor): 2704 Schurz Ave., Bronx, NY 10465. Missionary service of evangelization with the materially poor and homeless in the larger metropolitan New York area. Participants (married, single, Religious), 21 years of age and older; minimum full-time commitment, one year. Newsletter, two times a year.

Lay Mission-Helpers Association (1955): 1531 W. Ninth St., Los Angeles, CA 90015. Trains and assigns men and women for work in overseas apostolates for periods of two to three years. Approximately 700 members of the association have served in overseas assignments since its founding. Director, Rev. Michael Meyers. The **Mission Doctors Association** (same address) recruits, trains and sends Catholic physicians and their families to mission hospitals and clinics throughout the world for tours of two to three years.

Legion of Mary (1921, in Dublin, Ireland, by Frank Duff): P.O. Box 1313, St. Louis, MO 63188 (U.S. address); De Montfort House, Dublin 7, Ireland (headquarters). Enlists ordinary lay Catholic men and women, under the direction of local bishops and priests, for the work of conversion, conservation and consolation.

Movimiento Familiar Cristiano — USA (MFC) (1969): Movement of Catholic Hispanic families united in their efforts to promote the human and Christian virtues of the family so that it may become a force that forms persons, transmits the faith and contributes to the total development of the community. National presidents, Rodrigo and Lucero Agudelo, 3727 View Ct., Santa Rosa, CA 95403. Rev. Clemente Barron, C.P., is national spiritual director. Address: 651 North Sierra Madre Blvd., Pasadena, CA 91107.

National Catholic Conference for Seafarers, affiliated with the Apostleship of the Sea in the U.S. Pres., Rev. Sinclair Oubre, St, Mary's Church, 545 Savannah Ave., Port Arthur, TX 77640.

Pax Christi USA (1972): 348 E. 10th St., Erie, PA 16503. U.S. section of Pax Christi (see International Catholic Organizations). Founded to establish peacemaking as a priority for the American Catholic Church. *Pax Christi USA,* quarterly; membership, 11,500.

Volunteer Missionary Movement (1969): 5980 W. Loomis Rd., Milwaukee, WI 53129. Independent lay international mission organization with origins in the Catholic tradition but ecumenical and open to all Christian denominations. Members are involved in service-oriented ministry (usually for two years) in Africa, Central America and the U.S. Membership, 125, U.S.; over 1,000 worldwide. *Bridges,* quarterly.

Volunteers for Educational and Social Services (VESS), 3001 S. Congress Ave., Austin, TX. 78704. A program of the Texas Catholic Conference. Provides laity the opportunity to serve the Church in Texas for a year by ministering to needs of parishes, agencies and schools that are economically disadvantaged.

Center of Concern (1971): 3700 13th St., N.E., Washington, DC 20017. An independent, public-interest group engaged in social analysis, public education, advocacy and theological reflection relating to issues of global concern.

CATHOLIC YOUTH ORGANIZATIONS

Boy Scouts in the Catholic Church: The National Catholic Committee on Scouting (Eleanore Starr, Admin. .Sec., NCCS-BSA, P.O. Box 152079, Irving, TX 75015) works with the Boy Scouts of America in developing the character and spiritual life of members in units chartered to Catholic and non-Catholic organizations. National Committee Chairman, Frank Rossomondo, Jr., of Rockville, Maryland.

Camp Fire: The National Catholic Committee for Girl Scouts and Camp Fire, a standing committee of the National Federation for Catholic Youth Ministry, cooperates with Camp Fire Boys and Girls (4601 Madison Ave., Kansas City, MO 64112). To help young people learn and grow in their individual ways through participation in enjoyable activities.

Catholic Forester Youth Program, Catholic Order of Foresters: 355 Shuman Blvd., Naperville, IL 60566. To develop Christian leadership and promote the moral, intellectual, social and physical growth of its youth members. *Catholic Forester.* Membership: youth up to 16 years of age — over 19,000 in 835 local courts in U.S. High Chief Ranger, Bernard F. Milota.

Catholic Youth Organization (CYO): Name of parish-centered diocesan Catholic youth programs throughout the country. CYO promotes a program of spiritual, social and physical activities. The original CYO was organized in 1930 by Archbishop Bernard Sheil, auxiliary bishop of Chicago.

Columbian Squires (1925): 1 Columbus Plaza, New Haven, CT 06510. Junior organization of the Knights of Columbus. To train and develop leadership through active participation in a well-organized program of spiritual, service, social, cultural and athletic activities. Membership: Catholic young men, 12-18 years old. More than 22,000 in over 1,000 circles (local units) active in the U.S., Canada, Puerto Rico, Mexico, Guam and the Philippines. *Squires Newsletter,* monthly.

Girl Scouts: Girls from archdioceses and dioceses in the U.S. and its possessions participate in Girl Scouting through the collaboration of Girl Scouts of the U.S.A. (830 Third Ave., New York, NY 10022) with the National Catholic Committee for Girl Scouts and Camp Fire, a standing committee of the National Federation for Catholic Youth Ministry.

Holy Childhood Association (Pontifical Association of the Holy Childhood) (1843): 1720 Massachusetts Ave. N.W., Washington, DC 20036. The official children's mission-awareness society of the Church. Provides mission awareness for elementary school children under "HCA: Young Catholics in Mission," and financial assistance to children in more than 100 developing countries. Publishes mission and global education material for teachers and students, including *It's Our World,* student membership publication, four times a year in two grade levels. National Director, Rev. Francis W. Wright, C.S.Sp.

National Catholic Forensic League (1952): To develop articulate Catholic leaders through an interdiocesan program of speech and debate activities. *Newsletter,* quarterly. Membership: 850 schools; membership open to Catholic, private and public schools through the local diocesan league. Secretary-Treasurer, Richard Gaudette, 21 Nancy Rd., Milford, MA 01757.

National Catholic Young Adult Ministry Association (1982): 3700-A Oakview Terr. N.E., Washington, DC 20017. A national network of those who work with adults (18-35 years old) in the Church. President, Joan Weber.

National Christ Child Society Inc. (1887): 5101 Wisconsin Ave. N.W., Suite 304, Washington, DC 20016. Founder, Mary V. Merrick. A non-profit Catholic association of volunteers of all denominations dedicated to the service of needy children and youth regardless of race or creed. Membership: approximately 8,000 adult and junior members in 37 cities in U.S. President, Dr. Regis Louise Boyle.

National Federation for Catholic Youth Ministry, Inc. (1982): 3700-A Oakview Terr. NE, Washington, DC 20017. To foster the development of youth ministry in the United States through CYO and other expressions of ministry to, with, by and for youth. Executive Director, Fr. Len Wenke.

Young Christian Students: 7436 W. Harrison,

Forest Park, IL 60130. A student movement for Christian personal and social change. Membership: 500 in high schools and parishes.

COLLEGE SOCIETIES

Alpha Sigma Nu (1915): Marquette Univ., Brooks 201, Milwaukee, WI 53233 (national headquarters). National honor society of the 28 Jesuit colleges and universities of the U.S.; members chosen on the basis of scholarship, loyalty and service; 1,400 student and 30,000 alumni members. Member, Association of College Honor Societies. Gamma Pi Epsilon (1925) merged with Alpha Sigma Nu in 1973 to form society for men and women. Executive Director, Ann J. Panlener.

Delta Epsilon Sigma (1939): Barry University, Miami Shores, FL 33161. National scholastic honor society for students, faculty and alumni of colleges and universities with a Catholic tradition. *Delta Epsilon Sigma Journal,* three times a year. Membership: 52,000 in 116 chapters. Secretary, Dr. J. Patrick Lee.

Kappa Gamma Pi (1926): A national Catholic college honor society for graduates who, in addition to academic excellence, have shown outstanding leadership in extra-curricular activities. *Kappa Gamma Pi News,* five times a year. Membership: more than 30,000 in 135 colleges; 20 alumnae chapters in metropolitan areas. Executive Secretary, Marjorie Durbin, 2415 Hillcrest Dr., Stow, Ohio 44224.

Phi Kappa Theta: 3901 W. 86th St., Indianapolis, IN 46268. National social fraternity with a Catholic heritage. Merger (1959) of Phi Kappa Fraternity, founded at Brown Univ. in 1889, and Theta Kappa Phi Fraternity, founded at Lehigh Univ. in 1919. *The Temple Magazine,* quarterly, and newsletter, *The Sun.* Membership: 2,800 undergraduate and 44,000 alumni in 60 collegiate and 21 alumni chapters. Executive Director, Mark T. McSweeney.

National Catholic Student Coalition (1982): National coalition of Catholic campus ministry groups at state and private institutions of higher education. Formed after National Newman Club Federation and the National Federation of Catholic College Students dissolved in the 1960s. The U.S. affiliate of Pax Romana — IMCS (see International Catholic Organizations). Holds annual national leadership conference. Publishes *The Catholic Collegian,* four times a year. Membership: 140 campus groups. Executive administrator, David Klopfenstein, 300 College Park Ave., Dayton, Ohio 45469.

ASSOCIATIONS, MOVEMENTS, SOCIETIES IN THE U.S.

(Principal source: Almanac survey.)
See Index for other associations, movements and societies covered elsewhere.

Academy of American Franciscan History (1944), 1712 Euclid Ave., Berkeley, CA 97409. Dir., Rev. Dismas Bonner, O.F.M.

Albanian Catholic Institute "Daniel Dajani, S.J." (1992), University of San Francisco, Xavier Hall, San Francisco, CA 94117. To assist the rebuilding of the Catholic Church in Albania and to promote the dissemination of knowledge of Albania's national,

religious and cultural heritage. Director, Paul Bernadicou, S.J. *Albanian Catholic Bulletin,* annually; circulation 1,500 in North and South America, Europe, Australia, Japan and New Zealand. Editor, Gjon Sinishta.

Aid to the Church in Need (1947), U.S. office, P.O. Box 576, Deer Park, NY 11729. Assists the pastoral activities of the church in Third World countries, Eastern Europe and the former Soviet Union. *Mirror* (newsletter), 9 times a year.

American Benedictine Academy (1947). To

promote Benedictine values in contemporary culture. Pres., Jeanne Ranek, O.S.B., Our Lady of the Angels Monastery, Mt. Angel, OR 97362.

American Catholic Correctional Chaplains Association (1952), 220 in 300 institutions. Pres., Bro. Peter Donohue, C.F.X.; Sec., Sr. Dorothea Murphy, R.S.M., 1717 N.E. 9th St., Suite 123, Gainsville, FL 32609.

American Catholic Historical Association (1919), Catholic University of America, Washington, DC 20064. *The Catholic Historical Review,* quarterly. Sec.-Treas., Rev. Msgr. Robert Trisco.

American Catholic Philosophical Association (1926), The Catholic University of America, Washington, DC 20064. *American Catholic Philosophical Quarterly; Proceedings,* annually.

American Committee on Italian Migration (1952), 352 W. 44th St., New York, NY 10036; 6,000. *ACIM Newsletter* and *ACIM Nuova Via,* 6 times a year. Sec., Rev. Walter Tonelotto, C.S.

American Friends of the Vatican Library (1981), 157 Lakeshore Rd., Grosse Point Farms, MI 48236. Sponsored by the Catholic Library Association. To assist in supporting the Vatican Library: *AMICI,* newsletter.

Ancient Order of Hibernians in America, Inc. (1836); 120,000. *National Hibernian Digest,* bimonthly. Nat. Sec., Thomas McNabb, 31 Logan St., Auburn, NY 13021.

Apostleship of Prayer (1844-France; 1861-U.S.): 3 Stephen Ave., New Hyde Park, NY 11040. Promotes Daily Offering and Sacred Heart devotion.

Apostolate for Family Consecration (1975), Pope John Paul II Holy Family Center, Rt. 2, Box 700, Bloomingdale, OH 43910; 26,000 members. Family reinforcement by transforming neighborhoods into God-centered communities in the spirit of Pope John Paul II. Pres., Jerome F. Coniker.

Archconfraternity of Christian Mothers (Christian Mothers) (1881), 220 37th St., Pittsburgh, PA 15201; over 3,500 branches. Dir., Rev. Bertin Roll, O.F.M. Cap.

Archconfraternity of the Holy Ghost (1912), Holy Ghost Fathers, 2401 Bristol Pike, Bensalem, PA 19020 (U.S. headquarters).

Archdiocese for the Military Services Seminary Education Fund (1988), 962 Wayne Ave., Suite 500, Silver Spring, MD 20910.

Association for Religious and Value Issues in Counseling (1962), division of American Counseling Association. *Counseling and Values,* 3 times a year. Address, 5999 Stevenson Ave., Alexandria, VA 22304.

Association for Social Economics (formerly the Catholic Economic Association) (1941), Marquette University, Milwaukee, WI 53233; 1,300. *Review of Social Economy,* quarterly.

Association of Catholic Diocesan Archivists (1979): To work for establishment of an archival program in every American diocese. *ACDA Bulletin,* quarterly. Pres. (1994-95), Mr. John J. Treanor, 5150 Northwest Highway, Chicago, IL 60630.

Association of Catholic Trade Unionists (1937), 12 Holly Hills Dr., Woodstock, NY 12498. Chaplain, Rev. Vincent J. P. Fox.

Association of Marian Helpers (1944), Stockbridge, MA 01263; 1,200,000, mostly in U.S. *Marian Helpers Bulletin,* bimonthly. To promote vocations to Church service and support worldwide apostolates of Marians of the Immaculate Conception.

Beginning Experience (1973), 305 Michigan Ave., Detroit, MI 48226; 150 teams throughout the world. Weekend program to help divorced, widowed and separated start a new beginning in their lives. Exec. Dir., Sr. Tarianne DeYonker, O.P.

Calix Society (1947), 7601 Wayzata Blvd., Minneapolis, MN 55426; 2,000 members in U.S. and Canada; *Chalice,* bimonthly. Association of Catholic alcoholics maintaining their sobriety through affiliation with and participation in Alcoholics Anonymous. Sec.-Treas., Bill Fox.

Canon Law Society of America (1939), Catholic University, Washington, DC 20064. To further research and study in canon law; 1,850. Exec. Coord., Rev. Patrick Cogan, S.A.

Cardinal Mindszenty Foundation (CMF) (1958), P.O. Box 11321, St. Louis, MO 63105. To uphold and defend the Catholic Church, family life and freedom for all under God. Pres., Eleanor Schlafly.

Catholic Aid Association (1878), 3499 N. Lexington Ave., St. Paul, MN 55126; 80,000. *Catholic Aid News,* monthly. Fraternal life insurance society. Pres. F. L. Spanier.

Catholic Alumni Clubs International (1957): To advance social, cultural and spiritual well-being of members. Membership limited to single Catholics with professional education; 7,500 in 48 clubs in U.S. Pres., Guy A. DiMarino, 215 W. Wood St., Lowellville, OH 44436.

Catholic Answers (1982), P.O. Box 17490, San Diego, CA 92177. *This Rock,* monthly. Apologetics and evangelization organization. Founder and dir., Karl Keating.

Catholic Biblical Association of America (1936), Catholic University of America, Washington, DC 20064; 1,263. *The Catholic Biblical Quarterly; Old Testament Abstracts,* monograph series.

Catholic Book Publishers Association,Inc. (1987), 333 Glen Head Rd., Old Brookville, NY 11545. Sec., Charles A. Roth.

Catholic Commission on Intellectual and Cultural Affairs (CCICA) (1946), LaSalle University, Philadelphia, PA 19141; 350; Exec. Dir., Bro. Daniel Burke, F.S.C.

Catholic Committee of Appalachia (1970), 115 Main St., Box 953, Whitesburg, KY 41858.

Catholic Daughters of the Americas (1903), 10 W. 71st St., New York, NY 10023; 140,000. *Share Magazine.* Nat. Regent, Edna Jane Nolte.

Catholic Golden Age (1975): National Headquarters, Scranton, PA 18503; more than 1,000,000 members since its founding. *CGA World Magazine.* For Catholics over 50 years of age. Pres., Rev. Gerald N. Dino.

Catholic Guardian Society (1913), 1011 First Ave., New York, NY 10022. Exec. Dir., James P. O'Neill.

Catholic Home Bureau (1898), 1011 First Ave., New York, NY 10022. Exec. Dir., Sr. Una McCormack.

Catholic Home Study Service (1936), P.O. Box 363, Perryville, MO 63775. Provides instruction in the Catholic faith by mail free of charge. Director, Rev. Oscar Lukefahr, C.M.

Catholic Interracial Council of New York, Inc. (1934), 899 Tenth Ave., New York, NY 10019. To promote racial and social justice.

Catholic Knights of America (1877), 1850 Dalton St., Cincinnati, OH 45214; 7,800. *Catholic Knights of America Journal*, monthly. Fraternal insurance society.

Catholic Knights of Ohio (1891): 22005 Mastick Rd., Fairview Park, OH 44126; 12,000 in Ohio and Kentucky. *The Messenger*, monthly. Fraternal insurance society. Pres., Victor D. Huss.

Catholic Kolping Society of America (1923), 22515 Masonic Blvd., St. Clair Shores, MI 48082. *Kolping Banner*, monthly. International society concerned with spiritual, educational and physical development of members.

Catholic Lawyers' Guild. Organization usually on a diocesan basis, under different titles.

Catholic League (1943), 1200 N. Ashland Ave., Chicago, IL 60622. Exec. Dir., Most Rev. Alfred Abramowicz.

Catholic League for Religious and Civil Rights (1973), 1011 First Ave., Room 1670, New York, NY 10022; 15 local chapters throughout U.S. Serves Catholic community as an anti-defamation and civil rights agency. Pres., William A. Donohue.

Catholic Library Association (1921), 461 W. Lancaster Avenue, Haverford, PA 19041; 2,210. *Catholic Library World*, bimonthly.

Catholic Near East Welfare Association (1926), 1011 First Ave., New York, NY 10022. A papal agency for humanitarian and pastoral support, under the jurisdiction of the Congregation for the Oriental Churches. Missionary service for all Near and Middle East countries, India, Ethiopia, Eastern Europe and the former Soviet Union. Sec. Gen., Rev. Msgr. Robert L. Stern.

Catholic Order of Foresters (1883), 355 Shuman Blvd., Naperville, IL 60566; 150,000. *The Catholic Forester*, bimonthly. Fraternal insurance society. High Chief Ranger, Bernard F. Milota.

Catholic Pamphlet Society (1938), 100 Old Maryvale Dr., Cheektowago, NY 14525. Parish pamphlet and rack distributors. Dir., Rev. Msgr. Walter O. Kern.

Catholic Peace Fellowship (1964), 339 Lafayette St., New York, NY 10012; 3,500. *CPF Bulletin*. Peace education and direct action projects, development of the nonviolent tradition within the Catholic community; draft counseling and nonviolence training.

Catholic Press Association of the U.S., Inc. (1911), 119 N. Park Ave., Rockville Centre, NY 11570. *The Catholic Journalist*, monthly; *Catholic Press Directory*, annually. Pres., Arthur L. McKenna; exec. dir., Owen P. McGovern.

Catholic Theological Society of America (1946), Office of Executive Secretary, LaSalle University, Philadelphia, PA 19141; 1,400. *Proceedings*, annually. Pres. (1993-94), Gerard Sloyan.

Catholic Union of Texas, The K.J.T. (1889), 214

E. Colorado St., La Grange, TX 78945; 18,000. *Nasinec*, weekly, and *K. J. T. News*, monthly. Fraternal and insurance society. Pres., Laddie Matula, Sr.

Catholic War Veterans (1935), 441 N. Lee St., Alexandria, VA 22314; 500 posts, *Catholic War Veteran*, bimonthly.

Catholic Worker Movement (1933), 36 E. First St., New York, NY 10003. *The Catholic Worker*, 8 times a year. Lay apostolate founded by Peter Maurin and Dorothy Day; has Houses of Hospitality in over 60 U.S. cities and several communal farms in various parts of the country. Promotes pacifism, personalism, voluntary poverty.

Catholic Workman (Katolicky Delnik) (1891), P.O. Box 47, New Prague, MN 56071; 16,211. *Catholic Workman*, monthly. Fraternal and insurance society.

Catholics against Capital Punishment (1992), P.O. Box 3125, Arlington, VA 22203. Nat. coordinator, Frank McNeirney.

Catholics United for Spiritual Action, Inc. (CUSA) (1947), 63 Wall St., New York, NY 10005 (legal office); 1,200. A group- correspondence apostolate for the disabled. Admin. Leader, Miss Anna Marie Sopko, 176 W. 8th St., Bayonne, NJ 07002 (national central office).

Catholics United for the Faith (1968), 50 Washington Ave., New Rochelle, NY 10801; 23,000 worldwide, *Lay Witness*, monthly. Lay apostolic group concerned with spiritual and doctrinal formation of members. Documentary and Information Service. Pres., James Likoudis.

Central Association of the Miraculous Medal (1915), 475 E. Chelten Ave., Philadelphia, PA 19144. *Miraculous Medal*, quarterly. Dir., Rev. John W. Gouldrick, C.M.

Chaplains' Aid Association, Inc. (1917), 962 Wayne Ave., Silver Spring, MD 20910. To receive and administer funds toward education of seminarians to become priest-chaplains in military services. Pres., Most Rev. Joseph T. Dimino.

Christian Foundation for Children and Aging, One Elmwood Ave., Kansas City, KS 66103. Grassroots movement dedicated to improving the condition of poor children and aging around the world. Pres., Robert K. Hentzen.

Christophers, Inc., The (1945), 12 E. 48th St., New York, NY 10017. Founded by Rev. James Keller, M.M. Without formal organization, meetings or membership fees, The Christophers stimulate personal initiative and responsible action in line with Christian principles through broadcast of Christopher radio and TV programs; free distribution of *Christopher News Notes*, ten times a year; publication of a weekly Christopher column in over 200 newspapers; and other publications. Dir., Rev. John Catoir.

Citizens for Educational Freedom (1959): Nonsectarian group concerned with parents' right to educational choice by means of tuition tax credits and vouchers. Exec. dir., Robert S. Marlowe, 921 S. Walter Reed Dr., Suite 1, Arlington, VA 22204.

Confraternity of Bl. Junipero Serra (1989): P.O. Box 7125, Mission Hills, CA 91346; 3,500 in U.S. and foreign countries. Founded in Monterey diocese, California, to help promote process of canonization of Bl. Junipero Serra and increase spiritual development of members through emulation of his virtues. *Siempre Adelante,* newsletter, two times a year. Director, Rev. Thomas L. Davis, Jr.; Spiritual Dir., Rev. Noel F. Moholy, O.F.M.

Confraternity of Catholic Clergy (1976): Association of priests pledged to pursuit of personal holiness, loyalty to the Pope, theological study and adherence to authentic teachings of the Catholic faith. Sec., Rev. L. Dudley Day, O.S.A., 6310 Claremont Ave., Chicago, IL 60636.

Confraternity of the Immaculate Conception of Our Lady of Lourdes (1874), Box 561, Notre Dame, IN 46556. Distributors of Lourdes water.

Confraternity of the Most Holy Rosary: See Dominican Rosary Apostolate.

Convert Movement Our Apostolate (CMOA) (1945), formerly Convert Makers of America, c/o Our Lady of Grace Rectory, 430 Avenue W, Brooklyn, NY 11223. To train and assist lay persons on a parish level to discuss and present the Faith to interested persons. Dir., Msgr. Erwin A. Juraschek; Nat./Internatl. Coord., Mary A. LaCava.

Courage (1980), c/o St. Michael's Rectory, 424 W. 34th St., New York, NY 10001. To live chaste lives in accordance with the Church's teaching on homosexuality. Newsletter, 3 or 4 times a year. Nat. Dir., Rev. John F. Harvey, O.S.F.S.

Damien-Dutton Society for Leprosy Aid, Inc. (1944), 616 Bedford Ave., Bellmore, NY 11710; 25,000. *Damien Dutton Call,* quarterly. Provides medicine, rehabilitation and research for conquest of leprosy. Pres., Howard E. Crouch; Dir., Sr. Mary Augustine, S.M.S.M.

Daughters of Isabella (1897), P.O. Box 9585, New Haven, CT 06535; 100,000. To unite Catholic women into a fraternal order for spiritual benefits and to promote higher ideals within society.

Disaster Response Office (1990), Catholic Charities USA, 1731 King St., Suite 200, Alexandria, VA 22314. Promotes and facilitates Catholic disaster response in the U.S. Dir., Jane A. Gallagher.

Dominican Rosary Apostolate (1806), 141 E. 65th St., New York, NY 10021. Acting Dir., Rev. Kenneth A. France-Kelly, O.P.

Edith Stein Guild, Inc. (1955), Our Lady of Victory Church, 60 William St., New York, NY 10005; quarterly newsletter. Promotes Judaeo-Christian understanding, extends friendship to Catholics of Jewish background, spreads knowledge of life and writings of Bl. Edith Stein (Sister Benedicta of the Cross).

Enthronement of the Sacred Heart in the Home (1907), Box 111, Fairhaven, MA 02719.

Family Rosary, Inc., The (1942), Executive Park Drive, Albany, NY 12203. Founded by Father Patrick Peyton, C.S.C. Conducts worldwide Family Rosary Crusades to strengthen love and unity within families by prayer, especially the family rosary. Nat. Dir., Rev. Robert J. Brennan, C.S.C.

Federation of Diocesan Liturgical Commissions (FDLC) (1969), P.O. Box 29039, Washington, DC 20017. Voluntary association of personnel from diocesan liturgical commissions of the U.S. The main purpose is promotion of the liturgy as the heart of Christian life, especially in the parish community. Exec. Sec., Rev. Michael J. Spillane.

Fellowship of Catholic Scholars (1977), Prof. Ralph McInerny, president, Jacques Maritain Center, 714 Hesburgh Library, Notre Dame, IN 46556; over 1,000 members. Interdisciplinary research and publications of Catholic scholars in accord with the magisterium of the Catholic Church.

First Catholic Slovak Ladies' Association, USA (1892), 24950 Chagrin Blvd., Beachwood, OH 44122; 102,000. *Fraternally Yours,* monthly. Fraternal insurance society. Pres., Anna S. Granchay.

First Catholic Slovak Union (Jednota) (1890), FCSU Corporate Center, 6611 Rockside Rd., Independence, OH 44131; 96,206. *Jednota,* weekly. Exec. Sec., Margaret M. Bacho.

Foundations and Donors Interested in Catholic Activities, Inc. (FADICA), 1350 Connecticut Ave. N.W., Suite 303, Washington, DC 20036. To improve effectiveness of private philanthropy assisting the Catholic Church carry out its mission. Pres., Francis J. Butler.

Franciscan Apostolate of the Way of the Cross (1949), P.O. Box 23, Boston, MA 02112. Distributes religious materials to the sick and shut-in. Dir., Rev. Robert Lynch, O.F.M.

Franciscan Canticle, Inc. (1983), 13333 Palmdale Rd., Victorville, CA 92392. Community of men and women artists who use their gifts and talents to promote the work of God.

Free the Fathers (1983), 1120 Applewood Circle, Signal Mountain, TN 37377. To work for the freedom of bishops and priests imprisoned in China. Pres., John M. Davies.

Gabriel Richard Institute (1949), 2820 West Maple Rd., Suite No. 101, Troy, MI 48084. Conducts Christopher Leadership Course for development of leadership abilities with Christian purpose. Dir., Rev. Thomas J. Bresnahan; national manager, Dolores Ammar.

Guard of Honor of the Immaculate Heart of Mary (1932), 135 West 31st St., New York, NY 10001. An archconfraternity approved by the Holy See whose members cultivate devotion to the Blessed Virgin Mary, particularly through a daily Guard Hour of Prayer.

Guild of Our Lady of Ransom (1948), c/o St. Margaret Rectory, 800 Columbia Rd., Dorchester, MA 02125. Boston archdiocesan ministry for spiritual aid and rehabilitation of inmates of penal institutions. Exec. Dir., Rev. Thomas D. Conway.

Guild of St. Paul (1937), 230 Waller Ave., Lexington, KY 40503; For converts. Nat. Spir. Dir., Rev. Msgr. Leonard Nienaber.

Holy Name Society: Founded in 1274 by Blessed John Vercelli, master general of the Dominicans, to promote reverence for the Holy Name of Jesus; this is still the principal purpose of the society, which also develops lay apostolic programs in line with directives of the Second Vatican Council. Introduced in the U.S. by Dominican Father Charles H. McKenna in 1870-71, the society has about 5 million members on diocesan and parochial levels.

With approval of the local bishop and pastor, women as well as men may be members.

Holy Name Society, National Association (NAHNS) (1970), P.O. Box 26038, Baltimore, MD 21224. *Holy Name Newsletter*, monthly. Association of diocesan and parochial Holy Name Societies.

Hungarian Catholic League of America, Inc. (1945), 30 E. 30th St., New York, NY 10016. Member of the National Catholic Resettlement Council.

International Institute of the Heart of Jesus (1972), 7700 Blue Mound Rd., Milwaukee, WI 53213 (business office); Delegacion Latinoamericana, IIHJ, Casilla 118, Correo 35, Las Condes, Santiago, Chile (president's office). Promote awareness and appreciation of the mystery of the Heart of Christ and establish an international forum for the apostolate. Pres., Rev. Roger Vekemans, S.J.

Italian Catholic Federation, Central Council (1924), 1801 Van Ness Ave., Suite 330, San Francisco, CA 94109; 25,000; *Bollettino*, monthly.

John Carroll Society, The (1951), P.O. Box 29260, Washington, DC 20017. Chaplain, Rev. Peter Vaghi.

Judean Society, Inc., The (1966), 1075 Space Park Way No. 336, Mt. View, CA 94043. International organization for divorced Catholics. Foundress/Internatl. Dir., Frances A. Miller.

Knights of Peter Claver (1909), and **Knights of Peter Claver, Ladies Auxiliary** (1926), 1825 Orleans Ave., New Orleans, LA 70116. 35,000. *The Claverite*, biannually. Fraternal and aid society. National Chaplain, Most Rev. Curtis J. Guillory, S.V.D.

Knights of St. John, International Supreme Commandery (1886), 6517 Charles Ave., Parma, OH 44129; Sup. Sec., Brig. Gen Salvatore La Bianca.

Knights of the Immaculata (Militia Immaculatae, M.I.) (1917), 1600 W. Park Ave., Libertyville, IL 60048; canonically established with international headquarters in Rome. A pious association for evangelization and catechesis beginning with members' own inner renewal, through the intercession of the Blessed Virgin Mary.

Ladies of Charity of the United States of America (1960), 7800 Natural Bridge Rd., St. Louis, MO 63121; 40,000 in U.S. International Association founded by St. Vincent de Paul in 1617.

Latin Liturgy Association (1975), Office of Chairman, Prof. Anthony Lo Bello, Box 29, Dept. of Mathematics, Allegheny College, Meadville, PA 16335; 1,500. To promote the use of the Latin language and music in the approved rites of the Church. Quarterly journal.

Legatus (1987), 30 Frank Lloyd Wright Dr., P.O. Box 997, Ann Arbor, MI 48106; 347 members. To apply Church's moral teaching in business and personal lives of members. Legatus Newsletter, monthly.

Lithuanian Groups: Ateitininkai, members of Lithuanian Catholic Federation Ateitis (1910), 1209 Country Lane, Lemont, IL 60439; to promote Catholic action and uphold Lithuanian heritage among youth; *Ateitis*, bimonthly; Pres., Juozas Polikaitis. Knights of Lithuania (1913), educational-fraternal organization; *Vytis*, monthly; Pres., Frances R. Petkus, 800 Haldeman Ave., Dayton, OH 45404. Lithuanian Catholic Alliance (1886), 71-73 S. Washington St., Wilkes-Barre, PA 18701; 118 branches; *Garsas*, monthly; fraternal insurance organization; Pres., Thomas E. Mack. Lithuanian Roman Catholic Federation of America (1906), umbrella organization for Lithuanian parishes and organizations; *The Observer*, bimonthly; Pres., Saulius Kuprys, 4545 W. 63rd St., Chicago, IL 60629. Lithuanian Roman Catholic Priests' League (1909): religious-professional association, Pres., Rev. Albert Contons, 50 Orton-Marotta Way, Boston, MA 02127. Lithuanian Catholic Religious Aid, Inc. (1961), 351 Highland Blvd., Brooklyn, NY 11207; to assist Catholics in Lithuania; Chairman and Pres., Most Rev. Paul Baltakis.

Little Flower Mission League (1957), P.O. Box 25, Plaucheville, LA 71362. Sponsored by the Brothers of the Holy Eucharist. Dir., Bro. André M. Lucia, F.S.E.

Little Flower Society (1923), 1313 Frontage Rd.; Darien, IL 60559; 200,000 Nat. Dir., Rev. Robert E. Colaresi, O. Carm.

Liturgical Conference, The, 8750 Georgia Ave., Suite 123, Silver Spring, MD 20910. *Liturgy, Accent on Worship, Homily Service*. Education, research and publication programs for renewing and enriching Christian liturgical life. Ecumenical. Exec. Dir., Ralph R. Van Loon.

Loyal Christian Benefit Association (1890), P.O. Box 13005, Erie, PA 16514. Fraternal benefit and insurance society. *The Fraternal Leader*, quarterly.

Marian Movement of Priests (1972), P.O. Box 8, St. Francis, ME 04774 (U.S.); Via Mercalli, 23, 20122 Milano, Italy (internatl. headquarters); 4,000 clergy; 34,000 religious and laity (U.S.). Spiritual renewal through consecration to the Immaculate Heart of Mary. Pres. Rev. Albert G. Roux.

Mariological Society of America (1949), Sec., Rev. Thomas A. Thompson, S.M., Marian Library, Box 1390, University of Dayton, Dayton, OH 45469; 520. *Marian Studies*, annually. Founded by Rev. Juniper B. Carol, O.F.M., to promote greater appreciation of and scientific research in Marian theology.

Maryheart Crusaders, The (1964), 22 Button St., Meriden, CT 06450; 3,000. To reunite fallen-away Catholics and promote religious education for adults. Pres., Louise D'Angelo.

Men of the Sacred Heart (1964), Shrine of the Sacred Heart, Harleigh, PA 18225. Promote enthronement of Sacred Heart.

Missionary Association of Catholic Women (1916), 3501 S. Lake Dr., P.O. Box 07912, Milwaukee, WI 53207.

Missionary Vehicle Association, Inc. (MIVA America) (1971), 1241 Monroe St. N.E., Washington, DC 20017. To raise funds and distribute them annually as vehicle grants to missionaries working with the poor in Third World countries. Nat. Dir., Rev. Philip De Rea, M.S.C.

Morality in Media, Inc. (1962), 475 Riverside Dr., New York, NY 10115. Interfaith national organization. Newsletter, bimonthly. Works by constitutional means to curb the explosive growth of hard-core pornography and to turn back the tide of grossly offensive, indecent media. A major project is the National Obscenity Law Center which provides legal information for prosecutors and other attorneys. Pres., Robert W. Peters.

National Assembly of Religious Women (NARW): Founded as the National Assembly of Women Religious, 1970; title changed, 1980. A movement of feminist women committed to prophetic tasks of giving witness, raising awareness and engaging in public action and advocacy for justice in church and society. Address: 529 S. Wabash Ave., Suite 404, Chicago, IL 60605.

National Association for Lay Ministry (1977), 80 E. 78th St., Chanhassen, MN 55317; 600. Affirms lay people who respond to a call to ministry in the Church.

National Association of Church Personnel Administrators (1973), 100 E. 8th St., Cincinnati, OH 45202. Exec. Dir., Sr. Ann White, S.L.

National Association of Diocesan Ecumenical Officers, Network of Catholics involved in ecumenical and interreligious work. Pres., Rev. Vincent A. Heier, 462 N. Taylor St., St. Louis, MO 63108.

National Association of Pastoral Musicians (1976), 225 Sheridan St., N.W., Washington, DC 20011; 9,000. _Pastoral Music,_ six times a year. For clergy and musicians. Exec. Dir., Rev. Virgil C. Funk.

National Association of Priest Pilots (1964), Pres., Rev. John Hemann, 660 Bush Ave., Garner, IA 50438.

National Catholic Bandmasters' Association (1953), Box 1023, Notre Dame University, Notre Dame, IN 46556. Exec. Sec., Rev. George Wiskirchen, C.S.C.

National Catholic Cemetery Conference (1949), 710 N. River Rd., Des Plaines, IL 60016. Exec. Dir., Leo A. Droste.

National Catholic Conference for Interracial Justice (NCCIJ) (1960), 3033 Fourth St. N.E., Washington, DC 20017. Stresses moral dimension of civil rights, intercultural cooperation and interracial justice programming in each diocese/organization. Exec. Dir. Mr. Jerome B. Ernst.

National Catholic Conference of Airport Chaplains (1986), Chicago O'Hare International Airport, P.O. Box 66353, Chicago, IL 60666. Provides support and communication for Catholics performing pastoral ministry to airport and airline workers and Catholic travelers; affiliated with Bishops' Committee on Migration, NCCB. Pres., Rev. John A. Jamnicky.

National Catholic Council on Alcoholism and Related Drug Problems, 210 Noel Rd., Far Rockaway, NY 11693.

National Catholic Development Conference (1968), 86 Front St., Hempstead, NY 11550. Profes-

sional association of organizations and individuals engaged in raising funds for Catholic charitable activities. Pres., Peter A. Eltink; Exec. Dir., George T. Holloway.

National Catholic Ministry to the Bereaved (1990), 7835 Harvard Ave., Cleveland, OH 44105. Support ministry to the bereaved.

National Catholic Pharmacists Guild of the United States (1962): _The Catholic Pharmacist._ Exec. Dir., John P. Winkelmann, 1012 Surrey Hills Dr., St. Louis, MO 63117.

National Catholic Society of Foresters (1891), 446 E. Ontario St., Chicago, IL 60611; 57,534; _National Catholic Forester,_ quarterly. A fraternal insurance society.

National Catholic Stewardship Council (1962), 1275 K St. N.W., Suite 980, Washington, DC 20005. A professional association to promote the concept of Christian stewardship in dioceses and parishes. Nat. Dir., Matthew R. Paratore.

National Catholic Women's Union (1916), 3835 Westminster Pl., St. Louis, MO 63108; 10,500.

National Center for the Laity (1977), 1 E. Superior St., No. 311, Chicago, IL 60611. _Initiatives,_ six times a year. To promote and implement the vision of Vatican II: That the laity are the Church in the modern world as they attend to their occupational, family and neighborhood responsibilities.

National Center for Urban Ethnic Affairs (1971): P.O. Box 20, Cardinal Station, Washington, DC 20064. Research and action related to the Church's concern for cultural pluralism and urban neighborhoods. An affiliate of the USCC. Pres., Dr. John A. Kromkowski.

National Committee of Catholic Laymen, The (1977), 150 E. 35th St., Room 840, New York, NY 10016. Lobbying and publishing organization representing "orthodox" Catholics who strongly support Pope John Paul II; _catholic eye,_ monthly. Pres., J.P. McFadden.

National Conference of Catechetical Leadership (formerly, National Conference of Diocesan Directors of Religious Education) (1936): 3021 4th St. N.E., Washington, DC 20017; 987. To promote catechetical ministry at the national diocesan and parish levels. Exec. Dir., Neil A. Parent.

National Conference of Diocesan Vocation Directors (NCDVD) (1961), 1603 S. Michigan Ave., Suite 400, Chicago, IL 60616. To provide diocesan vocation personnel with information and services regarding: awareness and discernment of vocations to the diocesan or religious priesthood and the religious life for both men and women; formation of diocesan priesthood candidates. Exec. Dir., Rev. Jay F. O'Connor.

National Council for Catholic Evangelization (1983), 7494 Devon Lane, Manassas, VA 22111. To promote evangelization as the "primary and essential mission of the Church," in accordance with _Evangelii Nuntiandi,_ the 1975 apostolic exhortation of Pope Paul VI. Exec. Dir., Deacon Gordon Richard.

National Council of Catholic Men, 4712 Randolph Dr., Annandale, VA 22003. A federation of Catholic organizations through which Catholic men may be heard nationally on matters of common interest. NCCM is a constituent of the National Council of Catholic Laity.

National Council of Catholic Women (1920), 1275 K St. N.W., Suite 975, Washington, DC 20005. A federation of some 8,000 organizations of Catholic women in the U.S. *Catholic Woman,* bimonthly. NCCW unites Catholic organizations and individual Catholic women of the U.S., develops their leadership potential, assists them to act upon current issues in the Church and society, provides a medium through which Catholic women may speak and act upon matters of common interest, and relates to other national and international organizations in the solution of present-day problems. It is an affiliate of the World Union of Catholic Women's Organizations.

National Federation of Catholic Physicians' Guilds (1927), 850 Elm Grove Rd., Elm Grove, WI 53122; 3,500 in 82 autonomous guilds in U.S. and Canada, *Linacre Quarterly.* Exec. Dir., Robert H. Herzog.

National Federation of Priests' Councils (1968), 1337 West Ohio, Chicago, IL 60622. To give priests' councils a representative voice in matters of presbyteral, pastoral and ministerial concern to the U.S. and the universal Church. Pres., Rev. Thomas J. McCarthy.

National Federation of Spiritual Directors (1972). Pres., Rev. Robert M. Coerver, Holy Trinity Seminary, P.O. Box 140309, Irving, TX 75014.

National Guild of Catholic Psychiatrists, Inc. (1949). Integration of psychiatry and Roman Catholic theology. *The Bulletin.* Mailing address: Robert McAllister, M.D., Pres., P.O. Box 111, St. George, ME 04857.

National Institute for the Word of God (1972), 487 Michigan Ave. N.E., Washington, DC 20017. For renewed biblical preaching, Bible sharing and evangelization. Dir., Rev. John Burke, O.P.

National Organization for Continuing Education of Roman Catholic Clergy, Inc. (1973), 1337 W. Ohio St., Chicago, IL 60622. Membership: 157 dioceses, 81 religious provinces, 47 associates in U.S., 18 associates outside U.S. Pres., Rev. Francis S. Tebbe, O.F.M.; Exec. Dir., Bro. Paul A. Murray, C.F.X.

NETWORK (1971), 806 Rhode Island Ave. N.E., Washington, DC 20018. *NETWORK Connection,* bimonthly. A national Catholic social justice lobby. Nat. Coord., Kathy Thornton, R.S.M.

Nocturnal Adoration Society of the United States (1882), 184 E. 76th St., New York, NY 10021. Nat. Dir., Rev. Bernard J. Camire, S.S.S.

North American Academy of Liturgy, c/o Dr. David Truemper, Valparaiso Univ., Valparaiso, IN 46383. *Proceedings,* annually. Foster ecumenical and interreligious liturgical research, publication and dialogue on a scholarly level. Pres., Paul Bradshaw.

North American Conference of Separated and Divorced Catholics (1972), Exec. Dir., Dorothy J. Levesque, 80 St. Mary's Dr., Cranston, R.I. 02920.

Order of the Alhambra (1904), 4200 Leeds Ave., Baltimore, MD 21229. 7,800 in U.S. and Canada. Fraternal society dedicated to assisting retarded and handicapped children. Supreme Commander, Roger J. Reid.

Our Lady's Rosary Makers (1949), 4611 Poplar Level Rd., P.O. Box 37080, Louisville, KY 40233; 20,000 members. To supply missionaries with free rosaries for distribution throughout the world. *News Bulletin,* monthly. Pres., Harry Prestwood, Deacon.

Paulist National Catholic Evangelization Association (1977), 3031 Fourth St., N.E., Washington, DC 20017. *Share the Word,* bimonthly magazine. To work with unchurched and alienated Catholics; to develop, test and document contemporary ways in which Catholic parishes and dioceses can evangelize unchurched and inactive. Dir., Rev. Kenneth Boyack, C.S.P.

Perpetual Eucharistic Adoration, 660 Club View Dr., Los Angeles, CA 90024. Promote programs of Perpetual Eucharistic adoration/exposition in parishes throughout the world.

Philangeli (Friends of the Angels) (1949 in England; 1956 in U.S.), Viatorian Fathers, 1115 E. Euclid St., Arlington Heights, IL 60004.

Pious Union of Prayer (1898), St. Joseph's Home, P.O. Box 288, Jersey City, NJ 07303; 20,000. *St. Joseph's Messenger and Advocate of the Blind,* quarterly.

Polish Roman Catholic Union of America (1887): 984 N. Milwaukee Ave., Chicago, IL 60622. *Narod Polski,* bimonthly. Fraternal benefit society.

Pontifical Mission for Palestine (1949), c/o Catholic Near East Welfare Association, 1011 First Ave., New York, NY 10022. Office in Vatican City with field offices in Beirut, Lebanon; Jerusalem; Amman, Jordan. A papal relief agency for 2 million Palestinian refugees as well as other displaced and dispossessed peoples in the Middle East. Distributes food, clothing, other essentials; maintains medical clinics, orphanages, libraries, refugee camp schools and chapels. Pres., Rev. Msgr. Robert L. Stern.

Pontifical Missionary Union (1916), 366 Fifth Ave., New York, NY 10001. To promote mission awareness among clergy, religious, candidates to priestly and religious life, and others engaged in pastoral ministry of the Church. Nat. Dir., Most Rev. William J. McCormack.

Priests' Eucharistic League (1887), 5384 Wilson Mills Rd., Cleveland, OH 44143; 5,000. *Emmanuel,* 10 issues a year. Nat. Dir., Rev. Anthony Schueller, S.S.S.

Pro Ecclesia Foundation (1970), 509 Madison Ave., New York, NY 10022. *Pro Ecclesia,* quarterly, and books and pamphlets; twice-weekly cable TV program. To answer attacks against Church and promote Church teachings. Pres., Dr. Timothy A. Mitchell.

Pro Maria Committee (1952), 22 Second Ave., Lowell, MA 01854. Promote devotion to Our Lady of Beauraing (See Index).

Pro Sanctity Movement. A worldwide force of laity organized to spread God's call of all persons to holiness. Addresses: 205 S. Pine Dr., Fullerton, CA 92633; 730 E. 87th St., Brooklyn, NY 11236; 5310 S. 52nd St., Omaha, NE 68117.

Project Children (1975), P.O. Box 933, Greenwood Lake, NY 10925. Nonsectarian volunteer group; provide children of Northern Ireland with a six-week summer vacation with host families in the U.S.

The Providence Association of the Ukrainian Catholics in America (Ukrainian Catholic Fraternal Benefit Society) (1912), 817 N. Franklin St., Philadelphia, PA 19123. *America* (Ukrainian-English).

Queen of the Americas Guild, Inc. (1979), P.O. Box 851, 345 Kautz Rd., St. Charles, IL 60174; 3,000 members. To build English information center and hospice near Basilica in Mexico City and spread the message of Guadalupe. Pres., Frank E. Smoczynski. Moderator, Most Rev. Jerome J. Hastrich.

Raskob Foundation for Catholic Activities, Inc. (1945), Kennett Pike and Montchanin Rd., P.O. Box 4019, Wilmington, DE 19807. Pres., Gerard S. Garey.

Reparation Society of the Immaculate Heart of Mary, Inc. (1946), 100 E. 20th St., Baltimore, MD 21218. *Fatima Findings,* monthly. Dir. Rev. John Ryan, S.J.

Rosary for Life Organization, P.O. Box 40213, Memphis, TN 38174. Promotes two prayer events— Rosary Novena for Life held in springtime and Multination (formerly Worldwide) Rosary for Life held on a Saturday in October.

Sacred Heart League, Walls, MS 38686; 1,500,000. Promote devotion to the Sacred Heart. Its program services include the Sacred Heart Auto League for careful, prayerful driving and the Apostolate of the Printed Word. Pres., Rev. Robert Hess, S.C.J.

St. Ansgar's Scandinavian Catholic League (1910), 40 W. 13th St., New York, NY 10011; 1,000. *St. Ansgar's Bulletin,* annually. Prayers and financial support for Church in Scandinavia. Pres., Astrid M. O'Brien.

St. Anthony's Guild (1924), Paterson, NJ 07509; 100,000. Promotes devotion to St. Anthony of Padua and support for formation programs, infirm friars and ministries of the Franciscans of Holy Name Province. *The Anthonian,* quarterly. Dir., Rev. Kevin E. Mackin, O.F.M.

St. Gregory Foundation for Latin Liturgy (1989), 207 Adams St., Newark, NJ 07105. To promote within the Church in the U.S. the use of the Latin language in the Mass in accordance with the teachings of Vatican II. Founder and Pres., Rev. Peter M.J. Stravinskas.

St. Jude League (1929), 205 W. Monroe St., Chicago, IL 60606. *St. Jude Journal,* five times a year. Dir., Rev. Mark J. Brummel, C.M.F.

St. Margaret of Scotland Guild, Inc. (1938), Graymoor, Garrison, NY 10524; 743. Moderator, Bro. Pius MacIsaac, S.A.

St. Martin de Porres Guild (1935), 141 E. 65th St., New York, NY 10021. Acting Dir., Rev. Kenneth A. France-Kelly, O.P.

Serra International (1934), 22 W. Monroe St., Chicago, IL 60603; 19,500 members in 569 clubs in 30 countries. *Serran,* bimonthly. Fosters vocations to the priesthood, and religious life, trains Catholic lay leadership. Formally aggregated to the Pontifical Society for Priestly Vocations, 1951.

Slovak Catholic Federation (1911): Founded by Rev. Joseph Murgas to promote and coordinate religious activities among Slovak Catholic fraternal societies, religious communities and Slovak ethnic parishes in their effort to address themselves to the special needs of Slovak Catholics in the U.S. and Canada. Pres., Rev. Msgr. Edward M. Matash, 317 Avenue "E," Bayonne, NJ 07002.

Slovak Catholic Sokol (1905), 205 Madison St., Passaic, NJ 07055; 43,000. *Slovak Catholic Falcon,* weekly. Pres., George J. Kostelnik.

Society for the Propagation of the Faith (1822), 366 Fifth Ave., New York, NY 10001; established in 174 dioceses. Church's principal instrument for promoting mission awareness and generating financial support for the missions. General fund for ordinary and extraordinary subsidies for all mission dioceses. *Mission,* 4 times a year; *Director's Newsletter,* monthly. Is subject to Congregation for the Evangelization of Peoples. Nat. Dir., Most Rev. William J. McCormack.

Society of St. Monica (1986): 215 Falls Ave., Cuyahoga Falls, OH 44221; more than 10,000 members worldwide. Confident, daily prayer for the return of inactive Catholics and Catholics who have left the Church. *The Monican,* quarterly. Founder and spiritual director, Rev. Dennis M. McNeil.

Society of St. Peter Apostle (1889), 366 Fifth Ave., New York, NY 10001; 174 dioceses. Church's central fund for support of seminaries, seminarians and novices in all mission dioceses. Nat. Dir., Most Rev. William J. McCormack.

Society of the Divine Attributes (1974). Contemplative prayer society; 3,000 members worldwide (lay, clerical and religious). Spir. Dir. Rev. Ronald D. Lawler, O.F.M. Cap., 2905 Castlegate Ave., Pittsburgh, PA 15226.

Spiritual Life Institute of America (1960), Box 219, Crestone, CO 81131. *Desert Call,* seasonal. An eremetical movement to foster the contemplative spirit in America. Founder, Rev. William McNamara, O.C.D. Second foundation: *Nova Nada,* Primitive Wilderness Hermitage, Kemptville, Nova Scotia, Canada B0W 1Y0.

Theresians of the United States (1961), 2577 N. Chelton Rd., Suite 207, Colorado Springs, CO 80909. Spiritual, educational and ministerial organization of Christian women. Exec. Dir., Sr. Rose Ann Barmann, O.S.B. International division: **Theresian World Ministry** (1971), same address as above. Contact Person, Agnes Pino.

United Societies of U.S.A. (1903), 613 Sinclair St., McKeesport, PA 15132; 3,900 members. *Prosvita-Enlightenment,* monthly newspaper.

United States Catholic Historical Society (1884), P.O. Box 16229, Baltimore, MD 21210; 1,277. *U.S. Catholic Historian,* quarterly (published by Our Sunday Visitor, Huntington, IN 46750). Preserve U.S. Catholic history and culture, Pres. Dr. Brian Butler.

Western Catholic Union (1877), W.C.U. Bldg., 510 Maine St., Quincy, IL 62301; 25,025 members. *Western Catholic Union Record,* quarterly.

Women for Faith and Family (1984), P.O. Box 8326, St. Louis, MO 63132; 50,000 women associates worldwide (40,000 in U.S.). *Voices,* quarterly. To provide Catholic women with a means of expressing unity with the teachings of the Catholic Church through the "Affirmation for Catholic Women." Dir., Helen Hull Hitchcock.

World Apostolate of Fatima (The Blue Army USA) (1952), Mountain View Rd. (P.O. Box 976), Washington, NJ 07882. Promote Fatima message. *Soul, Alma Mariana,* bimonthlies; *Hearts Aflame,* quarterly. Exec. Dir., Rev. Frederick L. Miller.

Young Ladies' Institute (1887), P.O. Box 640687, San Francisco, CA 94164; 13,000. *Voice of YLI,* bimonthly. Grand Sec., Miss Carol Marshall.

Young Men's Institute (1883), 50 Oak St., San Francisco, CA 94102; 4,500. *Institute Journal,* bimonthly. Grand Sec., S. J. Welch.

KNIGHTS OF COLUMBUS

The Knights of Columbus, which originated as a fraternal benefit society of Catholic men, was founded by Father Michael J. McGivney and chartered by the General Assembly of Connecticut Mar. 29, 1882.

In line with their general purpose to be of service to the Church, the Knights are active in many apostolic works and community programs.

Since January, 1947, the Knights have sponsored a program of Catholic advertising in secular publications with national circulation. This has brought some 7.5 million inquiries and led to more than 800,000 enrollments in courses in the Catholic faith.

K. of C. scholarship funds — two at the Catholic University of America, another for disbursement at other Catholic colleges in the U.S., one at Canadian colleges and others for the Philippines, Mexico and Puerto Rico — have provided college educations for about 1,700 students since 1914. With funding from the Knights of Columbus, a North American Campus of the John Paul II Institute for Studies on Marriage and Family — a pontifical graduate school affiliated with Lateran University — opened in 1988 at the Dominican House of Studies, Washington, D.C.

The order promotes youth activity through sponsorship of the Columbian Squires and through cooperation with other organized youth groups.

Recent programs undertaken by the Knights include: promotion of vocations to the priesthood and religious life; extensive support of seminaries, houses of formation, and candidates for the priesthood and religious life; promotion of rosary devotion with free distribution of more than 100,000 rosaries a year; promotion of wider and more frequent use of the sacrament of Penance; securing aid for private schools; efforts to halt the killing of the unborn; assistance to the retarded and other disadvantaged people.

The Knights have formed an association with the Bishops in the United States, Canada and Mexico to help protect the lives of the unborn and to disseminate information on responsible family planning. Assistance also has been provided to the Eternal Word Television Network to help spread positive values over the airwaves and to Morality in Media to assist that organization in its battle to contain the spread of pornography.

In 1992, local units of the Knights contributed more than $95 million to charitable and benevolent causes, and gave nearly 42 million hours of community service.

K. of C. membership, as of 1992, was over 1.5 million in more than 10,000 councils in the U.S., Canada, the Philippines, Mexico, Puerto Rico, Panama, Guatemala, Guam, the Dominican Republic, the Virgin Islands and the Bahamas.

The Knights publication, *Columbia,* has the largest circulation (over 1.5 million) of any Catholic monthly in North America.

Virgil C. Dechant is Supreme Knight.

International headquarters are located at One Columbus Plaza, New Haven, CT 06510.

HUMAN DEVELOPMENT CAMPAIGN

The Campaign for Human Development was inaugurated by the U.S. Catholic Conference in November, 1969, to combat injustice, oppression, alienation and poverty in this country by funding self-help programs begun and carried out by the poor or by the poor and non-poor working together, and by seeking a re-evaluation of the priorities of individuals, families, the Church and the civic community with respect to the stewardship of God-given goods. The campaign got under way with a collection taken up in all parishes throughout the country on Nov. 22, 1970. Seventy-five per cent of the money contributed in this and subsequent annual collections was placed in a national fund principally for funding self-help projects and also for educational purposes; 25 percent remained in the dioceses where it was collected. From 1970 to 1993, the campaign has distributed approximately $182 million to more than 3,000 self-help projects. National office: 3211 Fourth St. N.E., Washington, D.C. 20017.

MARRIAGE ENCOUNTER

Marriage Encounter brings couples together for a weekend program of events directed by a team of several couples and a priest, for the purpose of developing their abilities to communicate with each other in their life together as husband and wife. This purpose is served by direction in techniques given by the team and by private dialogue of each couple. The address of National Marriage Encounter is 4704 Jamerson Pl., Orlando, FL 32807. The national office of Worldwide Marriage Encounter is located at 1908 E. Highland Ave., Suite A, San Bernardino, CA 92404.

COMMUNICATIONS

CATHOLIC PRESS STATISTICS

The *1993 Catholic Press Directory*, published by the Catholic Press Association, reported a total of 679 periodicals in North America with a circulation of 27,493,219. The figures included 198 newspapers with a circulation of 5,956,318; 297 magazines with a circulation of 16,941,170; 144 newsletters with a circulation of 3,806,602, and 40 other-language periodicals (newspapers and magazines) with a circulation of 789,129.

Newspapers in the U.S.

There were 185 newspapers in the United States, with a circulation 5,811,616. Six of these had national circulation; 165 were diocesan newspapers; 14 were Eastern rite publications.

National newspapers included: *National Catholic Register,* founded 1900; *Our Sunday Visitor,* founded 1912; *National Catholic Reporter,* founded 1964; *Catholic Twin Circle,* founded 1967 and *The Wanderer.*

The oldest Catholic newspaper in the United States is *The Pilot* of Boston, established in 1829 (under a different title).

Other Diocesan Newspapers: There were three other diocesan newspapers located outside continental North America (Samoa, U.S. Virgin Islands, West Indies), with a circulation of 22,200.

Magazines in U.S.

The *Catholic Press Directory* reported 273 magazines in the U.S. with a circulation of 16,038,066. In addition, there were 143 newsletters, circulation, 3,795,602.

America and *Commonweal* are the only weekly and biweekly magazines, respectively, of general interest.

The monthly magazines with the largest circulation are *Columbia* (1,437,658), the official organ of the Knights of Columbus, and *Catholic Digest* (589,834).

Other-Language Publications: There were an additional 28 publications (newspapers and magazines) in the U.S. in languages other than English with a circulation of 486,729.

Canadian Statistics

There were 10 newspapers in Canada with a circulation of 122,502. These included two national newspapers (*The Catholic Register,* founded 1857; *Catholic New Times,* founded 1976) and 8 diocesan. There were 24 magazines with a circulation of 903,104; one newsletter with a circulation of 11,000; and 12 publications in languages other than English, circulation, 302,400.

CATHOLIC NEWSPAPERS AND MAGAZINES IN THE U.S.

(Sources: *Catholic Press Directory; The Catholic Journalist;* Almanac survey; Catholic News Service.)

Abbreviation code: a, annual; bm, bimonthly; m, monthly; q, quarterly; w, weekly.

Newspapers

Acadiana Catholic, m; 1408 Carmel Ave., Lafayette, LA 70502; Lafayette diocese.

A.D. Times, biweekly; Dewberry and Madison Aves., Bethlehem, PA 18017; Allentown diocese.

Agua Viva, m; P.O. Box 16318, Las Cruces, NM 88004; Las Cruces diocese.

Alaskan Shepherd, 6 times a year; 1312 Peger Rd., Fairbanks, AK 99709; Fairbanks diocese.

America (Ukrainian-English), 3 times a week; 817 N. Franklin St., Philadelphia, PA 19123. Providence Association of Ukrainian Catholics in America.

Anchor, The w; P.O. Box 7, Fall River, MA 02722; Fall River diocese.

Arkansas Catholic, w; P.O. Box 7417, Little Rock, AR 72217. Little Rock diocese.

Arlington Catholic Herald, w; 200 N. Glebe Rd., Suite 614, Arlington, VA 22203; Arlington diocese.

Bayou Catholic, The, w; P.O. Box 9077, Houma, LA 70361; Houma-Thibodaux diocese.

Beacon, The, w; P.O. Box 1887, Clifton, NJ 07015. Paterson diocese.

Bishop's Bulletin, m; P.O. Box 665, Yankton, SD 57078. Sioux Falls diocese.

Byzantine Catholic World, biweekly; 925 Liberty Ave., Pittsburgh, PA 15222; Pittsburgh Byzantine archdiocese.

Catholic Accent, w; P.O. Box 850, Greensburg, PA 15601; Greensburg diocese.

Catholic Advance, The, w; 424 N. Broadway, Wichita, KS 67202; Wichita diocese.

Catholic Advocate, The, w; 37 Evergreen Pl., E. Orange, NJ 07018; Newark archdiocese.

Catholic Bulletin, w; 244 Dayton Ave., St. Paul, MN 55102; St. Paul and Minneapolis archdiocese.

Catholic Calendar, semi-monthly; 4029 Avenue G, Lake Charles, LA 70601; one page in local newspaper twice a month; Lake Charles diocese.

Catholic Chronicle, biweekly; P.O. Box 1866, Toledo, OH 43603; Toledo diocese.

Catholic Commentary, biweekly; P.O. Box 2239, Anchorage, AK 99510; supplement in local newspaper; Anchorage archdiocese.

Catholic Commentator, The, biweekly; P.O. Box 14746, Baton Rouge, LA 70898; Baton Rouge diocese.

Catholic Courier, w; 1150 Buffalo Rd., Rochester, NY 14624. Rochester diocese.

Catholic East Texas, biweekly; 1920 Sybil Lane, Tyler, TX 75703. Tyler diocese.

Catholic Exponent, biweekly; P.O. Box 6787, Youngstown, OH 44501; Youngstown diocese.

Catholic Free Press, w; 47 Elm St., Worcester, MA 01609; Worcester diocese.

Catholic Herald, The, m; 514 El Paso Blvd., Manitou Springs, CO 80829; Colorado Springs diocese.

Catholic Herald, w; P.O. Box 07913, Milwaukee, WI 53207; Milwaukee archdiocese.

Catholic Herald — Madison Edition, w; P.O. Box 5913, Madison, WI 53705.

Catholic Herald — Superior Edition, w; P.O. Box 969, Superior, WI 54880.

Catholic Herald, w; 5890 Newman Ct., P.O. Box 19312, Sacramento, CA 95819; Sacramento diocese.

Catholic Hungarian's Sunday, w; 1739 Mahoning Ave., Youngstown, OH 44509.

Catholic Key, w; P.O. Box 419037, Kansas City, MO 64141; Kansas City-St. Joseph diocese.

Catholic Lantern, m; P.O. Box 4237, Stockton, CA 95204; Stockton diocese.

Catholic Light, biweekly; P.O. Box 708, Scranton, PA 18501; Scranton diocese.

Catholic Lighthouse, m; P.O. Box 4070, Victoria, TX 77903; Victoria diocese.

Catholic Mentor, The, P.O. Box 90883, Nashville, TN 37209.

Catholic Messenger, w; P.O. Box 460, Davenport, IA 52805; Davenport diocese.

Catholic Mirror The, semimonthly; P.O. Box 10372, Des Moines, IA 50306. Des Moines diocese.

Catholic Missourian, w; P.O. Box 1107, Jefferson City, MO 65102; Jefferson City diocese.

Catholic New York, w; P.O. Box 5133, New York, NY 10150; New York archdiocese.

Catholic News and Herald, The, w; 1524 E. Morehead St., Charlotte, NC 28207. Charlotte diocese.

Catholic Observer, biweekly; Box 1570, Springfield, MA 01101; Springfield diocese.

Catholic Outlook, m; 2830 E. 4th St., Duluth, MN 55812; Duluth diocese.

Catholic Post, The, w; P.O. Box 1722, Peoria, IL 61656; Peoria diocese.

Catholic Register, biweekly; 126C Logan Blvd., Hollidaysburg, PA 16648; Altoona-Johnstown diocese.

Catholic Review, w; P.O. Box 777, Baltimore, MD 21201; Baltimore archdiocese.

Catholic Sentinel, w; P.O. Box 18030, Portland, OR 97218; Portland archdiocese, Baker diocese.

Catholic Spirit, The, biweekly; P.O. Box 13327, Capitol Sta., Austin, TX 78711; Austin diocese.

Catholic Spirit, The, w; P.O. Box 951, Wheeling, WV 26003; Wheeling-Charleston diocese.

Catholic Standard, w; P.O. Box 4464, Washington, DC 20017; Washington archdiocese.

Catholic Standard and Times, w; 222 N. 17th St., Philadelphia, PA 19103; Philadelphia archdiocese.

Catholic Star Herald, w; 1845 Haddon Ave., Camden, NJ 08101; Camden diocese.

Catholic Sun, The, semimonthly; 400 E. Monroe, Phoenix, AZ 85004; Phoenix diocese.

Catholic Sun, The, w; 421 S. Warren St., Syracuse, NY 13202; Syracuse diocese.

Catholic Telegraph, w; 100 E. 8th St., Cincinnati, OH 45202; Cincinnati archdiocese.

Catholic Times, w; P.O. Box 636, Columbus, OH 43216; Columbus diocese.

Catholic Times, w; 1520 Court St., Saginaw, MI 48602. Lansing diocese.

Catholic Times, w; 514 E. Lawrence St., Springfield, IL 62703; Springfield diocese.

Catholic Today, m; P.O. Box 31, Tucson, AZ 85702; Tucson diocese.

Catholic Transcript, w; 785 Asylum Ave., Hartford, CT 06105; Hartford archdiocese.

Catholic Twin Circle, w; 15760 Ventura Blvd., Suite 1201, Encino, CA 91436.

Catholic Universe Bulletin, biweekly; 1027 Superior Ave. N.E., Cleveland, OH 44114; Cleveland diocese.

Catholic Virginian, biweekly; Box 26843, Richmond, VA 23261; Richmond diocese.

Catholic Voice, The, biweekly; 2918 Lakeshore Ave., Oakland, CA 94610; Oakland diocese.

Catholic Voice, The, biweekly; P.O. Box 4010, Omaha, NE 68104; Omaha archdiocese.

Catholic Week, w; P.O. Box 349, Mobile, AL 36601; Mobile archdiocese.

Catholic Weekly, The, w; 1520 Court St., Saginaw, MI 48602; editions for Saginaw, Gaylord and Lansing dioceses.

Catholic Weekly, The, w; P.O. Box 1405, Saginaw, MI 48605. Gaylord diocese.

Catholic Witness, The, biweekly; P.O. Box 2555, Harrisburg, PA 17105; Harrisburg diocese.

Catolico de Texas, El, m; P.O. Box 190347, Dallas, TX 75219; Dallas diocese.

Central Washington Catholic, 6 times a year; 5301-A Tieton Dr., Yakima, WA 98908. Yakima diocese.

Challenge, The, semimonthly; 2530 Victory Pkwy., Cincinnati, OH 45206. St. Maron diocese.

Chicago Catolico, El, m; 1144 W. Jackson Blvd., Chicago, IL 60607; Chicago archdiocese.

Chronicle of Catholic Life, m; 514 El Paso Blvd. Manitou Springs, CO 80829; Pueblo diocese.

Church Today, twice a month; P.O. Box 7417, Alexandria, LA 71306; Alexandria and Shreveport dioceses.

Church World, w; Industry Rd., P.O. Box 698, Brunswick, ME 04011; Portland diocese.

Clarion Herald, biweekly; P.O. Box 53247, New Orleans, LA 70153; New Orleans archdiocese.

Common Sense, w; 1325 Jefferson Ave., Memphis, TN 38104; Memphis diocese.

Community, w; P.O. Box 24000, Jacksonville, FL 32241; one-page weekly in Sunday editions of two daily newspapers; St. Augustine diocese.

Compass, The, w; P.O. Box 23825, Green Bay, WI 54305; Green Bay diocese.

Courier, The, m; P.O. Box 949, Winona, MN 55987; Winona diocese.

Criterion, The, w; P.O. Box 1717, Indianapolis, IN 46206; Indianapolis archdiocese.

Cross Roads, 26 times a year; 1310 Leestown Rd., Lexington, KY 40508. Lexington diocese.

Dakota Catholic Action, m (exc. May and Aug.); P.O. Box 1137, Bismarck, ND 58502; Bismarck diocese.

Darbininkas (The Worker) (Lithuanian), w; 341 Highland Blvd., Brooklyn, NY 11207; Lithuanian Franciscans.

Denver Catholic Register, w; 200 Josephine St., Denver, CO 80206; Denver archdiocese.

Dialog, The, w; P.O. Box 2208, Wilmington, DE 19899; Wilmington diocese.

Diocese of Orange Bulletin, m; 2811 E. Villa Real Dr., Orange, CA 92667.

Diocese of Van Nuys Newsletter, bm; 18024 Parthenia St., Northridge, CA 91325.
Draugas (Lithuanian), daily; 4545 W. 63rd St., Chicago, IL 60629; Lithuanian Catholic Press Society.

East Texas Catholic, biweekly; P.O. Box 222, Port Neches, TX 77651; Beaumont diocese.
Eastern Catholic Life, biweekly; 445 Lackawanna Ave., W. Paterson, NJ 07424; Passaic Byzantine eparchy.
Eastern Oklahoma Catholic, biweekly; Box 520, Tulsa, OK 74101; Tulsa diocese.
Eternal Flame (Armenian-English) 110 E. 12th St., New NY 10003.
Evangelist, The, w; 40 N. Main Ave., Albany, NY 12203; Albany diocese.

Fairfield County Catholic, m; 238 Jewett Ave., Bridgeport, CT 06606; Bridgeport diocese.
Florida Catholic, The, w; P.O. Box 3551, Orlando, FL 32802; Orlando diocese. Publishes editions for Miami archdiocese and Palm Beach, Pensacola-Tallahassee, St. Petersburg and Venice dioceses.
Florida Catholic — Miami Edition, w; P.O. Box 38-1059, Miami, FL 33238.
Florida Catholic — Palm Beach Edition, w; 9995 N. Military Trail, Palm Beach Gardens, FL 33410.
Florida Catholic — Pensacola-Tallahassee Edition, w; 9945 Hillview Rd., Pensacola, FL 32514.
Florida Catholic — St. Petersburg Edition, w; P.O. Box 43022, Tampa, FL 33679.
Florida Catholic — Venice Edition, w; 1000 Pinebrook Rd., Venice, FL 34292.
Four County Catholic, m; 1595 Norwich New London Turnpike, Uncasville, CT 06382. Norwich diocese.

Georgia Bulletin, w; 680 W. Peachtree St. N.W., Atlanta, GA 30308; Atlanta archdiocese.
Glasilo KSKJ (Amerikanski Slovenec) (Slovenian), biweekly; 708 E. 159th, Cleveland, OH 44110; American Slovenian Catholic Union.
Globe, The, w; 1825 Jackson St., Sioux City, IA 51105; Sioux City diocese.
Gulf Pine Catholic, w; P.O. Box 1189, Biloxi, MS 39533; Biloxi diocese.

Hawaii Catholic Herald, biweekly; 1184 Bishop St., Honolulu, HI 96813; Honolulu diocese.
Heraldo Catolico, El (Spanish), biweekly; P.O. Box 19312, Sacramento, CA 95819; Sacramento diocese.
Hlas Naroda (Voice of the Nation) (Czech-English), w; 2340 61st Ave., Cicero, IL 60650.
Horizons, semi-monthly; 1900 Carlton Rd., Parma, OH 44134; Parma diocese.

Idaho Register, 3 times a month; 303 Federal Way, Boise, ID 83705; Boise diocese.
Inland Catholic, m; P.O. Box 2788, San Bernardino, CA 92406. San Bernardino diocese.
Inland Register, every 3 weeks; P.O. Box 48, Spokane, WA 99210; Spokane diocese.
Inside Passage, biweekly; 419 6th St., Juneau, AK 99801; Juneau diocese.

Intermountain Catholic, w; P.O. Box 2489, Salt Lake City, UT 84110; Salt Lake City diocese.

Jednota (Slovak-Eng.), w; 661 Rockside Rd., Independence, OH 44131; First Catholic Slovak Union.

Lake Shore Visitor, w; P.O. Box 10668, Erie, PA 16514; Erie diocese.
Leaven, The, w; 12615 Parallel Parkway, Kansas City, KS 66109; Kansas City archdiocese.
Long Island Catholic, The, w; P.O. Box 9009, Rockville Centre, NY 11571; Rockville Centre diocese.

Message, The, w; P.O. Box 4169, Evansville, IN 47724; Evansville diocese.
Messenger, The, w; P.O. Box 327, Belleville, IL 62222; Belleville diocese.
Messenger, The, w; P.O. Box 18068, Covington, KY 41018; Covington diocese.
Michigan Catholic, The, w; 305 Michigan Ave., Detroit, MI 48226; Detroit archdiocese.
Mirror, The, w; P.O. Box 847, Springfield, MO 65801; Springfield-Cape Girardeau diocese.
Mississippi Today, w; P.O. Box 2130, Jackson, MS 39225; Jackson diocese.
Monitor, The, w; P.O. Box 3095, Trenton, NJ 08619; Trenton and Metuchen dioceses.
Montana Catholic, The, m; P.O. Box 1729, Helena, MT 59624; Helena diocese.

Narod Polski (Polish Nation) (Polish-Eng.) semi-monthly; 984 Milwaukee Ave., Chicago, IL 60622.
National Catholic Register, w; 15760 Ventura Blvd., Suite 1201, Encino, CA 91436.
National Catholic Reporter, w; P.O. Box 419281, Kansas City, MO 64141.
New Catholic Explorer, w (biweekly Jan., July, Aug.); 402 S. Independence Blvd., Romeoville, IL 60441. Joliet diocese.
New Catholic Miscellany, The, w; 119 Broad St., Charleston, SC 29401; Charleston diocese.
New Earth, The, m; 244 Dayton Ave., St. Paul, MN 55102. Fargo diocese.
New Star, The, biweekly; 2208 W. Chicago Ave., Chicago, IL 60622; St. Nicholas of Chicago Ukrainian diocese.
New World, The, w; 1144 W. Jackson Blvd., Chicago, IL 60607; Chicago archdiocese.
Newsletter, The, 6 times a year; 215 N. Westnedge, Kalamazoo, MI 49001; Kalamazoo diocese.
NC Catholic, 32 times a year; 300 Cardinal Gibbons Dr., Raleigh, NC 27606. Raleigh diocese.
North Country Catholic, w; P.O. Box 326, Ogdensburg, NY 13669; Ogdensburg diocese.
North Texas Catholic, w; 800 West Loop 820 South, Fort Worth, TX 76108; Fort Worth diocese.
Northwest Indiana Catholic, w; 9292 Broadway, Merrillville, IN 46410; Gary diocese.
Northwestern Kansas Register, w; P.O. Box 1038, Salina, KS 67402; Salina diocese.
Nuevo Amanecer (Spanish), m; 653 Hicks St., Brooklyn, NY 11231; for Hispanic Catholic community of Brooklyn diocese.

Observer, The, m; P.O. Box 2079, Monterey, CA 93942; Monterey diocese.

Observer, The, twice a month; 921 W. State St., Rockford, IL 61102; Rockford diocese.

One Voice, w; P.O. Box 10822, Birmingham, AL 35202; Birmingham diocese.

Our Northland Diocese, biweekly; P.O. Box 610, Crookston, MN 56716; Crookston diocese.

Our Sunday Visitor, w; 200 Noll Plaza, Huntington, IN 46750; national.

People of God, m; 4000 St. Joseph Pl. N.W., Albuquerque, NM 87120; Santa Fe archdiocese.

Pilot, The, w; 49 Franklin St., Boston, MA 02110; Boston archdiocese.

Pittsburgh Catholic, The, w; 100 Wood St., Suite 500, Pittsburgh, PA 15222; Pittsburgh diocese.

Polish American Journal, m; 1275 Harlem Rd., Cheektowaga, NY 14206.

Prairie Catholic, m; 1400 6th North St., New Ulm, MN 56073. New Ulm diocese.

Pregonero, El (Spanish), w; 5001 Eastern Ave., Hyattsville, MD 20782. Washington archdiocese.

Progress, The, w; 910 Marion St., Seattle, WA 98104; Seattle archdiocese.

Providence Visitor, The, w; 184 Broad St., Providence, RI 02903. Providence diocese.

Record, The, w; 1200 S. Shelby St., Louisville, KY 40203; Louisville archdiocese.

Redwood Crozier, The, m; 547 B St., Santa Rosa, CA 95401; Santa Rosa diocese.

Rio Grande Catholic, The, 14 times a year; 499 St. Matthew St., El Paso, TX 79907.

Rockford Catolico (Spanish), m; 1144 W. Jackson Blvd., Chicago, IL 60607; Rockford diocese.

St. Cloud Visitor, w; P. O. Box 1068, St. Cloud, MN 56302; St. Cloud diocese.

St. Louis Review, w; 462 N. Taylor Ave., St. Louis, MO 63108; St. Louis archdiocese.

Seasons, 5800 Weiss St., Saginaw, MI 48603.

Slovak Catholic Falcon (Slovak-English), w; 205 Madison St., P.O.Box 899, Passaic, NJ 07055; Slovak Catholic Sokol.

Sooner Catholic, The, biweekly; P.O. Box 32180, Oklahoma City, OK 73123; Oklahoma City archdiocese.

Sophia, q; 7 V.F.W. Parkway, Roslindale, MA 02131; Newton Melkite eparchy.

South Plains Catholic, biweekly; P.O. Box 98700, Lubbock, TX 79499; Lubbock diocese.

South Texas Catholic, w; 1200 Lantana St., Corpus Christi, TX 78407; Corpus Christi diocese.

Southern Cross, semimonthly; P.O. Box 81869, San Diego, CA 92138; San Diego diocese.

Southern Cross, The, w; P.O. Box 948, Waynesboro, GA 30830; Savannah diocese.

Southern Nebraska Register, w; P.O. Box 80329, Lincoln, NE 68501; Lincoln diocese.

Southwest Catholic, m; 4029 Avenue G, Lake Charles, LA 70601 Lake Charles diocese.

Southwest Kansas Register, biweekly; P.O. Box 137, Dodge City, KS 67801; Dodge City diocese.

Sower (Ukrainian and English), biweekly; 161 Glenbrook Rd., Stamford, CT 06902. Stamford Ukrainian diocese.

Steubenville Register, biweekly; P.O. Box 160, Steubenville, OH 43952; Steubenville diocese.

Sunday Visitor, The, w; P.O. Box 1603, Lafayette, IN 47902; Lafayette diocese.

Tablet, w; 653 Hicks St., Brooklyn, NY 11231; Brooklyn diocese.

Tennessee Register, The, biweekly; 2400 21st Ave. S., Nashville, TN 37212; Nashville diocese.

Texas Catholic, biweekly; P.O. Box 190347, Dallas, TX 75219; Dallas diocese.

Texas Catholic Herald, The, semi-monthly; 1700 San Jacinto St., Houston, TX 77002; Galveston-Houston diocese.

Tidings, 8 times a year; 153 Ash St., Manchester, NH 03104.

Tidings, The, w; 1530 W. 9th St., Los Angeles, CA 90015; Los Angeles archdiocese, Orange diocese.

Times Review, The, w; P.O. Box 4004, La Crosse, WI 54602; La Crosse diocese.

Today's Visitor, w; P.O. Box 11169, Fort Wayne, IN 46856; Fort Wayne-S. Bend diocese.

Today's Catholic, biweekly; P.O. Box 28410, San Antonio, TX 78228; San Antonio archdiocese.

UNIREA, The Union (Romanian and English), m; 4309 Olcott Ave., East Chicago, IN 46312.

Upper Peninsula Catholic, biweekly; P.O. Box 548, Marquette, MI 49855; Marquette diocese.

Valley Catholic, m; 900 Lafayette St., Suite 301, Santa Clara, CA 95050; San Jose diocese.

Vermont Catholic Tribune, biweekly; 351 North Ave., Burlington, VT 05401; Burlington diocese.

Vida Nueva (Spanish), w; 1530 W. 9th St., Los Angeles, CA 90015.

Visitante de Puerto Rico, El (Spanish), w; Apartado 41305, Est Minillas, San Juan, PR 00940. Puerto Rican Catholic Conference.

Voice of the Southwest, m; P.O. Box 1338, Gallup, NM 87305; Gallup diocese.

Voz Catolica, La (Spanish); m; 9401 Biscayne Blvd., Miami, FL 33138; Miami archdiocese.

Wanderer, The, w; 201 Ohio St., St. Paul, MN 55107.

The Way (Ukrainian-Eng.), biweekly; 827 N. Franklin St., Philadelphia, PA 19123; Philadelphia archeparchy.

West Nebraska Register, w; P.O. Box 608, Grand Island, NE 68802; Grand Island diocese.

West River Catholic, m; P.O. Box 678, Rapid City, SD 57709; Rapid City diocese.

West Texas Angelus, m; P.O. Box 1829, San Angelo, TX 76902; San Angelo diocese.

West Texas Catholic, biweekly; P.O. Box 5644, Amarillo, TX 79117; Amarillo diocese.

Western Kentucky Catholic, m; 600 Locust St., Owensboro, KY 42301; Owensboro diocese.

Western New York Catholic, m; 795 Main St., Buffalo, NY 14203; Buffalo diocese.

Witness, The, w; P.O. Box 917, Dubuque, IA 52004; Dubuque archdiocese.

Wyoming Catholic Register, m; P.O. Box 1308, Cheyenne, WY 82003; Cheyenne diocese.

Magazines

Action News, q; 6160 North Cicero Ave., Chicago, IL 60646; Pro-Life Action League.

AIM (Aids in Ministry), q; P.O. Box 2703, Schiller Park, IL 60176.

Albanian Catholic Bulletin (Buletini Katolik Shqiptar), a; University of San Francisco, Xavier Hall, San Francisco, CA 94117.

Alma Mariana, bm; Mountain View Rd., Box 976, Washington, NJ 07882.

America, w; 106 W. 56th St., New York, NY 10019. Jesuits of U.S. and Canada.

American Benedictine Review, q; Assumption Abbey, Box A, Richardton, ND 58652.

American Catholic Philosophical Quarterly (formerly The New Scholasticism), Institute of Philosophical Studies, Univ. of Dallas, Irving, TX 75062. American Catholic Philosophical Assn.

American Midland Naturalist, q; Notre Dame, IN 46556.

Anthonian, The, q; Paterson, NJ 07509; St. Anthony's Guild.

Anthropological Quarterly; 620 Michigan Ave. N.E., Washington, DC 20064.

Apostolate of Our Lady, m; 315 Clay St., Carey, OH 43316; Our Lady of Consolation National Shrine.

Apostolate of the Little Flower, bm; P.O. Box 5280, San Antonio, TX 78201; Discalced Carmelite Fathers.

Association of Marian Helpers Bulletin, q; Eden Hill Stockbridge, MA 01263. Congregation of Marians of the Immaculate Conception.

Atchison Benedictines, q; Mount St. Scholastica Convent, 801 S. 8th St., Atchison, KS 66002.

Ateitis (The Future) (Lithuanian), bm; 7235 S. Sacramento Ave., Chicago, IL 60629; for youth.

Augustinian Heritage, two times a year; 214 Ashwood Rd., P.O. Box 476, Villanova, PA 19085.

Augustinian Journey, m; 101 Barry Rd., Worcester, MA 01609.

Benedictines, semiannually; Mt. St. Scholastica, Atchison, KS 66002.

Bible Today, The, bm; Liturgical Press, Collegeville, MN 56321.

Biblical Theology Bulletin, q; St. John's Univ., Theology Dept., Jamaica, NY 11439.

BLUEPRINT for Social Justice, 10 times a year; Twomey Center for Peace through Justice, Loyola University, Box 12, New Orleans, LA 70118.

Bolletino, m; 1801 Van Ness Ave., Suite 330, San Francisco, CA 94109; Central Council of Italian Catholic Federation.

Brothers, 5 times a year; 30 Montgomery Circle, New Rochelle, NY 10804; National Assembly of Religious Brothers.

Caelum et Terra, q; P.O. Box 2568, Manasses, VA 22110.

Carmelite Digest, q; P.O. Box 3180, San Jose, CA 95156.

Carmelite Review, The, m; Aylesford, 8433 Bailey Rd., Darien, IL 60561. Canadian-American Province of Carmelite Order.

Catechist, The, 8 times a year; 330 Progress Rd., Dayton, OH 45449.

Catechumenate: A Journal of Christian Initiation, 6 times a year; 1800 N. Hermitage Ave., Chicago, IL 60622.

Catholic Aid News, m; 3499 N. Lexington Ave., St. Paul, MN 55126.

Catholic Answer, The, bm; 200 Noll Plaza, Huntington, IN 46750.

Catholic Biblical Quarterly; Catholic University of America, Washington, DC 20064; Catholic Biblical Assn.

Catholic Cemetery, The, m; 710 N. River Rd., Des Plaines, IL 60016; National Catholic Cemetery Conference.

Catholic Digest, m; P.O. Box 64090, St. Paul, MN 55164.

Catholic Family Media Guide, 10 times a year; P.O. Box 369, Durand, IL 61024.

Catholic Forester Magazine, bm; 425 W. Shuman Blvd., Naperville, IL 60566; Catholic Order of Foresters.

CGA World, q; P.O. Box 3598, Scranton, PA 18505. Catholic Golden Age.

Catholic Health World, semimonthly; 4455 Woodson Rd., St. Louis, MO 63134. Catholic Health Association.

Catholic Heritage, bm; 200 Noll Plaza, Huntington, IN 46750. Our Sunday Visitor.

Catholic Historical Review, q; 620 Michigan Ave. N.E., Washington, DC 20064.

Catholic Journalist, The, m; 119 N. Park Ave., Rockville Centre, NY 11570; Catholic Press Association.

C.K. of A. Journal, m; 1850 Dalton St., Cincinnati, OH 45214; Catholic Knights of America.

Catholic Lawyer, q; St. John's University, Jamaica, NY 11439; St. Thomas More Institute for Legal Research.

Catholic Library World, 4 times a year; 461 W. Lancaster Ave., Haverford, PA 19041; Catholic Library Association.

Catholic Near East Magazine, bm; 1011 First Ave., New York, NY 10022; Catholic Near East Welfare Assn.

Catholic Parent, bm; 200 Noll Plaza, Huntington, IN 46750. Our Sunday Visitor.

Catholic Pharmacist, q; 1012 Surrey Hills Dr., St. Louis, MO 63117; National Catholic Pharmacists Guild.

Catholic Press Directory, a; 119 N. Park Ave. Rockville Centre, NY 11570; Catholic Press Assn.

Catholic Quote, m; Valparaiso, NE 68065; Rev. Jerome Pokorny.

Catholic Review (Braille, tape, large print), m; 154 E. 23rd St., New York, NY 10010; Xavier Society for the Blind.

Catholic Singles Magazine, two times a year; 8408 S. Muskegon, Chicago, IL 60617.

Catholic Telephone Guide, a; 210 North Ave., New Rochelle, NY 10801.

Catholic University of America Law Review, q; Washington, DC 20064.

Catholic War Veteran, bm; 419 N. Lee St., Alexandria, VA 22314.

Catholic Woman, bm; 1275 K St. N.W., Suite 975, Washington, DC 20005. National Council of Catholic Women.

Catholic Women's Network, bm; 877 Spinosa Dr., Sunnyvale, CA 94087.

Catholic Worker, 8 times a year; 36 E. First St., New York, NY 10003. Catholic Worker Movement.

Catholic Workman, m; 111 W. Main, P.O. Box 47, New Prague, MN 56071.

Catholic World, bm; 997 Macarthur Blvd., Mahwah, NJ 07430.

Catholic World Report, The, 11 times a year; 2515 McAllister St., San Francisco, CA 94118. Ignatian Press.

Celebration, m; 207 Hillsboro Dr., Silver Spring, MD 20902; National Catholic Reporter Publishing Co.

Charism; 3 times a year; 4435 E. Patterson Rd., Dayton, OH 45430; Society of Mary.

Charities USA, q; 1731 King St., Suite 200, Alexandria, VA 22314.

Chicago Studies, 3 times a year; P.O. Box 665, Mundelein, IL 60060; Civitas Dei Foundation.

Christian Beginnings, 5 times a year; 200 Noll Plaza, Huntington, IN 46750. Our Sunday Visitor.

Christian Renewal News, 4 times a year; 411 First St., Flllmore, CA 93015. Apostolate of Christian Renewal.

Christopher News Notes, 10 times a year; 12 E. 48th St., New York, NY 10017; The Christophers.

Church, q; 299 Elizabeth St., New York, NY 10012; National Pastoral Life Center.

Cistercian Studies Quarterly; Abbey of Our Lady of New Clairvaux, P.O. Box 80, Vina, CA 96092; international review of monastic and contemplative spirituality, history and theology.

Columban Mission, m (exc. June, Aug.); St. Columbans, NE 68056; Columban Fathers.

Columbia, m; One Columbus Plaza, P.O. Drawer 1670, New Haven, CT 06507; Knights of Columbus.

Columbian, The, semimonthly; 188 W. Randolph St., Chicago, IL 60601.

Comboni Missions, q; 8108 Beechmont Ave., Cincinnati, OH 45255.

Commitment, q; 1200 Varnum St. N.E., Washington, DC 20017; National Catholic Conference for Interracial Justice.

Common Life, q; Edmundite Center, Fairholt-S. Prospect St., Burlington, VT 05401.

Commonweal, biweekly; 15 Dutch St., New York, NY 10038.

Communio — International Catholic Review, q; P.O. Box 4557, Washington, D.C. 20017.

Company, q; 3441 N. Ashland Ave., Chicago, IL 60657. National Jesuit Magazine.

Consecrated Life, semi-annually; P.O. Box 41007, Chicago, IL 60641; Institute on Religious Life. English edition of *Informationes,* official publication of Congregation for Institutes of Consecrated Life and Societies of Apostolic Life.

Contact, q; 555 Albany Ave., Amityville, NY 11701; Sisters of St. Dominic.

Continuum, 3 times a year; 3700 W. 103rd St., Chicago, IL 60655.

Cord, The, m; P.O. Drawer F, St. Bonaventure, NY 14778; Franciscan Institute.

Counseling and Values, 3 times a year; College of Education, Univ. of Iowa, Iowa City, IA 52242.

Crescat, 3 times a year; Belmont Abbey, Belmont, NC 28012; Benedictine Monks.

Crisis, 11 times a year; 1511 K St. N.W., Suite 525, Washington, DC 20005. Journal of lay Catholic opinion.

Critic, The, 4 times a year; 205 W. Monroe St., Chicago, IL 60606. Thomas More Assn.

Crusader's Almanac, The, biannually; 1400 Quincy St. N.E., Washington, DC 20017; Commissariat of the Holy Land.

CUA Magazine, 3 times a year; 620 Michigan Ave. N.E., Washington, DC 20064.

Deaf Blind Weekly, The (Braille), w; 154 E. 23rd St., New York, NY 10010; Xavier Society for the Blind.

DeSales World, The, 4 times a year; 2220 Kentmere Pkwy., P.O. Box 1452, Wilmington, DE 19899.

Desert Call, q; Box 219, Crestone, CO 81131; Spiritual Life Institute of America.

Diaconate, bm; P.O. Box 19113, Tampa, FL 33686.

Diakonia, 3 times a year; Univ. of Scranton, Scranton, PA 18510.

Divine Word Missionaries, q; Techny, IL 60082.

Earth Matters, 4 times a year; 4625 NW Beaver Dr., Des Moines, IA 50310. National Catholic Rural Life Conference.

Ecumenical Trends, m (exc. Aug.); Graymoor Ecumenical and Interreligious Institute, 475 Riverside Dr., Room 1960, New York, NY 10115.

Ecumenist, The, 6 times a year; Paulist Press, 997 MacArthur Blvd., Mahwah, NJ 07430.

Eglute (The Little Fir Tree) (Lithuanian), m; Putnam, CT 06260; Srs. of Immaculate Conception. For children ages 5-10.

Emmanuel, 10 times a year; 5384 Wilson Mills Rd., Cleveland, OH 44143; Congregation of Blessed Sacrament.

Extension, 9 times a year; 35 E. Wacker Dr., Suite 400, Chicago, IL 60601; Catholic Church Extension Society.

Faith and Reason, q; 2101 Shenandoah Shores Rd., Front Royal, VA 22630.

Family, The, - A Catholic Perspective, The, m; 50 St. Paul Ave., Boston, MA 02130; Daughters of St. Paul.

Family Friend, q; P.O. Box 11563, Milwaukee, WI 53211; Catholic Family Life Insurance.

Fidelity, m; 206 Marquette Ave., South Bend, IN 46617.

Flame, The, 4 times a year; Barry Univ., 11300 N.E. 2nd Ave., Miami Shores, FL 33161.

F.M.A. Focus, q; P.O. Box 598, Mt. Vernon, NY 10551; Franciscan Mission Associates.

Franciscan Studies, a; St. Bonaventure, NY 14778; Franciscan Institute.

Franciscan Way, q; 100 Franciscan Way, Steubenville, OH 43952.

Fraternal Leader, q; P.O. Box 13005; Erie, PA 16514; Loyal Christian Benefit Association.

Fraternally Yours (Zenska Jednota) (Eng.-Slovak), m; 24950 Chagrin Blvd., Beachwood, OH 44122; First Catholic Slovak Ladies Assn.

Friar Lines, q; 58 W. 88th St., New York, NY 10024. Franciscan Friars of Holy Name Province.

Garsas (The Sound) (Lithuanian-English), m; 71-73 S. Washington St., Wilkes-Barre, PA 18701; Lithuanian Catholic Alliance.

Glenmary Challenge, The, q; P.O. Box 465618, Cincinnati, OH 45246; Glenmary Home Missioners.

God's Word Today, m; P. O. Box 60488, St. Paul, MN 55164. Univ. of St. Thomas.

Good News, m; 2875 S. James Dr., New Berlin, WI 53151.

Good News for Children, 28 times during school year; 330 Progress Rd., Dayton, OH 45449.

Good Shepherd (Dobry Pastier) (Slovak and English), a; 8200 McKnight Rd., Pittsburgh, PA 15237; Slovak Catholic Federation of America.

Guide to Religious Ministries, A, a; 210 North Ave., New Rochelle, NY 10801.

Health Progress, m; 4455 Woodson Rd., St. Louis, MO 63134; Catholic Health Association.

Hearts Aflame, q; P.O. Box 976, Washington, NJ 07882. For youth (13-20).

Homiletic and Pastoral Review, m; 86 Riverside Dr., New York, NY 10024.

Horizon, 4 times a year; 1603 S. Michigan Ave. No. 400, Chicago, IL 60616.

Horizons, 2 times a year; Villanova University, Villanova, PA 19085. College Theology Society.

Human Development, q; Jesuit Educational Center, 400 Washington St., Hartford, CT 06106.

Human Life Issues, q; University of Steubenville, Steubenville, OH 43952.

Idea Ink, q; P.O. Box 295, Lodi, WI 53555.

In a Word, m; Bay Saint Louis, MS 39520; Society of the Divine Word.

Information From, six times a year; 3031 Fourth St. N.E., Washington, DC 20017. Paulist National Catholic Evangelization Association.

Inner Horizons, q; 50 St. Paul's Avenue, Jamaica Plain, Boston, MA 02130; Daughters of St. Paul.

Inspiration, q; Institute of Formative Spirituality, Duquesne University, Pittsburgh, PA 15282.

Institute Journal, bm; 50 Oak St., San Francisco, CA 94102; Young Men's Institute.

International Philosophical Quarterly; Fordham University, Bronx, NY 10458.

International Review, q; Human Life Center, Franciscan University of Steubenville, Steubenville, OH 43952.

Jesuit Blackrobe, semiannually; 3601 W. Fond du Lac Ave., Milwaukee, WI 53216.

Jesuit Bulletin, 4 times a year; 4511 W. Pine Blvd., St. Louis, MO 63108; Jesuit Seminary Aid Association.

Josephite Harvest, The, q; 1130 N. Calvert St., Baltimore, MD 21202; Josephite Missionaries.

Journal of Texas Catholic History and Culture, a; 3001 S. Congress Ave., Austin, TX 78704.

Jurist, The, semiannually; Catholic University of America, Washington, DC 20064; Department of Canon Law.

Justice Journal, bm; 328 W. Kellogg Blvd., St. Paul, MN 55102.

Key to Happiness, m; 86 Riverside Dr., New York, NY 10024. Catholic Views Broadcast.

Kinship, q; P.O. Box 2264, Owensboro, KY 42302; Glenmary Sisters.

Knights of St. John, q; 6517 Charles Ave., Cleveland, OH 44129.

Kolping Banner, m; 115-14 227th St., Cambria Heights., NY 11411; Catholic Kolping Society.

Kosmos Magazine, 6 times a year; 3700 Oakview Terr. N.E., Washington, DC 20017.

Laivas (Lithuanian), q; 4545 W. 63rd St., Chicago, IL 60629.

Law Briefs, 12 times a year; 3211 Fourth St. N.E. Washington, DC 20017; Office of General Counsel, USCC.

Leaflet Missal, 16160 S. Seton Dr., S. Holland, IL 60473.

Leaves, bm; 23715 Ann Arbor Trail, Dearborn Heights, MI 48127; Mariannhill Mission Society.

Liguorian, m; 1 Liguori Dr., Liguori, MO 63057; Redemptorists.

Linacre Quarterly; 850 Elm Grove Rd., Elm Grove, WI 53122; National Federation of Catholic Physicians Guilds.

Listening, 4 times a year; 814 Thayer Ave., Silver Spring, MD 20910. National Catholic Office for the Deaf.

Liturgia y Cancion (Spanish and English), q; 5536 NE Hassalo, Portland, OR 97213. Oregon Catholic Press.

Liturgy, q; 8750 Georgia Ave., Suite 123, Silver Spring, MD 20910. Liturgical Conference.

Liturgy Planner, The, q; 6414 N.E. Alameda, Portland, OR 97213.

Living City, m; P.O. Box 837, Bronx, NY 10465; Focolare Movement.

Living Faith, q; 10300 Watson Rd., St. Louis, MO 63127.

Living Light, The, q; 3211 Fourth St. N.E., Washington, DC 20017; Department of Education, USCC.

Living Prayer, bm; Beckley Hill, R.R. 2, Box 4784, Barre, Vt. 05641.

Marian Library Studies, a; Marian Library, Dayton, OH 45469.

Marian Studies, a; Marian Library, Dayton, OH 45469; Mariological Society of America (proceedings).

Marriage Encounter, m; 955 Lake Dr., St. Paul, MN 55120; International Marriage Encounter.

Maryknoll, m; Maryknoll, NY 10545; Catholic Foreign Mission Society.

Mary's Shrine, 2 times a year; Michigan Ave. and 4th St. N.E., Washington, DC 20017. Basilica of National Shrine of the Immaculate Conception.

Matrimony, q; 215 Santa Rosa Pl., Santa Barbara, CA 93109. Worldwide Marriage Encounter.

Medical Mission News, q; 10 W. 17th St., New York, NY 10011; Catholic Medical Mission Board, Inc.

Medjugorje Magazine, q; P.O. Box 99, Bloomingdale, IL 60108.

Men of Malvern, bm; Malvern, PA 19355; Laymen's Retreat League of Philadelphia.

Merciful Love, q; 5654 E. Westover, No. 103, P.O. Box 24, Fresno, CA 93727.

Mercy Health Services Perspectives, q; 34605 Twelve Mile Rd., Farmington Hills, MI 48331.

Mid-America, 3 times a year; Loyola University, Chicago, IL 60626.

Miesiecznik Franciszkanski (Polish), m; 165 E. Pulaski St., Pulaski, WI 54162; Franciscan Fathers.

Migration World, 5 times a year; 209 Flagg Pl., Staten Island, NY 10304; Center for Migration Studies.

Miraculous Medal, q; 475 E. Chelten Ave., Philadelphia, PA 19144; Central Association of the Miraculous Medal.

Mission, 4 times a year; 366 Fifth Ave., New York, NY 10001; Society for Propagation of the Faith.

Mission, q; 1663 Bristol Pike, Bensalem, PA 19020; Sisters of the Blessed Sacrament.

Mission Helper, The, q; 1001 W. Joppa Rd., Baltimore, MD 21204; Mission Helpers of the Sacred Heart.

Missionhurst, 6 times a year; 4651 N. 25th St., Arlington, VA 22207; Immaculate Heart of Mary Mission Society, Inc.

Mission of the Immaculata, The, 10 times a year; 1600 W. Park Ave., Libertyville, IL 60048; Conventual Franciscan Friars.

Modern Liturgy, 10 times a year; 160 E. Virginia St., No. 290, San Jose, CA 95112.

Modern Schoolman, The, q; 221 N. Grand Blvd., St. Louis, MO 63103; St. Louis University Philosophy Department.

Momentum, 4 times a year; Suite 100, 1077 30th St., N.W., Washington, DC 20007; National Catholic Educational Association.

Mountain Spirit, The, 6 times a year; 322 Crab Orchard Rd., Lancaster, KY 40446; ecumenical; Christian Appalachian Project.

My Daily Visitor, bm; 200 Noll Plaza, Huntington, IN 46750; Our Sunday Visitor, Inc.

My Friend, 10 times a year; 50 St. Paul's Ave., Jamaica Plain, Boston, MA 02130; for children, ages 6-12.

NAMRP Quarterly, P.O. Box 4711, Columbia, SC 29240. National Apostolate with Mentally Retarded Persons.

National Catholic Forester, q; 446 E. Ontario, Chicago, IL 60611.

National Directory of Catholic Higher Education, a; 210 North Ave., New Rochelle, NY 10801.

National Jesuit News, m; 1424 16th St. N.W., Suite 300, Washington, D.C. 20036.

Network, bm, 806 Rhode Island Ave. N.E., Washington, DC 20018; Network.

New Covenant, m; Our Sunday Visitor, Inc., 200 Noll Plaza, Huntington, IN 46750.

New Heaven/New Earth, m; 107 S. Greenlawn Ave., South Bend, IN 46617.

New Oxford Review, 10 issues a year; 1069 Kains Ave., Berkeley, CA 94706.

New Theology Review, q; 1935 W. 4th St., Wilmington, DE 19805.

North American Voice of Fatima, bm; 1023 Swann Rd., Youngstown, NY 14174.

Notebook, The, 4 times a year; 31 Chesterfield Rd., Stamford, CT 06902. Catholic Movement for Intellectual and Cultural Affairs.

Notre Dame Magazine, 4 times a year; Notre Dame Univ., Notre Dame, IN 46556.

Nova-Voice of Ministry, bm; 2875 S. James Dr., New Berlin, WI 53151 (editorial office, P.O. Box 19113, Tampa, FL 33686).

Oblate World and Voice of Hope, bm; 486 Chandler St., P.O. Box 680, Tewksbury, MA 01876; Oblates of Mary Immaculate.

Observer, The, m; 4545 W. 63rd St., Chicago, IL 60629; Lithuanian Roman Catholic Federation of America.

Old Testament Abstracts, 3 times a year; Catholic University of America, Washington, DC 20064.

Origins, 48 times a year; 3211 Fourth St. N.E., Washington, DC 20017; Catholic News Service.

Our Lady's Digest, q; Box 777, Twin Lakes, WI 53181; La Salette Fathers.

Padres' Trail, 4 times a year; Box 645, St. Michael, AZ 86511; Franciscan Fathers.

Parable, q; 3001 S. Congress, Austin, TX 78704; Volunteers for Educational and Social Services.

Parish Communication, q; P.O. Box 215, Weston, VT 05161.

Parish Family Digest, bm; 200 Noll Plaza, Huntington, IN 46750.

Passage, bm; 143 Schleigel Blvd., Amityville, NY 11701.

Passionists' Compassion, The, q; 526 Monastery Pl., Union City, NJ 07087.

Pastoral Life, m; Route 224, Canfield, OH 44406; Society of St. Paul.

Pastoral Music, bm; 225 Sheridan St., N.W. Washington, DC 20011; National Association of Pastoral Musicians.

Paulist Magazine, twice a year; 997 Macarthur Blvd. Mahwah, NJ 07430.

Pax Christi USA, q; 348 E. 10th St., Erie, PA 16503.

Philosophy Today, q; De Paul University, 2323 Seminary Pl., Chicago, IL 60614; Philosophy Department.

PIME World Magazine, m (exc. July-Aug.); 17330 Quincy St., Detroit, MI 48221; PIME Missionaries.

Pope Speaks, The, bm; Our Sunday Visitor, Inc., 200 Noll Plaza, Huntington, IN 46750.

Prayers for Worship, q; 2875 S. James Dr., New Berlin, WI 53151.

Praying, 6 times a year; 115 E. Armour Blvd., Kansas City, MO 64111.

Priest, The, m; 200 Noll Plaza, Huntington, IN 46750; Our Sunday Visitor, Inc.

Pro Ecclesia Magazine, q; 509 Madison Ave. New York, NY 10022. Pro Ecclesia Foundation.

Probe, bm (Sept.-June); 529 S. Wabash Ave., Room 404, Chicago, IL 60605; National Assembly of Religious Women.

Proceedings, a; Catholic Univ. of America, 403

Adm. Bldg., Washington, DC 20064; American Catholic Philosophical Assn.

Queen of All Hearts, bm; 26 S. Saxon Ave., Bay Shore, NY 11706; Montfort Missionaries.

Reign of the Sacred Heart, q; 6889 S. Lovers Lane, Hales Corners, WI 53130.

Religion Teacher's Journal, m (Sept.-May); P.O. Box 180, Mystic, CT 06355.

Renascence, q; Marquette University, Milwaukee, WI 53233.

Report on U.S. Catholic Overseas Mission, biannually; 3029 Fourth St. N.E.; Washington, DC 20017. United States Catholic Mission Association.

Response, The, a; 4121 Harewood Rd. N.E., Washington, DC 20017; International Liaison of Lay Volunteers.

Review for Religious, bm; Room 428, 3601 Lindell Blvd., St. Louis, MO 63108.

Review of Politics, q; Box B, Notre Dame, IN 46556.

Review of Social Economy, 4 times a year; Marquette University, Milwaukee, WI 53233. Association for Social Economics.

Revista Maryknoll (Spanish-English), m; Maryknoll, NY 10545; Catholic Foreign Mission Society of America.

Roze Maryi (Polish), m; Eden Hill, Stockbridge, MA 01263; Marian Helpers Center.

Sacred Music, q; 548 Lafond Ave., St. Paul, MN 55103.

St. Anthony Messenger, m; 1615 Republic St., Cincinnati, OH 45210; Franciscan Friars.

St. Joseph's Messenger and Advocate of the Blind, q; St. Joseph Home, 541 Pavonia Ave., Jersey City, NJ 07303.

Salesian Missions of St. John Bosco, q; 148 Main St., New Rochelle, NY 10802.

Salt, m; 205 W. Monroe St., Chicago, IL 60606; Claretians.

San Francisco Catholic, m; 441 Church St., San Francisco, CA 94114; San Francisco archdiocese.

Scalabrinians, 4 times a year; 209 Flagg Pl., Staten Island, NY 10304.

SC News, q; Nazareth, KY 40048; Sisters of Charity of Nazareth.

School Guide, a; 210 North Ave., New Rochelle, NY 10801.

SCRC Vision, The, m; 2810 Artesia Blvd., Redondo Beach, CA 90278; Southern California Renewal Communities.

Serenity, q; 601 Maiden Choice Lane, Baltimore, MD 21228; Little Sisters of the Poor.

Serran, The, bm; 22 W. Monroe St., No. 1600, Chicago, IL 60603; Serra International.

Share the Word, bm; 3031 Fourth St. N.E., Washington, DC 20017; Paulist Catholic Evangelization Association.

Silent Advocate, q; St. Rita School for the Deaf, 1720 Glendale-Milford Rd., Cincinnati, OH 45215.

Sister Miriam Teresa League of Prayer Bulletin, q; League Headquarters, Convent Station, NJ 07961.

Sisters Today, bm; Liturgical Press, Collegeville, MN 56321.

Social Justice Review, bm; 3835 Westminster Pl., St. Louis, MO 63108; Catholic Central Union of America.

Social Thought, q; 1731 King St., Alexandria, VA 22314; Catholic Charities USA.

Soul, bm; Mountain View Rd., Washington, NJ 07882; World Apostolate of Our Lady of Fatima.

Spinnaker, 5 times a year; 610 W. Elm, Monroe, MI 48161; IHM Sisters.

Spirit, biannually; Seton Hall University, South Orange, NJ 07079.

Spirit, w; 1884 Randolph Ave., St. Paul, MN 55105. For teens.

Spirit and Life, 6 times a year; 800 N. Country Club Rd., Tucson, AZ 85716; Benedictine Srs. of Perpetual Adoration.

Spiritual Life, q; 2131 Lincoln Rd. N.E., Washington, DC 20002; Discalced Carmelite Friars.

Spirituality Today (formerly Cross and Crown), q; 3642 Lindell Blvd., St. Louis, MO 63108; Dominican Fathers.

Star, 10 times a year; 22 W. Kiowa, Colorado Springs, CO 80903.

Studies in the Spirituality of Jesuits, 5 times a year; 3700 W. Pine Blvd., St. Louis, MO 63108.

Sunday by Sunday, w; 1884 Randolph Ave., St. Paul, MN 55105.

Sword Magazine, 2 times a year; 120 Monroe Ave., Cresskill, NJ 07626; Carmelite Fathers.

Synthesis, q; P.O. Box 247, Bolton, MA 01740.

Theological Studies, q; 37th and O Sts. NW, Washington, DC 20057.

Theology Digest, q; 3634 Lindell Blvd., St. Louis, MO 63108; St. Louis Univesity.

This Rock, m; P.O. Box 17181, San Diego, CA 92177.

Thomist, The, q; 487 Michigan Ave. N.E., Washington, DC 20017; Dominican Fathers.

Thought, q; Fordham University Press, Box L, Bronx, NY 10458; Fordham University.

Today's Catholic Teacher, m (Sept.-May); 330 Progress Rd., Dayton, OH 45449.

Today's Liturgy, q; 5536 NE Hassalo, Portland, OR 97213.

Today's Parish, m (Sept.-May); P.O. Box 180, Mystic, CT 06355.

Tracings, q; Gamelin St., Holyoke, MA 01040; Sisters of Providence.

Trinity Missions Magazine, q; 9001 New Hampshire Ave., Silver Springs, MD 20903.

TV Prayer Guide, 2 times a year; 19 Second Ave., P.O. Box 440, Pelham, NY 10803.

Ultreya Magazine, 8 times a year; 4500 W. Davis St., P.O. Box 210226, Dallas, TX 75211. Cursillo Movement.

L'Union (French), q; 1 Social St., Woonsocket, RI 02895.

Universitas, q; 221 N. Grand, Room 39, St. Louis, MO 63103; St. Louis University.

U.S. Catholic, m; 205 W. Monroe St., Chicago, IL 60606; Claretians.

U.S. Catholic Historian, q; 200 Noll Plaza, Huntington, IN 46750.

Venture, 28 times during school year; 330 Progress Rd., Dayton, OH 45449, Intermediate grades.

Verelk (Armenian-English), bimonthly; 1327 Pleasant Ave., Los Angeles, CA 90033.

Vision (Spanish-English), P.O. Box 28185, San Antonio, TX 78228. Mexican American Cultural Center.

Visions, 28 times during school year; 330 Progress Rd., Dayton, OH 45449. For junior high school students.

Vocations and Prayer, q; 9815 Columbus Ave., Sepulveda, CA 91343. Rogationist Fathers.

Waif's Messenger, q; 1140 W. Jackson Blvd., Chicago, IL 60607; Mission of Our Lady of Mercy.

Way of St. Francis, bm; 109 Golden Gate Ave., San Francisco, CA 94102; Franciscan Friars of California, Inc.

Wheeling Jesuit College, 3 times a year; 316 Washington Ave., Wheeling, WV 26003.

Word Among Us, The, m; P.O. Box 6003, Gaithersburg, MD 20884.

Word/USA, 2 times a year; Box 577, Techny, IL 60082. Chicago province, Society of the Divine Word.

World Lithuanian Catholic Directory, 50 Orton Marotta Way, S. Boston, MA 02127.

Worship, 6 times a year; St. John's Abbey, Collegeville, MN 56321.

You! Magazine, 10 times a year; 29800 Agoura Rd., Suite 102, Agoura Hills, CA 91301. Catholic youth magazine.

Newsletters

Act, 10 times a year; 22 Kano Court, Ft. Myers, FL 33912; Christian Family Movement.

ADRIS Newsletter, q; Department of Theological Studies, St. Louis University, St. Louis, MO 63103. Association for the Development of Religious Information Services.

Angel Guardian Herald, 3 times a year; 6301 12th Ave., Brooklyn, NY 11219.

Archdiocesan Bulletin, bm; 827 N. Franklin St., Philadelphia, PA 19123; Philadelphia archeparchy.

At-one-ment, m; Graymoor Ecumenical Institute, Garrison, NY 10524.

Aylesford Carmelite Newsletter, q. P.O. Box 65, Darien, Ill. 60559.

Baraga Bulletin, The, q; 444 S. 4th St., P.O. Box 550, Marquette, MI 49855.

Benedictine Orient, bm; 2400 Maple Ave., Lisle, IL 60532.

Bringing Religion Home, m; 205 W. Monroe St., Chicago, IL 60606.

Call Board, The, 12 times a year; 1501 Broadway, Suite 518, New York, NY 10036; Catholic Actors' Guild.

Capuchin Benefactors Newsletter, 4 times a year; 210 W. 31st St., New York, NY 10001.

Caring Community, The, m; 115 E. Armour Blvd., Kansas City, MO 64111.

Catechist's Connection, The, 10 times a year;

115 E. Armour Blvd., Kansas City, MO 64111.

Catholic Communicator, The, q; 9 Loudoun St. S.E., Leesburg, VA 22075; Catholic Home Study Institute.

Catholic Insight, 20 times a year; 200 Noll Plaza, Hungtinton, IN 46750. Our Sunday Visitor.

Catholic League Newsletter, m; 6324 W. North Ave., Wauwatosa, WI 53212; Catholic League for Religious and Civil Rights.

Catholic Trends, biweekly; 3211 Fourth St. N.E., Washington, DC 20017; Catholic News Service.

Catholic Update, m; 1615 Republic St., Cincinnati, OH 45210.

C.F.C. Newsletter, 5 times a year; 30 Montgomery Circle, New Rochelle, NY 10804. Christian Brothers.

Chariscenter USA Newsletter, 6 times a year; P.O. Box 628, Locust Grove, VA 22508.

Christ the King Seminary Newsletter, 4 times a year; 711 Knox Rd., Box 607, E. Aurora, NY 14052.

Christian Foundation for Children and Aging (Newsletter), 4 times a year; 1 Elmwood Ave., Kansas City, KS 66103.

Clarion, The, 5 times a year; Box 159, Alfred, ME 04002; Brothers of Christian Instruction.

Comboni Mission Newsletter, q; 8108 Beechmont Ave., Cincinnati, OH 45255.

Commentary, 8 times a year; 1010 11th St., Suite 200, Sacramento, CA 95814.

Consolata Missionaries, bm; P.O. Box 5550, Somerset, NJ 08875.

Context, 22 issues a year; 205 W. Monroe St., Chicago, IL 60606.

CRS News, q; 209 W. Fayette St., Baltimore, MD 21201. Catholic Relief Services.

Cross Roads, 8 times a year; 300 College Park Ave., Dayton, OH 45469. Catholic Campus Ministry Association.

CRUX of the News, w; 3 Enterprise Dr., Albany, NY 12204.

Damien-Dutton Call, q; 616 Bedford Ave., Bellmore, NY 11710.

Dimensions, m; 86 Front St., Hempstead, NY 11550; National Catholic Development Conference.

Diocesan Newsletter, The, m; P.O. Box 2279, Brownsville, TX 78522; Brownsville diocese.

Educating in Faith, q; 2021 H St. N.W., Washington, DC 20006. Catholic Negro-American Mission Board.

Environment and Art Letter, m; 1800 N. Hermitage Ave., Chicago, IL 60622.

Escoge la Vida!, bm; 4345 SW 72nd Ave., Suite E, Miami, FL 33155. Vida Humana Internacional.

Eucharistic Minister, m; 115 E. Armour, P.O. Box 419493, Kansas City, MO 64141.

Fatima Findings, m; 100 E. 20th St., Baltimore, MD 21218; Reparation Society of the Immaculate Heart of Mary.

Fellowship of Catholic Scholars Newsletter, q; Jacques Maritain Center, 714 Hesburgh Library, Notre Dame, IN 46556.

Fonda Tekakwitha News, P.O. Box 627, Fonda, NY 12068.

Food for the Poor, 3 times a year; 550 SW 12th Ave., Deerfield Beach, FL 33442.

Franciscan Reporter, annually; 3140 Meramec St., St. Louis, MO 63118.

Franciscan World Care, 6 times a year; P.O. Box 29034, Washington, D.C. 20017. Franciscan Mission Service of North America.

Friar News, biweekly; 58 W. 88th St., New York, NY 10024; Franciscan Friars of Holy Name Province.

Frontline Report, bm; 23 Bliss Ave., Tenafly, NJ 07670.

Fund Raising Forum, m; 86 Front St., Hempstead, NY 11550; National Catholic Development Conference.

Generation, m; 205 W. Monroe St., Chicago, IL 60606.

Glenmary Bridge, The, 5 times a year; P.O. Box 465618, Cincinnati, OH 45246.

Good News NEWS, The, bm; 2115 Summit Ave., No. 8001, St. Paul, MN 55105.

Graymoor Today, m; Graymoor, Garrison, NY 10524.

Guadalupe Missioners Newsletter, m; 4714 W. 8th St., Los Angeles, CA 90005.

Happiness, q; 567 Salem End Rd., Framingham, MA 01701; Sons of Mary, Health of the Sick.

Harmony, 4 times a year; 800 N. Country Club Rd., Tucson, AZ 85716 . Benedictine Srs. of Perpetual Adoration.

Haz Todo Con Amor, m; 499 St. Matthew St., El Paso, TX 79907; El Paso diocese.

Holy Name Newsletter, m; P.O. Box 26038, Baltimore, MD 21224. National Association of the Holy Name Society.

HLI Reports, m; 7845 Airpark Rd., Suite E, Gaithersburg, MD 20879. Human Life International.

Initiatives, 6 times a year; 1 East Superior St., No. 311, Chicago, IL 60611; National Center for the Laity.

In Between, 5 times a year; 1257 E. Siena Hts. Dr., Adrian, MI 49221; Adrian Dominican Sisters.

Insight, bm; 912 Market St., La Crosse, WI 54601. Franciscan Sisters of Perpetual Adoration.

It's Our World, 4 times during school year; 1720 Massachusetts Ave. N.W., Washington, DC 20036. Young Catholics in Mission (Holy Childhood Association).

Land of Cotton, q; 2048 W. Fairview Ave., Montgomery, AL 39196; City of St. Jude.

Law Reports, 4 times a year; 4455 Woodson Rd., St. Louis, MO 63134; Catholic Health Association.

Laywitness, m; 50 Washington Ave., New Rochelle, NY 10801; Catholics United for the Faith.

Legatus, m; 30 Frank Lloyd Wright Dr., Ann Arbor, MI 48105.

Life Insight, m; 3211 Fourth St. N.E., Washington, DC 20017; Committee for Pro-Life Activities, NCCB.

Light, The, m; 721 Second St. N.E., Washington, DC 20002.

Markings, m; 205 W. Monroe St., Chicago, IL 60606.

Medical Mission Sisters News, 4 times a year; 8400 Pine Road, Philadelphia, PA 19111.

Messenger of St. Joseph's Union, The, 3 times a year; 108 Bedell St., Staten Island, NY 10309.

Missionaries of Africa Report, q; 1624 21st St. N.W., Washington, DC 20009; Society of Missionaries of Africa (White Fathers).

Mission Messenger, The, m; P.O. Box 610, Thoreau, NM 87323; St. Bonaventure Indian Mission and School.

Mission Update, bm; 3029 Fourth St., N.E., Washington, DC 20017; U.S. Catholic Mission Association.

Mustard Seed, 3 times a year, and **Mustard Seed Update,** 3 times a year; 1615 Vine St., Cincinnati, OH 45210; Franciscans Network.

NCPD National Update, q; P.O. Box 29113, Washington, DC 20017; National Catholic Office for Persons with Disabilities.

NCSC News, q; 1275 K St. N.W., Suite 980, Washington, DC 20005. National Catholic Stewardship Council.

Nevada Catholic Newsletter, m; P.O. Box 1211, Reno, NV 89504; Reno-Las Vegas diocese.

News and Views, q; 3900 Westminster Pl.; St. Louis, MO 63108; Sacred Heart Program.

Newsletter of the Bureau of Catholic Indian Missions, 10 times a year; 2021 H St. N.W., Washington, DC 20006.

Nuestra Parroquia (Spanish-English), m; 205 W. Monroe St., Chicago, IL 60606. Claretians.

Oblates, bm; 15 S. 59th St., Belleville, IL 62223; Missionary Oblates of Mary Immaculate.

Overview, m; 205 W. Monroe St., Chicago, IL 60606; Thomas More Assn.

Pacer, m; 500 17th Ave., Seattle, WA 98124; Providence Medical Center.

Palabra Entre Nosotros, La, m; P.O. Box 826, Gaithersburg, MD 20884.

Paulist, q; 86 Dromore Rd., Scarsdale, NY 10583.

Perpetual Eucharistic Adoration Newsletter, 3 times a year; P.O. Box 84595, Los Angeles, CA 90073.

Piarist Newsletter, 2 times a year; 1339 Monroe St. N.E., Washington, DC 20017.

Pilgrim, q; Jesuit Fathers, Auriesville, NY 12016; Shrine of North American Martyrs.

Priestly Heart Newsletter, 5337 Genessee St., Bowmansville, NY 14026. Apostleship of Prayer.

Program Supplement, 18 times a year; Columbus Plaza, New Haven, CT 06507; Knights of Columbus.

Quarterly, The, 2021 H St. N.W., Washington, DC 20006; Commission for Catholic Missions Among the Colored People and the Indians.

Religious Life, m (bm, May-Aug.); P.O. Box 41007, Chicago, IL 60641; Institute on Religious Life.

RSCJ Newsletter, bm; 785 Centre St., Newton, MA 02158. Religious of Sacred Heart.

SCJ News, 9 times a year; P.O. Box 289, Hales Corners, WI 53130; Sacred Heart Fathers and Brothers.

Sacred Heart Newsletter, 2 times a year; 5337 Genesee, Bowmansville, NY 14026.

St. Anthony's Newsletter, 10 times a year; Mt. St. Francis, IN 47146.

SSM Network, q; 1031 Bellevue Ave., St. Louis, MO 63117. Sisters of St. Mary.

Spiritual Book Associates, 8 times a year; Notre Dame, IN 46556.

Squires Newsletter, m; One Columbus Plaza, New Haven, CT 06507; Columbian Squires.

Star of the Chaldeans, The, bm; 25585 Berg Rd., Southfield, MI 48034; St. Thomas the Apostle Chaldean Eparchy.

Tekakwitha Conference Newsletter (Cross and Feather News), q; P.O. Box 6768, Great Falls, MT 59406.

Theresian, The, 4 times a year; 5326 E. Pershing Ave., Scottsdale, AZ 85254.

Thirsting for Justice, q; 3211 Fourth St. N.E. Washington, DC 20017; Campaign for Human Development.

Total Stewardship Newsnotes, q; 1633 N. Cleveland Ave., Chicago, IL 60614; National Catholic Conference for Total Stewardship.

Touchstone, 4 times a year; 1337 W. Ohio St., Chicago, IL 60622; National Federation of Priests' Councils.

Trinity Review, m; P.O. Box 700, Jefferson, MD 21755.

UCIP Information, q; Post Box 197, 1211 Geneva 20, Switzerland; International Catholic Union of the Press.

Unda USA Newsletter, 4 times a year; 901 Irving Ave., Dayton, OH 45409.

U.S. Parish, m; 205 W. Monroe St., Chicago, IL 60606.

Vision/Camillian Newsletter — National Association of Catholic Chaplains, bm; 3501 S. Lake Dr., Milwaukee, WI 53207.

Visions, 2 times a year; Victory Noll, P.O. Box 109, Huntington, IN 46750; Our Lady of Victory Missionary Sisters.

Vocation News, q; 26 Brentford Ct., Camarillo, CA 93010.

Voices, q; P.O. Box 8326, St. Louis, MO 63132; Women for Faith and Family.

Washington Theological Union Newsletter, 3 times a year; 9001 New Hampshire Ave., Silver Spring, MD 20903.

Wooden Bell, The, 4 times a year; 209 W. Fayette St., Baltimore, MD 21201. Catholic Relief Services.

Woodstock Report, q; Georgetown Univ., Washington, DC 20057. Woodstock Theological Center.

Word One, 5 times a year; 205 W. Monroe St., Chicago, IL 60606; Claretians.

Xaverian Missions Newsletter, six times a year; 101 Summer St., Holliston, MA 01746; Xaverian Missionary Fathers.

Your Edmundite Missions Newsletter, bm; 1428 Broad St., Selma, AL 36701; Southern Missions of Society of St. Edmund.

Youth Update, m; 1615 Republic St., Cincinnati, OH 45210.

Zeal Newsletter, 3 times a year; P.O. Box 86, Allegany, NY 14706; Franciscan Sisters of Allegany.

BOOKS

The Official Catholic Directory, annual; P.J. Kenedy and Sons, Reed Reference Publishing Co., 121 Chanlon Rd., New Providence, NJ 07974. First edition, 1817.

The Catholic Almanac, annual; Our Sunday Visitor, Inc., 200 Noll Plaza, Huntington, Ind., 46750, publisher; editorial offices, P.O. Box 3765, Wallington, N.J. 07057. First edition, 1904.

BOOK CLUBS

Catholic Book Club (1928), 106 W. 56th St., New York, NY 10019. Sponsors the Campion Award.

Catholic Digest Book Club (1954), 475 Riverside Dr., New York, NY 10115.

Spiritual Book Associates (1934), Notre Dame, IN 46556.

Thomas More Book Club (1939), Thomas More Association, 205 W. Monroe St., Sixth Floor, Chicago, Ill. 60606.

FOREIGN CATHOLIC PERIODICALS

Principal source: Catholic Almanac survey. Included are English-language Catholic periodicals published outside the U.S.

African Ecclesial Review (AFER), bm; Gaba Publications, P.O. Box 4002, Eldoret, Kenya.

Australasian Catholic Record, q; St. Patrick's Seminary, Manly, New South Wales, Australia.

Christ to the World, bm; Via di Propaganda 1- C, 00187, Rome, Italy.

Christian Orient, q; P.B. 1 Vadavathoor, Kottayam 686010, Kerala, India.

Doctrine and Life, m; Dominican Publications, 49 Parnell Sq., Dublin 1, Ireland.

Downside Review, q; Downside Abbey, Stratton on Fosse, Bath, BA3 4RH, England.

East Asian Pastoral Review, q; East Asian Pastoral Institute, P.O. Box 221 U.P. Campus, 1101 Quezon City, Philippines.

Furrow, The, m; St. Patrick's College, Maynooth, Ireland.

Heythrop Journal, q; Heythrop College, 11 Cavendish Sq., London W1M, OAN, England (Editorial Office). Published by Blackwell Publishers, 108 Cowley Rd., Oxford, OX4 1JF, U.K.

Holy Land Review, q; P.O. Box 186, 91001 Jerusalem, Israel. Illustrated.

Irish Biblical Studies, The, q; Union Theological College, Belfast BT7 1JT, N. Ireland.

Irish Theological Quarterly, q; St. Patrick's College, Maynooth, Ireland.

L'Osservatore Romano, w; Vatican City. (See Index.)

Louvain Studies, q; St. Michielsstraat 6, B-3000, Leuven, Belgium.

Lumen Vitae (French, with English summaries), q; International Center for Studies in Religious Education, 186, rue Washington, B-1050 Brussels, Belgium.

Maynooth Review, The, q; St. Patrick's College, Maynooth, Ireland.

Mediaeval Studies, annual; Pontifical Institute of Mediaeval Studies, 59 Queen's Park Crescent East, Toronto, Ont., Canada M5S 2C4.

Month, m; 114 Mount St., London, WIY 6AH, England.

Music and Liturgy, 6 times a year; The Editor, 30, North Terrace, Mildenhall, Suffolk 1P28 7AB, England.

New Blackfriars, m; edited by English Dominicans, Blackfriars, Oxford, OX1 3LY, England.

Omnis Terra (English Edition), m; Pontifical Missionary Union, Congregation for the Evangelization of Peoples, Via di Propaganda 1/c, 00187 Rome, Italy.

One in Christ, q; Edited at: Turvey Abbey, Turvey, Beds. MK43 8DE, England.

Priests and People (formerly The Clergy Review), 11 times a year; 1 King Street Cloisters, Clifton Walk, London W6 0QZ, England.

Recusant History, biannual; Catholic Record Society, 12 Melbourne Pl., Wolsingham, Durham DL13 3EH, England.

Religious Life Review, bm; Dominican Publications, 42 Parnell Sq., Dublin 1, Ireland.

Scripture in Church, q; Dominican Publications, 42 Parnell Sq., Dublin 1, Ireland.

Social Studies, q; St. Patrick's College, Maynooth, Ireland.

Spearhead, 5 times a year; Gaba Publications, P.O. Box 4002, Eldoret, Kenya.

Tablet, The, w; 1 King Street Cloisters, Clifton Walk, London W6 0QZ, England.

Teilhard Review, The, 3 times a year; The Teilhard Centre, 3 Priory Farm Court, Lavenham, Suffolk CO10 9RW, England.

Way, The, q; 114 Mount St., London W1Y 6AN, England.

CATHOLIC NEWS AGENCIES

(Sources: International Catholic Union of the Press, Geneva; Catholic Press Association, U.S.)

Argentina: Agencia Informativa Catolica Argentina (AICA), av. Rivadavia, 413, 40 Casilla de Correo Central 2886, 1020 Buenos Aires.

Austria: Katholische Presse-Agentur (Kathpress), Singerstrasse 7/6/2, 1010 Vienna 1.

Belgium: Centre d'Information de Presse (CIP), 35 Chaussée de Haecht, 1030 Brussels.

Bolivia: Agencia Noticias Fides, ANF, Casilla 5782, La Paz.

ERBOL, Casilla 5946, La Paz.

Chile: Agencia informativa y de comunicaciones (AIC Chile), Brasil 94, Santiago.

Croatia: Christian Information Service, Marulicev 14, PP 434, 410001 Zagreb.

Germany: Katholische Nachrichten Agentur (KNA), Adenauer Allee 134, 5300 Bonn 1.

Greece: Agence TYPOS Rue Acharnon 246, Athens 815.

Hong Kong: UCA-News, P.O. Box 69626, Kwun Tong (Hong Kong).

Hungary: Magyar Kurir, Milkszath ter 1, 1088, Budapest.

India: South Asian Religious News (SAR-News), PB 6236, Mazagaon, Bombay 400 010.

Italy: Servizio Informazioni Religiosa (SIR), Via di Porta Cavalleggeri 143, I-00165 Roma.

Centrum Informationis Catolicae (CIC-Roma), via Delmonte de la Farina, 30/4, 00186 Roma.

Peru: ACI-PRENSA, A.P. 040062, Lima.

Switzerland: Katholische Internationale Presse-Agentur (KIPA), Case Postale 1054 CH 1701, Fribourg.

Centre International de Reportages et d'-Information Culturelle (CIRIC), Chemin Clochetons 8, P.O. Box 1000, Lausanne.

United States of America: Catholic News Service (CNS), 3211 Fourth St. N.E., Washington, DC 20017

Zaire: Documentation et Information Africaine (DIA), B.P. 2598, Kinshasa I.

Missions: Agenzia Internationale Fides (AIF), Palazzo di Propagande Fide, Via di Propaganda I-c, 00187 Rome, Italy.

U.S. PRESS SERVICES

Catholic News Service (CNS), established in 1920 (NC News Service), provides a worldwide daily news report by satellite throughout the U.S. and Canada and by wire and computer links into several foreign countries, and by mail to other clients, serving Catholic periodicals and broadcasters including Vatican Radio in about 40 countries. CNS also provides feature and photo services and a weekly religious education package, "Faith Alive!" It publishes "Origins," a weekly documentary service, and "Catholic Trends," a fortnightly newsletter, the weekly TV and Movie Guide and Movie Guide Monthly. CNS maintains a full-time bureau in Rome. It is a division of the United States Catholic Conference, with offices at 3211 Fourth St. N.E., Washington, DC 20017. The director and editor-in-chief is Thomas N. Lorsung.

Religious News Service (RNS) is an editorially independent wire service covering Catholic, Protestant and Jewish news. The service is available by mail, by computer, and New York Times syndication. RNS also offers a photo service. The service was started in 1934 and is today the country's only interfaith news service. RNS has stringers throughout the U.S. and key spots around the globe, including the Vatican, Israel, Central America, South Africa, and Europe. Mailing address: P.O. Box 1015, Radio City Station, New York, NY 10101. The executive editor is Judy Weidman.

Spanish-Language Service: A weekly news summary provided by Catholic News Service is used by a number of Catholic newspapers. Some papers carry features of their own in Spanish.

RADIO, TELEVISION, THEATRE

Radio and Television

Christopher Radio Program: 14-minute interview series, "Christopher Closeup," weekly, on 90 stations; "Christopher Minutes," daily, on 700 stations. Address: 12 E. 48th St., New York, NY 10017.

Christopher TV Series, "Christopher Closeup": Originated in 1952. Half-hour and quarter-hour interviews in color, weekly, on 400 commercial and cable stations, CTNA, American Forces Network outlets. Address: 12 E. 48th St., New York, NY 10017.

Journeys Thru Rock (Radio): Produced in cooperation with the Department of Communication, NCCB/USCC. A 15-minute weekly program currently employing a youth-oriented music and commentary format; heard on more than 950 stations (ABC).

Sacred Heart Program (Radio, TV): Originated in 1939, operated by the Jesuits. Produces and syndicates nationally one TV program and three radio programs each week on approximately 800 stations. Address: 3900 Westminster Place, St. Louis, MO 63108.

Religious Specials (TV): The NCCB/USCC Catholic Communications Campaign produces two one-hour Catholic specials a year and additional seasonal liturgical services. The specials use a variety of formats and are broadcast on the ABC and NBC television networks.

Theatre

Catholic University Drama Department: Established in 1937. Offers B.A., M.A. and M.F.A. degree programs in playwriting, directing and acting. Produces four or five plays in The Hartke Theatre and four to six plays in the Callan and Lab Theatres each year. Affiliated with National Players and Olney Theatre. Chairman of the department, William H. Graham. Address: Catholic University of America, Washington, DC 20064.

Catholic Actors' Guild of America, Inc.: Established in 1914 to provide material and spiritual assistance to people in the theatre. Has more than 500 members; publishes *The Call Board.* Address: 1501 Broadway, Suite 510, New York, NY 10036.

Communications Services

Black Catholic Televangelization Network: Consists of production organizations that promote the evangelization of the Black community and share the gifts of Black Catholics. The member production groups are: *Black and Catholic,* the television magazine; This Far by Faith (Radio); *Search for a Black Christian Heritage; The Catholic African World Network,* Rev. Clarence Williams, C.Pp.S., is president. Address: 5247 Sheridan Ave., Detroit, MI 48213.

Catholic Views Broadcasts, Inc., 86 Riverside Dr., New York, NY 10024. Produces weekly 15-minute radio program *Views of the News.* Also operates Catholic community TV stations in Chicago, Minneapolis and St. Louis.

Clemons Productions, Inc.: Produces "That's the Spirit," a family show. Available to dioceses, organizations or channels. Address: P.O. Box 7466, Greenwich, CT 06830.

Eternal Word Television Network (EWTN), 5817 Old Leeds Rd., Birmingham, AL 35210. America's largest religious cable network; features 24 hours of spiritual-growth programming for the entire family. Offers documentaries, weekly teaching series and talk shows, including the award-winning "Mother Angelica Live." Also features live Church events from around the world and devotional programs such as "The Holy Rosary." Mother M. Angelica, P.C.P.A., foundress.

Father Justin Rosary Hour (Polish): Station F — Box 217, Buffalo, NY 14212. Founded in 1931. Rev. Cornelian Dende, O.F.M. Conv., director. Aired over more than 45 stations in U.S. and Canada. Cassette recordings and printed copies of programs available.

Family Theater Productions: Founded by Father Peyton. Video cassettes, films for TV. Address: 7201 Sunset Blvd., Hollywood, CA 90046.

Franciscan Communications/Winston Press: An award-winning producer of video and print resources for pastoral ministry and publisher of religious education material for schools and parish catechetical programs. Address: 1229 South Santee St., Los Angeles, CA 90015.

Hispanic Telecommunications Network, Inc. (HTN): Produces *Nuestra Familia,* a national weekly Spanish-language TV series and *VideoValores,* adult religious education and evangelization video tapes. Address: 130 Lewis St., San Antonio, TX 78212.

ITP-Paulist Communications: Full service video production in syndication to dioceses, religious communities and church groups. Free services to broadcasters include public announcements, seasonal programming and weekly music and news programs. Creators of *Sunday to Sunday* weekly TV scripture series. Address: 818 Roeder Rd., Suite 600, Silver Spring, MD 20910.

Mary Productions: Originated in 1950. Offers royalty-free scripts for stage, film, radio and tape production. Audio and video tapes of lives of the saints and historical characters. Traveling theatre company. Address: Mary Productions, 212 Oakdale Dr., Tomaso Plaza, Middletown, NJ 07748.

Oblate Media and Communication Corporation: Producers, Broadcast syndicators and distributors of Catholic and value-centered video and audio programming. Address: 1944 Innerbelt Business Center Dr., St. Louis, MO 63114.

Passionist Communications, Inc.: Present Sunday Mass on TV seen in U.S. and available to dioceses and channels; publish "TV Prayer Guide," semi-annually. Address: 19 Second Ave., P.O. Box 440, Pelham, NY 10803.

Paulist Productions: Producers and distributors of the INSIGHT Film Series (available for TV) and educational film series. Address: P.O. Box 1057, Pacific Palisades, CA 90272.

VISN: Interfaith cable TV network. Policies shaped by consortium of 28 members representing 54 faith groups from Roman Catholic, Jewish, Protestant and Eastern Orthodox traditions. Address:

National Interfaith Cable Coalition, Suite 915, 74 Trinity Place, New York, NY 10006.

Catholic Telecommunications Network of America (CTNA): A private satellite network established in 1981 by the U.S. Catholic Bishops. Provides telecommunications services that inform, educate and respond to the pastoral needs of the Church. CTNA currently serves 199 affiliates (dioceses, hospitals, colleges and religious communities) and over 425 receiving sites across the U.S. CTNA reported that, starting in January, 1994, programming would be available directly to parishes. Address: 3211 Fourth St., N.E., Fifth Floor, Washington, DC 20017.

Catholic Television Network (CTN): Instructional TV operations have been established in the following archdioceses and dioceses. Archdioceses are indicated by an asterisk.

Boston,* Mass.: Rev. Francis McFarland, Director, P.O. Box 9109, Newtonville, MA 02158.

Brooklyn, NY: Rev. Msgr. Michael J. Dempsey, Director, 1712 10th Ave., 11215.

Chicago,*IL: Mr. Joseph Loughlin, Director, 155 E. Superior. 60611.

Corpus Christi, TX: Mr. Martin L. Wind, 1200 Lantania St., Corpus Christi, TX 78409.

Dallas, TX: Ms. Patricia Martin, 3725 Blackburn. 75219.

Detroit,* MI: Mr. Ned McGrath, Director, 305 Michigan Ave., Detroit, Mich. 48226.

Los Angeles,* CA: Mr. Tom Mossman, 1530 W. Ninth St. 90015.

New York,* NY: Mr. Michael Lavery, Director, 215 Seminary Ave., Yonkers, NY 10704.

Oakland, San Jose, San Francisco,* CA (Bay Area): Mr. Brian Coyne, 324 Middlefield Rd., Menlo Park, CA 94025.

Orange, CA: Msgr. Michael A. Harris, Director, 22062 Antonio FWY, Rancho Santa Margarita, CA 92688.

Orlando, FL: Ms. Carol Stanton, P.O. Box 2728, Orlando, FL 32802.

Rockville Centre, NY: Rev. Msgr. Thomas Hartman, Director, 1345 Admiral Lane, Uniondale, NY 11553.

San Bernardino, CA: Ms. Clare Colella, Director, Caritas Communications, 1450 N. "D" St., San Bernardino, CA 92405.

Wichita, KS: Mr. Robert Voboril, 424 N. Broadway, Wichita, KS 67202.

Youngstown, OH: Rev. James Korda, P.O. Box 430, Canfield, OH 44406.

Unda-USA: A national professional Catholic association for broadcasters and other allied communicators in church ministry; organized in 1972. It succeeded the Catholic Broadcasters Association of America which in 1948 had replaced the Catholic Forum of the Air organized in 1938. It is a member of the international Catholic association for radio and television known as Unda (the Latin word for "wave," symbolic of air waves of communication). Subgroups include Catholic Television Network, the Association of Catholic TV/Radio Syndicators, the Catholic Telecommunications Network of America and the USCC Communications Dept. Unda-USA publishes a newsletter four times a year for members, sponsors an annual general assembly and presents the Gabriel Awards annually for excellence in broadcasting. President, Sister Angela Ann Zukowski, M.H.S.H. Address: Unda-USA, 901 Irving Ave., Dayton, OH 45409.

The Catholic Communications Foundation (CCF) was established by the Catholic Fraternal Benefit Societies in 1966 to lend support and assistance to development of the communications apostolate of the Church. The CCF promotes the development of diocesan communications capabilities and funds a scholarship program at the Annual Institute for Religious Communications. CCF officers include Bishop Anthony G. Bosco, chairman of the board. Address: P.O. Box 374, Pawling, NY 12564.

HONORS AND AWARDS

PONTIFICAL ORDERS

The Pontifical Orders of Knighthood are secular orders of merit whose membership depends directly on the pope.

Supreme Order of Christ (Militia of Our Lord Jesus Christ): The highest of the five pontifical orders of knighthood, the Supreme Order of Christ was approved Mar. 14, 1319, by John XXII as a continuation in Portugal of the suppressed Order of Templars. Members were religious with vows and a rule of life until the order lost its religious character toward the end of the 15th century. Since that time it has existed as an order of merit. Paul VI, in 1966, restricted awards of the order to Christian heads of state.

Order of the Golden Spur (Golden Militia): Although the original founder is not certainly known, this order is one of the oldest knighthoods. Indiscriminate bestowal and inheritance diminished its prestige, however, and in 1841 Gregory XVI replaced it with the Order of St. Sylvester and gave it the title of Golden Militia. In 1905 St. Pius X res-

tored the Order of the Golden Spur in its own right, separating it from the Order of St. Sylvester. Paul VI, in 1966, restricted awards of the order to Christian heads of state.

Order of Pius IX: Founded by Pius IX June 17, 1847, the order is awarded for outstanding services for the Church and society, and may be given to non-Catholics as well as Catholics. The title to nobility formerly attached to membership was abolished by Pius XII in 1939. In 1957 Pius XII instituted the Class of the Grand Collar as the highest category of the order; in 1966, Paul VI restricted this award to heads of state "in solemn circumstances." The other three classes are of Knights of the Grand Cross, Knight Commanders with and without emblem, and Knights. The new class was created to avoid difficulties in presenting papal honors to Christian or non-Christian leaders of high merit.

Order of St. Gregory the Great: First established by Gregory XVI in 1831 to honor citizens of the Papal States, the order is conferred on persons who are distinguished for personal character and reputation, and for notable accomplishment. The order has civil and military divisions, and three classes of knights.

Order of St. Sylvester: Instituted Oct. 31, 1841, by Gregory XVI to absorb the Order of the Golden Spur, this order was divided into two by St. Pius X in 1905, one retaining the name of St. Sylvester and the other assuming the title of Golden Militia. Membership consists of three degrees: Knights of the Grand Cross, Knight Commanders with and without emblem, and Knights.

PAPAL MEDALS

Pro Ecclesia et Pontifice: This decoration ("For the Church and the Pontiff") had its origin in 1888 as a token of the golden sacerdotal jubilee of Leo XIII; he bestowed it on those who had assisted in the observance of his jubilee and on persons responsible for the success of the Vatican Exposition. The medal, cruciform in shape, bears the likenesses of Sts. Peter and Paul, the tiara and the papal keys, the words *Pro Ecclesia et Pontifice,* and the name of the present pontiff, all on the same side; it is attached to a ribbon of yellow and white, the papal colors. Originally, the medal was issued in gold, silver or bronze. It is awarded in recognition of service to the Church and the papacy.

Benemerenti: Several medals ("To a well-deserving person") have been conferred by popes for exceptional accomplishment and service. The medals, which are made of gold, silver or bronze, bear the likeness and name of the reigning pope on one side; on the other, a laurel crown and the letter "B."

These two medals may be given by the pope to both men and women. Their bestowal does not convey any title or honor of knighthood.

ECCLESIASTICAL ORDER

Equestrian Order of the Holy Sepulchre of Jerusalem: The order traces its origin to Godfrey of Bouillon who instituted it in 1099. It took its name from the Basilica of the Holy Sepulchre where its members were knighted. After the fall of the Latin Kingdom of Jerusalem and the consequent departure of the knights from the Holy Land, national divisions were established in various countries.

The order was reorganized by Pius IX in 1847 when he reestablished the Latin Patriarchate of Jerusalem and placed the order under the jurisdiction of its patriarch. In 1888, Leo XIII confirmed permission to admit women — Ladies of the Holy Sepulchre — to all degrees of rank. Pius X reserved the office of grand master to himself in 1907; Pius XII gave the order a cardinal patron in 1940 and, in 1949, transferred the office of grand master from the pope to the cardinal patron. Pope John XXIII approved updated constitutions in 1962; the latest statutes were approved by Paul VI in 1977.

The purposes of the order are strictly religious and charitable. Members are committed to sustain and aid the charitable, cultural and social works of the Catholic Church in the Holy Land, particularly in the Latin Patriarchate of Jerusalem.

The order is composed of knights and ladies grouped in three classes: class of Knights of the Collar and Ladies of the Collar; Class of Knights (in four grades); Class of Ladies (in four grades). Members are appointed by the cardinal grand master according to procedures outlined in the constitution.

Under the present constitution the order is divided into national lieutenancies, largely autonomous, with international headquarters in Rome. Cardinal Giuseppe Caprio is the grand master of the order.

There are seven lieutenancies of the order in the United States and one in Puerto Rico. Address of Vice Governor General: F. Russell Kendall, 309 Knipp Rd., Houston, TX 77024.

ORDER OF MALTA

The Sovereign Military Hospitaller Order of St. John of Jerusalem of Rhodes and of Malta traces its origin to a group of men who maintained a Christian hospital in the Holy Land in the 11th century. The group was approved as a religious order — the Hospitallers of St. John — by Paschal II in 1113.

The order, while continuing its service to the poor, principally in hospital work, assumed military duties in the twelfth century and included knights, chaplains and sergeants-at-arms among its members. All the knights were professed monks with the vows of poverty, chastity and obedience. Headquarters were located in the Holy Land until the last decade of the 13th century and on Rhodes after 1308 (whence the title, Knights of Rhodes).

After establishing itself on Rhodes, the order became a sovereign power like the sea republics of Italy and the Hanseatic cities of Germany, flying its own flag, coining its own money, floating its own navy, and maintaining diplomatic relations with many nations.

The order was forced to abandon Rhodes in 1522 after the third siege of the island by the Turks under Sultan Suliman I. Eight years later, the Knights were given the island of Malta, where they remained as a bastion of Christianity until near the end of the 18th century. Headquarters have been located in Rome since 1834.

The title of Grand Master of the Order, in abeyance for some time, was restored by Leo XIII in 1879. A more precise definition of both the religious and the sovereign status of the order was embodied in a new constitution of 1961 and a code issued in 1966.

The four main classifications of members are: Knights of Justice, who are religious with the vows of poverty, chastity and obedience; Knights of Obedience, who make a solemn promise to strive for Christian perfection; Knights of Honor and Devotion and of Grace and Devotion — all of noble lineage; and Knights of Magistral Grace. There are also chaplains, Dames and Donats of the order.

The order, with five grand priories, four sub-priories and 38 national associations, is devoted to hospital and charitable works of all kinds in some 100 countries.

Under the provisions of international law, the order maintains full diplomatic relations with the Holy See — on which, in its double nature, it depends as a religious Order, but of which, as a sovereign Order of Knighthood, it is independent — and 53 countries throughout the world.

The Grand Master, who is the head of the order, has the title of Most Eminent Highness with the rank of Cardinal. He must be of noble lineage and under solemn vows for a minimum period of 10 years, if under 50.

The present Grand Master is Fra' Andrew Willoughby Ninian Bertie, member of the British aristocracy, who was elected for life Apr. 8, 1988, by the Council of State. His election was approved by the Pope.

The address of headquarters of the order is Via Condotti, 68, Palazzo Malta, 00187 Rome, Italy. U.S. addresses: American Association, 1011 First Ave., New York, NY 10022; Western Association of U.S.A., 465 California St., Suite 812, San Francisco, CA 94104; Federal Association of U.S.A., 1730 M St. N.W., Suite 301; Washington, DC 20036.

AMERICAN CATHOLIC AWARDS

Most of the awards listed below are presented annually. Recipients for 1992/1993 are given where available; an asterisk indicates that the award has not been presented recently. See earlier editions of the Almanac for award winners of previous years. See also Index for other awards.

Aquinas Medal (1956), by the American Catholic Philosophical Association for outstanding contributions to the field of Catholic philosophy. Ralph McInerny (1993).

Bellarmine Medal (1955), by Bellarmine College (Louisville, Ky.), to persons in national or international affairs who, in controversial matters, exemplify the characteristics of St. Robert Bellarmine in charity, justice and temperateness. Lech Walesa (1990).

Berakah Award (1976), by the North American Academy of the Liturgy, to recognize distinguished contribution to the professional work of liturgy by a liturgist or person of an allied vocation. Mary Collins, O.S.B. (1993).

Borromeo Award (1960), by Carroll College (Helena, Mont.), for zeal, courage and devotion in the spirit of St. Charles Borromeo. Most Rev. Elden F. Curtiss (1991); Priests of the Helena diocese (1992).

Brent Award (1976), by the Diocese of Arlington, Va., for distinguished service to others. Mary Ellen Bork (1993).

Campion Award (1955), by the Catholic Book Club for distinguished service in Catholic letters. Rev. J. Bryan Hehir (1993).

Cardinal Gibbons Medal (1949) by the Alumni Association of The Catholic University of America for distinguished and meritorious service to the Church, the United States or The Catholic University of America. Rev. William J. Byron, S.J. (1991); George J. Quinn (1992).

Cardinal Spellman Award, see John Courtney Murray Award.

Cardinal Wright Award (1980), by the Fellowship of Catholic Scholars to a Catholic adjudged to have done an outstanding service for the Church. Rev. Mr. Owen Lee, C.S.B. (1993).

Cardinal O'Boyle Award, by the Fellowship of Catholic Scholars. Awarded intermittently to a Catholic for his or her defense of the faith. Rev. John C. Ford, S.J. (1988), Mother M. Angelica (1991).

Caritas Medal (1992), by St. John's University (Jamaica, N.Y.) for humanitarian service to the people of New York City. Sister Mary Rose McGeady (1992).

Christian Culture Award (1941), by Assumption University (Canada) to outstanding exponents of Christian ideals. Janet E. Smith, Ph.D. (1993).

College of New Rochelle Pope John XXIII Award* (1963), by College of New Rochelle (N.Y.) to those whose lives are witness "to the centrality of human dignity in the creation of peace." Mary Shea Giordano (1988).

Damien-Dutton Award (1953), by the Damien-Dutton Society for service toward conquest of leprosy or for the promotion of better understanding of social problems connected with the disease. Dr. C. Job, India (1993).

Edith Stein Award (1955), by the Edith Stein Guild for service toward better understanding between Christians and Jews. Cardinal John O'Connor (1991).

Emmanuel D'Alzon Medal (1954), by Assumptionists to persons exemplifying the ideals of their founder. Raymond J. Marion (1990).

Father McKenna Award (1950), by the National Association of the Holy Name Society. Awarded biennially to recognize a member of the clergy for service to the society. Rev. Thomas J. Dzurenda (1992).

Fidelitas Medal (1949), by Orchard Lake Schools (Sts. Cyril and Methodius Seminary, St. Mary's College, St. Mary's Preparatory), to an outstanding American Catholic of Polish descent for fidelity in serving God and country. Mr. Edward G. Dykla (1993).

Franciscan International Award (1958), by the Conventual Franciscan Friars of the Franciscan Retreat Center (Prior Lake, Minn.) to an individual or group exemplifying the ideals of St. Francis of Assisi. Poor Clare Sisters (1993).

Gaudium Medal, The* (1982, as The Compostela Award), by the Oratory of St. Philip Neri in the Diocese of Brooklyn to men and women whose lives represent the noblest ideals of the human tradition of fidelity to justice, truth, beauty and peace.

George M. Cohan Award (1970), by the Catholic Actors Guild of America, Inc., Jose Ferrer (1989), Chita Rivera (1990), Gwen Verdon (1991). Other awards presented by the organization include: **St. Genesius Award,** Father John Catoir (1990); **Fred Allen Humanitarian Award,** Vincent Gardenia (1991).

Good Samaritan Award (1968), by the National Catholic Development Conference to recognize the concern for one's fellowman exemplified by the parable of the Good Samaritan. Sister Margaret Dillier, S.C.N. (1992).

Hoey Awards* (1942), by the Catholic Interracial Council of New York, to persons who have worked to combat racism and have promoted social and interracial justice.

Honor et Veritas Award (1959), by the Catholic War Veterans to outstanding Americans. Rear Adm. Roberta L. Hazard, USN (1991).

Howard R. Marraro Prize (1973), by the American Catholic Historical Association for a book on Italian history or Italo-American history or relations. Martha D. Pollack (1992).

Insignis Medal (1951), by Fordham University for extraordinary distinction in the service of God and humanity. The Jesuits of El Salvador (1990).

John Courtney Murray Award (1972), by the Catholic Theological Society for distinguished achievement in theology. Originated in 1947 as the Cardinal Spellman Award. Margaret A. Farley (1992).

John Gilmary Shea Prize (1944), by the American Catholic Historical Association for scholarly works on the history of the Catholic Church broadly considered. David J. O'Brien (1992).

Laetare Medal (1883), by Notre Dame University. Donald R. Keough (1993).

Lumen Christi Award (1978), by the Catholic Church Extension Society to persons making an outstanding contribution in service to the American home missions. Harry Blue Thunder (1992).

The Manhattan College De La Salle Medal, by Manhattan College, for significant contribution to the moral, cultural and educational life of the nation. Edmund T. Pratt, Jr. (1993).

Marianist Award (1949), by the University of Dayton for outstanding service in America to the Mother of God (until 1966); for outstanding contributions to mankind (from 1967); for outstanding scholarship by a Roman Catholic (from 1986). Monica Helwig (1993).

Marian Library Medal (1953), by the Marian Library of the University of Dayton. Awarded annually (until 1967) to encourage books in English on the Blessed Virgin Mary. Awarded every four years (from 1971), at the time of an International Mariological Congress, to a scholar for Mariological studies. Paul Melada, O.F.M. (1991).

Mendel Medal (1928), by Villanova University. Named in honor of Gregor Mendel, Augustinian priest, and awarded to outstanding scientists who, by their standing before the world as scientists, have demonstrated that there is no intrinsic conflict between true science and true religion. Dr. Philip A. Sharp (1993).

The Patronal Medal (1974), by the Catholic University of America in cooperation with the National Shrine of the Immaculate Conception for outstanding contributions to the Catholic Church and in promoting interest and devotion to Mary, patroness of the University. Mother M. Angelica (1990).

Paulist Award for Lay Evangelization (1979), by the Paulist Fathers to Catholic laity for significant contribution in ministry of evangelizing inactive Catholics and the unchurched in the U.S. Carmilita Kenny (1991).

Pax Christi Award (1963), by St. John's University

(Collegeville, Minn.), to honor persons of strong faith whose lives exemplify the importance of spiritual values and concern for the welfare of others. Abbot Jerome Theisen, O.S.B. (1992).

Peter Guilday Prize* (1972), by the American Catholic Historical Association for articles accepted by the editors of the *Catholic Historical Review* which are the first scholarly publications of their authors.

Poverello Medal (1949), by The Franciscan University of Steubenville (Ohio), "in recognition of great benefactions to humanity, exemplifying in our age the Christ-like spirit of charity which filled the life of St. Francis of Assisi." Admiral (ret.) Ferdinand Mahfood (1992).

Regina Medal (1959), by the Catholic Library Association for outstanding contributions to children's literature. Jane Yolen (1992).

Role of Law Award (1973), by the Canon Law Society of America, to recognize a canon lawyer who embodies a pastoral attitude and is committed to research and study. Rev. Ladislaus Örsy, S.J. (1992).

St. Elizabeth Ann Seton Medal (1976), by St. John's University (Jamaica, N.Y.), to an American Catholic laywoman who exemplifies the qualities and virtues of America's first native-born saint. Margaret Grace (1993).

St. Francis de Sales Award (1958), by the Catholic Press Association for distinguished contribution to Catholic journalism. Rev. John Catoir (1993).

St. Vincent de Paul Medal (1948), by St. John's University (Jamaica, N.Y.), for outstanding service to Catholic charities. Thomas A. DeStefano (1992).

Serra Award of the Americas* (1947), by the Academy of American Franciscan History for service to Inter-American good will. (In abeyance; may be revived later.)

Signum Fidei Medal (1942), by the Alumni Association of La Salle University (Phila.) for noteworthy contributions to the advancement of humanitarian principles in keeping with Christian tradition. Rev. Reggie White (1993).

Sword of Loyola (1964), by Loyola University, Chicago, to person or persons exemplifying Ignatius of Loyola's courage, dedication and service. Rev. Timothy S. Healy, S.J. (1990); Sargent and Eunice Kennedy Shriver (1991).

U.S. Catholic Award (1978), by the editors of *U.S. Catholic* magazine for furthering the cause of women in the Church. Rev. Andrew M. Greeley (1993).

DEATHS SEPTEMBER 1992 TO SEPTEMBER 1993

Ackerman, Bishop Richard Henry, C.S.Sp., 89, Nov. 18, 1992, Covington, Ky.; bishop of Covington, 1960 to 1978 when he retired.

Ahr, Bishop George W., 88, May 5, 1993, Lawrenceville, N.J.; bishop of Trenton, 1950 to 1980 when he retired.

Allison, Davey, 32, July 13, 1993, Charlotte, N.C., from injuries suffered in a helicopter crash; stock car race driver.

Antonelli, Cardinal Ferdinando Giuseppe, O.F.M., 96, July 12, 1993, Rome, Italy; cardinal from 1973.

Baggio, Cardinal Sebastiano 79, Mar. 21, 1993, Rome, Italy; chamberlain of the Holy Roman Church; sub-dean of the College of Cardinals; cardinal from 1969.

Baudouin, King, 62, July 31, 1993, while vaca-

tioning in Motril, Spain; King of Belgium from 1951; abdicated for several days in 1990 rather than sign a bill legalizing abortion.

Beltritti, Patriarch Giacomo, 82, Nov. 1, 1992, Jerusalem, Israel; Latin rite patriarch of Jerusalem, 1970 to 1987 when he retired.

Bishop, Mrs. Claire Huchet, 94, Mar. 11, 1993, Paris France; leader in Catholic-Jewish relations.

Brennan, Frank H., Sr., 70, Sept. 15, 1992, Norwalk, Conn.; pioneer in Catholic-Jewish Relations.

Chavez, Cesar Estrada, 66, Apr. 23, 1993, San Luis, Arizona; promoter of farmworkers' rights; president of United Farm Workers of America.

Cosgrove, Bishop William M., 76, Dec. 11, 1992,

Belleville, Il.; bishop of Belleville, 1976 to 1981 when he retired because of ill health.

Daly, Patrick, 48, Dec. 17, 1992, Brooklyn, N.Y.; Brooklyn school principal killed when caught in crossfire at Brooklyn housing project.

Danglymayr, Bishop Augustine, 93, Sept. 18, 1992, Muenster, Tex.; auxiliary bishop of Dallas, 1942-62.

Del Mestri, Cardinal Guido, 82, Aug. 2, 1993, Nuremberg, Germany; born Banja Luka, Yugoslavia (now Bosnia-Herzegovina); Italian citizen; longtime papal diplomat; cardinal from 1991.

Dolinay, Archbishop Thomas V., 69, Apr. 13, 1993, Pittsburgh, Pa.; metropolitan archbishop of Byzantine Rite Archdiocese of Pittsburgh from 1991.

Ellis, Msgr. John Tracy, 87, Oct. 16, 1992, Washington, D.C.; leading church historian; author.

Fagan, Harry A., 52, Dec. 9, 1992, New York, NY; co-founder and managing director of the National Pastoral Life Center.

Finlay, Rev. James C., S.J., 70, Dec. 5, 1992, New York, NY; president of Fordham Univ. from 1972-84.

Fisher, Bishop Carl A., S.S.J., 47, Sept. 2, 1993, Los Angeles, Calif.; auxiliary bishop of Los Angeles from 1986; first black bishop in western U.S.

Foster, Vincent W., Jr., 48, July 20, 1993, Washington, D.C., of a self-inflicted gunshot wound; deputy White House legal counsel.

Fuerst, Rev. Adrian, O.S.B., 76, Dec. 4, 1992, St. Meinrad, Ind.; researcher with CARA.

Ghattas, Bishop Ignatius, B.S.O., 71, Oct. 11, 1992, Cleveland, Ohio; bishop of Newton for Greek Melkites from 1990.

Glinka, Sister Mary Ann, O.S.F., 50, Mar. 19, 1993, Baltimore, Md.; murdered in convent during burglary.

Gray, Cardinal Gordon, 82, July 19, 1993, Edinburgh, Scotland; archbishop of St. Andrews and Edinburgh, 1951 to 1985 when he retired; cardinal from 1969.

Griffiths, Bede, O.S.B., 87, May 13, 1993, Shantivanam, India; English-born internationally known theologian; author; founder of experimental monastery in India; Anglican; received into Church, 1932.

Hayes, Helen, 92, March 17, 1993, Nyack, N.Y.; award-winning actress; called First Lady of the American Theater.

Healy, Timothy S., S.J., 69, Dec. 30, 1992, Newark, N. J.; educator; head of New York Public Library from 1989; former president of Georgetown University.

Honsberger, Mother Mary Claudia, 80, June 12, 1993, Immaculata, Pa.; teacher, administrator and writer; former mother general of the Sisters Servants of the Immaculate Heart of Mary.

John, Harry, 73, Dec. 19, 1992, Milwaukee, Wis.; philanthropist; founder of De Rance Foundation.

Karlon, Sister Madeleine Sophie, M.M., 84, Feb. 13, 1993, Maryknoll, N.Y.; missionary in China (until 1949), among Chinese in Hong Kong and, from 1954, in New York's Chinatown.

Leonard, Msgr. George, 63, Jan. 20, 1993, England; former director of communications for the Catholic Bishops' Conference of England and Wales.

Leonard, Msgr. Thomas, 63, May 15, 1993, Springfield, Pa.; NCCB-USCC official; associate general secretary 1978-82.

Lyke, Archbishop James P., 53, Dec. 27, 1992, Atlanta, Ga.; only active black archbishop; archbishop of Atlanta from 1991.

McDonald, Donald, 72, Mar. 16, 1993, Santa Barbara, Calif.; former editor of Davenport diocesan newspaper and dean of Marquette University College of Journalism.

Magrath, Frank J., 62, Dec. 13, 1992, Miami, Fla.; director since 1966 of Miami-based regional office of the National Conference of Christians and Jews.

Mallon, Rev. Vincent T., M.M., 70, Dec. 18, 1992, Maryknoll, N.Y.; former missionary in Peru; former member of Vatican Congregation for the Clergy.

Martin, Cardinal Jacques, 84, Sept 27, 1992, Vatican City; prefect of the papal household, 1969-86; cardinal from 1988.

Miragliotta, Sal J., 71, Jan. 27, 1993, Washington, D.C.; researcher for New York Times for 27 years; Catholic News Service librarian 1976-86.

Olivares, Luis, C.M.F., 59, Mar. 18, 1993, Los Angeles, Calif; aided El Salvadoran refugees, granting them sanctuary in his parish in Los Angeles.

O'Neill, John J., 72, Oct. 18, 1992, northern Virginia; first director of U.S. Bishops' Office of Research, Plans and Programs.

Oesterreicher, Msgr. John M., 89, Apr. 18, 1993, Livingston, N.J.; convert from Judaism; pioneer in Catholic-Jewish relations; author.

Ott, Bishop Stanley J., 65, Nov. 28, 1992, Baton Rouge, La.; bishop of Baton Rouge from 1983.

Picachy,Cardinal Lawrence T., 76, Nov. 29, 1992, Calcutta, India; retired archbishop of Calcutta; cardinal from 1976.

Posados Ocampo, Cardinal Juan Jesus, 67, May 24, 1993, at Guadalajara, Mexico, airport; shot to death by drug terrorists; archbishop of Guadalajara; cardinal from 1991.

Riquet, Rev. Michel, S.J., 94, Mar. 5, 1993, Paris, France; French resistance fighter during World War II; popular preacher and author.

Russell, Bishop John J., 95, Mar. 17, 1993, Richmond, Va.; bishop of Charleston, 1950 to 1958; bishop of Richmond, 1958 to 1973 when he retired.

Scheiber, Richard P., 66, Dec. 29, 1992, Huntington, Ind.; newspaperman, Knights of Columbus official.

Schuck, Bishop James A., O.F.M., 80, Jan. 31, 1993, Denville, NJ; bishop of Prelacy of Cristalandia, Brazil from 1959 to 1988 when he retired.

Schuster, Rev. George, S.D.S., 67, Nov. 27, 1992, Sacramento, Calif.; editor and business manager of the Catholic Herald, Sacramento diocesan newspaper.

Sellinger, Rev. Joseph A., S.J., 72, Apr. 19, 1993, Baltimore, Md.; president of Loyola College in Maryland for almost 30 years.

Shea, Sister Mary Gemma, M.M., 98, Jan. 8, 1993, Maryknoll, N.Y.; last survivor of seven founding members of Maryknoll Sisters.

Unterkoefler, Bishop Ernest L., 75, Jan. 4, 1993, Charleston, S.C.; bishop of Charleston from 1965 to 1990, when he retired.

Weiss, Vincent A., 82, Nov. 28, 1992, Trenton, N.J.; founding editor of The Monitor; Trenton diocesan newspaper.

Yanitelli, Victor, S.J., 78, Jan. 2, 1993, New York, N.Y.; educator, pastor; president of St. Peter's College, Jersey City, 1965-78.

Zhu Hongsheng, Rev. Vincent, S.J., 77, July 6, 1993, Shanghai, China; Chinese dissident; served several prison sentences rather than join the government approved and controlled Catholic organization.